Signature

MICROSOFT®

Word 2007

Nita Rutkosky
Pierce College at Puyallup, Puyallup, Washington

Audrey Rutkosky Roggenkamp
Pierce College at Puyallup, Puyallup, Washington

Managing Editor Sonja Brown
Project Manager Linda Lynch
Cover and Text Designer Leslie Anderson
Desktop Production John Valo, Desktop Solutions
Proofreaders Joy McComb, Carol McLean
Indexer Nancy Fulton

Acknowledgments: The editors and authors wish to thank the following instructors for their valuable contributions as testers of the chapter exercises and activities:

- Janice Davidson, Office Administration, Lambton College, Sarnia, Ontario, Canada
- Jeanette McCarthy, Computer Information Systems and Office Technology, Solano College, Fairfield, CA

ISBN 978-0-76383-218-6 (Hardcover Text)
ISBN 978-0-76383-214-8 (Hardcover Text and CD)
ISBN 978-0-76383-022-9 (Softcover Text)
ISBN 978-0-76383-026-7 (Softcover Text and CD)

875 Montreal Way
St. Paul, MN 55102
E-mail: educate@emcp.com
Web site: www.emcp.com

Printed in the United States of America

16 15 14 13 12 11 10 09 08 3 4 5 6 7 8 9 10

Contents

Introduction

When students prepare for a successful business career, they need to acquire the skills and qualifications essential to becoming a productive member of the business community. Microcomputer systems are prevalent in business offices, and students will encounter employment opportunities that require a working knowledge of computers and computer software. Microcomputers, along with the appropriate software, are used by businesses in a variety of capacities. One of the most popular uses is word processing—the creation of all types of documents, including letters, contracts, group mailings, newsletters, and brochures.

Word processing certainly belongs in the business world, but it is also a popular application for home computer use. People will want to learn word processing to write personal correspondence, keep personal records, provide support for a homebased business or cottage industry, write term papers and reports, and much more.

This textbook offers students the opportunity to learn word processing for employment purposes or home use and to utilize a microcomputer as a word processor. The Microsoft Word 2007 program, together with a microcomputer system, must be available for students to practice the features of the program. Word 2007 needs to be installed on each hard drive or on a network system. To install the program properly, please refer to the Word or Microsoft Office documentation.

This textbook instructs students in the theories and practical applications of one of the most popular word processing programs—Microsoft Word 2007. The textbook is designed to be used in beginning through advanced word processing classes and provides approximately 80 to 120 hours of instruction. No prior knowledge of word processing is required. After successfully completing a course using this textbook, students will be able to

- Create and edit memos, letters, and reports of varying complexity
- Format and customize a range of document types and styles
- Add and modify graphics and other visual elements to enhance written communication
- Organize content into tables, lists, and other structures that promote reader understanding and efficient management in a collaborative work environment
- Plan, research, write, revise, and publish documents to meet specific information needs

Textbook Structure

This textbook is divided into six units. Units 1–3 cover foundation, entry-level word processing skills. Units 4–6 cover intermediate- to advanced-level skills. The chapters within each unit contain the following elements:

- Performance Objectives, identifying the specific learning goals of the chapter.
- Introductory material, providing an overview of new concepts and features.
- Step-by-step exercises, organized into groups, providing students with the opportunity to practice using features immediately after they read about them.
- Chapter Summary, reviewing the main points of the chapter.
- Commands Review, listing the major commands learned in the chapter.
- Reviewing Key Points, a short-answer self-check of chapter concepts.
- Applying Your Skills, offering computer skill assessment exercises that students complete without step-by-step guidance.

Performance Assessments at the end of each unit include the following:

- *Assessing Proficiencies.* Practical computer simulation exercises that require students to make decisions about document preparation and formatting, providing ample opportunity to apply new features as well as to practice previously learned material.
- *Creating Original Documents.* Writing activities that provide students with the opportunity to compose and format business documents, requiring the demonstration of problem-solving, critical, and creative abilities as well as hands-on computer skills.

Completing Computer Exercises

Some computer exercises in the chapters require students to access and use an existing file saved on the Student Resources CD that accompanies this textbook. The files are contained in individual folders for each chapter. A CD icon and folder name displayed on the opening page of each chapter and each set of unit assessments indicates that students need to copy a folder of files from the CD before beginning the activities. Detailed instructions on how to copy and delete folders are provided in the *Getting Started* section that follows this section. For added convenience, the instructions are repeated inside the back cover of the book.

Approved Courseware for Teaching Microsoft Certified Application Specialist Skills

The logo on the cover of this textbook signifies that Microsoft has approved this book as courseware that teaches the skills students need to pass the Word 2007 Microsoft Certified Application Specialist certification exams. These skills and the corresponding page numbers of each related instruction in the text are listed on the page that precedes the first chapter of each unit.

The Microsoft Certified Application Specialist program tests and validates a student's skills, thereby supplying objective proof to an employer or prospective employer that the student knows how to use a program efficiently and productively. Practice tests for the Microsoft Certified Application Specialist exams are included as part of the SNAP Training and Assessment program, described below. For more information on the Microsoft Certified Application Specialist program, visit www.microsoft.com/learning/msbc.

Student and Instructor Ancillaries Available with This Text

Student Resources CD. Packaged with the textbook is a Student Resources CD containing all of the files required for completing computer exercises in the book, as well as model answers in PDF format for all of the intrachapter exercises that students print. To view the model answers and compare them with their own work, students will need Adobe® Acrobat® Reader installed on their computers. A free download of the software is available at www.adobe.com.

Signature Series Resource Center at www.emcp.net/SignatureWord07XP. The Signature Series Resource Center provides a wealth of Web-based resources for students and teachers, including course syllabi, study aids, vital Web links, numerous tests and quizzes, a wide variety of performance tests, and PowerPoint presentations.

SNAP Training and Assessment. A Web-based program designed to optimize skill-based learning for all of the programs of Microsoft Office 2007, SNAP is comprised of:

- a learning management system that creates a virtual classroom on the Web, allowing the instructor to schedule tutorials and tests and to employ an electronic gradebook;
- more than 200 interactive, multi-media tutorials, aligned to textbook chapters, that can be used for direct instruction or remediation;

- a test bank of 1,800 performance skill items that simulate the operation of Microsoft Office and allow the instructor to assign pre-tests, to administer chapter post-tests, and to create practice tests to help students prepare for Microsoft Certified Application Specialist certification exams; and
- approximately 6,000 concept items that can be used in combined concepts/application courses to monitor student understanding of technical and computer literacy knowledge.

Curriculum Planner and Resources. Instructor support for the Signature Word Series has been expanded to include a *Curriculum Planner and Resources* binder with CD. This all-in-one print resource includes course and lesson planning resources such as Lesson Blueprints, teaching hints, and sample course syllabi; presentation resources such as PowerPoint presentations (on Instructor's CD within the binder) and handouts; and assessment resources including an overview of assessment venues, live program and PDF model answers for intrachapter exercises, and live program and annotated PDF model answers for end-of-chapter and end-of-unit assessments. Contents of the *Curriculum Planner and Resources* binder are also available on the password-protected Instructor's section of the Internet Resource Center for this title at www.emcp.com.

Computerized Test Generator. Instructors can use ExamView test generating software and the provided bank of multiple choice items to create customized Web-based or print tests.

Class Connection Web Course Management Tool. The Class Connection is a set of files compatible with both WebCT and Blackboard platforms for traditional and distance learning. Using this product creates a personalized Web site for the course and provides supplementary content, communication via e-discussions and online group conferences, and testing resources. Content items include a syllabus; assignments, quizzes, and tests; performance exams; course links; and study aids.

System Requirements

This text is designed for the student to complete projects and assessments on a computer running a standard installation of Microsoft Office 2007, Professional Edition, and the Microsoft Windows XP operating system with Service Pack 2 or later. To effectively run this suite and operating system, your computer should be outfitted with the following:

- 500 MHz processor or higher; 256 MB RAM or higher
- DVD or CD-ROM drive
- 2 GB of available hard-disk space
- 1024 by 768 monitor resolution
  Note: Screen captures in this book were created using 1024 by 768 resolution; screens with higher resolution may look different.
- Computer mouse or compatible pointing device

About the Authors

Nita Rutkosky began teaching business education courses at Pierce College in Puyallup, Washington, in 1978. Since then she has taught a variety of software applications to students in postsecondary Information Technology certificate and degree programs. In addition to Benchmark Office 2007 texts, she has co-authored *Marquee Office* 2007, *Using Computers in the Medical Office: Microsoft Word, Excel, and PowerPoint* 2003, as well as textbooks on most earlier versions of Microsoft Office, keyboarding, WordPerfect, desktop publishing, and voice recognition for Paradigm Publishing, Inc.

Audrey Rutkosky Roggenkamp has been teaching courses in the Business Information Technology department at Pierce College in Puyallup including keyboarding, skill building, and Microsoft Office programs. In addition to titles in the Benchmark Office 2007 series, she has co-authored *Using Computers in the Medical Office* and *Marquee Office* 2007 for Paradigm Publishing, Inc.

What Is the Microsoft Business Certification Program?

The Microsoft Business Certification program enables candidates to show that they have something exceptional to offer—proven expertise in Microsoft Office programs. The two certification tracks allow candidates to choose how they want to exhibit their skills, either through validating skills within a specific Microsoft product or taking their knowledge to the next level and combining Microsoft programs to show that they can apply multiple skill sets to complete more complex office tasks. Recognized by businesses and schools around the world, over 3 million certifications have been obtained in over 100 different countries. The Microsoft Business Certification Program is the only Microsoft-approved certification program of its kind.

What is the Microsoft Certified Application Specialist Certification?

CERTIFIED

Application Specialist

The Microsoft Certified Application Specialist Certification exams focus on validating specific skill sets within each of the Microsoft® Office system programs. Candidates can choose which exam(s) they want to take according to which skills they want to validate. The available Application Specialist exams include:

- Using Microsoft® Windows Vista™
- Using Microsoft® Office Word 2007
- Using Microsoft® Office Excel® 2007
- Using Microsoft® Office PowerPoint® 2007
- Using Microsoft® Office Access 2007
- Using Microsoft® Office Outlook 2007

What is the Microsoft Certified Application Professional Certification?

Microsoft CERTIFIED

Application Professional

The Microsoft Certified Application Professional Certification exams focus on a candidate's ability to use the 2007 Microsoft® Office system to accomplish industry-agnostic functions, for example, Budget Analysis and Forecasting, or Content Management and Collaboration. The available Application Professional exams currently include:

- Organizational Support
- Creating and Managing Presentations
- Content Management and Collaboration
- Budget Analysis and Forecasting

What do the Microsoft Business Certification Vendor of Approved Courseware logos represent?

Microsoft CERTIFIED *Application Specialist* | Approved Courseware

Microsoft CERTIFIED *Application Professional* | Approved Courseware

The logos validate that the courseware has been approved by the Microsoft® Business Certification Vendor program and that these courses cover objectives that will be included in the relevant exam. It also means that after utilizing this courseware, you may be prepared to pass the exams required to become a Microsoft Certified Application Specialist or Microsoft Certified Application Professional.

For more information:

To learn more about Microsoft Certified Application Specialist or Professional exams, visit www.microsoft.com/learning/msbc.

To learn about other Microsoft Certified Application Specialist or Professional approved courseware from Paradigm Publishing, visit www.emcp.com/microsoft-certified-courseware.

The availability of Microsoft Certified Application exams varies by Microsoft Office program, program version, and language. Visit www.microsoft.com/learning for exam availability.

Getting Started

As you work your way through this textbook, you will learn functions and commands for Microsoft Office Word 2007, one of the applications included in the Microsoft Office 2007 suite. Word 2007 is a word processing program. To operate it, you will need access to a microcomputer system.

Identifying Computer Hardware

The computer equipment you will need to operate Word 2007 is referred to as ***hardware***. You will need access to a microcomputer system that consists of the following six components, shown in Figure G.1: a central processing unit (CPU), monitor, keyboard, printer, mouse, and drives. Each component is described below. If you are not sure what equipment you will be operating, check with your instructor.

Figure G.1 Microcomputer System

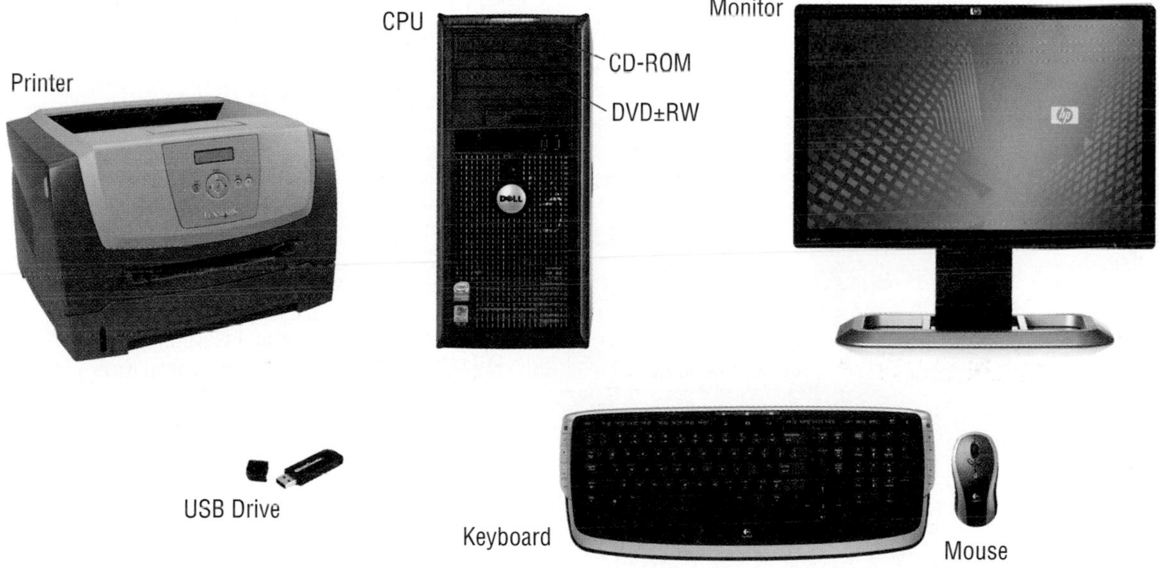

CPU

The CPU is the intelligence of the computer. All processing occurs in it. The CPU is made up of silicon chips containing miniaturized circuitry, which are placed on boards that plug into slots within the CPU. When the computer is given an instruction, the instruction is processed through the circuitry in the CPU.

Monitor

A monitor looks like a television screen. It displays both the information of the program being run by the computer and the text being input at the keyboard. The quality of a monitor's visual display varies depending on the type of monitor and the level of resolution. Monitors can also vary in size, generally ranging from a 14-inch screen up to a 21-inch screen or larger.

Keyboard

A keyboard is used to input information into the computer. Keyboards for microcomputers vary in the number and location of the keys. Microcomputers have alphabetic and numeric keys positioned in the same location as the keys on a typewriter. The symbol keys, however, may be placed in a variety of locations, depending on the manufacturer. In addition to letters, numbers, and symbols, most microcomputer keyboards contain function keys, arrow keys, and a numeric keypad. Figure G.2 shows a keyboard.

Figure G.2 Microcomputer Keyboard

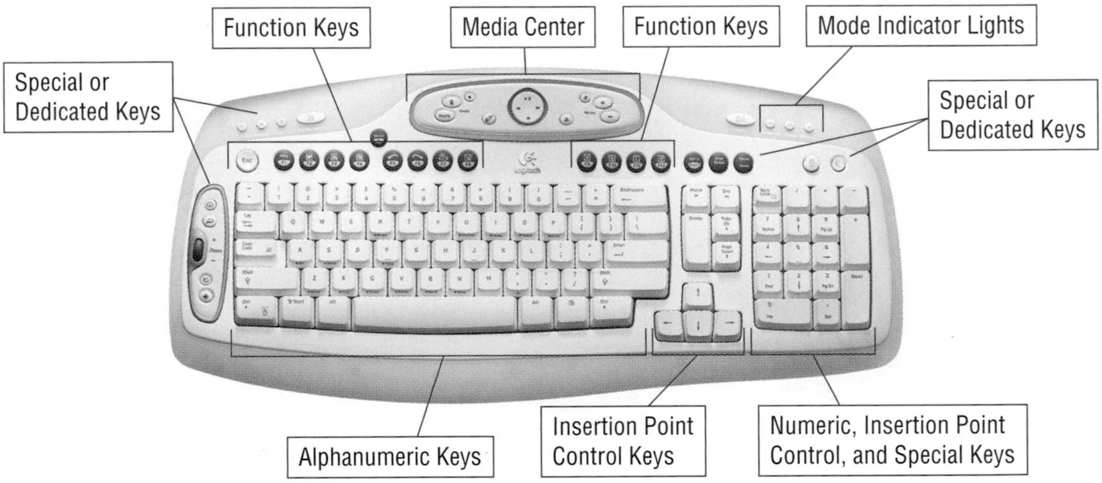

The 12 keys at the top of a keyboard, labeled with the letter F followed by a number, are called ***function keys***. Use these keys to perform functions in Word. To the right (and sometimes to the left) of the regular keys is a group of ***special*** or ***dedicated keys***. These keys are labeled with specific functions that will be performed when you press the key. Below the special keys are arrow keys. Use these keys to move the insertion point in the document screen.

In the upper right corner of the keyboard are three mode indicator lights. When you select certain modes, a light appears on the keyboard. For example, if you press the Caps Lock key, which disables the lowercase alphabet, a light appears next to Caps Lock. Similarly, pressing the Num Lock key will disable the special functions on the numeric keypad, which is located at the right side of the keyboard, and turn on the Num Lock mode indicator light.

Disk Drives

Depending on the computer system you are using, Microsoft Office 2007 is installed on a hard drive or as part of a network system. Whether you are using Word 2007 on a hard drive or network system, you will need to have available a digital video disc (DVD) or compact disk (CD) drive and a USB drive or other storage medium. You will insert the CD that accompanies this textbook in the DVD or CD drive and then copy folders from the CD to your storage medium. You will also save documents you complete at the computer to folders on your storage medium.

Printer

A document you create in Word is considered ***soft copy***. If you want a hard copy of a document, you need to print it. To print documents, you will need to access a printer, which will probably be either a laser printer or an ink-jet printer. A laser printer uses a laser beam combined with heat and pressure to print documents while an ink-jet printer prints a document by spraying a fine mist of ink on the page.

Mouse

Many functions in Word are designed to operate more efficiently with a mouse. A mouse is an input device that sits on a flat surface next to the computer. You can operate a mouse with your left or right hand. When you move the mouse on the flat surface, a corresponding mouse pointer moves on the screen. Figure G.1 shows an illustration of a mouse.

Using the Mouse

You can execute commands in Word 2007 using a keyboard or a mouse. The mouse may have two or three buttons on top, which you tap to execute specific functions and commands. To use the mouse, rest it on a flat surface or a mouse pad. Put your hand over it with your palm resting on top of the mouse and your wrist resting on the table surface.

To use the mouse, you need to understand four terms—point, click, double-click, and drag. With the mouse, you may need to *point* to a specific command, button, or icon. To point means to position the mouse pointer on the desired item. With the mouse pointer positioned on the desired item, you may need to *click* one of the buttons on the mouse. To click means to quickly tap a mouse button once. To complete two steps at one time, such as choosing and then executing a function, you may need to *double-click* a mouse button. To double-click means to tap the left mouse button twice in quick succession. To *drag* with the mouse means to press and hold the left mouse button, move the mouse pointer to a specific location, and then release the button.

Using the Mouse Pointer

The mouse pointer changes appearance depending on the function being performed or where the pointer is positioned. The mouse pointer may appear as one of the following images:

- I-beam pointer—the mouse pointer appears as an I-beam (called the I-beam pointer) in a document. It can be used to move the insertion point or select text.
- arrow pointer—the mouse pointer appears as an arrow pointing up and to the left (called the arrow pointer) when it is moved to the Title bar, Quick Access toolbar, or ribbon, or to an option in a dialog box. For example, to open a new document with the mouse, you will position the I-beam pointer on the Office button located in the upper left corner of the screen until the pointer turns into an arrow pointer, and then you will click the left mouse button. At the drop-down list that displays, you can make a selection by positioning the arrow pointer on the desired option and then clicking the left mouse button.

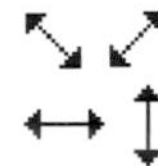

- double-headed arrow—the mouse pointer becomes a double-headed arrow (either pointing left and right, pointing up and down, or pointing diagonally) when you perform certain functions, such as changing the size of an object.

- four-headed arrow—in certain situations, such as when you move an object or image, the mouse pointer becomes a four-headed arrow. The four-headed arrow indicates that you can move the object left, right, up, or down.

- hourglass—when the computer is processing a request or when you are loading a program, the mouse pointer may appear with an hourglass beside it. The hourglass image means "please wait." When the process is completed, the hourglass image is removed.

- hand—the mouse pointer displays as a hand with a pointing index finger when you have accessed certain functions, such as the Help feature. It indicates that more information is available about the item.

Choosing Commands

In Word, you can use several methods to choose a command. A command is an instruction that tells the program to do something. You can choose a command using the mouse or the keyboard. When Word is open, the ribbon displays at the top of the screen. The ribbon contains buttons, arranged in tabs, for completing tasks. To choose a button on the Quick Access toolbar or in the ribbon, position the tip of the mouse arrow pointer on a button and then click the left mouse button.

Word provides access keys you can press to use a command in a program. Press the Alt key on the keyboard to display KeyTips that identify the access key you need to press to execute a command. For example, press the Alt key in a document and KeyTips display, as shown in Figure G.3. Continue pressing access keys until you execute the desired command. For example, if you want to begin spell checking a document, you would press the Alt key, press the R key on the keyboard to display the Review tab, and then press the S key on the keyboard.

Figure G.3 Access Key KeyTips

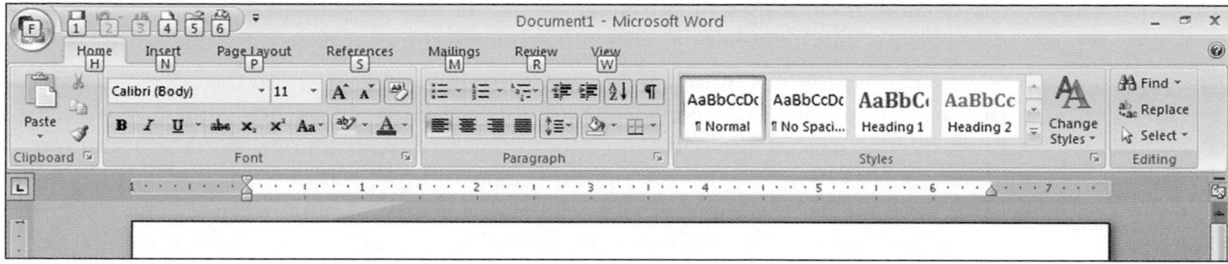

Choosing Commands from Drop-Down Lists

To choose a command from a drop-down list with the mouse, position the mouse pointer on the desired option and then click the left mouse button. To make a selection from a drop-down list with the keyboard, type the underlined letter in the desired option.

Some options at a drop-down list may be gray shaded (dimmed), indicating that the option is currently unavailable. If an option at a drop-down list displays preceded by a check mark, the check mark indicates that the option is currently active. If an option at a drop-down list displays followed by an ellipsis (...), a dialog box will display when that option is chosen.

Choosing Options from a Dialog Box

A dialog box contains options for applying formatting to a document or to data in a document. Some dialog boxes display with tabs along the top, which provide additional options. For example, the Font dialog box, shown in Figure G.4, contains two tabs—the Font tab and the Character Spacing tab. The tab that displays in front is the

Figure G.4 Font Dialog Box

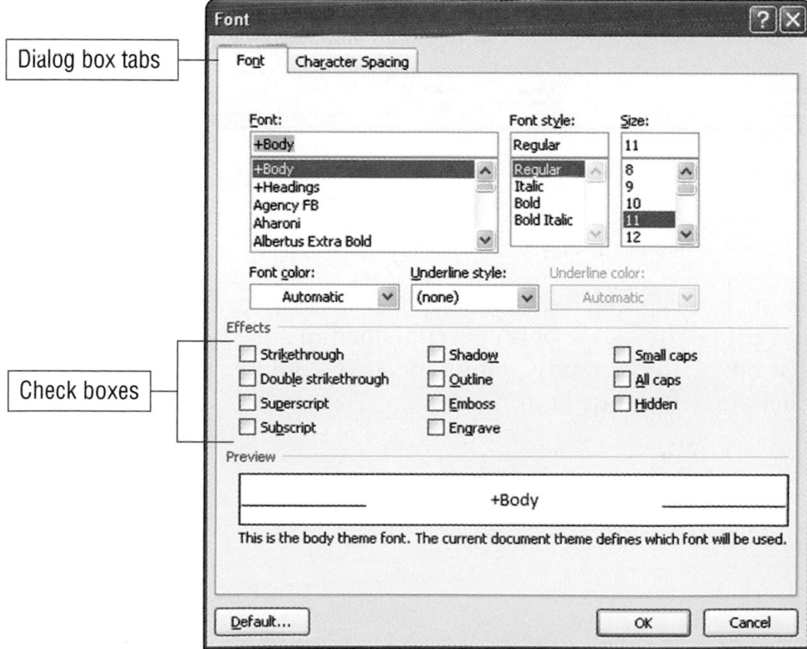

active tab. To make a tab active using the mouse, position the arrow pointer on the desired tab and then click the left mouse button. If you are using the keyboard, press Ctrl + Tab or press Alt + the underlined letter on the desired tab.

To choose options from a dialog box with the mouse, position the arrow pointer on the desired option and then click the left mouse button. If you are using the keyboard, press the Tab key to move the insertion point forward from option to option. Press Shift + Tab to move the insertion point backward from option to option. You can also hold down the Alt key and then press the underlined letter of the desired option. When an option is selected, it displays with a blue background or surrounded by a dashed box called a marquee. A dialog box contains one or more of the following elements: text boxes, list boxes, check boxes, option buttons, spin boxes, and command buttons.

Text Boxes

Text boxes are options in a dialog box that require you to enter text. For example, the boxes below the *Find what* and *Replace with* options at the Find and Replace dialog box, shown in Figure G.5, are text boxes. In a text box, you type text or edit existing text. You can edit text in a text box in the same manner you would edit text in a document. (You will learn to edit text in a document in Chapter 1.) Use the Left and Right Arrow keys on the keyboard to move the insertion point without deleting text and use the Delete key or Backspace key to delete text.

Figure G.5 Find and Replace Dialog Box

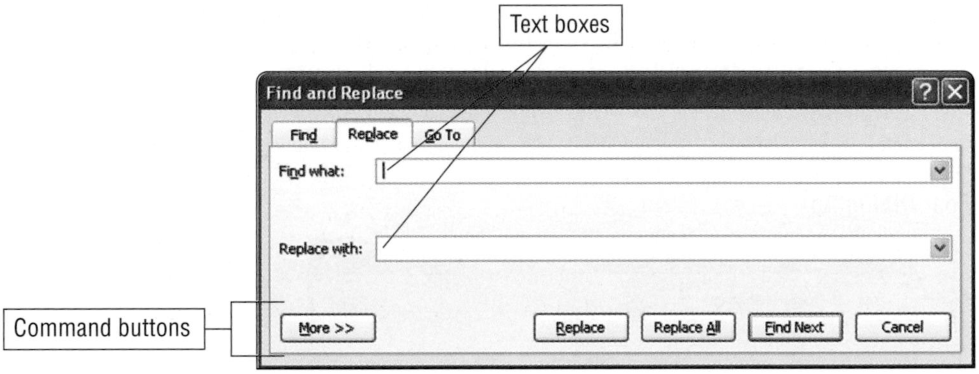

List Boxes

Some dialog boxes, such as the Open dialog box, shown in Figure G.6, contain a list box. The list of files below the *Look in* option is contained in a list box. To make a selection from a list box with the mouse, move the arrow pointer to the desired option and then click the left mouse button.

Figure G.6 **Open Dialog Box**

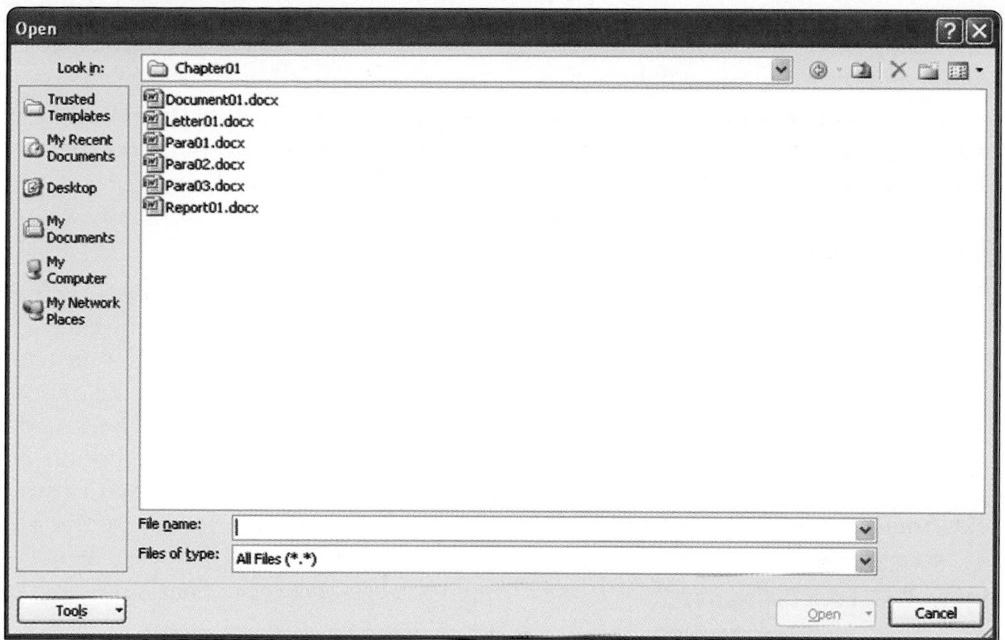

Some list boxes contain a scroll bar. This scroll bar displays at the right side of the list box (a vertical scroll bar) or at the bottom of the list box (a horizontal scroll bar). You can use a vertical scroll bar or a horizontal scroll bar to move through the list if the list is longer than the box. To move down through a list on a vertical scroll bar, position the arrow pointer on the down-pointing arrow and hold down the left mouse button. To scroll up through the list in a vertical scroll bar, position the arrow pointer on the up-pointing arrow and hold down the left mouse button. You can also move the arrow pointer above the scroll box and click the left mouse button to scroll up the list or move the arrow pointer below the scroll box and click the left mouse button to move down the list. To move through a list with a horizontal scroll bar, click the left-pointing arrow to scroll to the left of the list or click the right-pointing arrow to scroll to the right of the list.

To make a selection from a list using the keyboard, move the insertion point into the box by holding down the Alt key and pressing the underlined letter of the desired option. Press the Up and/or Down Arrow keys on the keyboard to move through the list.

In some dialog boxes, not enough room is available for a list box. In these dialog boxes, options are inserted in drop-down list boxes. Options that contain a drop-down list box display with a down-pointing arrow. For example, the *Underline style* option in the Font dialog box, shown in Figure G.4, contains a drop-down list. To display the list, click the down-pointing arrow to the right of the *Underline style* option box. If you are using the keyboard, press Alt + U.

Check Boxes

Some dialog boxes contain options preceded by a box. A check mark may or may not appear in the box. The Font dialog box, shown in Figure G.4, displays a variety of check boxes within the *Effects* section. If a check mark appears in the box, the option is active (turned on). If the check box does not contain a check mark, the option is inactive (turned off). Any number of check boxes can be active. For example, in the Font dialog box, you can insert a check mark in any or all of the boxes in the *Effects* section and these options will be active.

To make a check box active or inactive with the mouse, position the tip of the arrow pointer in the check box, and then click the left mouse button. If you are using the keyboard, press Alt + the underlined letter of the desired option.

Option Buttons

The Print dialog box, shown in Figure G.7, contains options in the *Print range* section preceded by option buttons. Only one option button can be selected at any time. When an option button is selected, a green circle displays in the button. To select an option button with the mouse, position the tip of the arrow pointer inside the option button, and then click the left mouse button. To make a selection with the keyboard, hold down the Alt key, and then press the underlined letter of the desired option.

Figure G.7 Print Dialog Box

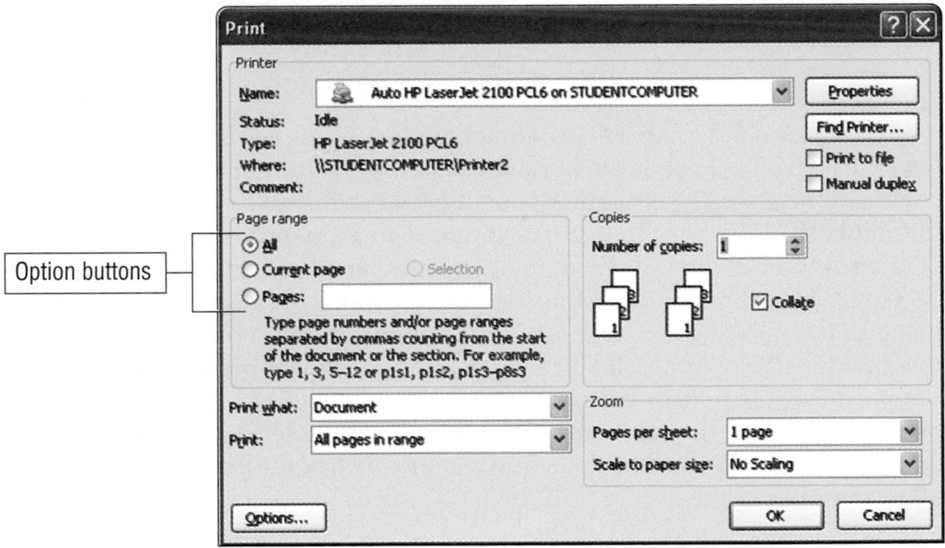

Spin Boxes

Some options in a dialog box contain measurements or numbers you can increase or decrease. These options are generally located in a spin box. For example, the Paragraph dialog box, shown in Figure G.8, contains spin boxes located after the *Left*, *Right*, *Before*, and *After* options. To increase a number in a spin box, position the tip of the arrow pointer on the up-pointing arrow to the right of the desired option, and then click the left mouse button. To decrease the number, click the down-pointing arrow. If you are using the keyboard, press Alt + the underlined letter of the desired option, and then press the Up Arrow key to increase the number or the Down Arrow key to decrease the number.

Figure G.8 Paragraph Dialog Box

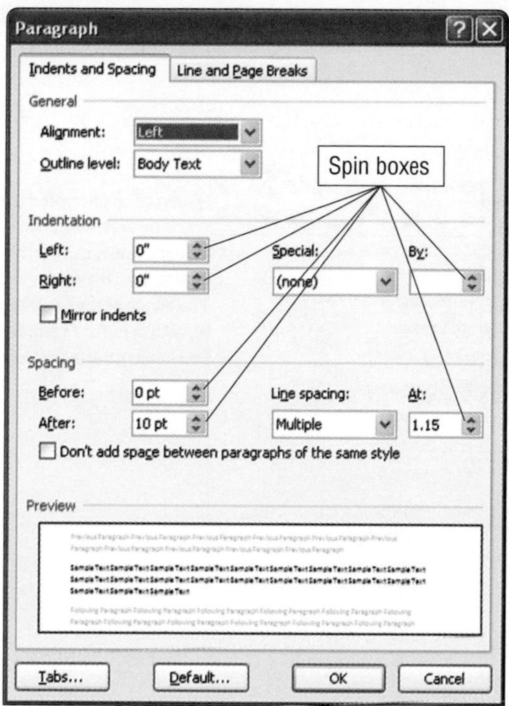

Command Buttons

In the Find and Replace dialog box, shown in Figure G.5, the boxes along the bottom of the dialog box are called command buttons. Use a command button to execute or cancel a command. Some command buttons display with an ellipsis (...). A command button that displays with an ellipsis opens another dialog box when chosen. To choose a command button with the mouse, position the arrow pointer on the desired button, and then click the left mouse button. To choose a command button with the keyboard, press the Tab key until the desired command button contains the marquee and then press the Enter key.

Choosing Commands with Keyboard Shortcuts

Word offers a variety of keyboard shortcuts you can use to executive specific commands. Keyboard shortcuts generally require two or more keys. For example, the keyboard shortcut to display the Open dialog box is Ctrl + O. To use this keyboard shortcut, hold down the Ctrl key, type the letter O on the keyboard, and then release the Ctrl key. For a list of keyboard shortcuts, refer to the Help files.

Choosing Commands with Shortcut Menus

Word includes shortcut menus that display commands and options related to the position of the mouse pointer or the insertion point. To display a shortcut menu, click the *right* mouse button or press Shift + F10. For example, if you position the mouse pointer in a paragraph of text in a document and then click the *right* mouse button or press Shift + F10, the shortcut menu shown in Figure G.9 displays in the document.

Figure G.9 **Shortcut Menu**

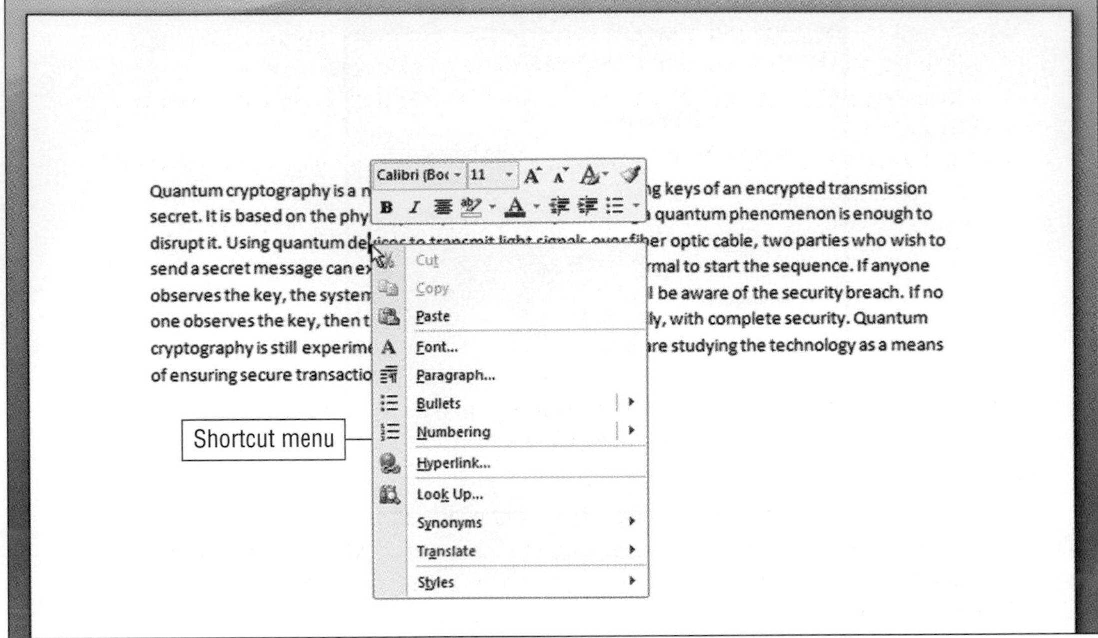

To select an option from a shortcut menu with the mouse, click the desired option. If you are using the keyboard, press the Up or Down Arrow key until the desired option is selected, and then press the Enter key. To close a shortcut menu without choosing an option, click anywhere outside the shortcut menu or press the Esc key.

Completing Computer Exercises

Some computer exercises in this textbook require you to open an existing document. These exercise documents are saved on the Student Resources CD that accompanies this textbook. The documents and files you need for each chapter are saved in individual folders. Before beginning a chapter, copy the necessary folder from the CD to your storage medium.

The Student Resources CD also contains model answers in PDF format for the exercises within (but not at the end of) each chapter so you can check your work. To access the PDF files, you will need to have Adobe Acrobat Reader installed on your computer's hard drive. A free download of the program is available at www.adobe.com.

Copying a Folder

As you begin working in a chapter, copy the chapter folder from the CD to your storage medium using the My Computer window by completing the following steps:

1. Insert the CD that accompanies this textbook in the CD drive.
2. Insert your storage medium in the appropriate drive.
3. At the Windows XP desktop, open the My Computer window by clicking the Start button and then clicking *My Computer* at the Start menu.

4. Double-click the CD drive in the contents pane (probably displays as *Signature Word 2007 Student CD* followed by the drive letter).
5. Double-click the StudentDataFiles folder in the contents pane.
6. Click once on the desired chapter folder name to select it.
7. Click the Copy this folder hyperlink in the *File and Folder Tasks* section of the task pane.
8. At the Copy Items dialog box, click the drive where your storage medium is located and then click the Copy button.
9. After the folder is copied to your storage medium, close the My Computer window by clicking the Close button (the button marked with a white *X* on a red background) that displays in the upper right corner of the window.

Deleting a Folder

If storage is limited on your storage medium, you may want to delete any previous chapter folders. Do this in the My Computer window by completing the following steps:

1. Insert your storage medium in the appropriate drive.
2. At the Windows XP desktop, open the My Computer window by clicking the Start button and then clicking *My Computer* at the Start menu.
3. Double-click the drive where your storage medium is located in the contents pane.
4. Click the chapter folder in the list box.
5. Click the Delete this folder hyperlink in the *File and Folder Tasks* section of the task pane.
6. At the message asking if you want to remove the folder and all its contents, click the Yes button.
7. If a message displays asking if you want to delete a read-only file, click the Yes to All button.
8. Close the My Computer window by clicking the Close button (marked with a white *X* on a red background) that displays in the upper right corner of the window.

Viewing or Printing the Exercise Model Answers

If you want to access the PDF model answer files, first make sure that Adobe Acrobat Reader is installed on your hard drive. Double-click the ExerciseModelAnswers(PDF) folder, double-click the desired chapter folder name, and double-click the appropriate file name to open the file. You can view and/or print the file to compare it with your own completed exercise file.

Customizing the Quick Access Toolbar

Word 2007 contains a Quick Access toolbar that displays at the top of the screen. By default, this toolbar contains three buttons—Save, Undo, and Redo. Before beginning chapters in this textbook, customize the Quick Access toolbar by adding three additional buttons—New, Open, and Quick Print. To add these three buttons to the Word Quick Access toolbar, complete the following steps:

1. Open Word.
2. Click the Customize Quick Access Toolbar button that displays at the right side of the toolbar.
3. At the drop-down list, click *New*. (This adds the New button to the toolbar.)

4. Click the Customize Quick Access Toolbar button and then click *Open* at the drop-down list. (This adds the Open button to the toolbar.)
5. Click the Customize Quick Access Toolbar button and then click *Quick Print* at the drop-down list. (This adds the Quick Print button to the toolbar.)

Customizing Settings

Before beginning computer exercises in this textbook, you may need to customize the monitor settings and turn on the display of file extensions. Exercises in the chapters in this textbook assume that the monitor display is set to 1024 by 768 pixels and that the display of file extensions is turned on. To change the monitor display to 1024 by 768, complete the following steps:

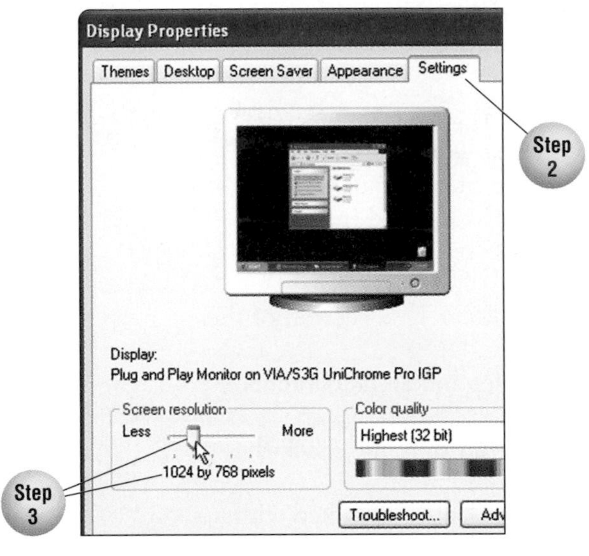

1. At the Windows XP desktop, right-click on any empty location on the desktop and then click Properties at the shortcut menu.
2. At the Display Properties dialog box, click the Settings tab.
3. Using the mouse, drag the slide bar button in the *Screen resolution* section to the left or right until *1024 by 768* displays below the slider bar.
4. Click the Apply button.
5. Click the OK button.

To turn on the display of file extensions, complete the following steps:

1. At the Windows XP desktop, click the Start button and then click *My Computer.*
2. At the My Computer window, click *Tools* on the Menu bar and then click *Folder Options* at the drop-down list.

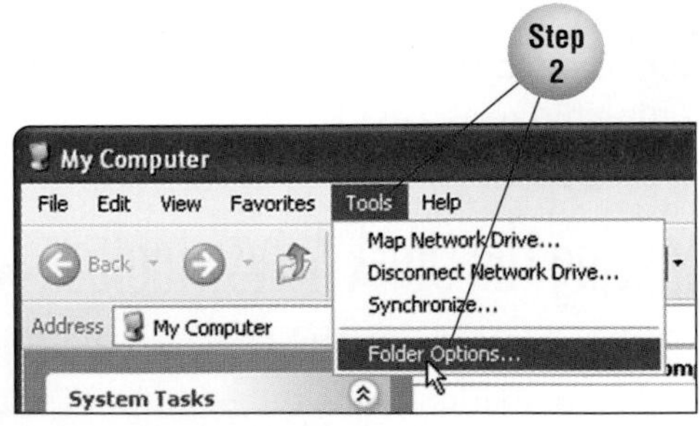

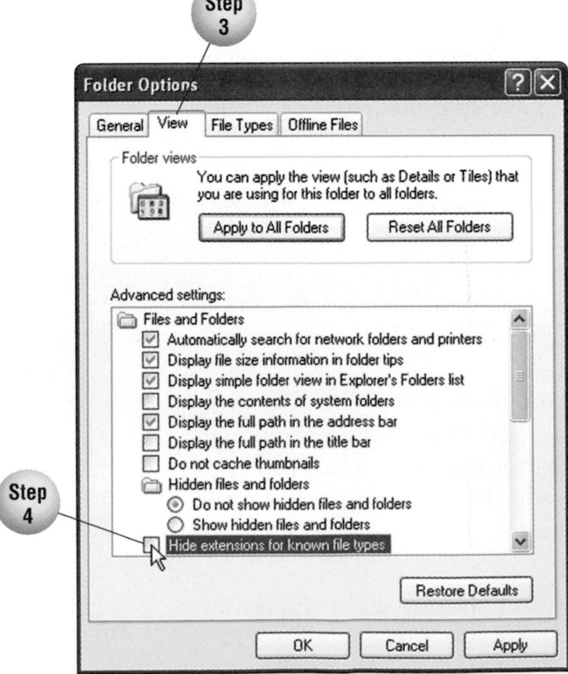

3. At the Folder Options dialog box, click the View tab.
4. Click the *Hide extensions for known file types* check box to remove the check mark.
5. Click the Apply button.
6. Click the OK button.

Unit 1

Preparing Documents

- Creating, Printing, and Editing Documents
- Formatting Characters
- Aligning and Indenting Paragraphs
- Customizing Paragraphs
- Proofing Documents
- Unit 1 Performance Assessments

Signature Microsoft® Word 2007

Microsoft Certified Application Specialist Skills—Unit 1

Reference No.	Skill	Pages
1	**Creating and Customizing Documents**	
1.1	Create and format documents	
1.1.2	Apply Quick Styles to documents	41-43
1.1.3	Format documents using themes	44-46
1.1.4	Customize themes	45-46
1.4	Personalize Word	
1.4.2	Change research options	130-132
2	**Formatting Content**	
2.1	Format text and paragraphs	
2.1.1	Apply styles	41-66
2.1.3	Format characters	29-48
2.1.4	Format paragraphs	55-67
2.1.5	Set and clear tabs	89-96
2.2	Manipulate text	
2.2.1	Cut, copy, and paste text	96-103
4	**Organizing Content**	
4.2	Use tables and lists to organize content	
4.2.1	Create tables and lists	67-72
5	**Reviewing Documents**	
5.1	Navigate documents	
5.1.1	Move in a document quickly using the Find and Go To commands	13-15

Chapter 1

Creating, Printing, and Editing Documents

Tutorial 1.1
Creating a Document and Using Help

Performance Objectives

Upon successful completion of Chapter 1, you will be able to:

- Open Microsoft Word
- Create, save, name, print, open, and close a Word document
- Exit Word and Windows
- Edit a document
- Move the insertion point within a document
- Scroll within a document
- Select text in a document
- Use the Undo and Redo buttons
- Use the Help feature

In this chapter, you will learn to create, save, name, print, open, close, and edit a Word document. Before continuing, make sure you read the *Getting Started* section presented at the beginning of this book. This section contains information about computer hardware and software, using the mouse, executing commands, and customizing settings.

Note: Before beginning computer exercises for this chapter, copy to your storage medium the Chapter01 folder from the CD that accompanies this textbook. Steps on how to copy a folder are presented on the inside back cover of this textbook. Do this for each chapter before starting the chapter's exercises.

Opening Microsoft Word

QUICK STEPS

Open Word
1. Click Start button.
2. Point to *All Programs*, then *Microsoft Office*.
3. Click *Microsoft Office Word 2007*.

start

Microsoft Office 2007 contains a word processing program named Word that you can use to create, save, edit, and print documents. The steps to open Word may vary depending on your system setup. Generally, to open Word, you would click the Start button on the Taskbar at the Windows desktop, point to *All Programs*, point to *Microsoft Office*, and then click *Microsoft Office Word* 2007.

Creating, Saving, Printing, and Closing a Document

When Microsoft Word is open, a blank document displays as shown in Figure 1.1. The features of the document screen are described in Table 1.1.

Figure 1.1 Blank Document Screen

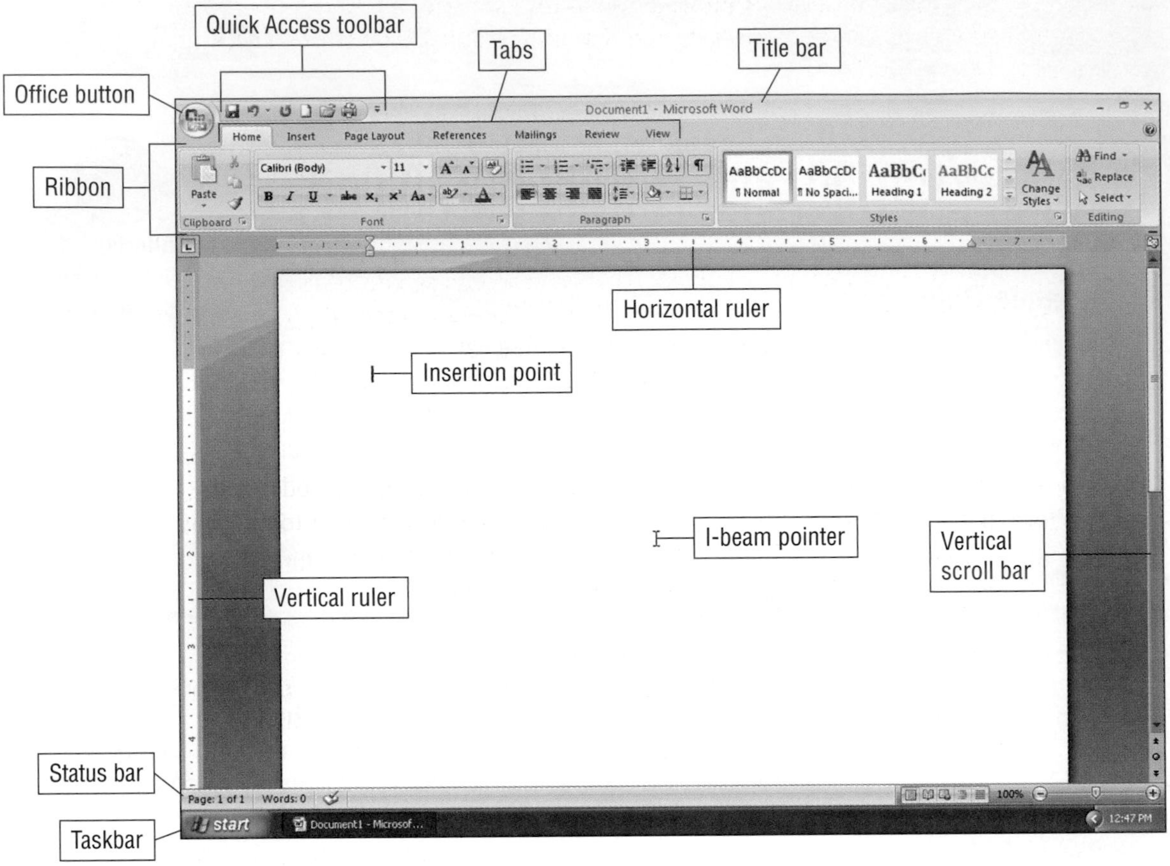

Table 1.1 Microsoft Word Screen Features

Feature	***Description***
Office Button	Displays as the Microsoft Office logo and, when clicked, displays a list of options along with the most recently opened documents
Quick Access Toolbar	Contains buttons for commonly used commands
Title Bar	Displays document name followed by program name
Tabs	Contain commands and features organized into groups
Ribbon	Area containing the tabs and commands divided into groups
Horizontal Ruler	Used to set margins, indents, and tabs
Vertical Ruler	Used to set top and bottom margins
I-beam Pointer	Used to move the insertion point or to select text
Insertion Point	Indicates location of next character entered at the keyboard
Vertical Scroll Bar	Used to view various parts of the document
Status Bar	Displays number of pages and words, View buttons, and the Zoom slider bar

At a blank document, you can type information to create a document. A document is any piece of writing that conveys information—for example, a letter, report, term paper, table, and so on. As you type text, you will notice that Word contains the following helpful features:

- **Word Wrap:** You do not need to press the Enter key at the end of each line because Word wraps text from one line to the next. A word is wrapped to the next line if it begins before the right margin and continues past the right margin. You need to press Enter only to end a paragraph, create a blank line, or end a short line.
- **AutoCorrect:** Word automatically corrects certain words as you type them. For example, if you type *adn* instead of the word *and*, Word automatically corrects your typing when you press the spacebar after the word. AutoCorrect also superscripts the letters that follow an ordinal number. For example, if you type 2nd and then press the spacebar or Enter key, Word will convert this ordinal number to 2nd.
- **Automatic Spell Checker:** By default, Word automatically inserts a red wavy line below words that are not contained in its Spelling dictionary or automatically corrected by AutoCorrect. This underlining may include misspelled words, proper names, some terminology, and some foreign words. If you type a word that is not recognized by the Spelling dictionary, leave it as you have written it if the word is correct. However, if the word is incorrect, you have two choices—you can delete the word and then type it correctly, or you can position the I-beam pointer on the word, click the *right* mouse button, and then click the correct spelling in the pop-up list that displays.
- **Automatic Grammar Checker:** Word also includes an automatic grammar checker. If the grammar checker detects a sentence that contains a grammatical error, Word inserts a green wavy line below the sentence. You can leave the sentence as written or position the I-beam pointer on the sentence, click the *right* mouse button, and choose from the pop-up list of possible corrections.
- **Spacing Punctuation:** Typically, Word uses Calibri, a proportional typeface, as the default typeface. (You will learn more about typefaces in Chapter 2.) When you type text in a proportional typeface, space once (rather than twice) after end-of-sentence punctuation such as a period, question mark, or exclamation point, and after a colon. Because proportional typeface is set closer together, extra white space at the end of a sentence or after a colon is not needed.
- **Option Buttons:** As you insert or edit text in a document, an option button may pop up. The button that appears varies with the action you are completing. If you type a word that is corrected by AutoCorrect, if you create an automatic list, or if Word applies autoformatting to text, the AutoCorrect Options button appears. Click this button to undo the specific automatic action. If you paste text in a document, the Paste Options button appears near the text. Click this button to display options for controlling how the pasted text is formatted.
- **AutoComplete:** Microsoft Word and other Office applications include an AutoComplete feature that inserts an entire item when you type a few identifying characters. For example, type the letters *Mond* and *Monday* displays in a ScreenTip above the letters. Press the Enter key or press F3 and Word inserts *Monday* in the document.

Using the New Line Command

A Word document is based on a template that applies default formatting. Two default formats are 1.15-point line spacing and 10 points of spacing after a paragraph. Each time you press the Enter key, Word inserts 10 points of spacing and begins a new paragraph. If you want to move the insertion point down to the next line without including the additional 10 points of spacing, use the New Line command Shift + Enter.

Exercise 1A

Creating a Document

1. Follow the instructions in this chapter to open Microsoft Word.
2. At the blank document, type the information shown in Figure 1.2 with the following specifications:
   a. Correct any errors highlighted by the spell checker as they occur.
   b. Space once after end-of-sentence punctuation.
   c. To insert the word *Wednesday* located toward the end of the document, type Wedn and then press F3. (This illustrates the AutoComplete feature.)
   d. To insert the word *November*, type Nove and then press the Enter key. (This again illustrates the AutoComplete feature.)
   e. Press Shift + Enter after typing *November 17, 2010*. (This moves the insertion point to the next line without adding 10 points of additional spacing.)
   f. When typing the last line (the line containing the ordinal numbers), type the ordinal number text and AutoCorrect will automatically convert the letters in the ordinal numbers to superscript.
3. When you are finished typing the text, press the Enter key once.

Figure 1.2 Exercise 1A

Keystroke identification is a new area of biometric technology that measures an individual's typing rhythms, which are virtually impossible to falsify. The system compares a typing sample obtained on a specialized keyboard with a sample stored in a database. In addition to analyzing the person's typing speed and accuracy, the system measures dwell time, which is the amount of time the person depresses a given key, and flight time, which is the amount of time between the person's keystrokes. This type of identification system, which requires only specialized software run on an otherwise ordinary computer, offers the advantages of being unobtrusive, fairly low tech, and inexpensive. One limitation of keystroke identification systems is the lack of uniformity among keyboards, which results in variations in measurements. Currently, no company has announced a commercial use for this technology, but a company that provides Web site filtering software has begun developing a product.

This document was written Wednesday, November 17, 2010.
Please insert as the 4th and 5th paragraphs of the 7th section.

Saving a Document

Save a document if you want to use it in the future. You can use a variety of methods to do so, such as clicking the Save button on the Quick Access toolbar, clicking the Office button and then clicking *Save As* at the drop-down list, or using the keyboard shortcut Ctrl + S. Clicking the Save button on the Quick Access toolbar and clicking the Office button followed by *Save As* at the drop-down list both display the Save As dialog box, shown in Figure 1.3. In this box, type a name for the document and then press Enter or click the Save button located in the lower right corner of the dialog box.

Save a Document
1. Click Save button on Quick Access toolbar.
2. Type document name.
3. Click Save button.

Save

Office

Figure 1.3 **Save As Dialog Box**

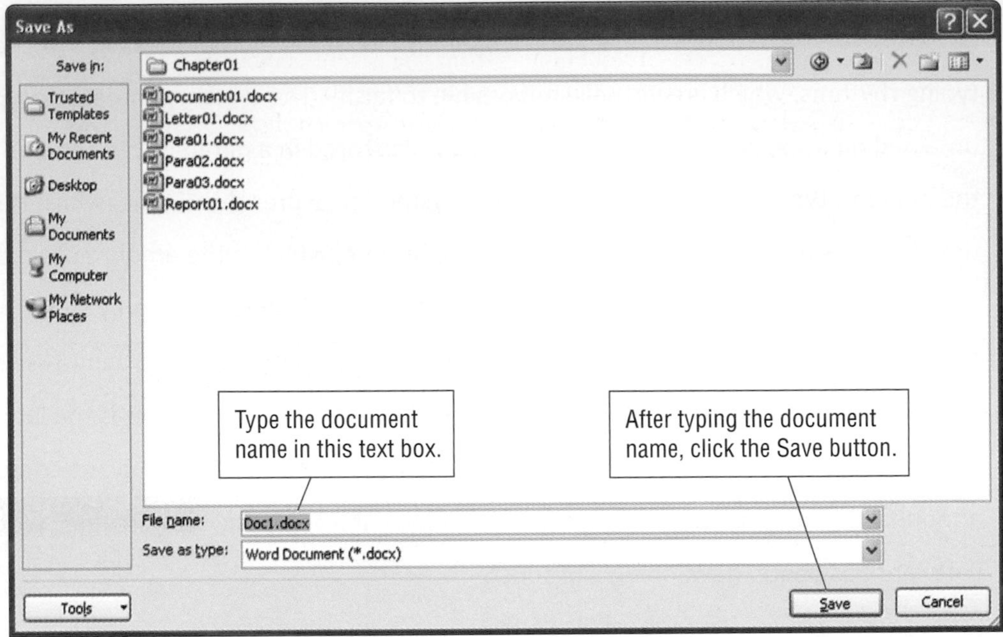

Naming a Document

Document names created in Word and other suite applications can be a maximum of 255 characters in length, including drive letter and any folder names, and may include spaces. File names cannot include any of the following characters:

forward slash (/)	question mark (?)
backslash (\)	quotation mark (")
greater than sign (>)	colon (:)
less than sign (<)	semicolon (;)
asterisk (*)	pipe symbol (|)

Print a Document
Click Quick Print button on Quick Access toolbar.
OR
1. Click Office button.
2. Click Print.
3. Click OK.

Quick Print

Printing a Document

You will need to print many of the computer exercises you will be creating. A document printed on paper is referred to as ***hard copy;*** a document displayed on the screen is referred to as ***soft copy***. You can send a document immediately to the printer by clicking the Quick Print button on the Quick Access toolbar. (If the Quick Print button does not display on the Quick Access toolbar, click the Customize Quick Access Toolbar button at the right side of the toolbar and then click *Quick Print* at the drop-down list.) You can also print by clicking the Office button and then clicking *Print* at the drop-down list, or by pressing the keyboard shortcut Ctrl + P, which displays the Print dialog box. At this dialog box, click OK to send the document to the printer.

Closing a Document

When you save a document, it is saved on your storage medium but remains on the document screen. To remove the document from the screen, click the Office button and then click *Close* at the drop-down list, or use the keyboard shortcut Ctrl + F4. When you close a document, it is removed and a blank screen displays. At this screen, you can open a previously saved document, create a new document, or exit the Word program.

Close a Document
1. Click Office button.
2. Click Close.

Exercise 1B

Saving, Printing, and Closing a Document

1. Save the document you created in Exercise 1A and name it **C01Ex01** (for Chapter 1, Exercise 1) by completing the following steps:
   a. Click the Save button on the Quick Access toolbar.

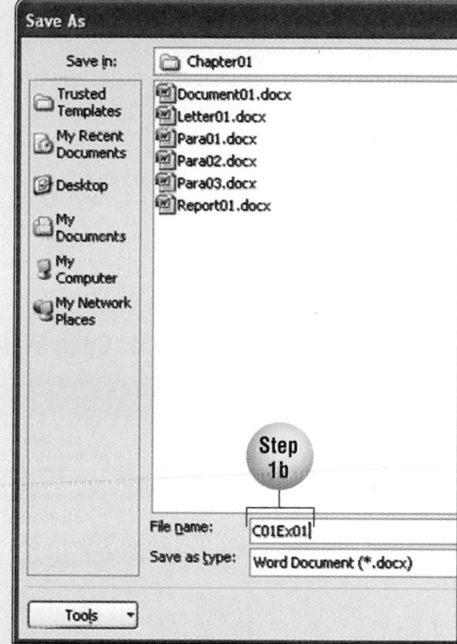

   b. At the Save As dialog box, type **C01Ex01** and then press Enter.
2. Print the document by clicking the Quick Print button on the Quick Access toolbar.
3. Close the document by clicking the Office button and then clicking *Close* at the drop-down list.

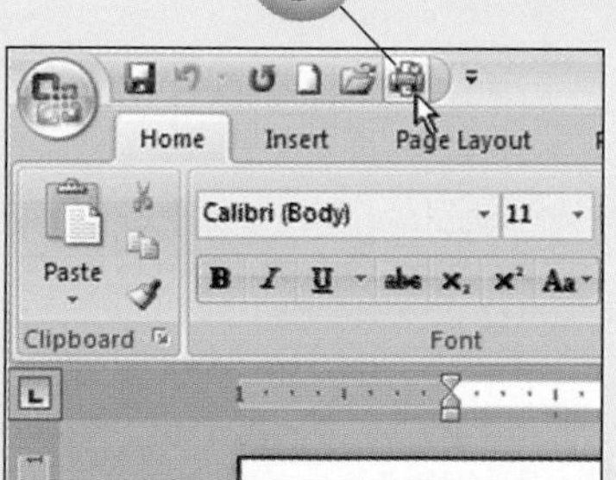

QUICK STEPS

Create New Document
Click New button on Quick Access toolbar.
OR
1. Click Office button.
2. Click *New*.
3. Click *Blank document* option.
OR
Press Ctrl + N.

Open a Document
Click Open button on Quick Access toolbar.
OR
1. Click Office button.
2. Click *Open*.
3. Double-click document name.

Open

Creating a New Document

After you close a document and a blank screen displays, you can create a new document. To do this, first display a blank document by clicking the New button on the Quick Access toolbar or clicking the Office button and then clicking *New*. (If the New button does not display on the Quick Access toolbar, click the Customize Quick Access Toolbar button that displays at the right side of the toolbar and then click *New* at the drop-down list.) At the New Document dialog box, click the *Blank document* option. You can also open a new document using the keyboard shortcut Ctrl + N.

Opening a Document

After you save and close a document, you can open it at the Open dialog box, shown in Figure 1.4. To display this dialog box, click the Open button on the Quick Access toolbar, click the Office button and then click *Open*, or use the keyboard shortcut Ctrl + O. (If the Open button does not display on the Quick Access toolbar, click the Customize Quick Access Toolbar button that displays at the right side of the toolbar and then click *Open* at the drop-down list.) At the Open dialog box, double-click the document name. The names of the most recently opened documents display at the right side of the Office button drop-down list. Click a document at the right side of the drop-down list to open it.

Figure 1.4 Open Dialog Box

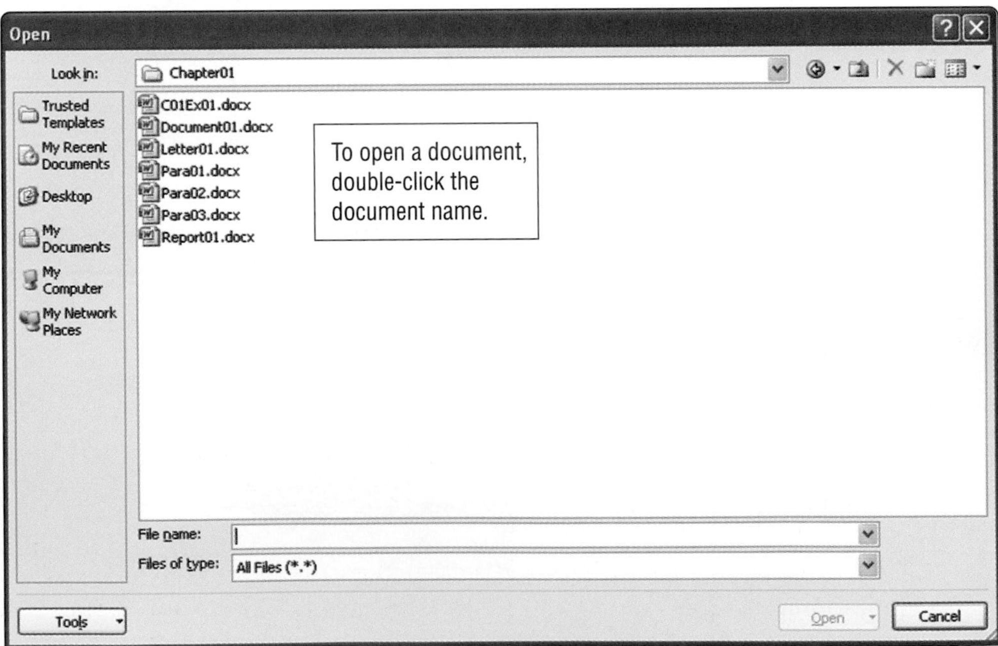

Pinning Documents

When you click the Office button a drop-down list displays with the nine most recently opened documents displayed at the right side of the list. If you want a document to remain in the list, "pin" the document to the drop-down list by clicking the pin button that displays at the right side of the document name. This changes the dimmed gray stick pin to a green stick pin. To "unpin" the document, click the pin button to change it from a green pin to a gray pin.

Exercise 2A

Opening a Document

1. Open the **Document01.docx** document by completing the following steps:
   a. Click the Open button on the Quick Access toolbar.
   b. At the Open dialog box, make sure the Chapter01 folder on your storage medium is the active folder.
   c. Double-click **Document01.docx**.
2. With the insertion point positioned at the beginning of the document, type the text shown in Figure 1.5. After typing the text, press the Enter key.

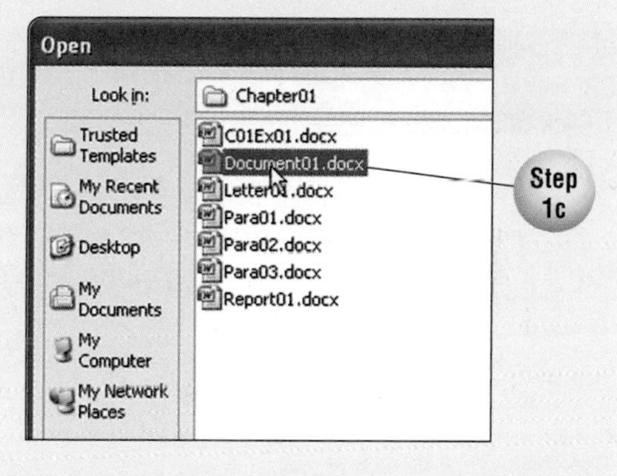

Figure 1.5 Exercise 2A

Quantum Cryptography

One of the problems inherent in encryption is the fact that if the randomly generated key is intercepted, the later encrypted transmission can be unraveled. The key must be agreed upon and sent by parties at both ends of a connection (such as a secure connection between you and your banking institution), otherwise the key is not secure. If a spying program gets that key, the security is broken for the duration of the connection.

Saving a Document with Save As

If you open a previously saved document and want to give it a new name, use the *Save As* option from the Office button drop-down list rather than the *Save* option. When you click *Save As*, the Save As dialog box displays. At this dialog box, type the new name for the document and then press the Enter key.

Save a Document with Save As
1. Click Office button.
2. Click *Save As*.
3. Type document name.
4. Click Save button.

Exit Word
1. Click Office button.
2. Click Exit Word.
OR
Click Close button.

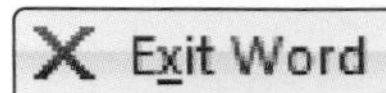

Close

Exiting Word

When you are finished working with Word and have saved all necessary information, exit Word by clicking the Office button and then clicking the Exit Word button (located at the bottom right side of the drop-down list). You can also exit the Word program by clicking the Close button located in the upper right corner of the screen.

Exercise 2B

Saving a Document Using Save As

1. With **Document01.docx** open, save the document with a new name by completing the following steps:
   a. Click the Office button and then click *Save As*.
   b. At the Save As dialog box, type C01Ex02.
   c. Press Enter.
2. Print the document by clicking the Quick Print button on the Quick Access toolbar.
3. Close the document by pressing Ctrl + F4.

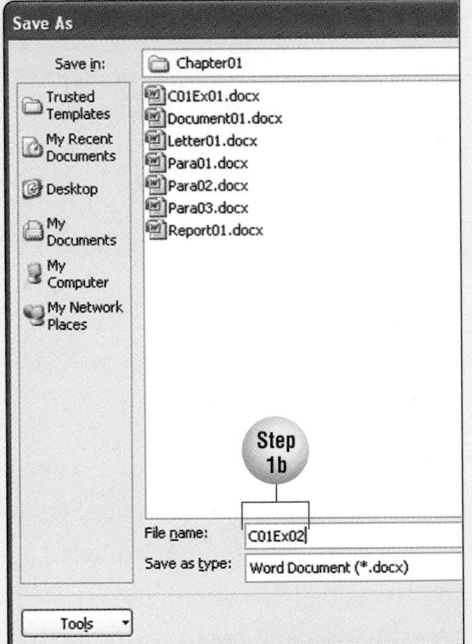

Editing a Document

You may need to change, or edit, documents that you create. To edit a document, use the mouse, the keyboard, or the mouse in combination with the keyboard to move the insertion point to specific locations in the document. To move the insertion point using the mouse, position the I-beam pointer where you want the insertion point to be located and then click the left mouse button.

In addition to moving the insertion point to a specific location, you can use the mouse to move the display of text on the document screen. Use the mouse with the ***vertical scroll bar***, located at the right side of the screen, to scroll through text in a document. Click the up scroll arrow at the top of the vertical scroll bar to scroll up through the document; click the down scroll arrow to scroll down through the document. A scroll box on the scroll bar indicates the location of the text on the document screen in relation to the remainder of the document. To scroll up one screen at a time, position the arrow pointer above the scroll box (but below the up scroll arrow) and then click the left mouse button. Position the arrow pointer below the scroll box and click the left button to scroll down a screen. If you hold down the left mouse button, the action becomes continuous. You can also position the arrow pointer on the scroll box, hold down the left mouse button, and then drag the scroll box along the scroll bar to reposition text on the document screen. As you drag the scroll box along the vertical scroll bar in a multi-page document, page numbers display in a box at the right side of the document screen. Scrolling in a document changes the text displayed but does not move the insertion point.

Exercise 3A

Scrolling in a Document

1. At a blank document, open **Report01.docx**. (This document is located in the Chapter01 folder you copied to your storage medium.)
2. Save the document with Save As and name it **C01Ex03**.
3. Position the I-beam pointer at the beginning of the first paragraph and then click the left mouse button.
4. Click the down scroll arrow on the vertical scroll bar several times. (This scrolls down lines of text in the document.) With the mouse pointer on the down scroll arrow, hold down the left mouse button and keep it down until the end of the document displays.
5. Position the mouse pointer on the up scroll arrow and hold down the left mouse button until the beginning of the document displays.
6. Position the mouse pointer below the scroll box and then click the left mouse button. Continue clicking the mouse button (with the mouse pointer positioned below the scroll box) until the end of the document displays.
7. Position the mouse pointer on the scroll box in the vertical scroll bar. Hold down the left mouse button, drag the scroll box to the top of the vertical scroll bar, and then release the mouse button. (Notice that the document page numbers display in a box at the right side of the document screen.)
8. Click on the title at the beginning of the document. (This moves the insertion point to the location of the mouse pointer.)

Moving the Insertion Point to a Specific Page

Along with scrolling options, Word contains navigation buttons for moving the insertion point to specific locations within a document. These buttons display toward the bottom of the vertical scroll bar and include the Previous button, the Select Browse Object button, and the Next button. The names of the Previous and Next buttons and the tasks they complete vary depending on the last navigation selected. Click the Select Browse Object button and a palette of browsing choices displays. You will learn more about the Select Browse Object button in the next section.

Previous

Next

Select Browse Object

Word also includes a Go To option you can use to move the insertion point to a specific page within a document. To move the insertion point to a specific page, click the Find button arrow located in the Editing group in the Home tab and then click *Go To* at the drop-down list. At the Find and Replace dialog box with the Go To tab selected, type the page number in the *Enter page number* text box and then press Enter. Click the Close button to close the dialog box.

Browsing in a Document

Select Browse Object

As noted in the preceding section, the Select Browse Object button, located toward the bottom of the vertical scroll bar, allows you to select options for browsing through a document. Click this button and a palette of browsing choices displays. Use the options on the palette to move the insertion point to various features in a Word document. Position the arrow pointer on an option in the palette and the option name displays below the options. The options on the palette and their location vary depending on the last function performed.

Moving the Insertion Point with the Keyboard

To move the insertion point with the keyboard, use the arrow keys located to the right of the regular keyboard. You can also use the arrow keys on the numeric keypad. If you use these keys, make sure Num Lock is off. Use the arrow keys together with other keys to move the insertion point to various locations in the document, as shown in Table 1.2.

Table 1.2 **Insertion Point Movement Commands**

To move insertion point	***Press***
One character left	Left Arrow
One character right	Right Arrow
One line up	Up Arrow
One line down	Down Arrow
One word to the left	Ctrl + Left Arrow
One word to the right	Ctrl + Right Arrow
To end of a line	End
To beginning of a line	Home
To beginning of current paragraph	Ctrl + Up Arrow
To beginning of next paragraph	Ctrl + Down Arrow
Up one screen	Page Up
Down one screen	Page Down
To top of previous page	Ctrl + Page Up
To top of next page	Ctrl + Page Down
To beginning of document	Ctrl + Home
To end of document	Ctrl + End

When you move the insertion point with the keyboard, keep in mind that the Word commands use the following definitions: a word is any series of characters between spaces, a paragraph is any text that is followed by a stroke of the Enter key, and a page is text separated by a soft or hard page break. If you open a previously saved document, you can move the insertion point to where it was last located when the document was closed by pressing Shift + F5.

Exercise 3B

Moving the Insertion Point and Browsing in a Document

1. With **C01Ex03.docx** open, move the insertion point to page 3 by completing the following steps:
   a. Click the Find button arrow located in the Editing group in the Home tab and then click *Go To* at the drop-down list.
   b. At the Find and Replace dialog box with the Go To tab selected, make sure *Page* is selected in the *Go to what* list box, type **3** in the *Enter page number* text box, and then press Enter.
   c. Click the Close button to close the Find and Replace dialog box.

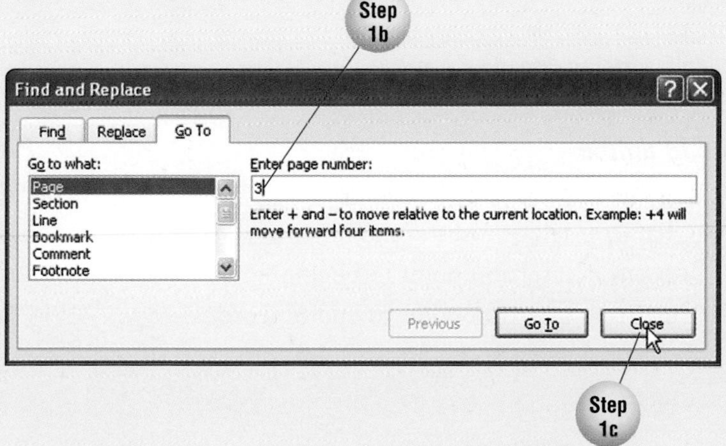

2. Click the Previous Page button located immediately above the Select Browse Object button on the vertical scroll bar. (This moves the insertion point to page 2.)
3. Click the Previous Page button again. (This moves the insertion point to page 1.)
4. Click the Next Page button located immediately below the Select Browse Object button on the vertical scroll bar. (This moves the insertion point to the beginning of page 2.)

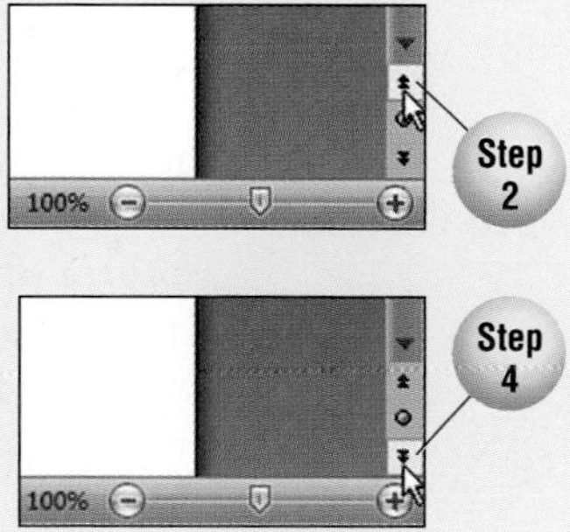

5. Move to the beginning of page 3 by completing the following steps:
   a. Click the Select Browse Object button.
   b. At the palette of browsing choices, click the *Browse by Page* choice. (This moves the insertion point to page 3.)
6. Press Ctrl + Home to move the insertion point to the beginning of the document.
7. Practice using the keyboard commands shown in Table 1.2 to move the insertion point within the document.
8. Close **C01Ex03.docx**.

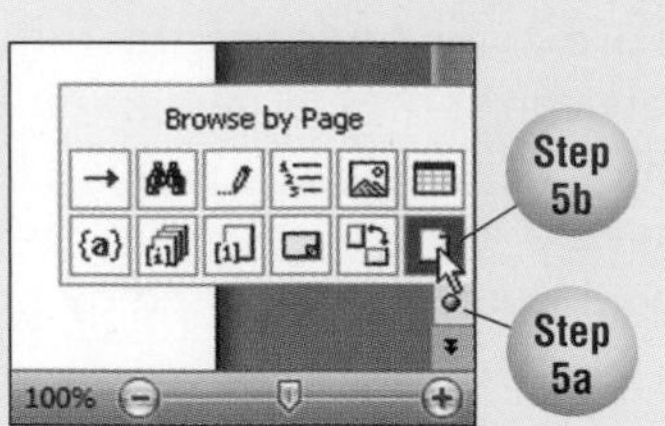

Inserting and Deleting Text

Editing a document may include inserting or deleting text. To insert text in a document, position the insertion point in the desired location and then type the text. By default, existing characters move to the right as you type the text. A number of options are available for deleting text. Some deletion commands are shown in Table 1.3.

Table 1.3 **Deletion Commands**

To delete	***Press***
Character right of insertion point	Delete key
Character left of insertion point	Backspace key
Text from insertion point to beginning of word	Ctrl + Backspace
Text from insertion point to end of word	Ctrl + Delete

Word Options

If you want to type over existing text rather than have it move to the right as you insert new text, you will need to turn on the Overtype mode. With the Overtype mode on, anything you type will replace existing text. To turn on the Overtype mode, click the Office button and then click the Word Options button located toward the bottom of the drop-down list. At the Word Options dialog box, click *Advanced* in the left panel. In the *Editing options* section, insert a check mark in the *Use overtype mode* check box if you want the Overtype mode always on in the document. Or, insert a check mark in the *Use the Insert key to control overtype mode* check box if you want to use the Insert key to turn Overtype mode on and off. After making your selection, click the OK button located in the lower right corner of the window.

Selecting Text

You can use the mouse or the keyboard to select a specific amount of text. Once you have selected the text, you can delete it or perform other Word functions that involve it. When text is selected, it displays with a blue background as shown in Figure 1.6. The Mini toolbar also displays, in a dimmed fashion, and it contains options for performing common tasks. Move the mouse pointer over the Mini toolbar and it becomes active. (You will learn more about the Mini toolbar in Chapter 2.)

Figure 1.6 Selected Text and Mini Toolbar

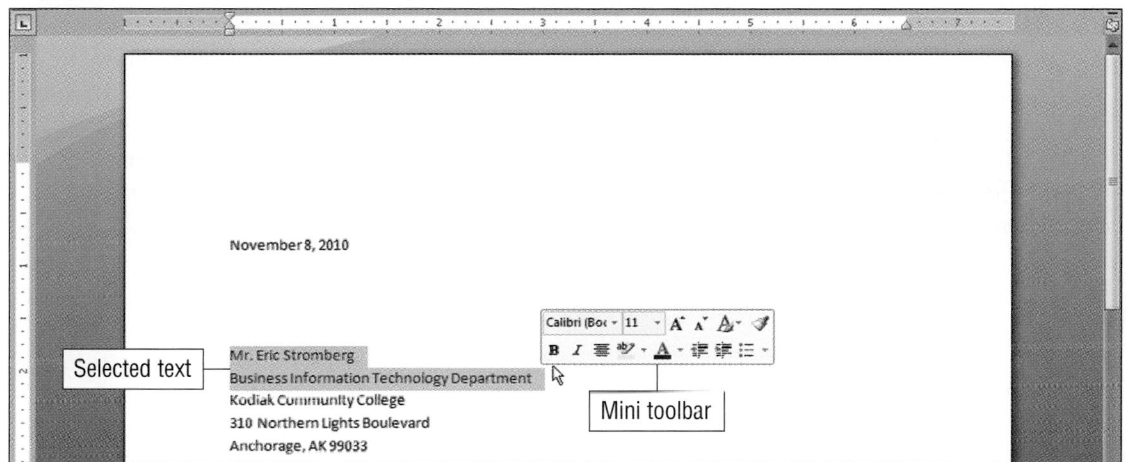

Selecting Text with the Mouse

Use the mouse to select a word, line, sentence, paragraph, or an entire document. Table 1.4 lists the steps to follow to select a specific amount of text. For example, to select a line, click in the selection bar. The selection bar is the space located toward the left side of the document screen between the left edge of the page and the text. When the mouse pointer is positioned in the selection bar, the pointer turns into an arrow pointing up and to the right.

Table 1.4 Selecting with the Mouse

To select	***Complete these steps using the mouse***
A word	Double-click the word.
A line of text	Click in the selection bar to the left of the line.
Multiple lines of text	Drag in the selection bar to the left of the lines.
A sentence	Hold down the Ctrl key, then click anywhere in the sentence.
A paragraph	Double-click in the selection bar next to the paragraph or triple-click anywhere in the paragraph.
Multiple paragraphs	Drag in the selection bar.
An entire document	Triple-click in the selection bar or click Select button in Editing group and then *Select All*.

To select sections of text other than a word, sentence, or paragraph, position the I-beam pointer on the first character of the text to be selected, hold down the left mouse button, drag the I-beam pointer to the last character of the text to be selected, and then release the mouse button. You can also select all text between the current insertion point and the I-beam pointer. To do this, position the insertion point where you want the selection to begin, hold down the Shift key, click the I-beam pointer at the end of the selection, and then release the Shift key. To cancel a selection using the mouse, click anywhere in the document screen outside the selected text.

Selecting Text with the Keyboard

To select a specific amount of text using the keyboard, turn on the Selection Mode by pressing the F8 function key. With the Selection Mode activated, use the arrow keys to select the desired text. If you want to cancel the selection, press the Esc key and then press any arrow key. You can customize the Status bar to display text indicating that the Selection Mode is activated. To do this, *right* click any blank location on the Status bar and then click Selection Mode at the shortcut menu. When you press F8 to turn on the Selection Mode, the words *Selection Mode* display on the Status bar. You can also select text with the commands shown in Table 1.5.

Table 1.5 **Selecting with the Keyboard**

To select	*Press*
One character to right	Shift + Right Arrow
One character to left	Shift + Left Arrow
To end of word	Ctrl + Shift + Right Arrow
To beginning of word	Ctrl + Shift + Left Arrow
To end of line	Shift + End
To beginning of line	Shift + Home
One line up	Shift + Up Arrow
One line down	Shift + Down Arrow
To beginning of paragraph	Ctrl + Shift + Up Arrow
To end of paragraph	Ctrl + Shift + Down Arrow
One screen up	Shift + Page Up
One screen down	Shift + Page Down
To end of document	Ctrl + Shift + End
To beginning of document	Ctrl + Shift + Home
Entire document	Ctrl + A

Exercise 4

Editing a Document

1. Open **Letter01.docx**. (This document is located in the Chapter01 folder you copied to your storage medium.)
2. Save the document with Save As and name it **C01Ex04**.
3. Delete the name, *Mr. Eric Stromberg*, and the department, *Business Information Technology Department*, using the mouse by completing the following steps:
   a. Position the I-beam pointer on the *M* in *Mr.* (in the address).
   b. Hold down the left mouse button and then drag the mouse down until *Mr. Eric Stromberg* and *Business Information Technology Department* are selected.
   c. Release the left mouse button.
   d. Press the Delete key.
4. Position the insertion point at the left margin of the line containing the text **Kodiak Community College**, type the name **Dr. Avery Reynolds**, and then press Shift + Enter.
5. Delete *Mr. Stromberg* in the salutation (after the word *Dear*) and then type **Dr. Reynolds**. (You choose the method for deleting.)
6. Delete the reference line, *Re: Pharmacy Tech Program*, using the Extend Selection key, F8, by completing the following steps:
   a. Position the insertion point on the *R* in *Re:*.
   b. Press F8 to turn on select.
   c. Press the Down Arrow key. (This selects the reference line and the blank line below it.)
   d. Press the Delete key.
7. Delete the first sentence in the first paragraph using the mouse by completing the following steps:
   a. Position the I-beam pointer anywhere in the sentence, *The North Pacific Computer Technology conference that we attended last week was very educational.*
   b. Hold down the Ctrl key and then click the left mouse button.
   c. Press the Delete key.
8. Delete the first sentence in the second paragraph (the sentence that reads, *Interest in the program has been phenomenal.*) using the keyboard by completing the following steps:
   a. Position the insertion point on the first letter of the sentence (the *I* in *Interest*).
   b. Hold down the Shift key and then press the Right Arrow key until the sentence is selected. Be sure to include the period at the end of the sentence and the space after the period.
   c. Press the Delete key.
9. Delete the third paragraph in the letter using the mouse by completing the following steps:
   a. Position the I-beam pointer anywhere in the third paragraph (the paragraph that begins, *The instructor for the Medical Coding course . . .*).
   b. Triple-click the left mouse button.
   c. Press the Delete key.
10. Save, print, and then close **C01Ex04.docx**.

Using the Undo and Redo Buttons

If you make a mistake and delete text that you did not intend to, or if you change your mind after deleting text and want to retrieve it, you can use the Undo or Redo buttons on the Quick Access toolbar. For example, if you type text and then click the Undo button, the text will be removed. You can undo text or commands. For example, if you add formatting such as bolding to text and then click the Undo button, the bolding is removed.

Undo

Redo

If you use the Undo button and then decide you do not want to reverse the original action, click the Redo button. For example, if you select and underline text and then decide to remove the underlining, click the Undo button. If you then decide you want the underlining back on, click the Redo button. Many Word actions can be undone or redone. Some actions, however, such as printing and saving, cannot be undone or redone.

Word maintains actions in temporary memory. If you want to undo an action performed earlier, click the Undo button arrow. This causes a drop-down list to display. To make a selection from this drop-down list, click the desired action. That action, along with any actions listed above it in the drop-down list, is undone.

Exercise 5

Deleting and Restoring Text with the Undo Button

1. Open **Para01.docx**. (This document is located in the Chapter01 folder you copied to your storage medium.)
2. Save the document with Save As and name it **C01Ex05**.
3. Make the changes indicated by the proofreaders' marks in Figure 1.7. (Proofreaders' marks are listed and described in Appendix A at the end of this textbook.)
4. Move the insertion point to the end of the document. Press the Backspace key until the last four words of the document (*or into a spreadsheet.*) are deleted. Be sure to delete the space before *or*.
5. Undo the deletion by clicking the Undo button on the Quick Access toolbar.
6. Redo the deletion by clicking the Redo button on the Quick Access toolbar.
7. Type a period after the word *presentation* to end the sentence.
8. Select the first sentence in the first paragraph and then delete it.
9. Select the second paragraph in the document and then delete it.
10. Undo the two deletions by completing the following steps:
    a. Click the down-pointing arrow to the right of the Undo button.
    b. Click the *second* Clear listed in the drop-down list. (This will redisplay the first sentence in the first paragraph and the second paragraph. The first sentence will be selected.)
11. With the first sentence of the paragraph selected, press the Delete key.
12. Save, print, and then close **C01Ex05.docx**.

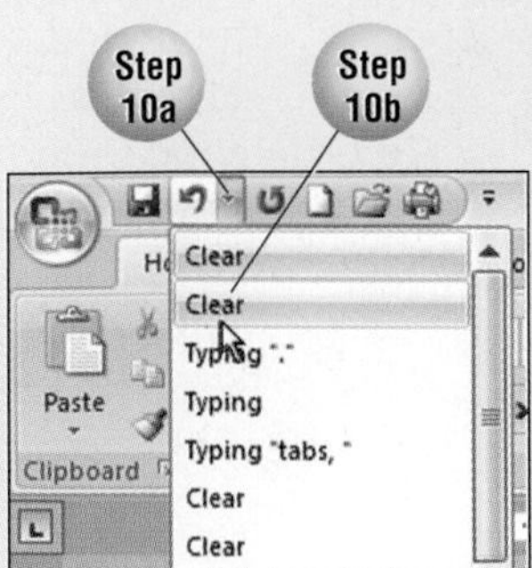

Figure 1.7 Exercise 5

Some commercial software vendors bundle and sell a group of software programs as a single package called a software suite, ~~also known as integrated software~~. Software suites typically include the four most widely used applications: word processing, database management, spreadsheet, and presentation ~~programs~~. Some, such as Microsoft Office, also include Web page authoring programs because the development of personal Web sites is becoming increasingly important to consumers. Suites are popular because buying a package is ~~cheaper~~ than purchasing each component program separately.

Software suites offer advantages other than price. Because the programs were developed using the same user interface, all programs in the suite ~~work~~ in a similar manner. A user who becomes familiar with one program can easily learn to use the others because the screen layouts, menus, buttons, icons, and toolbars are similar.

Another strong feature of suites is that they allow users to seamlessly integrate files from component programs. For example, information produced using a spreadsheet can be placed into a word processing document, or a database table can be imported into a slide show presentation or into a spreadsheet.

Using Help

Microsoft Word includes a Help feature that contains information about Word features and commands. This on-screen reference manual is similar to Windows Help and the Help features in Excel, PowerPoint, and Access. Click the Microsoft Office Word Help button (the circle with the question mark) located in the upper right corner of the screen or press the keyboard shortcut F1 to display the Word Help window. In this window, type a topic, feature, or question in the *Search* text box and then press Enter. Topics related to the search text display in the Word Help window. Click a topic that interests you. If the topic window contains a Show All hyperlink in the upper right corner, click this hyperlink and the topic options expand to show additional help information related to the topic. When you click the Show All hyperlink, it becomes the Hide All hyperlink.

Use Help Feature
1. Click Microsoft Office Word Help button.
2. Type topic or feature.
3. Press Enter.
4. Click desired topic.

Help

Exercise 6A

Using the Help Feature

1. At a blank document, click the Microsoft Office Word Help button located in the upper right corner of the screen.
2. At the Word Help window, type **selecting text** in the *Search* text box.

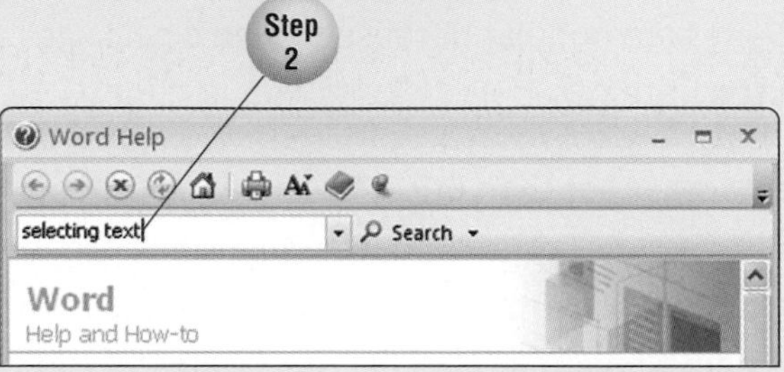

3. Press the Enter key.
4. When the list of topics displays, click the Select text hyperlink.

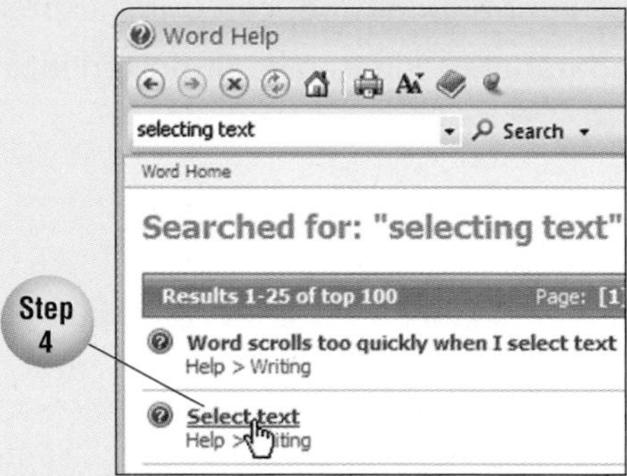

5. Click the Show All hyperlink that displays in the upper right corner of the window.
6. Read the information about selecting text.
7. Print the information by clicking the Print button located toward the top of the Word Help window.
8. At the Print dialog box, click the Print button.
9. Click the Close button to close the Word Help window.

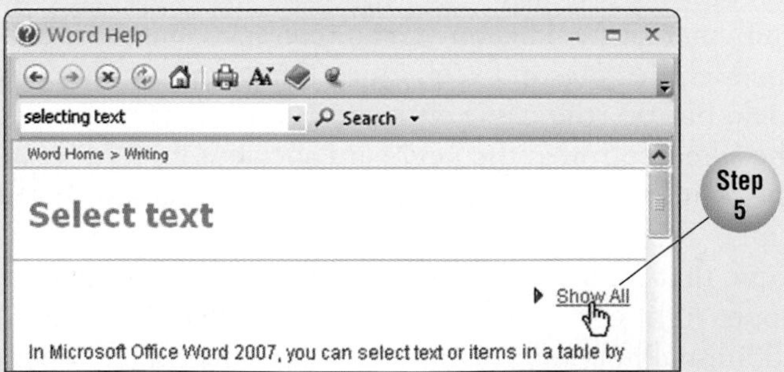

Getting Help in a Dialog Box

Dialog boxes contain a Help button you can click to display the Word Help window that is specific to the dialog box. This button is located in the upper right corner of the dialog box and displays as a question mark inside a square. Click this button and the Word Help window displays with topics related to the dialog box.

Dialog Box Help Button

Exercise 6B

Using a ScreenTip to Access Help

1. At a blank document, click the Office button and then click *Save As* at the drop-down list.
2. At the Save As dialog box, click the Help button located in the upper right corner of the dialog box.
3. At the Word Help window, click the *Save As* hyperlink.

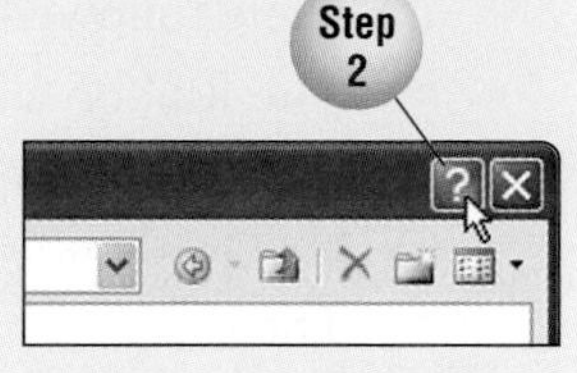

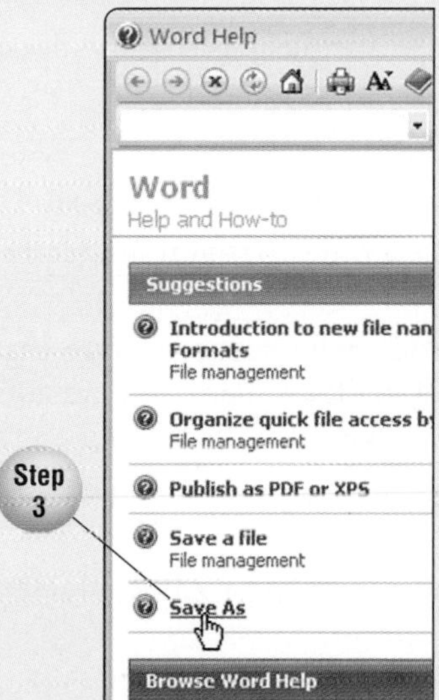

4. In the Save As list box, click *Microsoft Office Word*.
5. Read the information that displays about saving in Word and then click the Close button to close the Word Help window.
6. Close the Save As dialog box.

Chapter Summary

- Open Microsoft Word by clicking the Start button on the Taskbar, pointing to *All Programs*, pointing to *Microsoft Office*, and then clicking *Microsoft Office Word* 2007.
- The Office button displays as a Microsoft Office logo and, when clicked, displays a list of options and most recently opened documents.
- The Quick Access toolbar is located to the right of the Office button and contains buttons for commonly used commands.
- The Title bar is located to the right of the Quick Access toolbar and displays the document name followed by the program name.
- The Ribbon area contains tabs with commands and options divided into groups.
- The insertion point displays as a blinking vertical line and indicates the position of the next character to be entered in the document.
- The mouse displays on the screen as an I-beam pointer or as an arrow pointing up and to the left.
- Use the vertical scroll bar to view various parts of the document.
- The Status bar displays the number of pages and words, View buttons, and the Zoom slider bar.
- Word automatically wraps text to the next line as you type information. Press the Enter key only to end a paragraph, create a blank line, or end a short line.
- Word contains an AutoCorrect feature that automatically corrects certain words as they are typed.
- Word contains both an automatic spell checker feature that inserts a red wavy line below words not contained in the Spelling dictionary and an automatic grammar checker that inserts a green wavy line below a sentence containing a grammatical error.
- The AutoComplete feature inserts an entire item when you type a few identifying characters and then press Enter or F3.
- Document names can contain a maximum of 255 characters, including the drive letter and folder names, and may include spaces.
- The insertion point can be moved throughout the document without interfering with text by using the mouse, the keyboard, or the mouse in combination with the keyboard.
- You can move the insertion point by character, word, screen, or page, and from the first to the last character in a document. Refer to Table 1.2 for keyboard insertion point movement commands.
- The scroll box on the vertical scroll bar indicates the location of the text in the document screen in relation to the remainder of the document.
- Click the Select Browse Object button located at the bottom of the vertical scroll bar to display options for browsing through a document.
- You can delete text by character, word, line, several lines, or partial page using specific keys or by selecting text using the mouse or the keyboard.
- A specific amount of text can be selected using the mouse or the keyboard. Refer to Table 1.4 for information on selecting with the mouse and refer to Table 1.5 for information on selecting with the keyboard.
- Use the Undo button on the Quick Access toolbar if you change your mind after typing, deleting, or formatting text and want to undo the action. Use the Redo button to redo something that has been undone with the Undo button.

- Word's Help feature is an on-screen reference manual that contains information about all Word features and commands.
- Click the Microsoft Office Word Help button or press F1 to display the Word Help window. At this window, type a topic and then press Enter.
- Dialog boxes contain a Help button you can click to display the Word Help window with information specific to the dialog box.

Commands review

FEATURE	TAB, GROUP	BUTTON	QUICK ACCESS TOOLBAR	OFFICE BUTTON DROP-DOWN LIST	KEYBOARD SHORTCUT
Close document				Close	Ctrl + F4
Exit Word				Exit Word	
Find and Replace dialog box with Go To tab selected		Go To...			Ctrl + G
Word Help window					F1
New blank document				New, Blank document	Ctrl + N
Open dialog box				Open	Ctrl + O
Print dialog box				Print	Ctrl + P
Print document				Print, Quick Print	
Save document				Save	Ctrl + S
Select document	Home, Editing	Select			Ctrl + A

Reviewing key points

Completion: In the space provided at the right, indicate the correct term, command, or number.

1. This toolbar contains the Save button. ____________________
2. This button displays in the upper left corner of the screen with the Microsoft logo. ____________________

3. This is the area located toward the top of the screen that contains tabs with commands and options divided into groups. ____________
4. This bar, located toward the bottom of the screen, displays number of pages and words, View buttons, and the Zoom slider bar. ____________
5. This feature automatically corrects certain words as you type them. ____________
6. This feature inserts an entire item when you type a few identifying characters and then press Enter or F3. ____________
7. This is the keyboard shortcut to display the Print dialog box. ____________
8. This is the keyboard shortcut to close a document. ____________
9. This is the keyboard shortcut to display a new blank document. ____________
10. Use this keyboard command to move the insertion point to the beginning of the previous page. ____________
11. Press this key on the keyboard to delete the character left of the insertion point. ____________
12. Use this keyboard command to move the insertion point to the end of the document. ____________
13. Using the mouse, do this to select one word. ____________
14. To select various amounts of text using the mouse, you can click in this bar. ____________
15. This is the keyboard shortcut to display the Word Help window. ____________

Applying your skills

Assessment 1 Type a Document

1. At a blank document, type the text in Figure 1.8. (Correct any errors highlighted by the spell checker as they occur and remember to space once after end-of-sentence punctuation.)
2. Save the document with the name **C01A01**.
3. Print and then close **C01A01.docx**.

Figure 1.8 Assessment 1

Productivity software improves efficiency and performance on the job and at home and is the largest category of application software for individual use. Employment notices appearing in newspapers and magazines often identify required computer skills, such as word processing or spreadsheet expertise. Some employment notices even specify that an applicant must be certified in a particular application, such as Word, Excel, or Access. Certified applicants often receive priority consideration over those without such qualifications. In-depth knowledge and skill in using productivity software applications can make a potential employee more valuable to a business, organization, or agency.

Assessment 2 Edit a Document Containing Proofreaders' Marks

1. Open **Para02.docx**.
2. Save the document with Save As and name it **C01A02**.
3. Make the changes indicated by the proofreaders' marks in Figure 1.9.
4. Save, print, and then close **C01A02.docx**.

Figure 1.9 Assessment 2

Editing is
lc
The process of altering the contents of an existing document is called editing. Editing
when
occurs anytime something is inserted, deleted, or modified within a document. Editing features allow users to make changes until they are satisfied with the content. Perhaps the most valued word processing editing feature is a spell checker, which matches each word in a document to a word list or dictionary. A spell checker is not context-sensitive. It will not flag words that have been spelled correctly but used incorrectly.
and

No ¶ A grammar checker checks a document for common errors in grammar, usage, and mechanics. Grammar checkers are no substitute for careful review by a knowledgeable editor, but they can be useful for identifying such problems as run-on sentences, sentence fragments, and misused apostrophes.
double negatives,

Assessment 3 Edit a Document Containing Proofreaders' Marks

1. Open **Para03.docx**.
2. Save the document with Save As and name it **C01A03**.
3. Make the changes indicated by the proofreaders' marks in Figure 1.10.
4. Save, print, and then close **C01A03.docx**.

Figure 1.10 Assessment 3

which is the

Word processing programs allow many different types of formatting, of the manipulation of text to change its appearance at the word, paragraph, or document level. Many word processing applications include text, paragraph, and document formatting.

programs

the

Text formatting features include the ability to change font type, size, color, and style (such as bold, italic, or underlined). Users can also adjust the leading (the space between lines) and kerning (the amount of space that appears between letters).

which is

which is

No ¶ Paragraph formatting changes the way a body of text flows on the page. Features related to the appearance of a paragraph include placing the text in columns or tables, aligning the text left, right, center, or justified within the margins; and double- or single-spacing lines.

spacing

No ¶ Document formatting lets users specify the form of a document as a whole, defining page numbers, headers, footers, paper size, and margin width. A style is a special shortcut feature that formats text in a single step. Styles allow users to apply text and paragraph formatting to a page, and the styles automatically apply those same attributes to other sections of text.

Many word processing programs include

then

document

Assessment 4 Compose a Document on Saving a Document

1. At a blank document, compose a paragraph explaining when you would use the Save As command when saving a document and the advantages to Save As.
2. Save the document with the name **C01A04**.
3. Print and then close **C01A04.docx**.

Assessment 5 Use Help to Learn About and Then Create a Document Describing Keyboard Shortcuts

1. Click the Microsoft Office Word Help button, type **keyboard shortcuts**, and then press Enter.
2. At the Word Help window, click the *Keyboard shortcuts for Microsoft Office Word* hyperlink.
3. At the keyboard shortcut window, click the *Show All* hyperlink.
4. Read through the information in the Word Help window.
5. Create a document describing four keyboard shortcuts.
6. Save the document with the name **C01A05**.
7. Print and then close **C01A05.docx**.

Chapter 2

Formatting Characters

Tutorial 2.1
Text Formatting
Tutorial 2.2
Adding Effects and Styles

Performance Objectives

Upon successful completion of Chapter 2, you will be able to:

- Change fonts and font effects
- Format selected text with buttons on the Mini toolbar
- Apply styles from Quick Styles sets
- Apply and customize Themes

Format refers to how a document looks on screen and when it is printed. As you learned in Chapter 1, Word uses a template to apply default formatting that affects a document's appearance. Some default settings include 11-point Calibri type, 1.15-point line spacing, 10-point spacing after each paragraph, and left aligned text. In this chapter, you will learn about character formatting, including how to change the typeface, type size, and typestyle, as well as how to apply font effects such as subscripting, superscripting, and highlighting.

Note: Before beginning computer exercises for this chapter, copy to your storage medium the Chapter02 folder from the CD that accompanies this textbook and then make Chapter02 the active folder.

Changing Fonts

The Font group in the Home tab, shown in Figure 2.1, contains a number of buttons you can use to apply character formatting to text in a document. Buttons in the top row change the font and the font size. Buttons in the bottom row apply typestyles such as bold or italic and font effects such as underlining, superscripting, and subscripting. You can remove all character formatting (as well as paragraph formatting) that has been applied to text by clicking the Clear Formatting button in the top row. To remove character formatting from selected text only, press the keyboard shortcut Ctrl + spacebar.

Clear Formatting

Figure 2.1 Font Group Buttons

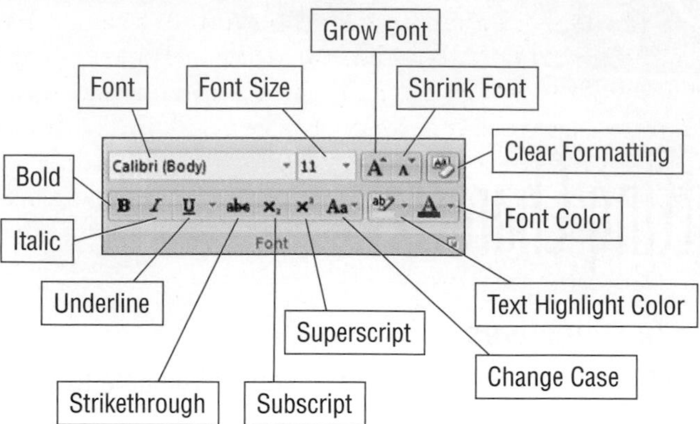

As noted earlier, 11-point Calibri type is Word's default font. You may want to change this default to some other font for reasons such as to change the mood of the document, enhance its visual appeal, or increase its readability. A font consists of three elements—typeface, type size, and typestyle.

A typeface is a set of characters with a common design and shape. It can be decorative or plain, monospaced or proportional. Word refers to typeface as **font**. A monospaced typeface allots the same amount of horizontal space for each character; a proportional typeface allots a varying amount of space for each character. Proportional typefaces are divided into two main categories: ***serif*** and ***sans serif***. A serif is a small line at the end of a character stroke. Because serifs help move the reader's eyes across the page, serif fonts are a good choice for text-intensive documents. Sans serif typefaces are often used for headings, headlines, and advertisements.

Microsoft Word 2007 includes six new typefaces designed for extended on-screen reading: Calibri (the default), Cambria, Candara, Consolas, Constantia, and Corbel. Calibri, Candara, and Corbel are sans serif typefaces; Cambria and Constantia are serif typefaces; and Consolas is monospaced. These six typefaces as well as some other popular typefaces are shown in Table 2.1.

Table 2.1 **Serif and Sans Serif Typefaces**

Serif Typefaces	*Sans Serif Typefaces*	*Monospaced Typefaces*
Cambria	Calibri	Consolas
Constantia	Candara	Courier
Times New Roman	Corbel	Letter Gothic
Bookman Old Style	Arial	

Type size is generally set in proportional size. The size of proportional type is measured vertically in units called ***points***. A point is approximately 1⁄72 of an inch—the higher the point size, the larger the characters. Within a typeface, various typestyles may be available. Typestyles are divided into four main categories: regular, bold, italic, and bold italic.

Use the Font button in the Font group to change the font and the Font Size button or the Shrink Font and Grow Font buttons to change the size. When you select text and then click the Font button arrow, a drop-down gallery displays font options. Hover your mouse pointer over a font option and the selected text in the document displays with the font applied. You can continue hovering your mouse pointer over different font options to see how the selected text displays in the specified font. The Font button drop-down gallery is an example of Word's ***live preview*** feature, which allows you to see how the font formatting affects your text without having to return to the document. The live preview feature is also available when you click the Font Size button arrow.

Change Font
1. Click Font button arrow.
2. Click desired font at drop-down gallery.

Change Font Size
1. Click Font Size button arrow.
2. Click desired font size at drop-down gallery.

Calibri

Font

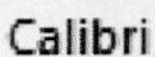

Font Size

Exercise 1A

Changing the Font

1. Open **Document02.docx**.
2. Save the document with Save As and name it **C02Ex01**.
3. Change the typeface to Cambria by completing the following steps:
   a. Select the entire document by pressing Ctrl + A. (You can also select all text in the document by clicking the Select button in the Editing group and then clicking *Select All* at the drop-down list.)
   b. Click the Font button arrow and then scroll down the Font drop-down gallery until *Cambria* displays. Hover the mouse pointer over *Cambria* to display a live preview of the text set in Cambria.
   c. Click the mouse button on *Cambria*.

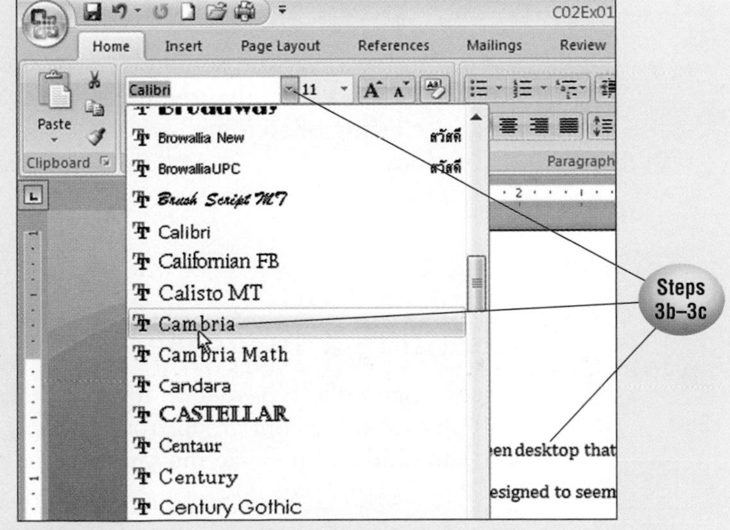

4. Change the type size to 14 points by completing the following steps:
   a. With the text in the document still selected, click the Font Size button arrow.
   b. At the drop-down gallery that displays, hover the mouse pointer over *14* and look at the live preview of the text in 14-point type.
   c. Click the left mouse button on *14*.
5. Deselect the text by clicking anywhere in the document screen outside the selected text.
6. Change the type size and typeface by completing the following steps:
   a. Press Ctrl + A to select the entire document.
   b. Click three times on the Shrink Font button in the Font group. (This decreases the size to 10 points.)
   c. Click twice on the Grow Font button. (This increases the size of the font to 12 points.)

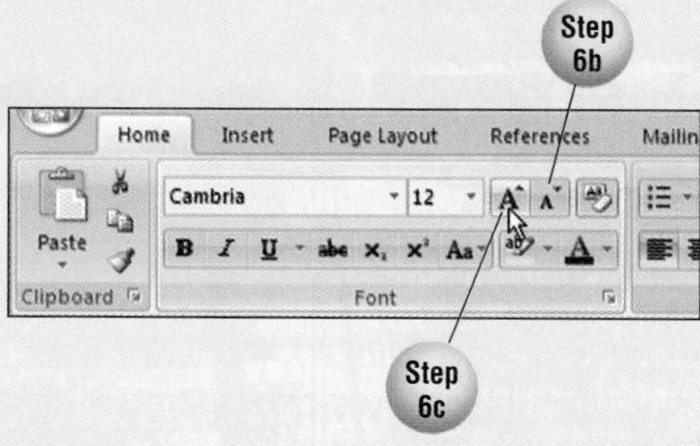

   d. Click the Font button arrow, scroll down the drop-down gallery, and then click *Constantia*. (The most recently used fonts display at the beginning of the document followed by a listing of all fonts.)
7. Save **C02Ex01.docx**.

Choosing a Typestyle

Bold Italic

Underline

Apply a particular typestyle to text with the Bold, Italic, or Underline buttons in the bottom row in the Font group. You can apply more than one style to text. For example, you can bold and italicize the same text or apply all three styles to the same text.

Exercise 1B

Applying Character Formatting to Text as You Type

1. With **C02Ex01.docx** open, press Ctrl + Home to move the insertion point to the beginning of the document.
2. Type a heading for the document by completing the following steps:
   a. Press the Caps Lock key.
   b. Click the Bold button in the Font group. (This turns on bold.)
   c. Click the Underline button in the Font group. (This turns on underline.)
   d. Type **GLOSSARY OF TERMS**.
   e. Select *GLOSSARY OF TERMS* and then click the Clear Formattting button in the Font group. (This removes all formatting from the text.)
   f. Return formatting to the text by clicking the Undo button on the Quick Access toolbar.

3. Press Ctrl + End to move the insertion point to the end of the document.
4. Type the text shown in Figure 2.2 with the following specifications:
   a. While typing the document, make the appropriate text bold as shown in the figure by completing the following steps:
      1) Click the Bold button in the Font group. (This turns on bold.)
      2) Type the text.
      3) Click the Bold button in the Font group. (This turns off bold.)
   b. While typing the document, italicize the appropriate text as shown in the figure by completing the following steps:
      1) Click the Italic button in the Font group.
      2) Type the text.
      3) Click the Italic button in the Font group.
5. After typing the text, press the Enter key.
6. Remove underlining from the title by selecting <u>*GLOSSARY OF TERMS*</u> and then clicking the Underline button in the Font group.
7. With the title *GLOSSARY OF TERMS* still selected, change the font size to 14 points.
8. Save **C02Ex01.docx**.

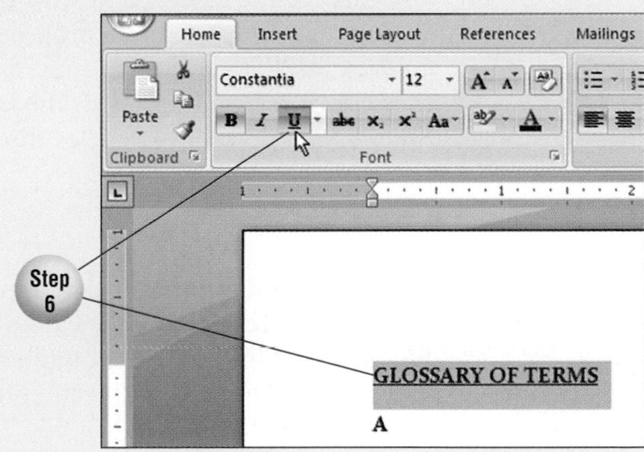

Figure 2.2 Exercise 1B

C

Carpal tunnel syndrome: A condition characterized by weakness, pain, or numbness of the hand(s), caused by compression of the median nerve as it passes through the wrist; the *syndrome* is associated with repetitive motion such as typing or using the computer mouse.

Cell: In a spreadsheet, the *intersection* of one row and one column into which text, numbers, formulas, links, or other elements may be entered.

Clip art: Professionally designed graphic images sold for use in *word processing* and other types of documents; collections are sometimes included in a software program.

Choosing a Font Effect

Strikethrough

Subscript

Superscript

Apply font effects with some of the buttons in the bottom row in the Font group. Use the Strikethrough button to draw a line through selected text. This has a practical application in some legal documents in which deleted text must be retained in the document. Use the Subscript button to create text that is lowered slightly below the text line, such as the chemical formula H_2O. Use the Superscript button to create text that is raised slightly above the text line, such as the mathematical equation four to the third power (written as 4^3).

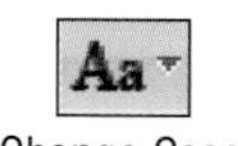

Change Case

Change the case of text with the Change Case button drop-down list. Click the Change Case button and a drop-down list displays with the options *Sentence case.*, *lowercase*, *UPPERCASE*, *Capitalize Each Word*, and *tOGGLE cASE*. You can also change the case of selected text with the keyboard shortcut Shift + F3. Each time you press Shift + F3, selected text cycles through the case options.

Text Highlight Color

Font Color

In addition to buttons that apply typestyles, the bottom row in the Font group includes the Text Highlight Color button and the Font Color button. Use the Text Highlight Color button to highlight specific text in a document and use the Font Color button to change the color of text.

Using Keyboard Shortcuts

Several buttons in the Font group have keyboard shortcuts. For example, you can press Ctrl + B to turn on bold, or press Ctrl + I to turn on italic. Position the mouse pointer on a button and an enhanced ScreenTip displays with the name of the button, the keyboard shortcut (if there is one), a description of the action performed by the button, and, in some cases, access to the Word Help window. Table 2.2 identifies the keyboard shortcuts available for buttons in the Font group.

Table 2.2 **Font Button Keyboard Shortcuts**

Font Group Button	*Keyboard Shortcut*
Font	Ctrl + Shift + F
Font Size	Ctrl + Shift + P
Grow Font	Ctrl + Shift + >
Shrink Font	Ctrl + Shift + <
Bold	Ctrl + B
Italic	Ctrl + I
Underline	Ctrl + U
Subscript	Ctrl + =
Superscript	Ctrl + Shift + +
Change Case	Shift + F3

Formatting with the Mini Toolbar

When you select text, the Mini toolbar displays in a dimmed fashion above the selected text. Hover the mouse pointer over the Mini toolbar and it becomes active. Click a button on the Mini toolbar to apply formatting to selected text.

If you do not want the Mini toolbar to display when you select text, you can turn it off. To do this, click the Office button and then click the Word Options button that displays in the lower right corner of the drop-down list. At the Word Options dialog box with the *Popular* option selected in the left panel, click the *Show Mini Toolbar on selection* check box to remove the check mark.

Exercise 1C

Applying Font Effects

1. With **C02Ex01.docx** open, move the insertion point to the beginning of the term *Clip art*, press the Enter key, and then press the Up Arrow key. Type the text shown in Figure 2.3. Create the superscript numbers by clicking the Superscript button, typing the number, and then clicking the Superscript button.
2. Change the case of text by completing the following steps:
   a. Select the title *GLOSSARY OF TERMS*.
   b. Click the Change Case button in the Font group and then click *Capitalize Each Word* at the drop-down list. (Change the uppercase O in *Of* to a lowercase *o*.)

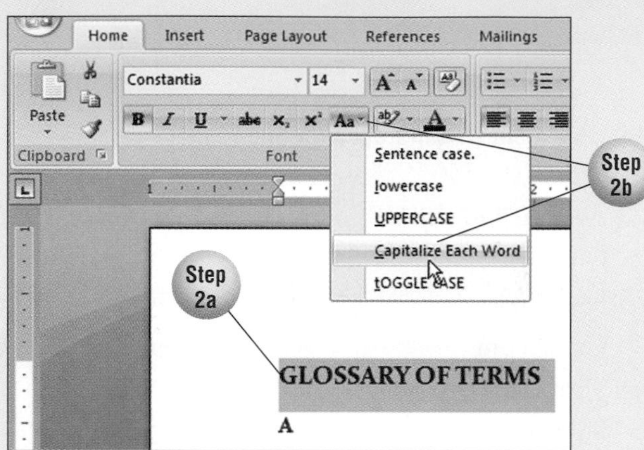

3. Strike through text by completing the following steps:
   a. Select the commas and words *, generally created using the Java programming language,* located in the *Applet* definition.
   b. Click the Strikethrough button in the Font group.

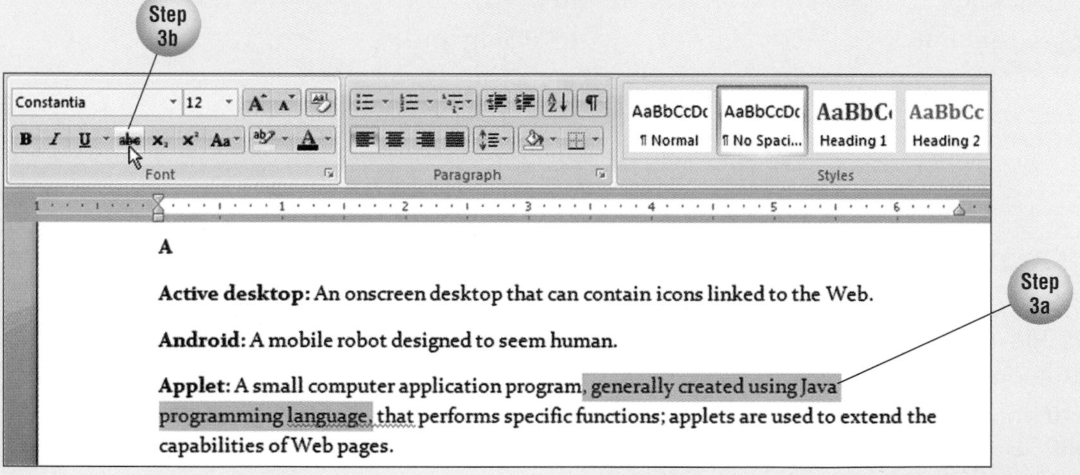

4. Change the font color by completing the following steps:
   a. Press Ctrl + A to select the entire document.
   b. Click the Font Color button arrow.
   c. Click Dark Blue (the second color from right in the *Standard Colors* section) at the drop-down gallery.
   d. Click outside the selected area to deselect text.

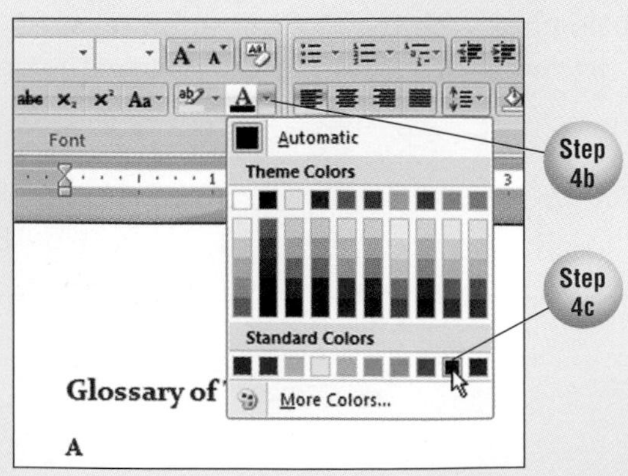

5. Highlight text in the document by completing the following steps:
   a. Click the Text Highlight Color button in the Font group. (This causes the mouse pointer to display as an I-beam pointer with a pen attached.)
   b. Select the term *Beta version* and the definition that follows.

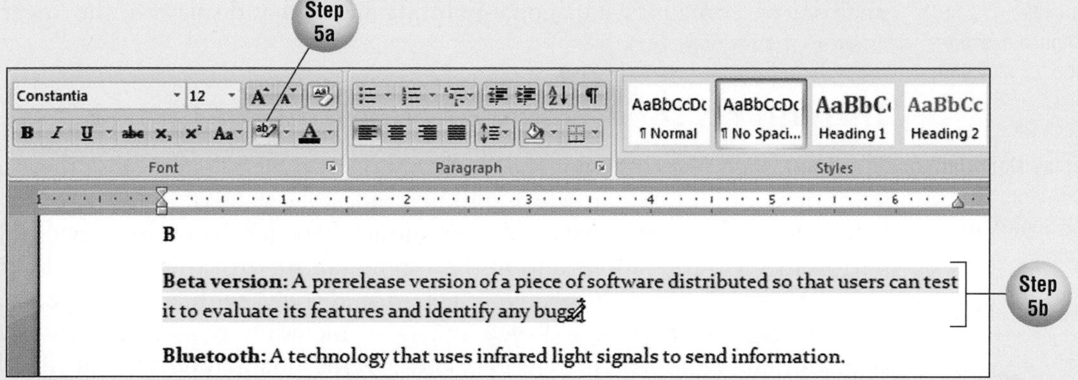

   c. Click the Text Highlight Color button arrow and then click a green color (you decide which green).
   d. Select the term *Cell* and the definition that follows.
   e. Click the Text Highlight Color button arrow and then click the yellow color that displays in the upper left corner of the drop-down gallery.
   f. Click the Text Highlight Color button to turn off highlighting.
6. Change the case of the title by selecting *Glossary of Terms* and then pressing Shift + F3. (This changes the case of the title text to uppercase.)
7. Apply italic formatting using the Mini toolbar by completing the following steps:
   a. Select the word *robot* located in the *Android* definition. (When you select the word, the Mini toolbar displays.)
   b. Click the Italic button on the Mini toolbar.
   c. Select the words *infrared light signals* located in the *Bluetooth* definition and then click the Italic button on the Mini toolbar.

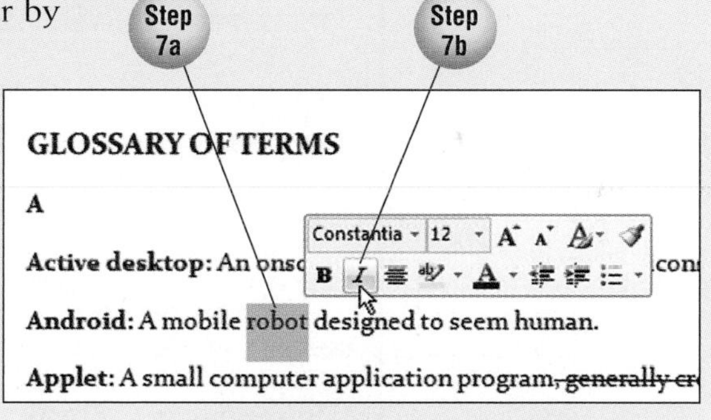

8. Save **C02Ex01.docx**.

Figure 2.3 Exercise 1C

Chinese abacus: Pebbles strung on a rod inside a frame. Pebbles in the upper part of an abacus correspond to 5×10^0, or 5, for the first column; 5×10^1, or 50, for the second column; 5×10^2, or 500, for the third column; and so on.

QUICK STEPS

Change Fonts
1. Click Font group dialog box launcher.
2. Choose desired options at dialog box.
3. Click OK.

Display Nonprinting Characters
Click Show/Hide ¶ button.
OR
Press Ctrl + Shift + *.

Show/Hide ¶

Changing Fonts at the Font Dialog Box

In addition to using the Font group buttons to apply font formatting, you can use options at the Font dialog box, shown in Figure 2.4, to change the typeface, type size, and typestyle of text as well as to apply font effects. Display the Font dialog box by clicking the Font group dialog box launcher. The dialog box launcher is a small square containing a diagonal-pointing arrow that displays in the lower right corner of the Font group.

Turning on the Display of Nonprinting Characters

The Font dialog box contains the *Hidden* option in the *Effects* section of the dialog box. With this option, you can select and then hide specific text. If you want to view the hidden text, turn on the display of nonprinting characters by clicking the Show/Hide ¶ button in the Paragraph group in the Home tab or with the keyboard shortcut Ctrl + Shift + *. When it is active, the button displays with an orange background. Hidden text displays with a dotted underline, including nonprinting characters such as paragraph symbols, tab symbols, and spacing characters. To redisplay hidden text, click the Show/Hide ¶ button to make it active, select the text, display the Font dialog box, and then remove the check mark from the *Hidden* option.

Figure 2.4 Font Dialog Box

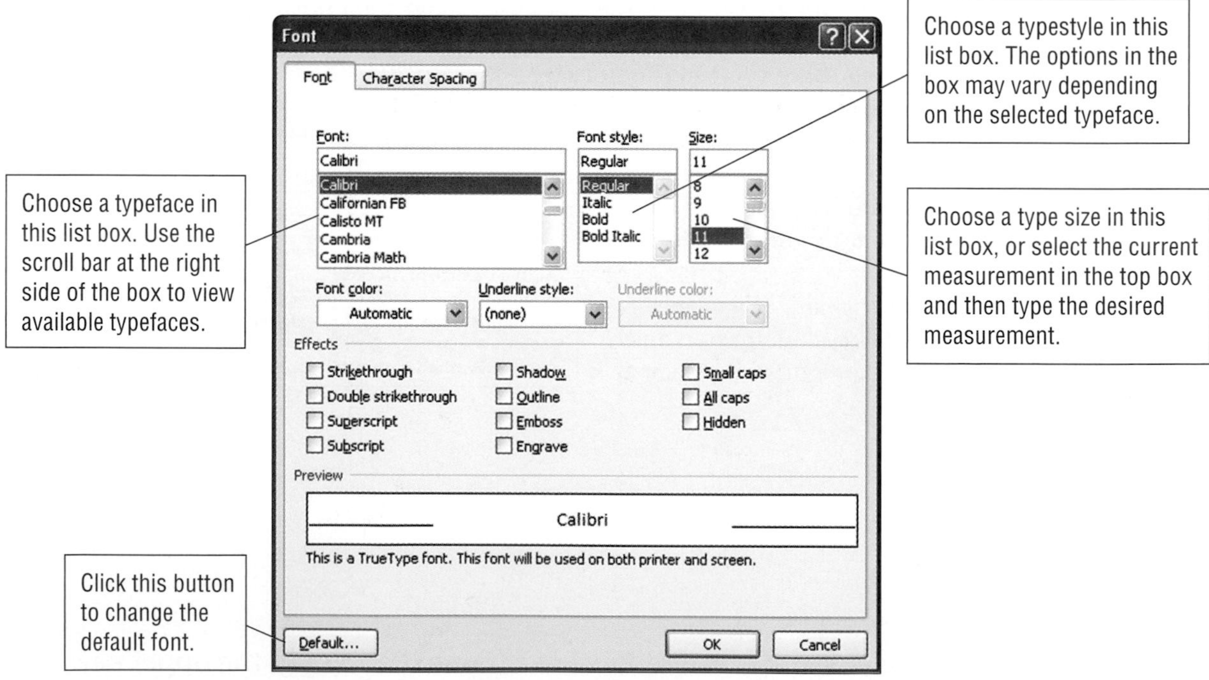

Exercise 1D

Changing the Font at the Font Dialog Box

1. With **C02Ex01.docx** open, press Ctrl + End to move the insertion point to the end of the document. (Make sure the insertion point is positioned below the last line of text.)
2. Type **Submitted by Marcus Jackson** and then press the Enter key.
3. Type **Monday, October 11, 2010**.
4. Change the font to 13-point Times New Roman and the font color to dark red by completing the following steps:
   a. Press Ctrl + A to select the entire document.
   b. Click the Font group dialog box launcher.
   c. At the Font dialog box, click the down-pointing arrow at the right side of the *Font* list box to scroll down the list box and then click *Times New Roman*.
   d. Click in the *Size* text box and then type **13**.
   e. Click the down-pointing arrow at the right side of the *Font color* list box and then click Dark Red at the color gallery (first option from the left in the *Standard Colors* section).
   f. Click OK to close the dialog box.

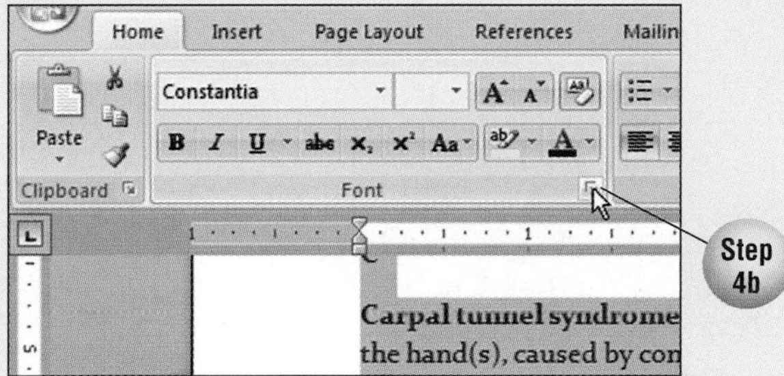

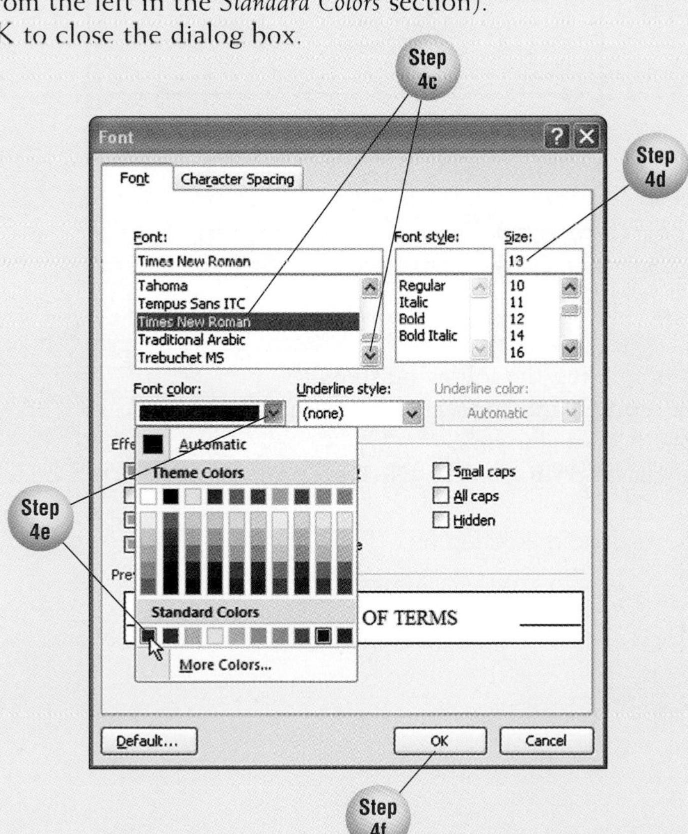

5. Double underline text by completing the following steps:
   a. Select *Monday, October 11, 2010.*
   b. Click the Font group dialog box launcher.
   c. At the Font dialog box, click the down-pointing arrow at the right side of the *Underline style* option box and then click the double-line option at the drop-down list.
   d. Click OK to close the dialog box.

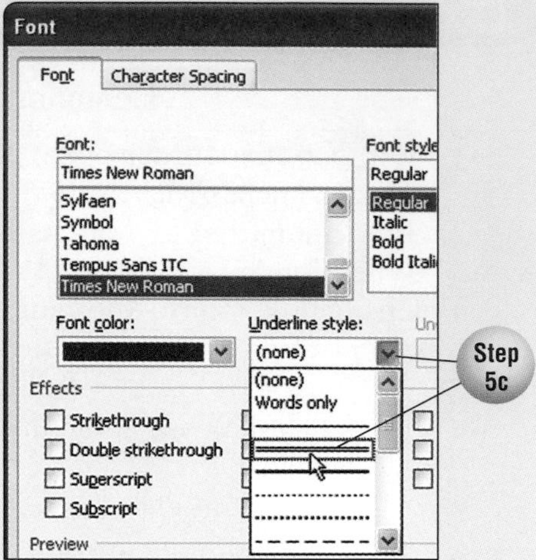

6. Change text to small caps by completing the following steps:
   a. Select the text *Submitted by Marcus Jackson* and *Monday, October 11, 2010.*
   b. Display the Font dialog box.
   c. Click the *Small caps* option in the *Effects* section. (This inserts a check mark in the check box.)
   d. Click OK to close the dialog box.

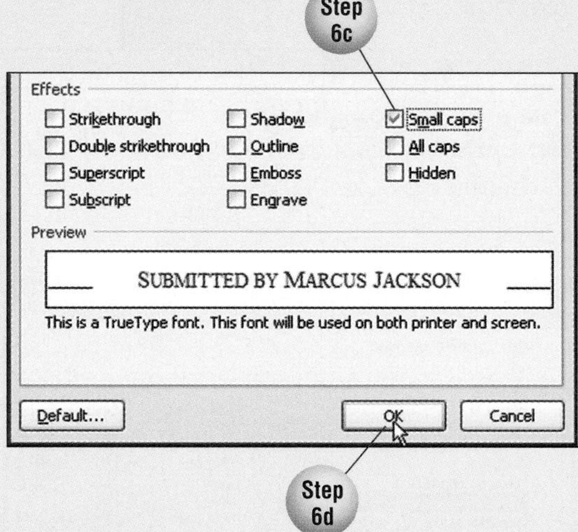

7. Hide text by completing the following steps:
   a. Select the term *Chinese abacus* and the definition that follows.
   b. Display the Font dialog box.
   c. Click the *Hidden* option in the *Effects* section. (This inserts a check mark in the check box.)
   d. Click OK to close the dialog box.

8. Click the Show/Hide ¶ button in the Paragraph group in the Home tab to turn on the display of nonprinting characters. (The hidden text is now visible and displays with a dotted underline.)
9. Redisplay the hidden text by completing the following steps:
   a. Select the term *Chinese abacus* and the definition that follows.
   b. Display the Font dialog box.
   c. Click the *Hidden* option in the *Effects* section to remove the check mark.
   d. Click OK to close the dialog box.
10. Click the Show/Hide ¶ button to turn off the display of nonprinting characters.
11. Save, print, and then close C02Ex01.docx.

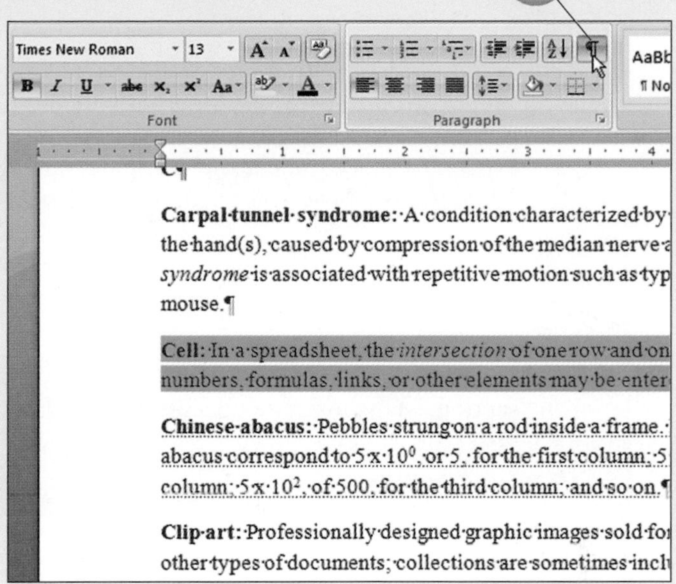

Applying Styles from a Quick Styles Set

Apply a Style
1. Position insertion point in paragraph of desired text.
2. Click More button in Styles group.
3. Click desired style.

Change Quick Styles Set
1. Click Change Styles button.
2. Point to Style Set.
3. Click desired set.

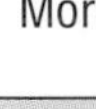
More

Word contains a number of predesigned formats grouped into style sets called Quick Styles. Four of the styles in the default Quick Styles set display in the Styles group in the Home tab. You can display additional styles by clicking the More button that displays at the right side of the four styles. This displays a drop-down gallery of style choices. To apply a style, position the insertion point in the paragraph of text to which you want the style applied, click the More button at the right side of the styles in the Styles group, and then click the desired style at the drop-down gallery.

As noted earlier, Word applies some default formatting to documents, including 10 points of spacing after paragraphs and a line spacing of 1.15. You can remove this default formatting as well as any character formatting applied to text in your document by applying the No Spacing style to your text. This style is one of the styles that displays in the Styles group in the Home tab.

Changing the Quick Styles Set

To change to a different Quick Styles set, click the Change Styles button in the Styles group in the Home tab and then point to Style Set. This displays a side menu with Quick Styles sets. Click the desired set, and the style formatting changes in the styles that display in the Styles group.

Exercise 2A

Applying Quick Styles

1. Open **Document03.docx**.
2. Save the document with Save As and name it **C02Ex02**.
3. Remove the 10 points of spacing after paragraphs and change the line spacing to 1 by completing the following steps:
   a. Press Ctrl + A to select the entire document.
   b. Click the No Spacing style in the Styles group in the Home tab.

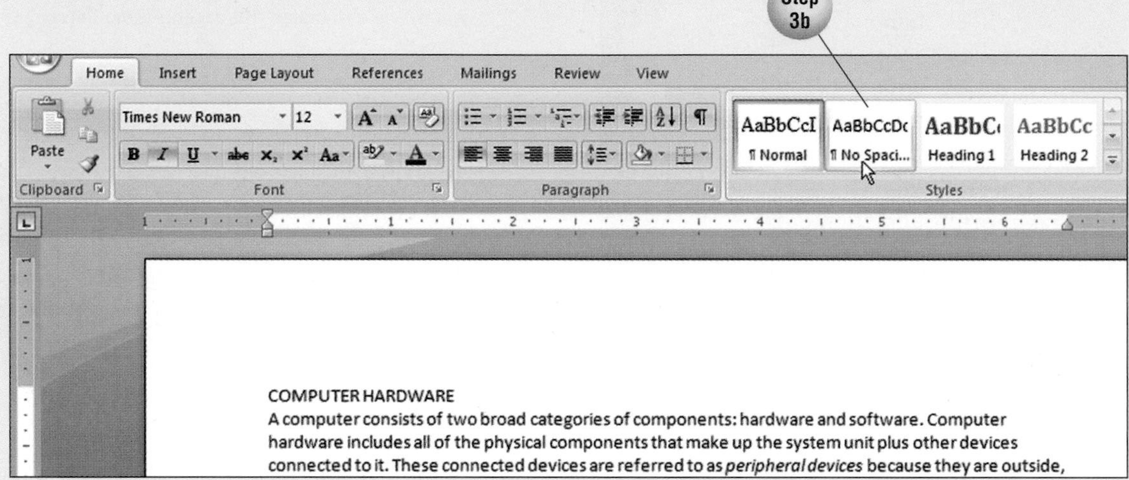

4. Position the insertion point on any character in the title *COMPUTER HARDWARE* and then click the Heading 1 style that displays in the Styles group.

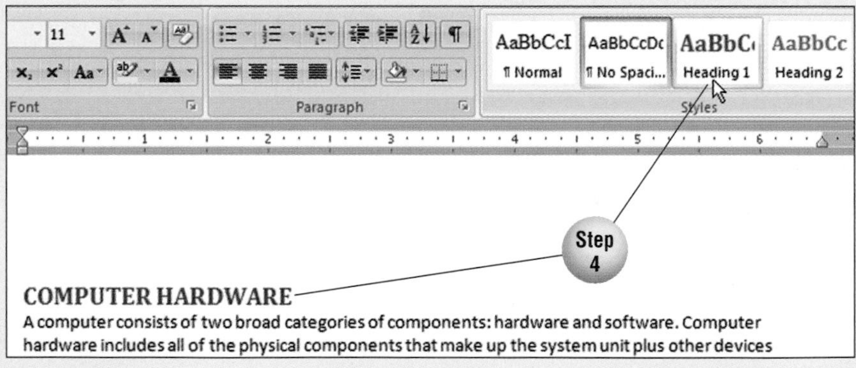

5. Position the insertion point on any character in the heading *System Unit* and then click the Heading 2 style that displays in the Styles group.

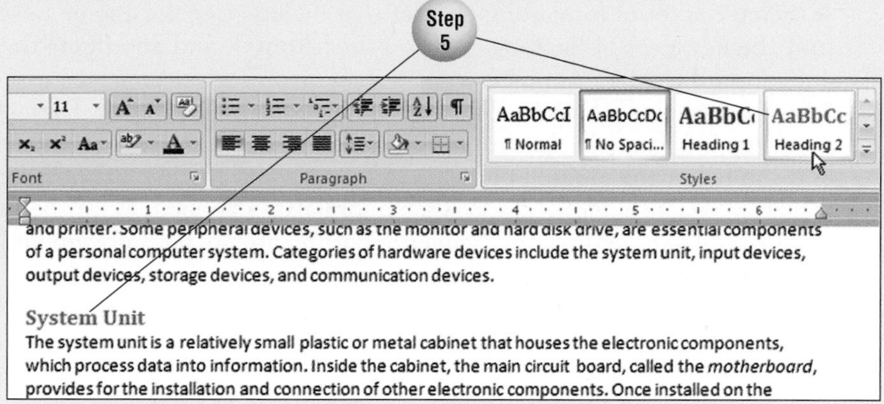

6. Position the insertion point on any character in the heading *Input Devices* and then click the Heading 2 style in the Styles group.
7. Position the insertion point on any character in the heading *Output Devices* and then click the Heading 2 style in the Styles group.
8. Click the Change Styles button in the Styles group, point to Style Set, and then click *Modern*. (Notice how the Heading 1 and Heading 2 formatting changes.)

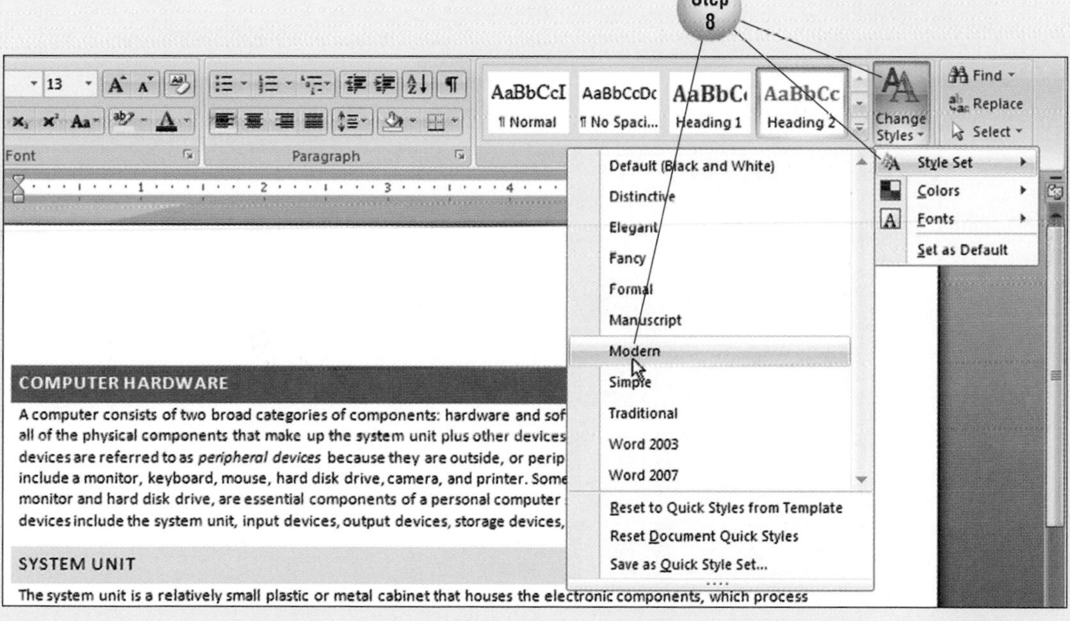

9. Save and then print **C02Ex02.docx**.

QUICK STEPS

Apply a Theme
1. Click Page Layout tab.
2. Click Themes button.
3. Click desired theme.

Applying a Theme

Word provides a number of themes you can use to format text in your document. A theme is a set of formatting choices that includes a color theme (a set of colors), a font theme (a set of heading and body text fonts), and an effects theme (a set of lines and fill effects). Applying a theme can give your documents a professional look. To apply a theme, click the Page Layout tab and then click the Themes button in the Themes group. At the drop-down gallery that displays, click the desired theme. You can hover the mouse pointer over a theme and the live preview feature will display your document with the theme formatting applied. With the live preview feature, you can see how the theme formatting affects your document before you make your final choice.

Exercise 2B

Applying a Theme to Text in a Document

1. With **C02Ex02.docx** open, click the Page Layout tab and then click the Themes button in the Themes group.
2. At the drop-down gallery, hover your mouse pointer over each theme and notice how the text formatting changes in your document.
3. Click the *Concourse* theme.

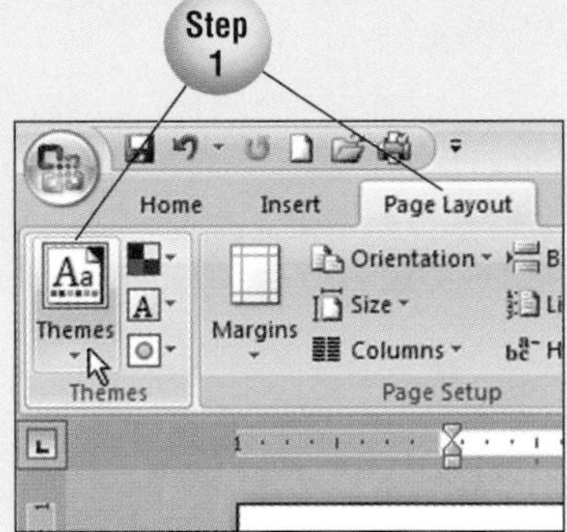

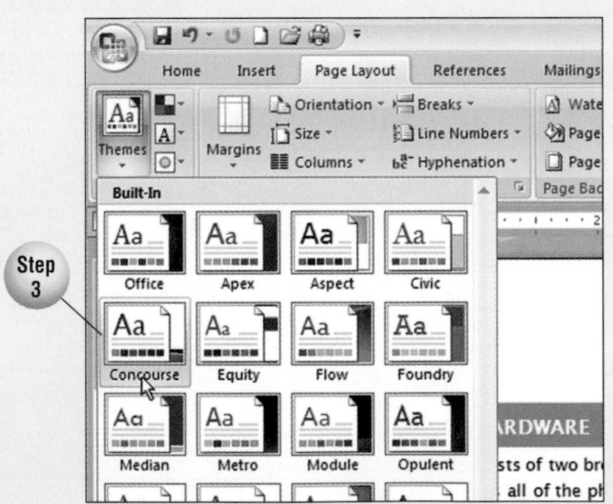

4. Save and then print **C02Ex02.docx**.

Customizing Themes

You can customize a theme with the three buttons that display at the right side of the Themes button. A theme contains specific color formatting, which you can change with options from the Theme Colors button in the Themes group. Click this button, and a drop-down gallery displays with named color schemes. The names of the color schemes correspond to the names of the themes. Each theme applies specific fonts, which you can change with options from the Theme Fonts button in the Themes group. Click this button and a drop-down gallery displays with font choices. Each font group in the drop-down gallery contains two choices. The first choice in the group is the font that is applied to headings and the second choice is the font that is applied to body text in the document. If you are formatting a document containing graphics with lines and fills, you can apply a specific theme of effects with options at the Theme Effects drop-down gallery.

Change Theme Color

1. Click Page Layout tab.
2. Click Theme Colors button.
3. Click desired theme color.

Change Theme Fonts

1. Click Page Layout tab.
2. Click Theme Fonts button.
3. Click desired theme font.

Change Theme Effect

1. Click Page Layout tab.
2. Click Theme Effects button.
3. Click desired theme effect.

Theme Colors

Theme Fonts

Theme Effects

Exercise 2C

Customizing a Theme

1. With **C02Ex02.docx** open, click the Theme Colors button in the Themes group and then click *Foundry* at the drop-down gallery. (Notice how the colors in the title and headings change.)
2. Click the Theme Fonts button and then click the *Aspect* option. (Notice how the document text font changes.)

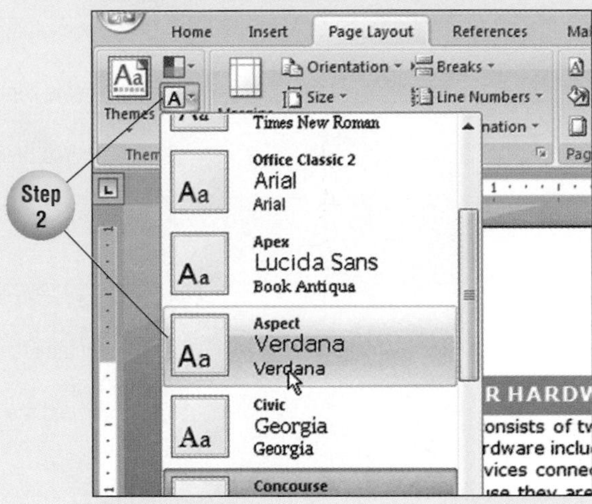

3. Save, print, and then close **C02Ex02.docx**.

Adjust Character Spacing
1. Click Font group dialog box launcher.
2. Click Character Spacing tab.
3. Change desired option.
4. Click OK.

Adjusting Character Spacing

Each typeface is designed with a specific amount of space between characters. You can change this character spacing with options at the Font dialog box with the Character Spacing tab selected, as shown in Figure 2.5. To display this dialog box, click the Font group dialog box launcher located in the lower right corner in the Font group. At the Font dialog box, click the Character Spacing tab.

Figure 2.5 Font Dialog Box with Character Spacing Tab Selected

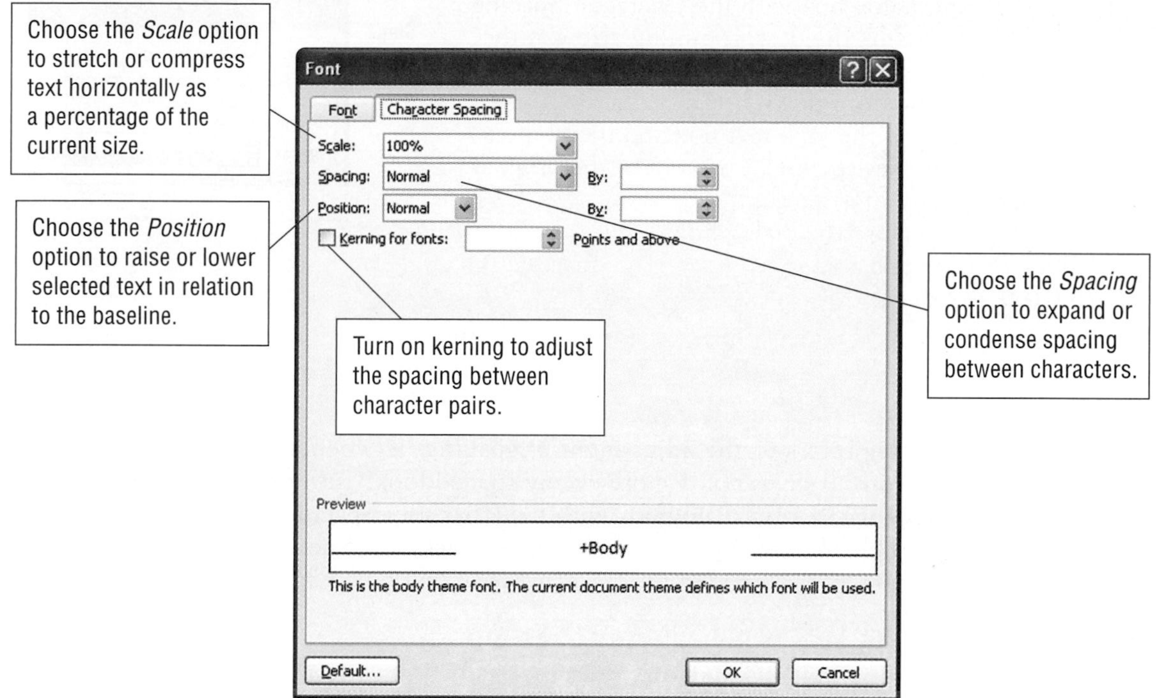

Choose the *Scale* option to stretch or compress text horizontally as a percentage of the current size. You can choose a percentage from 1 to 600. Expand or condense the spacing between characters with the *Spacing* option. Choose either the *Expanded* or *Condensed* option and then enter the desired percentage amount in the *By* text box. Raise or lower selected text in relation to the baseline with the *Position* option. Choose either the *Raised* or *Lowered* option and then enter the percentage amount in the *By* text box.

Exercise 3A

Adjusting Character Spacing and Scaling and Turning on Kerning

1. Open **Notice01.docx**.
2. Save the document with Save As and name it **C02Ex03**.
3. Compress text horizontally by completing the following steps:
    a. Select the entire document.
    b. Display the Font dialog box by clicking the Font group dialog box launcher.

c. At the Font dialog box with the Character Spacing tab selected, click the down-pointing arrow at the right side of the *Spacing* option and then click *Expanded* at the drop-down list.
d. Select 100% in the *Scale* text box and then type 97. (This compresses text to 97 percent of the original horizontal spacing.)
e. Click OK to close the dialog box.
f. Deselect the text.
4. Save **C02Ex03.docx**.

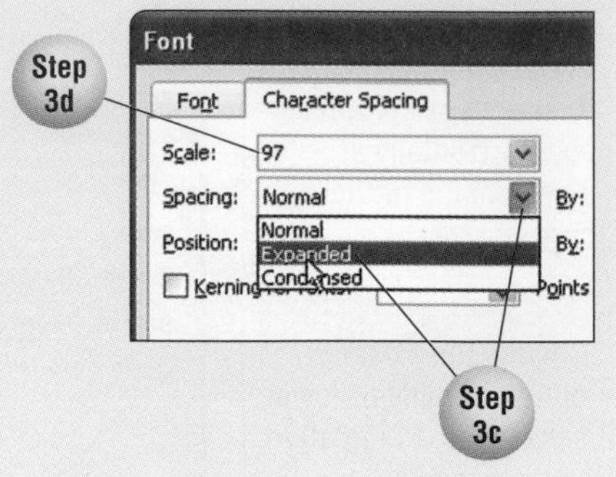

Kerning refers to the adjustment of spacing between certain character combinations. It gives text a more evenly spaced look. Turn on automatic kerning by displaying the Font dialog box with the Character Spacing tab selected and then inserting a check mark in the *Kerning for fonts* check box. Specify the beginning point size that you want kerned in the *Points and above* text box. Click OK to close the dialog box.

Exercise 3B

Kerning Text

1. With **C02Ex03.docx** open, adjust character spacing and turn on kerning by completing the following steps:
   a. Select the entire document.
   b. Click the Font group dialog box launcher.
   c. At the Font dialog box, click the Font tab and then change the *Font* to *Bookman Old Style* and the *Size* to *14*.
   d. Click the Character Spacing tab.
   e. Click the down-pointing arrow at the right side of the *Scale* option and then click 100% at the drop-down list.
   f. Click the down-pointing arrow at the right side of the *Spacing* option and then click *Normal* at the drop-down list.
   g. Click in the *Kerning for fonts* check box. (This inserts a check mark in the check box and also inserts *14* in the *Points and above* text box.)
   h. Click OK to close the dialog box.
   i. Deselect the text.
2. Save, print, and then close **C02Ex03.docx**.

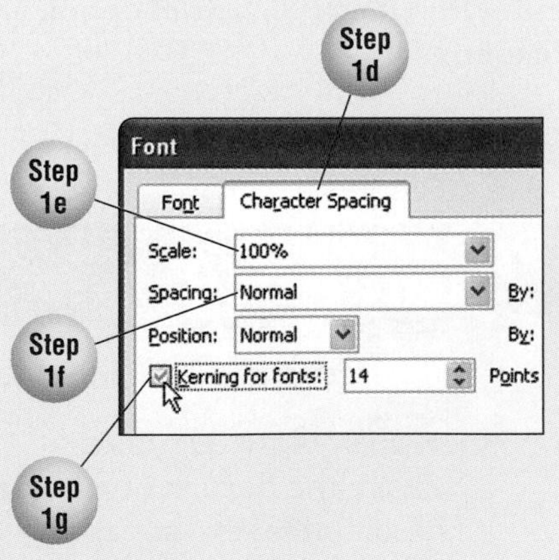

Chapter Summary

- The appearance of a document on the document screen and how it looks when printed is called the format.
- The top row in the Font group in the Home tab contains buttons for changing the font and font size. The bottom row contains buttons for applying typestyles and effects.
- A font consists of three elements: typeface, type size, and typestyle.
- A typeface (font) is a set of characters with a common design and shape. Typefaces are either monospaced, allotting the same amount of horizontal space to each character, or proportional, allotting a varying amount of space for each character. Proportional typefaces are divided into two main categories: serif and sans serif.
- Type size is measured in point size—the higher the point size, the larger the characters.
- A typestyle is a variation of style within a certain typeface. You can apply typestyle formatting with buttons in the Font group.
- With buttons in the Font group, you can apply font effects such as superscript, subscript, and strikethrough.
- Some buttons in the Font group have corresponding keyboard shortcuts. Refer to Table 2.2 for a list of these shortcuts.
- The Mini toolbar automatically displays above selected text. Use buttons on this toolbar to apply formatting to selected text. Turn off the Mini toolbar by removing the check mark from the *Show Mini Toolbar on selection* option in the Word Options dialog box with the *Popular* option selected.
- With options at the Font dialog box, you can change the font, font size, and font style and apply specific effects. Display this dialog box by clicking the Font group dialog box launcher.
- Click the Show/Hide ¶ button in the Paragraph group in the Home tab or press Ctrl + Shift + * to turn on the display of nonprinting characters. With the display of nonprinting characters turned on, hidden text will display with a dotted underline in the document.
- A Word document contains a number of predesigned formats grouped into style sets called Quick Styles. Change to a different Quick Styles set by clicking the Change Styles button in the Styles group in the Home tab, pointing to Style Set, and then clicking the desired set.
- Word provides a number of themes, which are a set of formatting choices that include a color theme (a set of colors), a font theme (a set of heading and body text fonts), and an effects theme (a set of lines and fill effects). Apply a theme and change theme colors, fonts, and effects with buttons in the Themes group in the Page Layout tab.
- Adjust character spacing and turn on kerning with options at the Font dialog box with the Character Spacing tab selected.

Commands review

FEATURE	RIBBON TAB, GROUP	BUTTON	KEYBOARD SHORTCUT
Bold text	Home, Font	B	Ctrl + B
Change case of text	Home, Font	Aa	Shift + F3
Change Quick Styles set	Home, Styles		
Character spacing	Home, Font		
Clear all formatting	Home, Font		
Clear character formatting			Ctrl + spacebar
Decrease font size	Home, Font	A	Ctrl + <
Display nonprinting characters	Home, Paragraph	¶	Ctrl + Shift + *
Font	Home, Font	Calibri (Body)	
Font color	Home, Font	A	
Font dialog box	Home, Font		Ctrl + Shift + F
Highlight text	Home, Font	ab	
Increase font size	Home, Font	A	Ctrl + >
Italicize text	Home, Font	I	Ctrl + I
Strikethrough text	Home, Font	abc	
Subscript text	Home, Font	x_2	Ctrl + =
Superscript text	Home, Font	x^2	Ctrl + Shift + +
Theme Colors	Page Layout, Themes		
Theme Fonts	Page Layout, Themes	A	
Themes	Page Layout, Themes	Aa	
Underline text	Home, Font	U	Ctrl + U

Reviewing key points

Completion: In the space provided at the right, indicate the correct term, command, or number.

1. The Bold button is located in this group in the Home tab. ____________________
2. A font consists of a typeface, a typestyle, and this. ____________________
3. Proportional typefaces are divided into two main categories, serif and this. ____________________
4. This is the keyboard shortcut to italicize selected text. ____________________
5. Click this button in the Font group to remove all formatting from selected text. ____________________
6. This term refers to text that is raised slightly above the regular text line. ____________________
7. This automatically displays above selected text. ____________________
8. Click this to display the Font dialog box. ____________________
9. Click this button in the Paragraph group in the Home tab to turn on the display of nonprinting characters. ____________________
10. A Word document contains a number of predesigned formats grouped into style sets called this. ____________________
11. Apply a theme and change theme colors, fonts, and effects with buttons in the Themes group in this tab. ____________________
12. Adjust character spacing at this dialog box with the Character Spacing tab selected. ____________________

Applying your skills

Assessment 1 Create and Format a Utility Program Document

1. At a blank document, type the document shown in Figure 2.6.
2. Bold, italicize, and underline the text as shown.
3. Save the completed document with the name **C02A01**.
4. Print **C02A01.docx**.
5. Select the entire document and then change to a serif typeface.
6. With the entire document still selected, display the Font dialog box with the Character Spacing tab selected, change the *Spacing* option to *Expanded* (by 1 point), turn on kerning, and then close the dialog box.
7. Select *Utility Programs*, remove underlining, change to uppercase letters, and then deselect the text.
8. Remove the bolding from the text *Antivirus software:*, *Backup utility:*, *File compression utility:*, *Device driver:*, and *Uninstaller utility:* and insert underlining instead. (Do not underline the colon [:] after each utility.)
9. Select and then hide the utility *Backup utility:* and the sentence that follows it.
10. Select and then hide the last sentence in the last paragraph (the sentence that begins *Several companies produce software . . .*).
11. Turn on the display of nonprinting characters, unhide the utility *Backup utility:* and the sentence that follows it.
12. Turn off the display of nonprinting characters.
13. Save, print, and then close **C02A01.docx**.

Assessment 2 Format a Memo

1. Open **Memo01.docx**.
2. Save the memo with Save As and name it **C02A02**.
3. Select the book title, *Managing Network Security*, remove the underlining, and then add italics.
4. Select the book title, *Network Management*, remove the underlining, and then add italics.
5. Select the book title, *Internet Security*, remove the underlining, and then add italics.
6. Select the book title, *Protecting and Securing Data*, remove the underlining, and then add italics.
7. Select and bold the headings *DATE:*, *TO:*, *FROM:*, and *SUBJECT:*.
8. Select the subject *Network and Internet Books* and change the case of the text to uppercase.
9. Insert your initials at the end of the document where you see the *XX*. Change the document name after your initials from **Memo01.docx** to **C02A02.docx**.
10. Select the entire document and then change to the *Cambria* font.
11. Save, print, and then close **C02A02.docx**.

Figure 2.6 Assessment 1

<u>**Utility Programs**</u>

A *utility program* performs a single maintenance or repair task and is useful for correcting many of the problems that computer users are likely to encounter. Some of the most popular kinds of utility programs include the following:

Antivirus software: This type of software program protects the computer system from a virus attack.

Backup utility: This utility makes a backup copy of files on a separate disk.

File compression utility: Use this utility to reduce the size of files so they take up less disk space.

Device driver: This utility allows hardware devices, such as disk drives and printers, to work with the computer system.

Uninstaller utility: Remove programs and related system files with this utility.

An operating system typically includes several utility programs that are preinstalled at the factory. Users can also purchase and install additional utilities programs of their choice. Several companies produce software suites containing a variety of utility programs.

Assessment 3 Format a Training Announcement

1. Open **Notice02.docx**.
2. Save the document with Save As and name it **C02A03**.
3. Select the entire document.
4. Change the font to 16-point Candara bold, the font color to red, and apply the *Shadow* effect.
5. Save, print, and then close **C02A03.docx**.

Assessment 4 Create and Format a Memo

1. At a blank document, type the memo shown in Figure 2.7 in a traditional-style memo (refer to Appendix B at the end of this textbook for information on typing a memo). Italicize, superscript, and subscript text as shown in the memo.
2. After typing the memo, select the entire memo, and then change the font to 12-point Constantia. (If neccessary, realign the headings in the memo.)
3. Save the memo with the name **C02A04**.
4. Print and then close **C02A04.docx**.

Figure 2.7 Assessment 4

DATE: February 22, 2010; TO: Jolie Anderson; FROM: Ronald Chen; SUBJECT: STATISTICAL ANALYSIS

I have been running an analysis on the areas mentioned in your February 16 memo. Completing the computations has brought up the following questions:

With smaller section ratios of r^1 and r^2 (.10 to .25)[1], what will be the yield increase?

What is the interaction effect on the scores of X_1, X_2, and X_3?

Chapter 3

Aligning and Indenting Paragraphs

Tutorial 3.1
Enhancing a Document
Tutorial 3.2
Using Formatting Features

Performance Objectives

Upon successful completion of Chapter 3, you will be able to:

- Change the alignment of text in paragraphs
- Indent text in paragraphs
- Increase and decrease spacing before and after paragraphs
- Repeat the last action
- Automate formatting with Format Painter
- Change line spacing in a document
- Apply numbering and bullet formatting to text
- Reveal and compare formatting

As you learned previously, a paragraph in Word is any amount of text followed by the press of the Enter key. Word provides a variety of options for formatting text in a paragraph. In this chapter, you will learn to change text alignment in a paragraph, indent text, change the line spacing, and insert numbers and bullets. You will also learn how to apply formatting with Format Painter and how to reveal and compare paragraph formatting.

Note: Before beginning computer exercises for this chapter, copy to your storage medium the Chapter03 folder from the CD that accompanies this textbook and then make Chapter03 the active folder.

QUICK STEPS

Change Paragraph Alignment
Click desired alignment button in Paragraph group.
OR
1. Click Paragraph group dialog box launcher.
2. Click *Alignment* option down-pointing arrow.
3. Click desired alignment.
4. Click OK.

Changing Paragraph Alignment

The Paragraph group in the Home tab contains a number of buttons that you can use to format paragraphs in a document. The four buttons in the bottom row change the alignment of text within a paragraph. In a Word document, paragraphs are aligned at the left margin and ragged at the right margin by default. You can change this alignment to center, right, or justified alignment with the alignment buttons in the Paragraph group or with keyboard shortcuts. The keyboard shortcuts and the alignment buttons in the Paragraph group are shown in Table 3.1.

Table 3.1 Paragraph Alignment Buttons and Commands

To align text	*Paragraph Group Button*	*Shortcut Command*
At the left margin		Ctrl + L
Between margins		Ctrl + E
At the right margin		Ctrl + R
At the left and right margins		Ctrl + J

You can change the text alignment before you type a paragraph, or you can change the alignment of an existing paragraph. If you change the alignment before typing text, the alignment formatting is inserted in the paragraph mark. As you type text and press Enter, the paragraph formatting is continued. For example, if you click the Center button in the Paragraph group, type a paragraph of text, and then press the Enter key, the center alignment formatting is still active and the insertion point displays in the middle of the left and right margins.

To return to the default alignment (left aligned), click the Align Text Left button in the Paragraph group. You can also return all paragraph formatting to the default with the keyboard shortcut Ctrl + Q. This keyboard shortcut removes paragraph formatting from selected text. If you want to remove all formatting—character and paragraph—from selected text, click the Clear Formatting button in the Font group.

To change the alignment of existing text in a paragraph, position the insertion point anywhere within the paragraph. You do not need to select the entire paragraph. To change the alignment of several adjacent paragraphs in a document, select a portion of the first paragraph through a portion of the last paragraph. You do not need to select all of the text in the paragraphs.

Displaying Formatting Marks

Show/Hide ¶

As you learned in Chapter 2, you can turn on the display of nonprinting characters by clicking the Show/Hide ¶ button in the Paragraph group in the Home tab. When you make a formatting change to a paragraph, the formatting is inserted in the paragraph mark, which is visible if the display of nonprinting characters is turned on. By default, all nonprinting characters display on the screen when you click the Show/Hide ¶ button. You can turn on the display of specific characters only by using options at the Word Options dialog box with *Display* selected, as shown in Figure 3.1. Display this dialog box by clicking the Office button, clicking the Word Options button, and then clicking *Display* in the left panel. Insert a check mark in the check boxes in the *Always show these formatting marks on the screen* section to select those nonprinting characters that you want to display.

Figure 3.1 Word Options Dialog Box with Display Option Selected

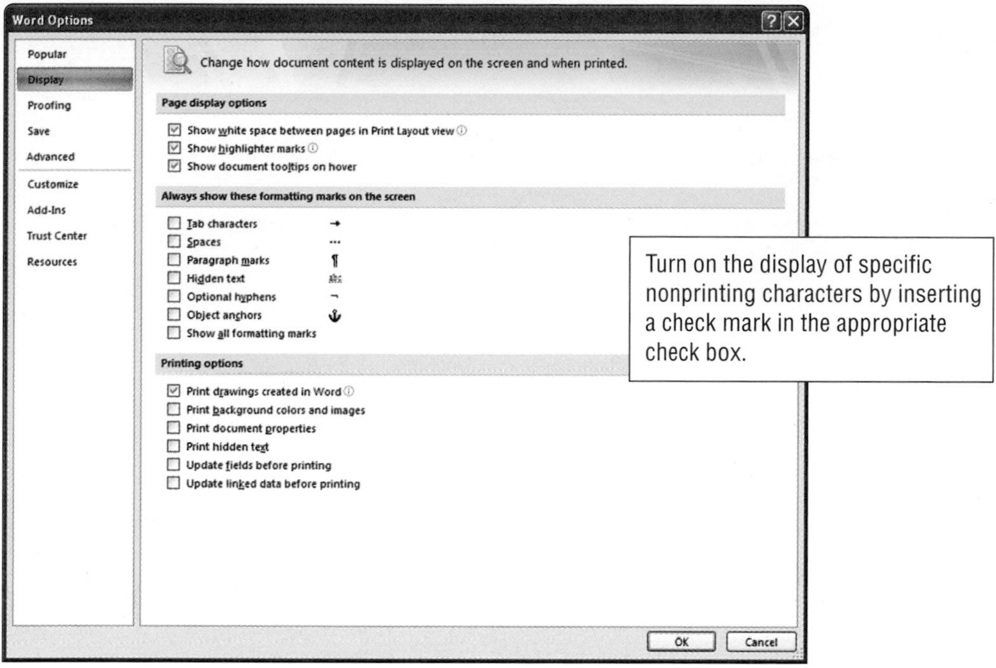

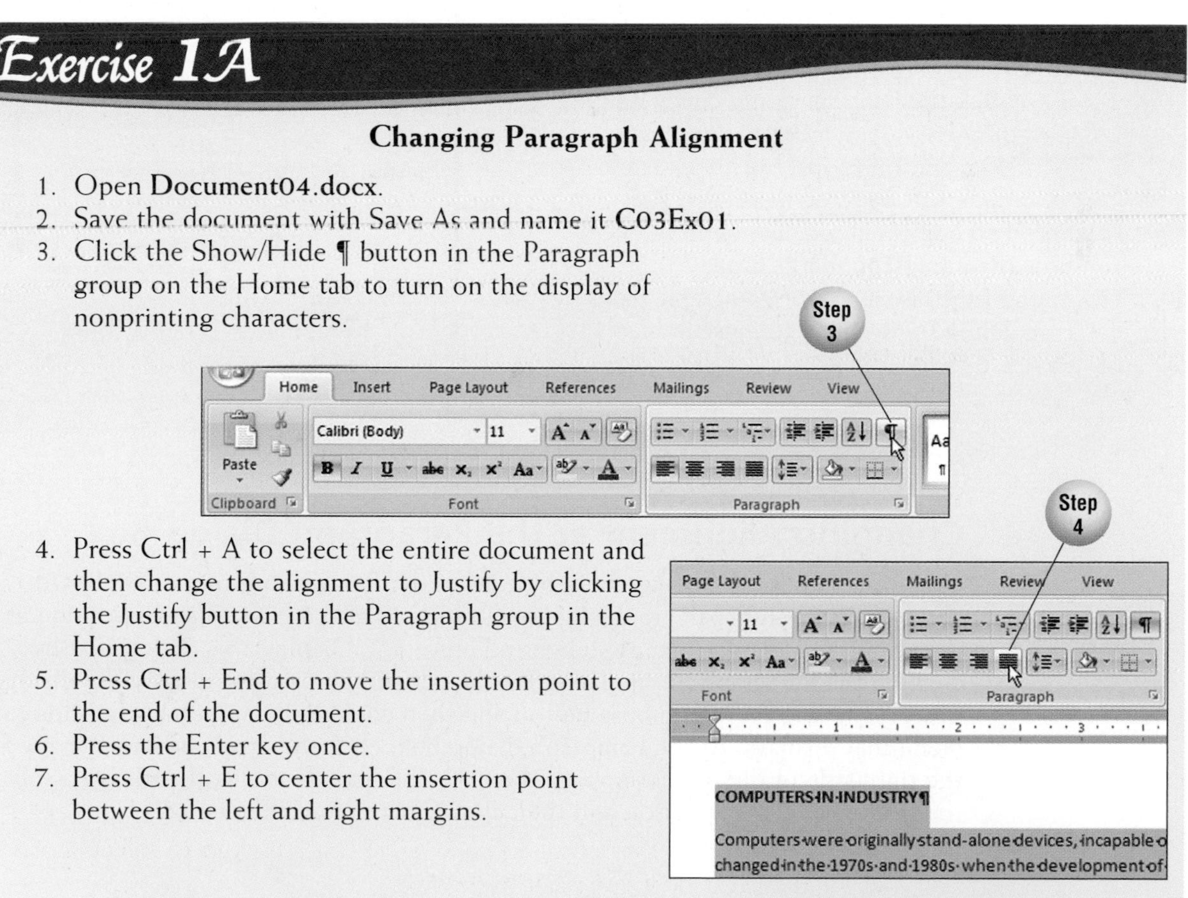

Exercise 1A

Changing Paragraph Alignment

1. Open **Document04.docx**.
2. Save the document with Save As and name it **C03Ex01**.
3. Click the Show/Hide ¶ button in the Paragraph group on the Home tab to turn on the display of nonprinting characters.
4. Press Ctrl + A to select the entire document and then change the alignment to Justify by clicking the Justify button in the Paragraph group in the Home tab.
5. Press Ctrl + End to move the insertion point to the end of the document.
6. Press the Enter key once.
7. Press Ctrl + E to center the insertion point between the left and right margins.

8. Type **Prepared by Christian Samora**.
9. Press Shift + Enter and then type **Edited by Martina Sanchez**.

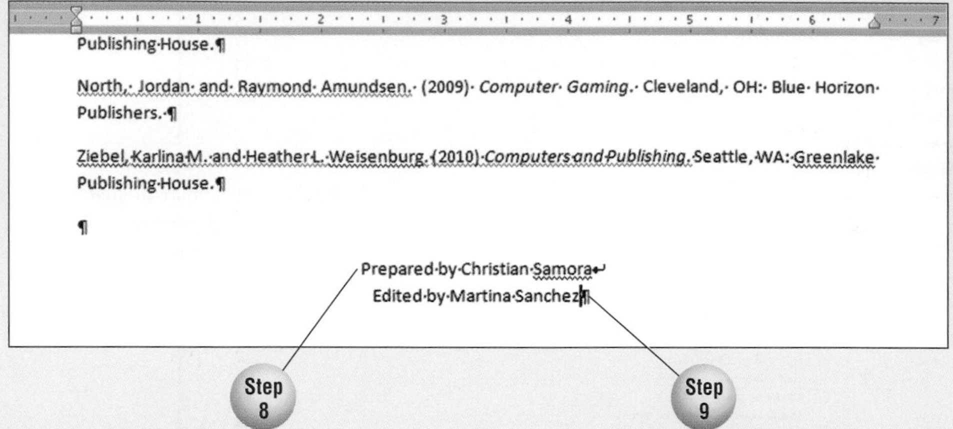

10. Click the Show/Hide ¶ button in the Paragraph group in the Home tab to turn off the display of nonprinting characters.
11. Turn on the display of paragraph marks only by completing the following steps:
    a. Click the Office button and then click the Word Options button located toward the bottom right side of the drop-down list.
    b. At the Word Options dialog box, click the *Display* option in the left panel.
    c. Click the *Paragraph marks* check box in the *Always show these formatting marks on the screen* section to insert a check mark.
    d. Click OK to close the dialog box.
12. Scroll through the document and notice how the paragraph marks display.
13. Turn off the display of the paragraph marks by completing steps similar to those in Step 11.
14. Save **C03Ex01.docx**.

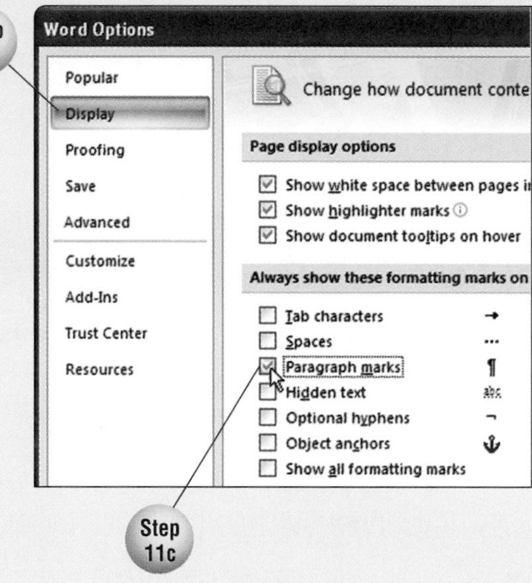

Changing Alignment at the Paragraph Dialog Box

In addition to using the alignment buttons in the Paragraph group or keyboard shortcuts to change paragraph alignment, you can also use the *Alignment* option at the Paragraph dialog box, as shown in Figure 3.2. Display this dialog box by clicking the Paragraph group dialog box launcher. You can also display the dialog box by clicking the *right* mouse button and then clicking Paragraph at the shortcut menu that displays. At the Paragraph dialog box, click the down-pointing arrow at the right side of the *Alignment* option box. At the drop-down list that displays, click the desired alignment option and then click OK to close the dialog box.

Figure 3.2 Paragraph Dialog Box with Alignment Options Displayed

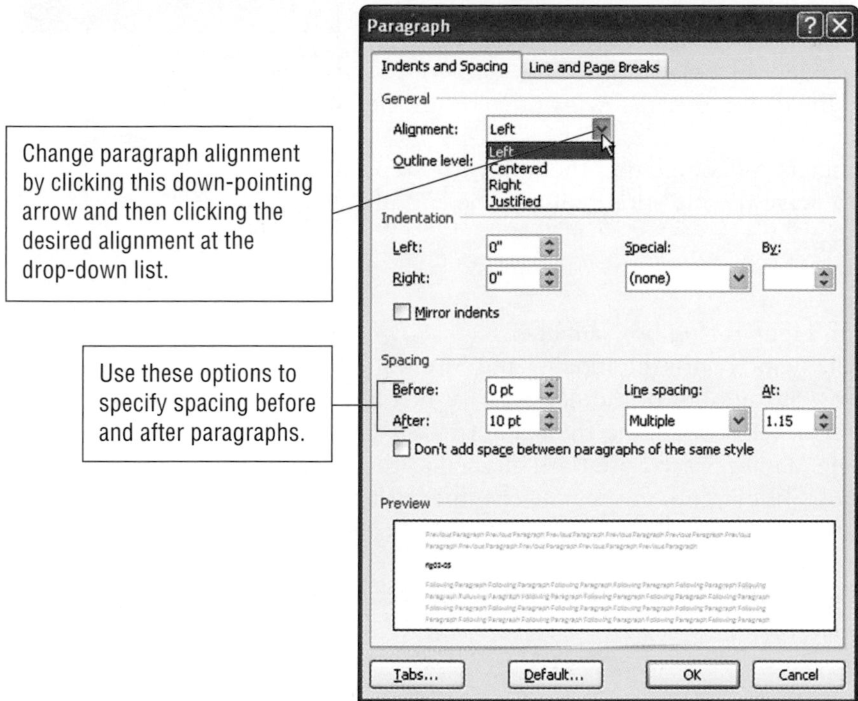

Exercise 1B

Changing Paragraph Alignment at the Paragraph Dialog Box

1. With C03Ex01.docx open, change the paragraph alignment by completing the following steps:
   a. Select the entire document.
   b. Click the Paragraph group dialog box launcher.

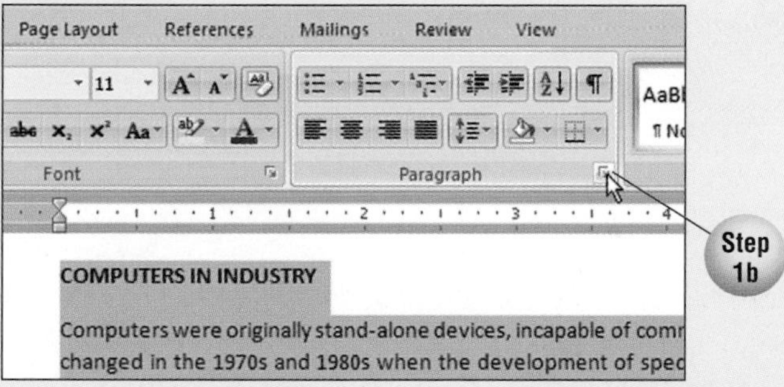

c. At the Paragraph dialog box with the Indents and Spacing tab selected, click the down-pointing arrow at the right of the *Alignment* list box and then click *Left*.

d. Click OK to close the dialog box.
e. Deselect the text.

2. Change paragraph alignment by completing the following steps:
   a. Press Ctrl + End to move the insertion point to the end of the document.
   b. Position the insertion point on any character in the text *Prepared by Christian Samora*.
   c. Click the Paragraph group dialog box launcher.
   d. At the Paragraph dialog box with the Indents and Spacing tab selected, click the down-pointing arrow at the right of the *Alignment* list box and then click *Right*.
   e. Click OK. (The line of text containing the name *Christian Samora* and the line of text containing the name *Martina Sanchez* are both aligned at the right because you used the New Line command, Shift + End, to separate the lines of text without creating a new paragraph.)
3. Save **C03Ex01.docx**.

Indenting Text in Paragraphs

QUICK STEPS

Indent Text in Paragraphs
Drag indent marker(s) on Ruler.
OR
Press keyboard shortcut.
OR
1. Click Paragraph group dialog box launcher.
2. Insert measurement in *Left*, *Right*, and/or *By* text box.
3. Click OK.

View Ruler

By now you are familiar with Word's word wrap feature, which ends lines and wraps the insertion point to the next line. You can indent the first line of text in a paragraph, indent all text in a paragraph, or indent the second and subsequent lines of a paragraph (called a hanging indent). You can indent text from the left margin, the right margin, or both. Several methods are available for indenting text: using buttons in the Paragraph group in either the Home tab or the Page Layout tab, using markers on the Ruler, using options at the Paragraph dialog box with the Indents and Spacing tab selected, or using keyboard shortcuts. The various methods for indenting text are shown in Table 3.2. The indent markers and Alignment button on the Ruler are shown in Figure 3.3. To display the Ruler, click the View Ruler button located at the top of the vertical scroll bar.

Figure 3.3 Ruler and Indent Markers

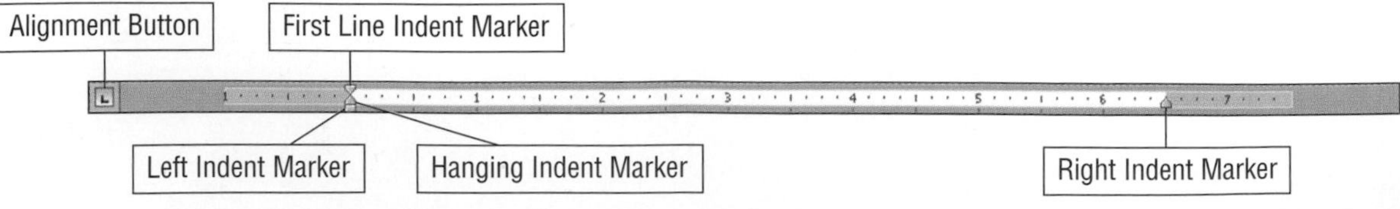

Table 3.2 **Methods for Indenting Text**

Indent	***Methods for Indenting***
First line of paragraph	• Press the Tab key. • Display Paragraph dialog box, click the down-pointing arrow to the right of the *Special* list box, click *First line*, and then click OK. • Drag the first line indent marker on the Ruler. • Click the Alignment button located at the left side of the Ruler until the First Line Indent button displays and then click on the Ruler at the desired location.
Text from left margin	• Click the Increase Indent button in the Paragraph group in the Home tab to increase the indent or click the Decrease Indent button to decrease the indent. • Display the Paragraph dialog box, type the desired indent measurement in the *Left* measurement box, and then click OK. • Drag the left indent marker on the Ruler. • Press Ctrl + M to increase the indent or press Ctrl + Shift + M to decrease the indent. • Insert a measurement in the Indent Left measurement box in the Paragraph group in the Page Layout tab.
Text from right margin	• Display the Paragraph dialog box, type the desired indent measurement in the *Right* measurement box, and then click OK. • Drag the right indent marker on the Ruler. • Insert a measurement in the Indent Right measurement box in the Paragraph group in the Page Layout tab.
All lines of text except the first (called a hanging indent)	• Display the Paragraph dialog box, click the down-pointing arrow at the right side of the *Special* list box, click *Hanging*, and then click OK. • Press Ctrl + T. (Press Ctrl + Shift + T to remove hanging indent.) • Click the Alignment button located at the left side of the Ruler until the Hanging Indent button displays and then click on the Ruler at the desired location.

Exercise 1C

Indenting Paragraphs

1. With **C03Ex01.docx** open, indent the first line of text in paragraphs by completing the following steps:
   a. Select the first two paragraphs of text in the document (the text after the title *COMPUTERS IN INDUSTRY* and before the heading *Telecommunications*).
   b. Make sure the Ruler displays. If it does not, click the View Ruler button located at the top of the vertical scroll bar.
   c. Position the mouse pointer on the First Line Indent marker on the Ruler, hold down the left mouse button, drag the marker to the 0.5-inch mark, and then release the mouse button.
   d. Position the insertion point on any character in the paragraph below the *Telecommunications* heading and then drag the First Line Indent marker on the Ruler to the 0.5-inch mark.
   e. Indent the first line of the paragraph below the *Publishing* heading and the *News Services* heading.
   f. Indent the first line of the first paragraph and the first line of the third paragraph in the *Television and Film* heading.
2. The second paragraph in the *Television and Film* section is a quote and needs to be indented from the left and right margins by completing the following steps:
   a. Position the insertion point anywhere within the second paragraph in the *Television and Film* section (the paragraph that begins *The film* Jurassic Park *brought . . .*).
   b. Click the Paragraph group dialog box launcher.
   c. At the Paragraph dialog box, select the current measurement in the *Left* measurement box, and then type **0.5**.
   d. Select the current measurement in the *Right* measurement box and then type **0.5**.
   e. Click OK or press Enter.
3. Create a hanging indent for the first paragraph in the *REFERENCES* section by positioning the insertion point anywhere in the first paragraph below *REFERENCES* and then pressing Ctrl + T.
4. Create a hanging indent for the second paragraph in the *REFERENCES* section by completing the following steps:
   a. Position the insertion point anywhere in the second paragraph in the *REFERENCES* section.
   b. Click the Alignment button located at the left side of the Ruler until the Hanging Indent button displays.
   c. Click on the 0.5-inch mark on the Ruler.

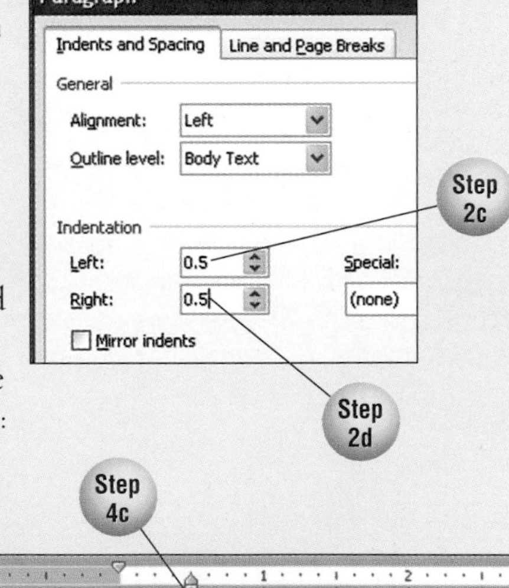

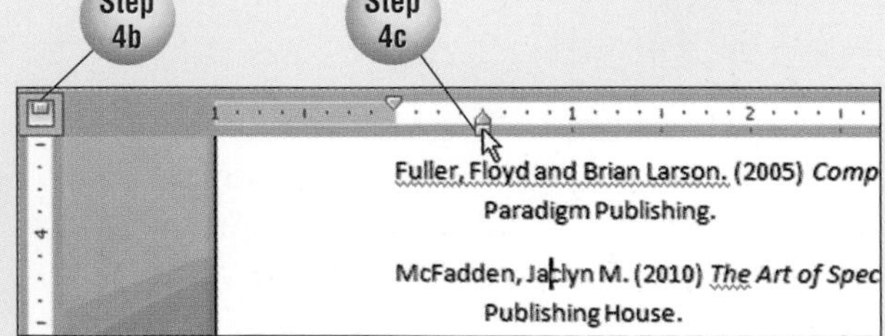

5. Create a hanging indent for the third and fourth paragraphs in the REFERENCES section by completing the following steps:
   a. Select a portion of the third and fourth paragraphs.
   b. Click the Paragraph group dialog box launcher.
   c. At the Paragraph dialog box with the Indents and Spacing tab selected, click the down-pointing arrow at the right side of the *Special* list box and then click *Hanging* at the drop-down list.
   d. Click OK or press Enter.
6. Save **C03Ex01.docx**.

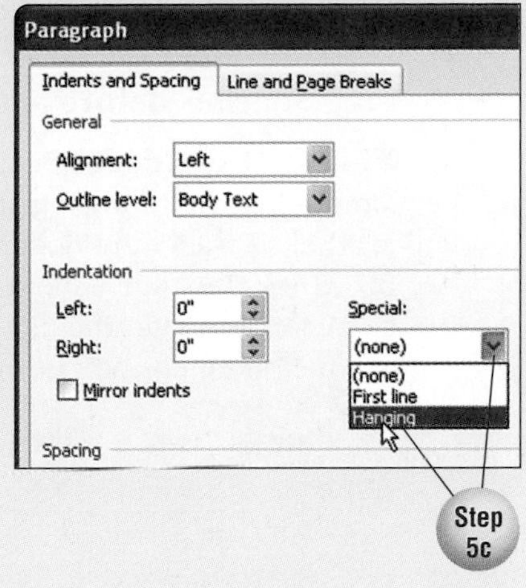

Spacing Before and After Paragraphs

As you learned earlier, the insertion of 10 points of spacing after a paragraph is one of Word's default settings. You can remove this spacing, increase it, or decrease it. You can also insert spacing above a paragraph. To change spacing before or after a paragraph, use the Spacing Before and Spacing After measurement boxes located in the Paragraph group in the Page Layout tab or the *Before* and/or *After* options at the Paragraph dialog box with the Indents and Spacing tab selected.

Spacing before or after a paragraph is part of that paragraph, and it will be moved, copied, or deleted with the paragraph. If a paragraph, such as a heading, contains spacing before it and the paragraph falls at the top of a page, Word ignores the spacing.

Spacing before or after paragraphs is added in points. A vertical inch contains approximately 72 points. To add spacing before or after a paragraph, click the Page Layout tab, select the current measurement in the Spacing Before or the Spacing After measurement box, and then type the desired number of points. You can also click the up- or down-pointing arrows at the right side of the Spacing Before and Spacing After measurement boxes to increase or decrease the amount of spacing.

QUICK STEPS

Change Paragraph Spacing
1. Click Page Layout tab.
2. Change spacing with Spacing Before and/or Spacing After measurement boxes.

OR

1. Click Page Layout tab.
2. Click Paragraph group dialog box launcher.
3. Insert measurement in *Before* and/or *After* measurement box.
4. Click OK.

Repeat Last Action
Press F4
OR
Press Ctrl + Y.

Repeating the Last Action

If you apply formatting to a selection of text and then want to apply the same formatting to other text in the document, consider using the Repeat command. To use this command, apply the desired formatting, move the insertion point to the next location where you want the formatting applied, and press the F4 function key or press Ctrl + Y.

Exercise 1D

Spacing Before and After Paragraphs and Repeating Last Action

1. With **C03Ex01.docx** open, change the spacing after paragraphs to 6 points by completing the following steps:
   a. Select the entire document.
   b. Click the Page Layout tab.
   c. Click once on the down-pointing arrow at the right side of the Spacing After measurement box in the Paragraph group (this inserts *6 pt* in the box).

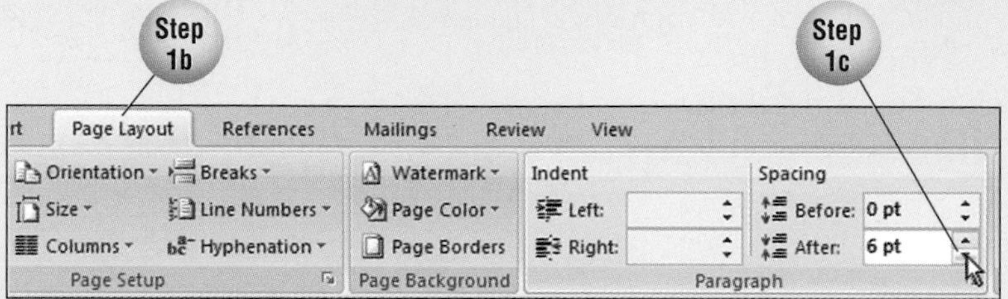

2. Add 18 points of spacing above and 12 points of spacing after the two titles by completing the following steps:
   a. Position the insertion point on any character in the title *COMPUTERS IN INDUSTRY*.
   b. Click three times on the up-pointing arrow at the right side of the Spacing Before measurement box (this changes the measurement to *18 pt*).
   c. Click once on the up-pointing arrow at the right side of the Spacing After measurement box (this changes the measurement to *12 pt*).

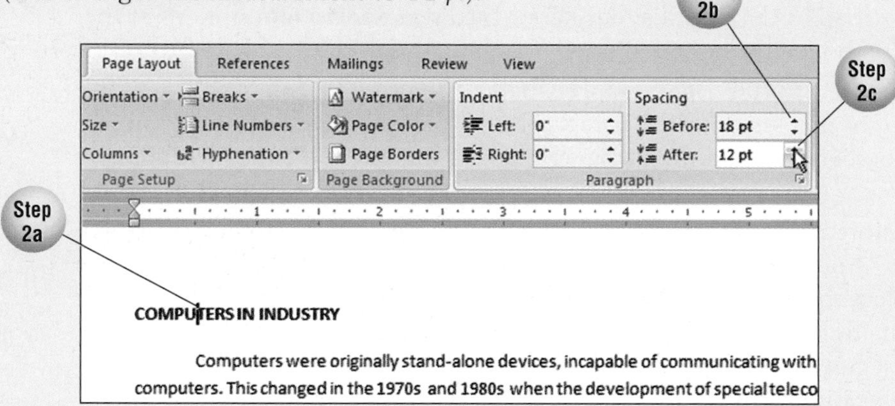

   d. Position the insertion point on any character in the title *REFERENCES* and then press F4 (this is the Repeat command).
3. Save **C03Ex01.docx**.

Formatting with Format Painter

The Clipboard group in the Home tab contains a button for copying character formatting to different locations in the document. This button, called the Format Painter, displays as a paintbrush. To use the Format Painter button, position the insertion point on a character containing the desired character formatting, click the Format Painter button, and then select text to which you want the character formatting applied. When you click the Format Painter button, the mouse I-beam pointer displays with a paintbrush attached. If you want to apply character formatting a single time, click the Format Painter button once. If you want to apply the character formatting in more than one location in the document, double-click the Format Painter button. After selecting and applying formatting, click the Format Painter button to turn it off or press the Esc key.

Format with Format Painter
1. Format text.
2. Double-click Format Painter button.
3. Select text.
4. Click Format Painter button.

Format Painter

Exercise 1E

Formatting Headings with the Format Painter

1. With **C03Ex01.docx** open, click the Home tab.
2. Select the entire document and then change the font to 12-point Cambria.
3. Select the title *COMPUTERS IN INDUSTRY*, click the Center button in the Paragraph group, and then change the font to 16-point Candara bold.
4. Apply 16-point Candara bold formatting to the *REFERENCES* heading by completing the following steps:
   a. Click on any character in the title *COMPUTERS IN INDUSTRY*.
   b. Click once on the Format Painter button in the Clipboard group.

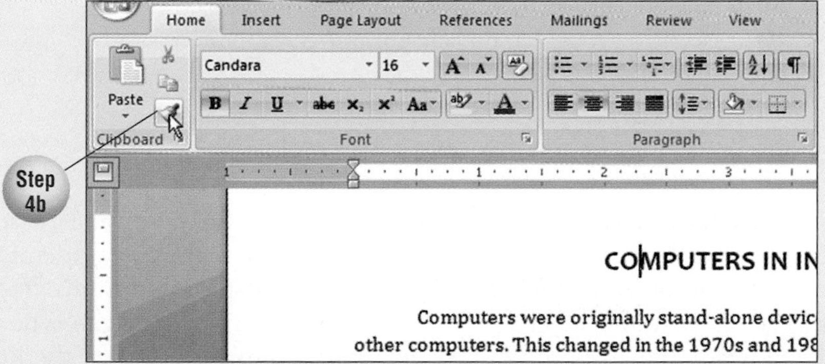

   c. Press Ctrl + End to move the insertion point to the end of the document and then select the heading *REFERENCES*. (This applies the 16-point Candara bold formatting and centers the text.)
5. Select the heading *Telecommunications* and then change the font to 14-point Candara bold.

6. Use the Format Painter button and apply 14-point Candara bold formatting to the other headings by completing the following steps:
   a. Position the insertion point on any character in the heading *Telecommunications*.
   b. Double-click the Format Painter button in the Clipboard group.
   c. Using the mouse, select the heading *Publishing*.
   d. Using the mouse, select the heading *News Services*.
   e. Using the mouse, select the heading *Television and Film*.
   f. Click once on the Format Painter button in the Clipboard group. (This turns off the feature.)
   g. Deselect the heading.
7. Save **C03Ex01.docx**.

QUICK STEPS

Change Line Spacing
1. Click Line Spacing button in Paragraph group.
2. Click *Spacing* option at drop-down list.

OR

Press keyboard shortcut.

OR

1. Click Paragraph group dialog box launcher.
2. Click *Line Spacing* option down-pointing arrow.
3. Click desired line spacing option.
4. Click OK.

OR

1. Click Paragraph group dialog box launcher.
2. Type line measurement in *At* text box.
3. Click OK.

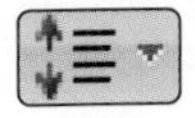
Line Spacing

Changing Line Spacing

The default line spacing in a Word document is 1.15. In some documents, you may want to change to another line spacing such as single, 1.5 spacing, or double spacing. Change line spacing by using the Line Spacing button in the Paragraph group in the Home tab, keyboard shortcuts, or options from the Paragraph dialog box. The keyboard shortcuts for changing line spacing are shown in Table 3.3.

Table 3.3 **Line Spacing Keyboard Shortcuts**

Press	***To change line spacing to***
Ctrl + 1	single spacing
Ctrl + 2	double spacing
Ctrl + 5	1.5 line spacing

To change line spacing at the Paragraph dialog box, use the *Line spacing* option or the *At* option. If you click the down-pointing arrow at the right side of the *Line spacing* option, a drop-down list displays with a variety of spacing options. To change the line spacing to double, click *Double* at the drop-down list. You can type a specific line spacing measurement in the *At* text box. For example, to change the line spacing to 1.75, type **1.75** in the *At* text box.

Exercise 1F

Changing Line Spacing

1. With **C03Ex01.docx** open, change the line spacing for all paragraphs to double spacing by completing the following steps:
   a. Select the entire document.
   b. Click the Line spacing button in the Paragraph group in the Home tab.
   c. Click 2.0 at the drop-down list.
2. With the entire document still selected, press Ctrl + 5. (This changes the line spacing to 1.5.)
3. Change the line spacing to 1.4 using the Paragraph dialog box by completing the following steps:
   a. With the document still selected, click the Paragraph group dialog box launcher.
   b. At the Paragraph dialog box, make sure the Indents and Spacing tab is selected, click inside the *At* text box, and then type **1.4**. (This text box is located to the right of the *Line spacing* list box.)
   c. Click OK or press Enter.
   d. Deselect the text.
4. Save, print, and then close **C03Ex01.docx**.

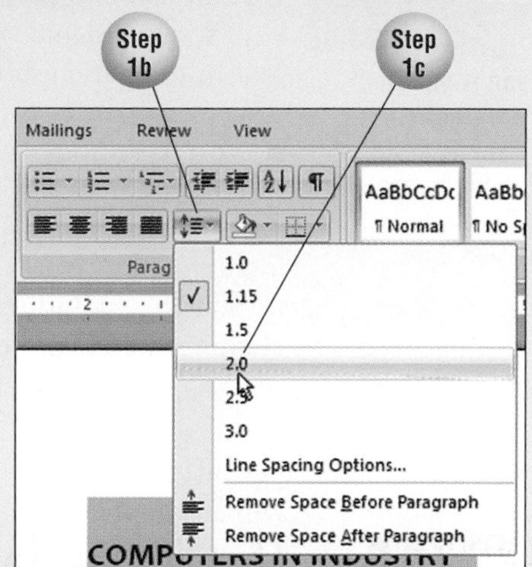

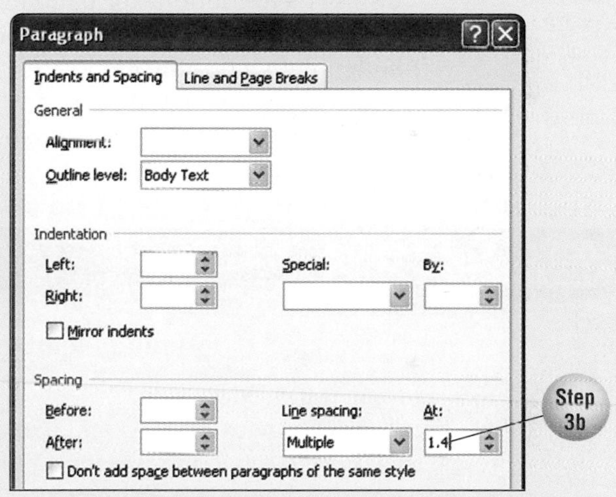

Applying Numbering and Bullets

Use buttons in the Paragraph group to automatically number paragraphs or insert bullets before them. Use the Bullets button to insert bullets before specific paragraphs and use the Numbering button to insert numbers.

Bullets

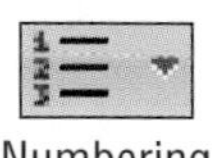

Numbering

Numbering Paragraphs

Type Numbered Paragraphs
1. Type **1.**
2. Press spacebar.
3. Type text.
4. Press Enter.

If you type **1.**, press the spacebar, type a paragraph of text, and then press the Enter key, Word indents the number approximately 0.25 inch and then hang indents the text in the paragraph approximately 0.5 inch from the left margin. In addition, Word insets 2. at the beginning of the next paragraph, indented 0.25 inch from the left margin. Continue typing items, and Word inserts the next number in the list. To turn off numbering, press the Enter key twice or click the Numbering button in the Paragraph group. (You can also remove all paragraph formatting from a paragraph, including automatic numbering, with the keyboard shortcut Ctrl + Q. Remove all formatting including character and paragraph formatting from selected text by clicking the Clear Formatting button in the Font group.)

If you press the Enter key twice between numbered paragraphs, the automatic number is removed. To turn it back on, type the next number in the list (and the period) followed by a space, type the paragraph of text, and then press Enter. Word will automatically indent the number and hang indent the text.

When the AutoFormat feature inserts numbering and indents text, the AutoCorrect Options button displays. Click this button and a drop-down list displays with options for undoing and/or stopping the automatic numbering. An AutoCorrect Options button also displays when AutoFormat inserts automatic bulleting in a document.

Exercise 2A

Typing Numbered Paragraphs

1. Open **Document05.docx**.
2. Save the document with Save As and name it **C03Ex02**.
3. Press Ctrl + End to move the insertion point to the end of the document and then type the text shown in Figure 3.4. When you type the numbered paragraphs, complete the following steps:
   a. Type **1.** and then press the spacebar. (This indents the number and the period 0.25 inch from the left margin and moves the insertion point 0.5 inch from the left margin. Also, the AutoCorrect Options button displays. Use this button if you want to undo or stop automatic numbering.)
   b. Type the paragraph of text and then press the Enter key. (This moves the insertion point down to the next line, inserts 2. indented 0.25 inch from the left margin, and indents the insertion point 0.5 inch from the left margin.
   c. Continue typing the remaining text. (Remember, you do not need to type the paragraph number and period—these are automatically inserted.)
   d. After typing the last question, press the Enter key twice. (This turns off paragraph numbering.)
4. Save **C03Ex02.docx**.

Figure 3.4 Exercise 2A

Research and Writing

1. Describe the components of a computer's central processing unit (CPU).
2. Identify at least four methods for inputting information into a computer.
3. Identify at least three methods for outputting information from a computer.
4. Explain the difference between read-only memory (ROM) and random-access memory (RAM).
5. Describe at least three types of network systems.

If you do not want automatic numbering in a document, turn off the feature at the AutoCorrect dialog box with the AutoFormat As You Type tab selected, as shown in Figure 3.5. To display this dialog box, click the Office button and then click the Word Options button that displays toward the bottom of the drop-down list. At the Word Options dialog box, click *Proofing* in the left panel and then click the AutoCorrect Options button that displays in the *AutoCorrect options* section of the dialog box. At the AutoCorrect dialog box, click the AutoFormat As You Type tab and then click the *Automatic numbered lists* check box to remove the check mark. Click OK to close the AutoCorrect dialog box and then click OK to close the Word Options dialog box.

Figure 3.5 AutoCorrect Dialog Box with the AutoFormat As You Type Tab Selected

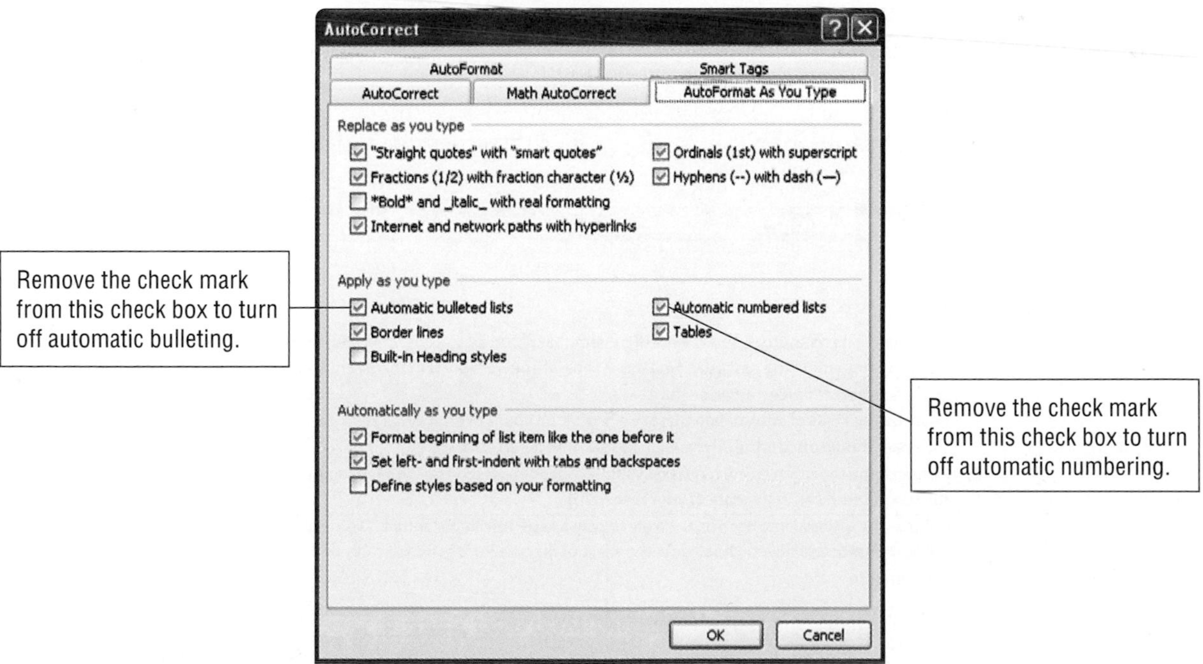

Create Numbered Paragraphs
1. Select text.
2. Click Numbering button in Paragraph group in Home tab.

You can also automate the creation of numbered paragraphs with the Numbering button in the Paragraph group. To use this button, type the text (do not type the number) for each paragraph to be numbered, select the paragraphs to be numbered, and then click the Numbering button in the Paragraph group. You can insert or delete numbered paragraphs in a document.

Exercise 2B

Inserting Paragraph Numbering

1. With **C03Ex02.docx** open, apply numbers to paragraphs by completing the following steps:
   a. Select the three paragraphs of text in the *Activities* section.
   b. Click the Numbering button in the Paragraph group.
2. Add the paragraph shown in Figure 3.6 between paragraphs 2 and 3 in the *Activities* section by completing the following steps:
   a. Position the insertion point immediately to the right of the period at the end of the second paragraph.
   b. Press Enter.
   c. Type the paragraph shown in Figure 3.6.

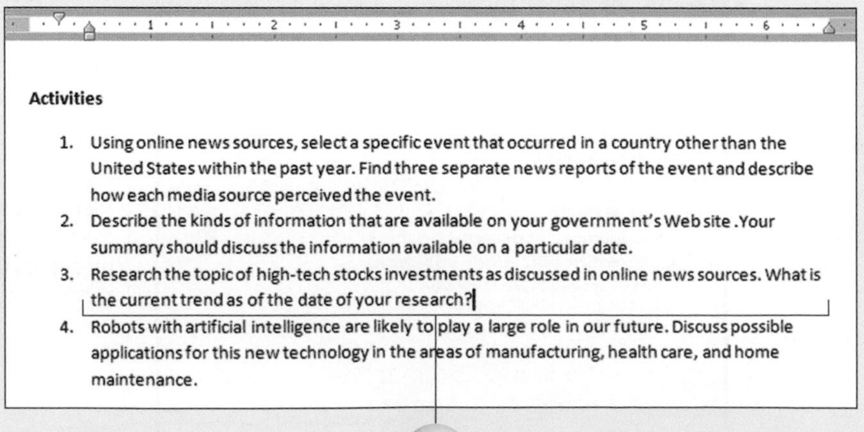

Activities

1. Using online news sources, select a specific event that occurred in a country other than the United States within the past year. Find three separate news reports of the event and describe how each media source perceived the event.
2. Describe the kinds of information that are available on your government's Web site .Your summary should discuss the information available on a particular date.
3. Research the topic of high-tech stocks investments as discussed in online news sources. What is the current trend as of the date of your research?
4. Robots with artificial intelligence are likely to play a large role in our future. Discuss possible applications for this new technology in the areas of manufacturing, health care, and home maintenance.

3. Save **C03Ex02.docx**.

Figure 3.6 Exercise 2B

Research the topic of high-tech stocks investments as discussed in online news sources. What is the current trend as of the date of your research?

Bulleting Paragraphs

Type Bulleted Paragraphs

1. Type *, >, or - symbol.
2. Press spacebar.
3. Type text.
4. Press Enter.

In addition to automatically numbering paragraphs, Word's AutoFormat feature creates bulleted paragraphs. Figure 3.7 shows an example of bulleted paragraphs. Word automatically creates bulleted lists with hanging indents when you begin a paragraph with one of the following symbols: *, >, or -. Type one of the symbols, press the spacebar, type text, and then press Enter. The AutoFormat feature inserts a bullet approximately 0.25 inch from the left margin and indents the text following the bullet another 0.25 inch. The type of bullet inserted depends on the type of character entered. For example, if you use the asterisk (*) symbol, a round bullet is inserted, and an arrow bullet is inserted if you type the greater than symbol (>). The automatic bulleting feature, like the automatic numbering feature, can be turned off at the AutoCorrect dialog box with the AutoFormat As You Type tab selected.

Figure 3.7 Bulleted Paragraphs

- This is a paragraph preceded by a bullet. A bullet indicates a list of items or topics.
- This is another paragraph preceded by a bullet. You can easily create bulleted paragraphs by typing certain symbols before the text or with the Bullets button in the Paragraph group.

Exercise 2C

Typing Bulleted Paragraphs

1. With **C03Ex02.docx** open, press Ctrl + End to move the insertion point to the end of the document and then press the Enter key once.
2. Type the text shown in Figure 3.8. Create the bulleted paragraphs by completing the following steps:
   a. With the insertion point positioned at the left margin of the first paragraph to contain a bullet, type the greater than symbol (>).
   b. Press the spacebar once.
   c. Type the text of the first bulleted paragraph.
   d. Press the Enter key once and then continue typing the text after the bullets.
3. After typing the last bulleted paragraph, press the Enter key twice (this turns off bullets).
4. Save **C03Ex02.docx**.

Figure 3.8 Exercise 2C

Technology Objectives

- Define the terms "input" and "processing."
- Categorize input devices for personal computers and explain their functions.
- Identify the main components of the system unit and explain their functions.
- Explain the four basic operations of a machine cycle.
- Describe the different types of computer memory and their functions.

Create Bulleted Paragraphs
1. Select text.
2. Click Bullets button in Paragraph group in Home tab.

Another way to create bulleted paragraphs is with the Bullets button in the Paragraph group. To create bulleted paragraphs using the Bullets button, type the text (do not type the bullet) of the paragraphs, select the paragraphs, and then click the Bullets button in the Paragraph group.

Exercise 2D

Inserting Bullets Using the Bullets Button

1. With **C03Ex02.docx** open, insert bullets before the six paragraphs of text below the paragraph in the *Internet Research* section by completing the following steps:
   a. Select the paragraphs of text in the *Internet Research* section from *Author's name (if known)* through *URL in angle brackets* < >.
   b. Click the Bullets button in the Paragraph group. (Because the last bullet you inserted was an arrow bullet, an arrow is inserted before the selected text.)
2. Save, print, and then close **C03Ex02.docx**.

Step 1b

Step 1a

Internet Research

Conduct Internet searches to find information to complete the report summarizing your research results. Be sure to documen which is recommended by the Modern Language Association (

Author's name (if known)

Title of document, in quotation marks

Title of Internet page or online periodical, in italics (if not titled organization that created and maintains the page)

Date of publication (for an article) or date site was last update

Date you accessed the site

URL, in angle brackets < >

Revealing Formatting

To identify formatting that has been applied to specific text in a document, access the Reveal Formatting task pane, shown in Figure 3.9. The Reveal Formatting task pane displays font, paragraph, and section formatting applied to text where the insertion point is positioned or to selected text. Display the Reveal Formatting task pane with the keyboard shortcut Shift + F1. Generally, a minus symbol precedes *Font* and *Paragraph* and a plus symbol precedes *Section* in the *Formatting of selected text* section of the Reveal Formatting task pane. Click the minus symbol to hide any items below a heading and click the plus symbol to reveal items. Some of the items below headings in the *Formatting of selected text* section are hyperlinks. Click a hyperlink and a dialog box displays with the specific option.

Figure 3.9 Reveal Formatting Task Pane

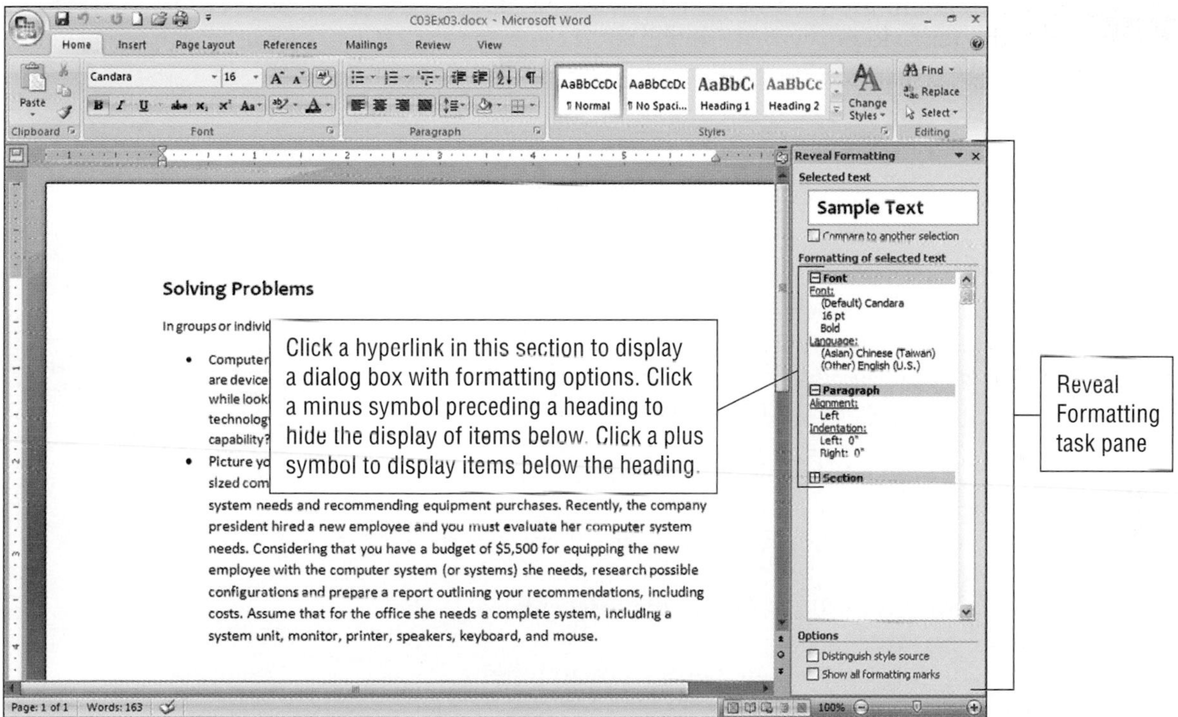

Exercise 3A

Revealing Formatting

1. Open **Quiz01.docx**.
2. Save the document with Save As and name it **C03Ex03**.
3. Press Shift + F1 to display the Reveal Formatting task pane.
4. Click anywhere in the heading *Solving Problems* and then notice the formatting information that displays in the Reveal Formatting task pane.
5. Click in the bulleted paragraph and notice the formatting information that displays in the Reveal Formatting task pane.

Compare Formatting

1. Display Reveal Formatting task pane.
2. Click or select text.
3. Click *Compare to another selection* check box.
4. Click or select text.

Comparing Formatting

In addition to using the Reveal Formatting task pane to identify formatting, you can use it to compare the formatting of two text selections to identify differences. To compare formatting, select the first text sample to be compared, click the *Compare to another selection* check box, and then select the second text sample. Any differences between the two selections display in the *Formatting differences* list box.

Exercise 3B

Comparing Formatting

1. With **C03Ex03.docx** open, make sure the Reveal Formatting task pane displays. If it does not, turn it on by pressing Shift + F1.
2. Select the first bulleted paragraph (the paragraph that begins *Computers currently offer both . . .*).
3. Click the *Compare to another selection* check box to insert a check mark.
4. Select the second bulleted paragraph (the paragraph that begins *Picture yourself working in the . . .*).
5. Determine the formatting differences by reading the information in the *Formatting differences* list box. (The list box displays *11 pt -> 12 pt* below the Font hyperlink, indicating that the difference is point size.)
6. Format the second bulleted paragraph so the text is set in 11-point size.
7. Click the *Compare to another selection* check box to remove the check mark.
8. Select the word *visual* that displays in the first sentence in the first bulleted paragraph.
9. Click the *Compare to another selection* check box to insert a check mark.
10. Select the word *audio* that displays in the first sentence of the first bulleted paragraph.
11. Determine the formatting differences by reading the information in the *Formatting differences* list box.
12. Format the word *audio* so it matches the formatting of the word *visual*.
13. Click the *Compare to another selection* check box to remove the check mark.
14. Close the Reveal Formatting task pane by clicking the Close button (contains an X) that displays in the upper right corner of the task pane.
15. Save, print, and then close **C03Ex03.docx**.

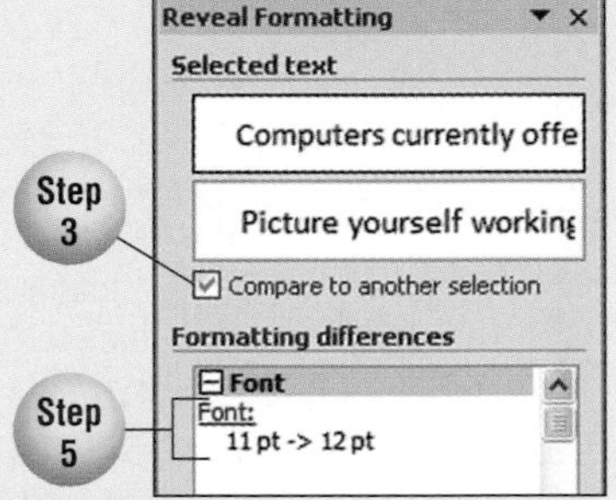

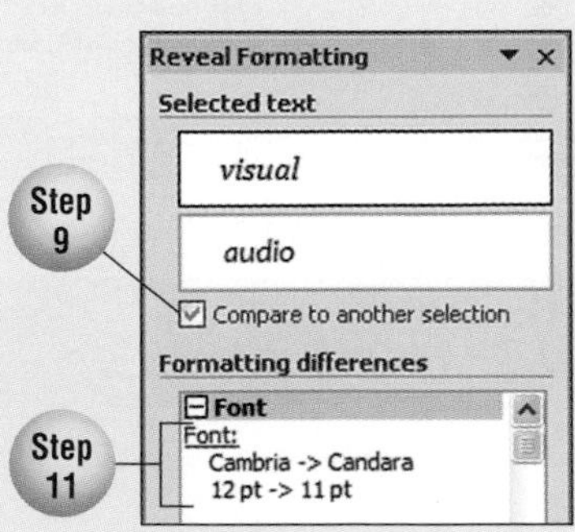

Chapter Summary

- In Word, a paragraph is any amount of text followed by a paragraph mark (a stroke of the Enter key). Word inserts into the paragraph mark any paragraph formatting that is turned on.
- By default, paragraphs in a Word document are aligned at the left margin and ragged at the right margin. Change this default alignment with buttons in the Paragraph group, at the Paragraph dialog box, or with keyboard shortcuts for left, center, right, or fully aligned.
- To turn on or off the display of nonprinting characters such as paragraph marks, click the Show/Hide ¶ button in the Paragraph group in the Home tab.
- Indent text in paragraphs with indent buttons in the Paragraph group in the Home tab, indent buttons in the Paragraph group in the Page Layout tab, keyboard shortcuts, options at the Paragraph dialog box, markers on the Ruler, or use the Alignment button on the Ruler. Refer to Table 3.2 for a description of the various methods for indenting text.
- Increase or decrease spacing before and after paragraphs using the Spacing Before and Spacing After measurement boxes in the Paragraph group in the Page Layout tab or using the *Before* and/or *After* options at the Paragraph dialog box.
- Repeat the last action by pressing the F4 function key or pressing Ctrl + Y.
- Use the Format Painter button in the Clipboard group in the Home tab to copy character formatting that you have already applied to text in different locations in the document.
- Change line spacing with the Line Spacing button in the Paragraph group in the Home tab, keyboard shortcuts, or options at the Paragraph dialog box.
- Number paragraphs with the Numbering button in the Paragraph group in the Home tab and insert bullets before paragraphs with the Bullets button.
- Display the Reveal Formatting task pane to display formatting applied to text. Use the *Compare to another selection* option in the task pane to compare the formatting of two text selections to determine how the formatting differs.

Commands review

FEATURE	RIBBON TAB, GROUP	BUTTON	KEYBOARD SHORTCUT
Bullets	Home, Paragraph		
Center align text	Home, Paragraph		Ctrl + E
Clear all formatting	Home, Font		
Clear paragraph formatting			Ctrl + Q
Format Painter	Home, Clipboard		Ctrl + Shift + C
Justify align text	Home, Paragraph		Ctrl + J
Left align text	Home, Paragraph		Ctrl + L
Line spacing	Home, Paragraph		Ctrl + 1 (single) Ctrl + 2 (double) Ctrl + 5 (1.5)
Numbering	Home, Paragraph		
Paragraph dialog box	Home, Paragraph Page Layout, Paragraph		
Repeat last action			F4 or Ctrl + Y
Reveal Formatting task pane			Shift + F1
Right align text	Home, Paragraph		Ctrl + R
Spacing after paragraph	Page Layout, Paragraph	After: 0 pt	
Spacing before paragraph	Page Layout, Paragraph	Before: 0 pt	

Reviewing key points

Completion: In the space provided at the right, indicate the correct term, command, or number.

1. Click this button in the Paragraph group to turn on the display of nonprinting characters. ____________
2. This is the default paragraph alignment. ____________
3. Return all paragraph formatting to normal with this keyboard shortcut. ____________
4. Click this button in the Paragraph group in the Home tab to align text at the right margin. ____________
5. In this type of paragraph, the first line of text remains at the left margin and the remaining lines of text are indented to the first tab. ____________
6. Use this button in the Clipboard group in the Home tab to copy character formatting already applied to text in different locations in the document. ____________
7. Repeat the last action by pressing F4 or with this keyboard shortcut. ____________
8. Change line spacing to1.5 with this keyboard shortcut. ____________
9. The Numbering button is located in this group in the Home tab. ____________
10. Automate the creation of bulleted paragraphs with this button in the Home tab. ____________
11. This button displays when the AutoFormat feature inserts numbers. ____________
12. Bulleted lists with hanging indents are automatically created when you begin a paragraph with the asterisk symbol (*), the hypen (-), or this symbol. ____________
13. You can turn off automatic numbering and bullets at the AutoCorrect dialog box with this tab selected. ____________
14. Press these keys to display the Reveal Formatting task pane. ____________

Applying your skills

Assessment 1 Create and Format a Training Announcment

1. At a blank document, click the No Spacing style in the Styles group and then type the text shown in Figure 3.10 with the following specifications:
   a. Center and right align text as indicated.
   b. After typing the text, select the centered text and change the font to 18-point Constantia bold.
   c. Select the right aligned text and change the font to 10-point Constantia bold.
   d. Increase paragraph spacing after each line of text by 12 points.
2. Save the document and name it **C03A01**.
3. Print and then close **C03A01.docx**.

Figure 3.10 Assessment 1

DATA SECURITY
Technical Support Training
Building C, Room 250
Thursday, April 22, 2010
3:00 - 5:30 p.m.

Technical Support Department
Support and Services Team

Assessment 2 Format a Document on Buying a Handheld Computer

1. Open **Document06.docx**.
2. Save the document with Save As and name it **C03A02**.
3. Select the second through the fifth paragraphs of text below the title and then indent the left and right margins 0.5 inch.
4. Select the first sentence of each of the indented paragraphs and apply bold formatting.
5. Apply the Heading 2 style to the title of the document.
6. Change the style set to *Modern*.
7. Apply the *Civic* theme.
8. Center the title.
9. Save and then print **C03A02.docx**.
10. Select the indented paragraphs of text and then click the Bullets button.
11. Display the Paragraph dialog box, change the *Left* indent to 0.25", make sure the hanging indent is set at 0.25", and then close the dialog box.
12. Save, print, and then close **C03A02.docx**.

Assessment 3 Create and Format a Bibliography

1. At a blank document, create the document shown in Figure 3.11 with the following specifications:
   a. Change the line spacing to double.
   b. Center, bold, and italicize text as indicated.
   c. Create hanging paragraphs as indicated.
   d. Change the alignment of paragraphs to justified.
2. Save the document and name it **C03A03**.
3. Print and then close **C03A03.docx**.

Figure 3.11 Assessment 3

BIBLIOGRAPHY

Albright, Anthony A. (2009). *Managing Telecommunications*, 2nd edition (pp. 24-33). Salt Lake City, UT: Blue Ridge Publishing Company.

Brown-Smythe, Lillian N. (2010). *Creating and Maintaining Local Area Networks* (pp. 19-22). Boston, MA: Northampton Publishers.

Lopez, Valentina C. (2009). *The Future of Nanotechnology* (pp. 43-51). Philadelphia, PA: Greenleaf Press.

Okada, David G. (2010). *Electronic Commerce*, 2nd edition (pp. 38-42). New Orleans, LA: Pontchartrain Publishing, Inc.

Assessment 4 Format a Travel Document

1. Open **Document07.docx**.
2. Save the document with Save As and name it **C03A04**.
3. Move the insertion point to the end of the document and then type the text shown in Figure 3.12.
4. Select the entire document and then add 6 points of spacing after paragraphs.
5. Change the style set to *Formal*.
6. Apply the Heading 1 style to the title *Hawaiian Adventures* and apply the Heading 2 style to the three headings in the document (*Rainy Day Activities*, *Kauai Sights*, and *Photo Opportunities*.
7. Apply the *Flow* theme.
8. Select the second through the fifth paragraphs of text in the *Rainy Day* section and then apply bullet formatting.
9. Bold the first word (and the colon) that begins the four bulleted paragraphs.
10. Select the paragraphs of text in the *Kauai Sights* section and then apply bullet formatting.

11. Insert the following paragraph of text between paragraphs 2 and 3 in the *Kauai Sights* section: **Tree tunnel: Fragrant eucalyptus trees provide a canopy of green en route to Koloa and Poipu.**
12. Bold the text followed by a colon that begins each paragraph in the *Kauai Sights* section.
13. Select the bulleted text below the *Photo Opportunities* heading and then increase the left paragraph indentation to 2.1 inch.
14. Save, print, and then close **C03A04.docx**.

Figure 3.12 Assessment 4

Photo Opportunities

- Hanalei Pier and Bay
- Green Waioli Huiia Church
- Lumahai Beach
- Coconut Grove
- Fern Grotto
- Sleeping Giant

Chapter 4

Customizing Paragraphs

Tutorial 4.1
Adding Borders and Shading and Working with Tabs
Tutorial 4.2
Working with Text

Performance Objectives

Upon successful completion of Chapter 4, you will be able to:

- Insert paragraph borders and shading
- Apply custom borders and shading
- Sort paragraph text
- Set, clear, and move tabs on the Ruler and at the Tabs dialog box
- Cut, copy, and paste text in a document
- Copy and paste text between documents

In the last chapter, you learned some of the options Word provides for formatting text in a paragraph. In this chapter, you will learn additional options, including how to apply borders and shading, sort paragraphs, and manipulate tabs both on the Ruler and at the Tabs dialog box. You will also learn to perform edits, such as selecting and then deleting, moving, or copying text, using buttons in the Home tab or keyboard shortcuts.

Note: Before beginning computer exercises for this chapter, copy to your storage medium the Chapter04 folder from the CD that accompanies this textbook and then make Chapter04 the active folder.

Inserting Paragraph Borders and Shading

Borders

Shading

Every paragraph you create in Word is surrounded by an invisible frame. You can apply a border to that frame. You can apply the border to a specific side of the paragraph or to all sides. You can also customize the type of border line and add shading to fill the border. Two methods are available for adding borders and shading to paragraphs: You can use the Borders and Shading buttons in the Paragraph group, or you can use options from the Borders and Shading dialog box.

QUICK STEPS

Insert Paragraph Border
1. Select text.
2. Click Borders button arrow.
3. Click desired border at drop-down list.

Inserting Paragraph Borders

When you add a border to a paragraph of text, the border expands and contracts as you insert or delete text from the paragraph. You can create a border around a single paragraph or around multiple paragraphs. One method for creating a border is to use options from the Borders button in the Paragraph group. The name of the button changes depending on the last border option selected. Click the Borders button arrow, and a drop-down list displays as shown in Figure 4.1.

Figure 4.1 Borders Drop-down List

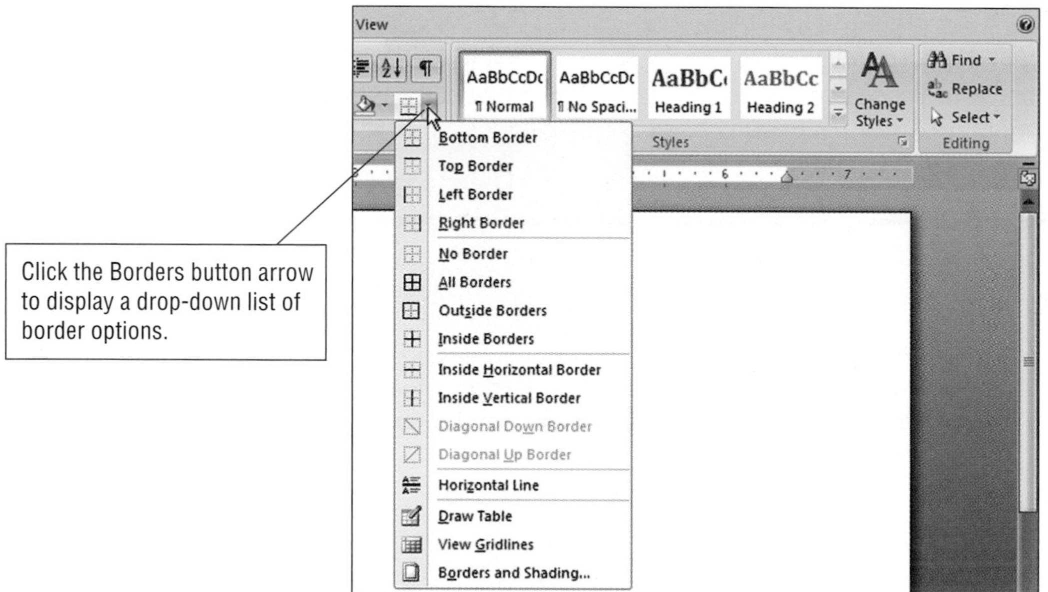

At the drop-down list, click the option that will insert the desired border. For example, to insert a border at the bottom of the paragraph, click the *Bottom Border* option. Clicking an option adds the border to the paragraph where the insertion point is located. To add a border to more than one paragraph, select the paragraphs first and then click the desired border option.

Exercise 1A

Adding Borders to Paragraphs of Text

1. Open **Quiz02.docx** and save the document with the name **C04Ex01**.
2. Make the following changes to the document.
   a. Select the entire document, change the font to 12-point Cambria, and then deselect the text.
   b. Center the title *CHAPTER 3 QUIZ*.

3. Insert a border above and below the title by completing the following steps:
   a. Position the insertion point on any character in the title *CHAPTER 3 QUIZ*.
   b. Click the Borders button arrow and then click *Bottom Border* at the drop-down list.
   c. Click the Borders button arrow and then click *Top Border* at the drop-down list.
4. Insert an outside border to specific text by completing the following steps:
   a. Select the text (including the multiple-choice options) for the first item.
   b. Click the Borders button arrow and then click *Outside Borders* at the drop-down list.

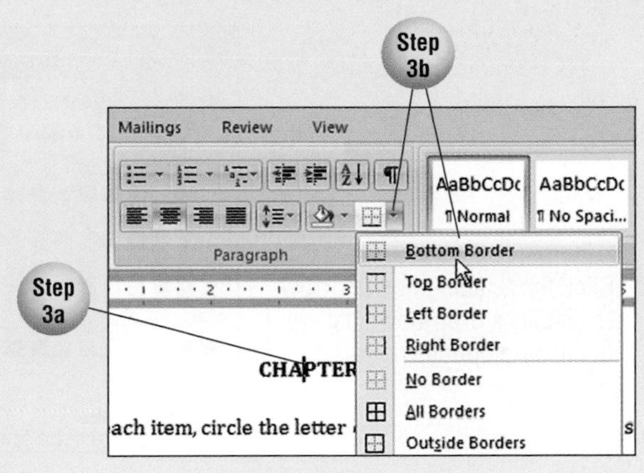

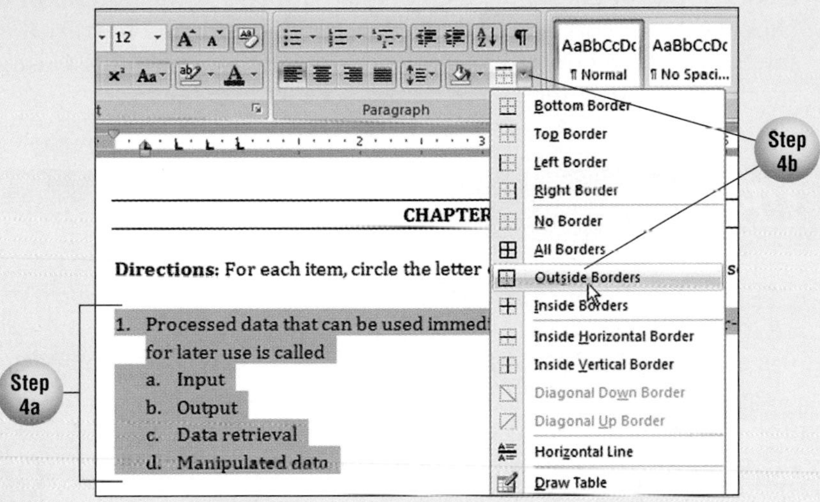

5. Select the text (including the multiple-choice options) for the second item and then press the Repeat command, F4. (This command repeats the last function.)
6. Select each of the remaining items and multiple-choice options and press F4.
7. Save **C04Ex01.docx**.

Adding Paragraph Shading

With the Shading button in the Paragraph group, you can add shading to text in a document. Select text you want to shade and then click the Shading button. This applies a background color behind the text. Click the Shading button arrow, and a drop-down gallery of shading colors displays as shown in Figure 4.2.

Apply Paragraph Shading
1. Select text.
2. Click Shading button arrow.
3. Click desired shade in drop-down gallery.

Figure 4.2 Shading Drop-down Gallery

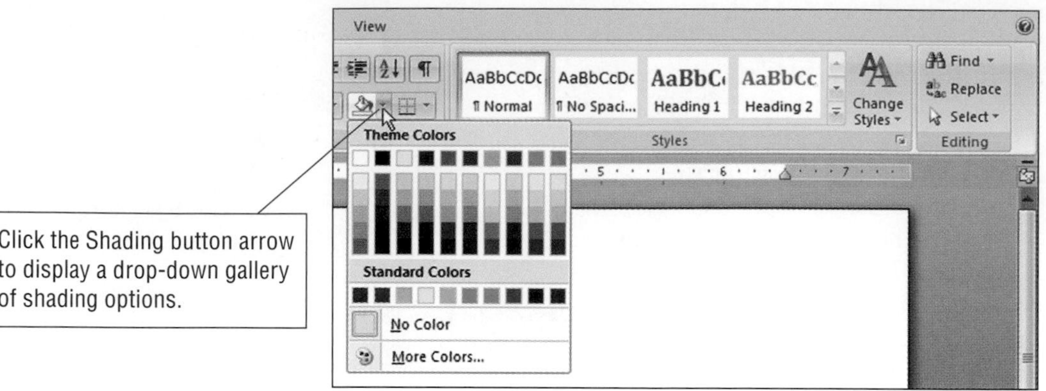

The shading colors are arranged in color themes. Choose one of the theme colors or one of the standard colors that displays at the bottom of the gallery, or click the *More Colors* option to display the Colors dialog box. At this dialog box with the Standard tab selected, click the desired color or click the Custom tab and then specify a custom color.

Exercise 1B

Applying Shading to Paragraphs

Step 1b

1. With **C04Ex01.docx** open, apply paragraph shading by completing the following steps:
   a. Position the insertion point on any character in the title *CHAPTER 3 QUIZ*.
   b. Click the Shading button arrow and then click the *Olive Green, Accent 3, Lighter 40%* option.
2. Apply shading to item one text by completing the following steps:
   a. Position the insertion point on any character in the item one text.
   b. Click the Shading button arrow and then click the *Olive Green, Accent 3, Lighter 80%* option. (Clicking this option applies shading to the item one text but not to the multiple-choice options.)
3. Use the Repeat command, F4, to apply the same formatting to the remaining item text (not the multiple-choice options).
4. Save, print, and then close **C04Ex01.docx**.

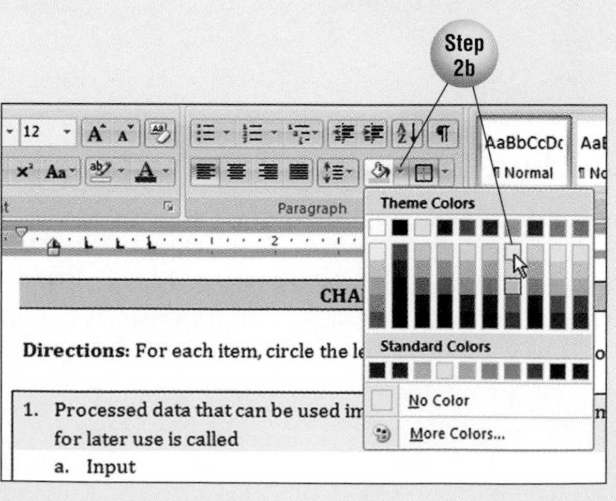

Customizing Borders and Shading

If you want to further customize paragraph borders and shading, use options at the Borders and Shading dialog box. Display this dialog box by clicking the Borders button arrow and then clicking *Borders and Shading* at the drop-down list. With the Borders tab selected, as shown in Figure 4.3, the Borders and Shading dialog box contains options for specifying the border style, color, and width. Click the Shading tab, and the dialog box displays as shown in Figure 4.4 with options for applying a fill color and pattern.

QUICK STEPS

Customize Borders

1. Click Borders button arrow.
2. Click *Borders and Shading* at drop-down list.
3. Specify desired border, style, color, and width.
4. Click OK.

Customize Shading

1. Click Borders button arrow.
2. Click *Borders and Shading* at drop-down list.
3. Click Shading tab.
4. Specify desired shading.
5. Click OK.

Figure 4.3 Borders and Shading Dialog Box with the Borders Tab Selected

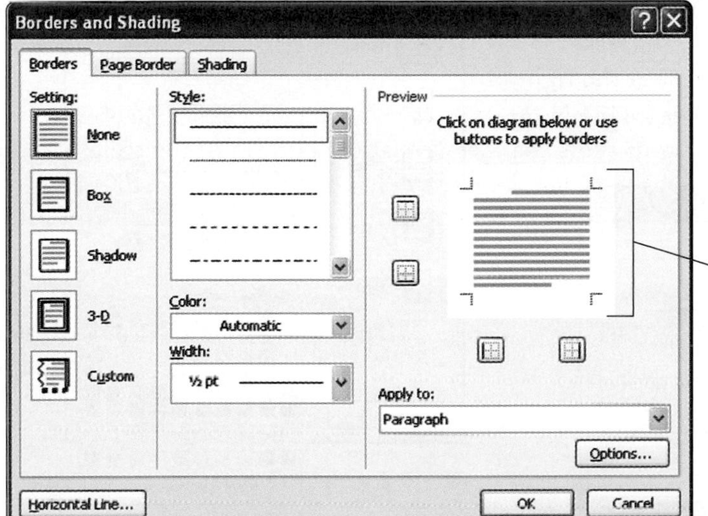

Click the sides, top, or bottom of this preview area to insert or remove a border.

Figure 4.4 Borders and Shading Dialog Box with the Shading Tab Selected

Click this down-pointing arrow to display a drop-down list of shading options.

Exercise 2A

Adding a Customized Border and Shading to a Document

1. Open **Document08.docx** and then save the document with the name **C04Ex02**.
2. Insert a custom border and add shading to a heading by completing the following steps:
   a. Move the insertion point to any character in the heading *International Correspondence*.
   b. Click the Borders button arrow and then click *Borders and Shading* at the drop-down list.
   c. At the Borders and Shading dialog box with the Borders tab selected, click the down-pointing arrow at the right side of the *Color* option box and then click Dark Blue in the *Standard Colors* section.

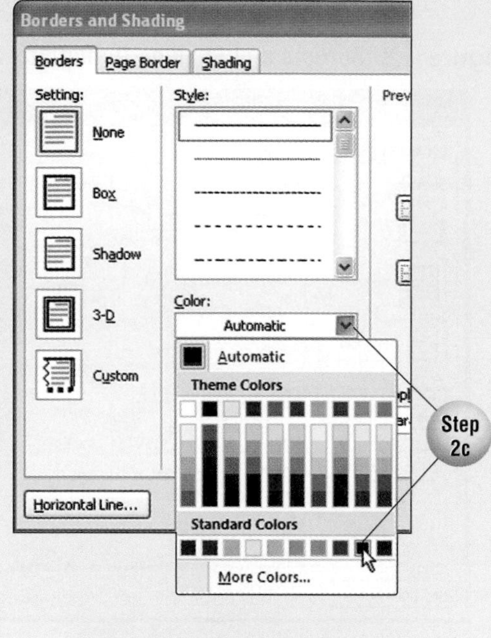

   d. Click the down-pointing arrow at the right of the *Width* option box and then click *1 pt* at the drop-down list.

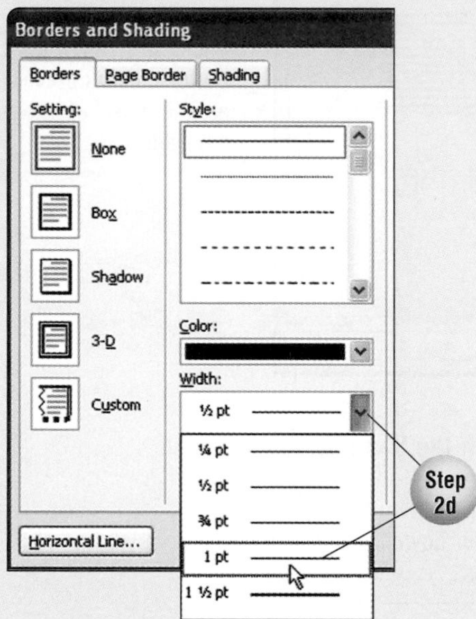

   e. Click the top border of the box in the *Preview* section of the dialog box.

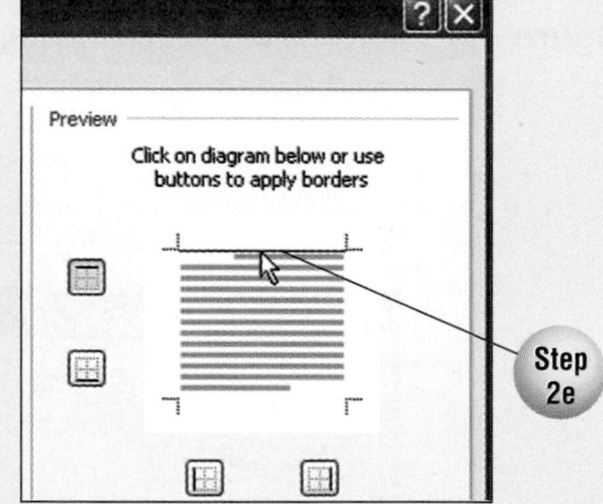

f. Click the down scroll arrow in the *Style* list box and then click the first thick-thin line combination.
g. Click the down-pointing arrow at the right side of the *Color* option box and then click Dark Blue in the *Standard Colors* section.
h. Click the bottom border of the box in the *Preview* section of the dialog box.

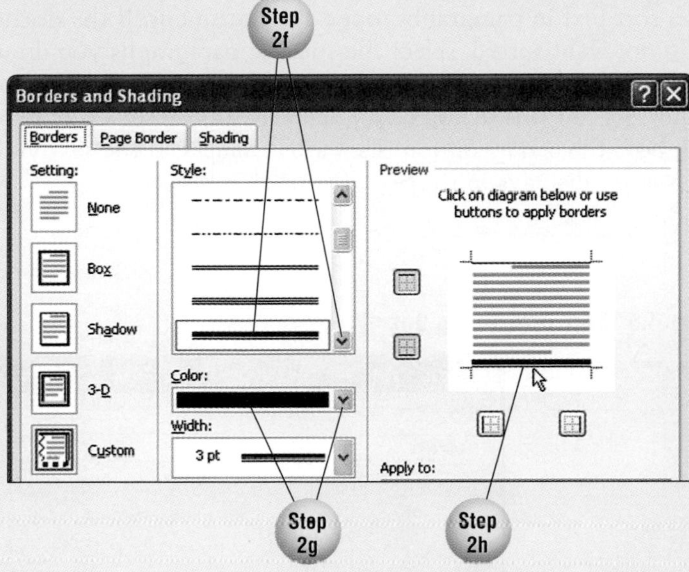

i. Click the Shading tab.
j. Click the down-pointing arrow at the right side of the *Fill* option box and then click *Olive Green, Accent 3, Lighter 60%*.
k. Click OK to close the dialog box.

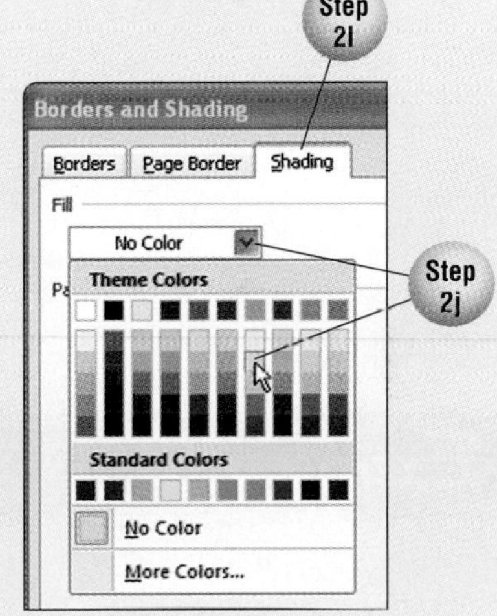

3. Use Format Painter to apply the same border and shading formatting to the remaining headings by completing the following steps:
   a. Position the insertion point on any character in the heading *International Correspondence*.
   b. Double-click the Format Painter button in the Clipboard group in the Home tab.
   c. Select the heading *International Addresses*.
   d. Select the heading *Canadian Codes and Provinces*.
   e. Select the heading *Canadian Codes and Territories*.
   f. Click the Format Painter button once.
4. Save **C04Ex02.docx**.

Sort Text in Paragraphs
1. Select desired paragraphs.
2. Click Sort button.
3. Make any needed changes at Sort Text dialog box.
4. Click OK.

Sort

Sorting Text in Paragraphs

You can sort text that is arranged in paragraphs alphabetically by the first character. This character can be a number, symbol (such as $ or #), or letter. You can type the paragraphs you want to sort at the left margin or indent them to a tab stop. Unless you select specific paragraphs to be sorted, Word sorts the entire document.

To sort text in paragraphs, open the document. If the document contains text you do not want sorted, select the specific paragraphs you do want sorted. Click the Sort button in the Paragraph group, and the Sort Text dialog box displays as shown in Figure 4.5. At this dialog box, click OK. If you select text and then display the dialog box, the *Sort by* option is set at *Paragraphs*. If the text you select is numbers, then *Numbers* displays in the Sort Text dialog box.

Figure 4.5 Sort Text Dialog Box

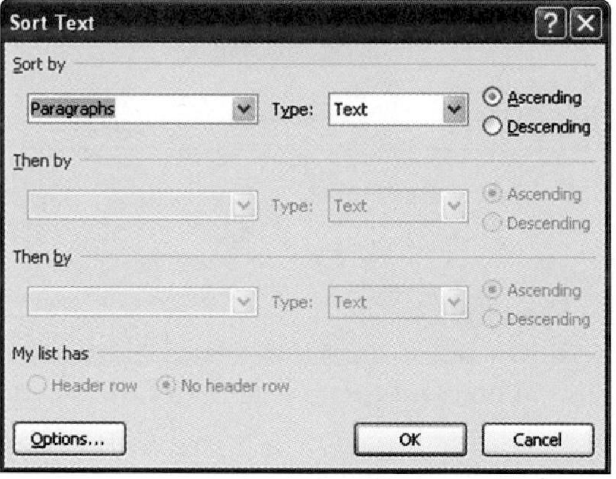

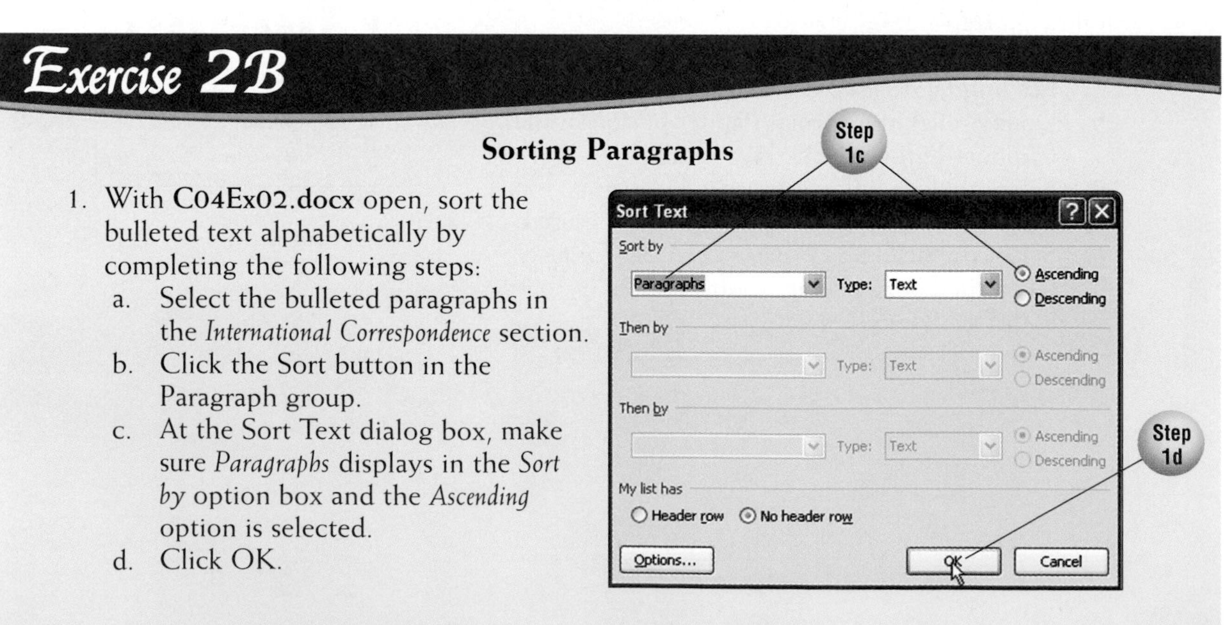

Exercise 2B

Sorting Paragraphs

1. With **C04Ex02.docx** open, sort the bulleted text alphabetically by completing the following steps:
   a. Select the bulleted paragraphs in the *International Correspondence* section.
   b. Click the Sort button in the Paragraph group.
   c. At the Sort Text dialog box, make sure *Paragraphs* displays in the *Sort by* option box and the *Ascending* option is selected.
   d. Click OK.

2. Sort the numbered paragraphs by completing the following steps:
    a. Select the numbered paragraphs in the *International Addresses* section.
    b. Click the Sort button in the Paragraph group.
    c. Click OK at the Sort Text dialog box.
3. Follow the steps outlined above to sort alphabetically the Canadian provinces and then the Canadian territories.
4. Save, print, and then close **C04Ex02.docx**.

Manipulating Tabs on the Ruler

When you work with a document, Word offers a variety of default settings. One of these defaults is a left tab set every 0.5 inch. For some documents, these default tabs are appropriate; for others, you may want to create your own tabs. You can set tabs on the Ruler or at the Tabs dialog box.

Use the Ruler to set, move, and delete tabs. If the Ruler is not visible, click the View Ruler button located at the top of the vertical scroll bar. The Ruler displays left tabs set every 0.5 inch. These default tabs are indicated by tiny vertical lines along the bottom of the Ruler. With a left tab, text aligns at the left edge of the tab. The other types of tabs that can be set on the Ruler are center, right, decimal, and bar. Use the Alignment button that displays at the left side of the Ruler to specify tabs. Each time you click the Alignment button, a different tab or paragraph alignment symbol displays. Table 4.1 shows the tab alignment button and what type of tab each will set.

Table 4.1 **Tab Alignment Symbols**

Alignment Button	***Type of Tab***
L	Left tab
┴	Center tab
┘	Right tab
┴.	Decimal tab
|	Bar tab

Set Tabs on Ruler
1. Click Alignment button on Ruler.
2. Click desired location on Ruler.

Setting Tabs

To set a left tab on the Ruler, make sure the left alignment symbol (see Table 4.1) displays in the Alignment button. Position the arrow pointer just below the tick mark (on the Ruler) where you want the tab symbol to appear and then click the left mouse button once. When you set a tab on the Ruler, Word automatically deletes any default tabs to the left. You can set a center, right, decimal, or bar tab on the Ruler in a similar manner. When you set tabs on the Ruler, a dotted guideline displays to help align tabs.

Before setting a tab on the Ruler, click the Alignment button at the left side of the Ruler until the appropriate tab symbol is displayed and then set the tab. If you change the tab symbol in the Alignment button, the symbol remains until you change it again or you exit Word. If you exit and then reenter Word, the tab symbol returns to the default of left tab.

If you want to set a tab at a specific measurement on the Ruler, hold down the Alt key, position the arrow pointer at the desired position, and then hold down the left mouse button. This displays two measurements on the Ruler. The first measurement displays the location of the arrow pointer on the Ruler in relation to the left edge of the page. The second measurement is the distance from the location of the arrow pointer on the Ruler to the right margin. With the left mouse button held down, position the tab symbol at the desired location, and then release the mouse button and the Alt key.

If you change tab settings and then type tabbed text using the New Line Command Shift + Enter, the tab formatting is stored in the paragraph mark at the end of the typed text. If you want to make changes to the tab settings for text in the columns, position the insertion point anywhere within the columns (all of the text in the columns does not have to be selected) and then make the changes.

Exercise 3A

Setting Left, Center, and Right Tabs on the Ruler

1. At a blank document, type TRAINING centered and bolded as shown in Figure 4.6.
2. Press the Enter key and then return the paragraph alignment back to left and turn off bold.
3. Set a left tab at the 0.5-inch mark, a center tab at the 3.25-inch mark, and a right tab at the 6-inch mark by completing the following steps:
   a. Click the Show/Hide ¶ button in the Paragraph group in the Home tab to turn on the display of nonprinting characters.
   b. Make sure the Ruler is displayed. (If not, click the View Ruler button located at the top of the vertical scroll bar.)

c. Make sure the left tab symbol displays in the Alignment button at the left side of the Ruler.
d. Position the arrow pointer on the 0.5-inch mark on the Ruler and then click the left mouse button.
e. Position the arrow pointer on the Alignment button at the left side of the Ruler and then click the left mouse button until the center tab symbol displays (see Table 4.1).

f. Position the arrow pointer below the 3.25-inch mark on the Ruler. Hold down the Alt key and then the left mouse button. Make sure the first measurement on the Ruler displays as 3.25″ and then release the mouse button and the Alt key.

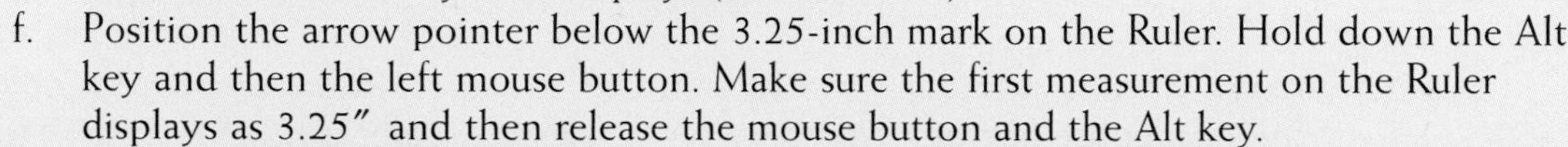

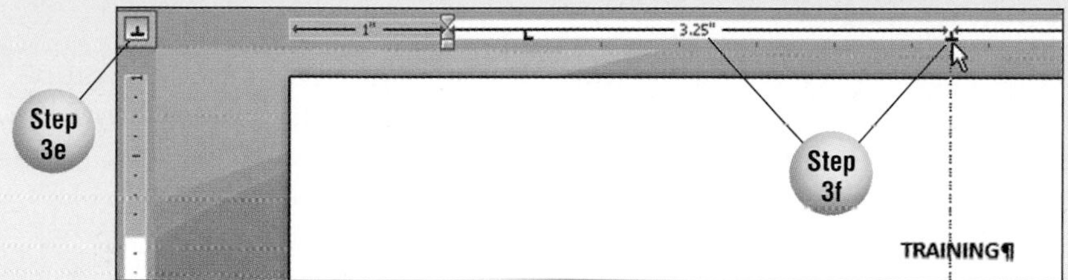

g. Position the arrow pointer on the Alignment button at the left side of the Ruler and then click the left mouse button until the right tab symbol displays (see Table 4.1).
h. Position the arrow pointer below the 6-inch mark on the Ruler. Hold down the Alt key and then the left mouse button. Make sure the first measurement on the Ruler displays as 6″ and then release the mouse button and the Alt key.

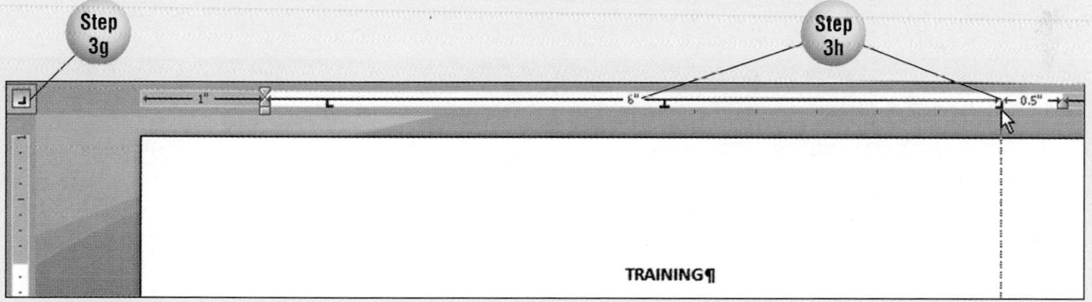

4. Type the text in columns as shown in Figure 4.6. Press the Tab key before typing each column entry and press Shift + Enter after typing the text in the third column.
5. After typing the last column entry, press the Enter key twice.
6. Press Ctrl + Q to remove paragraph formatting (tab settings).
7. Click the Show/Hide ¶ button to turn off the display of nonprinting characters.
8. Save the document and name it **C04Ex03**.

Figure 4.6 Exercise 3A

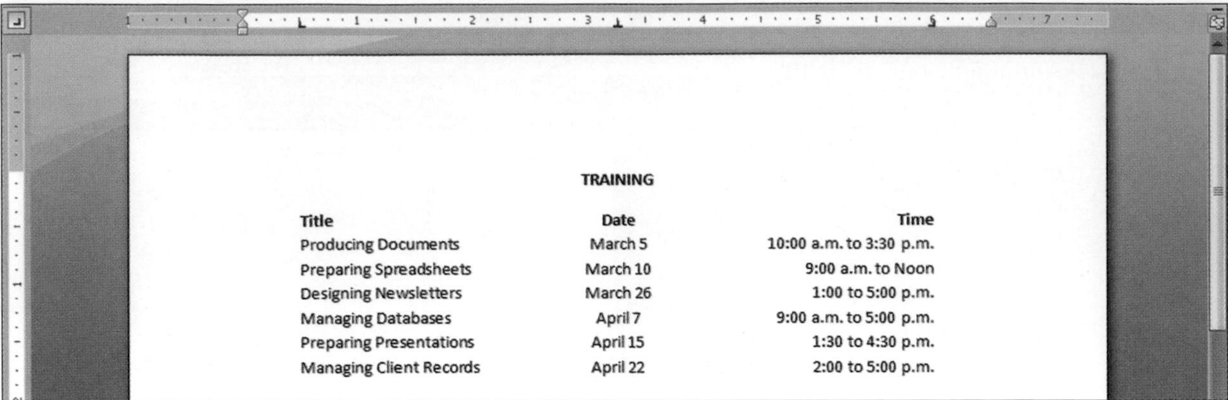

TRAINING

Title	Date	Time
Producing Documents	March 5	10:00 a.m. to 3:30 p.m.
Preparing Spreadsheets	March 10	9:00 a.m. to Noon
Designing Newsletters	March 26	1:00 to 5:00 p.m.
Managing Databases	April 7	9:00 a.m. to 5:00 p.m.
Preparing Presentations	April 15	1:30 to 4:30 p.m.
Managing Client Records	April 22	2:00 to 5:00 p.m.

Moving Tabs

After a tab has been set on the Ruler, it can be moved to a new location. To move a tab, position the arrow pointer on the tab symbol on the Ruler, hold down the left mouse button, drag the symbol to the new location on the Ruler, and then release the mouse button.

Deleting Tabs

To delete a tab from the Ruler, position the arrow pointer on the tab symbol you want deleted, hold down the left mouse button, drag the symbol down into the document, and then release the mouse button.

Exercise 3B

Moving Tabs

1. With **C04Ex03.docx** open, position the insertion point on any character in the first entry in the tabbed text.
2. Position the arrow pointer on the left tab symbol at the 0.5-inch mark, hold down the left mouse button, drag the left tab symbol to the 1-inch mark on the Ruler, and then release the mouse button. *(Hint: Use the Alt key to help you precisely position the tab symbol.)*
3. Position the arrow pointer on the right tab symbol at the 6-inch mark, hold down the left mouse button, drag the right tab symbol to the 5.5-inch mark on the Ruler, and then release the mouse button. *(Hint: Use the Alt key to help you precisely position the tab symbol.)*
4. Save **C04Ex03.docx**.

Step 2

Manipulating Tabs at the Tabs Dialog Box

Use the Tabs dialog box, shown in Figure 4.7, to set tabs at a specific measurement. You can also use the Tabs dialog box to set tabs with preceding leaders and to clear one tab or all tabs. To display the Tabs dialog box, click the Paragraph group dialog box launcher. At the Paragraph dialog box, click the Tabs button located in the bottom left corner of the dialog box.

QUICK STEPS

Set Tabs at Tabs Dialog Box

1. Click Paragraph group dialog box launcher.
2. Click Tabs button.
3. Specify tab positions, alignments, and leader options.
4. Click OK.

Figure 4.7 Tabs Dialog Box

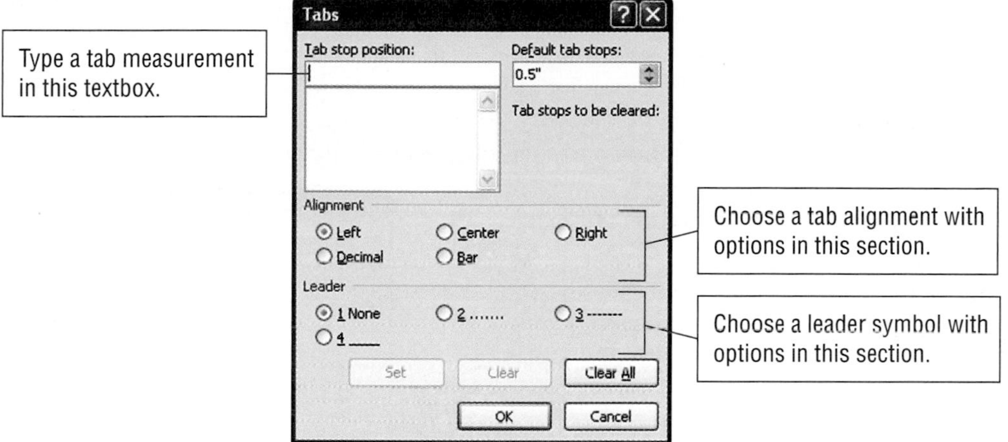

Clearing Tabs

At the Tabs dialog box, you can clear an individual tab or all tabs. To clear all tabs, click the Clear All button. To clear an individual tab, specify the tab position and then click the Clear button.

Setting Tabs

At the Tabs dialog box, you can set a left, right, center, or decimal tab as well as a bar tab. (For an example of a bar tab, refer to Figure 4.8.) You can also set a left, right, center, or decimal tab with preceding leaders. To change the type of tab at the Tabs dialog box, display the dialog box and then click the desired tab in the *Alignment* section. Type the desired measurement for the tab in the *Tab stop position* measurement box.

Exercise 3C

Setting Left Tabs and a Bar Tab at the Tabs Dialog Box

1. With **C04Ex03.docx** open, press Ctrl + End to move the insertion point to the end of the document.
2. Type the title **NEW EMPLOYEE TRAINING** bolded and centered as shown in Figure 4.8, press the Enter key, change the paragraph alignment back to Left, and turn off bold.
3. Display the Tabs dialog box and then set left tabs and a bar tab by completing the following steps:
   a. Click the Paragraph group dialog box launcher.
   b. At the Paragraph dialog box, click the Tabs button located in the lower left corner of the dialog box.
   c. Make sure *Left* is selected in the *Alignment* section of the dialog box.
   d. Type **1.75** in the *Tab stop position* measurement box.
   e. Click the Set button.
   f. Type **4** in the *Tab stop position* text box and then click the Set button.
   g. Type **3.25** in the *Tab stop position* text box, click *Bar* in the *Alignment* section, and then click the Set button.
   h. Click OK to close the Tabs dialog box.

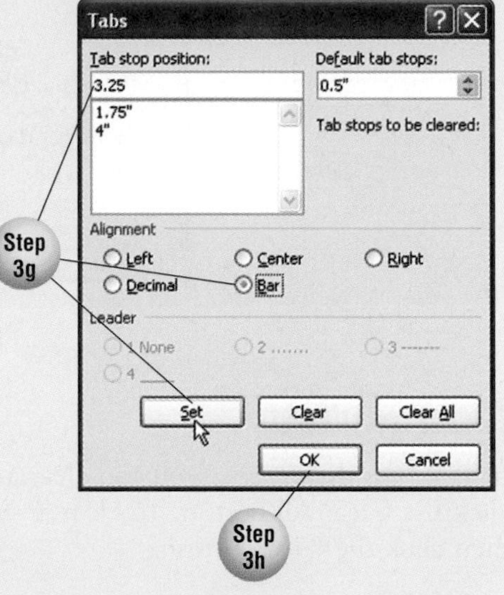

4. Type the text in columns as shown in Figure 4.8. Press the Tab key before typing each column entry and press Shift + Enter to end each line.
5. After typing *February* **23**, complete the following steps:
   a. Press the Enter key.
   b. Clear tabs by displaying the Tabs dialog box, clicking the Clear All button, and then clicking OK.
   c. Press the Enter key.
6. Remove the 10 points of spacing after the last entry in the text by completing the following steps:
   a. Position the insertion point on any character in the *January* **18** entry.
   b. Click the Page Layout tab.
   c. Click twice on the down-pointing arrow at the right side of the *Spacing After* measurement box. (This changes the measurement to *0 pt*.)
7. Save **C04Ex03.docx**.

Figure 4.8 Exercise 3C

NEW EMPLOYEE TRAINING

January 5	February 8
January 7	February 16
January 12	February 18
January 18	February 23

Setting Leader Tabs

The four types of tabs can also be set with leaders. Leaders are useful in a table of contents or other material where you want to direct the reader's eyes across the page. Figure 4.9 shows an example of leaders. Leaders can be periods (.), hyphens (-), or underlines (_). To add leaders to a tab, click the type of leader desired in the *Leader* section of the Tabs dialog box.

Exercise 3D

Setting a Left Tab and a Right Tab with Dot Leaders

1. With **C04Ex03.docx** open, press Ctrl + End to move the insertion point to the end of the document.
2. Type the title **CONTENTS** bolded and centered as shown in Figure 4.9.
3. Press the Enter key and then return the paragraph alignment back to left and turn off bold.
4. Set a left tab and then a right tab with dot leaders by completing the following steps:
    a. Click the Paragraph group dialog box launcher.
    b. Click the Tabs button located in the lower left corner of the Paragraph dialog box.
    c. At the Tabs dialog box, make sure *Left* is selected in the *Alignment* section of the dialog box.
    d. With the insertion point positioned in the *Tab stop position* measurement box, type **1** and then click the Set button.
    e. Type **5.5** in the *Tab stop position* measurement box.
    f. Click *Right* in the *Alignment* section of the dialog box.
    g. Click 2 ...... in the *Leader* section of the dialog box and then click the Set button.
    h. Click OK to close the dialog box.
5. Type the text in columns as shown in Figure 4.9. Press the Tab key before typing each column entry and press Shift + Enter to end each line.
6. Save, print, and then close **C04Ex03.docx**.

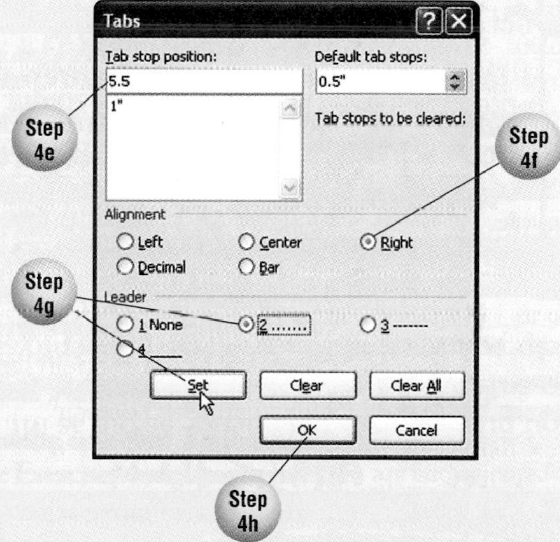

Figure 4.9 Exercise 3D

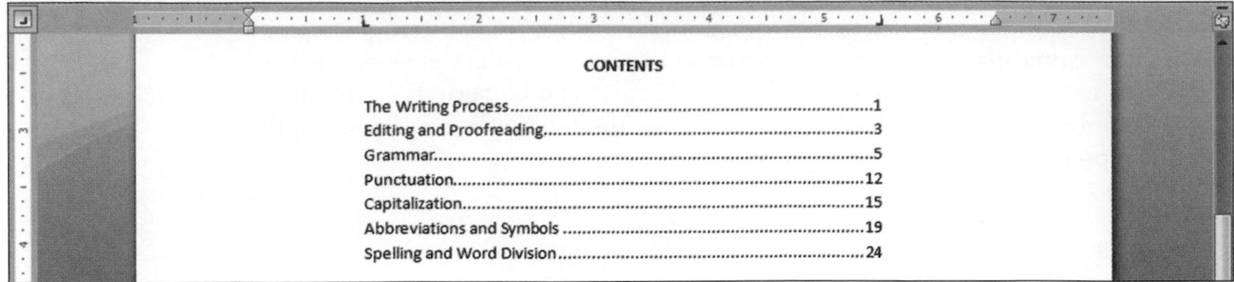

CONTENTS

Cutting, Copying, and Pasting Text

When you edit a document, you may need to delete specific text, move it to a different location, or copy it to various locations in the document. You can complete these activities using buttons in the Clipboard group in the Home tab.

Deleting Selected Text

Cut

Word offers several methods for deleting text from a document. To delete a single character, you can use either the Delete key or the Backspace key. To delete more than a single character, select the text and then press the Delete key on the keyboard, or click the Cut button in the Clipboard group. If you press the Delete key, the text is deleted permanently. (You can restore deleted text with the Undo button on the Quick Access toolbar.) The Cut button in the Clipboard group removes the selected text from the document and inserts it in the ***Clipboard***. Word's Clipboard is a temporary area of memory. The Clipboard holds text while it is being moved or copied to a new location in the document or to a different document.

Move Selected Text
1. Select text.
2. Click Cut button.
3. Move to desired location.
4. Click Paste button.

Paste

Cutting and Pasting Text

To move text to a different location in the document, select the text, click the Cut button in the Clipboard group, position the insertion point at the location where you want the text inserted, and then click the Paste button in the Clipboard group.

You can also move selected text with a shortcut menu. To do this, select the text and then position the insertion point inside the selected text until it turns into an arrow pointer. Click the *right* mouse button and then click Cut at the shortcut menu. Position the insertion point where you want the text inserted, click the *right* mouse button, and then click Paste at the shortcut menu. Keyboard shortcuts are also available for cutting and pasting text. Use Ctrl + X to cut text and Ctrl + V to insert text.

When selected text is cut from a document and inserted in the Clipboard, it stays in the Clipboard until other text is inserted in the Clipboard. For this reason, you can paste text from the Clipboard more than just once. For example, if you cut text to the Clipboard, you can paste this text in different locations within the document or other documents as many times as desired.

Exercise 4A

Moving Selected Text

1. Open **Document09.docx** and save the document with the name **C04Ex04**.
2. Move a paragraph by completing the following steps:
   a. Select the *Spacing:* paragraph.
   b. Click the Cut button in the Clipboard group in the Home tab.

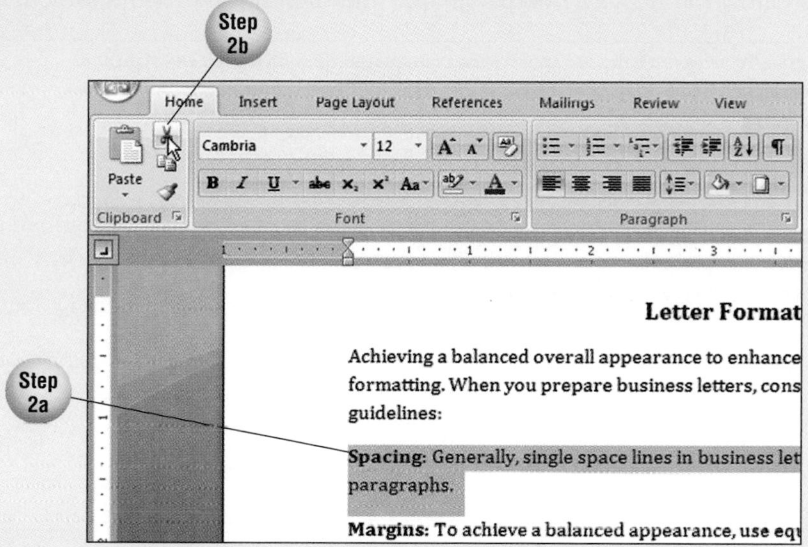

   c. Position the insertion point at the beginning of the *Justification:* paragraph.
   d. Click the Paste button in the Clipboard group. (If the first and second paragraphs are not separated by a blank line, press the Enter key once.)
3. Following the steps outlined above, move the *Margins:* paragraph before the *Date Line:* paragraph.
4. Save **C04Ex04.docx**.

Moving Text by Dragging with the Mouse

You can also use the mouse to move text. To do this, select text to be moved and then position the I-beam pointer inside the selected text until it turns into an arrow pointer. Hold down the left mouse button, drag the arrow pointer (which displays as an arrow with a gray box attached) to the location where you want to insert the selected text, and then release the button.

Move Text with Mouse
1. Select text.
2. Position mouse pointer in selected text.
3. Hold down left mouse button and drag to desired location.

Exercise 4B

Moving Text by Dragging with the Mouse

1. With **C04Ex04.docx** open, use the mouse to select the *Date Line:* paragraph.
2. Move the I-beam pointer inside the selected text until it becomes an arrow pointer.
3. Hold down the left mouse button, drag the arrow pointer (which displays with a small gray box attached) so that the insertion point, which displays as a grayed vertical bar, is positioned below the *Attention Line:* paragraph, and then release the mouse button.

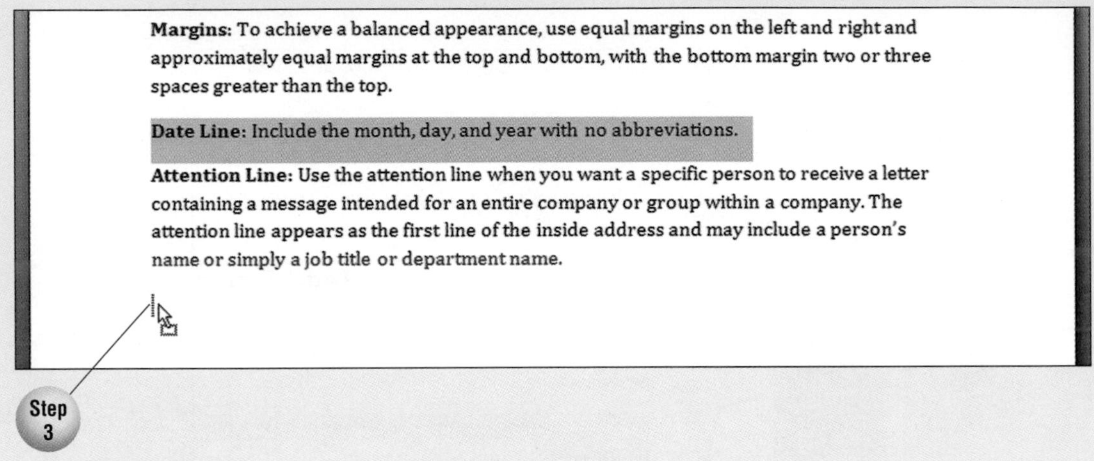

4. Deselect the text.
5. Save **C04Ex04.docx**.

Using the Paste Options Button

Paste Options

When you paste selected text, the Paste Options button displays in the lower right corner of the text. Click this button and a drop-down list displays, as shown in Figure 4.10. Use options from this drop-down list to specify how you want the pasted text formatted in the document. By default, pasted text retains the formatting of the selected text. You can choose to match the formatting of the pasted text with the formatting where the text is pasted, paste only the text without retaining formatting, or apply a style to pasted text.

Figure 4.10 Paste Options Button Drop-Down List

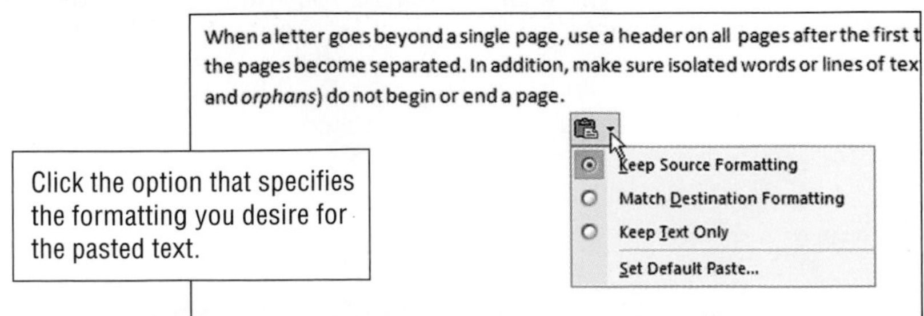

Exercise 4C

Using the Paste Options Button

1. With **C04Ex04.docx** open, open **Para04.docx**.
2. Press Ctrl + A to select the entire document and then click the Cut button in the Clipboard group.
3. Close **Para04.docx** without saving the changes.
4. Move the insertion point to the end of the document.
5. Click the Paste button in the Clipboard group.
6. Click the Paste Options button that displays at the end of the paragraph and then click the *Match Destination Formatting* option. (This changes the font so it matches the paragraphs before the pasted paragraphs.)

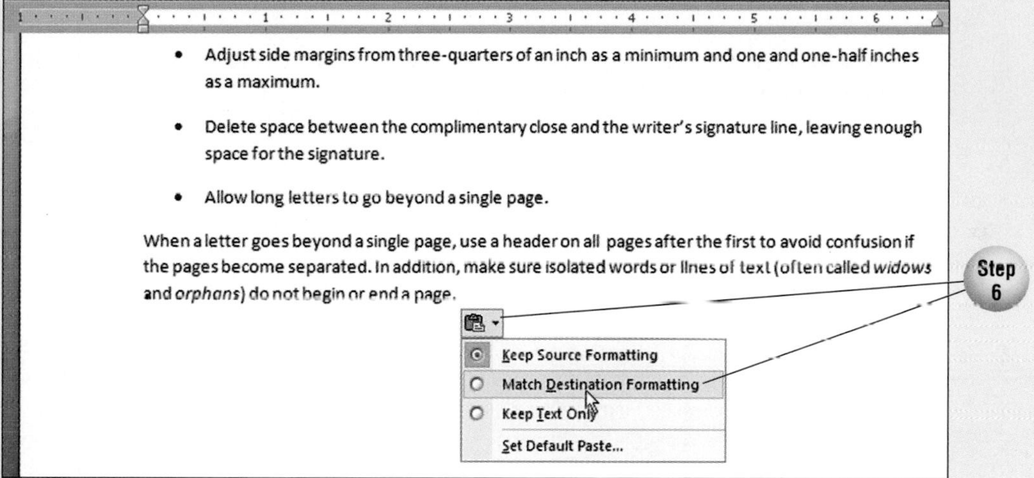

7. Apply paragraph shading of your choosing to the title of the document. (Make sure the title is readable through the shading.)
8. Save, print, and then close **C04Ex04.docx**.

Copying and Pasting Text

Copy Selected Text
1. Select text.
2. Click Copy button.
3. Move to desired location.
4. Click Paste button.

Copy

Copying selected text can be useful in documents that contain repetitive portions of text. You can use this function to insert duplicate portions of text in a document instead of retyping the text. After you have selected text, copy it to a different location with the Copy and Paste buttons in the Clipboard group in the Home tab or by using the mouse. You can also use the keyboard shortcut Ctrl + C to copy text.

Exercise 5A

Copying Text

1. Open **Notice02.docx** and save the document with the name **C04Ex05**.
2. Make the following changes to the document:
   a. Press Ctrl + A to select the entire document.
   b. Change the line spacing to single.
   c. Change the spacing after paragraphs from *10 pt* to *3 pt*. (You will need to select *10 pt* in the measurement box and then type 3.)
   d. Change the font to 12-point Candara bold.
   e. Press Ctrl + End to move the insertion point to the end of the document and then press the Enter key.
3. Copy the text in the document to the end of the document by completing the following steps:
   a. Press Ctrl + A to select the entire document.
   b. Click the Copy button in the Clipboard group.
   c. Move the insertion point to the end of the document.
   d. Click the Paste button in the Clipboard group.

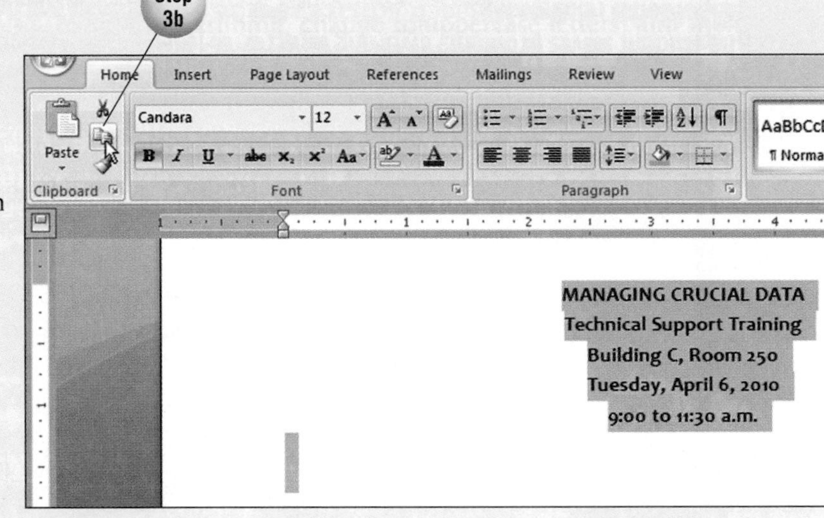

4. Copy the text again at the end of the document. To do this, position the insertion point at the end of the document, and then click the Paste button in the Clipboard group. (This inserts a copy of the text from the Clipboard.)
5. Save **C04Ex05.docx**.

To use the mouse to copy text, select the text and then position the I-beam pointer inside the selected text until it becomes an arrow pointer. Hold down the left mouse button and hold down the Ctrl key. Drag the arrow pointer (displays with both a small gray box and a box containing a plus symbol) to the location where you want to insert the copied text (make sure the insertion point, which displays as a grayed vertical bar, is positioned in the desired location), and then release the mouse button and then the Ctrl key.

Exercise 5B

Copying Selected Text Using the Mouse

1. With **C04Ex05.docx** open, select all of the text in the document using the mouse.
2. Move the I-beam pointer inside the selected text until it becomes an arrow pointer.
3. Hold down the Ctrl key and then the left mouse button. Drag the arrow pointer (displays with a box with a plus symbol inside) to the end of the document, release the mouse button, and then the Ctrl key.
4. Deselect the text.
5. Make sure all text fits on one page. If not, consider deleting any extra blank lines.
6. Save, print, and then close C04Ex05.docx.

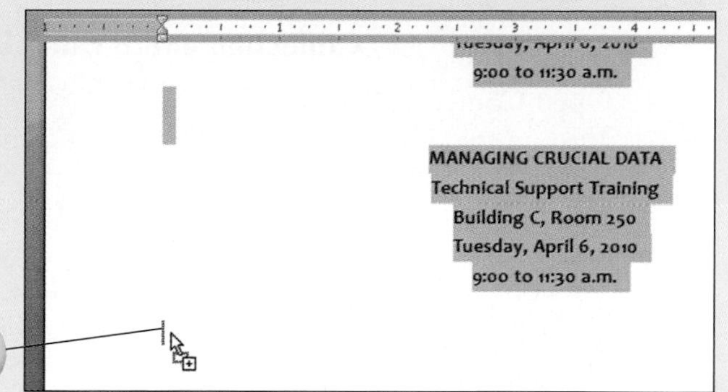

Using the Clipboard

Use Clipboard
1. Click Clipboard group dialog box launcher.
2. Select and copy desired text.
3. Move to desired location.
4. Click desired option in Clipboard task pane.

Use the Clipboard to collect and paste multiple items. You can collect up to 24 different items and then paste them in various locations. To display the Clipboard task pane, click the Clipboard group dialog box launcher located in the lower right corner of the Clipboard group. The Clipboard task pane displays at the left side of the screen in a manner similar to that shown in Figure 4.11.

Select text or an object you want to copy and then click the Copy button in the Clipboard group. Continue selecting text or items and clicking the Copy button. To insert an item, position the insertion point in the desired location and then click the button in the Clipboard task pane representing the item. If the copied item is text, the first 50 characters display beside the button in the Clipboard task pane. When all desired items are inserted, click the Clear All button to remove any remaining

Figure 4.11 Clipboard Task Pane

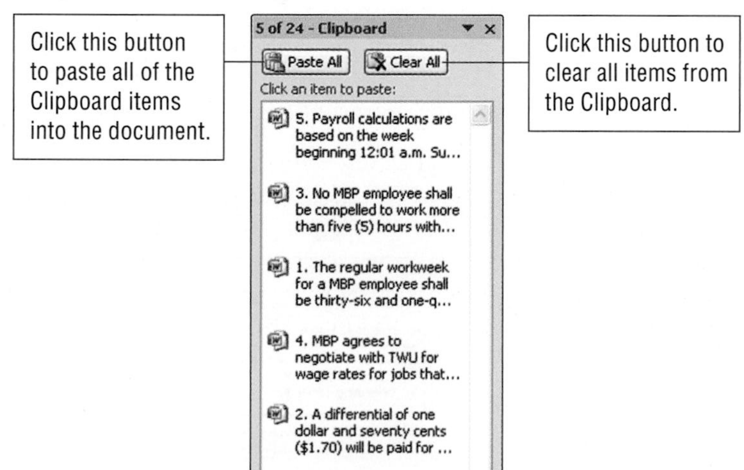

items. As noted earlier, the Clipboard provides temporary storage. When you turn off your computer, any items remaining in the Clipboard are deleted. To save Clipboard content permanently, save it as a separate document.

Exercise 6A

Collecting and Pasting Paragraphs of Text

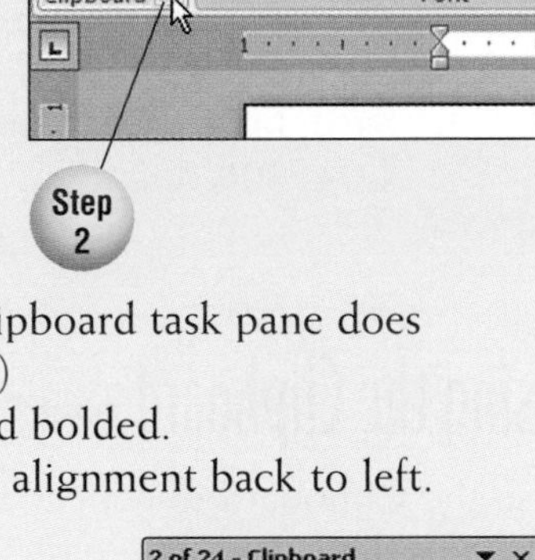

1. Open **ContItems01.docx.**
2. Turn on the display of the Clipboard task pane by clicking the Clipboard group dialog box launcher. (If the Clipboard task pane list box contains any text, click the Clear All button located towards the top of the task pane.)
3. Select paragraph 1 in the document (the *1.* is not selected) and then click the Copy button in the Clipboard group.
4. Select paragraph 3 in the document (the 3. is not selected) and then click the Copy button in the Clipboard group.
5. Close **ContItems01.docx.**
6. Paste the paragraphs by completing the following steps:
   a. Press Ctrl + N to display a new blank document. (If the Clipboard task pane does not display, click the Clipboard group dialog box launcher.)
   b. Type **CONTRACT NEGOTIATION ITEMS** centered and bolded.
   c. Press the Enter key, turn off bold, and return the paragraph alignment back to left.
   d. Click the Paste All button in the Clipboard task pane to paste both paragraphs in the document.
   e. Click the Clear All button in the Clipboard task pane.
7. Open **Contract01.docx.**
8. Select and then copy each of the following paragraphs:
   a. Paragraph 2 in the *Wages* section.
   b. Paragraph *4* in the *Wages* section.
   c. Paragraph *1* in the *Workweek* section.
   d. Paragraph 3 in the *Workweek* section.
   e. Paragraph *5* in the *Workweek* section.
9. Close **Contract01.docx.**
10. Make sure the insertion point is positioned at the end of the document and then paste the paragraphs by completing the following steps:
    a. Click the button in the Clipboard task pane representing paragraph 2. (When the paragraph is inserted in the document, the paragraph number changes to 3.)
    b. Click the button in the Clipboard task pane representing paragraph *4*.
    c. Click the button in the Clipboard task pane representing paragraph 3.
    d. Click the button in the Clipboard task pane representing paragraph *5*.
11. Click the Clear All button located toward the top of the Clipboard task pane.
12. Close the Clipboard task pane.
13. Save the document and name it **C04Ex06.**
14. Print and then close **C04Ex06.docx.**

Using Paste Special

Use options at the Paste Special dialog box, shown in Figure 4.12, to specify the format for pasted text. Display this dialog box by clicking the Paste button arrow in the Clipboard group and then clicking *Paste Special* at the drop-down list. The options in the *As* list box vary depending on the cut or copied text or object and the source application. For example, in Exercise 6b you will select and copy text from one document to another and paste the text without the formatting.

Figure 4.12 Paste Special Dialog Box

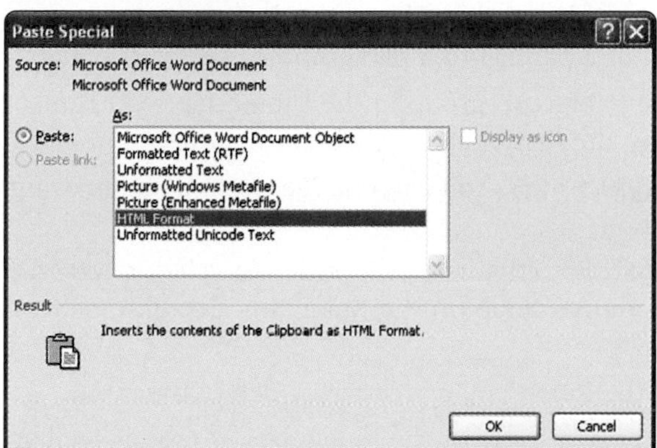

Exercise 6B

Copying Text Using the Paste Special Dialog Box

1. With **C04Ex06.docx** open, press Ctrl + End to move the insertion point to the end of the document and then press the Enter key once.
2. Open the document named **TeamMembers.docx**.
3. Press Ctrl + A to select the entire document and then click the Copy button.
4. Close **TeamMembers.docx**.
5. At the **C04Ex06.docx** document, click the Paste button arrow and then click *Paste Special* at the drop-down list.
6. At the Paste Special dialog box, click *Unformatted Text* in the *As* list box.
7. Click OK to close the dialog box.
8. Select and then bold the title *Negotiating Team*.
9. Select the names below the title and then click the Bullets button.
10. Save, print, and then close **C04Ex06.docx**.

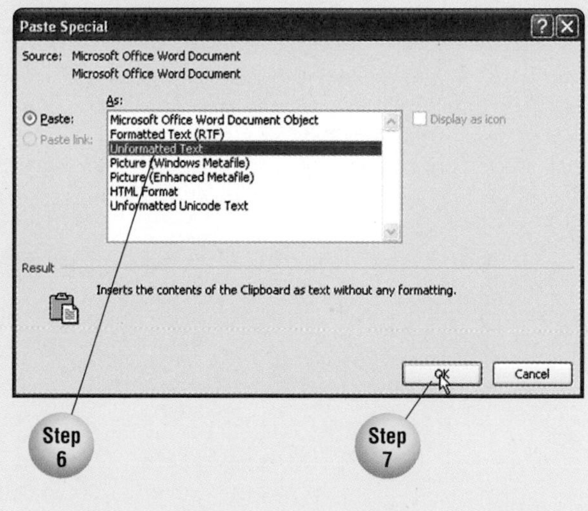

Chapter Summary

- A paragraph created in Word contains an invisible frame, and you can insert a border around this frame. Click the Borders button arrow to display a drop-down list of border choices.
- Apply shading to text by clicking the Shading button arrow and then clicking the desired color at the drop-down gallery.
- Use options at the Borders and Shading dialog box with the Borders tab selected to add a customized border to a paragraph or selected paragraphs and use options with the Shading tab selected to add shading or a pattern to a paragraph or selected paragraphs.
- With the Sort button in the Paragraph group in the Home tab, you can sort text arranged in paragraphs alphabetically by the first character, which includes numbers, symbols, or letters.
- By default, tabs are set every 0.5 inch. You can change these defaults using the Ruler or with options at the Tabs dialog box.
- Use the Alignment button at the left side of the Ruler to select a left, right, center, decimal, or bar tab. When you set a tab on the Ruler, any default tabs to the left are automatically deleted.
- After a tab has been set on the Ruler, you can move or delete the tab.
- At the Tabs dialog box, you can set any of the four types of tabs as well as a bar at a specific measurement. You can also set tabs with preceding leaders and clear one tab or all tabs. Preceding leaders can be periods, hyphens, or underlines.
- Cut, copy, and paste text using buttons in the Clipboard group or with keyboard shortcuts.
- When selected text is pasted, the Paste Options button displays in the lower right corner of the text with options for specifying how you want information pasted in the document.
- With the Office Clipboard, you can collect up to 24 items and then paste them in various locations in a document.

Commands review

FEATURE	RIBBON TAB, GROUP	BUTTON, OPTION	KEYBOARD SHORTCUT
Borders	Home, Paragraph	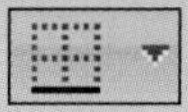	
Borders and Shading dialog box	Home, Paragraph	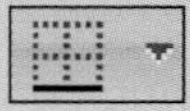 , Borders and Shading	
Clear character and paragraph formatting	Home, Font		
Clear paragraph formatting			Ctrl + Q
Clipboard task pane	Home, Clipboard		
Copy text	Home, Clipboard		Ctrl + C
Cut text	Home, Clipboard		Ctrl + X
New Line command			Shift + Enter
Paragraph dialog box	Home, Paragraph Page Layout, Paragraph		
Paste text	Home, Clipboard		Ctrl + V
Shading	Home, Paragraph		
Sort Text dialog box	Home, Paragraph		
Tabs dialog box	Home, Paragraph	 , Tabs	

Reviewing key points

Completion: In the space provided at the right, indicate the correct term, symbol, or command.

1. The Borders button is located in this group in the Home tab. ____________
2. Use options at this dialog box with the Borders tab selected to add a customized border to a paragraph or selected paragraphs. ____________
3. Sort text arranged in paragraphs alphabetically by the first character, which includes numbers, symbols, or this. ____________
4. By default, each tab is set apart from the other by this measurement. ____________
5. This is the default tab type. ____________
6. When setting tabs on the Ruler, choose the tab type with this button. ____________
7. Press these keys to end a line with the New Line command. ____________
8. Tabs can be set on the Ruler or here. ____________
9. This group in the Home tab contains the Cut, Copy, and Paste buttons. ____________
10. This is the keyboard shortcut to paste text. ____________
11. To copy selected text with the mouse, hold down this key while dragging selected text. ____________
12. With this task pane, you can collect up to 24 items and then paste the items in various locations in the document. ____________

Applying your skills

Assessment 1 Format an Abbreviations Document

1. Open **Document10.docx** and save the document with the name **C04A01**.
2. Type the text shown in Figure 4.13 immediately below the *R.N. Registered Nurse* text. Make sure you tab to the correct tab stop and press the Enter key to end each line.
3. Apply the Heading 1 style to the title *Abbreviations* and apply the Heading 2 style to the two headings *Personal Names* and *Academic, Professional, and Religious Designations*.
4. Change the style set to *Formal*.
5. Apply the *Module* theme.

6. Select the columns of text in the *PERSONAL NAMES* section and then drag the left tab at the 1-inch mark on the Ruler to the 0.5 inch mark and drag the left tab at the 3.5-inch mark on the Ruler to the 1.5-inch mark.
7. Select the columns of text in the *ACADEMIC, PROFESSIONAL, AND RELIGIOUS DESIGNATIONS* section and then complete the following:
   a. Sort the text.
   b. Drag the left tab at the 1-inch mark on the Ruler to the 0.5-inch mark.
   c. Move the left tab at the 3.5-inch mark on the Ruler to the 1.5-inch mark.
8. Apply a top border to the title *ABBREVIATIONS* (in the same color as the bottom border) and apply shading of your choosing.
9. Apply shading to the other two headings in the document.
10. Save, print, and then close **C04A01.docx**.

Figure 4.13 Assessment 1

M.D.	Doctor of Medicine
Ed.D.	Doctor of Education
D.D.S.	Doctor of Dental Science
D.D.	Doctor of Divinity

Assessment 2 Type and Format a Table of Contents Document

1. At a blank document, type the document shown in Figure 4.14 with the following specifications:
   a. Change the font to 11-point Cambria.
   b. Bold and center the title as shown.
   c. Before typing the text in columns, display the Tabs dialog box, and then set left tabs at the 1-inch mark and the 1.5-inch mark, and a right tab with dot leaders at the 5.5-inch mark.
2. Save the document with the name **C04A02**.
3. Print **C04A02.docx**.
4. Select the text in columns and then move the tab symbols on the Ruler as follows:
   a. Delete the left tab symbol that displays at the 1.5-inch mark.
   b. Set a new left tab at the 0.5-inch mark.
   c. Move the right tab at the 5.5-inch mark to the 6-inch mark.
   d. Deselect the text.
5. Apply paragraph borders and shading of your choosing to enhance the visual appeal of the document.
6. Save, print, and then close **C04A02.docx**.

Figure 4.14 **Assessment 2**

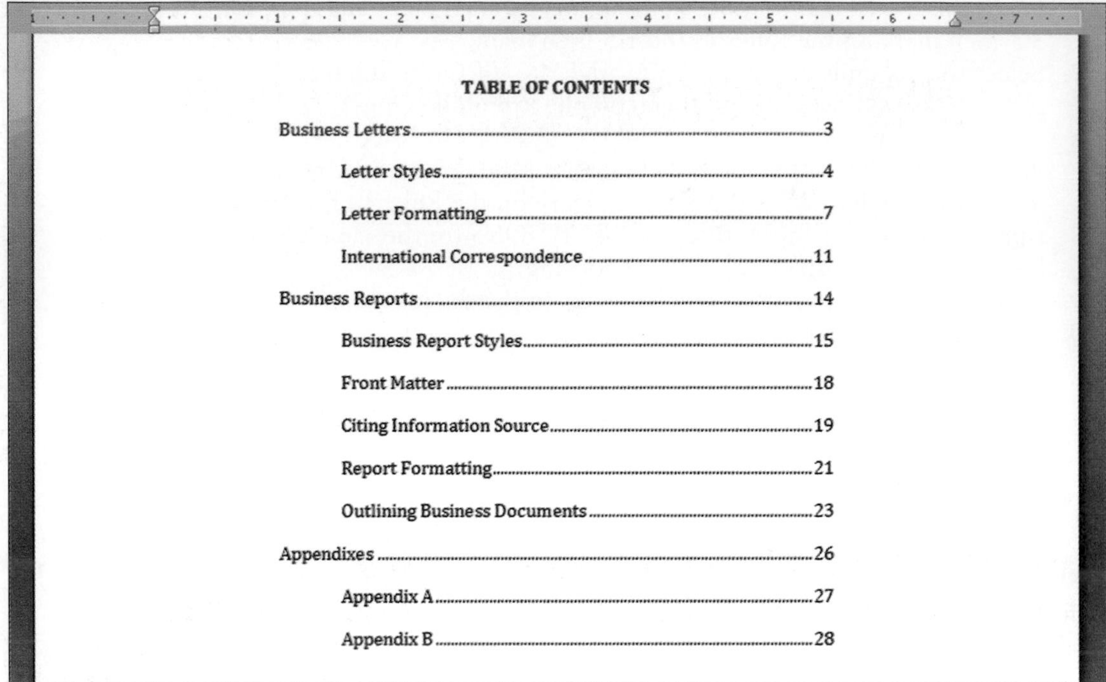
TABLE OF CONTENTS

Business Letters........3
Letter Styles........4
Letter Formatting........7
International Correspondence........11
Business Reports........14
Business Report Styles........15
Front Matter........18
Citing Information Source........19
Report Formatting........21
Outlining Business Documents........23
Appendixes........26
Appendix A........27
Appendix B........28

Assessment 3 Type an Employee List

1. At a blank document, create the document shown in Figure 4.15 with the following specifications:
   a. Change the font to 12-point Candara.
   b. Bold text as shown in the figure.
   c. When typing the text in columns, set a left tab for the first column, a center tab for the second column, and a right tab for the third column. (You determine the tab measurements.)
   d. Apply shading as shown in the figure.
   e. Remove the 10 points of spacing below the title *MOBILE BAY PRODUCTS*.
2. Save the document and name it **C04A03**.
3. Print and then close **C04A03.docx**.

Figure 4.15 Assessment 3

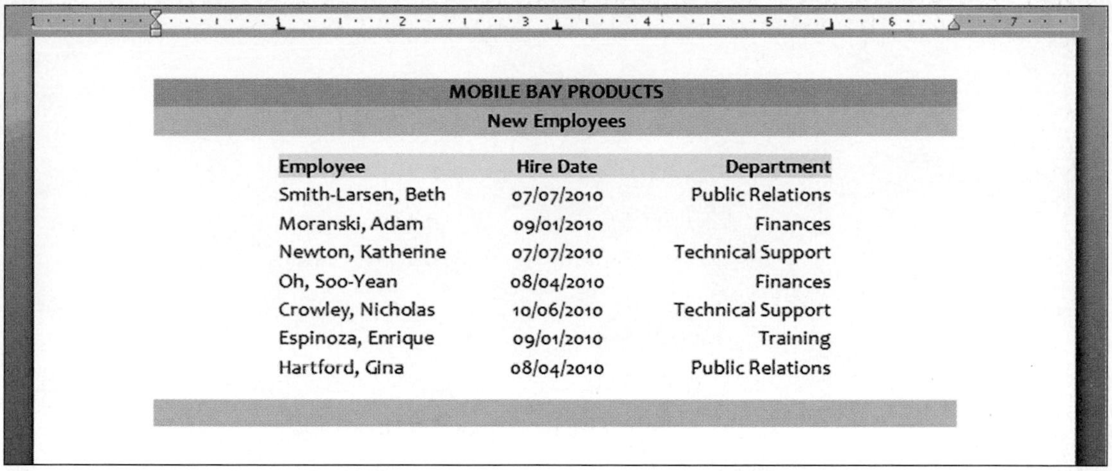

MOBILE BAY PRODUCTS		
New Employees		
Employee	**Hire Date**	**Department**
Smith-Larsen, Beth	07/07/2010	Public Relations
Moranski, Adam	09/01/2010	Finances
Newton, Katherine	07/07/2010	Technical Support
Oh, Soo-Yean	08/04/2010	Finances
Crowley, Nicholas	10/06/2010	Technical Support
Espinoza, Enrique	09/01/2010	Training
Hartford, Gina	08/04/2010	Public Relations

Assessment 4 Format a Beta Testing Agreement Document

1. Open **Agreement01.docx** and save the document with the name **C04A04**.
2. Select and then delete the paragraph that begins *Licensee agrees that Software includes . . . .*
3. Move the paragraph that begins *This Agreement shall be governed, construed and . . .* above the paragraph that begins *In consideration of the mutual covenants . . . .*
4. Open **Document11.docx**.
5. Turn on the display of the Clipboard task pane.
6. Select and then copy the first paragraph.
7. Select and then copy the second paragraph.
8. Select and then copy the third paragraph.
9. Select and then copy the fifth paragraph.
10. Close **Document11.docx**.
11. With **C04A04.docx** open, turn on the display of the Clipboard task pane.
12. Paste the paragraph that begins *Licensee shall comply with . . .* above the paragraph that begins *In consideration of the mutual . . . .*
13. Paste the paragraph that begins *This Agreement constitutes the entire . . .* above the line of text that begins *Stylus Enterprises:*.
14. Paste the paragraph that begins *IN WITNESS WHEREOF, parties hereto . . .* above the line of text that begins *Stylus Enterprises:*.
15. Clear all items from the Clipboard task pane and then close it.
16. Apply border and shading to enhance the visual appeal of the agreement.
17. Save, print, and then close **C04A04.docx**.

Chapter 5

Proofing Documents

Tutorial 5.1
Proofreading a Document
Tutorial 5.2
Getting Document Information

Performance Objectives

Upon successful completion of Chapter 5, you will be able to:

- Complete a spelling and grammar check on text in a document
- Create a custom dictionary and change the default dictionary
- Display synonyms and antonyms for specific words using the Thesaurus
- Display document word, paragraph, and character counts
- Use the translation feature to translate words from English to other languages
- Search for and request specific information from online sources

Word includes a number of proofing tools to help create thoughtful and well-written documents. In addition to using a spell checker, grammar checker, and Thesaurus, you can display information about a document's readability. With options at the Research task pane you can translate words from English to other languages and search for and request specific information from online sources. In this chapter you will learn how to use these proofing tools as well as how to create a custom dictionary.

Note: Before beginning computer exercises for this chapter, copy to your storage medium the Chapter05 folder from the CD that accompanies this textbook and then make Chapter05 the active folder.

QUICK STEPS

Check Spelling and Grammar

1. Click Review tab.
2. Click Spelling & Grammar button.
3. Change or ignore error.
4. Click OK.

Checking the Spelling and Grammar in a Document

Two tools for creating professional, polished-looking documents are a spell checker and a grammar checker. Word's spell checker finds misspelled words and offers replacement words. It also finds duplicate words and irregular capitalizations. When you spell check a document, the spell checker compares the words in your document to the words in its dictionary. If the spell checker finds a match, it passes over the word. If it does not find a match, the spell checker stops and selects the following:

- a misspelled word, when the misspelling does not match another word that exists in the dictionary
- typographical errors (such as transposed letters)
- double word occurrences (such as *and and*)

- irregular capitalization
- some proper names
- jargon and some technical terms

Word's grammar checker searchs a document for errors in grammar, punctuation, and word usage. Word's spell checker and the grammar checker can help you create a well-written document, but they do not replace the need for proofreading.

Before checking the spelling or grammar of a document you are working in, save the document first; or, open a saved document and then complete these basic steps:

1. Click the Review tab.
2. Click the Spelling and Grammar button. (You can also press the keyboard shortcut F7.)
3. If the spell checker detects an error, it selects the misspelled word and displays a Spelling and Grammar dialog box, similar to the one shown in Figure 5.1. The sentence that contains the misspelled word displays in the *Not in Dictionary:* text box. If the grammar checker detects a grammatical error, it selects the sentence with the error and displays a Spelling and Grammar dialog box, similar to the one shown in Figure 5.2.
4. If a misspelled word is selected, replace the word with the correct spelling, tell Word to ignore it and continue checking the document, or add the word to a custom dictionary. If a sentence containing a grammatical error is selected, it displays in the top text box in the Spelling and Grammar dialog box. Choose to ignore or change errors found by the grammar checker.
5. When the spelling and grammar check is complete, the message *The spelling and grammar check is complete* displays. Click OK to close the message box or press Enter.

Figure 5.1 Spelling and Grammar Dialog Box with Spelling Error Selected

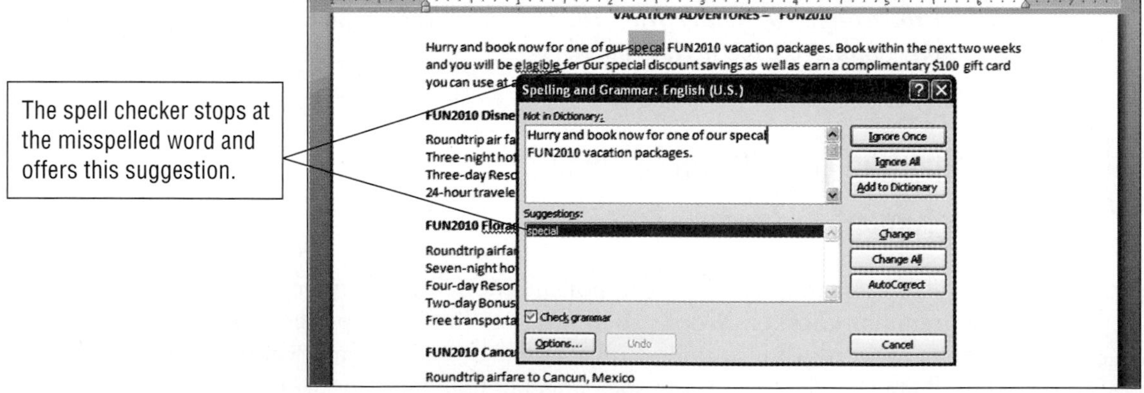

Figure 5.2 Spelling and Grammar Dialog Box with Grammar Error Selected

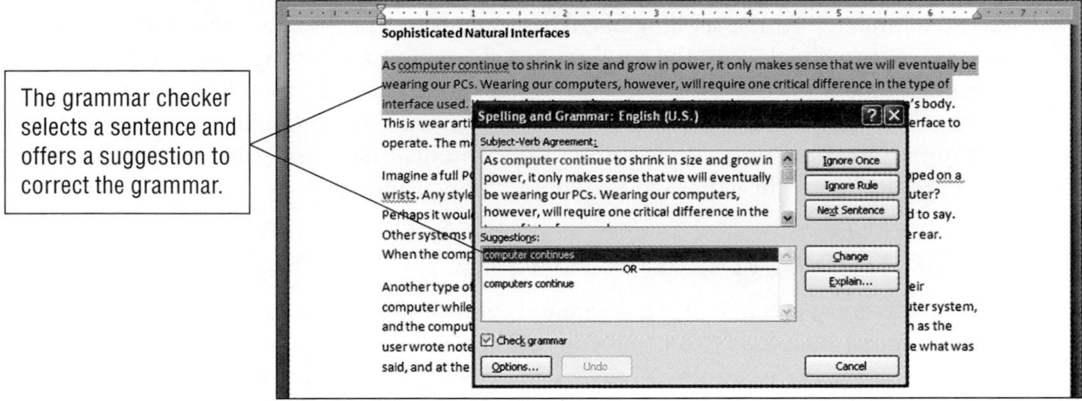

When a word or sentence is selected during a spelling or grammar check, you need to determine if the word or sentence should be corrected or ignored. Word provides buttons at the right side and bottom of the Spelling and Grammar dialog box to help you make decisions. The buttons that display vary depending on the type of error selected. These buttons and their functions are described in Table 5.1.

Table 5.1 Spelling and Grammar Dialog Box Buttons

Button	Function
Ignore Once	During spell checking, skips that occurrence of the word; during grammar checking, leaves currently selected text as written.
Ignore All	During spell checking, skips that occurrence of the word and all other occurrences of the word in the document.
Ignore Rule	During grammar checking, leaves currently selected text as written and ignores the current rule for remainder of the grammar check.
Add to Dictionary	Adds selected word to the main spell check dictionary.
Change	Replaces selected word in sentence with selected word in *Suggestions* list box.
Change All	Replaces selected word in sentence with selected word in *Suggestions* list box and all other occurrences of the word.
AutoCorrect	Inserts selected word and correct spelling of word in AutoCorrect dialog box.
Explain	During grammar checking, displays grammar rule information about the selected text.
Undo	Reverses most recent spelling and grammar action.
Next Sentence	Accepts manual changes made to sentence and then continues grammar checking.
Options	Displays a dialog box with options for customizing a spelling and grammar check.

Spell Checking a Document

Word completes both a spelling check and grammar check on a document by default. If you want to check only the spelling in a document and not the grammar, remove the check mark from the *Check grammar* check box located in the lower left corner of the Spelling and Grammar dialog box. If you want to complete a spelling and grammar check on only a portion of a document, first select the text you want checked and then click the Spelling and Grammar button.

Editing while Spell Checking

While you are spell checking a document, you can temporarily leave the Spelling and Grammar dialog box to make corrections in the document and then resume spell checking. For example, suppose while spell checking you notice a sentence that you want to change. To correct the sentence, you would move the mouse pointer to the location in the sentence where you want to make the change, click the left mouse button, and make the change. To resume spell checking, you would click the Resume button, which formerly displayed as the Ignore Once button.

Change Spelling Options

1. Click Office button, Word Options.
2. Click *Proofing*.
3. Specify options.
4. Click OK.

Changing Spelling Options

Click the Options button at the Spelling and Grammar dialog box, and the Word Options dialog box displays with the *Proofing* option selected, as shown in Figure 5.3. (You can also display the Word Options dialog box by clicking the Office button, clicking the Word Options button at the bottom of the drop-down list, and then clicking *Proofing* in the left panel of the dialog box.) Use options at this dialog box to customize spell checking by identifying what you want the spell checker to check or ignore. You can also create or edit a custom dictionary.

Figure 5.3 Word Options Dialog Box with Proofing Selected

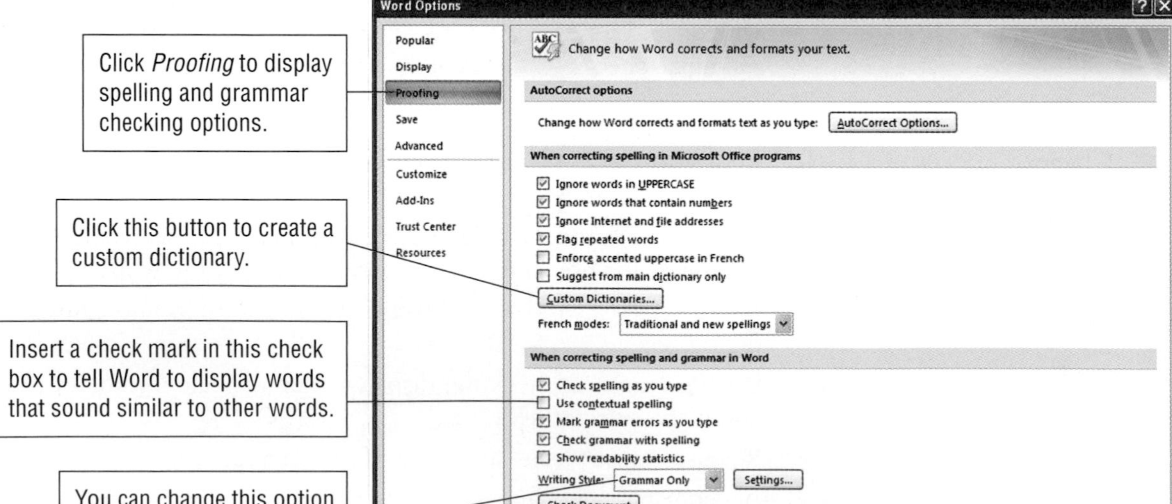

Exercise 1

Spell Checking a Document with Words in Uppercase and with Numbers

1. Open **SpellCheck01.docx** and save the document with the name **C05Ex01**.
2. Check spell checking options by completing the following steps:
   a. Click the Office button.
   b. Click the Word Options button located at the bottom of the drop-down list.
   c. At the Word Options dialog box, click the *Proofing* option in the left panel.
   d. Make sure the *Ignore words in UPPERCASE* check box and the *Ignore words that contain numbers* check box each contain a check mark.
   e. Click OK to close the dialog box.

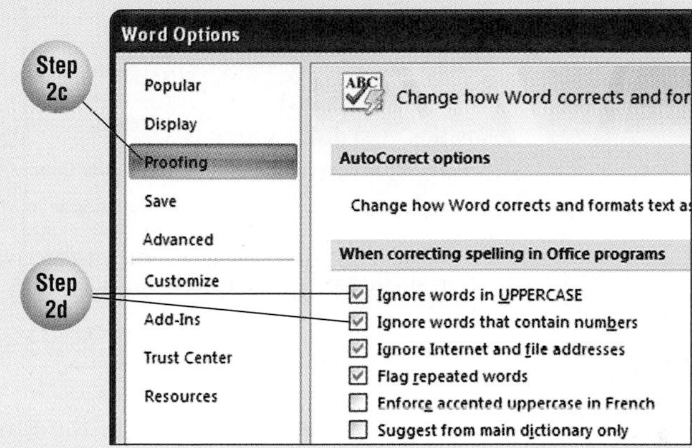

3. Complete a spelling check on the document by completing the following steps:
   a. Click the Review tab.
   b. Click the Spelling & Grammar button in the Proofing group.
   c. When the spell checker selects the word *specal*, the proper spelling is selected in the *Suggestions* list box. Click the Change button (or Change All button) to correct the misspelling.
   d. When the spell checker selects the word *elagible*, the proper spelling is selected in the *Suggestions* list box. Click the Change button.

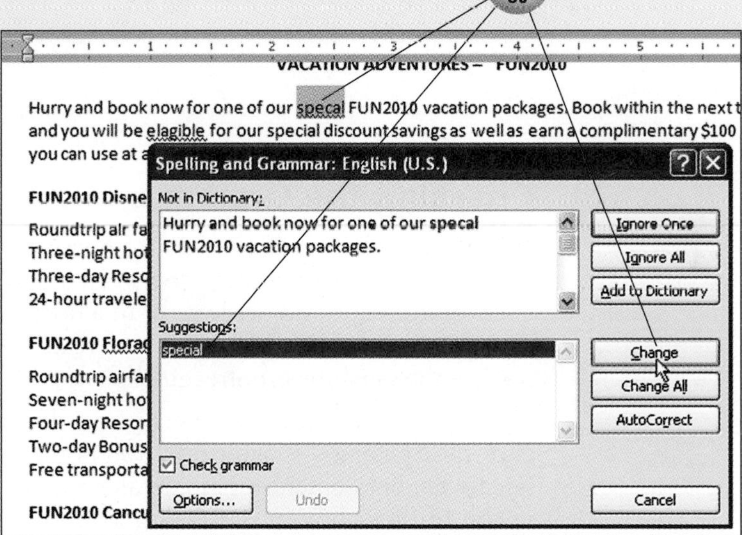

e. When the spell checker selects *itnte*, the proper spelling of *into* is included in the *Suggestions* list box but it is not selected. Click *into* in the *Suggestions* list box and then click the Change button.
f. When the spell checker selects *Florada*, the proper spelling is selected in the *Suggestions* list box. Click the Change button.
g. When the spell checker selects *accomodations*, the proper spelling is selected in the *Suggestions* list box. Click the Change button.

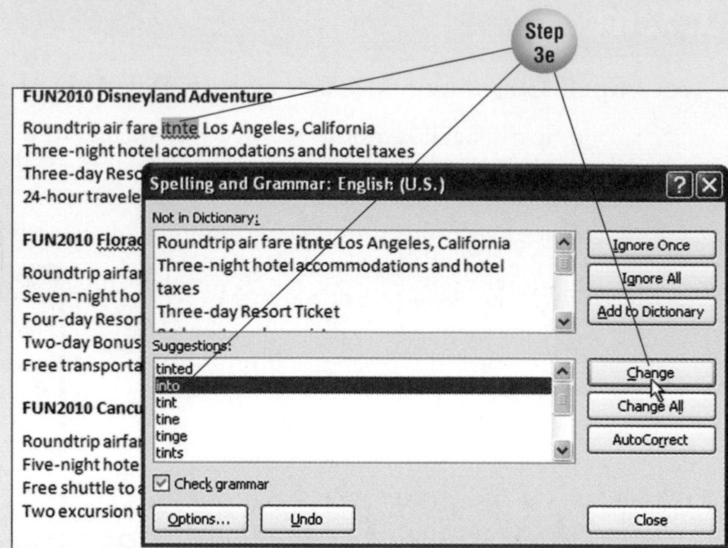

h. When the grammar checker selects the paragraph of text below the heading *FUN2010 Cancun Adventure*, click the Ignore Rule button.
i. When the message displays telling you that the spelling and grammar check is complete, click the OK button.

4. Save, print, and then close **C05Ex01.docx**.

Checking the Grammar in a Document

Word's grammar checking feature allows you to search a document for errors in grammar, style, punctuation, and word usage. Like the spell checker, the grammar checker does not find every error in a document and may stop at correct phrases. The grammar checker can help you create a well-written document, but it does not replace the need for proofreading.

To complete a grammar check on a document, click the Review tab and then click the Spelling & Grammar button in the Proofing group. The grammar checker selects the first sentence that contains a grammatical error and displays the sentence in the top text box in the dialog box. A suggested correction displays in the *Suggestions* text box. You can choose to ignore or change errors found by the grammar checker. When the grammar checker is finished, the open document displays on the screen with the changes made during the check are inserted in it. By default, a spelling check is completed on a document during a grammar check.

The grammar checker checks a document for a variety of grammar and style errors. In some situations, you may want the grammar checker to ignore a particular grammar or style rule. To tell the grammar checker to ignore a rule, click the Ignore Rule button the first time the text breaking that particular grammar or style rule displays. If the grammar checker selects a sentence that contains a grammar or style error and you want the sentence left as written, click the Next Sentence button. This tells the grammar checker to leave the current sentence unchanged and move to the next sentence.

When a sentence with a grammar error displays in the Spelling and Grammar dialog box, click the Explain button and the Word Help window displays with information about the specific grammar rule. Read this information carefully. Some suggestions may not be valid, and a problem identified by the grammar checker may not be a problem. After reading the information in the Word Help window, click the Close button located in the upper right corner of the window.

Exercise 2A

Checking Grammar in a Document

1. Open **GrammarCheck01.docx** and save the document with the name **C05Ex02**.
2. Check the grammar in the document by completing the following steps:
   a. Click the Review tab.
   b. Click the Spelling & Grammar button in the Proofing group.
   c. When the grammar checker selects the sentence that begins *As computer continue to . . .* and displays *computer continues* and *computers continue* in the *Suggestions* text box, click the Explain button.
   d. Read the information about Subject-Verb Agreement that displays in the Word Help window and then click the Close button located in the upper right corner of the window.
   e. Click *computers continue* in the *Suggestions* list box and then click the Change button.

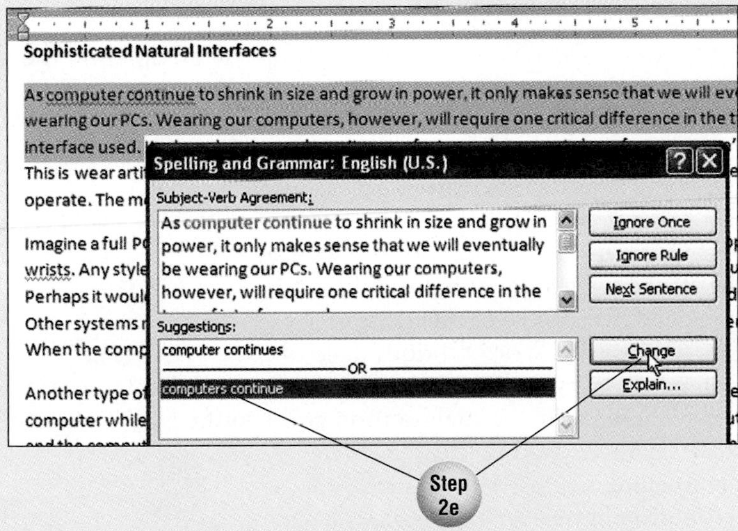

   f. The grammar checker selects the sentence that begins *Keyboards, mice, and monitors are . . .* and displays *too* in the *Suggestions* list box.
   g. Click the Explain button, read the information on commonly confused words that displays in the Word Help window, and then close the window.
   h. With *too* selected in the *Suggestions* list box, click the Change button.
   i. When the grammar checker selects the sentence that begins *Imagine a full PC system the size . . .*, click *on a wrist* in the *Suggestions* list box and then click the Change button.
   j. At the message telling you that the spelling and grammar check is complete, click OK.
3. Save **C05Ex02.docx**.

Change Grammar Checking Options

1. Click Office button, Word Options.
2. Click *Proofing*.
3. Specify options.
4. Click OK.

Changing Grammar Checking Options

You can customize the type of grammar checking you complete on a document by using options in the *When correcting spelling and grammar in Word* section of the Word Options dialog box with *Proofing* selected. Insert a check mark in the check box preceding those options you want active in a document and remove the check mark from the check boxes preceding those you want inactive.

Consider making active the *Use contextual spelling* option when you are proofing a document that contains words that sound similar but have different meanings, such as *to* and *too* and *there* and *their*. When this feature is active, Word inserts a wavy blue line below words that sound similar to other words.

By default, the grammar checker checks only the grammar in a document. The *Writing Style* option in the Word Options dialog box with *Proofing* selected has a default setting of *Grammar Only*. You can change this default setting to *Grammar & Style*. To determine what style issues the grammar checker will select, click the Settings button and the Grammar Settings dialog box displays with grammar options. Insert a check mark for those options you want active and remove the check mark from those options you want inactive during a grammar check.

Exercise 2B

Changing Grammar Settings

1. With **C05Ex02.docx** open, change grammar settings by completing the following steps:
   a. Click the Office button.
   b. Click the Word Options button located at the bottom of the drop-down list.
   c. At the Word Options dialog box, click the *Proofing* option in the left panel.
   d. Click the *Use contextual spelling* check box to insert a check mark.
   e. Click the down-pointing arrow at the right side of the *Writing Style* option box and then click *Grammar & Style* at the drop-down list.
   f. Click the Recheck Document button.
   g. At the message that displays, click Yes.
   h. Click OK to close the Word Options dialog box.
2. Complete grammar and style check on the document by completing the following steps:
   a. Press Ctrl + Home to move the insertion point to the beginning of the document.
   b. Make sure the Review tab is selected.
   c. Click the Spelling & Grammar button in the Proofing group.
   d. When the grammar checker selects the sentence that begins *This is wear artificial intelligence . . .* and inserts *where* in the *Suggestions* list box, click the Change button.

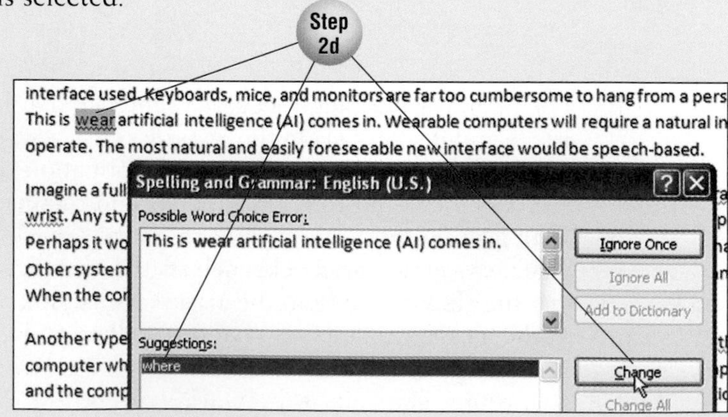

e. When the grammar checker selects the sentence that begins *Imagine a full PC system the size . . .*, click the Explain button. Read the information on verb use that displays in the Word Help window, close the window, and then click the Ignore Once button.
f. When the grammar checker selects the sentence that begins *When the computer speaks only . . .* and inserts *speaks*, in the *Suggestions* list box, click the Change button.
g. When the grammar checker selects the sentence that begins *Someone might want to talk to their . . .* and inserts *his or her* in the *Suggestions* list box, click the Change button.
h. At the message telling you that the spelling and grammar check is complete, click OK.

3. Save and then print **C05Ex02.docx**.

Displaying Readability Statistics

After you have completed a spelling and grammar check, you can display a document's readability statistics at the Readability Statistics dialog box. Figure 5.4 shows the dialog box and the readability statistics for **C05Ex02.docx**. Readability statistics provide useful information about the level of writing in a document, including the number of words, characters, paragraphs, and sentences in the document; the average number of sentences per paragraph, words per sentence, and characters per word. Readability statistics also include other information about a document's readability, such as the percentage of passive sentences, the Flesch Reading Ease score, and the Flesch-Kincaid grade level rating. You can control the display of readability statistics with the *Show readability statistics* check box in the Word Options dialog box with *Proofing* selected.

Show Readability Statistics
1. Click Office button, Word Options.
2. Click *Proofing*.
3. Click *Show readability statistics* check box.
4. Click OK.
5. Complete spelling and grammar check.

Figure 5.4 Readability Statistics Dialog Box

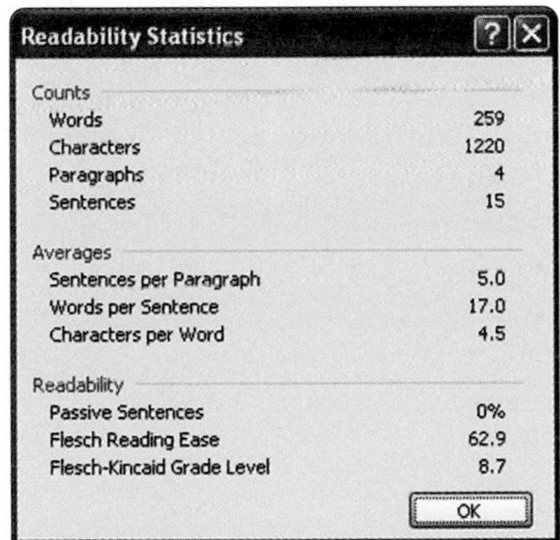

The Flesch Reading Ease score is based on the average number of syllables per word and the average number of words per sentence. The higher the score, the greater the number of people who will be able to understand the text in the document. Standard writing, such as newspapers and magazines, is generally given a score of 60 to 70. The Flesch-Kincaid Grade Level is based on the average number of syllables per word and the average number of words per sentence. The score indicates a grade level. Standard writing is generally written at the seventh or eighth grade level.

Exercise 2C

Displaying Readability Statistics

1. With **C05Ex02.docx** open, display readability statistics for the document by completing the following steps:
   a. Click the Office button and then click the Word Options button.
   b. At the Word Options dialog box, click *Proofing* in the left panel.
   c. Click the *Show readability statistics* check box to insert a check mark.
   d. Click OK to close the Word Options dialog box.
   e. Make sure the Review tab is selected and then click the Spelling & Grammar button.
   f. Look at the readability statistics that display in the Readability Statistics dialog box and then click OK to close the dialog box.

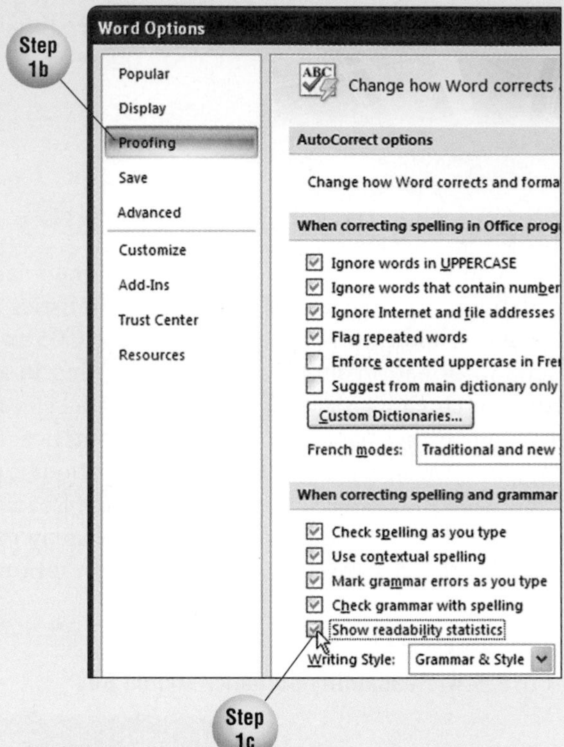

2. Change the grammar options back to the default by completing the following steps:
   a. Click the Office button and then click the Word Options button.
   b. At the Word Options dialog box, click *Proofing* in the left panel.
   c. Click the *Use contextual spelling* check box to remove the check mark.
   d. Click the *Show readability statistics* check box to remove the check mark.
   e. Click the down-pointing arrow at the right side of the *Writing Style* option box and then click *Grammar Only* at the drop-down list.
   f. Click OK to close the Word Options dialog box.
3. Save and then close **C05Ex02.docx**.

Creating a Custom Dictionary

When Word completes a spelling check on a document, it uses the default CUSTOM.DIC custom dictionary. You can add or remove words from this default dictionary. In a multiple-user environment, you might also consider creating your own custom dictionary and then selecting it as the default. In this way, multiple users can create their own dictionaries to use when spell checking a document.

To create a custom dictionary, display the Word Options dialog box with *Proofing* selected, and then click the Custom Dictionaries button. Clicking this button displays the Custom Dictionaries dialog box, shown in Figure 5.5. At this dialog box, click the New button to display the Create Custom Dictionary dialog box. Type a name for the dictionary in the *File name* text box and then press Enter. The new dictionary name will display in the *Dictionary List* box in the Custom Dictionaries dialog box. You can use more than one dictionary when spell checking a document. Insert a check mark in the check box next to any dictionary you want to use.

QUICK STEPS

Create Custom Dictionary
1. Click Office button, Word Options.
2. Click *Proofing.*
3. Click Custom Dictionaries button.
4. Click New button.
5. Type name for dictionary, press Enter.

Figure 5.5 Custom Dictionaries Dialog Box

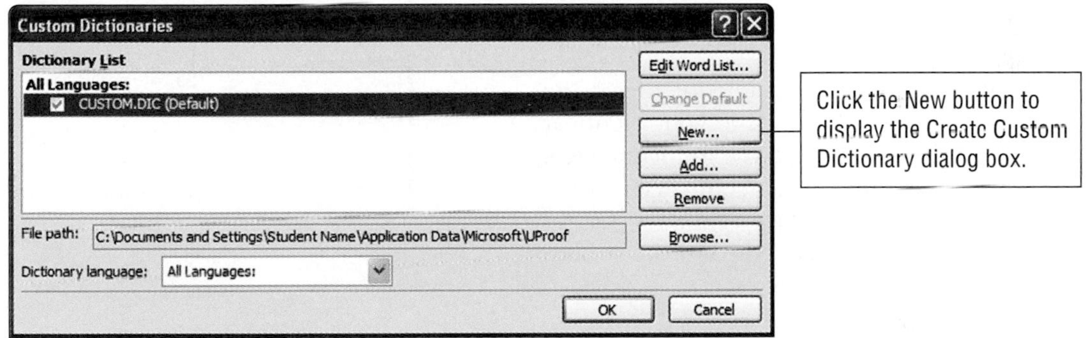

Changing the Default Dictionary

At the Custom Dictionaries dialog box, the default dictionary displays in the *Dictionary List* box followed by *(Default)*. You can change this default by clicking the desired dictionary name in the list box and then clicking the Change Default button.

Removing a Dictionary

Remove a custom dictionary with the Remove button at the Custom Dictionaries dialog box. To do this, display the Custom Dictionaries dialog box, click the dictionary name in the *Dictionary List* box, and then click the Remove button. You are not prompted to confirm the removal of the dictionary so make sure you select the correct name before clicking the Remove button.

Remove Custom Dictionary
1. Click Office button, Word Options.
2. Click *Proofing.*
3. Click Custom Dictionaries button.
4. Click custom dictionary name.
5. Click Remove.
6. Click OK.

Exercise 3A

Creating a Custom Dictionary and Changing the Default Dictionary

1. Open **Document12.docx**, notice the wavy red lines indicating words that are not recognized by the spell checker (that is, words not in the custom dictionary) and then close the document.
2. At a blank document, create a custom dictionary, add words to it, and then change the default dictionary by completing the following steps:
   a. Click the Office button and then click the Word Options button at the bottom of the drop-down list.
   b. At the Word Options dialog box, click *Proofing* in the left panel.
   c. Click the Custom Dictionaries button.
   d. At the Custom Dictionaries dialog box, click the New button.
   e. At the Create Custom Dictionary dialog box, type your first and last names (without a space between) in the *File name* text box and then press Enter.
   f. At the Custom Dictionaries dialog box, add a word to your dictionary by completing the following steps:
      1) Click your dictionary name in the *Dictionary List* box.
      2) Click the Edit Word List button.

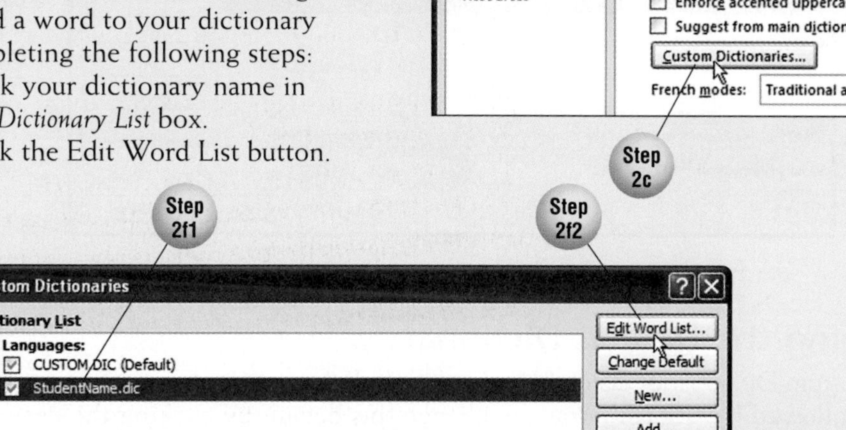

      3) At your custom dictionary dialog box, type **nano** in the *Word(s)* text box.
      4) Click the Add button.

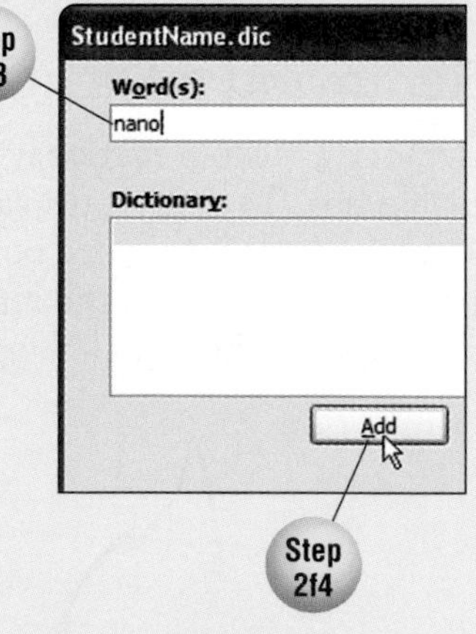

   g. Complete the steps outlined in 2f3 and 2f4 to add the following words:
      nanotubes
      nanotubules
      Nantero
   h. When you have added the words, click the OK button to close the dialog box.

i. At the Custom Dictionaries dialog box with your dictionary name selected in the *Dictionary List* box, click the Change Default button. (Notice that the word *(default)* displays after your custom dictionary.)

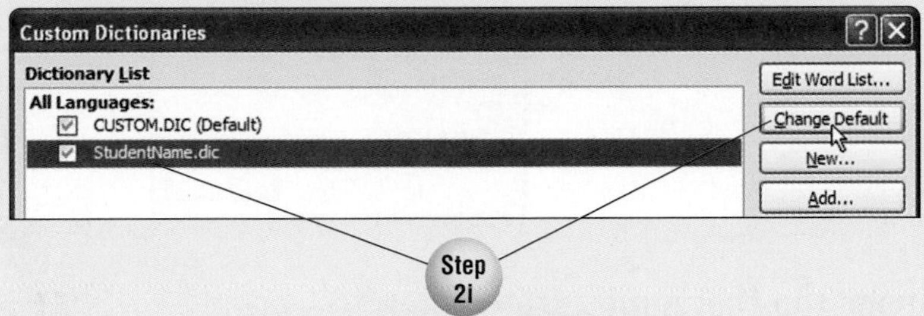

j. Click OK to close the Custom Dictionaries dialog box.
k. Click OK to close the Word Options dialog box.

3. Open **Document12.docx** and then save the document and name it **C05Ex03**.
4. Complete a spelling and grammar check on your document. (The spell checker will not stop at the words you added to your custom dictionary.)
5. Save and then print **C05Ex03.docx**.
6. Change the default dictionary and then remove your custom dictionary by completing the following steps:
   a. Click the Office button and then click the Word Options button at the bottom of the drop-down list.
   b. At the Word Options dialog box, click *Proofing* in the left panel.
   c. Click the Custom Dictionaries button.
   d. At the Custom Dictionaries dialog box, click CUSTOM.DIC in the *Dictionary List* box.
   e. Click the Change Default button. (This changes the default back to the CUSTOM.DIC dictionary.)
   f. Click your dictionary name in the *Dictionary List* box.
   g. Click the Remove button.
   h. Click OK to close the Custom Dictionaries dialog box.
   i. Click OK to close the Word Options dialog box.

Displaying Word Count

The Status bar displays the total number of words in your document. If you want to display more information, such as the number of pages, paragraphs, and lines, display the Word Count dialog box, shown in Figure 5.6. Display this dialog box by clicking the word count section of the Status bar or by clicking the Review tab and then clicking the Word Count button in the Proofing group. If you want to count the words in a portion of the document only, select the text first.

Display Word Count
Click Word Count section of Status bar.
OR
1. Click Review tab.
2. Click Word Count button.

Word Count

Figure 5.6 Word Count Dialog Box

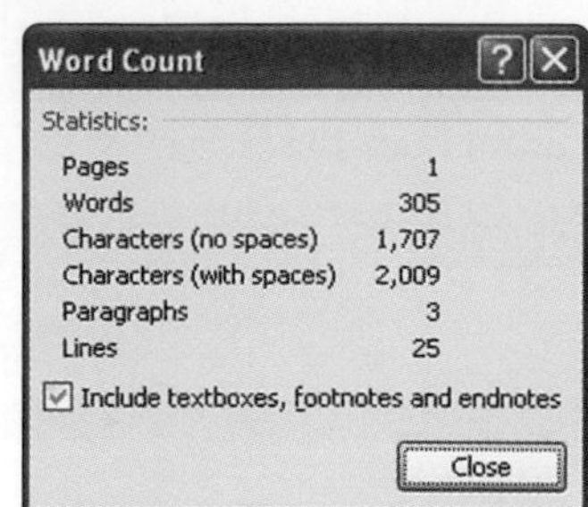

Using the Thesaurus

Use Thesaurus

1. Click Review tab.
2. Click Thesaurus button.
3. Type word in *Search for* text box.
4. Press Enter.

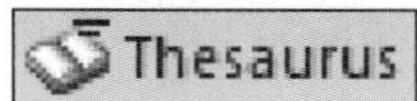

With Word's Thesaurus feature you can find synonyms, antonyms, and related words for a particular word. Synonyms are words that have the same or nearly the same meaning; antonyms are words that have opposite meanings. Word may display antonyms as well as synonyms for some words. With the Thesaurus, you can improve the clarity of business documents.

To use the Thesaurus, click the Review tab and then click the Thesaurus button in the Proofing group. (You can also use the keyboard shortcut Shift +F 7.) This displays the Research task pane. Click in the *Search for* text box located toward the top of the Research task pane, type the word for which you want to find synonyms or antonyms, and then press Enter or click the Start searching button (the button marked with a white arrow on a green background). A list of synonyms and antonyms displays in the task pane list box. Figure 5.7 shows the Research task pane with synonyms for the word *twist* displayed.

Figure 5.7 Research Task Pane

Type a word in this text box and press Enter. Synonyms and antonyms for the word display in the list box below.

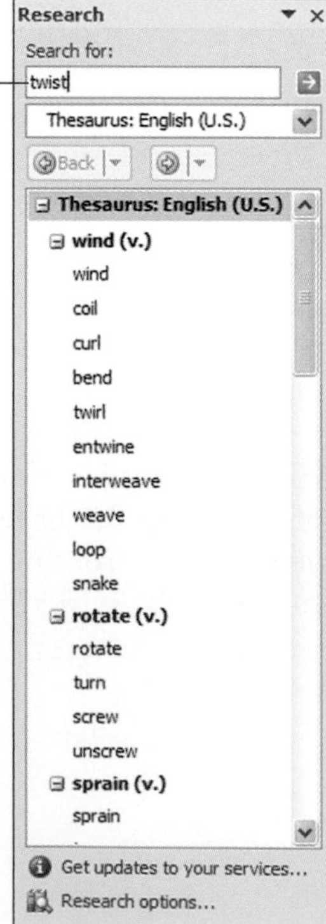

Depending on the word you are looking up, the words that display in the Research task pane list box may be followed by *(n.)* for *noun*, *(adj.)* for *adjective*, or *(adv.)* for *adverb*. When antonyms display, they are at the end of the list of related synonyms and they are followed by the word *(Antonym)*.

The Thesaurus provides synonyms for the selected word along with a list of related synonyms. For example, the task pane list box shown in Figure 5.7 displays several main synonyms for *twist,* and each is preceded by a minus symbol in a square. The minus symbol indicates that the list of related synonyms is displayed. Click the minus symbol and the list of related synonyms is removed from the task pane list box and the minus symbol changes to a plus symbol. If a synonym displays preceded by a plus symbol, click this symbol to show the list of related synonyms.

As you look up synonyms and antonyms for various words, you can display the list for previous words by clicking the Previous search button (contains a left arrow and the word *Back*) located above the Research task pane list box (see Figure 5.7). Click the Next search button to display the next search in the sequence. You can also click the down-pointing arrow at the right side of the Next search button to display a list of words for which you have looked up synonyms and antonyms.

Exercise 3B

Displaying Word Count and Using Thesaurus

1. With **C05Ex03.docx** open, click the word count section of the Status bar.

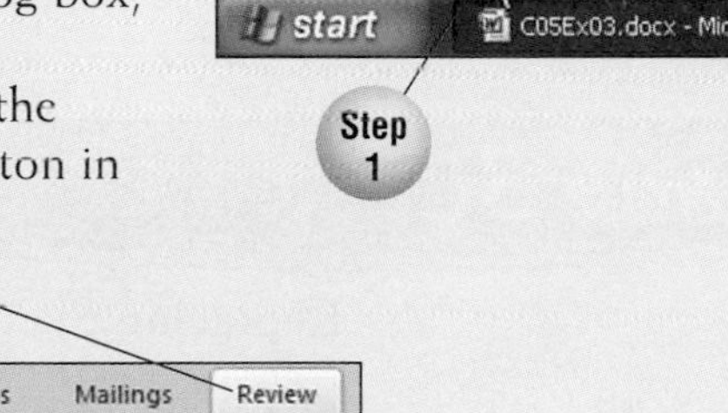

2. After reading the statistics in the Word Count dialog box, click the Close button.
3. Redisplay the Word Count dialog box by clicking the Review tab and then clicking the Word Count button in the Proofing group.

4. Click the Close button to close the Word Count dialog box.
5. Change the word *twist* in the first paragraph to *interweave* using the Thesaurus by completing the following steps:
   a. Select the word *twist* located in the last sentence of the first paragraph.
   b. Click the Review tab.

c. Click the Thesaurus button in the Proofing group.
d. At the Research task pane, hover the mouse pointer over the synonym *interweave*, click the down-pointing arrow that displays at the right of the word, and then click *Insert* at the drop-down list.

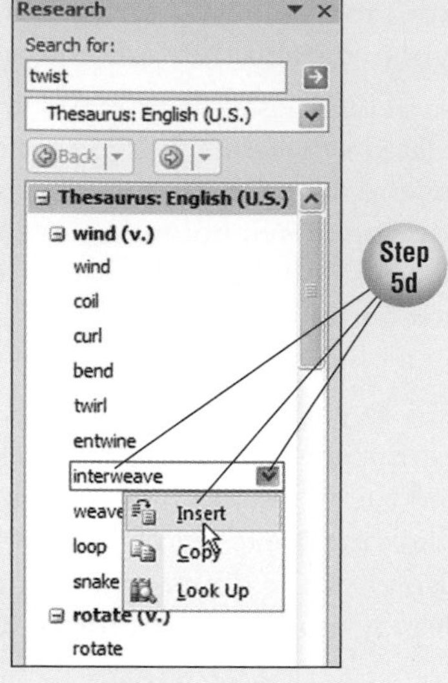

6. Follow similar steps to make the following changes using the Thesaurus:
   a. Change *fashion* in the first paragraph to *mold*.
   b. Change *perform* in the second sentence of the second paragraph to *execute*.
7. Close the Research task pane by clicking the Close button located in the upper right corner of the task pane.
8. Save **C05Ex03.docx**.

Displaying Synonyms Using a Shortcut Menu

Another method for displaying synonyms for a word is to use a shortcut menu. To do this, position the mouse pointer on the word and then click the *right* mouse button. At the shortcut menu that displays, point to Synonyms and then click the desired synonym at the side menu. Click the Thesaurus option at the bottom of the side menu to display synonyms and antonyms for the word in the Research task pane.

Exercise 3C

Replacing Synonyms Using a Shortcut Menu

1. With **C05Ex03.docx** open, position the mouse pointer on the word *thrilling* located in the second sentence from the end of the document.
2. Click the *right* mouse button.
3. At the shortcut menu that displays, point to Synonyms and then click *exciting* at the side menu.
4. Change the word *a* that displays before *exciting* to *an*.
5. Save, print, and then close **C05Ex03.docx**.

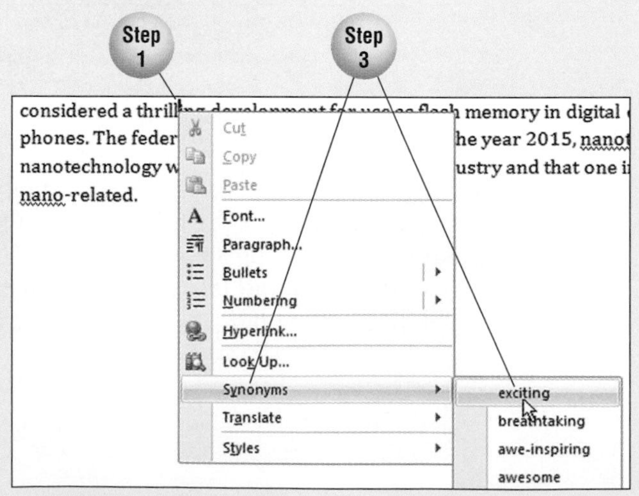

Researching and Requesting Information

Along with the Thesaurus, the Research task pane offers options for translating text and searching for and requesting specific information from online sources. The Research task pane displays when you click the Research, Thesaurus, or Translate buttons in the Proofing group in the Review tab. You can also display the Research task pane by holding down the Alt key and then clicking anywhere in the open document.

Translate

QUICK STEPS

Translate Text
1. Click Review tab.
2. Click Research button.
3. Type word in *Search for* text box.
4. Click down-pointing arrow at right of resource list.
5. Click translation.
6. If necessary, specify *From* language and *To* language.

Translating Text

At the Research task pane, you can translate words from one language into another; however, the translation feature must be installed before you can use it. To translate a word, type the word in the *Search for* text box of the Research task pane. In the *Translation* list box, specify the languages you are translating to and from. For example, to translate *computer* from English to Spanish, type **computer** in the *Search for* text box. Click the down-pointing arrow at the right of the *To* list box in the *Translation* section and then click *Spanish (International Sort)* at the drop-down list. The translation displays in the task pane, as shown in Figure 5.8.

Figure 5.8 Research Task Pane Displaying a Translation

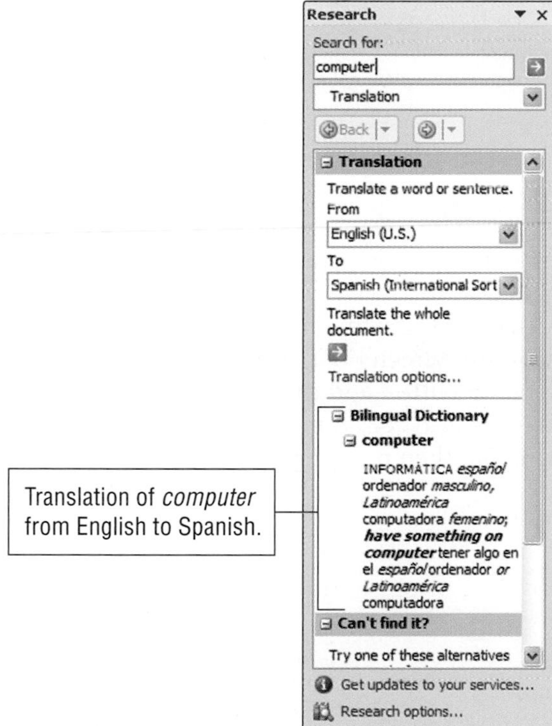

Exercise 4A

Translating Words

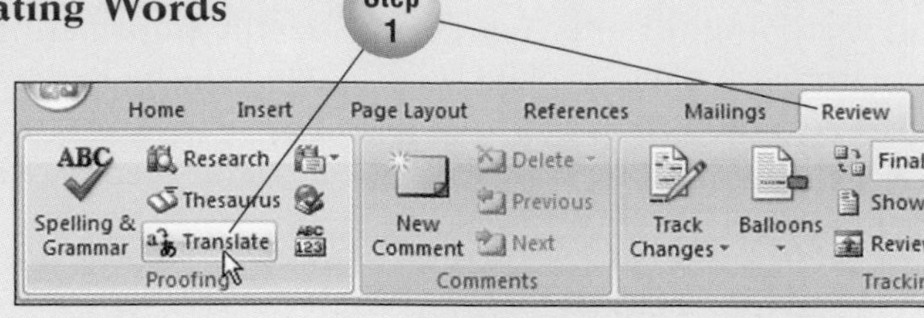

1. At a blank document, use the Translation feature to translate *document* from English to Spanish and from English to French. Begin by clicking the Review tab and then clicking the Translate button in the Proofing group.
2. At the Research task pane, click in the *Search for* text box and then type **document**.
3. Make sure that *English (U.S.)* displays in the *From* option box. (If it does not, click the down-pointing arrow at the right of the *From* option and then click *English (U.S.)* at the drop-down list.)
4. Click the down-pointing arrow to the right of the *To* option and then click *Spanish (International Sort)* at the drop-down list.
5. Click the down-pointing arrow to the right of the *To* option and then click *French (France)* at the drop-down list.
6. Click the Research button in the Proofing group in the Review tab to close the Research task pane.

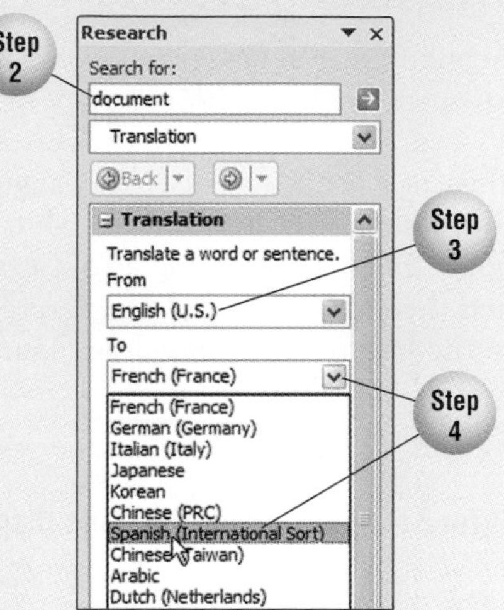

QUICK STEPS

Use Translation ScreenTip
1. Click Review tab.
2. Click Translation ScreenTip button.
3. Click desired transition language at drop-down list.
4. Hover mouse pointer over word.

Translation ScreenTip

Using Translation ScreenTips

The Proofing group in the Review tab includes a Translation ScreenTip button you can use to display the translation of a word. To translate with it, click the button and then click the translation language. Hover the mouse pointer over a word and the translation of the word displays in a ScreenTip above the word. To turn off the feature, click the Translation ScreenTip button and then click *Turn Off Translation ScreenTip* at the drop-down list. You can also access translation ScreenTips by right-clicking anywhere in the document and then pointing to *Translate*.

Exercise 4B

Using Translation ScreenTips

1. Open **Document13.docx** and save the document with the name **C05Ex04**.
2. Translate the term *Central* into Spanish by completing the following steps:
   a. Click the Review tab.
   b. Click the Translation ScreenTip button in the Proofing group and then click *Spanish (International Sort)* at the drop-down list.

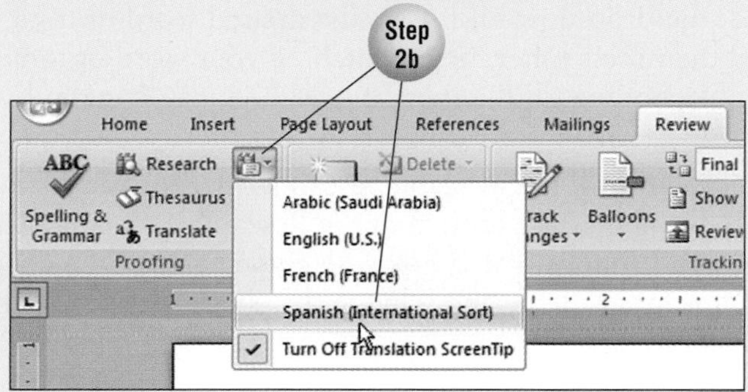

   c. Hover the mouse pointer over the word *Central* in the table. Look at the translation that displays in the ScreenTip. Type one of the Spanish terms in the Spanish column.

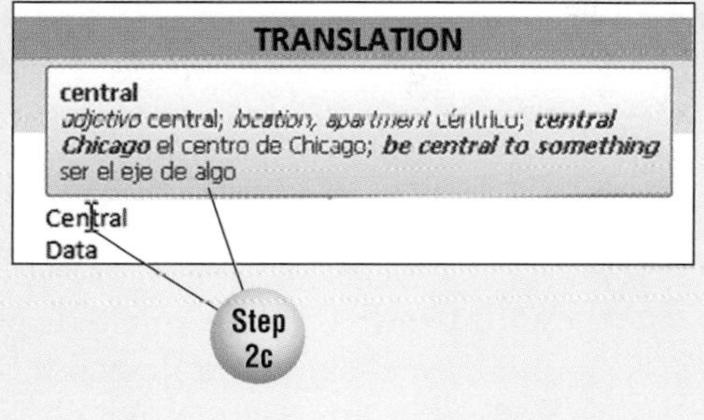

   d. Complete steps similar to those in Step 2c to display Spanish translations of the remaining terms. Type one of the Spanish terms in the appropriate cell in the table. If a ScreenTip displays more than one translation, choose one to type in the cell. Type the term without any accents or special symbols.
3. Use the Translation ScreenTip to translate terms into French by completing the following steps:
   a. Click the Translation ScreenTip button in the Proofing group and then click *French (France)* at the drop-down list.
   b. Hover the mouse pointer over the word *Central* in the table and then choose one of the French terms and type it in the French column.
   c. Complete steps similar to those in Step 3b to display French translations for the remaining terms. If a ScreenTip displays more than one translation, choose one to type in the cell. Type the term without any accents or special symbols.
4. Turn off the translation ScreenTip by clicking the Translation ScreenTip button in the Proofing group and then clicking *Turn Off Translation ScreenTip* at the drop-down list.
5. Save **C05Ex04.docx**.

Request Information from Online Sources

1. Click Review tab.
2. Click Research button.
3. Type word or topic.
4. Specify resources.
5. Click Start searching button.

Searching for and Requesting Information

The Research task pane also contains options that you can use to search for and request specific information from online sources. The online resources available to you depend on the locale to which your system is set, authorization information indicating that you are allowed to download the information, and your Internet service provider.

Determine which resources are available by clicking the down-pointing arrow at the right of the resources option box (the option box located below the *Search for* text box). The drop-down list includes reference books, research sites, business and financial sites, and other services. If you want to use a specific reference in your search, click it at the drop-down list, type the desired word or topic in the *Search for* text box, and then press Enter. Items matching your word or topic display in the task pane list box. Depending on the item, the list box may contain hyperlinks you can click to access additional information on the Internet.

You can control the available research options by clicking the Research options hyperlink located at the bottom of the Research task pane. Clicking this link displays the Research Options dialog box where you can insert a check mark before those items you want available and remove the check mark from those items you do not want available.

Exercise 4C

Researching and Requesting Information

Note: Your computer must be connected to the Internet to complete this exercise.

1. With **C05Ex04.docx** open, display the Research task pane by clicking the Review tab and then clicking the Research button in the Proofing group.
2. Search for information in a dictionary on the term *avatar* by completing the following steps:
   a. Click in the *Search for* text box or select any text that displays in the text box and then type **avatar**.
   b. Click the down-pointing arrow to the right of the resources option box (the down-pointing arrow immediately below the Start searching button).
   c. At the drop-down list of resources, click *Encarta Dictionary: English (North America)*. If this reference is not available, click any other dictionary available to you.
3. Search for information on the term *avatar* in an encyclopedia by completing the following steps:
   a. Make sure *avatar* displays in the *Search for* text box.
   b. Click the down-pointing arrow at the right of the resources option box and then click an encyclopedia listed in the *All Research Sites* section of the list box.
   c. Look at the information that displays in the task pane list box and then click a hyperlink that interests you.
   d. After reading the information that displays in your Web browser, close the browser window.

Inserting Research Information

Some of the information that displays in the Research task pane can be inserted directly into your document; other information you can copy and paste into your document. For example, if you look up stock prices, an *Insert Stock Price* option is available for inserting the stock table in your document. If information you want to include in your document displays in your browser, select it, click Edit on the browser's menu bar, and then click *Copy* at the drop-down list. Make your document active, click the Home tab, and then click the Paste button.

Exercise 4D

Researching and Inserting Information

1. With **C05Ex04.docx** open, press Ctrl + End to move the insertion point to the end of the document.
2. Make sure the Research task pane is open. (If not, click the Review tab and then click the Research button.)
3. Search for stock information and then insert the information in your document by completing the following steps:
   a. Select any text that displays in the *Search for* text box and then type **IBM**.
   b. Click the down-pointing arrow at the right of the resources option box and then click *MSN Money Stock Quotes*.
   c. Click the Insert Price button in the task pane. (This inserts the current stock price in your document.)
   d. Press the Enter key twice.
   e. Select IBM in the *Search for* text box, type **MSFT** and then press Enter.
   f. Click the Insert Price button in the task pane.
   g. Press the Enter key twice.

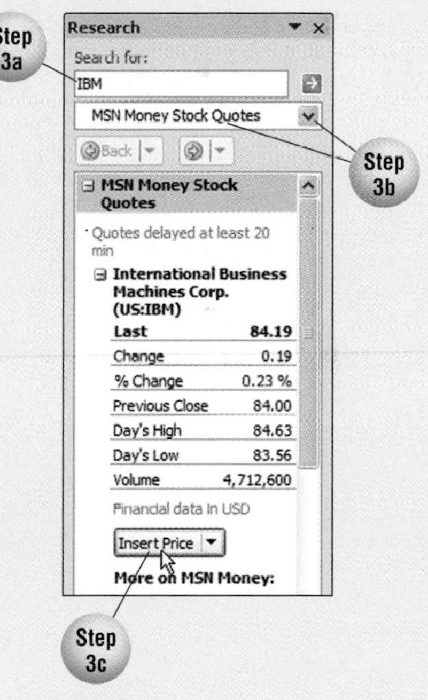

4. Search for a company profile and insert the profile in your document by completing the following steps:
   a. Click the down-pointing arrow at the right side of the resources option box and then click *Thomson Gale Company Profiles*.
   b. Click the Click to read full profile hyperlink that displays below the company profile.
   c. Select the company profile information that displays in the Web browser window.
   d. Click Edit on the Menu bar and then click *Copy*. (If the Menu bar does not display, click the Tools button and then click *Menu bar* at the drop-down list.)
   e. Click the button on the Taskbar representing your Word document.
   f. Make sure the insertion point is positioned a double space below the Microsoft stock price.
   g. Click the Home tab.
   h. Click the Paste button.
   i. Close the Web browser window.
   j. Close the Research task pane.
5. Save, print, and then close **C05Ex04.docx**.

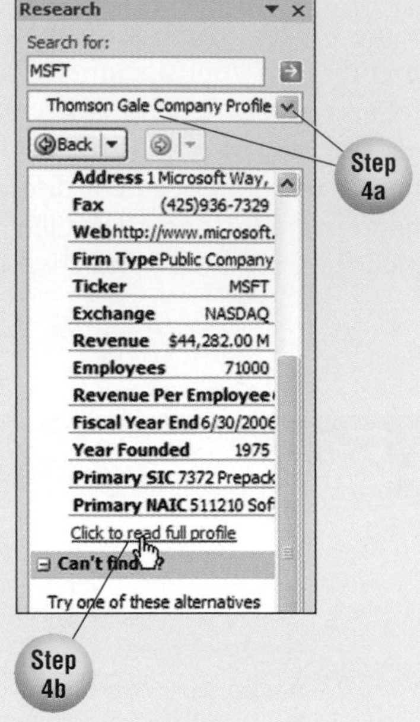

Chapter Summary

- The spell checker matches the words in your document with the words in its dictionary. If a match is not found, the word is selected and possible corrections are suggested.
- When checking the spelling or grammar in a document, you can temporarily leave the Spelling and Grammar dialog box, make corrections in the document, and then resume checking.
- Customize spell checking options at the Word Options dialog box with *Proofing* selected in the left panel.
- With the grammar checker, you can search a document for correct grammar, style, punctuation, and word usage.
- When the grammar checker detects a grammar error, you can display information about the error by clicking the Explain button at the Spelling and Grammar dialog box.
- Customize grammar checking with options in the *When correcting spelling and grammar in Word* section of the Word Options dialog box with *Proofing* selected.
- Turn on the *Use contextual spelling* option if you want Word to insert a wavy blue line below words that sound similar to other words. During a spelling and grammar check, Word will stop at a word with a wavy blue line and offer alternate words.
- To display readability statistics on a document, insert a check mark in the *Show readability statistics* check box in the Word Options dialog box with *Proofing* selected and then complete a spelling and grammar check.
- Word uses the CUSTOM.DIC custom dictionary when spell checking a document. Add your own custom dictionary at the Custom Dictionaries dialog box. Display this dialog box by clicking the Custom Dictionaries button at the Word Options dialog box with *Proofing* selected.
- The Word Count dialog box displays the number of pages, words, characters, paragraphs, and lines in a document. Display this dialog box by clicking the word count section of the Status bar or clicking the Word Count button in the Proofing group in the Review tab.
- Use the Thesaurus to find synonyms and antonyms for words in your document. Display synonyms and antonyms at the Research task pane or by right-clicking a word and then pointing to Synonyms at the shortcut menu.
- Use options at the Research task pane to translate words from a variety of languages and to search for and request specific information from online sources.

Commands review

FEATURE	RIBBON TAB, GROUP	BUTTON	KEYBOARD SHORTCUT
Spelling and Grammar dialog box	Review, Proofing	ABC	F7
Word Options dialog box		, Word Options	
Word Count dialog box	Review, Proofing	ABC 123	
Research task pane	Review, Proofing	Research	
Research task pane for synonyms and antonyms	Review, Proofing	Thesaurus	Shift + F7
Research task pane for translating words	Review, Proofing	Translate	
Translation ScreenTip	Review, Proofing		

Reviewing key points

Completion: In the space provided at the right, indicate the correct term, symbol, or command.

1. Click this tab to display the Proofing group. __________
2. Click this button in the Spelling and Grammar dialog box to replace the selected word with the word in the *Suggestions* list box. __________
3. Click this button in the Spelling and Grammar dialog box to display the Word Help window with information about the selected text. __________
4. During spell checking, click this button to skip the occurrence of the word and all other occurrences of the word in the document. __________
5. This is the keyboard shortcut to display the Spelling and Grammar dialog box. __________

6. To display options for customizing spelling and grammar checking, click the Office button, click the Word Options button, and then click this option in the left panel. ______________________
7. Consider making this option active in the Word Options dialog box when correcting a document that contains words that sound similar but have different meanings. ______________________
8. This is the default setting for the *Writing Style* option at the Word Options dialog box with *Proofing* selected. ______________________
9. This readability score is based on the average number of syllables per word and average number of words per sentence. ______________________
10. When completing a spelling check on a document, Word uses this custom dictionary by default. ______________________
11. The Research task pane displays when you click the Research button, the Thesaurus button, or this button. ______________________

Applying your skills

Assessment 1 Complete a Spelling and Grammar Check and Format a Style Document on Numbers

1. Open **SpellCheck02.docx** and save the document with the name **C05A01**.
2. Complete a spelling and grammar check on the document.
3. Apply the Heading 1 style to the title *NUMBERS* and apply the Heading 2 style to the two headings *Time Expressions* and *Dates*.
4. Change the style set to *Formal*.
5. Select the indented text in the *Time Expressions* section and then apply bullets.
6. Select the indented text in the *Dates* section and then apply bullets.
7. Save, print, and then close **C05A01.docx**.

Assessment 2 Complete a Spelling and Grammar Check and Proofread a Business Letter

1. Open **Letter02.docx** and save the document with the name **C05A02**.
2. Complete a spelling and grammar check on the document. (Proper names are spelled correctly.)
3. After completing the spelling and grammar check, proofread the letter and make necessary changes. (The letter contains mistakes that the spell and grammar checker will not select.)
4. Select the entire document and then change the font to 12-point Candara.
5. Save, print, and then close **C05A02.docx**.

Assessment 3 Complete a Spelling, Grammar, and Style Check on a Document Using Contextual Spelling

1. Open **GrammarCheck02.docx** and save the document with the name **C05A03**.
2. Display the Word Options dialog box with *Proofing* selected, insert a check mark in the *Use contextual spelling* check box, change the *Writing Style* option to *Grammar & Style*, and then close the dialog box.
3. Complete a spelling and grammar check on the document.
4. Apply formatting to enhance the visual appeal of the document.
5. Display the Word Options dialog box with *Proofing* selected, remove the check mark from the *Use contextual spelling* check box, change the *Writing Style* option to *Grammar Only*, and then close the dialog box.
6. Save, print, and then close **C05A03.docx**.

Assessment 4 Create and Format a Document Featuring Translated Terms

1. At a blank document, use the translation feature to find the Spanish and French translations for the following terms:

    Memory
    Logic
    Navigate
    Register
    System
    Utility
    Voice

2. Type the English words followed by the Spanish and French translations. Set the text in columns and then apply formatting to enhance the visual appeal of the document.
3. Save the document with the name **C05A04**.
4. Print and then close **C05A04.docx**.

Performance Assessments

UNIT 1

Preparing Documents

ASSESSING PROFICIENCIES

In this unit, you have learned to create, edit, save, and print Word documents; use writing tools such as the spell checker, grammar checker, and Thesaurus; and format characters and paragraphs.

Note: Before beginning computer assessments, copy to your storage medium the Unit01PA folder from the CD that accompanies this textbook and then make Unit01PA the active folder.

Assessment 1 Format an Online Shopping Document

1. Open **OnlineShopping.docx** and save the document with the name **U01PA01**.
2. Select the entire document and then change the font to 12-point Cambria.
3. Apply 14-point Calibri bold formatting to the two titles (*ONLINE SHOPPING* and *REFERENCES*) and the three headings (*Advantages of Online Shopping*, *Online Shopping Venues*, and *Online Shopping Safety Tips*).
4. Center the titles *ONLINE SHOPPING* and *REFERENCES*.
5. Select the second through the fifth paragraphs in the *Advantages of Online Shopping* section and then apply bullet formatting.
6. Select the first sentence of each of the bulleted paragraphs and apply bold formatting.
7. Select and then sort in ascending order the numbered paragraphs in the *Online Shopping Safety Tips* section.
8. Apply a hanging indent to the paragraphs of text below the *REFERENCES* title.
9. Apply *Aqua, Accent 5, Lighter 60%* paragraph shading and a bottom border line to the two titles.
10. Apply *Aqua, Accent 5, Lighter 80%* paragraph shading and a bottom border line to the three headings in the document.
11. Save, print, and then close **U01PA01.docx**.

Assessment 2 Format a Corporate Report

1. Open **Document19.docx** and save the document with the name **U01PA02**.
2. Make the following changes to the document:
   a. Change the bullets in the *Compensation Philosophy* section to custom bullets of your choosing.
   b. Apply the Heading 1 style to the title *Compensation Committee Report*.
   c. Apply the Heading 2 style to the two headings *Compensation Philosophy* and *Competitive Compensation*.
   d. Change the style set to *Fancy*.
   e. Select the entire document and then remove italic formatting.
   f. Apply the *Urban* theme.
   g. Apply the *Flow* theme colors.
3. Save, print, and then close **U01PA02.docx**.

Assessment 3 Create and Format a Training Announcement

1. At a blank document, click the No Spacing style in the Styles group in the Home tab and then type the text shown in Figure U1.1 with the following specifications:
   a. Center and right-align text as indicated.
   b. After typing the text, select the centered text and change the font to 20-point Candara bold and the font color to dark blue.
   c. Select the right-aligned text and change the font to 12-point Candara bold and the font color to dark blue.
   d. Select the centered text and then change the line spacing to 2.
2. Save the document with the name **U01PA03**.
3. Print and then close **U01PA03.docx**.

Figure U1.1 Assessment 3

Managing Data
Tuesday, March 9, 2010
Corporate Headquarters
Conference Room A
8:30 - 10:30 p.m.

Training Department
Technical Support Team

Assessment 4 Format a Software Document

1. Open **Document14.docx** and save the document with the name **U01PA04**.
2. Select the entire document and then make the following changes:
   a. Change the spacing after paragraphs to zero points.
   b. Change the line spacing to 1.5.
   c. Change the font to 12-point Constantia.
3. Indent the paragraphs that begin with bold text 0.5 inch from the left and right margins.
4. Select the title and then change the font to 14-point Constantia bold.
5. Apply *Dark Blue, Text 2, Lighter 60%* paragraph shading to the title.
6. Insert a double border line above the title and a single border line below the title.
7. Save, print, and then close **U01PA04.docx**.

Assessment 5 Format a Travel Document

1. Open **Document20.docx** and save the document with the name **U01PA05**.
2. Move the insertion point to the end of the document and then type the text shown in Figure U1.2.
3. Select the entire document and then add 6 points of spacing after paragraphs.
4. Apply the Heading 1 style to the title.
5. Apply the Heading 2 style to the two headings *Fast Facts* and *Special Highlights*.
6. Change the style set to *Traditional*.
7. Apply the *Solstice* theme.
8. Select the paragraphs of text in the *Fast Facts* section and then apply paragraph numbering.
9. Insert the following paragraph between paragraphs 3 and 4: **Ski School: The Cedar Meadows Ski School employs over 225 certified ski instructors and offers a variety of programs.**
10. Bold the words (and the colon) that begin the six numbered paragraphs.
11. Save, print, and then close **U01PA05.docx**.

Figure U1.2 Assessment 5

Special Highlights

- 4,800 acres
- 79 trails
- 25 lifts
- Largest bi-state ski resort
- 3,500-foot vertical drop and 5.5-mile mountain descent
- 250 inches annual snowfall

Assessment 6 Set Tabs and Create a Training Costs Document

1. At a blank document, create the document shown in Figure U1.3. Set a left tab for the text in the first column and set right tabs for the text in the second and third columns.
2. After typing the text, make the following changes:
   a. Select the title and change the font size to 14 points.
   b. Apply *Purple, Accent 4, Lighter 60%* paragraph shading to the title.
   c. Apply *Purple, Accent 4, Lighter 80%* paragraph shading to the subtitle.
   d. Move the insertion point to the end of the document on the line below the text and then apply the *Purple, Accent 4, Lighter 80%* paragraph shading.
3. Save the document with the name **U01PA06**.
4. Print and then close **U01PA06.docx**.

Figure U1.3 Assessment 6

SMITH-ALLEN ENTERPRISES

Training Costs

Human Resources	$20,250	$23,500
Production	21,230	18,075
Ancillary Services	1,950	3,400
Sales and Marketing	10,375	9,500
Finances	15,300	17,200

Assessment 7 Set Tabs and Create a Vacation Packages Document

1. At a blank document, create the document shown in Figure U1.4. Set a left tab for the text in the first column and set a right tab with leaders for the text in the second column.
2. After typing the text, make the following changes:
   a. Apply the Heading 1 style to the title *Rates and Packages*.
   b. Apply the Heading 2 style to the headings *Value Season*, *Peak Season*, and *Holiday Season*.
   c. Change the style set to *Traditional*.
   d. Change the theme fonts to *Aspect*.
3. Save the document with the name **U01PA07**.
4. Print and then close **U01PA07.docx**.

Figure U1.4 Assessment 7

Rates and Packages

Value Season

Hotel Room .... $90 to $115

One-Bedroom Suite .... $115 to $140

Two-Bedroom Suite .... $145 to $170

Peak Season

Hotel Room .... $100 to $130

One-Bedroom Suite .... $130 to $160

Two-Bedroom Suite .... $165 to $195

Holiday Season

Hotel Room .... $140 to $150

One-Bedroom Suite .... $160 to $175

Two-Bedroom Suite .... $180 to $200

Assessment 8 Customize Grammar Checking and Check Spelling and Grammar in a Document

1. Open **SpellGrammarCheck.docx** and save the document with the name **U01PA08**.
2. Display the Word Options dialog box with *Proofing* selected, insert a check mark in the *Use contextual spelling* check box, change the *Writing Style* option to *Grammar & Style*, and then close the dialog box.
3. Complete a spelling and grammar check on the document.
4. Apply formatting to enhance the visual appeal of the document.
5. Display the Word Options dialog box with *Proofing* selected, remove the check mark from the *Use contextual spelling* check box, change the *Writing Style* option to *Grammar Only*, and then close the dialog box.
6. Save, print, and then close **U01PA08.docx**.

CREATING ORIGINAL DOCUMENTS

The activities in Assessments 9, 10, and 11 give you the opportunity to practice your writing skills as well as demonstrate your mastery of the important Word features presented in this unit. Use correct grammar, precise word choices, and clear sentence construction. Follow the steps below to improve your writing skills.

THE WRITING PROCESS

Plan: Gather ideas, select the information to include, and choose the order in which to present it.

Checkpoints

- What is the purpose?
- What information do readers need to reach your intended conclusion?

Write: Keeping the reader in mind and following the information plan, draft the document using clear, direct sentences that say what you mean.

Checkpoints

- What are the subpoints for each main thought?
- How can you connect paragraphs so the reader moves smoothly from one idea to the next?

Revise: Improve what you have written by changing, deleting, rearranging, or adding words, sentences, and paragraphs.

Checkpoints

- Is the meaning clear?
- Do the ideas follow a logical order?
- Have you included any unnecessary information?
- Have you built your sentences around strong verbs and nouns?

Edit: Check spelling, sentence construction, word use, punctuation, and capitalization.

Checkpoints

- Can you spot any redundancies or clichés?
- Can you reduce any phrases to an effective word (for example, change *the fact that* to *because*)?
- Have you used commas only where there is a strong reason for doing so?
- Did you proofread the document for errors that your spell checker cannot identify?

Publish: Prepare a final copy that could be reproduced and shared with others.

Checkpoints

- Which design elements, for example, bolding and different fonts, would help highlight important ideas or sections?
- Would charts or other graphics help clarify meaning?

Assessment 9 Create and Format an Announcement

Situation: You work in the Public Relations Department at Coleman Development Corporation, and your supervisor has asked you to prepare an announcement about the appointment of the new corporate president using the following information:

- The Board of Trustees has appointed Stephanie Branson as president of Coleman Development Corporation.
- She has 25 years of experience in the land management field and has spent the past 11 years as president of Lancaster, Inc.
- The selection process began over six months ago and included several interviews with board members and visitations by board members to Lancaster. An open house is planned for Friday, August 20, 2010, from 1:30 to 5:00 p.m., in the corporation's conference room.

Include a title for the announcement. Name the announcement **U01PA09**. Print and then close the document.

Assessment 10 Create and Format a Word Commands Document

Situation: You work in the training department at Crossroads Industries, and your supervisor has asked you to prepare a brief summary of some Word commands for use in Microsoft Word training classes. She has asked you to include the following information:

- A brief explanation of how to move the insertion point to a specific page.
- Keyboard commands to move the insertion point to the beginning and to the end of a line and to the beginning and end of a document.
- Commands to delete text from the insertion point to the beginning of a word and from the insertion point to the end of a word.
- Steps to select a word, a sentence, a paragraph, and an entire document using the mouse.
- Keyboard command to select the entire document.

Save the document with the name **U01PA10**. Print and then close the document.

Assessment 11 Prepare a Document Illustrating Font Use

Situation: You work as the assistant to the public relations manager at your local Chamber of Commerce. The manager wants to maintain a consistent style for articles published in the Chamber's monthly newsletter. He wants you to explore the use of various handwriting, decorative, and plain fonts. He would like you to choose two handwriting fonts, two decorative fonts, and two plain fonts and then prepare a document illustrating the use of each of these fonts. Save the document with the name **U01PA11**. Print and then close the document.

Unit 2

Formatting and Managing Documents

- Formatting Pages
- Customizing Page Formatting
- Inserting Elements and Navigating in a Document
- Maintaining Documents
- Managing and Printing Documents
- Unit 2 Performance Assessments

Signature Microsoft® Word 2007

Microsoft Certified Application Specialist Skills—Unit 2

Reference No.	Skill	Pages
1	**Creating and Customizing Documents**	
1.1	Create and format documents	
1.1.1	Work with templates	241-242
1.1.5	Format document backgrounds	165-168
1.1.6	Insert blank pages or cover pages	175-177
1.2	Lay out documents	
1.2.1	Format pages	150-179
1.2.3	Create and format columns	157-162
1.3	Make documents and content easier to find	
1.3.4	Insert document navigation tools	211-217
2	**Formatting Content**	
2.2	Manipulate text	175-177
2.2.2	Find and replace text	184-192
2.3	Control pagination	
2.3.1	Insert and delete page breaks	173-174
2.3.2	Create and modify sections	155-161
3	**Working with Visual Content**	
3.3.3	Insert and modify drop caps	204
4	**Organizing Content**	
4.5	Merge documents and data sources	
4.5.3	Create a single envelope or label	259-265
5	**Reviewing Documents**	
5.1	Navigate documents	
5.1.2	Change window views	248-254
6	**Sharing and Securing Content**	
6.1	Prepare documents for sharing	
6.1.1	Save to appropriate formats	236-240

Chapter 6

Formatting Pages

SNAP

Tutorial 6.1
Using Document Views
Tutorial 6.2
Managing Text

Performance Objectives

Upon successful completion of Chapter 6, you will be able to:

- Change document views
- Change margins, page orientation, and paper size in a document
- Format pages at the Page Setup dialog box
- Insert section breaks
- Create and format text in columns
- Hyphenate words automatically and manually
- Insert line numbers in a document
- Insert a watermark, page color, and page border

A Word document generally displays in Print Layout view. You can change this default view with buttons in the view area on the Status bar or with options in the View tab. A Word document also has default top, bottom, left, and right margins of 1 inch. You can change these default margins with the Margins button in the Page Setup group in the Page Layout tab or with options at the Page Setup dialog box. You can apply formatting to a portion of a document only by inserting a continuous section break or a section break that begins a new page. Inserting a section break is useful when you want to arrange text in columns. With Word's hyphenation feature, you can hyphenate words at the end of lines to create a less ragged right margin. You can also insert a variety of page formatting elements in your documents, including a watermark, page background color, and page borders.

Note: Before beginning computer exercises for this chapter, copy to your storage medium the Chapter06 folder from the CD that accompanies this textbook and then make Chapter06 the active folder.

Changing the View

Zoom Out

Zoom In

By default, a Word document displays in Print Layout view. In this view, the document displays on the screen as it will appear when printed. Other views are available such as Draft and Full Screen Reading. Change views with buttons in the view area on the Status bar or with options in the View tab. Figure 6.1 identifies the buttons in the view area on the Status bar. Along with the view buttons, the Status bar also contains a Zoom slider bar (see Figure 6.1). Drag the button on the Zoom slider bar to increase or decrease the display size or click the Zoom Out button to decrease size and click the Zoom In to increase size.

Figure 6.1 Viewing Buttons and Zoom Slider Bar

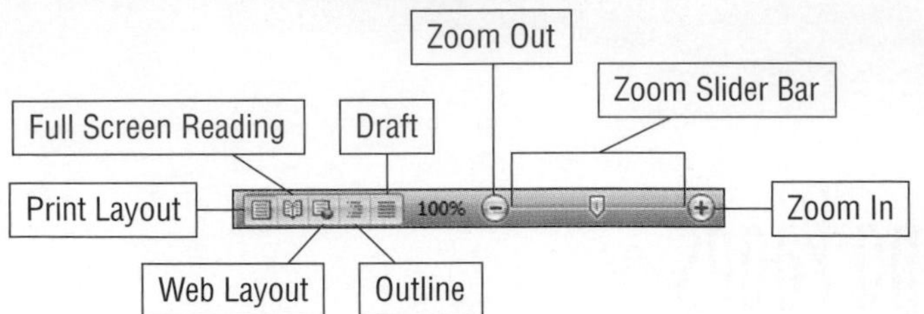

Draft

Displaying a Document in Draft View

Change to Draft view and the document displays in a format for efficient editing and formatting. In this view, margins and features such as headers and footers do not display on the screen. Change to Draft view by clicking the Draft button in the view area on the Status bar or click the View tab and then click the Draft button in the Document Views group.

Display Document in Full Screen Reading View
Click Full Screen Reading button in view area on Status bar.
OR
1. Click View tab.
2. Click Full Screen Reading button.

Full Screen Reading

Displaying a Document in Full Screen Reading View

The Full Screen Reading view displays a document in a format for easy viewing and reading. Change to Full Screen Reading view by clicking the Full Screen Reading button in the view area on the Status bar or by clicking the View tab and then clicking the Full Screen Reading button in the Document Views group.

You can navigate in Full Screen Reading view using the keys on the keyboard, as shown in Table 6.1. You can also navigate in Full Screen Reading view with options from the View Options button that displays toward the top right side of the screen or with the Next Screen and Previous Screen buttons located at the top of the window and also located at the bottom of each page.

You can customize the Full Screen Reading view with options from the View Options drop-down list. Display this list by clicking the View Options button located in the upper right corner of the Full Screen Reading window.

Table 6.1 **Keyboard Commands in Full Screen Reading View**

Press this key to	***Complete this action***
Page Down key or spacebar	Move to the next page or section
Page Up key or Backspace key	Move to the previous page or section
Right Arrow key	Move to next page
Left Arrow key	Move to previous page
Home	Move to first page in document
End	Move to last page in document
Esc	Return to previous view

Exercise 1A

Changing Views

1. Open **Report01.docx** and save the document with the name **C06Ex01**.
2. Click the Draft button located in the view area on the Status bar.
3. Using the mouse, drag the Zoom slider bar button to the left to decrease the size of the document display to approximately 60%. (The percentage displays at the left side of the Zoom Out button.)
4. Drag the Zoom slider bar button back to the middle until *100%* displays at the left side of the Zoom Out button.
5. Click the Print Layout button in the view area on the Status bar.
6. Click the Full Screen Reading button located in the view area on the Status bar.
7. Click the View Options button located toward the top of the viewing window and then click *Show Two Pages* at the drop-down list.
8. Click the Next Screen button to display the next two pages in the viewing window.

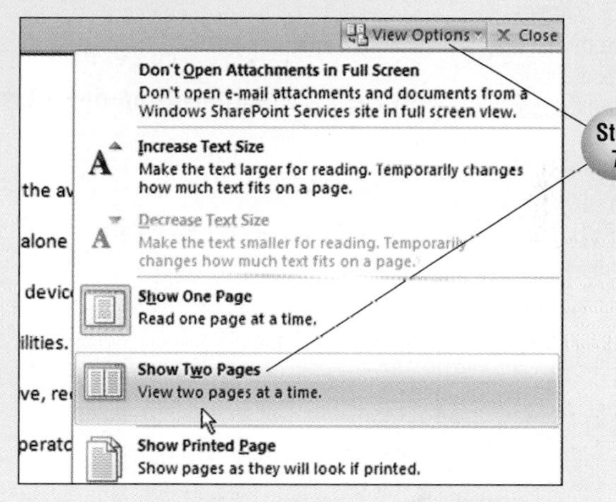

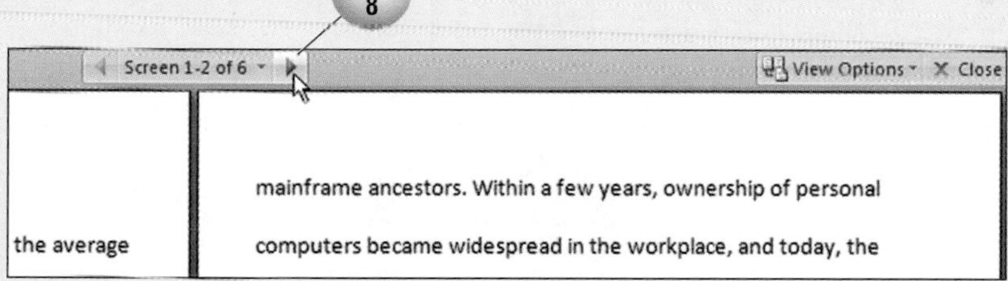

9. Click the Previous Screen button to display the previous two pages.
10. Click the View Options button located toward the top of the viewing window and then click *Show One Page* at the drop-down list.
11. Practice navigating using the keyboard commands shown in Table 6.1.
12. Increase the size of the text by clicking the View Options button and then clicking the *Increase Text Size* option.
13. Press the Home key to display the first viewing page.
14. Decrease the size of the text by clicking the View Options button and then clicking the *Decrease Text Size* option.
15. Click the Close button located in the upper right corner of the screen.

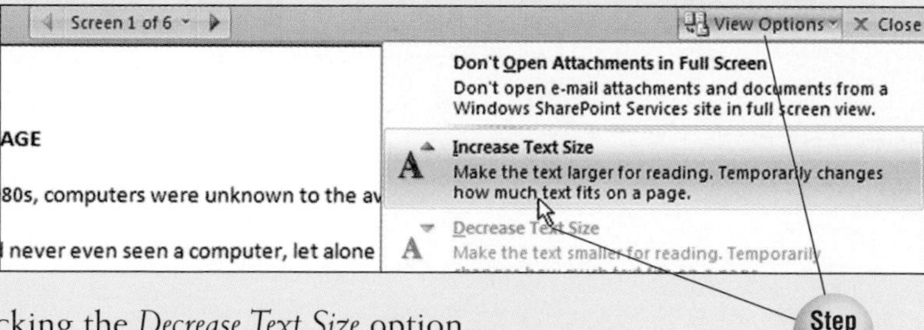

Changing Page Setup

The Page Setup group in the Page Layout tab contains a number of buttons that you can use to change the setup of pages in a document. With these buttons, you can perform actions such as changing the margins, page orientation, page size, and inserting page breaks. As you will learn in the next chapter you can also use the three buttons in the Pages group in the Insert tab to insert a page break, a blank page, or a cover page.

QUICK STEPS

Change Margins
1. Click Page Layout tab.
2. Click Margins button.
3. Click desired margin option.

Changing Margins

Change page margins with options at the Margins drop-down list, shown in Figure 6.2. To display this list, click the Page Layout tab and then click the Margins button in the Page Setup group. To change the margins, click one of the preset options that display in the drop-down list.

Figure 6.2 Margins Drop-down List

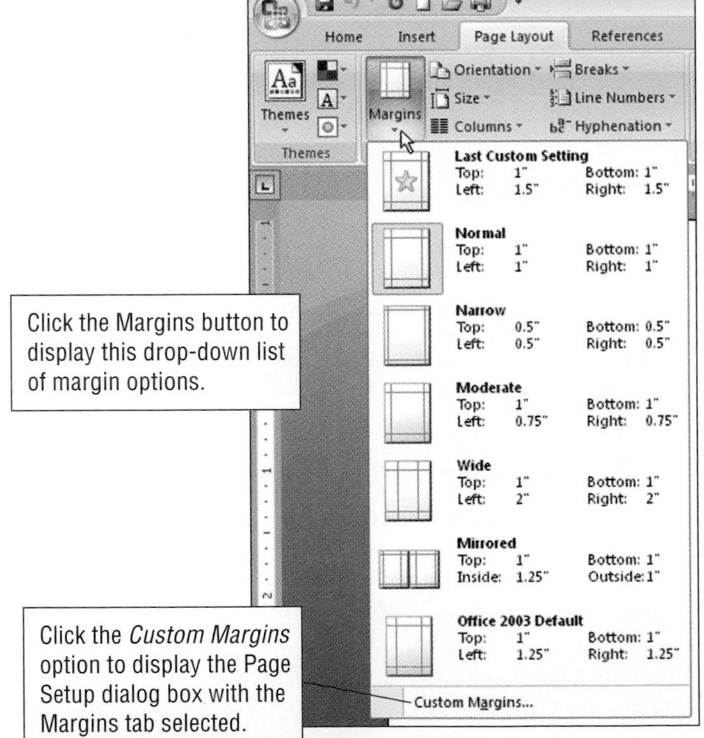

Exercise 1B

Changing Margins

1. With **C06Ex01.docx** open, make the following changes to the document:
   a. Center the title *THE COMPUTER ADVANTAGE*.
   b. Select the entire document, change the line spacing to single, and then deselect the text.
2. Click the Page Layout tab.
3. Click the Margins button in the Page Setup group and then click the *Office 2003 Default* option.
4. Save **C06Ex01.docx**.

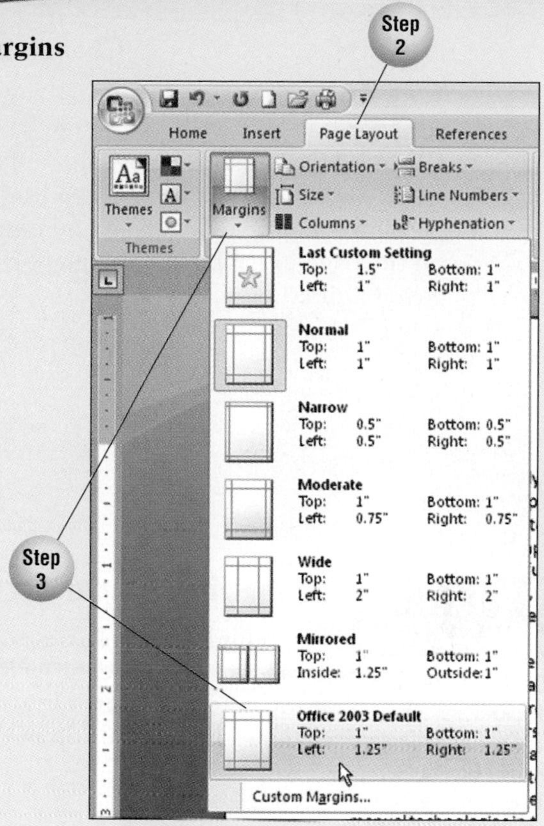

Changing Page Orientation

Click the Orientation button in the Page Setup group in the Page Layout tab, and two options for orienting pages in a document display—Portrait and Landscape. In Portrait orientation, which is the default, the page is 11 inches tall and 8.5 inches wide. In Landscape orientation, the page is 8.5 inches tall and 11 inches wide. When you change the page orientation, the page margins change automatically.

Change Page Orientation
1. Click Page Layout tab.
2. Click Orientation button.
3. Click desired orientation.

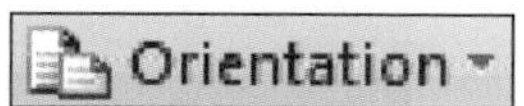

Exercise 1C

Changing Page Orientation

1. With **C06Ex01.docx** open, make sure the Page Layout tab is selected.
2. Click the Orientation button in the Page Setup group.
3. Click *Landscape* at the drop-down list.
4. Scroll through the document and notice how the text displays on the page in Landscape orientation.
5. Save **C06Ex01.docx**.

Change Page Size
1. Click Page Layout tab.
2. Click Size button.
3. Click desired size option.

Changing Page Size

The template Word uses to apply default formatting is based on a page size of 8.5 inches wide and 11 inches tall. You can change this default setting with options at the Size drop-down list, shown in Figure 6.3. Display this drop-down list by clicking the Size button in the Page Setup group in the Page Layout tab.

Figure 6.3 Size Drop-down List

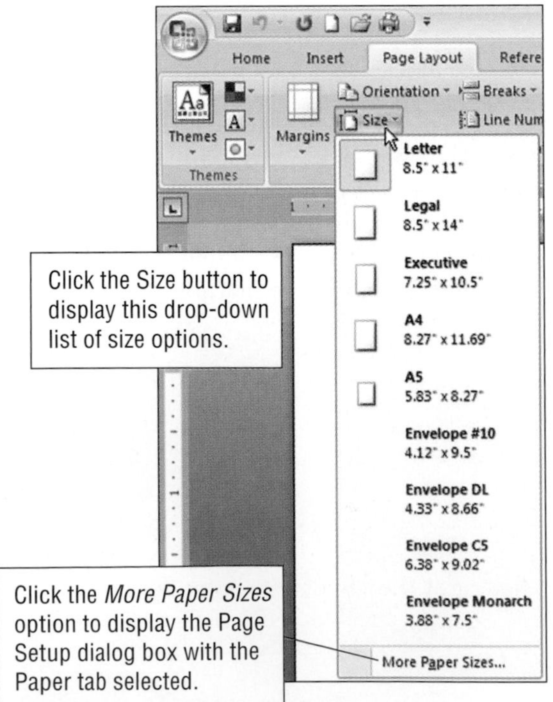

Exercise 1D

Changing Page Size

1. With **C06Ex01.docx** open, make sure the Page Layout tab is selected.
2. Click the Orientation button in the Page Setup group and then click *Portrait* at the drop-down list. (This changes the orientation back to the default.)
3. Click the Size button in the Page Setup group.
4. Click the A5 option (displays with 5.83″× 8.27″ below A5). If this option is not available, choose an option with a similar size.

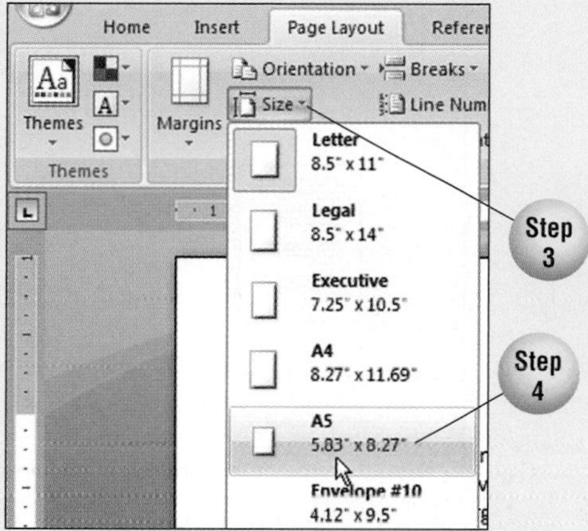

5. Scroll through the document and notice how the text displays on the page.
6. Click the Size button and then click *Legal* (displays with 8.5″× 14″ below Legal).
7. Scroll through the document and notice how the text displays on the page.
8. Click the Size button and then click *Letter* (displays with 8.5″× 11″ below Letter). (This returns the size back to the default.)
9. Save **C06Ex01.docx**.

Changing Margins at the Page Setup Dialog Box

The Margins button drop-down list provides you with a number of preset margins. If these margins do not fit your needs, you can set specific margins at the Page Setup dialog box with the Margins tab selected, as shown in Figure 6.4. Display this dialog box by clicking the Page Setup group dialog box launcher or by clicking the Margins button and then clicking *Custom Margins* at the bottom of the drop-down list.

To change margins, select the current measurement in the *Top*, *Bottom*, *Left*, or *Right* measurement box and then type the new measurement. You can also increase a measurement by clicking the up-pointing arrow at the right side of the measurement box. Decrease a measurement by clicking the down-pointing arrow. As you change the margin measurements at the Page Setup dialog box, the sample page in the *Preview* section illustrates the effects of the margin changes.

Change Margins at Page Setup Dialog Box

1. Click Page Layout tab.
2. Click Page Setup group dialog box launcher.
3. Specify desired margins.
4. Click OK.

Figure 6.4 Page Setup Dialog Box with Margins Tab Selected

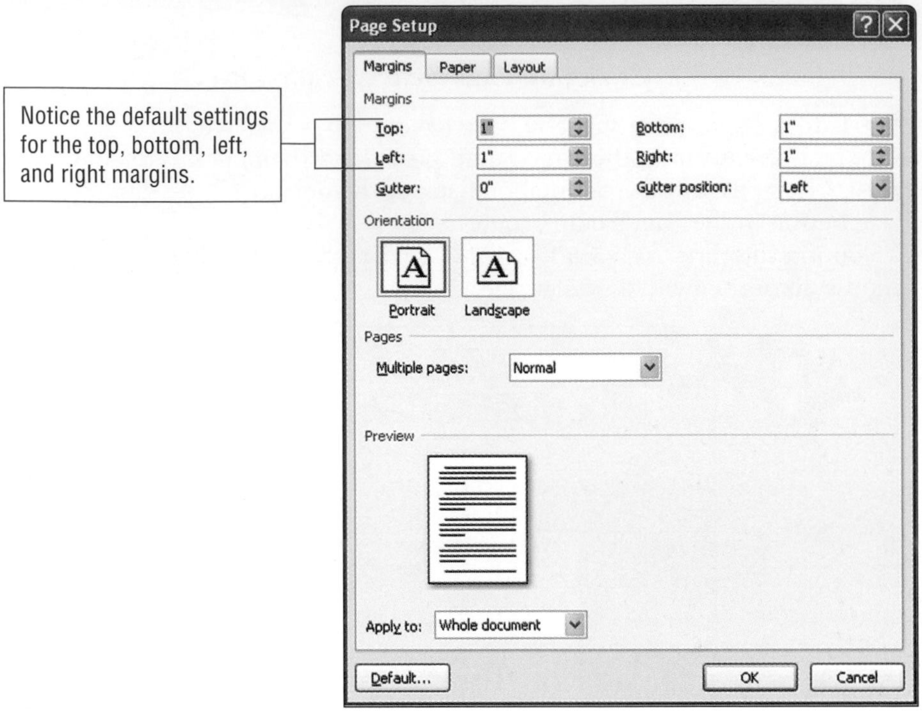

Notice the default settings for the top, bottom, left, and right margins.

Change Page Size at Page Setup Dialog Box

1. Click Page Layout tab.
2. Click Size button.
3. Click *More Paper Sizes* at drop-down list.
4. Specify desired size.
5. Click OK.

Changing Paper Size at the Page Setup Dialog Box

The Size button drop-down list contains a number of preset page sizes. If these sizes do not fit your needs, you can specify page size at the Page Setup dialog box with the Paper tab selected. Display this dialog box by clicking the Size button in the Page Setup group and then clicking *More Paper Sizes,* which displays at the bottom of the drop-down list.

Exercise 1E

Changing Margins at the Page Setup Dialog Box

1. With **C06Ex01.docx** open, make sure the Page Layout tab is selected.
2. Click the Page Setup group dialog box launcher.
3. At the Page Setup dialog box with the Margins tab selected, click the down-pointing arrow at the right side of the *Top* measurement box until 0.5″ displays.
4. Click the down-pointing arrow at the right side of the *Bottom* measurement box until 0.5″ displays.
5. Select the current measurement in the *Left* measurement box and then type **0.75**.
6. Select the current measurement in the *Right* measurement box and then type **0.75**.
7. Click OK to close the dialog box.
8. Click the Size button in the Page Setup group and then click *More Paper Sizes* at the drop-down list.
9. At the Page Setup dialog box with the Paper tab selected, click the down-pointing arrow at the right side of the *Paper size* option and then click *A4* at the drop-down list.
10. Click OK to close the dialog box.
11. Scroll through the document and notice how the text displays on the page.
12. Click the Size button in the Page Setup group and then click *Letter* at the drop-down list.
13. Save, print, and then close **C06Ex01.docx**.

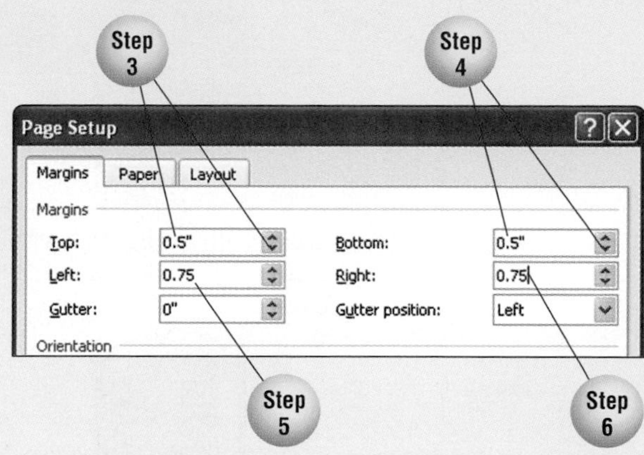

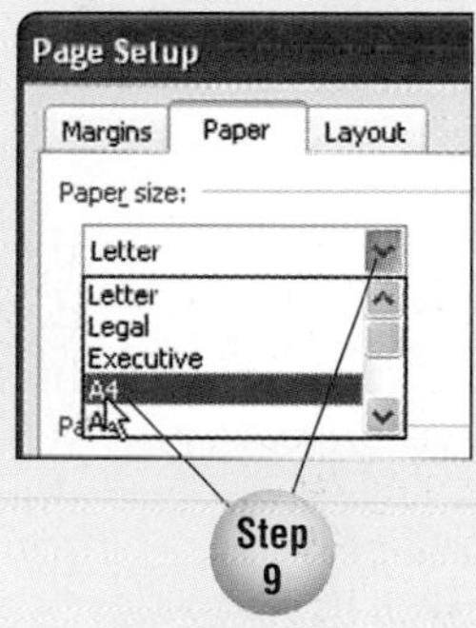

Inserting a Section Break

Insert Section Break
1. Click the Page Layout tab.
2. Click Breaks button.
3. Click section break type in drop-down list.

You can change the layout and formatting of specific portions of a document by inserting section breaks. For example, you can insert section breaks and then change margins for the text between the section breaks. If you want to format specific text in a document into columns, insert a section break.

Insert a section break in a document by clicking the Page Layout tab, clicking the Breaks button in the Page Setup group, and then clicking the desired option in the *Section Breaks* section of the drop-down list, shown in Figure 6.5. You can insert a section break that begins a new page or a continuous section break that does not insert a page break. A continuous section break separates the document into sections but does not insert a page break. Click one of the other three options in the *Section Breaks* section of the Breaks drop-down list if you want to insert a section break that begins a new page.

Figure 6.5 **Breaks Button Drop-down List**

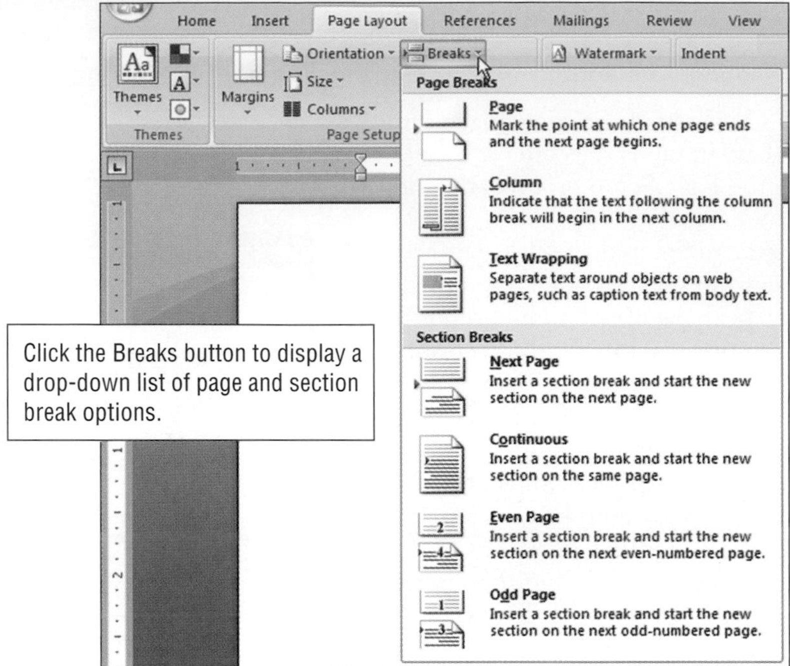

A section break inserted in a document is not visible in Print Layout view. Click the Draft button and a section break displays in the document as a double row of dots with the words *Section Break* in the middle. Depending on the type of section break you insert, text follows *Section Break*. For example, if you insert a continuous section break, the words *Section Break (Continuous)* display in the middle of the row of dots. If you delete a section break, the text that follows the section break takes on the formatting of the text preceding the break.

Exercise 2A

Inserting a Continuous Section Break

1. Open **Report02.docx** and save the document with the name **C06Ex02**.
2. Center the title *COMPUTERS IN COMMUNICATIONS.*
3. Delete text by completing the following steps:
   a. Position the insertion point at the beginning of the title *COMPUTERS IN ENTERTAINMENT* located at the bottom of page 1.
   b. Select text from the beginning of the title to the end of the document and then press the Delete key.

4. Insert a continuous section break by completing the following steps:
   a. Move the insertion point to the beginning of the *Telecommunications* heading.
   b. Click the Page Layout tab.
   c. Click the Breaks button in the Page Setup group and then click *Continuous* in the *Section Breaks* section of the drop-down list.

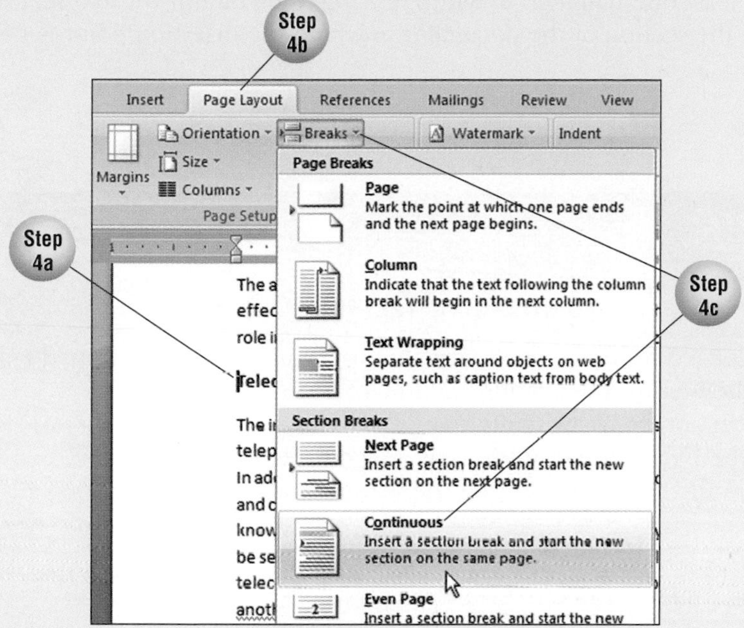

5. Click the Draft button in the view area on the Status bar and then notice the section break that displays across the screen.
6. Click the Print Layout button in the view area on the Status bar.
7. With the insertion point positioned at the beginning of the *Telecommunications* heading, change the left and right margins to 1.5 inches. (The margin changes affect only the text after the continuous section break.)
8. Save and then print **C06Ex02.docx**.

Creating Columns

When you are preparing any document that contains text, the document's readability is an important consideration. As you learned in the last chapter, readability refers to the ease with which a person can read and understand groups of words. Line length in a document can enhance or detract from the readability of the text. If the length is too long, the reader may lose his or her place on the line and have a difficult time moving to the next line below. To improve the readability of documents such as newsletters or reports, you may want to set the text in columns. One commonly used type of column is the newspaper column, which is typically used for text in newspapers, newsletters, and magazines. In newspaper columns, text flows up and down in the document.

Create Columns
1. Click Page Layout tab.
2. Click Columns button.
3. Click on desired number of columns.

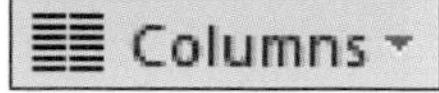

You can set text in columns with the Columns button in the Page Setup group in the Page Layout tab or with options from the Columns dialog box. The Columns button creates columns of equal width. To create columns with varying widths, use the Columns dialog box. A document can include as many columns as space permits on the page. Word determines how many columns can be included based on page width, margin width, and the size and spacing of the columns. Columns must be at least one-half inch in width. Changes in column width affect the entire document or the section of the document in which the insertion point is positioned.

Exercise 2B

Formatting Text into Columns

1. With **C06Ex02.docx** open, make sure the insertion point is positioned below the section break and then return the left and right margins to 1 inch.
2. Delete the section break by completing the following steps:
   a. Click the Draft button in the view area on the Status bar.
   b. Position the insertion point on the section break.

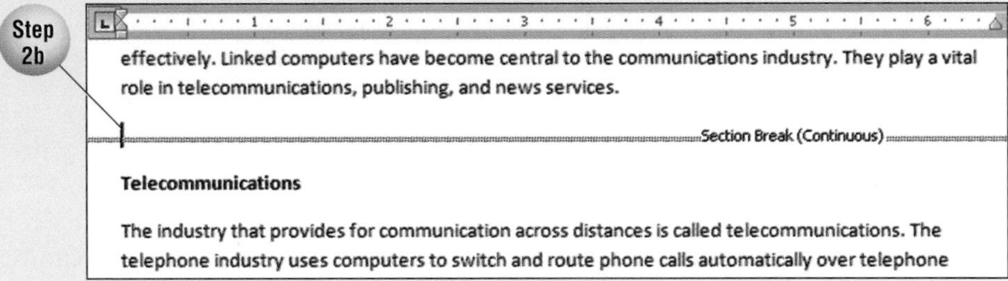

   c. Press the Delete key.
   d. Click the Print Layout button in the view area on the Status bar.
3. Select the entire document and then change the font to 12-point Cambria.
4. Move the insertion point to the beginning of the first paragraph of text in the document and then insert a continuous section break.
5. Format the text into columns by completing the following steps:
   a. Make sure the insertion point is positioned below the section break.
   b. Click the Page Layout tab.
   c. Click the Columns button in the Page Setup group.
   d. Click *Two* at the drop-down list.
6. Save **C06Ex02.docx**.

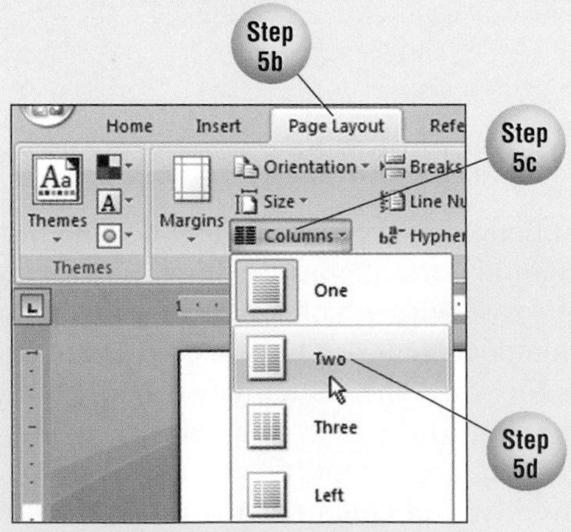

Creating Columns with the Columns Dialog Box

You can use the Columns dialog box to create newspaper columns that are equal or unequal in width. To display the Columns dialog box, shown in Figure 6.6, click the Columns button in the Page Setup group in the Page Layout tab and then click *More Columns* at the drop-down list.

Figure 6.6 Columns Dialog box

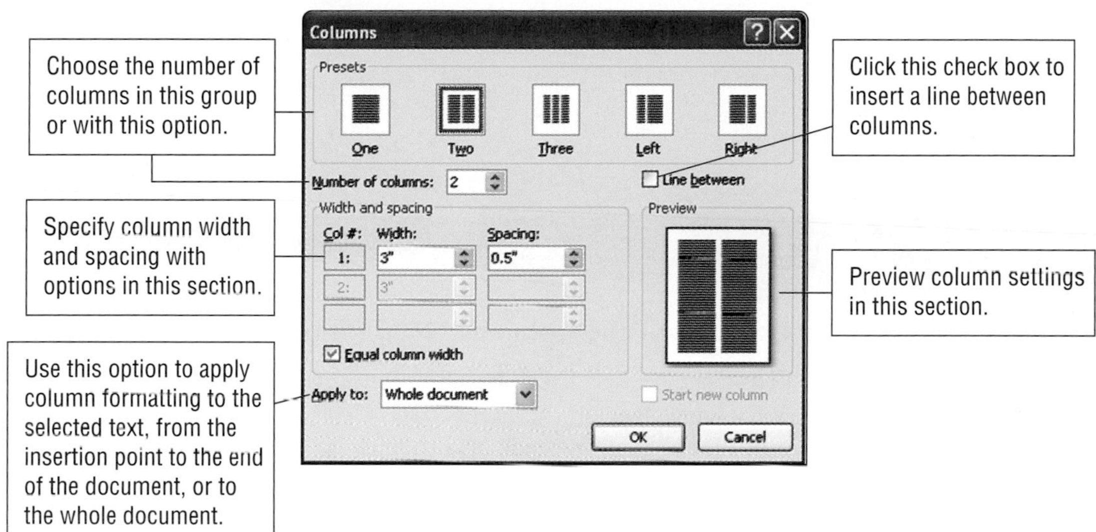

Using options at the Columns dialog box, you can specify the style and number of columns, enter your own column measurements, and create unequal columns. You can also insert a line between columns. By default, column formatting is applied to the whole document. With the *Apply to* option at the bottom of the Columns dialog box, you can change this from *Whole document* to *This point forward*. With the *This point forward* option, a section break is inserted and the column formatting is applied to text from the location of the insertion point to the end of the document or until other column formatting is encountered. The *Preview* section of the dialog box displays an example of how the columns will appear in your document.

Create Columns with Columns Dialog Box

1. Click Page Layout tab.
2. Click Columns button.
3. Click *More Columns* at the drop-down list.
4. Specify columns options.
5. Click OK.

Removing Column Formatting

To remove column formatting using the Columns button, position the insertion point in the section containing columns, click the Page Layout tab, click the Columns button, and then click *One* at the drop-down list. You can also remove column formatting at the Columns dialog box by selecting the *One* option in the *Presets* section.

Insert Column Break
1. Position insertion point at desired location.
2. Click Page Layout tab.
3. Click Breaks button.
4. Click *Column* at drop-down list.

Inserting a Column Break

When Word formats text into columns, it automatically breaks the columns to fit the page. At times, column breaks may appear in an undesirable location. You can insert a column break by positioning the insertion point where you want the column to end, clicking the Page Layout tab, clicking the Breaks button, and then clicking *Column* at the drop-down list. You can also insert a column break with the keyboard shortcut Ctrl + Shift + Enter.

Exercise 2C

Formatting Columns at the Columns Dialog Box

1. With **C06Ex02.docx** open, delete the section break by completing the following steps:
   a. Click the Draft button in the view area on the Status bar.
   b. Position the insertion point on the section break and then press the Delete key.
   c. Click the Print Layout button in the view area on the Status bar.
2. Remove column formatting by clicking the Columns button in the Page Setup group in the Page Layout tab and then clicking *One* at the drop-down list.
3. Format text in columns by completing the following steps:
   a. Position the insertion point at the beginning of the first paragraph of text in the document.
   b. Click the Columns button in the Page Setup group and then click *More Columns* at the drop-down list.
   c. At the Columns dialog box, click *Two* in the *Presets* section.
   d. Click the up-pointing arrow at the right of the *Spacing* option box to display 0.6″.
   e. Click the *Line between* check box to insert a check mark.
   f. Click the down-pointing arrow at the right side of the *Apply to* option box and then click *This point forward* at the drop-down list.
   g. Click OK to close the dialog box.

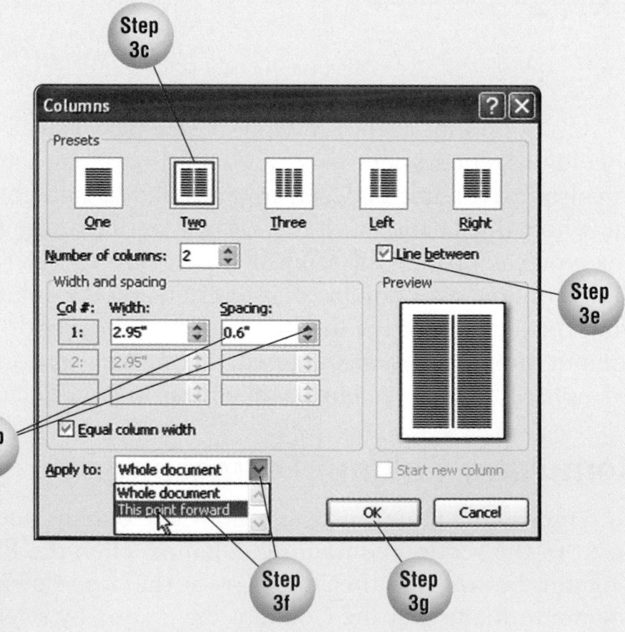

4. Insert a column break by completing the following steps:
   a. Position the insertion point at the beginning of the *News Services* heading.
   b. Click the Breaks button in the Page Setup group and then click *Column* at the drop-down list.
5. Save and then print **C06Ex02.docx**.

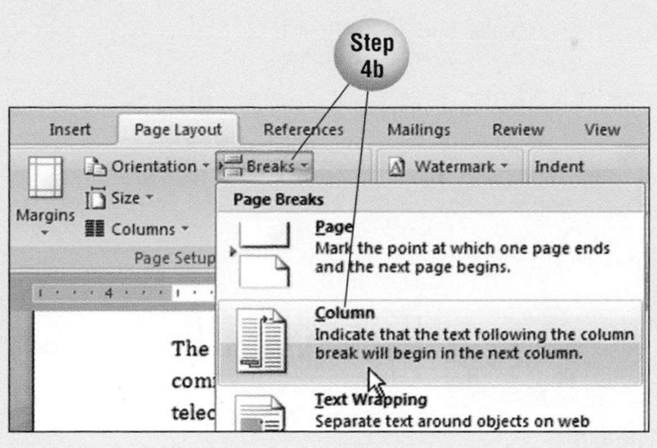

Balancing Columns on a Page

In documents that contain text formatted into columns, Word automatically lines up (balances) the last line of text at the bottom of each column, except on the last page. Text in the first column of the last page may flow to the end of the page, while the text in the second column may end far short of the end of the page. You can balance columns by inserting a continuous section break at the end of the text.

Exercise 2D

Formatting and Balancing Columns of Text

1. With **C06Ex02.docx** open, delete the column break by completing the following steps:
   a. Position the insertion point at the beginning of the *News Services* heading.
   b. Click the Draft button in the view area on the Status bar.
   c. Position the insertion point on the column break.

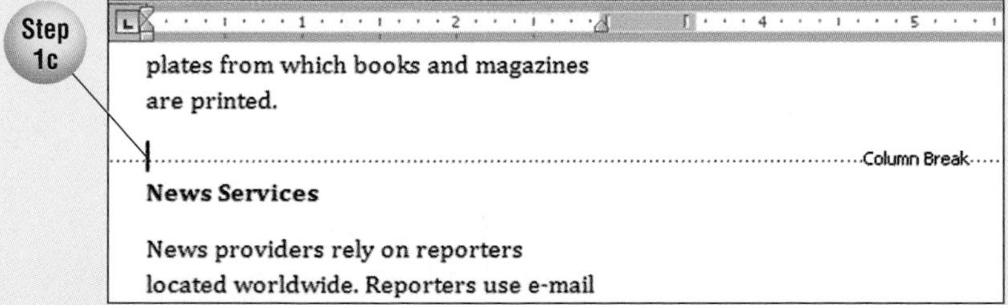

   d. Press the Delete key.
   e. Click the Print Layout button in the view area on the Status bar.
2. Select the entire document and then change the font to Constantia.
3. Move the insertion point to the end of the document and then balance the columns by clicking the Page Layout tab, clicking the Breaks button, and then clicking *Continuous* at the drop-down list.

4. Apply the *Red, Accent 2, Lighter 60%* paragraph shading to the title *COMPUTERS IN COMMUNICATIONS*.
5. Apply the *Red, Accent 2, Lighter 80%* paragraph shading to each of the headings in the document.
6. Save **C06Ex02.docx**.

Hyphenating Words

QUICK STEPS

Automatic Hyphenation
1. Click Page Layout tab.
2. Click Hyphenation button.
3. Click *Automatic* at drop-down list.

Manual Hyphenation
1. Click Page Layout tab.
2. Click Hyphenation button.
3. Click *Manual* at drop-down list.
4. Click Yes or No to hyphenate indicated words.
5. When complete, click OK.

In some Word documents, especially documents that have left and right margins wider than 1 inch or text set in columns, the right margin may appear quite ragged. To improve the display of line text, consider hyphenating long words that fall at the end of the text line. With Word's hyphenation feature, you can hyphenate words in a document automatically or manually.

Automatically Hyphenating Words

To hyphenate words automatically, click the Page Layout tab, click the Hyphenation button in the Page Setup group, and then click *Automatic* at the drop-down list. Scroll through the document and check to see if hyphens display in appropriate locations within the words. If after hyphenating words in a document you want to remove all hyphens, immediately click the Undo button on the Quick Access toolbar.

Manually Hyphenating Words

If you want to control where a hyphen appears in a word, choose manual hyphenation. To do this, click the Page Layout tab, click the Hyphenation button in the Page Setup group, and then click *Manual* at the drop-down list. This displays the Manual Hyphenation dialog box, shown in Figure 6.7. (The word in the *Hyphenate at* text box will vary.) At this dialog box, click Yes to hyphenate the word as indicated in the *Hyphenate at* text box, click No if you do not want the word hyphenated, or click Cancel to cancel hyphenation. Continue clicking Yes or No at the Manual Hyphenation dialog box. At the message indicating hyphenation is complete, click OK.

Figure 6.7 Manual Hyphenation Dialog Box

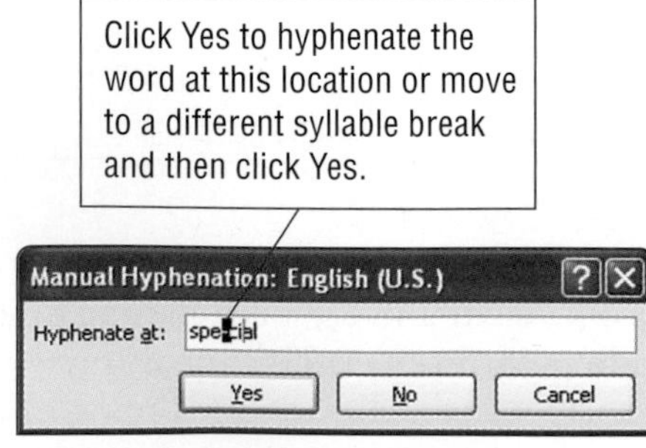

At the Manual Hyphenation dialog box, you can reposition the hyphen in the *Hyphenate at* text box. Word displays the word with syllable breaks indicated by a hyphen. The position at which the word will be hyphenated displays as a blinking black bar. If you want to hyphenate at a different location in the word, position the blinking black bar where you want the hyphen and then click Yes.

Exercise 2E

Automatically and Manually Hyphenating Words

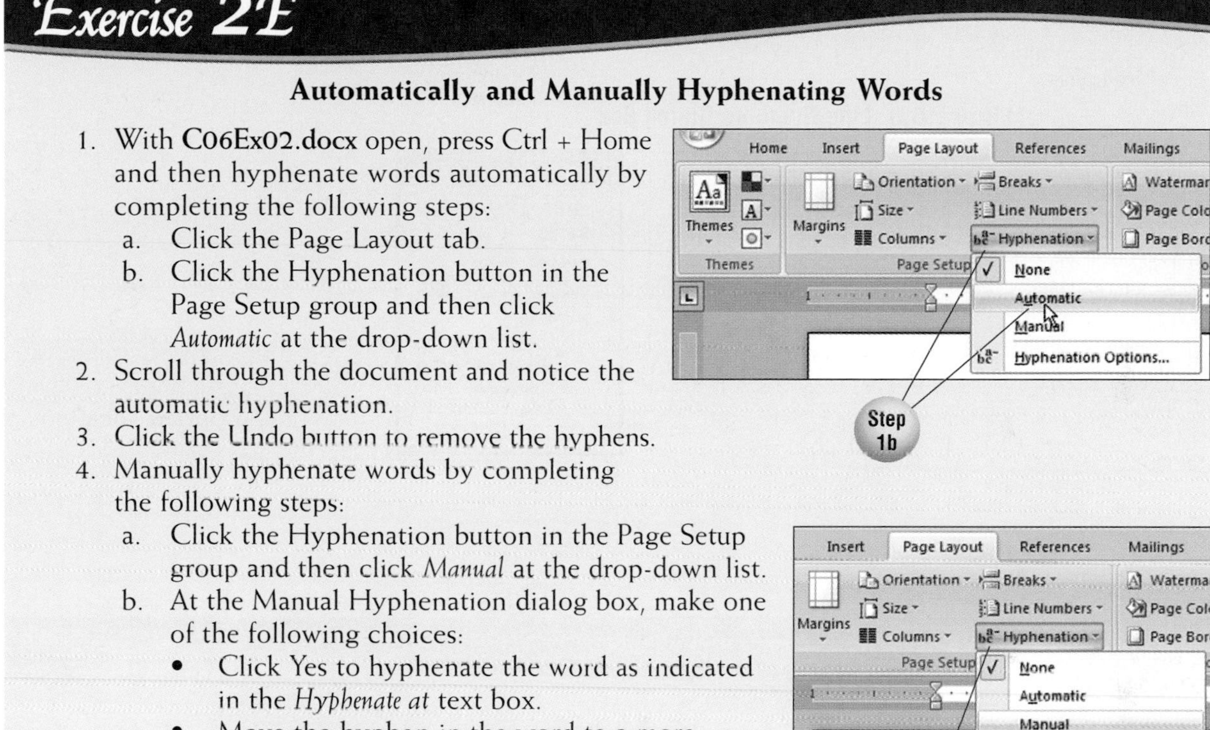

1. With **C06Ex02.docx** open, press Ctrl + Home and then hyphenate words automatically by completing the following steps:
   a. Click the Page Layout tab.
   b. Click the Hyphenation button in the Page Setup group and then click *Automatic* at the drop-down list.
2. Scroll through the document and notice the automatic hyphenation.
3. Click the Undo button to remove the hyphens.
4. Manually hyphenate words by completing the following steps:
   a. Click the Hyphenation button in the Page Setup group and then click *Manual* at the drop-down list.
   b. At the Manual Hyphenation dialog box, make one of the following choices:
      - Click Yes to hyphenate the word as indicated in the *Hyphenate at* text box.
      - Move the hyphen in the word to a more desirable location and then click Yes.
      - Click No if you do not want the word hyphenated.
   c. Continue clicking Yes or No at the Manual Hyphenation dialog box.
   d. At the hyphenation complete message, click OK.
5. Save **C06Ex02.docx**.

Inserting Line Numbers

You can use the Line Numbers button in the Page Setup group in the Page Layout tab to insert line numbers in a document. Numbering lines has practical applications for certain legal papers and for reference purposes. To number lines in a document, click the Page Layout tab, click the Line Numbers button in the Page Setup group, and then click the desired line number option at the drop-down list.

QUICK STEPS

Insert Line Numbers

1. Click Page Layout tab.
2. Click Line Numbers button.
3. Click desired line number option.

OR

1. Click Page Layout tab.
2. Click Line Numbers button.
3. Click *Line Numbering Options* at drop-down list.
4. Click Line Numbers button.
5. Specify line numbering options at dialog box.
6. Click OK.
7. Click OK.

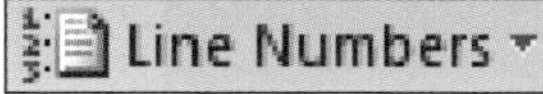

If you want more control over inserting line numbers in a document, click the Line Numbers button and then click *Line Numbering Options* at the drop-down list. At the Page Setup dialog box with the Layout tab selected, click the Line Numbers button that displays at the bottom of the dialog box. This displays the Line Numbers dialog box, shown in Figure 6.8. Use options at this dialog box to insert line numbering and to specify the starting number, where line numbers are printed, the interval between printed line numbers, and whether line numbers are consecutive or start over at the beginning of each page.

Figure 6.8 Line Numbers Dialog Box

Click this check box to turn on line numbering and make the remaining options active. Use options at this dialog box to customize how line numbers appear in the document.

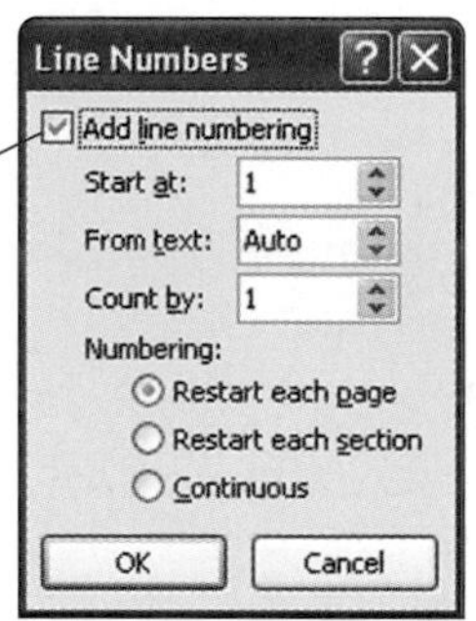

Exercise 2F

Inserting Line Numbers

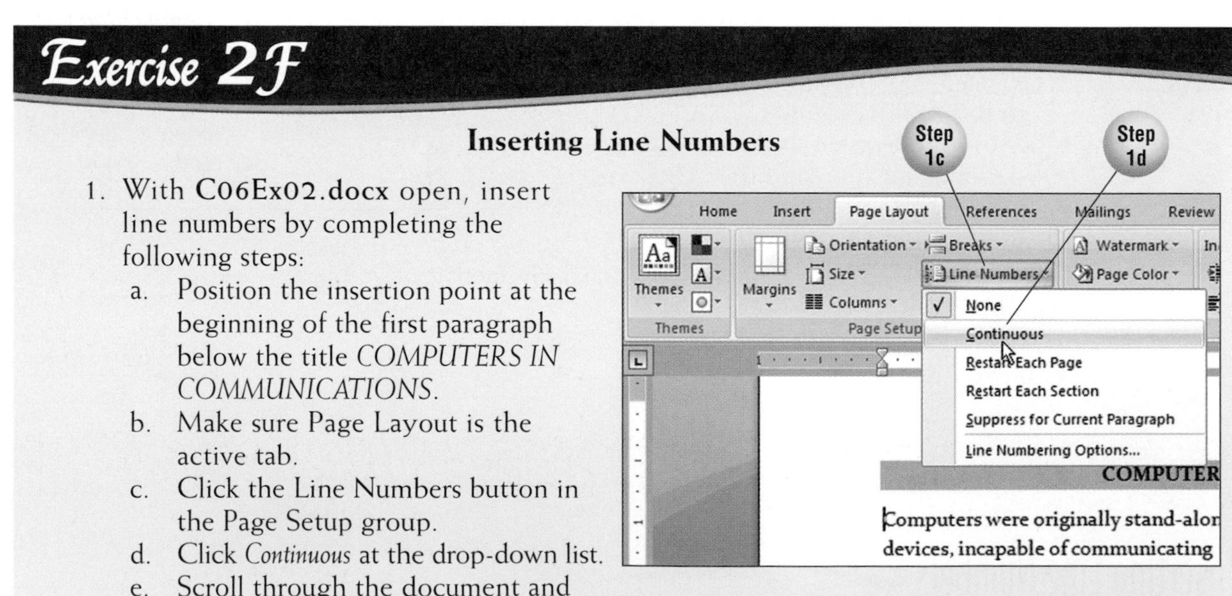

1. With C06Ex02.docx open, insert line numbers by completing the following steps:
   a. Position the insertion point at the beginning of the first paragraph below the title *COMPUTERS IN COMMUNICATIONS*.
   b. Make sure Page Layout is the active tab.
   c. Click the Line Numbers button in the Page Setup group.
   d. Click *Continuous* at the drop-down list.
   e. Scroll through the document and notice how the numbers appear in the document.
   f. Turn off line numbering by clicking the Line Numbers button and then clicking *None*.
2. Insert line numbers at the Line Numbers dialog box by completing the following steps:
   a. With the insertion point positioned at the beginning of the first paragraph below the title *COMPUTERS IN COMMUNICATIONS*, click the Line Numbers button and then click *Line Numbering Options* at the drop-down list.

b. At the Page Setup dialog box with the Layout tab selected, click the Line Numbers button that displays at the bottom of the dialog box.
c. At the Line Numbers dialog box, click the *Add line numbering* option.
d. Click the up-pointing arrow at the right side of the *Count by* option to display 2 in the text box.
e. Click OK to close the Line Numbers dialog box.
f. Click OK to close the Page Setup dialog box.
3. Scroll through the document and notice the appearance of the line numbers.
4. Remove line numbering by clicking the Line Numbers button and then click *None* at the drop-down list.
5. Save, print, and then close **C06Ex02.docx**.

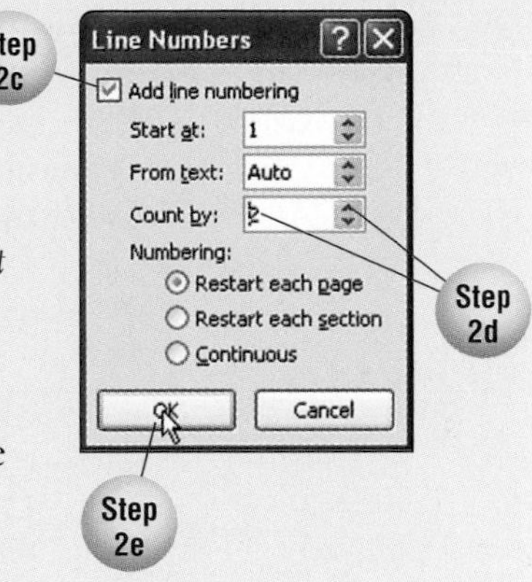

Inserting a Watermark

A watermark is a lightened image that displays behind text in a document. Word provides a number of predesigned watermarks that you can insert in a document. Display these watermarks by clicking the Watermark button in the Page Background group in the Page Layout tab. Scroll through the list of watermarks and then click the desired option.

Changing Page Color

Use the Page Color button in the Page Background group to apply background color to a document. This background color is intended for viewing a document on screen or on the Web. The color is visible on the screen but does not print. Insert a page color by clicking the Page Color button and then clicking the desired color at the color palette.

Insert Watermark
1. Click Page Layout tab.
2. Click Watermark button.
3. Click desired option at drop-down list.

Change Page Color
1. Click Page Layout tab.
2. Click Page Color button.
3. Click desired option at color palette.

Exercise 3A

Inserting a Watermark and Page Color

1. Open **Report03.docx** and save the document with the name **C06Ex03**.
2. Make the following changes to the document:
   a. Apply the Heading 1 style to the two titles in the document *SECTION 1: UNAUTHORIZED ACCESS* and *SECTION 2: INFORMATION THEFT*.
   b. Apply the Heading 2 style to all of the headings in the document.
   c. Change the style set to *Formal*.

3. With **C06Ex03.docx** open, insert a watermark by completing the following steps:
   a. Move the insertion point to the beginning of the document.
   b. Click the Page Layout tab.
   c. Click the Watermark button in the Page Background group.
   d. At the drop-down list, click the *CONFIDENTIAL 1* option.

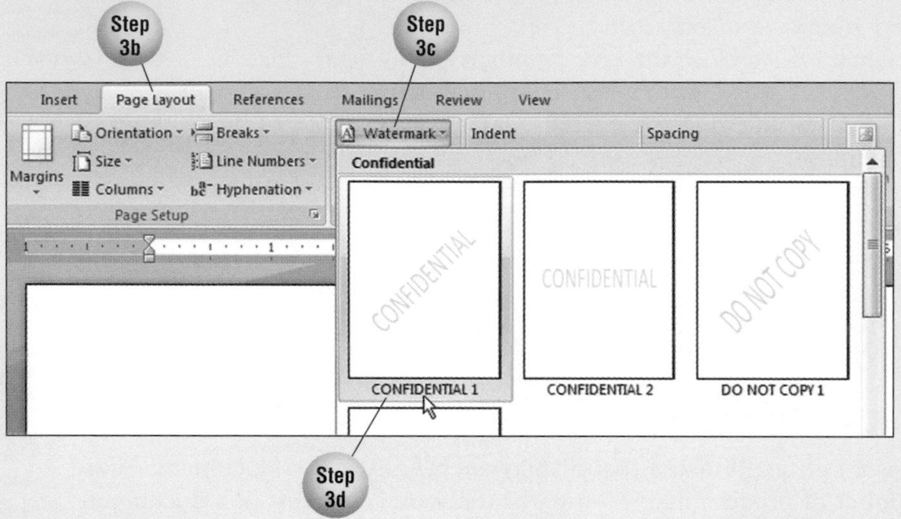

4. Scroll through the document and notice how the watermark displays behind the text.
5. Remove the watermark and insert a different one by completing the following steps:
   a. Click the Watermark button in the Page Background group and then click *Remove Watermark* at the drop-down list.
   b. Click the Watermark button and then click *DO NOT COPY 1* at the drop-down list.
6. Scroll through the document and notice how the watermark displays.
7. Move the insertion point to the beginning of the document.
8. Click the Page Color button in the Page Background group and then click *Aqua, Accent 5, Lighter 80%* at the color palette.
9. Save **C06Ex03.docx**.

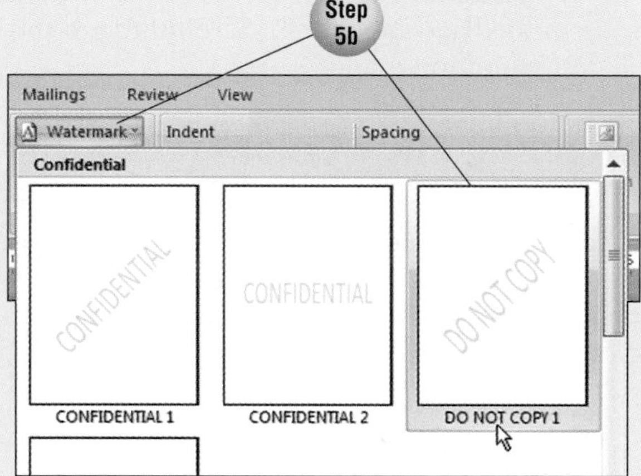

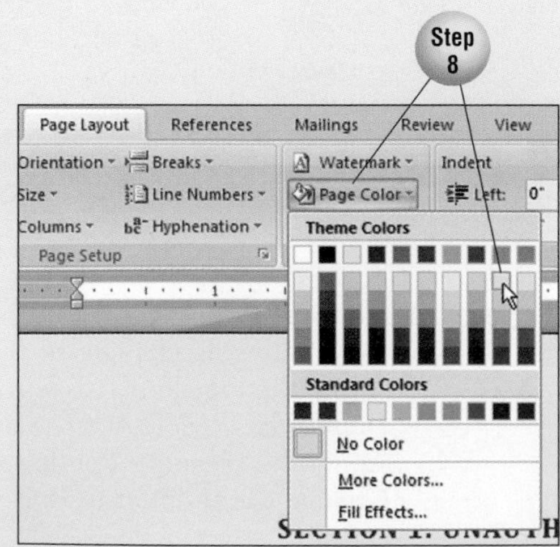

Inserting a Page Border

To improve the visual appeal of a document, consider inserting a page border. When you insert a page border in a multiple-page document, the border prints on each page. To insert a page border, click the Page Borders button in the Page Background group in the Page Layout tab. This displays the Borders and Shading dialog box with the Page Border tab selected, as shown in Figure 6.9. At this dialog box, you can specify the border style, color, and width.

The dialog box includes an option for inserting a page border that contains an image. To display the images available, click the down-pointing arrow at the right side of the *Art* list box. Scroll down the drop-down list and then click the desired image. (This feature may need to install the first time you use it.)

Insert Page Border

1. Click Page Layout tab.
2. Click Page Borders button.
3. Specify desired options at dialog box.

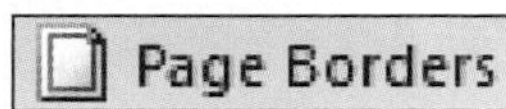

Figure 6.9 Borders and Shading Dialog Box with Page Border Tab Selected

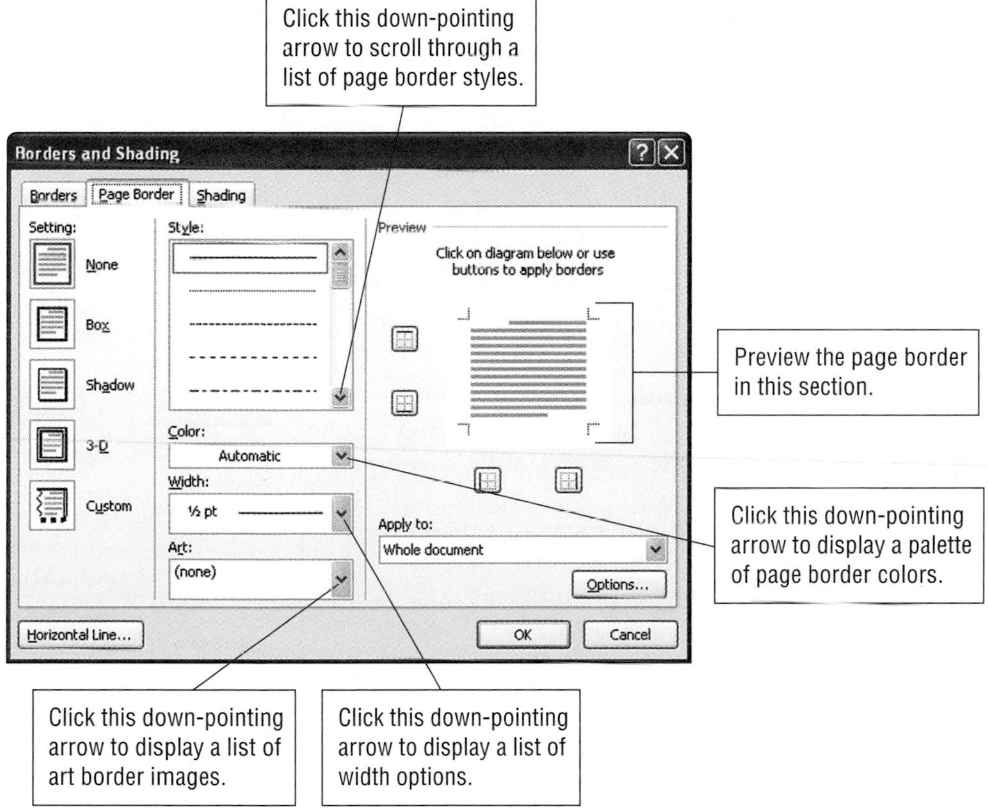

Exercise 3B

Inserting a Page Border

1. With **C06Ex03.docx** open, remove the page color by clicking the Page Color button in the Page Background group and then clicking *No Color* at the color palette.
2. Insert a page border by completing the following steps:
   a. Click the Page Borders button in the Page Background group in the Page Layout tab.
   b. Click the *Box* option in the *Setting* section.
   c. Scroll down the list of line styles in the *Style* list box until the end of the list displays and then click the third line from the end.
   d. Click the down-pointing arrow at the right of the *Color* list box and then click *Red, Accent 2, Darker 50%* at the color palette.
   e. Click OK to close the dialog box.

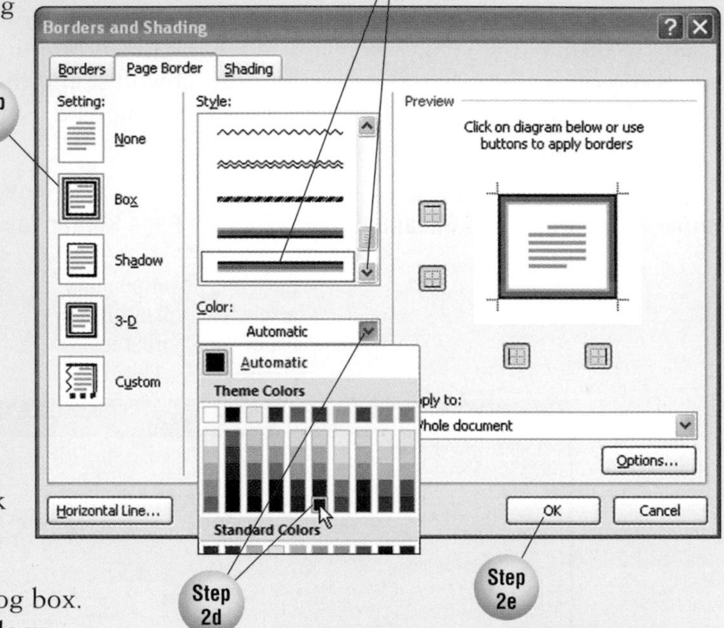

3. Save and then print **C06Ex03.docx**.
4. Insert an image page border by completing the following steps:
   a. Click the Page Borders button in the Page Background group.
   b. Click the down-pointing arrow at the right side of the *Art* list box and then click the border image shown at the right.
   c. Click OK to close the dialog box.
5. Save, print, and then close **C06Ex03.docx**.

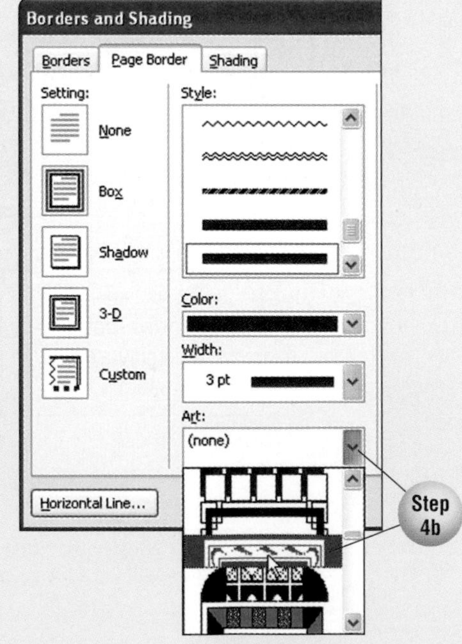

Chapter Summary

- You can change the document view with buttons in the view area on the Status bar or with options in the View tab.
- Print Layout is the default view, which you can change to other views such as Draft view or Full Screen Reading view.
- The Draft view displays the document in a format for efficient editing and formatting.
- Use the Zoom slider bar to change the percentage of the display.
- Full Screen Reading view displays a document in a format for easy viewing and reading.
- Navigate in Full Screen Reading view using keys on the keyboard or with the Next and Previous buttons.
- By default, a Word document contains 1-inch top, bottom, left, and right margins. Change margins with preset margin settings at the Margins drop-down list or with options at the Page Setup dialog box with the Margins tab selected.
- The default page orientation is Portrait, which you can change to Landscape with the Orientation button in the Page Setup group in the Page Layout tab.
- The default page size is 8.5 by 11 inches, which can be changed with options at the Size drop-down list or options at the Page Setup dialog box with the Paper tab selected.
- Insert a section break in a document to apply formatting to a portion of a document. You can insert a continuous section break or a section break that begins a new page. View a section break in Draft view because section breaks are not visible in Print Layout view.
- Set text in columns to improve readability of documents such as newsletters or reports. Format text in columns using the Columns button in the Page Setup group in the Page Layout tab or with options at the Columns dialog box.
- Remove column formatting with the Columns button in the Page Layout tab or at the Columns dialog box. Balance column text on the last page of a document by inserting a continuous section break at the end of the text.
- Improve the display of text lines by hyphenating long words that fall at the end of the line. You can automatically or manually hyphenate words in a document.
- Number lines in a document with options from the Line Numbers button drop-down list or with options at the Line Numbers dialog box.
- A watermark is a lightened image that displays behind text in a document. Use the Watermark button in the Page Background group in the Page Layout tab to insert a watermark.
- Insert page color in a document with the Page Color button in the Page Background group. Page color is designed for viewing a document on screen and does not print.
- Click the Page Borders button in the Page Background group and the Borders and Shading dialog box with the Page Border tab selected displays. Use options at this dialog box to insert a page border or an image page border in a document.

Commands review

FEATURE	RIBBON TAB, GROUP	BUTTON, OPTION
Borders and Shading dialog box with Page Border tab selected	Page Layout, Page Background	Page Borders
Columns	Page Layout, Page Setup	Columns
Columns dialog box	Page Layout, Page Setup	Columns, More Columns
Continuous section break	Page Layout, Page Setup	Breaks, Continuous
Draft view	View, Document Views	
Full Screen Reading view	View, Document Views	
Hyphenate words automatically	Page Layout, Page Setup	Hyphenation, Automatic
Hyphenate words manually	Page Layout, Page Setup	Hyphenation, Manual
Line numbers	Page Layout, Page Setup	Line Numbers
Margins	Page Layout, Page Setup	
Orientation	Page Layout, Page Setup	Orientation
Page color	Page Layout, Page Background	Page Color
Page Setup dialog box with Margins tab selected	Page Layout, Page Setup	, *Custom Margins*; or Page Setup group dialog box launcher
Page Setup dialog box with Paper tab selected	Page Layout, Page Setup	Size, *More Paper Sizes*
Page size	Page Layout, Page Setup	Size
Print Layout view	View, Document Views	
Section break	Page Layout, Page Setup	Breaks
Watermark	Page Layout, Page Background	Watermark

Reviewing key points

Completion: In the space provided at the right, indicate the correct term, symbol, or command.

1. This view displays a document in a format for efficient editing and formatting. ____________________
2. This view displays a document in a format for easy viewing and reading. ____________________
3. This is the default measurement for the top, bottom, left, and right margins. ____________________
4. This is the default page orientation. ____________________
5. Set specific margins at this dialog box with the Margins tab selected. ____________________
6. View a section break in this view. ____________________
7. Format text into columns with the Columns button located in this group in the Page Layout tab. ____________________
8. Balance column text on the last page of a document by inserting this type of break at the end of the text. ____________________
9. If you hyphenate words in a document and then decide to remove the hyphens, immediately click this button. ____________________
10. A lightened image that displays behind text in a document is called this. ____________________
11. The Page Borders button displays in this group in the Page Layout tab. ____________________

Applying your skills

Assessment 1 Apply Formatting to a Computers in Industry Report

1. Open **Document04.docx** and save the document with the name **C06A01**.
2. Apply the Heading 1 style to the titles *COMPUTERS IN INDUSTRY* and *REFERENCES*.
3. Apply the Heading 2 style to the headings in the report.
4. Change the style set to *Formal*.
5. Hang indent the paragraphs of text below the *REFERENCES* title.
6. Change the top, left, and right margins to 1.25 inches.
7. Manually hyphenate the text in the document.
8. Insert the SAMPLE 1 watermark in the document. (You will need to scroll down the list box to display this watermark.)
9. Insert a page border of your choosing.
10. Save, print, and then close **C06A01.docx**.

Assessment 2 Apply Formatting to a Data Security Training Notice

1. Open **Notice01.docx** and save the document with the name **C06A02**.
2. Change the font for the entire document to 12-point Candara.
3. Set the title in 14-point Candara bold and center it.
4. Change the page orientation to *Landscape*.
5. Change the left and right margins to 1.8 inches and the top margin to 2.3 inches.
6. Insert the ASAP 1 watermark in the document.
7. Insert a page border of your choosing.
8. Save, print, and then close **C06A02.docx**.

Assessment 3 Apply Formatting to a Computer Viruses and Security Report

1. Open **Report04.docx** and save the document with the name **C06A03**.
2. Select text from the title *SECTION 4: HARDWARE AND SOFTWARE SECURITY RISKS* to the end of the document and then press the Delete key.
3. Select the entire document, change the font to 12-point Cambria, and then deselect the text.
4. Change the top margin to 1.5 inches.
5. Format the text from the first paragraph to the end of the document into two columns with 0.6 inch and a line between columns.
6. Manually hyphenate the text in the document.
7. Balance the columns on the second page.
8. Center the title and change the font size of the title to 14 points. Add shading to the title and insert a double-line bottom border and a single-line top border.
9. Apply shading to the headings in the document and apply a single-line bottom border to each heading.
10. Save, print, and then close **C06A03.docx**.

Chapter 7

Customizing Page Formatting

Tutorial 7.1
Numbering Pages
Tutorial 7.2
Using Headers and Footers
Tutorial 7.3
Searching within a Document

Performance Objectives

Upon successful completion of Chapter 7, you will be able to:

- Insert a page break, blank page, and cover page
- Insert page numbering
- Insert and edit predesigned headers and footers
- Use the Click and Type feature
- Vertically align text

In Chapter 6, you learned how to format pages in a Word document by changing margin sizes, page orientation, and paper size; setting text in columns; hyphenating words; and inserting graphic elements. In this chapter, you will learn how to insert other elements such as cover pages, blank pages, page breaks, page numbers, and headers and footers. You will also learn how to align text vertically and how to use Word's Click and Type feature, which allows you to insert text in specific locations in a document, and Word's Find and Replace feature, which allows you to search for specific text or formatting and replace it with other text or formatting.

Note: Before beginning computer exercises for this chapter, copy to your storage medium the Chapter07 folder from the CD that accompanies this textbook and then make Chapter07 the active folder.

Inserting Page Elements

Insert Page Break
1. Click Insert tab.
2. Click Page Break button
OR
Press Ctrl + Enter.

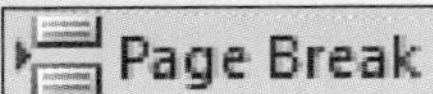

The Pages group in the Insert tab contains three buttons that you can use to insert and then format or modify elements in a document. With these buttons, you can insert a page break, a blank page, and a predesigned cover page.

Inserting a Page Break

Word assumes that you are using standard-sized paper, which is 8.5 inches wide and 11 inches long. With default top and bottom margins of 1 inch, a Word document contains approximately 9 inches of text on a page. At approximately the 10-inch mark, Word automatically inserts a page break. You can insert your own page break in a document with the keyboard shortcut Ctrl + Enter, or with the Page Break button in the Pages group in the Insert tab.

A page break automatically inserted by Word is considered a *soft* page break; a page break that you insert is considered a *hard* page break. A soft page break adjusts automatically when you add or delete text from a document. A hard page break does not adjust and is therefore less flexible than a soft page break. If you add or delete text from a document with a hard page break, check the break to determine whether it is still in a desirable location. If you are working in Draft view, a hard page break displays as a row of dots with the words Page Break in the center. To delete a page break, position the insertion point immediately below the page break and then press the Backspace key or position the insertion point above the page break and then press the Delete key. In Draft view, position the insertion point on the page break and then press the Delete key.

Exercise 1A

Inserting Page Breaks

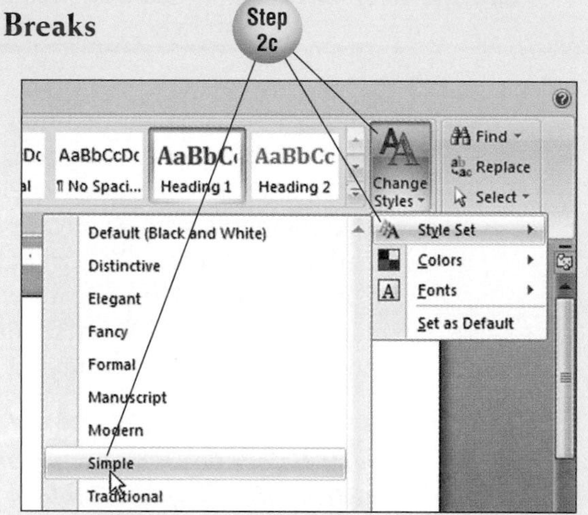

1. Open **Report03.docx** and save the document with the name **C07Ex01**.
2. Make the following formatting changes:
   a. Apply the Heading 1 style to the two titles: *SECTION 1: UNAUTHORIZED ACCESS* and *SECTION 2: INFORMATION THEFT*.
   b. Apply the Heading 2 style to the six headings: *User IDs and Passwords*, *System Backdoors*, *Spoofing*, *Spyware*, *Wireless Device Security*, and *Data Browsing*.
   c. Change the style set to *Simple*. (*Hint: Use the* Change Styles *button in the Styles group in the Home tab.*)
3. Insert a page break by completing the following steps:
   a. Position the insertion point at the beginning of the title *SECTION 2: INFORMATION THEFT* (located on page 2).
   b. Click the Insert tab and then click the Page Break button in the Pages group.
4. Move the insertion point to the beginning of the heading *Spyware* and then press Ctrl + Enter to insert a page break.
5. Scroll through the document and notice the page breaks. Delete the page break above *Spyware* by positioning the insertion point immediately right of the period that ends the paragraph in the *Spoofing* paragraph and then pressing the Delete key twice.
6. Save **C07Ex01.docx**.

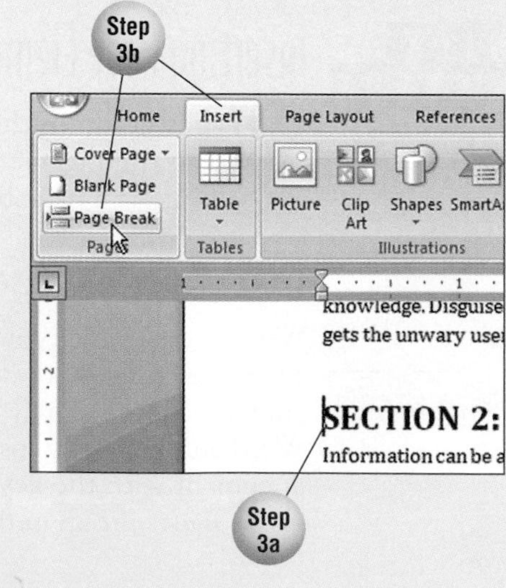

Inserting a Blank Page

Click the Blank Page button in the Pages group in the Insert tab to insert a blank page at the position of the insertion point. Inserting a blank page can be useful as a spaceholder in a document when you want to insert an illustration, graphic, or figure.

Insert Blank Page
1. Click Insert tab.
2. Click Blank Page button.

Insert Cover Page
1. Click Insert tab.
2. Click Cover Page button.
3. Click desired cover page at drop-down list.

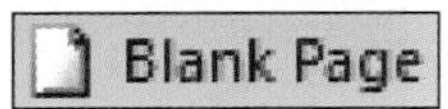

Inserting a Cover Page

If you are preparing a document for distribution to others, or if you simply want to improve a document's visual appeal, consider inserting a cover page. With the Cover Page button in the Pages group in the Insert tab, you can insert a predesigned, formatted cover page and then type text in specific locations on the page to personalize it. Click the Cover Page button and a drop-down list displays, similar to the one shown in Figure 7.1. The drop-down list provides a visual representation of each cover page option. Scroll through the list and then click the cover page you want to use.

These predesigned cover pages contain location placeholders where you can enter specific information. For example, a cover page might contain the placeholder *[Type the document title]*. Click anywhere in the placeholder and then type the desired text. The first time you click placeholder text, all of the text is selected. If you have typed text in a placeholder text, clicking in the text will position the insertion point at that location. If you want to delete the entire placeholder, click the placeholder tab and then press the Delete key. To delete the text but not the placeholder, select only the text in the placeholder and then press the Delete key.

Figure 7.1 Cover Page Drop-down List

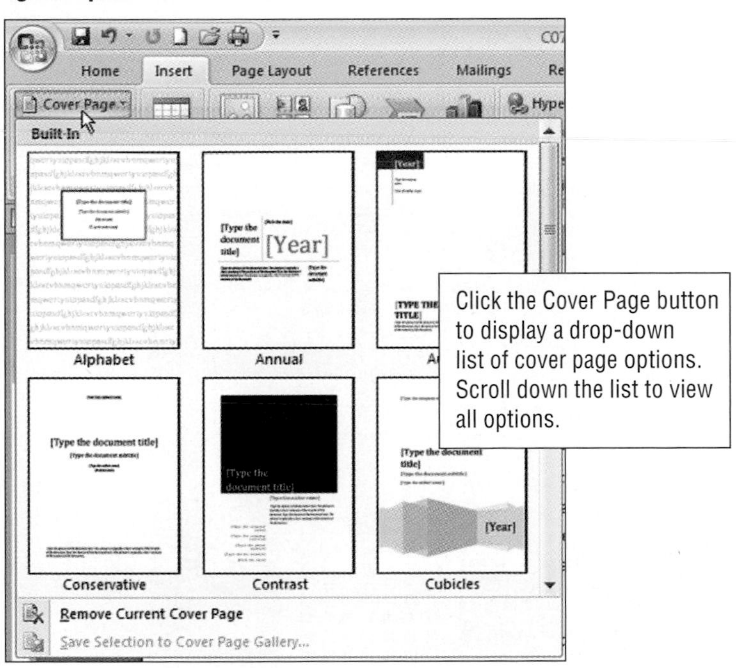

Exercise 1B

Inserting a Blank Page and a Cover Page

1. With **C07Ex01.docx** open, create a blank page by completing the following steps:
   a. Move the insertion point to the beginning of the heading *Spoofing* (located on the first page).
   b. Click the Insert tab.
   c. Click the Blank Page button in the Pages group.
2. Insert a cover page by completing the following steps:
   a. Press Ctrl + Home to move the insertion point to the beginning of the document.
   b. Click the Cover Page button in the Pages group.
   c. At the drop-down list, scroll down and then click the *Motion* cover page.
   d. Click anywhere in the placeholder text [Year], click the down-pointing arrow that displays at the right side of the placeholder, and then click the Today button that displays at the bottom of the drop-down calendar.

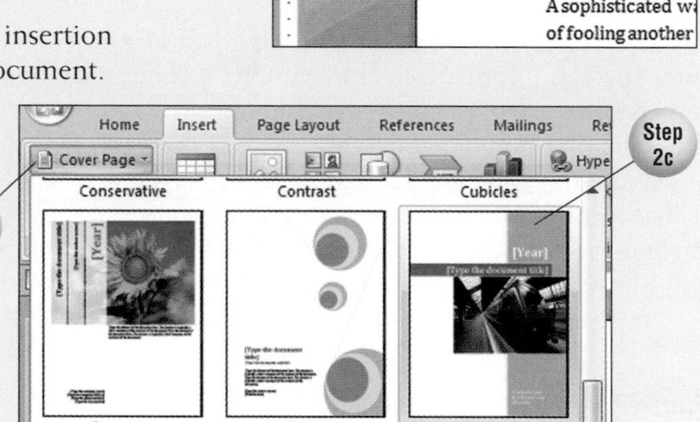

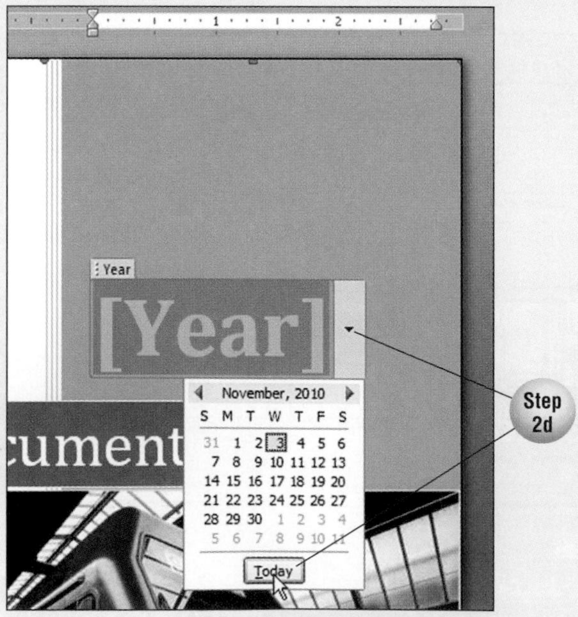

e. Click anywhere in the placeholder text *[Type the document title]* and then type **Computer Security**.

f. Scroll down the page and then click the placeholder text *[Type the author name]* and then type your first and last names.

g. Click the placeholder text *[Type the company name]* and then type **Madison Security Systems**.

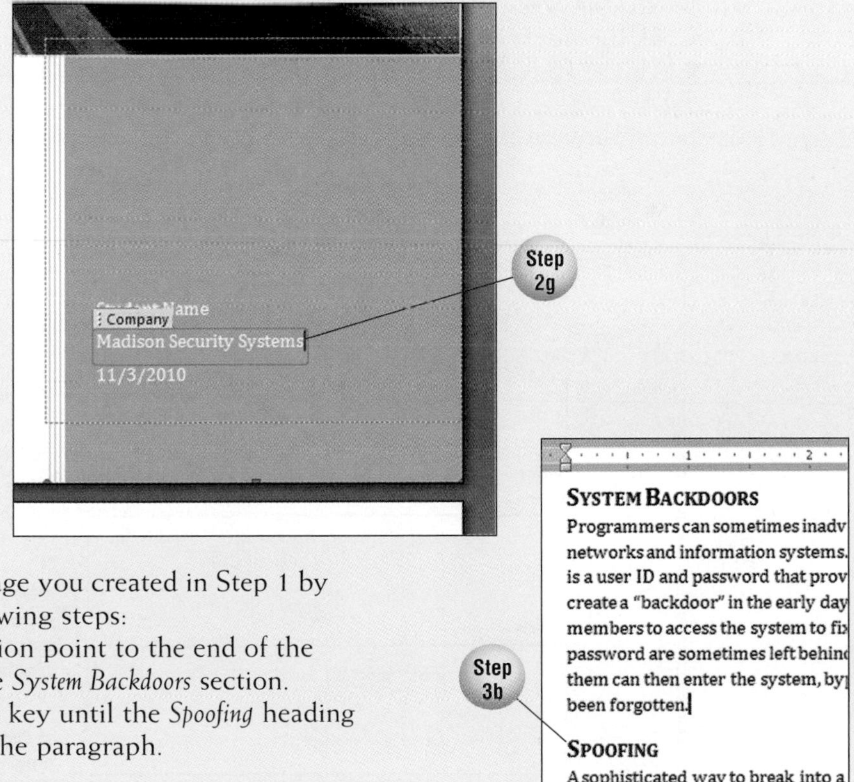

3. Remove the blank page you created in Step 1 by completing the following steps:
   a. Move the insertion point to the end of the paragraph in the *System Backdoors* section.
   b. Press the Delete key until the *Spoofing* heading displays below the paragraph.
4. Save **C07Ex01.docx**.

QUICK STEPS

Insert Page Numbering
1. Click Insert tab.
2. Click Page Number button.
3. Click desired option at drop-down list.

Inserting Predesigned Page Numbering

Word, by default, does not print page numbers on document pages. If you want to insert page numbers in a document, use the Page Number button in the Header & Footer group in the Insert tab. When you click the Page Number button, a drop-down list displays with options for specifying where on the page you want the page number inserted. Point to an option at this list, and a drop-down list displays of predesigned page formats. Scroll through the options in the drop-down list and then click the desired option. You can remove page numbering from a document by clicking the Page Number button and then clicking *Remove Page Numbers* at the drop-down list.

Exercise 1C

Inserting Predesigned Page Numbering

1. With **C07Ex01.docx** open, insert page numbering by completing the following steps:
   a. Move the insertion point to the beginning of the title *SECTION 1: UNAUTHORIZED ACCESS.*
   b. Click the Insert tab.
   c. Click the Page Number button in the Header & Footer group and then point to *Top of Page.*
   d. Scroll through the drop-down list and then click the *Brackets* 2 option.

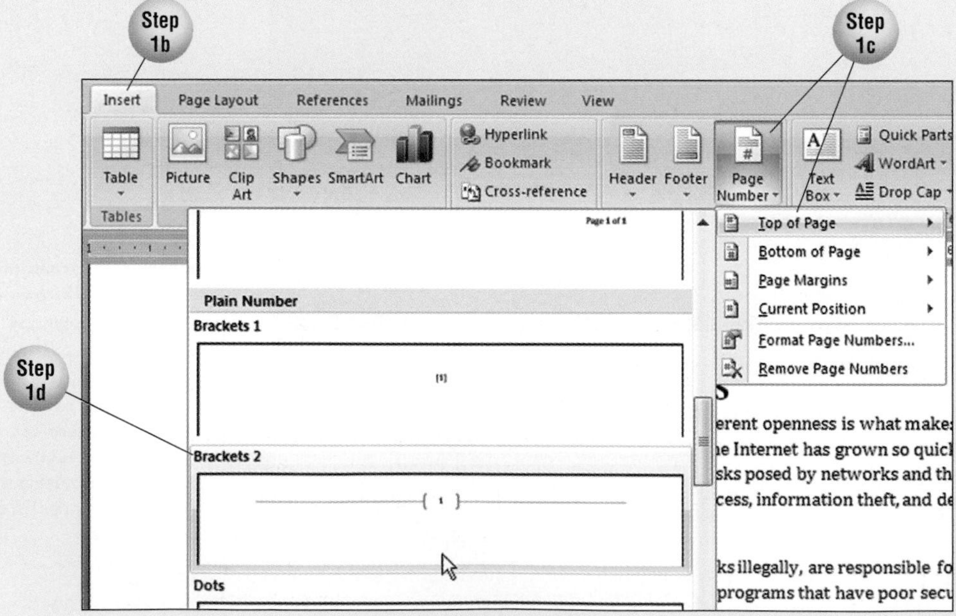

2. Double-click in the document and then scroll through it to view the page numbering that displays at the top of each page except the cover page. (The cover page and text are divided by a section break. Word considers the cover page as page 1 but does not include the numbering on the page.)

3. Remove the page numbering by clicking the Insert tab, clicking the Page Number button, and then clicking *Remove Page Numbers* at the drop-down list.
4. Click the Page Number button, point to *Bottom of Page*, scroll down the drop-down list, and then click the *Circle* option.

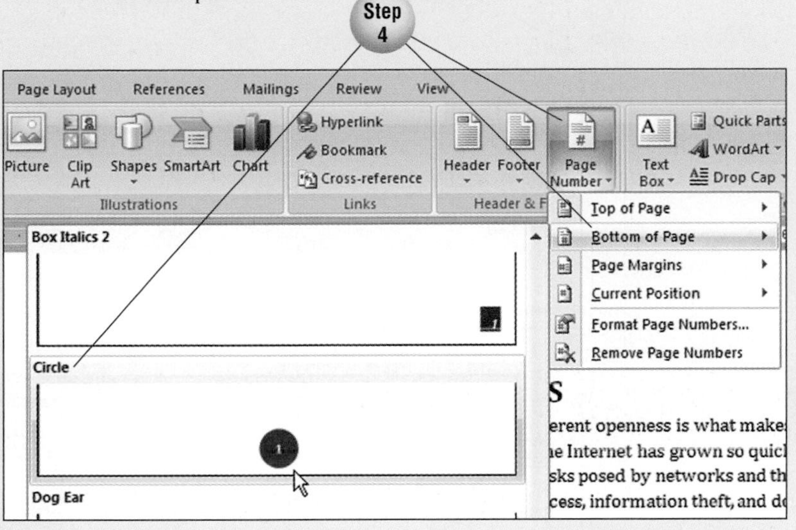

5. Double-click in the document and view page numbering.
6. Save, print, and then close **C07Ex01.docx**.

Inserting Predesigned Headers and Footers

Insert Predesigned Header
1. Click Insert tab.
2. Click Header button.
3. Click desired option at drop-down list.
4. Type text in specific placeholders in header.

Text that appears at the top of every page of a multi-page document is called a ***header***; text that appears at the bottom of every page is referred to as a ***footer***. Headers and footers are common in manuscripts, textbooks, reports, and other publications. You can insert a predesigned header in a document by clicking the Insert tab and then clicking the Header button in the Header & Footer group. This displays the Header drop-down list, shown in Figure 7.2. At this list, click the predesigned header you want to use, and the header is inserted in the document. The header is visible in Print Layout view but not in Draft view.

A predesigned header or footer, like a predesigned cover page, may contain location placeholders where you can enter specific information. For example, a header might contain the placeholder *[Type the document title]*. Click anywhere in the placeholder and then type the desired text. The first time you click placeholder text, all of the text is selected. If you have typed text in placeholder, clicking in the text will position the insertion point at that location. If you want to delete the entire placeholder, click the placeholder tab and then press the Delete key. To delete the text but not the placeholder, select only the text in the placeholder and then press the Delete key.

Figure 7.2 Header Drop-down List

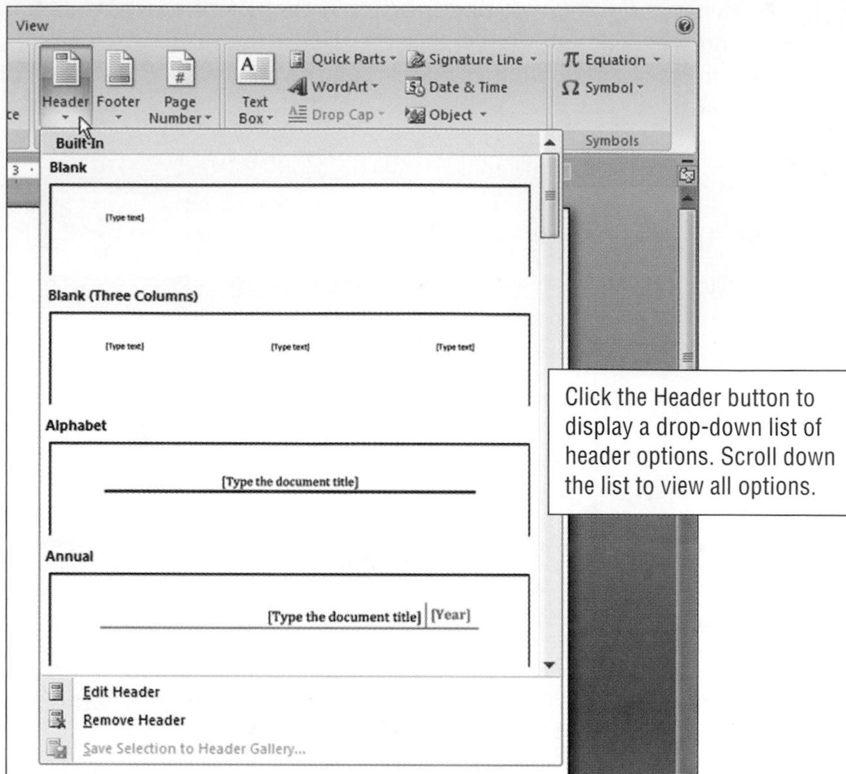

Exercise 2A

Inserting a Predesigned Header in a Document

1. Open **Report01.docx** and save the document with the name **C07Ex02**.
2. Change the top margin by completing the following steps:
   a. Click the Page Layout tab.
   b. Click the Margins button in the Page Setup group and then click *Custom Margins* at the drop-down list.
   c. Type 1.5 in the *Top* measurement box.
   d. Click OK.

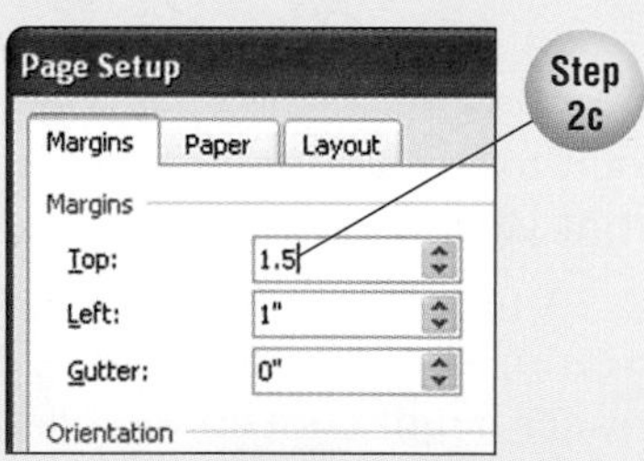

3. Make the following changes to the document:
   a. Apply the Heading 1 style to the title *THE COMPUTER ADVANTAGE*.
   b. Apply the Heading 2 style to the five headings: *Speed*, *Accuracy*, *Versatility*, *Storage*, and *Communications*.
   c. Change the style set to *Formal*.
   d. Move the insertion point to the beginning of the heading *Speed* (located at the bottom of page 1) and then insert a page break by clicking the Insert tab and then clicking the Page Break button in the Pages group.
   e. Move the insertion point to the beginning of the heading *Communications* (located at the bottom of page 3) and then insert a page break by pressing Ctrl + Enter.

4. Press Ctrl + Home to move the insertion point to the beginning of the document and then insert a header by completing the following steps:
   a. Click the Insert tab.
   b. Click the Header button in the Header & Footer group.
   c. Scroll to the bottom of the drop-down list that displays and then click *Tiles*.

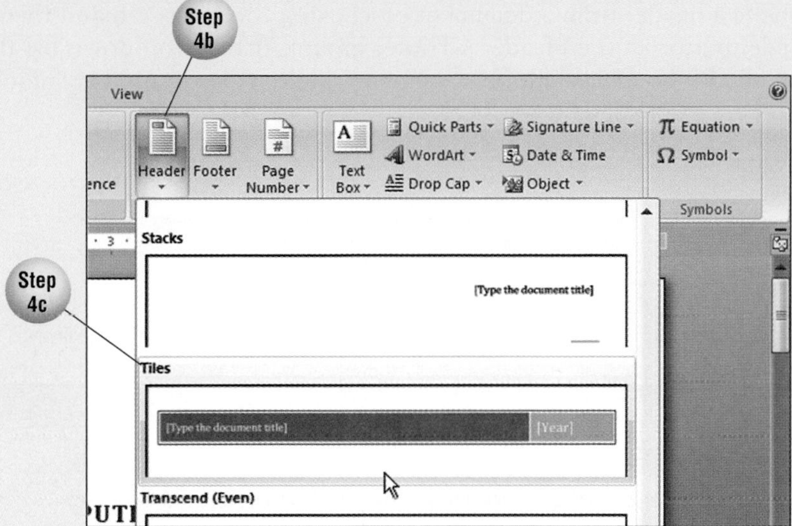

   d. Click anywhere in the placeholder text *[Type the document title]* and then type **The Computer Advantage**.

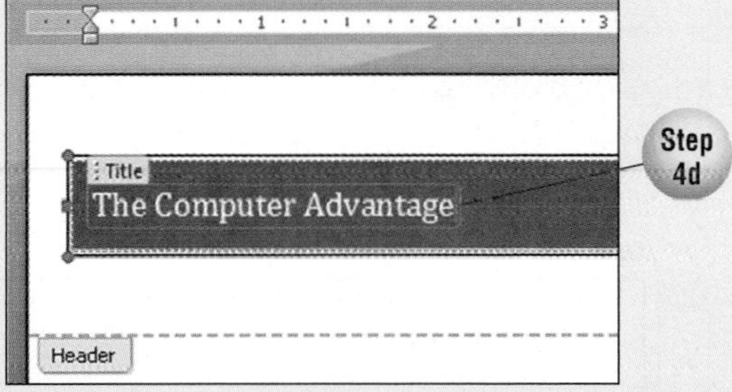

   e. Click anywhere in the placeholder text *[Year]* and then type the current year.
   f. Double-click in the document text. (This makes the document text active and dims the header.)
5. Scroll through the document to see how the header will print.
6. Save and then print **C07Ex02.docx**.

Insert Predesigned Footer
1. Click Insert tab.
2. Click Footer button.
3. Click desired option at drop-down list.
4. Type text in specific placeholders in footer.

Insert a predesigned footer in the same way you would insert a header. Click the Footer button in the Header & Footer group in the Insert tab, and a drop-down list displays similar to the Header drop-down list shown in Figure 7.2. Click the desired footer, and the predesigned footer formatting is applied to the document.

Removing a Header or Footer

Remove a header from a document by clicking the Insert tab and then clicking the Header button in the Header & Footer group. At the drop-down list that displays, click the *Remove Header* option. Complete similar steps to remove a footer.

Exercise 2B

Removing a Header and Inserting a Predesigned Footer

1. With **C07Ex02.docx** open, press Ctrl + Home to move the insertion point to the beginning of the document.
2. Remove the header by clicking the Insert tab, clicking the Header button in the Header & Footer group, and then clicking the *Remove Header* option at the drop-down list.

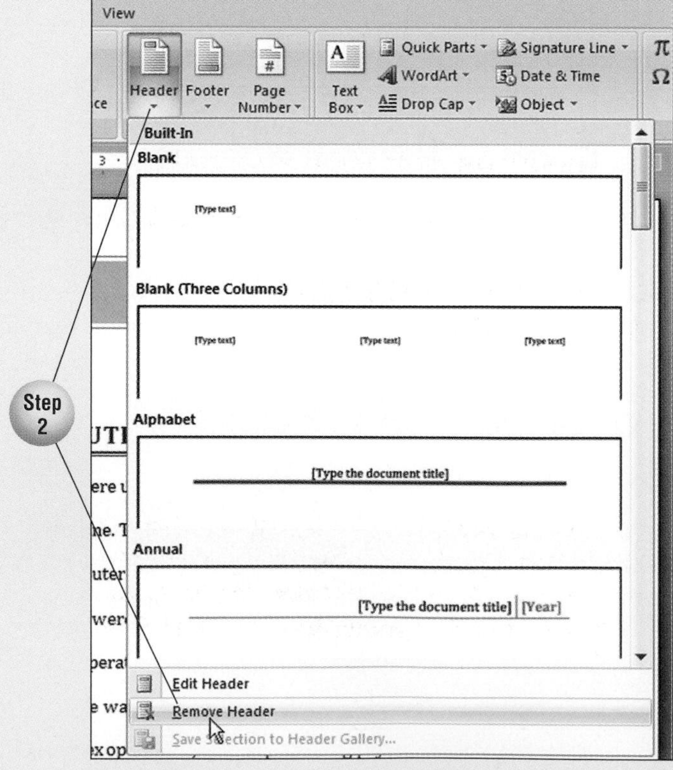

3. Insert a footer in the document by completing the following steps:
   a. Click the Footer button in the Header & Footer group.
   b. Click *Alphabet* at the drop-down list.

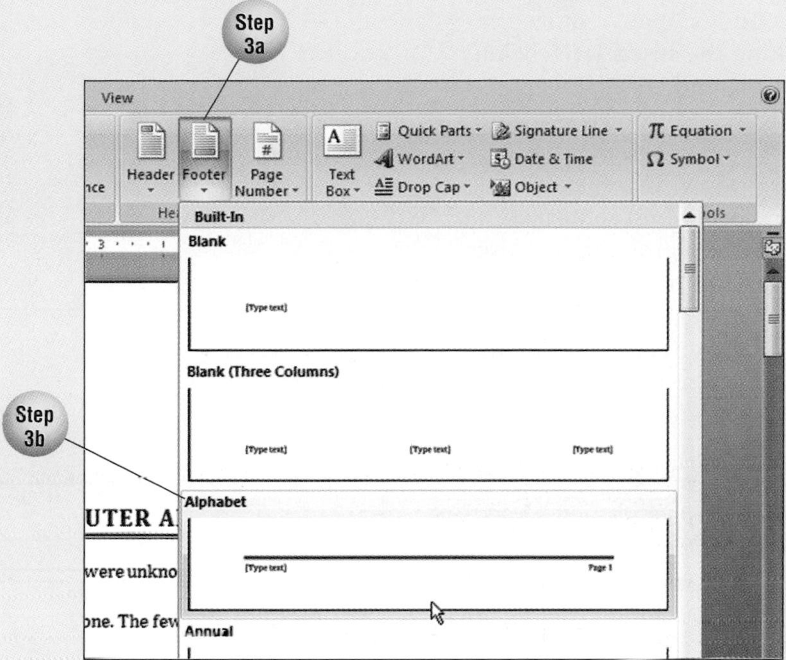

   c. Click anywhere in the placeholder text *[Type text]* and then type **The Computer Advantage**.

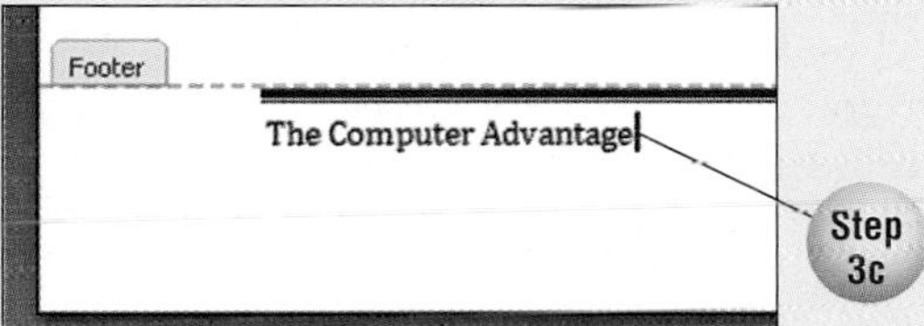

   d. Double-click in the document text. (This makes the document text active and dims the header.)
4. Scroll through the document to see how the footer will print.
5. Save and then print **C07Ex02.docx**.

Editing a Predesigned Header or Footer

Predesigned headers and footers contain elements such as page numbers and the document title. You can change the formatting of an element by clicking it and then applying the desired formatting. You can also select and then delete an element. In Print Layout view, you can display the header or footer pane for editing by double-clicking a header or footer.

Exercise 2C

Formatting and Deleting Header and Footer Elements

1. With **C07Ex02.docx** open, remove the footer by clicking the Insert tab, clicking the Footer button, and then clicking *Remove Footer* at the drop-down list.
2. Insert and then format a header by completing the following steps:
   a. Click the Header button in the Header & Footer group in the Insert tab, scroll in the drop-down list, and then click *Motion (Odd Page)*. (This header inserts the document title as well as the page number.)
   b. Delete the document title from the header by clicking anywhere in the text *The Computer Advantage*, selecting the text, and then pressing the Delete key.
   c. Double-click in the document text.
3. Insert and then format a footer by completing the following steps:
   a. Click the Insert tab.
   b. Click the Footer button, scroll down the drop-down list, and then click *Motion (Odd Page)*.
   c. Select the date that displays in the footer and then type **The Computer Advantage**. (If the placeholder *[Pick the date]* displays instead of the date, click in the placeholder and then type **The Computer Advantage**.)
   d. Select the text you just typed (*The Computer Advantage*) and then click the Home tab.
   e. Turn on bold and change the font size to 12.
   f. Double-click in the document text.
4. Scroll through the document to see how the header and footer will print.
5. Save, print, and then close **C07Ex02.docx**.

Finding and Replacing Text and Formatting

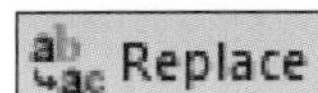

With Word's Find feature you can search in a document for specific characters or types of formatting. With the Find and Replace feature, you can search for specific characters or types of formatting and replace them with other characters or formatting. The Find button and the Replace button are located in the Editing group in the Home tab.

Finding Text

Find Text
1. Click Home tab.
2. Click Find button.
3. Type find text.
4. Click Find Next button.

With the Find feature, you can search a document for specific text. To use this feature, click the Find button in the Editing group in the Home tab or use the keyboard shortcut Ctrl + F. This displays the Find and Replace dialog box with the Find tab selected, as shown in Figure 7.3. Type the text you want to find in the *Find what* text box. Click the Find Next button, and Word searches for and selects the first occurrence of the text in the document. Make corrections to the text if needed and then search for the next occurrence by clicking the Find Next button again. Click the Cancel button to close the Find and Replace dialog box. If the Find and Replace dialog box is in the way of specific text, drag the dialog box to a different location.

Figure 7.3 Find and Replace Dialog Box with Find Tab Selected

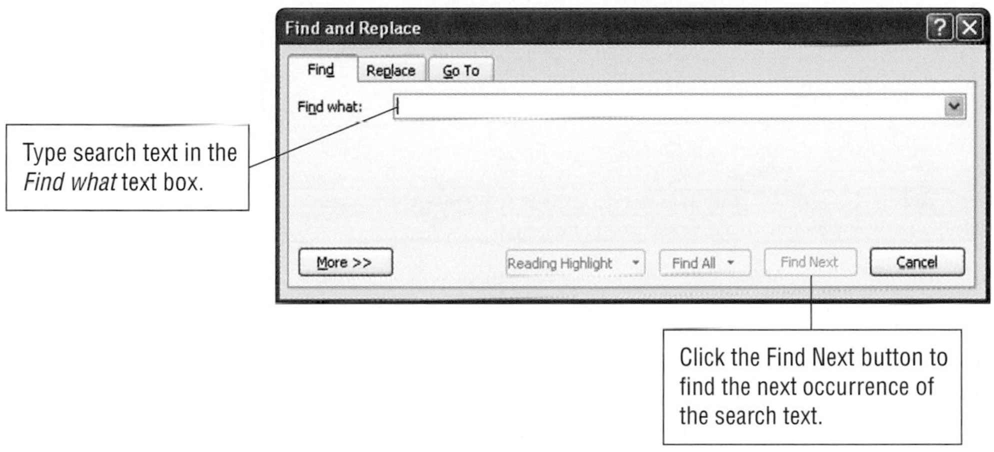

Highlighting Find Text

You can use the Find feature to highlight specific text in a document. Highlighting can help you easily scan a document for every occurrence of the specific text. To find and highlight text, click the Find button, type the text you want highlighted in the *Find what* text box, click the Reading Highlight button, and then click *Highlight All* at the drop-down list. All occurrences of the text in the document are highlighted. To remove highlighting, click the Reading Highlight button and then click *Clear Highlighting* at the drop-down list.

Exercise 3A

Finding Text and Finding and Highlighting Text

1. Open **Lease01.docx** and save the document with the name **C07Ex03**.
2. Find all occurrences of *lease* by completing the following steps:
   a. Click the Find button in the Editing group in the Home tab.
   b. At the Find and Replace dialog box with the Find tab selected, type **lease** in the *Find what* text box.
   c. Click the Find Next button.

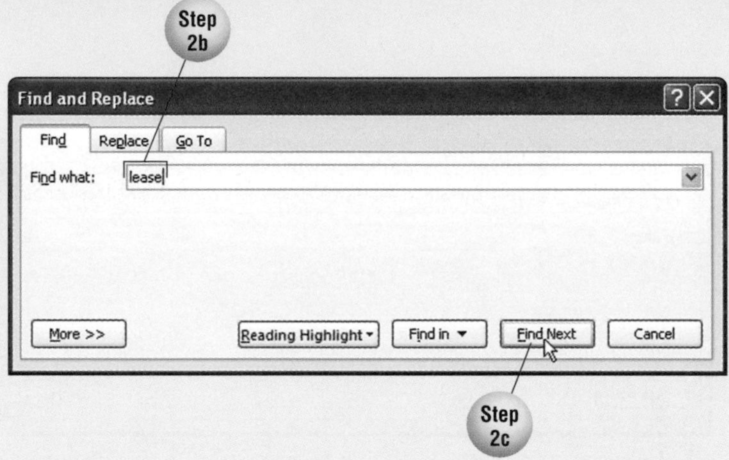

   d. Continue clicking the Find Next button until a message displays telling you that Word has finished searching the document. At this message, click OK.
3. Highlight all occurrences of *Premises* in the document by completing the following steps:
   a. At the Find and Replace dialog box with the Find tab selected, select the text in the *Find what* text box and then type **Premises**.
   b. Click the Reading Highlight button and then click *Highlight All* at the drop-down list.
   c. Click in the document to make it active and then scroll through the document and notice the occurrences of highlighted text.
   d. Click in the dialog box to make it active.
   e. Click the Reading Highlight button and then click *Clear Highlighting* at the drop-down list.
4. Click the Close button to close the Find and Replace dialog box.

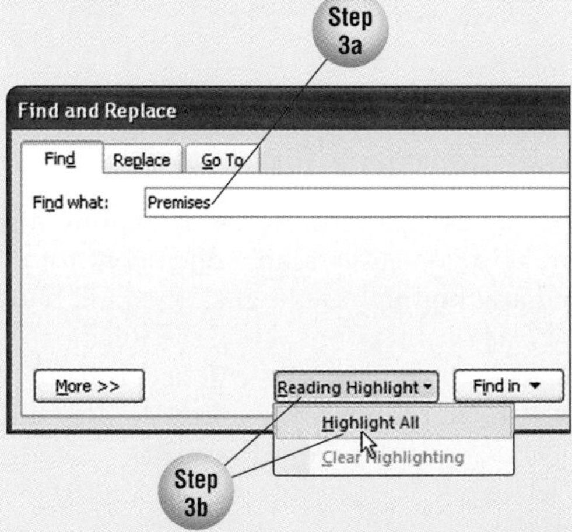

Finding and Replacing Text

To find and replace text, click the Replace button in the Editing group in the Home tab or use the keyboard shortcut Ctrl + H. Either action displays the Find and Replace dialog box with the Replace tab selected, as shown in Figure 7.4. Type the text you want to find in the *Find what* text box, press the Tab key, and then type the replacement text.

Find and Replace Text
1. Click Home tab.
2. Click Replace button.
3. Type find text.
4. Press Tab key.
5. Type replace text.
6. Click Replace or Replace All button.

Figure 7.4 Find and Replace Dialog Box with the Replace Tab Selected

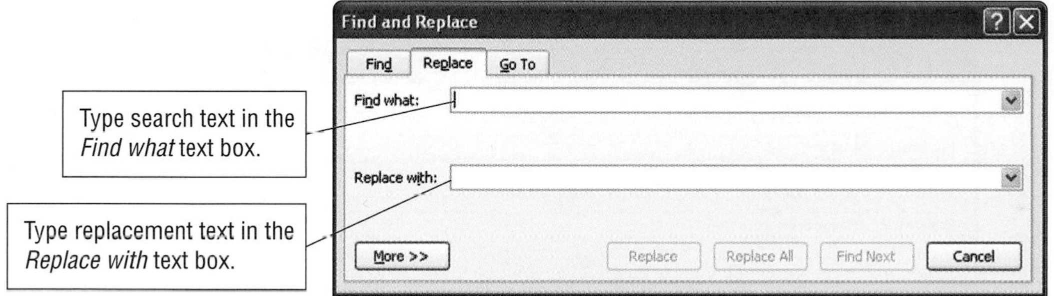

Type search text in the *Find what* text box.

Type replacement text in the *Replace with* text box.

The Find and Replace dialog box contains several command buttons. Click the Find Next button to tell Word to find the next occurrence of the characters. Click the Replace button to replace the characters and find the next occurrence. If you know that you want all occurrences of the characters in the *Find what* text box replaced with the characters in the *Replace with* text box, click the Replace All button. This replaces every occurrence from the location of the insertion point to the beginning or end of the document (depending on the search direction). Click the Cancel button to close the Find and Replace dialog box. If you make a mistake when replacing text, close the Find and Replace dialog box and then click the Undo button on the Quick Access toolbar.

Exercise 3B

Finding and Replacing Text

1. With **C07Ex03.docx** open, make sure the insertion point is positioned at the beginning of the document.
2. Find all occurrences of *Lessor* and replace with *Maggie Branson* by completing the following steps:
   a. Click the Replace button in the Editing group in the Home tab.
   b. At the Find and Replace dialog box with the Replace tab selected, type **Lessor** in the *Find what* text box.
   c. Press the Tab key to move the insertion point to the *Replace with* text box.
   d. Type **Maggie Branson**.
   e. Click the Replace All button.

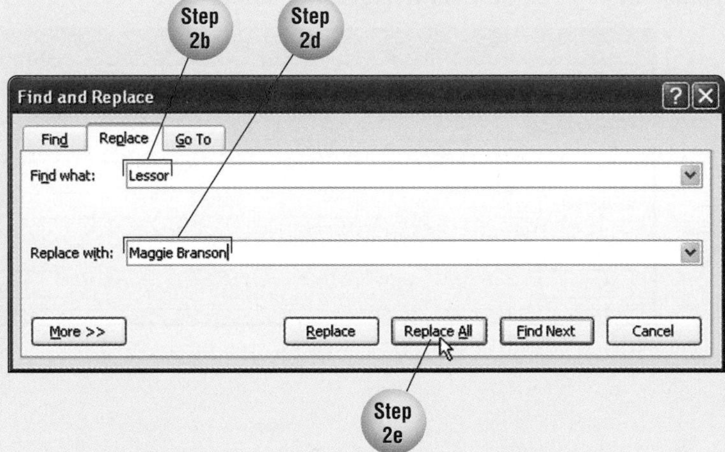

   f. At the message *Word has completed its search of the document and has made 13 replacements*, click OK. (Do not close the Find and Replace dialog box.)
3. With the Find and Replace dialog box still open, complete the steps outlined in Step 2 to find all occurrences of *Lessee* and replace with *Lee Gardella*.
4. Close the Find and Replace dialog box.
5. Save **C07Ex03.docx**.

Choosing Check Box Options

The Find and Replace dialog box contains a variety of search option check boxes that you can choose to complete a search. To display these options, click the More button located at the bottom of the dialog box. Clicking the More button expands the Find and Replace dialog box, as shown in Figure 7.5. Table 7.1 describes each option in the expanded dialog box and what the result of clicking that option will be. To remove the display of options, click the Less button. (The Less button was previously the More button.)

Figure 7.5 Expanded Find and Replace Dialog Box

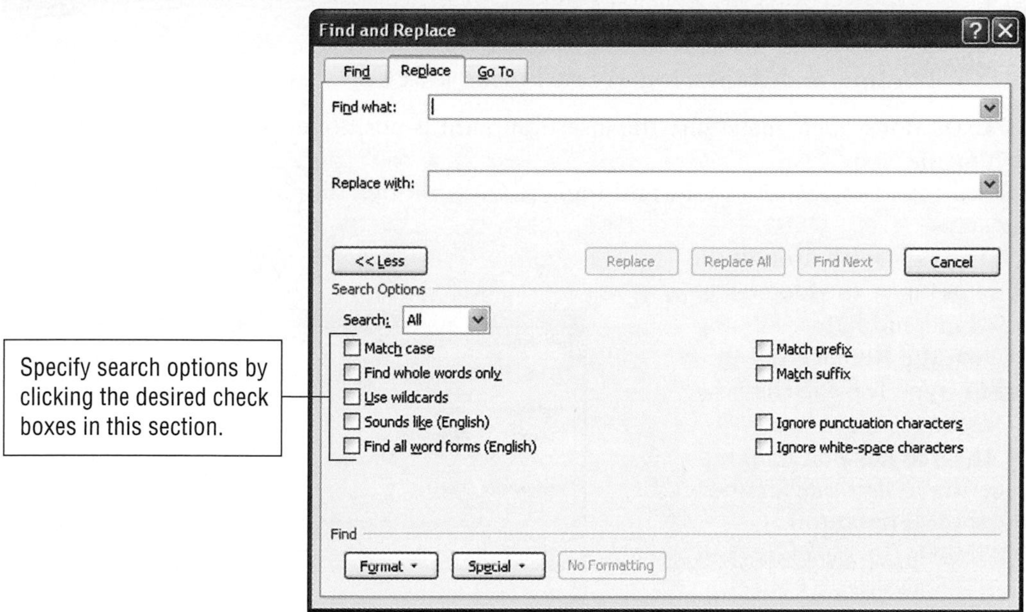

Table 7.1 **Options Available at the Expanded Find and Replace Dialog Box**

Choose this option	***To***
Match case	Exactly match the case of the search text. For example, if you search for *Book* and select the *Match case* option, Word will stop at *Book* but not *book* or *BOOK*.
Find whole words only	Find a whole word, not a part of a word. For example, if you search for *her* and do not select *Find whole words only*, Word will stop at *there*, *here*, *hers*, etc.
Use wildcards	Search for wildcards, special characters, or special search operators.
Sounds like	Match words that sound alike but are spelled differently such as *know* and *no*.
Find all word forms	Find all forms of the word entered in the *Find what* text box. For example, if you enter *hold*, Word will stop at *held* and *holding*.
Match prefix	Find only those words that begin with the letters in the *Find what* text box. For example, if you enter *per*, Word will stop at words such as *perform* and *perfect* but skip words such as *super* and *hyperlink*.
Match suffix	Find only those words that end with the letters in the *Find what* text box. For example, if you enter *ly*, Word will stop at words such as *accurately* and *quietly* but skip over words such *catalyst* and *lyre*.
Ignore punctuation characters	Ignore punctuation within characters. For example, if you enter *US* in the *Find what* text box, Word will stop at *U.S.*
Ignore white-space characters	Ignore spaces between letters. For example, if you enter *F B I* in the *Find what* text box, Word will stop at FBI.

Exercise 3C

Finding and Replacing Word Forms and Suffixes

1. With **C07Ex03.docx** open, make sure the insertion point is positioned at the beginning of the document.
2. Find all word forms of the word *lease* and replace with *rent* by completing the following steps:
   a. Click the Replace button in the Editing group in the Home tab.
   b. At the Find and Replace dialog box with the Replace tab selected, type **lease** in the *Find what* text box.
   c. Press the Tab key and then type **rent** in the *Replace with* text box.
   d. Click the More button.
   e. Click the *Find all word forms* option. (This inserts a check mark in the check box.)
   f. Click the Replace All button.
   g. At the message telling you that Replace All is not recommended with Find All Word Forms, click OK.

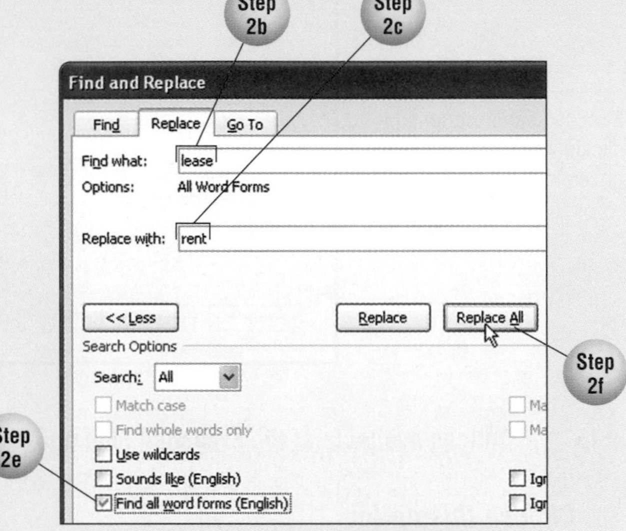

   h. At the message *Word has completed its search of the document and has made 5 replacements*, click OK.
   i. Click the *Find all word forms* option to remove the check mark.
3. Find the word *less* and replace with the word *minus* and specify that you want Word to find only those words that end in *less* by completing the following steps:
   a. At the expanded Find and Replace dialog box, select the text in the *Find what* text box and then type **less**.
   b. Select the text in the *Replace with* text box and then type **minus**.
   c. Click the *Match suffix* check box to insert a check mark and tell Word to find only words that end in *less*.
   d. Click the Replace All button.

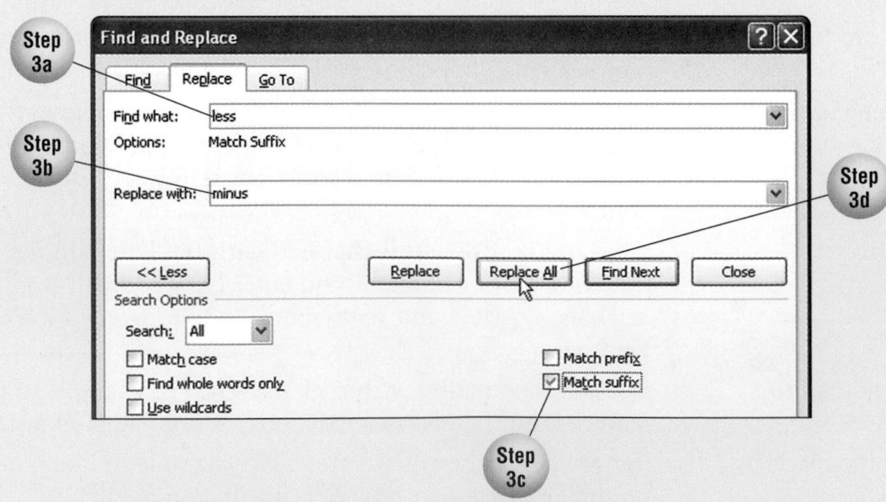

e. At the message telling you that two replacements were made, click OK.
f. Click the *Match suffix* check box to remove the check mark.
g. Click the Less button.
h. Close the Find and Replace dialog box.

4. Save **C07Ex03.docx**.

Finding and Replacing Formatting

At the Find and Replace dialog box with the Replace tab selected, you can select options to search for characters with specific formatting and replace them with other characters or formatting. To specify formatting in the Find and Replace dialog box, click the More button and then click the Format button that displays toward the bottom of the dialog box. At the pop-up list that displays, identify the type of formatting you want to find.

Exercise 3D

Finding and Replacing Fonts

1. With **C07Ex03.docx** open, make sure the insertion point is positioned at the beginning of the document.
2. Find text set in 11-point Calibri bold dark orange and replace it with text set in 12-point Cambria bold dark blue by completing the following steps:
   a. Click the Replace button in the Editing group.
   b. At the Find and Replace dialog box, press the Delete key. (This deletes any text that displays in the *Find what* text box.)
   c. Click the More button. (If a check mark displays in any of the check boxes, click the option to remove the check mark.)
   d. With the insertion point positioned in the *Find what* text box, click the Format button located toward the bottom of the dialog box and then click Font at the pop-up list.

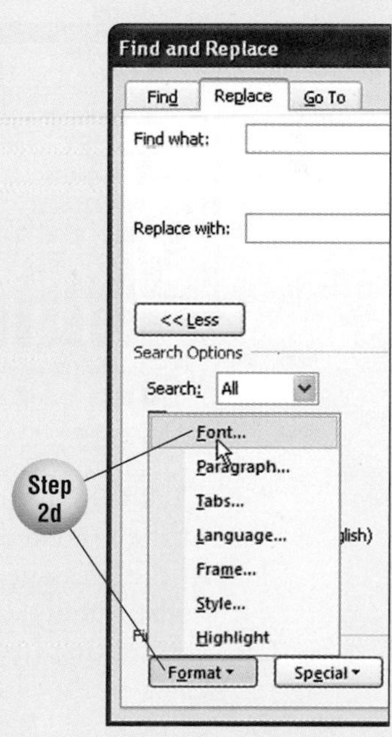

e. At the Find Font dialog box, click *Calibri* in the Font list box, *Bold* in the Font style list box, *11* in the Size list box, and change the Font color to dark orange (*Orange, Accent 6, Darker 50%*).

f. Click OK to close the Find Font dialog box.

g. At the Find and Replace dialog box, click inside the *Replace with* text box. (Make sure the text box does not contain any text.)

h. Click the Format button located toward the bottom of the dialog box and then click Font at the pop-up list.

i. At the Replace Font dialog box, click *Cambria* in the Font list box, *Bold* in the Font style list box, *12* in the Size list box, and change the font color to *Dark Blue* (second color option from the right in the Standard Colors section).

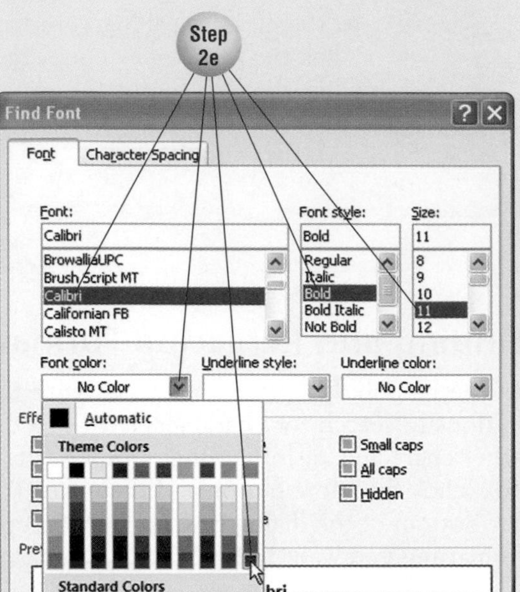

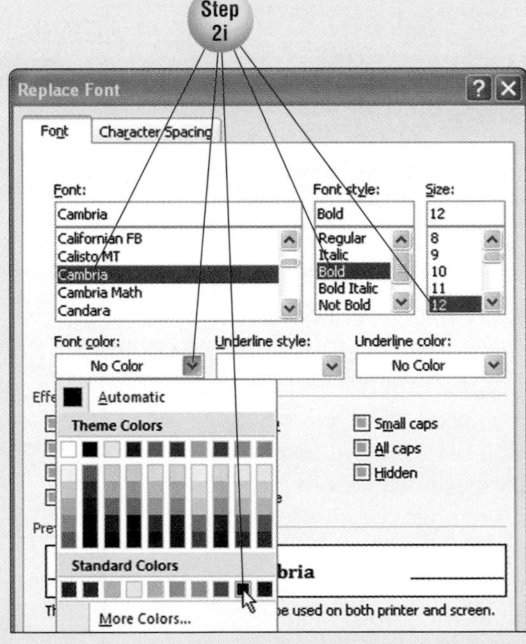

j. Click OK to close the Replace Font dialog box.

k. At the Find and Replace dialog box, click the Replace All button.

l. At the message telling you that the search of the document is complete and 13 replacements were made, click OK.

3. Clear formatting from the Find and Replace dialog box by completing the following steps:
   a. Click in the *Find what* text box and then click the No Formatting button.
   b. Click in the *Replace with* text box and then click the No Formatting button.
   c. Close the Find and Replace dialog box.
4. Save, print, and then close **C07Ex03.docx**.

Using the Click and Type Feature

Use Click and Type
1. Hover mouse at left margin, between left and right margin, or at right margin.
2. Double-click left mouse button.

Word contains a Click and Type feature that you can use to position the insertion point at a specific location and alignment in the document. To use Click and Type, make sure the document displays in Print Layout view and then hover the mouse pointer at the location where you want the insertion point positioned. As you move the mouse pointer, you will notice that the pointer displays with varying horizontal lines representing the alignment. Double-click the mouse button and the insertion point is positioned at the location of the mouse pointer.

If the horizontal lines do not display next to the mouse pointer when you double-click the mouse button, a left tab is set at the position of the insertion point. If you want to change the alignment and not set a tab, make sure the horizontal lines display near the mouse pointer before double-clicking the mouse. You can turn off the Click and Type feature by clicking the Office button and then clicking Word Options. Click the *Advanced* option in the left panel, click the *Enable click and type* check box to remove the check mark, and then click OK.

Exercise 4A

Using Click and Type

1. At a blank document, create the centered text shown in Figure 7.6 by completing the following steps:
   a. Position the I-beam pointer between the left and right margins at about the 3.25-inch mark on the horizontal ruler and the top of the vertical ruler.
   b. When the center alignment lines display below the I-beam pointer, double-click the left mouse button.
   c. Type the centered text shown in Figure 7.6. Press Shift + Enter to end each text line.

2. Change to right alignment by completing the following steps:
   a. Position the I-beam pointer near the right margin at approximately the 1.5-inch mark on the vertical ruler until the right alignment lines display at the left side of the I-beam pointer.
   b. Double-click the left mouse button.
   c. Type the right-aligned text shown in Figure 7.6. Press Shift + Enter to end the text line.
3. Select the centered text and then change the font to 14-point Constantia bold and the line spacing to double.
4. Select the right aligned text, change the font to 10-point Constantia bold, and then deselect the text.
5. Save the document and name it **C07Ex04**.

Figure 7.6 **Exercise 4**

MICROSOFT WORD TRAINING
Formatting Company Documents
Thursday, January 28, 2010
Technology Department Training Center
8:30 a.m. to 11:30 p.m.

Sponsored by
Culver Training Services

Vertically Align Text
1. Click Page Layout tab.
2. Click Page Setup group dialog box launcher.
3. Click Layout tab.
4. Click desired alignment.
5. Click OK.

Vertically Aligning Text

Text in a Word document is aligned at the top of the page by default. You can change this alignment with the *Vertical alignment* option at the Page Setup dialog box with the Layout tab selected, as shown in Figure 7.7. Display this dialog box by clicking the Page Layout tab, clicking the Page Setup group dialog box launcher, and then clicking the Layout tab at the Page Setup dialog box.

Figure 7.7 **Page Setup Dialog Box with Layout Tab Selected**

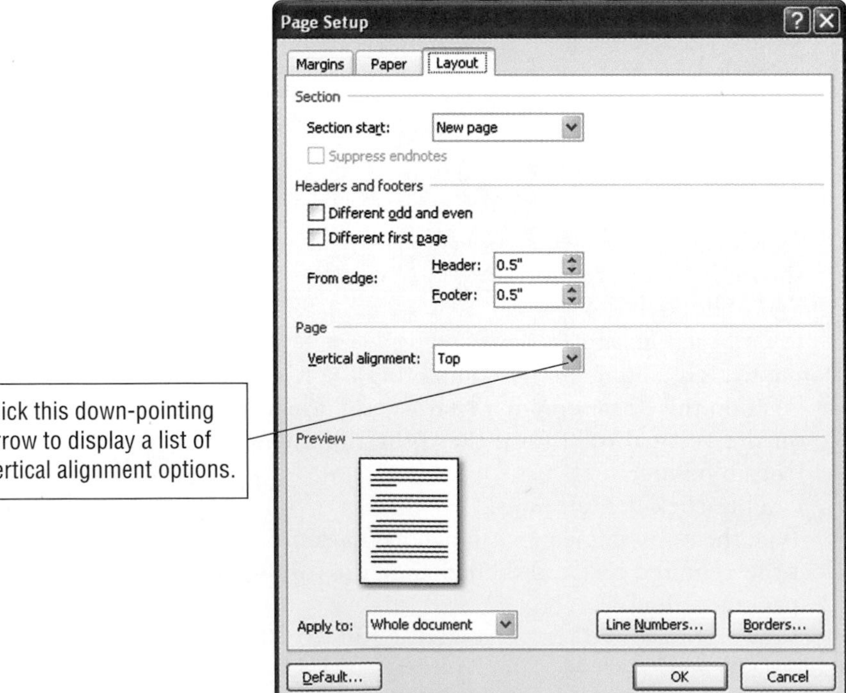

The *Vertical alignment* option in the Page Setup dialog box contains four choices: *Top*, *Center*, *Justified*, and *Bottom*. The default setting is *Top*, which aligns text at the top of the page. Choose *Center* if you want text centered vertically on the page. The *Justified* option aligns text between the top and the bottom margins. The *Center* option positions text in the middle of the page vertically, while the *Justified* option adds space between paragraphs of text (not within) to fill the page from the top to bottom margins. If you center or justify text, it does not display as centered or justified on the screen in the Draft view, but it does display centered or justified in the Print Layout view. Choose the *Bottom* option to align text in the document vertically along the bottom of the page.

Exercise 4B

Vertically Centering Text

1. With **C07Ex04.docx** open, click the Page Layout tab and then click the Page Setup group dialog box launcher.
2. At the Page Setup dialog box, click the Layout tab.
3. Click the down-pointing arrow at the right side of the *Vertical alignment* option box and then click *Center* at the drop-down list.
4. Click OK to close the dialog box.
5. Save, print, and then close **C07Ex04.docx**.

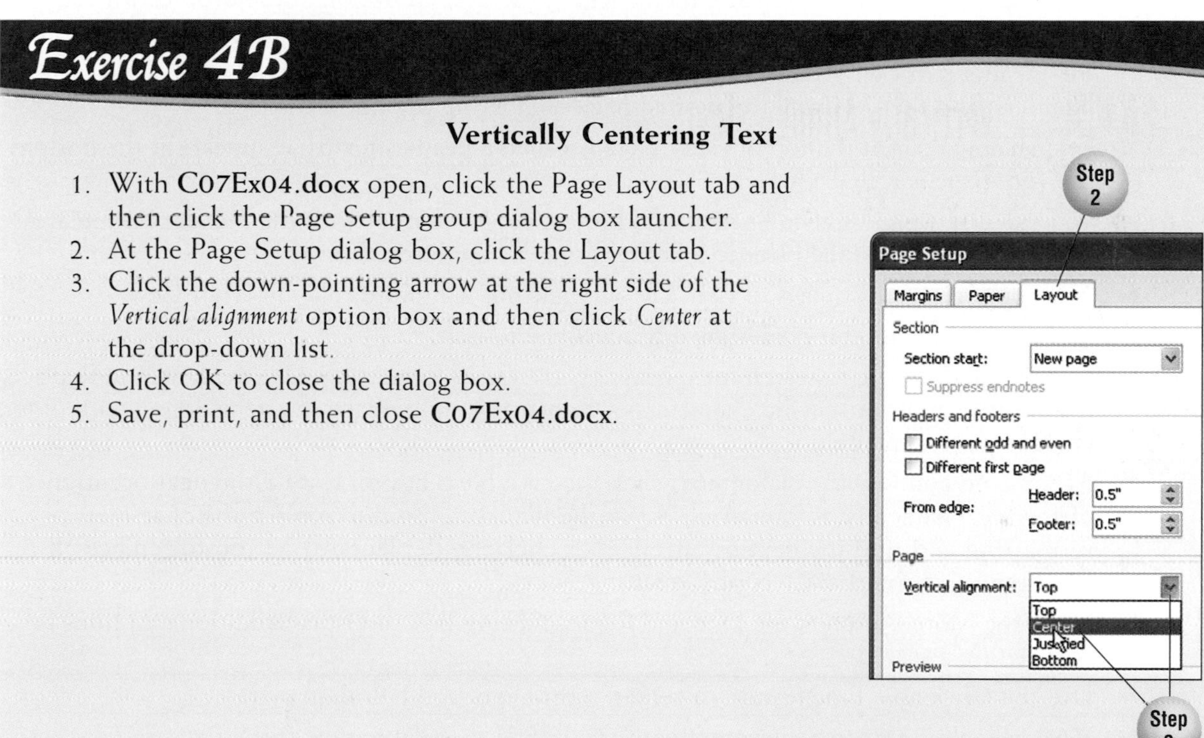

Chapter Summary

- The page break that Word inserts automatically is a soft page break. A page break that you insert is a hard page break. Insert a hard page break with the Page Break button in the Pages group in the Insert tab or by pressing Ctrl + Enter.
- Insert a blank page in a document by clicking the Blank Page button in the Pages group in the Insert tab.
- Insert a predesigned and formatted cover page by clicking the Cover Page button in the Pages group in the Insert tab and then clicking the desired option at the drop-down list.
- Insert predesigned and formatted page numbering by clicking the Page Number button in the Header & Footer group in the Insert tab, specifying the desired location of the page numbers, and then clicking the desired page numbering option.
- Text that appears at the top of every page is called a header; text that appears at the bottom of every page is called a footer.
- You can insert predesigned headers and footers in a document with the Header button and the Footer button in the Header & Footer group in the Insert tab.
- A header or footer displays in Print Layout view but will not display in Draft view.
- You can remove or edit predesigned headers and footers.
- Use the Find feature to search for specific characters or formatting. Use the Find and Replace feature to search for specific characters or formatting and replace the items found with other characters or formatting.
- At the Find and Replace dialog box, click the Find Next button to find the next occurrence of specific characters or formatting. Click the Replace button to replace the characters or formatting and find the next occurrence; or click the Replace All button to replace all occurrences of the characters or formatting.
- Click the More button at the Find and Replace dialog box to display additional options for completing a search.
- Use the Click and Type feature to center, right-align, and left-align text.
- Vertically align text in a document with the *Vertical alignment* option at the Page Setup dialog box with the Layout tab selected.

Commands review

FEATURE	RIBBON TAB, GROUP	BUTTON	KEYBOARD SHORTCUT
Blank page	Insert, Pages	Blank Page	
Cover page	Insert, Pages	Cover Page	
Find and Replace dialog box with Find tab selected	Home, Editing	Find	Ctrl + F
Find and Replace dialog box with Replace tab selected	Home, Editing	Replace	Ctrl + H
Footer	Insert, Header & Footer		
Header	Insert, Header & Footer		
Page numbering	Insert, Header & Footer		
Page Setup dialog box	Page Layout, Page Setup		

Reviewing key points

Completion: In the space provided at the right, indicate the correct term, symbol, or command.

1. Press these keys on the keyboard to insert a page break. ____________
2. The Cover Page button is located in the Pages group in this tab. ____________
3. A predesigned cover page generally contains these, which are locations where you can enter specific information. ____________
4. The Page Number button is located in this group in the Insert tab. ____________
5. Text that appears at the top of every page is called this. ____________
6. A footer displays in Print Layout view, but not this view. ____________
7. The Find button is located in this group in the Home tab. ____________
8. This is the keyboard shortcut to display the Find and Replace dialog box with the Replace tab selected. ____________
9. If you want to replace every occurrence of what you are searching for in a document, click this button at the Find and Replace dialog box. ____________
10. Click this option at the Find and Replace dialog box if you are searching for a word and all of its forms. ____________
11. Use this feature to position the insertion point at a specific location and alignment in a document. ____________
12. Vertically align text with the *Vertical alignment* option at the Page Setup dialog box with this tab selected. ____________

Applying your skills

Assessment 1 Format and Insert a Cover Page in a Document

1. Open **Document04.docx** and save the document with the name **C07A01**.
2. Select text from the beginning of the title *REFERENCES* (located on the second page) to the end of the document and then delete the selected text.
3. Apply the Heading 1 style to the title of the document and apply the Heading 2 style to the headings in the document.
4. Change the style set to *Modern*.
5. Change the theme colors to *Concourse*.
6. Insert a page break at the beginning of the heading *NEWS SERVICES*.
7. Move the insertion point to the beginning of the document and then insert the *Mod* cover page.
8. Insert the following text in the specified placeholders:
   a. Type *Computers in Industry* in the *[Type the document title]* placeholder.
   b. Delete the *[Type the document subtitle]* placeholder. (*Hint: To delete a placeholder, click in the placeholder text, click the placeholder tab, and then press the Delete key.*)
   c. Delete the *[Abstract]* placeholder.
   d. Type your first and last names in the *[Type the author name]* placeholder.
   e. Insert the date in the *[Pick the date]* placeholder.
9. Move the insertion point to any character in the title *COMPUTERS IN INDUSTRY* in the main document (not in the cover page) and then insert the *Outline Circle 3* page numbering at the bottom of the pages (the page numbering will not appear on the cover page).
10. Save, print, and then close **C07A01.docx**.

Assessment 2 Format and Insert a Header and Footer in a Report

1. Open **Report04.docx** and save the document with the name **C07A02**.
2. Apply the Heading 1 style to the two titles in the document and apply the Heading 2 style to the five headings in the document.
3. Change the style set to *Fancy*.
4. Select the entire document and then remove the italic formatting.
5. Apply the *Apex* theme.
6. Insert a page break at the beginning of the title *SECTION 4: HARDWARE AND SOFTWARE SECURITY RISKS*.
7. Move the insertion point to the beginning of the document and then insert the *Pinstripes* header. Type **Computer Security** in the *[Type the document title]* placeholder.
8. Insert the *Pinstripes* footer and type your first and last names in the *[Type text]* placeholder.
9. Change the theme colors to *Oriel*.
10. Save and then print **C07A02.docx**.
11. Remove the header and footer.
12. Insert the *Austere (Odd Page)* footer and then make the following changes:
    a. Select and then delete the *[Type the company name]* placeholder.
    b. Select the text and page number in the footer and then change the font to 10-point Constantia bold.
13. Insert the DRAFT 1 watermark in the document.
14. Insert a page border of your choosing to the document.
15. Save, print, and then close **C07A02.docx**.

Assessment 3 Find and Replace Text in a Real Estate Agreement

1. Open **Agreement02.docx** and save the document with the name **C07A03**.
2. Find all occurrences of BUYER (matching the case) and replace with Craig Metzner. (If the *Find what* and/or *Replace with* options contain any formatting, delete the formatting.)
3. Find all occurrences of SELLER (matching the case) and replace with Carol Winters.
4. Find all word forms of the word *buy* and replace with *purchase*.
5. Search for 14-point Tahoma bold formatting in dark red and replace with 12-point Constantia bold formatting in black.
6. Clear the formatting from the Find and Replace dialog box.
7. Insert page numbers at the bottom of each page.
8. Save, print, and then close **C07A03.docx**.

Assessment 4 Create a Notice Using Click and Type

1. At a blank document, use the Click and Type feature to create the document shown in Figure 7.8.
2. Select the centered text and then change the font to 16-point Candara bold in dark blue.
3. Select the right-aligned text and then change the font to 12-point Candara bold in dark blue.
4. Change the vertical alignment of the text to *Center*.
5. Save the document and name it **C07A04**.
6. Print and then close **C07A04.docx**.

Figure 7.8 **Assessment 4**

Securing Company Data

Systems for Backing up Crucial Data

Tuesday, February 9, 2010

Corporate Training Center

1:30 to 4:00 p.m.

Sponsored by
Madison Security Systems

Chapter 8

CHAPTER08

Inserting Elements and Navigating in a Document

SNAP

Tutorial 8.1
Inserting Elements into a Document
Tutorial 8.2
Navigating in a Document and Creating Hyperlinks

Performance Objectives

Upon successful completion of Chapter 8, you will be able to:

- Insert symbols and special characters
- Insert a drop cap
- Insert the date and time
- Insert a file into an open document
- Navigate in a document using Document Map, Thumbnails, bookmarks, hyperlinks, and cross-references
- Insert hyperlinks to a location in the same document, a different document, and a file in another program

You can insert a variety of elements into a Word document to serve a variety of purposes. In this chapter, you will learn to insert symbols, special characters, and drop caps to add visual appeal. You will learn to insert the date and/or time in a number of formats to identify when a document was created and automatically update the information to reflect when a document was revised. You will learn how to insert one file into another to efficiently combine the content of two documents, and you will learn how to insert hyperlinks, bookmarks, and cross-references to provide additional information for readers and to allow for more efficient navigation within a document.

Note: Before beginning computer exercises for this chapter, copy to your storage medium the Chapter08 folder from the CD that accompanies this textbook and then make Chapter08 the active folder.

QUICK STEPS

Insert a Symbol
1. Click Insert tab.
2. Click Symbol button.
3. Click desired symbol in drop-down list.

OR

1. Click Insert tab.
2. Click Symbol button.
3. Click *More Symbols*.
4. Select desired font.
5. Double-click desired symbol.
6. Click Close.

Inserting Symbols and Special Characters

You can use the Symbol button in the Symbols group in the Insert tab to insert special symbols in a document. Click the button to display a drop-down list with the most recently inserted symbols and a *More Symbols* option. Click one of the symbols that displays in the list to insert it in the document or click the *More Symbols* option to display the Symbol dialog box, shown in Figure 8.1. At the Symbol dialog box, double-click the symbol you want to insert and then click Close; or, click the symbol you want to insert, click the Insert button, and then click Close.

Figure 8.1 Symbol Dialog Box with Symbols Tab Selected

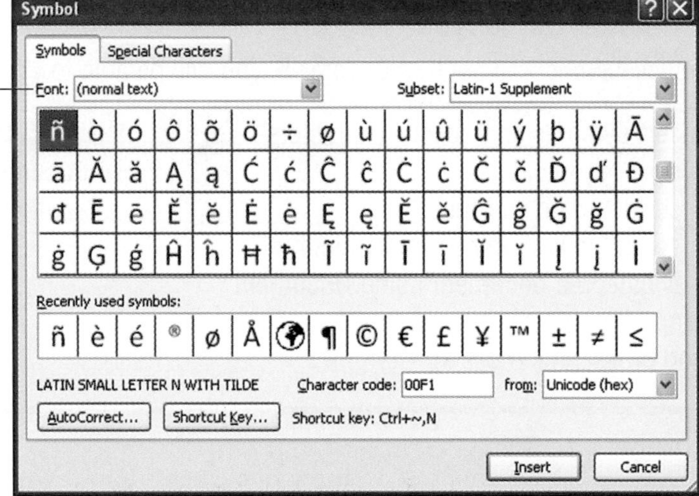

At the Symbol dialog box with the Symbols tab selected, you can change the font by using the *Font* option. When you change the font, different symbols display in the dialog box. Click the Special Characters tab, and a list of special characters displays along with the keyboard shortcuts to create them.

Exercise 1A

Inserting Symbols and Special Characters

1. Open **Document14.docx** and save the document with the name **C08Ex01**.
2. Press Ctrl + End to move the insertion point to the end of the document.
3. Press the Enter key once, type **Created by:**, and then press the spacebar once.
4. Type the first name **Rueben**.
5. Insert the last name *Cedeño* by completing the following steps:
   a. Type **Cede**.
   b. Click the Insert tab.
   c. Click the Symbol button in the Symbols group.
   d. Click *More Symbols* at the drop-down list.

e. At the Symbol dialog box, make sure the *Font* option displays as *(normal text)* and then double-click the ñ symbol (first symbol from the left in the twelfth row).
f. Click the Close button.
g. Type **o**.

6. Press Shift + Enter.
7. Insert the computer laptop symbol (💻) by completing the following steps:
   a. Click the Symbol button and then click *More Symbols*.
   b. At the Symbol dialog box, click the down-pointing arrow at the right side of the *Font* option and then click *Wingdings* at the drop-down list. (You will need to scroll down the list to display this option.)
   c. Double-click 💻 (eleventh symbol from the left in the second row).

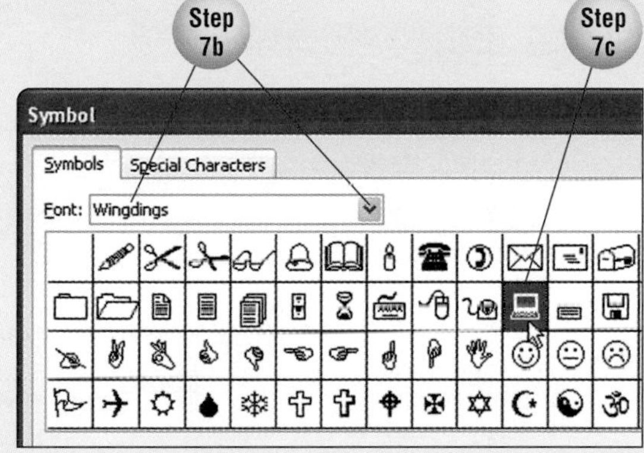

   d. Click the Close button.
8. Type **Madison Security Systems**.
9. Insert the registered trademark symbol (®) by completing the following steps:
   a. Click the Symbol button and then click *More Symbols*.
   b. At the Symbol dialog box, click the Special Characters tab.
   c. Double-click the ® symbol (tenth option from the top).

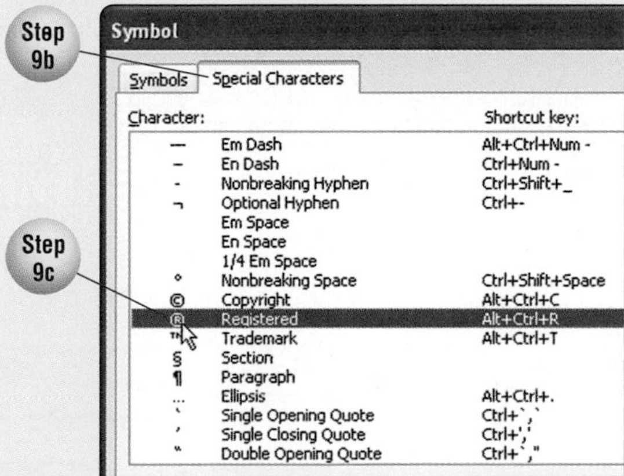

   d. Click the Close button.
   e. Press Shift + Enter.
10. Select the computer laptop symbol (💻) and then change the font size to 18.
11. Save **C08Ex01.docx**.

Create Drop Cap
1. Click Insert tab.
2. Click Drop Cap button.
3. Click desired type in drop-down list.

Creating a Drop Cap

A drop cap is a design element often used to enhance the appearance of text. A drop cap is the first letter of the first word of a paragraph enlarged and set into the paragraph to extend (drop) more than one line space. Drop caps identify the beginning of major sections or parts of a document. They generally look best when they are used in paragraphs that contain text set in a proportional font. You can create a drop cap with the Drop Cap button in the Text group in the Insert tab. You can choose to set the drop cap in the paragraph or in the margin. At the Drop Cap dialog box, you can specify the font, the number of lines you want the letter to drop, and the distance you want the letter positioned from the text of the paragraph. To drop cap the first word in a paragraph, select the word and then click the Drop Cap button.

Exercise 1B

Inserting a Drop Cap

1. With **C08Ex01.docx** open, create a drop cap by completing the following steps:
   a. Position the insertion point on the first word of the first paragraph of text (*Productivity*).
   b. Click the Insert tab.
   c. Click the Drop Cap button in the Text group.
   d. Click *In margin* at the drop-down gallery.

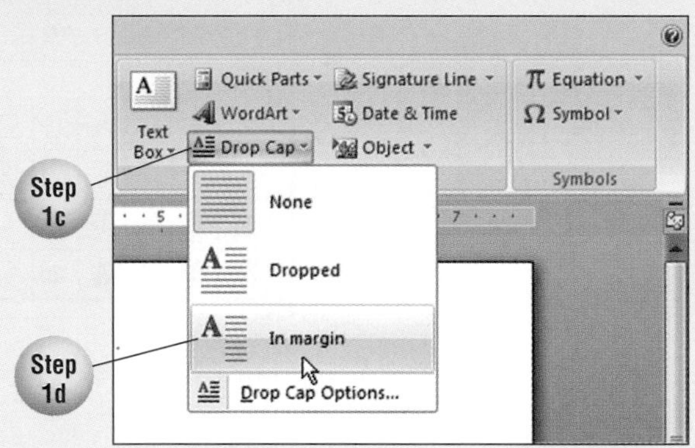

2. To see how a drop cap's size and location affect the visual appeal of the document, make the drop smaller and change its location by completing the following steps:
   a. With the *P* selected in the word *Productivity*, click the Drop Cap button in the Text group and then click *None* at the drop-down gallery.
   b. Click the Drop Cap button and then click *Drop Cap Options* at the drop-down gallery.
   c. At the Drop Cap dialog box, click *Dropped* in the *Position* section.
   d. Change the font to Times New Roman.
   e. Change the *Lines to drop* option to 2.
   f. Click OK to close the dialog box.
   g. Click outside the drop cap to deselect it.
3. Save **C08Ex01.docx**.

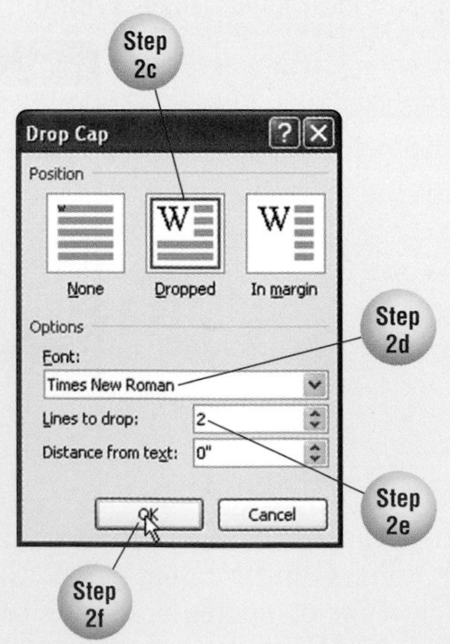

Inserting the Date and Time

Insert Date and Time
1. Click Insert tab.
2. Click Date and Time button.
3. Click option in list box.
4. Click OK.

Use the Date & Time button in the Text group in the Insert tab to insert the current date and time into a document. Click this button and the Date and Time dialog box displays, as shown in Figure 8.2 (the date that displays on your screen will vary from the one you see in the figure). At the Date and Time dialog box, click the desired date and/or time format in the *Available formats* list box.

Figure 8.2 Date and Time Dialog Box

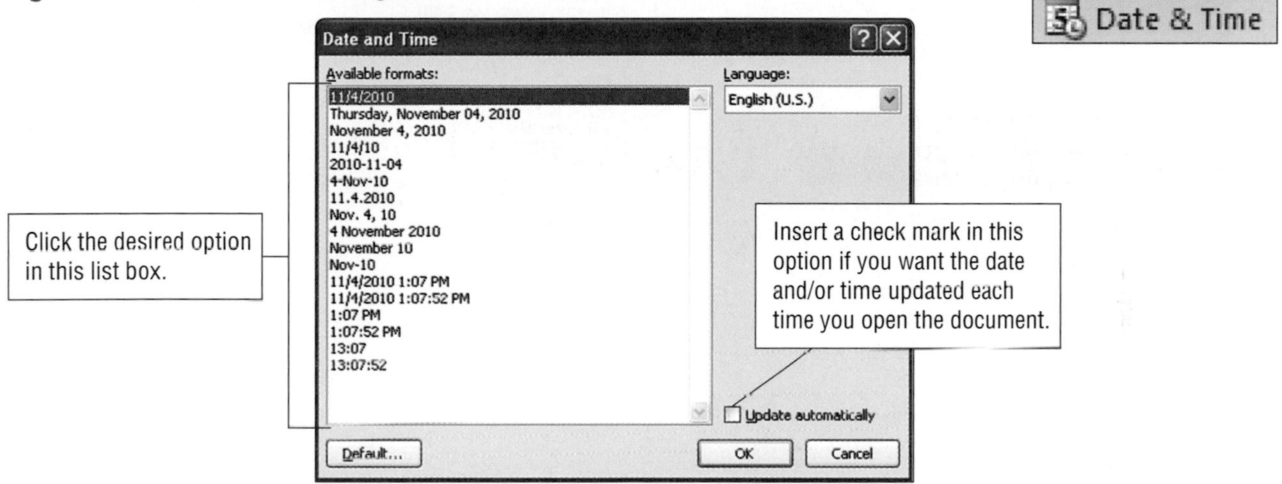

If the *Update automatically* check box at the bottom of the dialog box does not contain a check mark, the date and/or time that you click are inserted in the document as normal text that can be edited in the usual manner. You can also insert the date and/or time as a field. The advantage to inserting the date or time as a field is that you can update the field with the Update Field keyboard shortcut F9. Insert a check mark in the *Update automatically* check box to insert the date and/or time as a field. You can also insert the date as a field using the keyboard shortcut Alt + Shift + D, and insert the time as a field with the keyboard shortcut Alt + Shift + T.

Exercise 1C

Inserting the Date and Time

1. With **C08Ex01.docx** open, press Ctrl + End and make sure the insertion point is positioned below the company name.
2. Insert the current date by completing the following steps:
   a. Click the Date & Time button in the Text group in the Insert tab.
   b. At the Date and Time dialog box, click the third option from the top in the *Available formats* group.
   c. Click in the *Update automatically* check box to insert a check mark.
   d. Click OK to close the dialog box.
3. Press Shift + Enter.
4. Insert the current time by pressing Alt + Shift + T.
5. Save **C08Ex01.docx**.
6. Update the time by clicking the time and then pressing F9.
7. Save and then print **C08Ex01.docx**.

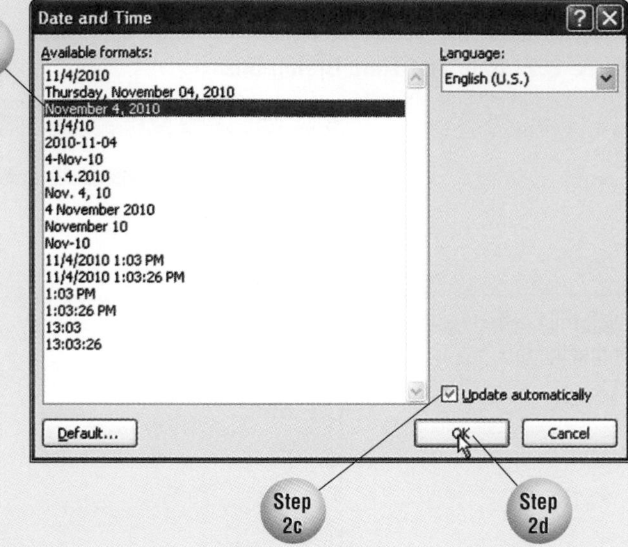

QUICK STEPS

Insert a File
1. Open document.
2. Click Insert tab.
3. Click Object button arrow.
4. Click *Text from File*.
5. Navigate to desired folder.
6. Double-click document name.

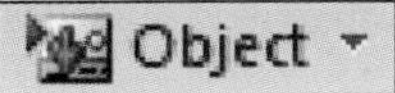

Inserting a File

If you want to insert the contents of one document into another, use the Object button in the Text group in the Insert tab. With the document into which you are inserting content open, click the Object button arrow and then click *Text from File* to display the Insert File dialog box. This dialog box is similar to the Open dialog box. Navigate to the desired folder and then double-click the document you want to insert in the open document.

Exercise 1D

Inserting a File

1. With **C08Ex01.docx** open, insert a file into the open document by completing the following steps:
   a. Move the insertion point to the blank line above the text *Created by: Rueben Cedeño.*
   b. Click the Insert tab.
   c. Click the Object button arrow in the Text group.
   d. Click *Text from File* at the drop-down list.
   e. At the Insert File dialog box, navigate to the Chapter08 folder and then double-click **Document15.docx**.

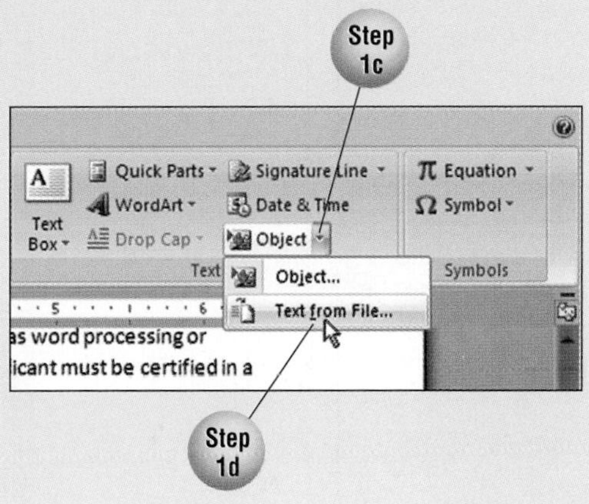

2. Make the following changes to the document:
   a. Apply the Heading 2 style to the two headings in the document.
   b. Select the four paragraphs of text in the *Personal-use Software* section that each begin with bolded text and then click the Bullets button in the Paragraph group.
   c. Change the top margin to 1.5 inch.
   d. Change the style set to *Formal.*
   e. Apply the *Aspect* theme.
   f. Insert page numbering centered at the bottom of each page.
3. Save, print, and then close **C08Ex01.docx**.

Navigating in a Document

QUICK STEPS

Navigate with Document Map
1. Click View tab.
2. Click Document Map check box.
3. Click desired heading in navigation pane.

In Chapter 1 you learned to scroll in a document and use navigation buttons to move the insertion point to specific locations. Word provides a number of other features and methods you can use to navigate in a document. Two such features are the Document Map feature and the Thumbnails feature. You can also navigate in a document by inserting bookmarks, cross-references, and hyperlinks. The Document Map and Thumbnails buttons are located in the Show/Hide group in the View tab; the Bookmark, Cross-reference, and Hyperlink buttons are located in the Links group in the Insert tab.

Navigating Using the Document Map

To navigate using the Document Map feature, click the View tab and then click the Document Map check box in the Show/Hide group. Clicking the Document Map check box displays a navigation pane at the left side of the screen, as shown in Figure 8.3. The Document Map navigation pane displays any headings formatted with styles or text that looks like a heading, such as a short line set in a larger type size. Navigate to a specific location in the document by clicking the heading in the navigation pane.

Figure 8.3 **Document Map Navigation Pane**

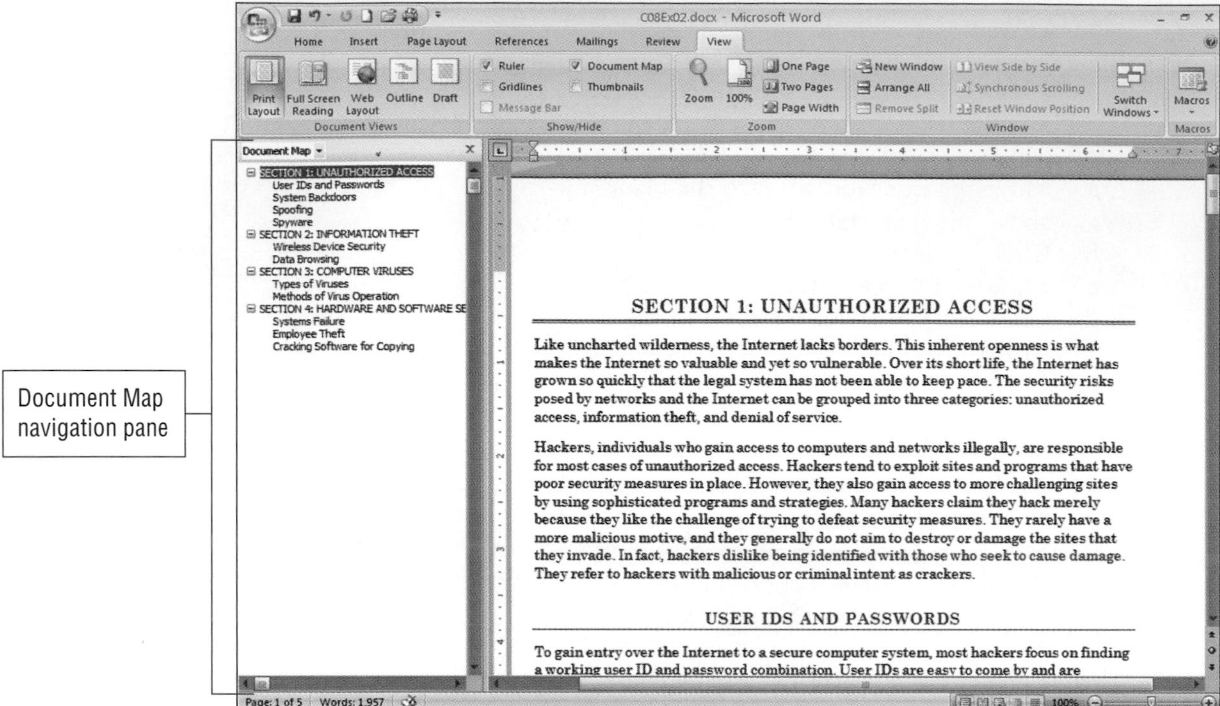

Exercise 2A

Navigating Using Document Map

1. Open **Report03.docx** and save the document with the name **C08Ex02**.
2. Press Ctrl + End and then insert a file by completing the following steps:
   a. Click the Insert tab.
   b. Click the Object button arrow in the Text group.
   c. Click *Text from File* at the drop-down list.
   d. At the Insert File dialog box, navigate to the Chapter08 folder and then double-click **Report04.docx**.
3. Make the following changes to the document:
   a. Apply the Heading 1 style to the four section titles in the document.
   b. Apply the Heading 2 style to all of the headings in the document.
   c. Change the style set to *Formal*.
   d. Apply the *Oriel* theme to the document.

4. Navigate in the document using Document Map by completing the following steps:
   a. Click the View tab.
   b. Click the Document Map check box in the Show/Hide group to insert a check mark. (This displays the navigation pane at the left side of the screen.)
   c. Click the *SECTION 2: INFORMATION THEFT* title in the navigation pane.

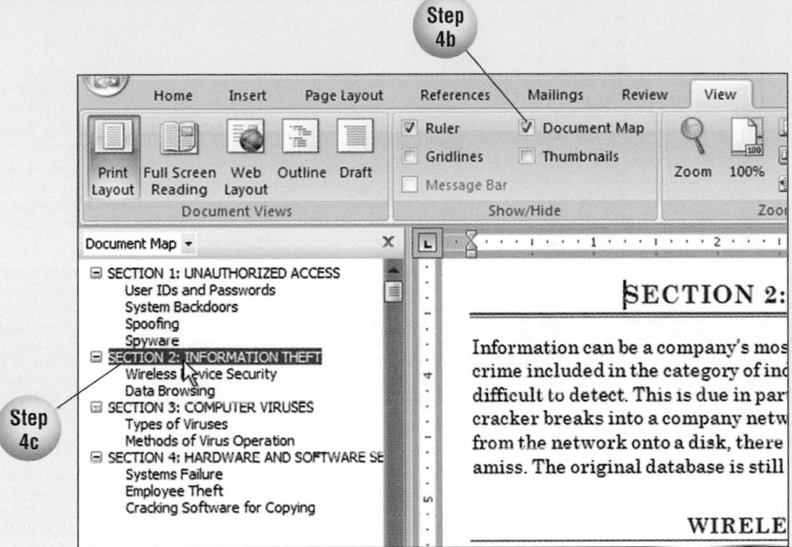

   d. Click the *SECTION 4: HARDWARE AND SOFTWARE SECURITY RISKS* title in the navigation pane.
   e. Click *Spoofing* in the navigation pane.
5. Click the Document Map check box in the Show/Hide group in the View tab to remove the check mark.
6. Save **C08Ex02.docx**.

Navigating Using Thumbnails

To navigate in a document using the Thumbnails feature, click the View tab and then click the Thumbnails check box in the Show/Hide group. Clicking the Thumbnails check box displays a thumbnail (a miniature representation) of each page in the navigation pane at the left side of the screen, as shown in Figure 8.4. You can switch between the Thumbnails and Document Map features by clicking the Switch Navigation Window button that displays at the top of the navigation pane and then clicking the desired option at the drop-down list. Close the navigation pane by clicking the Thumbnails check box to remove the check mark or by clicking the Close button located in the upper right corner of the pane.

Navigate with Thumbnails
1. Click View tab.
2. Click Thumbnails check box.
3. Click desired thumbnail in navigation pane.

Figure 8.4 Thumbnails Navigation Pane

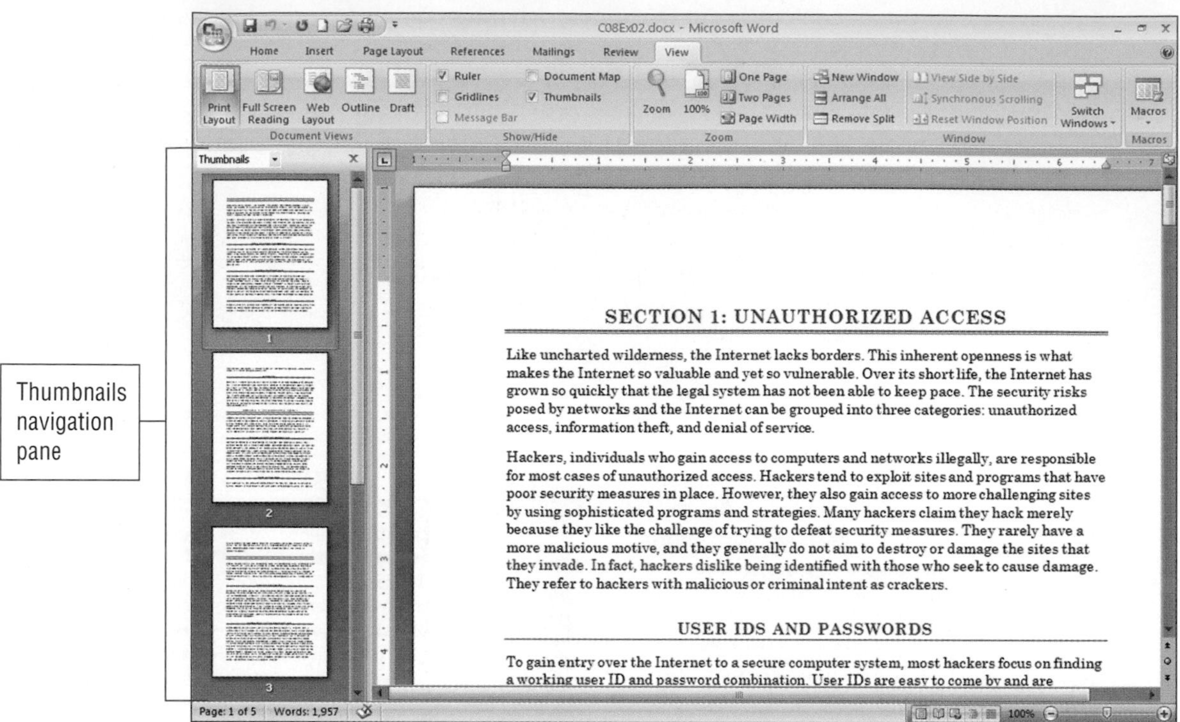

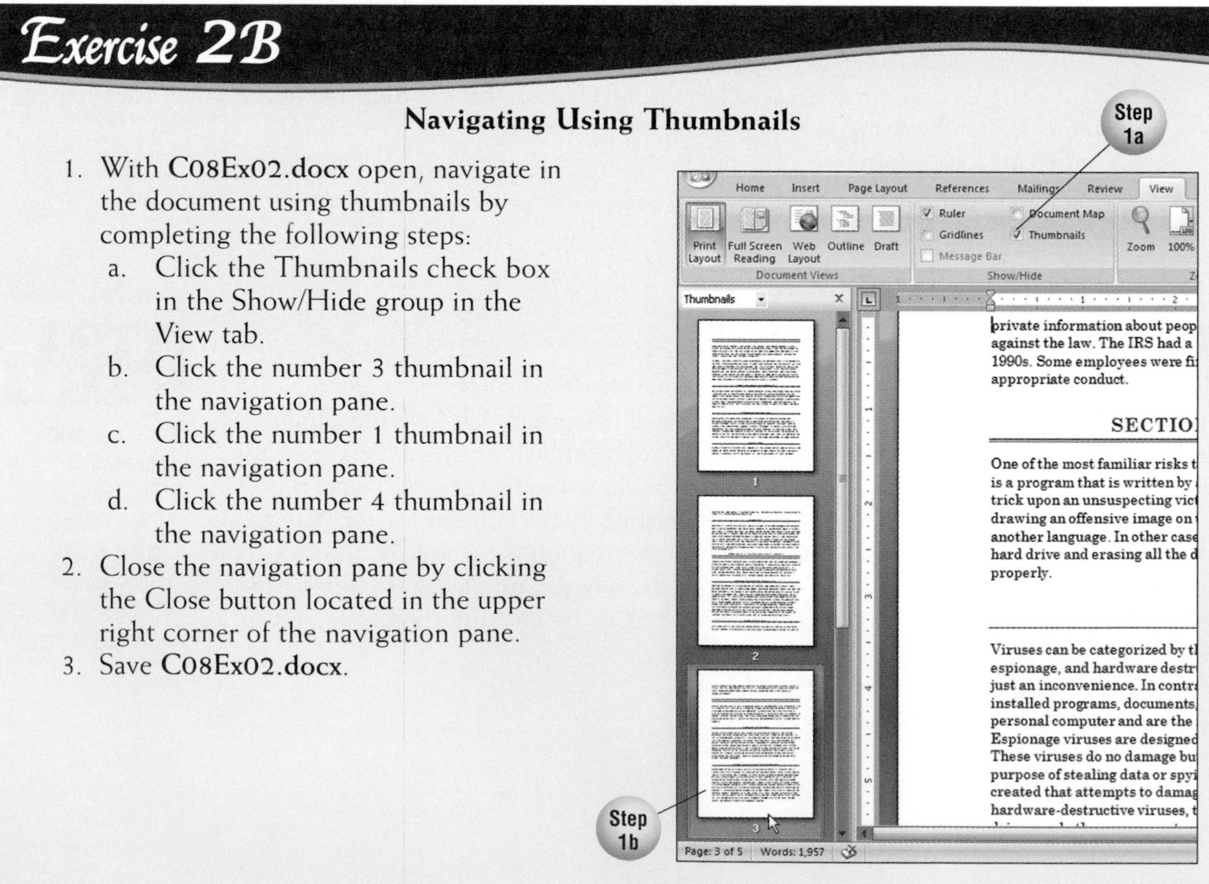

Exercise 2B

Navigating Using Thumbnails

1. With **C08Ex02.docx** open, navigate in the document using thumbnails by completing the following steps:
   a. Click the Thumbnails check box in the Show/Hide group in the View tab.
   b. Click the number 3 thumbnail in the navigation pane.
   c. Click the number 1 thumbnail in the navigation pane.
   d. Click the number 4 thumbnail in the navigation pane.
2. Close the navigation pane by clicking the Close button located in the upper right corner of the navigation pane.
3. Save **C08Ex02.docx**.

Navigating with Bookmarks

In a long document, you may find marking a specific location useful to allow you to quickly move the insertion point to that location. Use the Bookmark button to create bookmarks for locations in a document. To create a bookmark, position the insertion point at the desired location, click the Insert tab, and then click the Bookmark button in the Links group. This displays the Bookmark dialog box, shown in Figure 8.5. Type a name for the bookmark in the *Bookmark name* text box and then click the Add button. Repeat these steps as many times as needed to insert the desired bookmarks. Give each bookmark a unique and meaningful name. A bookmark name must begin with a letter; it can contain numbers but not spaces. Use the underscore character if you want to separate words in a bookmark name.

Create a Bookmark
1. Position insertion point at desired location.
2. Click Insert tab.
3. Click Bookmark button.
4. Type name for bookmark.
5. Click Add button.

Navigate with Bookmarks
1. Click Insert tab.
2. Click Bookmark button.
3. Double-click desired bookmark name.

OR
1. Click Insert tab.
2. Click Bookmark button.
3. Click bookmark name.
4. Click Go To button.

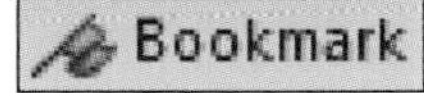

Figure 8.5 Bookmark Dialog Box

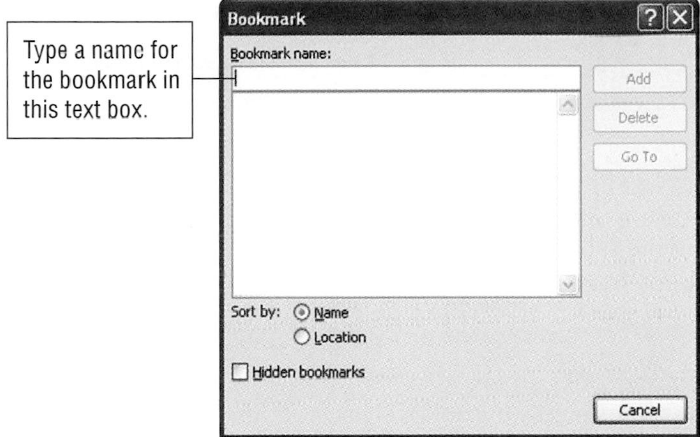

By default, bookmarks that you insert are not visible in the document. You can turn on the display of bookmarks at the Word Options dialog box with *Advanced* selected. Display this dialog box by clicking the Office button and then clicking the Word Options button. At the Word Options dialog box, click the *Advanced* option in the left panel. Click the *Show bookmarks* check box in the *Show document content* section to insert a check mark. Complete similar steps to turn off the display of bookmarks. A bookmark displays in the document as an I-beam marker.

You can also create a bookmark for selected text. To do this, select the text first and then complete the steps to create a bookmark. When you create a bookmark for selected text, a left bracket ([) indicates the beginning of the selected text and a right bracket (]) indicates the end of selected text. The bookmark brackets do not print.

Exercise 2C

Inserting Bookmarks

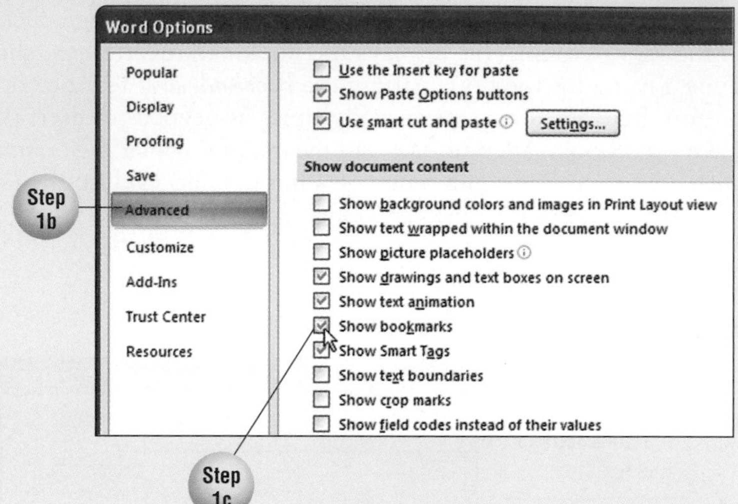

1. With **C08Ex02.docx** open, turn on the display of bookmarks by completing the following steps:
   a. Click the Office button and then click the Word Options button that displays at the bottom of the drop-down list.
   b. At the Word Options dialog box, click *Advanced* in the left panel.
   c. Click the *Show bookmarks* check box in the *Show document content* section to insert a check mark.
   d. Click OK to close the dialog box.
2. Insert a bookmark by completing the following steps:
   a. Move the insertion point to the beginning of the first paragraph in the document (below the title SECTION 1: UNAUTHORIZED ACCESS).
   b. Click the Insert tab.
   c. Click the Bookmark button in the Links group.
   d. At the Bookmark dialog box, type **Access** in the *Bookmark name* text box.
   e. Click the Add button.

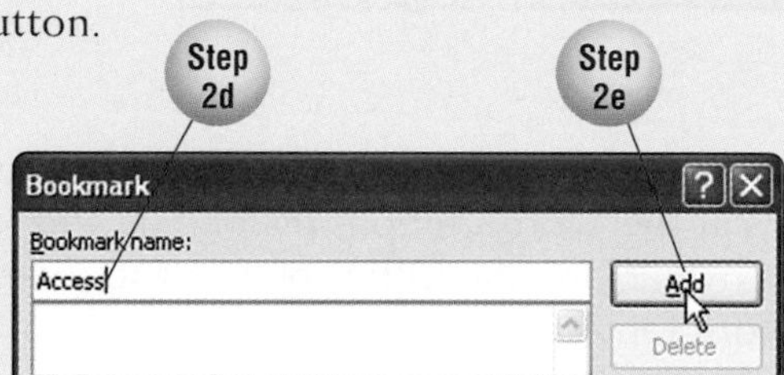

3. Insert a bookmark named *Viruses* at the beginning of the first paragraph in the TYPES OF VIRUSES section.
4. Insert a bookmark named *Electrical* at the beginning of the first paragraph in the SYSTEMS FAILURE section.
5. Save **C08Ex02.docx**.

After you have inserted bookmarks in a document, you can move the insertion point to a specific bookmark. To do this, display the Bookmark dialog box and then double-click the bookmark name. You can also click the Bookmark name and then click the Go To button. When Word stops at the location of the bookmark, click the Close button to close the dialog box. If you move the insertion point to a bookmark created with selected text, Word moves the insertion point to the bookmark and selects the text. You can delete bookmarks in the Bookmark dialog box by clicking the bookmark name in the list box and then clicking the Delete button.

Exercise 2D

Navigating Using Bookmarks and Deleting Bookmarks

1. With **C08Ex02.docx** open, navigate to the Viruses bookmark by completing the following steps:
   a. If necessary, click the Insert tab.
   b. Click the Bookmark button in the Links group.
   c. At the Bookmark dialog box, click *Viruses* in the list box.
   d. Click the Go To button.

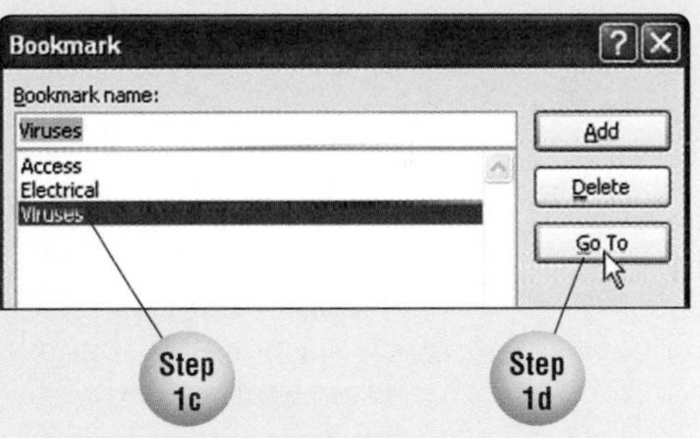

2. With the Bookmark dialog box open, navigate to the Access bookmark by double-clicking *Access* in the list box.
3. With the Bookmark dialog box open, delete the *Electrical* bookmark by clicking *Electrical* in the list box and then clicking the Delete button.
4. Click the Close button to close the Bookmark dialog box.
5. Save **C08Ex02.docx**.

Inserting Hyperlinks

A hyperlink in a document can serve a number of purposes: Click it to navigate to a specific location in the document, to display a different document, to open a file in a different program, to create a new document, or to link to an e-mail address. Insert a hyperlink by clicking the Hyperlink button located in the Links group in the Insert tab. This displays the Insert Hyperlink dialog box, shown in Figure 8.6. You can also display the Insert Hyperlink dialog box by pressing Ctrl + K. At this dialog box, identify what you want to link to and the location of the link. Click the ScreenTip button to customize the hyperlink ScreenTip.

Insert Hyperlink
1. Click Insert tab.
2. Click Hyperlink button.
3. Make desired changes at the Insert Hyperlink dialog box.
4. Click OK.

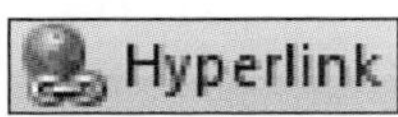

Figure 8.6 Insert Hyperlink Dialog Box

Type the text you want to display in the hyperlink.

Click this button to edit the hyperlink ScreenTip.

Click a button in this group to indicate the hyperlink location.

Insert Hyperlink

Link to: Text to display: ScreenTip...

Existing File or Web Page | Look in: Chapter08 | Bookmark... | Target Frame...

Place in This Document | Current Folder | Browsed Pages | Recent Files

Create New Document

E-mail Address

C08Ex01.docx
C08Ex02.docx
Document14.docx
Document15.docx
Document16.docx
Document17.docx
Document18.docx
Document19.docx
ExcelAuditorFees.xlsx
MSSPresentation.pptx

Address:

OK Cancel

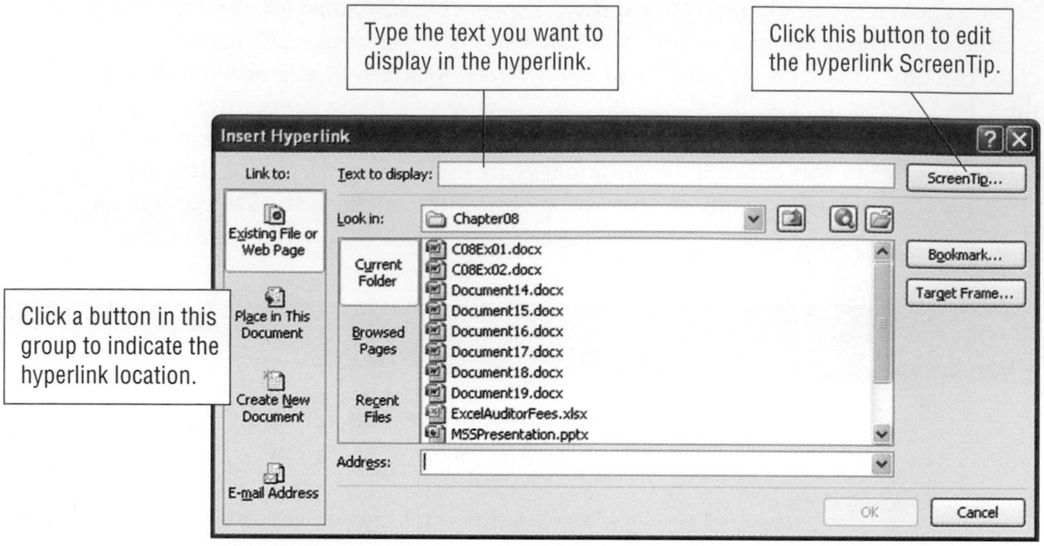

Linking to a Place in the Document

To create a hyperlink to another location in the document, you need to mark the location either by applying heading styles to text or by inserting bookmarks. To hyperlink to a heading or bookmark in a document, display the Insert Hyperlink dialog box and then click the Place in This Document button in the *Link to* group. This displays text with heading styles applied and bookmarks in the *Select a place in this document* list box. Click the desired heading style or bookmark name, and the heading or bookmark name displays in the *Text to display* text box. You can leave the text as displayed or you can select the text and then type the text you want to appear in the document.

Navigate to a hyperlink by hovering the mouse over the hyperlink text, holding down the Ctrl key, and then clicking the left mouse button. When you hover the mouse over hyperlink text, a ScreenTip displays with the name of the heading or bookmark. If you want specific information to display in the ScreenTip, click the ScreenTip button in the Insert Hyperlink dialog box, type the desired text in the Set Hyperlink ScreenTip dialog box, and then click OK.

Exercise 2E

Inserting a Hyperlink to a Location in the Document

1. With **C08Ex02.docx** open, insert a hyperlink to a location in the document by completing the following steps:
   a. Position the insertion point immediately right of the period that ends the first paragraph of text in the *SECTION 4: HARDWARE AND SOFTWARE SECURITY RISKS* section.
   b. Press the spacebar once.
   c. If necessary, click the Insert tab.
   d. Click the Hyperlink button.
   e. At the Insert Hyperlink dialog box, click the Place in This Document button in the *Link to* group.
   f. Scroll down the *Select a place in this document* list box and then click *Access,* which displays below *Bookmarks* in the list box.
   g. Select the text that displays in the *Text to display* text box and then type **Click to view types of unauthorized access**.

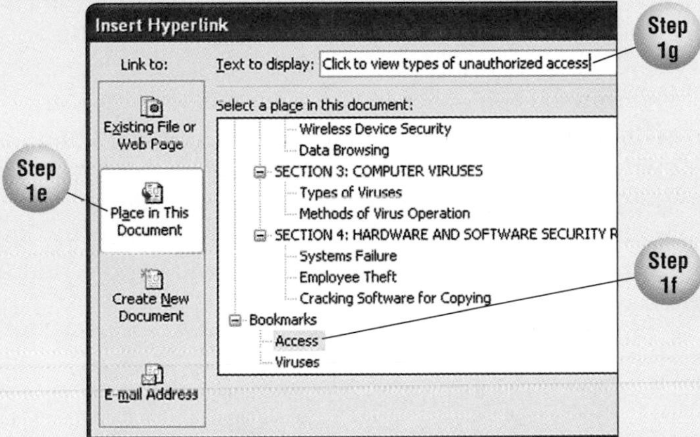

   h. Click the ScreenTip button located in the upper right corner of the dialog box. At the Set Hyperlink ScreenTip dialog box, type **View types of unauthorized access to computers** and then click OK.

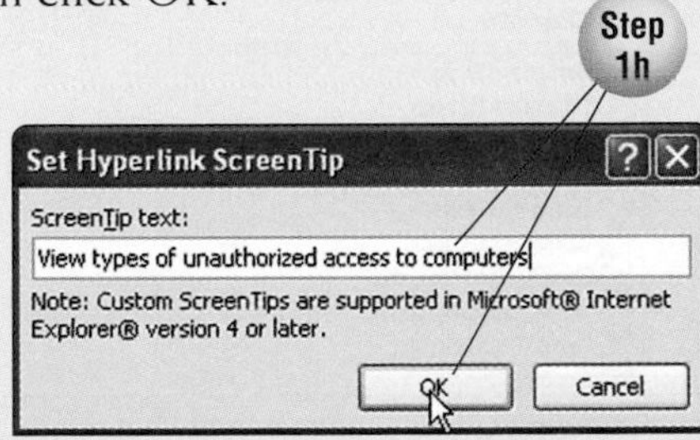

   i. Click OK to close the Insert Hyperlink dialog box.
2. Navigate to the hyperlinked location by hovering the mouse over the *Click to view types of unauthorized access* hyperlink, holding down the Ctrl key, and then clicking the left mouse button.
3. Save **C08Ex02.docx**.

Linking to a File in Another Program

In some situations, you may want to provide information to your readers from a variety of sources. You may want to provide information in a Word document, an Excel spreadsheet, or a PowerPoint presentation. To link a Word document to a file in another application, display the Insert Hyperlink dialog box and then click the Existing File or Web Page button in the *Link to* group. Use the *Look in* option to navigate to the folder containing the desired file and then click the file. Make other changes in the Insert Hyperlink dialog box as needed and then click OK.

Exercise 2F

Inserting a Hyperlink to a PowerPoint Presentation

1. The **C08Ex02.docx** contains information used by Madison Security Systems. The company also has a PowerPoint presentation that contains similar information. Link the document with the presentation by completing the following steps:
   a. Press Ctrl + End to move the insertion point to the end of the document.
   b. If necessary, click the Insert tab.
   c. Click the Hyperlink button in the Links group.
   d. Click the Existing File or Web Page button in the *Link to* group.
   e. Click the down-pointing arrow at the right side of the *Look in* list box and then navigate to the Chapter08 folder on your storage medium.
   f. Click the presentation named **MSSPresentation.pptx** in the list box.
   g. Select the text in the *Text to display* text box in the dialog box and then type **Computer Viruses Presentation**.
   h. Click OK to close the Insert Hyperlink dialog box.

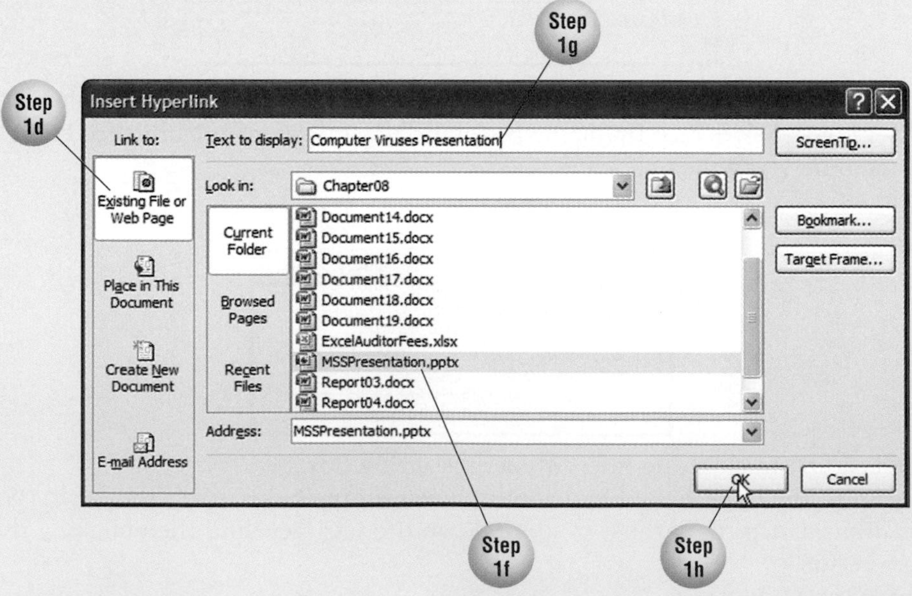

2. View the PowerPoint presentation by completing the following steps:
   a. Position the mouse pointer over the Computer Viruses Presentation hyperlink, hold down the Ctrl key, and then click the left mouse button.
   b. Click the button on the Taskbar representing the PowerPoint presentation.
   c. At the PowerPoint presentation, click the Slide Show button in the view area on the Status bar.
   d. Click the left mouse button to advance each slide.
   e. Click the left mouse button at the black screen that displays the message *End of slide show, click to exit.*
   f. Close the presentation and PowerPoint by clicking the Close button (contains an X) that displays in the upper right corner of the screen.
3. Save **C08Ex02.docx**.

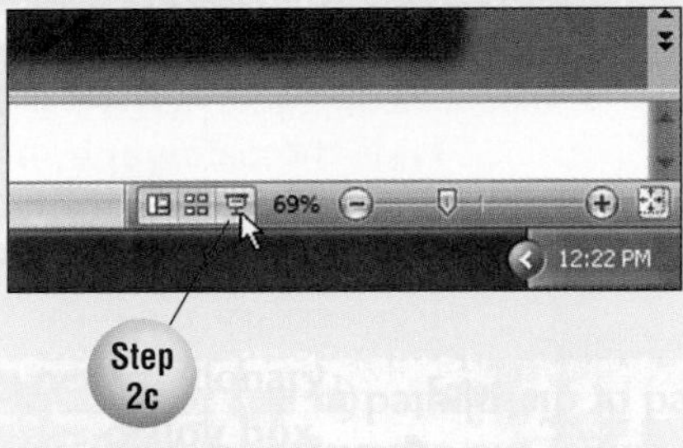

Creating a Cross-Reference

Insert a Cross-reference
1. Type introductory text.
2. Click Insert tab.
3. Click Cross-reference button.
4. Identify reference type, where to refer, and specific text.
5. Click Insert.
6. Click Close.

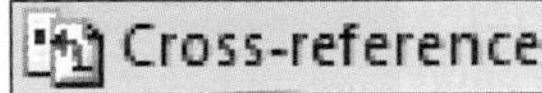

A cross-reference in a Word document refers the reader to another location within the document. Cross-referencing is useful in a long document or in a document that contains related information. You can insert a reference to an item such as a heading, figure, or table. For example, you can insert a cross-reference that refers readers to another location with more information about the topic or that refers readers to a specific table or page. Cross-references are inserted in a document as hyperlinks.

To insert a cross-reference, you type introductory text, click the Insert tab, and then click the Cross-reference button in the Links group. Clicking the Cross-reference button displays the Cross-reference dialog box, similar to the one shown in Figure 8.7. At the Cross-reference dialog box, identify the reference type (what you are referencing), where the reader should refer, and the specific text.

The reference identified in the Cross-reference dialog box displays immediately after the introductory text. To move to the specified reference, hold down the Ctrl key, position the mouse pointer over the introductory text (pointer turns into a hand), and then click the left mouse button.

Figure 8.7 Cross-reference Dialog Box

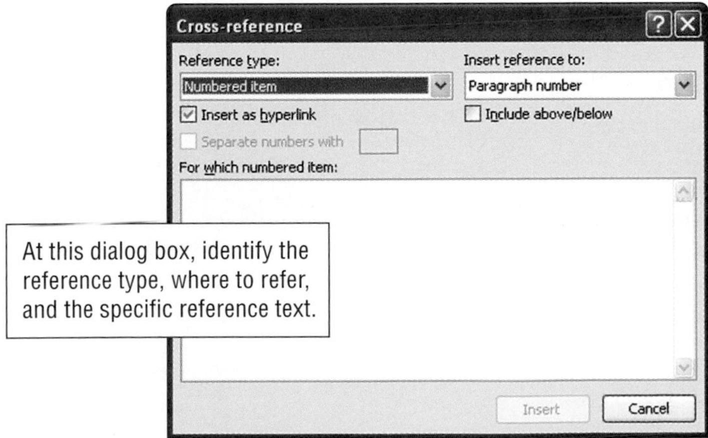

Exercise 2G

Inserting and Navigating with Cross-references

1. With **C08Ex02.docx** open, insert a cross-reference in the document by completing the following steps:
   a. Move the insertion point so it is positioned immediately right of the period that ends the paragraph in the *TYPES OF VIRUSES* section.
   b. Press the spacebar once and then type (**For more information, refer to**.
   c. Press the spacebar once.
   d. If necessary, click the Insert tab.
   e. Click the Cross-reference button in the Links group.
   f. At the Cross-reference dialog box, click the down-pointing arrow at the right side of the *Reference type* list box and then click *Heading* at the drop-down list.
   g. Click *Data Browsing* in the *For which heading* list box.
   h. Click the Insert button.
   i. Click the Close button to close the dialog box.
   j. At the document, type a period followed by the right parenthesis.

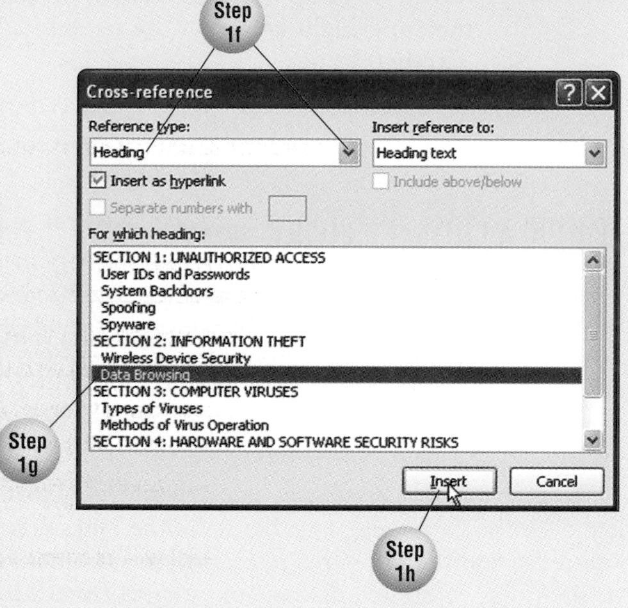

2. Move to the reference text by holding down the Ctrl key, positioning the mouse pointer over *Data Browsing* until the pointer turns into a hand, and then clicking the left mouse button.
3. Save **C08Ex02.docx**.
4. Apply the following formatting to the document:
   a. Insert page numbering that prints at the top right margin on each page.
   b. Insert the Puzzle [Odd Page] footer. Click the *[Type the company name]* placeholder and then type **Madison Security Systems**.
   c. Insert the Pinstripes cover page and insert the following in the specified placeholders:
      [Type the document title] = **Computer Security**
      [Type the document subtitle] = (Delete this placeholder)
      [Pick the date] = Insert today's date.
      [Type the author name] = Your first and last names
5. Save and then print **C08Ex02.docx**.
6. Turn off the display of bookmarks by completing the following steps:
   a. Click the Office button and then click the Word Options button that displays at the bottom of the drop-down list.
   b. At the Word Options dialog box, click *Advanced* in the left panel.
   c. Click the *Show bookmarks* check box in the *Show document content* section to remove the check mark.
   d. Click OK to close the dialog box.
7. Close **C08Ex02.docx**.

Chapter Summary

- Insert symbols with options at the Symbol dialog box with the Symbols tab selected; insert special characters with options at the Symbol dialog box with the Special Characters tab selected.
- To enhance the appearance of text, use drop caps to identify the beginning of major sections or parts of a paragraph. Create drop caps with the Drop Cap button in the Text group in the Insert tab.
- Click the Date & Time button in the Text group in the Insert tab to display the Date and Time dialog box. Insert the date or time with options at this dialog box or with keyboard shortcuts. If the date or time is inserted as a field, update the field with the Update Field key, F9.
- Insert a document into an open document by clicking the Insert tab, clicking the Object button arrow, and then clicking *Text from File* at the drop-down list. At the Insert File dialog box, double-click the desired document.
- Navigate in a document by turning on the Document Map or Thumbnails feature or by inserting bookmarks, hyperlinks, or cross-references.
- The Document Map and Thumbnails buttons are located in the View tab.
- Insert bookmarks with options at the Bookmark dialog box.
- Insert hyperlinks in a document with options at the Insert Hyperlink dialog box. You can insert a hyperlink to a location in the document, to a different document, to a file in another program, or to a web page on the Internet.
- Create a cross-reference with options at the Cross-reference dialog box.

Commands review

FEATURE	RIBBON TAB, GROUP	BUTTON	KEYBOARD SHORTCUT
Symbol dialog box	Insert, Symbols	Symbol	
Drop cap	Insert, Text	Drop Cap	
Date and Time dialog box	Insert, Text	Date & Time	
Insert date			Alt + Shift + D
Insert time			Alt + Shift + T
Update field			F9
Insert file	Insert, Text	Object	
Document Map	View, Show/Hide	Document Map	
Thumbnails	View, Show/Hide	Thumbnails	
Bookmark dialog box	Insert, Links	Bookmark	
Insert Hyperlink dialog box	Insert, Links	Hyperlink	Ctrl + K
Cross-reference dialog box	Insert, Links	Cross-reference	

Reviewing key points

Completion: In the space provided at the right, indicate the correct term, symbol, or command.

1. The Symbol button is located in this tab. ____________
2. Click this option at the Symbol button drop-down list to display the Symbol dialog box. ____________
3. The first letter of the first word of a paragraph that is set into a paragraph is called this. ____________
4. This is the keyboard shortcut to insert the current date. ____________
5. This is the keyboard shortcut to insert the current time. ____________
6. The Date & Time button is located in this group in the Insert tab. ____________
7. This is the Update Field keyboard shortcut. ____________
8. Display the Insert File dialog box by clicking the Object button arrow in the Insert tab and then clicking this option. ____________
9. The Document Map and Thumbnails features are available in this tab. ____________
10. Click the Document Map check box to insert a check mark and this displays at the left side of the document. ____________
11. Turn on the display of bookmarks in a document with the *Show bookmarks* check box in this dialog box with *Advanced* selected. ____________
12. The Bookmark button is located in this group in the Insert tab. ____________
13. Navigate to a hyperlink by hovering the mouse over the hyperlink text, holding down this key, and then clicking the left mouse button. ____________
14. To link a Word document to a file in another application, click this button in the *Link to* group in the Insert Hyperlink dialog box. ____________
15. Cross-references are inserted in a document as this. ____________

Applying your skills

Assessment 1 Apply Headers and Footers to Employee Orientation Documents

1. Open **Document16.docx** and save the document with the name **C08A01**.
2. Press Ctrl + End to move the insertion point to the end of the document and then insert the file named **Document17.docx**.
3. Press Ctrl + End to move the insertion point to the end of the document and then type **Séverin Technologies®**.
4. Press Shift + Enter and then insert the current date.
5. Press Shift + Enter and then insert the current time.
6. Create a drop cap with the first letter of the first paragraph of text (the word *Acceptance*) and specify that the drop cap is dropped two lines.
7. Make the following changes to the document:
   a. Insert a page break at the beginning of the title *EMPLOYEE PERFORMANCE* located on the second page.
   b. Apply the Heading 1 style to the two titles in the document *PROBATIONARY PERIODS* and *EMPLOYEE PERFORMANCE*.
   c. Apply the Heading 2 style to the four headings *Types of Appointments*, *Work Performance Standards*, *Performance Evaluation*, and *Employment Records*.
   d. Change the style set to *Simple*.
   e. Apply the *Foundry* theme.
   f. Center the two titles.
   g. Add 12 points of space after the first title (*PROBATIONARY PERIODS*).
   h. Insert the Pinstripes header and type **Employee Handbook** in the *[Type the document title]* placeholder.
   i. Insert the Pinstripes footer and insert **Séverin Technologies** in the *[Type text]* placeholder.
8. Save, print, and then close **C08A01.docx**.

Assessment 2 Format and Navigate in Corporate Report Documents

1. Open **Document18.docx** and save the document with the name **C08A02**.
2. Move the insertion point to the end of the document and then insert the document named **Document19.docx**.
3. Apply the following formatting (you choose the specific formatting):
   a. Apply heading styles of your choosing to the titles and headings.
   b. Apply a style set.
   c. Apply a theme.
   d. Insert a header and/or footer.
   e. Insert a cover page.
4. Turn on the display of bookmarks.
5. Move the insertion point to the end of the third paragraph in the document (the paragraph that begins *The Audit Committee selects . . .*) and then insert a bookmark named **Audit**.
6. Move the insertion point to the end of the first paragraph in the *Fees to Independent Auditor* section—following the *(Excel Worksheet)* text—and then insert a bookmark named **Audit_Fees**.
7. Move the insertion point to the end of the last paragraph of text in the document and then insert a bookmark named **Compensation**.
8. Navigate in the document using the bookmarks.
9. Move the insertion point to the end of the first paragraph in the *Committee Responsibilities* section and then insert a hyperlink to the *Audit_Fees* bookmark.
10. Select the text *(Excel Worksheet)* that displays at the end of the first paragraph in the *Fees to Independent Auditors* section and then insert a hyperlink to the Excel file named **ExcelAuditorFees.xlsx** that is located in the Chapter08 folder on your storage medium.
11. Click the *(Excel Worksheet)* hyperlink and then print the Excel worksheet that displays by clicking the Quick Print button on the Quick Access toolbar. (If the toolbar does not contain the Quick Print button, click the Office button, point to Print, and then click Quick Print.) Close the Excel program.
12. Save, print, and then close **C08A02.docx**.

Chapter 9

Maintaining Documents

Tutorial 9.1
Managing Folders and Documents and Using Templates

Performance Objectives

Upon successful completion of Chapter 9, you will be able to:

- Create and rename a folder
- Select, delete, copy, move, rename, and print documents
- Move a document from one folder into another
- Create a document using a Word template

Nearly every company that conducts business maintains a filing system. The system may consist of paper documents, folders, and file cabinets, or it may consist of electronic files and folders stored on a computer hard drive or other storage medium. Whatever type of system a business uses, the daily maintenance of files is important to the company's operations. In this chapter, you will learn to maintain files (documents) in Word, including how to create folders and copy, move, and rename documents. You will also learn how to create a document using a Word template.

Note: Before beginning computer exercises for this chapter, copy to your storage medium the Chapter09 folder from the CD that accompanies this textbook and then make Chapter09 the active folder.

Maintaining Documents

Many file (document) management tasks in Word can be completed at either the Open or the Save As dialog box. These tasks include copying, moving, printing, and renaming documents; opening multiple documents; and creating new folders and renaming existing folders.

Create a Folder
1. Display Open dialog box.
2. Click Create New Folder button.
3. Type folder name.
4. Press Enter.

Create New Folder

Creating a Folder

Word documents, like paper documents, are grouped logically and placed in *folders*. The main folder on a storage medium is called the *root* folder, and you can create additional folders within the root folder. At both the Open and Save As dialog boxes, documents display in the list box preceded by the document icon; folders display preceded by the folder icon. You can create a new folder by clicking the Create New Folder button located on either dialog box toolbar. At the New Folder dialog box, shown in Figure 9.1, type a name for the folder and then press Enter. The new folder becomes the active folder. A folder name can contain a maximum of 255 characters. Numbers, spaces, and symbols (except those symbols listed in Chapter 1 in the "Naming a Document" section) can be used in the folder name.

Figure 9.1 New Folder Dialog Box

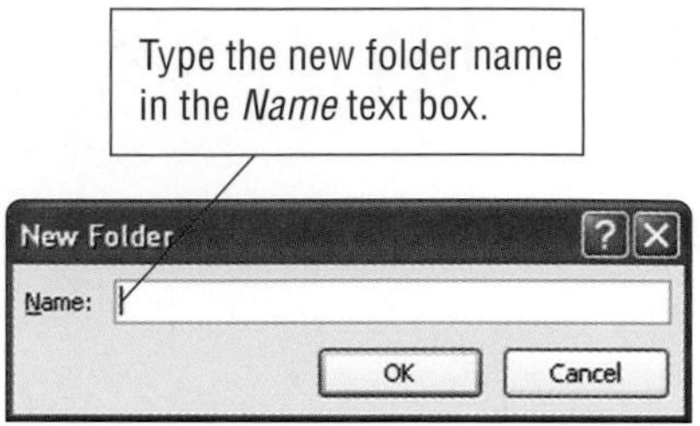

Up One Level

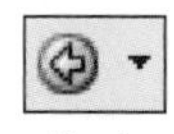
Back

If you want to make the previous folder the active folder, click the Up One Level button on the dialog box toolbar. Clicking this button makes active the folder up one level from the current folder. When you click the Up One Level button, the Back button becomes active. Click this button and the previously active folder becomes active again.

Exercise 1A

Creating a Folder

1. Create a folder named Contracts on your storage medium by completing the following steps:
   a. Display the Open dialog box and open the Chapter09 folder on your storage medium.
   b. Click the Create New Folder button located on the dialog box toolbar.
   c. At the New Folder dialog box, type **Contracts**.
   d. Click OK. (The Contracts folder becomes the active folder.)

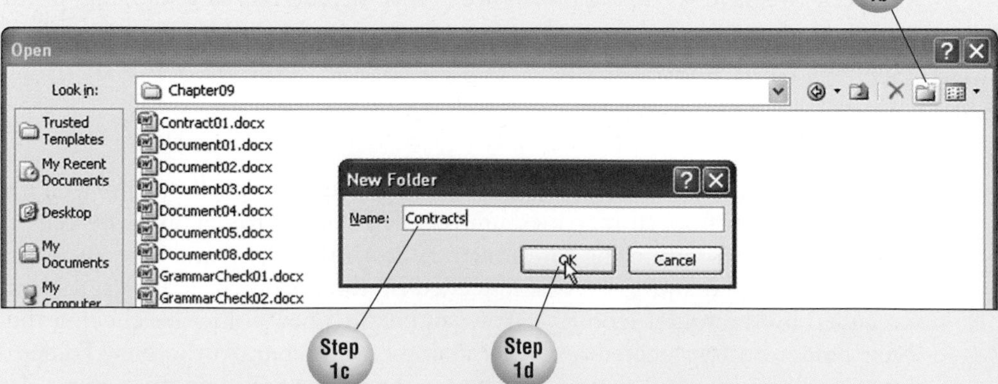

2. Change back to the Chapter09 folder by clicking the Up One Level button on the dialog box toolbar.

Renaming a Folder

Rename a Folder
1. Display Open dialog box.
2. Right-click folder.
3. Click Rename.
4. Type new name.
5. Press Enter.

As you organize files and folders, you may decide to rename a folder. You can rename a folder using the Tools button in the Open or Save As dialog box or using a shortcut menu. To rename a folder using the Tools button, display the Open or the Save As dialog box, click the folder you want to rename, click the Tools button located in the lower left corner of the dialog box, and then click *Rename* at the drop-down list. Clicking *Rename* selects the folder name and inserts a border around it. Type the new name for the folder and then press Enter. To rename a folder using a shortcut menu, display the Open dialog box, right-click the folder you want to rename, and then click Rename at the shortcut menu. Type a new name for the folder and then press Enter.

Exercise 1B

Renaming a Folder

1. With the Open dialog box open, right-click the *Contracts* folder name in the list box.
2. Click Rename at the shortcut menu.
3. Type **Documents** and then press Enter.

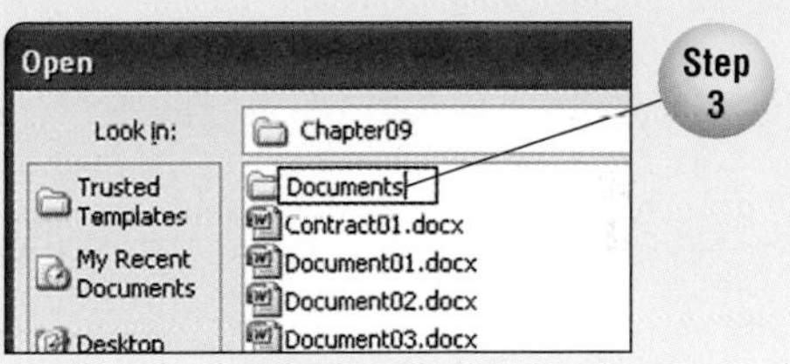

Selecting Documents

You can complete document management tasks on one or more selected documents. To select one document, display the Open dialog box and then click the desired document. To select several adjacent documents (documents that display next to each other), click the first document, hold down the Shift key, and then click the last document. To select documents that are not adjacent, click the first document, hold down the Ctrl key, click any other desired documents, and then release the Ctrl key.

Deleting Documents

Delete a Document
1. Display Open dialog box.
2. Click document name.
3. Click Delete button.
4. Click Yes.

Delete

At some point, you may want to delete certain documents from your storage medium or from any other drive or folder in which you may be working. To delete a document, display the Open or Save As dialog box, select the document, and then click the Delete button on the dialog box toolbar. At the dialog box asking you to confirm the deletion, click Yes. To delete a document using a shortcut menu, right-click the document name in the list box, click Delete at the shortcut menu, and then click Yes at the confirmation dialog box.

Deleting to the Recycle Bin

When you delete a document from your storage medium, it is deleted permanently. (Recovery programs are available, however, that will help you recover deleted text. If you accidentally delete a document or documents from a storage medium such as a USB flash drive, do not do anything more with the drive until you can run a recovery program.) In contrast, documents deleted from the hard drive are automatically sent to the Windows Recycle Bin. If you accidentally delete a document to the Recycle Bin, it can be easily restored. To free space on the drive, empty the Recycle Bin periodically. Restoring a document from or emptying the contents of the Recycle Bin is done at the Windows desktop (not in Word). To empty the Recycle Bin, complete the following steps:

1. Display the Windows desktop. If you are just beginning, turn on the computer and Windows will open. If you are currently working in Word, click the Minimize button at the right side of the Title bar. The Minimize button is marked with a single underline symbol (_).
2. At the Windows desktop, double-click the *Recycle Bin* icon (usually located at the left side of the desktop).
3. At the Recycle Bin dialog box, click File and then Empty Recycle Bin.
4. At the question asking if you are sure you want to empty the Recycle Bin, click Yes.

If you want to empty only specific documents from the Recycle Bin, hold down the Ctrl key while clicking the documents to be emptied. Position the mouse pointer on one of the selected documents, click the *right* mouse button, and then click Delete at the shortcut menu. At the question asking if you want to delete the selected documents, click Yes.

A document or selected documents can also be restored from the Recycle Bin. To do this, complete the following steps:

1. At the Windows desktop, double-click the *Recycle Bin* icon.
2. At the Recycle Bin dialog box, click the document to be restored. (If you are restoring more than one document, hold down the Ctrl key while clicking the desired documents.)
3. Click File and then Restore.

At the Recycle Bin dialog box, you can also restore a document by positioning the mouse pointer on the document to be restored, clicking the *right* mouse button, and then clicking Restore at the shortcut menu.

If you minimized the Word program by clicking the Minimize button, you can maximize (display the Word screen) the Word program on the desktop by clicking the Microsoft Word button (displays with the name of the document) located on the Taskbar (at the bottom of the screen).

Exercise 1C

Selecting and Deleting Documents

1. Open **Document04.docx** and save the document with the name **C09Ex01**.
2. Close **C09Ex01.docx**.
3. Delete **C09Ex01.docx** by completing the following steps:
   a. Display the Open dialog box.
   b. Click **C09Ex01.docx** to select it.
   c. Click the Delete button on the dialog box toolbar.

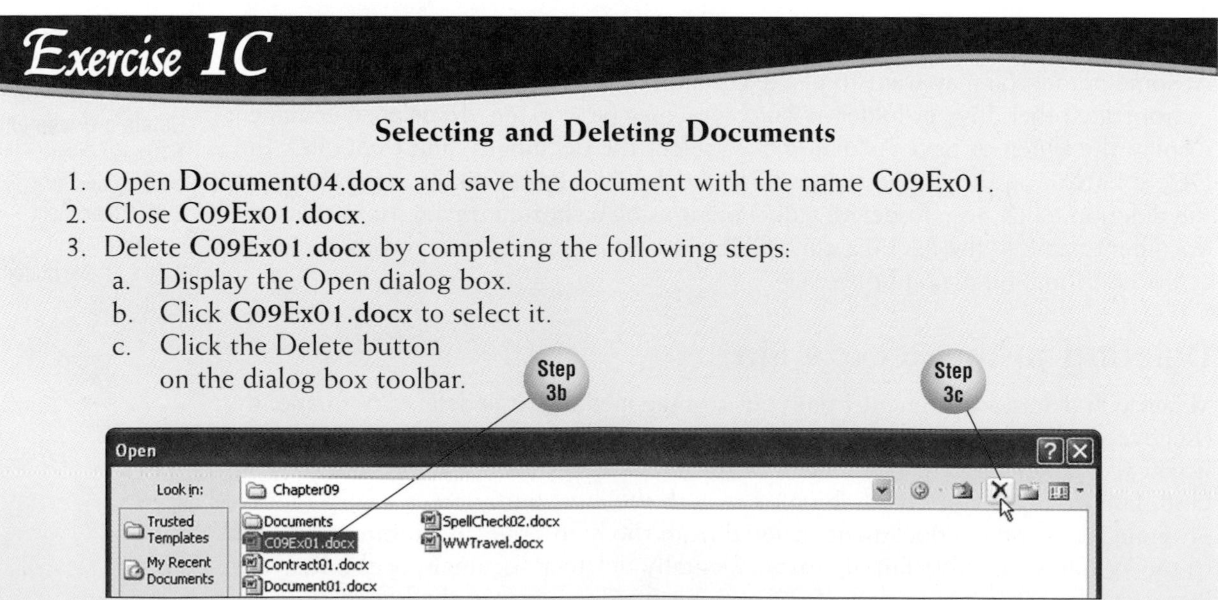

d. At the question asking if you want to delete **C09Ex01.docx**, click Yes.
4. Delete selected documents by completing the following steps:
   a. At the Open dialog box, click **Report01.docx**.
   b. Hold down the Shift key and then click **Report03.docx**.
   c. Position the mouse pointer on a selected document and then click the *right* mouse button.
   d. At the shortcut menu that displays, click Delete.
   e. At the question asking if you want to delete the items, click Yes.
5. Open **Document03.docx** and save the document with the name **ComputerHardware**.
6. Save a copy of the **ComputerHardware.docx** document in the Documents folder by completing the following steps:
   a. With **ComputerHardware.docx** open, click the Office button and then click *Save As*.
   b. At the Save As dialog box, double-click the Documents folder located at the beginning of the Chapter09 folder list box (folders are listed before documents).
   c. Click the Save button located in the lower right corner of the dialog box.
7. Close **ComputerHardware.docx**.
8. Display the Open dialog box and then click the Up One Level button to return to the Chapter09 folder.

Copying and Moving Documents

You can copy a document to another folder without opening the document first. To do this, use the Copy and Paste options from the shortcut menu at the Open or Save As dialog box. You can copy a document or selected documents into the same folder. When you do this, Word names the document(s) "Copy of xxx" (where *xxx* is the current document name).

You can also remove a document from one folder and insert it in another folder using the Cut and Paste options from the shortcut menu at the Open dialog box. To do this, display the Open dialog box, position the arrow pointer on the document to be removed (cut), click the *right* mouse button, and then click Cut at the shortcut menu. Navigate to the desired folder, position the arrow pointer in a white area in the list box, click the *right* mouse button, and then click Paste at the shortcut menu.

Copy or Move a Document
1. Display Open dialog box.
2. Right-click document name.
3. Click Copy or Cut.
4. Navigate to desired folder.
5. Right-click blank area.
6. Click Paste.

Exercise 1D

Copying Documents

1. At the Open dialog box with Chapter09 the active folder, copy a document to another folder by completing the following steps:
   a. Position the arrow pointer on **Document02.docx**, click the *right* mouse button, and then click Copy at the shortcut menu.
   b. Change to the Documents folder by double-clicking *Documents* at the beginning of the list box.
   c. Position the arrow pointer in any white area (not on a document name) in the list box, click the *right* mouse button, and then click Paste at the shortcut menu.

2. Change back to the Chapter09 folder by clicking the Up One Level button located on the dialog box toolbar.
3. Copy several documents to the Documents folder by completing the following steps:
   a. Click once on **Document01.docx**. (This selects the document.)
   b. Hold down the Ctrl key, click **Document04.docx**, click **Document05.docx**, and then release the Ctrl key.
   c. Position the arrow pointer on one of the selected documents, click the *right* mouse button, and then click Copy at the shortcut menu.
   d. Double-click the Documents folder.
   e. Position the arrow pointer in any white area in the list box, click the *right* mouse button, and then click Paste at the shortcut menu.
4. Click the Up One Level button to return to the Chapter09 folder.
5. Move **Quiz01.docx** to the Documents folder by completing the following steps:
   a. Position the arrow pointer on **Quiz01.docx**, click the *right* mouse button, and then click Cut at the shortcut menu.
   b. Double-click Documents to make it the active folder.
   c. Position the arrow pointer in the white area in the list box, click the *right* mouse button, and then click Paste at the shortcut menu.
6. Click the Up One Level button to return to the Chapter09 folder.

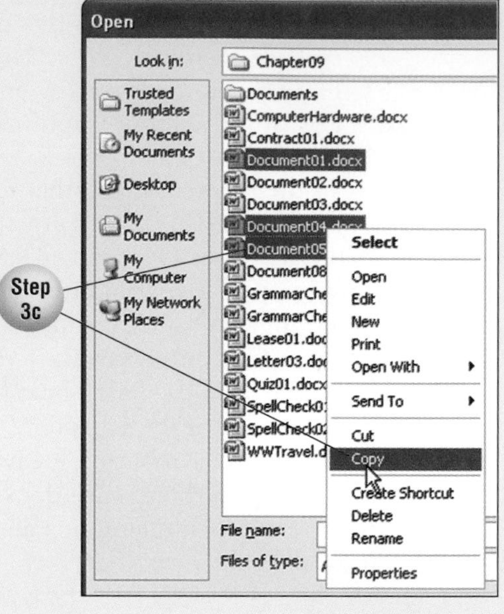

QUICK STEPS

Rename a Document
1. Display Open dialog box.
2. Click document name.
3. Click Tools, *Rename*.
4. Type new name.
5. Press Enter.

Renaming Documents

At the Open dialog box, you can use the *Rename* option from the Tools button drop-down list to give a document a different name. The *Rename* option changes the name of the document but keeps it in the same folder. To use *Rename,* display the Open dialog box, click once on the document to be renamed, click the Tools button, and then click *Rename* at the drop-down list. When you click *Rename*, a black border surrounds the document name and the name is selected. Type the new name and then press Enter. You can also rename a document by right-clicking the document name at the Open dialog box and then clicking Rename at the shortcut menu. Type the desired name for the document and then press the Enter key.

Exercise 1E

Renaming Documents

1. Rename a document located in the Documents folder by completing the following steps:
   a. At the Open dialog box with the Chapter09 folder open, double-click the Documents folder to make it active.
   b. Click once on **Document04.docx** to select it.
   c. Click the Tools button located in the lower left corner of the dialog box.
   d. Click *Rename* at the drop-down list.
   e. Type **Computers.docx** and then press the Enter key.
2. Click the Up One Level button to return to the Chapter09 folder.

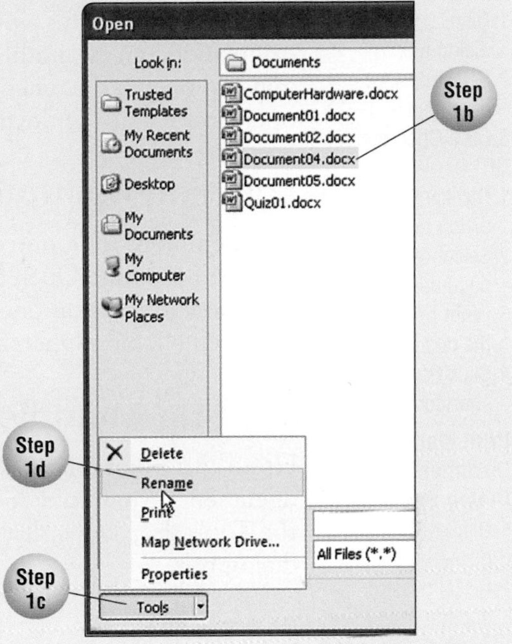

Delete a Folder
1. Display Open dialog box.
2. Click folder name.
3. Click Delete button.
4. Click Yes.

Deleting a Folder

As you learned earlier in this chapter, you can delete a selected document or documents. You can also delete a folder and all its contents in the same manner.

Exercise 1F

Deleting a Folder

1. At the Open dialog box, click the Documents folder to select it.
2. Click the Delete button on the dialog box toolbar.

3. At the question asking if you want to remove the folder and its contents, click Yes.

3. Scroll through the document and notice how the pages display.
4. Redisplay the white spaces at the top and bottom of pages by positioning the mouse pointer on any thin, black, horizontal line separating pages until the pointer turns into the *Show White Space* icon and then double-clicking the left mouse button.
5. Save **C10Ex01.docx**.

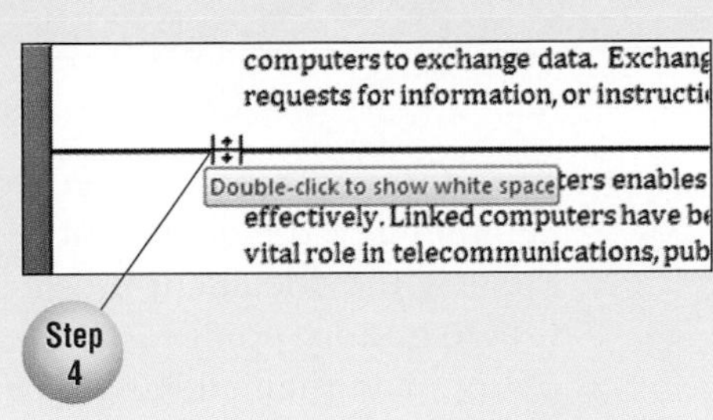

Previewing a Document

Before printing a document, you may want to view it as it will appear when printed. To do this, display the document in Print Preview by clicking the Office button, pointing to the *Print* option, and then clicking *Print Preview* in the side menu. The page on which the insertion point is located displays on the screen in a manner similar to that shown in Figure 10.3. With options in the Print Preview tab, you can send the document to the printer, change the page setup, change the zoom display, and customize the preview window.

Preview a Document
1. Click Office button.
2. Point to *Print*.
3. Click Print Preview.

Figure 10.3 Document in Print Preview

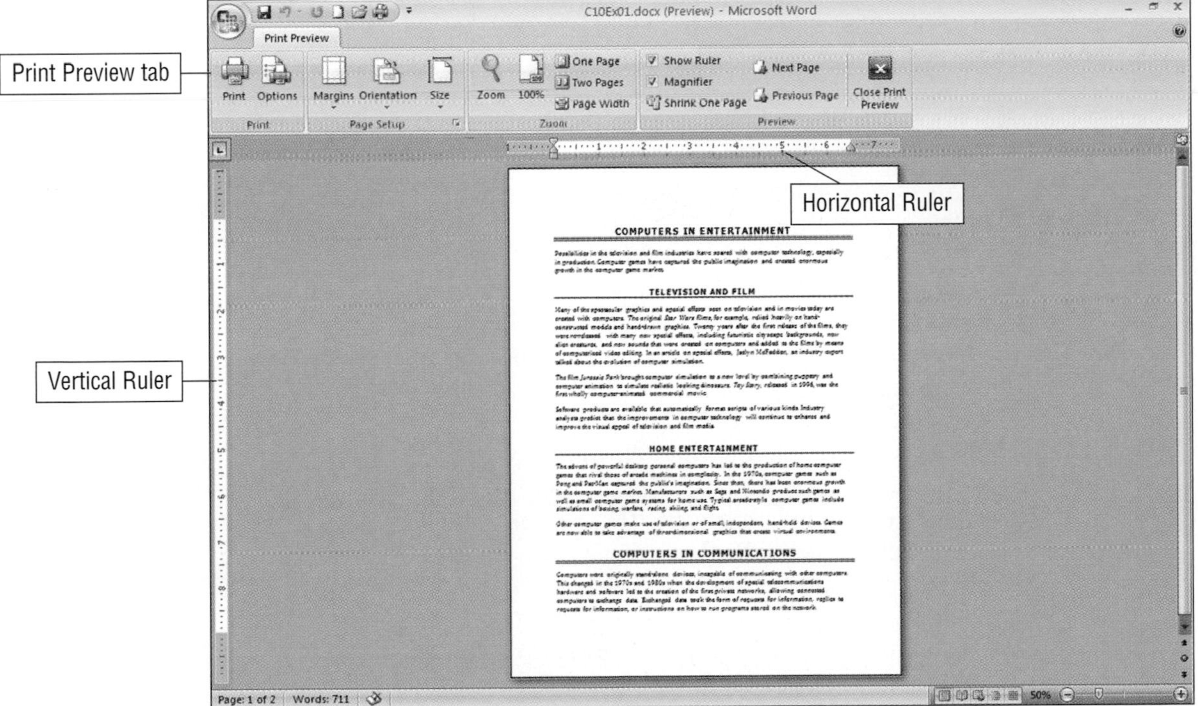

Exercise 1F

Previewing the Document

1. With **C10Ex01.docx** open, press Ctrl + Home to move the insertion point to the beginning of the document.
2. Preview the document by clicking the Office button, pointing to the *Print* option, and then clicking *Print Preview* at the side menu.
3. Click the Two Pages button in the Zoom group in the Print Preview tab. (This displays the first two pages in the document.)

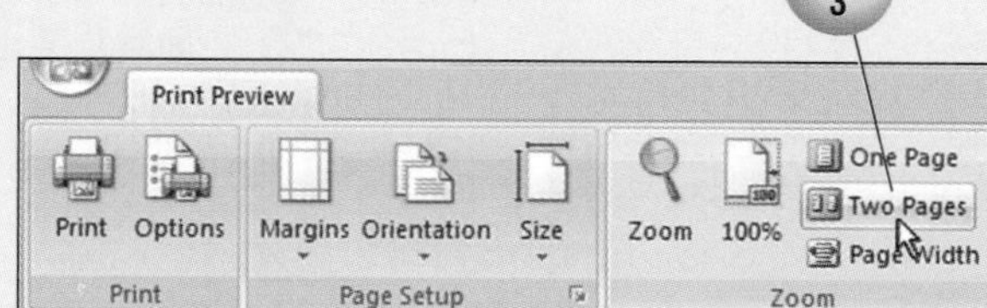

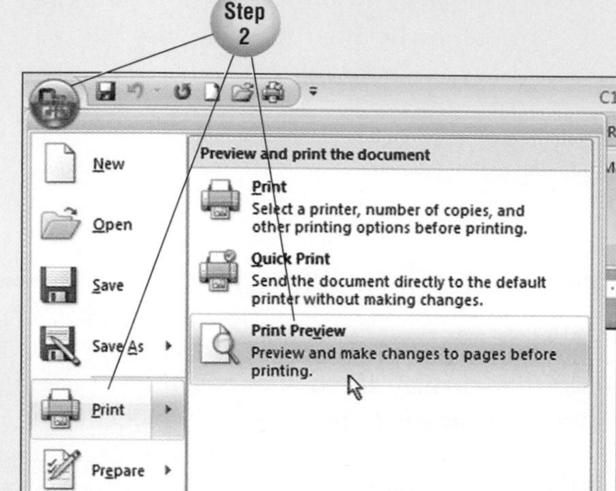

4. Click the One Page button in the Zoom group to display only the first page in the document.
5. Click the Next Page button in the Preview group. (This displays the second page.)
6. Click the Previous Page button in the Preview group. (This displays the first page.)
7. Change the page orientation by clicking the Orientation button in the Page Setup group and then clicking *Landscape* at the drop-down list.
8. After looking at the page in landscape orientation, return to portrait orientation. To do this, click the Orientation button in the Page Setup group and then click *Portrait* at the drop-down list.

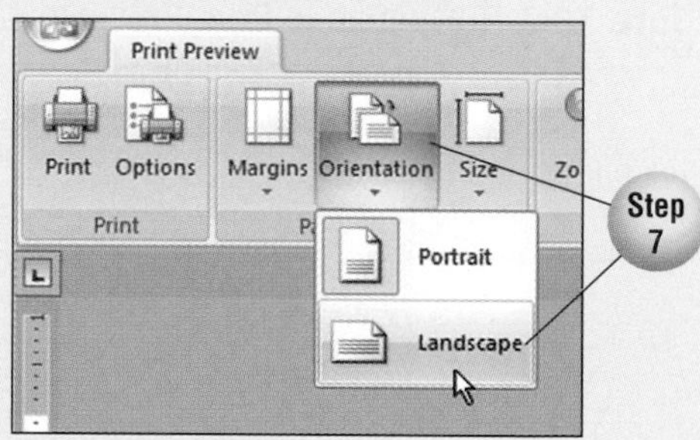

9. Change margin size by completing the following steps:
   a. Click the Margins button in the Page Setup group and then click *Custom Margins* at the drop-down list.
   b. At the Page Setup dialog box with the Margins tab selected, change the top margin to 1.25."
   c. Click OK to close the dialog box.

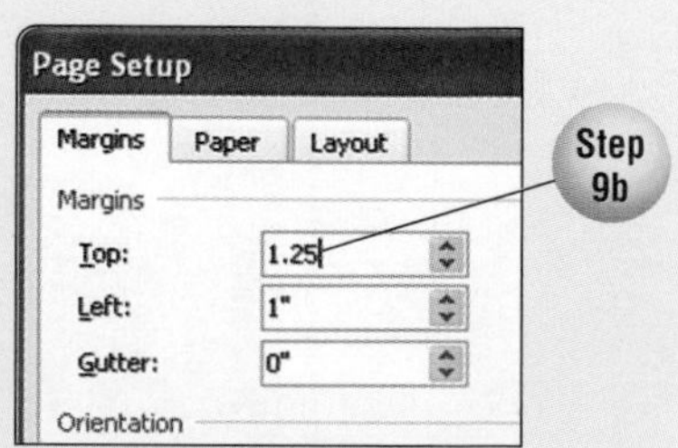

10. Change the Zoom by completing the following steps:
    a. Click the Zoom button in the Zoom group.
    b. At the Zoom dialog box, click the 75% option.
    c. Click OK to close the dialog box.
    d. After viewing the document in 75% view, click the Zoom button.
    e. At the Zoom dialog box, click the *Whole page* option.
    f. Click OK to close the dialog box.
11. Click the Close Print Preview button.
12. Save **C10Ex01.docx**.

Printing Documents

In Chapter 1, you learned to print the document displayed on the document screen at the Print dialog box. By default, one copy of all pages of the currently open document prints. With options at the Print dialog box, you can specify the number of copies to print and also specific pages for printing. To display the Print dialog box, shown in Figure 10.4, click the Office button and then click *Print* or press Ctrl + P.

Figure 10.4 Print Dialog Box

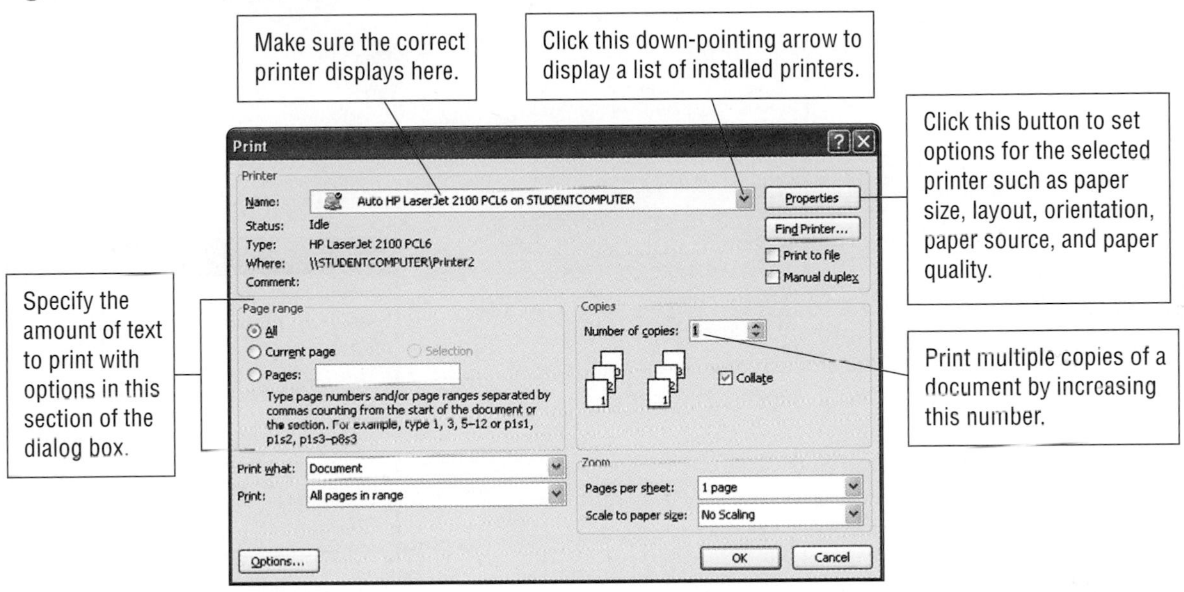

Printing Specific Text or Pages

The *Page range* section of the Print dialog box contains options you can use to specify the amount of text you want printed. With the default setting of *All*, all pages of the current document are printed. Choose the *Current page* option to print only the page on which the insertion point is located. If you want to select and then print a portion of the document, choose the *Selection* option. With this option, only the text that you have selected in the current document prints. (This option is dimmed unless text is selected in the document.)

With the *Pages* option, you can identify a specific page, multiple pages, or a range of pages to print. If you want specific multiple pages printed, use a comma (,) to indicate *and* and use a hyphen (-) to indicate *through*. For example, to print pages 2 and 5, you would type **2,5** in the *Pages* text box. To print pages 6 through 10, you would type **6-10**.

Exercise 1G

Printing Specific Text and Pages

1. With **C10Ex01.docx** open, select the heading *Television and Film* and the three paragraphs that follow it.
2. Press Ctrl + P.
3. At the Print dialog box, click the *Selection* option in the *Page range* section.

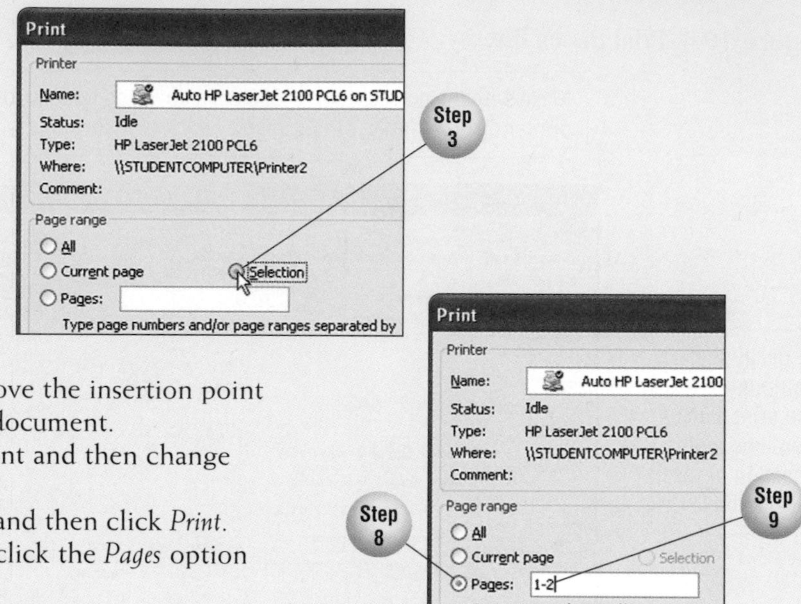

4. Click OK.
5. Press Ctrl + Home to move the insertion point to the beginning of the document.
6. Select the entire document and then change the line spacing to *1.5*.
7. Click the Office button and then click *Print*.
8. At the Print dialog box, click the *Pages* option in the *Page range* section.
9. Type 1-2 in the *Pages* text box.
10. Click OK.

Printing Multiple Copies

If you want to print more than one copy of a document, use the *Number of copies* option at the Print dialog box. If you print several copies of a document that has multiple pages, Word collates the pages as they print. For example, if you print two copies of a three-page document, pages 1, 2, and 3 print, and then the pages print a second time. Printing collated pages is helpful for assembly but takes more printing time. To reduce printing time, you can tell Word *not* to print collated pages. To do this, remove the check mark from the *Collate* option at the Print dialog box. With the check mark removed, Word will print all copies of the first page, then all copies of the second page, and so on.

Exercise 1H

Printing Multiple Copies of a Specific Page

1. With **C10Ex01.docx** open, press Ctrl + P.
2. Type **2** in the *Number of copies* text box.
3. Click the *Pages* option in the *Page range* section.
4. Type **1,3**.
5. Click the *Collate* check box in the *Copies* section to remove the check mark.
6. Click OK.
7. Save and then close **C10Ex01.docx**.

Creating and Printing Envelopes

Word provides options to automate the creation of envelopes. To create an envelope, display the Envelopes and Labels dialog box with the Envelopes tab selected, as shown in Figure 10.5. Display this dialog box by clicking the Mailings tab and then clicking the Envelopes button in the Create group. At the dialog box, type the delivery address in the *Delivery address* text box and the return address in the *Return address* text box. You can send the envelope directly to the printer by clicking the Print button or insert the envelope in an open document by clicking the Add to Document button.

QUICK STEPS

Create Envelope

1. Click Mailings tab.
2. Click Envelopes button.
3. Type delivery address.
4. Click in *Return address* text box.
5. Type return address.
6. Click Add to Document button or Print button.

Figure 10.5 Envelopes and Labels Dialog Box with Envelopes Tab Selected

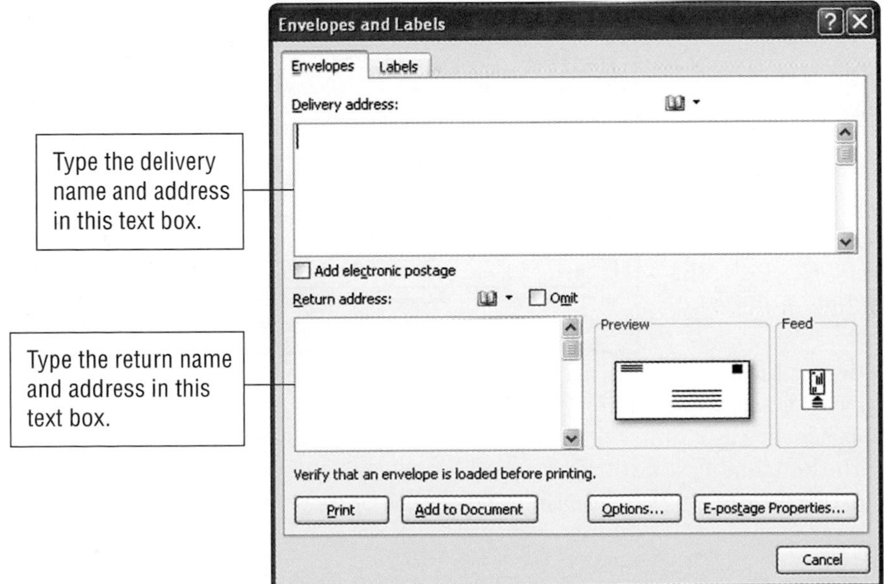

If you enter a return address and then click the Print button, Word displays the question *Do you want to save the new return address as the default return address?* Click Yes if you want the current return address available for future envelopes. Click No if you do not want the current return address used as the default. If a default return address displays in the *Return address* section of the dialog box, you can tell Word to omit the return address when printing the envelope by clicking the *Omit* check box to insert a check mark.

The Envelopes and Labels dialog box contains a *Preview* sample box and a *Feed* sample box. The *Preview* sample box shows how the envelope will appear when printed, and the *Feed* sample box shows how to insert the envelope into the printer.

When you address envelopes, consider following the general guidelines issued by the United States Postal Service (USPS). The USPS guidelines suggest using all capital letters with no commas or periods for return and delivery addresses. USPS guidelines also suggest using abbreviations for street designations (such as *ST* for *STREET* and *AVE* for *Avenue*). Figure 10.6 shows a delivery and return address following the USPS guidelines. For a complete list of address abbreviations, visit the USPS Web site.

Exercise 2

Printing an Envelope

1. At a blank document, create an envelope that prints the delivery address and return address shown in Figure 10.6. Begin by clicking the Mailings tab.
2. Click the Envelopes button in the Create group.
3. At the Envelopes and Labels dialog box with the Envelopes tab selected, type the delivery address shown in Figure 10.6 (the one containing the name *CRYSTAL BERGMAN*). (Press the Enter key to end each line in the name and address.)
4. Click in the *Return address* text box. (If any text displays in the *Return address* text box, select and then delete it.)
5. Type the return address shown in Figure 10.6 (the one containing the name *JOSEPH DEROUSSE*). (Press the Enter key to end each line in the name and address.)
6. Click the Add to Document button.
7. At the message *Do you want to save the new return address as the default return address?*, click No.
8. Save the document with the name **C10Ex02**.
9. Print and then close **C10Ex02.docx**. *(Note: Manual feed of the envelope may be required. Please check with your instructor.)*

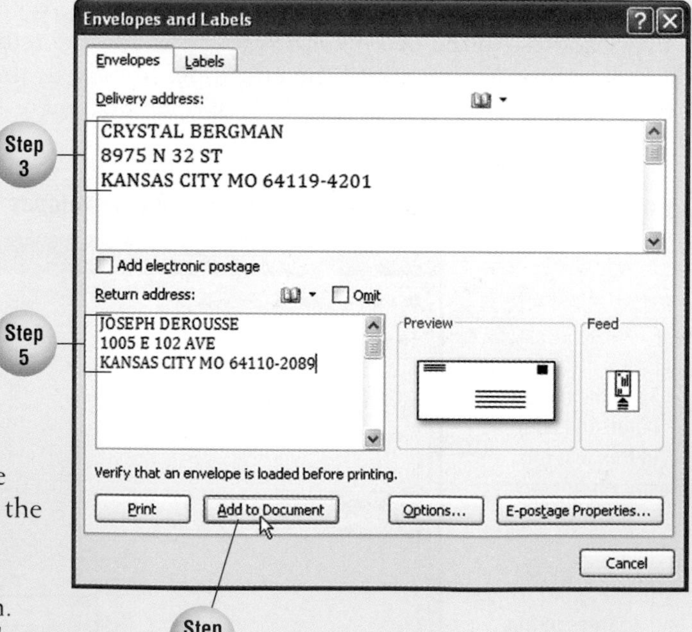

Figure 10.6 Exercise 2

JOSEPH DEROUSSE
1005 E 102 AVE
KANSAS CITY MO 64110-2089

CRYSTAL BERGMAN
8975 N 32 ST
KANSAS CITY MO 64119-4201

If you open the Envelopes and Labels dialog box in a document that contains a name and address with each line ending with a press of the Enter key (not Shift + Enter), Word automatically inserts the name and address in the *Delivery address* section of the dialog box. To automatically insert a delivery address, open a document containing a name and address and then display the Envelopes and Labels dialog box. The name and address are inserted in the *Delivery address* section as they appear in the letter and may not conform to the USPS guidelines. The USPS guidelines for addressing envelopes are only suggestions, not requirements.

Exercise 3A

Creating an Envelope in an Existing Document

1. Open **Letter07.docx**.
2. Click the Mailings tab.
3. Click the Envelopes button in the Create group.
4. At the Envelopes and Labels dialog box with the Envelopes tab selected, make sure the delivery address contained in Letter07.docx displays properly in the *Delivery address* section.
5. If any text displays in the *Return address* section, insert a check mark in the *Omit* check box (located to the right of the *Return address* option). (This tells Word not to print the return address on the envelope.)
6. Click the Print button.

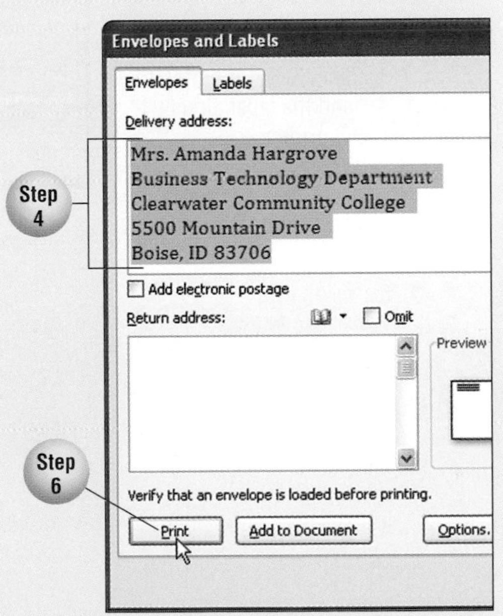

QUICK STEPS

Create Labels
1. Click Mailings tab.
2. Click Labels button.
3. Type desired address(es).
4. Click New Document button or Print button.

Creating and Printing Labels

Use Word's labels feature to print text on mailing labels, file labels, disk labels, or other types of labels. The feature includes a variety of predefined labels you can purchase at an office supply store. To create a sheet of mailing labels with the same name and address using the default options, click the Labels button in the Create group in the Mailings tab. At the Envelopes and Labels dialog box with the Labels tab selected as shown in Figure 10.7, type the desired address in the *Address* text box. Click the New Document button to insert the mailing label in a new document or click the Print button to send the mailing label directly to the printer. If you open the Envelopes and Labels dialog box with the Labels tab selected in a document that contains a name and address with each line ending with a press of the Enter key (not Shift + Enter), Word automatically inserts the name and address in the *Address* section of the dialog box.

Figure 10.7 Envelopes and Labels Dialog Box with Labels Tab Selected

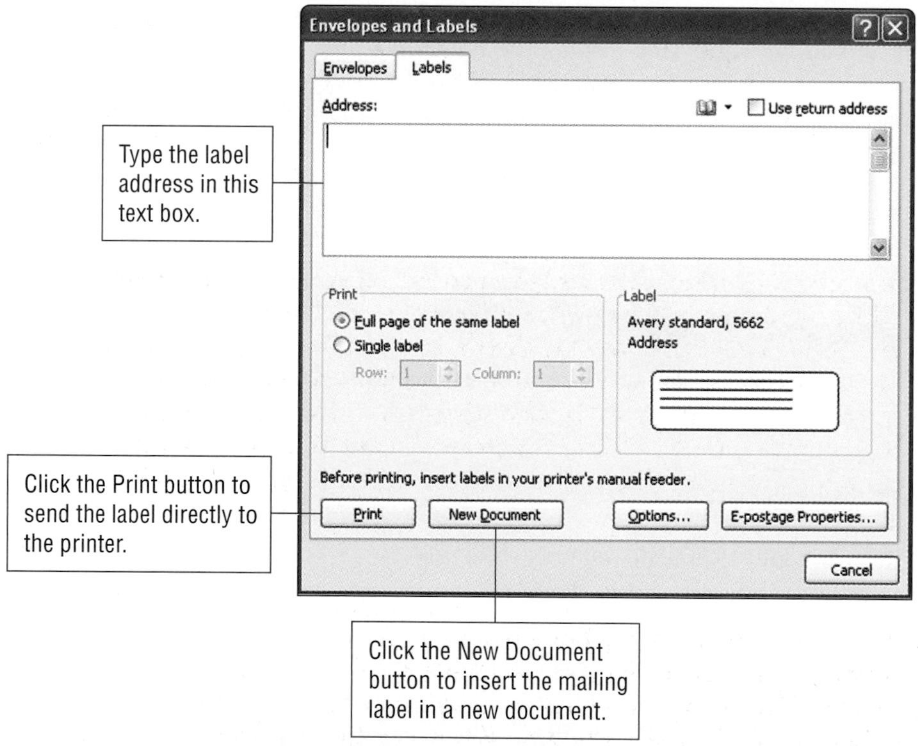

Exercise 3B

Creating Mailing Labels

1. With **Letter07.docx** open, create mailing labels with the delivery address. Begin by clicking the Mailings tab.
2. Click the Labels button in the Create group.
3. At the Envelopes and Labels dialog box with the Labels tab selected, make sure the delivery address displays properly in the *Address* section.
4. Click the New Document button.
5. Save the mailing label document with the name **C10Ex03**.
6. Print and then close **C10Ex03.docx**.
7. Close **Letter07.docx**.

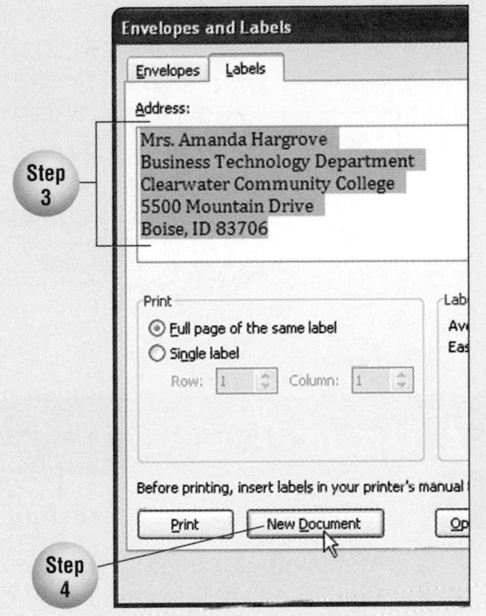

To create a sheet of mailing labels with a different name and address in each label, start with a blank document, display the Envelopes and Labels dialog box with the Labels tab selected, and then click the New Document button. The Envelopes and Labels dialog box is removed from the screen and the document displays with label forms. The insertion point is positioned in the first label form. Type the name and address in this label and then press the Tab key to move the insertion point to the next label. Pressing Shift + Tab moves the insertion point back to the preceding label.

Changing Label Options

Click the Options button at the Envelopes and Labels dialog box with the Labels tab selected, and the Label Options dialog box displays, as shown in Figure 10.8. At the Label Options dialog box, choose the type of printer, the desired label product, and the product number. This dialog box also displays information about the selected label such as type, height, width, and paper size. When you select a label, Word automatically determines label margins. If, however, you want to customize these default settings, click the Details button.

Figure 10.8 Label Options Dialog Box

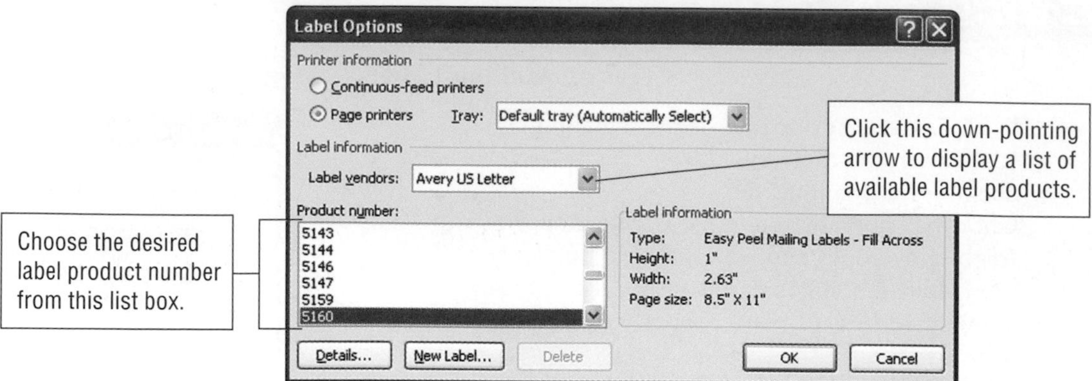

Exercise 4

Creating Customized Mailing Labels

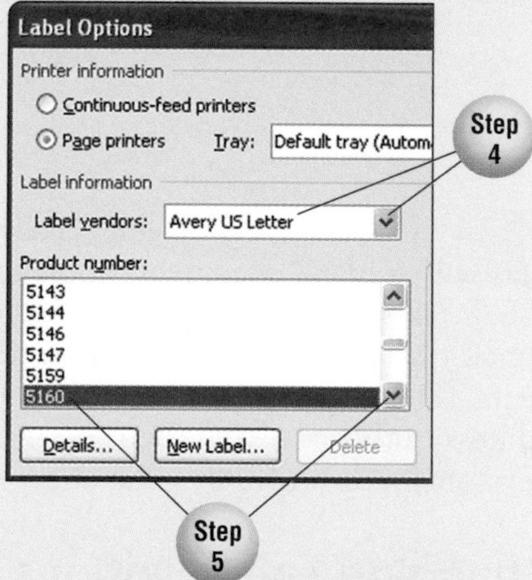

1. At a blank document, click the Mailings tab.
2. Click the Labels button in the Create group.
3. At the Envelopes and Labels dialog box with the Labels tab selected, click the Options button.
4. At the Label Options dialog box, click the down-pointing arrow at the right side of the *Label vendors* option and then click *Avery US Letter* at the drop-down list.
5. Scroll down the *Product number* list box and then click *5160*.
6. Click OK or press Enter.
7. At the Envelopes and Labels dialog box, click the New Document button.
8. At the document, type in the first label the first name and address shown in Figure 10.9.
9. Press the Tab key twice to move the insertion point to the next label and then type the second name and address shown in Figure 10.9.
10. Press the Tab key twice to move the insertion point to the next label and then type the third name and address shown in Figure 10.9.
11. Press the Tab key once (this moves the insertion point to the label below the label containing the name *DEBRA FOSTER*).
12. Type the fourth name and address shown in Figure 10.9. Continue in this manner until you have typed all the names and addresses.
13. Save the document and name it **C10Ex04**.
14. Print and then close **C10Ex04.docx**.
15. At the blank document, close the document without saving changes.

Figure 10.9 **Exercise 4**

DEBRA FOSTER 9054 N 23 ST BOISE ID 83709	CHARLES MOZONNE 12003 203 SE BOISE ID 83799	CASSANDRA REID 9045 VISTA AVE BOISE ID 83719
BEN AND JILL NYE 6013 FAIRVIEW AVE BOISE ID 83720	MARK CHAVEZ 805 ORCHARD ST BOISE ID 83720	KARL KNOWLES 23102 HARRISON BLVD BOISE ID 83722

Chapter Summary

- Move among open documents on your screen by clicking the button on the Taskbar representing the desired document or by clicking the View tab, clicking the Switch Windows button in the Window group, and then clicking the desired document name.
- View a portion of all open documents by clicking the View tab and then clicking the Arrange All button in the Window group.
- Use the Minimize, Maximize, and Restore buttons in the upper right corner of the window to reduce or increase the size of the active window.
- Divide a window into two panes by clicking the View tab and then clicking the Split button in the Window group. This enables you to view different parts of the same document at one time.
- View the contents of two open documents side by side by clicking the View tab and then clicking the View Side by Side button in the Window group.
- By default, synchronous scrolling is turned on when you view documents side by side. If you want to scroll through each document individually, click the Synchronous Scrolling button to turn off the feature.
- If you have changed the size of side-by-side document windows, click the Reset Window Position button to reset the document windows so they are displayed equally on the divided screen.
- Use buttons in the Zoom group in the View tab to increase or decrease the visual display of a document.
- In Print Layout view, you can remove the white space at the top and bottom of pages.
- Preview a document to display how the document will appear when printed. Use options and buttons in the Print Preview tab to customize the view and to format text in the document.
- Customize a print job with options at the Print dialog box. Use the *Page range* section to specify the amount of text you want to print; use the *Pages* option to identify a specific page, multiple pages, or a range of pages you want to print; and use the *Number of copies* option to print more than one copy of a document.
- At the Envelopes and Labels dialog box with the Envelope tab selected, you can use Word's envelope feature to create and print an envelope.
- If you open the Envelopes and Labels dialog box in a document that contains a name and address with each line ending with a press of the Enter key (not Shift + Enter), that information is automatically inserted in the *Delivery address* text box in the dialog box.
- Use Word's labels feature to print text on mailing labels, file labels, disk labels, or other types of labels.

Commands review

FEATURE	RIBBON TAB, GROUP	BUTTON, OPTION	KEYBOARD SHORTCUT
Arrange all documents	View, Window	Arrange All	
Minimize document			
Maximize document			
Restore			
Split window	View, Window	Split	
View documents side by side	View, Window	View Side by Side	
Synchronous scrolling	View, Window	Synchronous Scrolling	
Reset window position	View, Window	Reset Window Position	
Zoom dialog box	View, Zoom		
100% display	View, Zoom		
One Page view	View, Zoom	One Page	
Two Pages view	View, Zoom	Two Pages	
Page Width view	View, Zoom	Page Width	
Preview document		, Print, Print Preview	
Print dialog box		, Print	Ctrl + P
Envelopes and Labels dialog box with Envelopes tab selected	Mailings, Create		
Envelopes and Labels dialog box with Labels tab selected	Mailings, Create		

Reviewing key points

Completion: In the space provided at the right, indicate the correct term, command, or number.

1. To determine which documents are open, click the View tab and then click this button in the Window group. ____________________
2. Click this button in the Window group in the View tab to arrange all open documents so a portion of each document displays. ____________________
3. Click this button and the active document fills the editing window. ____________________
4. Click this button and the active document reduces to a button on the Taskbar. ____________________
5. The split bar is the small gray horizontal bar located above the up scroll arrow on this bar. ____________________
6. To display documents side by side, click this button in the Window group in the View tab. ____________________
7. If you are viewing documents side by side and decide you want to scroll in one and not the other, click this button in the Window group in the View tab. ____________________
8. When viewing documents side by side, click this button in the Window group in the View tab to reset document windows so they display equally on the divided screen. ____________________
9. This group in the View tab contains options for changing the display of the document to one page or two pages. ____________________
10. To remove white space on the document from the top and bottom of pages, double-click this icon. ____________________
11. Display a document in this view to determine how a document will appear when printed. ____________________
12. Type this in the *Pages* text box in the *Page range* section of the Print dialog box to print pages 3 through 6 of the open document. ____________________
13. Type this in the *Pages* text box in the *Page range* section of the Print dialog box to print page 4 and 9 of the open document. ____________________
14. The Envelopes button is located in the Create group in this tab. ____________________
15. If you open the Envelopes and Labels dialog box in a document containing a name and address, the name and address are automatically inserted in this section of the dialog box. ____________________

Applying your skills

Assessment 1 Arrange Documents

1. Open **Agreement01.docx**, **Document03.docx**, and **Report03.docx**.
2. Make **Document03.docx** the active document.
3. Make **Agreement01.docx** the active document.
4. Arrange all of the windows.
5. Make **Report03.docx** the active document and then minimize it.
6. Minimize the remaining documents.
7. Restore **Agreement01.docx**.
8. Restore **Document03.docx**.
9. Restore **Report03.docx**.
10. Maximize and then close **Agreement01.docx** and then maximize and close **Report03.docx**.
11. Maximize **Document03.docx** and then save the document and name it **C10A01**.
12. Open **ComputerHardware.docx**.
13. View the **C10A01.docx** document and **ComputerHardware.docx** document side by side.
14. Scroll through both documents simultaneously. Notice the formatting differences between the two documents. Change the font, font size, and paragraph shading in **C10A01.docx** so they match the formatting in **ComputerHardware.docx**.
15. Make **ComputerHardware.docx** active and then close it.
16. Save, print, and then close **C10A01.docx**.

Assessment 2 Create an Envelope

1. At a blank document, create an envelope with the text shown in Figure 10.10.
2. Save the envelope document with the name **C10A02**.
3. Print and then close **C10A02.docx**.

Figure 10.10 Assessment 2

SHAWN FINNEGAN
3078 SIXTH AVE
SALT LAKE CITY UT 84119

DR DAVID TOMOLLA
12039 CHAMBER ST
SALT LAKE CITY UT 84110

Assessment 3 Create Mailing Labels

1. Create mailing labels with the names and addresses shown in Figure 10.11. Use a label option of your choosing. (You may need to check with your instructor before choosing an option.)
2. Save the document with the name **C10A03**.
3. Print and then close **C10A03.docx**.
4. At the blank document, close the document without saving changes.

Figure 10.11 Assessment 3

LINDA GOULD 3210 CRANSTON ST PROVIDENCE RI 02903	ROBERT ALBRIGHT 10228 123 ST NE PROVIDENCE RI 02908	TRAVIS KANE 5532 S BROAD ST PROVIDENCE RI 02905
CHARLES WHITE 887 N 42 ST PROVIDENCE RI 02903	RAY PETROVICH 12309 45 AVE N PROVIDENCE RI 02904	BLAINE ISHAM 12110 141 ST SE PROVIDENCE RI 02907

Performance Assessments

UNIT 

Formatting and Managing Documents

ASSESSING PROFICIENCIES

In this unit, you have learned to format the pages of a document by changing page margins, orientation, and size. You have learned to improve the visual display of a document by inserting a cover page, page color, page border, drop cap, and watermark. You have learned to insert other elements such as special symbols and characters, page numbers, headers and footers, and the date and time. You have also learned how to hyphenate words, navigate within a document, insert hyperlinks, and maintain and print documents.

Note: Before beginning computer assessments, copy to your storage medium the Unit02PA folder from the CD that accompanies this textbook and then make Unit02PA the active folder.

Assessment 1 Format a Corporate Report

1. Open **Document21.docx** and save the document with the name **U02PA01**.
2. Move the insertion point to the beginning of the heading *Manufacturing* and then insert the file named **Document22.docx**.
3. Apply the Heading 1 style to the title and the Heading 2 style to the headings in the document.
4. Change the style set to *Formal*.
5. Apply the *Paper* theme.
6. Insert a continuous section break at the beginning of the first paragraph (the paragraph that begins *Terra Energy Corporation is a . . .*).
7. Format the text below the section break into two columns.
8. Balance the columns on the second page.
9. Create a drop cap with the first letter of the first word *Terra* that begins the first paragraph of text and make the drop cap two lines in height.
10. Manually hyphenate words in the document.
11. Insert page numbering that prints at the bottom center of each page.
12. Insert the Motion cover page and type the appropriate text in the text placeholders.
13. Save, print, and then close **U02PA01.docx**.

Assessment 2 Create and Format an Announcement

1. At a blank document, use the Click and Type feature to create the document shown in Figure U2.1.
2. Select the centered text and then change the font to 20-point Cambria and the font color to dark orange (*Orange, Accent 6, Darker 50%*).
3. Select the right-aligned text and then change the font to 14-point Cambria and the font color to dark orange (*Orange, Accent 6, Darker 50%*).
4. Change the vertical alignment of the text to *Center*.
5. Insert a page border and, if possible, change the color of the border to dark orange (*Orange, Accent 6, Darker 50%*).
6. Save the document with the name **U02PA02**.
7. Print **U02PA02.docx**
8. Change the page orientation to landscape.
9. Save, print, and then close **U02PA02.docx**.

Figure U2.1 Assessment 2

INVESTMENT SERVICES PANEL DISCUSSIONS

Fiduciary Responsibility in Retirement Plans

Best Practices in Technology

Redefining Investment Advice

Small Business Succession Planning

Sponsored by
Qualité Group®

Assessment 3 Format a Computer Security Report

1. Open **Report04.docx** and save the document with the name **U02PA03**.
2. Apply the following formatting:
   a. Apply the Heading 1 style to the two titles and the Heading 2 style to the five headings.
   b. Change the style set to *Modern*.
   c. Apply the *Concourse* theme.
   d. Insert the Conservative footer.
3. Move to the end of the paragraph in the *Types of Viruses* section, press the spacebar, and then type **(Pie Chart)**.
4. If necessary, turn on the display of bookmarks. (Do this at the Word Options dialog box with *Advanced* selected in the left panel.)
5. Move the insertion point to the end of the paragraph in the *Types of Viruses* section (following the *(Pie Chart)* text), press the spacebar, and then insert a bookmark named **Types**.

6. Move the insertion point to the end of the first paragraph in the *Methods of Virus Operation* section and then insert a bookmark named **Effects**.
7. Move the insertion point to the end of the second paragraph in the *Methods of Virus Operation* section and then insert a bookmark named **Infection**.
8. Navigate in the document using the bookmarks.
9. Move the insertion point to the end of the first paragraph in the *SECTION 4: HARDWARE AND SOFTWARE SECURITY RISKS* section and then insert a hyperlink to the *Effects* bookmark.
10. Select the text *(Pie Chart)* that you inserted at the end of the paragraph in the *Types of Viruses* section and then insert a hyperlink to the Excel file named **Viruses.xlsx**, located in the Unit02 folder on your storage medium.
11. Click the (Pie Chart) hyperlink and then print the Excel worksheet that displays by clicking the Quick Print button on the Quick Access toolbar. (If the toolbar does not contain the Quick Print button, click the Office button, point to *Print*, and then click *Quick Print*.) Close the Excel program.
12. Insert the DRAFT1 watermark in the document.
13. Save, print, and then close **U02PA03.docx**.

Assessment 4 Create a Business Letter using a Template

1. Open the *Equity Letter* template at the New Document dialog box and then insert the following information in the specified fields:

[Pick the date]	(Insert today's date)
Name	**Click in the name that displays below the date, select the name, and then type your first and last names.**
Sender company name	**Mobile Bay Products**
Sender company address	**700 Michigan Avenue, Mobile, AL 36606**
Recipient name	**Dr. Erin Sutton**
Recipient address	**5110 Third Avenue, Prichard, AL 36610**
Salutation	**Dear Dr Sutton.**

2. Delete the three paragraphs of text in the body of the letter and then insert **Letter04.docx.** (Press the Delete key once to remove the blank space above the complimentary close.)
3. Insert the following information in the specified fields:

Closing	**Sincerely,**
Sender title	**President**

4. Save the document with the name **U02PA04**.
5. Print and then close **U02PA04.docx**.

Assessment 5 Format an Employment Document

1. Open **Document16.docx** and save the document with the name **U02PA05**.
2. Change the top, left, and right margins to 1.25 inches.
3. Apply the Heading 1 style to the title *PROBATIONERY PERIODS* and the Heading 2 style to the heading *Types of Appointments*.
4. Change the style set to *Simple*.
5. Insert a page break at the beginning of the text *Reappointment*.
6. Move the insertion point to the end of the document and then insert the current date and time.
7. Insert the Alphabet header and type **Employee Handbook** for the document title.
8. Insert the Alphabet footer and type **Probationary Periods** in the *[Type text]* placeholder.
9. Save, print, and then close **U02PA05.docx**.

Assessment 6 Create an Envelope

1. At a blank document, create an envelope with the text shown in Figure U2.2.
2. Save the envelope document with the name **U02PA06**.
3. Print and then close **U02PA06.docx**.

Figure U2.2 Assessment 6

Dr. Erin Sutton
5110 Third Avenue
Prichard, AL 36610

Mrs. Violet Kohlberg
12032 145th Street East
Mobile, AL 36607

Assessment 7 Create Mailing Labels

1. Create mailing labels with the name and address for Dr. Erin Sutton shown in Figure U2.2, using a label vendor and product of your choosing.
2. Save the document with the name **U02PA07**.
3. Print and then close **U02PA07.docx**.

CREATING ORIGINAL DOCUMENTS

The activities in Assessments 8, 9, and 10 give you the opportunity to practice your writing skills as well as demonstrate your mastery of some of the important Word features presented in this unit. When composing the documents, use correct grammar, precise word choices, and clear sentence construction.

Assessment 8 Format a Computer Guidelines Company Document

Situation: You work in the Technology Support Department at Mobile Bay Products, and your supervisor has asked you to format a document providing computer use guidelines. Open **ComputerGuidelines.docx**, save the document with the name **U02PA08**, and then format it by applying or inserting at least the following elements: a style set; a heading style; a header, footer, and/or page numbers; and a cover page. Save, print, and then close **U02PA08.docx**. Use one of the Word letter templates and write a letter to your instructor describing how you formatted the U02PA08.docx document, including the reasons you choose specific formatting. Save the completed letter with the name **U02PA08Letter**. Print and then close **U02PA08Letter.docx**.

Assessment 9 Create a Calendar using a Calendar Template

Situation: You are responsible for monitoring employee vacation days and decide to use a Word calendar template to record the information. Look for calendar templates offered at the Microsoft Office Online site (accessed at the New Document dialog box). Download a calendar for the next year that allows you to enter information. In the appropriate calendar months (use months for the next year) enter the following data on employee vacation days:

- Mariah Brown, first two weeks of June
- Jaden Holland, second week of July
- Maddie O'Hara, last two weeks of July
- Evan Noland, first week of August

Save the completed calendar document with the name **U02PA09**. Print only those pages containing the months of June, July, and August and then close **U02PA09.docx**.

Assessment 10 Research and Prepare a Netiquette Report

Situation: Your supervisor at Mobile Bay Products wants to provide employees with a document that describes *netiquette* ("Internet etiquette" rules). She has asked you to research the topic and then create a document that will be distributed to employees. Use the Internet (or any other resource available to you) and search for information on "rules of netiquette." Locate at least two sources that provide information on netiquette. Using the information you locate, create a document that describes netiquette rules and apply formatting to enhance the document's visual appeal. Save the document with the name **U02PA10**. Print and then close **U02PA10.docx**.

Unit 3

Enhancing Documents

- Inserting Images
- Inserting Shapes and WordArt
- Creating Tables
- Enhancing Tables
- Creating Charts
- Unit 3 Performance Assessments

Signature Microsoft® Word 2007

Microsoft Certified Application Specialist Skills—Unit 3

Reference No.	Skill	Pages
3	**Working with Visual Content**	
3.1	Insert illustrations	
3.1.1	SmartArt graphics	291-298
3.1.2	Pictures from files and clip art	279-289
3.1.3	Shapes	305-311
3.2	Format illustrations	
3.2.1	Format text wrapping	280, 282-284, 287
3.2.2	Format by sizing, cropping, scaling, and rotating	281-284, 288
3.2.3	Apply picture styles	280-281, 284, 289
3.2.4	Set contrast, brightness, and coloration	280, 284
3.2.5	Add text to SmartArt graphics and shapes	292-293, 297
3.2.6	Compress pictures	280, 285
3.3	Format text graphically	
3.3.1	Insert and modify WordArt	318-323
3.3.2	Insert pull quotes	289-291
3.4	Insert and modify text boxes	
3.4.1	Insert text boxes	312-316
3.4.2	Format text boxes	312-316
3.4.3	Link text boxes	313-316
4	**Organizing Content**	
4.2	Use tables and lists to organize content	
4.2.1	Create tables and lists	331-369
4.2.2	Sort content	370-371
4.3	Modify tables	
4.3.1	Apply table styles to tables	339-340
4.3.2	Modify table properties and options	341-356
4.3.3	Merge and split table cells	356-357
4.3.4	Perform calculations in tables	371-375
4.3.5	Change the position and direction of cell contents	363

Chapter 11

CHAPTER11

Inserting Images

Tutorial 11.1
Adding Images and Shapes
Tutorial 11.2
Inserting and Formatting Images

Performance Objectives

Upon successful completion of Chapter 11, you will be able to:

- Insert, format, and customize pictures
- Insert, format, and customize clip art images
- Insert and customize pull quotes
- Create and format SmartArt diagrams
- Create and format SmartArt organizational charts

Inserting images and pull quotes into your documents can further increase their visual appeal and attract readers' attention. In this chapter, you will learn to insert these elements and display data in a more visual way by creating a SmartArt graphic. The SmartArt feature provides a number of predesigned diagrams and organizational charts.

Note: Before beginning computer exercises for this chapter, copy to your storage medium the Chapter11 folder from the CD that accompanies this textbook and then make Chapter11 the active folder.

Inserting an Image

You can insert a picture or clip art image into a Word document by using buttons in the Illustrations group in the Insert tab, shown in Figure 11.1. Click the Picture button to display the Insert Picture dialog box where you can specify the desired picture file you want to insert or click the Clip Art button to display the Clip Art task pane where you can choose from a variety of available images.

Figure 11.1 Insert Tab Illustrations Group Buttons

Use buttons in this group in the Insert tab to insert images in a document.

Inserting a Picture

QUICK STEPS

Insert Picture
1. Click Insert tab.
2. Click Picture button.
3. Navigate to desired folder.
4. Double-click desired picture in Insert Picture dialog box.

To insert a picture in a document, click the Insert tab and then click the Picture button in the Illustrations group. At the Insert Picture dialog box, navigate to the folder that contains the picture you want to insert and then double-click the picture. After you have inserted the picture, you can use buttons in the Picture Tools Format tab to format and customize it. In addition to inserting a picture you have saved to your storage medium, you can insert a picture from a Web page. To do this, open the Web page, open the document you want to insert the picture into, and then drag the picture from the Web page to the document. If the picture is linked, the link displays in your document rather than the image.

Customizing and Formatting an Image

When you insert an image in a document, the image is selected and the Picture Tools Format tab, shown in Figure 11.2, becomes active. Use buttons in this tab to format the image. With buttons in the Adjust group, you can recolor the picture or clip art image and change its brightness and contrast. You can reset the picture or clip art back to its original color or change to a different image. You can also compress the size of the image file with the Compress Pictures button.

With buttons in the Picture Styles group, you can apply a predesigned style to your image, change the image border, or apply other effects to the image. With options in the Arrange group, you can position the image on the page, specify how text will wrap around it, align the image with other elements in the document, and rotate the image. With the Crop button in the Size group, you can remove any unnecessary parts of the image and specify the image size with the Shape Height and Shape Width measurement boxes.

Figure 11.2 Picture Tools Format Tab

Exercise 1

Inserting a Picture

1. At a blank document, click the Insert tab and then click the Picture button in the Illustrations group.
2. At the Insert Picture dialog box, navigate to the Chapter11 folder on your storage medium and then double-click *Olympics.jpg*.

3. Click the Picture Shape button in the Picture Styles group and then click the second option from the left in the third row in the *Flowchart* section (*Flowchart Magnetic Disk*).
4. Click the Picture Effects button in the Picture Styles group, point to *Bevel*, and then click the second option from the left in the first row of the *Bevel* section (*Relaxed Inset*).

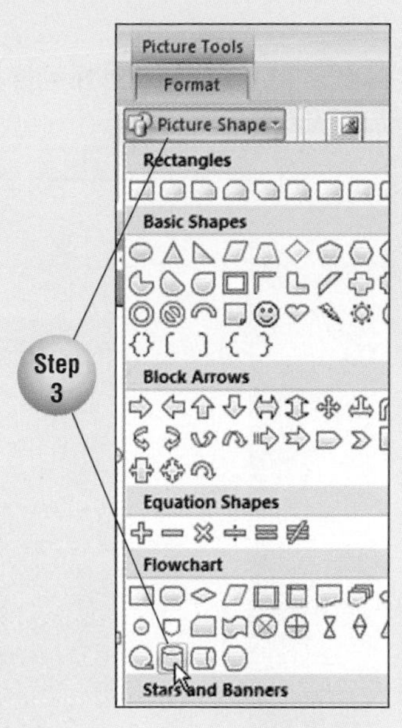

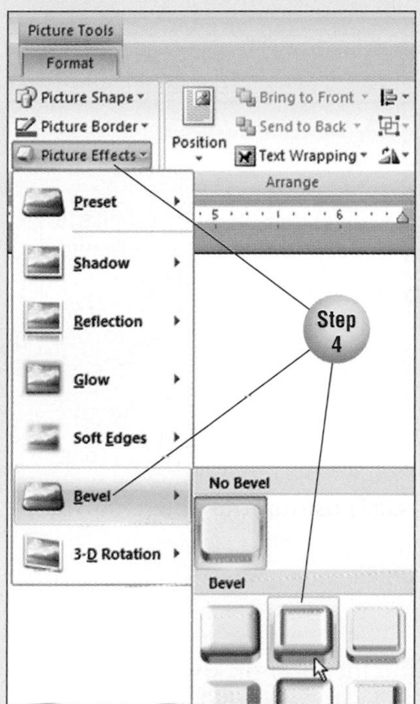

5. Click the Picture Effects button in the Picture Styles group, point to *Glow*, and then click the first option from the left in the bottom row in the *Glow Variations* section (*Accent color 1, 18 pt glow*).
6. Click outside the picture to deselect it.
7. Save the document with the name **C11Ex01**.
8. Print and then close **C11Ex01.docx**.

Sizing an Image

You can change the size of an image with the Shape Height and Shape Width measurement boxes in the Size group in the Picture Tools Format tab or with the sizing handles that display around a selected image, as shown in Figure 11.3. To increase or decrease an image's size with a sizing handle, position the mouse pointer on a handle until the pointer turns into a double-headed arrow and then hold down the left mouse button. Drag the sizing handle in to decrease or out to increase the size of the image and then release the mouse button. Use the middle sizing handles at the left or right side of the image to make the image wider or thinner. Use the middle sizing handles at the top or bottom of the image to make the image taller or shorter. Use the sizing handles at the corners of the image to change both the width and height at the same time.

Figure 11.3 Selected Image

Drag the rotation handle to rotate the image.

Use the sizing handles to increase or decrease the size of the image.

Moving an Image

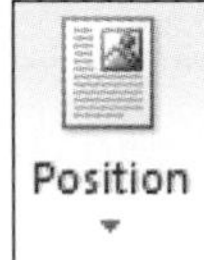

Move an image to a specific location on the page with options from the Position button drop-down gallery. The Position button is located in the Arrange group in the Picture Tools Format tab. When you choose an option at the Position button drop-down gallery, the image is moved to the specified location on the page and the text wraps around the image.

You can also move an image by dragging it to the desired location. Before dragging an image, however, you must first choose how the text will wrap around it by clicking the Text Wrapping button in the Arrange group and then clicking the desired wrapping style at the drop-down list. After choosing a wrapping style, move the image by positioning the mouse pointer on the image border until the arrow pointer turns into a four-headed arrow. Hold down the left mouse button, drag the image to the desired position, and then release the mouse button.

A third way to move an image is with the arrow keys on the keyboard. To move the image in small increments (called *nudging*), hold down the Ctrl key while pressing an arrow key. To help precisely position an image, consider turning on gridlines. Do this by clicking the Align button in the Arrange group in the Picture Tools Format tab and then clicking Show Gridlines.

To rotate an image, use the rotation handle (see Figure 11.3) or the Rotate button in the Arrange group. To use the rotation handle, position the mouse pointer on the round, green rotation handle until the pointer displays as a circular arrow. Hold down the left mouse button, drag in the desired direction, and then release the mouse button.

Exercise 2

Inserting and Customizing a Picture

1. At a blank document, press the Enter key two times and then type the centered text shown in Figure 11.4.
2. Select the text and then change the font to 18-point Franklin Gothic Heavy and the text color to dark blue.
3. Press Ctrl + Home to move the insertion point to the beginning of the document.
4. Insert a picture by completing the following steps:
   a. Click the Insert tab.
   b. Click the Picture button in the Illustrations group.
   c. At the Insert Picture dialog box, navigate to your Chapter11 folder.
   d. Double-click *Mountain.jpg* in the list box.
5. Crop the picture by completing the following steps:
   a. Click the Crop button in the Size group.
   b. Position the mouse pointer on the bottom, middle crop handle (which displays as a short black line) until the pointer turns into the crop tool (which displays as a small, black T).
   c. Hold down the left mouse button, drag up to just below the mountain as shown at the right, and then release the mouse button.
   d. Click the Crop button in the Size group to turn off the feature.

6. Increase the size of the picture by selecting the current measurement in the Shape Width measurement box, typing **6**, and then pressing Enter.
7. Position the picture by clicking the Position button in the Arrange group and then clicking the middle option in the top row in the *With Text Wrapping* section (*Position in Top Center with Square Text Wrapping*).

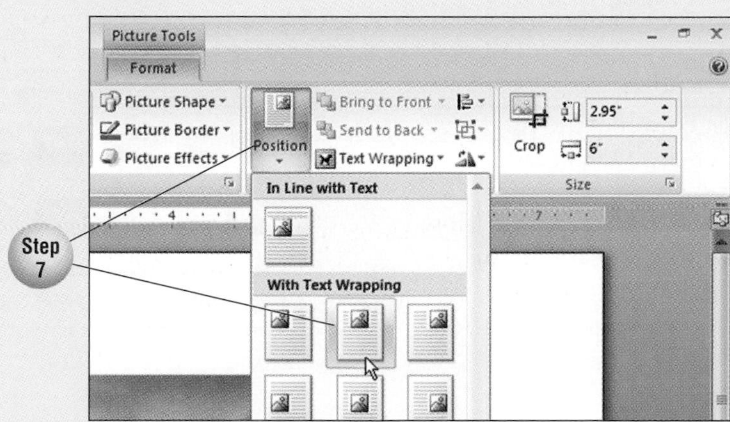

8. Move the picture behind the text by clicking the Text Wrapping button in the Arrange group and then clicking *Behind Text* at the drop-down list.
9. Rotate the image by clicking the Rotate button in the Arrange group and then clicking *Flip Horizontal* at the drop-down list.

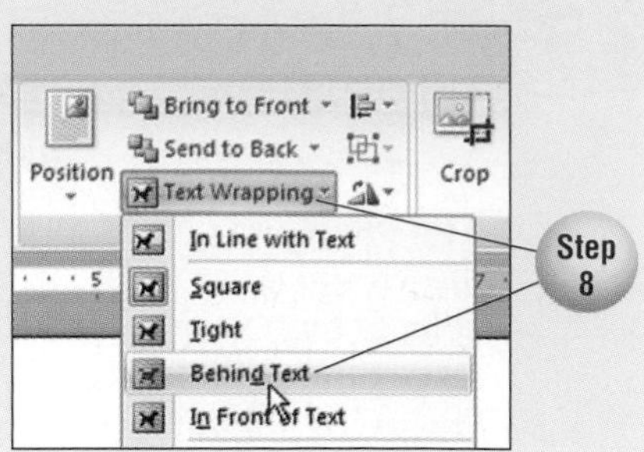

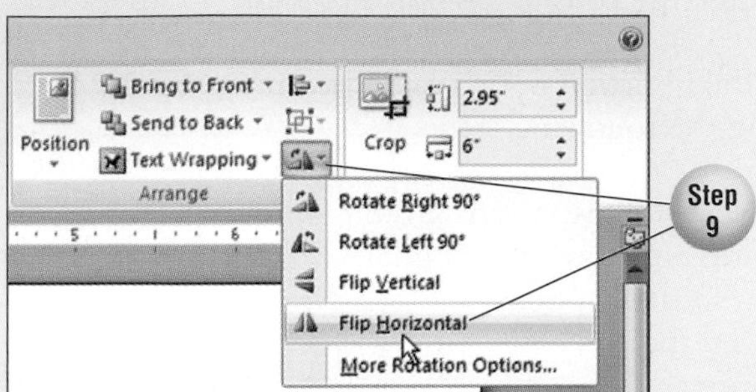

10. Change the picture color by clicking the Recolor button in the Adjust group and then clicking the second option from the left in the *Light Variations* section (*Accent color 1 Light*).
11. After looking at the coloring, return the image to the original color by clicking the Recolor button in the Adjust group and then clicking the *No Recolor* option.
12. Click the Brightness button in the Adjust group and then click *+10%* at the drop-down gallery.

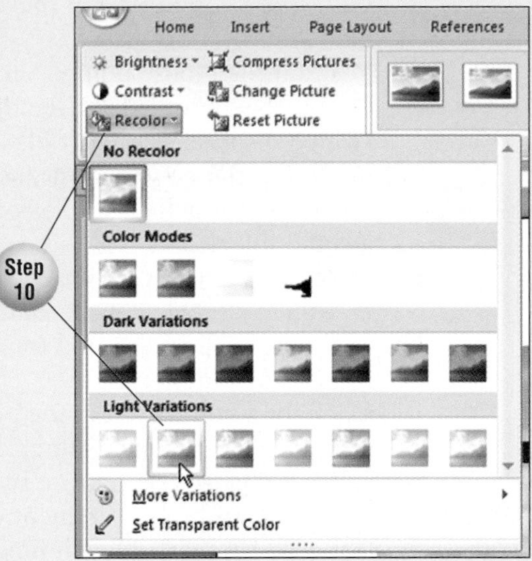

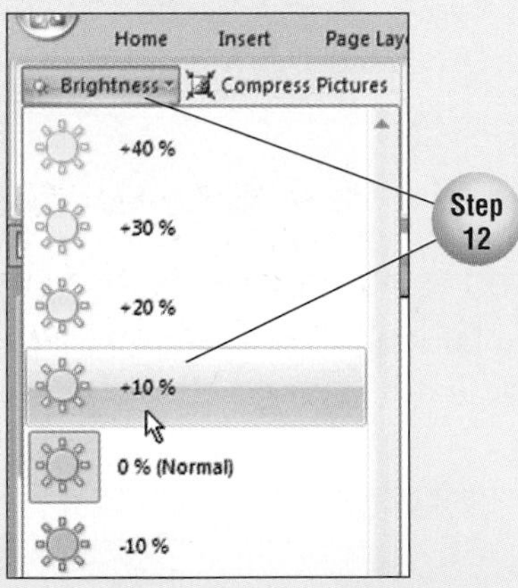

13. Click the Contrast button in the Adjust group and then click *-10%* at the drop-down gallery.
14. Apply a picture style by clicking the More button at the right side of the picture styles and then clicking *Soft Edge Rectangle* (first image from the left in the second row).

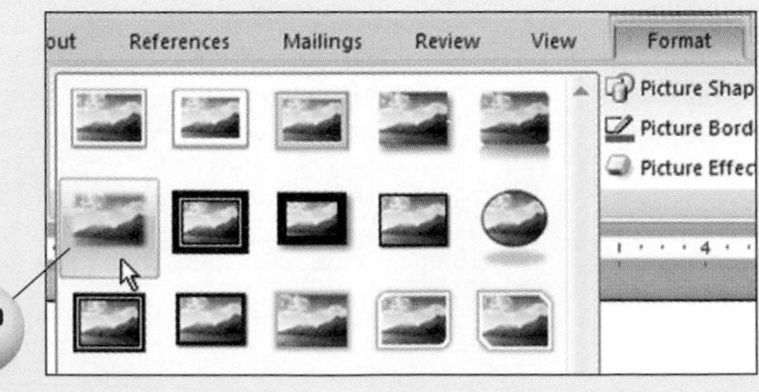

15. Compress the picture by completing the following steps:
    a. Click the Compress Pictures button in the Adjust group.
    b. At the Compress Pictures dialog box, click the *Apply to selected pictures only* check box to insert a check mark.
    c. Click OK.
16. Click outside the picture to deselect it.
17. Save the document with the name **C11Ex02**.
18. Print and then close **C11Ex02.docx**.

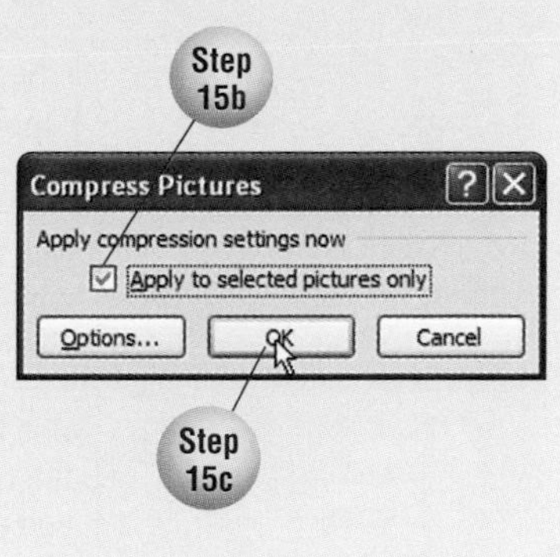

Figure 11.4 Exercise 2

BLUE MOUNTAIN SPA AND RESORT

Special Summer Rates

Complimentary Breakfast Buffet

June 1 through August 31

Inserting a Clip Art Image

Microsoft Office includes a gallery of media images you can insert in a document, including clip art, photographs, and movie images, as well as sound clips. To insert an image in a Word document, click the Insert tab and then click the Clip Art button in the Illustrations group. This displays the Clip Art task pane at the right side of the screen, as shown in Figure 11.5.

Insert Clip Art Image

1. Click Insert tab.
2. Click Clip Art button.
3. Type search word or topic.
4. Press Enter.
5. Click desired image.

Figure 11.5 Clip Art Task Pane

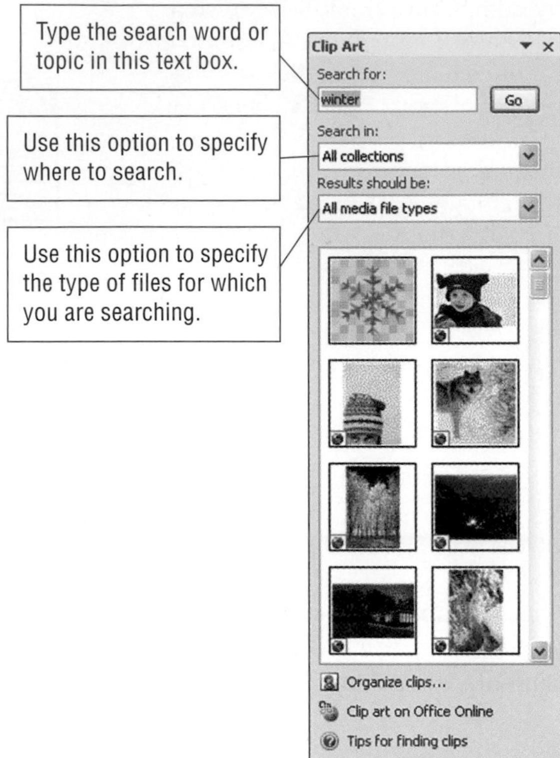

To view all picture, sound, and motion files available in the gallery, make sure the *Search for* text box in the Clip Art task pane does not contain any text and then click the Go button. Scroll through the images that display until you find one you want to use and then click the image to insert it in the document. Use buttons in the Picture Tools Format tab (see Figure 11.2) to format and customize the clip art image.

If you are searching for a specific type of image, click in the *Search for* text box, type a category, and then click the Go button. For example, if you want to find images related to business, click in the *Search for* text box, type **business**, and then click the Go button. Clip art images related to business display in the viewing area of the task pane. If you are connected to the Internet, Word will search for images matching the word or topic at the Microsoft Office Online Web site. You can drag a clip art image from the Clip Art task pane to your document.

Exercise 3

Inserting and Formatting a Clip Art Image

1. Open **Notice03.docx** and save the document with the name **C11Ex03**.
2. Select the text and then change the font to 20-point Harrington bold and the text color to blue.
3. Press Ctrl + Home to move the insertion point to the beginning of the document.

4. Insert a clip art image by completing the following steps:
    a. Click the Insert tab and then click the Clip Art button in the Illustrations group.
    b. At the Clip Art task pane, select any text that displays in the *Search for* text box, type **winter**, and then press Enter.
    c. Click the computer image in the list box as shown at the right.
    d. Close the Clip Art task pane by clicking the Close button (the button marked with an X) located in the upper right corner of the task pane.
5. Click the Text Wrapping button in the Arrange group and then click *Square* at the drop-down list.
6. Click in the Shape Height measurement box, type 2.3, and then press Enter.
7. Nudge the image down slightly by holding down the Ctrl key and pressing the down arrow key until the top of the image aligns with the top of the first line of text.
8. Click outside the image to deselect it.
9. Save, print, and then close **C11Ex03.docx**.

Unless the Clip Art task pane default setting has been customized, the task pane displays all media images and sound clips found in all available locations. You can narrow the search for clip art images to specific locations or to specific images. To do this, change the *Search in* option at the Clip Art task pane from the default setting *All collections* to *My Collections*, *Office Collections*, or *Web Collections*. The *Results should be* option has a default setting of *Selected media file types*. Click the down-pointing arrow at the right side of this option to display media types. To search for a specific media type, remove the check mark before all options at the drop-down list except for the desired type. For example, if you are searching only for photograph images, remove the check mark before Clip Art, Movies, and Sound.

Exercise 4A

Inserting an Image

1. Open **Report03.docx** and save the document with the name **C11Ex04**.
2. Apply the Heading 1 style to the two titles and apply the Heading 2 style to the six headings in the document.
3. Change the style set to *Modern*. (*Hint: Do this with the Change Styles button in the Styles group in the Home tab.*)
4. Insert a clip art image by completing the following steps:
    a. Move the insertion point so it is positioned at the beginning of the first paragraph of text (the sentence that begins *Like uncharted wilderness . . .*).
    b. Click the Insert tab.

c. Click the Clip Art button in the Illustrations group.
d. At the Clip Art task pane, click the down-pointing arrow at the right side of the *Results should be* option box and then click in the *Photographs*, *Movies*, and *Sounds* check boxes to remove the check marks. (The *Clip Art* check box should be the only one with a check mark.)

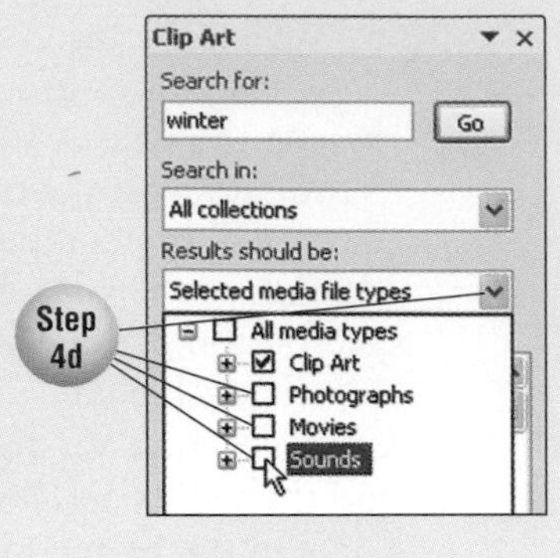

e. Select any text that displays in the *Search for* text box, type **computer**, and then press Enter.
f. Click the computer image in the list box as shown at the right.

g. Click the down-pointing arrow at the right side of the *Results should be* option box and then click in the *All media types* check box to insert a check mark.
h. Close the Clip Art task pane by clicking the Close button (the button marked with an X) located in the upper right corner of the task pane.

5. Crop the clip art image by completing the following steps:
   a. Click the Crop button in the Size group.
   b. Position the mouse pointer on the top, middle crop handle (which displays as a short black line) until the pointer turns into the crop tool.
   c. Hold down the left mouse button, drag down to just above the top of the computer as shown at the right, and then release the mouse button.
   d. Click the Crop button in the Size group to turn off the feature.

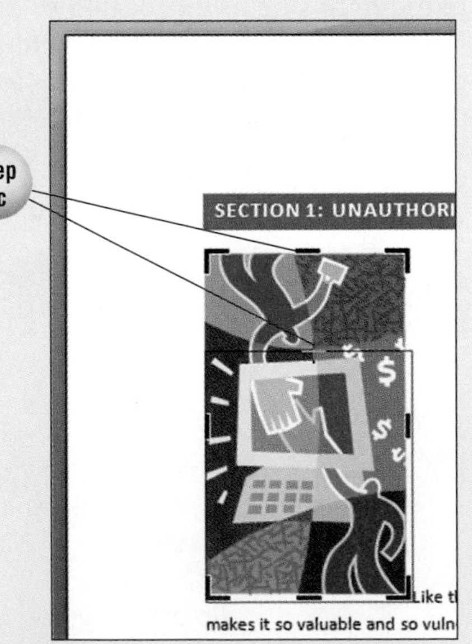

6. Decrease the size of the picture by clicking in the Shape Height measurement box, typing 1.5, and then pressing Enter.
7. Change the text wrapping by clicking the Text Wrapping button in the Arrange group and then clicking *Square* at the drop-down list.
8. Rotate the image by clicking the Rotate button in the Arrange group and then clicking *Flip Horizontal* at the drop-down list.
9. Change the picture color by clicking the Recolor button in the Adjust group and then clicking the second option from the left in the *Light Variations* section (*Accent color 1 Light*).

10. Click the Picture Effects button in the Picture Styles group, point to *Shadow*, and then click the *Offset Right* option (first option from the left in the second row in the *Outer* section).
11. Click outside the clip art image to deselect it.
12. Save **C11Ex04.docx**.

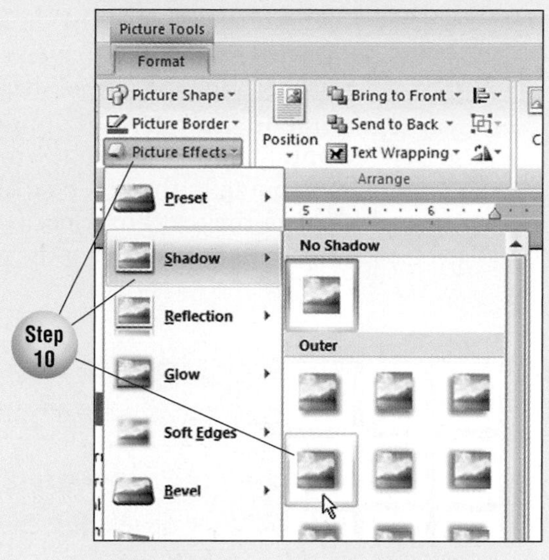

Inserting and Customizing a Pull Quote

QUICK STEPS

Inserting Pull Quote
1. Click Insert tab.
2. Click Text Box button.
3. Click desired pull quote style at drop-down list.

Use a pull quote in a document such as an article to attract readers' attention. A pull quote is a quote that is "pulled" from an article, enlarged, and displayed in a strategic or attractive location on the page. Some advantages to using pull quotes are that they reinforce important concepts, summarize your message, and break up blocks of text to make them easier to read. You can insert a pull quote in a document by using one of the predesigned text boxes that Word provides. Display the available pull quote text boxes by clicking the Insert tab and then clicking the Text Box button in the Text group. Click the desired pull quote text box from the drop-down list, and the text box is inserted in the document. Type the quote you have selected inside the text box and then format the text and/or customize the text box. Use buttons in the Text Box Tools Format tab, shown in Figure 11.6, to format and customize the built-in text box.

Figure 11.6 Text Box Tools Format Tab

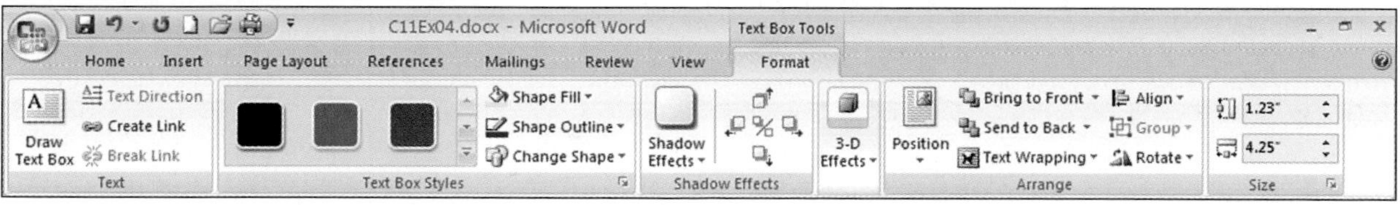

With options in the Text group in the Text Box Tools Format tab, you can draw a text box, change the direction of text in a text box, and link text boxes. Apply predesigned styles to a text box with options in the Text Box Styles group. You can also change the shape, shape fill, and shape outline. Add and customize shadows and 3-D effects with options in the Shadow Effects and 3-D Effects groups. Use options in the Arrange group to position the text box on the page, specify text wrapping in the text box, align the text box with other objects in the document, and rotate the text box. Specify the image size with the Shape Height and Shape Width measurement boxes in the Size group.

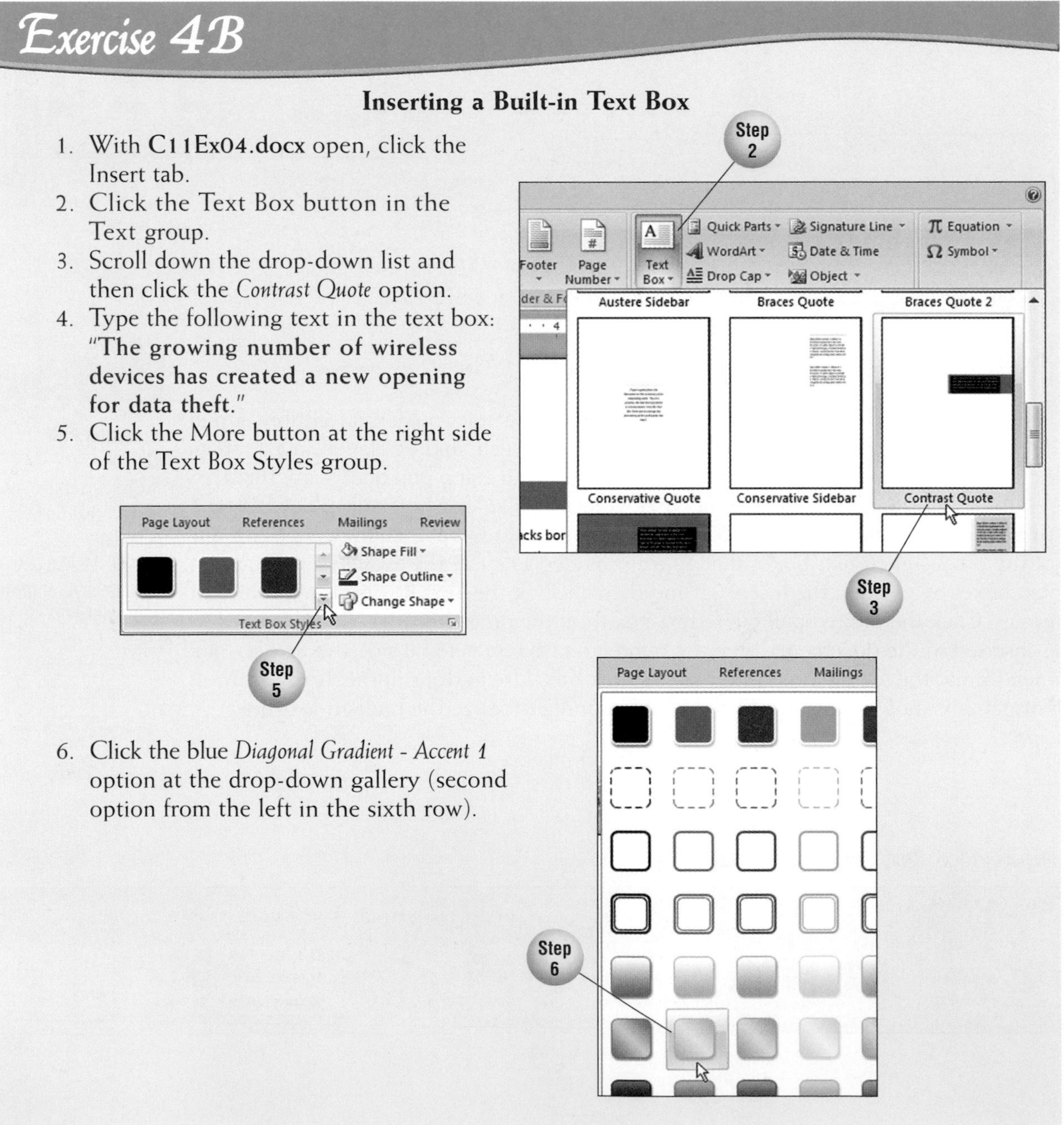

Exercise 4B

Inserting a Built-in Text Box

1. With **C11Ex04.docx** open, click the Insert tab.
2. Click the Text Box button in the Text group.
3. Scroll down the drop-down list and then click the *Contrast Quote* option.
4. Type the following text in the text box: "**The growing number of wireless devices has created a new opening for data theft.**"
5. Click the More button at the right side of the Text Box Styles group.
6. Click the blue *Diagonal Gradient - Accent 1* option at the drop-down gallery (second option from the left in the sixth row).

7. Click the Shadow Effects button in the Shadow Effects group and then click the *Shadow Style 5* option in the *Drop Shadow* section (first option from the left in the second row).

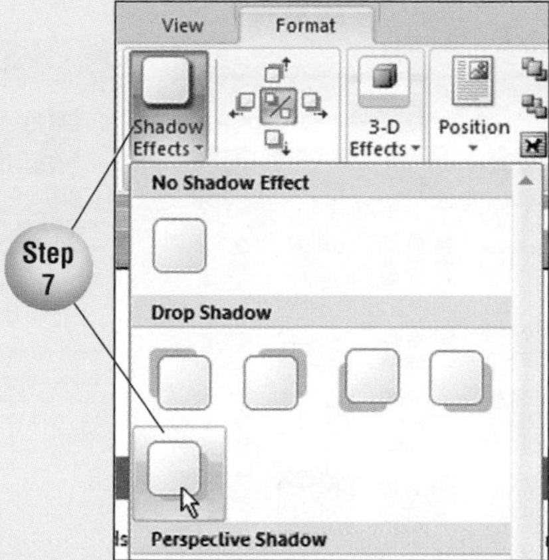

8. Position the mouse pointer on the border of the selected text box until the pointer turns into a four-headed arrow and then drag the text box so it is positioned as shown below.

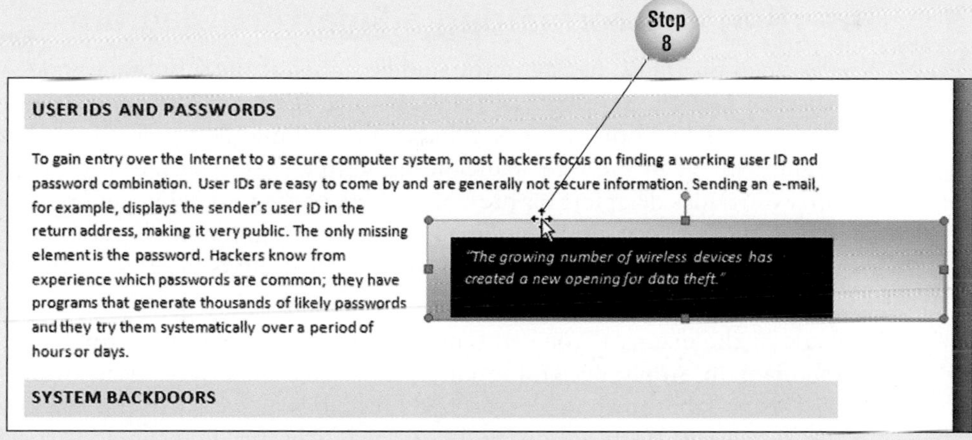

9. Save, print, and then close **C11Ex04.docx**.

Creating SmartArt

With Word's SmartArt feature you can insert diagrams and organizational charts in a document. SmartArt offers a variety of predesigned diagrams and organizational charts that are available at the Choose a SmartArt Graphic dialog box, shown in Figure 11.7. At this dialog box, *All* is selected in the left panel, and all available predesigned diagrams display in the middle panel.

Figure 11.7 Choose a SmartArt Graphic Dialog Box

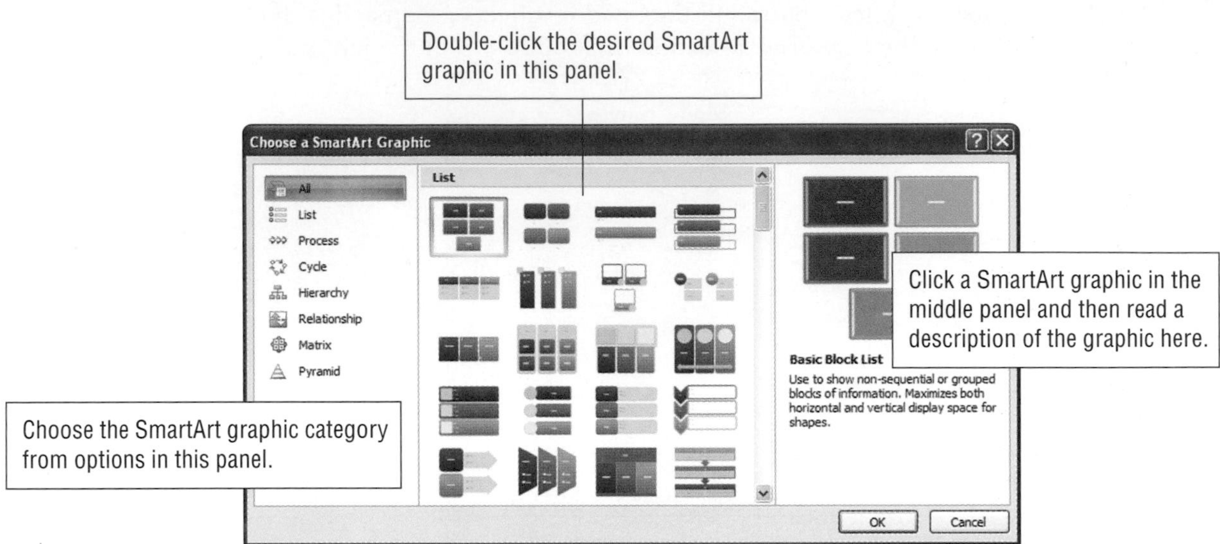

Insert a SmartArt Diagram
1. Click Insert tab.
2. Click SmartArt button.
3. Double-click desired diagram.

Inserting and Formatting a SmartArt Diagram

Predesigned diagrams display in the middle panel of the Choose a SmartArt Graphic dialog box. Use the scroll bar at the right side of the middle panel to scroll down the list of diagram choices. Click a diagram in the middle panel, and the name of the diagram displays in the right panel along with a description of the diagram type. SmartArt includes diagrams for presenting a list of data; showing data processes, cycles, and relationships; and presenting data in a matrix or pyramid. Double-click a diagram in the middle panel of the dialog box and the diagram is inserted in the document.

When the diagram is inserted in the document, a text pane may display at the left side of the diagram. You can type text in the diagram in the text pane or directly in the diagram. Apply design formatting to a diagram with options in the SmartArt Tools Design tab, shown in Figure 11.8. This tab is active when the diagram is inserted in the document. With options and buttons in this tab, you can add objects, change the diagram layout, apply a style to the diagram, and reset the diagram back to the original formatting.

Figure 11.8 SmartArt Tools Design Tab

Exercise 5A

Inserting and Formatting a Diagram

1. At a blank document, insert the diagram shown in Figure 11.9 by completing the following steps:
   a. Click the Insert tab.
   b. Click the SmartArt button in the Illustrations group.
   c. At the Choose a SmartArt Graphic dialog box, click *Process* in the left panel and then double-click the *Alternating Flow* diagram (last option in the top row).
   d. If a *Type your text here* text pane does not display at the left side of the diagram, click the Text Pane button in the Create Graphic group to display the pane.
   e. With the insertion point positioned after the top bullet in the *Type your text here* text pane, type **Design**.
   f. Click *[Text]* that displays below *Design* and then type **Mock-up**.
   g. Continue clicking occurrences of *[Text]* and typing text so the text pane displays as shown at the right.
   h. Close the text pane by clicking the Close button (marked with an X) that displays in the upper right corner of the pane. (You can also click the Text Pane button in the Create Graphic group.)
   i. Click inside the diagram border but outside any shape. (This deselects any shapes but keeps the diagram selected.)

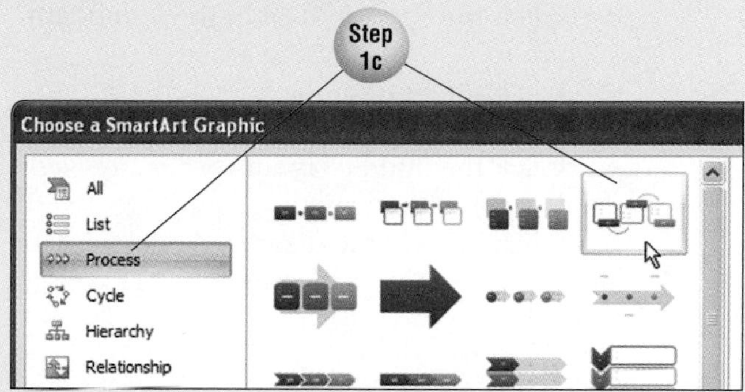

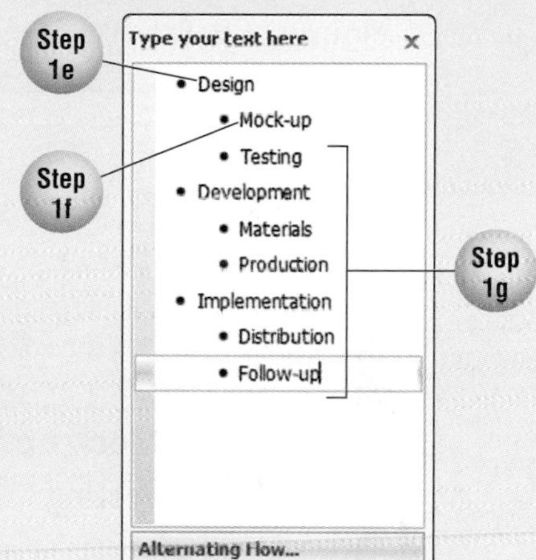

2. Change the diagram colors by clicking the Change Colors button in the SmartArt Styles group and then clicking the first option in the *Colorful* section (*Colorful - Accent Colors*).
3. Apply a style by clicking the More button that displays at the right side of the SmartArt Styles group and then clicking the second option from the left in the top row of the *3-D* section (*Inset*).

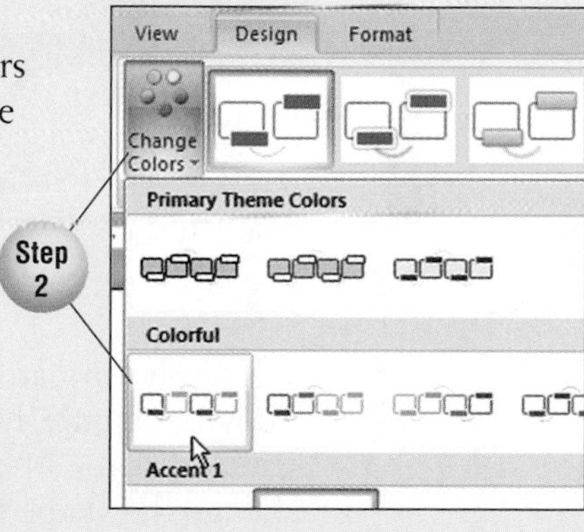

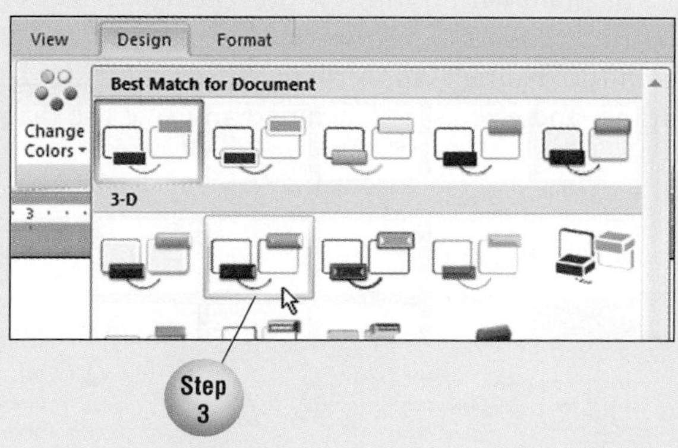

4. Copy the diagram and then change the layout by completing the following steps:
   a. Click the Home tab.
   b. Click the Copy button in the Clipboard group.
   c. Press Ctrl + End, press the Enter key once, and then press Ctrl + Enter to insert a page break.
   d. Click the Paste button in the Clipboard group.
   e. Click the bottom diagram.
   f. Click the SmartArt Tools Design tab.
   g. Click the middle layout (*Continuous Block Process*) in the Layouts group.
   h. Click outside the diagram to deselect it.
5. Save the document and name it **C11Ex05**.

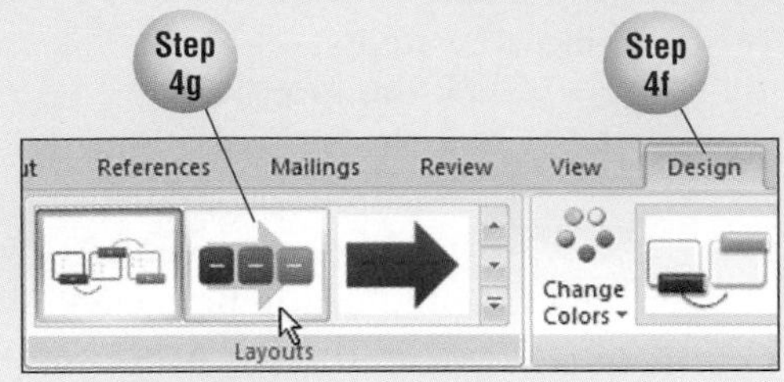

Figure 11.9 Exercise 5A

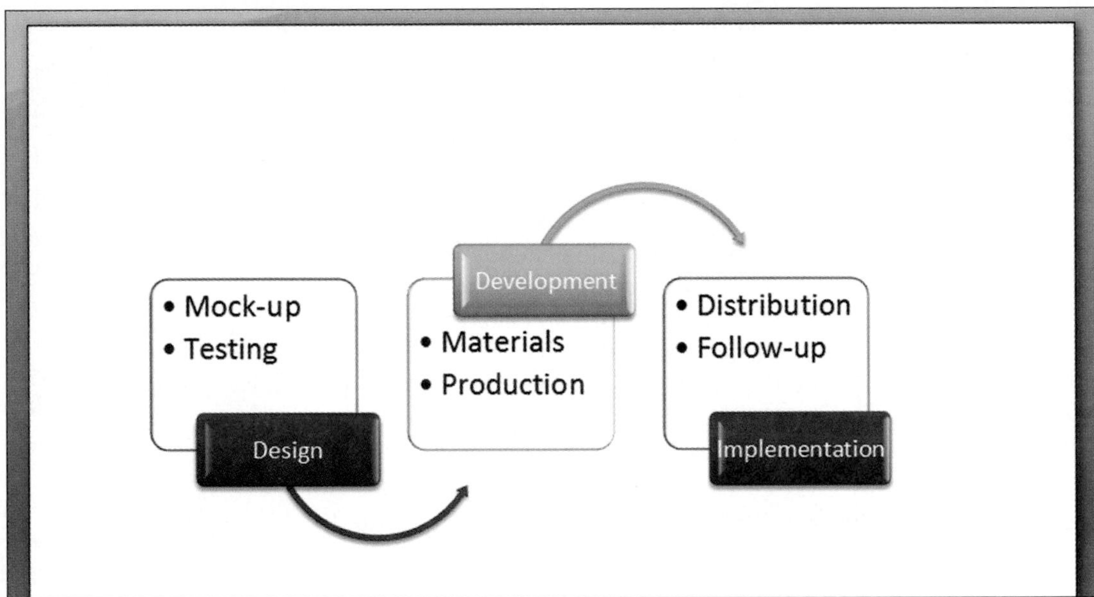

Apply formatting to a diagram with options in the SmartArt Tools Format tab, shown in Figure 11.10. With options and buttons in this tab, you can change the size and shape of objects in the diagram; apply shape styles and WordArt styles; change the shape fill, outline, and effects; and arrange and size the diagram.

Figure 11.10 SmartArt Tools Format Tab

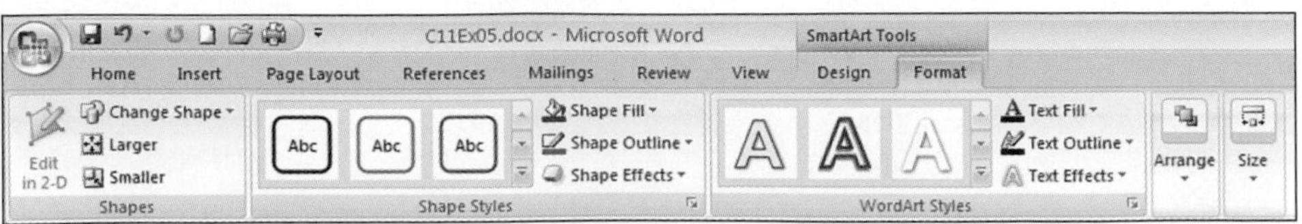

Arranging and Moving a SmartArt Diagram

Before moving a SmartArt diagram, you must select a text wrapping style. Select a text wrapping style with the Arrange button in the SmartArt Tools Format tab. Click the Arrange button, click the Position button, and then click the desired position at the drop-down gallery. You can also choose a text wrapping style by clicking the Arrange button, clicking *Text Wrapping*, and then clicking the desired wrapping style at the drop-down list. Move the diagram by positioning the arrow pointer on the diagram border until the pointer turns into a four-headed arrow, holding down the left mouse button, and then dragging the diagram to the desired location.

Exercise 5B

Formatting Diagrams

1. With **C11Ex05.docx** open, format shapes by completing the following steps:
   a. Click the diagram on the first page to select it (light turquoise border surrounds the diagram).
   b. Click the SmartArt Tools Format tab.
   c. Click the rectangle shape containing the word *Design*.
   d. Hold down the Shift key and then click the shape containing the word *Development*.
   e. With the Shift key still down, click the shape containing the word *Implementation*. (All three shapes should now be selected.)
   f. Click the Change Shape button in the Shapes group.
   g. Click the seventh shape from the left in the second row of the *Block Arrows* section (the Pentagon shape).
   h. With the shapes still selected, click the Larger button in the Shapes group.
   i. With the shapes still selected, click the Shape Outline button arrow in the Shape Styles group and then click the *Red, Accent* 2 color.

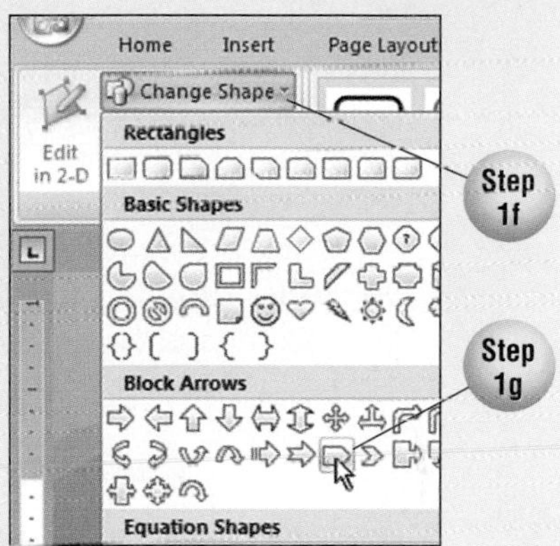

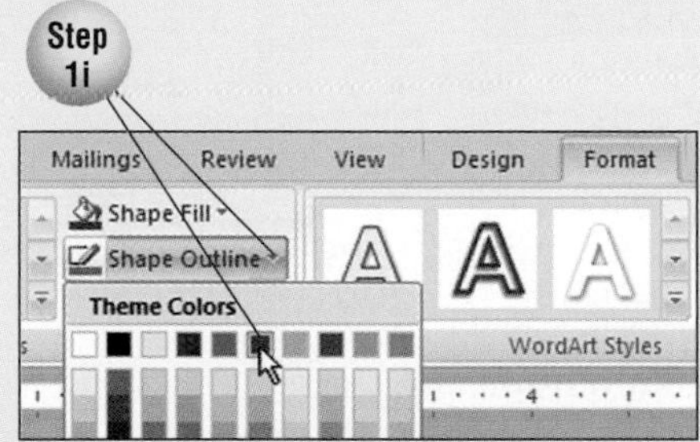

   j. Click inside the diagram border but outside any shape. (This deselects the shapes but keeps the diagram selected.)
2. Change the size of the diagram by completing the following steps:
   a. Click the Size button located at the right side of the tab.
   b. Select the current measurement in the Height measurement box, type **4**, and then press Enter.

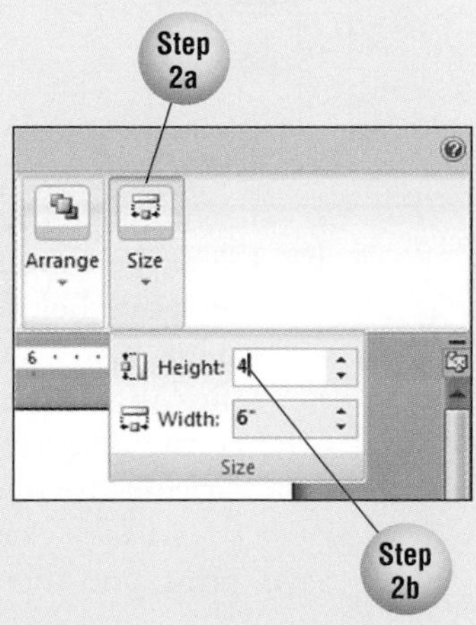

3. Position the diagram by completing the following steps:
   a. Click the Arrange button located toward the right side of the tab.
   b. Click the Position button.
   c. Click the middle option in the second row of the *With Text Wrapping* section (the *Position in Middle Center with Square Text Wrapping* option).
4. Format the bottom diagram by completing the following steps:
   a. Press Ctrl + End to move to the end of the document and then click in the bottom diagram to select it.
   b. Hold down the Shift key and then click each of the three shapes.
   c. Click the More button at the right side of the styles in the WordArt Styles group.
   d. Click the last WordArt style in the lower right corner of the drop-down gallery (*Fill - Accent 1, Metal Bevel, Reflection*).
   e. Click the Text Outline button arrow in the WordArt Styles group and then click the light blue color in the *Standard Colors* section (the seventh color from the left).
   f. Click the Text Effects button in the WordArt Styles group, point to *Glow* at the drop-down list, and then click the last option in the top row.

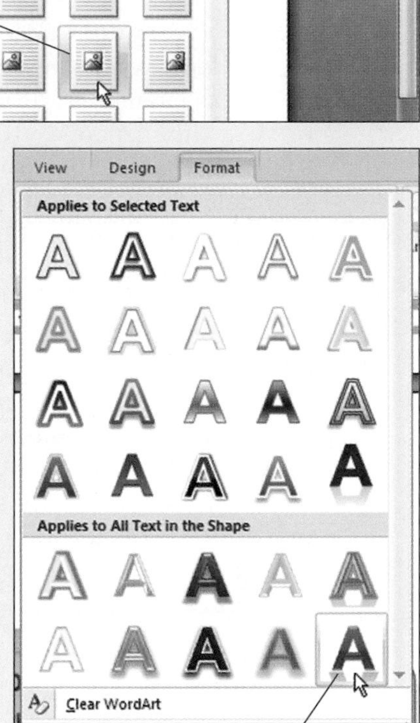

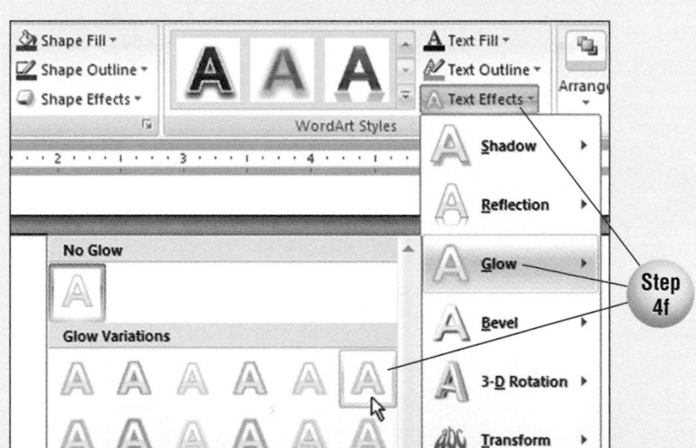

   g. Click inside the diagram border but outside any shape.
   h. Click the third shape (containing the title *Implementation*) and then change the fill color by clicking the Shape Fill button arrow and then clicking *Purple, Accent 4, Lighter 40%* color.
   i. Click inside the diagram border but outside the shape.
5. Arrange the diagram by clicking the Arrange button, clicking the Position button, and then clicking the middle option in the second row of the *With Text Wrapping* section (the *Position in Middle Center with Square Text Wrapping* option).
6. Save, print, and then close **C11Ex05.docx**.

Creating an Organizational Chart with SmartArt

If you need to visually illustrate hierarchical data, consider creating an organizational chart with a SmartArt option. To display organizational chart SmartArt options, click the Insert tab and then click the SmartArt button in the Illustrations group. At the Choose a SmartArt Graphic dialog box, click *Hierarchy* in the left panel. Organizational chart options display in the middle panel of the dialog box. Double-click the desired organizational chart, and the chart is inserted in the document. Type text in a chart by selecting the shape and then typing text in the shape, or you can type text in the *Type your text here* window that displays at the left side of the diagram. Format a SmartArt organizational chart with options and buttons in the SmartArt Tools Design tab similar to the one shown in Figure 11.8 and the SmartArt Tools Format tab similar to the one shown in Figure 11.10.

Insert an Organizational Chart

1. Click Insert tab.
2. Click SmartArt button.
3. Click Hierarchy.
4. Double-click desired organizational chart.

Exercise 6

Creating and Formatting an Organizational Chart

1. At a blank document, create the organizational chart shown in Figure 11.11. To begin, click the Insert tab.
2. Click the SmartArt button in the Illustrations group.
3. At the Choose a SmartArt Graphic dialog box, click *Hierarchy* in the left panel of the dialog box and then double-click the first option in the middle panel, *Organization Chart*.
4. If a *Type your text here* pane displays at the left side of the organizational chart, close the pane by clicking the Text Pane button in the Create Graphic group.
5. Delete one of the boxes in the organizational chart by clicking the border of the box in the lower right corner to select it and then pressing the Delete key. (Make sure that the selection border that surrounds the box is a solid line and not a dashed line. If a dashed line displays, click the box border again. This should change it to a solid line.)
6. With the bottom right box selected, click the Add Shape button arrow and then click the *Add Shape Below* option.
7. Click *[Text]* in the top box, type **Susan Garner**, press the Enter key, and then type **President**. Click in each of the remaining boxes and type the text as shown in Figure 11.11.
8. Click the More button located at the right side of the styles in the SmartArt Styles group and then click the *Inset* style in the *3-D* section (second option from the left in the top row of the *3-D* section).
9. Click the Change Colors button in the Quick Styles group and then click the *Colorful Range - Accent Colors 4 to 5* in the *Colorful* section (fourth option from the left in the *Colorful* section).

Step 3

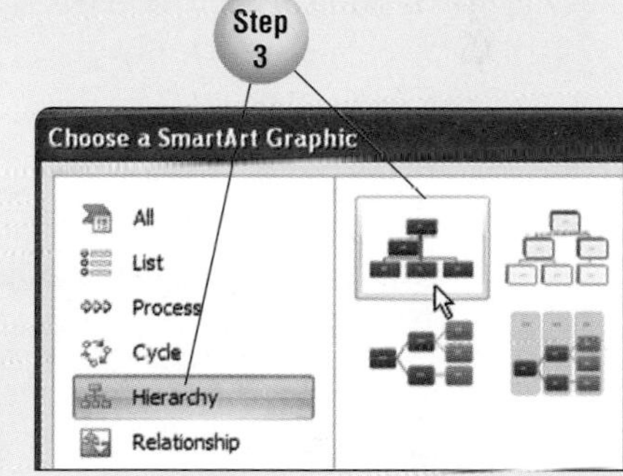

Step 6

Home Insert Page Layo
Add Bullet
Right to Left
Layout
Promote
Demote
Text Pane
Add Shape
Add Shape After
Add Shape Before
Add Shape Above
Add Shape Below
Add Assistant

Step 9

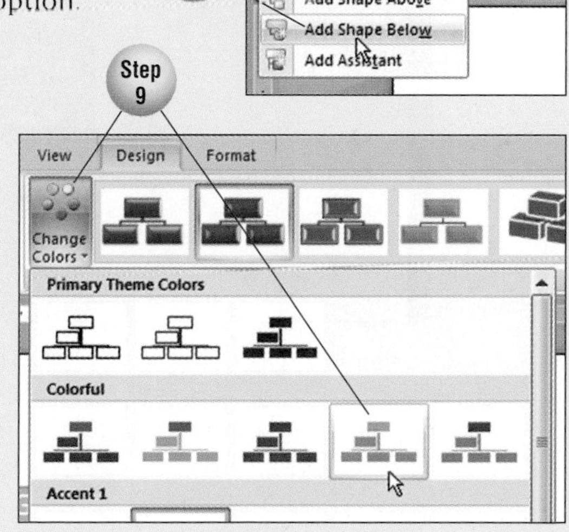

10. Click the SmartArt Tools Format tab.
11. Click the tab (displays with a right- and left-pointing triangle) that displays at the left side of the diagram border. (This displays the *Type your text here* window.)
12. Using the mouse, select the text that displays in the *Type your text here* window.
13. Click the Change Shape button in the Shapes group and then click the *Round Same Side Corner Rectangle* option (second option from the *right* in the top row).
14. Click the Shape Outline button in the Quick Styles group and then click the dark blue color (second color from the *right* in the *Standard Colors* section).
15. Click the Size button located at the right side of the ribbon and then click the up arrow to change the *Height* to 4″ and the *Width* to 6.5″.
16. Close the *Type your text here* window by clicking the Close button (marked with an *X*) located in the upper right corner of the window.
17. Click outside the chart to deselect it.
18. Save the document with the name **C11Ex06**.
19. Print and then close the **C11Ex06.docx**.

Figure 11.11 Exercise 6

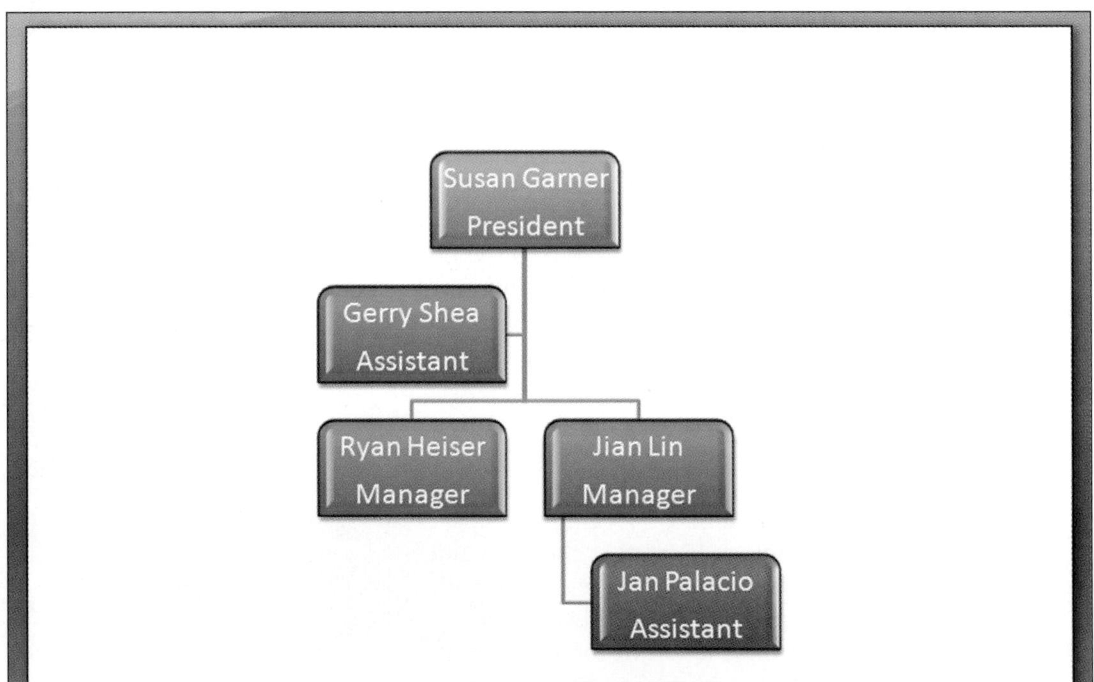

Chapter Summary

- Insert an image such as a picture or clip art with buttons in the Illustrations group in the Insert tab.
- To insert a picture, click the Insert tab, click the Picture button, navigate to the desired folder at the Insert Picture dialog box, and then double-click the picture.
- Customize and format an image with options and buttons in the Picture Tools Format tab.
- Size an image with the Shape Height and Shape Width measurement boxes in the Picture Tools Format tab or with the sizing handles that display around a selected image.
- Move an image with options from the Position button drop-down gallery located in the Picture Tools Format tab or by choosing a text wrapping style and then moving the image by dragging it with the mouse.
- You can also move an image using the arrow keys on the keyboard. Hold down the Ctrl key while pressing an arrow key on the keyboard to move the image in small increments.
- To insert a clip art image, click the Insert tab, click the Clip Art button, and then click the desired image in the Clip Art task pane.
- To search for specific types of clip art images, type the desired topic in the *Search for* text box in the Clip Art task pane.
- By default, the Clip Art task pane displays all available media images. Narrow the search to specific locations by clicking the down-pointing arrow at the right side of the *Results should be* option and then removing the check mark from any option you do not want searched.
- Insert a pull quote in a document with a built-in text box by clicking the Insert tab, clicking the Text Box button, and then clicking the desired built-in text box at the drop-down list.
- Format a pull quote with options in the Text Box Tools Format tab.
- Use the SmartArt feature to insert predesigned diagrams and organizational charts in a document.
- Choose a SmartArt diagram at the Choose a SmartArt Graphic dialog box. Display this dialog box by clicking the Insert tab and then clicking the SmartArt button in the Illustrations group.
- Format a SmartArt diagram or organizational chart with options and buttons in the SmartArt Tools Design tab and the SmartArt Tools Format tab.
- To move a SmartArt diagram, first choose a position or a text wrapping style with the Arrange button in the SmartArt Tools Format tab.

Commands review

FEATURE	RIBBON TAB, GROUP	BUTTON
Insert Picture dialog box	Insert, Illustrations	
Clip Art task pane	Insert, Illustrations	
Pull quote (Built-in text box)	Insert, Text	
Choose a SmartArt Graphic dialog box	Insert, Illustrations	

Reviewing key points

Completion: In the space provided at the right, indicate the correct term, symbol, or command.

1. Insert an image in a document with buttons in this group in the Insert tab. ________________
2. Click the Picture button in the Insert tab, and this dialog box displays. ________________
3. Customize and format an image with options and buttons in this tab. ________________
4. Size an image with the sizing handles that display around the selected image or with these boxes in the Picture Tools Format tab. ________________
5. To move an image in small increments, hold down this key while pressing an arrow key on the keyboard. ________________
6. Click the Clip Art button in the Insert tab, and this displays at the right side of the screen. ________________
7. Display available pull quote text boxes by clicking the Insert tab and then clicking this button in the Text group. ________________
8. Format a pull quote with options in this tab. ________________
9. The SmartArt button is located in this tab. ________________
10. Click the SmartArt button and this dialog box displays. ________________
11. Insert a SmartArt diagram in a document and this tab is active. ________________
12. If you need to visually illustrate hierarchical data, consider creating this with the SmartArt feature. ________________

Applying your skills

Assessment 1 Create a Flyer with a Picture and Text

1. At a blank document, press the Enter key three times, type **Ocean View Condominiums**, press the Enter key, and then type **1-888-555-6570**.
2. Press Ctrl + Home and then insert the picture **Ocean.jpg** with the following specifications:
   a. Change the position to *Position in top Center with Square Text Wrapping*.
   b. Change the text wrapping to *Behind Text*.
   c. Change the width to 4.5 inches.
   d. Change the brightness to -10%.
   e. Change the contrast to +20%.
3. Select the text, change the font to 26-point Script MT Bold and the text color to white, and then center the text.
4. Save the document with the name **C11A01**.
5. Print and then close **C11A01.docx**.

Assessment 2 Insert a Clip Art Image in a Data Security Training Notice

1. Open **Notice01.docx** and save the document with the name **C11A02**.
2. Center the title and change the font for the title to 18-point Calibri bold.
3. Select the text in the document (excluding the title) and then change the font size to 12 points.
4. Insert a computer clip art image of your choosing and then format, size, and position the clip art so it displays attractively in the document.
5. Save, print, and then close **C11A02.docx**.

Assessment 3 Format Columns and Insert a Pull Quote in a Document

1. Open **Document23.docx** and save the document with the name **C11A03**.
2. Apply the Heading 1 style to the title of the report and apply the Heading 2 style to the five headings in the report.
3. Change the style set to *Traditional*.
4. Format the text from the first paragraph to the end of the document into two columns.
5. Select the title *COMMERCIAL LIFE CYCLE*, increase the spacing after the title to 12 points, and then center the title.
6. Insert the *Contrast Sidebar* built-in text box and then make the following customizations:
   a. Type the following text in the text box: "**The commercial software life cycle is repeated every time a new version of a program is needed.**"
   b. Select the text in the text box and then change the font size to 12.
   c. Change the shape fill to *Blue, Accent 1, Lighter 40%*.
7. Save, print, and then close **C11A03.docx**.

Assessment 4 Create and Format a SmartArt Diagram

1. At a blank document, create the SmartArt diagram shown in Figure 11.12 with the following specifications:
   a. Use the *Pyramid List* diagram.
   b. Apply the *Inset* SmartArt style.
   c. Change the color to purple (*Colorful Range - Accent Colors 4 to 5*).
   d. Apply light green shape fill color to the bottom shape, light blue fill color to the middle shape, and red fill color to the top shape.
   e. Type the text in each shape as shown in Figure 11.12.
2. Save the document with the name **C11A04**.
3. Print and then close **C11A04.docx**.

Figure 11.12 Assessment 4

Assessment 5 Create and Format a SmartArt Organizational Chart

1. At a blank document, create the organizational chart shown in Figure 11.13 with the following specifications:
   a. Use the *Hierarchy* organizational chart.
   b. Select the top text box and insert a shape above.
   c. Select the top right text box and then add a shape below.
   d. Apply the *Colorful Range - Accent Colors 2 to 3* option.
   e. Increase the height to 4.5 inches and the width to 6.5 inches.
   f. Type the text in each text box as shown in Figure 11.13.
   g. Position the organizational chart in the middle of the page.
2. Save the document with the name **C11A05**.
3. Print and then close **C11A05.docx**.

Figure 11.13 Assessment 5

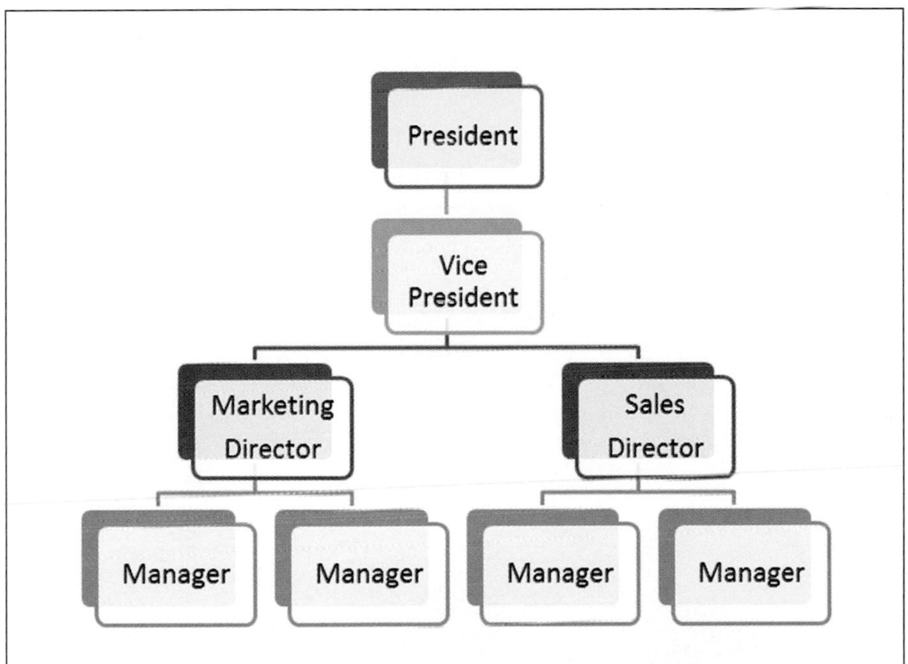

Chapter 12

Inserting Shapes and WordArt

Tutorial 12.1
Inserting and Formatting Objects
Tutorial 12.2
Creating and Customizing WordArt

Performance Objectives

Upon successful completion of Chapter 12, you will be able to:

- Draw and format shapes
- Draw and format text boxes
- Link text boxes
- Select objects
- Insert, format, and customize WordArt

In earlier chapters you learned to insert symbols, special characters, drop caps, and images to enhance the visual appeal of your documents. Other elements you can use to improve a document's visual appeal include shapes, text boxes, and WordArt. With the Shapes button in the Illustrations group in the Insert tab, you can draw a variety of shapes. You can then customize those shapes with options in the Drawing Tools Format tab. You can use the Text Box button, also in the Insert tab, to draw and insert a text box in your document, and you can customize the text box with options in the Text Box Tools Format tab. You can also use the WordArt feature to distort or modify text to conform to a variety of shapes.

Note: Before beginning computer exercises for this chapter, copy to your storage medium the Chapter12 folder from the CD that accompanies this textbook and then make Chapter12 the active folder.

QUICK STEPS

Draw a Shape
1. Click Insert tab.
2. Click Shapes button.
3. Click desired shape in drop-down list.
4. Drag in document to create shape.

Drawing Shapes

With the Shapes button in the Insert tab, you can draw a variety of objects such as lines, basic geometric shapes, block arrows, flowchart shapes, callouts, stars, and banners. When you click a shape at the drop-down list, the mouse pointer displays as a set of crosshairs (plus sign). Click in the document to insert the shape or position the crosshairs where you want the shape to begin, hold down the left mouse button, drag to create the shape, and then release the mouse button. This inserts the shape in the document and also displays the Drawing Tools Format tab, shown in Figure 12.1. Use buttons in this tab to replace the shape with another shape, apply a style to the shape, position or arrange the shape, or change the size of the shape. This tab contains many of the same options and buttons contained in both the Picture Tools Format tab and the Text Box Tools Format tab.

Figure 12.1 Drawing Tools Format Tab

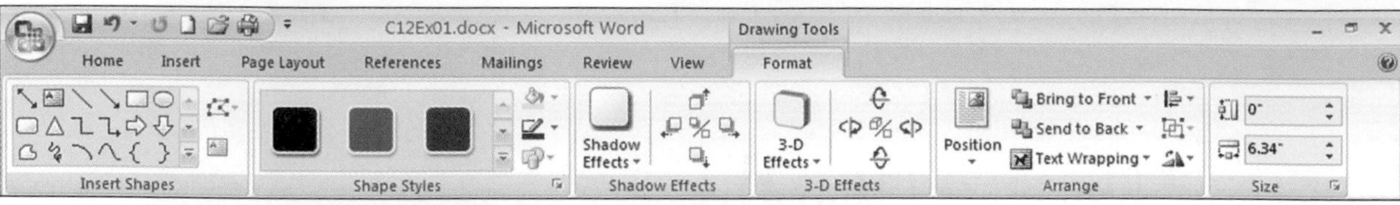

Drawing Lines

The Shapes button drop-down list includes lines and enclosed shapes. To draw a line, click an option in the *Lines* group. When the mouse pointer changes to crosshairs, position the crosshairs in the document and then drag to draw the line. If you want to draw a straight horizontal or vertical line, hold down the Shift key while dragging with the mouse.

Exercise 1

Drawing and Customizing a Line

1. At a blank document, type and format the text shown in Figure 12.2 by completing the following steps:
   a. Type **Greenland Systems**.
   b. Select the text, change the font to 28-point Copperplate Gothic Bold, the font color to olive green (*Olive Green, Accent 3, Darker 25%*), and then center the text.
   c. Deselect the text.
2. Insert and format the line below the text as shown in Figure 12.2 by completing the following steps:
   a. Click the Insert tab.
   b. Click the Shapes button and then click the third option from the left in the *Lines* section (*Double Arrow*).
   c. Hold down the Shift key and then drag to create a horizontal line that is approximately 6.5 inches in length (see Figure 12.2).
   d. With the line selected, click the More button at the right side of the Shape Styles group and then click the fourth option from the left in the fourth row (*Compound Outline - Accent 3*).

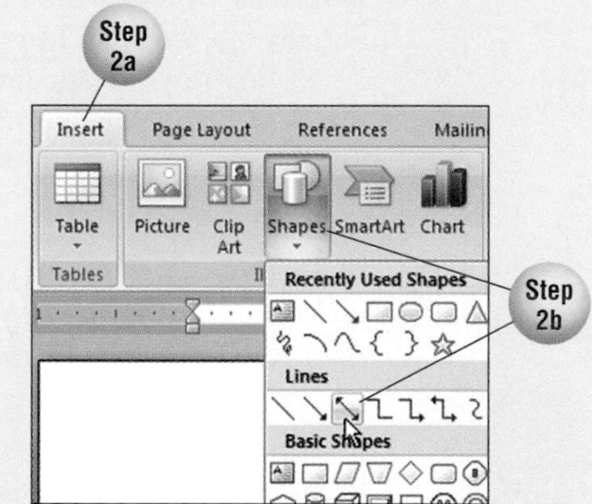

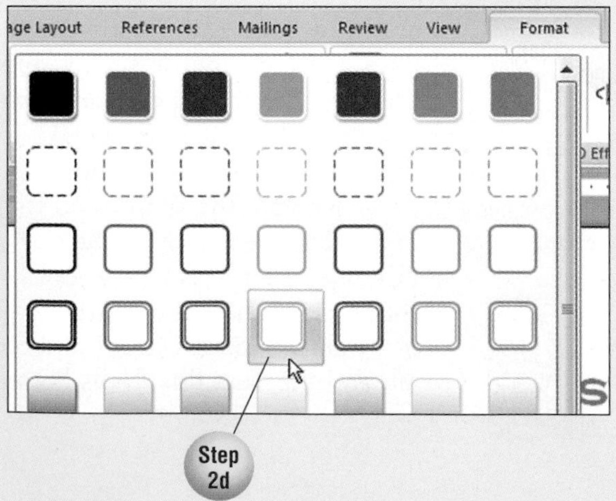

e. Click the Shape Outline button arrow in the Shape Styles group and then click the same olive green color you selected for the text (*Olive Green, Accent 3, Darker 25%*).

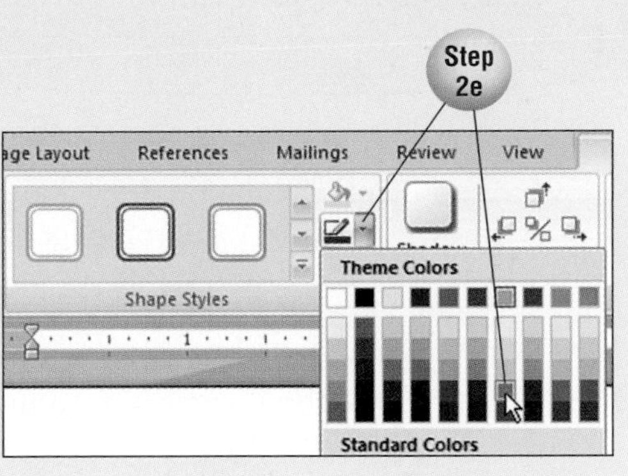

f. Click the Shadow Effects button in the Shadow Effects group and then click the last option in the top row in the *Drop Shadow* section (*Shadow Style 4*).

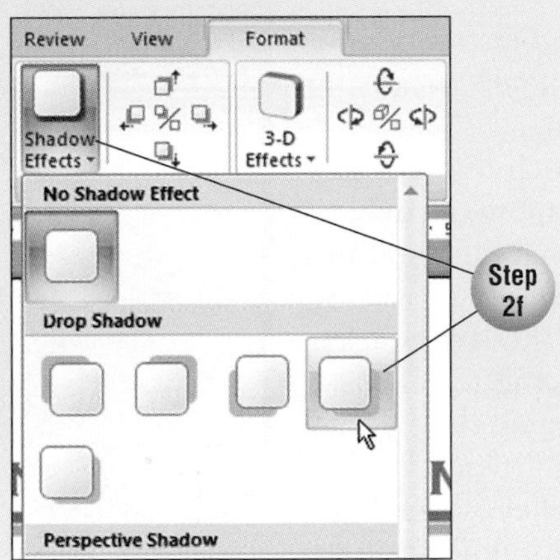

3. Click outside the line to deselect it.
4. Save the document with the name C12Ex01.
5. Print and then close C12Ex01.docx.

Figure 12.2 Exercise 1

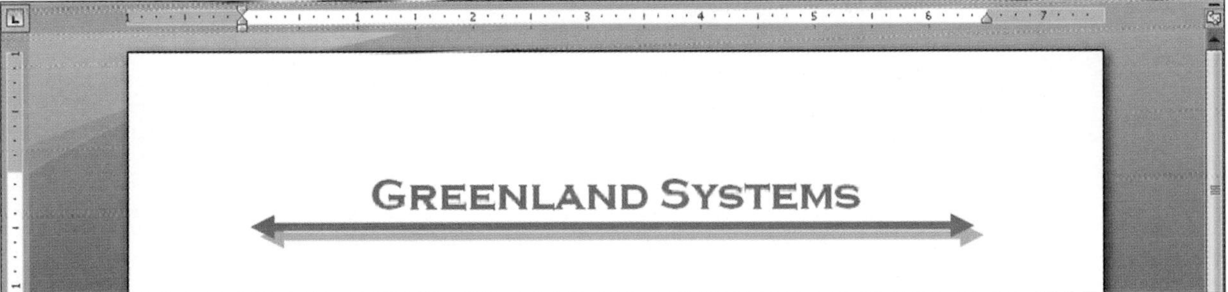

Drawing Enclosed Shapes

If you choose a shape in the *Lines* section of the Shapes button drop-down list, the shape you draw is considered a ***line drawing.*** If you choose an option in one of the other sections of the drop-down list, the shape you draw is considered an ***enclosed shape.*** When you draw an enclosed shape, you can maintain the shape's proportions by holding down the Shift key while dragging to create the shape. For example, to draw a square, choose the *Rectangle* shape and then hold down the Shift key while drawing the shape. To draw a circle, choose the *Oval* shape and then hold down the Shift key while drawing the shape.

Exercise 2A

Drawing Arrow Shapes

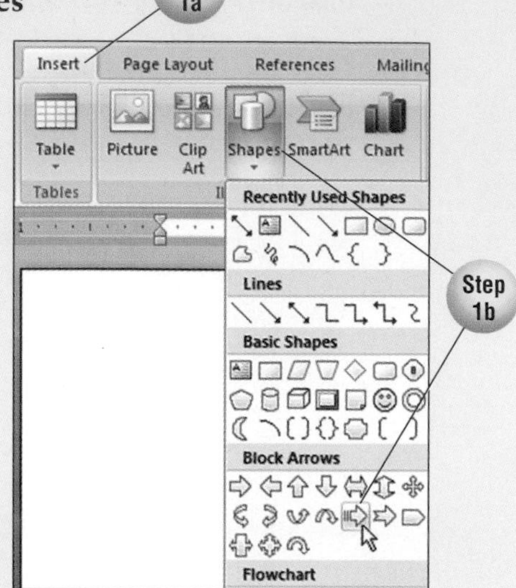

1. At a blank document, draw and format the shapes shown in Figure 12.3 (on page 311). Begin by pressing the Enter key twice and then draw an arrow shape by completing the following steps:
   a. Click the Insert tab.
   b. Click the Shapes button in the Illustrations group and then click the *Striped Right Arrow* shape in the *Block Arrows* section.
   c. Position the mouse pointer (which displays as crosshairs) in the document at approximately the 1-inch mark on the horizontal ruler and the 0.5-inch mark on the vertical ruler.
   d. Hold down the Shift key and the left mouse button, drag to the right until the tip of the arrow is positioned at approximately the 5.5-inch mark on the horizontal ruler, and then release the mouse button and the Shift key.
2. Format the arrow by completing the following steps:
   a. Click in the Shape Height measurement box in the Size group and then type **2.4**.
   b. Click in the Shape Width measurement box in the Size group, type **4.5**, and then press Enter.
   c. Click the More button at the right side of the Shape Styles group and then click the green *Linear Up Gradient - Accent 3* option at the drop-down gallery (fourth option from the left in the fifth row).

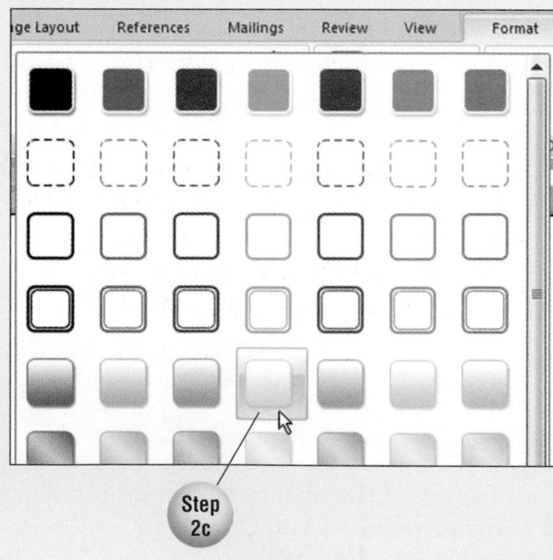

d. Click the 3-D Effects button in the 3-D Effects group and then click *3-D Style 6* in the *Perspective* section.

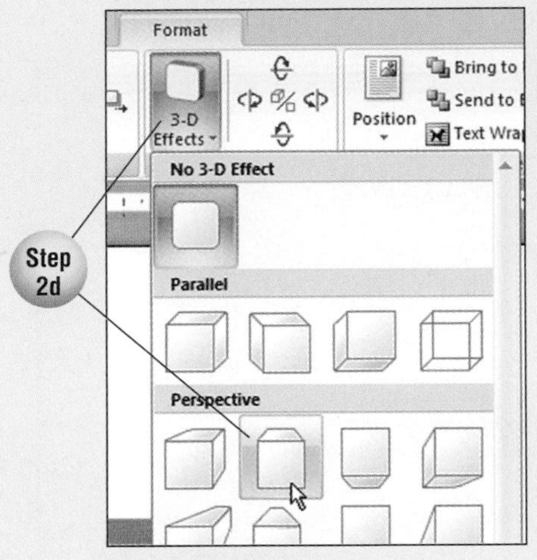

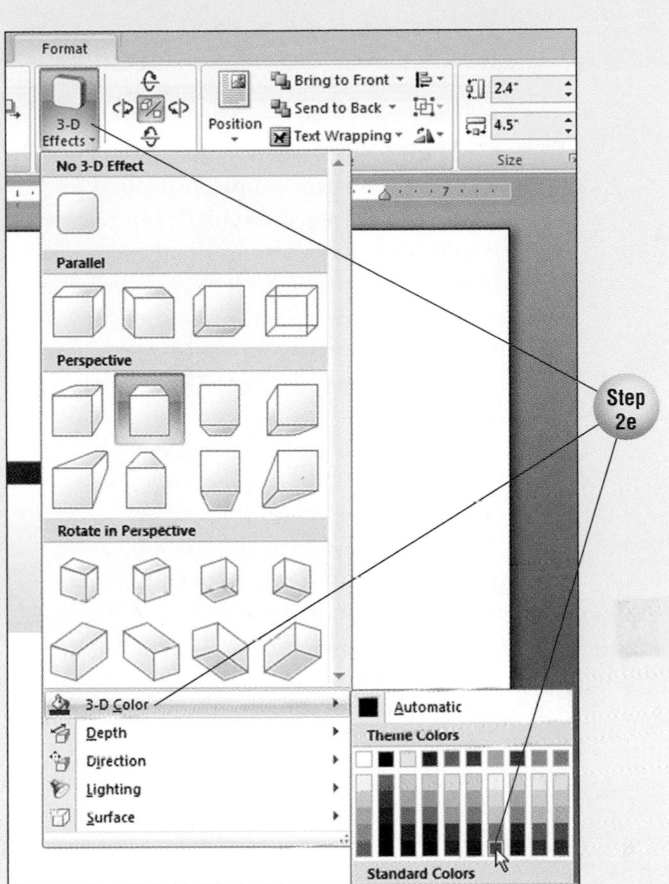

e. Click the 3-D Effects button, point to *3-D Color*, and then click the *Olive Green, Accent 3, Darker 50%* color.

3. Save the document with the name **C12Ex02**.

Copying Shapes

Once you have drawn a shape, you can copy it to another location in the document. To do this, select the shape and then click the Copy button in the Clipboard group in the Home tab. Position the insertion point at the location where you want to insert the copied image and then click the Paste button. You can also copy a selected shape by holding down the Ctrl key while dragging the shape to the desired location.

Copy a Shape

1. Select desired shape.
2. Click Copy button.
3. Position insertion point at desired location.
4. Click Paste button.

OR

1. Select desired shape.
2. Hold down Ctrl key.
3. Drag shape to desired location.

Exercise 2B

Copying a Shape

1. With **C12Ex02.docx** open, copy the arrow by completing the following steps:
   a. With the insertion point positioned in the arrow (the mouse pointer displays with a four-headed arrow attached), hold down the Ctrl key.
   b. Drag down until the outline of the copied arrow displays just below the top (original) arrow, release the Ctrl key, and then release the mouse button.
   c. Copy the arrow again by holding down the Ctrl key and then dragging the outline of the copied arrow just below the second arrow.
2. Flip the middle arrow by completing the following steps:
   a. Click the middle arrow to select it.
   b. If necessary, click the Drawing Tools Format tab.
   c. Click the Rotate button in the Arrange group and then click *Flip Horizontal* at the drop-down gallery.
3. Save **C12Ex02.docx**.

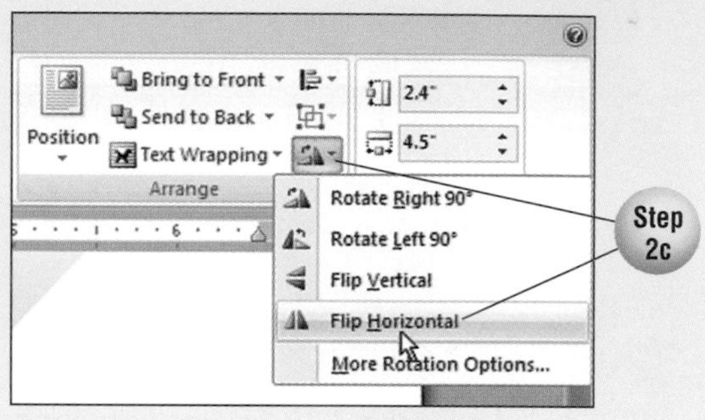

Insert Text in Shape
1. Click in desired shape.
2. Click Edit Text button in Drawing Tools Format tab.

Edit Text

Inserting Text in Shapes

You can insert text inside of an enclosed shape. To insert text, click the Edit Text button in the Insert Shapes group in the Drawing Tools Format tab. This moves the insertion point inside the shape, changes the border around the shape to a dashed blue line, and also makes the Text Box Tools Format tab active. Use options in this tab or options in any of the other tabs to make changes to the text in the shape. For example, change the text font by selecting the text, clicking the Home tab, and then choosing the desired font.

Exercise 2C

Inserting Text in a Shape

1. With **C12Ex02.docx** open, insert text in the top arrow by completing the following steps:
   a. Click the top arrow.
   b. Click the Edit Text button in the Insert Shapes group in the Drawing Tools Format tab.

c. Click the Home tab.
d. Change the font size to 16, turn on bold, and then change the font color to *Olive Green, Accent 3, Darker 50%*.
e. Click the Center button in the Paragraph group.
f. Type **Reliable**.
g. Click the Text Box Tools Format tab.
h. Click the Text Direction button in the Text group.

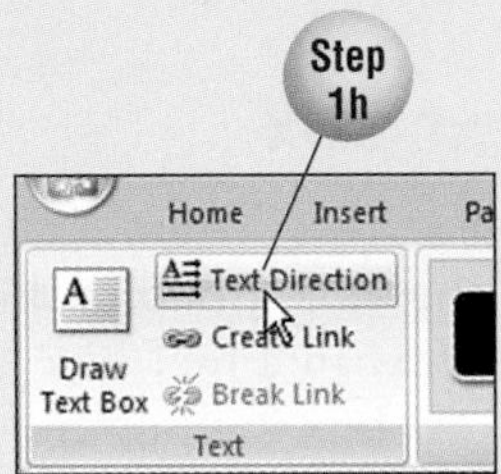

2. Complete steps similar to those in Step 1 to insert the word *Safe* in the middle arrow. (Click twice on the Text Direction button to insert *Safe* in the tip of the arrow.)
3. Complete steps similar to those in Step 1 to insert the word *Responsive* in the bottom arrow.
4. Save, print, and then close **C12Ex02.docx**.

Figure 12.3 Exercises 2A – 2C

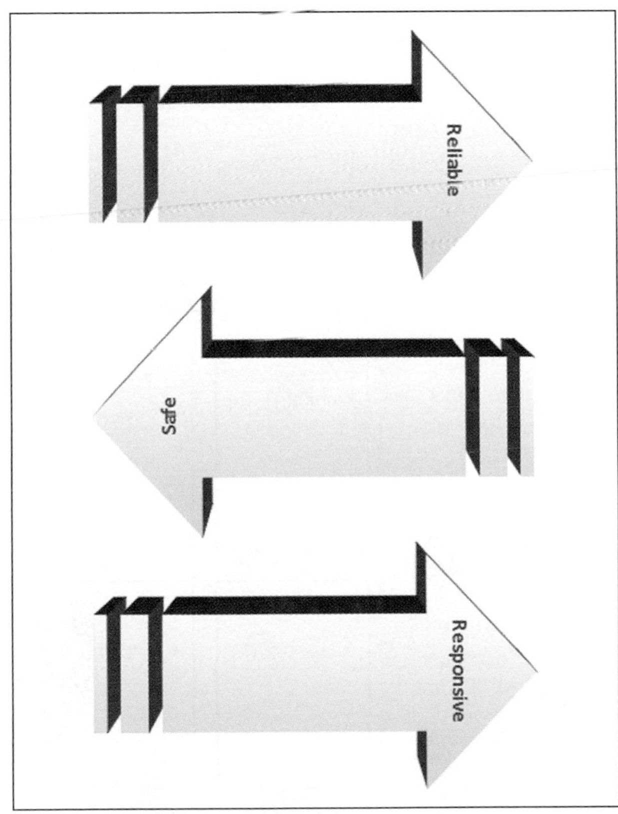

Draw a Text Box
1. Click Insert tab.
2. Click Text Box button in Text group.
3. Click *Draw Text Box.*
4. Drag in document to create box.

Drawing and Formatting a Text Box

As you learned in Chapter 11, you can use built-in text boxes provided by Word to insert a pull quote in a document. You can also draw your own text box in a document and then format and customize it. To draw a text box, click the Insert tab, click the Text Box button in the Text group, and then click *Draw Text Box* at the drop-down list. The mouse pointer displays as crosshairs. Position the crosshairs in the document and then drag to create the text box.

Formatting a Text Box

When you insert a text box in a document, the Text Box Tools Format tab becomes active. With options in the Text group in this tab, you can draw another text box, change the direction of text in a text box, and link text boxes. You can apply predesigned styles to a text box with options in the Text Box Styles group, and you can change the text box shape, shape fill, and shape outline. You can add and customize shadows and 3-D effects with options in the Shadow Effects and 3-D Effects groups. With options in the Arrange group, you can position the text box on the page, specify how text wraps around the text box, align the text box with other objects in the document, and rotate the text box. You can specify the text box size with the Shape Height and Shape Width measurement boxes in the Size group.

Exercise 3

Inserting a Text Box in a Shape

1. Open **Document24.docx** and save the document with the name **C12Ex03**.
2. Make the following changes to the document:
   a. Apply the Heading 1 style to the title and the Heading 2 style to the two headings.
   b. Change the style set to *Simple*.
   c. Center the title and add 12 points of spacing after it.
3. Insert and format a text box by completing the following steps:
   a. Click the Insert tab.
   b. Click the Text Box button in the Text group and then click *Draw Text Box* at the drop-down list.
   c. Draw a text box in the middle of the paragraph in the *Types of Viruses* section that is approximately 3 inches wide and 1 inch tall.
   d. Click the Text Wrapping button in the Arrange group in the Text Box Tools Format tab and then click *Tight* at the drop-down list.

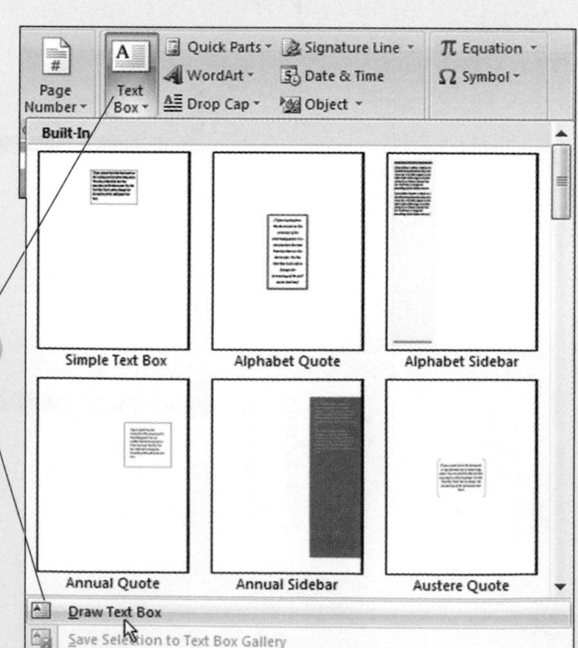

e. Click the More button at the right side of the text box styles in the Text Box Styles group and then click the second option from the left in the sixth row (*Diagonal Gradient - Accent 1*).

f. Click the Shadow Effects button in the Shadow Effects group and then click the second option from the left in the top row in the *Drop Shadow* section (*Shadow Style 2*).

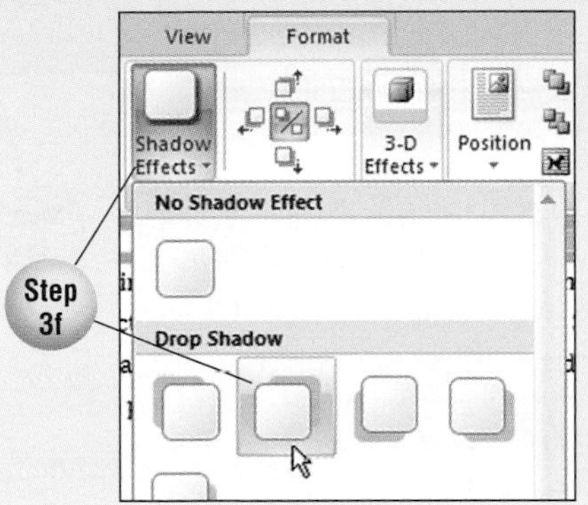

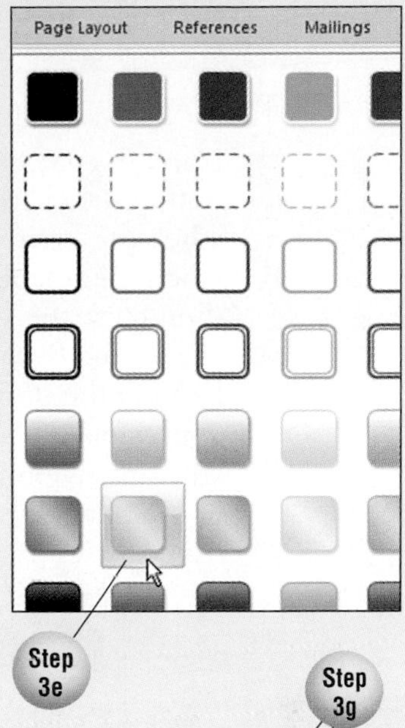

g. Click twice on the Nudge Shadow Up button in the Shadow Effects group and click three times on the Nudge Shadow Right button.

h. Click in the Shape Height measurement box in the Size group and then type 1.

i. Click in the Shape Width measurement box in the Size group, type 2.9, and then press Enter.

4. Insert text in the text box by completing the following steps:
   a. With the text box selected, type "**Viruses can cause effects that range from minor and annoying to highly destructive . . .** ".
   b. Select the text you just typed, click the Home tab, click the Italic button, and change the font size to 14 points.
5. If necessary, position the text box in the middle of the paragraph in the *Types of Viruses* section.
6. Save, print, and then close **C12Ex03.docx**.

Linking Text Boxes

You can create several text boxes and then have text flow from one text box to another by linking the text boxes. To do this, draw the desired text boxes and then select the first text box you want in the link. Click the Create Link button in the Text group in the Text Box Tools Format tab, and the mouse pointer displays with a link image attached. Click an empty text box to link it with the selected text box. To break a link between two boxes, select the first text box in the link, click the Break Link button in the Text group, and then click the linked text box. When you break a link, all of the text is placed in the selected text box.

QUICK STEPS

Link Text Boxes

1. Select first text box.
2. Click Create Text Box Link button.
3. Click empty text box.

Create Link

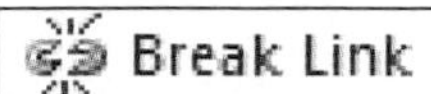

Exercise 4A

Linking Text Boxes

1. At a blank document, draw and format an arrow shape by completing the following steps:
   a. Click the Insert tab.
   b. Click the Shapes button in the Illustrations group and then click the sixth option from the left in the second row of the *Block Arrows* section (*Notched Right Arrow*).
   c. Drag in the document screen to create an arrow that is approximately 4.5 inches wide and 2.5 inches tall.
   d. Click the More button at the right side of the shape styles in the Shape Styles group and then click the sixth option from the left in the sixth row (*Diagonal Gradient - Accent 5*).

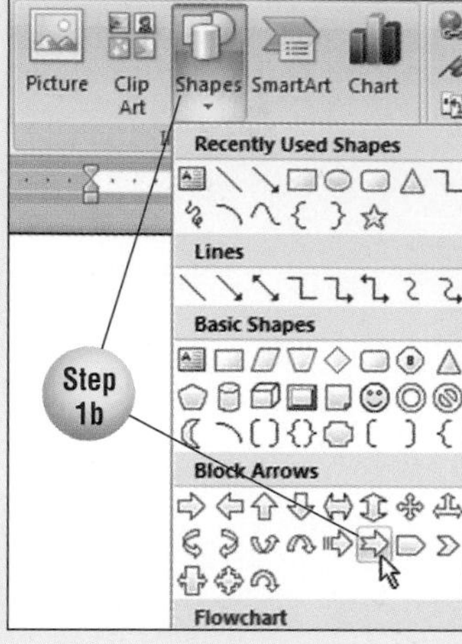

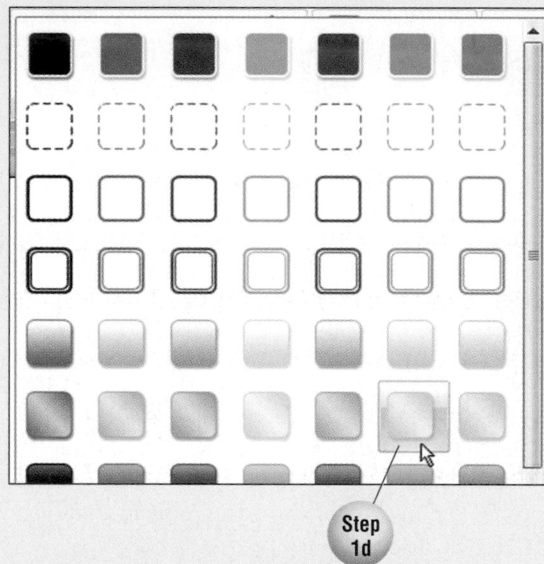

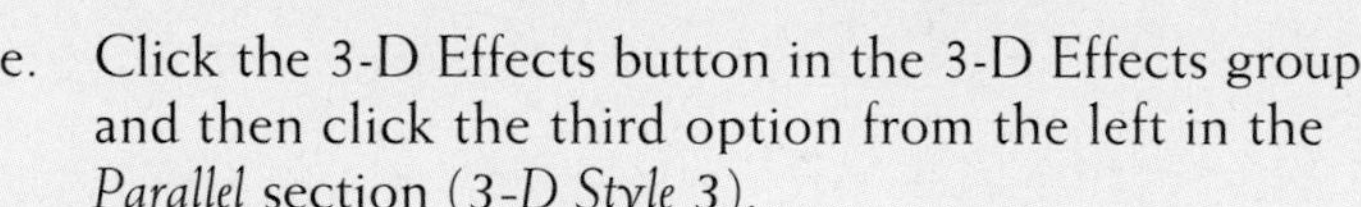

   e. Click the 3-D Effects button in the 3-D Effects group and then click the third option from the left in the *Parallel* section (*3-D Style 3*).
   f. Click in the Shape Height measurement box in the Size group and then type **2.5**.
   g. Click in the Shape Width measurement box in the Size group, type **4.5**, and then press Enter.

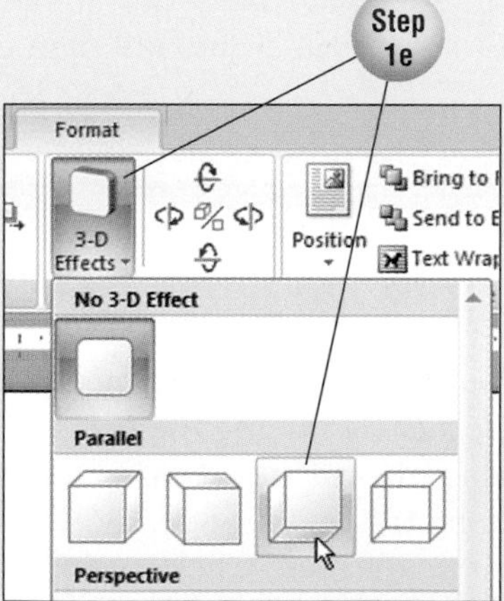

2. With the arrow selected, copy it by holding down the Ctrl key, dragging the arrow below the original arrow, and releasing the mouse button and then the Ctrl key.
3. With the bottom arrow selected, click the Rotate button in the Arrange group and then click *Flip Horizontal* at the drop-down list.

4. Insert a text box inside the top arrow and format the text box by completing the following steps:
   a. Click in the top arrow to select it.
   b. Click the Insert tab.
   c. Click the Text Box button in the Text group and then click *Draw Text Box* at the drop-down list.
   d. Draw a text box inside the arrow as shown below.

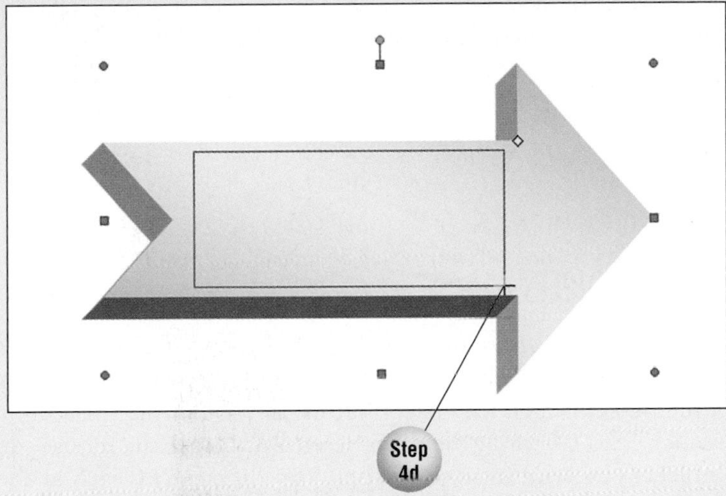

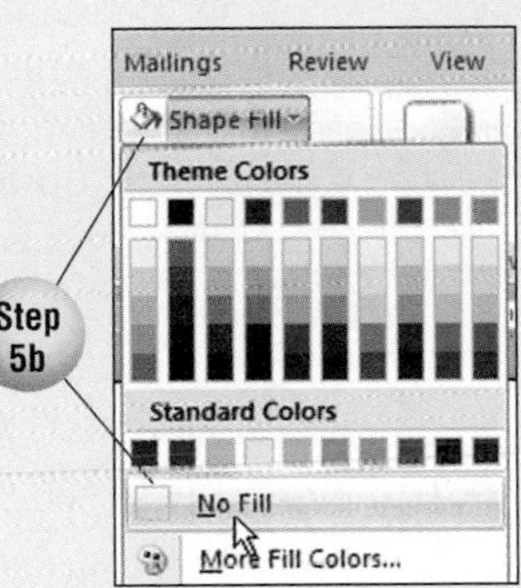

5. Format the text box by completing the following steps:
   a. Change the height measurement to 1 inch and the width measurement to 2.6 inches.
   b. Click the Shape Fill button arrow and then click *No Fill*.
   c. Make sure the text box is centered in the arrow.
6. With the text box selected, copy it to the bottom arrow by holding down the Ctrl key, dragging the text box inside the bottom arrow, releasing the mouse button and then releasing the Ctrl key.
7. Link the text boxes by completing the following steps:
   a. Click in the text box in the top arrow to select it.
   b. Click the Create Link button in the Text group.
   c. Click the text box in the second arrow.
8. With the top text box selected, make the following changes:
   a. Click the Home tab.
   b. Change the font size to 16 points, the font color to dark blue, and turn on bold.
   c. Change the line spacing to single.
   d. Click the Center button in the Paragraph group.
   e. Type **Let Leland Financial Services help you plan for retirement and provide you with information to determine your financial direction.** (The text will flow to the text box in the bottom arrow.)

9. Remove the border around the text boxes by completing the following steps:
   a. Click in the text box in the top arrow.
   b. With the top text box selected, click the Text Box Tools Format tab.
   c. Click the Shape Outline button arrow and then click *No Outline*.
   d. Click the bottom text box.
   e. Click the Shape Outline button arrow and then click *No Outline*.
10. Save the document with the name **C12Ex04**.

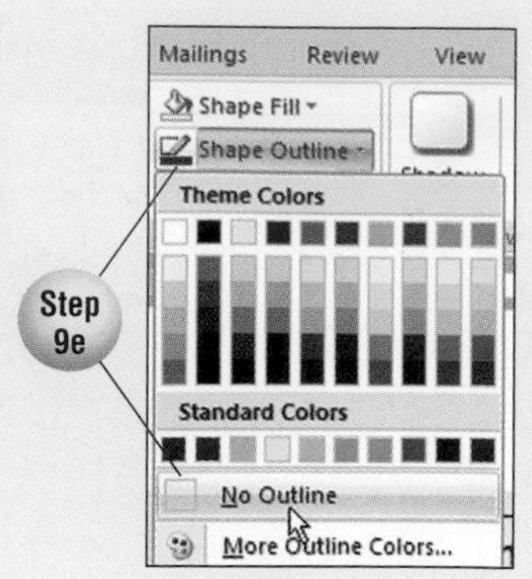

QUICK STEPS

Select Objects

1. Click Select button.
2. Click *Select Objects*.
3. Draw border around objects to select.

Selecting Objects

When a document contains a number of objects, you may need to select one or more of them to perform tasks such as formatting, moving, or aligning them. To select multiple objects, click the Select button in the Editing group in the Home tab and then click *Select Objects* at the drop-down list. Using the mouse, draw a border around the objects you want to select. When you click *Select Objects* at the drop-down list, the option in the drop-down list becomes active, and the mouse arrow at the left side of the option displays with an orange background. To turn off object selecting, click the Select button and then click *Select Objects*. (This removes the orange background from the mouse arrow at the left side of the option.)

You can resize a selected object horizontally, vertically, or diagonally from the center outward by holding down the Ctrl key and then dragging the sizing handle. Nudge a selected shape with the up, down, left, or right arrow keys on the keyboard.

Exercise 4B

Selecting, Moving, and Aligning Objects

1. With **C12Ex04.docx** open, select, align, and move the arrows and text boxes by completing the following steps:
   a. Click the Zoom Out button located at the left side of the Zoom slider bar until 60% displays at the left side of the button.
   b. Click the Home tab.
   c. Click the Select button in the Editing group and then click *Select Objects* at the drop-down list.

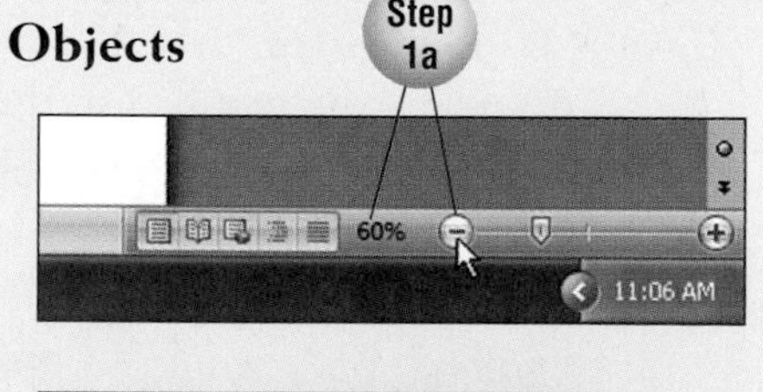

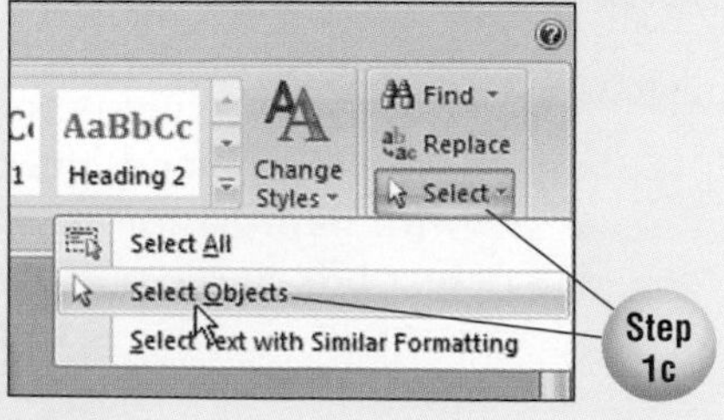

d. Using the mouse, draw a border around the two arrows. (When you release the mouse button, the arrows are selected as well as the text boxes inside the arrows.)

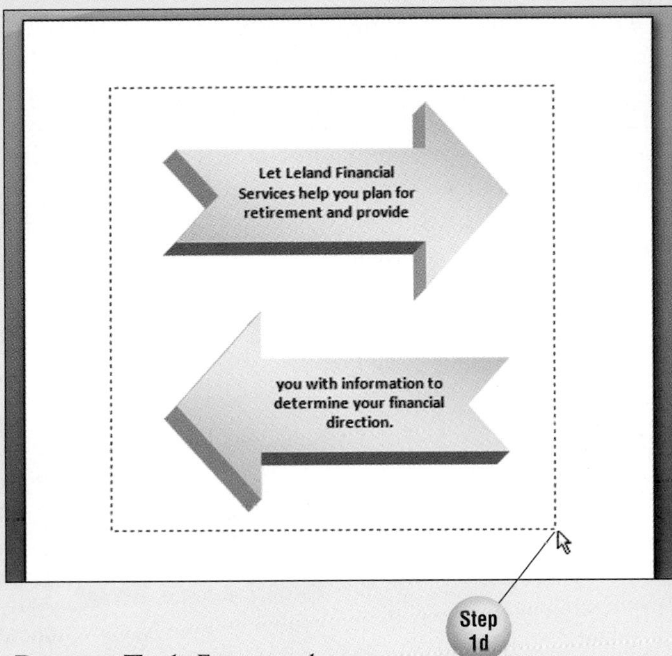

e. Click the Drawing Tools Format tab.
f. Click the Align button in the Arrange group and then click *Align Center* at the drop-down list.

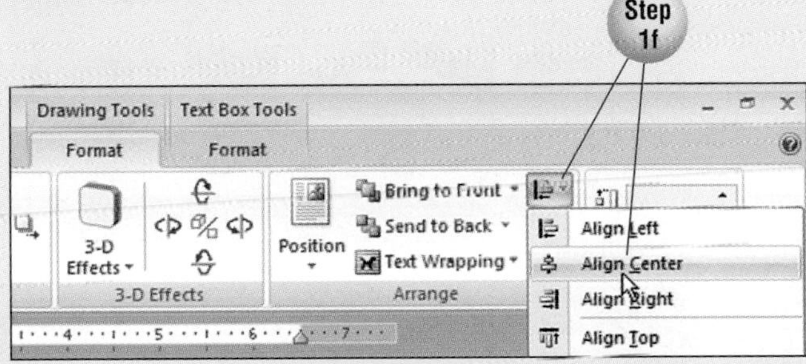

g. Position the mouse pointer on the border of the selected arrows until the pointer displays as a four-headed arrow and then drag the arrows down so they are positioned vertically in the middle of the page.
h. Click outside the selected objects.
2. Turn off object selecting by clicking the Select button in the Editing group and then clicking *Select Objects* at the drop-down list.
3. Click four times on the Zoom In button that displays at the right side of the Zoom slider bar. (This changes the zoom percentage to 100%.)
4. Save **C12Ex04.docx**.

Create WordArt Text
1. Click Insert tab.
2. Click WordArt button.
3. Click desired WordArt style.
4. Type WordArt text.
5. Click OK.

Creating WordArt Text

With the WordArt feature, you can distort or modify text to conform to a variety of shapes. This is useful for creating company logos, letterhead, flyer titles, or headings. To insert WordArt in a document, click the Insert tab and then click the WordArt button in the Text group. This displays the WordArt drop-down list, shown in Figure 12.4. When you click a WordArt style at this drop-down list, the Edit WordArt Text dialog box displays, as shown in Figure 12.5. At this dialog box, type the text that you want to become WordArt text and then click OK. When you click OK, the text is inserted as WordArt in the document, and the WordArt Tools Format tab, shown in Figure 12.6, becomes active.

Figure 12.4 WordArt Drop-down List

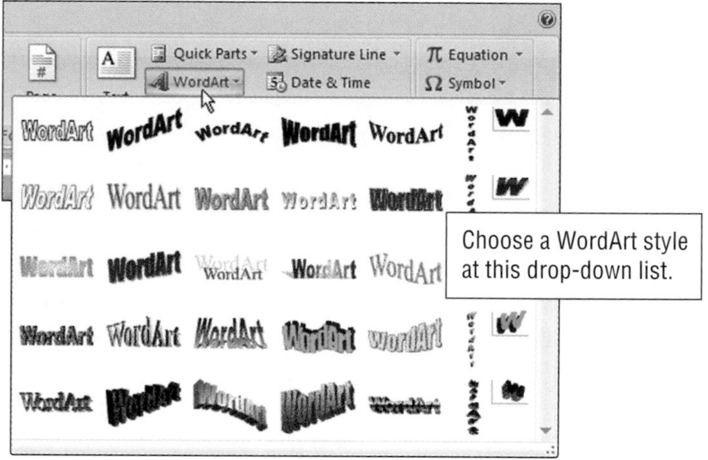

Figure 12.5 Edit WordArt Text Dialog Box

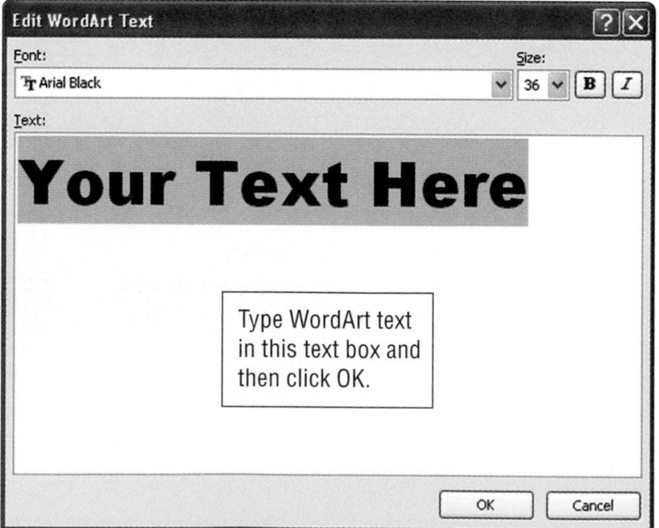

Editing WordArt Text

After you insert WordArt text in a document, you can edit and format the text with options and buttons in the WordArt Tools Format tab (see Figure 12.6). If you want to edit the WordArt text, make sure the WordArt is selected and then click the Edit Text button in the Edit group in the WordArt Tools Format tab. This displays the Edit WordArt Text dialog box. Make the desired changes to the text and then click OK.

Edit Text

The Text group in the WordArt Tools Format tab contains buttons for spacing WordArt text and for specifying its vertical and horizontal height. When you click the Spacing button, a drop-down list displays with the spacing options *Very Tight*, *Tight*, *Normal*, *Loose*, and *Very Loose*. Click the Even Height button to make both uppercase and lowercase letters the same height. Click the WordArt Vertical Text button to display the WordArt text vertically with the letters stacked on top of each other.

Even Height

WordArt Vertical Text

Figure 12.6 WordArt Tools Format Tab

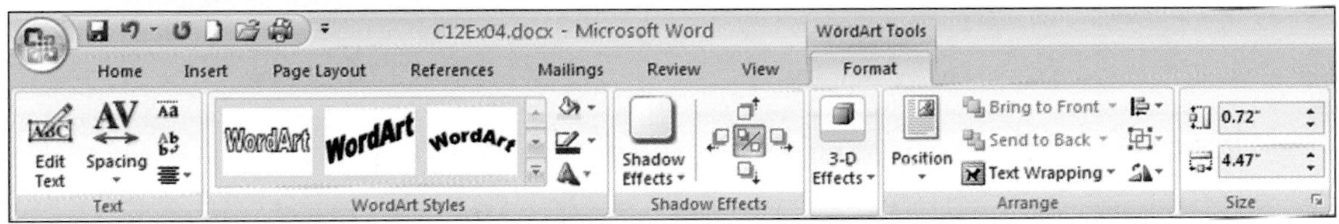

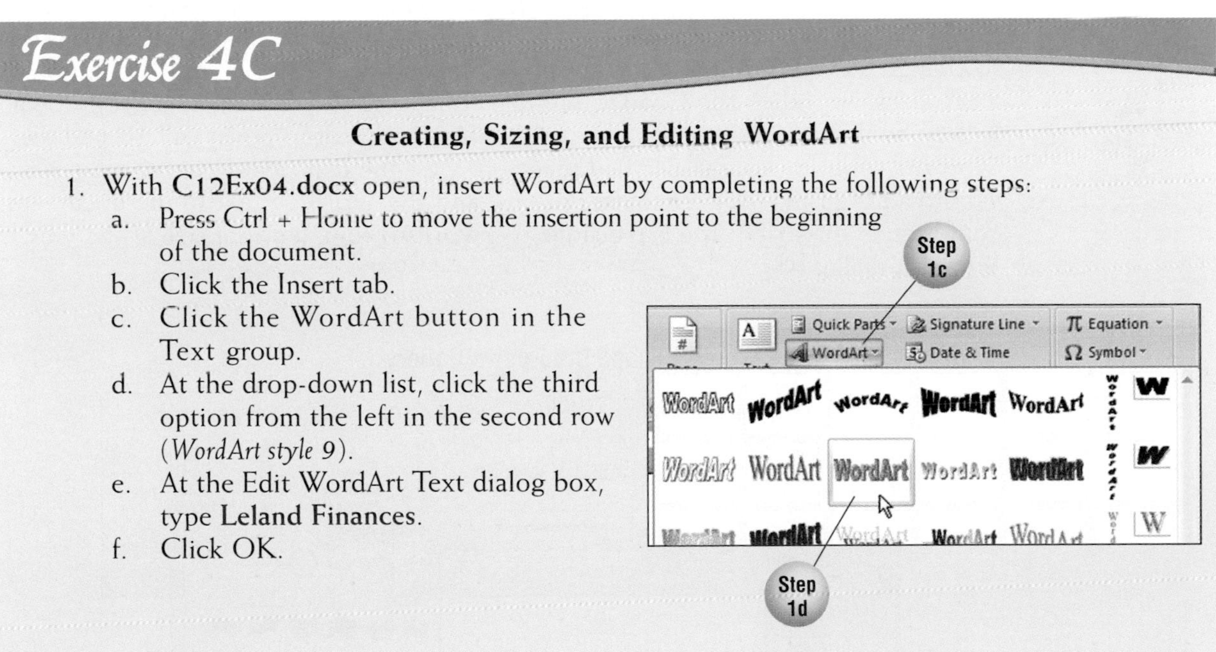

Exercise 4C

Creating, Sizing, and Editing WordArt

1. With **C12Ex04.docx** open, insert WordArt by completing the following steps:
   a. Press Ctrl + Home to move the insertion point to the beginning of the document.
   b. Click the Insert tab.
   c. Click the WordArt button in the Text group.
   d. At the drop-down list, click the third option from the left in the second row (*WordArt style 9*).
   e. At the Edit WordArt Text dialog box, type **Leland Finances**.
   f. Click OK.

2. Edit the WordArt text to change the company name to *Leland Financial Services* by completing the following steps:
   a. Click the Edit Text button in the Text group in the WordArt Tools Format tab.
   b. At the Edit WordArt Text dialog box, type **Leland Financial Services**.
   c. Click OK.
3. Click the Spacing button in the Text group and then click *Loose* at the drop-down list.
4. Click the Even Height button in the Text group. After viewing the text with all the letters the same height, return the text to the default by clicking the Even Height button again.
5. Save **C12Ex04.docx**.

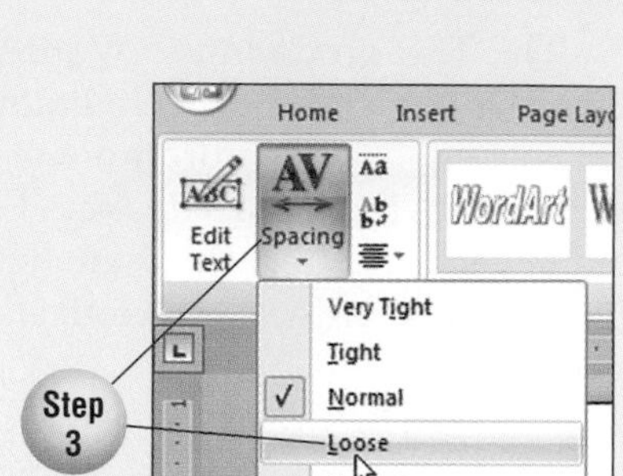

Customizing WordArt Styles

Change WordArt Shape

If you want to customize WordArt text, click the More button at the right side of the WordArt Styles group. A drop-down list displays with the same style options as the drop-down list that displays when you click the WordArt button in the Insert tab. Click an option at this drop-down list to change the WordArt style. Use the Shape Fill button to change the WordArt fill color and use the Shape Outline button to change the color of the WordArt outline. If you want WordArt text to conform to a certain shape, click the Change WordArt Shape button to display a drop-down gallery, as shown in Figure 12.7. Click an option in this drop-down gallery, and the WordArt conforms to the specified shape. To view the text in different shapes, you can hover your mouse over shape options, and the WordArt text in the document conforms to the shape. You can change the WordArt font and font size at the Edit WordArt dialog box.

Figure 12.7 Change WordArt Shape Drop-down Gallery

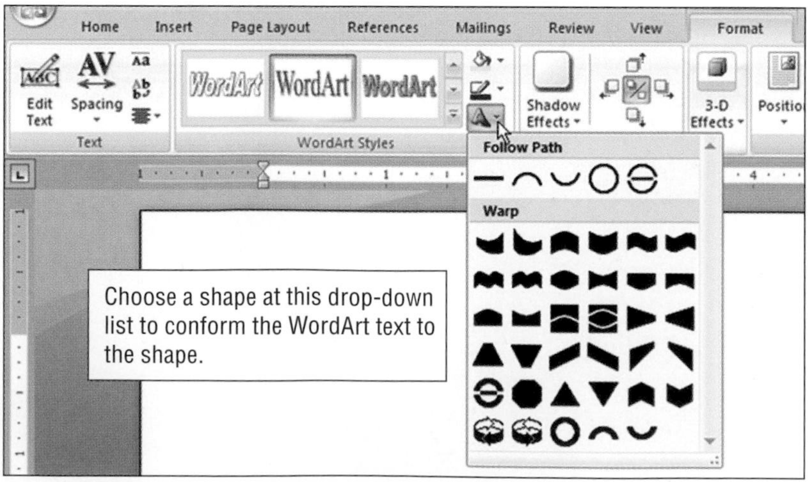

Sizing WordArt

If you want to change the size of WordArt, you can do so in one of two ways. When you select WordArt, sizing handles display around it. You can use these handles to increase or decrease the size of the WordArt text. You can also size WordArt with the Shape Height and Shape Width measurement boxes in the Size group in the WordArt Tools Format tab.

Exercise 4D

Modifying the WordArt Style

1. With **C12Ex04.docx** open and the WordArt text selected, change the WordArt style by clicking the More button at the right side of the styles in the WordArt Styles group and then clicking the second option from the left in the second row (*WordArt style 8*).
2. Click the Shape Fill button arrow in the WordArt Styles group and then click the aqua color (*Aqua, Accent 5, Lighter 60%*).

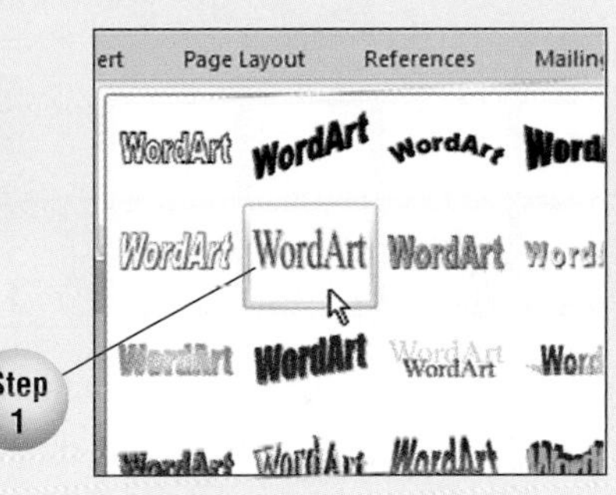

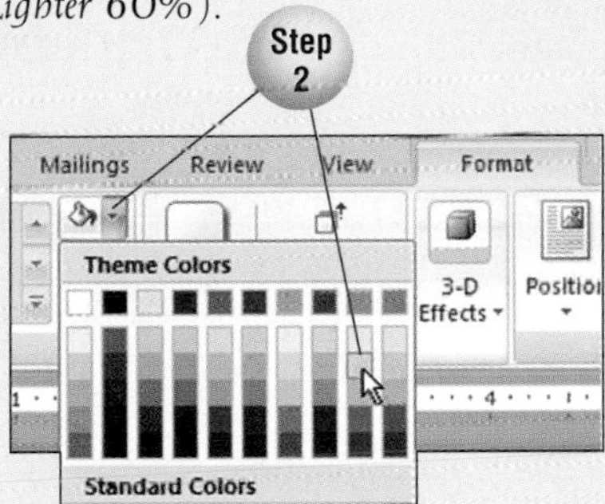

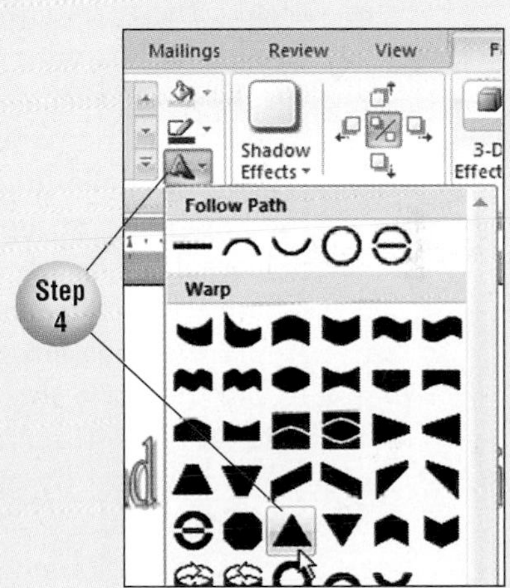

3. Click the Shape Outline button arrow in the WordArt Styles group and then click the aqua color (*Aqua, Accent 5, Darker 50%*).
4. Click the Change WordArt Shape button in the WordArt Styles group and then click the third option from the left in the fifth row of the *Warp* section (*Triangle Up*).
5. Increase the size of the WordArt by completing the following steps:
   a. Click in the Shape Height measurement box and then type **1**.
   b. Click in the Shape Width measurement box, type **6.5**, and then press Enter.
6. Save, print, and then close **C12Ex04.docx**

Shadow On/Off

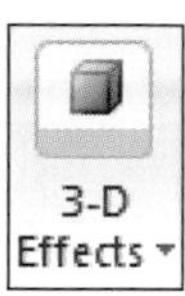

Applying Effects

Use the Shadow Effects button in the Shadow Effects group in the WordArt Tools Format tab to apply shadow effects such as a drop shadow or perspective shadow. Click the Shadow On/Off button that displays in the Shadow Effects group to turn shadowing on or off. Click the nudge buttons that display around the Shadow On/Off button to nudge the WordArt in small increments in a specific direction. Click the 3-D Effects button to apply a 3-D effect to WordArt or to tilt the WordArt a specific direction.

Arranging WordArt

Use buttons in the Arrange group in the WordArt Tools Format tab to position WordArt text on the page and to choose a text wrapping style. With buttons in this group, you can also align, group, or rotate WordArt text.

Exercise 5

Inserting and Modifying WordArt

1. Open **Document07.docx** and save the document with the name **C12Ex05**.
2. Make the following changes to the document:
   a. Delete the title *Hawaiian Adventures*.
   b. Apply the Heading 1 style to the two headings in the document (*Rainy Day Activities* and *Kauai Sights*).
   c. Select from the paragraph in the *Rainy Day Activities* section that begins with *Movies* through the paragraph that begins with *Theater* and then click the Bullets button in the Paragraph group in the Home tab.
   d. Select all of the paragraphs in the *Kauai Sights* section and click the Bullets button.
   e. Change the style set to *Modern*.
   f. Apply the *Concourse* theme.
   g. Apply the *Metro* theme colors.
   h. Change the left margin to 2.5 inches.
3. Insert WordArt text by completing the following steps:
   a. Press Ctrl + Home to move the insertion point to the beginning of the document.
   b. Click the Insert tab.
   c. Click the WordArt button in the Text group and then click the fourth option from the left in the third row (*WordArt style 16*).
   d. At the Edit WordArt Text dialog box, type **HAWAII** and then click OK.

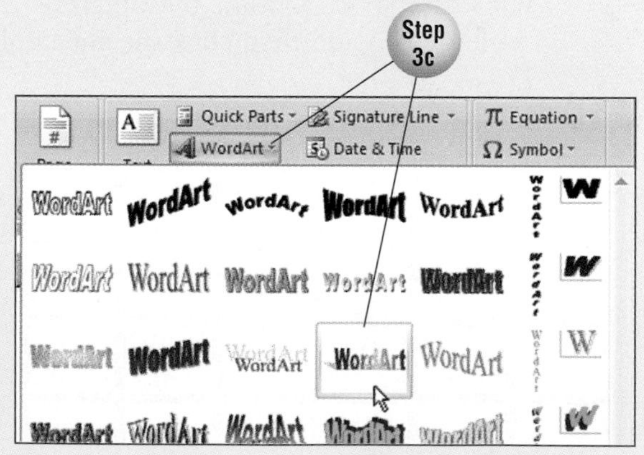

e. Click the WordArt Vertical Text button in the Text group.
f. Click the Shadow Effects button and then click the second option from the left in the top row in the *Drop Shadow* section (*Shadow Style 2*).
g. Click the Shadow Effects button, point to *Shadow Color,* and then click the green color (*Green, Accent 1, Darker 25%*) at the color palette.
h. Click the Text Wrapping button in the Arrange group and then click *Square* at the drop-down list.
i. Click in the Shape Height measurement box and then type **1.5**.
j. Click in the Shape Width measurement box, type **8**, and then press Enter.
k. After looking at the WordArt text with a shadow effect, apply a 3-D effect. To do this, click the 3-D Effects button in the WordArt Tools Format tab and then click the *Tilt Up* option.

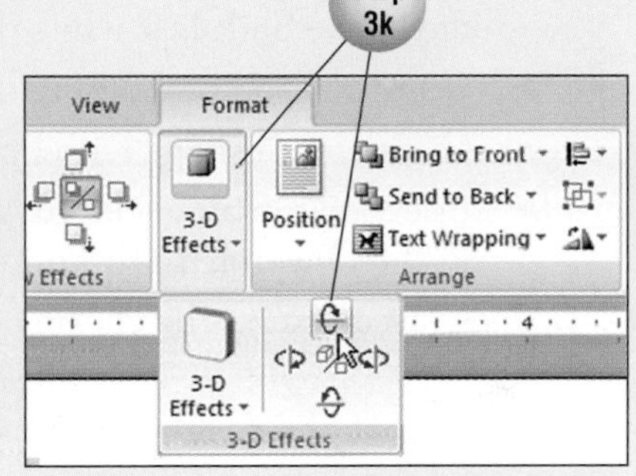

4. Position the WordArt by completing the following steps:
   a. Click the View tab.
   b. Click the One Page button in the Zoom group.
   c. With the WordArt text selected, drag and position it as shown in Figure 12.8.
   d. Click the 100% button in the Zoom group.
5. Make sure the document fits on one page. If necessary, delete blank lines to make the document fit.
6. Save, print, and then close **C12Ex05.docx**.

Figure 12.8 Exercise 5

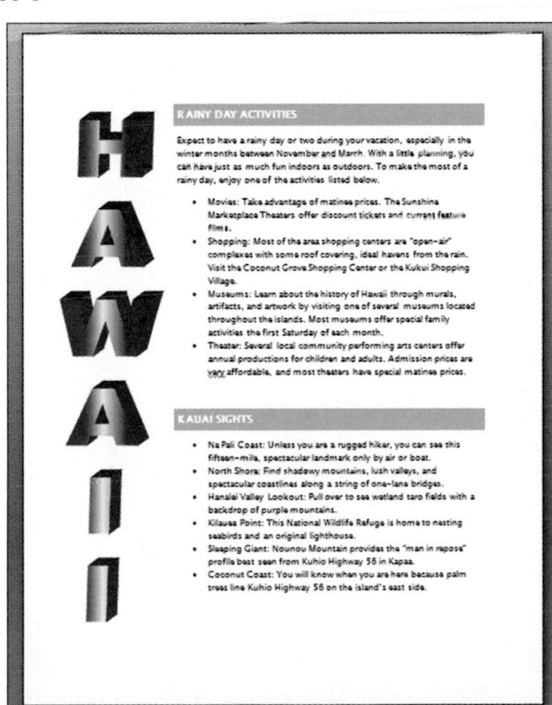

Chapter Summary

- Draw shapes in a document by clicking the Shapes button in the Illustrations group in the Insert tab, clicking the desired shape at the drop-down list, and then dragging in the document to draw the shape.
- With shape options at the Shapes button drop-down list, you can draw lines or enclosed shapes.
- When you draw a line, hold down the Shift key to draw a straight horizontal or vertical line. When you draw an enclosed shape, maintain the proportions of the shape by holding down the Shift key while dragging in the document to create the shape.
- Copy a shape by holding down the Ctrl key while dragging the selected shape.
- Customize a shape with options in the Drawing Tools Format tab.
- Insert text in an enclosed object by clicking the Edit Text button in the Insert Shapes group in the Drawing Tools Format tab.
- Draw a text box by clicking the Text Box button in the Text group in the Insert tab, clicking *Draw Text Box* at the drop-down list, and then clicking in the document or dragging in the document.
- Format and customize a text box with buttons in the Text Box Tools Format tab.
- Link drawn text boxes with the Create Link button in the Text group in the Text Box Tools Format tab. Break a link with the Break Link button in the Text group.
- Select multiple objects by clicking the Select button in the Editing group in the Home tab and then clicking *Select Objects* at the drop-down list. Draw a border around objects you want to select.
- Use WordArt to distort or modify text to conform to a variety of shapes.
- Customize WordArt with options in the WordArt Tools Format tab.
- Edit WordArt text by clicking the Edit Text button in the Edit group in the WordArt Tools Format tab.
- Size WordArt using the sizing handles that display around the selected WordArt or with the Shape Height and Shape Width measurement boxes in the WordArt Tools Format tab.
- Apply shadow and 3-D effects to WordArt text with buttons in the WordArt Tools Format tab.
- Use buttons in the Arrange group in the WordArt Tools Format tab to position WordArt text on the page.

Commands review

FEATURE	RIBBON TAB, GROUP	BUTTON	OPTION
Shapes	Insert, Illustrations		
Text box	Insert, Text		Draw Text Box
Link text box	Text Box Tools Format, Text	Create Link	
Select objects	Home, Editing	Select	Select Objects
WordArt	Insert, Text	WordArt	

Reviewing key points

Completion: In the space provided at the right, indicate the correct term, symbol, or command.

1. The Shapes button is located in this tab. ________________
2. Format text boxes with options and buttons in this tab. ________________
3. With options at the Shapes button drop-down list, you can draw lines or these. ________________
4. To draw a straight horizontal or vertical line, hold down this key while dragging in the document. ________________
5. To copy a selected shape, hold down this key while dragging the shape. ________________
6. To insert text inside of an enclosed shape, click this button in the Insert Shapes group in the Drawing Tools Format tab. ________________
7. Link text boxes using this button in the Text group. ________________
8. To select multiple objects in a document, click the Select button in the Editing group in the Home tab and then click this option. ________________
9. The WordArt button is located in this group in the Insert tab. ________________

10. This tab contains options for formatting WordArt. ____________

11. This group in the WordArt Tools Format tab contains buttons for spacing WordArt text and specifying the vertical and horizontal height of text. ____________

12. Use this button in the WordArt Tools Format tab to change the WordArt fill color. ____________

Applying your skills

Assessment 1 Create a Letterhead with Text and a Drawn Line

1. At a blank document, type the text *Blue Water Charters* shown in Figure 12.9 with the following specifications:
   a. Change the font to 56-point Freestyle Script bold and the font color to *Blue, Accent 1, Darker 25%*. (To change the font size to 56 points, you will need to select the current point size in the Font Size text box and then type **56**.)
   b. Center the text.
2. Draw the line below the text with the *Line* option at the Shapes drop-down list and then apply the following formatting:
   a. Apply the *Solid Fill, Compound Outline, Accent 1* shape style (second option from the left in the bottom row of the drop-down list).
   b. Apply the *Shadow style 4* shadow style (last option in the top row of the *Drop Shadow* section).
3. Save the document with the name **C12A01**.
4. Print and then close **C12A01.docx**.

Figure 12.9 Assessment 1

Blue Water Charters

Assessment 2 Create an Announcement with a Shape and Text Box

1. At a blank document, create the shape shown in Figure 12.10 with the following specifications:
   a. Use the *Bevel* shape.
   b. Change the height to 3.3 inches and the width to 5.7 inches.
   c. Change the shape style to *Diagonal Gradient - Accent* 2 (third option from the left in the sixth row of the drop-down list).
   d. Apply the *Shadow Style* 2 style (second option from the left in the top row of the *Drop Shadow* section).
2. Click the Edit Text button in the Insert Shapes group and then type the text inside the shape with the following specifications:
   a. Press the Enter key once.
   b. Click the Home tab and then change the font to 36-point Monotype Corsiva bold and the font color to red (*Red, Accent* 2, *Darker* 50%).
   c. Click the Center button and then type the text shown in Figure 12.10.
3. Save the document with the name **C12A02**.
4. Print and then close **C12A02.docx**.

Figure 12.10 Assessment 2

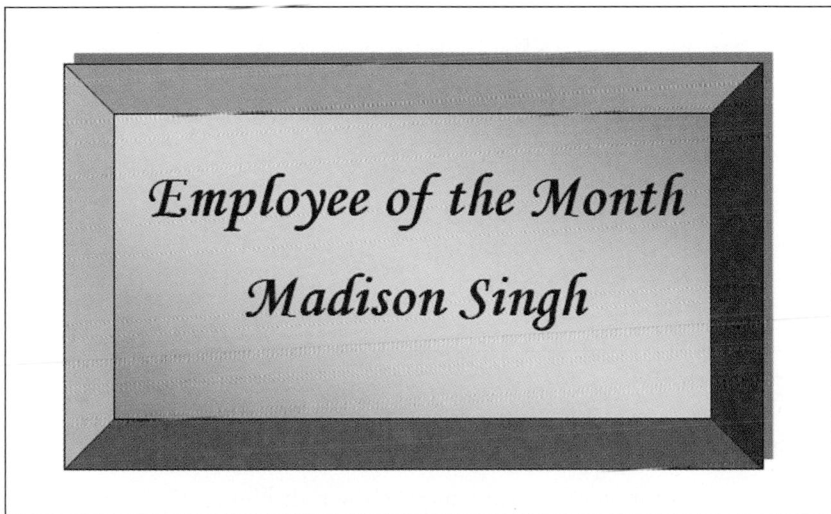

Assessment 3 Create a Flyer with Shapes and a Text Box

1. At a blank document, create the left circular arrow shown in Figure 12.11 with the following specifications:
   a. Draw the shape using the *Curved Right Arrow* shape.
   b. Change the height of the arrow to 4.2 inches and the width of the arrow to 2.5 inches.
   c. Apply the *Horizontal Gradient - Accent* 6 shape style (last option in the seventh row in the drop-down list).
   d. Change the shape outline color to dark orange (*Orange, Accent* 6, *Darker* 50%).
2. Copy the arrow to the right and then flip the arrow horizontally and then flip it vertically.
3. Move the arrows so they are positioned as shown in Figure 12.11.
4. Draw a text box inside the arrows that is 0.7 inches tall and 2.8 inches wide and then change the shape outline to *No Outline*.

5. Type the text inside the text box with the following specifications:
   a. Change the line spacing to single and change the spacing after to 0 points.
   b. Change the paragraph alignment to Center.
   c. Change the font to 20-point Franklin Gothic Heavy and the font color to dark orange (*Orange, Accent 6, Darker 50%*).
6. Make sure the arrows and text box are positioned as shown in Figure 12.11.
7. Save the document with the name **C12A03**.
8. Print and then close **C12A03.docx**.

Figure 12.11 Assessment 3

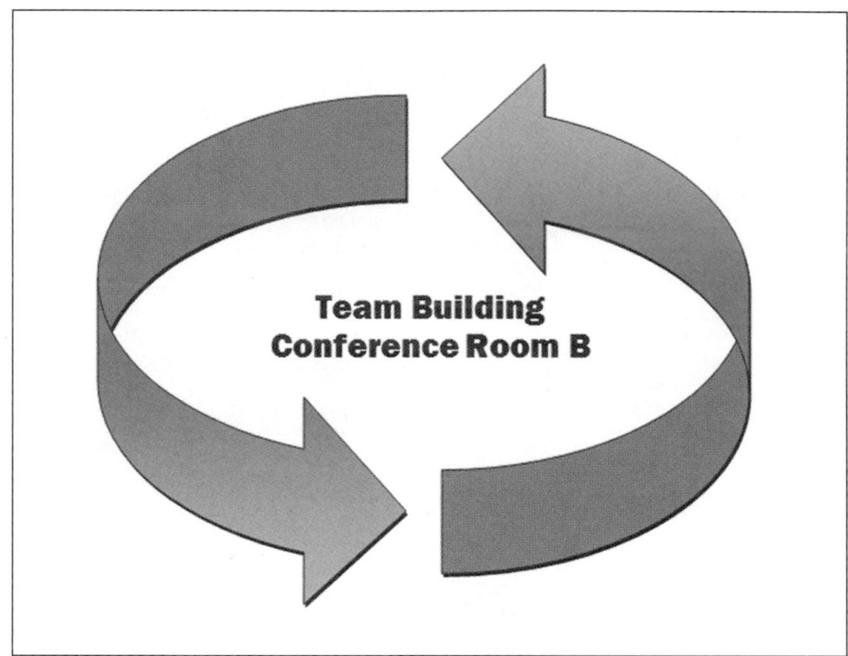

Assessment 4 Create a Banner with WordArt Text

1. At a blank document, create the document shown in Figure 12.12. Insert the WordArt text (Mountain Adventures) with the following specifications:
   a. Create the WordArt with *WordArt style* 20.
   b. Change the height to 1.3 inches and the width to 6.5 inches.
   c. Change the WordArt shape to *Inflate Top*.
   d. Apply the *3-D Style 1* 3-D effect.
2. Save the document with the name **C12A04**.
3. Print and then close **C12A04.docx**.

Figure 12.12 **Assessment 4**

Mountain Adventures

Assessment 5 Format and Insert WordArt Text in a Travel Document

1. Open **Document20.docx** and save the document with the name **C12A05**.
2. Create WordArt and format the text so it displays as shown in Figure 12.13. Make the following changes to the document text:
   a. Apply the Heading 1 style to the title and the Heading 2 style to the one heading in the document.
   b. Select the paragraphs of text below the *Fast Facts* heading and then apply bullets.
   c. Change the style set to *Traditional*.
   d. Change the theme to *Concourse*.
   e. Change the left margin to 2 inches.
3. Insert the WordArt text shown in Figure 12.13 with the following specifications:
   a. Create the WordArt with *WordArt style 11*.
   b. Change the text wrapping to *Square*.
   c. Click the WordArt Vertical Text button in the Text group.
   d. Change the height of the WordArt text to 0.8 inch and the width to 6.2 inches.
   e. Change the shape fill to *Turquoise, Accent 1, Lighter 40%*.
   f. Change the shape outline to *Turquoise, Accent 1, Darker 50%*.
   g. Change the shadow color to *Turquoise, Accent 1, Darker 50%*. (To change the shadow color, click the Shadow Effects button, point to *Shadow Color,* and then click the turquoise color at the color palette.)
   h. Drag the WordArt so it is positioned as shown in Figure 12.13.
4. Save, print, and then close **C12A05.docx**.

Figure 12.13 **Assessment 5**

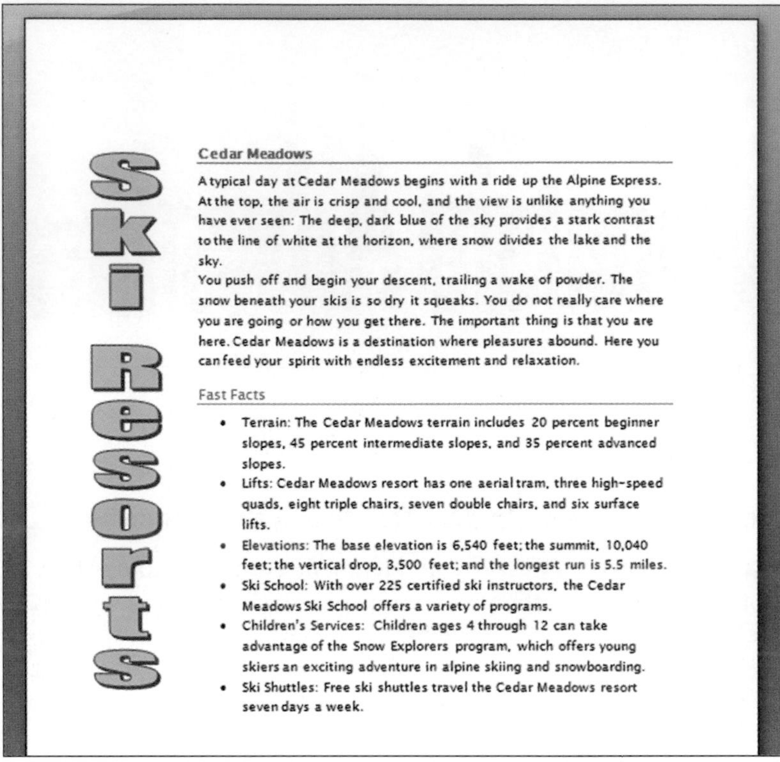

Ski Resorts

Cedar Meadows

A typical day at Cedar Meadows begins with a ride up the Alpine Express. At the top, the air is crisp and cool, and the view is unlike anything you have ever seen: The deep, dark blue of the sky provides a stark contrast to the line of white at the horizon, where snow divides the lake and the sky.

You push off and begin your descent, trailing a wake of powder. The snow beneath your skis is so dry it squeaks. You do not really care where you are going or how you get there. The important thing is that you are here. Cedar Meadows is a destination where pleasures abound. Here you can feed your spirit with endless excitement and relaxation.

Fast Facts

- Terrain: The Cedar Meadows terrain includes 20 percent beginner slopes, 45 percent intermediate slopes, and 35 percent advanced slopes.
- Lifts: Cedar Meadows resort has one aerial tram, three high-speed quads, eight triple chairs, seven double chairs, and six surface lifts.
- Elevations: The base elevation is 6,540 feet; the summit, 10,040 feet; the vertical drop, 3,500 feet; and the longest run is 5.5 miles.
- Ski School: With over 225 certified ski instructors, the Cedar Meadows Ski School offers a variety of programs.
- Children's Services: Children ages 4 through 12 can take advantage of the Snow Explorers program, which offers young skiers an exciting adventure in alpine skiing and snowboarding.
- Ski Shuttles: Free ski shuttles travel the Cedar Meadows resort seven days a week.

Assessment 6 Edit a Drawn Line in a Letterhead Document

1. Open **C12A01.docx** and save the document with the name **C12A06**.
2. Click the horizontal line to select it and then click the Shape Styles group dialog box launcher in the Drawing Tools Format tab. This displays the Format AutoShape dialog box with additional options for customizing the shape. Look over the options at this dialog box and then change the beginning and ending arrow style to *Diamond Arrow*. (Do this with options in the *Arrows* section of the Format AutoShape dialog box with the Colors and Lines tab selected.)
3. Save, print, and then close **C12A06.docx**.

Chapter 13

CHAPTER13

Tutorial 13.1
Working with Tables
Tutorial 13.2
Applying and Modifying Styles to a Table

Creating Tables

Performance Objectives

Upon successful completion of Chapter 13, you will be able to:

- Create and format a table
- Change the table design
- Draw a table
- Insert a Quick Table

Tables provide a systematic way to organize and display data in a document. With Word's Tables feature, you can organize data such as text, numbers, or formulas into columns and rows to create a variety of tables. In this chapter you will learn to create tables using several different methods, including inserting a Quick Table. You will also learn how to format data in a table and apply table styles.

Note: Before beginning computer exercises for this chapter, copy to your storage medium the Chapter13 folder from the CD that accompanies this textbook and then make Chapter13 the active folder.

QUICK STEPS

Create a Table
1. Click Insert tab.
2. Click the Table button.
3. Drag to create desired number of columns and rows.
4. Click the mouse button.

OR
1. Click Insert tab.
2. Click Table button.
3. Click *Insert Table.*
4. Specify number of columns and rows.
5. Click OK.

Creating a Table

A table is made up of information boxes called ***cells.*** A cell is the intersection between a column and a row. Cells can contain text, numbers, characters, graphics, or formulas. You can use Word's Tables feature to create cells and organize data in columns and rows. To create a table, click the Insert tab, click the Table button in the Tables group, drag down and to the right until the correct number of columns and rows display, and then click the mouse button.

Figure 13.1 shows a sample table with four columns and three rows. Various features of a Word table are identified in the figure, such as gridlines, end-of-cell markers, end-of-row markers, move table column markers, and the resize handle. In a Word table, nonprinting characters identify the end of a cell and the end of a row. The end-of-cell marker displays inside each cell, and the end-of-row marker displays at the end of each row of cells. To view these characters, click the Show/Hide ¶ button in the Paragraph group in the Home tab.

Figure 13.1 Table

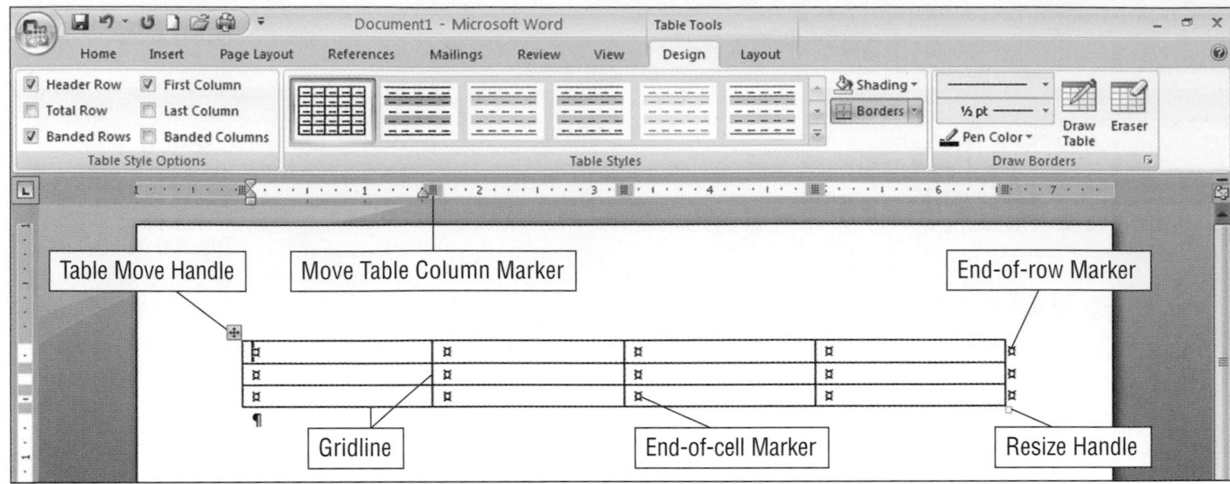

Cells in a table have a cell designation. The columns in a table are lettered from left to right, beginning with *A*; the rows in a table are numbered from top to bottom beginning with *1*. The cell in the upper left corner of the table is cell A1. The cell to the right of A1 is B1, the cell to the right of B1 is C1, and so on. When you create a table, the insertion point displays in cell A1 (in the upper left corner of the table).

When the insertion point is positioned in a cell in the table, the move table column markers display on the horizontal ruler (see Figure 13.1). If the horizontal ruler is not displayed, you can display it—and the markers—by clicking the View Ruler button located toward the top of the vertical scroll bar. These markers represent the end of a column and are useful when changing the width of columns.

Entering Text in Cells

With the insertion point positioned in a cell, type or edit the cell's contents. If the text you type does not fit on one line, it wraps to the next line within the same cell. Or, if you press Enter within a cell, the insertion point moves to the next line within that cell. The cell lengthens vertically to accommodate the text, and all cells in that row also lengthen.

Moving the Insertion Point within a Table

To move the insertion point to a different cell within a table using the mouse, click in the desired cell. To move the insertion point to different cells within a table using the keyboard, use the keyboard commands shown in Table 13.1.

Table 13.1 Insertion Point Movement within a Table Using the Keyboard

To move the insertion point	*Press these keys*
To next cell	Tab
To preceding cell	Shift + Tab
Forward one character	Right Arrow key
Backward one character	Left Arrow key
To previous row	Up Arrow key
To next row	Down Arrow key
To first cell in the row	Alt + Home
To last cell in the row	Alt + End
To top cell in the column	Alt + Page Up
To bottom cell in the column	Alt + Page Down

If you want to move the insertion point to a tab stop within a cell, press Ctrl + Tab. If the insertion point is located in the last cell of the table and you press the Tab key, Word adds another row to the table. You can insert a page break within a table by pressing Ctrl + Enter. The page break is inserted between rows, not within.

Exercise 1A

Creating a Table

1. At a blank document, turn on bold, and then type the title **TECHNICAL SUPPORT PERSONNEL** shown in Figure 13.2.
2. Turn off bold and then press the Enter key.
3. Create the table shown in Figure 13.2 by completing the following steps:
   a. Click the Insert tab.
   b. Click the Table button in the Tables group.
   c. Move the mouse pointer down and to the right until the number above the grid displays as 3 × 6 and then click the mouse button.
4. Type the text in the cells as indicated in Figure 13.2. Press the Tab key to move to the next cell or press Shift + Tab to move to the preceding cell. To indent the text in the cells in the middle column, press Ctrl + Tab to move the insertion point to a tab within the cells, and then type the text. (If you accidentally press the Enter key within a cell, immediately press the Backspace key. Do not press Tab after typing the text in the last cell. If you do, another row is inserted in the table. If this happens, immediately click the Undo button on the Quick Access toolbar.)
5. Save the table with the name **C13Ex01**.

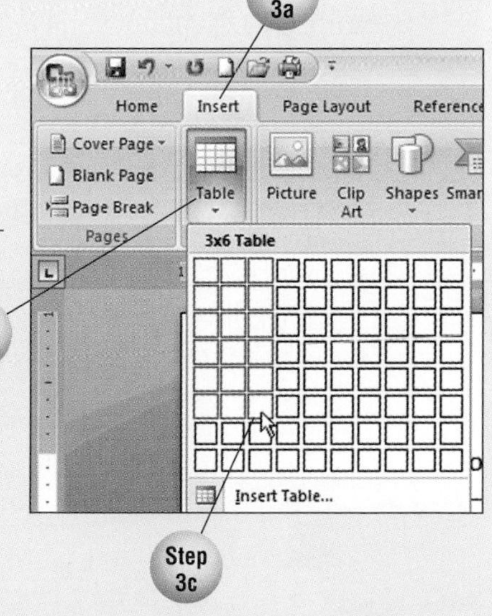

Figure 13.2 Exercise 1A

TECHNICAL SUPPORT PERSONNEL

Name	Title	Telephone Number
Alan Hubbard	Manager	555-3203 Ext. 5401
Debbie Morrissey	Assistant Manager	555-3312 Ext. 5320
Christopher Sorenson	Technician	555-3938 Ext. 5327
Donna Grabowski	Technician	555-3894 Ext. 5411
William Koehler	Technician	555-3809 Ext. 5388

You can also create a table with options at the Insert Table dialog box, shown in Figure 13.3. To display this dialog box, click the Insert tab, click the Table button in the Tables group, and then click *Insert Table* at the drop-down list. At the Insert Table dialog box, enter the desired number of columns and rows and then click OK.

Figure 13.3 Insert Table Dialog Box

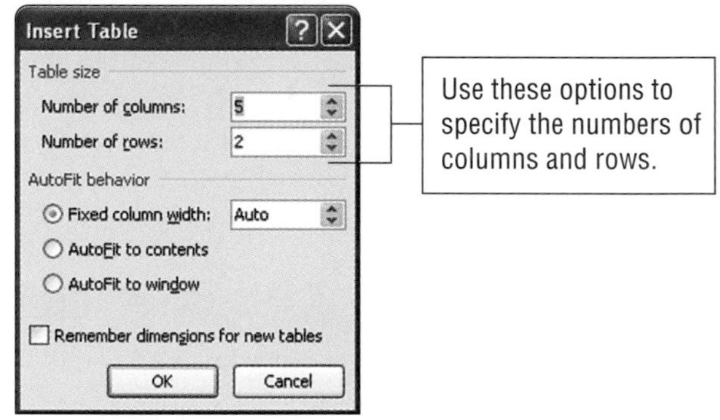

Exercise 1B

Creating a Table with the Insert Table Dialog Box

1. With **C13Ex01.docx** open, press Ctrl + End to move the insertion point below the table.
2. Press the Enter key twice.
3. Turn on bold and then type the title **HUMAN RESOURCES PERSONNEL** shown in Figure 13.4.
4. Turn off bold and then press the Enter key.
5. Insert the table by completing the following steps:
   a. Click the Insert tab.
   b. Click the Table button in the Tables group and then click *Insert Table* at the drop-down list.
   c. At the Insert Table dialog box, type **3** in the *Number of columns* text box. (The insertion point is automatically positioned in this text box.)
   d. Press the Tab key (this moves the insertion point to the *Number of rows* option).
   e. Type **6**.
   f. Click OK.

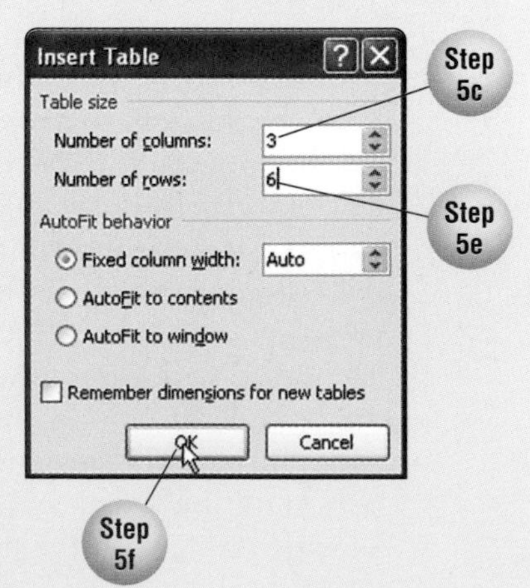

6. Type the text in the cells as indicated in Figure 13.4. Press the Tab key to move to the next cell or press Shift + Tab to move to the preceding cell. To indent the text in cells B1 through B6, press Ctrl + Tab to move the insertion point to a tab within cells, and then type the text.
7. Save **C13Ex01.docx**.

Figure 13.4 Exercise 1B

HUMAN RESOURCES PERSONNEL

Name	Title	Telephone Number
Melissa Clemensen	Manager	555-7463 Ext. 2100
Myong Han	Assistant Manager	555-7487 Ext. 2105
David Hoover	Assistant	555-7444 Ext. 2238
Joseph Reeves	Assistant	555-7601 Ext. 2311
Stephanie Tomasi	Assistant	555-7548 Ext. 2408

Selecting Cells

You can format data within a table in several ways. For example, you can change the alignment of text within cells or rows, or you can add character formatting such as bold, italic, and underlining. To format specific cells, rows, or columns, you must first select them.

Selecting in a Table with the Mouse

Use the mouse pointer to select a cell, column, row, or an entire table. Table 13.2 provides instructions for selecting specific portions of a table or the entire table with the mouse. The left edge of each cell, between the left column border and the end-of-cell marker or first character in the cell, is called the ***cell selection bar.*** When you position the mouse pointer in the cell selection bar, it turns into a black arrow pointing up and to the right (instead of the left). Each row in a table contains a ***row selection bar,*** which is the space just to the left of the left edge of the table. When you position the mouse pointer in the row selection bar, the mouse pointer turns into an arrow pointing up and to the right.

Table 13.2 **Selecting in a Table with the Mouse**

To select this	*Do this*
A cell	Position the mouse pointer in the cell selection bar at the left edge of the cell until it turns into a black arrow pointing up and to the right and then click the left mouse button.
A row	Position the mouse pointer in the row selection bar at the left edge of the table until it turns into an arrow pointing up and to the right and then click the left mouse button. To select nonadjacent rows, hold down the Ctrl key while selecting rows.
A column	Position the mouse pointer on the uppermost horizontal gridline of the table in the appropriate column until it turns into a short, down-pointing arrow and then click the left mouse button. To select nonadjacent columns, hold down the Ctrl key while selecting columns.
Adjacent cells	Position the mouse pointer in the first cell to be selected, hold down the left mouse button, drag the mouse pointer to the last cell to be selected, and then release the mouse button.
All cells in a table	Click the table move handle, or position the mouse pointer in any cell in the table, hold down the Alt key, and then double-click the left mouse button. You can also position the mouse pointer in the row selection bar for the first row at the left edge of the table until it turns into an arrow pointing up and to the right, hold down the left mouse button, drag down to select all rows in the table, and then release the left mouse button.
Text within a cell	Position the mouse pointer at the beginning of the text and then hold down the left mouse button as you drag the mouse across the text. (When a cell is selected, the cell background color changes to blue. When text within a cell is selected, only those lines containing text are selected.)

Selecting in a Table with the Keyboard

Another way to select specific cells within a table is to use the keyboard. Table 13.3 presents the commands for selecting specific portions of a table.

Table 13.3 **Selecting in a Table with the Keyboard**

To select	*Press*
The next cell's contents	Tab
The preceding cell's contents	Shift + Tab
The entire table	Alt + 5 (on numeric keypad with Num Lock off)
Adjacent cells	Hold down Shift key, then press an arrow key repeatedly.
A column	Position insertion point in top cell of column, hold down Shift key, then press down-pointing arrow key until column is selected.

If you want to select only the text within a cell rather than the entire cell, press F8 to turn on the *Extend* mode, and then move the insertion point with an arrow key. When a cell is selected, the cell background color changes to blue. When text within a cell is selected, only those lines containing text are selected. You can move text to a different cell by selecting the text and then dragging the selected text to a different cell.

Exercise 1C

Selecting Cells and Applying Formatting

1. With **C13Ex01.docx** open, select the heading *TECHNICAL SUPPORT PERSONNEL*, change the font to 14-point Candara, and then center the text.
2. Apply the same formatting to the heading *HUMAN RESOURCES PERSONNEL*.
3. Change the formatting for the entire top table by completing the following steps:
   a. Hover the mouse pointer over any cell in the top table until the table move handle displays in the upper left corner of the table.
   b. Position the mouse pointer over the table move handle until the pointer displays as a four-headed arrow and then click the left mouse button. (This selects the entire table.)
   c. Click the Home tab.
   d. Click the Font button arrow and then click *Candara* at the drop-down gallery. (You will need to scroll down the list.)
   e. Deselect the table by clicking in any cell in the table.

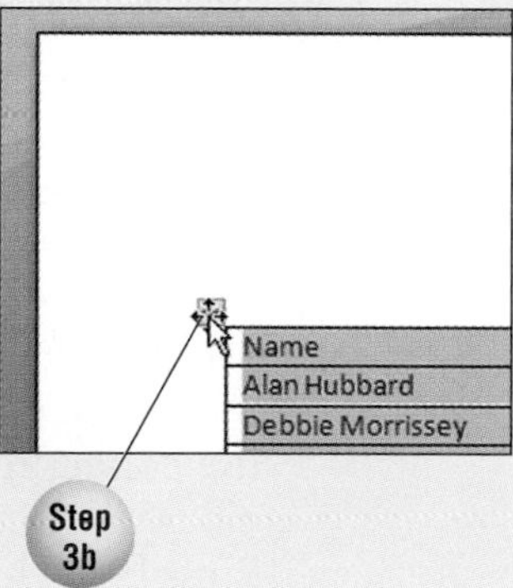

4. Center text in cells in the third column of the top table by completing the following steps:
   a. Position the mouse pointer in the cell below the heading Telephone Number (555-3203 Ext. 5401).
   b. Hold down the left mouse button, drag down to the bottom cell in the table (the cell containing the telephone number 555-3809 Ext. 5388).
   c. Make sure the Home tab is active and then click the Center button in the Paragraph group.

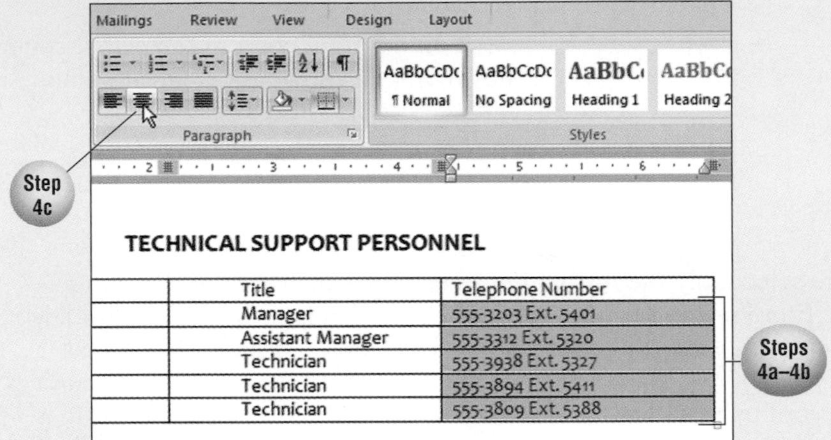

5. Apply formatting to the first row in the top table by completing the following steps:
   a. Position the mouse pointer in the row selection bar at the left side of the first row until the pointer turns into an arrow pointing up and to the right and then click the left mouse button. (This selects the entire first row of the top table.)
   b. Make sure the Home tab is active.
   c. Click the Bold button in the Font group.
   d. Click the Center button in the Paragraph group.
   e. Click the Shading button arrow and then click the dark red color (*Red, Accent 2, Darker 50%*). (This automatically changes the font color to white.)
6. Apply paragraph shading to rows in the top table by completing the following steps:
   a. Click immediately right of the name *Alan Hubbard*.
   b. Hold down the Shift key and then press the Right Arrow key on the keyboard until the entire row is selected.
   c. Click the Shading button arrow and then click the light red color (*Red, Accent 2, Lighter 80%*).
   d. Select the fourth row in the table (begins with the name *Christopher Sorenson*) by positioning the mouse pointer in the row selection bar at the left edge of the fourth row until the pointer turns into an arrow pointing up and to the right and then click the left mouse button.
   e. Press F4. (This is the Repeat command that repeats the last action.)
   f. Select the sixth row (begins with the name *William Koehler*) and then press F4.
7. Complete steps similar to those in Steps 6b-6c to apply red color (*Red, Accent 2, Lighter 60%*) to rows 3 and 5.
8. Complete steps similar to those in Steps 3 through 6 to apply formatting and shading to the bottom table *except* use purple colors for shading.
9. Save, print, and then close **C13Ex01.docx**.

Changing the Table Design

When you insert a table, the Table Tools Design tab, shown in Figure 13.5, becomes active. This tab contains options for applying and changing table styles. The tab also contains a button for applying borders, a button for applying shading, and a button for drawing a table.

Figure 13.5 Table Tools Design Tab

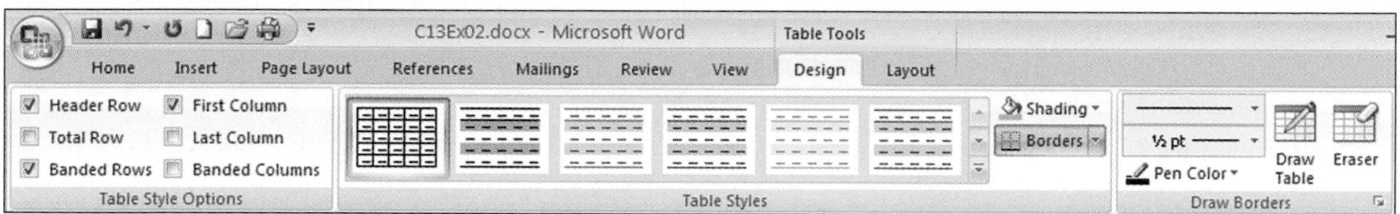

Applying Table Styles

Word provides a number of predesigned table styles that you can use to format your tables and add visual appeal. The Table Styles group in the Table Tools Design tab displays six styles. Word provides additional styles that you can view by clicking the More button that displays at the right side of the styles. Clicking the More button displays a drop-down gallery of style options. Hover the mouse pointer over an option, and the table in the document displays with the formatting applied.

With options in the Table Style Options group, also in the Table Tools Design tab, you can further refine predesigned style formatting that you have applied to your table. For example, if your table contains a total column, you can insert a check mark in the *Total Row* option. If your table contains data in the first column that you would like set off from the other columns of data, you can insert a check mark in the *First Column* check box. If you make a mistake while formatting a table, immediately click the Undo button on the Quick Access toolbar.

Exercise 2A

Creating a Table and Applying Styles

1. At a blank document, create the table shown in Figure 13.6 by completing the following steps:
   a. Type the heading *WOODRIDGE MANUFACTURING* centered and in bold.
   b. Type the subheading *YEARLY SALES* centered and in bold.
   c. Press the Enter key once after typing the subheading, change the paragraph alignment back to left, turn off bold, and then click the Insert tab.
   d. Click the Table button in the Tables group in the Insert tab, drag down and to the right until *5 × 8* displays above the grid.
   e. Type the text in the cells as shown in Figure 13.6.
2. Center the text in all of the columns except the first column by completing the following steps:
   a. Position the mouse pointer at the top of the second column until the pointer displays as a down-pointing black arrow, hold down the left mouse button, drag to the fifth column, and then release the mouse button.
   b. Press Ctrl + E.

3. Apply a table style by completing the following steps:
   a. Make sure the insertion point is positioned in a cell in the table and that the Table Tools Design tab is active.
   b. In the Table Styles Options group, make sure the *Header Row* and *Banded Rows* check boxes are checked and that all other check boxes are unchecked.
   c. Click the More button that displays at the right side of the table styles in the Table Styles group.
   d. Click the fourth option from the left in the fifth row from the top in the *Built-In* section (*Medium Shading 2 - Accent 3*).
4. Save the document with the name **C13Ex02**.
5. Print **C13Ex02.docx**.
6. With the document open, make the following changes:
   a. Make sure the Table Tools Design tab is active.
   b. Remove the check mark from the *Banded Rows* check box in the Table Style Options group.
   c. Insert a check mark in the *First Column* check box and in the *Banded Columns* check box.
   d. Make sure the *Header Row* check box contains a check mark.
7. Save **C13Ex02.docx**.

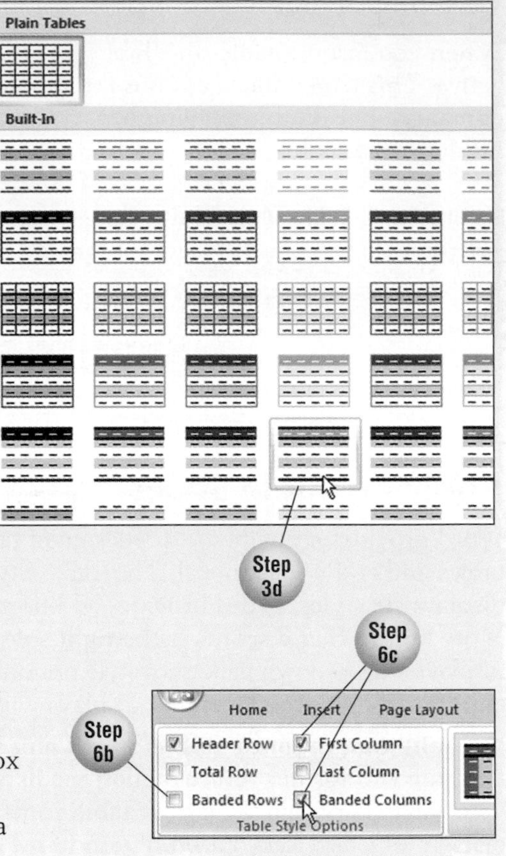

Figure 13.6 Exercise 2A

WOODRIDGE MANUFACTURING

YEARLY SALES

State	First Quarter	Second Quarter	Third Quarter	Fourth Quarter
Maine	$100,340	$105,249	$110,985	$123,679
New Hampshire	$105,674	$101,563	$100,257	$110,947
Massachusetts	$152,491	$162,490	$153,276	$160,054
Connecticut	$104,239	$97,639	$100,574	$106,379
New York	$203,549	$211,574	$199,548	$225,340
Pennsylvania	$189,542	$192,438	$200,459	$221,398
New Jersey	$175,463	$188,390	$173,429	$200,118

Applying Shading and Borders

You can apply shading or change the shading in a table with options from the Shading button drop-down gallery. Display this gallery by clicking the Shading button arrow in the Table Styles group. Click the Borders button arrow in the Table Styles group to display a drop-down gallery of border options. If you want further control over inserting a border in a table, click the *Borders and Shading* option from the drop-down list. This displays the Borders and Shading dialog box with the Borders tab selected, as shown in Figure 13.7. With options at this dialog box, you can choose a border, style, color, and width as well as specify where in the table to apply them.

QUICK STEPS

Apply Shading to Table
1. Click Table Tools Design tab.
2. Click Shading button arrow.
3. Click desired shading color.

Apply Borders to Table
1. Click Table Tools Design tab.
2. Click Borders button arrow.
3. Click desired border option at drop-down list.

OR
1. Click Table Tools Design tab.
2. Click Borders button arrow.
3. Click *Borders and Shading* at drop-down list.
4. Select desired border options.
5. Click OK.

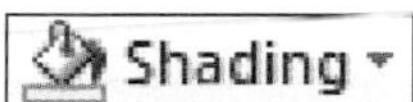

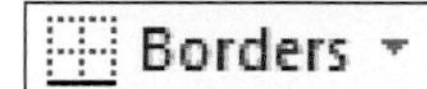

Figure 13.7 Borders and Shading Dialog Box with Borders Tab Selected

Choose a border line style, color, and width with options in this dialog box.

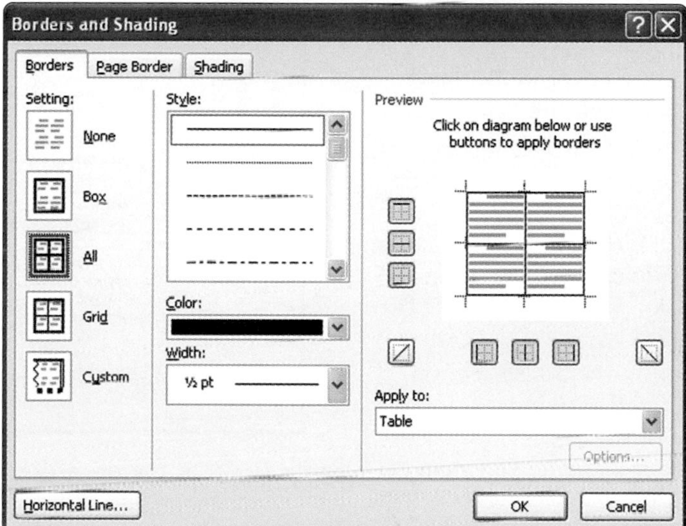

Exercise 2B

Customizing Shading and Borders

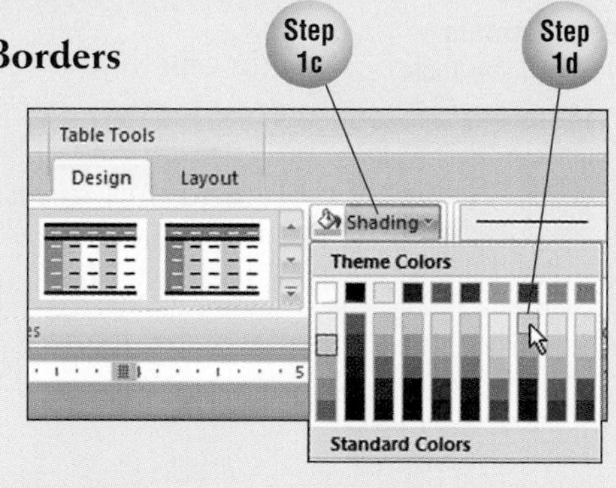

1. With **C13Ex02.docx** open, change cell shading by completing the following steps:
   a. Make sure the Table Tools Design tab is active.
   b. Select the cells in the second column *except* the first cell.
   c. Click the Shading button arrow in the Table Styles group.
   d. Click the light purple color (*Purple, Accent 4, Lighter 80%*) at the drop-down gallery.
   e. Select the cells in the fourth column *except* the first cell and then press F4.
   f. Select the cells in the third column *except* the first cell.
   g. Click the Shading button arrow in the Table Styles group.

h. Click the light green color (*Olive Green, Accent 3, Lighter 80%*) at the drop-down gallery.
i. Select the cells in the fifth column *except* the first cell and then press F4.

2. Change cell borders by completing the following steps:
   a. Select the first column in the table.
   b. Click the Borders button arrow in the Table Styles group and then click the *Left Border* option at the drop-down list.
   c. Select the fifth column in the table.
   d. Click the Borders button arrow in the Table Styles group and then click the *Right Border* option at the drop-down list.

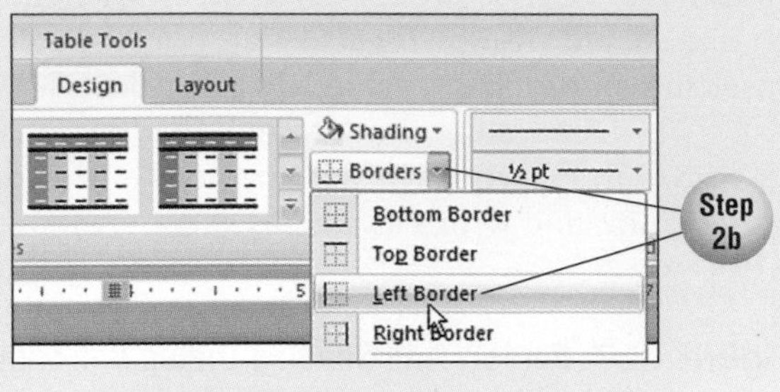

3. Customize cell borders by completing the following steps:
   a. Select the entire table by hovering the mouse pointer over the table and then clicking the table move handle.
   b. Click the Borders button arrow in the Table Styles group and then click the *Borders and Shading* option located at the bottom of the drop-down list.
   c. At the Borders and Shading dialog box with the Borders tab selected, click the down-pointing arrow at the right side of the *Color* option.
   d. Click the purple color at the drop-down list (*Purple, Accent 4, Darker 25%*).
   e. Click the *Box* option in the *Setting* section.
   f. Click OK to close the dialog box.
   g. Select the first row of the table.
   h. Click the Borders button arrow and then click *Bottom Border* at the drop-down list.

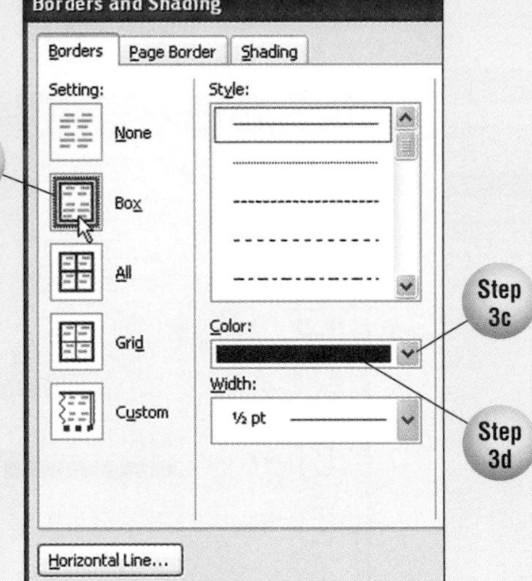

4. Save **C13Ex02.docx**.

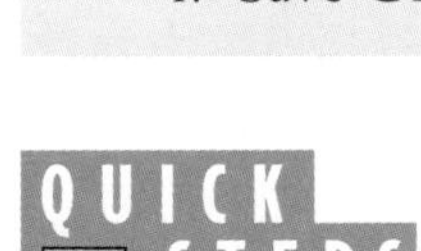

Draw Borders
1. Click Table Tools Design tab.
2. Click Draw Table button.
3. Select desired line style, weight, or color.
4. Draw along table gridlines and/or borders.

Drawing Borders

Another method for inserting borders in a table is to draw them with the pen pointer. To draw borders, click the Draw Table button in the Draw Borders group in the Table Tools Design tab. This changes the mouse pointer to a pen pointer. Draw along the table gridlines to insert a border or to change the color and weight of a border. The Draw Table button displays with an orange background when the button is active. Turn it off by clicking the button.

You can draw a border with a specific line style, weight, and color. Click the Line Style button arrow, and a drop-down list displays with a variety of border line styles. Click the Line Weight button arrow to display a list of line weight options. Change the color of the border line you draw by clicking the Pen Color button arrow and then clicking the desired color at the color palette.

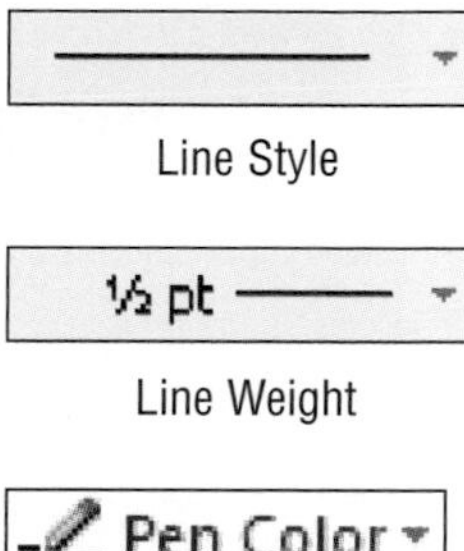

Exercise 2C

Drawing Borders and Lines

1. With **C13Ex02.docx** open, make sure the Table Tools Design tab is active.
2. Draw a double-line border by completing the following steps:
   a. Click the Line Style button arrow in the Draw Borders group and then click the first double-line option at the drop-down list. (This turns on the Draw Table button and changes the mouse pointer to a pen.)
   b. Click the Line Weight button arrow and then click *¾ pt* at the drop-down list.

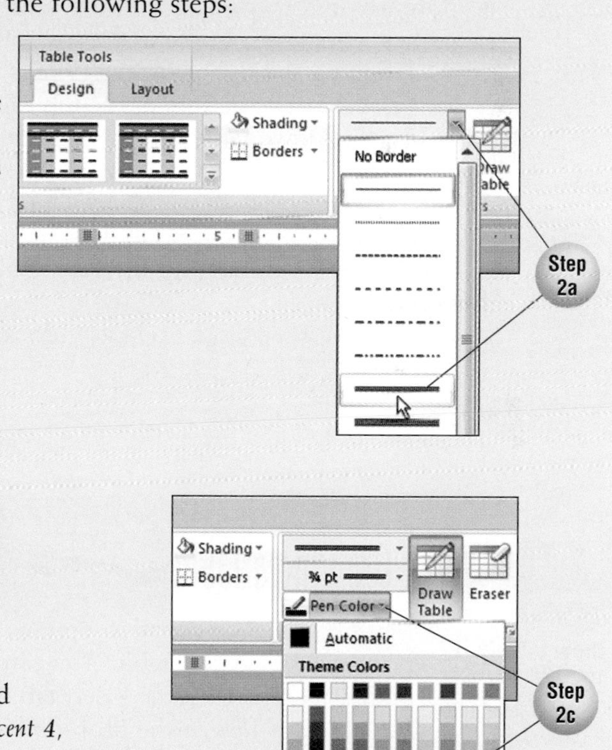

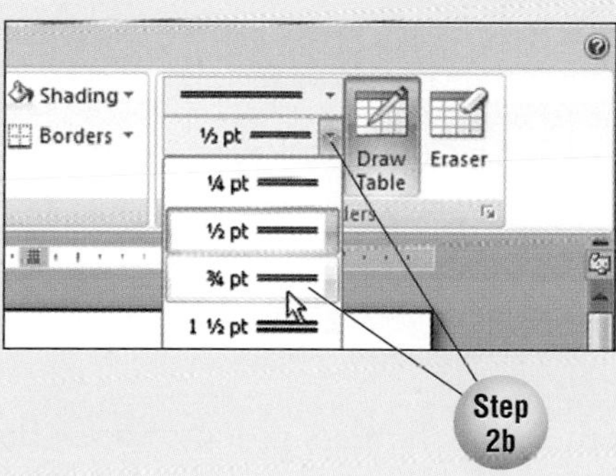

   c. Click the Pen Color button arrow and then click the purple color (*Purple, Accent 4, Darker 50%*).

d. Drag with the pen pointer along the bottom border of the first row from the first cell to the last cell in the row.

Step 2d

WOODRIDGE MANUFACTURING

YEARLY SALES

State	First Quarter	Second Quarter	Third Quarter	Fourth Quarter
Maine	$100,340	$105,2491	$110,985	$123,679
New Hampshire	$105,674	$101,563	$100,257	$110,947

3. Draw a single-line border between columns by completing the following steps:
   a. Click the Line Style button arrow and then click the single-line option that displays toward the top of the drop-down list.
   b. Click the Line Weight button arrow and then click *¼ pt* at the drop-down list.
   c. Draw along the right side of the cells in the second column from the bottom of the first row to the last row.
   d. Draw along the right side of the cells in the third column from the bottom of the top row to the last row.
   e. Draw along the right side of the cells in the fourth column from the bottom of the top row to the last row.
   f. Click the Draw Table button to deactivate it.

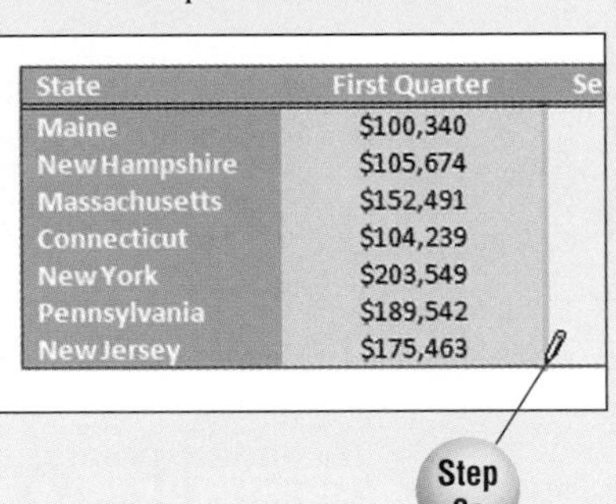

State	First Quarter	Se
Maine	$100,340	
New Hampshire	$105,674	
Massachusetts	$152,491	
Connecticut	$104,239	
New York	$203,549	
Pennsylvania	$189,542	
New Jersey	$175,463	

4. Select the heading and subheading in the document (*WOODRIDGE MANUFACTURING* and *YEARLY SALES*) and then change the font color to dark purple (*Purple, Accent 4, Darker 50%*). (Do this with the Font Color button in the Home tab.)
5. Save, print, and then close **C13Ex02.docx**.

Draw a Table
1. Click Insert tab.
2. Click Table button.
3. Click *Draw Table* at drop-down list.
4. Drag pen pointer in document to create table.

Drawing a Table

In Exercise 2C, you used options in the Draw Borders group to draw borders in and around an existing table. You can also use these options to draw an entire table. To draw a table, click the Insert tab, click the Table button in the Tables group, and then click *Draw Table* at the drop-down list. This turns the mouse pointer into a pen and also displays guidelines on the horizontal and vertical rulers that identify the location of the pen in the document. Drag the pen pointer in the document screen to create the table using the guidelines as a reference.

The first time you release the mouse button when drawing a table, the Table Tools Design tab becomes active. Use buttons in this tab to customize the table as well as to apply table styles, shading, and borders. If you make a mistake while drawing a table, click the Eraser button in the Draw Borders group (this changes the mouse pointer to an eraser) and then drag over any border lines you want to erase.

Exercise 3

Drawing a Table

1. At a blank document, draw the table shown in Figure 13.8 by completing the following steps:
   a. Click the Insert tab.
   b. Click the Table button in the Tables group and then click *Draw Table* at the drop-down list.
   c. Move the pen pointer to approximately the 2-inch marker on the horizontal ruler and the 1-inch marker on the vertical ruler. (Use the guidelines to position the pen.)
   d. Hold down the left mouse button, drag down and to the right until the guideline displays at approximately the 4.5-inch marker on the horizontal ruler and the 3-inch marker on the vertical ruler, and then release the mouse button.

   e. Click the Line Style button arrow and then click the first thick/thin line option at the drop-down list.
   f. Drag over each border of the table to change the border to a thick/thin line.
   g. Click the Line Style button arrow and then click the first double-line option at the drop-down list.

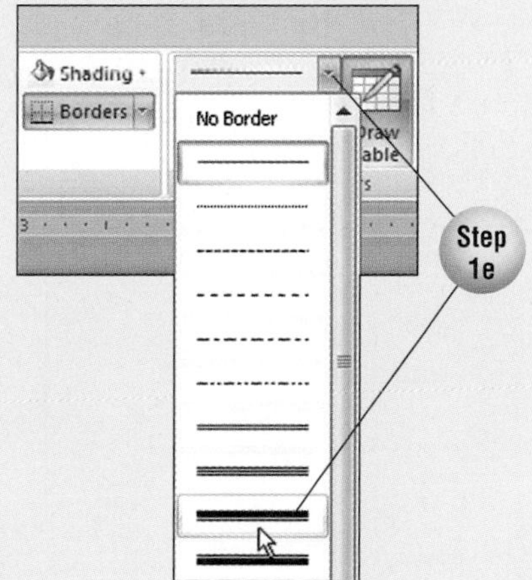

h. Drag to create the first row with the double-line border.
i. Click the Line Style button arrow and then click the single-line option.
j. Drag in the table to create the remaining rows and columns as shown in Figure 13.8. If you are not satisfied with a table border, click the Eraser button in the Draw Borders group and then drag across the border line you want to remove.
k. Click the Draw Table button to deactivate it.

2. Type the text in the table as shown in Figure 13.8.
3. Apply a table style by completing the following steps:
   a. In the Table Style Options group, insert a check mark in the *Header Row* and *Banded Rows* options and remove the check marks (if any) from the other options in the group.
   b. Click the More button that displays at the right side of the table styles in the Table Styles group.
   c. Click the second option from the left in the fifth row from the top in the *Built-In* section (*Medium Shading* 2 - *Accent 1*).
   d. Center the title in Row 1.
4. Save the document with the name **C13Ex03**.
5. Print and then close **C13Ex03.docx**.

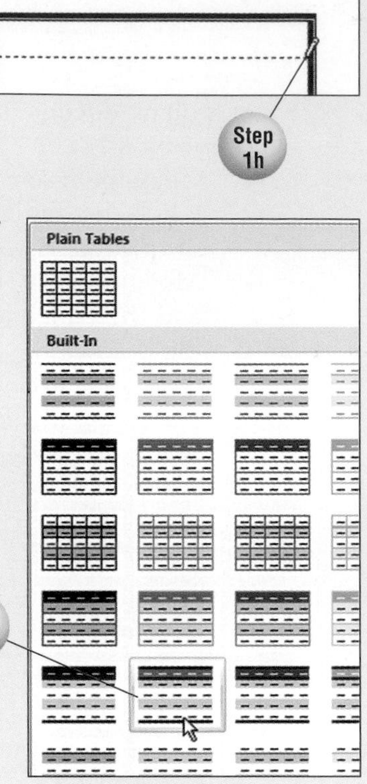

Figure 13.8 Exercise 3

WOODRIDGE MANUFACTURING	
Ethan Sanchez	President
Shawna Richards	Vice President
Jennifer Powell	Director
Chase Selden	Director
Lee Kazlowski	Director

Inserting a Quick Table

Word includes a Quick Tables feature you can use to insert predesigned tables in a document. To insert a quick table, click the Insert tab, click the Table button, point to *Quick Tables,* and then click the desired table at the side menu. When the quick table is inserted in the document, the Table Tools Design tab becomes active. Use options in this tab to further customize the table.

QUICK STEPS

Insert a Quick Table
1. Click Insert tab.
2. Click Table button.
3. Point to *Quick Tables* in drop-down list.
4. Click desired table at side menu.

Exercise 4

Inserting a Quick Table

1. At a blank document, click the Insert tab.
2. Click the Table button, point to *Quick Tables*, and then click *Calendar 3* at the side menu.

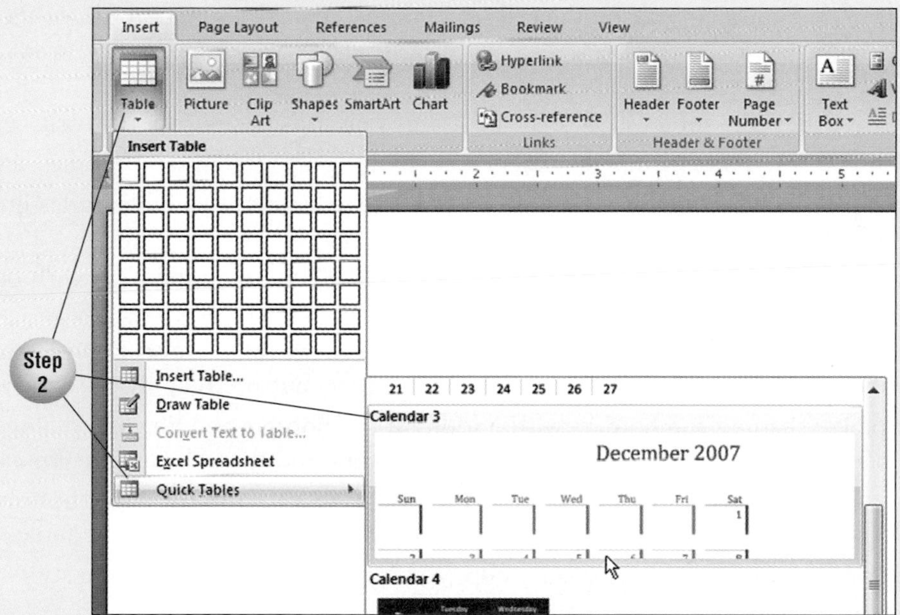

3. Edit text in each of the cells so the month, year, and days reflect the current date.
4. Save the completed monthly calendar with the name **C13Ex04**.
5. Print and then close **C13Ex04.docx**.

Chapter Summary

- Use the Tables feature to create columns and rows of information. A cell is the intersection between a column and a row.
- A table can contain text, characters, numbers, data, graphics, or formulas.
- Create a table by clicking the Insert tab, clicking the Table button in the Tables group, dragging the mouse pointer down and to the right until the desired number of columns and rows display in the grid, and then releasing the mouse button. You can also create a table with options at the Insert Table dialog box.
- Columns in a table are lettered from left to right beginning with A. Rows are numbered from top to bottom beginning with 1.
- The lines that form the cells of the table are called gridlines.
- To move the insertion point to different cells within the table using the mouse, click in the desired cell.
- To move the insertion point to different cells within the table using the keyboard, refer to Table 13.1.
- Position the mouse pointer on the cell selection bar, the row selection bar, or the top gridline of a column to select a cell, row, or column. Click the table move handle to select the entire table.
- Refer to Table 13.3 for a list of keyboard commands for selecting specific cells within a table.
- When you insert a table in a document, the Table Tools Design tab becomes active.
- Apply formatting to a table with the table styles available in the Table Styles group in the Table Tools Design tab.
- Further refine predesigned style formatting applied to columns and rows with options in the Table Style Options group in the Table Tools Design tab.
- Use the Shading button in the Table Styles group in the Table Tools Design tab to apply shading to a cell or selected cells and use the Borders button to apply borders.
- Customize shading and borders with options at the Borders and Shading dialog box. Display this dialog box by clicking the Borders button arrow and then clicking *Borders and Shading*.
- Draw a table in a document by clicking the Insert tab, clicking the Table button, and then clicking *Draw Table*. Using the mouse, drag in the document to create the table.
- With options in the Draw Borders group, you can change the border line style, weight, and color and turn the eraser on or off.
- Quick Tables are predesigned tables you can insert in a document by clicking the Insert tab, clicking the Table button, pointing to *Quick Tables*, and then clicking the desired option at the side menu.

Commands review

FEATURE	RIBBON TAB, GROUP	BUTTON, OPTION	KEYBOARD SHORTCUT
Create table	Insert, Tables	, drag in grid	
Insert Table dialog box	Insert, Tables	, Insert Table	
Move insertion point to next cell			Tab
Move insertion point to previous cell			Shift + Tab
Insert page break within a table			Ctrl + Enter
Draw a table	Insert, Tables	, Draw Table	
Insert Quick Table	Insert, Tables	, Quick Tables	

Reviewing key points

Completion: In the space provided at the right, indicate the correct term, symbol, or command.

1. The Table button is located in this tab. ____________
2. This term refers to the intersection between a row and a column. ____________
3. When you hover the mouse pointer over a table, this displays in the upper left corner of the table. ____________
4. Press this key to move the insertion point to the next cell. ____________
5. Press these keys to move the insertion point to the previous cell. ____________
6. The space just to the left of the left edge of the table is referred to as this. ____________
7. When you insert a table in a document, this tab is active. ____________
8. Click the Borders button arrow and then click *Borders and Shading,* and the Borders and Shading dialog box displays with this tab active. ____________
9. To draw borders in a table using the mouse, click this button in the Draw Borders group. ____________
10. To remove a border line, click this button in the Draw Borders group and then drag across the border. ____________
11. Use this feature to insert predesigned tables in a document. ____________

Applying your skills

Assessment 1 Create and Format a Table in a Letter

1. Open **Letter05.docx** and save the document with the name **C13A01**.
2. Move the insertion point to the blank line between the two paragraphs of text in the body of the letter and then create the table shown in Figure 13.9 with the following specifications:
   a. Create a table with three columns and eight rows.
   b. Select the entire table and then change the font to *Cambria*.
   c. Center, bold, and italicize the text in the first row.
   d. Bold the text in the cells below the *Name* heading.
   e. Apply blue fill to the first row (*Blue, Accent 1, Darker 50%*).
   f. Apply green fill to the second, fourth, sixth, and eighth rows (*Olive Green, Accent 3, Lighter 80%*).
   g. Apply blue fill to the third, fifth, and seventh rows (*Blue, Accent 1, Lighter 80%*).
3. Save, print, and then close **C13A01.docx**.

Figure 13.9 Assessment 1

Name	***Title***	***Department***
Shawn Kilpatrick	Chief Executive Officer	Administration
Gerald Palmer	President	Administration
Emily Higgins	Vice President	Administration
Ryan Keaton	Finances Manager	Finances
Jim Everson	Resources Coordinator	Purchasing
Isabelle Brown	Training Coordinator	Support and Training Services
Sandy Romano-Ellison	Public Relations Manager	Public Relations

Assessment 2 Create and Format a Tour Package Table

1. At a blank document, create the text and table shown in Figure 13.10 with the following specifications:
   a. Set the title *BAYSIDE TRAVEL – TOUR PACKAGES* in 16-point size.
   b. Create a table with four columns and five rows.
   c. Type the text in the cells as shown in Figure 13.10.
   d. Select *Header Row* and *Banded Rows* in the Table Style Options group and remove any other check marks from the check boxes in the group.
   e. Apply the *Medium Shading 1 - Accent 5* table style.
   f. Apply the *Orange, Accent 6, Lighter 80%* orange fill to rows three and five.
2. Save the document with the name **C13A02**.
3. Print and then close **C13A02.docx**.

Figure 13.10 Assessment 2

BAYSIDE TRAVEL – TOUR PACKAGES

Name	Duration	Costs	Discount
Hawaiian Fun in the Sun	5 days and 4 nights	From $709 to $1049	20% in March
Hawaiian Nights	8 days and 7 nights	From $1079 to $1729	10% March and April
Hawaiian Fun Tours	10 days and 9 nights	From $1999 to $2229	15% April and May
Hawaiian Island Tours	14 days and 13 nights	From $2499 to $3099	10% May and June

Assessment 3 Format a Contact List Table

1. Open **Table01.docx** and save the document with the name **C13A03**.
2. Apply formatting to enhance the visual appeal of the document.
3. Save, print, and then close **C13A03.docx**.

Assessment 4 Draw and Format an Employment Information Table

1. At a blank document, draw a table and then type the text shown below in the table.
2. Apply formatting to enhance the visual appeal of the table.
3. Save the document with the name **C13A04**.
4. Print and then close **C13A04.docx**.

JOBS IN DEMAND

Position	Weekly Income	Yearly Openings
Accountants/Auditors	$975	852
Financial Managers	$895	343
Loan Officers	$875	301
Registered Nurses	$852	1,550
Teachers, Elementary	$780	1,112
Teachers, Secondary	$750	1,258

Assessment 5 Create a Monthly Calendar with a Quick Table

1. Use Quick Table to create a monthly calendar for next month.
2. Apply any additional formatting to enhance the visual appeal of the calendar.
3. Save the document with the name **C13A05**.
4. Print and then close **C13A05.docx**.

Chapter 14

Enhancing Tables

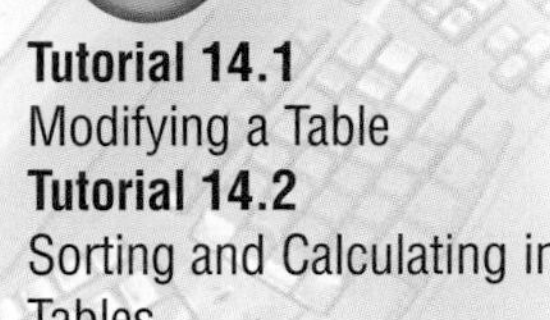

Tutorial 14.1
Modifying a Table
Tutorial 14.2
Sorting and Calculating in Tables

Performance Objectives

Upon successful completion of Chapter 14, you will be able to:

- Edit and format a table
- Change the table design and layout
- Sort text in a table
- Perform calculations on data in a table

In Chapter 13, you learned to create tables and format them by applying table styles, borders, and shading. In this chapter, you will learn how to enhance tables by changing the table layout; inserting and deleting columns and rows; merging and splitting cells; and changing cell size, cell alignment, and cell margins. You will also learn to sort text in a table and perform calculations on data in a table.

Note: Before beginning computer exercises for this chapter, copy to your storage medium the Chapter14 folder from the CD that accompanies this textbook and then make Chapter14 the active folder.

Changing Table Layout

When you insert a table in a document, the Table Tools Design tab becomes active. In Chapter 13, you learned how to use options in this tab to format tables. You can also format a table with options in the Table Tools Layout tab. To display the Table Tools Layout tab, shown in Figure 14.1, position the insertion point in a table and click the tab. Use options and buttons in the tab to select specific cells within the table, delete and insert rows and columns, merge and split cells, specify the height and width of cells, sort data in cells, and insert formulas. Some of these table layout options are also available at a shortcut menu that can be viewed by right-clicking a table.

Figure 14.1 Table Tools Layout Tab

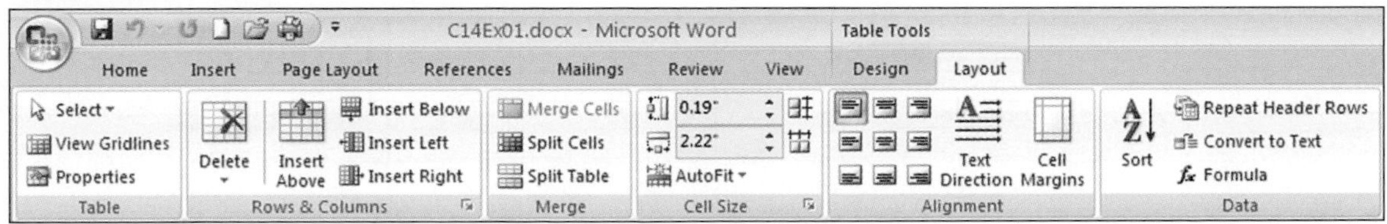

Selecting in a Table with the Select Button

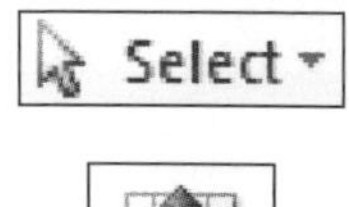

As you learned in Chapter 13, you can select a specific cell, column, or row in a table using either the mouse or the keyboard. You can also select in a table with the Select button, located in the Table group in the Table Tools Layout tab. To select with this button, position the insertion point in the desired cell, column, or row and then click the Select button. At the drop-down list that displays, specify what you want to select—the entire table or a column, row, or cell.

Inserting and Deleting Rows and Columns

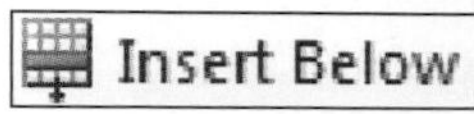

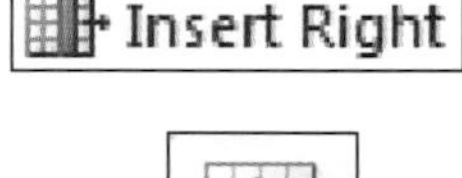

With buttons in the Rows & Columns group in the Table Tools Layout tab, you can insert rows or columns and delete rows or columns. Click the button in the group that inserts the row or column in the desired location, such as above, below, to the left, or to the right of a row or column that you have selected. To delete a row, column, or the entire table, click the Delete button and then click the option specifying what you want to delete.

Exercise 1A

Inserting and Deleting Columns, Rows, and a Table

1. Open **Table02.docx** and save the document with the name **C14Ex01**.
2. Insert a new row in the top table and type text in the new cells by completing the following steps:
   a. Click in the cell containing the name *Joseph Lundeen*.
   b. Click the Table Tools Layout tab.
   c. Click the Insert Above button in the Rows & Columns group.
   d. Type **Janelle Fisher** in the first cell of the new row, press the Tab key, and then type **$2,005,476** in the middle cell of the new row. Press the Tab key and then type **$1,057,422** in the third cell of the new row.

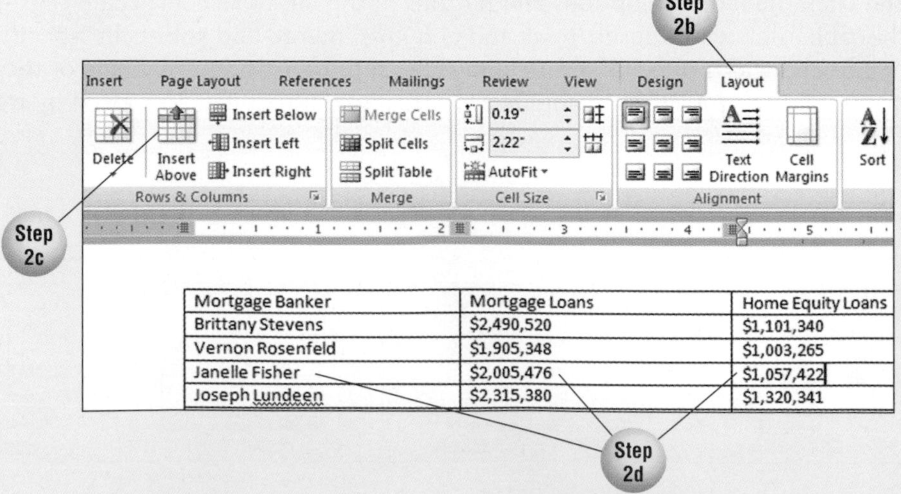

Mortgage Banker	Mortgage Loans	Home Equity Loans
Brittany Stevens	$2,490,520	$1,101,340
Vernon Rosenfeld	$1,905,348	$1,003,265
Janelle Fisher	$2,005,476	$1,057,422
Joseph Lundeen	$2,315,380	$1,320,341

3. Insert three new rows in the middle table and type text in the new cells by completing the following steps:
   a. Select the three rows of cells that begin with the names *Kimberly Gibson*, *Neville Lewis*, and *Ivy Talmadge*.
   b. Click the Insert Below button in the Rows & Columns group.
   c. Type the following text in the new cells:

      Chandra Hall **Horizon Mutual** **(712) 555-0331**
      Harrison Brooks **Mainland Bank** **(313) 555-8555**
      Richard Osaka **Meridian Savings** **(603) 555-9002**

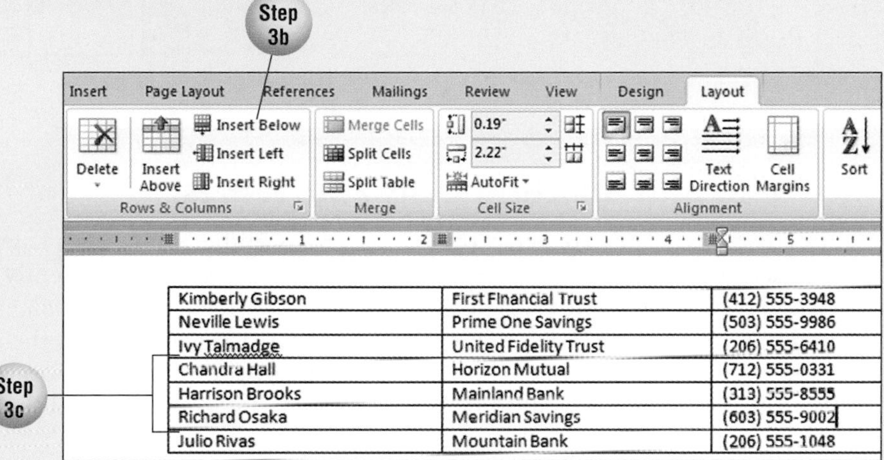

4. Delete a row in the middle table by completing the following steps:
   a. Click in the cell containing the name *Ivy Talmadge*.
   b. Click the Delete button in the Rows & Columns group and then click *Delete Rows* at the drop-down list.
5. Insert a new column in the middle table and type text in the new cells by completing the following steps:
   a. Click in the cell containing the text *First Financial Trust*.
   b. Click the Insert Left button in the Rows & Columns group.
   c. Type the following text in the new cells:

      B1 = **Vice President**
      B2 = **Loan Officer**
      B3 = **Manager**
      B4 = **Vice President**
      B5 = **President**
      B6 = **Loan Officer**

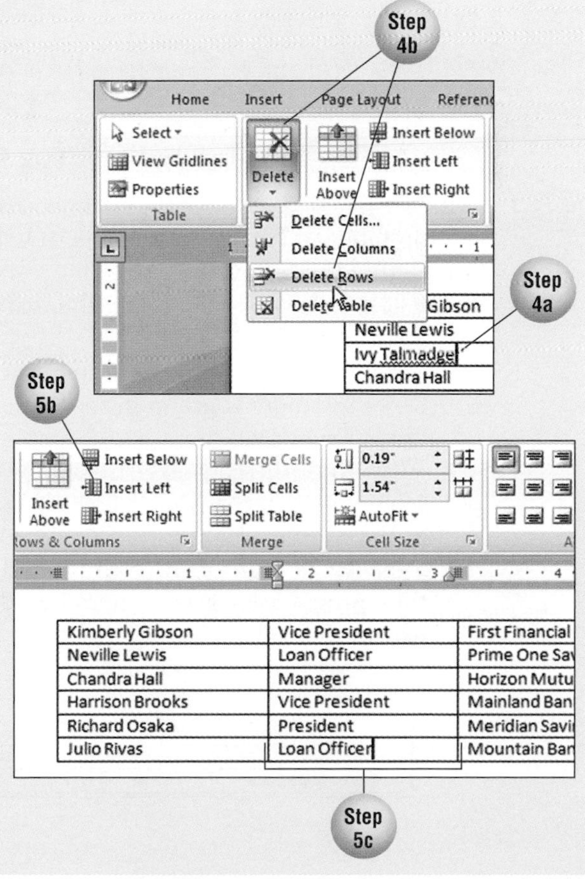

6. Delete the bottom table by completing the following steps:
   a. Click in any cell in the bottom table.
   b. Make sure the Table Tools Layout tab is active.
   c. Click the Delete button in the Rows & Columns group and then click *Delete Table* at the drop-down list.
7. Save **C14Ex01.docx**.

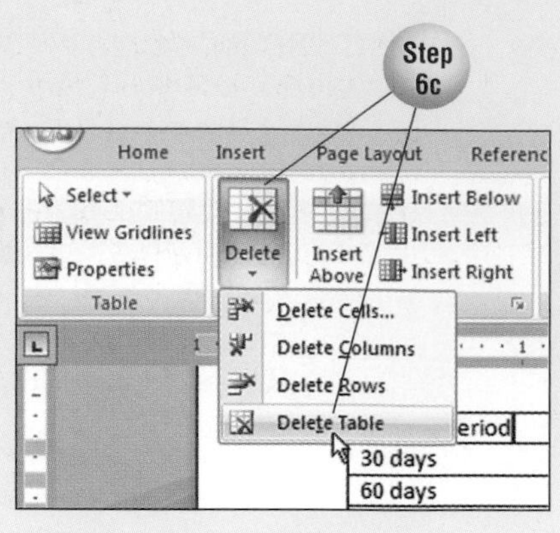

Merging and Splitting Cells and Tables

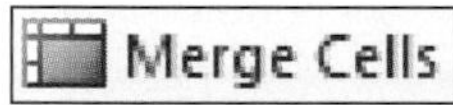

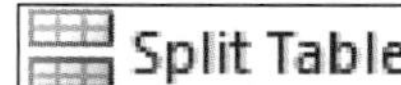

Click the Merge Cells button in the Merge group in the Table Tools Layout tab to merge selected cells and click the Split Cells button to split the currently active cell. When you click the Split Cells button, the Split Cells dialog box displays. At this dialog box, specify the number of columns or rows you want to split the active cell into. If you want to split one table into two tables, position the insertion point in a cell in the row that you want to be the first row in the new table and then click the Split Table button.

Exercise 1B

Merging and Splitting Cells and Splitting a Table

1. With **C14Ex01.docx** open, insert a new row in the top table and merge cells in the row by completing the following steps:
   a. Click in the cell containing the text *Mortgage Banker*.
   b. Click the Insert Above button in the Rows & Columns group in the Table Tools Layout tab.
   c. With all of the cells in the new row selected, click the Merge Cells button in the Merge group.
   d. Type **MORTGAGE BANKERS** and then press Ctrl + E to center align the text in the cell.

2. Insert rows and text in the bottom table and merge cells by completing the following steps:
   a. Click in the cell containing the text *Kimberly Gibson*.
   b. Make sure the Table Tools Layout tab is active.
   c. Click the Insert Above button twice. (This inserts two rows at the top of the table.)
   d. With the cells in the top row selected, click the Merge Cells button in the Merge group.
   e. Type **CONTACT INFORMATION, NORTH** and then press Ctrl + E to change the paragraph alignment to center.
   f. Type the following text in the four cells in the new second row.

      Name Title Company Telephone

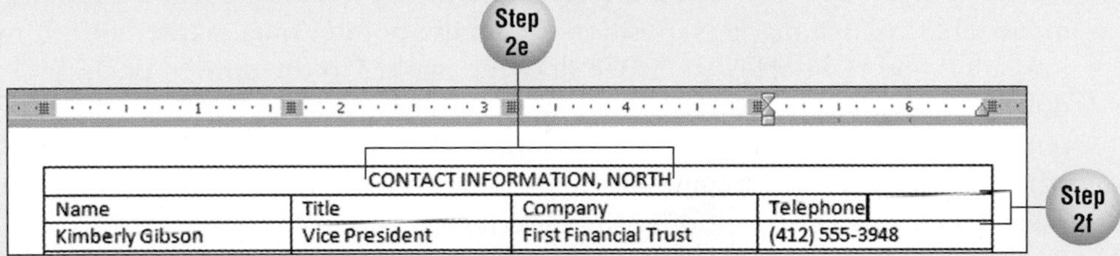

3. Split a cell by completing the following steps:
   a. Click in the cell containing the telephone number (412) 555-3948.
   b. Click the Table Tools Layout tab.
   c. Click the Split Cells button in the Merge group.
   d. At the Split Cells dialog box, click OK. (The telephone number will wrap to a new line. You will change this in the next exercise.)
   e. Click in the new cell.
   f. Type **Ext. 231** in the new cell.
4. Split the cell containing the telephone number (603) 555-9002 and then type **Ext. 782** in the new cell.
5. Split the bottom table into two tables by completing the following steps:
   a. Click in the cell containing the name *Harrison Brooks*.
   b. Click the Split Table button in the Merge group.
   c. Click in the cell containing the name *Harrison Brooks* (in the first row of the new table).
   d. Click the Insert Above button.
   e. With the new row selected, click the Merge Cells button.
   f. Type **CONTACT INFORMATION, SOUTH** in the new row and then press Ctrl + E to center align the text.
6. Insert a new row in the bottom table and type text in the new cells by completing the following steps:
   a. Click in the cell containing the name *Harrison Brooks*.
   b. Make sure the Table Tools Layout tab is active.
   c. Click the Insert Above button in the Rows & Columns group.
   d. Type **Name** in the first cell, type **Title** in the second cell, type **Company** in the third cell, and type **Telephone** in the fourth cell.
7. Save **C14Ex01.docx**.

Customizing Cell Size

Distribute Rows

Distribute Columns

When you create a table, the column width and row height are equal. You can customize the width of columns and the height of rows with buttons in the Cell Size group in the Table Tools Layout tab. Use the Table Row Height measurement box to increase or decrease the height of rows and use the Table Column Width measurement box to increase or decrease the width of columns. The Distribute Rows button distributes equally the height of selected rows, and the Distribute Columns button distributes equally the width of selected columns.

You can also change column width using the move table column markers on the horizontal ruler or by using the table gridlines. To change column width using the move table column markers, position the mouse pointer on a marker until it turns into a left and right arrow and then drag the marker to the desired position. Hold down the Shift key while dragging a table column marker, and the horizontal ruler remains stationary while the table column marker moves. Hold down the Alt key while dragging a table column marker, and measurements display on the horizontal ruler. To change column width using gridlines, position the arrow pointer on the gridline separating columns until the insertion point turns into a left and right arrow with a vertical line between and then drag the gridline to the desired position. If you want to see the column measurements on the horizontal ruler as you drag a gridline, hold down the Alt key.

Adjust row height in a manner similar to that used to adjust column width. You can drag the adjust table row marker on the vertical ruler or drag the gridline separating rows. Hold down the Alt key while dragging the adjust table row marker or the row gridline, and measurements display on the vertical ruler.

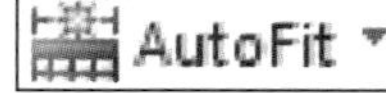

Use the AutoFit button in the Cell Size group to make the column widths in a table automatically fit the contents. To do this, position the insertion point in any cell in the table, click the AutoFit button in the Cell Size group, and then click *AutoFit Contents* at the drop-down list.

Exercise 1C

Changing Column Width and Row Height

1. With **C14Ex01.docx** open, change the width of the first column in the middle table by completing the following steps:
   a. Click in the cell containing the name *Kimberly Gibson*.
   b. Position the mouse pointer on the move table column marker that displays just right of the 1.5-inch marker on the horizontal ruler until the pointer turns into an arrow pointing left and right.
   c. Hold down the Shift key and then the left mouse button.
   d. Drag the marker to the 1.25-inch mark, release the Shift key, and then release the mouse button.

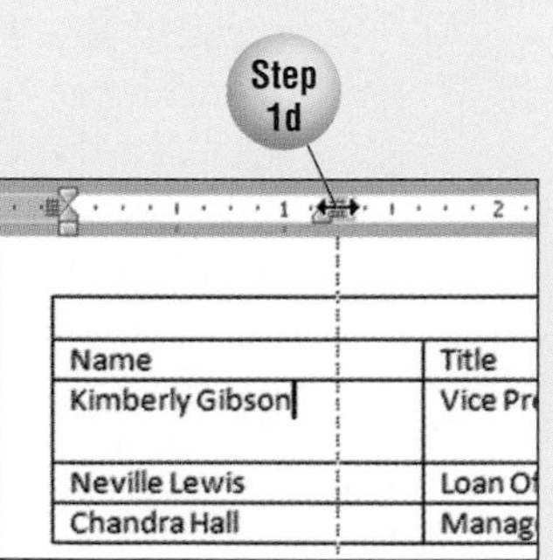

2. Complete steps similar to those in Step 1 to drag the move table column marker that displays just right of the 3-inch mark on the horizontal ruler to the 2.5-inch mark.

3. Change the width of the third column in the middle table by completing the following steps:
   a. Position the mouse pointer on the gridline separating the third and fourth columns until the pointer turns into a left and right arrow with a vertical double line between.
   b. Hold down the Alt key and then the left mouse button, drag the gridline to the left until the measurement for the third column on the horizontal ruler displays as *1.3"*, release the Alt key, and then release the mouse button. (If the Research task pane displays, click the Close button in the upper right corner of the task pane to close it.)
4. Position the mouse pointer on the gridline that separates the telephone number *(412) 555-3948* from the extension *Ext. 231* and then drag the gridline to the 5.25-inch mark on the horizontal ruler.
5. Click in the cell containing the text *Ext. 231* and then drag the right border of the middle table to the 6-inch mark on the horizontal ruler.
6. Click in any cell in the bottom table and then drag the column boundaries so they match the column boundaries in the middle table. (Use the guidelines that display when dragging boundaries to help you position the column boundaries.)
7. AutoFit the columns in the top table by completing the following steps:
   a. Click in any cell in the top table.
   b. Click the AutoFit button in the Cell Size group and then click *AutoFit Contents* at the drop-down list.

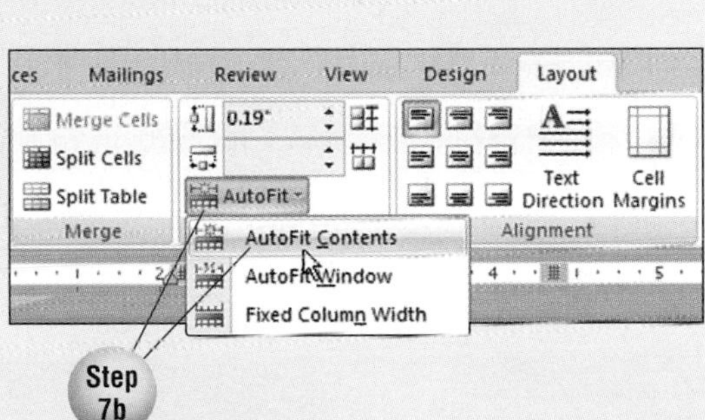

8. Increase the height of the first row in the top table by completing the following steps:
   a. Make sure the insertion point is located in one of the cells in the top table.
   b. Position the mouse pointer on the top adjust table row marker on the vertical ruler.
   c. Hold down the left mouse button and hold down the Alt key.
   d. Drag the adjust table row marker down until the first row measurement on the vertical ruler displays as *0.41"*, release the mouse button, and then release the Alt key.

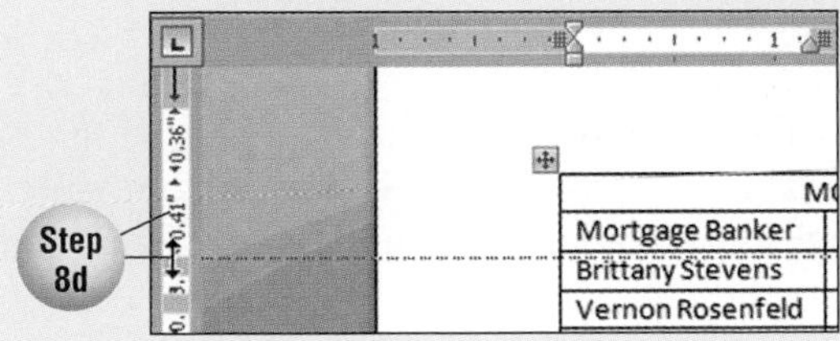

9. Increase the height of the first row in the middle table by completing the following steps:
   a. Click in any cell in the middle table.
   b. Position the arrow pointer on the gridline that displays at the bottom of the top row until the arrow pointer turns into an up- and down-pointing arrow with a vertical double line between.
   c. Hold down the left mouse button and then hold down the Alt key.
   d. Drag the gridline down until the first row measurement on the vertical ruler displays as 0.38″, release the mouse button, and then release the Alt key.

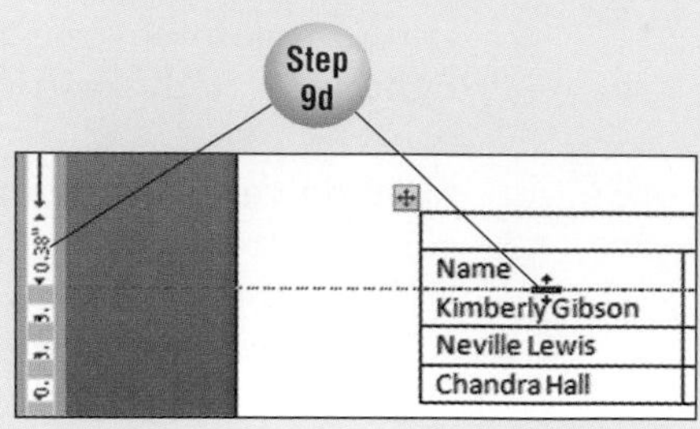

10. Complete steps similar to those in Step 9 to increase the height of the first row in the bottom table to 0.38 inch.
11. Save **C14Ex01.docx**.

Changing Cell Alignment

The Alignment group in the Table Tools Layout tab includes a number of buttons for specifying the horizontal and vertical alignment of text in cells. The buttons contain a visual representation of the alignment; you can also hover the mouse pointer over a button to determine the alignment.

You can also change the alignment of text in a cell with options at the Table Properties dialog box, with the Cell tab selected. Display this dialog box by clicking the Properties button in the Table group in the Table Tools Layout tab. Click the Cell tab, and the *Vertical alignment* section of the dialog box displays options to align text at the top, center, or bottom of cells.

Exercise 1D

Aligning Text in Cells

1. With **C14Ex01.docx** open, vertically align text in the top cell in the top table by completing the following steps:
   a. Click in the top cell in the top table (the cell containing the title *MORTGAGE BANKERS*).
   b. Click the Align Center button in the Alignment group in the Table Tools Layout tab.

2. Complete steps similar to those in Step 1 to vertically align text in the top cell in the middle table and the top cell in the bottom table.
3. Format and align text in the second row in the top table by completing the following steps:
   a. Select the second row in the top table.
   b. Press Ctrl + B.
   c. Click the Align Center button in the Alignment group.
4. Complete steps similar to those in Step 3 to format and align text in the second row in the middle table and the second row in the bottom table.

5. Apply a table style by completing the following steps:
   a. Click in any cell in the top table.
   b. Click the Table Tools Design tab.
   c. Insert or remove check marks from the options in the Table Style Options group so only *Header Row* and *Banded Rows* contain check marks in the check boxes.
   d. Click the More button that displays at the right side of the table styles in the Table Styles group.
   e. Scroll down the drop-down gallery and then click *Colorful List* (the first option from the left in the thirteenth row in the *Built-In* section).
   f. Click in the top cell in the table, click the Table Tools Layout tab, and then click the Align Center button in the Alignment group.
6. Complete steps similar to those in Step 5 to apply the *Colorful List - Accent 1* table style and change cell alignment in the middle table.
7. Complete steps similar to those in Step 5 to apply the *Colorful List - Accent* 2 table style and change cell alignment in the bottom table.
8. Center the cells below the *Mortgage Loans* heading in the top table and center the cells below the *Home Equity Loans* heading.
9. Save, print, and then close **C14Ex01.docx**.

Changing Cell Margin Measurements

Cells in a Word table have specific default margin settings. Top and bottom margins in a cell have a default measurement of 0 inches and left and right margins have a default setting of .08 inch. You can change these default settings with options at the Table Options dialog box, shown in Figure 14.2. Display this dialog box by clicking the Cell Margins button in the Alignment group in the Table Tools Layout tab. Use the options in the *Default cell margins* section to change the top, bottom, left, or right cell margin measurements.

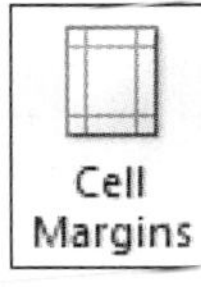

Figure 14.2 Table Options Dialog Box

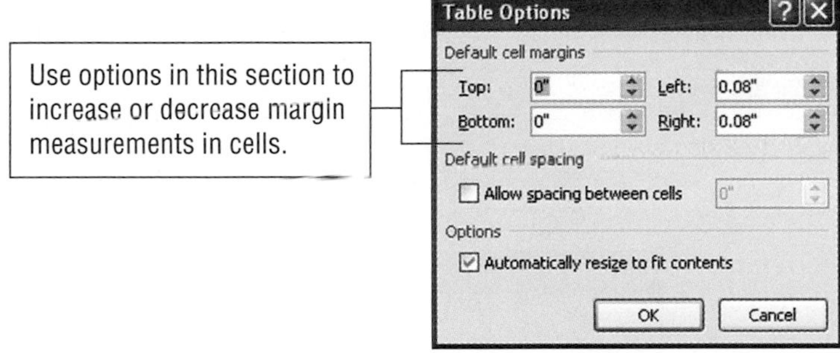

Changing the cell margins affects all cells in a table. If you want to change the cell margin measurements for one cell or for selected cells, position the insertion point in the cell or select the desired cells and then click the Properties button in the Table group in the Table Tools Layout tab. (You can also click the Cell Size group dialog box launcher.) At the Table Properties dialog box, click the Cell tab and then click the Options button that displays in the lower right corner of the dialog box. This displays the Cell Options dialog box, shown in Figure 14.3.

Figure 14.3 Cell Options Dialog Box

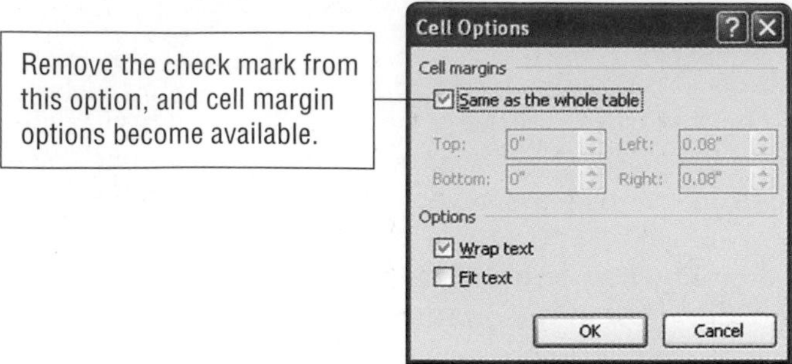

Before you can set new cell margin measurements, you must remove the check mark from the *Same as the whole table* option. When the check mark is removed from this option, the cell margin options become available. Specify the new cell margin measurements and then click OK to close the dialog box.

Exercise 2A

Changing Cell Margin Measurements

1. Open **Table03.docx** and save the document with the name **C14Ex02**.
2. Change the top and bottom margins for all cells in the table by completing the following steps:
   a. Position the insertion point in any cell in the table and then click the Table Tools Layout tab.
   b. Click the Cell Margins button in the Alignment group.
   c. At the Table Options dialog box, change the *Top* and *Bottom* measurements to 0.05″.
   d. Click OK to close the Table Options dialog box. 
3. Change the top and bottom cell margin measurements for the first row of cells by completing the following steps:
   a. Select the first row of cells (the cells containing *Name* and *Department*).
   b. Click the Properties button in the Table group.
   c. At the Table Properties dialog box, click the Cell tab.
   d. Click the Options button.
   e. At the Cell Options dialog box, remove the check mark from the *Same as the whole table* option.
   f. Change the *Top* and *Bottom* measurements to 0.1″.
   g. Click OK to close the Cell Options dialog box.
   h. Click OK to close the Table Properties dialog box.

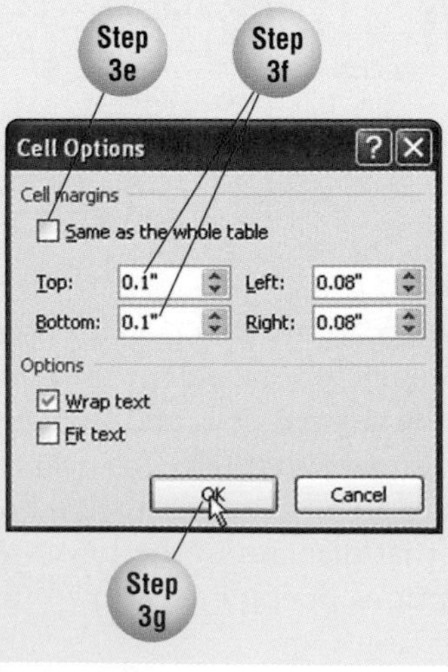

4. Change the left cell margin measurement for specific cells by completing the following steps:
   a. Select all rows in the table *except* the top row.
   b. Click the Cell Size group dialog box launcher.
   c. At the Table Properties dialog box, click the Cell tab.
   d. Click the Options button.
   e. At the Cell Options dialog box, remove the check mark from the *Same as the whole table* option.
   f. Change the *Left* measurement to 0.3″.
   g. Click OK to close the Cell Options dialog box.
   h. Click OK to close the Table Properties dialog box.
5. Save **C14Ex02.docx**.

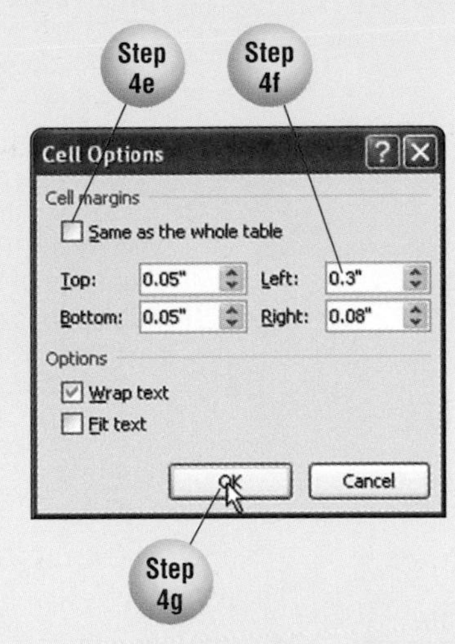

Changing Cell Direction

You can change the direction of text in a cell with the Text Direction button in the Alignment group in the Table Tools Layout tab. Each time you click the Text Direction button, the text in the cell rotates 90 degrees.

Changing Table Alignment

By default, a table aligns at the left margin. Change this alignment with options at the Table Properties dialog box, with the Table tab selected, as shown in Figure 14.4. To change the alignment, click the desired alignment option in the Alignment section of the dialog box.

Change Cell Direction
1. Click in desired cell.
2. Click Table Tools Layout tab.
3. Click Text Direction button until text is in desired position.

Change Table Alignment
1. Click in table.
2. Click Table Tools Layout tab.
3. Click Properties button.
4. Click Table tab.
5. Click desired alignment option.

Figure 14.4 Table Properties Dialog Box with Table Tab Selected

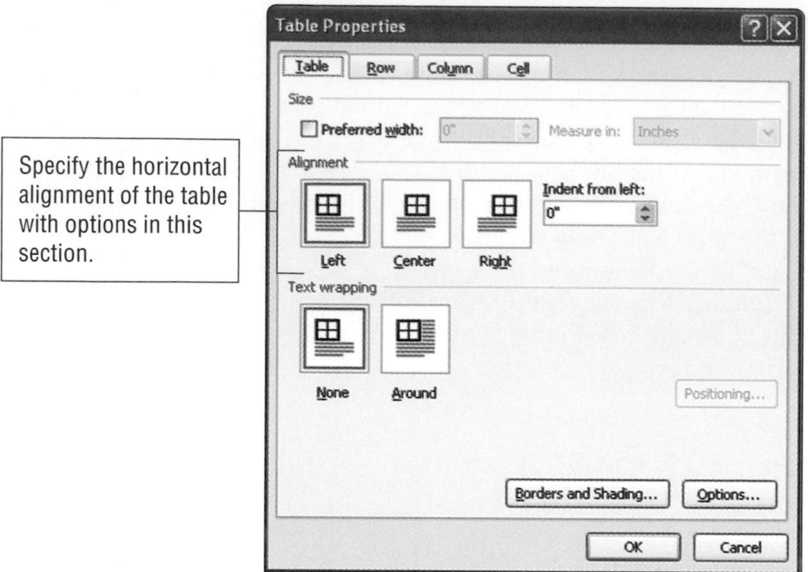

Exercise 2B

Changing Table Alignment

1. With **C14Ex02.docx** open, insert a new column and change text direction by completing the following steps:
   a. Click in any cell in the first column and then click the Table Tools Layout tab.
   b. Click the Insert Left button in the Rows & Columns group.
   c. With the cells in the new column selected, click the Merge Cells button in the Merge group.
   d. Type **Mobile Bay Products**.
   e. Click the Align Center button in the Alignment group.
   f. Click twice on the Text Direction button in the Alignment group.
   g. With Mobile Bay Products selected, click the Home tab, increase the font size to *14*, and, if necessary, turn on bold.

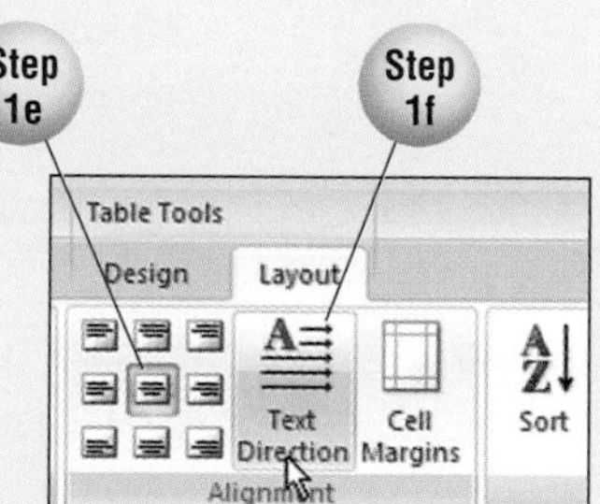

2. AutoFit the contents by completing the following steps:
   a. Click in any cell in the table.
   b. Click the Table Tools Layout tab.
   c. Click the AutoFit button in the Cell Size group and then click the *AutoFit Contents* at the drop-down list.

3. Change the table alignment by completing the following steps:
    a. Click the Properties button in the Table group in the Table Tools Layout tab.
    b. At the Table Properties dialog box, click the Table tab.
    c. Click the *Center* option in the *Alignment* section.
    d. Click OK.
4. Select the two cells containing the text *Name* and *Department* and then click the Align Center button in the Alignment group.
5. Save **C14Ex02.docx**.

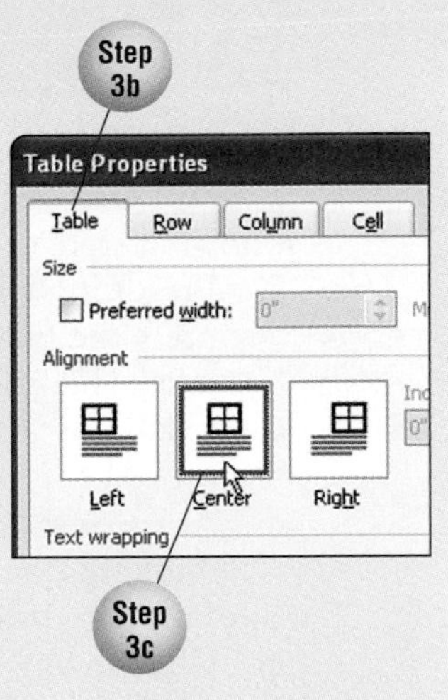

Changing Table Size with the Resize Handle

When you hover the mouse pointer over a table, a resize handle displays as a small, white square in the lower right corner of the table. Drag this resize handle to increase or decrease the size and proportion of the table.

Moving a Table

Position the mouse pointer in a table, and a table move handle displays in the upper left corner. Use this handle to move the table in the document. To move a table, position the mouse pointer on the table move handle until the pointer turns into a four-headed arrow, hold down the left mouse button, drag the table to the desired position, and then release the mouse button.

Change Table Size with Resize Handle

1. Hover mouse pointer over table.
2. Position mouse on resize handle in lower right corner of table.
3. Drag resize handle to increase or decrease size and proportion of table.

Move a Table

1. Position mouse pointer on table move handle until pointer displays as a four-headed arrow.
2. Drag table to desired position.
3. Release mouse button.

Exercise 2C

Resizing and Moving Tables

1. With **C14Ex02.docx** open, insert a table into the current document by completing the following steps:
   a. Press Ctrl + End to move the insertion point to the end of the document and then press the Enter key.
   b. Click the Insert tab.
   c. Click the Object button arrow in the Text group and then click *Text from File* at the drop-down list.
   d. At the Insert File dialog box, navigate to the Chapter14 folder and then double-click **Table04.docx.**
2. AutoFit the bottom table by completing the following steps:
   a. Click in any cell in the bottom table.
   b. Click the Table Tools Layout tab.
   c. Click the AutoFit button in the Cell Size group and then click *AutoFit Contents* at the drop-down list.
3. Format the bottom table by completing the following steps:
   a. Click the Table Tools Design tab.
   b. Click the More button that displays at the right side of the Table Styles group and then click the *Medium Shading 1 - Accent 5* style (sixth style from the left in the fourth row of the *Built-In* section).

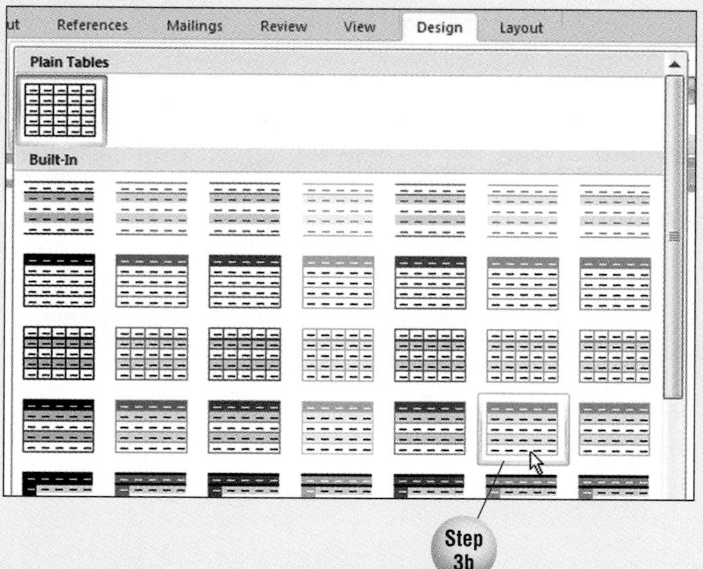

   c. Click the *First Column* check box to remove the check mark.
   d. Select the first and second rows, click the Table Tools Layout tab, and then click the Align Center button in the Alignment group.
   e. Select the second row and then press Ctrl + B to turn on bold.

4. Resize the bottom table by completing the following steps:
   a. Position the mouse pointer on the resize handle located in the lower right corner of the top table.
   b. Hold down the left mouse button, drag down and to the right until the width and height of the table increase approximately 1 inch, and then release the mouse button.

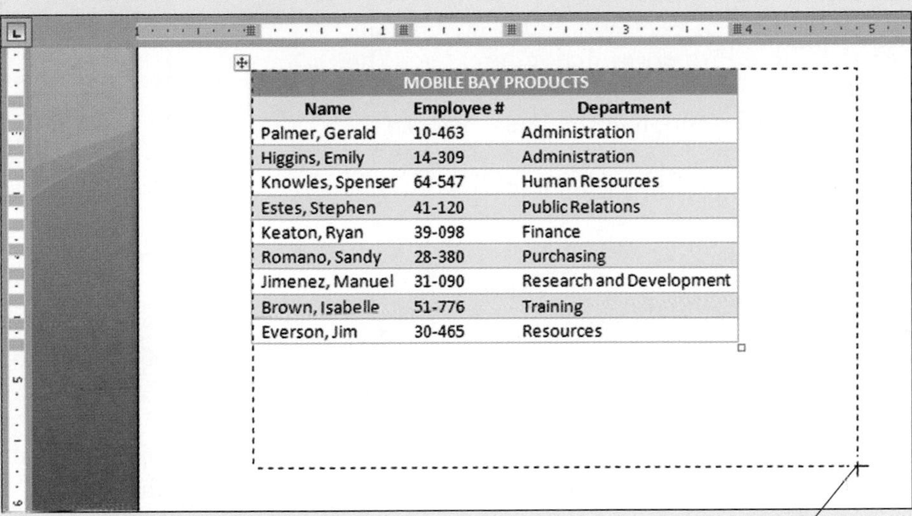

MOBILE BAY PRODUCTS		
Name	Employee #	Department
Palmer, Gerald	10-463	Administration
Higgins, Emily	14-309	Administration
Knowles, Spenser	64-547	Human Resources
Estes, Stephen	41-120	Public Relations
Keaton, Ryan	39-098	Finance
Romano, Sandy	28-380	Purchasing
Jimenez, Manuel	31-090	Research and Development
Brown, Isabelle	51-776	Training
Everson, Jim	30-465	Resources

5. Move the bottom table by completing the following steps:
   a. Hover the mouse pointer over the bottom table.
   b. Position the mouse pointer on the table move handle until the pointer displays with a four-headed arrow attached.
   c. Hold down the left mouse button, drag the table so it is positioned equally between the left and right margins, and then release the mouse button.

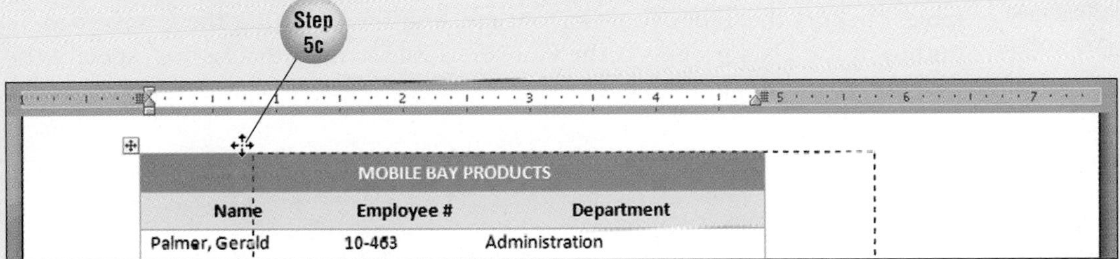

MOBILE BAY PRODUCTS		
Name	Employee #	Department
Palmer, Gerald	10-463	Administration

6. Select the cells in the column below the heading *Employee #* and then click the Align Top Center button in the Alignment group.

7. Center align text vertically in cells by completing the following steps:
   a. Select all of the cells in the three columns below the headings *Name*, *Employee #*, and *Department* (begin with the cell containing *Palmer, Gerald* and select through the cell containing *Resources*).
   b. Click the Properties button in the Table group.
   c. At the Table Properties dialog box, click the Cell tab.
   d. Click the *Center* option in the *Vertical alignment* section.
   e. Click OK to close the dialog box.
8. Save **C14Ex02.docx**.

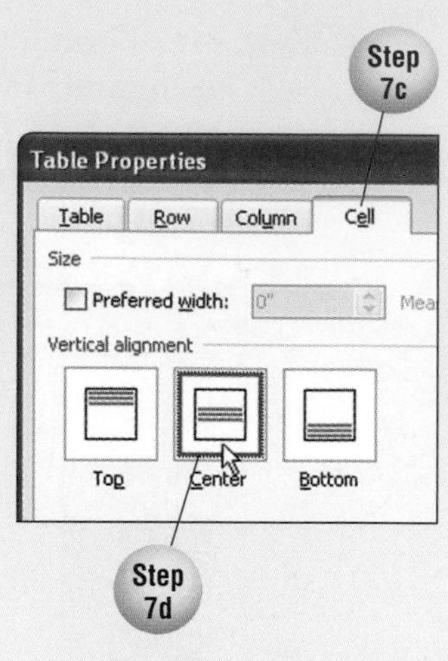

QUICK STEPS

Convert Text to Table

1. Select text.
2. Click Insert tab.
3. Click Table button.
4. Click *Convert Text to Table.*

Convert Table to Text

1. Position insertion point in any cell of table.
2. Click Table Tools Layout tab.
3. Click Convert to Text.
4. Specify desired separator at Convert Table to Text dialog box.
5. Click OK.

Convert to Text

Converting Text to a Table

You can create a table and then enter data in the cells, or you can create data and then convert it to a table. To convert text to a table, type the text and separate it with a separator character such as a comma or tab. The separator character identifies where you want text divided into columns. To convert text, select the text, click the Insert tab, click the Table button in the Tables group, and then click *Convert Text to Table* at the drop-down list.

Converting a Table to Text

You can convert a table to text by positioning the insertion point in any cell of the table, clicking the Table Tools Layout tab, and then clicking the Convert to Text button in the Data group. At the Convert Table to Text dialog box, specify the desired separator and then click OK.

Exercise 2D

Converting Text to a Table

1. With **C14Ex02.docx** open, press Ctrl + End to move the insertion point to the end of the document. (Make sure the insertion point is positioned approximately a double space below the bottom table.)
2. Insert the document named **List01.docx** into the current document.
3. Convert the text to a table by completing the following steps:
   a. Select the text you just inserted.
   b. Click the Insert tab.
   c. Click the Table button in the Tables group and then click *Convert Text to Table* at the drop-down list.
   d. At the Convert Text to Table dialog box, type 2 in the *Number of columns* text box.
   e. Click the *AutoFit to contents* option in the *AutoFit behavior* section.
   f. Click the *Commas* option in the *Separate text at* section.
   g. Click OK.

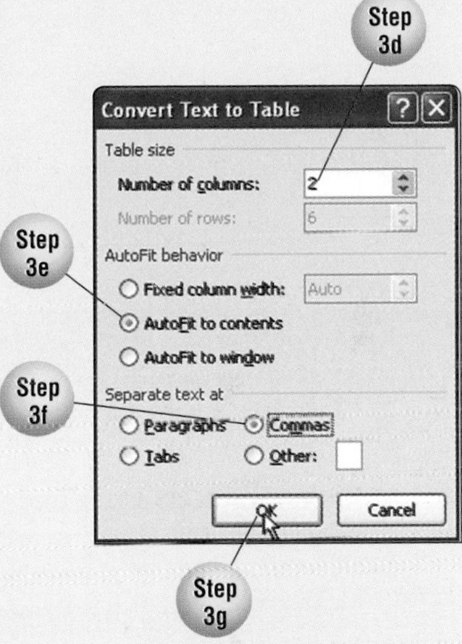

4. Select and merge the cells in the top row (the row containing the title *MOBILE BAY PRODUCTS*) and then change the alignment to Center.
5. Apply the *Medium Shading 1 - Accent 5* table style (sixth style from the left in the fourth row of the *Built-In* section) and remove the check mark from the *First Column* check box in the Table Style Options group in the Table Tools Design tab.
6. Drag the table so it is centered and positioned below the table above.
7. Apply the *Medium Shading 1 - Accent 5* style to the top table. Increase the width of the columns so the text *MOBILE BAY PRODUCTS* is visible and the text in the second and third columns displays on one line.
8. If necessary, drag the table so it is centered and positioned above the middle table. Make sure the three tables fit on one page.
9. Save and then print **C14Ex02.docx**.
10. Convert a table to text by completing the following steps:
    a. Select the middle table.
    b. Click the Copy button in the Clipboard group in the Home tab.
    c. Press Ctrl + N (this displays a blank document).
    d. Click the Paste button in the Clipboard group.
    e. Select the table and then click the Table Tools Layout tab.
    f. Click the Convert to Text button in the Data group.
    g. At the Convert Table to Text dialog box, click the *Tabs* option in the *Separate text with* section, and then click OK.
    h. Select and then bold the title *MOBILE BAY PRODUCTS*.
    i. Click the Quick Print button on the Quick Access toolbar.
    j. Close the document without saving it.

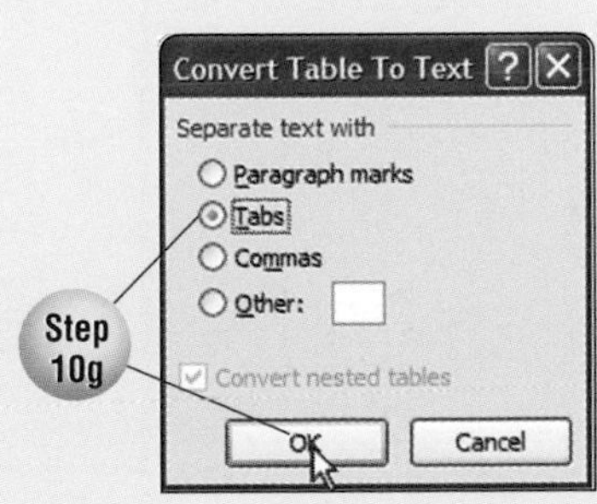

11. Save and then close **C14Ex02.docx**.

Sorting Text in a Table

QUICK STEPS

Sort Text in Tables
1. Select desired rows in table.
2. Click Sort button in Table Tools Layout tab.
3. Specify the column containing text to sort.
4. Click OK.

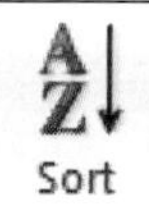

With the Sort button in the Data group in the Table Tools Layout tab, you can sort text in selected cells in a table in ascending alphabetic or numeric order. To sort text, select the desired rows in the table and then click the Sort button in the Data group. At the Sort dialog box, specify the column containing the text on which you want to sort, and then click OK.

Exercise 3A

Sorting Text in a Table

1. Open **Table05.docx** and save the document with the name **C14Ex03**.
2. Sort text in the top table by completing the following steps:
   a. Select all of the rows containing names (from *Kohler, Roger* through *Washington, Isaac*).
   b. Click the Table Tools Layout tab.
   c. Click the Sort button in the Data group.
   d. At the Sort dialog box, click OK. (This sorts the last names in the first column in alphabetical order.)

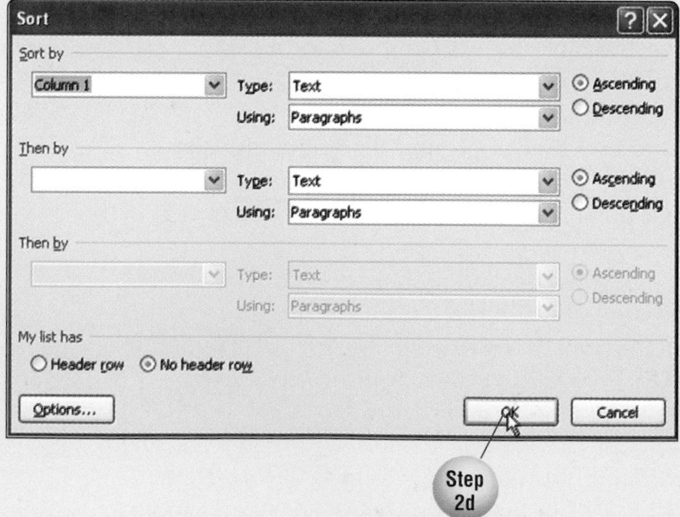

3. Re-sort the table by 2009 Sales by completing the following steps:
   a. With the rows still selected, click the Sort button in the Data group.
   b. At the Sort dialog box, click the down-pointing arrow at the right side of the *Sort by* option box and then click *Column 2* at the drop-down list.
   c. Click OK.
   d. Deselect the rows.
4. Save **C14Ex03.docx**.

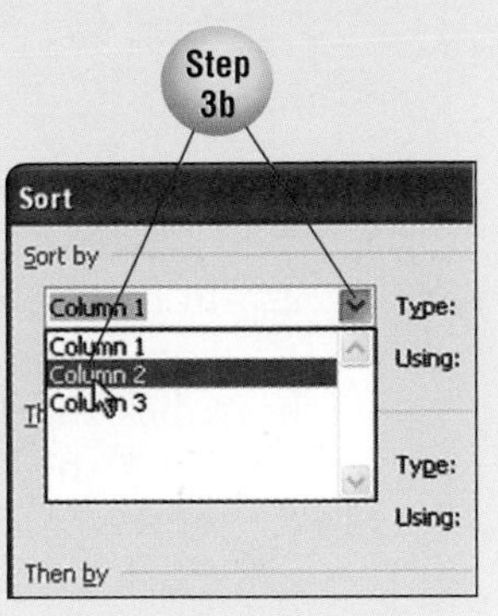

Performing Calculations in a Table

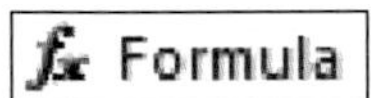

You can use the Formula button in the Data group in the Table Tools Layout tab to insert formulas that calculate data in a table. Numbers in the cells of a table can be added, subtracted, multiplied, and divided. In addition, you can calculate averages, percentages, and minimum and maximum values. Although you can calculate data in a Word table, an Excel worksheet is more suitable for complex calculations.

To perform a calculation on data in a table, position the insertion point in the cell where you want the result of the calculation inserted and then click the Formula button in the Data group in the Table Tools Layout tab. This displays the Formula dialog box, shown in Figure 14.5. At this dialog box, accept the default formula that displays in the *Formula* text box or type the desired calculation and then click OK.

Figure 14.5 Formula Dialog Box

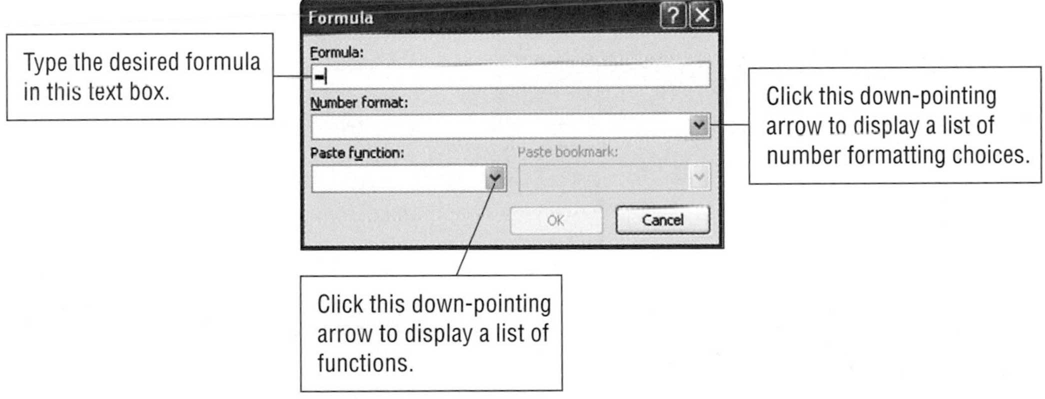

In the default formula, the **SUM** part of the formula is called a ***function.*** Word provides other functions you can use to write a formula. These functions are available with the *Paste function* option in the Formula dialog box. For example, you can use the AVERAGE function to average numbers in cells. Specify the numbering format with the *Number format* option at the Formula dialog box. For example, if you are calculating money amounts, you can specify that the calculated numbers display with no numbers or two numbers following the decimal point.

Exercise 3B

Inserting Formulas

1. With **C14Ex03.docx** open, insert a formula by completing the following steps:
   a. In the top table, click in cell B9 (the empty cell located immediately below the cell containing the amount $700,328).
   b. Click the Table Tools Layout tab.
   c. Click the Formula button in the Data group.
   d. At the Formula dialog box, make sure =*SUM(ABOVE)* displays in the *Formula* option box.
   e. Click the down-pointing arrow at the right side of the *Number format* option box and then click #,##0 at the drop-down list (top option in the list).
   f. Click OK to close the Formula dialog box.
   g. In the table, type a dollar sign ($) before the number just inserted in cell B9.

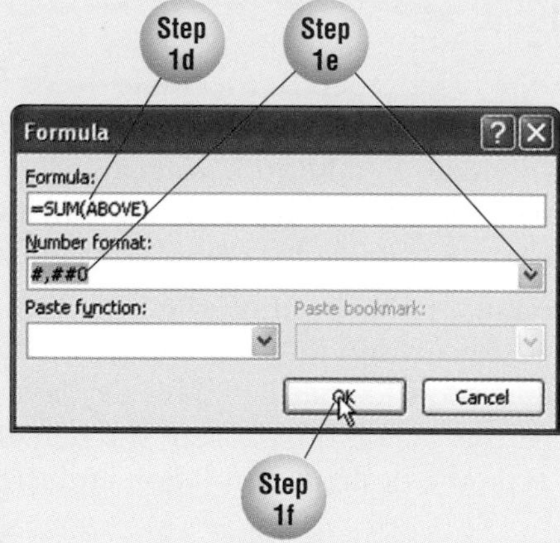

2. Complete steps similar to those in Steps 1c through 1g to insert the Sum formula in cell C9 (the empty cell located immediately below the cell containing the amount $675,329).
3. In the bottom table, complete steps similar to those in Steps 1c through 1g to insert Sum formulas that calculate totals in the cells in the *Total* row.
4. In the bottom table, complete steps similar to those in Steps 1c through 1g to insert in cell F2 (the cell below the *Total* heading) a Sum formula that calculates the total of cells in the row.
5. Insert a formula in the second cell below the *Total* heading (cell F3) by completing the following steps:
   a. Click in cell F3.
   b. Click the Formula button in the Data group.
   c. At the Formula dialog box, press the Backspace key to delete *ABOVE)*.
   d. Type LEFT).

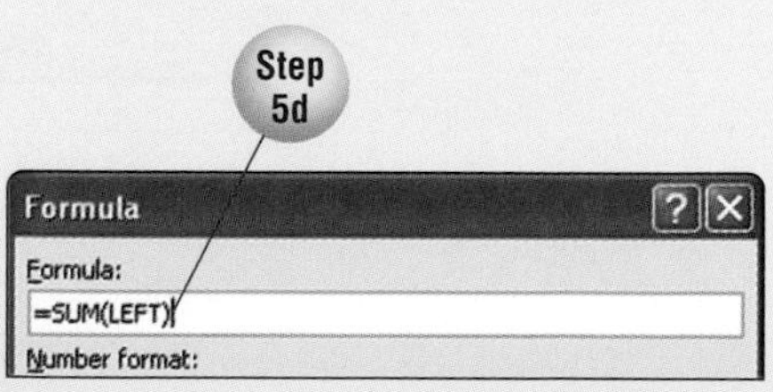

   e. Click the down-pointing arrow at the right side of the *Number format* option box and then click #,##0 at the drop-down list (top option in the list).
   f. Click OK to close the Formula dialog box.
   g. In the table, type a dollar sign ($) before the number just inserted in cell F3.
6. In the bottom table, complete steps similar to those in Steps 5b through 5g to insert Sum formulas that calculate totals of cells in the rows in the *Total* column.

7. Insert a formula that calculates the average of amounts by completing the following steps:
    a. Click in cell B10 in the top table. (Cell B10 is the empty cell immediately right of the cell containing the word *Average*.)
    b. Click the Formula button in the Data group.
    c. At the Formula dialog box, delete the formula in the *Formula* text box *except* the equals sign.
    d. With the insertion point positioned immediately right of the equals sign, click the down-pointing arrow at the right side of the *Paste function* option box and then click *AVERAGE* at the drop-down list.
    e. With the insertion point positioned between the left and right parentheses, type **B2:B8**.
    f. Click the down-pointing arrow at the right side of the *Number format* option box and then click #,##0 at the drop-down list (top option in the list).
    g. Click OK to close the Formula dialog box.
    h. Type a dollar sign ($) before the number just inserted in cell B10.
8. Complete steps similar to those in Steps 7b through 7h to insert in the top and bottom tables formulas that calculate averages. Insert formulas in the *Average* rows of both tables. (When inserting an average formula in a cell in the bottom table, identify only those amounts in row 2 through row 5.)
9. Insert a formula that calculates the maximum number by completing the following steps:
    a. Click in cell B11 (the empty cell immediately right of the cell containing the word *Top Sales*).
    b. Click the Formula button in the Data group.
    c. At the Formula dialog box, delete the formula in the *Formula* text box *except* the equals sign.
    d. With the insertion point positioned immediately right of the equals sign, click the down-pointing arrow at the right side of the *Paste function* option box and then click *MAX* at the drop-down list. (You will need to scroll down the list to display the *MAX* option.)
    e. With the insertion point positioned between the left and right parentheses, type **B2:B8**.
    f. Click the down-pointing arrow at the right side of the *Number format* option box and then click #,##0 at the drop-down list (top option in the list).
    g. Click OK to close the Formula dialog box.
    h. Type a dollar sign ($) before the number just inserted in cell B10.

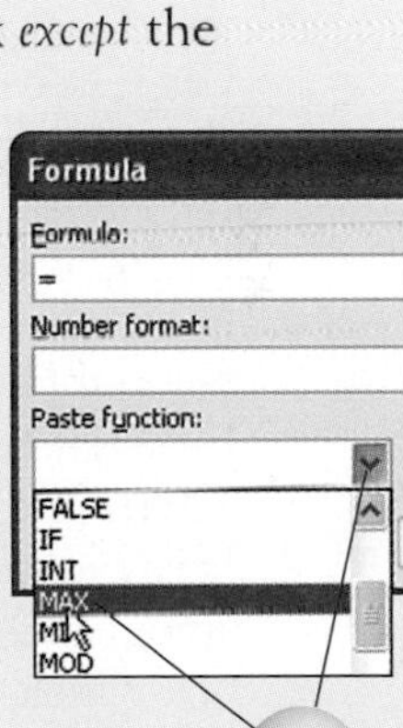

10. Complete steps similar to those in Steps 9b through 9h to insert the maximum number in cell C11.
11. Apply formatting to each table to enhance the visual appeal of the tables.
12. Save, print, and then close **C14Ex03.docx**.

Writing Formulas

In addition to using the functions provided in the Formula dialog box, you can write your own formulas. Use the four basic operators when you write a formula, including the plus sign (+) for addition, the minus sign (hyphen) for subtraction, the asterisk (*) for multiplication, and the forward slash (/) for division. If a calculation contains two or more operators, Word calculates from left to right. If you want to change the order of the calculations, use parentheses around the part of the calculation to be performed first.

Exercise 4A

Writing Formulas in Tables

1. Open **Table06.docx** and save the document with the name **C14Ex04**.
2. Write a formula in the top table that calculates the difference in amounts by completing the following steps:
   a. Click in cell D3 (the empty cell located immediately below the cell containing the heading *Difference*).
   b. Click the Table Tools Layout tab.
   c. Click the Formula button in the Data group.
   d. At the Formula dialog box, press the Backspace key to delete *SUM(LEFT)* that displays in the *Formula* option box. (Do not delete the equals sign.)
   e. Type **B3-C3**.
   f. Click OK to close the Formula dialog box.
3. Click in cell D4 and then complete steps similar to those in Steps 2c through 2g, except type **B4-C4** in the *Formula* text box in the Formula dialog box. (Amounts enclosed in parentheses indicate a negative amount.)
4. Insert the correct formula in the remaining cells in column D. (Make sure you change the cell designation for each formula. For example, type **B5-C5** when inserting the formula in cell D5.)
5. Write a formula in the bottom table that calculates the salary amounts by completing the following steps:
   a. Click in cell D3 (the empty cell located immediately below the cell containing the heading *Salary*).
   b. Click the Table Tools Layout tab.
   c. Click the Formula button in the Data group.
   d. At the Formula dialog box, press the Backspace key to delete *SUM(LEFT)* that displays in the *Formula* option box. (Do not delete the equals sign.)
   e. Type **C3*B3**.
   f. Click OK to close the Formula dialog box.
6. Click in cell D4 and then complete steps similar to those in Steps 5c through 5f, except type **C4*B4** in the *Formula* text box in the Formula dialog box.

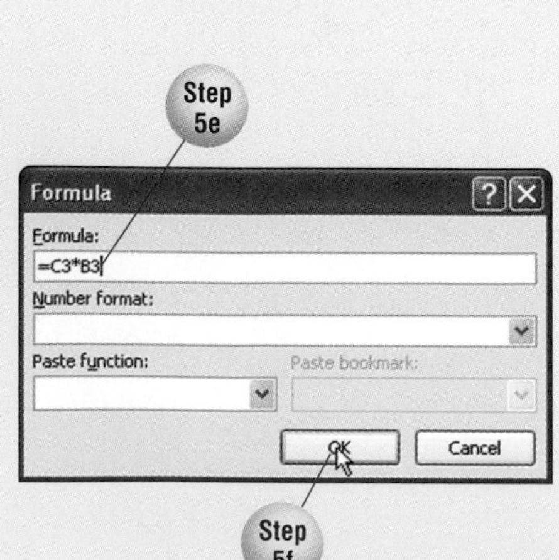

7. Insert the correct formula in the remaining cells in column D. (Make sure you change the cell designation for each formula. For example, type **C5*B5** when inserting the formula in cell D5.)
8. Make the following changes to the top table:
   a. AutoFit the contents of the table.
   b. Apply the *Medium Shading 2 - Accent 5* table style.
   c. Remove the check mark from the *First Column* check box in the Table Style Options group in the Table Tools Design tab.
   d. Select all of the cells containing amounts, click the Table Tools Layout tab, and then click the *Align Top Right* button in the Alignment group.
9. Make the following changes to the bottom table:
   a. AutoFit the contents of the table.
   b. Apply the *Medium Shading 2 - Accent 5* table style.
   c. Remove the check mark from the *First Column* check box in the Table Style Options group in the Table Tools Design tab.
   d. Select the cells containing amounts in the *Rate* and *Salary* columns, click the Table Tools Layout tab, and then click the Align Top Right button in the Alignment group.
   e. Select the hour numbers below the *Hours* heading and then click the Align Top Center button in the Alignment group.
10. Center each table between the left and right margins.
11. Save and then print **C14Ex04.docx**.

Recalculating a Formula

If you change numbers in cells that are part of a formula, recalculate the formula. To do this, select the result of the formula and then press the F9 function key. This recalculates the formula and inserts the new result in the cell. You can recalculate adjacent cells by selecting the cells and then pressing F9. You can also recalculate by selecting the result of the formula, clicking the Formula button in the Table Tools Layout tab, and then clicking OK at the Formula dialog box.

Exercise 4B

Recalculating Formulas

1. With **C14Ex04.docx** open, make the following changes to amounts in the top table:
   a. Change the amount in cell B4 from *$65,375.50* to *$94,375.50*.
   b. Change the amount in cell B6 from *$75,328.20* to *$68,947.00*.
2. Recalculate the amounts in cells D4 and D6 in the top table by completing the following steps:
   a. Click the number in cell D4 and then press the F9 function key.
   b. Click the number in cell D6 and then press the F9 function key.
3. Make the following changes to numbers in the bottom table:
   a. Change the number in cell B4 from *40* to *30*.
   b. Change the amount in cell C5 from *$38.00* to *$39.50*.
4. Recalculate the amounts in cells D4 and D5 in the bottom table by selecting cells D4 and D5 and then pressing the F9 function key.
5. Save, print, and then close **C14Ex04.docx**.

Chapter Summary

- Change the layout of a table with options and buttons in the Table Tools Layout tab.
- You can select a cell, row, column, or table using the Select button in the Table group in the Table Tools Layout tab.
- Insert and delete columns and rows with buttons in the Rows & Columns group in the Table Tools Layout tab.
- Merge selected cells with the Merge Cells button and split cells with the Split Cells button, both located in the Merge group in the Table Tools Layout tab.
- Change column width and row height using the height and width measurement boxes in the Cell Size group in the Table Tools Layout tab; by dragging move table column markers on the horizontal ruler, adjust table row markers on the vertical ruler, or gridlines in the table; or with the AutoFit button in the Cell Size group.
- Change alignment of text in cells with buttons in the Alignment group in the Table Tools Layout tab.
- Change cell margins with options at the Table Options dialog box.
- Change text direction in a cell with the Text Direction button in the Alignment group.
- Change the table alignment at the Table Properties dialog box with the Table tab selected.
- Use the resize handle to change the size of the table and use the table move handle to move the table.
- Convert text to a table with the *Convert Text to Table* option at the Table button drop-down list. Convert a table to text with the Convert to Text button in the Data group in the Table Tools Layout tab.
- Sort selected rows in a table with the Sort button in the Data group.
- Perform calculations on data in a table by clicking the Formula button in the Data group in the Table Tools Layout tab and then specifying the formula and number format at the Formula dialog box.
- Write a formula with basic operators including the plus sign for addition, the minus sign for subtraction, the asterisk for multiplication, and the forward slash for division.
- Recalculate a formula by clicking in the cell containing the result of the formula and then pressing the F9 function key or by clicking the Formula button in the Table Tools Layout tab and then clicking OK at the Formula dialog box.

Commands review

FEATURE	RIBBON TAB, GROUP	BUTTON	OPTION
Insert column left	Table Tools Layout, Rows & Columns	Insert Left	
Insert column right	Table Tools Layout, Rows & Columns	Insert Right	
Insert row above	Table Tools Layout, Rows & Columns		
Insert row below	Table Tools Layout, Rows & Columns	Insert Below	
Delete table	Table Tools Layout, Rows & Columns		Delete Table
Delete row	Table Tools Layout, Rows & Columns		Delete Rows
Delete column	Table Tools Layout, Rows & Columns		Delete Columns
Merge cells	Table Tools Layout, Merge	Merge Cells	
Split Cells dialog box	Table Tools Layout, Merge	Split Cells	
AutoFit table contents	Table Tools Layout, Cell Size	AutoFit	
Cell alignment	Table Tools Layout, Alignment		
Table Options dialog box	Table Tools Layout, Alignment		
Cell direction	Table Tools Layout, Alignment		
Convert text to table	Insert, Tables		Convert Text to Table
Convert table to text	Table Tools Layout, Data	Convert to Text	
Sort text in table	Table Tools Layout, Data		
Formula dialog box	Table Tools Layout, Data	*fx* Formula	

Reviewing key points

Completion: In the space provided at the right, indicate the correct term, command, or number.

1. Click this button in the Table Tools Layout tab to insert a column at the left side of the column containing the insertion point. ________________
2. One method for changing column width is dragging this on the horizontal ruler. ________________
3. Insert and delete columns and rows with buttons in this group in the Table Tools Layout tab. ________________
4. Click this button in the Table Tools Layout tab to merge the selected cell. ________________
5. Use this measurement box in the Table Tools Layout tab to increase or decrease the height of rows. ________________
6. Hold down this key while dragging a table column marker, and measurements display on the horizontal ruler. ________________
7. Use this button in the Cell Size group in the Table Tools Layout tab to make the column widths in a table automatically fit the contents. ________________
8. This is the default setting for the left and right margins in a cell. ________________
9. Change the table alignment at this dialog box with the Table tab selected. ________________
10. Hover the mouse pointer over a table, and this displays in the lower right corner of the table. ________________
11. Position the mouse pointer in a table, and this displays in the upper left corner. ________________
12. Click this button to display the *Convert Text to Table* option. ________________
13. The Sort button is located in this group in the Table Tools Layout tab. ________________
14. When writing a formula, this symbol indicates multiplication. ________________
15. When writing a formula, this symbol indicates division. ________________

Applying your skills

Assessment 1 Create and Format a Supply Request Form Table

1. At a blank document, create the table shown in Figure 14.6 with the following specifications:
   a. Create a table with five columns and eight rows.
   b. Insert three additional rows in the table.
   c. Merge the cells in the first row.
   d. Type the text in the cells as shown in Figure 14.6.
   e. Change the row height of the first row to 0.58 inch.
   f. Select the text in the first row and then change the font size to 22 points.
   g. Select rows 2 through 11 and then change the row height for the selected cells to 0.3 inch.
   h. Apply the *Medium Shading 2 - Accent 2* table style.
   i. Remove the check mark from the *First Column* option in the Table Style Options group.
   j. Change the alignment of the text in the first row to Align Center.
   k. Change the alignment of the text in the second row to Align Center and turn on bold.
2. Save the document with the name **C14A01**.
3. Print and then close **C14A01.docx**.

Figure 14.6 Assessment 1

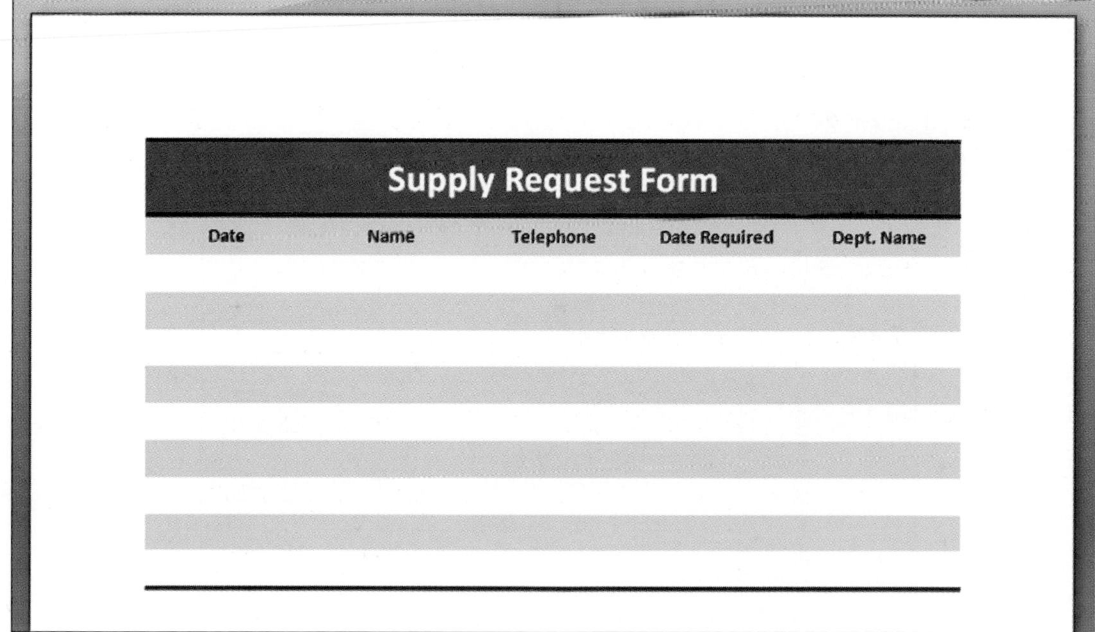

Assessment 2 Format a Transportation Services Table

1. Open **Table07.docx** and save the document with the name **C14A02**.
2. Format the table so it appears as shown in Figure 14.7, with the following specifications:
   a. Delete the row that begins with *City Travel 24-hour customer service*.
   b. Click in the cell containing the text *Edgewood City Transit*, insert four new rows above, and then type the following text in the new rows:

      Valley Rail Road
      Railway information (206) 555-8775
      Status hotline (206) 555-8740
      Travel information (206) 555-8442

   c. Select the cells containing the text *Railway information*, *Status hotline*, and *Travel information* and then change the left cell margin measurement to 0.3". *(Hint: Refer to Exercise 2A, Step 4.)*
   d. Select the two cells below City Travel Card (the cells containing indented text) and then change the left cell margin measurement to 0.3 inch.
   e. Select the three cells below Edgewood City Transit (the cells containing indented text) and then change the left cell margin measurement to 0.3 inch.
   f. Select the three cells below Mainline Bus (the cells containing indented text) and then change the left cell margin measurement to 0.3 inch.
   g. Insert a column at the left side of the first column and then merge the cells in the new column. Type the text **Edgewood Area Transportation Services**, change the text direction so it displays as shown in Figure 14.7, and then change the alignment to Align Center. With the text selected, change the font size to 18.
   h. Use the move table column marker to change the width of the first column to 1 inch.
   i. Change the width of the second column to approximately 2.2 inches, and then the width of the third column to approximately 1 inch. *(Hint: Hold down the Alt key while dragging the move table column marker on the horizontal ruler.)*
   j. Apply bold and italic to text as shown in Figure 14.7.
   k. Apply shading to cells as shown in Figure 14.7.
3. Position the table in the middle of the page.
4. Save, print, and then close **C14A02.docx**.

Figure 14.7 Assessment 2

	Service	Telephone
Edgewood Area Transportation Services	***City Travel Card***	
	City Travel office	(213) 555-6500
	Card inquiries	(213) 555-9005
	Valley Rail Road	
	Railway information	(206) 555-8775
	Status hotline	(206) 555-8740
	Travel information	(206) 555-8442
	Edgewood City Transit	
	Subway and bus information	(213) 555-5475
	Service status hotline	(213) 555-1194
	Travel information	(213) 555-9043
	Mainline Bus	
	Bus routes	(213) 555-4355
	Emergency hotline	(213) 555-5121
	Travel information	(213) 555-4550

Assessment 3 Create and Format a Training Costs Table

1. At a blank document, create the table shown in Figure 14.8, with the following specifications:
   a. Create a table with two columns and eight rows.
   b. Merge the cells in the top row and then change the alignment to Align Center.
   c. Type the text in the cells as shown in Figure 14.8.
   d. Right align the cells containing the money amounts as well as the blank line below the last amount (cells B2 through B8).
   e. AutoFit the contents of the cells.
   f. Apply the *Medium Shading 2 - Accent 4* table style.
   g. Change the font size to 14 for the text in cell A1.
   h. Use the resize handle located in the lower right corner of the table and increase the width and height of the table by approximately 1 inch.
2. Insert a formula in cell B8 that sums the amounts in cells B2 through B7.
3. Select the entire table and then change the vertical cell alignment to Center. *(Hint: Refer to Exercise 2C, Step 7.)*
4. Save the document with the name **C14A03**.
5. Print and then close **C14A03.docx**.

Figure 14.8 Assessment 3

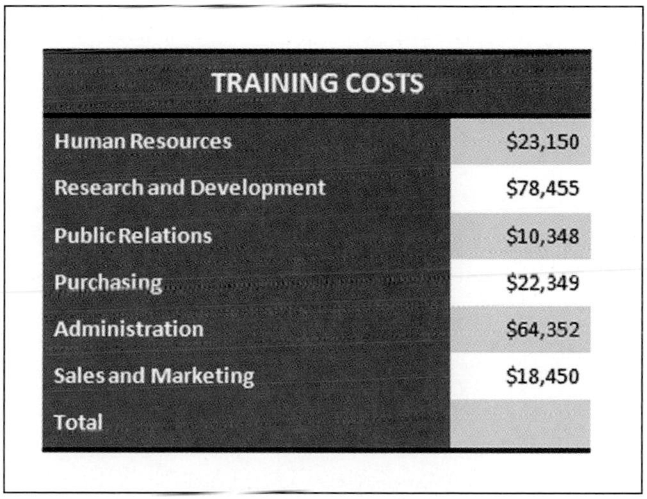

TRAINING COSTS	
Human Resources	$23,150
Research and Development	$78,455
Public Relations	$10,348
Purchasing	$22,349
Administration	$64,352
Sales and Marketing	$18,450
Total	

Assessment 4 Insert Formulas and Format a Training Department Table

1. Open **Table08.docx** and save the document with the name **C14A04**.
2. Insert formulas in the cells below the *Average* heading that calculate the averages of the numbers in the modules columns. Change the *Number format* to 0 at the Formula dialog box.
3. Change the number in cell B6 from 78 to 90 and change the number in cell B7 from 76 to 90. Recalculate the averages in cells E6 and E7.
4. Apply the *Medium Shading 2 - Accent 5* table style. Remove the check mark from the *First Column* check box in the Table Style Options group in the Table Tools Design tab.
5. Save, print, and then close **C14A04.docx**.

Assessment 5 Insert Formulas and Format a Financial Analysis Table

1. Open **Table09.docx** and save the document with the name **C14A05**.
2. Insert a formula in cell B13 that sums the amounts in cells B6 through B12.
3. Insert a formula in cell C13 that sums the amounts in cells C6 through C12.
4. Insert a formula in cell B14 that subtracts the amount in B13 from the amount in B4. (*Hint: The formula should look like this:* **=B4-B13**.)
5. Insert a formula in cell C14 that subtracts the amount in C13 from the amount in C4. (*Hint: The formula should look like this:* **=C4-C13**.)
6. Apply the *Medium Shading 2 - Accent 5* table style. Remove the check mark from the *First Column* check box in the Table Style Options group in the Table Tools Design tab.
7. Select the top two rows in the table and then change the alignment to Align Center.
8. Select the third row in the table and then change the alignment to Align Top Right.
9. Save, print, and then close **C14A05.docx**.

Chapter 15

CHAPTER15

Creating Charts

Tutorial 15.1
Working with Charts
Tutorial 15.2
Working with Organization Charts

Performance Objectives

Upon successful completion of Chapter 15, you will be able to:

- Create charts
- Change chart design
- Edit chart data
- Change chart layout and style
- Select and format chart elements
- Insert objects in charts
- Apply shapes and styles
- Position and size charts

In Chapters 13 and 14, you learned to create tables to organize data. Although tables provide an adequate way to present and display data, a chart can provide a more visual representation. Sometimes referred to as a ***graph,*** a chart is a picture of numeric data. If you have Microsoft Excel installed on your computer, you can create a chart in a Word document and use the chart design, formatting, and layout options provided in Excel. If you do not have Excel installed on your computer, Word uses the Microsoft Graph feature to create your chart. Exercises and assessments in this chapter assume that you have Excel installed on your computer.

Note: Before beginning computer exercises for this chapter, copy to your storage medium the Chapter15 folder from the CD that accompanies this textbook and then make Chapter15 the active folder.

Creating a Chart

In Word, you can create a variety of charts, including bar and column charts, pie charts, area charts, and much more. Table 15.1 describes the eleven basic chart types you can create in Word. To create a chart, click the Insert tab and then click the Chart button in the Illustrations group. This displays the Insert Chart dialog box, shown in Figure 15.1. At this dialog box, choose the type of chart you want to create from the list at the left side of the dialog box, click the chart style, and then click OK.

Table 15.1 **Types of Charts**

Area	An area chart emphasizes the magnitude of change, rather than the rate of change, over time. It also shows the relationship of parts to a whole by displaying the sum of the plotted values.
Bar	A bar chart shows individual figures at a specific time, or shows variations between components but not in relationship to the whole.
Bubble	A bubble chart compares sets of three values in a manner similar to a scatter chart, with the third value displayed as the size of the bubble marker.
Column	A column chart compares separate (noncontinuous) items as they vary over time.
Doughnut	A doughnut chart shows the relationship of parts of the whole.
Line	A line chart shows trends and change over time at even intervals. It emphasizes the rate of change over time rather than the magnitude of change.
Pie	A pie chart shows proportions and relationships of parts to the whole.
Radar	A radar chart emphasizes differences, amounts of change over time, and variations and trends. Each category has its own value axis radiating from the center point. Lines connect all values in the same series.
Stock	A stock chart shows five values for a stock—open, high, low, volume, and close.
Surface	A surface chart shows trends in values across two dimensions in a continuous curve.
XY (Scatter)	A scatter chart shows either the relationships among numeric values in several data series or plots the interception points between *x* and *y* values. It shows uneven intervals of data and is commonly used in scientific data.

Figure 15.1 Insert Chart Dialog Box

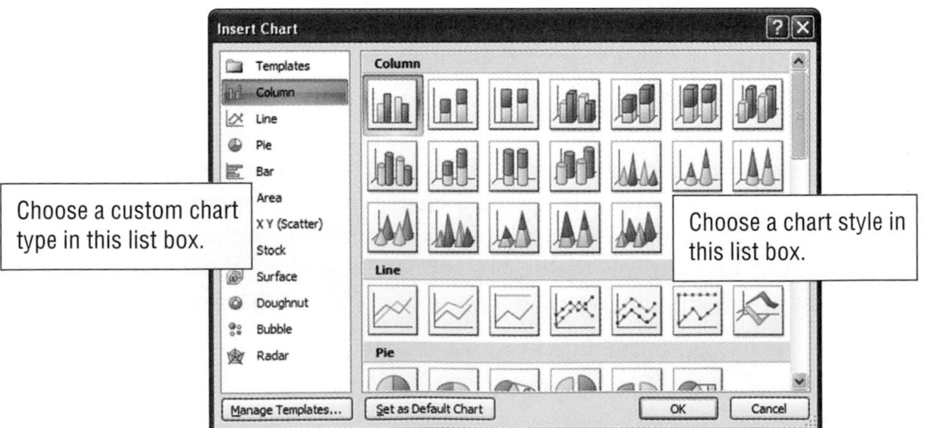

When you click OK, a sample chart is inserted in your Word document, and Excel opens with sample data, as shown in Figure 15.2. Type the desired data in the Excel worksheet cells over the existing data. To type data in the Excel worksheet, click in the desired cell, type the data, and then press the Tab key to make the next cell active. Press Shift + Tab to make the previous cell active or press Enter to make the cell below active. As you type data in the Excel worksheet, the entries are reflected in the chart in the Word document.

Insert a Chart
1. Click Insert tab.
2. Click Chart button.
3. Click desired chart style and type.
4. Enter data in Excel spreadsheet.
5. Close Excel.

The Excel cells that you use to create the chart are surrounded by a blue border. Below that border, the following message displays: "To resize chart data range, drag lower right corner of range." If you need to change the data range, position the mouse pointer on the bottom right corner of the border until the mouse pointer displays as a double-headed arrow pointing diagonally. Hold down the left mouse button and then drag up, down, left, or right until the border is in the desired location. You can also click in a cell immediately outside the border, and, when you insert data in the cell, the border expands.

When you have entered all the data in the worksheet, click the Close button that displays in the upper right corner of the screen (the top Close button). This closes the Excel window, expands the Word document window, and displays the chart in the document.

Close Window

Figure 15.2 Sample Chart

Enter data in cells in the Excel worksheet. The data entered is reflected in the Word document chart.

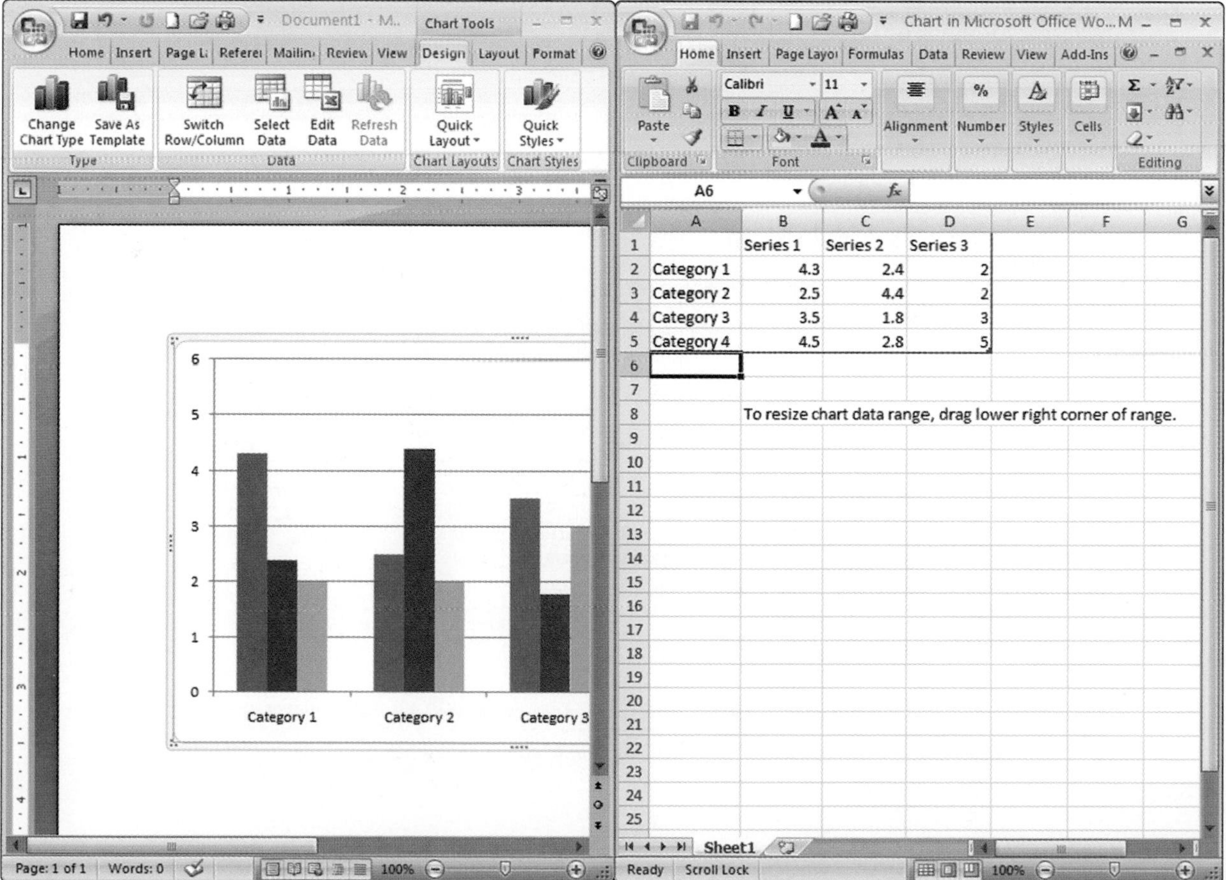

Exercise 1A

Creating a Column Chart

1. At a blank document, click the Insert tab and then click the Chart button in the Illustrations group.
2. At the Insert Chart dialog box with the first column chart selected, click OK.
3. In the Excel worksheet, position the mouse pointer on the bottom right corner of the border until the mouse pointer displays as a double-headed arrow pointing diagonally. Hold down the left mouse button, drag to the left until the border displays at the right side of column C, and then release the mouse button.

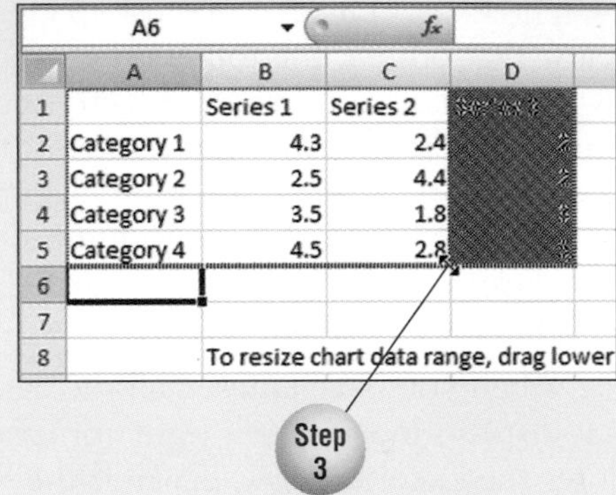

4. Type the text in the cells as shown in Figure 15.3 by completing the following steps:
   a. Click in cell B1 in the Excel worksheet and then type **1st Half**.
   b. Press the Tab key and then type **2nd Half** in cell C1.
   c. Press the Tab key. (This makes cell B2 active.)
   d. Continue typing the remaining data in the cells as indicated in Figure 15.3.
5. When you have entered all the data, click the Close button that displays in the upper right corner of the Excel window.
6. Save the document with the name **C15Ex01**.

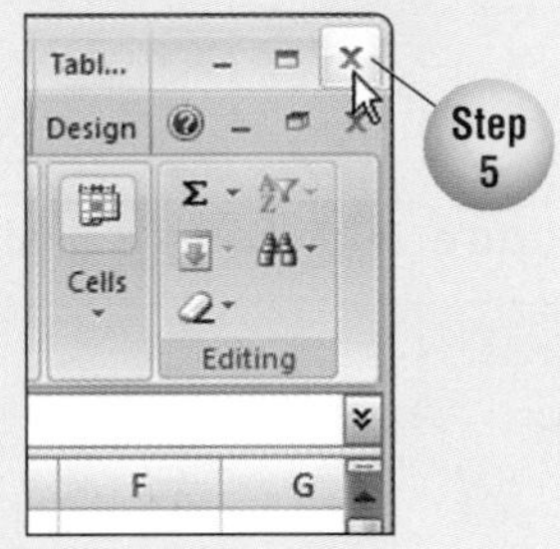

Figure 15.3 Exercise 1A

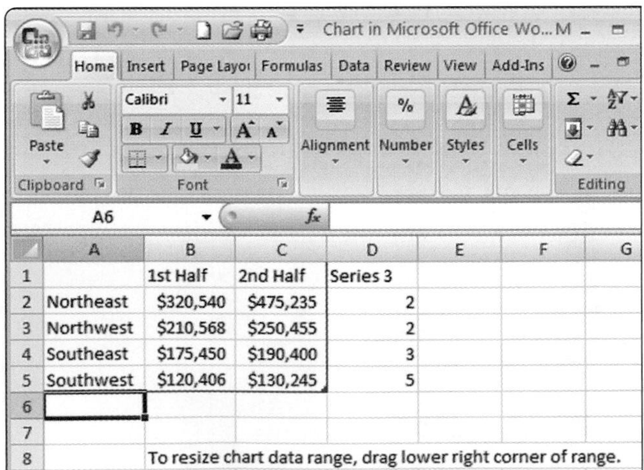

Changing Chart Design

When you insert a chart in a document, the Chart Tools Design tab, shown in Figure 15.4, becomes active. Use options in this tab to change the chart type, edit chart data, change the chart layout, or apply a chart style.

Figure 15.4 Chart Tools Design Tab

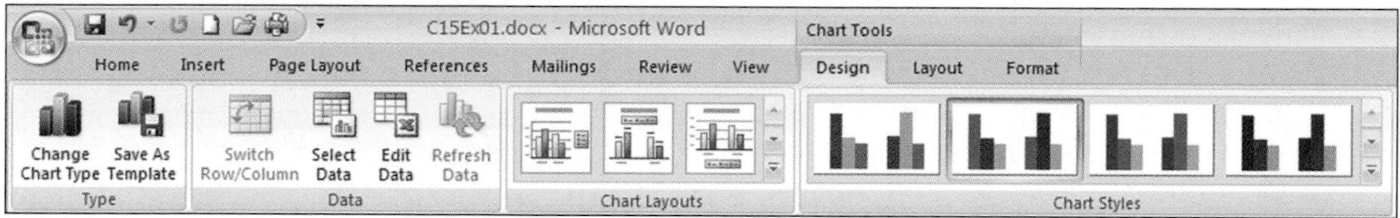

Changing the Chart Type

After you create a chart, you can change the chart type by clicking the Change Chart Type button in the Type group in the Chart Tools Design tab. This displays the Change Chart Type dialog box. This dialog box and the Insert Chart dialog box, shown in Figure 15.1, contain the same options. At the Change Chart Type dialog box, click the desired chart type in the panel at the left and click the desired chart style at the right.

Change Chart Type and Style

1. Make the chart active.
2. Click Chart Tools Design tab.
3. Click Change Chart Type button.
4. Click desired chart type.
5. Click desired chart style.
6. Click OK.

Saving a Chart as a Template

If you consistently create the same type of chart, you can save the formatting and layout of that chart type as a template. To do this, click the Save As Template button in the Type group in the Chart Tools Design tab. At the Save Chart Template dialog box, type a name for the template and then click Save.

Exercise 1B

Changing the Chart Type

1. Make sure **C15Ex01.docx** is open.
2. Click in the chart outside of any chart elements. (This displays a light turquoise border around the chart.)
3. Change the chart type by completing the following steps:
   a. Click the Chart Tools Design tab.
   b. Click the Change Chart Type button in the Type group.
   c. At the Change Chart Type dialog box, click the *Bar* option in the left panel.
   d. Click the *Clustered Bar in 3-D* option in the Styles group.
   e. Click OK to close the dialog box.
4. Save and then print **C15Ex01.docx**.
5. Return to a column chart by completing the following steps:
   a. Make sure the chart is active and then click the Change Chart Type button in the Type group.
   b. At the Change Chart Type dialog box, click the *Column* option in the left panel.
   c. Click the *3-D Clustered Column* option in the Styles group.

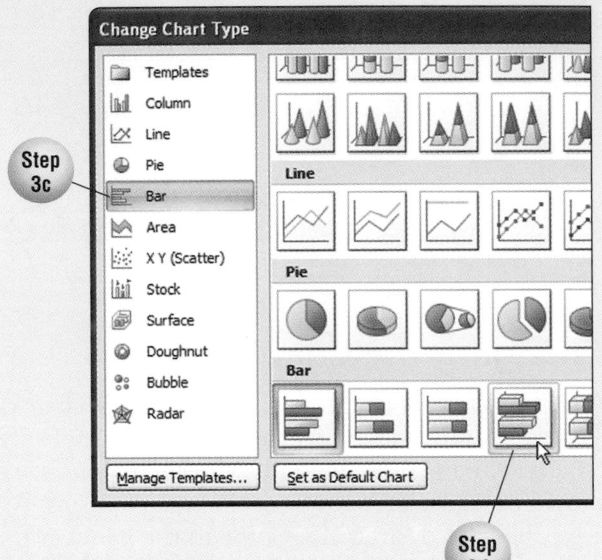

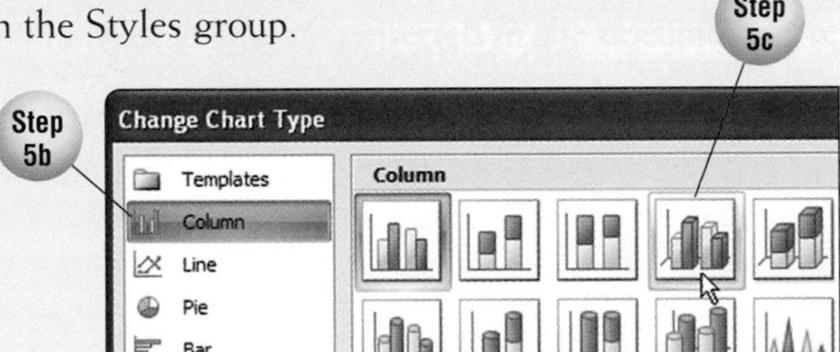

   d. Click OK to close the dialog box.
6. Save **C15Ex01.docx**.

Managing Data

Use options in the Data group in the Chart Tools Design tab to change the order of data in the chart, select specific data, edit data, or refresh the data. When you create a chart, the cells in the Excel worksheet are linked to the chart in the Word document. If you need to edit data in the chart, click the Edit Data button, and the Excel worksheet opens. Make the desired changes to cells in the Excel worksheet and then click the Close Window button.

Exercise 1C

Managing Data in a Chart

1. With **C15Ex01.docx** open, edit the data and switch the rows and columns by completing the following steps:
   a. Make sure the chart and the Chart Tools Design tab are active.
   b. Click the Edit Data button in the Data group.
   c. Click in cell B2 (the cell containing the amount $320,540), type 357975, and then press Enter. (When you press Enter, a dollar sign is automatically inserted in front of the number, and a thousands separator comma is inserted between 7 and 9.)
   d. With cell B3 active (the cell containing the amount $210,568), type 270568, and then press Enter.
   e. In the Word document, click the Switch Row/Column button in the Data group.

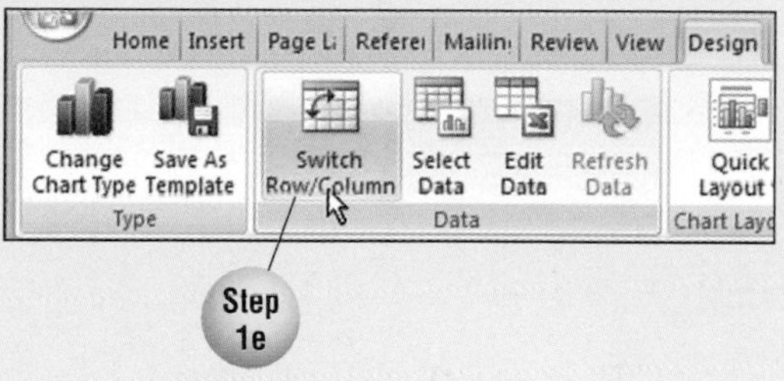

2. Click the Close button that displays in the upper right corner of the Excel window.
3. Save **C15Ex01.docx**.

Changing the Chart Layout and Style

Word's Chart feature provides a number of predesigned chart layouts and chart styles that you can apply to your chart. The Chart Layouts group displays three chart layouts. Click one of these layouts or click the More button and then click a layout at the drop-down list of additional layout options. The Chart Styles group displays four chart styles. Click one of these to apply a predesigned style to a chart or click the More button and then click a style at the drop-down list of additional style options.

Exercise 1D

Changing the Chart Layout and Style

1. With **C15Ex01.docx** open, change the chart layout by completing the following steps:
   a. Make sure the chart and the Chart Tools Design tab are active.
   b. Click the first layout option in the Chart Layouts group (*Layout 1*).

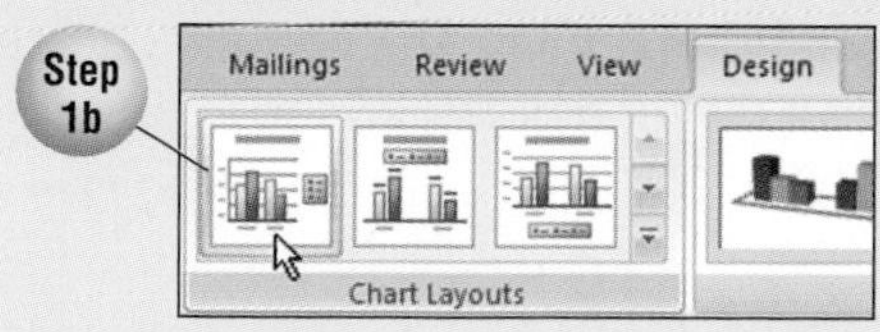

c. Click the text *Chart Title* that displays toward the top of the chart and then type **Division Sales**.
2. Change the chart style by completing the following steps:
   a. Click the More button that displays at the right side of the Chart Styles group.
   b. Click the second option from the left in the bottom row (*Style 42*).
3. Save, print, and then close **C15Ex01.docx**.

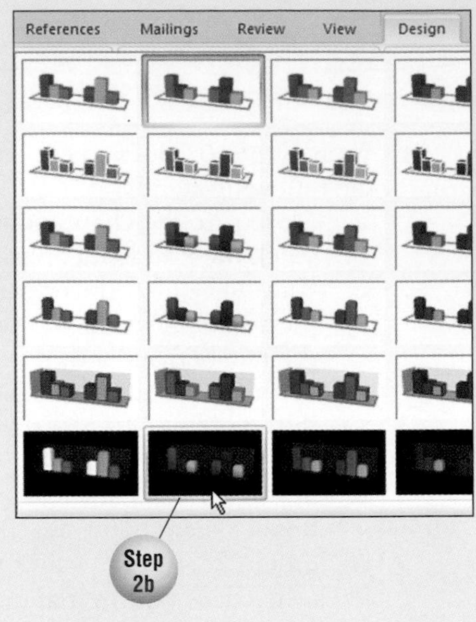

Formatting Chart Layout

Click the Chart Tools Layout tab, shown in Figure 15.5, and options display for changing and customizing chart elements. With options in this tab, you can format or modify specific chart elements, insert elements, add labels to the chart, customize the chart background, and add analysis items to the chart.

Figure 15.5 Chart Tools Layout Tab

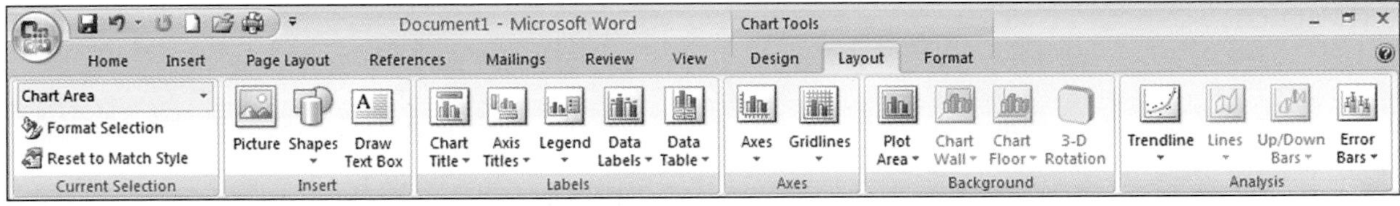

Selecting Elements

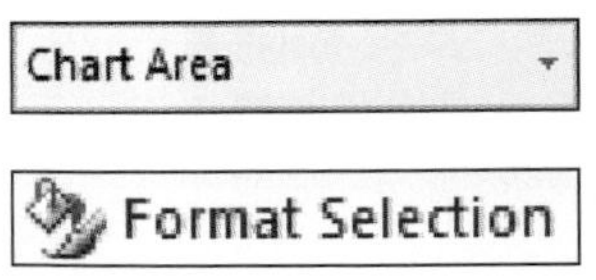

To format or modify a specific element in a chart, select the element first. You can select an element by clicking it or by clicking the Chart Elements button in the Current Selection group in the Chart Tools Layout tab. With the element selected, apply the desired formatting. Click the Format Selection button in the Current Selection group, and a dialog box displays with options for formatting the selected element.

Exercise 2A

Creating a Pie Chart

1. At a blank document, create a pie chart by completing the following steps:
   a. Click the Insert tab.
   b. Click the Chart button in the Illustrations group.
   c. At the Insert Chart dialog box, click the *Pie* option in the left panel and then click OK.

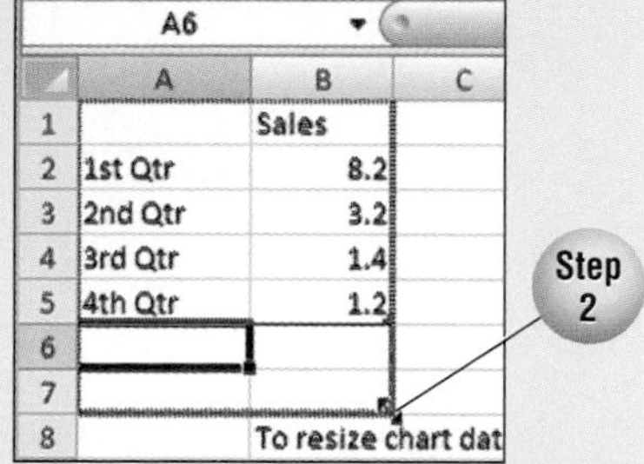

2. In the Excel worksheet, position the mouse pointer on the bottom right corner of the border until the mouse pointer displays as a double-headed arrow pointing diagonally. Hold down the left mouse button, drag down until the border displays at the bottom of row 7, and then release the mouse button.
3. Type the text in the cells as shown in Figure 15.6.
4. When all data is entered, click the Close button that displays in the upper right corner of the Excel window.
5. With the Chart Tools Design tab selected, click the More button at the right side of the Chart Styles group and then click the second option from the left in the fourth row (*Style 26*).
6. Customize the chart title by completing the following steps:
   a. Click the Chart Tools Layout tab.
   b. Click the Chart Elements button arrow in the Current Selection group and then click *Chart Title* at the drop-down list.
   c. Type **Training Budget Percentages**.
   d. Click the Chart Elements button arrow in the Current Selection group and then click *Legend* at the drop-down list.

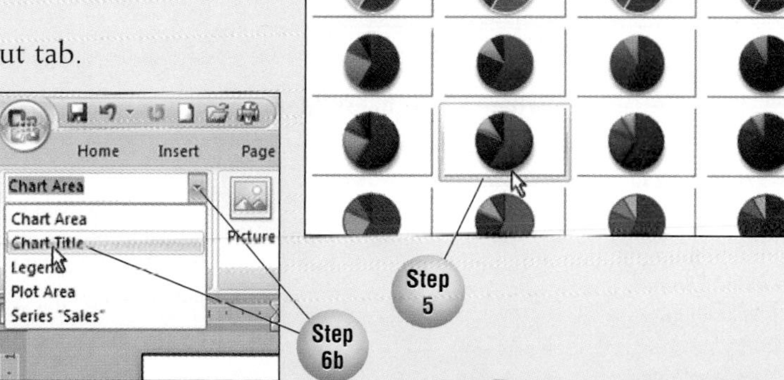

   e. Click the Format Selection button in the Current Selection group.
   f. At the Format Legend dialog box, click the *Fill* option at the left side of the dialog box.
   g. Click the *Solid fill* option in the *Fill* section of the dialog box.
   h. Click the button that displays at the right side of the *Color* option in the *Fill* section and then click the blue color (*Blue, Accent 1, Lighter 80%*).

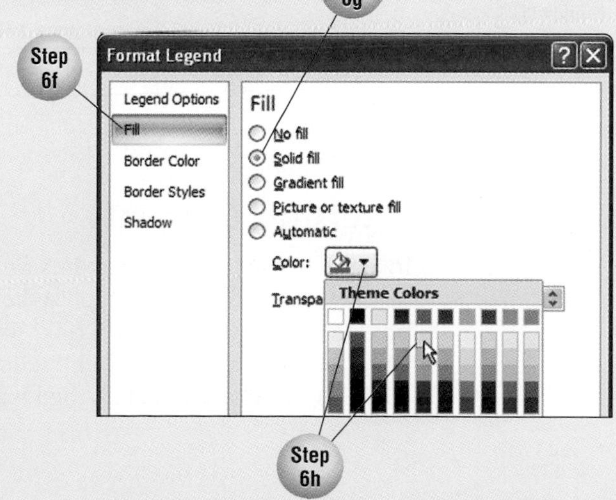

i. Click the *Shadow* option at the left side of the dialog box.
j. Click the down-pointing arrow at the right side of the *Presets* button in the *Shadow* group and then click the third option from the left in the second row in the *Outer* section (Offset Left).

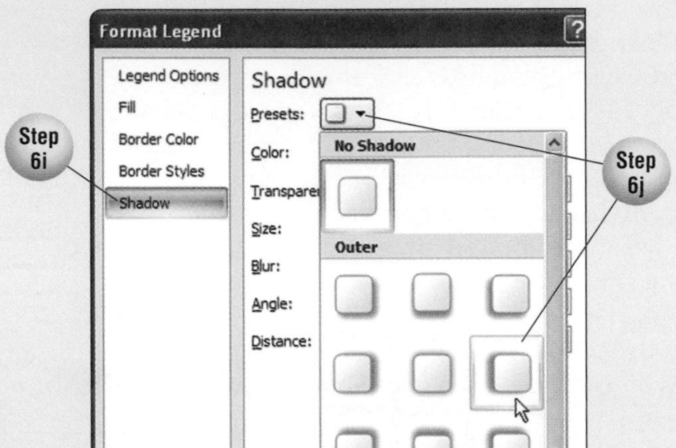

k. Click the Close button to close the Format Legend dialog box.
7. Save the document with the name **C15Ex02**.

QUICK STEPS

Insert Picture in Chart
1. Click Chart Tools Layout tab.
2. Click Picture button.
3. Navigate to desired folder.
4. Double-click desired picture.

Figure 15.6 Exercise 2A

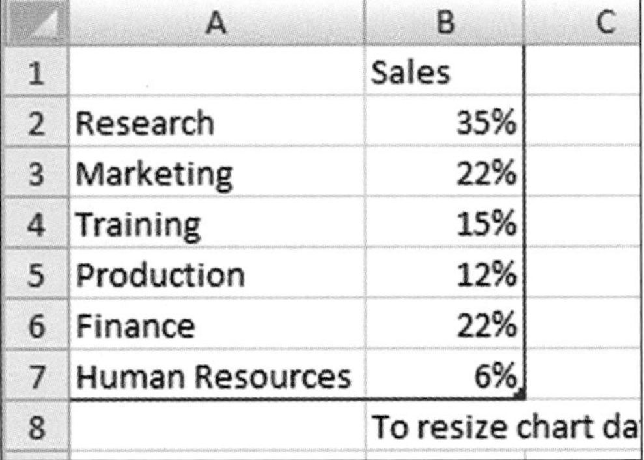

	A	B	C
1		Sales	
2	Research	35%	
3	Marketing	22%	
4	Training	15%	
5	Production	12%	
6	Finance	22%	
7	Human Resources	6%	
8		To resize chart da	

Inserting Elements

Insert elements, such as pictures or shapes, in a chart with buttons in the Insert group in the Chart Tools Layout tab. Click the Picture button, and the Insert Picture dialog box displays. At this dialog box, navigate to the folder that contains the picture you want to insert and then double-click the picture. Click the Shapes button to draw a shape in the chart and click the Draw Text Box button to insert a text box in the chart.

Exercise 2B

Inserting a Picture and Shape

1. With **C15Ex02.docx** open, insert a picture by completing the following steps:
   a. With the Chart Tools Layout tab active, click the Picture button in the Insert group.
   b. At the Insert Picture dialog box, navigate to the Chapter15 folder on your storage medium and then double-click **WELogo.jpg**.
   c. With the logo selected, decrease the size of the logo so it displays in the upper left corner of the chart as shown at the right.
   d. Click in the chart outside of any chart elements to deselect the logo.

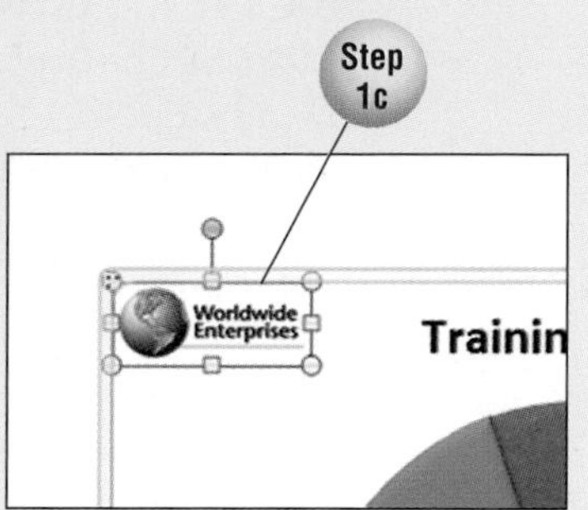

2. Insert a text box by completing the following steps:
   a. Make sure the chart is active and then click the Chart Tools Layout tab.
   b. Click the Draw Text Box button in the Insert group.
   c. Drag in the chart and draw a text box as shown at the right.
   d. Press Ctrl + B to turn on bold and then type **January, 2010**.
   e. Click in the chart outside the text box.
3. Save **C15Ex02.docx**.

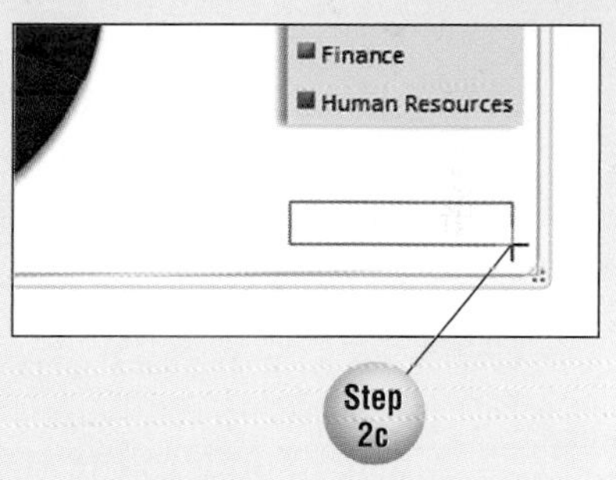

Positioning Labels

Use options in the Labels group in the Chart Tools Layout tab to insert and position labels in your chart. For example, click the Chart Title button, and a drop-down list displays with options for removing the chart title, centering the title and overlaying it on the chart, and displaying the title above the chart. You can also position a label by dragging it. To do this, select the label, position the mouse pointer over the selected label or over the label border until the pointer displays with a four-headed arrow attached, hold down the left mouse button, and then drag the label to the desired location.

Position Labels
1. Make the chart active.
2. Click Chart Tools Layout tab.
3. Click desired labels button.
4. Choose desired option at drop-down list.

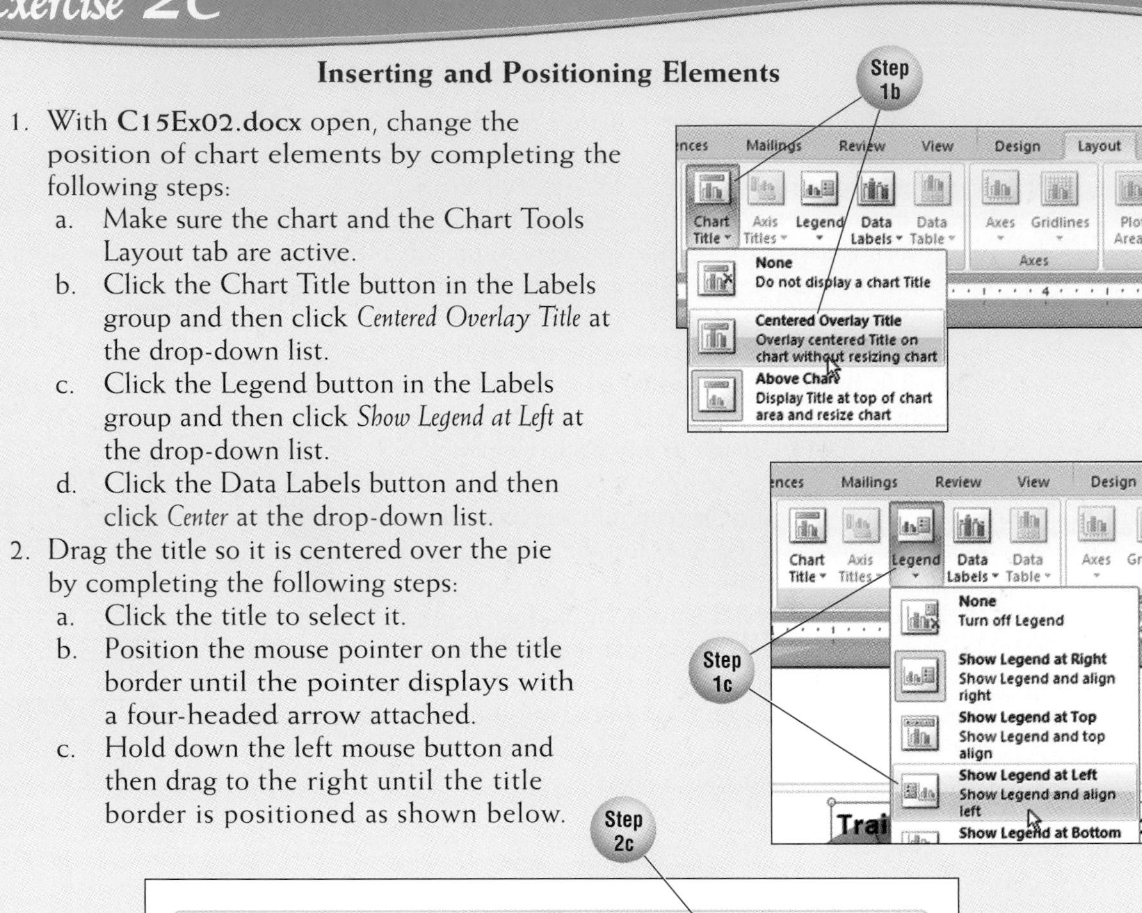

Exercise 2C

Inserting and Positioning Elements

1. With **C15Ex02.docx** open, change the position of chart elements by completing the following steps:
   a. Make sure the chart and the Chart Tools Layout tab are active.
   b. Click the Chart Title button in the Labels group and then click *Centered Overlay Title* at the drop-down list.
   c. Click the Legend button in the Labels group and then click *Show Legend at Left* at the drop-down list.
   d. Click the Data Labels button and then click *Center* at the drop-down list.
2. Drag the title so it is centered over the pie by completing the following steps:
   a. Click the title to select it.
   b. Position the mouse pointer on the title border until the pointer displays with a four-headed arrow attached.
   c. Hold down the left mouse button and then drag to the right until the title border is positioned as shown below.
3. Complete steps similar to those in Step 2 to drag the legend so it is centered between the left edge of the chart and the pie.
4. Save, print, and then close **C15Ex02.docx**.

Customizing Chart Backgrounds

You can further customize a chart with buttons in the Axes, Background, and Analysis groups. Use buttons in the Axes group to specify whether you want major and/or minor horizontal and vertical lines in the chart. With buttons in the Background group, you can format the chart wall and floor and rotate the chart. Depending on the type of chart you are customizing, some of the buttons in the Background group may not be active. Use buttons in the Analysis group to add analysis elements such as trend lines, up and down bars, and error bars.

Exercise 3A

Creating and Formatting a Line Chart

1. At a blank document, create a line chart by completing the following steps:
   a. Click the Insert tab.
   b. Click the Chart button in the Illustrations group.
   c. At the Insert Chart dialog box, click the *Line* option in the left panel.
   d. Click the fourth option from the left in the *Line* section (*Line with Markers*).
   e. Click OK to close the dialog box.
2. In the Excel worksheet, position the mouse pointer on the bottom right corner of the border until the mouse pointer displays as a double-headed arrow pointing diagonally. Hold down the left mouse button, drag left until the border displays at the right side of column B, and then release the mouse button.
3. Drag the bottom right corner down until the border displays at the bottom of row 7.
4. Type the text in cells as shown in Figure 15.7.
5. When you have entered all the data, click the Close button that displays in the upper right corner of the Excel window.
6. With the Chart Tools Design tab active, click the More button at the right side of the Chart Layouts group and then click the second option from the left in the second row (*Layout 5*).
7. Click the More button at the right side of the Chart Styles group and then click the third option from the left in the third row (*Style 19*).
8. Click the text *Axis Title* that displays at the left side of the chart and then type **City of Edgewood**.
9. Customize the chart title by completing the following steps:
   a. Click the Chart Tools Layout tab.
   b. Click the Chart Elements button arrow in the Current Selection group and then click *Chart Title* at the drop-down list.
   c. Click the Format Selection button in the Current Selection group.
   d. At the Format Chart Title dialog box, make sure the *Fill* option at the left side of the dialog box is selected.
   e. Click the *Solid fill* option in the *Fill* section of the dialog box.
   f. Click the button that displays at the right side of the *Color* option in the *Fill* section and then click the blue color (*Blue, Accent 1, Lighter 80%*).
   g. Click the *Shadow* option at the left side of the dialog box.

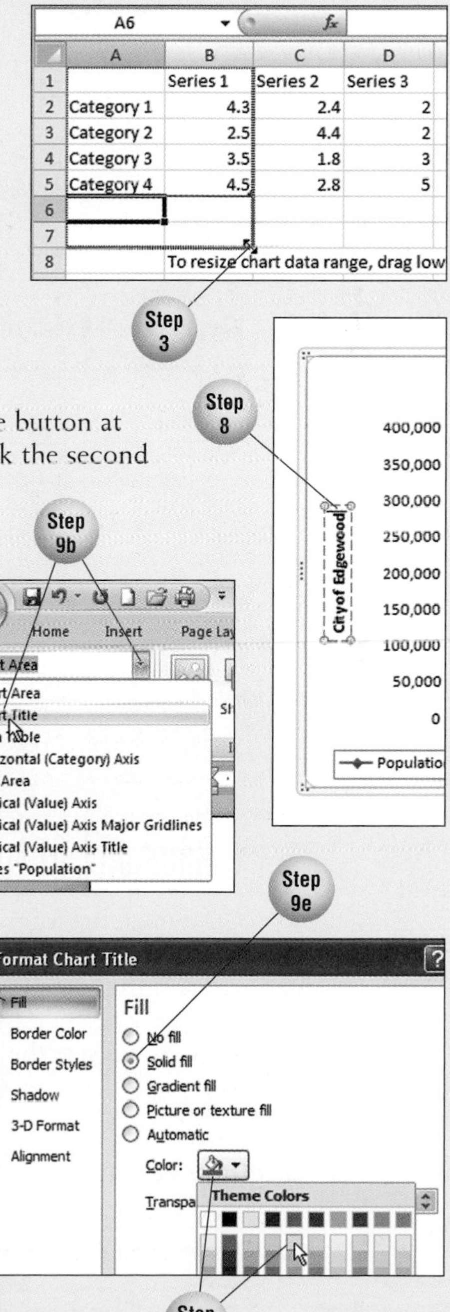

h. Click the down-pointing arrow at the right side of the *Presets* button in the *Shadow* group and then click the first option from the left in the first row in the *Outer* section (*Offset Diagonal Bottom Right*).

i. Click the Close button to close the Format Chart Title dialog box.

10. Click the Gridlines button in the Axes group, point to *Primary Vertical Gridlines*, and then click *Major Gridlines* at the side menu.
11. Click the Lines button in the Analysis group and then click *Drop Lines* at the drop-down list.
12. Save the document with the name **C15Ex03**.

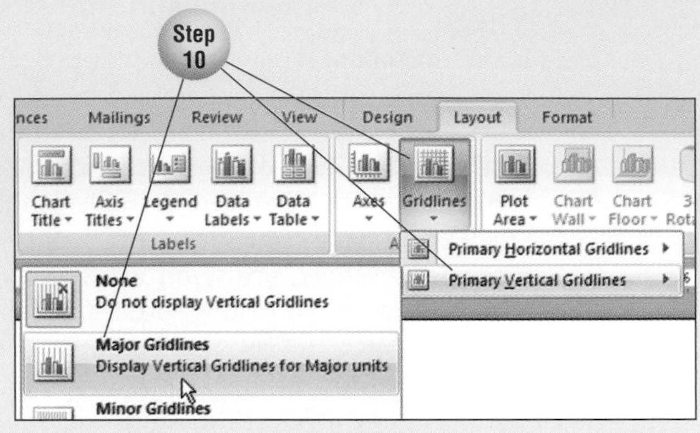

Figure 15.7 Exercise 3A

	A	B	C	D
1		Population	Series 2	Series 3
2	1960	200,450	2.4	2
3	1970	250,438	4.4	2
4	1980	175,340	1.8	3
5	1990	225,488	2.8	5
6	2000	300,540		
7	2010	350,230		
8		To resize chart data range, drag lowe		

Changing Chart Formatting

Customize the format of a chart and chart elements with options in the Chart Tools Format tab, shown in Figure 15.8. This tab and the Chart Tools Layout tab both contain the same Current Selection group. With the other options in the tab, you can apply a predesigned style to a shape, a predesigned WordArt style to text, or arrange and size the chart.

Figure 15.8 Chart Tools Format Tab

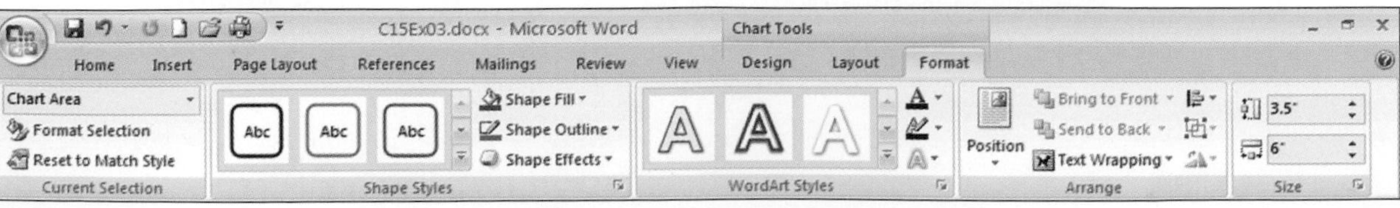

Applying Shape and WordArt Styles

The Shape Styles group in the Chart Tools Format tab contains buttons that you can use to apply predesigned styles to shapes inserted in your chart. Click the More button at the right side of the styles in the group, and a drop-down gallery of shape styles displays. Use the buttons that display at the right side of the Shape Styles group to apply fill, an outline, and an effect to a selected shape. The WordArt Styles group contains predesigned styles you can apply to text in a chart. Use the buttons that display at the right side of the WordArt Styles group to apply fill, an outline, or an effect to text in a chart.

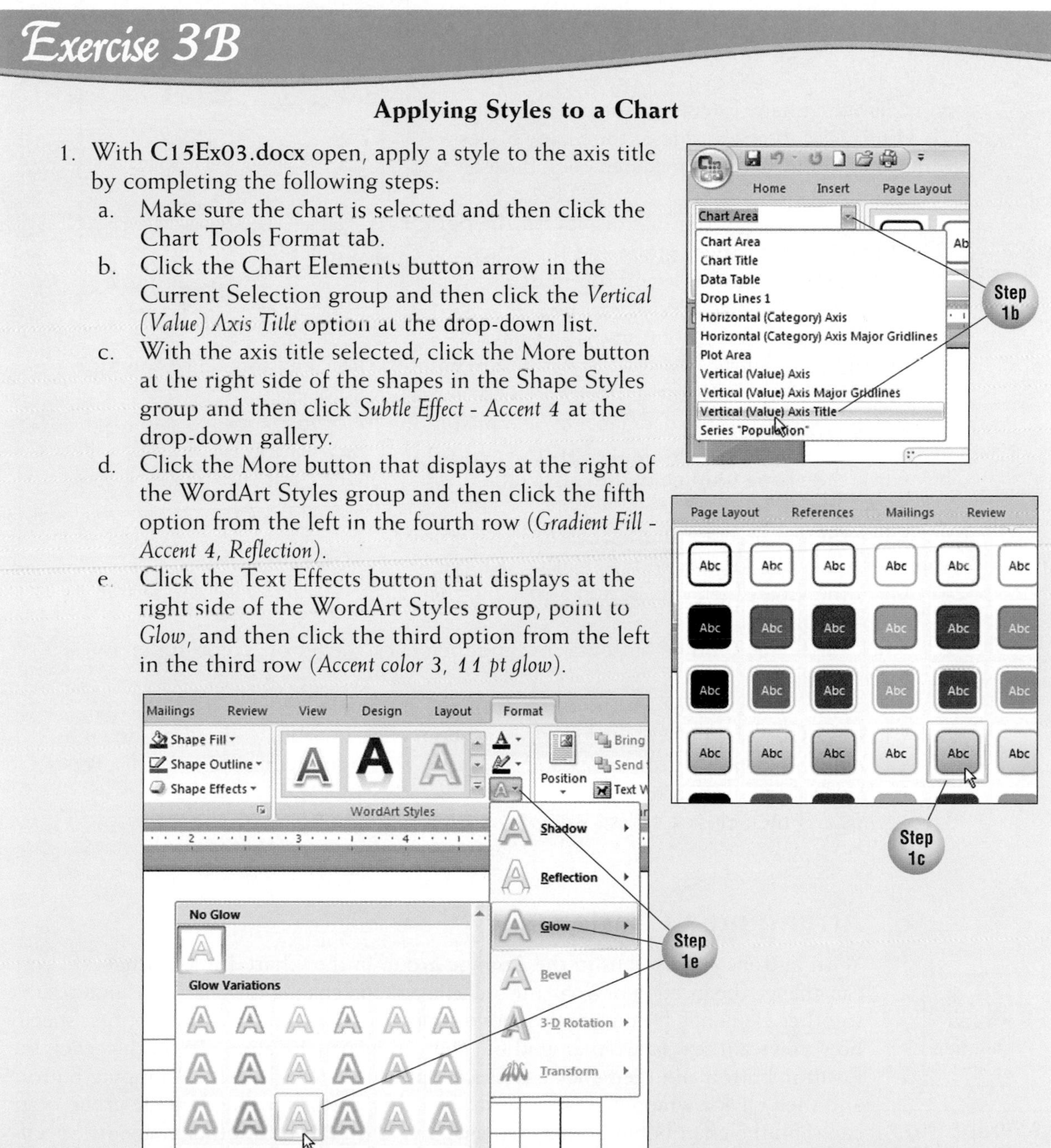

Exercise 3B

Applying Styles to a Chart

1. With **C15Ex03.docx** open, apply a style to the axis title by completing the following steps:
   a. Make sure the chart is selected and then click the Chart Tools Format tab.
   b. Click the Chart Elements button arrow in the Current Selection group and then click the *Vertical (Value) Axis Title* option at the drop-down list.
   c. With the axis title selected, click the More button at the right side of the shapes in the Shape Styles group and then click *Subtle Effect - Accent 4* at the drop-down gallery.
   d. Click the More button that displays at the right of the WordArt Styles group and then click the fifth option from the left in the fourth row (*Gradient Fill - Accent 4, Reflection*).
   e. Click the Text Effects button that displays at the right side of the WordArt Styles group, point to *Glow*, and then click the third option from the left in the third row (*Accent color 3, 11 pt glow*).

2. Apply a style and style effect to the chart title by completing the following steps:
   a. Click the chart title to select it.
   b. Click the *Subtle Effect - Accent 4* style that displays in the Shape Styles group.

   c. Click the Shape Effects button arrow that displays at the right side of the Shape Styles group, point to *Bevel*, and then click *Circle* at the side menu.
   d. Click the More button that displays at the right of the WordArt Styles group and then click the fifth option from the left in the fourth row (*Gradient Fill - Accent 4, Reflection*).
   e. Click the Text Effects button that displays at the right side of the WordArt Styles group, point to *Glow*, and then click the third option from the left in the third row (*Accent color 3, 11 pt glow*).
3. Apply a style outline to the data table by completing the following steps:
   a. Click the Chart Elements button arrow and then click *Data Table* at the drop-down list.
   b. Click the Shape Outline button arrow that displays at the right side of the Shape Styles group.
   c. Click the purple color in the *Standard Colors* section.
4. Apply a style outline to the vertical axis by completing the following steps:
   a. Click the Chart Elements button arrow and then click *Vertical (Value) Axis* at the drop-down list.
   b. Click the Shape Outline button arrow and then click the purple color in the *Standard Colors* section.
5. Apply a shape fill to the plot area by completing the following steps:
   a. Click the Chart Elements button arrow and then click *Plot Area* at the drop-down list.
   b. Click the Shape Fill button arrow and then click the light green color that displays in the *Standard Colors* section.
6. Save, print, and then close **C15Ex03.docx**.

Arranging a Chart

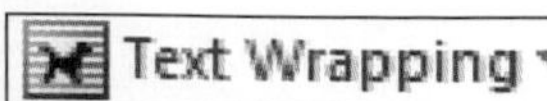

With buttons and options in the Arrange group in the Chart Tools Format tab, you can change the location of a chart in a document and change the chart's position relative to other elements. If you want to move a chart in a document, you must first specify how you want text to wrap around the chart in its new location. To do this, click the Position button and then click a position option or click the Text Wrapping button and then click a wrapping style. With the other buttons in the Arrange group, you can send the chart behind other elements, move it in front of other elements, specify the alignment, or rotate the chart.

Sizing a Chart

You can increase or decrease the size of a chart by selecting the chart and then dragging a sizing handle. You can also size a chart to specific measurements with the Shape Height and Shape Width measurement boxes in the Size group in the Chart Tools Format tab. Change the height or width by clicking the up- or down-pointing arrows that display at the right side of the measurement box or click the current measurement in the box and then type a specific measurement.

Change Chart Height and/or Width
1. Make the chart active.
2. Click Chart Tools Format tab.
3. Insert desired height and width in the Shape Height and Shape Width measurement boxes.

Shape Height

Shape Width

Exercise 4

Creating and Formatting a Doughnut Chart

1. At a blank document, create a doughnut chart by completing the following steps:
   a. Click the Insert tab.
   b. Click the Chart button in the Illustrations group.
   c. At the Insert Chart dialog box, click the *Doughnut* option in the left panel and then click OK.
2. In the Excel worksheet, type the text in cells as shown in Figure 15.9.
3. When you have entered all of the data, click the Close button that displays in the upper right corner of the Excel window.
4. With the Table Tools Design tab selected, click the More button at the right side of the Chart Styles group and then click the second option from the left in the fourth row (*Style 26*)
5. Insert a picture logo by completing the following steps:
   a. Click the Chart Tools Layout tab.
   b. Click the Picture button in the Insert group.
   c. At the Insert Picture dialog box, navigate to the Chapter15 folder on your storage medium and then double-click the *FCTLogo.jpg* file.
   d. With the logo selected, decrease the size of the logo so it displays in the upper left corner of the chart as shown at the right.
   e. Deselect the logo.

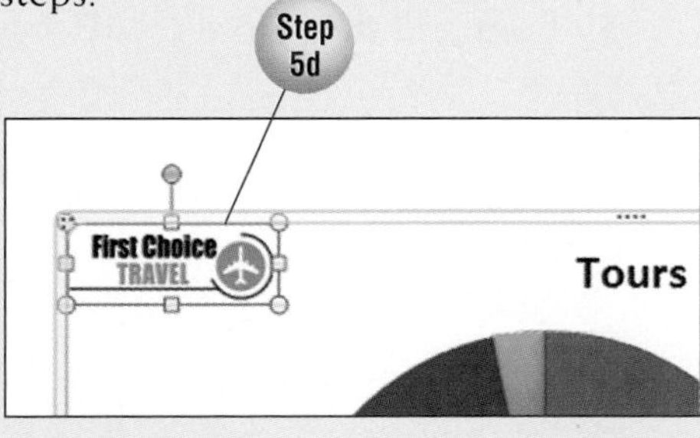

6. Insert data labels by clicking the Data Labels button in the Labels group and then clicking *Show* at the drop-down list.
7. Apply a WordArt style to the chart title by completing the following steps:
   a. Click the Chart Tools Format tab.
   b. Click the chart title to select it.

c. Click the More button in the WordArt Styles group and then click the fourth option from the left in the third row (*Gradient Fill - Accent 1*).

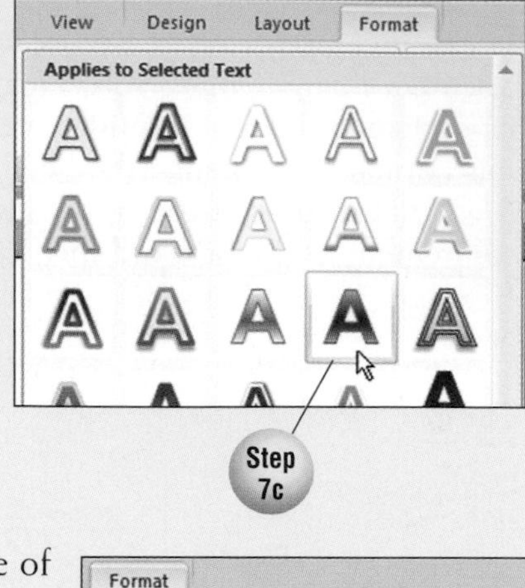

8. Add a shape style to the legend by completing the following steps:
   a. Click the legend to select it.
   b. Click the More button in the Shape Styles group and then click the second option from the left in the fourth row (*Subtle Effect - Accent 1*).
9. Increase the size of the doughnut by completing the following steps:
   a. Click the Chart Elements button arrow and then click *Plot Area* at the drop-down list.
   b. Drag the lower right sizing handle to increase the size of the doughnut.
   c. Drag the doughnut so it is better centered in the chart area.
10. Select the chart area and then change text wrapping by clicking the Text Wrapping button in the Arrange group and then clicking *Square* at the drop-down list.

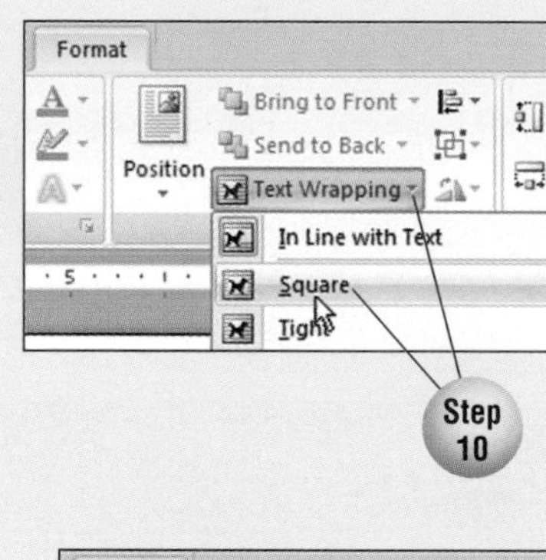

11. Increase the height of the chart by clicking in the Shape Height measurement box in the Size group, typing **4**, and then pressing Enter.
12. Increase the width of the chart by clicking in the Shape Width measurement box, typing **6.5**, and then pressing Enter.
13. Position the chart by clicking the Position button in the Arrange group and then clicking the second option from the left in the second row of the *With Text Wrapping* section (*Position in Middle Center with Square Text Wrapping*).

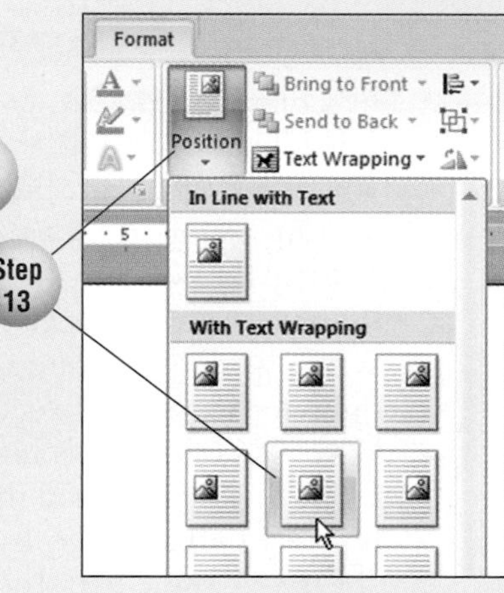

14. Save the document with the name **C15Ex04**.
15. Print and then close **C15Ex04.docx**.

Figure 15.9 Exercise 4

	A	B	C
1		Tours	
2	Europe	38	
3	Asia	25	
4	Australia	15	
5	Africa	12	
6	Antarctica	3	
7			
8		To resize chart data	

Chapter Summary

- A chart is a visual presentation of data. You can create a chart with the Chart button in the Insert tab.
- At the Insert Chart dialog box, choose one of eleven available chart types: area, bar, bubble, column, doughnut, line, pie, radar, stock, surface, or XY scatter charts.
- Enter data for a chart in an Excel worksheet. As you enter data, press Tab to make the next cell active, press Shift + Tab to make the previous cell active, and press Enter to make the cell below active.
- Use the Change Chart Type button in the Chart Tools Design tab to change the type of the existing chart.
- Cells in the Excel worksheet that are used to create a chart are linked to the chart in the Word document. Click the Edit Data button in the Chart Tools Design tab, make changes to text in the Excel worksheet, and the changes are reflected in the chart in the Word document.
- Select and modify chart elements with options in the Current Selection group in the Chart Tools Layout tab.
- Insert elements in a chart, such as pictures, shapes, and text boxes, with buttons in the Insert group in the Chart Tools Layout tab.
- Use options in the Labels group in the Chart Tools Layout tab to insert and position labels such as chart and axis tables, a legend, and data labels.
- Insert major and/or minor horizontal and vertical gridlines with buttons in the Axes group in the Chart Tools Layout tab.
- The Shape Styles group in the Chart Tools Format tab contains predesigned styles you can apply to shapes in a chart. The group also contains buttons for applying shape fill, outline, and effects. Use options in the WordArt Styles group to apply styles to text in a chart. Use buttons in the group to apply fill, outline, and effects to text.
- Use options in the Arrange group in the Chart Tools Format tab to position and arrange a chart in the document. To move a chart, choose a text wrapping style, and then drag the chart to the desired location.
- Change the height and width of the chart with buttons in the Size group in the Chart Tools Format tab.

Commands review

FEATURE	RIBBON TAB, GROUP	BUTTON, OPTION	KEYBOARD SHORTCUT
Insert Chart dialog box	Insert, Illustrations		
Make next cell active			Tab
Make previous cell active			Shift + Tab
Make cell below active			Enter
Change Chart Type dialog box	Chart Tools Design, Type		
Save Chart Template dialog box	Chart Tools Design, Type		
Insert Picture dialog box	Chart Tools Layout, Insert		

Reviewing key points

Completion: In the space provided at the right, indicate the correct term, symbol, or command.

1. When creating a chart, enter data in this. ____________
2. This is the number of chart types available at the Insert Chart dialog box. ____________
3. Use this type of chart to show proportions and relationships of parts to the whole. ____________
4. Use this type of chart to compare separate items as they vary over time. ____________
5. When a chart is first inserted in a document, this tab is active. ____________
6. Click this button to open the Excel worksheet containing the chart data. ____________
7. The Chart Elements button is located in this group in the Chart Tools Layout tab. ____________
8. Click the Picture button in the Insert group in the Chart Tools Layout tab, and this dialog box displays. ____________
9. This group in the Chart Tools Format tab contains predesigned styles you can apply to shapes in a chart. ____________

10. This group in the Chart Tools Format tab contains predesigned styles you can apply to chart text. ____________________

11. Control the position of a chart in a document with options and buttons in this group in the Chart Tools Format tab. ____________________

Applying your skills

Assessment 1 Create and Format a Column Chart

1. At a blank document, use the data in Figure 15.10 to create a column chart with the following specifications:
   a. Apply the *Layout 1* chart layout.
   b. Apply the *Style 16* chart style.
   c. Select the chart title text and then type **Sales by State**.
   d. Insert the **WELogo.jpg** logo picture in the chart and then size and move the logo so it is positioned in the upper right corner of the chart. (Make sure the logo is small enough that it does not overlap any chart elements.)
   e. Show the legend at the bottom of the chart. (Do this with the Legend button in the Labels group in the Chart Tools Layout tab.)
   f. Insert major and minor vertical primary gridlines.
   g. Select the legend and then apply the *Aqua, Accent 5, Lighter 80%* shape fill.
   h. Select the chart title, apply the *Aqua, Accent 5, Lighter 80%* shape fill, and then apply the *Gradient Fill - Accent 6, Inner Shadow* WordArt style.
2. Save the document with the name **C15A01**.
3. Print and then close **C15A01.docx**.

Figure 15.10 Assessment 1

	Sales 2007	Sales 2008	Sales 2009
Florida	$356,750	$400,790	$325,490
Georgia	$475,230	$385,675	$425,450
Alabama	$225,545	$300,245	$312,680

Assessment 2 Create and Format a Pie Chart

1. At a blank document, use the data in Figure 15.11 to create a pie chart with the following specifications:
   a. Apply the *Layout 6* chart layout.
   b. Apply the *Style 10* chart style.
   c. Select the chart title text and then type **Department Expenses**.
   d. Move the legend to the left side of the chart. (Select and then drag the legend so it is positioned between the left edge of the chart border and the pie.)
   e. Apply *Olive Green, Accent 3, Lighter 80%* shape fill to the chart area.
   f. Apply the glow shape effect *Accent color 3, 5 pt glow* in the chart area.
   g. Apply the WordArt style *Gradient Fill - Accent 1* to the chart title text.
   h. Change the chart height to 3 inches and the chart width to 4 inches.
   i. Select the plot area and then drag the pie so it is centered below the title. (Make sure the legend and pie do not overlap.)
   j. Position the chart centered at the top of the page. (Do this with the Position button in the Arrange group in the Chart Tools Format tab.)
2. Save the document with the name **C15A02**.
3. Print **C15A02.docx**.
4. With the chart selected, display the Excel worksheet and edit the data in the worksheet by changing the following:
   a. Change the *Salaries* percentage from 67% to 62%.
   b. Change the *Travel* percentage from 15% to 17%.
   c. Change the *Equipment* percentage from 11% to 14%.
5. Save, print, and then close **C15A02.docx**.

Figure 15.11 Assessment 2

Category	Percentage
Salaries	67%
Travel	15%
Equipment	11%
Supplies	7%

Assessment 3 Create and Format a Bar Chart

1. At a blank document, use the data in Figure 15.12 to create a bar chart with the following specifications:
   a. Change the bar chart type to *Clustered Bar in 3-D*.
   b. Apply the *Layout 9* chart layout.
   c. Apply the *Style 40* chart style.
   d. Show the data labels.
   e. Insert major primary horizontal gridlines.
   f. Increase the height of the chart to 4 inches and the width to 6.5 inches.
   g. Position the chart in the middle of the page.
2. Save the document with the name **C15A03**.
3. Print and then close **C15A03.docx**.

Figure 15.12 Assessment 3

	Sales in Millions
Africa	2.8
Asia	7.5
Europe	10.3
North America	12.2
South America	4.8

Assessment 4 Create and Format a Line Chart

1. At a blank document, use the data in Figure 15.13 to create a line chart with the following specifications:
   a. Choose the *Line with Markers* line chart type.
   b. Click the Switch Row/Column button. (The Excel chart must be open to switch the rows and columns.)
   c. Apply the *Layout 5* chart layout.
   d. Apply the *Style 26* chart style.
   e. Delete the *Axis Title* text that displays at the left side of the chart.
   f. Select the chart title text and then type **Population Comparison**.
   g. Insert major primary vertical gridlines.
   h. Insert drop lines. (Do this with the Lines button in the Analysis group.)
   i. Select the data table and then apply a blue shape outline.
   j. Select the plot area and then apply *Olive Green, Acent 3, Lighter 80%* shape fill.
   k. Select the chart area and then apply *Aqua, Accent 5, Lighter 60%* shape fill.
   l. With the chart area still selected, apply the *Cool Slant* bevel shape effect.
   m. Select the chart title and then apply the *Gradient Fill - Accent 1* WordArt style.
   n. Change the chart height to 4.5 inches and the chart width to 6.5 inches.
   o. Position the chart in the middle of the page.
2. Save the document with the name **C15A04**.
3. Print and then close **C15A04.docx**.

Figure 15.13 Assessment 4

	1960	1970	1980	1990	2000
Lanville	58,980	61,248	65,320	53,120	78,340
Mill Creek	68,458	70,538	55,309	64,328	70,537

Assessment 5 Create and Format a Chart

1. At a blank document, create a chart and chart type of your choosing with the data shown in Figure 15.14. You determine the design, layout, and format of the chart and chart elements. Insert a chart title with the text *Taxes*.
2. Save the document with the name **C15A05**.
3. Print and then close **C15A05.docx**.

Figure 15.14 Assessment 5

	Budgeted	Actual
City	$15,000	$17,350
County	$22,000	$24,100
Federal	$53,500	$48,750

Performance Assessments

UNIT 3

Enhancing Documents

ASSESSING PROFICIENCIES

In this unit, you have learned to improve the visual appeal of documents by inserting, customizing, and formatting pictures, clip art images, shapes, text boxes, and WordArt. You learned how to present data visually in SmartArt diagrams and charts. You also learned how to create, format, and customize tables and how to calculate data in tables.

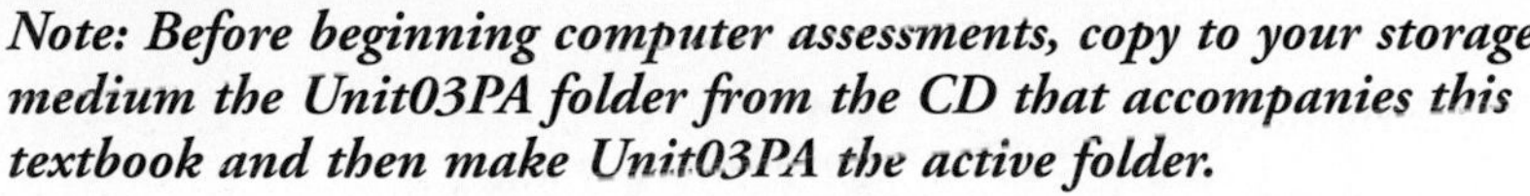

Note: Before beginning computer assessments, copy to your storage medium the Unit03PA folder from the CD that accompanies this textbook and then make Unit03PA the active folder.

Assessment 1 Format a Computers Report

1. Open **Report02.docx** and save the document with the name **U03PA01**.
2. Make the following changes to the document:
   a. Select text from the beginning of the title *COMPUTERS IN ENTERTAINMENT* (located at the bottom of page 1) to the end of the document and then press the Delete key.
   b. Apply the Heading 1 style to the title of the report and apply the Heading 2 style to the three headings in the report.
   c. Change the style set to *Simple*.
   d. Apply the *Civic* theme.
3. Format the text from the first paragraph to the end of the document into two columns.
4. Center the title *COMPUTERS IN COMMUNICATIONS* and change the spacing before to 6 points and the spacing after to 12 points.
5. Insert the Contrast Sidebar built-in text box and then make the following customizations:
   a. Type the following text in the text box: "**The linking of computers enables users to communicate and work together efficiently and effectively . . .** "
   b. Change the shape fill to *Orange, Accent 6, Darker 25%*.
6. Save, print, and then close **U03PA01.docx**.

Assessment 2 Create a Flyer with WordArt and a Clip Art Image

1. Create the flyer shown in Figure U3.1 with the following specifications:
   a. Insert the WordArt shape with *WordArt style 15* and then customize the WordArt by changing the shadow effect to *Shadow Style 1*, the shape to *Deflate Bottom*, and increasing the width of the WordArt to 6.5 inches and the height to 1 inch.
   b. Type the text shown in the figure in 22-point Calibri and bold and center the text.
   c. Insert the clip art image shown in the figure (use the keyword *buildings* to find the clip art) and then change the wrapping style to *Square*. Position and size the image as shown in the figure.
2. Save the document with the name **U03PA02**.
3. Print and then close **U03PA02.docx**.

Figure U3.1 **Assessment 2**

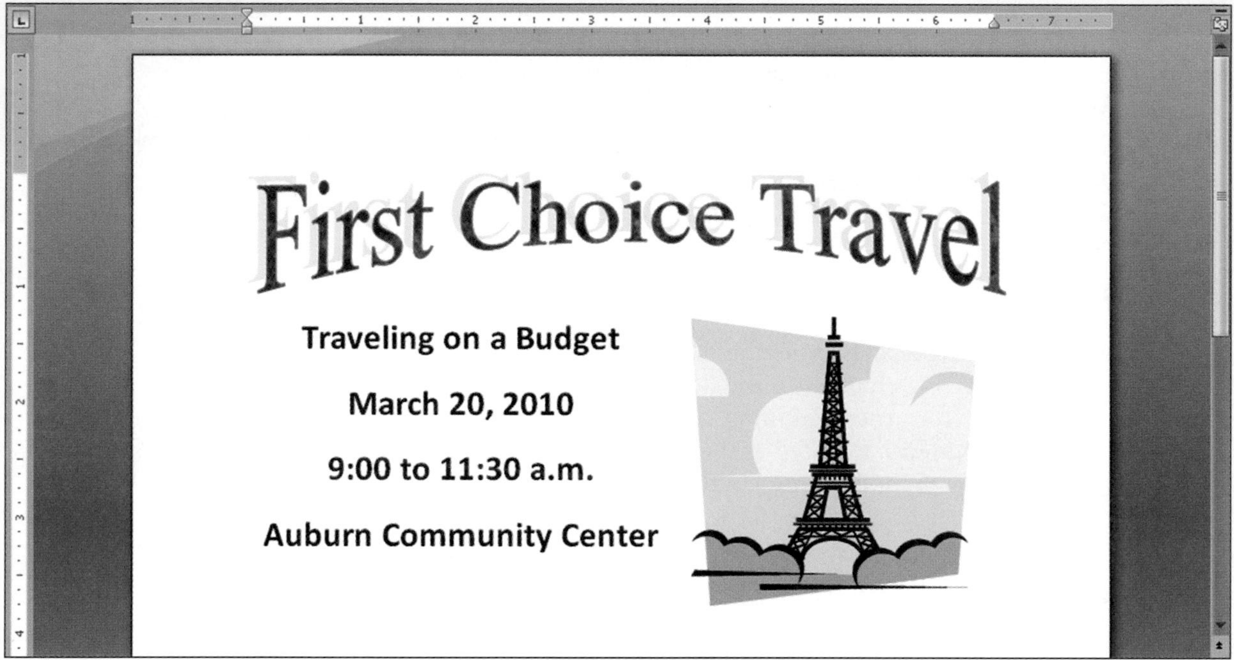

Assessment 3 Create and Format an Organizational Chart

1. Use SmartArt to create an organizational chart for the following text (in the order displayed). Apply formatting to enhance the chart's visual appeal.

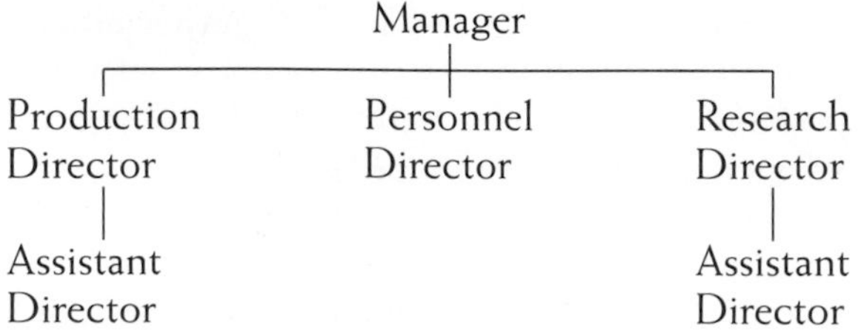

2. Save the completed document with the name **U03PA03**.
3. Print and then close **U03PA03.docx**.

Assessment 4 Create and Format a Radial Diagram

1. At a blank document, create the diagram shown in Figure U3.2 with the following specifications:
   a. Create the diagram using the *Basic Radial* diagram, insert two additional shapes, and then type text in the shapes as shown in the figure.
   b. Change the color to *Colorful Range - Accent Colors 3 to 4*.
   c. Apply the *Intense Effect* SmartArt style.
   d. Select all of the text in the diagram and then turn on bold.
   e. Increase the height to 4.5 inches and the width to 6.5 inches.
   f. Position the chart in the middle of the page.
2. Save the document with the name **U03PA04**.
3. Print and then close **U03PA04.docx**.

Figure U3.2 **Assessment 4**

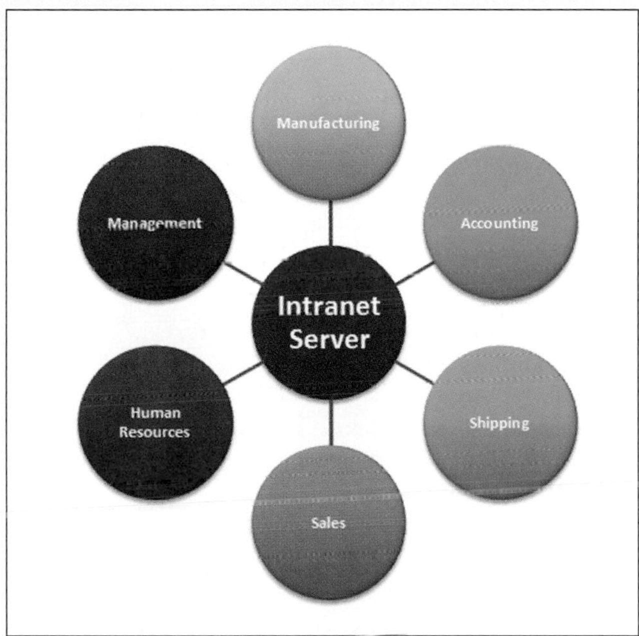

Assessment 5 Create and Format a Training Announcement

1. Create the announcement shown in Figure U3.3 with the following specifications:
   a. Use the *Bevel* shape in the *Basic Shapes* section of the Shapes drop-down list to create the shape.
   b. Apply the *Diagonal Gradient - Accent 3* style to the shape.
   c. Change the shape outline to white.
   d. Apply the *Shadow Style 2* shadow to the shape.
   e. Change the shape height to 2.8 inches and the shape width to 6 inches.
   f. Click the Edit Text button in the Insert Shapes group in the Drawing Tools Format tab. Change the font to 20-point Candara bold and the font color to dark blue, change the alignment to Center, and then type the text shown in Figure U3.3.
2. Save the completed document with the name **U03PA05**.
3. Print and then close **U03PA05.docx**.

Figure U3.3 **Assessment 5**

Assessment 6 Create an Announcement with a Picture and Text

1. At a blank document, insert the picture **River.jpg** located in the Unit03PA folder on your storage medium. (Insert the picture using the Picture button.)
2. Crop out a portion of the trees at the left and at the right and a portion of the hill at the top.
3. Change the brightness to +20%.
4. Specify that the picture should wrap behind text.
5. Insert the text *Riverside Apartments* on one line and *1-888-555-8800* on the second line.
6. Increase the size of the picture so it is easier to see and the size of the text so it is easier to read. Center the text and position it on the picture on top of the river so it is readable.
7. Save the document with the name **U03PA06**.
8. Print and then close **U03PA06.docx**.

Assessment 7 Create and Format a Table

1. At a blank document, create the table shown in Figure U3.4 with the following specifications:
   a. Merge and center cells as shown in the figure and then type the text as shown.
   b. Change the height of row 1 to 0.7 inch, the height of row 2 to 0.4 inch, and the height of the remaining rows to 0.3 inch.
   c. Change the font size to 16 points for the text in the first row.
   d. Align, center, and bold the text in the first three rows.
   e. Apply the shading as shown (use *Aqua, Accent 5, Lighter 40%* for the first and third rows and use *Aqua, Accent 5, Lighter 80%* for the second row).
2. Save the document with the name **U03PA07**.
3. Print and then close **U03PA07.docx**.

Figure U3.4 **Assessment 7**

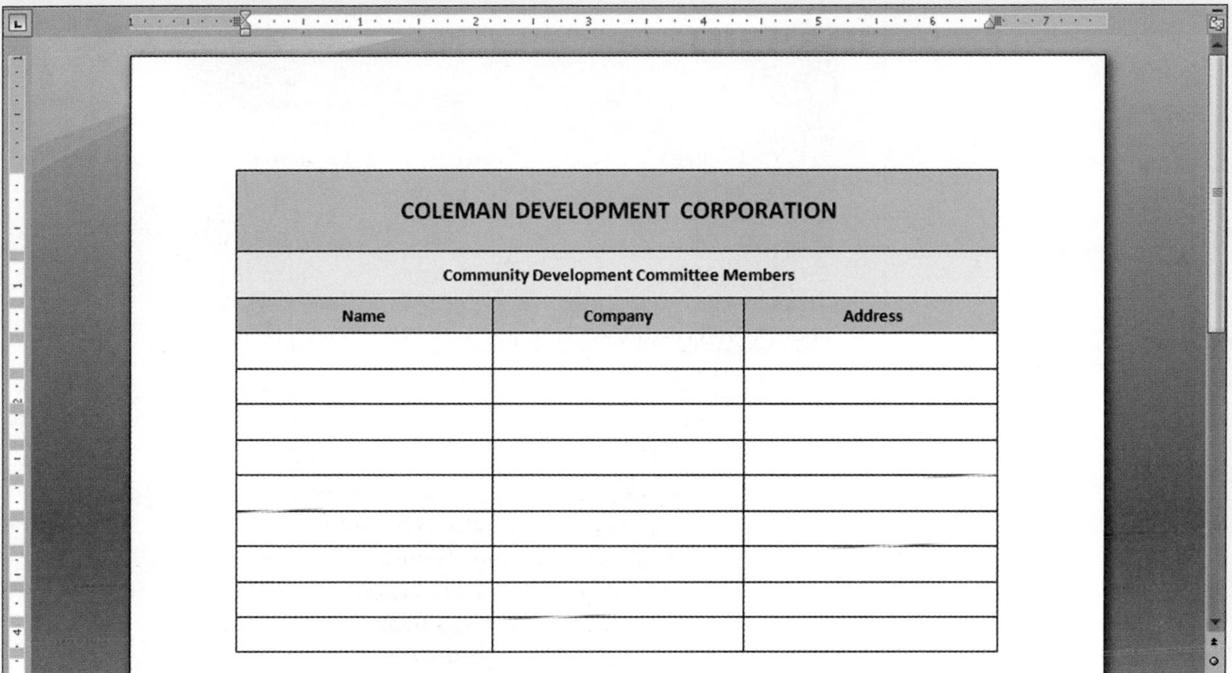

COLEMAN DEVELOPMENT CORPORATION		
Community Development Committee Members		
Name	Company	Address

Assessment 8 Format a Travel Table

1. Open **Table10.docx** and save the document with the name **U03PA08**.
2. Format the table so it displays as shown in Figure U3.5 with the following specifications:
   a. Select the entire table and then change the font to 14-point Candara.
   b. Change the column widths so the columns display as shown in the figure.
   c. Apply the *Medium Shading 2 - Accent 1* table style. Remove the check mark from the *First Column* option in the Table Style Options group.
   d. Align and center the text in the first two rows.
   e. Increase the font size of the text in row 1 to 20 points.
   f. Bold the text in rows 2 and 3.
   g. Slightly increase the height of rows 1 and 2 as shown in Figure U3.5.
   h. Center the text in row 3.
   i. Center the cells in the columns below the headings *Length* and *Estimated Cost*.
3. Drag the table so it is positioned in the middle of the page.
4. Save the document with the name **U03PA08**.
5. Print and then close **U03PA08.docx**.

Assessment 9 Calculate Averages in a Table

1. Open **Table11.docx** and save the document with the name **U03PA09**.
2. Insert formulas in the appropriate cells that calculate the averages of the quizzes.
3. AutoFit the contents of the table.
4. Apply a table style of your choosing to the table.
5. Appy any other formatting to improve the visual appeal of the table.
6. Save, print, and then close **U03PA09.docx**.

Figure U3.5 **Assessment 8**

BAYSIDE TRAVEL		
Family Fun Ski and Snowboard Vacations		
Package	**Length**	**Estimated Cost**
Lake Tahoe, Nevada	3 days, 2 nights	$229 to $259
Lake Tahoe, Nevada	7 days, 6 nights	$459 to $599
Sun Valley, Idaho	3 days, 2 nights	$249 to $279
Sun Valley, Idaho	7 days, 6 nights	$499 to $629
Jackson Hole, Wyoming	3 days, 2 nights	$239 to $269
Jackson Hole, Wyoming	7 days, 6 nights	$469 to $629

Assessment 10 Calculate Quantities and Totals in a Table

1. Open **Table12.docx** and save the document with the name **U03PA10**.
2. Insert in the appropriate cells formulas that multiply the quantity by the unit price. Insert in the bottom cell in the fourth column a formula that totals the amounts in the cells above.
3. Save, print, and then close **U03PA10.docx**.

Assessment 11 Create and Format a Column Chart

1. At a blank document, use the data in Figure U3.6 to create a column chart with the following specifications:
   a. Change the chart type to *3-D Clustered Column*.
   b. Apply the *Layout 3* chart layout.
   c. Apply the *Style 35* chart style.
   d. Select the chart title text and then type **2009 Sales**.
   e. Insert a small text box in the lower left corner of the chart and then type your first and last names.
   f. Insert major primary vertical gridlines.
   g. Select the chart area, apply *Orange, Accent 6, Lighter 60%* shape fill, and apply the *Offset Bottom* shadow shape effect.
   h. Select the chart title and then apply the *Gradient Fill - Accent 1* WordArt style.
   i. Change the chart height to 4 inches and the chart width to 6.5 inches.
   j. Position the chart in the middle of the page.
2. Save the document with the name **U03PA11**.
3. Print **U03PA11.docx**.
4. With the chart selected, display the Excel worksheet and edit the data in the worksheet by changing the following:
   a. Change the amount in cell C2 from *$285,450* to *$302,500*.
   b. Change the amount in cell C4 from *$180,210* to *$190,150*.
5. Save, print, and then close **U03PA11.docx**.

Figure U3.6 **Assessment 11**

Salesperson	First Half	Second Half
Bratton	$235,500	$285,450
Daniels	$300,570	$250,700
Hughes	$170,200	$180,210
Marez	$358,520	$376,400

Assessment 12 Create and Format a Pie Chart

1. At a blank document, use the data in Figure U3.7 to create a pie chart with the following specifications:
   a. Apply the *Layout 6* chart layout.
   b. Apply the *Style 26* chart style.
   c. Select the chart title text and then type **District Expenditures**.
   d. Move the legend to the left side of the chart.
   e. Select the chart area, apply *Purple, Accent 4, Lighter 80%* shape fill, and apply the *Accent color 4, 5 pt glow* glow shape effect.
   f. Select the legend, apply *Purple, Accent 4, Lighter 40%* shape fill, and apply the *Offset Left* shadow shape effect.
   g. Apply the WordArt style *Gradient Fill - Accent 4, Reflection* to the chart title text.
   h. Select the plot area and then increase the size of the pie so it better fills the chart area. (You may need to move the pie.)
   i. Select the legend and then move it so it is centered between the left edge of the chart and the pie.
   j. Position the chart centered at the top of the page.
2. Save the document with the name **U03PA12**.
3. Print and then close **U03PA12.docx**.

Figure U3.7 **Assessment 12**

	Percentage
Basic Education	42%
Special Needs	20%
Support Services	19%
Vocational	11%
Compensatory	8%

CREATING ORIGINAL DOCUMENTS

The activities in Assessments 13-16 give you the opportunity to practice your writing skills as well as demonstrate your mastery of the important Word features presented in this unit. When you compose the documents, use correct grammar, precise word choices, and clear sentence construction.

Assessment 13 Write Steps Describing How to Use SmartArt

Situation: You work in the Training Department of Coleman Development Corporation, and you are responsible for preparing a training document on how to use Word 2007. Because SmartArt is new in Word 2007, you need to write an explanation of the feature. Create a document that describes the SmartArt feature and the types of diagrams a user can create with it. Provide specific steps describing how to create an organizational chart using the *Organization Chart* diagram and specific steps describing how to create a *Radial Cycle* diagram. Save the completed document with the name **U03PA13**. Print and then close **U03PA13.docx**.

Assessment 14 Create an Expenditures Table

Situation: You are the vice president of Coleman Development Corporation, and you need to prepare a table showing the equipment expenditures for each department, as shown below:

COLEMAN DEVELOPMENT CORPORATION
Equipment Expenditures

Department	**Amount**
Personnel	$20,400
Research	$58,300
Finance	$14,900
Production	$90,100
Sales	$51,000
Marketing	$52,600

Create a table with the data and apply appropriate formatting to it. Save the document with the name **U03PA14**. Print and then close **U03PA14.docx**.

Assessment 15 Create a Column Chart

Situation: You decide that the data in the table you created in Assessment 14 would be easier to visualize if it were inserted in a chart. Using the information from the table, create a column chart and apply formatting to enhance its visual appeal. Save the completed document with the name **U03PA15**. Print and then close **U03PA15.docx**.

Assessment 16 Create a Store Letterhead

Situation: You work for Evergreen Sports, a sports equipment store that specializes in hiking gear. You have been asked to design letterhead for the store. When designing the letterhead, include an appropriate clip art image along with the following information:

Evergreen Sports
4500 Lowell Avenue
Portland, OR 99821
(503) 555-8220

Save the completed letterhead document with the name **U03PA16**. Print and then close **U03PA16.docx**.

Unit 4

Managing Data

- Merging Documents
- Sorting and Selecting
- Managing Lists
- Managing Page Numbers, Headers, and Footers
- Managing Shared Documents
- Unit 4 Performance Assessments

Signature Microsoft® Word 2007

Microsoft Certified Application Specialist Skills—Unit 4

Reference No.	Skill	Pages
1	**Creating and Customizing Documents**	
1.2	Lay out documents	
1.2.1	Format pages	489-494
1.2.2	Create and modify headers and footers (Not using Quick Parts)	489-503
2	**Formatting Content**	
2.3	Control Pagination	
2.3.2	Create and modify sections	502-503
4	**Organizing Content**	
4.2.	Use tables and lists to organize content	
4.2.2	Sort content	445-451
4.2.3	Modify list formats	465-478
4.5.	Merge documents and data sources	417-444
4.5.1.	Create merged documents	417-444
4.5.2.	Merge data into form letters	424-460
4.5.3.	Create envelopes and labels	425-428
5	**Reviewing Documents**	
5.2	Compare and merge document versions	527-532
5.2.1	Compare document versions	530-532
5.2.2	Merge document versions	530-532
5.2.3	Combine revisions from multiple authors	530-532
5.3	Manage track changes	
5.3.1	Display markup	523-524
5.3.2	Enable, disable, accept, and reject tracked changes	519-527
5.3.3	Change tracking options	512-527
5.4	Insert, modify, and delete comments	511-519

Chapter 16

Merging Documents

Tutorial 16.1
Automating Large Mailings
Tutorial 16.2
Using Fill In Fields and Creating Custom Mailing Labels

Performance Objectives

Upon successful completion of Chapter 16, you will be able to:

- Create and merge letters, envelopes, labels, and directories
- Create custom fields for a merge
- Edit main documents and data source files
- Input text during a merge
- Use the Mail Merge wizard to merge documents

Word includes a Mail Merge feature that you can use to create customized letters, envelopes, labels, directories, e-mail messages, and faxes. The Mail Merge feature is useful when you need to send the same letter to a number of people, but you want to personalize it and create an envelope or mailing label for each person. Mail Merge allows you to merge a main document, such as a letter, with a data source file, such as a database of names and addresses. In this chapter, you will use Mail Merge to create customized letters, envelopes, labels, and directories.

Note: Before beginning computer exercises for this chapter, copy to your storage medium the Chapter16 folder from the CD that accompanies this textbook and then make Chapter16 the active folder.

Completing a Merge

As noted above, a merge generally takes two files: a ***main document*** and a ***data source file***. The main document contains the standard text and/or the fields that identify where variable information will be inserted during the merge. The data source file contains the variable information that will be inserted into the main document.

Use the Start Mail Merge button in the Mailings tab, shown in Figure 16.1, to specify the type of main document you want to create; use the Select Recipients button to create a data source file or to choose an existing data source file.

Figure 16.1 **Mailings Tab**

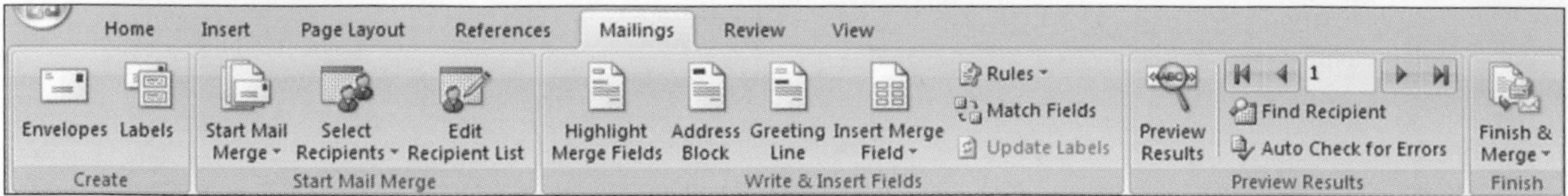

Create Data Source File

1. Click Mailings tab.
2. Click Select Recipients button.
3. Click *Type New List* in drop-down list.
4. Type data in predesigned or custom fields.
5. Click OK.

Creating a Data Source File

You begin a mail merge by clicking the Mailings tab, clicking the Start Mail Merge button, and selecting the type of main document that you want to create from the drop-down list. Before you actually create the main document though, you must determine the type of variable information you will need to insert into that document and create a data source file. Word provides predetermined field names for this purpose. Use these field names if they represent the data you are creating.

Variable information in a data source file is saved as a ***record.*** A record is a series of fields, and each record contains all of the information for one unit (for example, a person, family, customer, client, or business). A data source file is a series of records.

Create a data source file by clicking the Select Recipients button in the Start Mail Merge group in the Mailings tab and then clicking *Type New List* at the drop-down list. At the New Address List dialog box, shown in Figure 16.2, use the predesigned fields offered by Word and type the required data or edit the fields by deleting and/or inserting custom fields and then typing the data. When you have entered all the records, click OK. At the Save Address List dialog box, navigate to the desired folder, type a name for the data source file, and then click OK. Word saves a data source file as an Access database. You do not need Access on your computer to complete a merge with a data source file.

Figure 16.2 **New Address List Dialog Box**

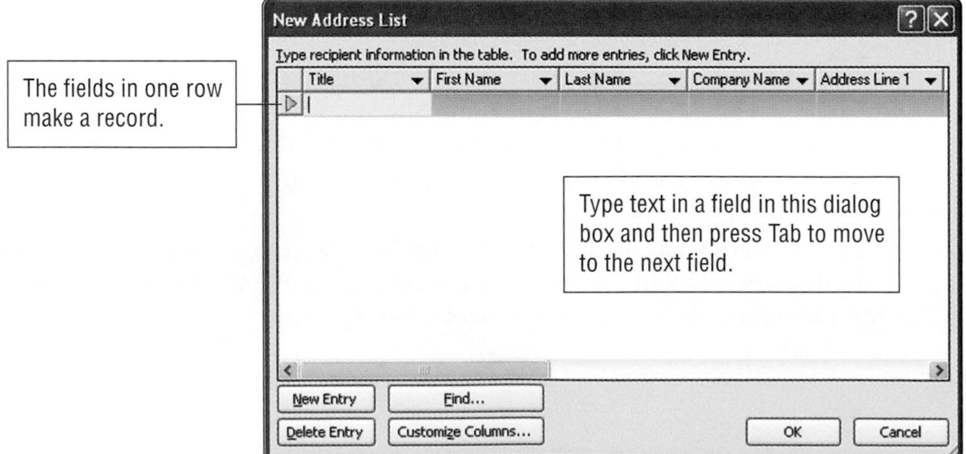

Exercise 1A

Creating a Data Source File

1. At a blank document, click the Mailings tab.
2. Click the Start Mail Merge button in the Start Mail Merge group and then click *Letters* at the drop-down list.

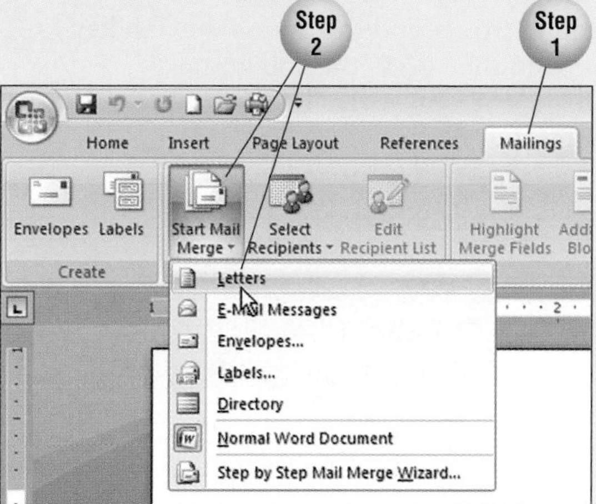

3. Click the Select Recipients button in the Start Mail Merge group and then click *Type New List* at the drop-down list.
4. At the New Address List dialog box, predesigned fields display in the *Field Names* list box. Delete the fields you do not need by completing the following steps:
   a. Click the Customize Columns button.
   b. At the Customize Address List dialog box, click *Company Name* to select it, and then click the Delete button.
   c. At the message asking if you are sure that you want to delete the field, click Yes.
   d. Complete steps similar to those in Steps 4b and 4c to delete the following fields:
      Country or Region
      Home Phone
      Work Phone
      E-mail Address
5. Insert a custom field by completing the following steps:
   a. At the Customize Address List dialog box, click the Add button.
   b At the Add Field dialog box, type **Membership** and then click OK.
   c. Click the OK button to close the Customize Address List dialog box.

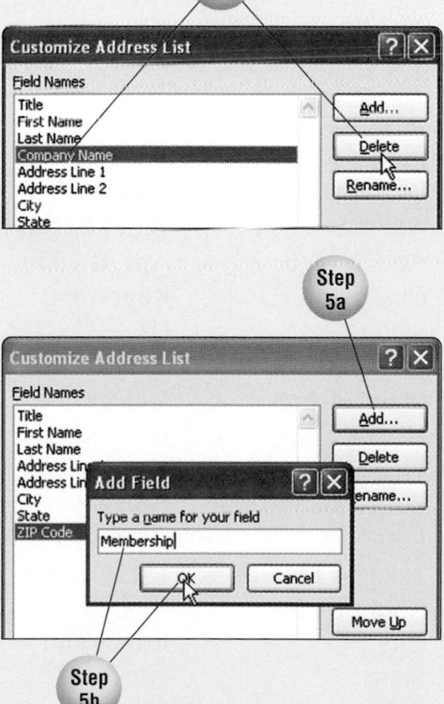

6. At the New Address List dialog box, enter the information for the first client shown in Figure 16.3 by completing the following steps:
   a. Click in the *Title* text box.
   b. Type **Mrs.** and then press the Tab key. (This moves the insertion point to the *First Name* field. You can also press Shift + Tab to move to the previous field.)
   c. Type **Barbara** and then press the Tab key.
   d. Type **Colburn** and then press the Tab key.
   e. Type **12309 Second Street** and then press the Tab key.
   f. Type **Apt. B-205** and then press the Tab key.
   g. Type **Edgewood** and then press the Tab key.
   h. Type **ID** and then press the Tab key.
   i. Type **83447**and then press the Tab key.
   j. Type **Gold** and then press the Tab key. (This makes the New Entry button active.)

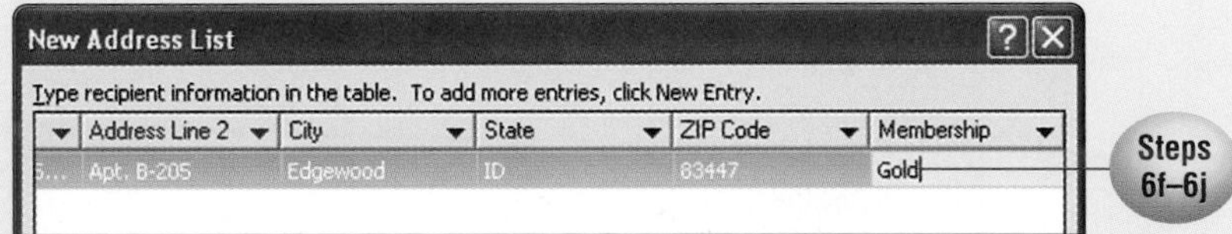

   k. With the insertion point positioned in the *Title* field, complete steps similar to those in Steps 6b through 6j to enter the information for the three other clients shown in Figure 16.3.
7. After entering all of the information for the last client in Figure 16.3 (Dr. Tracy Malone), click the OK button located in the bottom right corner of the New Address List dialog box.
8. At the Save Address List dialog box, navigate to the *Chapter16* folder on your storage medium, type C16Ex01DS in the *File name* text box, and then click the Save button.

Figure 16.3 Exercise 1A

Title	=	**Mrs.**	Title	=	**Mr.**
First Name	=	**Barbara**	First Name	=	**Brian**
Last Name	=	**Colburn**	Last Name	=	**Kosel**
Address Line 1	=	**12309 Second Street**	Address Line 1	=	**345 Rosewood Avenue**
Address Line 2	=	**Apt. B-205**	Address Line 2	=	(leave this blank)
City	=	**Edgewood**	City	=	**Edgewood**
State	=	**ID**	State	=	**ID**
ZIP Code	=	**83447**	ZIP Code	=	**83445**
Membership	=	**Gold**	Membership	=	**Platinum**
Title	=	**Mr.**	Title	=	**Dr.**
First Name	=	**Gordon**	First Name	=	**Tracy**
Last Name	=	**Costanzo**	Last Name	=	**Malone**
Address Line 1	=	**13115 132nd Street**	Address Line 1	=	**7485 North Collins**
Address Line 2	=	**Apt. 5**	Address Line 2	=	(leave this blank)
City	=	**Edgewood**	City	=	**Edgewood**
State	=	**ID**	State	=	**ID**
ZIP Code	=	**83445**	ZIP Code	=	**83447**
Membership	=	**Premium**	Membership	=	**Premium**

Creating a Main Document

Create Main Document
1. Click Mailings tab.
2. Click Start Mail Merge button.
3. Click desired document type at drop-down list.
4. Type main document text and insert fields as needed.

After creating and typing records in the data source file, you can type the main document. As you type, insert fields identifying where you want variable information to appear when the document is merged with the data source file. Use buttons in the Write & Insert Fields group to insert fields and field blocks in the main document.

Insert all of the fields required for the inside address of a letter with the Address Block button in the Write & Insert Fields group. Click this button, and the Insert Address Block dialog box displays with a preview of how the fields will be inserted in the document to create the inside address. The Insert Address dialog box also contains buttons and options for customizing the fields. Click OK and the «AddressBlock» field is inserted in the document. The «AddressBlock» field is an example of a composite field that groups a number of fields together.

Click the Greeting Line button, and the Insert Greeting Line dialog box displays with options for customizing how the fields are inserted in the document to create the greeting line. When you click OK at the dialog box, the «GreetingLine» composite field is inserted in the document.

If you want to insert an individual field from the data source file, click the Insert Merge Field button arrow and then click the desired field at the drop-down list containing the fields in the data source file. You can also click the Insert Merge Field button and then click the desired field at the Insert Merge Field dialog box.

Exercise 1B

Creating a Main Document

Note: If a message displays while you are completing exercises that indicates opening a document will run the SQL command, click Yes.

1. At a blank document, create the letter shown in Figure 16.4. Begin by clicking the *No Spacing* style in the Styles group in the Home tab.
2. Press the Enter key six times and then type **September 27, 2010**.
3. Press the Enter key five times and then insert address fields by completing the following steps:
   a. Click the Mailings tab and then click the Address Block button in the Write & Insert Fields group.
   b. At the Insert Address Block dialog box, click the OK button.
   c. Press the Enter key twice.

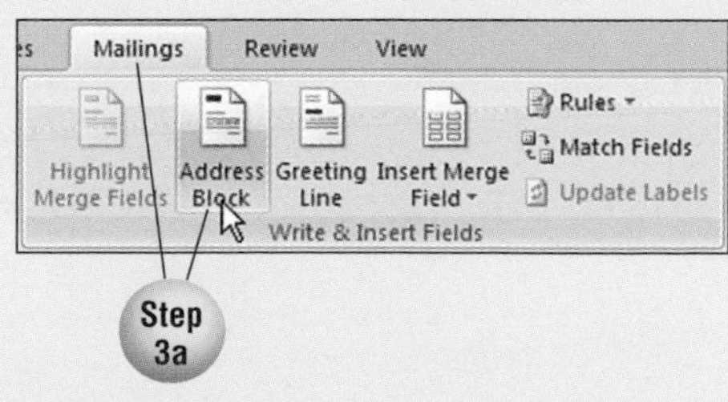

4. Insert greeting line fields by completing the following steps:
   a. Click the Greeting Line button in the Write & Insert Fields group.
   b. At the Insert Greeting Line dialog box, click the down-pointing arrow at the right of the option box containing the comma (the box to the right of the box containing *Mr. Randall*).
   c. At the drop-down list that displays, click the colon.

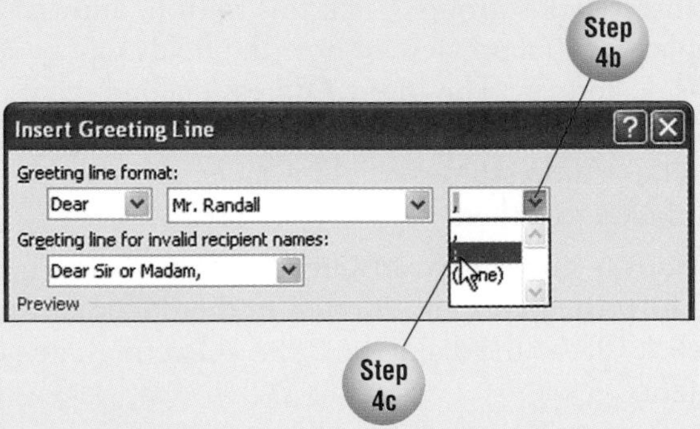

   d. Click OK to close the Insert Greeting Line dialog box.
   e. Press the Enter key twice.
5. Type the letter shown in Figure 16.4. When you reach the «Title» field, insert the field by clicking the Insert Merge Field button arrow and then clicking *Title* at the drop-down list.

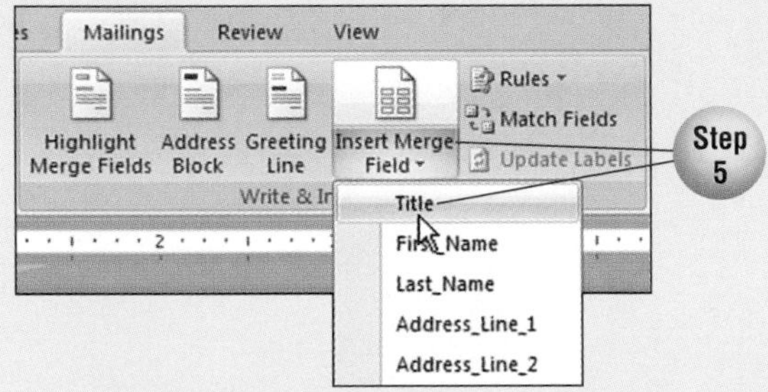

6. Press the spacebar and then insert the «Last_Name» field by clicking the Insert Merge Field button arrow and then clicking *Last_Name* at the drop-down list.
7. When you reach the «Membership» field insert the field by clicking the Insert Merge Field button arrow and then clicking *Membership* at the drop-down list.
8. Type the remainder of the letter shown in Figure 16.4. (Insert your initials instead of the *XX* at the end of the letter.)
9. Save the document with the name **C16Ex01MD**.

Figure 16.4 Exercise 1B

September 27, 2010

«AddressBlock»

«GreetingLine»

The next meeting of the Edgewood Volunteers Group will be Monday, October 11, at 7:00 p.m. The meeting was previously scheduled for the meeting hall in the community center but has been changed to the conference room at the library.

We will be discussing the annual holiday food drive. The director of the food bank will give a short presentation on the agency and how it serves the community. In addition to discussing the food drive, we will decide on additional community service activities.

In January, we will be printing our membership directory. Currently, «Title» «Last_Name», we have you listed as a «Membership» member. Please let us know if your membership or any of your personal information has changed. Also, we are interested in recruiting additional members so please call or e-mail us if you have a referral.

Sincerely,

Stacey Levine
Director

XX:C16Ex01MD.docx

Previewing a Merge

To view the main document as it will appear when merged with the first record in the data source file, click the Preview Results button in the Mailings tab. To view the main document merged with other records, use the navigation buttons in the Preview Results group. This group contains five buttons: First Record, Previous Record, Go to Record, Next Record, and Last Record. Click the button that will display the main document merged with the record you want to view. To use the Go to Record button, click the button, type the number of the desired record, and then press Enter. You can turn off the preview feature by clicking the Preview Results button.

First Record

Previous Record

Next Record

Last Record

Merge Documents
1. Click Finish & Merge button.
2. Click *Edit Individual Documents* at drop-down list.
3. Make sure *All* is selected in Merge to New Document dialog box.
4. Click OK.

Merging Documents

To complete the merge, click the Finish & Merge button in the Finish group in the Mailings tab. At the drop-down list that displays, you can choose to merge the records and create a new document, send the merged documents directly to the printer, or send the merged documents by e-mail.

To merge the documents and create a new document with the merged records, click the Finish & Merge button and then click *Edit Individual Documents* at the drop-down list. At the Merge to New Document dialog box, make sure *All* is selected in the *Merge records* section and then click OK. This merges the records in the data source file with the main document and inserts the merged documents in a new document.

Exercise 1C

Merging the Main Document with the Data Source File

1. With **C16Ex01MD.docx** open, preview the main document merged with the first record in the data source file by clicking the Preview Results button in the Mailings tab.
2. Click the Next Record button to view the main document merged with the second record in the data source file.

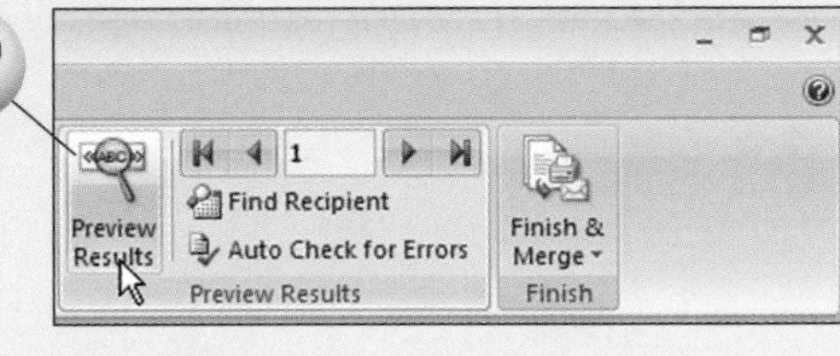

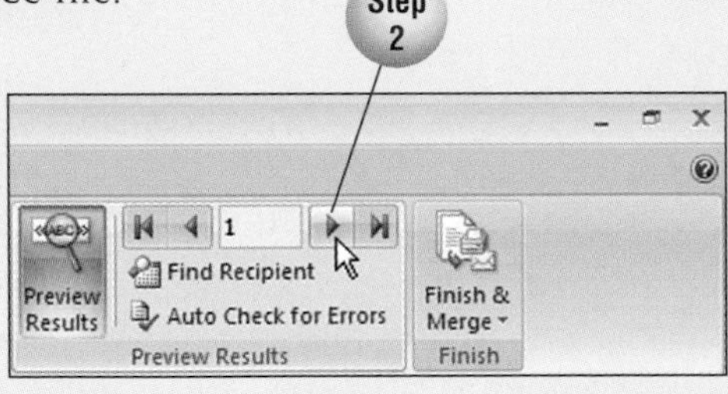

3. Click the Preview Results button to turn off the preview function.
4. Click the Finish & Merge button in the Finish group and then click *Edit Individual Documents* at the drop-down list.
5. At the Merge to New Document dialog box, make sure *All* is selected and then click OK.
6. Save the merged letters document with the name **C16Ex01Ltrs**.
7. Print **C16Ex01Ltrs.docx**. (This document will print four letters.)
8. Close **C16Ex01Ltrs.docx**.
9. Save and then close **C16Ex01MD.docx**.

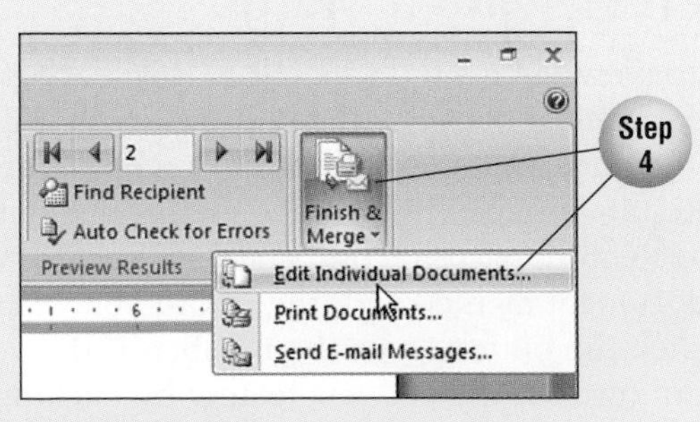

Merging Envelopes

If you create a letter as your main document and then merge it with a data source file, you will likely need properly addressed envelopes in which to send the letters. To create customized envelopes, prepare an envelope main document to be merged with the data source file. To do this, click the Mailings tab, click the Start Mail Merge button, and then click *Envelopes* at the drop-down list. This displays the Envelope Options dialog box, shown in Figure 16.5. At this dialog box, specify the desired envelope size, make any other changes, and then click OK.

Figure 16.5 Envelope Options Dialog Box

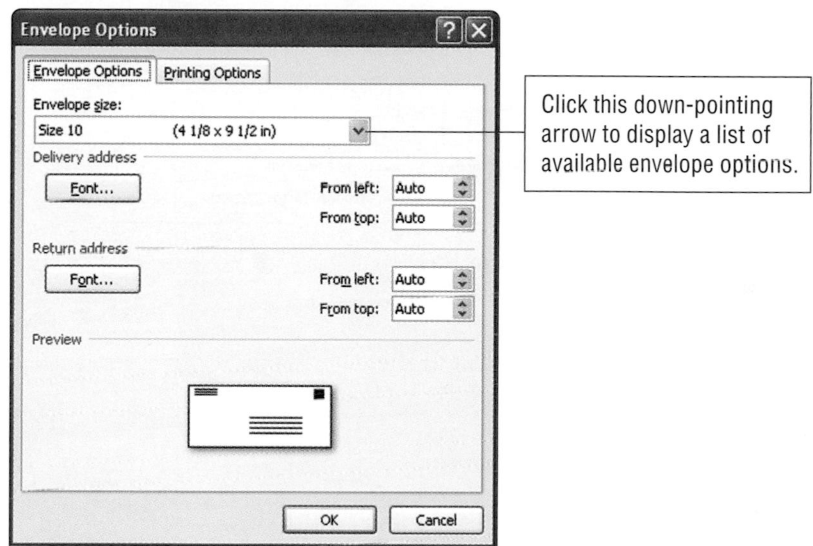

After selecting an envelope as the main document type, the next step in the envelope merge process is to create a data source file to merge with the envelope document or identify an existing file to use. To identify an existing data source file, click the Select Recipients button in the Start Mail Merge group, and then click *Use Existing List* at the drop-down list. At the Select Data Source dialog box, navigate to the folder that contains the data source file you want to use and then double-click the file.

With the data source file attached to the envelope main document, insert the appropriate fields. Click in the envelope approximately where the recipient's address should appear and a box with a dashed blue border displays. Click the Address Block button in the Write & Insert Fields group and then click OK at the Insert Address Block dialog box.

Exercise 2

Merging Envelopes

1. At a blank document, click the Mailings tab.
2. Click the Start Mail Merge button in the Start Mail Merge group and then click *Envelopes* at the drop-down list.

3. At the Envelope Options dialog box, make sure the envelope size is 10 and then click OK.
4. Click the Select Recipients button in the Start Mail Merge group and then click *Use Existing List* at the drop-down list.
5. At the Select Data Source dialog box, navigate to the Chapter16 folder on your storage medium and then double-click the data source file named **C16Ex01DS.mdb**.
6. In the envelope document click in the approximate location where the recipient's address will appear. (This causes a box with a dashed blue border to display. If you do not see this box, try clicking in a different location on the envelope.)

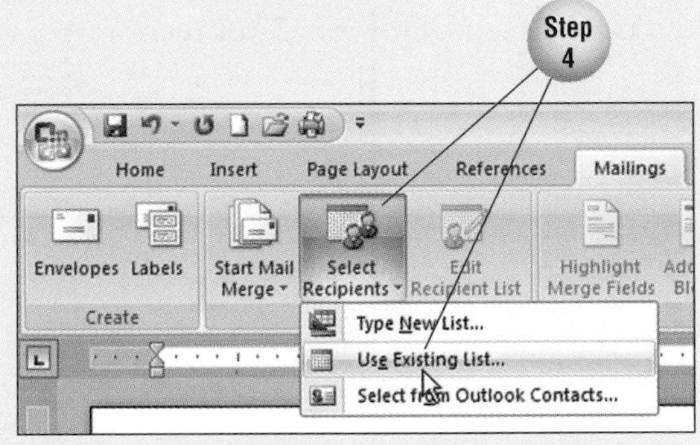

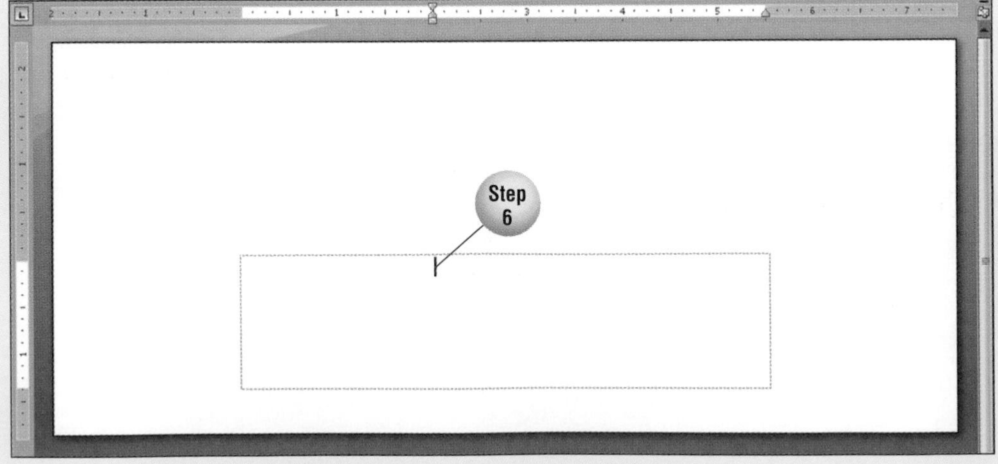

7. Click the Address Block button in the Write & Insert Fields group.
8. At the Insert Address Block dialog box, click the OK button.
9. Click the Preview Results button to view the envelope merged with the first record in the data source file.
10. Click the Preview Results button to turn it off.
11. Click the Finish & Merge button in the Finish group and then click *Edit Individual Documents* at the drop-down list.
12. At the Merge to New Document dialog box, make sure *All* is selected and then click OK.
13. Save the merged envelopes document with the name **C16Ex02Envs**.
14. Print **C16Ex02Envs.docx**. (This document will print four envelopes. Manual feed of envelopes may be required. Check with your instructor.)
15. Close **C16Ex02Envs.docx**.
16. Save the envelope main document with the name **C16Ex02MD**.
17. Close **C16Ex02MD.docx**.

Merging Labels

You can create mailing labels for records in a data source file in much the same way that you create envelopes. Click the Start Mail Merge button and then click *Labels* at the drop-down list. This displays the Label Options dialog box, shown in Figure 16.6. Make sure the label that you want to use is selected and then click OK to close the dialog box. Next, create the data source file or identify an existing data source file to use. With the data source file attached to the label main document, insert the appropriate fields and then complete the merge.

Figure 16.6 Label Options Dialog Box

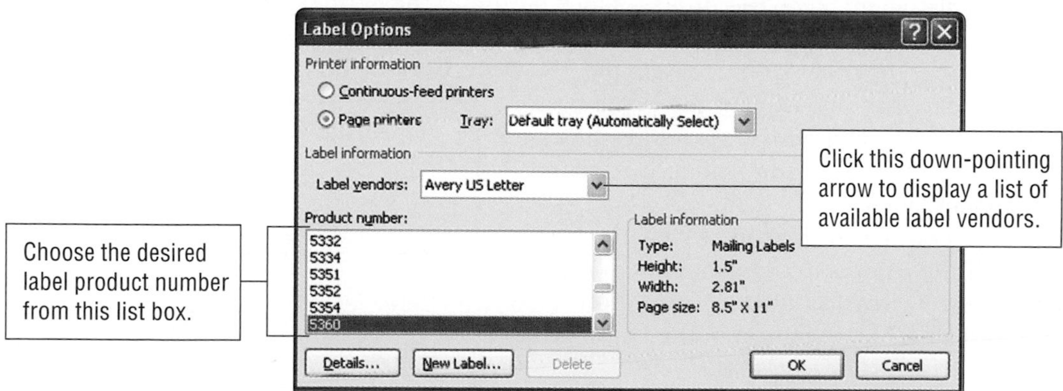

Exercise 3

Merging Mailing Labels

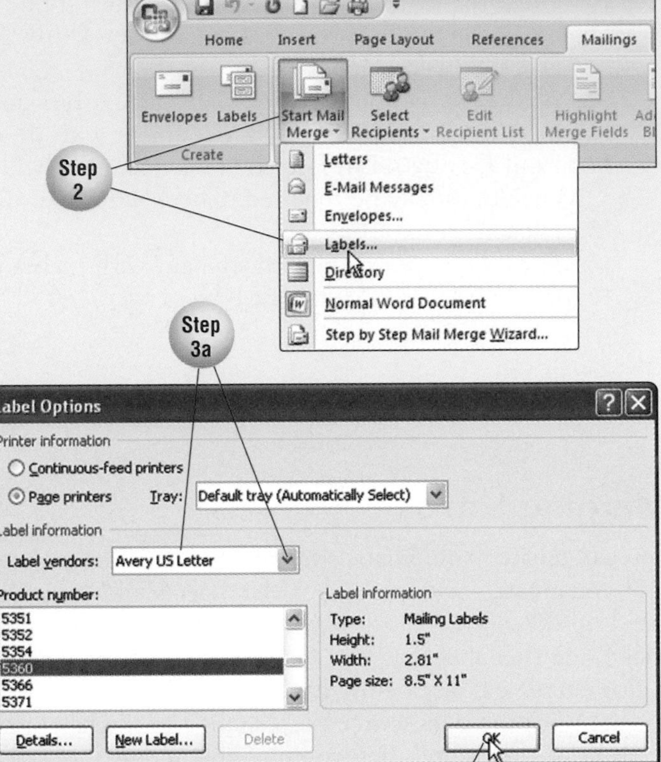

1. At a blank document, click the Mailings tab.
2. Click the Start Mail Merge button in the Start Mail Merge group and then click *Labels* at the drop-down list.
3. At the Label Options dialog box, complete the following steps:
   a. If necessary, click the down-pointing arrow at the right side of the *Label vendors* option and then click *Avery US Letter* at the drop-down list. (If this product vendor is not available, choose a vendor that offers labels that print on a full page.)
   b. Scroll in the *Product number* list box and then click *5360*. (If this option is not available, choose a label number that prints labels in two or three columns down a full page.)
   c. Click OK to close the dialog box.
4. Click the Select Recipients button in the Start Mail Merge group and then click *Use Existing List* at the drop-down list.
5. At the Select Data Source dialog box, navigate to the Chapter16 folder on your storage medium and then double-click the data source file named **C16Ex01DS.mdb**.
6. At the labels document, click the Address Block button in the Write & Insert Fields group.
7. At the Insert Address Block dialog box, click the OK button. (This inserts «AddressBlock» in the first label. The other labels contain the «Next Record» field.)
8. Click the Update Labels button in the Write & Insert Fields group. (This adds the «AddressBlock» field after each «Next Record» field in the second and subsequent labels.)

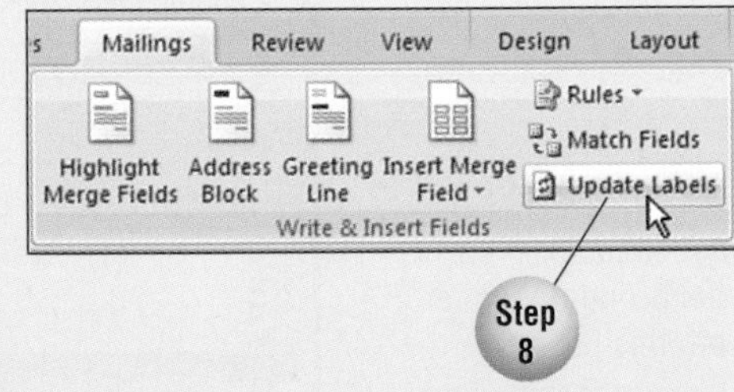

9. Click the Preview Results button to view the labels merged with the records in the data source file.
10. Click the Preview Results button to turn it off.
11. Click the Finish & Merge button in the Finish group and then click *Edit Individual Documents* at the drop-down list.
12. At the Merge to New Document dialog box, make sure *All* is selected and then click OK.
13. Save the merged labels document with the name **C16Ex03Labels**.
14. Print and then close **C16Ex03Labels.docx**.
15. Save the label main document with the name **C16Ex03MD**.
16. Close **C16Ex03MD.docx**.

Merging a Directory

When you merge letters, envelopes, or mailing labels, a new form is created for each record. For example, if the data source file merged with a letter contains eight records, eight letters are created. If the data source file merged with a mailing label contains twenty records, twenty labels are created. In some situations, you may want merged information to remain on the same page. This is useful, for example, when you want to create a list such as a directory or address list.

To create a merged directory, click the Start Mail Merge button and then click *Directory*. Create or identify an existing data source file and then insert the desired fields in the directory document. Set tabs if you want to insert text in columns.

Exercise 4

Merging a Directory

1. At a blank document, click the Mailings tab.
2. Click the Start Mail Merge button in the Start Mail Merge group and then click *Directory* at the drop-down list.

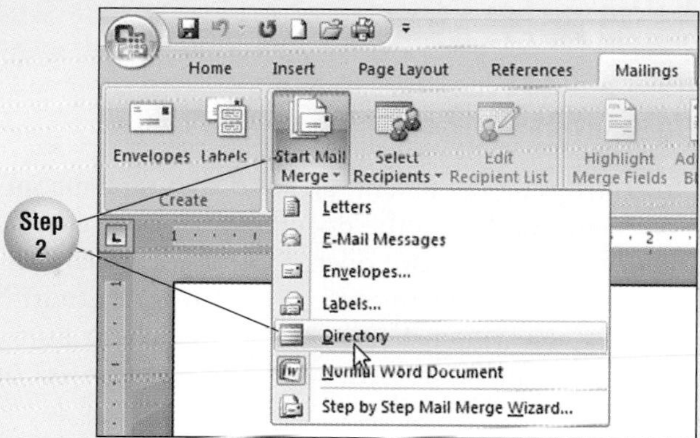

3. Click the Select Recipients button in the Start Mail Merge group and then click *Use Existing List* at the drop-down list.
4. At the Select Data Source dialog box, navigate to the Chapter16 folder on your storage medium and then double-click the data source file named **C16Ex01DS.mdb**.
5. At the document, set left tabs on the Ruler at the 1-inch mark, the 2.5-inch mark, and the 4-inch mark and then press the Tab key. (This moves the insertion point to the tab set at the 1-inch mark.)
6. Click the Insert Merge Field button arrow and then click *Last_Name* at the drop-down list.
7. Press the Tab key to move the insertion point to the 2.5-inch mark.
8. Click the Insert Merge Field button arrow and then click *First_Name* at the drop-down list.
9. Press the Tab key to move the insertion point to the 4-inch mark.
10. Click the Insert Merge Field button arrow and then click *Membership* at the drop-down list.
11. Press the Enter key once.
12. Click the Finish & Merge button in the Finish group and then click *Edit Individual Documents* at the drop-down list.
13. At the Merge to New Document dialog box, make sure *All* is selected and then click OK. (This merges the fields in the document.)
14. Press Ctrl + Home, press the Enter key once, and then press the Up Arrow key once.

15. Press the Tab key, turn on bold, and then type **Last Name**.
16. Press the Tab key and then type **First Name**.
17. Press the Tab key and then type **Membership**.

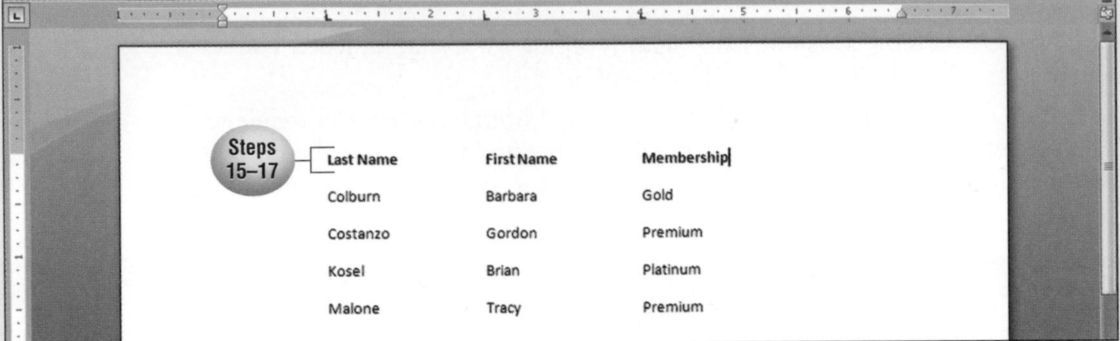

18. Save the directory document with the name **C16Ex04Directory**.
19. Print and then close the document.
20. Close the directory main document without saving it.

Edit Data Source File
1. Open main document.
2. Click Mailings tab.
3. Click Edit Recipient List button.
4. Make desired changes at Mail Merge Recipients dialog box.
5. Click OK.

Editing a Data Source File

If you need to edit a main document, do so in the usual manner: Open it, make the required changes, and then save the document. Because a data source file is actually an Access database file, you cannot open it in the usual manner. To open a data source file for editing, use the Edit Recipient List button in the Start Mail Merge group in the Mailings tab. When you click the Edit Recipient List button, the Mail Merge Recipients dialog box, shown in Figure 16.7, displays. Select or edit records at this dialog box.

Figure 16.7 Mail Merge Recipients Dialog Box

Select specific records by removing the check marks from those records you do not want included in the merge.

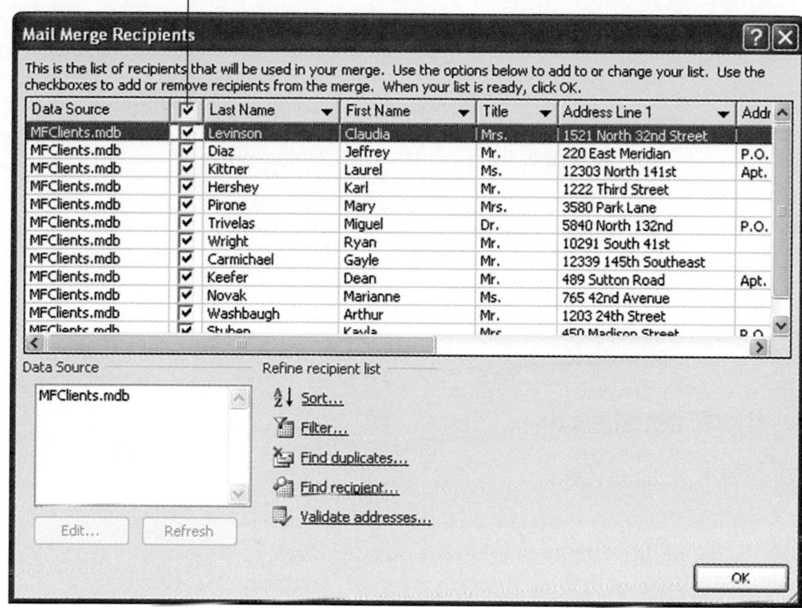

Selecting Specific Records

At the Mail Merge Recipients dialog box, the first field of each record is preceded by a check mark. If you do not want a specific record included in a merge, remove the check mark. In this way, you can select and then merge specific records in the data source file with the main document.

Exercise 5

Selecting Records and Merging Mailing Labels

1. At a blank document, create mailing labels for clients living in Lexington. Begin by clicking the Mailings tab.
2. Click the Start Mail Merge button in the Start Mail Merge group and then click *Labels* at the drop-down list.
3. At the Label Options dialog box, make sure *Avery US Letter* displays in the *Label products* option box, and *5360* displays in the *Product number* list box, and then click OK.
4. Click the Select Recipients button in the Start Mail Merge group and then click *Use Existing List* at the drop-down list.
5. At the Select Data Source dialog box, navigate to the Chapter16 folder on your storage medium and then double-click the data source file named **MFClients.mdb**.
6. Click the Edit Recipient List button in the Start Mail Merge group.

7. At the Mail Merge Recipients dialog box, complete the following steps:
   a. Click the check box located immediately left of the *Last Name* field to remove the check mark. (This removes all of the check marks from the check boxes.)
   b. Click the check box immediately left of each of the following last names: *Levinson*, *Kittner*, *Trivelas*, *Wright*, *Washbaugh*, and *Stuben*. (These are the clients who live in Lexington.)
   c. Click OK to close the dialog box.
8. At the labels document, click the Address Block button in the Write & Insert Fields group.
9. At the Insert Address Block dialog box, click the OK button.
10. Click the Update Labels button in the Write & Insert Fields group.
11. Click the Finish & Merge button in the Finish group and then click *Edit Individual Documents* at the drop-down list.
12. At the Merge to New Document dialog box, make sure *All* is selected and then click OK.
13. Save the merged labels document with the name **C16Ex05Labels**.
14. Print and then close **C16Ex05Labels.docx**.
15. Close the main labels document without saving it.

Editing Records

A data source file may need periodic editing to add or delete customer names, update fields, insert new fields, or delete existing fields. To edit a data source file, click the Edit Recipient List button in the Start Mail Merge group. At the Mail Merge Recipients dialog box, click the data source file name in the *Data Source* list box and then click the Edit button that displays below the list box. This displays the Edit Data Source dialog box, shown in Figure 16.8. At this dialog box, you can add a new entry, delete an entry, find a particular entry, and customize columns.

Figure 16.8 Edit Data Source Dialog Box

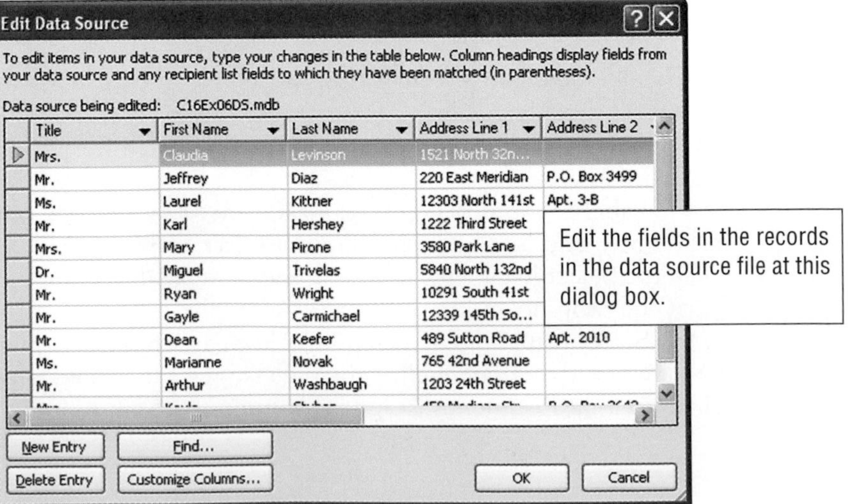

Exercise 6

Editing Records in a Data Source File

1. Make a copy of the **MFClients.mdb** file by completing the following steps:
   a. Display the Open dialog box and make Chapter16 the active folder.
   b. If necessary, change the *Files of type* option to *All Files (*.*)*.
   c. Right-click on the **MFClients.mdb** file and then click Copy at the pop-up list.
   d. Position the mouse pointer in a white portion of the Open dialog box list box (outside of any file name), click the *right* mouse button, and then click Paste at the pop-up list. (This inserts a copy of the file in the dialog box list box and names the file **Copy of MFClients.mdb**.)
   e. Right-click on the file name **Copy of MFClients.mdb** and then click Rename at the pop-up list.
   f. Type **C16Ex06DS.mdb** and then press Enter.
   g. Close the Open dialog box.
2. At a blank document, click the Mailings tab.
3. Click the Select Recipients button and then click *Use Existing List* from the drop-down list.
4. At the Select Data Source dialog box, navigate to the Chapter16 folder on your storage medium and then double-click the data source file named **C16Ex06DS.mdb**.
5. Click the Edit Recipient List button in the Start Mail Merge group.
6. At the Mail Merge Recipients dialog box, click *C16Ex06DS.mdb* that displays in the *Data Source* list box and then click the Edit button.

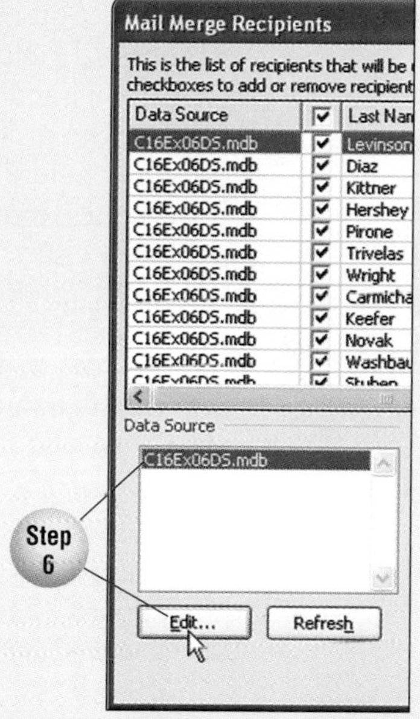

7. Delete the record for Dean Keefer by completing the following steps:
   a. Click the square that displays at the beginning of the row for Mr. Dean Keefer.
   b. Click the Delete Entry button.
   c. At the message asking if you want to delete the entry, click the Yes button.
8. Insert a new record by completing the following steps:
   a. Click the New Entry button in the dialog box.
   b. Type the following text in the new record in the specified fields:

      Title = **Mrs.**
      First Name = **Amanda**
      Last Name = **Montague**
      Address Line 1 = **632 Tenth Street**
      Address Line 2 = (none)
      City = **Lexington**
      State = **KY**
      ZIP Code = **40506**
      Home Phone = **859-555-2047**

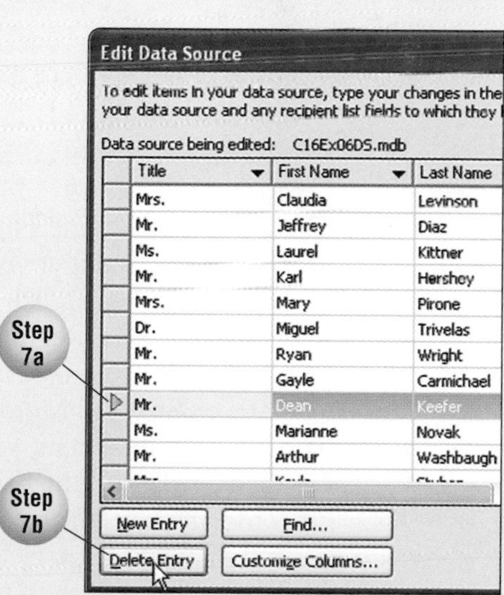

9. Insert a new field and type text in the field by completing the following steps:
   a. At the Edit Data Source dialog box, click the Customize Columns button.
   b. At the message asking if you want to save the changes made to the data source file, click Yes.
   c. At the Customize Address List dialog box, click *ZIP Code* in the *Field Names* list box. (This inserts a new field below the selected field.)
   d. Click the Add button.
   e. At the Add Field dialog box, type **Cell Phone** and then click OK.
   f. Change the order of the fields so the *Cell Phone* field displays after the *Home Phone* field. To move the *Cell Phone* field, make sure it is selected and then click the Move Down button.

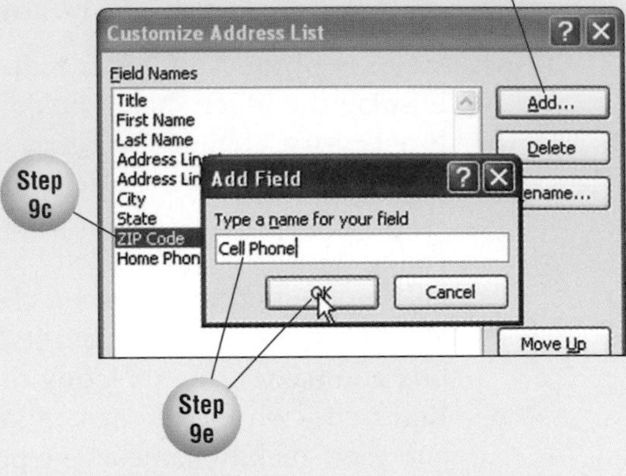

   g. Click OK to close the Customize Address List dialog box.
   h. At the Edit Data Source file, scroll to the right to display the *Cell Phone* field (last field in the file) and then type the following cell phone numbers (after typing each cell phone number, except the last number, press the Down Arrow key to make the next cell below active):
      Record 1 = **859-555-5879**
      Record 2 = **859-555-9902**
      Record 3 = **859-555-8349**
      Record 4 = **859-555-3849**
      Record 5 = **859-555-1200**
      Record 6 = **859-555-7522**
      Record 7 = **859-555-1233**
      Record 8 = **859-555-5628**
      Record 9 = **859-555-5890**
      Record 10 = **859-555-2903**
      Record 11 = **859-555-9703**
      Record 12 = **859-555-5563**
   i. Click OK to close the Edit Data Source dialog box.
   j. At the message asking if you want to update the recipient list and save changes, click Yes.
   k. At the Mail Merge Recipients dialog box, click OK.
10. Create a directory by completing the following steps:
   a. Click the Start Mail Merge button and then click *Directory* at the drop-down list.
   b. At the blank document, set left tabs on the horizontal ruler at the 1-inch mark, the 3.5-inch mark, and the 5-inch mark.
   c. Press the Tab key (this moves the insertion point to the first tab set at the 1-inch mark).
   d. Click the Insert Merge Field button arrow and then click *Last_Name* at the drop-down list.
   e. Type a comma and then press the spacebar.
   f. Click the Insert Merge Field button arrow and then click *First_Name* at the drop-down list.
   g. Press the Tab key, click the Insert Merge Field button arrow, and then click *Home_Phone* at the drop-down list.
   h. Press the Tab key, click the Insert Merge Field button arrow, and then click *Cell_Phone* at the drop-down list.

i. Press the Enter key once.
j. Click the Finish & Merge button in the Finish group and then click *Edit Individual Documents* at the drop-down list.
k. At the Merge to New Document dialog box, make sure *All* is selected and then click OK. (This merges the fields in the document.)

11. Press Ctrl + Home, press the Enter key once, and then press the Up Arrow key once.
12. Press the Tab key, turn on bold, and then type **Name**.
13. Press the Tab key and then type **Home Phone**.
14. Press the Tab key and then type **Cell Phone**.

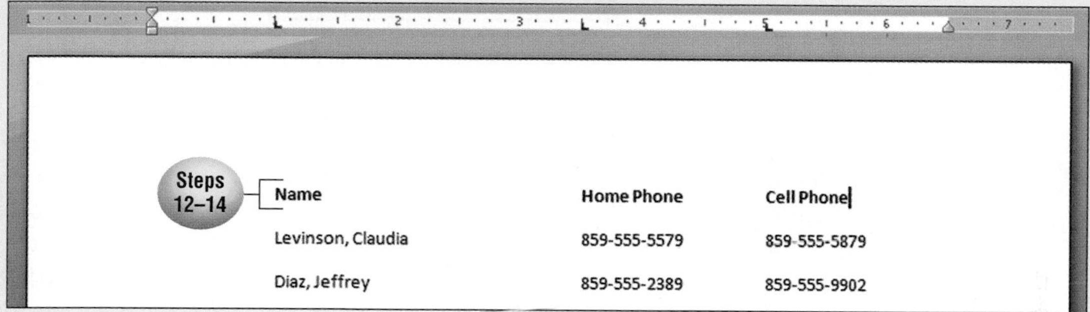

15. Save the directory document with the name **C16Ex06Directory**.
16. Print and then close the document.
17. Close the directory main document without saving it.

Inputting Text during a Merge

Word's Merge feature contains a large number of fields that you can insert in a main document. One such field, the *Fill-in* field, is used to input information with the keyboard during a merge. For information on the other Word fields, please refer to the on-screen help.

In some situations you may not need to keep all variable information in a data source file. For example, you may not need to keep variable information that changes regularly, such as a customer's monthly balance, a product price, and so on. Word lets you input variable information into a document during the merge using the keyboard. A Fill-in field is inserted in a main document by clicking the Rules button in the Write & Insert Fields group in the Mailings tab and then clicking *Fill-in* at the drop-down list. This displays the Insert Word Field: Fill-in dialog box, shown in Figure 16.9. At this dialog box, type a short message indicating what should be entered with the keyboard and then click OK. At the Microsoft Word dialog box, the message you entered displays in the upper left corner. Type the text you want to display in the document and then click OK. When you have added a Fill-in field or fields, save the main document in the normal manner. A document can contain any number of Fill-in fields.

Insert Fill-in Field in Main Document
1. Click Rules button.
2. Click *Fill-in* at drop-down list.
3. Type prompt text.
4. Click OK.
5. Type text to be displayed in document.
6. Click OK.

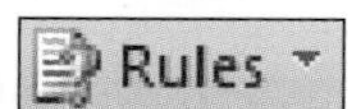

Figure 16.9 Insert Word Field: Fill-in Dialog Box

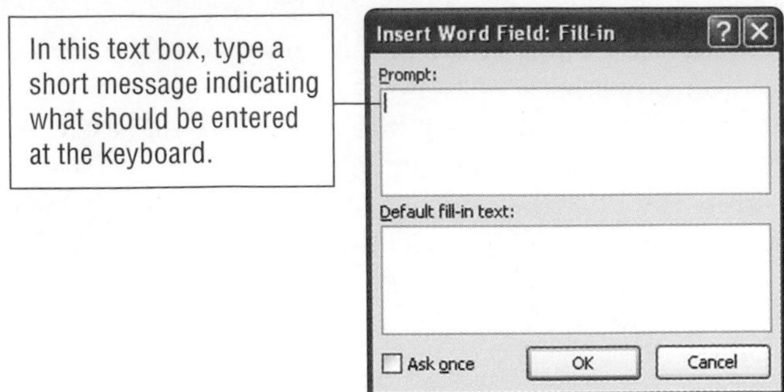

When you merge the main document with the data source file, the first record is merged and the Microsoft Word dialog box displays with the message you entered displayed in the upper left corner. Type the required information for the first record in the data source file and then click the OK button. Word displays the dialog box again. Type the required information for the second record in the data source file and then click OK. Continue in this manner until you have entered the required information for each record in the data source file. Word then completes the merge.

Exercise 7

Adding Fill-in Fields to a Main Document

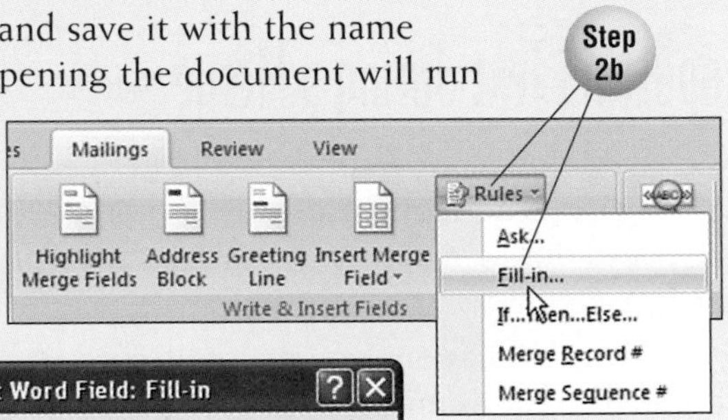

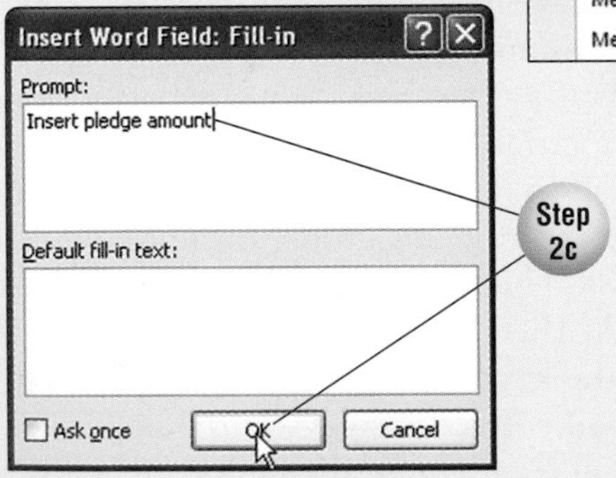

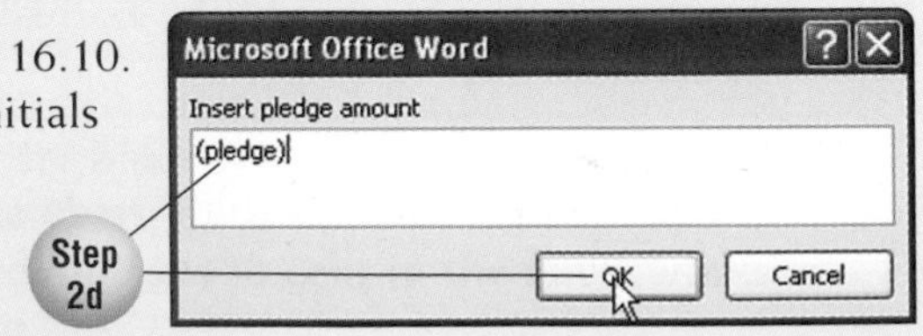

1. Open the document named **C16Ex01MD.docx** and save it with the name **C16Ex07MD**. (At the message indicating that opening the document will run the SQL command, click Yes.)
2. Change the second paragraph in the body of the letter to the paragraph shown in Figure 16.10. Insert the Fill-in field (pledge) by completing the following steps:
   a. Click the Mailings tab.
   b. Click the Rules button in the Write & Insert Fields group and then click *Fill-in* at the drop-down list.
   c. At the Insert Word Field: Fill-in dialog box, type **Insert pledge amount** in the *Prompt* text box and then click OK.
   d. At the Microsoft Office Word dialog box with *Insert pledge amount* displayed in the upper left corner, type **(pledge)** and then click OK.
   e. Continue typing the remaining text in Figure 16.10.
   f. Change the file name after your reference initials toward the bottom of the letter to C16Ex07MD.docx.
3. Save **C16Ex07MD.docx**.

4. Merge the main document with the data source file by completing the following steps:
    a. Click the Finish & Merge button and then click *Edit Individual Documents* at the drop-down list.
    b. At the Merge to New Document dialog box, make sure *All* is selected and then click OK.
    c. When Word merges the main document with the first record, a dialog box displays with the message *Insert pledge amount* and the text *(pledge)* selected. At this dialog box, type **$5,000** and then click OK.
    d. At the dialog box with the message *Insert pledge amount*, type **$2,500** (over $5,000) and then click OK.
    e. At the dialog box with the message *Insert pledge amount*, type **$5,000** (over $2,500) and then click OK.
    f. At the dialog box with the message *Insert pledge amount*, type **$10,000** (over $5,000) and then click OK.
5. Save the merged document with the name **C16Ex07Ltrs**.
6. Print and then close **C16Ex07Ltrs.docx**.
7. Save and then close **C16Ex07MD.docx**.

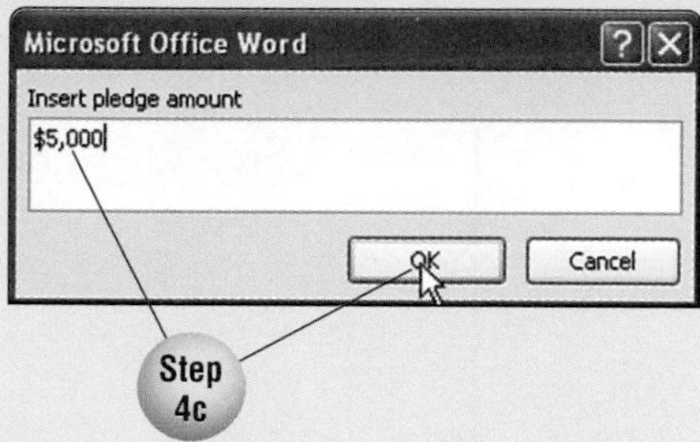

Figure 16.10 Exercise 7

As we prepare our budget for the next year, we need to confirm our members' pledges. According to our records, you have pledged (pledge) for 2011. Please contact us if you want to change this pledge.

Using the Mail Merge Wizard

The Mail Merge feature includes a Mail Merge wizard that guides you through the merge process. To access the Wizard, click the Mailings tab, click the Start Mail Merge button, and then click the *Step by Step Mail Merge Wizard* at the drop-down list. The first of six Mail Merge task panes displays at the right side of the screen. Completing the tasks at one task pane displays the next task pane. The options in each task pane may vary depending on the type of merge you are performing. Generally, you complete one of the following steps at each task pane:

Step 1: Select the type of document you want to create (letter, e-mail message, envelope, label, or directory).

Step 2: Specify whether you want to use the current document window to create the main document, start from a template, or start from an existing document.

Step 3: Specify whether you are typing a new list (for the variable information), using an existing list, or selecting from an Outlook contacts list. Depending on the choice you make, you may need to select a specific data source file or create a new data source file.

Step 4: Use the items in this task pane to help you prepare the main document. For example, if you are creating a letter, click the Address Block button in the Write & Insert Fields group in the Mailings tab, and the Wizard inserts the required codes in the main document for merging names and addresses. Click the Greeting Line button in the Write & Insert Fields group, and the Wizard inserts codes for a greeting. You can also click the More Fields button to display a list of fields that can be inserted in the document.

Step 5: Preview the merged documents.

Step 6: Complete the merge. At this step, you can send the merged document to the printer and/or edit the merged document.

Exercise 8

Preparing Form Letters Using the Mail Merge Wizard

1. At a blank document, click the Mailings tab, click the Start Mail Merge button in the Start Mail Merge group, and then click *Step by Step Mail Merge Wizard* at the drop-down list.
2. At the first Mail Merge task pane, make sure *Letters* is selected in the *Select document type* section and then click the Next: Starting document hyperlink located toward the bottom of the task pane.
3. At the second Mail Merge task pane, click the *Start from existing document* option in the *Select starting document* section.
4. Click the Open button in the *Start from existing* section of the task pane.
5. At the Open dialog box, navigate to the Chapter16 folder on your storage medium and then double-click **Letter06.docx**.
6. Click the Next: Select recipients hyperlink located toward the bottom of the task pane.
7. At the third Mail Merge task pane, click the Browse hyperlink that displays in the *Use an existing list* section of the task pane.
8. At the Select Data Source dialog box, navigate to the Chapter16 folder on your storage medium and then double-click **PRClients.mdb**.
9. At the Mail Merge Recipients dialog box, click OK.
10. Click the Next: Write your letter hyperlink that displays toward the bottom of the task pane.

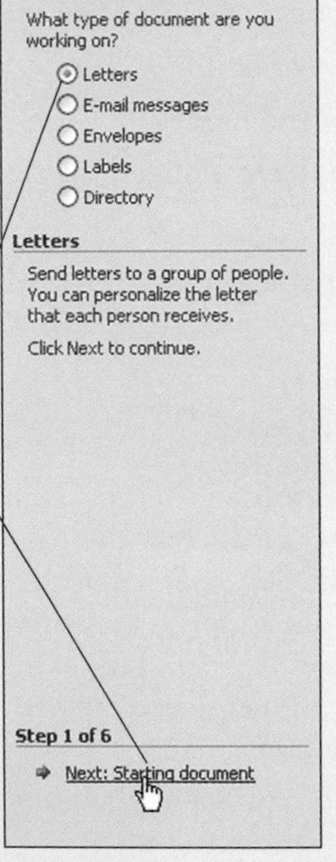

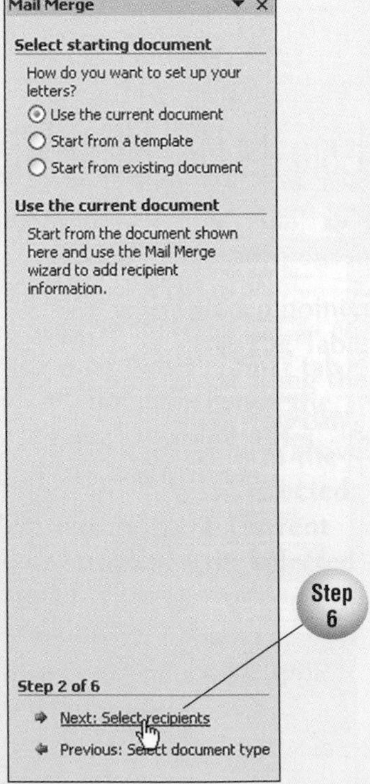

11. At the fourth Mail Merge task pane, enter fields in the form letter by completing the following steps:
    a. Position the insertion point a double-space above the first paragraph of text in the letter.
    b. Click the Address block hyperlink located in the *Write your letter* section of the task pane.

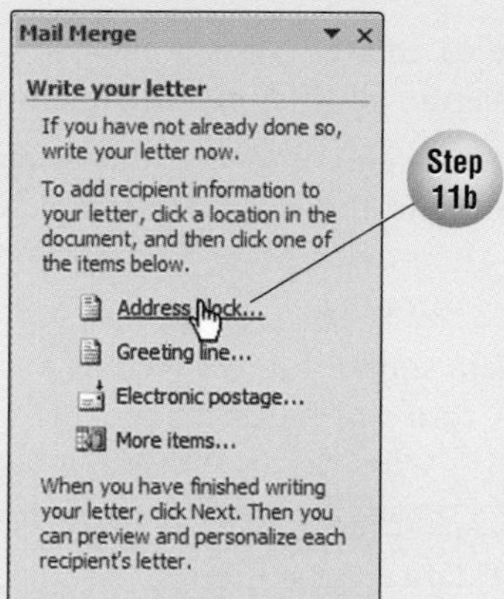

    c. At the Insert Address Block dialog box, click the OK button.
    d. Press the Enter key twice and then click the Greeting line hyperlink located in the *Write your letter* section of the task pane.
    e. At the Greeting Line dialog box, click the down-pointing arrow at the right of the option box containing the comma (the box to the right of the box containing *Mr. Randall*).
    f. At the drop-down list that displays, click the colon.
    g. Click OK to close the Greeting Line dialog box.
12. Click the Next: Preview your letters hyperlink located toward the bottom of the task pane.
13. At the fifth Mail Merge task pane, look over the letter that displays in the document window and make sure the information merged properly. If you want to see the letters for the other recipients, click the button in the Mail Merge task pane containing the two right-pointing arrows.
14. Click the Preview Results button in the Preview Results group to turn off the preview feature.
15. Click the Next: Complete the merge hyperlink that displays toward the bottom of the task pane.
16. At the sixth Mail Merge task pane, click the Edit individual letters hyperlink that displays in the *Merge* section of the task pane.
17. At the Merge to New Document dialog box, make sure *All* is selected and then click the OK button.
18. Save the merged letters document with the name **C16Ex08Ltrs**.
19. Print only the first two pages of **C16Ex08Ltrs.docx**. (This document contains seven pages.)
20. Close **C16Ex08Ltrs.docx**.
21. At the sixth Mail Merge task pane, close the letter main document without saving it.

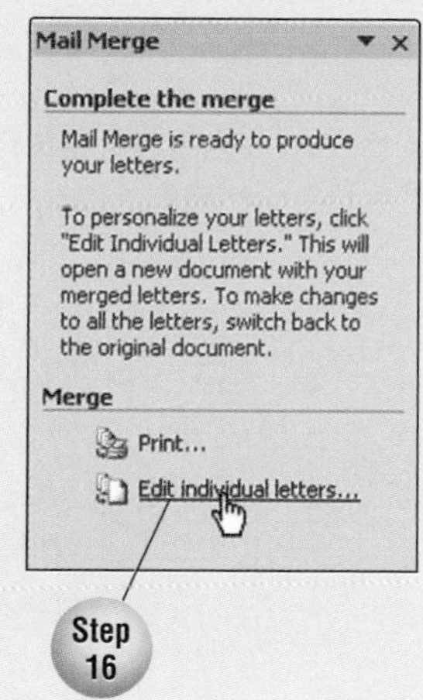

Chapter Summary

- Use the Mail Merge feature to create letters, envelopes, labels, directories, e-mail messages, and faxes for multiple recipients, all with personalized information.
- A merge generally takes two documents—the data source file, which contains information that varies for each recipient, and the main document, which contains standard text (text intended for all recipients) along with fields identifying where the variable information will be inserted during the merge process.
- Variable information in a data source file is saved as a record. A record contains all of the information for one unit. A series of fields makes one record, and a series of records makes a data source file.
- A data source file is saved as an Access database, but you do not need Access on your computer to complete a merge with a data source file.
- You can use predesigned fields when creating a data source file, or you can create your own custom fields at the Customize Address List dialog box.
- Use the Address Block button in the Write & Insert Fields group in the Mailings tab to insert all of the fields required for the inside address of a letter. This inserts the «AddressBlock» field, which is considered a composite field because it groups a number of fields together.
- Click the Greeting Line button in the Write & Insert Fields group in the Mailings tab to insert the «GreetingLine» composite field in the document.
- Click the Insert Merge Field button arrow in the Write & Insert Fields group in the Mailings tab to display a drop-down list of fields contained in the data source file.
- Click the Preview Results button in the Mailings tab to view the main document merged with the first record in the data source. Use the navigation buttons in the Preview Results group in the Mailings tab to display the main document merged with other records.
- Click the Finish & Merge button in the Mailings tab to complete the merge.
- Select specific records for merging by inserting or removing check marks preceding the desired records at the Mail Merge Recipients dialog box. Display this dialog box by clicking the Edit Recipient List button in the Mailings tab.
- Edit specific records in a data source file at the Edit Data Source dialog box. Display this dialog box by clicking the Edit Recipient List button in the Mailings tab, clicking the desired data source file name in the *Data Source* list box, and then clicking the Edit button.
- Use the *Fill-in* field in a main document to insert variable information with the keyboard during a merge.
- Word includes a Mail Merge wizard you can use to guide you through the process of creating letters, envelopes, labels, directories, and e-mail messages with personalized information.

Commands review

FEATURE	RIBBON TAB, GROUP	BUTTON, OPTION
New Address List dialog box	Mailings, Start Mail Merge	
Letter main document	Mailings, Start Mail Merge	, Letters
Envelopes main document	Mailings, Start Mail Merge	, Envelopes
Labels main document	Mailings, Start Mail Merge	, Labels
Directory main document	Mailings, Start Mail Merge	, Directory
Preview merge results	Mailings, Preview Results	
Mail Merge Recipients dialog box	Mailings, Start Mail Merge	
Address Block field	Mailings, Write & Insert Fields	
Greeting Line field	Mailings, Write & Insert Fields	
Insert merge fields	Mailings, Write & Insert Fields	
Fill-in merge field	Mailings, Write & Insert Fields	Rules, Fill-in
Mail Merge wizard	Mailings, Start Mail Merge	, Step by Step Mail Merge wizard

Reviewing key points

Completion: In the space provided at the right, indicate the correct term, command, or number.

1. A merge generally takes two files, a data source file and this. ______________
2. This term refers to all of the information for one unit in a data source file. ______________
3. Create a data source file by clicking this button in the Mailings tab and then clicking *Type New List* at the drop-down list. ______________
4. A data source file is saved as this type of file. ______________
5. Create your own custom fields in a data source file with options at this dialog box. ______________

6. Use this button in the Mailings tab to insert all of the required fields for the inside address in a letter. ____________________
7. The «GreetingLine» field is considered this type of field because it includes all of the fields required for the greeting line. ____________________
8. Click this button in the Mailings tab to display the first record merged with the main document. ____________________
9. To complete a merge, click this button in the Finish group in the Mailings tab. ____________________
10. Select specific records in a data source file by inserting or removing check marks from the records in this dialog box. ____________________
11. Use this field to insert variable information with the keyboard during a merge. ____________________
12. Click this option at the Mail Merge button drop-down list to begin the Mail Merge wizard. ____________________

Applying your skills

Assessment 1 Use Mail Merge to Create Letters

1. Look at the information shown in Figure 16.11 and Figure 16.12.
2. Use the Mail Merge feature to prepare four letters using the information shown in the figures (refer to Appendix C at the end of this textbook for information on formatting a business letter).
3. Name the data source file **C16A01DS**, name the main document **C16A01MD**, and name the merged letters document **C16A01Ltrs**.
4. Print and then close **C16A01Ltrs.docx**.
5. Save and then close **C16A01MD.docx**.

Figure 16.11 Assessment 1

Mrs. Tina Cardoza
2314 Magnolia Drive
P.O. Box 231
Augusta, ME 04336

Mr. Lucas Yarborough
12110 South 142nd Street
(leave this blank)
Augusta, ME 04332

Mrs. Lucille Alvarez
2554 Country Drive
(leave this blank)
Augusta, ME 04338

Mr. Daryl Gillette
120 Second Street
(leave this blank)
Augusta, ME 04330

Figure 16.12 Assessment 1

April 6, 2010

«AddressBlock»

«GreetingLine»

Now is the time to sign up for a sun-filled, fun-filled family vacation. We are offering three-day, seven-day, and ten-day fun-in-the-sun vacation packages to several southern destinations, including Los Angeles, Orlando, Miami, New Orleans, and Maui. Limited by a budget? No problem. We can find the perfect vacation for you and your family that fits within your budget.

We know we can create a vacation package that is as exciting and adventurous as your previous vacation. Right now, you can spend seven days and six nights in beautiful and tropical Maui, Hawaii, at the Pacific Beach Cabanas for under $700 per person including airfare! We also have a four-day, three-night vacation package to Orlando, Florida for less than $400 per person. To find out about these fabulous and affordable vacations, stop by our office and talk to a travel consultant or give us a call to book your next fun-and-sun family vacation.

Sincerely,

Megan Arigala

XX:C16A01MD.docx

Assessment 2 Use Mail Merge to Create Envelopes

1. Create an envelope main document and merge it with the **C16A01DS.mdb** data source file.
2. Save the merged envelopes document with the name **C16A02Envs**.
3. Print and then close **C16A02Envs.docx**. Close the envelope main document without saving it. (Manual feed of envelopes may be required. Check with your instuctor.)

Assessment 3 Use Mail Merge to Create Labels

1. Use the Mail Merge feature to prepare mailing labels for the names and addresses in the **C16A01DS.mdb** file.
2. Save the merged labels document with the name **C16A03Labels**.
3. Print and then close **C16A03Labels.docx**. Close the label main document without saving it.

Assessment 4 Edit Records and then Merge Letters with Fill-in Field

1. Open **C16A01MD.docx** and save the main document with the name **C16A04MD**.
2. Edit the **C16A01DS.mdb** data source file by making the following changes:
   a. Display the record for Mrs. Tina Cardoza and then change the last name from *Cardoza* to *Cordova*.
   b. Display the record for Mr. Daryl Gillette, change the street address from *120 Second Street* to *9843 22nd Southwest*, and change the ZIP code from *04330* to *04338*.
   c. Delete the record for Mr. Lucas Yarborough.
   d. Insert a new record with the following information:
      Mr. Curtis Jackson
      13201 North Fourth Street
      (leave blank)
      Augusta, ME 04336
3. At the main document, add the following sentence at the beginning of the second paragraph in the letter (insert a *Fill-in* field for *(vacation)* shown in the sentence below):
   Last summer we booked a fabulous (vacation) for you and your entire family.
4. Change the file name after your reference initials toward the bottom of the letter to **C16A04MD.docx**.
5. Merge the main document with the data source file and type the following text for each of the records:
   Record 1 = Ocean Vista Mexican cruise
   Record 2 = Disneyland California vacation
   Record 3 = Ocean Vista Caribbean cruise
   Record 4 = River Rafting Adventure vacation
6. Save the merged document with the name **C16A04Ltrs**.
7. Print and then close **C16A04Ltrs.docx**.
8. Save and then close **C16A04MD.mdb**.

Assessment 5 Use the Mail Merge Wizard to Create Envelopes

1. At a blank document, use the Mail Merge wizard to merge the records in the **PRClients.mdb** data source with an envelope main document. (Use the standard Size 10 envelope.)
2. Save the merged envelopes document with the name **C16A05Envs**.
3. Print only the first two envelopes in the document and then close **C16A05Envs.docx**.
4. Close the envelope main document without saving it.

Chapter 17

Sorting and Selecting

SNAP

Tutorial 17.1
Sorting Text and Data

Performance Objectives

Upon successful completion of Chapter 17, you will be able to:

- Sort text in paragraphs, columns, and tables
- Sort on more than one field
- Sort records in a data source file
- Select specific records in a data source file for merging

Word is primarily a word processing program, but it includes some basic database functions. For example, you can sort text that is set in paragraphs, columns, or a table; you can sort records in a data source file, and you can select specific records from a data source file to be merged with a main document.

Note: Before beginning computer exercises for this chapter, copy to your storage medium the Chapter17 folder from the CD that accompanies this textbook and then make Chapter17 the active folder.

Sort Text in Paragraphs
1. Select text.
2. Click Sort button.
3. Make any needed changes at the Sort Text dialog box.
4. Click OK.

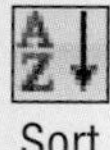

Sort

Sorting Text

In Word, you can sort text in paragraphs, text in columns within a table, or records in a data source file. As Table 17.1 shows, Word can perform three types of sorts: text, numbers, and date.

Sorting Text in Paragraphs

As you learned in Chapter 4, you can sort text arranged in paragraphs by the first character of the paragraph. This character can be a number or a symbol (such as $ or #). In an alphanumeric sort, Word sorts paragraphs beginning with a punctuation mark or special symbol first, followed by paragraphs beginning with a number, and then paragraphs beginning with a letter. Remember, in Word, a paragraph can be a single word or line followed by a press of the Enter key. If you sort paragraphs alphanumerically or numerically, Word treats dates as regular text. Unless you select specific paragraphs to be sorted, Word sorts an entire document.

To sort text arranged in paragraphs, select the text and then click the Sort button in the Paragraph group in the Home tab. This displays the Sort Text dialog box, shown in Figure 17.1, which contains sorting options. The default setting for the *Sort by* option is *Paragraphs*. This default setting changes depending on the text in

Table 17.1 **Types of Sorts**

Text	In a text sort, Word arranges text in the following order: text beginning with a special symbol, such as $ and #, first; text preceded by numbers second; and alphabetic by letter third. Word can also sort letters by case: text beginning with uppercase letters first, followed by text beginning with lowercase letters.
Numbers	In a numbers sort, Word arranges text in numeric order and ignores any alphabetic text. Only the numbers 0 through 9 and symbols pertaining to numbers are recognized. These symbols include $, %, ( ), a decimal point, a comma, and the symbols for the four basic operations: + (addition), - (subtraction), * (multiplication), and / (division). Word can sort numbers in ascending or descending order.
Date	In a date sort, Word chronologically sorts dates that are expressed in a common date format, such as 06-01-2010; 06/01/2010; June 1, 2010; or 1 June 2010. Word does not sort dates that include abbreviated month names without periods. Word does not sort dates that are expressed as a month, day, or year only. Like numeric sorts, date sorts can be in ascending or descending order.

the document. For example, if you are sorting text in a table, the *Sort by* option has a default setting of *Column 1*.

The *Type* option at the Sort Text dialog box has a default setting of *Text*. You can change this to *Number* or *Date*. Table 17.1 describes how Word sorts numbers and dates. When Word sorts paragraphs that are separated by more than a single space, the extra hard returns (a stroke of the Enter key) are removed and inserted at the beginning of the paragraphs selected for the sort.

Figure 17.1 Sort Text Dialog Box

Use options in this dialog box to specify the text on which you want to sort, the type of sort, and the sort order.

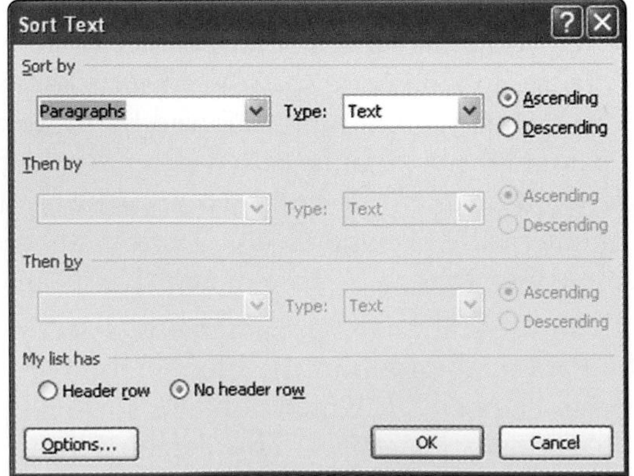

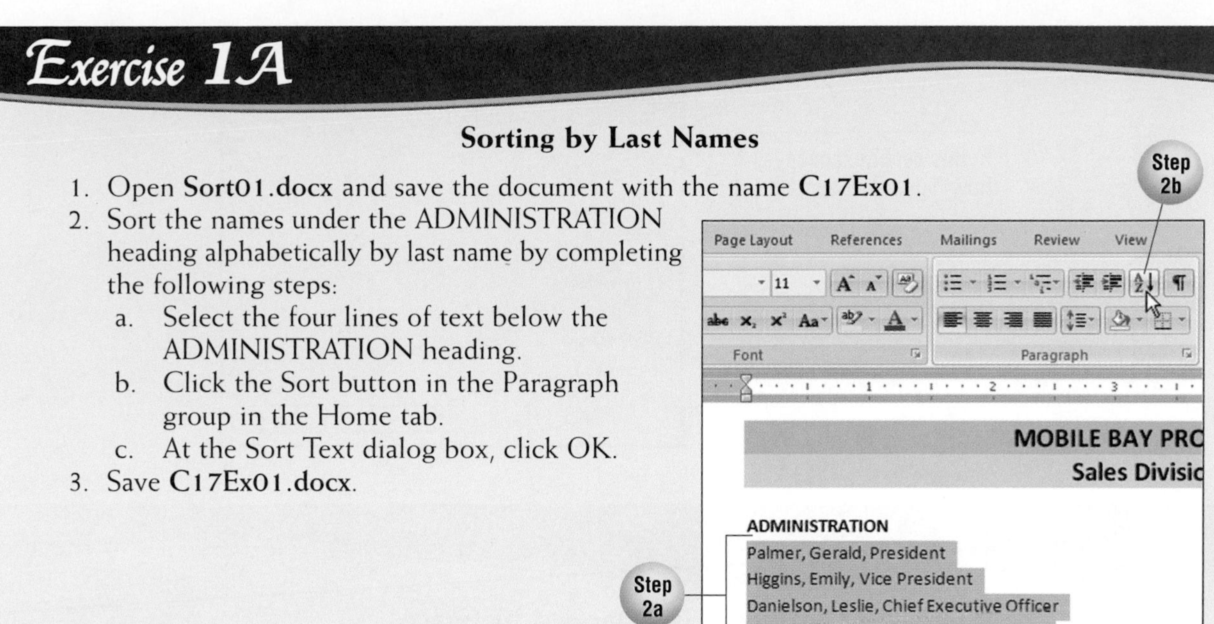

Exercise 1A

Sorting by Last Names

1. Open **Sort01.docx** and save the document with the name **C17Ex01**.
2. Sort the names under the ADMINISTRATION heading alphabetically by last name by completing the following steps:
   a. Select the four lines of text below the ADMINISTRATION heading.
   b. Click the Sort button in the Paragraph group in the Home tab.
   c. At the Sort Text dialog box, click OK.
3. Save **C17Ex01.docx**.

Changing Sort Options

Display Sort Options Dialog Box
1. Click Sort button.
2. Click Options button.

The *Sort by* options at the Sort Text dialog box will vary depending on the options selected in the Sort Options dialog box, shown in Figure 17.2. To display this dialog box, click the Options button in the Sort Text dialog box.

The *Separate fields at* section of the dialog box contains three options. The first option, *Tabs*, is the default setting. At this setting, Word assumes that the text to be sorted is divided by tabs. You can change this setting to *Commas* or *Other*. With the *Other* setting, you can specify which character that divides text to sort by. For example, suppose a document contains first and last names in paragraphs separated by a space and you want to sort by the last name. To do this, you would click *Other* at the Sort Options dialog box and then press the spacebar. This inserts a space, which is not visible, in the *Other* text box. If names are separated by a comma, click the *Commas* option.

The Sort Options dialog box contains two choices in the *Sort options* section. The first choice, *Sort column only*, sorts only the selected column. This choice is dimmed unless a column of text is selected. If a check mark appears in the *Case sensitive* check box, Word will sort text so that a word whose first letter is a capital letter is sorted before any word with the same first letter in lowercase. This option is available only if *Text* is selected in the *Type* option box at the Sort Text dialog box.

When you make changes at the Sort Options dialog box, those changes are reflected in the choices available with the *Sort by* option at the Sort Text dialog box. For example, if you click *Other* at the Sort Options dialog box and then press the spacebar, the choices for *Sort by* at the Sort Text dialog box will include *Word 1*, *Word 2*, *Word 3*, and so on.

Figure 17.2 Sort Options Dialog Box

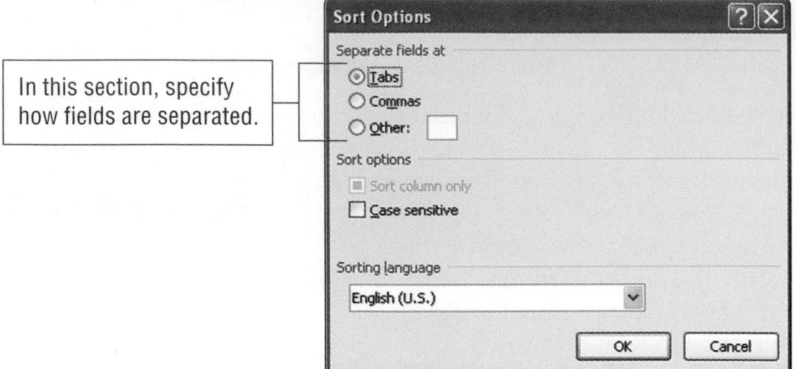

Exercise 1B

Sorting Text Separated by Spaces

1. With **C17Ex01.docx** open, sort the names of the technical support team alphabetically by last name by completing the following steps:
   a. Select the eight lines of text below the TECHNICAL SUPPORT TEAM heading.
   b. Click the Sort button.
   c. At the Sort Text dialog box, click the Options button.
   d. At the Sort Options dialog box, click *Other* and then press the spacebar. (This indicates the first and last names are separated by a space.)
   e. Click OK.
   f. At the Sort Text dialog box, click the down-pointing arrow at the right side of the *Sort by* option and then click *Word 2* at the drop-down list.
   g. Click OK.
2. Save **C17Ex01.docx**.

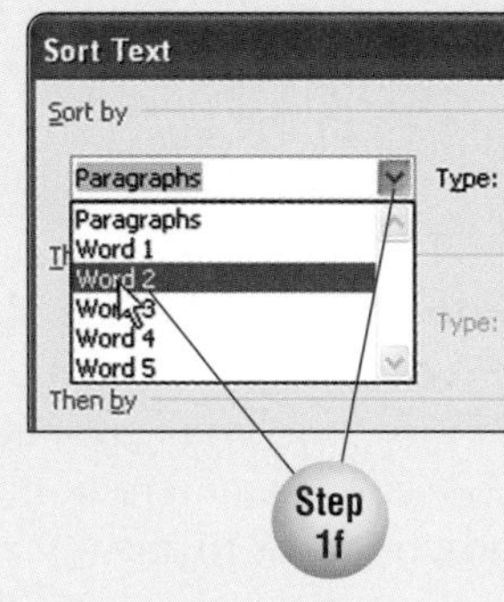

Sort Text in Columns
1. Select specific text.
2. Click Sort button.
3. Click Options button.
4. Specify *Tabs* as separator.
5. Click OK.
6. Make any needed changes at Sort Text dialog box.
7. Click OK.

Sorting Text in Columns

To sort text set in columns, the text must be separated with tabs. When Word sorts text in columns, it sorts by field. Word considers text typed at the left margin to be *Field 1*, text typed at the first tab stop *Field 2*, text typed at the second tab stop *Field 3*, and so on. To sort text arranged in columns, display the Sort Text dialog box and then click the Options button. At the Sort Options dialog box, make sure *Tabs* is selected in the *Separate fields at* section of the dialog box and then click OK. At the Sort Text dialog box, display the appropriate field number in the *Sort by* option box and then click OK.

When you sort text in columns, make sure the columns are separated by one tab only. If you press the Tab key more than once between columns, Word recognizes each tab as a separate column. In this case, the field number you specify may correspond to an empty column rather than the desired column.

Exercise 1C

Sorting Text in Columns

1. With **C17Ex01.docx** open, sort text in columns by completing the following steps:
   a. Select the seven lines of text set in columns that display below the headings *Employee*, *Department*, and *Hire Date*.
   b. Click the Sort button.
   c. Click the Options button.
   d. At the Sort Options dialog box, make sure the *Separate fields at* option is set at *Tabs* and then click OK to close the dialog box.
   e. At the Sort Text dialog box, make sure *Field 2* displays in the *Sort by* option box. (If not, click the down-pointing arrow at the right side of the *Sort by* option and then click *Field 2* at the drop-down list.)
   f. Click OK.

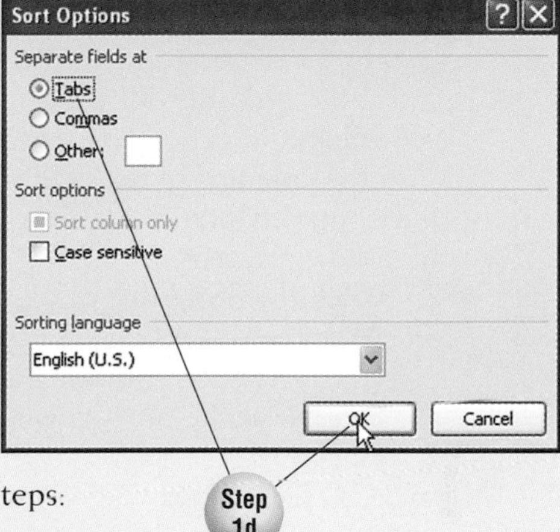

2. With the columns of text still selected, sort the third column of text by date by completing the following steps:
   a. Click the Sort button.
   b. Click the down-pointing arrow at the right side of the *Sort by* option and then click *Field 4* at the drop-down list.
   c. Click OK.
3. Save **C17Ex01.docx**.

Specifying a Header Row

In Exercise 1C, you identified columns by field numbers. You can also identify columns by heading. If the columns of text you are sorting contain column headings, you can specify this at the Sort Text dialog box by clicking the *Header row* option in the *My list has* section. Clicking the *Header row* option changes the sort options from field numbers to the column heading names. For example, in Exercise 1D, you will sort column text by department. To do this, you will select the columns of text including the header row, display the Sort Text dialog box, and then click the *Header row* option in the *My list has* section. When you click the down-pointing arrow at the right side of the *Sort by* option, the drop-down list displays the options *Employee*, *Department*, and *Hire Date* instead of field numbers. (The drop-down list will also contain the option *(Field 1)*, which identifies the left margin.)

Exercise 1D

Sorting Columns of Text with a Header Row

1. With **C17Ex01.docx** open, sort text in columns by department by completing the following steps:
   a. Select the eight lines of text set in columns beginning with the row containing the column headings *Employee*, *Department*, and *Hire Date*.
   b. Click the Sort button.

c. At the Sort Text dialog box, click the *Header row* option in the *My list has* section.
d. Click the Options button.
e. At the Sort Options dialog box, make sure the *Separate fields at* option is set at *Tabs* and then click OK to close the dialog box.
f. At the Sort Text dialog box, click the down-pointing arrow at the right side of the *Sort by* option and then click *Department* at the drop-down list.
g. Click OK.

2. With the columns of text still selected, sort the first column alphabetically by completing the following steps:
   a. Click the Sort button.
   b. At the Sort Text dialog box, click the *Header row* option in the *My list has* section.
   c. Click the down-pointing arrow at the right side of the *Sort by* option and then click *Employee* at the drop-down list.
   d. Click OK.
3. Save **C17Ex01.docx**.

Sorting on More than One Field

When sorting text, you can sort on more than one field. For example, in Exercise 1E you will sort the department entries alphabetically and then sort the employee names alphabetically within the departments. To do this, you specify the department column in the *Sort by* option and then specify the employee column in the *Then by* option.

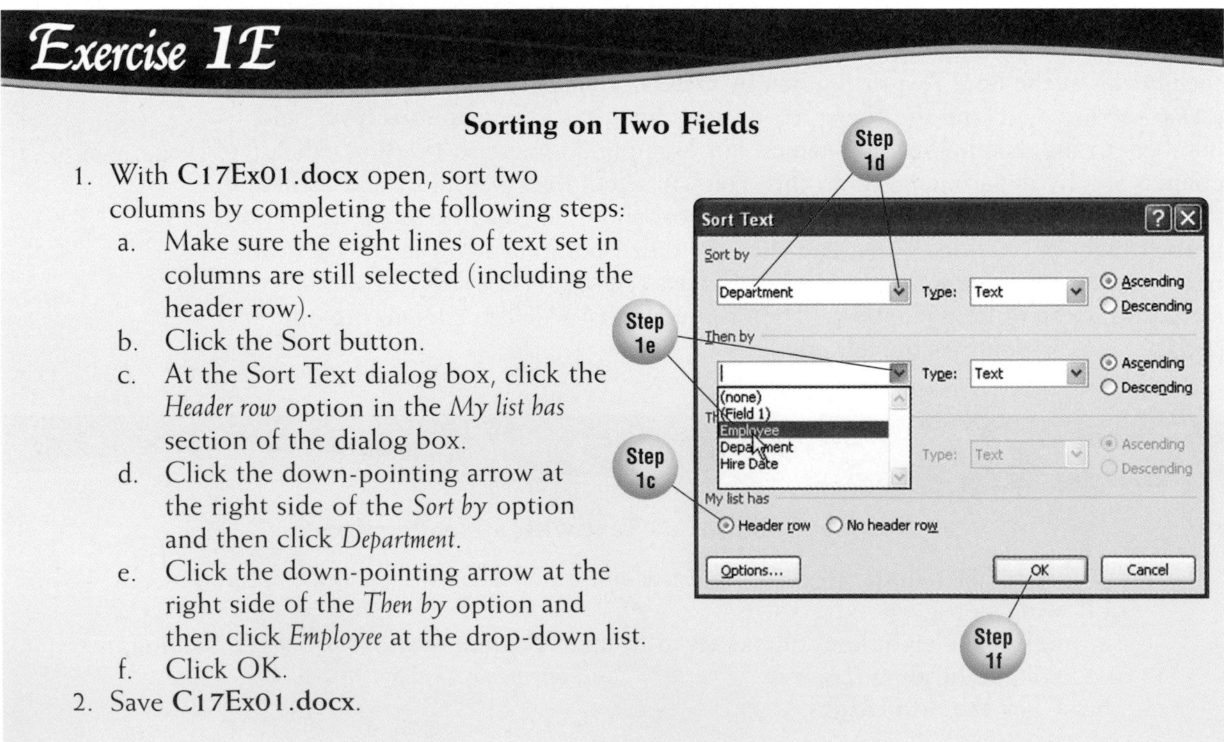

Exercise 1E

Sorting on Two Fields

1. With **C17Ex01.docx** open, sort two columns by completing the following steps:
   a. Make sure the eight lines of text set in columns are still selected (including the header row).
   b. Click the Sort button.
   c. At the Sort Text dialog box, click the *Header row* option in the *My list has* section of the dialog box.
   d. Click the down-pointing arrow at the right side of the *Sort by* option and then click *Department*.
   e. Click the down-pointing arrow at the right side of the *Then by* option and then click *Employee* at the drop-down list.
   f. Click OK.
2. Save **C17Ex01.docx**.

Sorting Text in Tables

You can sort text in columns within a table in much the same way that you sort columns of text separated by tabs. If a table contains a header, click the *Header row* option at the Sort dialog box. The Sort Text dialog box becomes the Sort dialog box when you are sorting in a table. If you want to sort only specific cells in a table, select the cells and then complete the sort.

Sort Text in Table
1. Position insertion point in table.
2. Click Sort button.
3. Make any needed changes at Sort dialog box.
4. Click OK.

Exercise 1F

Sorting Text in a Table

1. With **C17Ex01.docx** open, sort text in the first column of the table that displays toward the bottom of the page by completing the following steps:
   a. Position the insertion point in any cell in the table.
   b. Click the Sort button.
   c. At the Sort dialog box, make sure the *Header row* option is selected in the *My list has* section.
   d. Click the down-pointing arrow at the right side of the *Sort by* option and then click *Salesperson* at the drop-down list.
   e. Click OK.

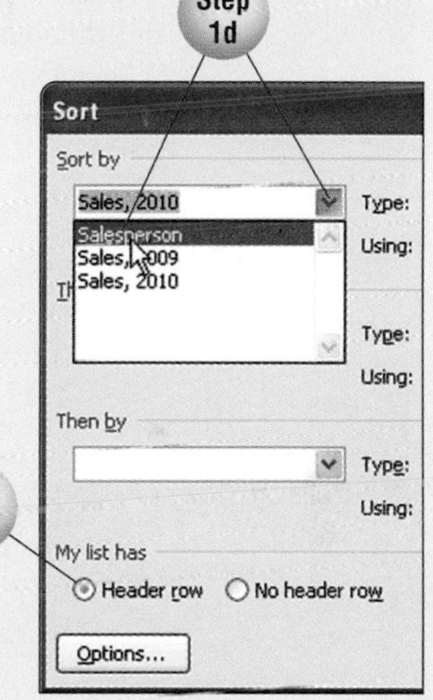

2. Sort the numbers in the second column in descending order by completing the following steps:
   a. Select all of the cells in the table except the cells in the first row.
   b. Click the Sort button.
   c. At the Sort dialog box, click the down-pointing arrow at the right side of the *Sort by* option and then click *Column 2* at the drop-down list.
   d. Click *Descending*.

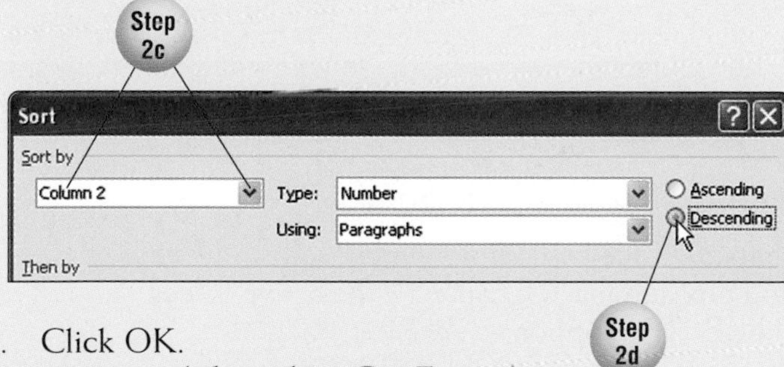

   e. Click OK.
3. Save, print, and then close **C17Ex01.docx**.

QUICK STEPS

Sort Records in Data Source
1. Click Mailings tab.
2. Click Select Recipients button.
3. Click *Use Existing List* at drop-down list.
4. Double-click desired file.
5. Click Edit Recipient List button.
6. At Mail Merge Recipients dialog box, sort by specific field by clicking field column heading.
7. Click OK.

Sorting Records in a Data Source

To sort records in a data source file, click the Mailings tab, click the Select Recipients button, and then click *Use Existing List*. At the Select Data Source dialog box, navigate to the folder that contains the data source file you want to use and then double-click the file. Click the Edit Recipient List button in the Start Mail Merge group in the Mailings tab, and the Mail Merge Recipients dialog box, shown in Figure 17.3 with data for Exercise 2A, displays.

Click the field column heading to sort data in ascending order in a specific field. To perform additional sorts, click the down-pointing arrow at the right side of the field column heading and then click the desired sort order.

Figure 17.3 Mail Merge Recipients Dialog Box

To sort on a specific field, click on the column heading.

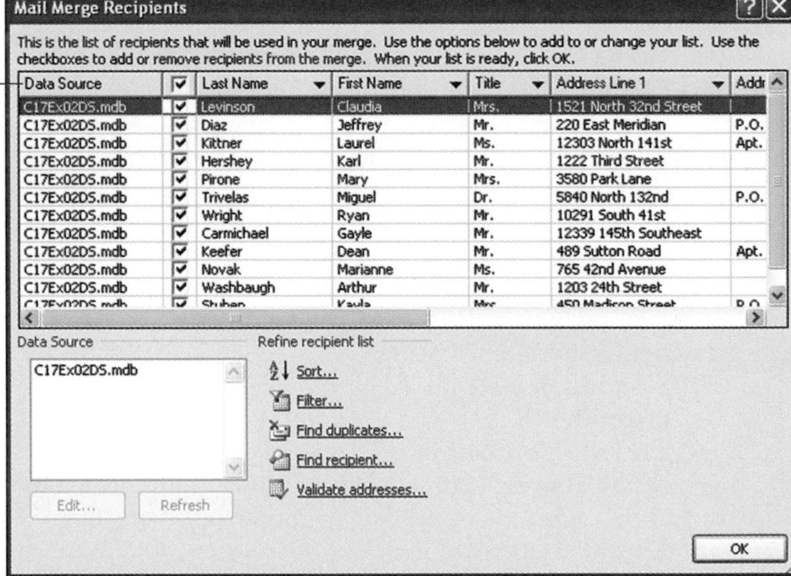

Exercise 2A

Sorting Data in a Data Source

1. Make a copy of the **MFClients.mdb** file by completing the following steps:
   a. Display the Open dialog box and make Chapter17 the active folder.
   b. If necessary, change the *Files of type* option to *All Files (*.*)*.
   c. Right-click on the **MFClients.mdb** file and then click Copy at the shortcut menu.
   d. Position the mouse pointer in a white portion of the Open dialog box list box (outside of any file name), click the *right* mouse button, and then click Paste at the shortcut menu. (This inserts a copy of the file in the dialog box list box and names the file **Copy of MFClients.mdb**.)
   e. Right-click on the file name **Copy of MFClients.mdb** and then click Rename at the shortcut menu.

f. Type **C17Ex02DS.mdb** and then press Enter.
g. Close the Open dialog box.

2. At a blank document, click the Mailings tab, click the Start Mail Merge button in the Start Mail Merge group, and then click *Labels* at the drop-down list.

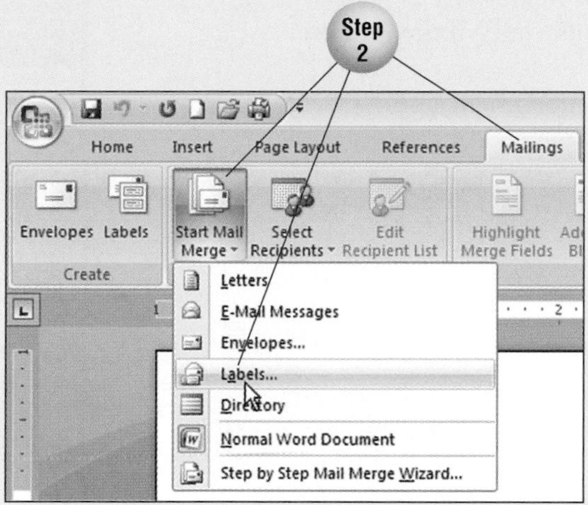

3. At the Label Options dialog box, click the down-pointing arrow at the right side of the *Label vendors* option and then click *Avery US Letter* at the drop-down list.
4. Scroll down the *Product number* list box, click *5360* in the *Product number* list box, and then click OK.

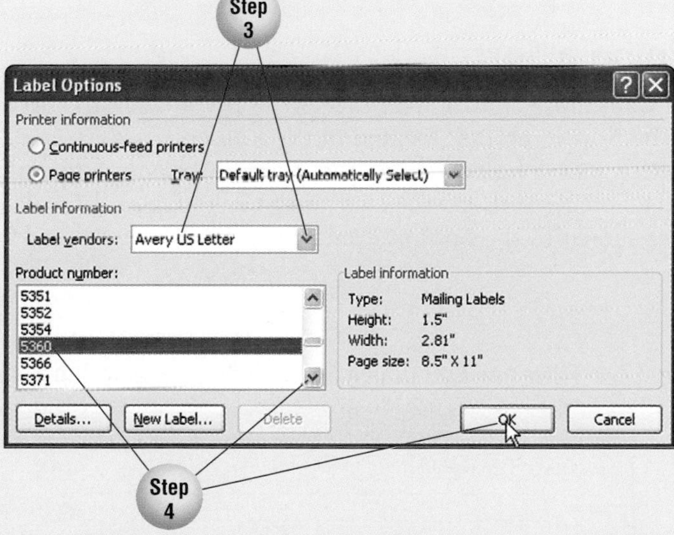

5. Click the Select Recipients button in the Start Mail Merge group and then click *Use Existing List* at the drop-down list.
6. At the Select Data Source dialog box, navigate to the Chapter17 folder on your storage medium and then double-click the data source file named **C17Ex02DS.mdb**.
7. Click the Edit Recipient List button.

8. At the Mail Merge Recipients dialog box, click the *Last Name* column heading. (This sorts the last names in ascending alphabetical order.)
9. Scroll to the right to display the *City* field and then click the *City* column heading.
10. Click OK to close the Mail Merge Recipients dialog box.
11. Save the labels main document and name it **C17Ex02MD**.

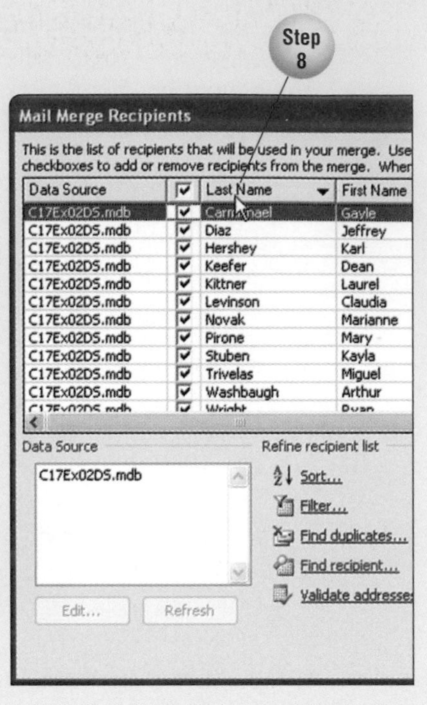

Refining a Sort

If you want more control over the sort or if you want to sort on more than one field, click the Sort hyperlink located in the *Refine recipient list* section of the Mail Merge Recipients dialog box. Clicking this hyperlink displays the Filter and Sort dialog box with the Sort Records tab selected, as shown in Figure 17.4. The options at the dialog box are similar to the options available at the Sort Text (and Sort) dialog box.

Figure 17.4 Filter and Sort Dialog Box with Sort Records Tab Selected

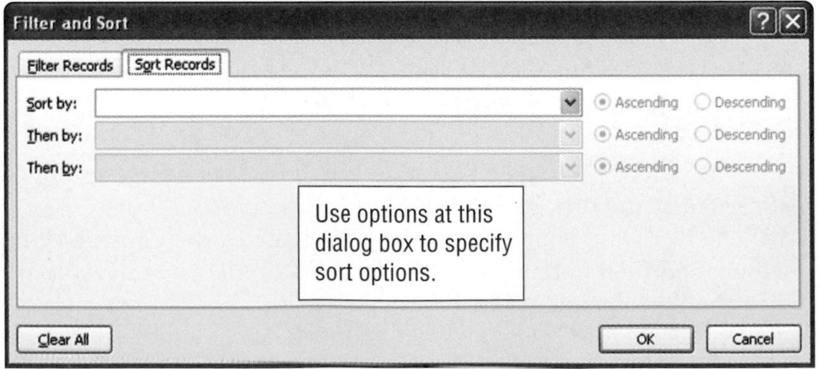

Exercise 2B

Refining a Sort

1. With **C17Ex02MD.docx** open, sort records by ZIP codes and then by last name by completing the following steps:
   a. Click the Edit Recipient List button.
   b. At the Mail Merge Recipients dialog box, click the Sort hyperlink located in the *Refine recipient list* section.
   c. At the Filter and Sort dialog box with the Sort Records tab selected, click the down-pointing arrow at the right side of the *Sort by* option box and then click *ZIP Code* at the drop-down list. (You will need to scroll down the list to display the *ZIP Code* field.)
   d. Make sure *Last Name* displays in the *Then by* option box.
   e. Click OK to close the Filter and Sort dialog box.

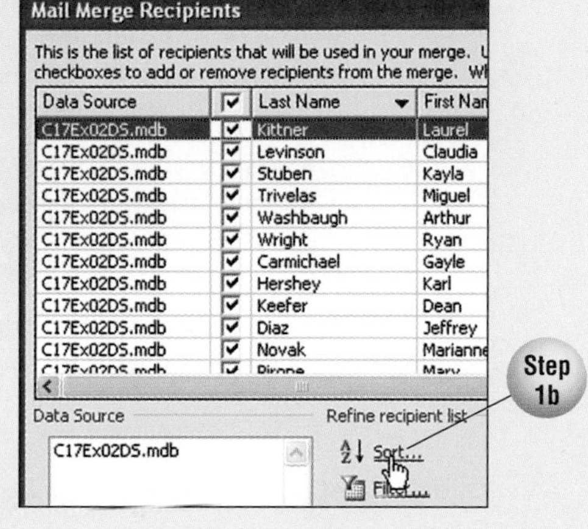

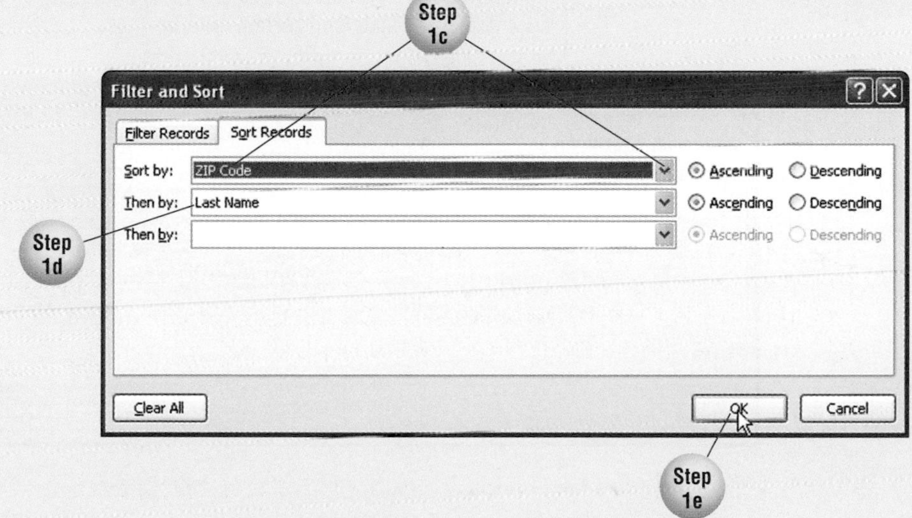

   f. Click OK to close the Mail Merge Recipients dialog box.
2. At the labels document, click the Address Block button in the Write & Insert Fields group.
3. At the Insert Address Block dialog box, click OK.
4. Click the Update Labels button in the Write & Insert Fields group.
5. Click the Finish & Merge button in the Finish group and then click *Edit Individual Documents* at the drop-down list.
6. At the Merge to New Document dialog box, make sure *All* is selected and then click OK.
7. Save the merged labels and name the document **C17Ex02Lbls01**.
8. Print and then close **C17Ex02Lbls01.docx**.
9. Save **C17Ex02MD.docx**.

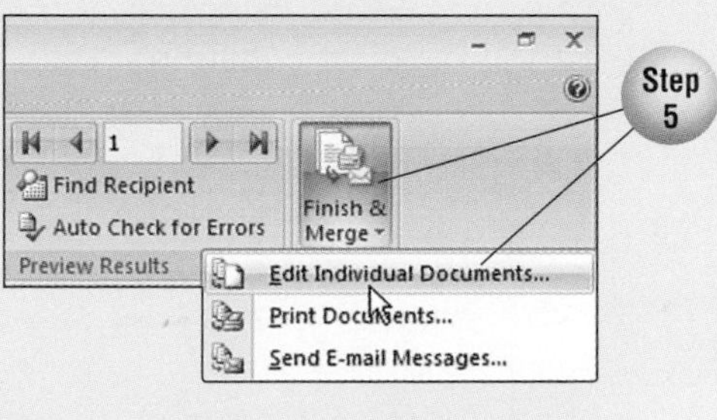

Selecting Records

If a data source file contains numerous records, situations may arise in which you want to merge the main document with only specific records in the data source. For example, you may want to send a letter to customers with a specific ZIP code or who live in a particular city. As you learned in Chapter 16, one method for selecting specific records is to display the Mail Merge Recipients dialog box and then insert or remove check marks from specific records.

Using check boxes to select specific records is useful when a data source contains a limited number of records, but this selection method may not be practical when a data source contains many records. In a large data source file, use options at the Filter and Sort dialog box with the Filter Records tab selected, as shown in Figure 17.5. To display this dialog box, click the Filter hyperlink that displays in the *Refine recipient list* section of the Mail Merge Recipients dialog box.

Figure 17.5 Filter and Sort Dialog Box with Filter Records Tab Selected

Use the *Field* option to specify which field you want to select and then use the *Comparison* and *Compare to* options to specify records matching certain criteria.

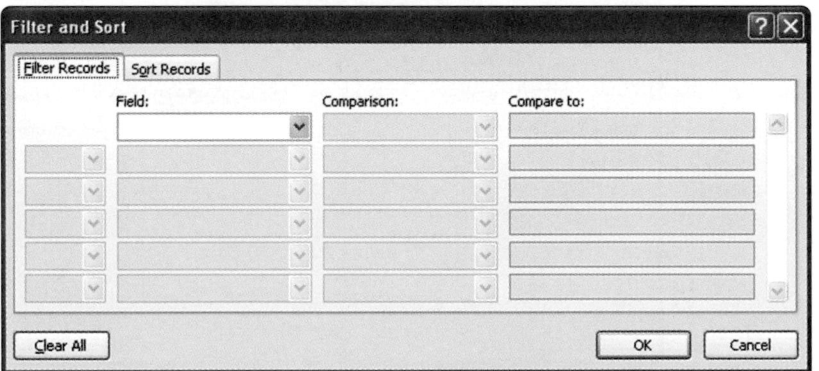

When you select a field from the *Field* drop-down list, Word automatically inserts *Equal to* in the *Comparison* option box. To make other comparisons, click the down-pointing arrow to the right of the *Comparison* option box. A drop-down list displays with these additional options: *Not equal to*, *Less than*, *Greater than*, *Less than or equal*, *Greater than or equal*, *Is blank*, and *Is not blank*. Use one of these options to create a select equation.

Exercise 2C

Selecting Records

1. With **C17Ex02MD.docx** open, find records with a ZIP code greater than *40400* by completing the following steps:
   a. Click the Edit Recipient List button.
   b. At the Mail Merge Recipients dialog box, click the <u>Filter</u> hyperlink in the *Refine recipient list* section of the dialog box.
   c. At the Filter and Sort dialog box, click the down-pointing arrow at the right side of the *Field* option and then click *ZIP Code* at the drop-down list. (You will need to scroll down the list to display *ZIP Code*. When *ZIP Code* is inserted in the *Field* option box, *Equal to* is inserted in the *Comparison* option box, and the insertion point is positioned in the *Compare to* text box.)
   d. Type **40400** in the *Compare to* text box.
   e. Click the down-pointing arrow at the right side of the *Comparison* option box and then click *Greater than* at the drop-down list.

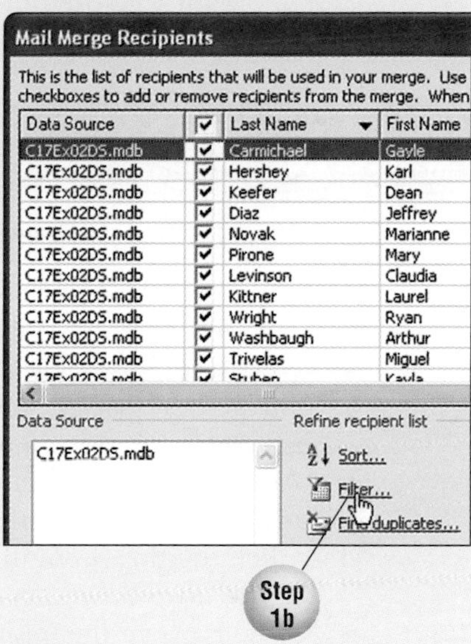

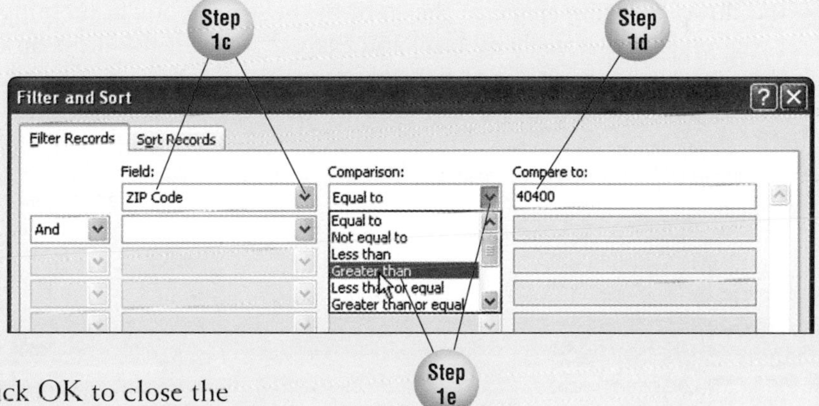

   f. Click OK to close the Filter and Sort dialog box.
   g. Click OK to close the Mail Merge Recipients dialog box.
2. At the labels document, click the Finish & Merge button in the Finish group and then click *Edit Individual Documents* at the drop-down list.
3. At the Merge to New Document dialog box, make sure *All* is selected and then click OK.
4. Save the merged labels and name the document **C17Ex02Lbls02**.
5. Print and then close **C17Ex02Lbls02.docx**.
6. Save **C17Ex02MD.docx**.

When you select a field from the *Field* option box, Word automatically inserts *And* in the first box at the left side of the dialog box. You can change this, if needed, to *Or*. With the *And* and *Or* options, you can specify more than one condition for selecting records. For example, in Exercise 2D, you will select all records for clients living in the cities of Paris or Winchester. If the data source file contained another field such as a specific financial plan for each customer, you could select all customers in a specific city who subscribe to a specific financial plan. For this situation, you would use the *And* option.

If you want to clear the current options at the Filter and Sort dialog box with the Filter Records tab selected, click the Clear All button. This clears any text from text boxes and leaves the dialog box on the screen. Click the Cancel button if you want to close the Filter and Sort dialog box without specifying any records.

Exercise 2D

Selecting Records with Specific Cities

1. With **C17Ex02MD.docx** open, find all records for recipients who live in the cities of *Paris* and *Winchester* by completing the following steps:
   a. Click the Edit Recipient List button.
   b. At the Mail Merge Recipients dialog box, click the Filter hyperlink in the *Refine recipient list* section of the dialog box.
   c. At the Filter and Sort dialog box, click the Clear All button that displays in the lower left corner of the dialog box.
   d. Click the down-pointing arrow at the right side of the *Field* option and then click *City* at the drop-down list. (You will need to scroll down the list to display this field.)
   e. Type **Paris** in the *Compare to* text box.
   f. Click the down-pointing arrow to the right of the option box containing the word *And* (at the left side of the dialog box) and then click *Or* at the drop-down list.
   g. Click the down-pointing arrow at the right side of the second *Field* option box and then click *City* at the drop-down list. (You will need to scroll down the list to display this field.)
   h. With the insertion point positioned in the second *Compare to* text box (the one below the box containing *Paris*), type **Winchester**.
   i. Click OK to close the Filter and Sort dialog box.

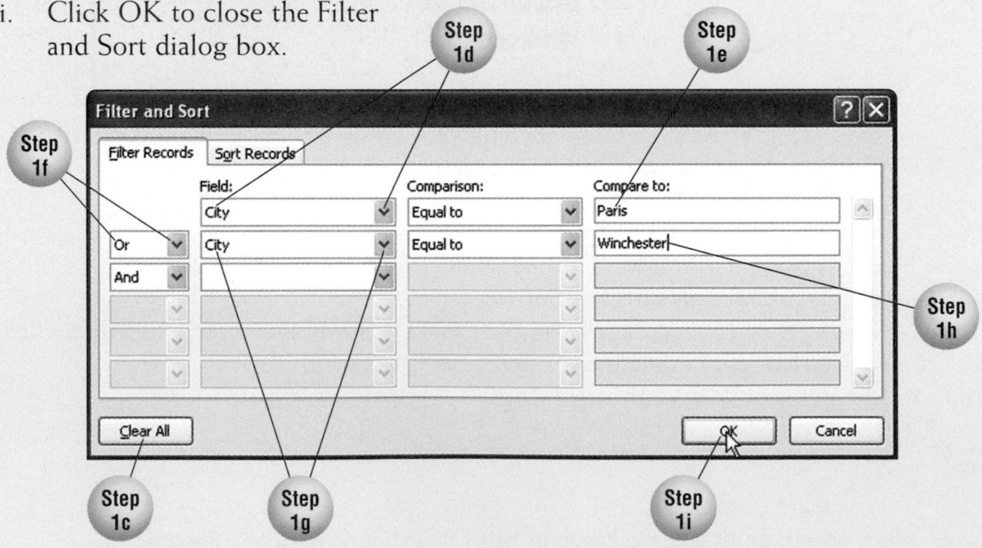

   j. Click OK to close the Mail Merge Recipients dialog box.
2. At the labels document, click the Finish & Merge button in the Finish group and then click *Edit Individual Documents* at the drop-down list.
3. At the Merge to New Document dialog box, make sure *All* is selected and then click OK.

4. Save the merged labels and name the document **C17Ex02Lbls03**.
5. Print and then close **C17Ex02Lbls03.docx**.
6. Save **C17Ex02MD.docx**.

Finding Records

The Find duplicates and Find recipient hyperlinks in the *Refine recipient list* section of the Mail Merge Recipients dialog box can be very useful for finding records in an extensive data source file. Use the Find duplicates hyperlink if you want to locate any duplicate records that appear in the data source file. If you need to find a specific record or records that meet a specific criterion, use the Find recipient hyperlink. The Validate addresses hyperlink in the *Refine recipient list* section is only available if you have installed address validation software. (Visit the Microsoft Office Web site to find more information about address validation add-ins.)

When you click the Find duplicates hyperlink, any duplicate records display in the Find Duplicates dialog box. At this dialog box, remove the check mark from the duplicate record you do not want to include in the merge. To find a specific record in a data source file, click the Find recipient hyperlink. At the Find Entry dialog box, type the text you want to find and then click the Find Next button. Continue clicking the Find Next button until a message displays telling you that there are no more entries that contain the text you typed. By default, Word searches for the specified text in all fields of all records in the data source file. You can limit the search by clicking the down-pointing arrow at the right side of the *This field* option box and then clicking the specific field. Type the find text in the *Find* text box and then click OK.

Exercise 2E

Finding Records

1. With **C17Ex02MD.docx** open, remove the filter by completing the following steps:
   a. Click the Edit Recipient List button.
   b. At the Mail Merge Recipients dialog box, click the Filter hyperlink in the *Refine recipient list* section.
   c. At the Filter and Sort dialog box, click the Clear All button that displays in the lower left corner of the dialog box.
   d. Click OK to close the Filter and Sort dialog box.
   e. At the Mail Merge Recipients dialog box, click the Find duplicates hyperlink in the *Refine recipient list* section.
   f. At the Find Duplicates dialog box, which indicates that there are no duplicate items, click OK.

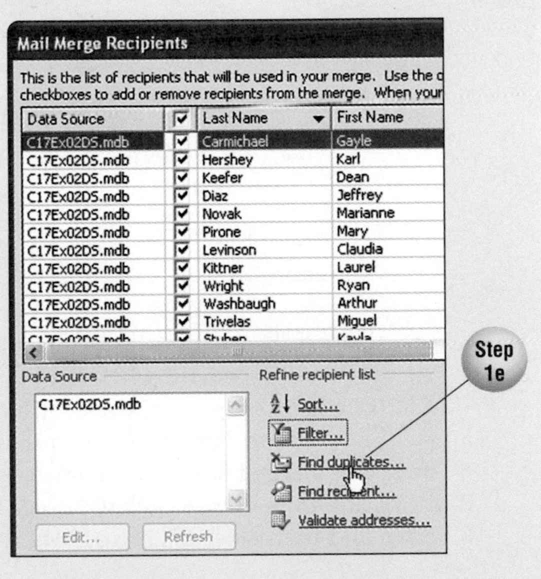

2. Find all records containing the ZIP code *40511* by completing the following steps:
   a. At the Mail Merge Recipients dialog box, click the Find recipient hyperlink in the *Refine recipient list* section.
   b. At the Find Entry dialog box, click the down-pointing arrow at the right side of the *This field* option box and then click *ZIP Code* at the drop-down list. (You will need to scroll down the list to display this option.)
   c. Click in the *Find* text box and then type **40511**.
   d. Click the Find Next button.
   e. When the first record is selected containing the ZIP code *40511*, click the Find Next button.
   f. Continue clicking the Find Next button until a message displays telling you that there are no more entries that contain the text you typed. At this message, click OK.
   g. Click the Cancel button to close the Find Entry dialog box.
3. Select and then merge records of those clients with a ZIP code of 40511 by completing the following steps:
   a. At the Mail Merge Recipients dialog box, click the Filter hyperlink in the *Refine recipient list* section of the dialog box.
   b. At the Filter and Sort dialog box, click the down-pointing arrow at the right side of the *Field* option and then click *ZIP Code* at the drop-down list. (You will need to scroll down the list to display this field.)
   c. Type **40511** in the *Compare to* text box.
   d. Click OK to close the Filter and Sort dialog box.

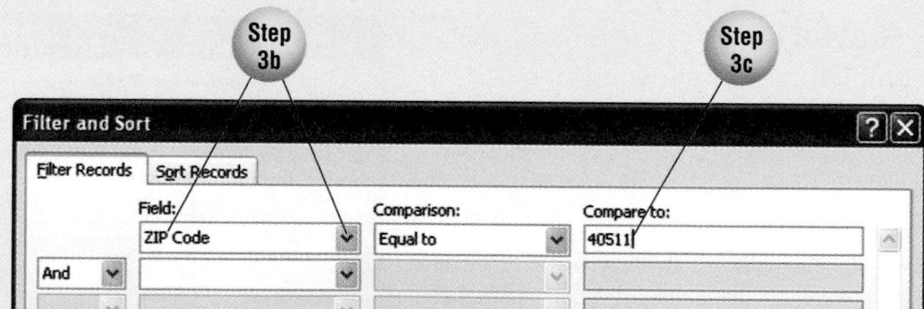

   e. Click OK to close the Mail Merge Recipients dialog box.
4. At the labels document, click the Finish & Merge button in the Finish group and then click *Edit Individual Documents* at the drop-down list.
5. At the Merge to New Document dialog box, make sure *All* is selected and then click OK.
6. Save the merged labels and name the document **C17Ex02Lbls04**.
7. Print and then close **C17Ex02Lbls04.docx**.
8. Save and then close **C17Ex02MD.docx**.

Chapter Summary

- Word is a word processing program that includes some basic database functions that you can use to alphabetize information, arrange numbers numerically, or select specific records from a data source.
- You can sort text in paragraphs, columns, or tables. You can also sort records in a data source file and select specific records for merging with a main document.
- Word can perform three types of sorts: text, numbers, and date.
- Unless specific text is selected, Word sorts text in the entire document.
- Use the Sort button in the Paragraph group in the Home tab to sort text in paragraphs, columns, and tables.
- The *Sort by* option at the Sort Text dialog box has a default setting of *Paragraphs*. This default setting changes depending on the text in the document.
- Click the Options button in the Sort Text dialog box to display the Sort Options dialog box. Use the *Separate fields at* section to specify the character that divides text to be sorted.
- To sort text in columns, the text must be separated with tabs. When Word sorts text set in columns, it considers the left margin *Field 1*, the first column *Field 2*, and so on.
- Use the *Header row* option in the *My list has* option in the Sort Text dialog box to sort all text in columns except the first row.
- You can sort on more than one field with the *Sort by* and *Then by* options at the Sort dialog box.
- You can sort text in the columns of a table much the same way you sort columns of text. The Sort Text dialog box becomes the Sort dialog box when you sort in a table.
- Sort records in a data source file at the Mail Merge Recipients dialog box. Sort by clicking the column heading. You can also sort by clicking the Sort hyperlink in the *Refine recipient list* section of the Mail Merge Recipients dialog box. This displays the Filter and Sort dialog box with the Sort Records tab selected.
- Select specific records in a data source file by inserting or removing check marks from the check boxes preceding records or with options at the Filter and Sort dialog box with the Filter Records tab selected. Display the dialog box by clicking the Filter hyperlink that displays in the *Refine recipient list* section.
- Use the *Comparison* option box to refine your search to records that meet specific criteria.
- Use the Find duplicates hyperlink in the *Refine recipient list* section of the Mail Merge Recipients dialog box to find duplicate records in a data source file and use the Find recipient hyperlink to search for records that match a specific criterion.

Commands review

FEATURE	RIBBON TAB, GROUP	BUTTON
Sort Text dialog box	Home, Paragraph	
Sort Options dialog box	Home, Paragraph	, Options
Filter and Sort dialog box with Sort Records tab selected	Mailings, Start Mail Merge	, Sort
Filter and Sort dialog box with Select Records tab selected	Mailings, Start Mail Merge	, Filter

Reviewing key points

Completion: In the space provided at the right, indicate the correct term, symbol, or command.

1. You can sort text in paragraphs, columns, or this. ________________
2. The three types of sorts you can perform in a document include text, numbers, and this. ________________
3. The Sort button is located in this group in the Home tab. ________________
4. Click the Sort button with paragraphs of text selected, and this dialog box displays. ________________
5. This is the default setting for the *Separate at* option at the Sort Options dialog box. ________________
6. When you sort text in columns, Word considers the left margin this field number. ________________
7. If you select column text, including the column headings, click this option in the *My list has* section of the Sort Text dialog box. ________________
8. With the insertion point positioned in a table, clicking the Sort button displays this dialog box. ________________
9. Click this at the Mail Merge Recipients dialog box to sort data in a specific column. ________________
10. Click this hyperlink at the Mail Merge Recipients dialog box, and the Filter and Sort dialog box displays with the Sort Records tab selected. ________________

11. Use this option at the Filter and Sort dialog box with the Filter Records tab selected to refine the search to records that meet specific criteria. ______________

12. Click this hyperlink in the Mail Merge Recipients dialog box to search for records that match a specific criterion. ______________

Applying your skills

Assessment 1 Sort Text in a McCormack Funds Document

1. Open **Sort02.docx** and save the document with the name **C17A01**.
2. Sort the nine lines of text below the *Executive Team* heading in ascending alphabetic order by last name.
3. Select the columns of text below the *New Employees* title and then sort the columns alphabetically by last name in the first column.
4. Sort the *Salesperson* column in the table located toward the bottom of the document in ascending order.
5. Save, print, and then close **C17A01.docx**.

Assessment 2 Sort Text in a Medical Health Services Document

1. Open **Sort03.docx** and save the document with the name **C17A02**.
2. Sort the columns of text below the *MEDICAL HEALTH SERVICES* title by clinic name in ascending order.
3. Sort the columns of text below the *EXECUTIVE TEAM* heading by last name in ascending order.
4. Sort the *Second Half Expenses* column in the table located toward the bottom of the document in descending order.
5. Save, print, and then close **C17A02.docx**.

Assessment 3 Create Labels for Key Life Customers

1. Make a copy of the **KLCustomers.mdb** file by completing the following steps:
   a. Display the Open dialog box and make Chapter17 the active folder.
   b. If necessary, change the *Files of type* option to *All Files (*.*)*.
   c. Right-click on the **KLCustomers.mdb** file and then click Copy at the shortcut menu.
   d. Position the mouse pointer in a white portion of the Open dialog box list box (outside of any file name), click the *right* mouse button, and then click Paste at the shortcut menu. (This inserts a copy of the file in the dialog box list box and names the file **Copy of KLCustomers.mdb**.)
   e. Right-click on the file name **Copy of KLCustomers.mdb** and then click Rename at the shortcut menu.
   f. Type **C17A03DS.mdb** and then press Enter.
   g. Close the Open dialog box.
2. Use the Mail Merge feature to create mailing labels with the *Avery US Letter 5360* label product. Use the existing data source **C17A03DS.mdb** for the labels.

3. Display the Mail Merge Recipients dialog box, sort records by ZIP code in ascending order and then by last name in ascending order, and then save the labels document with the name **C17A03Lbls**.
4. Print and then close **C17A03Lbls.docx**.
5. Close the labels main document without saving it.

Assessment 4 Create Labels for Key Life Boston Customers

1. Use the Mail Merge feature to create mailing labels with the *Avery US Letter 5360* label product. Use the existing data source **C17A03DS.mdb** for the labels.
2. Display the Mail Merge Recipients dialog box, display the Filter and Sort dialog box with the Filter Records tab selected, and then select only those customers living in Boston.
3. Complete the merge and then save the labels document with the name **C17A04Lbls**.
4. Print and then close **C17A04Lbls.docx**.
5. Close the labels main document without saving it.

Chapter 18

Managing Lists

Tutorial 18.1
Managing Lists
Tutorial 18.2
Working with Special Characters

Performance Objectives

Upon successful completion of Chapter 18, you will be able to:

- Insert custom numbers and bullets
- Define numbering formatting
- Define custom bullets
- Insert multilevel list numbering
- Define multilevel list numbering
- Insert special characters, hyphens, and nonbreaking spaces
- Find and replace special characters

Inserting a bullet before each item in a list draws a reader's attention to the list. Similarly, inserting numbers before a list of items in sequence emphasizes their order. You can insert numbers and bullets and create multiple-level bulleted or numbered paragraphs with buttons in the Paragraph group in the Home tab. Use options from these buttons' drop-down lists to customize bullets and numbers and to create customized multilevel numbering. In this chapter you will learn how to create and insert customized bullets and numbering; how to insert special characters such as intellectual property protection symbols, hyphens, and nonbreaking spaces; and how to search for and replace special characters.

Note: Before beginning computer exercises for this chapter, copy to your storage medium the Chapter18 folder from the CD that accompanies this textbook and then make Chapter18 the active folder.

Inserting Custom Numbers and Bullets

Numbering

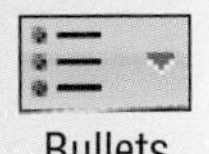

Bullets

In Chapter 3, you learned to number paragraphs and insert bullets automatically using the Numbering button and the Bullets button in the Paragraph group in the Home tab. After you insert numbers or bullets, you can customize them by clicking the Numbering button arrow or the Bullets button arrow and then choosing an option from the drop-down list.

Inserting Custom Numbers

As you learned earlier, you can insert numbers as you type text, or you can type text, select it, and then apply numbering formatting. Whether you insert numbers as you type text or click the Numbering button in the Paragraph group to apply number formatting after you type text, Word inserts Arabic numbers (1., 2., 3., and so on) in the document by default. You can change this default numbering by clicking the

Numbering button arrow and then clicking the option you desire at the Numbering drop-down gallery, shown in Figure 18.1.

With these options, you can also create a list with multiple levels or change the level of an existing numbered list. To do this, click the item or select the items you want to change, click the Numbering button arrow, and then point to *Change List Level*. At the side menu of numbering options, click the desired numbering level.

Figure 18.1 Numbering Gallery

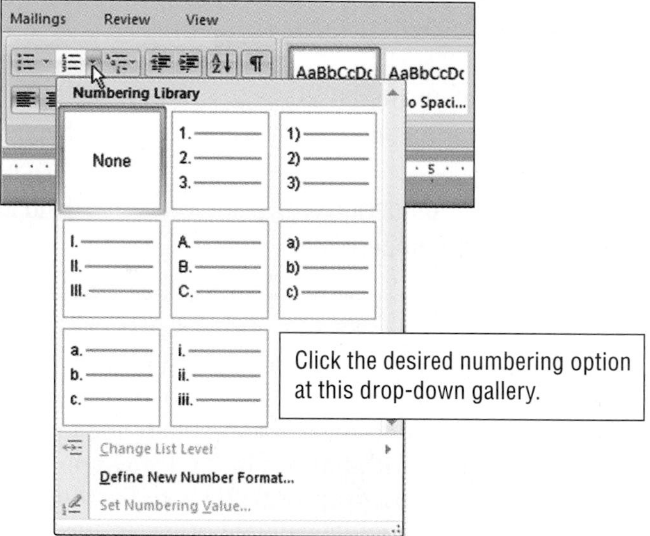

Exercise 1A

Inserting Custom Numbers

1. Open **Agenda01.docx** and save the document with the name **C18Ex01**.
2. Position the insertion point on any character in the title *TRAINING DEPARTMENT AGENDA* and then click the Heading 2 style in the Styles group in the Home tab.
3. Change the style set to *Traditional*.
4. Apply the *Concourse* theme.
5. Number the paragraphs in the document by completing the following steps:
   a. Select the paragraphs (excluding the title).
   b. Click the Home tab.

c. In the Paragraph group, click the Numbering button arrow.
d. At the Numbering drop-down gallery, click the option shown below (the location of the option in your drop-down gallery may vary).

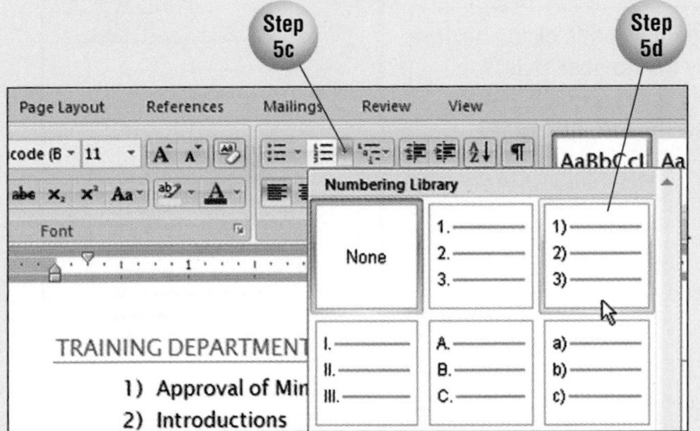

6. Add text to the agenda by completing the following steps:
   a. Position the insertion point immediately to the right of the text *Introductions*.
   b. Press the Enter key.
   c. Type **Organizational Overview**.
7. Select and then delete *Resources*.
8. Save and then print **C18Ex01.docx**.

Defining a Numbering Format

Define Numbering Formatting
1. Click Numbering button arrow.
2. Click *Define New Number Format* at drop-down gallery.
3. Choose the desired number formatting option.
4. Click OK.

In addition to using the default numbering format or a custom numbering format in the *Numbering Library* section in the Numbering button drop-down gallery, you can define your own numbering format with options at the Define New Number Format dialog box, shown in Figure 18.2. Display this dialog box by clicking the Numbering button arrow and then clicking *Define New Number Format* at the drop-down gallery. With options at the dialog box, you can specify the number style, font, and alignment and preview the formatting in the *Preview* section.

When you define a numbering format at the Define New Number Format dialog box, it is automatically included in the *Numbering Library* section in the Numbering button drop-down gallery. You can remove a numbering format from the drop-down gallery by right-clicking it and then clicking Remove at the shortcut menu.

Figure 18.2 Define New Number Format Dialog Box

Use options at this dialog box to specify the number style, font, format, and alignment and to preview the formatting.

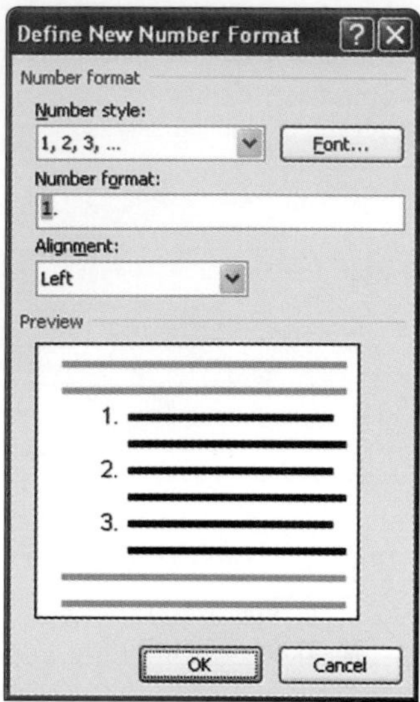

Exercise 1B

Defining a Numbering Format

1. With **C18Ex01.docx** open, define a new number format by completing the following steps:
   a. Position the insertion point on any character in the numbered text.
   b. Click the Numbering button arrow.
   c. Click *Define New Number Format* at the drop-down gallery.
   d. At the Define New Number Format dialog box, click the down-pointing arrow at the right of the *Number style* option and then click the 1st, 2nd, 3rd … option.

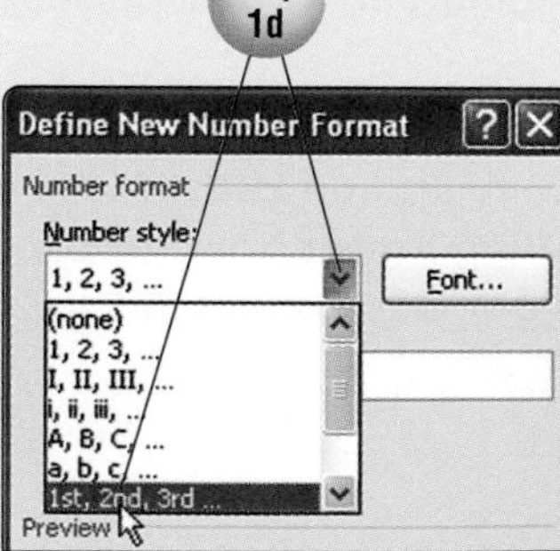

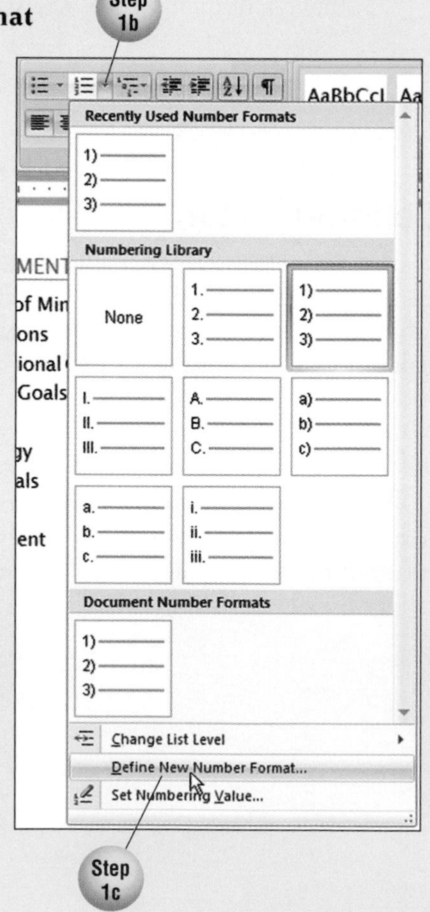

   e. Click the Font button that displays at the right side of the *Number style* list box.

f. At the Font dialog box, scroll down the *Font* list box and then click *Candara*.
g. Click *Bold* in the *Font style* list box.
h. Click OK to close the Font dialog box.
i. Click the down-pointing arrow at the right of the *Alignment* option box and then click *Right* at the drop-down list.

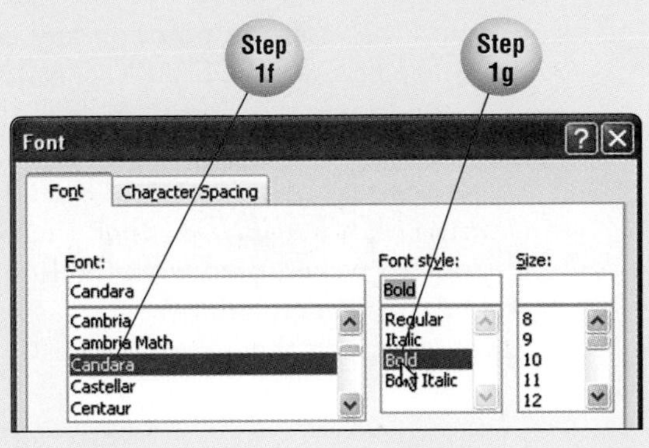

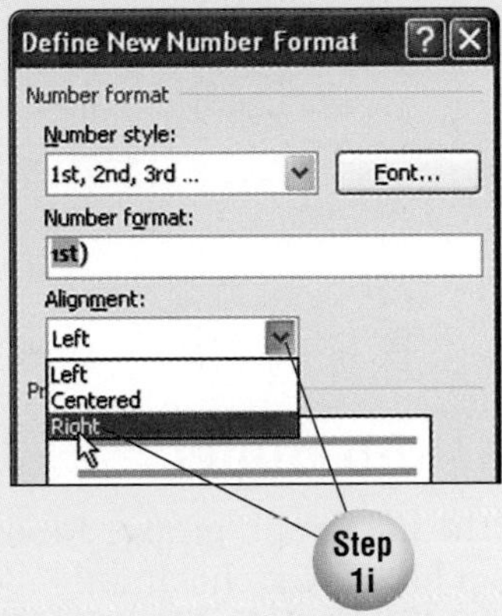

j. Click OK to close the Define New Number Format dialog box. (This applies the new formatting to the numbered paragraphs in the document.)

2. After looking at the numbering with the new formatting applied, define another number format by completing the following steps:
   a. With the insertion point positioned on any character in the numbered text, click the Numbering button arrow.
   b. Click *Define New Number Format* at the drop-down gallery.
   c. At the Define New Number Format dialog box, click the down-pointing arrow at the right of the *Number style* option and then click the *I, II, III, ...* option.
   d. Click the Font button that displays at the right side of the *Number style* list box.
   e. At the Font dialog box, click *Cambria* in the list box.
   f. Check to make sure *Bold* is selected in the *Font style* list box and then click OK to close the Font dialog box.
   g. At the Define New Number Format dialog box, make sure *Right* is selected in the *Alignment* option box and then click OK. (This applies the new formatting to the numbered paragraphs in the document.)
3. Insert a file into the current document by completing the following steps:
   a. Press Ctrl + End to move the insertion point to the end of the document.
   b. Click the Insert tab.
   c. Click the Object button arrow and then click *Text from File* at the drop-down list.
   d. At the Insert File dialog box, navigate to the Chapter18 folder and then double-click **Agenda02.docx**.

4. Position the insertion point on any character in the title *RESEARCH DEPARTMENT AGENDA*, click the Home tab, and then click the *Heading 2* style in the Styles group.
5. Select the text below the title *RESEARCH DEPARTMENT AGENDA*, click the Numbering button arrow, and then click the Roman numeral style that you defined.
6. Save, print, and then close **C18Ex01.docx**.

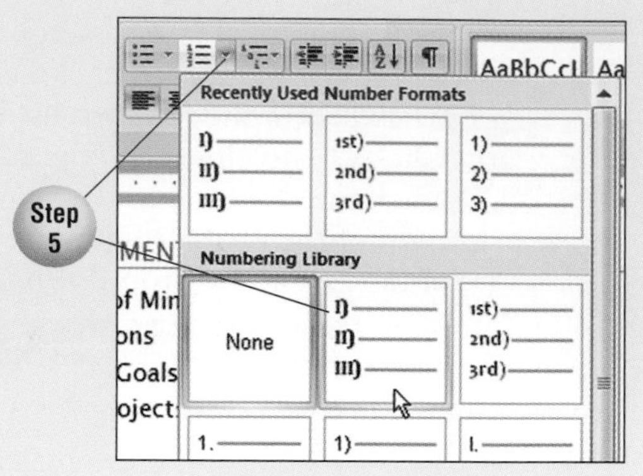

Define Custom Bullet
1. Click Bullets button arrow.
2. Click *Define New Bullet* at drop-down gallery.
3. Choose the desired bullet character.
4. Click OK.

Defining and Inserting Custom Bullets

When you click the Bullets button in the Paragraph group, a round bullet is inserted in the document. You can insert custom bullets by clicking the Bullets button arrow and then clicking the desired bullet at the drop-down gallery. This drop-down gallery displays the most recently used bullets along with an option for defining new bullets. Click the *Define New Bullet* option, and the Define New Bullet dialog box displays, as shown in Figure 18.3. With options at this dialog box, you can choose a symbol or picture bullet, change the font size of the bullet, and specify the alignment of the bullet. When you choose a custom bullet, consider matching the theme or mood of the document to maintain a consistent look or create a picture bullet to add visual interest.

Figure 18.3 Define New Bullet Dialog Box

Use options at this dialog box to choose a symbol or picture bullet and change the font size and alignment of the bullet.

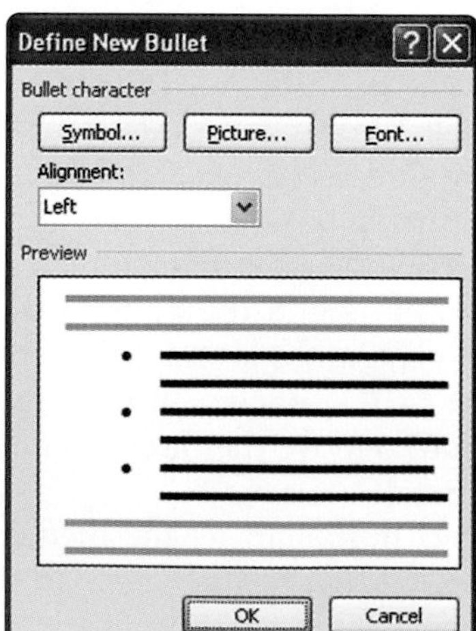

When you define a new bullet at the Define New Bullet dialog box, it is automatically included in the *Bullets Library* section in the Bullets button drop-down gallery. You can remove a bullet from the drop-down gallery by right-clicking the bullet and then clicking Remove at the shortcut menu.

As with a numbered list, you can change the level of a bulleted list. To do this, click the item or select the items you want to change, click the Bullets button arrow, and then point to *Change List Level*. At the side menu of bullet options that displays, click the desired bullet. With the *Change List Level* option, you can change a single-level list into a multilevel list. If you want to insert a line break in the list while the automatic bullets feature is on without inserting a bullet, press Shift + Enter. (You can also insert a line break in a numbered list without inserting a number by pressing Shift + Enter.)

Exercise 2

Defining and Inserting Custom Bullets

1. Open **Document07.docx** and save the document with the name **C18Ex02**.
2. Make the following changes to the document:
   a. Select the entire document and then change the line spacing to 1.15.
   b. Apply the Heading 1 style to the title *Hawaiian Adventures*.
   c. Apply the Heading 2 style to the two headings *Rainy Day Activities* and *Kauai Sights*.
   d. Change the style set to *Distinctive*.
   e. Change the theme to *Flow*.
3. Define and insert a picture bullet by completing the following steps:
   a. Select text in the *Rainy Day Activities* section from the paragraph that begins with *Movies* through the paragraph that begins with *Theater*.
   b. Click the Home tab.
   c. Click the Bullets button arrow and then click *Define New Bullet* at the drop-down gallery.

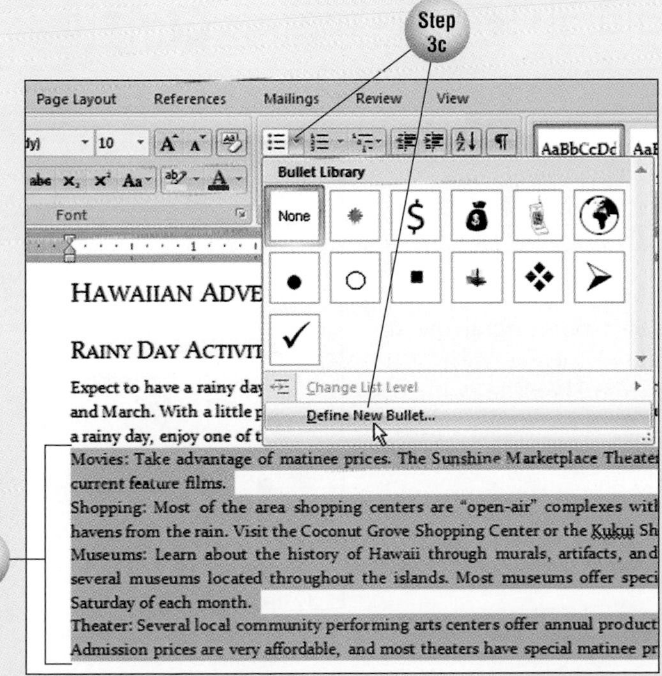

d. At the Define New Bullet dialog box, click the Picture button.
e. At the Picture Bullet dialog box, click the round, green bullet shown at the right.
f. Click OK to close the Picture Bullet dialog box.
g. Click OK to close the Define New Bullet dialog box. (This applies the new bullet to the selected paragraphs.)

4. Define and insert a symbol bullet by completing the following steps:
   a. Select the paragraphs of text below the heading *Kauai Sights*.
   b. Click the Bullets button arrow and then click *Define New Bullet* at the drop-down gallery.
   c. At the Define New Bullet dialog box, click the Symbol button.
   d. At the Symbol dialog box, click the down-pointing arrow at the right of the *Font* option, scroll down the drop-down list, and then click *Wingdings*.
   e. Click the thirteenth symbol from the left in the sixth row, as shown below (flower symbol).

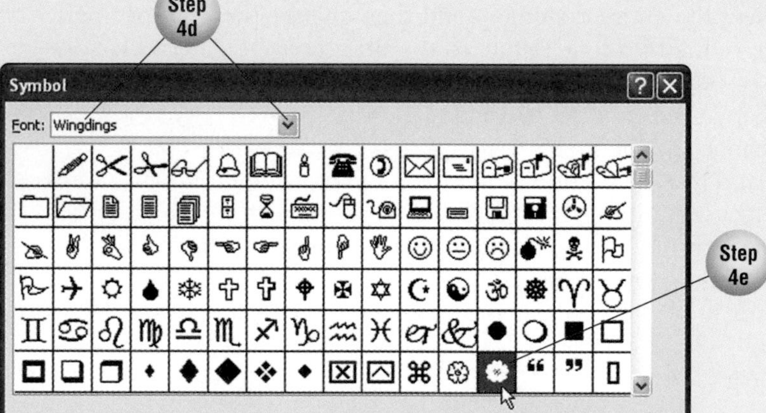

   f. Click OK to close the Symbol dialog box.
   g. At the Define New Bullet dialog box, click the Font button.
   h. At the Font dialog box, click *14* in the *Size* list box.
   i. Click the down-pointing arrow at the right side of the *Font color* option and then click the color *Green, Accent 5, Darker 50%*, shown at the right.
   j. Click OK to close the Font dialog box.
   k. At the Define New Bullet dialog box, click OK.

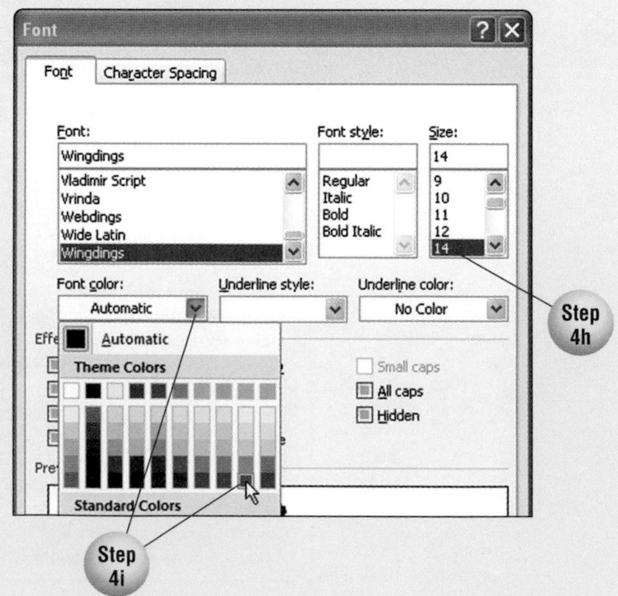

5. Remove from the Bullet Library the two bullets you have just defined by completing the following steps:
   a. Click the Bullets button arrow.
   b. Right-click the round, green picture bullet in the *Bullet Library* section and then click Remove at the shortcut menu.
   c. Click the Bullets button arrow.
   d. Right-click the flower symbol bullet in the *Bullet Library* section and then click Remove at the shortcut menu.
6. Save, print, and then close **C18Ex02.docx**.

Inserting Multilevel List Numbering

Insert Multilevel List Numbering
1. Click Multilevel List button.
2. Click desired style at drop-down gallery.

Multilevel List

Use the Multilevel List button in the Paragraph group in the Home tab to specify the type of numbering for paragraphs of text at the left margin, first tab, second tab, and so on. Apply predesigned multilevel numbering to text in a document by clicking the Multilevel List button and then clicking the desired numbering style at the drop-down gallery, shown in Figure 18.4. Some options at the Multilevel List drop-down gallery display with *Heading 1*, *Heading 2*, and so on, after the number. Click one of these options, and Word inserts the numbering and applies the heading styles to the text.

Figure 18.4 Multilevel List Drop-down Gallery

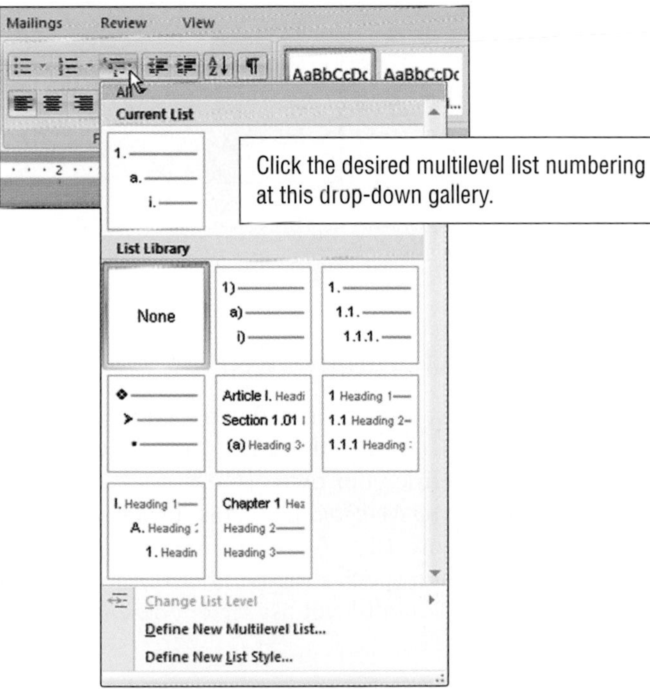

Exercise 3A

Inserting Multilevel List Numbering

1. Open **List02.docx** and save the document with the name **C18Ex03**.
2. Change tab settings by completing the following steps:
   a. Select the paragraphs of text below the title.
   b. Click the Paragraph group dialog box launcher.
   c. At the Paragraph dialog box, click the Tabs button located in the lower left corner of the dialog box.
   d. At the Tabs dialog box, select the 0.5″ measurement in the *Default tab stops* box and then type **0.25**.

Step 2b

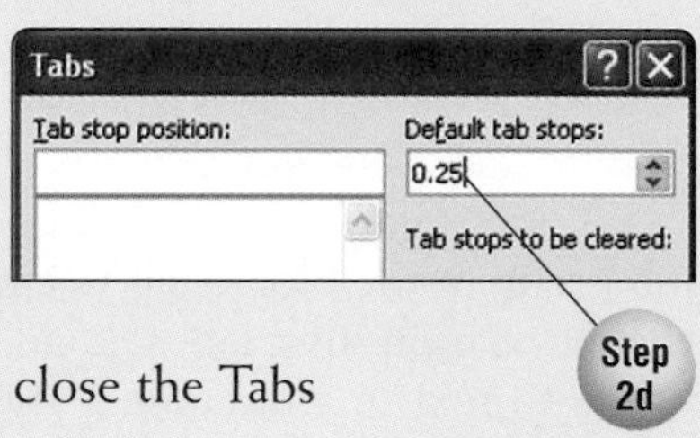

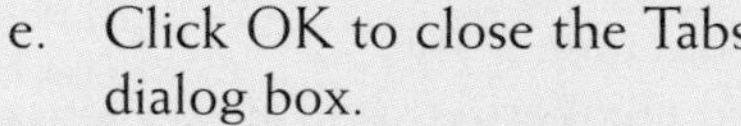

   e. Click OK to close the Tabs dialog box.
3. With the text still selected, apply multilevel numbering by completing the following steps:
   a. Click the Multilevel List button in the Paragraph group in the Home tab.
   b. At the drop-down gallery, click the middle option in the top row of the *List Library* section.
   c. Deselect the text.
4. Save and then print **C18Ex03.docx**.

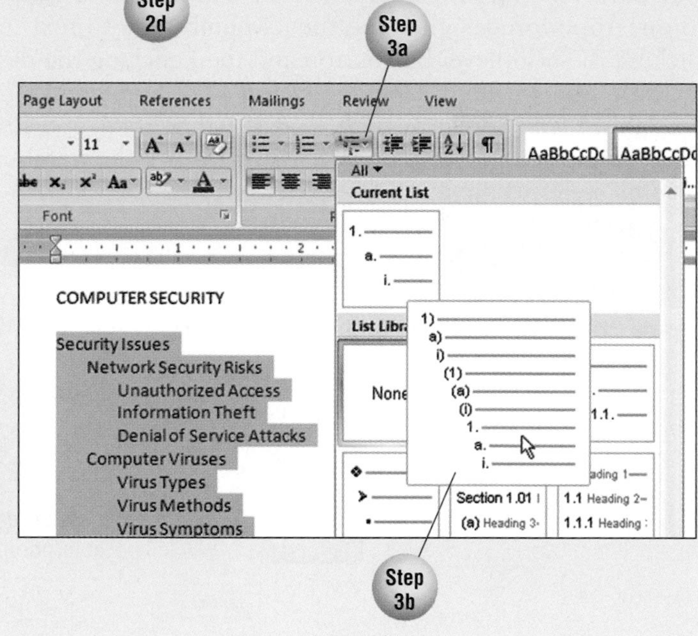

Define Multilevel List
1. Click Multilevel List button.
2. Click *Define New Multilevel List* at drop-down gallery.
3. Click desired level, number format, and/or position.
4. Click OK.

Defining a Multilevel List

The Multilevel List button drop-down gallery contains predesigned multiple-level numbering options. If the gallery does not contain the type of numbering you want to use, you can define your own. To do this, click the Multilevel List button and then click *Define New Multilevel List*. This displays the Define new Multilevel list dialog box, shown in Figure 18.5. At this dialog box, click a level in the *Click level to modify* option box and then specify the number format, style, position, and alignment. When you define a multilevel list style, you can mix numbers and bullets in the same list.

Figure 18.5 Define New Multilevel List Dialog Box

Click a level in this option box and then specify the number format, style, position, and alignment.

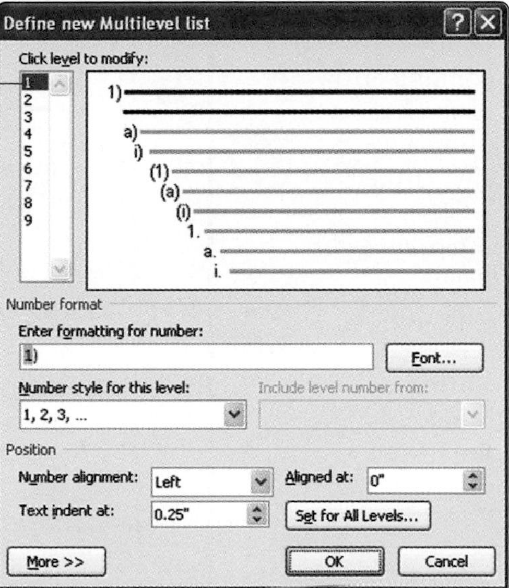

Exercise 3B

Defining a New Multilevel List

1. With **C18Ex03.docx** open, define a multilevel list by completing the following steps:
   a. Select the paragraphs of text below the title.
   b. Click the Multilevel List button in the Paragraph group in the Home tab.
   c. Click the *Define New Multilevel List* option at the drop-down gallery.
   d. At the Define new Multilevel list dialog box, make sure *1* is selected in the *Click level to modify* list box.
   e. Click the down-pointing arrow at the right side of the *Number style for this level* option and then click *A, B, C, ...* at the drop-down list.
   f. Click in the *Enter formatting for number* text box, delete any text that displays after *A*, and then type a period (.). (The entry in the text box should now display as *A.*)
   g. Click the up-pointing arrow at the right side of the *Aligned at* measurement box until *0.3″* displays in the measurement box.
   h. Click the up-pointing arrow at the right side of the *Text indent at* measurement box until *0.6″* displays in the measurement box.

i. Click 2 in the *Click level to modify* list box.
j. Click the down-pointing arrow at the right side of the *Number style for this level* option and then click *1, 2, 3, ...* at the drop-down list.
k. Click in the *Enter formatting for number* text box, delete any text that displays after the *1*, and then type a period (.).
l. Click the up-pointing arrow at the right side of the *Aligned at* measurement box until 0.6″ displays in the measurement box.
m. Click the up-pointing arrow at the right side of the *Text indent at* measurement box until 0.9″ displays in the measurement box.
n. Click 3 in the *Click level to modify* list box.
o. Click the down-pointing arrow at the right side of the *Number style for this level* option and then click *a, b, c, ...* at the drop-down list.
p. Make sure *a)* displays in the *Enter formatting for number* text box. (If not, delete any text that displays after the *a* and then type a right parenthesis.)
q. Click the up-pointing arrow at the right side of the *Aligned at* measurement box until 0.9″ displays in the measurement box.
r. Click the up-pointing arrow at the right side of the *Text indent at* measurement box until *1.2*″ displays in the measurement box.
s. Click OK to close the dialog box. (This applies the new multilevel numbering to the selected text.)
t. Deselect the text.

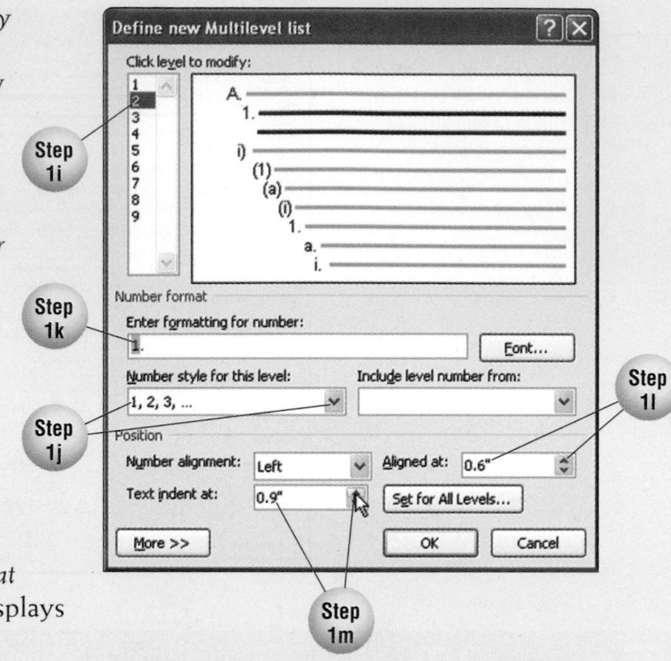

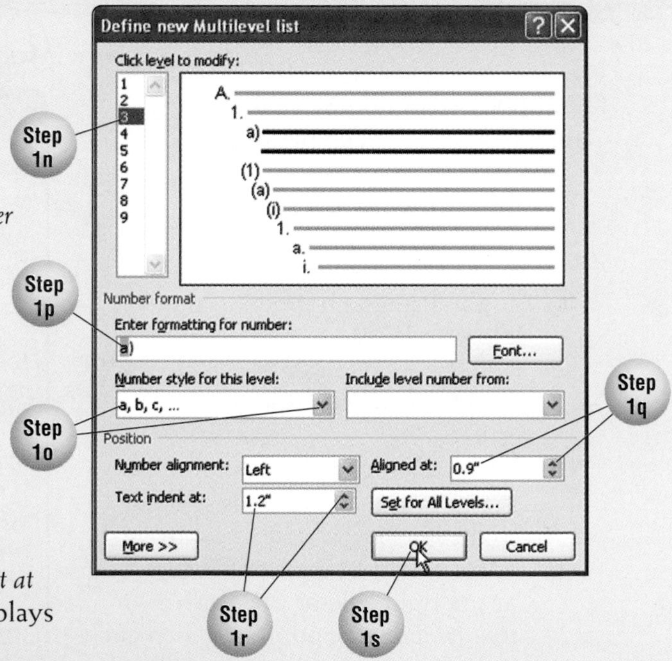

2. Make the following formatting changes to the document:
   a. Apply the Heading 1 style to the title *COMPUTER SECURITY*.
   b. Change the style set to *Formal*.
   c. Apply the *Solstice* theme.
3. With the document still open, make the following changes:
   a. Select and then delete *Network Sniffers* in the *Computer Protection* section.
   b. Move the insertion point immediately right of the text *Data Encryption*, press the Enter key, and then type **Passwords**.
4. Save **C18Ex03.docx**.

Typing a Multilevel List

You can select text and apply a multilevel list to it, or you can apply the list and then type the text. As you type text, press the Tab key to move to the next level or press Shift + Tab to move to the previous level.

Exercise 3C

Typing a Multilevel List

1. With **C18Ex03.docx** open, type the text shown in Figure 18.6 in a multilevel list by completing the following steps:
   a. Press Ctrl + End to move the insertion point to the end of the document and then press the Enter key.
   b. Type **NETWORKS** and then press the Enter key twice.
   c. Turn on the multilevel list you defined in Exercise 3B by clicking the Multilevel List button and then clicking the list (displays in the *Lists in Current Documents* section of the drop-down gallery).
   d. Type **Networking over the Web** as shown in Figure 18.6.

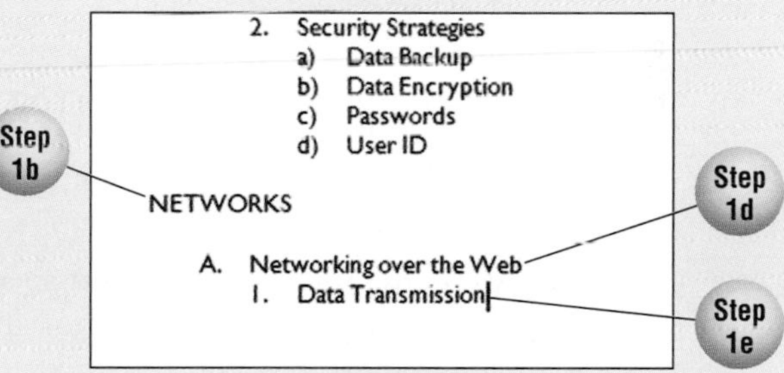

   e. Press the Enter key, press the Tab key, and then type **Data Transmission** as shown in Figure 18.6.
   f. Continue typing the text shown in Figure 18.6. Press the Tab key to indent text to the next level or press Shift + Tab to decrease the indent to the previous level. (The multilevel list will apply letter and number formatting.)
   g. Apply the Heading 1 style to the title *NETWORKS*.
2. Save, print, and then close **C18Ex03.docx**.

Figure 18.6 Exercise 3C

NETWORKS

Networking over the Web
- Data Transmission
  - Bandwidth
  - Analog and Digital Transmission
  - Parallel and Serial Transmission
- Communications Media
  - Wired Communications Media
  - Wireless Communications Media

Network Design
- Network Topologies
  - Bus Topologies
  - Star Topologies
  - Ring Topologies
  - Hybrid Topologies
- Network Hardware
  - Hubs
  - Repeaters
  - Routers
  - Gateways
  - Bridges

Inserting Special Characters

In Chapter 8, you learned how to insert symbols and special characters with options at the Symbol dialog box with the Symbols tab or the Special Characters tab selected. You can also insert special symbols and characters by typing a sequence of characters or by using keyboard shortcuts. Word creates some special characters automatically as you type text.

Inserting Intellectual Property Symbols

Among the symbols you can insert in Word are three intellectual property protection symbols: ©, ™, and ®. Insert the © symbol to identify copyrighted intellectual property, use the ™ symbol to identify a trademark, and use the ® symbol to identify a registered trademark. You can insert these symbols with options at the Symbol dialog box with the Special Characters tab selected, by typing a sequence of characters, or by using a keyboard shortcut. Insert a © symbol by typing (c) or pressing Alt + Ctrl + C, insert a ™ symbol by typing (tm) or pressing Alt + Ctrl + T, and insert a ® symbol by typing (r) or pressing Alt + Ctrl + R.

Exercise 4A

Inserting Intellectual Property Symbols

1. At a blank document, type the text shown in Figure 18.7. Insert the intellectual property symbols using the sequence of characters or the keyboard shortcuts. To insert (c), (tm), and (r) rather than the actual symbol, type the sequence of characters and then immediately click the Undo button. This changes the symbol back to the sequence of characters.
2. Save the document with the name **C18Ex04**.

Figure 18.7 Exercise 4A

INTELLECTUAL PROPERTY PROTECTION

A copyright protects original works in areas such as publishing, music, literature, and drama. Use the © symbol to identify copyrighted intellectual property. Create this symbol by typing (c), using the keyboard shortcut Alt + Ctrl + C, or by clicking the symbol in the Symbol dialog box with the Special Characters tab selected.

A trademark identifies a word, symbol, device, or name such as a brand name. Use the ™ symbol to identify a trademarked name or product. Create this symbol by typing (tm), using the keyboard shortcut Alt + Ctrl + T, or by clicking the symbol in the Symbol dialog box with the Special Characters tab selected.

A registered trademark is a trademark that has been registered with the U.S. Patent & Trademark Office. Use the ® symbol to identify a registered trademark. Create this symbol by typing (r), using the keyboard shortcut Alt + Ctrl + R, or by clicking the symbol in the Symbol dialog box with the Special Characters tab selected.

Inserting Hyphens

In Chapter 6, you learned how to use the Hyphenation button in the Page Setup group in the Page Layout tab to hyphenate words automatically or manually. In addition to inserting a regular hyphen in a document, you can insert an optional hyphen and a nonbreaking hyphen, as well as an en-dash and an em-dash. One method for inserting a regular hyphen is to press the hyphen key on the keyboard and use it to create compound words such as *fresh-looking* and *sister-in-law*. An optional hyphen is one inserted by Word when you automatically hyphenate a document. An optional hyphen will display only if the word falls at the end of the line and the word is divided between lines. Word removes the optional hyphen if the word is not divided between two lines. Optional hyphens display as a hyphen if you turn on the display of nonprinting characters.

You may not want some hyphenated text divided between lines. For example, you may not want a company name such as *Knowles-Myers Corporation* divided between *Knowles* and *Myers* on two lines. To avoid a break like this, you would insert a nonbreaking hyphen by clicking the *Nonbreaking Hyphen* option at the Symbol dialog box with the Special Characters tab selected or with the keyboard shortcut Ctrl + Shift + -.

In a written piece, an em-dash is used to indicate a break in a thought or a shift in tone. It is particularly useful in long sentences or sentences with a number of commas. For example, the sentence "The main focus of this document is on general-purpose, single-user computers—personal computers—that enable users to complete a variety of computing tasks." contains two em-dashes surrounding the words "personal computers." To create an em-dash in a Word document, type the word, type two hyphens, type the next word, and then press the spacebar. When you press the spacebar, Word automatically converts the two hyphens to an em-dash. If automatic formatting of em-dashes is turned off, you can insert an em-dash with the *Em Dash* option at the Symbol dialog box with the Special Characters tab selected or with the keyboard shortcut Alt + Ctrl + - (on the numeric keypad). (You must use the hyphen key in the numeric keypad rather than the hyphen key that is located between the zero key and the = key.)

An en-dash is used in a written piece to indicate inclusive dates, times, or numbers. For example, in the text 9:30–11:00 a.m., the numbers should be separated by an en-dash rather than a regular hyphen. Unlike em-dashes, Word does not automatically convert a hyphen to an en-dash. To create an en-dash, click the *En Dash* option at the Symbol dialog box with the Special Characters tab selected or with the keyboard shortcut Ctrl + - (on the numeric keypad).

Exercise 4B

Inserting Hyphens

1. With **C18Ex04.docx** open, press Ctrl + End, press the Enter key, and then type the text in Figure 18.8 with the following specifications:
   a. Type the en-dash between the times 9:00–10:30 a.m. by pressing Ctrl + - (on the numeric keypad).
   b. Create the em-dashes before and after *Excel, PowerPoint, and Access* by typing two hyphens.
   c. Insert a nonbreaking hyphen for Tri-State by pressing Ctrl + Shift + -.
2. Save **C18Ex04.docx**.

Figure 18.8 Exercise 4B

SOFTWARE TRAINING

The Microsoft® Office Word training is scheduled for Thursday, March 2, from 9:00–10:30 a.m. Additional training for other applications in the Office suite—Excel, PowerPoint, and Access—will be available during the month of April. Contact the Training Department for additional information. All Tri-State employees are eligible for the training.

Inserting Nonbreaking Spaces

Insert Nonbreaking Spaces
1. Click Insert tab.
2. Click Symbol button, *More Symbols.*
3. Click Special Characters tab.
4. Double-click Nonbreaking Space option.
5. Click Close.

OR

Press Ctrl + Shift + spacebar.

As you type text in a document, Word makes line-end decisions and automatically wraps text to the next line. In some situations, word wrap may break on two separate lines words or phrases that should remain together. To control where text is wrapped to the next line, consider inserting a nonbreaking space between words. Insert a nonbreaking space with the *Nonbreaking Space* option at the Symbol dialog box with the Special Characters tab selected or with the keyboard shortcut Ctrl + Shift + spacebar. If nonprinting characters are turned on, a normal space displays as a dot and a nonbreaking space displays as a degree symbol.

Exercise 4C

Inserting Nonbreaking Spaces

1. With **C18Ex04.docx** open, click the Show/Hide button in the Paragraph group in the Home tab.
2. Press Ctrl + End, press the Enter key, and then type the text in Figure 18.9. Insert nonbreaking spaces in the keyboard shortcuts by pressing Ctrl + Shift + spacebar before and after the plus symbol in the keyboard shortcuts.
3. Turn off the display of nonprinting characters.
4. Save and then print **C18Ex04.docx**.

Figure 18.9 Exercise 4C

KEYBOARD SHORTCUTS

Microsoft Word includes a number of keyboard shortcuts you can use to access features and commands. The ScreenTip for some buttons displays the keyboard shortcut you can use to execute the command. For example, hovering the mouse over the Font button causes the ScreenTip to display Ctrl + Shift + F as the keyboard shortcut. Additional Home tab Font group keyboard shortcuts include Ctrl + B to bold text, Ctrl + I to italicize text, and Ctrl + U to underline text. You can also press Ctrl + Shift + + to turn on superscript and press Ctrl + = to turn on subscript.

QUICK STEPS

Find and Replace Special Character

1. Click Replace button.
2. Click More button.
3. Click Special button.
4. Click desired character.
5. Click in *Replace with* text box.
6. Click Special button.
7. Click desired character.
8. Click *Replace All*.

Finding and Replacing Special Characters

You can use the Find feature to find special text and the Find and Replace feature to find special text and replace it with other text. You can also use these features to find special formatting, characters, or nonprinting elements in a document. To display a list of special characters and nonprinting elements, display the Find and Replace dialog box with either the Find or Replace tab selected, expand the dialog box, and then click the Special button. This displays a pop-up list similar to the one shown in Figure 18.10.

Figure 18.10 Special Button Pop-up List

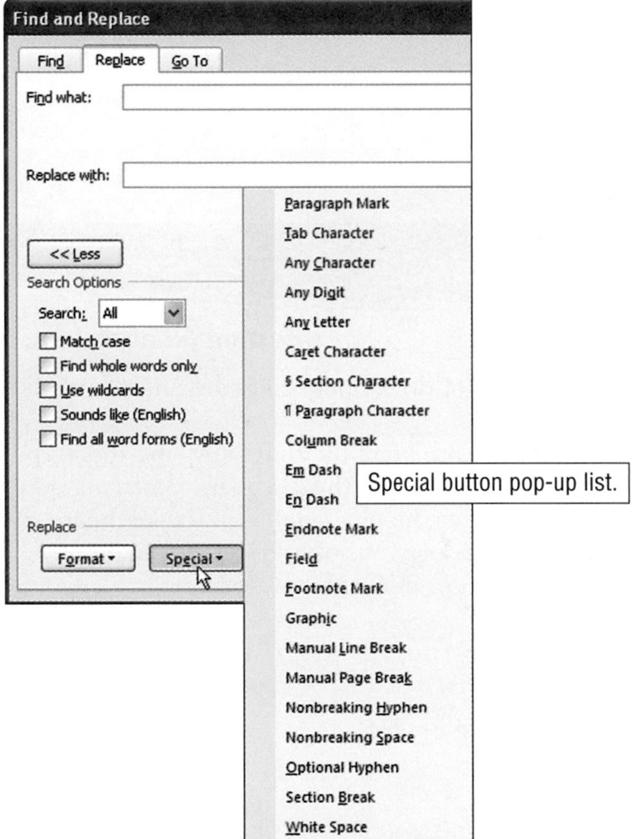

Exercise 4D

Finding and Replacing Nonbreaking Spaces

1. With **C18Ex04.docx** open, find all occurrences of nonbreaking spaces and replace them with regular spaces by completing the following steps:
    a. Press Ctrl + Home to move the insertion point to the beginning of the document.
    b. Click the Replace button in the Editing group in the Home tab.
    c. At the Find and Replace dialog box with the Replace tab selected, click the More button.

d. With the insertion point positioned in the *Find what* text box, click the Special button that displays toward the bottom of the dialog box.

e. At the pop-up list that displays, click Nonbreaking Space. (This inserts ^s in the *Find what* text box.)

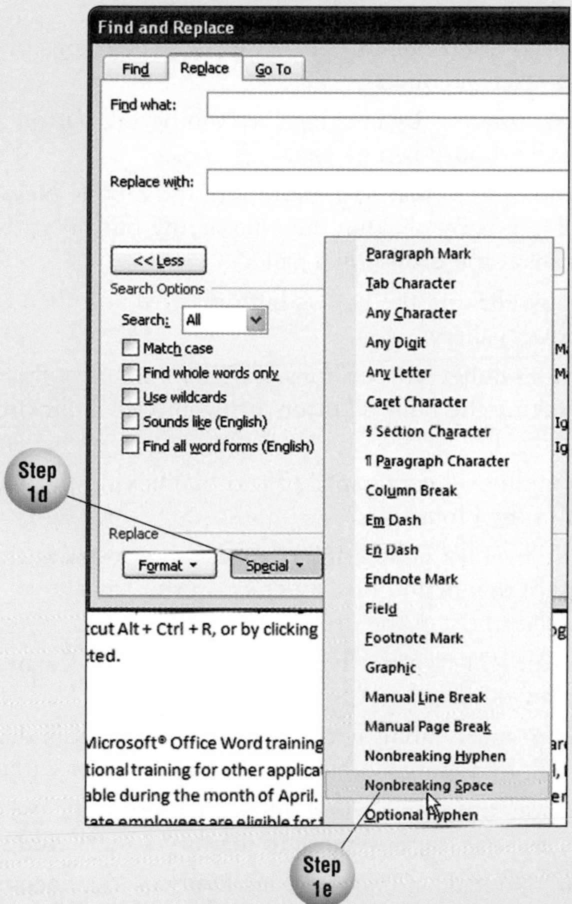

f. Click in the *Replace with* text box (make sure the text box does not contain any text) and then press the spacebar once. (This tells Word to find a nonbreaking space and replace it with a regular space.)

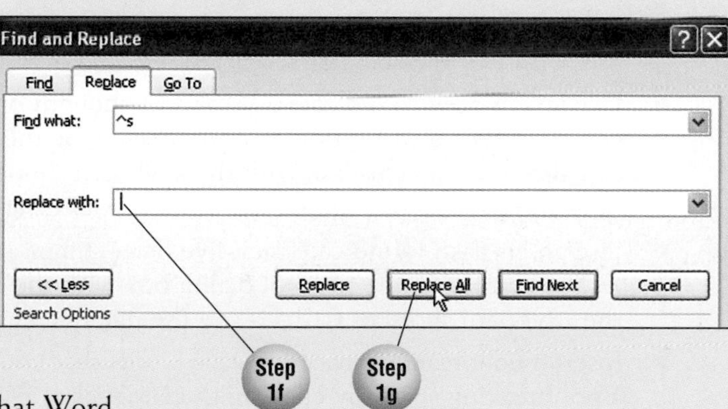

g. Click the Replace All button.

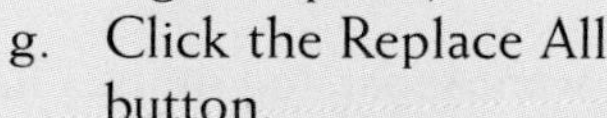

h. At the message telling you that Word completed the search and made the replacements, click OK.

i. Click the Less button.

j. Click the Close button to close the Find and Replace dialog box.

2. Save, print, and then close **C18Ex04.docx**.

Chapter Summary

- Use the Bullets button to insert bullets before specific paragraphs of text and use the Numbering button to insert numbers.
- Insert custom numbers or letters by clicking the Numbering button arrow and then clicking the desired option at the drop-down gallery.
- Define your own numbering format with options at the Define New Number Format dialog box. Display this dialog box by clicking the Numbering button arrow and then clicking *Define New Number Format* at the drop-down gallery.
- Insert custom bullets by clicking the Bullets button arrow and then clicking the desired option at the drop-down gallery.
- Define your own custom bullet with options at the Define New Bullet dialog box. Display this dialog box by clicking the Bullets button arrow and then clicking *Define New Bullet* at the drop-down gallery.
- Apply numbering to multilevel paragraphs of text by clicking the Multilevel List button in the Paragraph group in the Home tab.
- Define your own multilevel list numbering format with options at the Define new Multilevel list dialog box. Display this dialog box by clicking the Multilevel List button and then clicking *Define New Multilevel List* at the drop-down gallery.
- When you type a multilevel list, press the Tab key to move to the next level and press Shift + Tab to move to the previous level.
- Insert special characters and symbols with options at the Symbol dialog box with the Special Characters tab selected, by typing a sequence of characters, or with keyboard shortcuts.
- Use the © symbol to identify copyrighted intellectual property, use the ™ symbol to identify a trademark, and use the ® symbol to identify a registered trademark.
- You can insert regular, optional, and nonbreaking hyphens in a document, as well as en-dashes and em-dashes.
- Insert a nonbreaking hyphen by clicking the *Nonbreaking Hyphen* option at the Symbol dialog box with the Special Characters tab selected or with the keyboard shortcut Ctrl + Shift + -.
- Use an em-dash to indicate a break in a thought or a shift in tone in a sentence. To insert an em-dash, type a word, type two hyphens, type the next word, and press the spacebar. You can also insert an em-dash with the keyboard shortcut Alt + Ctrl + - (on the numeric keypad) or at the Symbol dialog box with the Special Characters tab selected.
- Use an en-dash to indicate inclusive dates, times, or numbers. To insert an en-dash, click the *En Dash* option at the Symbol dialog box with the Special Characters tab selected or with the keyboard shortcut Ctrl + - (on the numeric keypad).
- Insert a nonbreaking space between words that you do not want separated on two lines. Insert a nonbreaking space by clicking the *Nonbreaking Space* option at the Symbol dialog with the Special Characters tab selected or with the keyboard shortcut Ctrl + Shift + spacebar.
- Use the Find feature to find special characters or the Find and Replace feature to find special characters and replace them with other characters or text. Click the Special button at the Find and Replace dialog box to display a pop-up list of special characters.

Commands review

FEATURE	RIBBON TAB, GROUP	BUTTON, OPTION	KEYBOARD SHORTCUT
Numbering	Home, Paragraph		
Bullets	Home, Paragraph		
Multilevel List	Home, Paragraph		
Define New Number Format dialog box	Home, Paragraph	, Define New Number Format	
Define New Bullet dialog box	Home, Paragraph	, Define New Bullet	
Define new Multilevel list dialog box	Home, Paragraph	, Define New Multilevel List	
Symbol dialog box	Insert, Symbols	Symbol, More Symbols	
Copyright symbol ©			Alt + Ctrl + C
Trademark symbol ™			Alt + Ctrl + T
Registered symbol ®			Alt + Ctrl + R
Nonbreaking hyphen			Ctrl + Shift + -
Em-dash			Alt + Ctrl + - (on numeric keypad)
En-dash			Ctrl + - (on numeric keypad)
Nonbreaking space			Ctrl + Shift + spacebar
Find and Replace dialog box with Find tab selected	Home, Editing	Find	Ctrl + F
Find and Replace dialog box with Replace tab selected	Home, Editing	Replace	Ctrl + H

Reviewing key points

Completion: In the space provided at the right, indicate the correct term, symbol, or command.

1. The Numbering button is located in this group in the Home tab. ____________
2. Define your own numbering format with options at this dialog box. ____________
3. A bullet that you define at the Define New Bullet dialog box is automatically included in this section in the Bullets button drop-down gallery. ____________
4. Click this button to number paragraphs of text at the left margin, first tab, second tab, and so on. ____________
5. As you type a multilevel list, press these keys to move to the previous level. ____________
6. Type this sequence of characters on the keyboard to insert a copyright symbol. ____________
7. This is the keyboard shortcut to insert the ® symbol. ____________
8. Use this type of hyphen in a sentence to indicate a break in a thought or a shift in tone. ____________
9. Use this type of hyphen to indicate inclusive dates, times, and numbers. ____________
10. This is the keyboard shortcut for inserting a nonbreaking space. ____________
11. Click this button in the expanded Find and Replace dialog box to display a list of special characters. ____________

Applying your skills

Assessment 1 Insert Custom Bullets and Numbering in a Technology Document

1. Open **Document26.docx** and save the document with the name **C18A01**.
2. Apply the following formatting to the document.
   a. Apply the Heading 1 style to the title *ELECTRONIC TECHNOLOGY*.
   b. Apply the Heading 2 style to the headings *Technology Information Questions*, *Technology Timeline: Storage Devices and Media*, *Information Systems and Commerce* (located on page 2), and *Internet* (located on page 3).
   c. Change the style set to *Formal*.
   d. Change the theme to *Paper* and the theme color to *Flow*.
3. Select the questions below the *TECHNOLOGY INFORMATION QUESTIONS* heading and then insert check mark (✔) bullets.
4. Create a computer disk symbol bullet in 14-point font size and then apply the symbol bullet to the six paragraphs of text below the *TECHNOLOGY TIMELINE: STORAGE DEVICES AND MEDIA* heading. (You can find the disk symbol in the Wingdings font [thirteenth image from the left in the second row].)
5. Select the paragraphs of text below the heading *INFORMATION SYSTEMS AND COMMERCE*, click the Multilevel List button, and then click the middle option in the top row of the *List Library* section.
6. Select the paragraphs of text below the heading *INTERNET* and then apply the same multilevel list numbering.
7. Save and then print **C18A01.docx**.
8. Select the paragraphs of text below the heading *INFORMATION SYSTEMS AND COMMERCE* and then define a new multilevel list with the following specifications:
   a. Level 1 that inserts Arabic numbers (1, 2, 3) followed by a period and is aligned at 0 inch and indented at 0.25 inch.
   b. Level 2 that inserts capital letters (A, B, C) followed by a period and is aligned at 0.25 inch and indented at 0.5 inch.
   c. Level 3 that inserts Arabic numbers (1, 2, 3) followed by a right parenthesis and is aligned at 0.5 inch and indented at 0.75 inch.
   d. Make sure the new multilevel list numbering is applied to the selected paragraphs.
9. Select the paragraphs of text below the heading *INTERNET* and then apply the new multilevel list numbering.
10. Save, print, and then close **C18A01.docx**.

Assessment 2 Type a Corporate Report Document with Special Characters

1. At a blank document, type the text shown in Figure 18.11. Insert nonbreaking hyphens in the corporate name (Perez-Lin-Hyatt), insert en-dashes in the money amount ($20–25 million) and the meeting times (in the *Department Meetings* section), insert em-dashes around *an important indicator of current demand*, insert the ™ and © symbols correctly, and insert nonbreaking spaces within keyboard shortcuts.
2. Save the document with the name **C18A02**.
3. Print and then close **C18A02.docx**.

Figure 18.11 Assessment 2

Corporate Report

During 2009, Perez-Lin-Hyatt Industrial invested $28 million on capital expenditures and an additional $20–25 million on research and engineering. All major projects undergo a rigorous financial analysis to ensure they meet all investment return objectives. Employees completed two major projects at Perez-Lin-Hyatt including expansion of Asian and northern Europe markets. Major effort at Perez-Lin-Hyatt centered on development of product line extensions of our Tubular™ and ReedBit™ drill technology. The outlook for 2010 is encouraging. The backlog for our products—an important indicator of current demand—grew to a record $265 million at year-end 2009.

Perez-Lin-Hyatt Industrial Corporate Report©

Department Meetings

Finance: Tuesday, 9:30–11:00 a.m.

Purchasing: Wednesday, 3:00–4:30 p.m.

Training: Thursday, 8:30–9:30 a.m.

Keyboard Shortcuts

Word includes keyboard shortcuts you can use for creating, viewing, and saving documents. Press Ctrl + N to display a new blank document or press Ctrl + O to open a document. Use the shortcut Ctrl + W to close the currently open document. Additional keyboard shortcuts include pressing Alt + Ctrl + S to split the document window and pressing Alt + Shift + C to remove the document window split.

Chapter 19

Managing Page Numbers, Headers, and Footers

Tutorial 19.1
Creating Readable Documents

Performance Objectives

Upon successful completion of Chapter 19, you will be able to:

- Insert, format, and remove page numbers
- Insert, format, edit, and remove headers and footers
- Control widows and orphans and keep text together on a page
- Print sections of a document

As you learned earlier, Word provides predesigned page numbers, headers, and footers you can insert in a document. You can customize page numbers with options at the Page Number Format dialog box, and you can create and edit your own headers and footers with options in the Header & Footer Tools Design tab. In this chapter you will learn how to customize page numbers, create and customize headers and footers, control text flow on pages, and print sections of a document.

QUICK STEPS

Insert Page Numbers
1. Click Insert tab.
2. Click Page Number button.
3. Point to desired position.
4. Click desired predesigned page number option.

Remove Page Numbers
1. Click Insert tab.
2. Click Page Number button.
3. Click *Remove Page Numbers* at drop-down list.

Note: Before beginning computer exercises for this chapter, copy to your storage medium the Chapter19 folder from the CD that accompanies this textbook and then make Chapter19 the active folder.

Customizing Page Numbers

In Chapter 7, you learned to use the Page Number button in the Header & Footer group in the Insert tab to insert page numbers in a document. You inserted the numbers by clicking the Page Number button, pointing to the desired position on the page at the drop-down list, and then clicking a predesigned page number option. You removed page numbering from a document by clicking the Page Number button and then clicking the *Remove Page Numbers* option at the drop-down list.

When you insert page numbers, Word inserts Arabic numbers (1, 2, 3, and so on) by default and numbers pages sequentially beginning with number 1. You can customize these default settings with options at the Page Number Format dialog box, shown in Figure 19.1. To display this dialog box, click the Insert tab, click the Page Number button in the Header & Footer group, and then click *Format Page Numbers* at the drop-down list.

Figure 19.1 Page Number Format Dialog Box

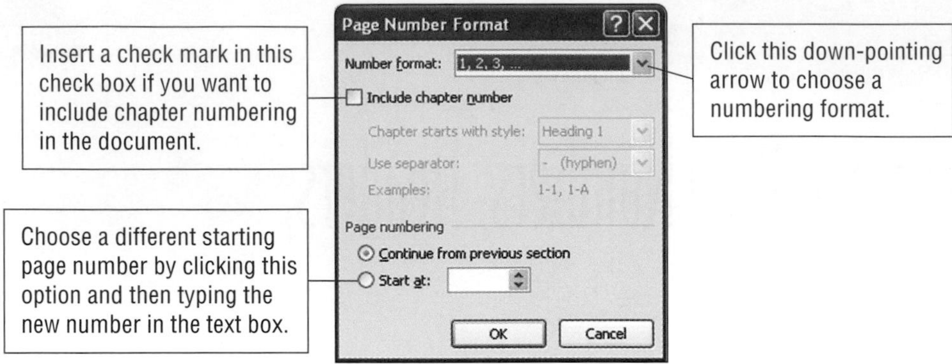

Click the *Number format* option in the Page Number Format dialog box to change numbering from Arabic numbers to one of the following options: Arabic numbers preceded and followed by hyphens (- 1 -, - 2 -, - 3 -, and so on), lowercase letters (a, b, c, and so on), uppercase letters (A, B, C, and so on), lowercase Roman numerals (i, ii, iii, and so on), or uppercase Roman numerals (I, II, III, and so on).

By default, page numbering begins with 1 and continues sequentially from 1 through all of the pages and sections in a document. You can change the beginning page number with the *Start at* option at the Page Number Format dialog box. To do this, click the *Start at* option and then type the desired beginning page number in the text box.

Exercise 1

Inserting Page Numbers

1. Open **Report03.docx** and save the document with the name **C19Ex01**.
2. Insert section breaks that begin new pages by completing the following steps:
   a. With the insertion point positioned at the beginning of the *SECTION 1: UNAUTHORIZED ACCESS* title, click the Page Layout tab.
   b. Click the Breaks button in the Page Setup group and then click *Next Page* in the *Section Breaks* section of the drop-down list.
   c. Move the insertion point to the beginning of the title *SECTION 2: INFORMATION THEFT*.
   d. Click the Breaks button in the Page Setup group and then click *Next Page* in the *Section Breaks* section of the drop-down list.

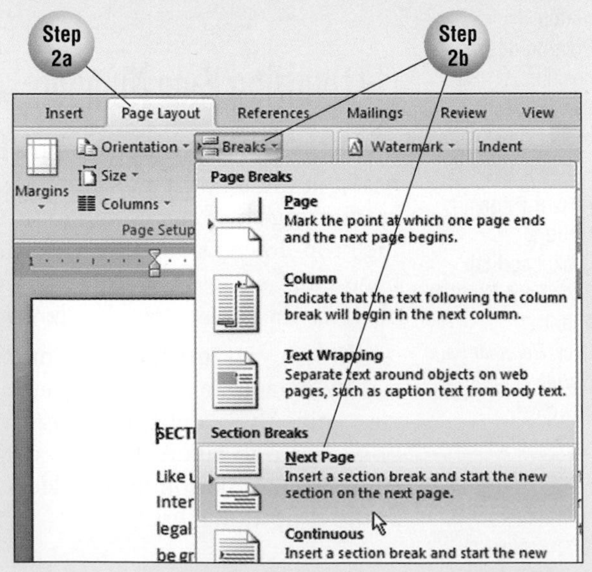

3. Insert a file by completing the following steps:
   a. Press Ctrl + Home to move the insertion point to the beginning of the document.
   b. Click the Insert tab.
   c. Click the Object button arrow and then click *Text from File* at the drop-down list.
   d. At the Insert File dialog box, navigate to the Chapter19 folder and then double-click **TableofContents.docx**.
4. Make the following changes to the document:
   a. Apply the Heading 1 style to the following titles:
      TABLE OF CONTENTS
      SECTION 1: UNAUTHORIZED ACCESS
      SECTION 2: INFORMATION THEFT
   b. Apply the Heading 2 style to the following headings:
      User IDs and Passwords
      System Backdoors
      Spoofing
      Spyware
      Wireless Device Security
      Data Browsing
   c. Change the style set to *Manuscript*.
5. Insert lowercase Roman numeral page numbering for the table of contents page by completing the following steps:
   a. Press Ctrl + Home.
   b. Click the Insert tab.
   c. Click the Page Number button in the Header & Footer group.
   d. Click *Format Page Numbers* at the drop-down list.
   e. At the Page Number Format dialog box, click the down-pointing arrow at the right side of the *Number format* option and then click *i, ii, iii, …* at the drop-down list.

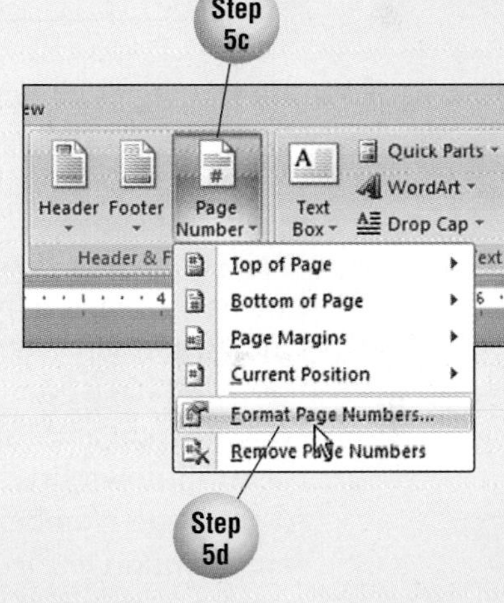

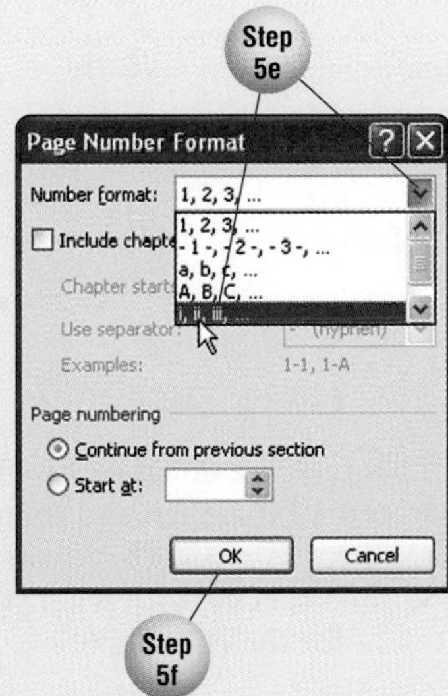

   f. Click OK to close the dialog box.

g. Click the Page Number button in the Header & Footer group, point to *Bottom of Page*, and then click the *Plain Number 2* option at the side menu.

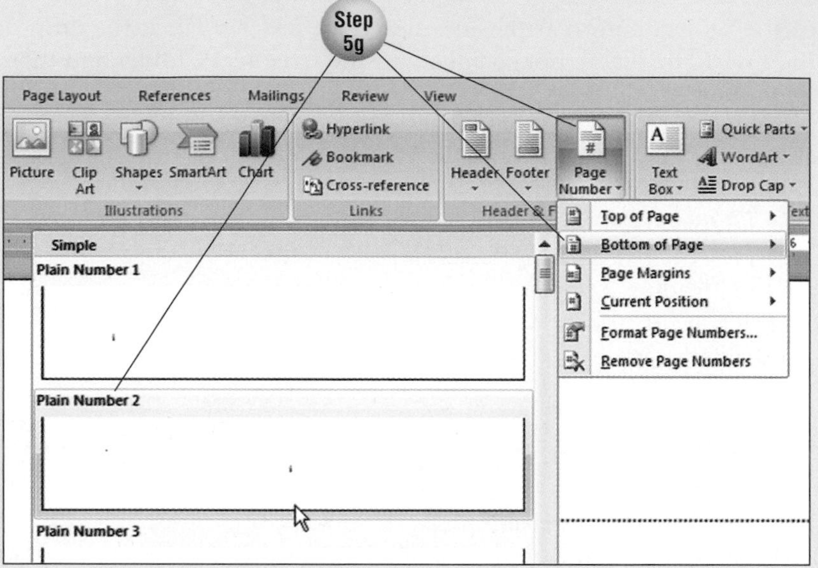

6. Start numbering beginning with 1 by completing the following steps:
   a. Double-click in the document to make the document active.
   b. Position the insertion point on any character in the title *SECTION 1: UNAUTHORIZED ACCESS*.
   c. Click the Insert tab.
   d. Click the Page Number button in the Header & Footer group and then click *Format Page Numbers* at the drop-down list.
   e. At the Page Number Format dialog box, click the *Start at* option in the *Page numbering* section. (This inserts a number 1 in the *Start at* text box.)
   f. Click OK to close the dialog box.
7. Save, print, and then close **C19Ex01.docx.**

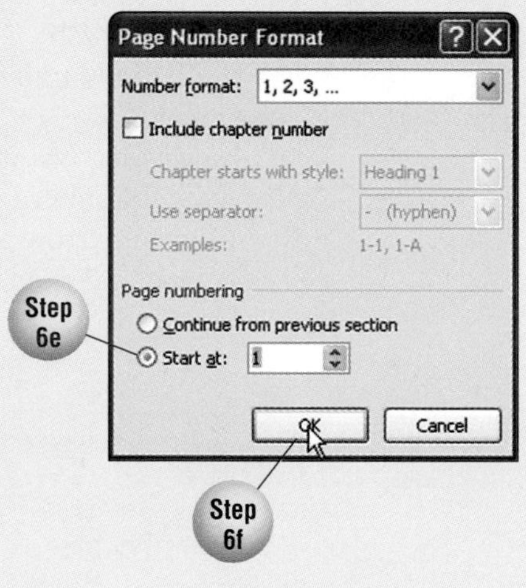

You can number chapters in a document with an option at the Multilevel List button drop-down list in the Home tab and then apply chapter numbering to the document. To do this, click the *Include chapter number* check box in the Page Number Format dialog box and then specify with what style the chapter starts and what separator you want to use for the page number.

Exercise 2

Inserting Chapter Numbering

1. Open **Report02.docx** and save the document with the name **C19Ex02**.
2. Press Ctrl + End to move the insertion point to the end of the document and then select and delete text from the beginning of the *REFERENCES* title to the end of the document.
3. Change the case of the first title by completing the following steps:
    a. Press Ctrl + Home to move the insertion point to the beginning of the document.
    b. Select the title *COMPUTERS IN COMMUNICATIONS*.
    c. Click the Change Case button in the Font group in the Home tab.
    d. Click the *Capitalize Each Word* option.
    e. Change the word *In* to *in*.

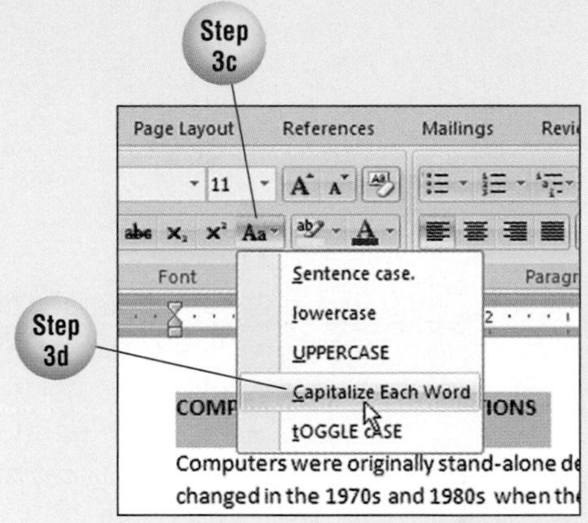

4. Complete steps similar to those in Step 3 to change the case of the other title in the document *COMPUTERS IN ENTERTAINMENT*.
5. Move the insertion point to the beginning of the title *Computers in Entertainment* and then insert a section break that begins a new page.
6. Apply the Heading 1 style to the two titles in the document and apply the Heading 2 style to the five headings in the document.
7. Change the style set to *Manuscript*.
8. Apply chapter multilevel list numbering by completing the following steps:
    a. Press Ctrl + Home to move the insertion point to the beginning of the document.
    b. If necessary, click the Home tab.
    c. Click the Multilevel List button in the Paragraph group.
    d. Click the last option in the *List Library* section of the drop-down gallery. (This inserts *Chapter 1* before the first title and *Chapter 2* before the second title.)

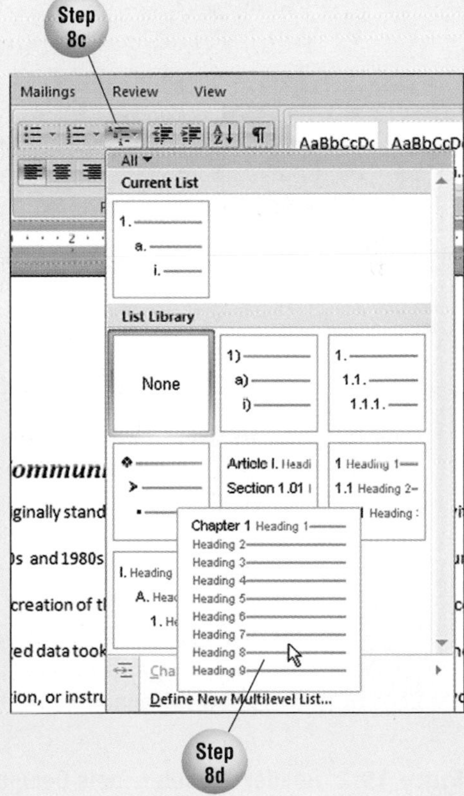

9. Insert chapter numbering in the document by completing the following steps:
    a. With the insertion point positioned at the beginning of the document, click the Insert tab.
    b. Click the Page Number button in the Header & Footer group and then click *Format Page Numbers* at the drop-down list.

c. At the Page Number Format dialog box, click the *Include chapter number* check box to insert a check mark.
d. Click OK.

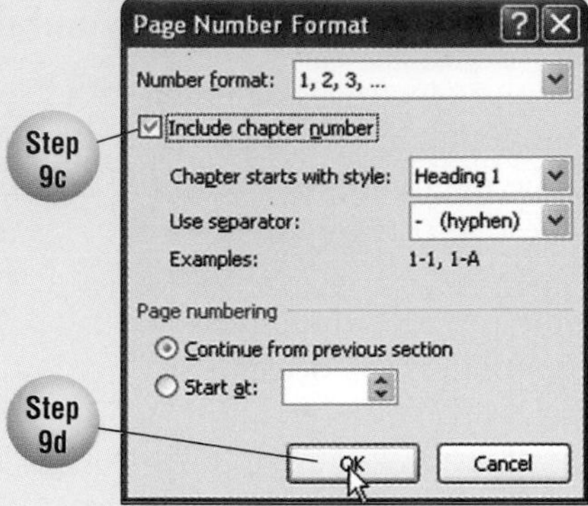

e. Click the Page Number button in the Header & Footer group, point to *Bottom of Page*, and then click the *Plain Number 2* option.
f. Double-click in the document.
g. Move the insertion point so it is positioned on any character in the second title *Chapter 2 Computers in Entertainment*.
h. Click the Insert tab.
i. Click the Page Number button in the Header & Footer group and then click *Format Page Numbers*.
j. At the Page Number Format dialog box, click the *Include chapter number* check box to insert a check mark.
k. Click OK to close the dialog box.

10. Scroll through the document and notice the chapter numbering. (The page number for the first page displays as *1-1* indicating page 1 of chapter 1. The numbering preceding the page number changes to 2 for the pages in the chapter 2 section.)
11. Save, print, and then close **C19Ex02.docx**.

Inserting Headers and Footers

In Chapter 7, you learned to insert predesigned headers with the Header button in the Insert tab and predesigned footers with the Footer button. If the predesigned headers and footers provided by Word do not meet your needs, you can create your own. To create a header, click the Insert tab, click the Header button in the Header & Footer group, and then click *Edit Header* at the drop-down list. This displays a Header pane in the document and also displays the Header & Footer Tools Design tab, shown in Figure 19.2. With options in this tab you can insert elements such as page numbers, pictures, and clip art; navigate to other headers or footers in the document; and position headers and footers on different pages in a document.

Figure 19.2 Header & Footer Tools Design Tab

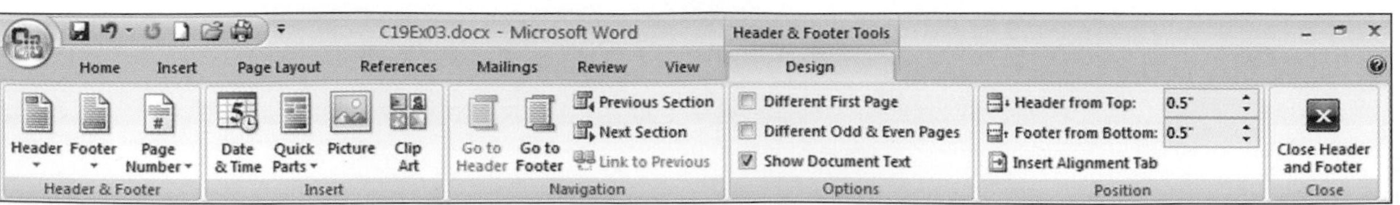

Inserting Elements in Headers and Footers

Use buttons in the Insert group in the Header & Footer Tools Design tab to insert elements into the header or footer such as the date and time, Quick Parts, pictures, and clip art images. Click the Date & Time button, and the Date and Time dialog box displays with options for inserting the current date as well as the current time. Click the Quick Parts button, and a drop-down list displays with options for inserting predesigned building blocks and fields. Click the Picture button, and the Insert Picture dialog box displays. At this dialog box, navigate to the desired folder and double-click the picture file. Click the Clip Art button, and the Clip Art task pane displays. At this task pane, you can search for and then insert an image into a header or footer.

Insert Element in Header
1. Click Insert tab.
2. Click Header button.
3. Click *Edit Header* at drop-down gallery.
4. Click desired elements.

Insert Element in Footer
1. Click Insert tab.
2. Click Footer button.
3. Click *Edit Footer* at drop-down gallery.
4. Click desired elements.

Date & Time

Picture

Clip Art

Exercise 3A

Inserting Elements in a Header and Footer

1. Open **EmployeeHandbook.docx** and save the document with the name **C19Ex03**.
2. Make the following changes to the document:
   a. Apply the Heading 1 style to the following titles:
      PROBATIONARY PERIODS
      EMPLOYEE PERFORMANCE
      COMPENSATION
   b. Apply the Heading 2 style to the following titles:
      Types of Appointments
      Work Performance Standards
      Performance Evaluation
      Employment Records
      Rate of Pay
      Direct Deposit Option
      Pay Progression
      Overtime
      Longevity Pay

Payment for Holidays
Shift Differential

c. Change the style set to *Formal*.
d. Change the left and right margins to 1.25 inches.

3. Insert a header by completing the following steps:
   a. Click the Insert tab.
   b. Click the Header button in the Header & Footer group.
   c. Click *Edit Header* at the drop-down list.
   d. With the insertion point positioned in the Header pane, click the Picture button in the Insert group in the Header & Footer Tools Design tab.

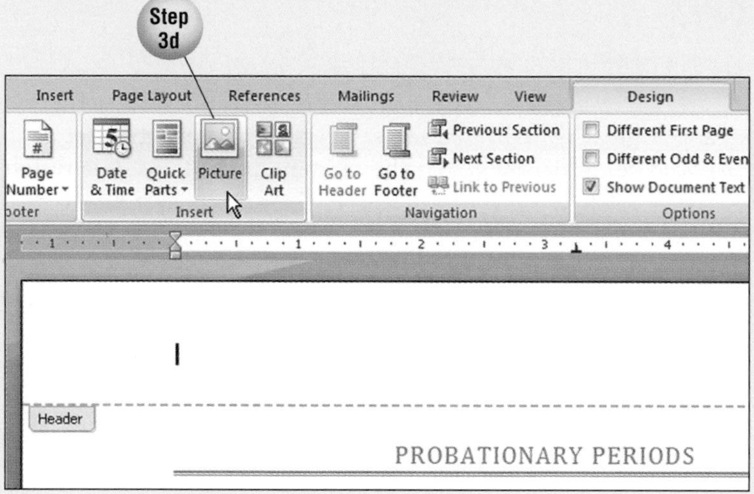

   e. At the Insert Picture dialog box, navigate to the Chapter19 folder on your storage medium and then double-click **WELogo.jpeg**.
   f. With the image selected, click in the Shape Height measurement box, type **0.6**, and then press Enter.
   g. Click the Text Wrapping button and then click *Tight* at the drop-down list.
   h. Drag the image up approximately one-third of an inch.
   i. Click to the right of the picture to deselect it.
   j. Press the Tab key. (This moves the insertion point to approximately the middle of the page.)
   k. Click the Header & Footer Tools Design tab.
   l. Click the Date & Time button in the Insert group.

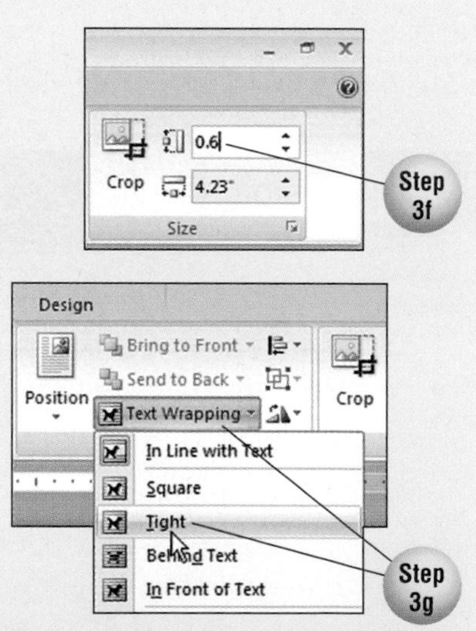

   m. At the Date and Time dialog box, click the twelfth option from the top (the option that displays the date in numbers and the time in hours and minutes) and then click OK to close the dialog box.
   n. Select the date and time text, click the Home tab, and then click the Bold button. Click the Font Size button arrow and then click *10* at the drop-down gallery.
   o. Double-click in the document to make the document active and dim the header.

4. Save **C19Ex03.docx**.

Navigating in Headers and Footers

If a document contains a header and footer or is divided into sections, use the buttons in the Navigation group in the Header & Footer Tools Design tab to navigate to various headers or footers. If a header pane is open, clicking the Go to Footer button will make active the footer on the same page. If a document is divided into sections, click the Previous Section or Next Section buttons to navigate between headers and footers.

Positioning a Header or Footer

Word inserts a header 0.5 inch from the top edge of the page and a footer 0.5 inch from the bottom of the page. You can change these default positions with buttons in the Position group in the Header & Footer Tools Design tab. Use the Header from Top and Footer from Bottom measurement boxes to adjust the position of the header or footer on the page.

By default, headers and footers contain two tab settings. A center tab is set at 3.25 inches, and a right tab is set at 6.5 inches. If the document contains default left and right margin settings of 1 inch, the center tab set at 3.25 inches is the center of the document, and the right tab set at 6.5 inches is at the right margin. If you make changes to the default margins, you may need to move the default tabs before inserting header or footer text at the center or right tabs. You can also set and position tabs with the Insert Alignment Tab button in the Position group. Click this button, and the Alignment Tab dialog box displays. Use options at this dialog box to change tab alignment and set tabs with leaders.

Exercise 3B

Positioning Headers and Footers

1. With **C19Ex03.docx** open, create a footer by completing the following steps:
   a. Click the Insert tab.
   b. Click the Footer button in the Header & Footer group and then click *Edit Footer* at the drop-down list.
   c. With the insertion point positioned in the footer pane, type your first and last names at the left margin.
   d. Press the Tab key. (This moves the insertion point to the center tab position.)

e. Click the Page Number button in the Header & Footer group, point to *Current Position*, and then click *Accent Bar 2* at the drop-down list.

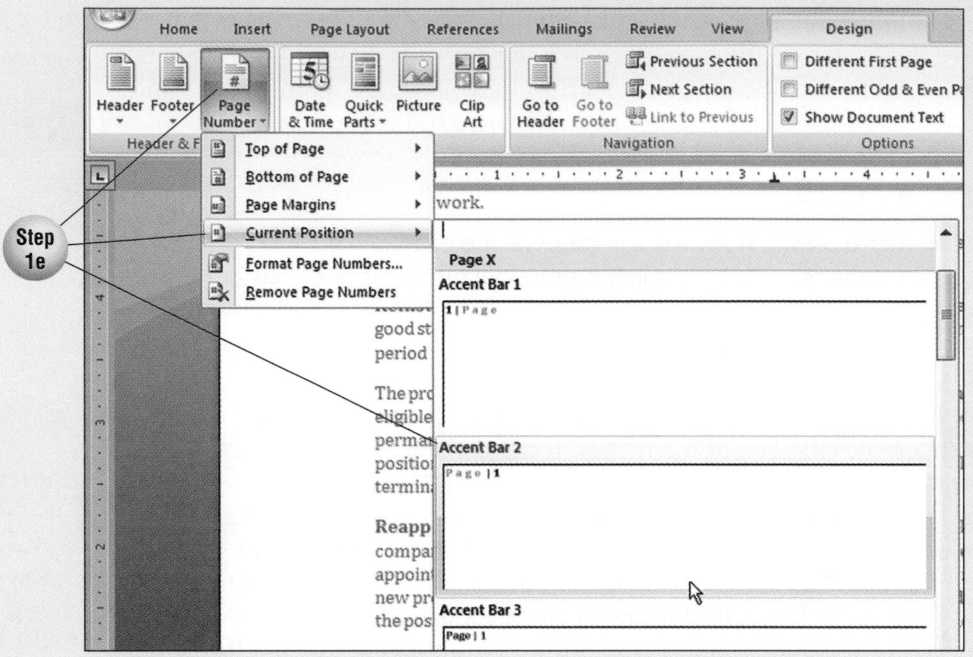

f. Press the Tab key and then type **C19Ex03.docx**.

g. Notice that the center tab and the right tab are off slightly because the left and right margins in the document are set at 1.25 inches instead of 1 inch. To correctly align the text, drag the Center tab marker to the 3-inch mark on the Ruler and drag the Right tab marker to the 6-inch mark on the Ruler. (If the Ruler is not visible, turn on its display by clicking the View Ruler button located at the top of the vertical scroll bar.)

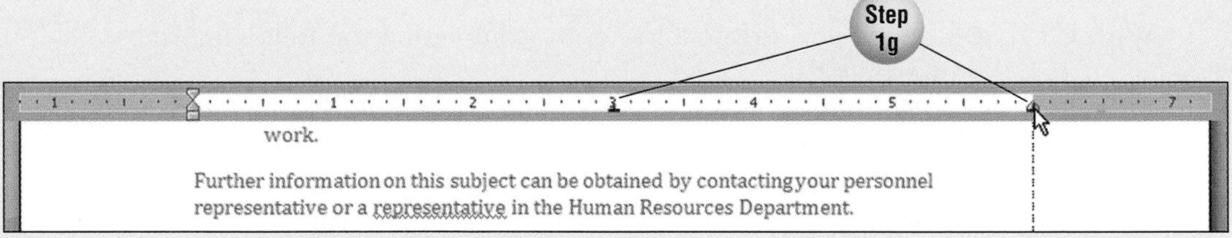

h. Select all of the footer text and then change the font to 10-point Cambria bold.

2. Edit the header by completing the following steps:
   a. Click the Header & Footer Tools Design tab.
   b. Click the Go to Header button in the Navigation group.
   c. Move the insertion point to the beginning of the date and then press the Tab key. (This right-aligns the text at the right margin.)
   d. Drag the Right tab marker to the 6-inch mark on the ruler.

Figure 20.3 Word Options Dialog Box with Popular Selected

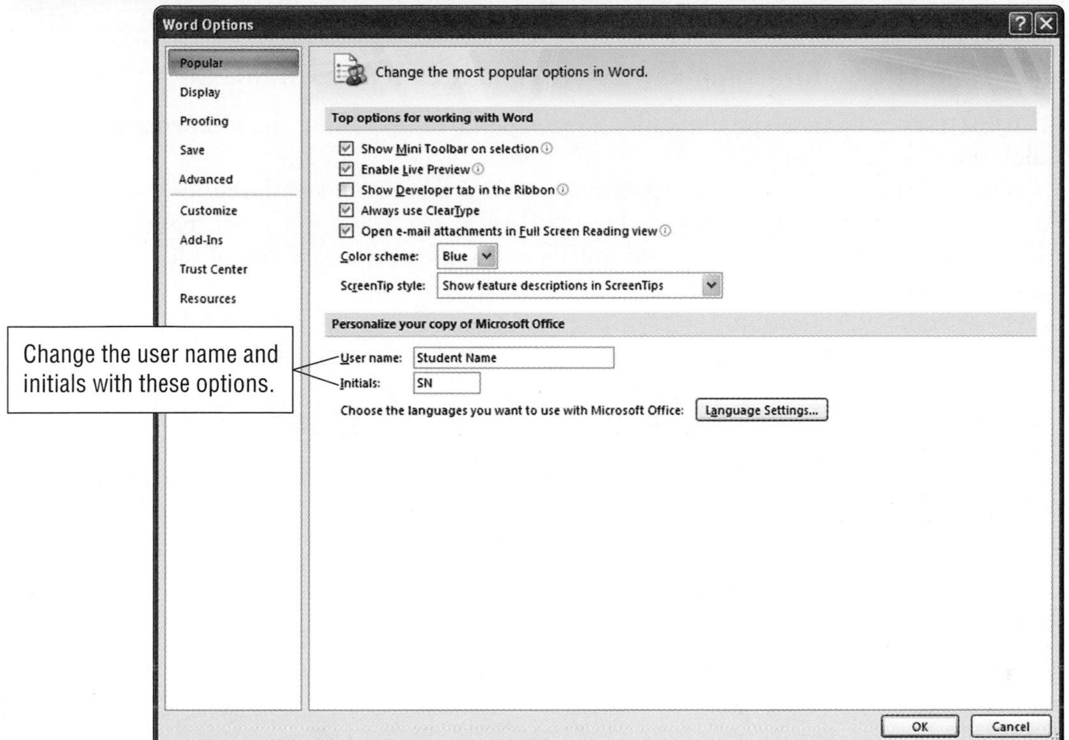

Printing Comments

You can print a document with the inserted comments or print just the comments. To print a document with the comments, display the Print dialog box, click the down-pointing arrow at the right side of the *Print what* option, and then click *Document showing markup* at the drop-down list. To print only comments, display the Print dialog box, click the down-pointing arrow at the right side of the *Print what* option, and then click *List of markup* at the drop-down list. This prints the contents of the Reviewing Pane, which may include tracked changes and changes to headers, footers, text boxes, footnotes, and endnotes, as well as comments.

Print Comments
1. Click Office button, *Print.*
2. Click down-pointing arrow at right of *Print what* option.
3. Click *Document showing markup* at drop-down list.
4. Click OK.

Delete a Comment
1. Click Review tab.
2. Click Next button until desired comment is selected.
3. Click Delete button.

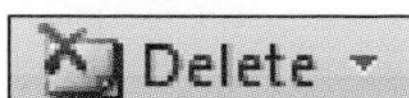

Deleting a Comment

You can delete a comment by clicking the Next button in the Comments group in the Review tab until the desired comment is selected and then clicking the Delete button. If you want to delete all comments in a document, click the Delete button arrow and then click *Delete All Comments in Document* at the drop-down list.

Exercise 1D

Changing User Information and Inserting and Deleting Comments

1. With **C20Ex01.docx** open, change the user information by completing the following steps:
   a. Click the Office button.
   b. Click the Word Options button that displays toward the bottom of the drop-down list.
   c. At the Word Options dialog box, make sure *Popular* is selected in the left panel.
   d. Make a note of the current name and initials in the *Personalize your copy of Microsoft Office* section.
   e. Select the name displayed in the *User name* text box and then type **Rene Johnson**.
   f. Select the initials displayed in the *Initials* text box and then type **RJ**.

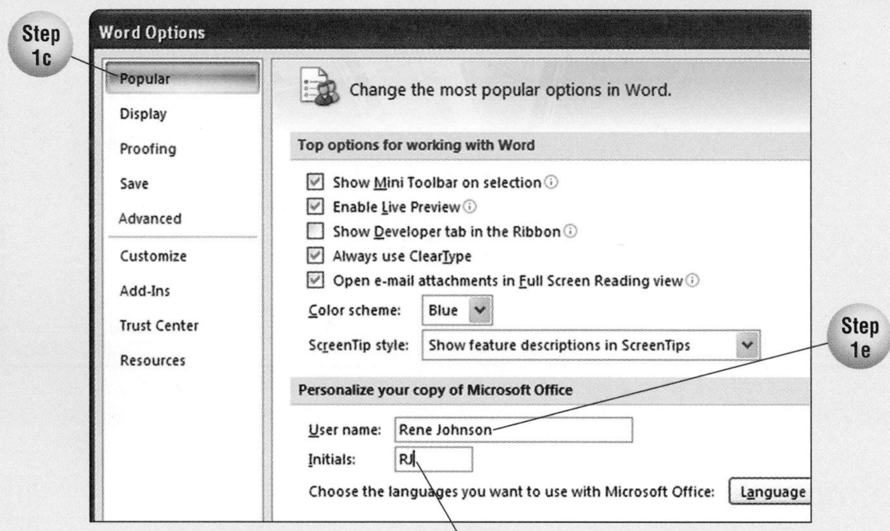

   g. Click OK to close the Word Options dialog box.
2. Insert a comment by completing the following steps:
   a. Move the insertion point to the end of the first paragraph of text in the *HOME ENTERTAINMENT* section.
   b. Press the spacebar once and then type **Examples?**.
   c. Make sure the Review tab is active and then select *Examples?*.
   d. Click the New Comment button in the Comments group.
   e. Type **Provide pictures of gaming systems.** in the Reviewing Pane.
   f. Click the Reviewing Pane button to close the pane.

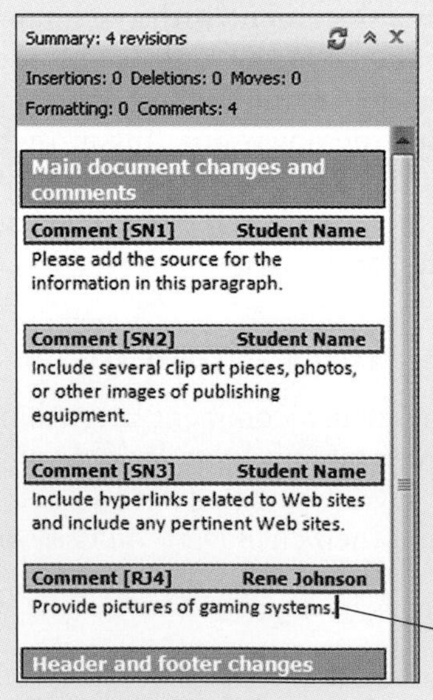

3. Print only the information in the Reviewing Pane by completing the following steps:
   a. Press Ctrl + P to display the Print dialog box.
   b. At the Print dialog box, click the down-pointing arrow at the right side of the *Print what* option and then click *List of markup* at the drop-down list.
   c. Click OK.

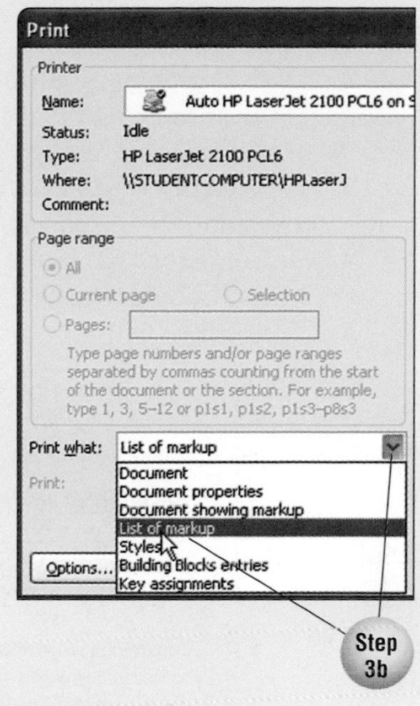

4. Delete a comment by completing the following steps:
   a. Press Ctrl + Home.
   b. If necessary, click the Review tab.
   c. Click the Next button in the Comments group.
   d. Click the Next button again.
   e. Click the Delete button in the Comments group.
5. Print only the information in the Reviewing Pane by completing Step 3.
6. Close the Reviewing Pane.
7. Change the user information back to the default by completing the following steps:
   a. Click the Office button and then click the Word Options button at the bottom of the drop-down list.
   b. At the Word Options dialog box with *Popular* selected, select *Rene Johnson* in the *User name* text box and then type the original name.
   c. Select the initials *RJ* in the *Initials* text box and then type the original initials.
   d. Click OK to close the dialog box.
8. Save and then close **C20Ex01.docx**.

Tracking Changes to a Document

Turn on Tracking
1. Click Review tab.
2. Click the Track Changes button.

OR

Press Ctrl + Shift + E.

If more than one person in a work group needs to review and edit a document, consider using Word's Track Changes feature. When Track Changes is turned on, Word tracks each deletion, insertion, or formatting change made to a document. For example, when you delete text, it is not removed from the document. Instead, it displays in a different color with a line through it. Word uses a different color (up to eight) for each person who makes changes to the document. In this way, anyone looking at the document can identify which user made which changes.

Turn on tracking by clicking the Review tab and then clicking the Track Changes button in the Tracking group. You can also turn on tracking by pressing Ctrl + Shift + E. Turn off tracking by completing the same steps. By default, Word displays changes such as deletions and insertions in the document. Word displays formatting changes, such as a change of font or font size, in the text and also by inserting a vertical line at the left margin to indicate where a formatting change has been made.

You can specify what tracking information displays in a document with options at the Balloons button drop-down list. To show all revisions in balloons at the right margin, click the *Show Revisions in Balloons* option at the Balloons button drop-down list. Click the *Show Only Comments and Formatting in Balloons* option at the drop-down list, and insertions and deletions display in the text while comments and formatting changes display in balloons at the right margin.

Exercise 2A

Tracking Changes in a Document

1. Open **Agreement03.docx** and save the document with the name **C20Ex02**.
2. Turn on tracking by clicking the Review tab and then clicking the Track Changes button in the Tracking group.
3. Type **BUILDING** between *THIS* and *AGREEMENT* in the first paragraph of text. (The text you type displays in the document underlined and in red.)
4. Delete *thirty* (30) in the second paragraph. (The deleted text displays in the document as strikethrough text.)
5. Type **sixty (60)**.

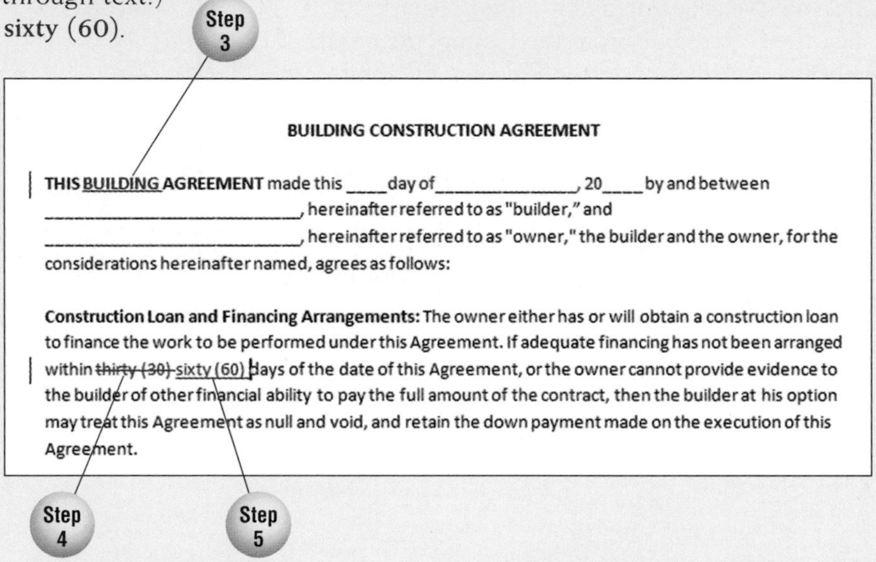

Step 3

BUILDING CONSTRUCTION AGREEMENT

THIS BUILDING AGREEMENT made this ____day of_______________, 20____by and between ____________________________, hereinafter referred to as "builder," and ____________________________, hereinafter referred to as "owner," the builder and the owner, for the considerations hereinafter named, agrees as follows:

Construction Loan and Financing Arrangements: The owner either has or will obtain a construction loan to finance the work to be performed under this Agreement. If adequate financing has not been arranged within ~~thirty (30)~~ sixty (60) days of the date of this Agreement, or the owner cannot provide evidence to the builder of other financial ability to pay the full amount of the contract, then the builder at his option may treat this Agreement as null and void, and retain the down payment made on the execution of this Agreement.

Step 4 Step 5

6. Move a paragraph of text by completing the following steps:
   a. Select the paragraph of text that begins with *Supervision of Work:* including the blank line below the paragraph.
   b. Press Ctrl + X to cut the text. (The text stays in the document and displays in red with strikethrough characters.)
   c. Position the insertion point at the beginning of the word *Start* (in the paragraph that begins *Start of Construction and Completion:*).
   d. Press Ctrl + V to insert the cut text. (This inserts the text in green with a double underline in the new location and also changes the text in the original location to green with double-strikethrough characters.)
7. Turn off tracking by clicking the Track Changes button in the Tracking group.
8. Display revisions in balloons by clicking the Balloons button in the Tracking group and then clicking *Show Revisions in Balloons* at the drop-down list.
9. After looking at the revisions in balloons, click the Balloons button and then click *Show All Revisions Inline* at the drop-down list.
10. Save **C20Ex02.docx**.

You can display information about tracked changes by positioning the mouse pointer on a change. After approximately one second, a box displays above the change listing the author of the change, the date, time, and type of change (for example, whether it was a deletion or insertion). You can also display information on tracked changes by displaying the Reviewing Pane. Each change is listed separately in the pane. Use the arrow keys at the right side to scroll through the pane and view each change.

Change User Information

1. Click Review tab.
2. Click the Track Changes button arrow.
3. Click *Change User Name* at drop-down list.
4. Type desired name in *User name* text box.
5. Type desired initials in *Initials* text box.

Changing User Information

In the Distinguishing Comments from Other Users section earlier in this chapter, you learned how to change the user name and initials at the Word Options dialog box. You can also display the Word Options dialog box with *Popular* selected by clicking the Track Changes button arrow and then clicking *Change User Name* at the drop-down list.

Exercise 2B

Changing User Information and Tracking Changes

1. With **C20Ex02.docx** open, change the user information by completing the following steps:
   a. If necessary, click the Review tab.
   b. Click the Track Changes button arrow and then click *Change User Name*.

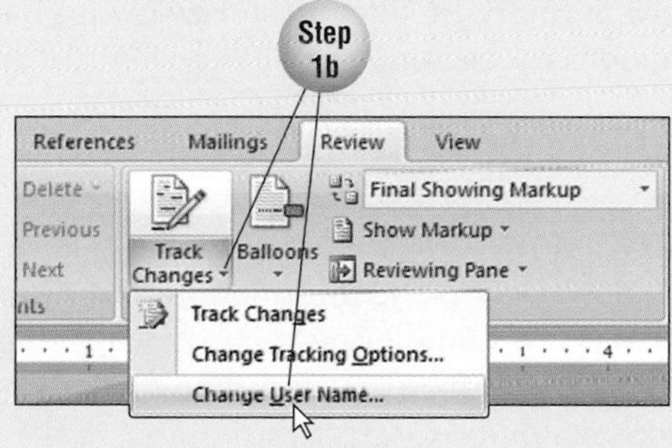

   c. At the Word Options dialog box with *Popular* selected, select the name in the *User name* text box and then type **Lorrie Carter**.
   d. Select the initials in the *Initials* text box and then type **LC**.
   e. Click OK to close the dialog box.
2. Make additional changes to the contract and track the changes by completing the following steps:
   a. Click the Track Changes button to turn on tracking.
   b. Select the title *BUILDING CONSTRUCTION AGREEMENT* and then change the font size to 14.

c. Delete the text *at his option* located in the second sentence in the second paragraph. (Your tracking color may vary from what you see below.)

d. Delete the text *and Completion* that displays in the beginning text in the fourth paragraph.

Construction Loan and Financing Arrangements: The owner either has or will obtain a construction loan to finance the work to be performed under this Agreement. If adequate financing has not been arranged within ~~thirty (30)~~ sixty (60) days of the date of this Agreement, or the owner cannot provide evidence to the builder of other financial ability to pay the full amount of the contract, then the builder ~~at his option~~ may treat this Agreement as null and void, and retain the down payment made on the execution of this Agreement.

Supervision of Work: Owner agrees that the direction and supervision of the working force, including subcontractors, rests exclusively with the builder, or his/her duly designated agent, and owner agrees not to issue any instructions to, or otherwise interfere with, same.

Start of Construction ~~and Completion~~: The builder shall commence construction of the residence as soon as practical after the signing of this Agreement and adequate financial arrangements satisfactory to the builder have been made.

Step
2d

e. Delete *thirty* (30) in the paragraph that begins *Builder's Right to Terminate the Contract:* (located on the second page).

f. Type **sixty (60)**.

g. Select the text *IN WITNESS WHEREOF* that displays toward the bottom of the document and then turn on bold.

3. Click the Review tab and then click the Track Changes button to turn off tracking.
4. Click the Reviewing Pane button to turn on the display of the pane and then use the up- and down-pointing arrow at the right side of the Reviewing Pane to review the changes.
5. View the changes in balloons by clicking the Balloons button and then clicking *Show Revisions in Balloons*.
6. Close the Reviewing Pane and then scroll through the document and view the changes in the balloons.
7. Click the Balloons button and then click *Show All Revisions Inline* at the drop-down list.
8. Change the user information back to the information that displayed before you typed *Lorrie Carter* and the initials *LC* by completing the following steps:
   a. Click the Track Changes button arrow and then click *Change User Name*.
   b. At the Word Options dialog box, select *Lorrie Carter* in the *User name* text box and then type the original name.
   c. Select the initials *LC* in the *Initials* text box and then type the original initials.
   d. Click OK to close the dialog box.
9. Print the document with the markups by completing the following steps:
   a. Press Ctrl + P to display the Print dialog box.
   b. At the Print dialog box, make sure the *Print what* option displays as *Document showing markup* and then click OK.
10. Save **C20Ex02.docx**.

Displaying for Review

By default, Word displays all tracked changes and comments in a document. You can change this default setting at the Display for Review button drop-down list. If you change the default setting *Final Showing Markup* to *Final*, the document displays with all changes incorporated in it. If you select *Original showing markup*, the original document displays with the changes tracked. Select *Original*, and the original document displays without any changes. These four options at the Display for Review button drop-down list allow you to view a document at various stages in the editing process.

Showing Markup

You can customize which tracked changes display in a document with options at the Show Markup button drop-down list. If you want to show only one particular type of tracked change, remove the check marks before all options except the desired one. For example, if you want to view only formatting changes and not other types of changes such as insertions and deletions, remove the check mark before each option except *Formatting*. If the changes of more than one reviewer have been tracked in a document, you can choose to view only the changes of a particular reviewer. To do this, click the Show Markup button, point to *Reviewer* at the bottom of the drop-down list, and then click the *All Reviewer* check box to remove the check mark. Click the Show Markup button, point to *Reviewers*, and then click the check box before the desired reviewer.

Exercise 2C

Changing the Display for Review and Showing Markup

1. With **C20Ex02.docx** open, change the display for review by completing the following steps:
   a. If necessary, click the Review tab.
   b. Click the Display for Review button and then click *Final*. (This displays the document with the changes included.)
   c. Click the Display for Review button and then click *Original*. (This displays the original document before any changes were made.)
   d. Click the Display for Review button and then click *Final Showing Markup*.

Step 1b

2. Display only those changes made by Lorrie Carter by completing the following steps:
   a. Click the Show Markup button in the Tracking group and then point to *Reviewers*.
   b. Click the *All Reviewers* check box to remove the check mark. (This also removes the drop-down list.)
   c. Click the Show Markup button, point to *Reviewers*, and then click *Lorrie Carter*.
   d. Scroll through the document and observe that only changes made by Lorrie Carter display in the document.
   e. Return the display to all reviewers by clicking the Show Markup button, pointing to *Reviewers*, and then clicking *All Reviewers*.

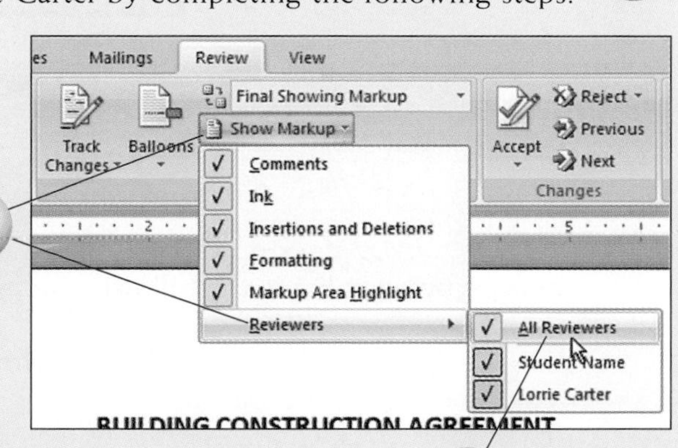

3. Save **C20Ex02.docx**.

Customizing Track Changes Options

Default settings determine how tracked changes display in a document. For example, inserted text displays in red type with an underline below the text, and deleted text displays in red type with strikethrough characters. Text that has been moved displays both in the original location in green type with double-strikethrough characters and in the new location in green type with a double underline below the text. You can customize these options and others at the Track Changes Options dialog box, shown in Figure 20.4. With options at this dialog box, you can customize the display of markup text, moved text, table cell highlighting, formatting, and balloons.

Figure 20.4 Track Changes Options Dialog Box

Change how markups display with options in this section.

Exercise 2D

Customizing Track Changes Options

1. With **C20Ex02.docx** open, customize track changes options by completing the following steps:
   a. If necessary, click the Review tab.
   b. Click the Track Changes button arrow and then click *Change Tracking Options*.
   c. At the Track Changes Options dialog box, click the down-pointing arrow at the right side of the *Insertions* option and then click *Double underline* at the drop-down list.

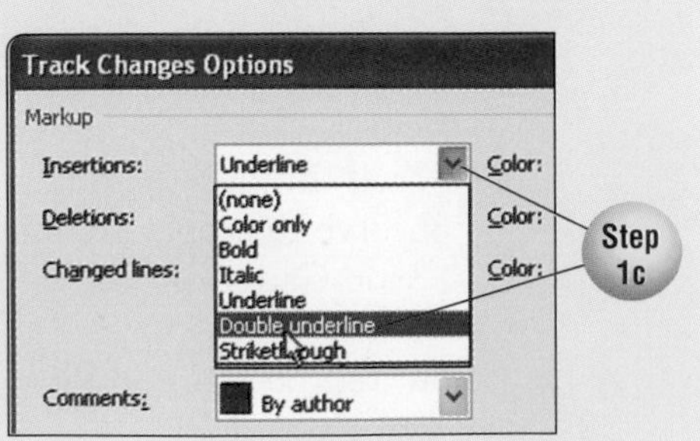

d. Click the down-pointing arrow at the right side of the *Insertions* color option box and then click *Green* at the drop-down list. (You will need to scroll down the list to display this color.)
e. Click the down-pointing arrow at the right side of the *Moved from* color option box and then click *Dark Blue* at the drop-down list.
f. Click the down-pointing arrow at the right side of the *Moved to* color option box and then click *Violet* at the drop-down list. (You will need to scroll down the list to display this color.)
g. Click OK to close the dialog box.

2. Save **C20Ex02.docx**.

Navigating to Revisions

Earlier in this chapter, you learned to use the Next and Previous buttons in the Comments group in the Review tab to navigate between comments inserted in a document. Similarly, you can use the Next and Previous buttons in the Changes group in the Review tab to navigate to revisions in a document. Click the Next button, and Word selects the next revision in the document. Click the Previous button to select the preceding revision. If you turn on Track Changes and then move text, revision balloons that contain a small Go button in the lower right corner display identifying the deleted (cut) text and the inserted (pasted) text. Click the Go button in either of the balloons to move the insertion point to the other balloon.

Accepting and Rejecting Revisions

You can accept or reject changes made to a document. Click the Accept button to accept the change and move to the next change. Click the Reject button to reject the change and move to the next. Click the Reject button arrow, and a drop-down list displays with options to reject the change and move to the next change, reject the change, reject all changes shown, or reject all changes in the document. Similar options are available at the Accept button arrow drop-down list.

Exercise 2E

Accepting and Rejecting Changes

1. With **C20Ex02.docx** open, display all tracked changes *except* formatting changes by completing the following steps:
   a. Click the Show Markup button and then click *Formatting* at the drop-down list.
   b. Scroll through the document and notice that the vertical line at the left side of the formatting locations has been removed.
   c. Click the Show Markup button and then click *Formatting* at the drop-down list. (This inserts a check mark in the check box.)

2. Navigate to tracked changes by completing the following steps:
    a. Press Ctrl + Home to move the insertion point to the beginning of the document.
    b. Click the Next button in the Changes group to select the first change.
    c. Click the Next button again to select the second change.
    d. Click the Previous button to select the first change.

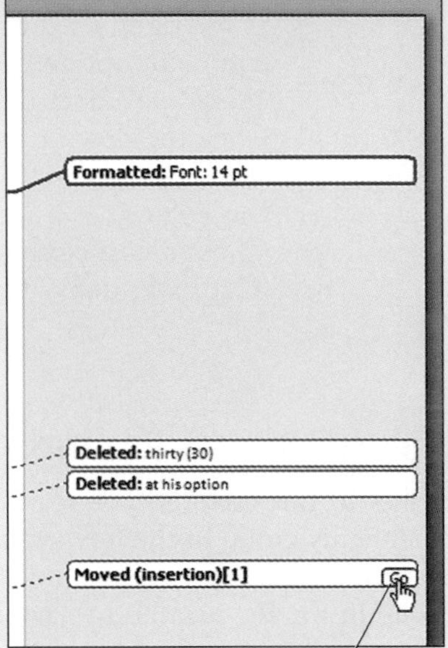

3. Navigate between the original location of the moved text and the new location by completing the following steps:
    a. Press Ctrl + Home to move the insertion point to the beginning of the document.
    b. Click the Balloons button and then click *Show Revisions in Balloons*.
    c. Scroll to the right to display the right edge of the balloons and then click the Go button that displays in the lower right corner of the Moved balloon. (This selects the text in the Moved up balloon.)
    d. Click the Go button in the lower right corner of the Moved up balloon. (This selects the text in the Moved balloon.)
    e. Click the Balloons button and then click *Show All Revisions Inline*.
4. Press Ctrl + Home to move the insertion point to the beginning of the document.
5. Display and then accept only formatting changes by completing the following steps:
    a. Click the Show Markup button in the Tracking group and then click *Comments* at the drop-down list. (This removes the check mark and the drop-down list.)
    b. Click the Show Markup button and then click *Ink*.
    c. Click the Show Markup button and then click *Insertions and Deletions*.
    d. Click the Show Markup button and then click *Markup Area Highlight* (Formatting is now the only option containing a check mark.)
    e. Click the Accept button arrow and then click *Accept All Changes Shown* at the drop-down list. (This accepts only the formatting changes in the document because those are the only changes showing.)
6. Display all changes by completing the following steps:
    a. Click the Show Markup button and then click *Comments* at the drop-down list.
    b. Click the Show Markup button and then click *Ink*.
    c. Click the Show Markup button and then click *Insertions and Deletions*.
    d. Click the Show Markup button and then click *Markup Area Highlight*.
7. Press Ctrl + Home to move the insertion point to the beginning of the document.
8. Reject the change inserting the word *BUILDING* by clicking the Next button in the Changes group and then clicking the Reject button. (This rejects the change and moves to the next revision in the document.)
9. Click the Accept button to accept the change deleting *thirty* (30).

10. Click the Accept button to accept the change inserting *sixty* (60).
11. Click the Reject button to reject the change deleting the words *at his option*.
12. Accept all remaining changes by clicking the Accept button arrow and then clicking *Accept All Changes in Document* at the drop-down list.
13. Return Track Changes options to the default settings by completing the following steps:
    a. If necessary, click the Review tab.
    b. Click the Track Changes button arrow and then click *Change Tracking Options*.
    c. At the Track Changes Options dialog box, click the down-pointing arrow at the right side of the *Insertions* option and then click *Underline* at the drop-down list.
    d. Click the down-pointing arrow at the right side of the *Insertions* color option box and then click *By author* at the drop-down list. (You will need to scroll up the list to display this color.)
    e. Click the down-pointing arrow at the right side of the *Moved from* color option box and then click *Green* at the drop-down list. (You may need to scroll down the list to display this color.)
    f. Click the down-pointing arrow at the right side of the *Moved to* color option box and then click *Green* at the drop-down list.
    g. Click OK to close the dialog box.
14. Check to make sure all tracked changes are accepted or rejected by completing the following steps:
    a. Click the Reviewing Pane button in the Tracking group.
    b. Check the summary information that displays at the top of the Reviewing Pane and make sure that a zero follows all of the options.
    c. Close the Reviewing Pane.
15. Save, print, and then close **C20Ex02.docx**.

Comparing Documents

Word contains a legal blackline option that you can use to compare two documents and display the differences as tracked changes in a third document. To use this option, click the Review tab, click the Compare button in the Compare group, and then click *Compare* at the drop-down list. This displays the Compare Documents dialog box, shown in Figure 20.5. At this dialog box, click the Browse for Original button. At the Open dialog box, navigate to the folder that contains the first of the two documents you want to compare and then double-click the document. Click the Browse for Revised button in the Compare Documents dialog box, navigate to the folder containing the second of the two documents you want to compare, and then double-click the document.

Figure 20.5 Compare Documents Dialog Box

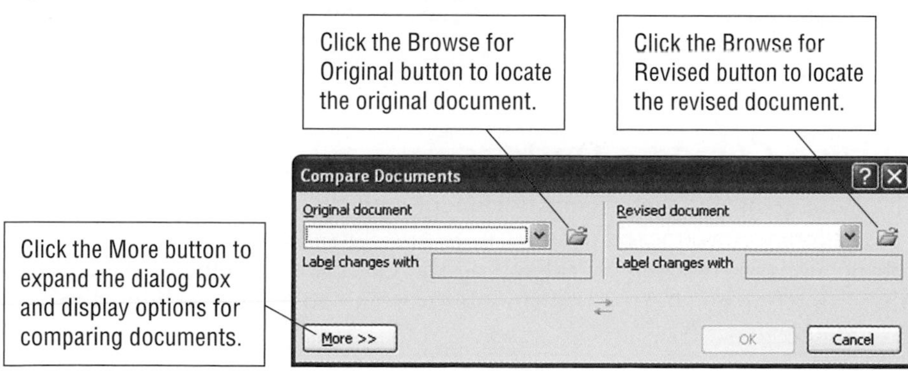

When you click OK at the Compare Documents dialog box, the compared document displays with the changes tracked. Other windows may also display depending on the option selected at the Show Source Documents button drop-down list. You may see just the compared document, or you may see the compared document plus the Reviewing Pane, original document, and/or revised document.

Exercise 3A

Comparing Documents

1. Close any open documents.
2. Click the Review tab.
3. Click the Compare button and then click *Compare* at the drop-down list.

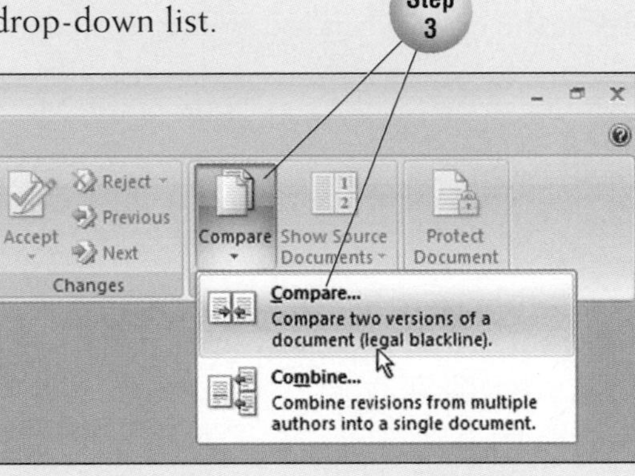

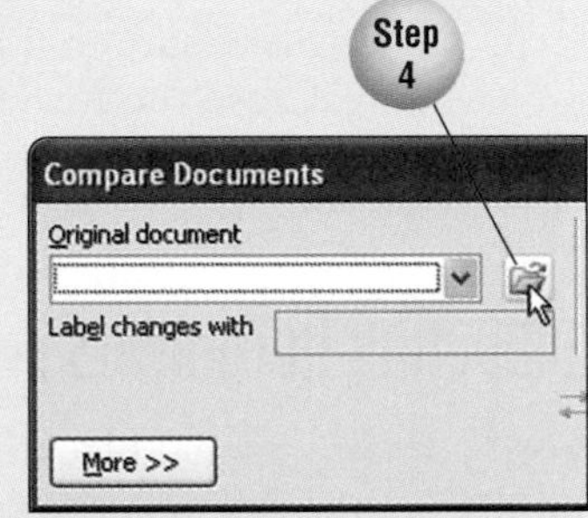

4. At the Compare Documents dialog box, click the Browse for Original button.
5. At the Open dialog box, navigate to the Chapter20 folder on your storage medium and then double-click **Lease02.docx**.
6. At the Compare Documents dialog box, click the Browse for Revised button.
7. At the Open dialog box, double-click **EditedLease02.docx**.
8. Click the OK button. (If the original and revised documents display along with the compared document, click the Show Source Documents button and then click *Hide Source Documents* at the drop-down list.)
9. With the compared document active, print the document showing markups.
10. Click the Office button and then click *Close*. At the message asking if you want to save changes, click the No button.

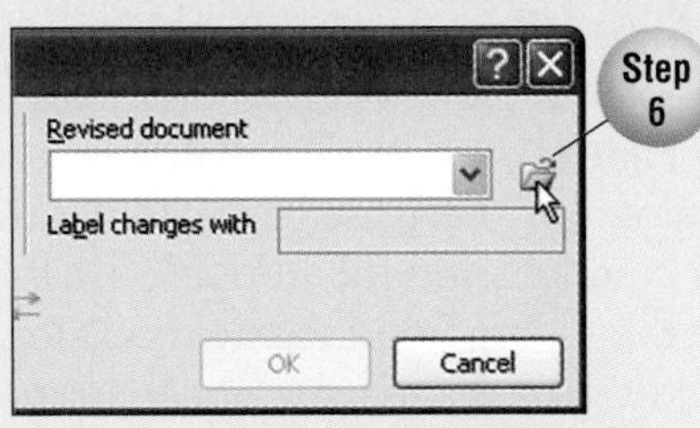

Customizing Compare Options

By default, Word compares the original document with the revised document and displays the differences as tracked changes in a third document. You can change this default setting along with others by expanding the Compare Documents dialog box. Expand the dialog box by clicking the More button, and additional options display, as shown in Figure 20.6.

Control the level of comparisons that Word makes between the original and revised documents with options in the *Comparison settings* section of the dialog box. The *Show changes at* option in the *Show changes* section of the dialog box has a default setting of *Word level*. At this setting, Word shows changes to whole words rather than individual characters within the word. For example, if you deleted the letters *ed* from the end of a word, Word would display the entire word as a change rather than just the *ed*. If you want to show changes by character, click the *Character level* option. By default, Word displays differences between compared documents in a new document. With options in the *Show changes* section, you can change this to *Original document* or *Revised document*. If you change options in the expanded Compare Documents dialog box, the selected options will be the defaults the next time you open the dialog box.

Figure 20.6 Expanded Compare Documents Dialog Box

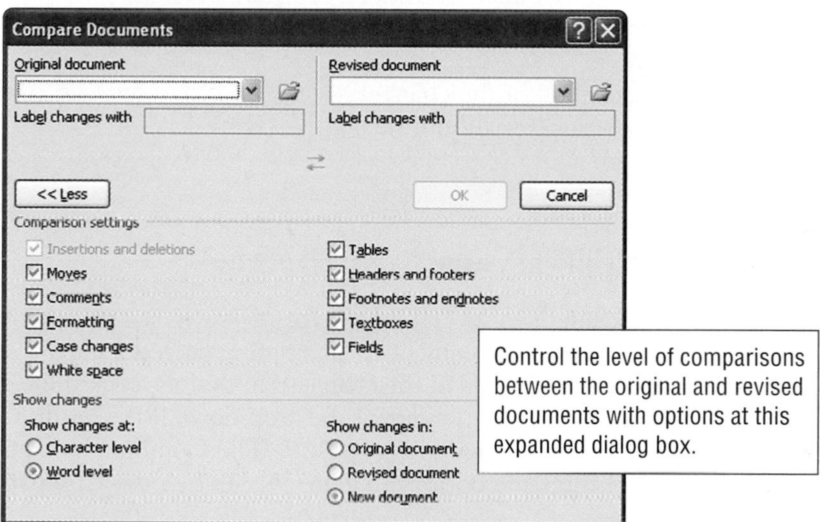

Exercise 3B

Customizing Compare Options and Comparing Documents

1. Close any open documents.
2. Click the Review tab.
3. Click the Compare button and then click *Compare* at the drop-down list.
4. At the Compare Documents dialog box, click the Browse for Original button.
5. At the Open dialog box, navigate to the Chapter20 folder on your storage medium and then double-click **Lease02.docx**.
6. At the Compare Documents dialog box, click the Browse for Revised button.
7. At the Open dialog box, double-click **EditedLease02.docx**.
8. At the Compare Documents dialog box, click the More button.
9. Click the *Moves* check box and then click the *Formatting* check box to remove the check marks.

10. Click the OK button.
11. Print the document showing markups.
12. Close the document without saving it.
13. Return the options to the default settings by completing the following steps:
    a. Close any open documents.
    b. Click the Review tab.
    c. Click the Compare button and then click *Compare* at the drop-down list.
    d. At the Compare Documents dialog box, click the Browse for Original button.
    e. At the Open dialog box, double-click **Lease02.docx**.
    f. At the Compare Documents dialog box, click the Browse for Revised button.
    g. At the Open dialog box, double-click **EditedLease02.docx**.
    h. At the Compare Documents dialog box, click the *Moves* check box to insert a check mark and then click the *Formatting* check box to insert a check mark.
    i. Click the Less button.
    j. Click the OK button.
14. At the new document, accept all of the changes.
15. Print and then close the document without saving the changes.

Combining Documents

If you send a document to several people for review, you can insert each person's changes into the original document by combining each document with the original until you have incorporated all of the changes. To do this, click the Compare button in the Review tab and then click *Combine* at the drop-down list. This displays the Combine Documents dialog box, shown in Figure 20.7. The Combine Documents dialog box contains many of the same options that are available in the Compare Documents dialog box.

Figure 20.7 Combine Documents Dialog Box

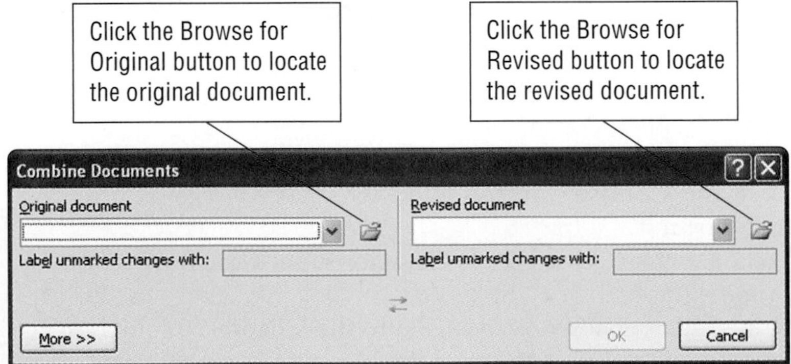

Click the Browse for Original button, navigate to the desired folder, and then double-click the original document. Click the Browse for Revised button, navigate to the desired folder, and then double-click one of the documents containing revisions. You can also click the down-pointing arrow at the right side of the *Original document* text box or the *Revised document* text box to display a drop-down list of the most recently selected documents.

Control how changes are combined with options in the expanded Combine Documents dialog box. By default, Word merges the changes in the revised document into the original document. You can change this default setting with options in the *Show changes in* section. You can choose to merge changes into the revised document or to merge changes into a new document.

Exercise 4A

Combining Documents

1. Close all open documents.
2. Click the Review tab.
3. Click the Compare button in the Compare group and then click *Combine* at the drop-down list.
4. At the Combine Documents dialog box, click the More button to expand the Combine Documents dialog box.
5. Click the *Original Document* option in the *Show changes in* section.
6. Click the Browse for Original button.
7. At the Open dialog box, navigate to the Chapter20 folder on your storage medium and then double-click **OriginalLease.docx**.
8. At the Combine Documents dialog box, click the Browse for Revised button.
9. At the Open dialog box, double-click **LeaseReviewer1.docx**.
10. Click the OK button.
11. At the message telling you that Word can only store one set of formatting changes in the final merged document, make sure *Your document (OriginalLease.docx)* is selected and then click the Continue with Merge button.
12. Save the document with Save As and name it **C20Ex04**.

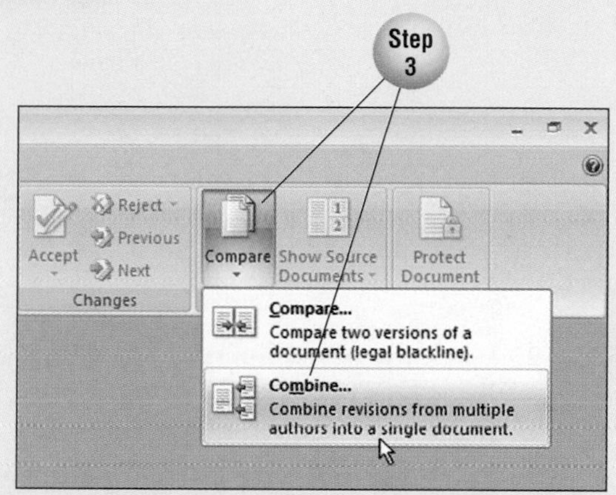

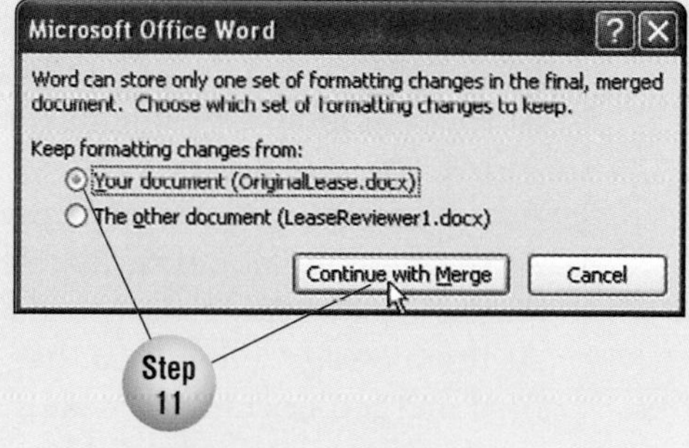

Showing Source Documents

With the Show Source Documents button in the Compare group in the Review tab, you can specify which source documents to display. Click this button to display a drop-down list with the options *Hide Source Documents*, *Show Original*, *Show Revised*, and *Show Both*. With the *Hide Source Documents* option selected, the original and revised documents do not display on the screen; only the combined document displays. If you choose the *Show Original* option, the original document displays in a side pane at the right side of the document. Synchronous scrolling is selected, so scrolling in one document results in scrolling in the other. Choose the *Show Revised* option, and the revised document displays in the panel at the right. Choose the *Show Both* option to display the original document in a panel at the right side of the screen and the revised document in a panel below the original document panel.

Exercise 4B

Combining and Showing Documents

1. With **C20Ex04.docx** open, click the Show Source Documents button in the Compare group, if necessary, and then click *Hide Source Documents*. (This displays the original document with the combined document changes shown as tracked changes.)

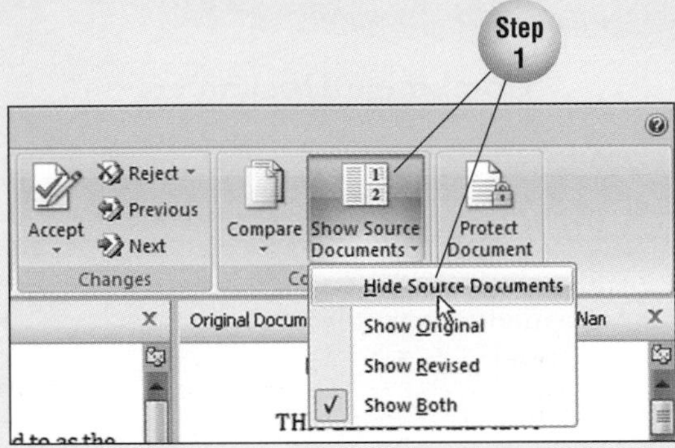

2. Click the Show Source Documents button and then click *Show Original* at the drop-down list. (This displays the original document at the right and the original document with tracked changes in the middle.)
3. Click the Show Source Documents button and then click *Show Revised*.
4. Click the Show Source Documents button and then click *Show Both*. Scroll in the original document and notice that the combined document and the revised document also scroll simultaneously.
5. Click the Show Source Documents button and then click *Hide Source Documents*.
6. Click the Review tab, click the Compare button, and then click *Combine* at the drop-down list.
7. At the Combine Documents dialog box, click the Browse for Original button.
8. At the Open dialog box, double-click **C20Ex04.docx**.
9. At the Combine Documents dialog box, click the Browse for Revised button.
10. At the Open dialog box, double-click **LeaseReviewer2.docx**.
11. At the Combine Documents dialog box, click the OK button.
12. At the message telling you that Word can only store one set of formatting changes in the final merged document, make sure *Your document (C20Ex04.docx)* is selected, and then click the Continue with Merge button.
13. Save **C20Ex04.docx**.
14. Print the document showing markups.
15. Accept all changes to the document.
16. Save, print, and then close **C20Ex04.docx**.

Chapter Summary

- Insert a comment in a document by clicking the New Comment button in the Comments group in the Review tab. When you click the New Comment button, a comment balloon displays at the right margin. If any previous settings have been applied, the Reviewing Pane, rather than a comment balloon, may display.
- Turn the display of the Reviewing Pane on and off with the Reviewing Pane button in the Tracking group in the Review tab.
- You can insert comments in the Reviewing Pane or in comment balloons. Insert a comment in a balloon by clicking the Balloons button in the Tracking group in the Review tab.
- Navigate through comments using the Previous and Next buttons in the Comments group in the Review tab.
- Edit a comment in the Reviewing Pane by displaying the pane and then making desired changes to the comment. Edit a comment in a comment balloon by turning on the display of balloons, clicking in the desired comment balloon, and then making desired changes.
- Display information about tracked changes, such as author's name, date, time, and the type of change, by positioning the mouse pointer on a change. After approximately one second, a box displays with the information. You can also display information on tracked changes by displaying the Reviewing Pane.
- If changes are made to a document by another person with different user information, the changes display in a different color. Change user name and initials at the Word Options dialog box with *Popular* selected.
- Print a document along with the inserted comments or choose to print just the comments and not the document.
- Delete a comment by clicking the Next button in the Comments group in the Review tab until the desired comment is selected and then clicking the Delete button in the Comments group.
- Use the Track Changes feature when more than one person is reviewing a document and making editing changes to it. Turn on tracking by clicking the Track Changes button in the Tracking group in the Review tab.
- Control how editing markings display in a document with the Display for Review button in the Tracking group in the Review tab. Control the marking changes that Word displays in a document with options at the Show Markup button drop-down list.
- Change Track Changes default settings with options at the Track Changes Options dialog box. Display this dialog box by clicking the Track Changes button arrow in the Tracking group and then clicking *Change Tracking Options* at the drop-down list.
- Move to the next change in a document by clicking the Next button in the Changes group in the Review tab or click the Previous button to move to the previous change.
- Use the Accept and Reject buttons in the Changes group in the Review tab to accept or reject revisions made in a document.
- Use the Compare button in the Compare group in the Review tab to compare two documents and display the differences between the documents as tracked changes.
- Customize options for comparing documents at the expanded Compare Documents dialog box. Click the More button to expand the dialog box.

- If you send a document to several people for review, you can combine changes made by each person with the original document until all changes are incorporated in the original document. Combine documents with options at the Combine Documents dialog box.
- Customize options for combining documents at the expanded Combine Documents dialog box. Click the More button to expand the dialog box.
- Specify which source documents to display by clicking the Show Source Documents button arrow in the Compare group in the Review tab and then clicking the desired option at the drop-down list.

Commands review

FEATURE	RIBBON TAB, GROUP	BUTTON, OPTION	KEYBOARD SHORTCUT
Comment	Review, Comments		
Reviewing Pane	Review, Tracking	Reviewing Pane	
Balloons	Review, Tracking		
Delete comment	Review, Comments	Delete	
Next comment	Review, Comments	Next	
Previous comment	Review, Comments	Previous	
Track changes	Review, Tracking		Ctrl + Shift + E
Display for review	Review, Tracking	Final Showing Markup	
Show markup	Review, Tracking	Show Markup	
Track Changes Options dialog box	Review, Tracking	, Change Tracking Options	
Next revision	Review, Changes	Next	
Previous revision	Review, Changes	Previous	
Accept changes	Review, Changes		
Reject changes	Review, Changes	Reject	
Compare Documents dialog box	Review, Compare	, Compare	
Combine Documents dialog box	Review, Compare	, Combine	
Show source documents	Review, Compare		

Reviewing key points

Completion: In the space provided at the right, indicate the correct term, command, or number.

1. Insert a comment into a document by clicking this button in the Comments group in the Review tab. ____________
2. Navigate to comments by using these two buttons in the Comments group in the Review tab. ____________
3. If a document contains comments, print only the comments by choosing this option at the Print dialog box *Print what* drop-down list. ____________
4. Display information on tracked changes in this pane. ____________
5. Change user information with options at this dialog box. ____________
6. Turn on the tracking feature by clicking the Track Changes button in this group in the Review tab. ____________
7. Change tracking default settings with options at this dialog box. ____________
8. This is the keyboard shortcut to turn on tracking. ____________
9. This is the default setting for the Display for Review button. ____________
10. With track changes on, moved text, by default, displays in this color. ____________
11. Customize tracking options at this dialog box. ____________
12. Click the *Combine* option at the Compare button drop-down list and this dialog box displays ____________
13. Specify which source document to display with options at this button's drop-down list. ____________

Applying your skills

Assessment 1 Insert Comments and Track Changes in a Computer Virus and Security Report

1. Open **Report06.docx** and save the document with the name **C20A01**.
2. Insert a comment at the end of the paragraph in the *TYPES OF VIRUSES* section. To do this, type the word **Update**, select it, and then create a comment with the following text: *Insert information on the latest virus.*
3. Insert a comment at the end of the last paragraph in the *METHODS OF VIRUS OPERATION* section. To do this, type the words **Company Example**, select the words, and then create a comment with the following text: *Include information on the latest virus to affect our company*.

4. Insert a comment at the end of the last paragraph in the document. To do this, type the word **Information**, select it, and then create a comment with the following text: *Include information about laws related to copying software.*
5. Turn on tracking and then make the following changes:
    a. Edit the first sentence in the document so it reads *The computer virus is one of the most familiar forms of risk to computer security.*
    b. Insert the word **computer's** between *the* and *motherboard* in the last sentence in the first paragraph of the document.
    c. Delete the word *real* in the second sentence of the *TYPES OF VIRUSES* section and then type **significant**.
    d. Select and then delete the last sentence in the *Methods of Virus Operation* section (the sentence that begins *A well-known example of a logic bomb was the . . .*).
    e. Turn off tracking.
6. Display the Word Options dialog box with *Popular* selected and then change the *User name* to **Stacey Phillips** and the *Initials* to **SP**.
7. Turn on tracking and then make the following changes:
    a. Delete the words *or cracker* located in the seventh sentence in the *TYPES OF VIRUSES* section.
    b. Delete the word *garner* in the first sentence in the CHAPTER 2: SECURITY RISKS section and then type **generate**.
    c. Select and then move the *EMPLOYEE THEFT* section below the *CRACKING SOFTWARE FOR COPYING* section.
    d. Turn off tracking.
8. Display the Word Options dialog box with *Popular* selected and then change the *User name* back to the original name and *Initials* back to the original initials.
9. Print the document showing markups.
10. Accept all of the changes in the document *except* the change moving the *EMPLOYEE THEFT* section below the *CRACKING SOFTWARE FOR COPYING* section.
11. Save, print, and then close the document.

Assessment 2 Compare Documents

1. Compare **Report09.docx** with **EditedReport09.docx** and insert the changes into a new document.
2. Save the compared document and name it **C20A02.docx**.
3. Print the list of markups only (not the document).
4. Reject the changes made to the bulleted text and the changes made to the last paragraph in the *DISASTER RECOVERY PLAN* section and accept all other changes.
5. Number the pages at the bottom center of each page.
6. Save, print, and then close the document.

Assessment 3 Combine Documents

1. Open **Legal01.docx** and save the document with the name **C20A03**.
2. Close **C20A03.docx**.
3. At a blank screen, combine **C20A03.docx** (the original document) with **Legal01Reviewer1.docx** (the revised document) into the original document.
4. Save **C20A03.docx**.
5. Combine **C20A03.docx** (the original document) with **Legal01Reviewer2.docx** (the revised document) into the original document.
6. Save **C20A03.docx**.
7. Print the list of markups only (not the document).
8. Accept all changes to the document.
9. Save, print, and then close the document.

Assessment 4 Change Tracking Options and Track Changes Made to a Table

1. Open **MBPSales.docx** and save the document with the name **C20A04**.
2. You can track changes made to a table and customize the Track Changes options for the table. Display the Track Changes Options dialog box and experiment with the options in the *Table Cell Highlighting* section and then make the following changes:
   a. Change the color for inserted cells to light purple.
   b. Change the color for deleted cells to light green.
3. Turn on Track Changes and then make the following changes:
   a. Insert a new row at the beginning of the table.
   b. Merge the cells in the new row.
   c. Type **Mobile Bay Products** in the merged cell.
   d. Delete the *Barclay, Kurt* row.
   e. Insert a new row below *Tanaka, Diana* and then type **Caswell, Martin** in the first cell, **$495,678** in the second cell, and **$475,850** in the third cell.
   f. Turn off tracking.
4. Save and then print the document with markups.
5. Accept all of the changes.
6. Display the Track Changes Options dialog box and then return the inserted cells color back to *Light Blue* and the deleted cells color back to *Pink*.
7. Save, print, and then close **C20A04.docx**.

Assessment 5 Insert Comments and Track Changes in a Travel Document

1. Open **FCTDocument.docx** and save the document with the name **C20A05**.
2. Display the Track Changes Options dialog box, change the *Use Balloons (Print and Web Layout)* option to *Always*, and then make the following changes:
   a. Change the balloon width to 2 inches.
   b. Display balloons at the left margin.
   c. Change the paper orientation to *Force Landscape*.
3. Insert the following comments:
   a. Type the text **Country names** at the end of the paragraph in the *African Study Adventure* section, select the text, and then insert the comment **Ask Jan if she wants to include specific country names.**
   b. Type the word **Examples** at the end of the paragraph in the *Custom Groups* section, select the word, and then insert the comment **Please provide custom program examples.**
4. Turn on tracking and then make the following changes:
   a. Insert the word *Travel* between *Comprehensive* and *Itineraries* in the *Comprehensive Itineraries* heading.
   b. Change the number 25 in the *Small Groups* section to 20.
   c. Delete the words *make sure* in the *Accommodations and Meals* section and then type **ensure**.
   d. Turn off tracking.
5. Save the document and then print the list of markups only (not the document).
6. Accept the changes.
7. Return the options at the Track Changes Option dialog box back to the default settings.
8. Save the document, print only the document, and then close the document.

Performance Assessments

UNIT 4

UNIT04

Managing Data

ASSESSING PROFICIENCIES

In this unit, you have learned to prepare customized letters, envelopes, labels, and directories and to sort text in paragraphs, columns, tables, and data source files. You learned how to select specific records from a data source file and merge the specific records with a main document. You also learned how to customize bullets, numbers, and lists; insert and customize headers and footers; insert comments; and track changes.

Note: Before beginning computer assessments, copy to your storage medium the Unit04PA folder from the CD that accompanies this textbook and then make Unit04PA the active folder.

Assessment 1 Use Mail Merge to Create Letters to Customers

1. Look at the information shown in Figure U4.1 and Figure U4.2.
2. Use the Mail Merge feature to prepare six letters using the information shown in the figures. (Before typing the letter, click the No Spacing style in the Styles group in the Home tab.)
3. Name the data source file **U04PA01DS**, name the main document **U04PA01MD**, and name the merged letters document **U04PA01Ltrs**.
4. Print and then close **U04PA01Ltrs.docx**.
5. Save and then close **U04PA01MD.docx**.

Figure U4.1 Assessment 1

Mr. Roy Heitzman
5043 Pleasant Street
Grand Rapids, MI 49518

Mr. and Mrs. Lawrence Nesbitt
11023 South 32nd Street
Kentwood, MI 49506

Ms. Julia Quintero
905 Randall Road
Kentwood, MI 49509

Mr. Darren Butler
23103 East Avenue
Grand Rapids, MI 49523

Ms. Lola Rose-Simmons
3312 South Meridian
Grand Rapids, MI 49510

Mr. Samuel McClelland
660 Grove Street
Grand Rapids, MI 49507

Figure U4.2 Assessment 1

September 15, 2010

«AddressBlock»

«GreetingLine»

Because you are a valued customer of Motorway Autos, we are offering you a free oil change with your next 15,000-, 36,000-, or 60,000-mile car service appointment. Mention the free offer the next time you schedule a service appointment and the oil change is on us!

For the entire month of October, we are offering fantastic deals on new 2011 models. If you buy a new car from us, we will offer you top trade-in dollars for your used car. Along with our low, low prices, we are also offering low-interest and, in some cases, no-interest loans. Come in and talk with one of our sales representatives to see if you qualify for these special loans.

Please come down to visit our showroom and check out the best-priced automobiles in the region. We are open for your convenience Monday through Friday from 8:00 a.m. to 8:00 p.m., Saturdays from 9:00 a.m. to 6:00 p.m., and Sundays from 9:00 a.m. to 5:00 p.m.

Sincerely,

Dusty Powell
Director of Sales

XX:U04PA01MD.docx

Assessment 2 Use Mail Merge to Create Envelopes

1. Use the Mail Merge feature to prepare envelopes for the letters you created in Assessment 1.
2. Specify **U04PA01DS.mdb** as the data source document.
3. Save the merged envelope document with the name **U04PA02Envs**.
4. Print and then close **U04PA02Envs.docx**. (Check with your instructor before printing.)
5. Close the envelope main document without saving it.

Assessment 3 Edit Data Source and Main Document and Merge Letters

1. Open **U04PA01MD.docx** (at the SQL message, click Yes) and then save the main document with the name **U04PA03MD**.
2. Edit the **U04PA01DS.mdb** data source file by making the following changes:
   a. Display the record for Mr. Darren Butler and then change the street address from *23103 East Avenue* to *715 South Fifth Street*.
   b. Add *and Mrs.* in the title for Mr. Samuel McClelland. (The title field should display as *Mr. and Mrs.*).
   c. Delete the record for Ms. Lola Rose-Simmons.
   d. Insert a new record with the following information:
      Ms. Glenda Jefferson
      5048 Burton Street
      Grand Rapids, MI 49503
3. At the main document, add the sentence shown in Figure U4.3 to the end of the third paragraph in the body of the letter and include fill-in fields as shown in parentheses in the figure.
4. Save **U04PA03MD.docx**.
5. Merge the records to a new document. At the dialog boxes asking for the number of automobiles and the percents, type the following:
   Record 1: Number = **two automobiles** Percent = **2%**
   Record 2: Number = **one automobile** Percent = **1%**
   Record 3: Number = **one automobile** Percent = **1%**
   Record 4: Number = **three automobiles** Percent = **3%**
   Record 5: Number = **two automobiles** Percent = **2%**
   Record 6: Number = **one automobile** Percent = **1%**
6. Save the merged document with the name **U04PA03Ltrs**.
7. Print and then close **U04PA03Ltrs.docx**.
8. Save and then close **U04PA03MD.mdb**.

Figure U4.3 Assessment 3

According to our records, you have purchased (Number) from us. This qualifies you for a special bonus of up to (Percent) off the purchase of a new automobile.

Assessment 4 Use Mail Merge to Create Labels

1. Use the Mail Merge feature to create mailing labels with the Avery US Letter 5360 label product. Use the existing data source **U04PA03DS.mdb** for the labels.
2. Display the Mail Merge Recipients dialog box, display the Filter and Sort dialog box with the Select Records tab selected, and then select only those customers living in Grand Rapids.
3. Complete the merge and then save the labels document with the name **U04PA04Lbls**.
4. Print and then close **U04PA04Lbls.docx**.
5. Close the labels main document without saving it.

Assessment 5 Sort Data in Columns and a Table

1. Open **Sort04.docx** and save the document with the name **U04PA05**.
2. Sort the columns of text below the *CONTACTS* title in ascending order by last name.
3. Sort the amounts in the *Home Equity Loans* column in the table in descending order.
4. Save, print, and then close **U04PA05.docx**.

Assessment 6 Create and Apply Custom Bullets and a Multilevel List

1. Open **MBPStockAwards.docx** and save the document with the name **U04PA06**.
2. Apply the Title style to the title *Mobile Bay Products*.
3. Apply the Heading 1 style to the headings *Stock Awards* and *Employee Stock Plan*.
4. Change the style set to *Traditional*.
5. Select the bulleted paragraphs of text and then define a new picture bullet of your choosing.
6. Select the lines of text below the *Employee Stock Plan* heading and then apply a multilevel list (the middle option in the top row of the *List Library* section of the Multilevel List button drop-down gallery).
7. With the text still selected, define a new multilevel list that inserts capital letters followed by a period (A., B., C.) for level 2 and inserts Arabic numbers followed by a period (1., 2., 3.) for level 3. (Make sure the new multilevel list applies to the selected text.)
8. Save, print, and then close **U04PA06.docx**.

Assessment 7 Keep Text Together and Insert Footers in a Report

1. Open **Report10.docx** and save the document with the name **U04PA07**.
2. Select the entire document and then change the line spacing to 2.0.
3. Change the top margin to 1.5 inches.
4. Apply the Heading 1 style to the two titles in the document *FUTURE OF COMPUTER ETHICS* and *REFERENCES*.
5. Apply the Heading 2 style to the five headings in the document.
6. Hang indent the paragraphs of text below the title *REFERENCES*.
7. Change the style set to *Modern*.
8. Change the theme to *Civic*.
9. Keep the heading *SELF-REPLICATING ROBOTS* together with the paragraph of text that follows it.
10. Keep the heading *REFERENCES* together with the paragraph of text that follows it.
11. Create an odd page footer that prints the document title at the left margin and the page number at the right margin and create an even page footer that prints the page number at the left margin and the document title at the right margin.
12. Save, print, and then close **U04PA07.docx**.

Assessment 8 Keep Text Together and Insert Footers in Different Sections in a Report

1. Open **Report11.docx** and save the document with the name **U04PA08**.
2. Change the left and right margins to 1.25 inches (the *Office 2003 Default*).

3. Insert a section break that begins a new page at the title *COMPUTER OUTPUT DEVICES*.
4. Apply the Title style to the two titles in the document *COMPUTER INPUT DEVICES* and *COMPUTER OUTPUT DEVICES*.
5. Apply the Heading 1 style to the six headings in the document.
6. Change the style set to *Formal*.
7. Keep the heading *MOUSE* together with the following paragraph.
8. Create a footer for the first section in the document that prints *Computer Input Devices* at the left margin, the page number in the middle, and your first and last names at the right margin. (Drag the footer center tab marker to 3 inches on the Ruler and drag the right tab marker to 6 inches.)
9. Edit the footer for the second section so it prints *Computer Output Devices* instead of *Computer Input Devices*.
10. Save, print, and then close **U04PA08.docx**.

Assessment 9 Insert Comments and Track Changes in a Report

1. Open **Report07.docx** and save the document with the name **U04PA09**.
2. Type the word **Source** at the end of the first paragraph in the report, select the word, and then insert the comment **Include the source where you found this definition.**
3. Type the word **Examples** at the end of the first paragraph in the *Online Shopping Venues* section, select the word, and then insert the comment **Include at least two of the most popular online shopping stores.**
4. Turn on tracking and then make the following changes:
   a. Delete the words *and most are eliminating paper tickets altogether* that display at the end of the last sentence in the second paragraph.
   b. Edit the heading *ADVANTAGES OF ONLINE SHOPPING* so it displays as *ONLINE SHOPPING ADVANTAGES*.
   c. Bold the first sentence of each of the bulleted paragraphs on the first page.
   d. Turn off tracking.
5. Display the Word Options dialog box with *Popular* selected and then change the *User name* to **Colleen Burton** and the *Initials* to **CB**.
6. Turn on tracking and then make the following changes:
   a. Delete the word *conveniences* in the first paragraph in the *ONLINE SHOPPING ADVANTAGES* section and then type **advantages**.
   b. Insert the following bulleted text between the third and fourth bulleted paragraphs on the second page: **Keep thorough records of all transactions.**
   c. Turn off tracking.
7. Display the Word Options dialog box with *Popular* selected and then change the *User name* back to the original name and *Initials* back to the original initials.
8. Accept all of the changes in the document *except* the change deleting the words *and most are eliminating paper tickets altogether*.
9. Save, print, and then close **U04PA09.docx**.

Assessment 10 Combine Documents

1. Open **Document27.docx** and save the document with the name **U04PA10**.
2. Close **U04PA10.docx**.
3. At a blank document, combine **U04PA10.docx** (the original document) with **Document27_SP.docx** (the revised document) into the original document.
4. Save **U04PA10.docx**.

5. Combine **U04PA10.docx** (the original document) with **Document27_CL.docx** (the revised document) into the original document.
6. Save **U04PA10.docx**.
7. Print the document showing markups.
8. Accept all changes to the document.
9. Make the following changes to the document:
   a. Change the style set to *Modern*.
   b. Apply the *Concourse* theme.
   c. Insert the Mod (Odd Page) footer.
   d. Insert the *SAMPLE 1* watermark in the document.
10. Save, print, and then close the document.

CREATING ORIGINAL DOCUMENTS

The activity in Assessment 11 gives you the opportunity to practice your writing skills as well as demonstrate your mastery of some of the important Word features presented in this unit. When you compose the document, use correct grammar, precise word choices, and clear sentence construction.

Assessment 11 Use Mail Merge to Create Letters to Volunteers

Situation: You are a volunteer coordinator for the Kentwood School District, and you have been asked to write a letter to the new reading volunteers listed below, thanking them for their interest in volunteering for the reading literacy program and inviting them to an orientation on Tuesday, September 28, 2010, from 7:00 to 8:30 p.m. In the letter, explain that during this orientation volunteers will learn more about the reading program, including the program goals, which students will be served by the program, what reading levels are included in the program, the time commitment required of volunteers, and the materials needed for the program. Use the Mail Merge feature to compose the main document letter and create a data source file with the names and addresses below. Save the data source file with the name **U04PA11DS.mdb** and the letter main document with the name **U04PA11MD.docx**. Merge the main document with the records in the data source file and name the merged document **U04PA11**. Print and then close the **U04PA11.docx** and then save and close the **U04PA11MD.docx**.

Ms. Karen Lyons
9023 South 42nd Street
Kentwood, MI 48933

Mr. Bryan Hamilton
11023 12th Northeast
Kentwood, MI 48920

Mr. Richard Ulrich
453 Silverdale Road
Kentwood, MI 48930

Mrs. Lindsay Childers
8931 133rd Place Northwest
Kentwood, MI 48933

Mr. Juan Nunez
8329 Branchwood Drive
Kentwood, MI 48933

Ms. Lisa Taua
1129 Military Road South
Kentwood, MI 48930

Unit 5

Customizing Documents and Features

- Inserting and Customizing Quick Parts
- Customizing AutoCorrect and Word Options
- Customizing Themes
- Formatting with Styles
- Protecting and Preparing Documents
- Unit 5 Performance Assessments

Signature Microsoft® Word 2007

Microsoft Certified Application Specialist Skills—Unit 5

Reference No.	Skill	Pages
1	**Creating and Customizing Documents**	
1.1	Create and format documents	
1.1.2	Apply Quick Styles to documents	612-613
1.1.3	Format documents using themes	593-612
1.1.4	Customize themes	593-607
1.3	Make documents and content easier to find	
1.3.3	Modify document properties	640-642
1.4	Personalize Word	
1.4.1	Customize Word options	569-586
2	**Formatting Content**	
2.1	Format text and paragraphs	
2.1.2	Create and modify styles	616-626
4	**Organizing Content**	
4.1	Structure content by using Quick Parts	
4.1.1	Insert building blocks in documents	548-560
4.1.2	Save frequently used data as building blocks	552-559
4.1.3	Insert formatted headers and footers from Quick Parts	551-562
4.1.4	Insert fields from Quick Parts	561-563
6	**Sharing and Securing Content**	
6.1	Prepare documents for sharing	
6.1.2	Identify document features not supported by previous versions using the compatibility checker	652-653
6.1.3	Remove inappropriate or private information using Document Inspector	643-645
6.2	Control document access	
6.2.1.	Restrict permissions to documents	646
6.2.2.	Mark documents as final	652-653
6.2.3	Set passwords	637-639
6.2.4	Protect documents	631-637
6.3	Attach digital signatures	
6.3.1	Authenticate documents using digital signatures	647-649
6.3.2	Insert a line for a digital signature	649-651

Chapter 21

Inserting and Customizing Quick Parts

Tutorial 21.1
Working with Building Blocks
Tutorial 21.2
Working with Quick Parts

Performance Objectives

Upon successful completion of Chapter 21, you will be able to:

- Sort and insert building blocks
- Create, edit, and modify building blocks
- Delete building blocks
- Insert fields from Quick Parts
- Update fields

Word offers a number of features to help you streamline the formatting of documents. In this chapter you will learn how to use predesigned building blocks to build a document. You will also learn how to create, save, and edit your own building blocks as well as how to insert fields in a document and update them.

Note: Before beginning computer exercises for this chapter, copy to your storage medium the Chapter21 folder from the CD that accompanies this textbook and then make Chapter21 the active folder.

Inserting Quick Parts

Quick Parts

Word includes a variety of tools you can use to insert data such as text, fields, objects, or other items in a document to help build it. To view some of the tools available, click the Quick Parts button in the Text group in the Insert tab. Clicking the Quick Parts button displays a drop-down list of options for inserting document properties, fields, and predesigned building blocks. The drop-down list also includes an option to connect to the Microsoft Online site to access additional predesigned content and an option for saving selected data to the Quick Parts gallery.

Inserting Building Blocks

Building blocks are tools you can use to develop or "build" a document. Word provides a number of these reusable pieces of content that you can insert in a document. You can also create your own and save them for future use. To insert one of Word's predesigned building blocks into a document, click the Insert tab, click the Quick Parts button in the Text group, and then click *Building Blocks Organizer* at the drop-down list. This displays the Building Blocks Organizer dialog box, shown in Figure 21.1. On the left, the dialog box displays four columns of information about the building blocks: the building block name, the gallery to which the building block belongs, the building block's category, and the template in which the building block is stored. When you click the name of a building block, the dialog box also displays a preview of the building block, its name, and a brief description of the building block.

Figure 21.1 Building Blocks Organizer Dialog Box

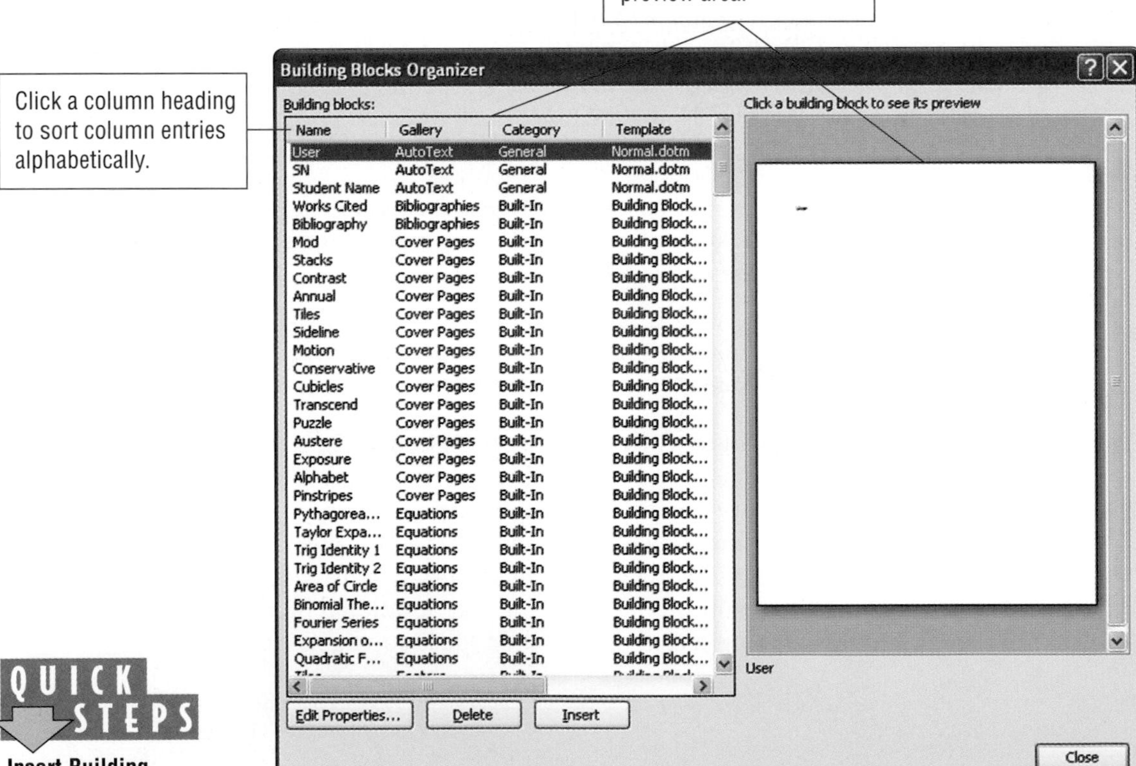

Insert Building Block

1. Click Insert tab.
2. Click Quick Parts button.
3. Click *Building Blocks Organizer*.
4. Click desired building block.
5. Click Insert button.
6. Click Close.

The Building Blocks Organizer dialog box provides a single location where you can view all of the predesigned building blocks available in Word. You used building blocks in previous chapters when you inserted elements such as predesigned cover pages, headers, footers, page numbering, and watermarks into a document. You used various buttons in the Insert tab to insert these elements. At the Building Blocks Organizer dialog box, you can conveniently view and insert all available building blocks.

Sorting Building Blocks

When you open the Building Blocks Organizer dialog box, the building blocks display in a list box sorted by the Gallery column. You can sort the building blocks by other columns by clicking the column heading. For example, to sort building blocks alphabetically by name, click the Name column heading.

Sort Building Blocks
1. Click Insert tab.
2. Click Quick Parts button.
3. Click *Building Blocks Organizer.*
4. Click desired column heading.

Exercise 1

Inserting Predesigned Building Blocks

1. Open **Report06.docx** and save the document with the name **C21Ex01**.
2. Make the following changes to the document:
   a. Insert a continuous section break at the beginning of the first paragraph below the title CHAPTER 1: COMPUTER VIRUSES.
   b. Insert a section break that begins a new page at the beginning of the title CHAPTER 2: SECURITY RISKS located in the middle of the second page.
   c. Insert a continuous section break at the beginning of the first paragraph below the title CHAPTER 2: SECURITY RISKS.
   d. Change the line spacing to 1.15 for the entire document.
   e. Format the section below the first title CHAPTER 1: COMPUTER VIRUSES into two equally spaced columns.
   f. Balance the columns of text on the second page.
   g. Format the section below the second title CHAPTER 2: SECURITY RISKS into two equally spaced and balanced columns.
3. Sort the building blocks and then insert a table of contents building block by completing the following steps:
   a. Press Ctrl + Home, press Ctrl + Enter to insert a page break, and then press Ctrl + Home again.
   b. With the insertion point positioned at the beginning of the new page (first page), click the Insert tab.
   c. Click the Quick Parts button in the Text group and then click *Building Blocks Organizer* at the drop-down list.

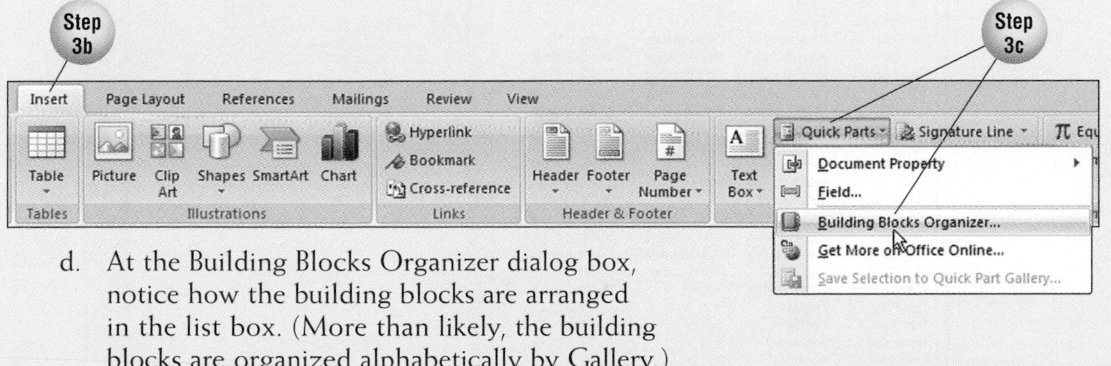

   d. At the Building Blocks Organizer dialog box, notice how the building blocks are arranged in the list box. (More than likely, the building blocks are organized alphabetically by Gallery.)

e. Click the Name column heading. (This sorts the building blocks alphabetically by name; however, some blank building blocks may display at the beginning of the list box.)
f. Scroll down the list box and then click *Automatic Table 1*. (You may see only a portion of the name. Click the name, and the full name as well as a description of the building block display in the dialog box below the preview.)
g. Click the Insert button that displays toward the bottom of the dialog box. (This inserts a Contents page at the beginning of the page and uses the titles and headings in the document to create the table of contents.)

4. Apply the Heading 1 style to the title *CONTENTS* by completing the following steps:
   a. Click on any character in the title *CONTENTS*.
   b. Click the Home tab.
   c. Click the Heading 1 style in the Styles group.
5. Insert a sidebar building block by completing the following steps:
   a. Position the insertion point at the beginning of the title CHAPTER 1: COMPUTER VIRUSES.
   b. Click the Insert tab.
   c. Click the Quick Parts button in the Text group.
   d. Click *Building Blocks Organizer* at the drop-down list.
   e. At the Building Blocks Organizer dialog box, scroll down the list box and then click *Tiles Sidebar* in the Name column. (This displays the sidebar in the preview section of the dialog box.)

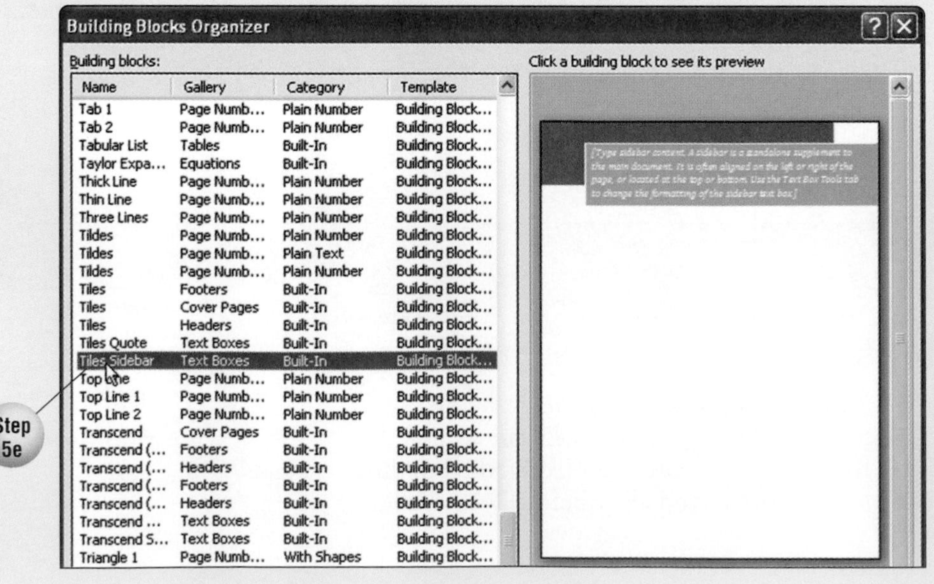

f. Click the Insert button that displays toward the bottom of the dialog box.
g. With the pull quote placeholder text selected, type "**Although accurate estimates are difficult to pinpoint, businesses certainly lose millions of dollars a year in stolen computer hardware and software.**"
h. Select the text you just typed, change the font size to 14 points, and then deselect the text.

6. Insert a footer building block by completing the following steps:
   a. Click the Insert tab, click the Quick Parts button, and then click *Building Blocks Organizer*.
   b. Scroll down the Building Blocks Organizer list box, click the *Tiles* footer, and then click the Insert button.
   c. Click the placeholder text *[Type the company address]* and then type **Northland Security Systems**. 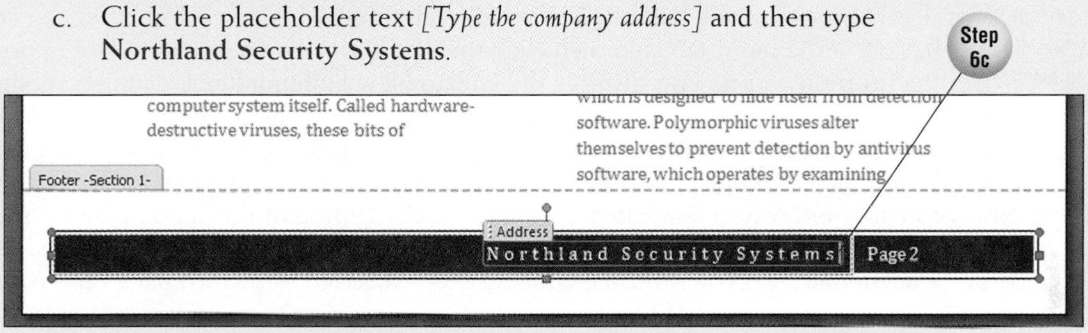
   d. Double-click in the document.
7. Insert a cover page building block by completing the following steps:
   a. Press Ctrl + Home to move the insertion point to the beginning of the document.
   b. Click the Insert tab, click the Quick Parts button, and then click *Building Blocks Organizer*.
   c. Scroll down the Building Blocks Organizer list box, click the *Tiles* cover page, and then click the Insert button.
   d. Click the placeholder text *[TYPE THE COMPANY NAME]* and then type **Northland Security Systems**.
   c. Click the placeholder text *[Type the document title]* and then type **Computer Security**.
   f. Click the placeholder text *[Type the document subtitle]* and then type **Computer Viruses and Security Risks**.
   g. If a name displays below the document subtitle in the Author placeholder, select the name and then type your first and last names.
   h. Click the placeholder text *[Year]* and then type the current year.
8. Scroll through the document and look at each page. The sidebar, footer, and cover page building blocks you inserted have similar formatting and are part of the *Tiles* group. Using building blocks from the same group provides consistency in a document and gives a document a polished and professional appearance.
9. Save, print, and then close **C21Ex01.docx**.

Save Content to Quick Part Gallery
1. Select desired data.
2. Click Insert tab.
3. Click Quick Parts button.
4. Click *Save Selection to Quick Part Gallery.*
5. Type name and description of building block.
6. Click OK.

Saving Content to the Quick Part Gallery

If you find yourself typing and formatting the same data regularly, consider saving the data as a building block. Saving frequently created data as a building block saves you time and reduces the potential for errors that might occur each time you type data or apply formatting. When you save data as a building block, it becomes available in the Building Blocks Organizer dialog box as well as the Quick Parts drop-down gallery. Before you create your own building blocks, click the Quick Parts button in the Insert group to display a drop-down list of choices. Create your own building block and then click the Quick Parts button. Your building block displays at the beginning of the drop-down gallery.

To save data as a building block, select the desired data, click the Quick Parts button in the Insert tab, and then click the *Save Selection to Quick Part Gallery* option at the drop-down list. This displays the Create New Building Block dialog box, shown in Figure 21.2. You can also display this dialog box by selecting the desired data and then pressing Alt + F3. At the Create New Building Block dialog box, type a name for the building block, decide whether to insert the building block in the General category or create a new category, provide a description of the building block, identify where to save the building block, and decide if you want only the content inserted in a document or if you want the building block inserted in its own paragraph or page.

Figure 21.2 Create New Building Block Dialog Box

At this dialog box, type the building block name, specify the gallery and category, and write a description of the building block.

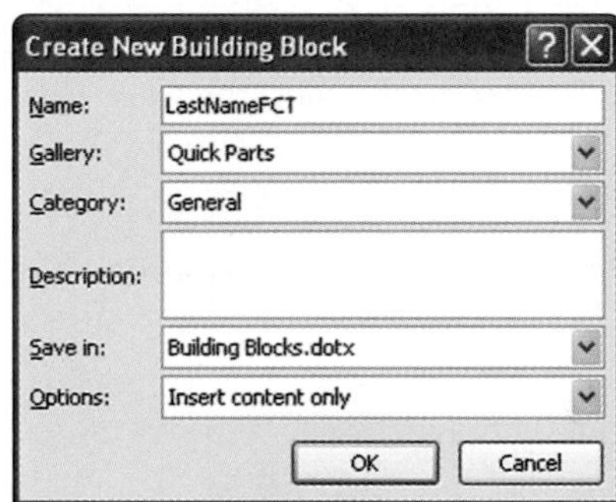

By default, building blocks you create are saved in the *Building Blocks.dotx* template. Click the down-pointing arrow at the right side of the *Save in* option, and a drop-down list displays with the default choice of *Building Blocks.dotx* as well as *Normal.dotm*. Saving a building block in either of these templates makes it available each time you open Word. In a public environment such as a school, you may not be able to save data to a template. Before completing Exercise 2, check with your instructor to determine if you can save your building blocks. At the completion of Exercise 3, you will be instructed to delete the building blocks you created.

Exercise 2A

Creating a Building Block

1. As an employee of First Choice Travel, you type letters regularly. You decide that saving the company's letterhead as a building block will help you "build" a letter more efficiently. Complete the following steps to save the letterhead as a building block:
   a. Open **FCTLetterhead.docx**.
   b. Press Ctrl + A to select the entire document (picture image, text, and border line).
   c. Click the Insert tab.
   d. Click the Quick Parts button and then click *Save Selection to Quick Part Gallery* at the drop-down list.

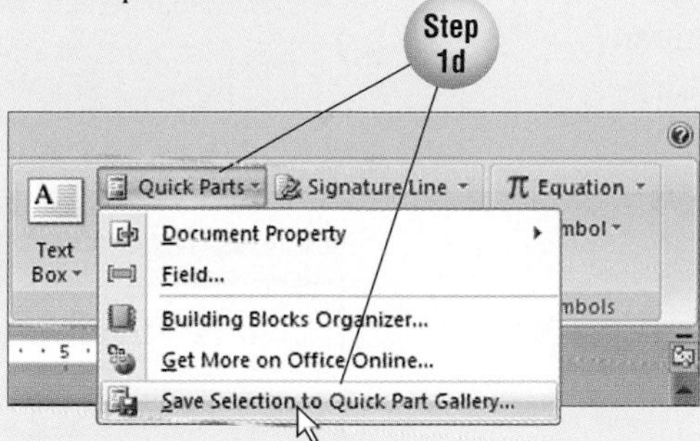

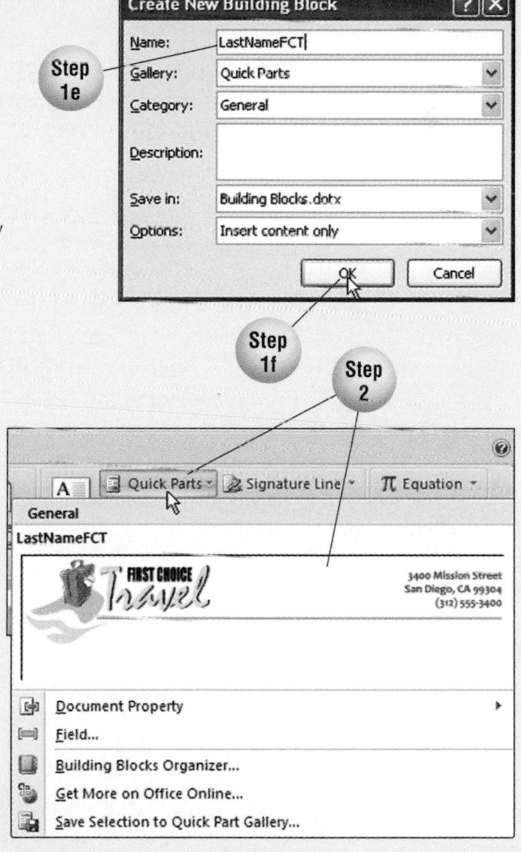

   e. At the Create New Building Block dialog box, type your last name and then type FCT.
   f. Click OK to close the dialog box.
2. Click the Quick Parts button in the Text group and notice that the letterhead now appears in the drop-down gallery.
3. Click in the document screen to remove the drop-down gallery.
4. Close **FCTLetterhead.docx** without saving it.
5. For many documents you create at First Choice Travel, you generally insert footer information. Because you are going to use the information regularly, you decide to save it as a building block by completing the following steps:
   a. Open **FCTFooter.docx**.
   b. Select the entire document and then press Alt + F3.
   c. At the Create New Building Block dialog box, type your last name and then type FCTFooter.
   d. Click OK to close the dialog box.
6. Click the Quick Parts button in the Text group and notice that both the letterhead and footer now appear in the drop-down gallery.
7. Click in the document screen to remove the gallery.
8. Close **FCTFooter.docx** without saving it.

In Exercise 2A, you opened a previously created document and saved it as a building block. You can also type text, insert objects, and apply formatting to a document and then save the data as a building block.

Exercise 2B

Typing Text and Saving It as a Building Block

1. You correspond regularly with Pacific Sky Cruise Lines, so you decide to type the company name and address and save the text as a building block by completing the following steps:
   a. At a blank document, type the company name and address below. (Press Shift + Enter at the end of the first and second lines of text. Do not press Enter after typing the third line.)

      Pacific Sky Cruise Lines
      120 Montgomery Boulevard
      Los Angeles, CA 97032

   b. Press Ctrl + A to select the entire document and then change the font to 11-point Candara.
   c. With the text still selected, click the Insert tab, click the Quick Parts button, and then click *Save Selection to Quick Part Gallery*.
   d. At the Create New Building Block dialog box, type your last name and then type **PacificSky**.
   e. Click OK to close the dialog box.

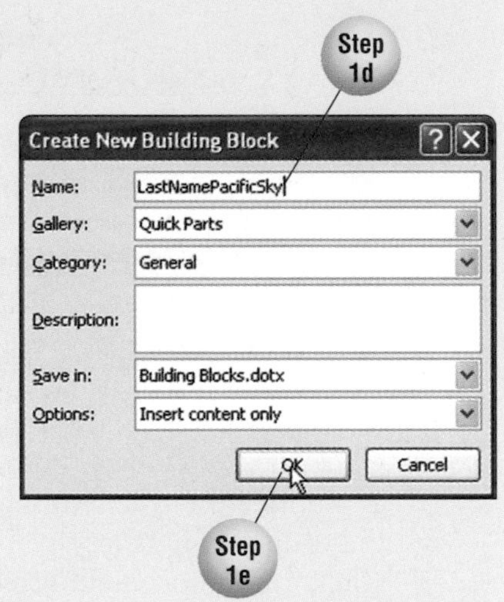

2. Create a building block with your name and company title by completing the following steps:
   a. Press Ctrl + End to move the insertion point to the end of the document.
   b. Press the Enter key.
   c. Type your first and last names.
   d. Press Shift + Enter to move the insertion point to the next line.
   e. Type **Travel Consultant**.
   f. Select your first and last names and title *Travel Consultant*, click the Insert tab, click the Quick Parts button, and then click *Save Selection to Quick Part Gallery*.
   g. At the Create New Building Block dialog box, type your last name and then type **Title**.
   h. Click OK to close the dialog box.
3. Close the document without saving it.

Editing Building Block Properties

You can make changes to the properties of a building block with options at the Modify Building Block dialog box. This dialog box contains the same options that are available at the Create New Building Block dialog box. Display the Modify Building Block dialog box by opening the Building Blocks Organizer dialog box, clicking the desired building block in the list box, and then clicking the Edit Properties button. You can also display this dialog box for a building block that displays in the drop-down gallery. To do this, click the Quick Parts button, right-click on the building block that displays in the drop-down gallery, and then click *Edit Properties* at the shortcut menu.

Make desired changes to the options in the Modify Building Block dialog box and then click OK. At the message that displays asking if you want to redefine the building block entry, click Yes.

Edit Building Blocks

1. Click Insert tab.
2. Click Quick Parts button, *Building Blocks Organizer*.
3. Click desired building block.
4. Click Edit Properties button.
5. Make desired changes.
6. Click OK.

OR

1. Click Insert tab.
2. Click Quick Parts button.
3. Right-click desired building block in drop-down gallery.
4. Click *Edit Properties* at shortcut menu.
5. Make desired changes.
6. Click OK.

Exercise 2C

Editing Building Block Properties

1. At a blank document, click the Insert tab, click the Quick Parts button, and then click *Building Blocks Organizer* at the drop-down list.
2. At the Building Blocks Organizer dialog box, make sure the building blocks are displayed in the list box in alphabetical order by name. (If not, click the Name column heading.)
3. Scroll down to the names of the four building blocks you created that begin with your last name.
4. Notice that the letterhead building block name *FCT* does not provide information about the content of the building block. Edit the building block properties by completing the following steps:
   a. Click the building block that begins with your last name followed by FCT.
   b. Click the Edit Properties button located at the bottom of the dialog box.
   c. At the Modify Building Block dialog box, click in the *Name* text box and then add *Letterhead* to the end of the name.
   d. Click in the *Description* text box and then type **Inserts the First Choice Travel letterhead including the company name and address.**
   e. Click OK to close the dialog box.

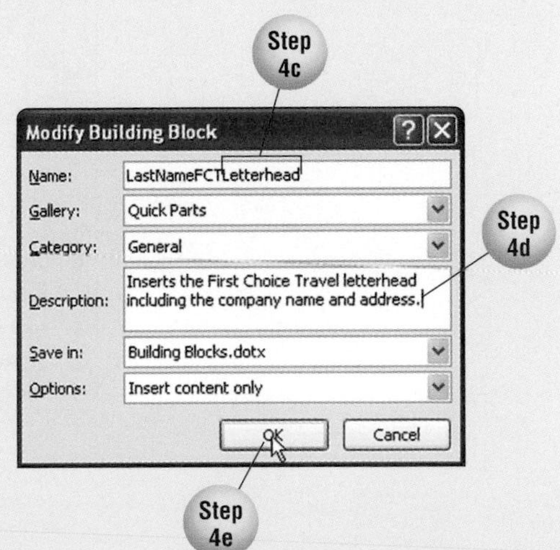

f. At the message asking if you want to redefine the building blocks entry, click Yes.

5. Edit the building block that begins with your last name followed by *PacificSky* and then insert the following text in the *Description* text box: **Inserts Pacific Sky Cruise Lines name and address.**
6. Close the Building Blocks Organizer dialog box.

QUICK STEPS

Insert Custom Building Block

1. Click Insert tab.
2. Click Quick Parts button.
3. Click desired building block at drop-down gallery.

OR

1. Click Insert tab.
2. Click Quick Parts button, *Building Blocks Organizer*.
3. Click desired building block.
4. Click Insert button.
5. Click Close.

Inserting Custom Building Blocks

As noted in an earlier section, a building block you create is available at the Building Blocks Organizer dialog box as well as in the Quick Parts drop-down gallery. Insert your building block by clicking the Quick Parts button and then clicking the building block at the drop-down gallery, or by displaying the Building Blocks Organizer dialog box, clicking the desired building block, and then clicking the Insert button.

You can specify where you want the building block inserted by clicking the Quick Parts button, right-clicking the building block in the drop-down gallery, and then choosing the desired location at the shortcut menu, shown in Figure 21.3.

Figure 21.3 Quick Parts Button Drop-down Gallery Shortcut Menu

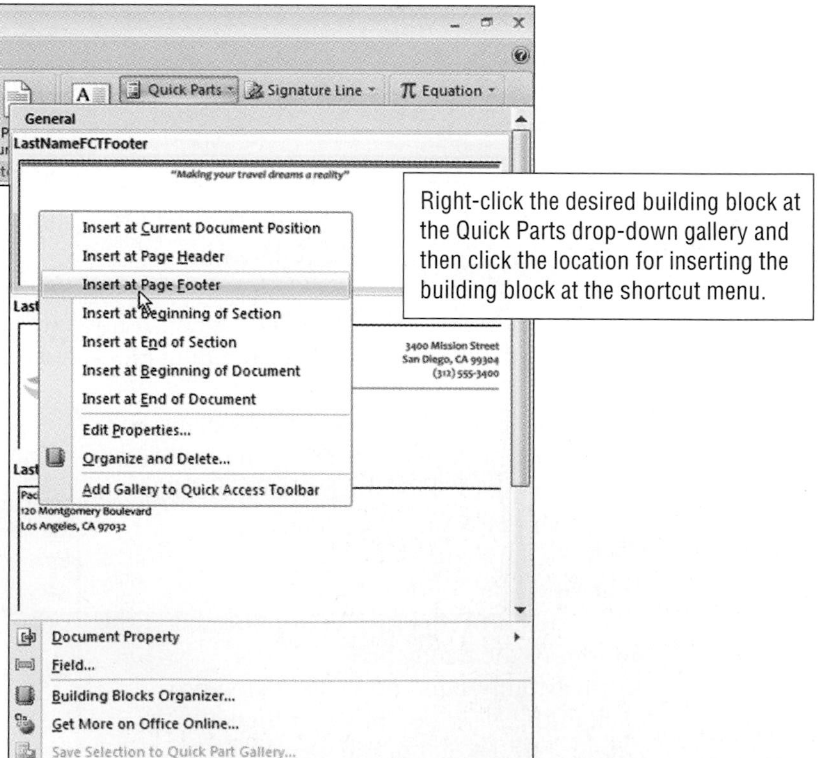

Exercise 2D

Inserting Custom Building Blocks

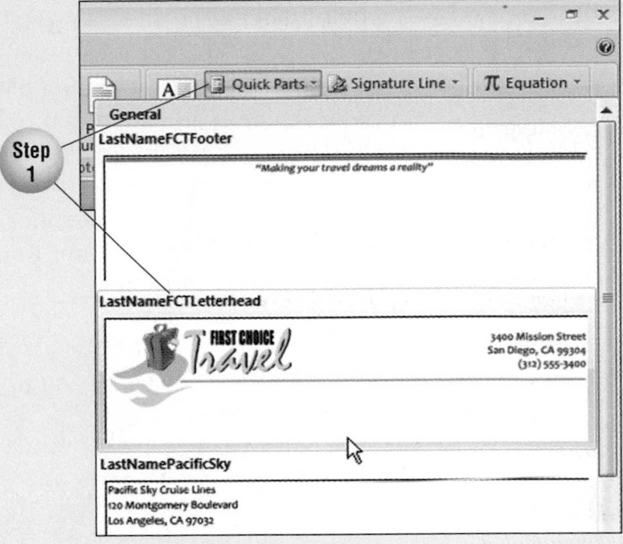

1. At a blank document, insert the letterhead building block you created by clicking the Insert tab, clicking the Quick Parts button, and then clicking the First Choice Travel letterhead at the drop-down gallery.
2. Type today's date and then press the Enter key twice.
3. Type **Mrs. Jody Lancaster** and then press Shift + Enter.
4. Insert the Pacific Sky Cruise Lines name and address building block by clicking the Quick Parts button and then clicking the building block at the drop-down gallery.
5. With the insertion point positioned below the city, state, and ZIP code, insert a letter document by completing the following steps:
   a. Make sure the Insert tab is selected
   b. Click the Object button arrow and then click *Text from File*.
   c. At the Insert File dialog box, navigate to the Chapter21 folder and then double-click **PacificSkyLetter01.docx**.
   d. Press Ctrl + End to move to the end of the document, type **Sincerely**, and then press the Enter key twice.
6. Insert your name and title building block by clicking the Quick Parts button and then clicking your name in the drop-down gallery. (You may need to scroll down the gallery to display this building block.)
7. Insert the footer building block you created by clicking the Quick Parts button, right-clicking the footer building block, and then clicking Insert at Page Footer in the shortcut menu.
8. Select the text in the document (excluding the text in the letterhead and footer) and then change the font to 11-point Candara.
9. Save the completed letter with the name **C21Ex02**.
10. Print and then close **C21Ex02.docx**.

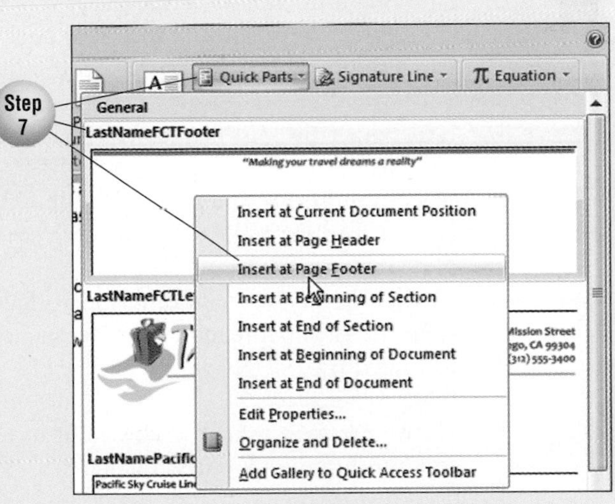

QUICK STEPS

Modify a Building Block
1. Insert desired building block.
2. Make corrections or changes.
3. Select modified building block.
4. Click Insert tab.
5. Click Quick Parts button, *Save Selection to Quick Part Gallery*.
6. Type original name, category, and gallery for building block.
7. Click OK.
8. Click Yes.

Modifying Building Blocks

You can insert a building block in a document, make corrections or changes to it, and then save it with the same name or a different name. Save a building block with the same name when you want to update the building block to reflect any changes. Save the building block with a new name if you want to use an existing building block as a basis for beginning to creating a new building block.

To save a modified building block with the same name, insert the building block in the document and then make the desired modifications. Select the building block data, click the Insert tab, click the Quick Parts button, and then click *Save Selection to Quick Part Gallery*. At the Create New Building Block dialog box, type the original name, category, and gallery for the building block and then click OK. At the message asking if you want to redefine the building block entry, click Yes.

Exercise 3A

Modifying Building Blocks

1. At First Choice Travel, you have been promoted from travel consultant to senior travel consultant. You decide to modify your name and title building block by completing the following steps:
   a. At a blank document, click the Insert tab, click the Quick Parts button, and then click your name and title building block in the drop-down gallery.
   b. Edit your title so it displays as *Senior Travel Consultant*.
   c. Select your name and title, click the Quick Parts button, and then click the *Save Selection to Quick Part Gallery* option.
   d. At the Create New Building Block dialog box, type the original name (your last name followed by *Title*).
   e. Click OK.
   f. At the message asking if you want to redefine the building block entry, click Yes.

2. Because most of the correspondence you send to Pacific Sky Cruise Lines is addressed to Jody Lancaster, you decide to include her name before the company name and address by completing the following steps:
   a. Click the Insert tab, click the Quick Parts button, and then click the Pacific Sky Cruise Lines name and address building block at the drop-down gallery.

b. Position the insertion point at the beginning of the company name *Pacific Sky Cruise Lines*, type **Mrs. Jody Lancaster**, and then press Shift + Enter.

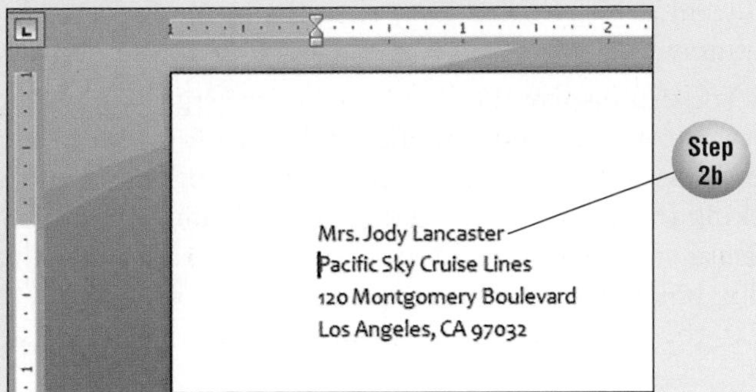

c. Select the name, company name, and address.
d. Click the Quick Parts button and then click the *Save Selection to Quick Part Gallery* option.
e. At the Create New Building Block dialog box, type the original name (your last name followed by *PacificSky*).
f. Click OK.
g. At the message asking if you want to redefine the building block entry, click Yes.

3. Close the document without saving it.
4. Create a business letter by completing the following steps:
   a. Click the New button on the Quick Access toolbar (or press Ctrl + N).
   b. At the blank document, insert the First Choice Travel letterhead building block.
   c. Type today's date and then press the Enter key twice.
   d. Insert the building block that includes Jody Lancaster's name as well as the cruise line name and address.
   e. Insert the file named **PacificSkyLetter02.docx** located in the Chapter21 folder on your storage medium. *(Hint: Do this with the Object button in the Text group on the Insert tab.)*
   f. Type **Sincerely**, and then press the Enter key twice.
   g. Insert the building block that contains your name and title.
   h. Insert the footer building block you created by clicking the Quick Parts button, right-clicking the footer building block, and then clicking Insert at Page Footer in the shortcut menu.
5. Select the text in the document (excluding the text in the letterhead and footer) and then change the font to 11-point Candara.
6. Save the completed letter with the name **C21Ex03**.
7. Print and then close **C21Ex03.docx**.

QUICK STEPS

Delete Building Block
1. Click Insert tab.
2. Click Quick Parts button, *Building Blocks Organizer*.
3. Click desired building block.
4. Click Delete button.
5. Click Yes.
6. Click Close.

OR

1. Click Insert tab.
2. Click Quick Parts button.
3. Right-click desired building block in drop-down gallery.
4. Click *Organize and Delete* at shortcut menu.
5. Click Delete button.
6. Click Yes.
7. Click Close.

Deleting Building Blocks

When you no longer use a building block that you created, consider deleting it. To do this, display the Building Blocks Organizer dialog box, click the building block you want to delete, and then click the Delete button. At the message asking if you are sure you want to delete the selected building block, click Yes.

You can display the Building Blocks Organizer dialog box by clicking the Quick Parts button and then clicking *Building Blocks Organizer* at the drop-down list. You can also display the dialog box with the building block you want to delete selected by clicking the Quick Parts button, right-clicking the building block, and then clicking *Organize and Delete* at the shortcut menu. This displays the Building Blocks Organizer dialog box with the building block selected. Click the Delete button and then answer yes to the confirmation question.

Exercise 3B

Deleting Building Blocks

1. At a blank document, delete the FCTLetterhead building block (that is preceded by your last name) by completing the following steps:
   a. Click the Insert tab and then click the Quick Parts button.
   b. Right-click the FCTLetterhead building block (preceded by your last name) and then click Organize and Delete.
   c. At the Building Blocks Organizer dialog box with the building block selected, click the Delete button.
   d. At the message that displays asking if you are sure you want to delete the selected building block, click Yes.
2. Complete steps similar to those in Step 1 to delete the three other building blocks you created (the FCTFooter, PacificSky, and Title that are all preceded by your last name).
3. Close the Building Blocks Organizer dialog box.
4. Close the document without saving it.

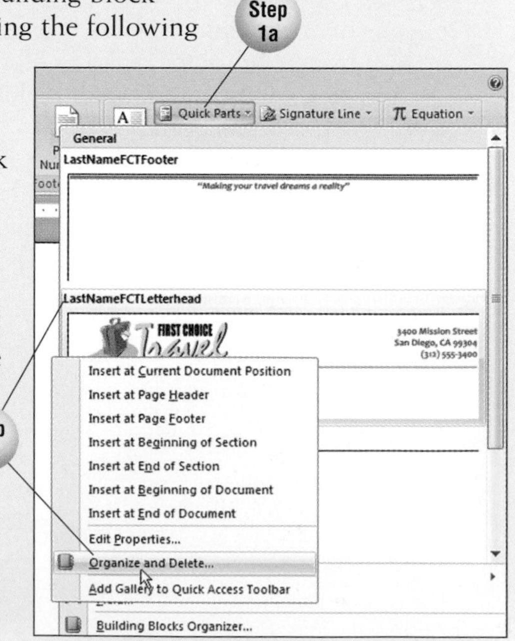

Inserting Fields

Insert Field
1. Click Insert tab.
2. Click Quick Parts button.
3. Click *Field* at drop-down list.
4. Click desired field.
5. Click OK.

Fields are placeholders for data that change and thus need to be updated and for data that change when a main document is merged with a data source file. You have inserted fields in documents when you merged main documents with data source files, inserted the date and time in a document, and inserted page numbering in a document. Word provides buttons for inserting many of the types of fields you may want to enter into a document. You can also insert a field in a document with options at the Field dialog box, shown in Figure 21.4. This dialog box contains a list of all available fields. Just as the Building Blocks Organizer dialog box is a single location for accessing all building blocks, the Field dialog box is a single location for accessing fields. To display the Field dialog box, click the Insert tab, click the Quick Parts button in the Text group, and then click *Field* at the drop-down list. At the Field dialog box, click the desired field in the *Field names* list box and then click OK.

Figure 21.4 Field Dialog Box

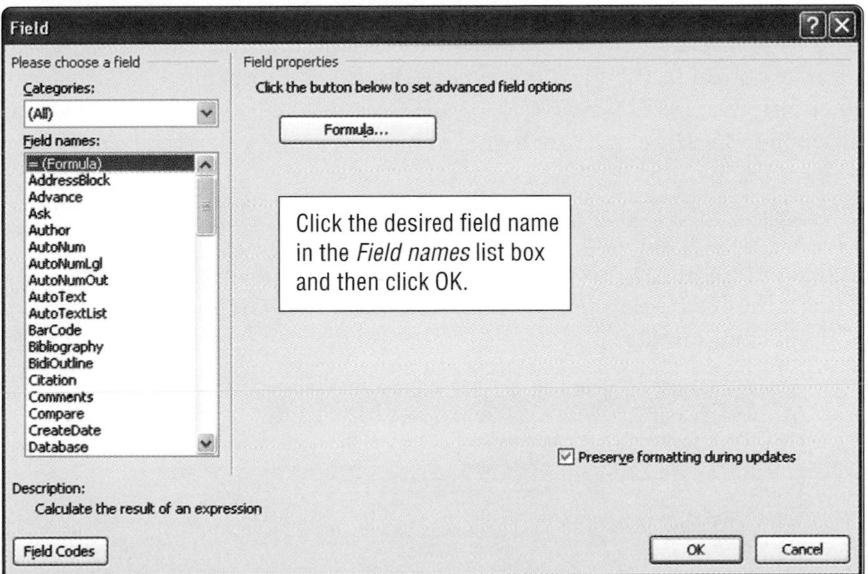

Exercise 4A

Inserting Fields

1. Open **Lease02.docx** and save the document with the name **C21Ex04**.
2. Press Ctrl + End to move the insertion point to the end of the document and then press the Enter key twice.
3. Insert a field for the current file name by completing the following steps:
   a. Click the Insert tab.
   b. Click the Quick Parts button and then click *Field* at the drop-down list.

c. At the Field dialog box, scroll down the *Field names* list box and then double-click *FileName*. (This inserts the current file name in the document and closes the Field dialog box.)

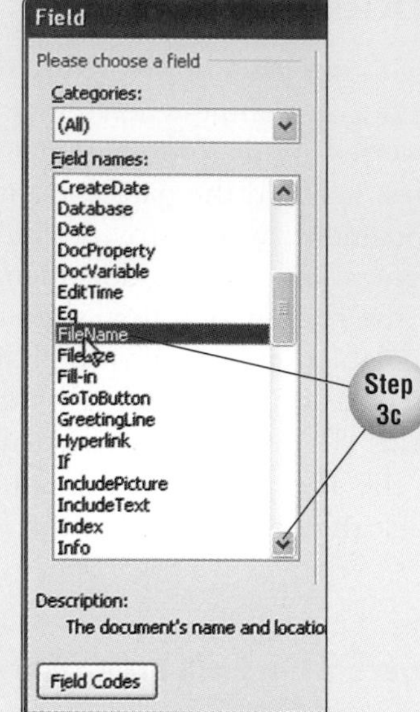

4. Insert a field that inserts the date the file is printed by completing the following steps:
   a. Press the Enter key.
   b. Click the Quick Parts button and then click *Field* at the drop-down list.
   c. At the Field dialog box, scroll down the *Field names* list box and then double-click *PrintDate*. (The date and time will display with zeros. The correct date and time will display when you send the document to the printer.)

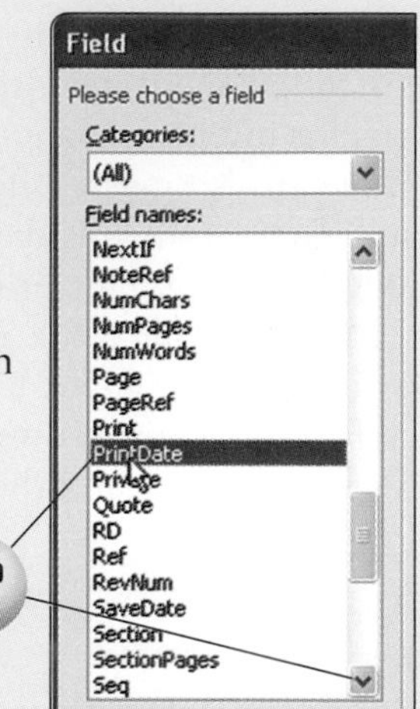

5. Insert a header and then insert a field in the header by completing the following steps:
   a. Click the Header button in the Header & Footer group and then click *Edit Header* at the drop-down list.
   b. At the header pane, press the Tab key twice. (This moves the insertion point to the right tab at the right margin.)
   c. Click the Insert tab.
   d. Click the Quick Parts button and then click *Field* at the drop-down list.
   e. At the Field dialog box, scroll down the *Field name* list box and then click *Date*.
   f. Click the date in the *Date formats* list box that will insert the date in figures followed by the time (hours and minutes).

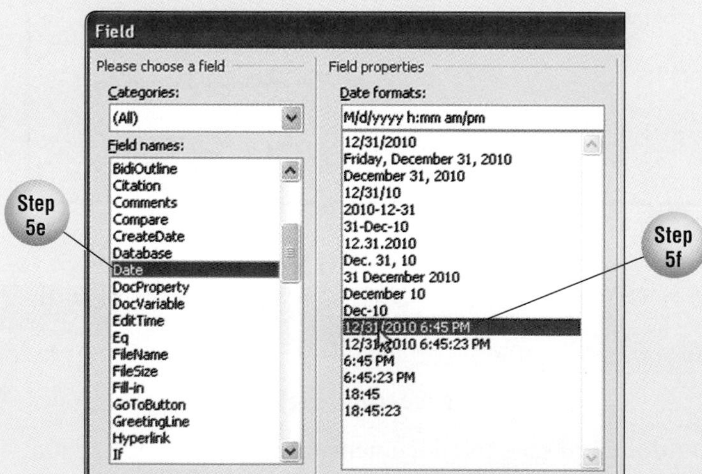

   g. Click OK to close the dialog box.
   h. Double-click in the document.
6. Save and then print **C21Ex04.docx**.

Updating a Field

Word automatically updates the fields in a document when you open the document. For example, open **C21Ex04.docx**, and the time in the header is automatically updated. You can manually update a field three ways: by clicking the field and then clicking the Update tab, by clicking the field and then pressing F9, or by right-clicking the field and then clicking Update at the shortcut menu. You can also update all fields in a document except headers, footers, and text boxes by pressing Ctrl + A to select the document and then pressing F9.

Update a Field
1. Click field.
2. Click Update tab.

OR
1. Click field.
2. Press F9.

OR
1. Right-click field.
2. Click Update at shortcut menu.

Exercise 4B

Updating Fields

1. With **C21Ex04.docx** open, update the time in the header by completing the following steps:
   a. Double-click the header.
   b. Click the date and time and then click the Update tab.
   c. Double click in the document.
2. Save the document with Save As and name it **C21Lease**.
3. Press Ctrl + A to select the entire document and then press F9.
4. Save, print, and then close **C21Lease.docx**.

Chapter Summary

- Word provides a number of predesigned building blocks you can use to help build a document.
- Insert building blocks at the Building Blocks Organizer dialog box. Display the dialog box by clicking the Quick Parts button in the Insert tab and then clicking *Building Blocks Organizer* at the drop-down list.
- The Building Blocks Organizer dialog box provides a single location where you can view all available predesigned and custom designed building blocks.
- Sort building blocks at the Building Blocks Organizer dialog box by clicking the desired column heading.
- You can save selected data as a new building block by selecting the text, clicking the Quick Parts button in the Insert tab, and then clicking *Save Selection to Quick Part Gallery*. At the Create New Building Block dialog box, specify a name, category, building block description, and location for saving the building block.
- By default, building blocks you create are saved in the *Building Blocks.dotx* template.
- Insert a building block by displaying the Building Blocks Organizer dialog box, clicking the desired building block, and then clicking the Insert button. You can also insert a custom building block by clicking the Insert tab, clicking the Quick Parts button, and then clicking the custom building block at the drop-down gallery.
- Edit a building block with options at the Modify Building Block dialog box. Display this dialog box by displaying the Building Blocks Organizer dialog box, clicking the desired building block, and then clicking the Edit Properties button.
- A building block you create is available at the Building Blocks Organizer dialog box as well as in the Quick Parts drop-down gallery.
- Delete a building block by displaying the Building Blocks Organizer dialog box, clicking the building block, clicking the Delete button, and then clicking Yes at the confirmation question.
- Fields are placeholders for data that you can insert with options at the Field dialog box, which provides a single location for accessing all fields provided by Word. Display the Field dialog box by clicking the Quick Parts button and then clicking *Field*.
- Fields in a document are updated automatically when you open the document. You can update a field manually by clicking the field and then clicking the Update tab, pressing F9, or right-clicking the field and then clicking *Update*.

Commands review

FEATURE	RIBBON TAB, GROUP	BUTTON, OPTION	KEYBOARD SHORTCUT
Building Blocks Organizer dialog box	Insert, Text	Quick Parts, Building Blocks Organizer	
Create New Building Block dialog box	Insert, Text	Select text, Quick Parts, Save Selection to Quick Part Gallery	Alt + F3
Field dialog box	Insert, Text	Quick Parts, Field	

Reviewing key points

Completion: In the space provided at the right, indicate the correct term, symbol, or command.

1. The Quick Parts button is located in this tab. ____________________
2. This dialog box provides a single location where you can view all of the predesigned building blocks. ____________________
3. By default, building blocks you create are saved in this template. ____________________
4. Save selected data as a building block by clicking the Quick Parts button and then clicking this option. ____________________
5. Make changes to the properties of a building block with options at this dialog box. ____________________
6. A building block you create is available at this drop-down gallery. ____________________
7. Delete building blocks at this dialog box. ____________________
8. To display the Field dialog box, click the Insert tab, click this button, and then click *Field* at the drop-down list. ____________________
9. You can manually update a field by pressing this key on the keyboard. ____________________

Applying your skills

Assessment 1 Insert Building Blocks and Fields in a Report

1. Open **Report12.docx** and save the document with the name **C21A01**.
2. Make the following changes to the document:
   a. Select the entire document and then change the spacing after paragraphs to 6 points.
   b. Press Ctrl + Home and then press Ctrl + Enter to insert a page break.
   c. Apply the Heading 1 style to the two titles *PROPERTY PROTECTION ISSUES* and *REFERENCES*.
   d. Apply the Heading 2 style to the three headings in the document.
   e. Change the style set to *Formal*.
   f. Change the theme to *Flow*.
   g. Change the theme colors to *Foundry*.
   h. Apply a hanging indent to the paragraphs of text below the title *REFERENCES*.
   i. Indent the second paragraph in the *Fair Use* section 0.5 inch from the left and right margins.
3. Press Ctrl + Home to move the insertion point to the beginning of the document and then insert the *Automatic Table 2* table of contents building block.
4. Insert the Pinstripes header building block, make sure the *Title* placeholder is selected, and then type **Woodland Legal Services**.
5. Double-click in the document.
6. Insert the Pinstripes footer building block, click the *[Type text]* placeholder, and then type **Property Protection Issues**.
7. Double-click in the document.
8. Press Ctrl + Home and then insert the Pinstripes cover page building block. Click the *[Type the document subtitle]* placeholder and then type **Property Protection Issues**. Click the *[Pick the date]* and then insert today's date. Click the *[Type the company name]* placeholder and then type your school's name. Click the Author placeholder (if a name displays below the company name, click in the name and then click the Author placeholder tab) and then type your first and last name.
9. Press Ctrl + End to move the insertion point to the end of the document and then insert a field that will insert the file name.
10. Press Shift + Enter and then insert a field that will insert the current date and time.
11. Save, print, and then close **C21A01.docx**.

Assessment 2 Create Building Blocks and Prepare a Letter

1. Open the **NSSLetterhead.docx**, create a building block with the data in the document, and name the building block with your last name followed by NSSLetterhead. Close **NSSLetterhead.docx**.
2. Open the **NSSFooter.docx**, create a building block with the data in the document, and name the building block with your last name followed by NSSFooter. Close **NSSFooter.docx**.
3. At a blank document, type **Sincerely**, and then press the Enter key twice. Type your first and last names, press Shift + Enter, and then type **Vice President**. Select the text and then create a building block named with your last name followed by *CClose* (for complimentary close). Close the document without saving it.
4. Use the building blocks you created to prepare a letter by completing the following steps:
   a. At a blank document, insert the letterhead building block you created.
   b. Type today's date and then press the Enter key twice.
   c. Insert the file named **NSSLetter01.docx**.
   d. Insert the complimentary close building block you created.
   e. Insert as a footer the footer building block you created containing the border line and Northland Security Systems' address.
5. Save the completed letter with the name **C21A02**.
6. Print and then close **C21A02.docx**.
7. At a blank document, delete the building blocks you created.

Chapter 22

Customizing AutoCorrect and Word Options

Tutorial 22.1
Using AutoCorrect
Tutorial 22.2
Using Word Options

Performance Objectives

Upon successful completion of Chapter 22, you will be able to:

- Add words to and delete words from the AutoCorrect dialog box
- Insert symbols in the AutoCorrect dialog box
- Use the AutoCorrect Options button
- Customize the Quick Access toolbar
- Customize Word options

Word offers a number of features to help you customize documents as well as streamline their formatting. In this chapter you will learn how to customize Word's AutoCorrect feature by inserting and deleting characters at the AutoCorrect dialog box. You will also learn how to use the AutoCorrect Options button, customize the Quick Access toolbar, and customize Word options.

Note: Before beginning computer exercises for this chapter, copy to your storage medium the Chapter22 folder from the CD that accompanies this textbook and then make Chapter22 the active folder.

Customizing AutoCorrect

Word's AutoCorrect feature corrects certain words automatically as you type them. You can add words to AutoCorrect while you are spell checking a document, or you can add, delete, or change words at the AutoCorrect dialog box, which displays with the full name AutoCorrect: English (U.S.). To display the AutoCorrect dialog box with the AutoCorrect tab selected, as shown in Figure 22.1, click the Office button and then click the Word Options button. At the Word Options dialog box, click *Proofing* in the left panel and then click the AutoCorrect Options button.

Figure 22.1 AutoCorrect Dialog Box with AutoCorrect Tab Selected

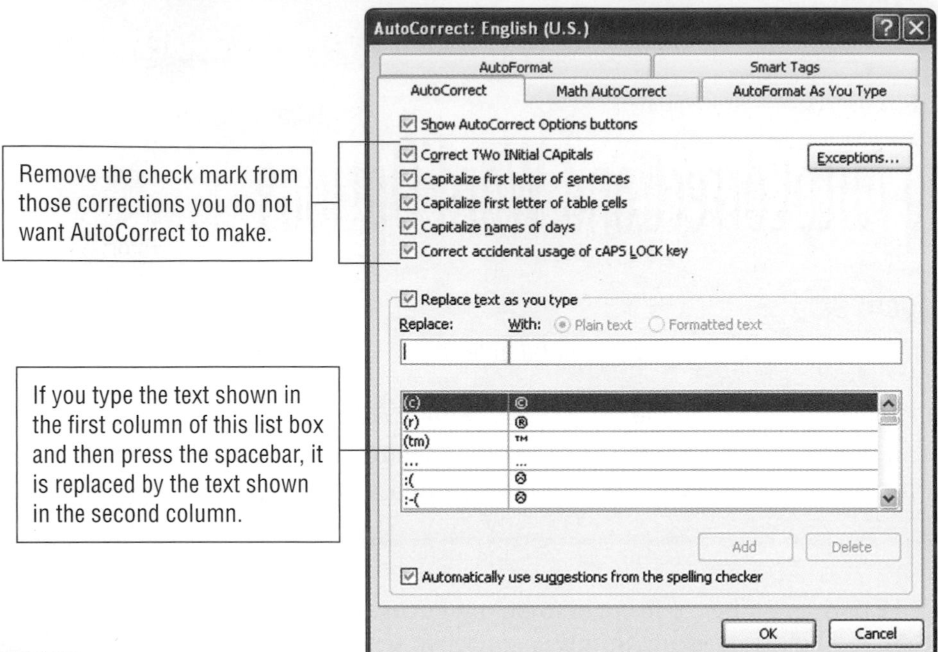

Insert Word(s) to AutoCorrect
1. Click Office button, Word Options.
2. Click *Proofing*.
3. Click AutoCorrect Options button.
4. Click AutoCorrect tab.
5. Type misspelled or abbreviated word.
6. Press Tab.
7. Type correctly spelled word or complete word(s).
8. Click Add button.
9. Click OK.

Adding Words to AutoCorrect

You can add commonly misspelled words or frequently made typographical errors to AutoCorrect. For example, if you consistently type *relavent* instead of *relevant*, you can add *relavent* to AutoCorrect and tell AutoCorrect to correct it as *relevant*. You can also add an abbreviation to AutoCorrect that when typed AutoCorrect will replace with the entire word (or words). For example, in Exercise 1A, you will add *fav* and the replacement text *Family Adventure Vacations* to AutoCorrect. Subsequently, when you type *fav* and then press the spacebar, AutoCorrect will insert *Family Adventure Vacations*. You can also control the capitalization of the word (or words) AutoCorrect inserts by controlling the capitalization of the abbreviation. For example, in Exercise 1A, you will add *Ky* to AutoCorrect. When you type *Ky* and then press the spacebar, AutoCorrect will insert *Kyrgyzstan*. If you want to insert KYRGYZSTAN in the document, you type KY and then press the spacebar.

Exercise 1A

Adding Text to AutoCorrect

1. At a blank document, click the Office button and then click the Word Options button located in the lower right corner of the drop-down list.
2. At the Word Options dialog box, click *Proofing* in the left panel.
3. Click the AutoCorrect Options button in the *AutoCorrect options* section.
4. At the AutoCorrect dialog box with the AutoCorrect tab selected, make sure the insertion point is positioned in the *Replace* text box. If not, click in the *Replace* text box.

5. Type **fav**.
6. Press the Tab key (this moves the insertion point to the *With* text box) and then type **Family Adventure Vacations**.
7. Click the Add button. (This adds *fav* and *Family Adventure Vacations* to AutoCorrect and also selects *fav* in the *Replace* text box.)

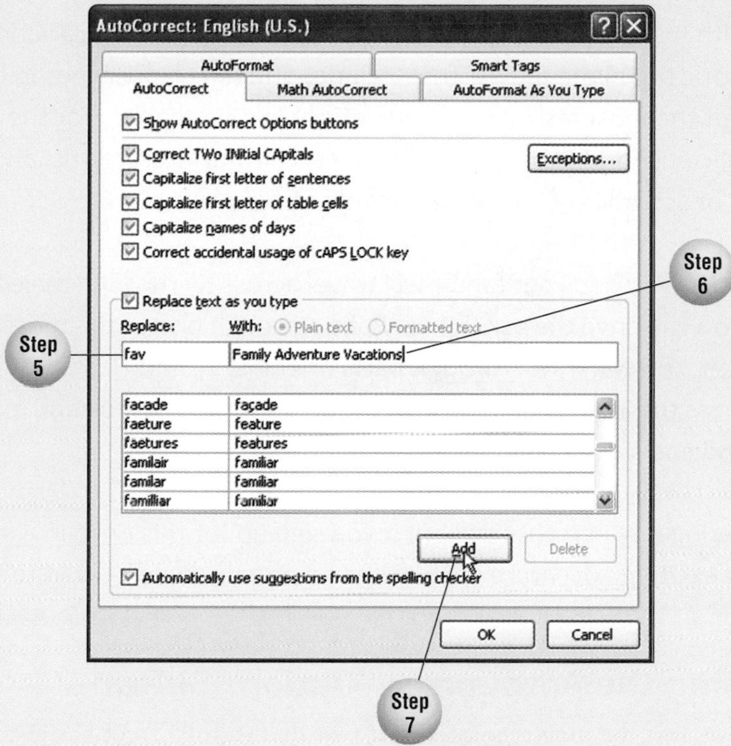

8. Type **Ky** in the *Replace* text box. (The text *fav* is removed automatically when you begin typing *Ky*.)
9. Press the Tab key and then type **Kyrgyzstan**.
10. Click the Add button.
11. With the insertion point positioned in the *Replace* text box, type **Tj**.
12. Press the Tab key and then type **Tajikistan**.
13. Click the Add button.
14. With the insertion point positioned in the *Replace* text box, type **Uz**.
15. Press the Tab key and then type **Uzbekistan**.
16. Click the Add button.
17. With the insertion point positioned in the *Replace* text box, type **fct**.
18. Press the Tab key and then type **First Choice Travel**.
19. Click the Add button.
20. With the insertion point positioned in the *Replace* text box, type **osr**.
21. Press the Tab key and then type **Old Silk Road**.
22. Click the Add button.
23. Click OK to close the AutoCorrect dialog box and then click OK to close the Word Options dialog box.
24. Open **FCTLetterhead.docx** and save the document with the name **C22Ex01**.
25. Press Ctrl + End and then type the text shown in Figure 22.2. Type the text exactly as shown. AutoCorrect will correct words as you type.
26. Save **C22Ex01.docx**.

Figure 22.2 **Exercise 1A**

CHINA, KY, TJ, UZ

osr Adventure

fct is partnering with fav to provide adventurous and thrilling family vacations. Our first joint adventure is an exotic trip along the osr that includes stunning landscapes in China, Ky, Tj, and Uz. The osr is one of the most fascinating destinations in Asia. Sign up for the osr Adventure and experience delicious food, comfortable facilities, cultural interactions, abundant wildlife, and a wide variety of activities of interest to people of all ages.

During the 20-day trip, you and your family will travel across Ky through majestic mountains and open plains. You will drive the osr of Tash Rabat through one of the most spectacular regions of Tien Shan. You will travel through parts of China, Tj, and Uz visiting museums and local bazaars, witness the Tien Shan Mountains at their most beautiful, and experience the sights of Samarkand and sleepy Bukhara.

fct and fav are offering a 15 percent discount if you sign up for this once-in-a-lifetime trip to travel the osr. This exciting adventure is limited to 30 people so don't wait to sign up!

Using the AutoCorrect Options Button

AutoCorrect

If you rest the mouse pointer near text that AutoCorrect has just corrected, a small blue box displays below the text. Move the mouse pointer to this blue box, and the AutoCorrect Options button displays. Click this button, and a drop-down list displays with three options. You can choose to change the corrected text back to the original spelling, tell AutoCorrect to stop automatically correcting occurrences of that specific text, or display the AutoCorrect dialog box. If the AutoCorrect Options button does not display, you will need to turn the feature on. To do this, display the AutoCorrect dialog box with the AutoCorrect tab selected, click the *Show AutoCorrect Options buttons* check box to insert a check mark, and then click OK to close the dialog box.

Exercise 1B

Using the AutoCorrect Options Button

1. With **C22Ex01.docx** open, select and then delete the last paragraph.
2. With the insertion point positioned a double space below the second paragraph of text, type the text shown in Figure 22.3. (AutoCorrect will automatically change *Ameria* to *America*. You will change this in the next step.)
3. Change the spelling of *America* back to *Ameria* by completing the following steps:
   a. Position the mouse pointer over *America* until a blue box displays below the word.
   b. Position the mouse pointer on the blue box until the AutoCorrect Options button displays.

c. Click the AutoCorrect Options button and then click the *Change back to "Ameria"* option.

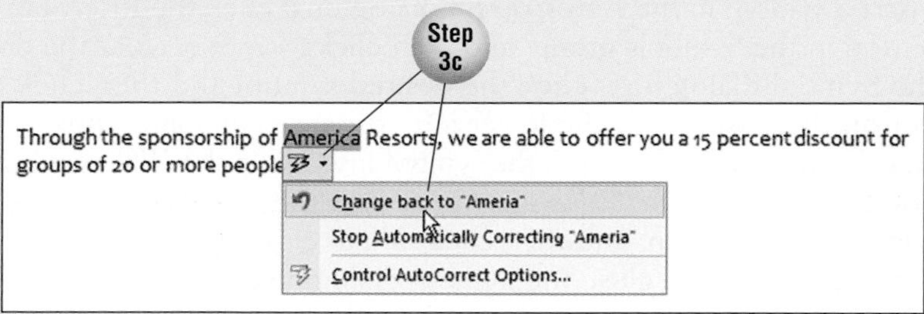

4. Save and then print **C22Ex01.docx**.

Figure 22.3 Exercise 1B

Through the sponsorship of Ameria Resorts, we are able to offer you a 15 percent discount for groups of 20 or more people.

Inserting Symbols Automatically

AutoCorrect recognizes and replaces symbols as well as text. Several symbols included in AutoCorrect display in the AutoCorrect dialog box, listed first in the *Replace* text box. Table 22.1 lists these symbols along with the characters you type to insert them.

Table 22.1 AutoCorrect Symbols Available at the AutoCorrect Dialog Box

Type	***To Insert***
(c)	©
(r)	®
(tm)	™
...	. . .
:) or :-)	☺
:| or :-|	😐
:(or :-(	☹
-->	→
<--	←
==>	➔
<==	🡐
<=>	⇔

Insert Symbol to AutoCorrect
1. Click Insert tab.
2. Click Symbol button, *More Symbols.*
3. Click desired symbol.
4. Click AutoCorrect button.
5. Type text used to insert symbol.
6. Click Add button.
7. Click OK.
8. Click Close button.

Along with the symbols provided by Word, you can insert other symbols in the AutoCorrect dialog box with the AutoCorrect button in the Symbol dialog box. To insert a symbol in the AutoCorrect dialog box, click the Insert tab, click the Symbol button in the Symbols group, and then click *More Symbols* at the drop-down list. At the Symbol dialog box, click the desired symbol and then click the AutoCorrect button that displays in the lower left corner of the dialog box. This displays the AutoCorrect dialog box with the symbol inserted in the *With* text box and the insertion point positioned in the *Replace* text box. Type the text you will use to insert the symbol, click the Add button, and then click OK to close the AutoCorrect dialog box. Click the Close button to close the Symbol dialog box.

Exercise 1C

Inserting Symbols Using AutoCorrect

1. With **C22Ex01.docx** open, move the insertion point so it is positioned immediately right of the last *s* in *Resorts* and then type **(r)**. (This inserts the registered trademark.)
2. Move the insertion point immediately left of the *1* in *15* and then type **==>**. (This inserts the ➔ symbol.)
3. Move the insertion point immediately right of the *t* in *discount* and then type **<==**. (This inserts the 🡐 symbol.)
4. Insert the pound currency unit symbol (£) in AutoCorrect by completing the following steps:
   a. Click the Insert tab.
   b. Click the Symbol button and then click *More Symbols* at the drop-down list.
   c. At the Symbol dialog box, make sure that *(normal text)* displays in the *Font* option box. If it does not, click the down-pointing arrow at the right side of the *Font* option box and then click *(normal text)* at the drop-down list (first option in the list).
   d. Scroll down the list of symbols and then click the pound currency unit symbol £ (third symbol from the left in the seventh row).
   e. Click the AutoCorrect button located in the lower left corner of the dialog box.
   f. At the AutoCorrect dialog box, type **pcu** in the *Replace* text box and then click the Add button.
   g. Click OK to close the AutoCorrect dialog box and then the Close button to close the Symbol dialog box.

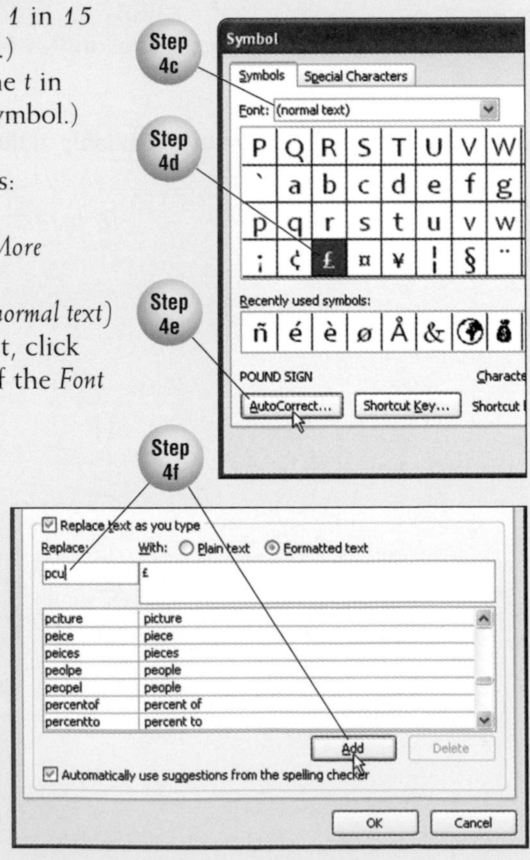

5. Press Ctrl + End to move the insertion point to the end of the document and then press the Enter key twice. (The insertion point should be positioned a double space below the last paragraph of text.)
6. Type the text shown in Figure 22.4. Create the pound currency unit symbol by typing **pcu** and then pressing the spacebar. Press the Backspace key once and then type **1,999**.
7. Save **C22Ex01.docx**.

Figure 22.4 Exercise 1C

Individual price:
$3,299 (US)
£1,999 (UK)

Individual price for groups of 10 or more:
$3,099 (US)
£1,599 (UK)

Deleting AutoCorrect Text

You can delete text from the AutoCorrect dialog box. To do this, display the dialog box, click the desired word or words in the list box, and then click the Delete button.

Exercise 1D

Deleting Text from AutoCorrect

1. With **C22Ex01.docx** open, delete *fav* from AutoCorrect by completing the following steps:
   a. Click the Office button and then click the Word Options button that displays at the bottom of the drop-down list.
   b. At the Word Options dialog box, click *Proofing* in the left panel.
   c. Click the AutoCorrect Options button in the *AutoCorrection options* section.
   d. At the AutoCorrect dialog box, type **fav** in the *Replace* text box. (This selects the entry in the list box.)
   e. Click the Delete button.
2. Complete steps similar to those in Step 1 to delete the following AutoCorrect entries: *fct*, *Ky*, *osr*, *pcu*, *Tj*, and *Uz*.
3. Click OK to close the AutoCorrect dialog box.
4. Click OK to close the Word Options dialog box.
5. Save and then close **C22Ex01.docx**.

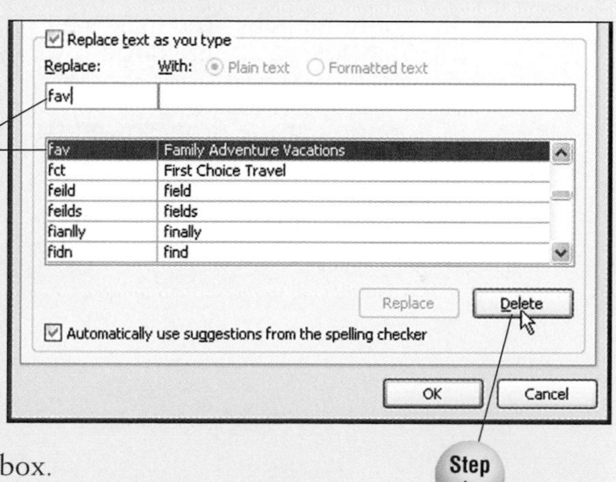

QUICK STEPS

Customize Quick Access Toolbar
1. Click Customize Quick Access Toolbar button.
2. Insert check mark before desired button(s).
3. Remove check mark before undesired button(s).

Customize Quick Access Toolbar

Customizing the Quick Access Toolbar

As its name implies, the Quick Access toolbar provides quick access to buttons for some of the most commonly performed tasks. By default, it contains the Save, Undo, and Redo buttons. In the Getting Started section of this textbook, you were instructed to add three more commonly used buttons to the toolbar—New, Open, and Quick Print. You can easily add or remove buttons for other basic functions to and from the Quick Access toolbar with options at the Customize Quick Access Toolbar drop-down list, shown in Figure 22.5. Display this list by clicking the Customize Quick Access Toolbar button that displays at the right side of the toolbar. Insert a check mark before the buttons you want displayed on the toolbar and remove the check mark from those you do not want to appear.

Figure 22.5 Customize Quick Access Toolbar Button Drop-down List

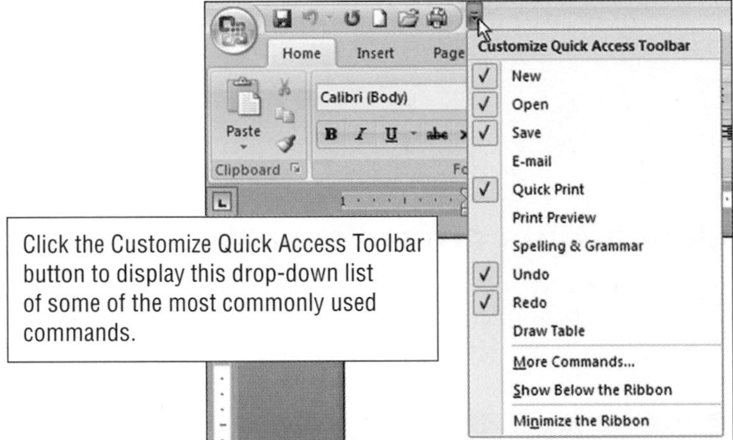

The Customize Quick Access Toolbar button drop-down list includes an option for minimizing the ribbon and an option for moving the location of the Quick Access toolbar. Click the *Minimize the Ribbon* option, and the ribbon is minimized, displaying only the tabs. You may want to minimize the ribbon to view more of your document on the screen. By default, the Quick Access toolbar is positioned above the ribbon. You can move the toolbar below the ribbon by clicking the *Show Below the Ribbon* option at the drop-down list.

Exercise 2A

Customizing the Quick Access Toolbar

1. Open **Report01.docx** and save the document with the name **C22Ex02**.
2. Make the following changes to the document:
   a. Apply the Heading 1 style to the title and the Heading 2 style to the five headings.
   b. Change the style set to *Formal*.
   c. Insert page numbering by clicking the Insert tab, clicking the Page Number button, pointing to *Bottom of Page*, and then clicking the *Accent Bar 2* option (you will need to scroll down the list to display this option).
   d. Double-click in the document.
3. Add a Print Preview button to the Quick Access toolbar by clicking the Customize Quick Access Toolbar button that displays at the right side of the toolbar and then clicking *Print Preview* at the drop-down list.
4. Minimize the ribbon by clicking the Customize Quick Access Toolbar button and then clicking the *Minimize the Ribbon* option at the drop-down list.
5. Click the Print Preview button on the Quick Access toolbar.
6. Scroll through the document to see how it will appear when printed and then click the Print Preview button on the Quick Access toolbar to return to the Print Layout view.
7. Redisplay the ribbon by clicking the Customize Quick Access Toolbar button and then clicking *Minimize the Ribbon* to remove the check mark.
8. Move the Quick Access toolbar by clicking the Customize Quick Access Toolbar button and then clicking *Show Below the Ribbon* at the drop-down list.
9. Move the Quick Access toolbar back to the default position by clicking the Customize Quick Access Toolbar button and then clicking *Show Above the Ribbon* at the drop-down list.
10. Save **C22Ex02.docx**.

Adding Buttons from Tabs

You can add buttons or commands from a tab to the Quick Access toolbar. To do this, click the tab, right-click on the desired button or command, and then click Add to Quick Access Toolbar at the shortcut menu. You can add buttons from tabs but you cannot add the contents of most lists. For example, you cannot add the Indent or Spacing measurements boxes in the Page Layout tab. You can add the command but not the measurement box.

Add Buttons to Quick Access Toolbar from Tabs

1. Right-click desired button in tab.
2. Click Add to Quick Access Toolbar at shortcut menu.

Exercise 2B

Inserting Buttons from Tabs on the Quick Access Toolbar

1. With **C22Ex02.docx** open, add buttons to the Quick Access toolbar by completing the following steps:
   a. Click the Page Layout tab.
   b. Right-click the Margins button in the Page Setup group and then click Add to Quick Access Toolbar at the shortcut menu.

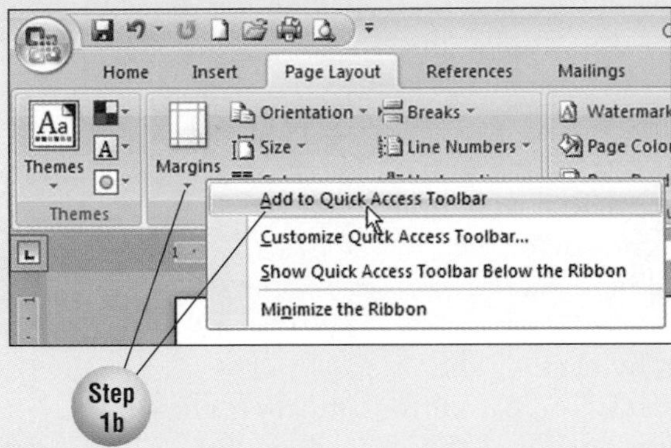

   c. Right-click the Themes button in the Themes group and then click Add to Quick Access Toolbar at the shortcut menu.
2. Change the top margin by completing the following steps:
   a. Click the Margins button on the Quick Access toolbar and then click *Custom Margins* at the drop-down list.
   b. At the Page Setup dialog box, change the top margin measurement to 1.5″ and then close the dialog box.
3. Change the theme by clicking the Themes button on the Quick Access toolbar and then clicking *Module* at the drop-down list.
4. Save and then print page 1 of **C22Ex02.docx**.

Customizing with Options at the Word Options Dialog Box

The Customize Quick Access Toolbar button drop-down list contains ten of the most commonly used buttons. You can, however, insert many other buttons on the toolbar. To display the buttons available, click the Customize Quick Access Toolbar button and then click *More Commands* at the drop-down list. This displays the Word Options dialog box with *Customize* selected in the left panel, as shown in Figure 22.6.

Figure 22.6 Word Options Dialog Box with Customize Selected

Click the desired command in the list box at the left, click the Add button, and the command displays in the list box at the right.

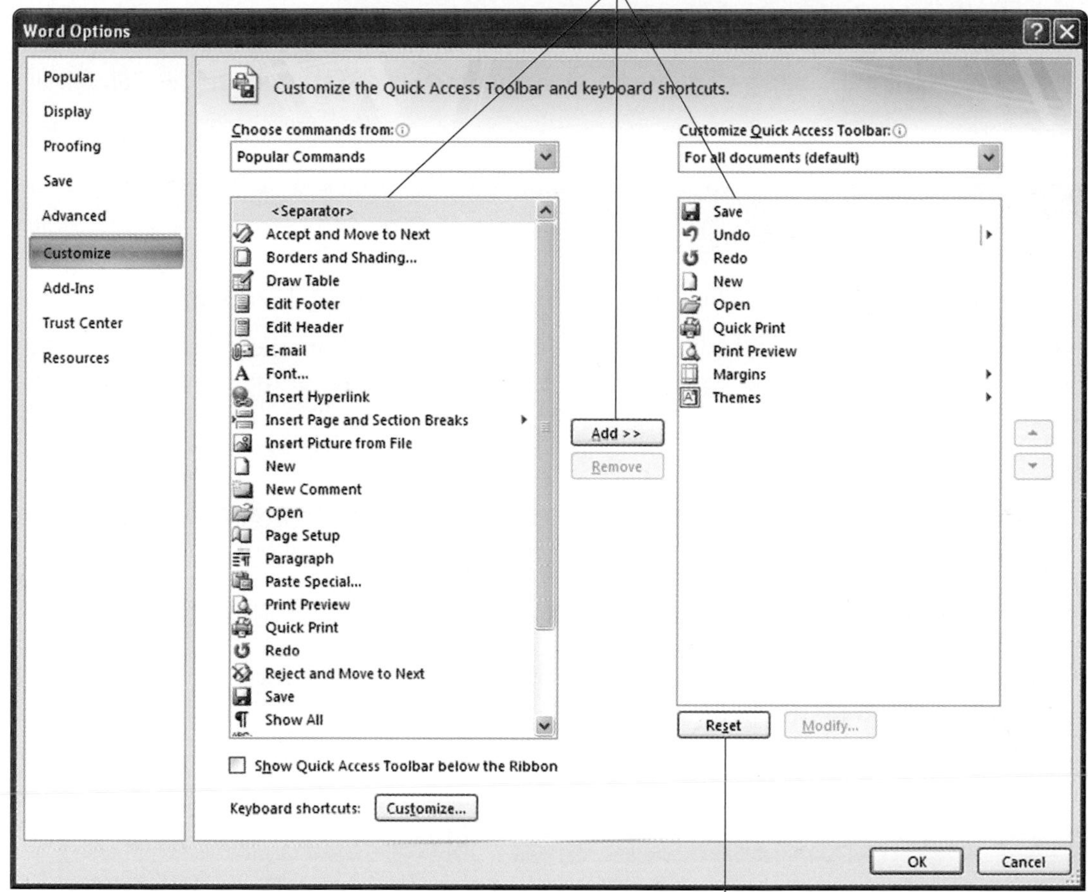

Click the Reset button to reset the Quick Access toolbar to the default buttons.

To reset the Quick Access toolbar to the default (Save, Undo, and Redo buttons), click the Reset button that displays toward the bottom of the dialog box. At the message asking if you are sure you want to restore the Quick Access toolbar shared between all documents to its default contents, click Yes.

You can customize the Quick Access toolbar for all documents or for a specific document. To customize the toolbar for the currently open document, display the Word Options dialog box with *Customize* selected, click the down-pointing arrow at the right side of the Customize Quick Access Toolbar option, and then click the *For (document name)* option where the name of the currently open document displays.

The *Choose commands from* option at the Word Options dialog box has a default setting of *Popular Commands*. At this setting, the list box below the option displays

QUICK STEPS

Add Buttons to Quick Access Toolbar from Word Options Dialog Box

1. Click Customize Quick Access Toolbar button.
2. Click *More Commands* at drop-down list.
3. Click desired command at left list box.
4. Click Add button.
5. Click OK.

only a portion of all of the commands available to insert as a button on the Quick Access toolbar. To display all of the commands available, click the down-pointing arrow at the right side of the *Choose commands from* option box and then click *All Commands*. The drop-down list also contains options for specifying commands that are not currently available on a tab (in the ribbon section of the screen), as well as commands from the Office button drop-down list and various tabs.

To add a button, click the desired command in the list box at the left side of the commands list box and then click the Add button that displays between the two list boxes. Continue adding all desired buttons and then click OK to close the dialog box.

Exercise 2C

Inserting and Removing Buttons from the Quick Access Toolbar

1. With **C22Ex02.docx** open, reset the Quick Access toolbar by completing the following steps:
   a. Click the Customize Quick Access Toolbar button that displays at the right side of the Quick Access toolbar and then click *More Commands* at the drop-down list.
   b. At the Word Options dialog box, click the Reset button that displays toward the bottom of the dialog box.
   c. At the message asking if you are sure you want to restore the Quick Access toolbar shared between all documents to its default contents, click Yes.
   d. Click OK to close the dialog box.
2. Insert buttons on the Quick Access toolbar for the currently open document by completing the following steps:
   a. Click the Customize Quick Access Toolbar button and then click *More Commands*.
   b. At the Word Options dialog box, click the down-pointing arrow at the right side of the Customize Quick Access Toolbar option and then click *For C22Ex02.docx* at the drop-down list.

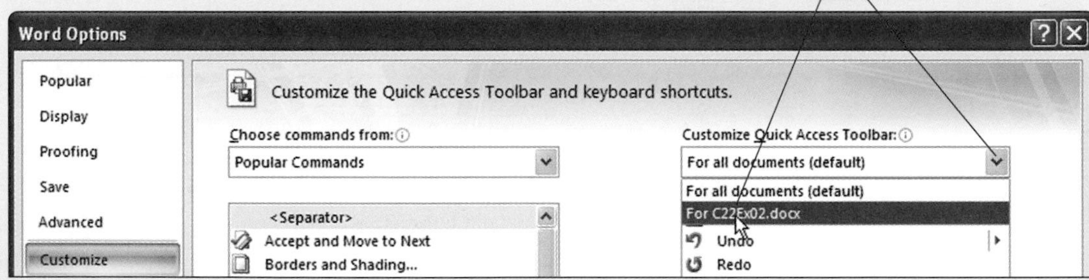

   c. Click the down-pointing arrow at the right side of the *Choose commands from* option box and then click *All Commands*.

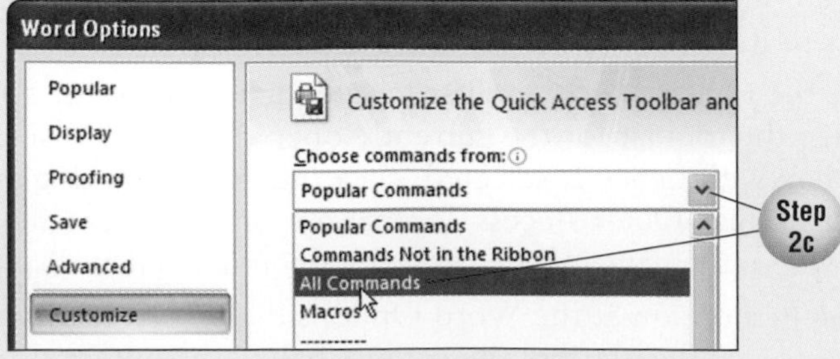

d. Scroll down the list box and then click the first *Close* command (commands are listed in alphabetical order).
e. Click the Add button that displays between the two list boxes.
f. Scroll down the list box and then click *Footer*.
g. Click the Add button.
h. Click OK to close the dialog box.
i. Check the Quick Access toolbar and notice the two buttons now display along with the default buttons.

3. Change the theme color by clicking the Page Layout tab, clicking the Theme Colors button, and then clicking *Office* at the drop-down gallery.
4. Remove page numbering from the document by completing the following steps:
   a. Click the Insert tab.
   b. Click the Page Number button in the Header & Footer group.
   c. Click *Remove Page Numbers* at the drop-down list.
5. Insert a footer by completing the following steps:
   a. Click the Footer button on the Quick Access toolbar.
   b. Click *Alphabet* at the drop-down list.

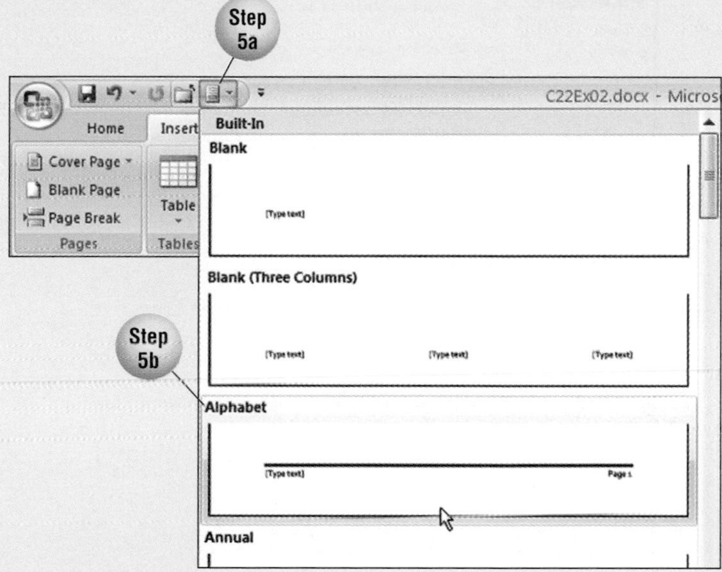

   c. Click in the *[Type text]* placeholder and then type your first and last names.
   d. Double-click in the document.
6. Save and then print **C22Ex02.docx**.
7. Close the document by clicking the Close button on the Quick Access toolbar.
8. Insert the New button on the Quick Access toolbar by clicking the Customize Quick Access Toolbar button and then clicking *New* at the drop-down list.
9. Complete steps similar to those in Step 8 to insert the Open button and the Quick Print button on the Quick Access toolbar.

QUICK STEPS

Customize Word Options
1. Click Office button, Word Options.
2. Click desired option in left panel.
3. Make desired customization choices.
4. Click OK to close Word Options dialog box.

Customizing Word Options

Throughout the chapters in this book, you have made changes to some of the Word options available at the Word Options dialog box. To display this dialog box, click the Office button and then the Word Options button located at the bottom of the drop-down list. By default, the Word Options dialog box displays with *Popular* selected in the left panel, as shown in Figure 22.7. With options in this dialog box, you can customize options for working with Word, including turning the Mini toolbar on or off, turning the display of live galleries on or off, and changing user information. By default, a document you open as an e-mail attachment opens in Full Screen Reading view. If you remove the check mark from the *Open e-mail attachments in Full Screen Reading view*, your e-mail attachment document will open in Print Layout view.

Figure 22.7 Word Options Dialog Box with Popular Selected

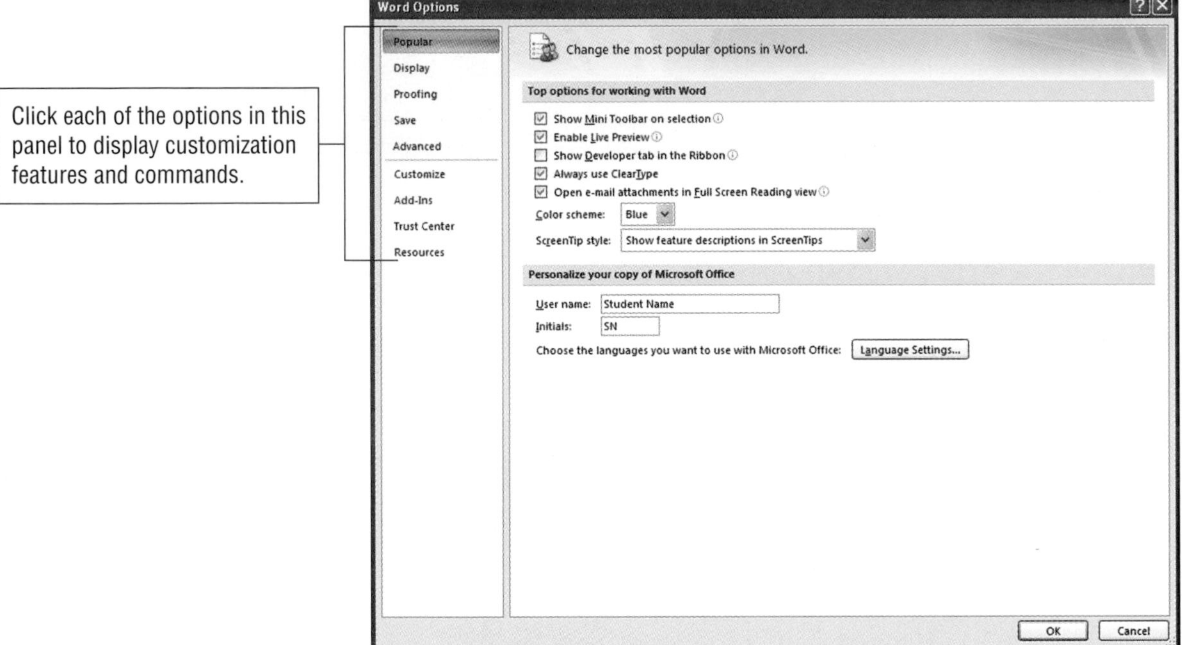

The Word Options dialog box, like many other dialog boxes in Word, contains a Help button in the upper right corner. Click this Help button, and the Word Help window displays with information about the options in the dialog box.

Exercise 3A

Customizing Popular and Display Options

1. Open **FCTDocument.docx** and save the document with the name **C22Ex03**.
2. Customize Word options by completing the following steps:
   a. Click the Office button and then click the Word Options button that displays at the bottom of the drop-down list.
   b. At the Word Options dialog box with *Popular* selected in the left panel, click the *Show Mini Toolbar on selection* check box to remove the check mark.
   c. Click the *Enable Live Preview* check box to remove the check mark.
   d. Click the *Open e-mail attachments in Full Screen Reading view* to remove the check mark.
   e. Select the current name in the *User name* text box and then type **Sylvia Porter**.
   f. Select the current initials in the *Initials* text box and then type **SP**.
   g. Click OK to close the dialog box.
3. Select text in the document and notice that the Mini toolbar does not display because you turned off the feature.
4. With the text still selected, click the Font button arrow and then hover the mouse pointer over the font options that display at the drop-down gallery. Because you turned off the live gallery feature, the text in your document does not display the font over which your mouse pointer is hovering.
5. Change to Full Screen Reading view by completing the following steps:
   a. Click the Full Screen Reading button in the view area on the Status bar.
   b. In the Full Screen Reading view, click the View Options button that displays in the upper right corner of the dialog box and notice that the top option *Don't Open Attachments in Full Screen* contains a check mark because you inserted a check mark in the *Open e-mail attachments in Full Screen Reading view* check box in the Word Options dialog box.
   c. Click the Close button that displays in the upper right corner of the screen.
6. Read information about the options in the Word Options dialog box with *Popular* selected by completing the following steps:
   a. Click the Office button and then click the Word Options button.
   b. Click the Help button that displays in the upper right corner of the dialog box (the button with the white question mark on a blue background).

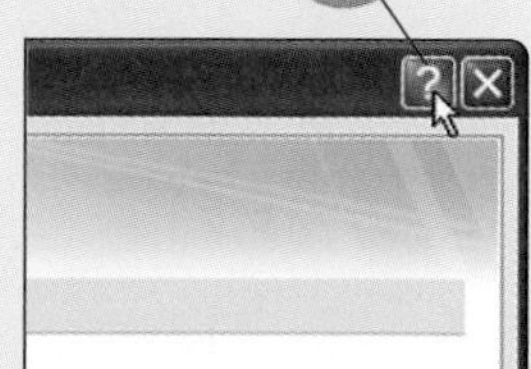

c. Scroll through the Word Help window and read the information that displays about the options in the dialog box.
d. Click the Close button to close the Word Help window.
e. Click OK to close the Word Options dialog box.
7. Insert a user name field by completing the following steps:
   a. Press Ctrl + End to move the insertion point to the end of the document.
   b. Click the Insert tab.
   c. Click the Quick Parts button in the Text group and then click *Field* at the drop-down list.
   d. At the Field dialog box, scroll to the bottom of the *Field names* list box and then double-click *UserName*.
8. Save **C22Ex03.docx**.

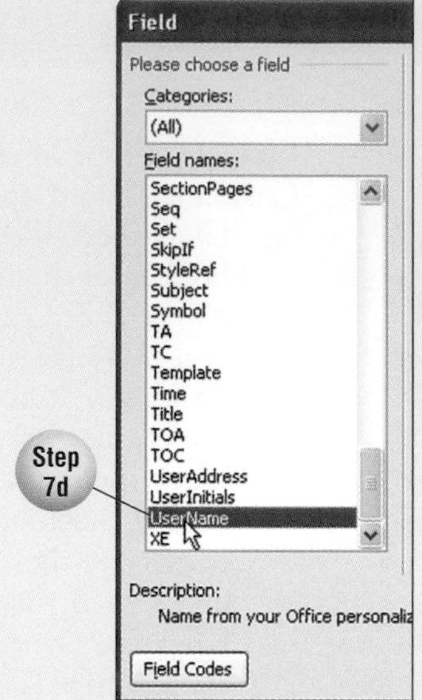

Click the *Display* option, and the Word Options dialog box displays options for specifying how document content appears on the screen and when it is printed. In a previous chapter, you learned how to turn on and off the display of white space that separates pages in Print Layout view by double-clicking the white space or the line separating the pages. You can also turn on or off the display of white space between pages with the *Show white space between pages in Print Layout view* option at the dialog box. Likewise, you can turn on or off the display of highlighting and ScreenTips that display when you hover the mouse over an option or button. Click the Help button in the upper right corner of the dialog box to display the Word Help window with information about these options in the dialog box.

Click the *Proofing* option, and the Word Options dialog box displays options for customizing AutoCorrect and the spelling and grammar checker. Again, you used some of these options in previous chapters. Click the Help button to display information about these options in the dialog box.

Click the *Save* option, and the Word Options dialog box displays options for customizing how documents are saved. You can change the format in which files are saved from the default *Word Document (*.docx)* to other formats, such as a previous version of Word, Word template, Web page, plain text, or previous versions of Microsoft Works. These save options are also available with the *Save as type* option at the Save As dialog box. The difference is that changing the file save format with the *Save files in this format* option at the Word Options dialog box with *Save* selected changes the default for all future documents saved.

Exercise 3B

Customizing Save Options

1. With **C22Ex03.docx** open, click the Office button and then click the Word Options button.
2. At the Word Options dialog box, click the *Display* option in the left panel.
3. Click the Help button located in the upper right corner of the dialog box.
4. Read through the information in the Word Help window.
5. Click the Close button to close the Word Help window.
6. Click the *Proofing* option that displays in the left panel.
7. Click the Help button, read the information that displays in the Word Help window, and then close the window.
8. Click the *Save* option that displays in the left panel.
9. Change the default file location by completing the following steps:
   a. Make a note of the current default file location.
   b. Click the Browse button that displays at the right side of the *Default file location* option box.

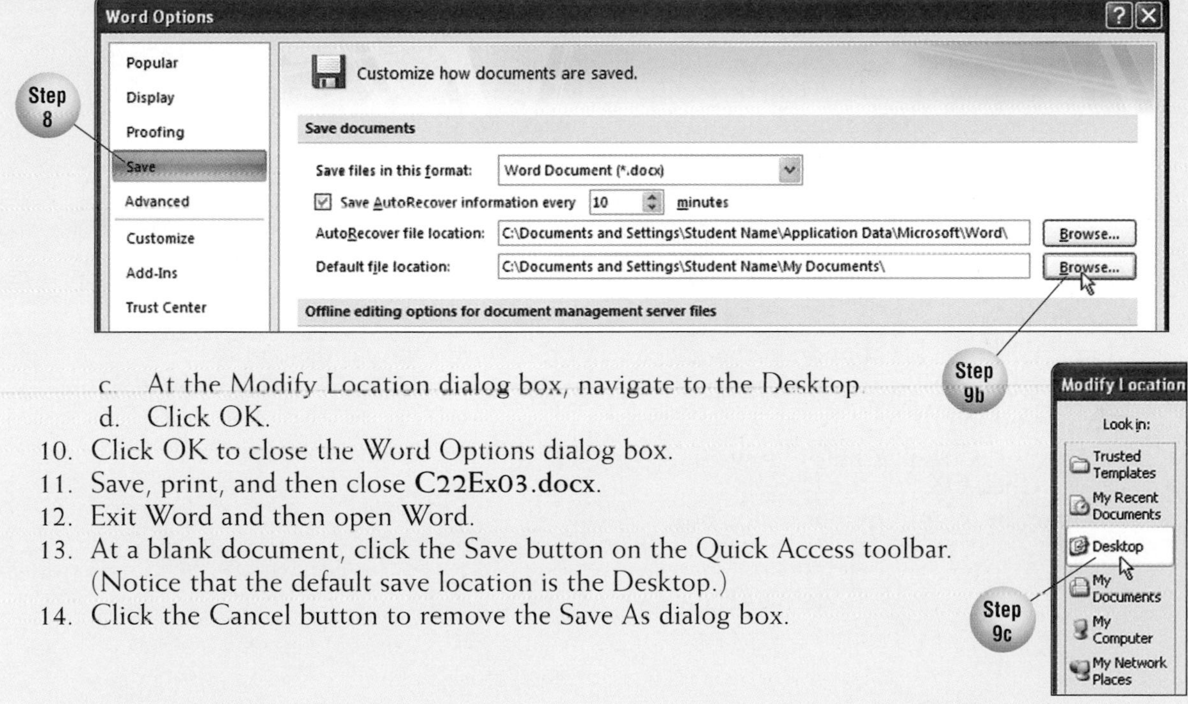

   c. At the Modify Location dialog box, navigate to the Desktop.
   d. Click OK.
10. Click OK to close the Word Options dialog box.
11. Save, print, and then close **C22Ex03.docx**.
12. Exit Word and then open Word.
13. At a blank document, click the Save button on the Quick Access toolbar. (Notice that the default save location is the Desktop.)
14. Click the Cancel button to remove the Save As dialog box.

With the *Advanced* option selected, the Word Options dialog box displays a number of sections for customizing Word, including a section for changing editing options, a section for specifying what document content to show, a section for customizing the display and printing of a document, as well as a number of other sections. To learn more about all of the options in this dialog box, click the Help button and then read the information about each option in the Word Help window.

Click the *Customize* option, and the Word Options dialog box displays with information for customizing the Quick Access toolbar and keyboard shortcuts. You worked with this dialog box in a previous section that included information on customizing the Quick Access toolbar.

If you click the *Add-Ins* option at the Word Options dialog box side panel, the dialog box displays add-ins, which are supplemental options that add custom commands and specialized features to Office 2007 applications.

With the *Trust Center* option selected in the left panel of the Word Options dialog box, hyperlinks display providing navigation to privacy and security information, including the Word privacy statement, the Microsoft Online privacy statement, the Customer Experience Improvement Program, and the Windows security center.

Click *Resources,* the last option in the left panel of the Word Options dialog box, and options display for displaying online resources and maintaining the health and reliability of Office programs.

Exercise 3C

Returning Options to Default

1. At a blank document, click the Office button and then click the Word Options button.
2. At the Word Options dialog box with *Popular* selected in the left panel, click the *Show Mini Toolbar on selection* check box to insert a check mark.
3. Click the *Enable Live Preview* check box to insert a check mark.
4. Click the *Open e-mail attachments in Full Screen Reading view* to insert a check mark.
5. Select the current name in the *User name* text box and then type the original name.
6. Select the current initials in the *Initials* text box and then type the original initials.
7. Change the default file location back to the original setting by completing the following steps:
   a. Click the *Save* option in the left panel of the Word Options dialog box.
   b. Click the Browse button that displays at the right side of the *Default file location* option box.
   c. At the Modify Location dialog box, navigate to the original location.
   d. Click OK.
8. Close the Word Options dialog box.

Chapter Summary

- You can add words to AutoCorrect while you spell check a document or at the AutoCorrect dialog box.
- Display the AutoCorrect dialog box by clicking the Office button, clicking the Word Options button, clicking *Proofing*, and then clicking the AutoCorrect Options button.
- Use the AutoCorrect Options button that displays when you hover the mouse over corrected text to change corrected text back to the original spelling, stop the automatic correction of specific text, or display the AutoCorrect dialog box.
- The AutoCorrect dialog box contains several symbols you can insert in a document by typing specific text or characters.
- You can insert a symbol from the Symbol dialog box into the AutoCorrect dialog box. To do this, display the Symbol dialog box, click the desired symbol, and then click the AutoCorrect button.
- Customize the Quick Access toolbar with options from the Customize Quick Access Toolbar button drop-down list.
- With options at the Customize Quick Access Toolbar button drop-down list, you can minimize the ribbon and change the location of the Quick Access toolbar.
- Add a button or command to the Quick Access toolbar by right-clicking the desired button or command and then clicking *Add to Quick Access Toolbar* at the shortcut list.
- You can customize the Quick Access toolbar with options at the Word Options dialog box with *Customize* selected.
- You can customize the Quick Access toolbar for all documents or for a specific document.
- The *Choose commands from* option at the Word Options dialog box with *Customize* selected has a default setting of *Popular Commands*. Change this option to *All Commands* to display all buttons and options available for adding to the Quick Access toolbar.
- Customize Word options at the Word Options dialog box.

Commands review

FEATURE	RIBBON TAB, GROUP	BUTTON, OPTION
AutoCorrect dialog box		Office button, Word Options, Proofing, AutoCorrect Options
Symbol dialog box	Insert, Symbols	Symbol, More Symbols
Word Options dialog box		Office button, Word Options

Reviewing key points

Completion: In the space provided at the right, indicate the correct term, symbol, or command.

1. This feature corrects certain words automatically as you type them. ____________
2. Use this button, which displays when you hover the mouse over corrected text, to change corrected text back to the original spelling. ____________
3. Type these characters to insert the ☺ symbol in a document. ____________
4. Type these characters to insert the ➔ symbol. ____________
5. Add or remove some basic buttons to and from the Quick Access toolbar with options at this drop-down list. ____________
6. Add a button to the Quick Access toolbar by right-clicking the desired button and then clicking this option at the shortcut menu. ____________
7. Click the Customize Quick Access Toolbar button and then click *More Commands* and this dialog box displays. ____________
8. This is the default setting for the *Choose commands from* option at the Word Options dialog box. ____________
9. Change user name and initials at the Word Options dialog box with this option selected in the left panel. ____________
10. Change the default file location at the Word Options dialog box with this option selected in the left panel. ____________

Applying your skills

Assessment 1 Insert and Format Text in a Medical Plan Document

1. Open **Document28.docx** and save the document with the name **C22A01**.
2. Add the following text to AutoCorrect:
   a. Insert *kl* in the *Replace* text box and insert *Key Life Health Plan* in the *With* text box.
   b. Insert *m* in the *Replace* text box and insert *medical* in the *With* text box.

3. With the insertion point positioned at the beginning of the document, type the text shown in Figure 22.8.
4. Make the following changes to the document:
   a. Apply the Heading 1 style to the title.
   b. Apply the Heading 2 style to the four headings in the document.
   c. Change the style set to *Formal*.
   d. Change the theme to *Civic*.
5. Insert the Puzzle (Odd Page) footer building block, click the *[Type the company name]* placeholder, type **kl**, and then press the spacebar. (This inserts *Key Life Health Plan* in the placeholder.)
6. Delete the text *Confidential* that displays in the footer.
7. Double-click in the document.
8. Press Ctrl + End to move the insertion point to the end of the document and then insert the *FileName* field.
9. Press Shift + Enter and then insert the *PrintDate* field. (You choose the date format.)
10. Move the insertion point to the beginning of the heading *Quality Assessment*, display the Paragraph dialog box with the Line and Page Breaks tab selected, insert a check mark in the *Keep with next* check box, and then close the dialog box.
11. Save and then print **C22A01.docx**.
12. Delete the two entries you made at the AutoCorrect dialog box.
13. Close **C22A01.docx**.

Figure 22.8 Assessment 1

kl

How the Plan Works

When you enroll in kl, you and each eligible family member selects a plan option. A kl option includes a main m clinic, any affiliated satellite clinics, and designated hospitals. Family members may choose different m plan options and can easily change options.

Some m plan options do not require you to choose a primary care physician. This means a member may self-refer for specialty care within that m plan option. However, kl encourages members to establish an ongoing relationship with a primary care physician and develop a valuable partnership in the management of their m care.

kl provides coverage for emergency m services outside the service area. If the m emergency is not life threatening, call your primary care physician to arrange for care before going to an emergency facility. If you have a life-threatening emergency, go directly to the nearest appropriate facility. Any follow-up care to emergency m services must be coordinated within your plan option.

Assessment 2 Create a Vacation Document with AutoCorrect and Special Symbols

1. At a blank document, add the following text to AutoCorrect:
   a. Insert *Pt* in the *Replace* text box and insert *Patagonia* in the *With* text box.
   b. Insert *Ft* in the *Replace* text box and insert *Futaleufu* in the *With* text box.
   c. Insert the Euro currency symbol (€) in the *With* text box (do this through the Symbol dialog box) and type **eu** in the *Replace* text box. (The Euro currency symbol is located toward the bottom of the Symbol dialog box list box with (normal text) selected.)
2. Type the text shown in Figure 22.9. Create the smiley face icon by typing :) and then pressing the spacebar. (To insert the Euro currency symbol, type **eu** and then press the spacebar. Press the Backspace key once and then type the amount.)
3. Save the document with the name **C22A02**.
4. Save, print, and then close **C22A02.docx**.
5. Delete the *eu*, *Ft*, and *Pt* AutoCorrect entries.

Figure 22.9 Assessment 2

LUXURY FAMILY ADVENTURE VACATIONS

Sign up today for one of our exciting luxury family adventure vacations, created for families who enjoy a multitude of outdoor activities and a bit of luxury. Our Chile luxury vacation combines whitewater rafting, hiking, kayaking, and horseback riding into one fun-filled week of adventure travel in beautiful Pt, Chile.

More than a family rafting trip, we'll make sure you are exposed to all that the Ft Valley has to offer including whitewater rafting on the Ft River, which contains sections for all levels of ability and experience; hiking up some of the beautiful tributaries of the Ft River; and horseback riding across beautiful valleys past the base of snow-peaked mountains.

Pt, Chile, provides a wide variety of opportunities for active travel that the whole family can enjoy. You can feel confident that we will take care of all of the details so that your experience is a mix of fun, comfort, and relaxation. ☺

Price for single occupancy:
$2,899
€2,675

Price for double occupancy:
$2,699
€2,450

Price for triple occupancy:
$2,499
€2,100

Assessment 3 Create a Report on Word Options and Customization Features

1. Display the Word Options dialog box and determine how to do the following:
   a. Change the color scheme. (Popular)
   b. Change the number of minutes for saving AutoRecover information. (Save)
   c. Change the number of recent documents that display in the Open button drop-down list. (Advanced)
   d. Display the File Locations dialog box and modify the location of documents and templates. (Advanced)
2. At a blank document, create a report that describes how to do the following:
   a. Steps to change the color scheme to Silver.
   b. Steps to change the minutes for saving AutoRecover information to 5 minutes.
   c. Steps to change the number of recent documents that display in the Open button drop-down list to 15.
   d. Steps to display the File Locations dialog box.
3. Use the Help feature to learn how to customize the Status bar and then add to your report steps that describe how to add track changes and caps lock notification in the Status bar.
4. Format your document to improve its visual appeal.
5. Save the document with the name **C22A03**.
6. Print and then close **C22A03.docx**.

Chapter 23

Customizing Themes

SNAP
Tutorial 23.1
Customizing Themes

Performance Objectives

Upon successful completion of Chapter 23, you will be able to:

- Create custom theme colors and theme fonts and apply theme effects
- Save a custom theme
- Apply, edit, and delete custom themes
- Reset to the template theme

The Microsoft Office suite offers themes to help you maintain consistent formatting both within and across documents, creating a professional and polished look. You can use the themes provided by Office or create your own custom themes. In this chapter, you will learn how to customize theme colors and fonts and save custom themes. You will also learn how to edit and delete custom themes and then reset options to the default template theme.

Note: Before beginning computer exercises for this chapter, copy to your storage medium the Chapter23 folder from the CD that accompanies this textbook and then make Chapter23 the active folder.

Customizing Themes

As you learned in Chapter 1, documents you create in Word are based on a template called the Normal.dotm template. This template provides default layout and formatting instructions and specifies the themes and styles that Word applies to your documents. This default template includes a number of built-in or predesigned themes, some of which you have been using throughout the chapters of this textbook to apply color, change fonts, and add effects to content in documents. The built-in themes that are available in Microsoft Word are also available in Excel, PowerPoint, and Outlook. Having these themes available across applications allows you to "brand" business files, such as documents, workbooks, and presentations, with a consistent and uniform appearance.

A theme is a combination of colors, fonts, and effects. Within a theme, you can change one or all of these elements with the buttons in the Themes group in the Page Layout tab. You can use the default theme, named *Office*, change to one of the other built-in themes, or create your own custom theme. You can also download additional themes by clicking the Page Layout tab, clicking the Themes button, and then clicking *More Themes on Microsoft Online*. A theme that you create displays in the

QUICK STEPS

Create Custom Theme Colors

1. Click Page Layout tab.
2. Click Theme Colors button.
3. Click *Create New Theme Colors.*
4. Select new background, accent, or hyperlink colors.
5. Type name for custom color theme.
6. Click Save button.

Theme Colors

Theme Fonts

Themes drop-down gallery under the *Custom* section. To create a custom theme, change the color, font, and/or effects of a predesigned theme.

The buttons in the Themes group in the Page Layout tab display a visual representation of the current theme. For example, the Themes button displays an uppercase and lowercase *A* with a row of small colored squares below them. If you change the theme colors, the change is reflected in these squares on the Themes button and in the four squares on the Theme Colors button. If you change theme fonts, the *As* on the Themes button and the uppercase *A* on the Theme Fonts button reflect the change.

Creating Custom Theme Colors

To create custom theme colors, click the Page Layout tab, click the Theme Colors button, and then click *Create New Theme Colors* at the drop-down gallery. This displays the Create New Theme Colors dialog box, shown in Figure 23.1. A color theme includes four text and background colors, six accent colors, and two hyperlink colors, as shown in the *Theme colors* section of the dialog box. Change a color in the list box by clicking the color button at the right side of the color option and then clicking the desired color in the color palette.

Figure 23.1 Create New Theme Colors Dialog Box

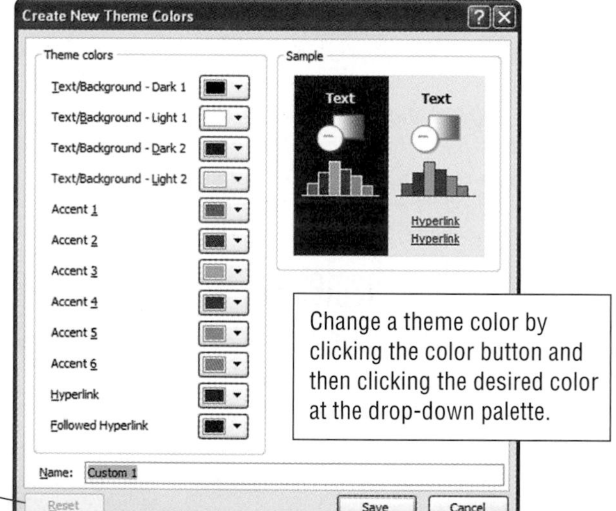

After you have made all desired changes to the theme colors, click in the *Name* text box, type a name for the custom theme colors, and then click the Save button. This saves the custom theme colors and also applies the color changes to the currently open document. Display the custom theme colors by clicking the Theme Colors button in the Themes group in the Page Layout tab. Your custom theme colors will display toward the top of the drop-down gallery in the *Custom* section, as shown in Figure 23.2.

Figure 23.2 Theme Colors Drop-down Gallery with Custom Theme

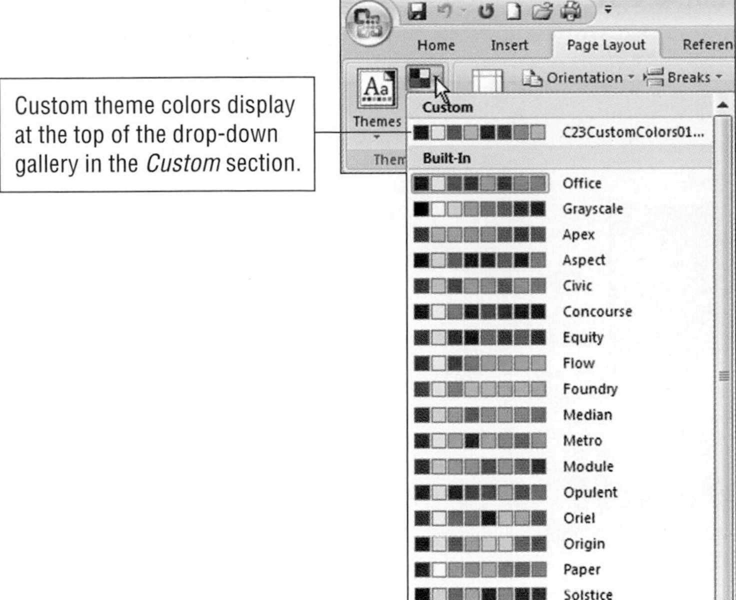

Resetting Custom Colors

If you change the colors at the Create New Theme Colors dialog box and then decide you do not like the changes, click the Reset button located in the lower left corner of the dialog box. Clicking this button resets the colors back to the default *Office* template colors.

Exercise 1A

Creating Custom Theme Colors

Note: If you are running Word 2007 on a computer connected to a network in a public environment such as a school, you may not be able to save themes to the hard drive. Before beginning Exercise 1A, check with your instructor.

1. At a blank document, create custom theme colors by completing the following steps:
   a. Click the Page Layout tab.
   b. Click the Theme Colors button in the Themes group and then click the *Create New Theme Colors* option at the drop-down gallery.
   c. At the Create New Theme Colors dialog box, click the color button that displays at the right side of the *Text/Background - Light 1* option and then click Dark Red in the color palette (the first color from the left in the *Standard Colors* section).

Step 1c

d. Click the color button that displays at the right side of the *Accent 1* option and then click Yellow in the color palette (the fourth color from the left in the *Standard Colors* section).

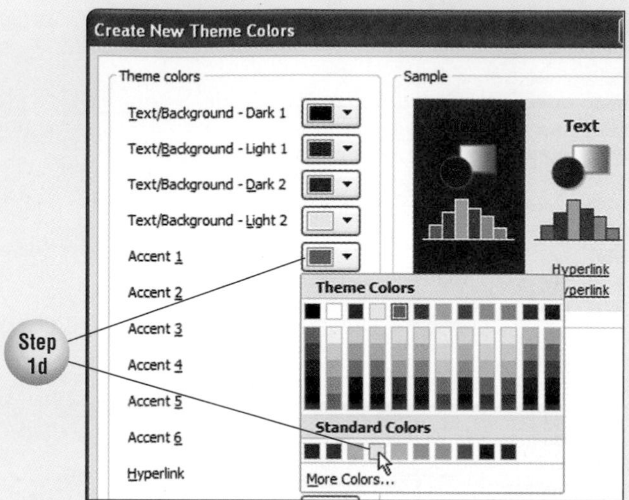

2. After viewing the colors you have chosen in the *Sample* section at the right of the dialog box, start over by completing the following steps:
   a. Click the Reset button located in the lower left corner of the dialog box.

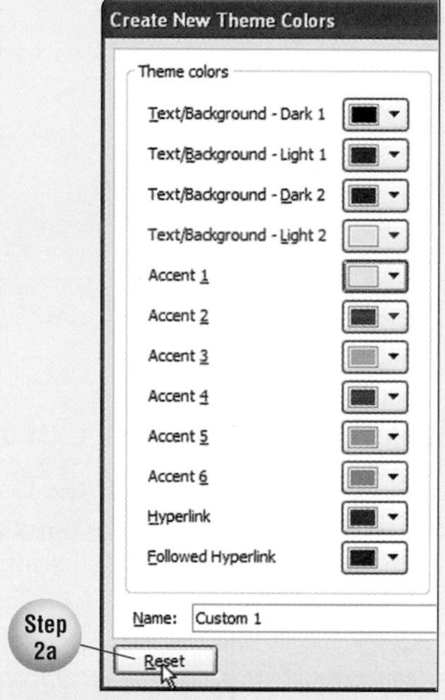

   b. Click the color button that displays at the right side of the *Accent 2* option and then click *Aqua, Accent 5, Lighter 40%* in the color palette.

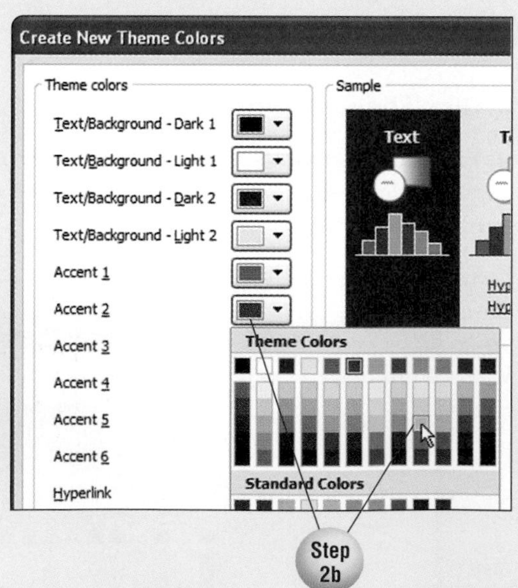

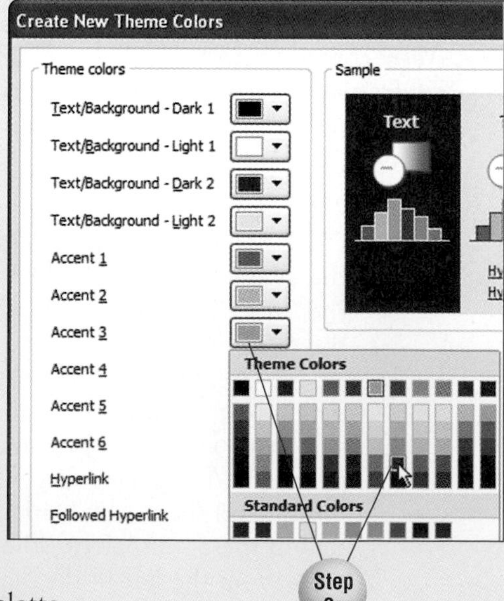

   c. Click the color button that displays at the right side of the *Accent 3* option and then click *Purple, Accent 4, Darker 25%* in the color palette.

d. Click the color button that displays at the right side of the *Accent 6* option and then click *Aqua, Accent 5, Lighter 40%* in the color palette.
3. Save the custom colors by completing the following steps:
   a. Select the current text in the *Name* text box.
   b. Type **C23CustomColors01** and then type your last name.

Step 3b

Name: C23CustomColors01LastName

Reset Save Cancel

Step 3c

   c. Click the Save button.
4. Close the document without saving it.

Applying Custom Theme Colors

After you create custom theme colors, you can apply them to your document by clicking the Theme Colors button in the Themes group in the Page Layout tab and then clicking the custom theme colors that display toward the top of the drop-down gallery in the *Custom* section.

Exercise 1B

Applying Custom Theme Colors

1. Open **Document24.docx** and save the document with the name **C23Ex01**.
2. Apply the Heading 1 style to the title and the Heading 2 style to the two headings.
3. Change the style set to *Formal*.
4. Insert a pull quote by completing the following steps:
   a. Click the Insert tab.
   b. Click the Quick Parts button and then click *Building Blocks Organizer*.
   c. At the Building Blocks Organizer dialog box, click the *Name* column heading to alphabetize the building blocks by name.
   d. Scroll down the list box and then click *Tiles Sidebar*.
   e. Click the Insert button.
   f. With the insertion point positioned in the pull quote text box, type "**Viruses can create effects that range from minor and annoying to highly destructive . . .** "
5. Apply your custom theme colors by completing the following steps:
   a. Click the Page Layout tab.
   b. Click the Theme Colors button in the Themes group.
   c. Click the custom theme colors named *C23CustomColors01LastName* that displays toward the top of the drop-down gallery in the *Custom* group.
6. Save **C23Ex01.docx**.
7. Print page 1 of **C23Ex01.docx** and then close the document.

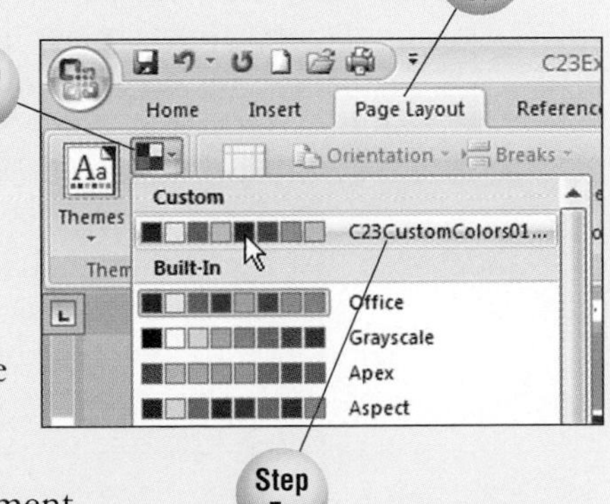

Choosing Colors at the Colors Dialog Box

When you click a color button in the Create New Theme Colors dialog box, color sets display in columns in a color palette. If you want more control over colors (i.e., you want to use a color at a percentage other than those listed in a column), click the *More Colors* option that displays at the bottom of the color palette. This displays the Colors dialog box, which contains two tabs, a Standard tab and a Custom tab. With the Standard tab selected, click the desired color option that displays in the honeycomb. With the Custom tab selected, click the desired color in the color square and fine tune the color by dragging the slider button (right-pointing triangle) on the vertical slider bar that displays at the right side of the color square. You can also enter numbers in the *Red*, *Green*, and *Blue* text boxes in the dialog box.

Exercise 1C

Choosing Custom Colors

1. At a blank document, create custom theme colors by completing the following steps:
   a. Click the Page Layout tab.
   b. Click the Theme Colors button in the Themes group and then click the *Create New Theme Colors* option at the drop-down gallery.
   c. At the Create New Theme Colors dialog box, change the *Text/Background - Light 1* color by completing the following steps:
      1) Click the color button that displays at the right side of the *Text/Background - Light 1* option and then click the *More Colors* option at the bottom of the color palette.
      2) At the Colors dialog box, click the Standard tab if necessary.
      3) Click the dark green color at the left edge of the honeycomb, as shown at the right.
      4) Click OK to close the Colors dialog box.
   d. Change the *Accent 2* color by completing the following steps:
      1) Click the *Accent 2* color button.
      2) At the color palette, click the dark green color that displays in the *Recent Colors* row.
   e. Change the *Accent 3* color by completing the following steps:
      1) Click the *Accent 3* color button and then click the *More Colors* option.
      2) At the Colors dialog box, click the Standard tab if necessary.
      3) Click the yellow color in the lower portion of the honeycomb, as shown at the right.
      4) Click OK to close the Colors dialog box.

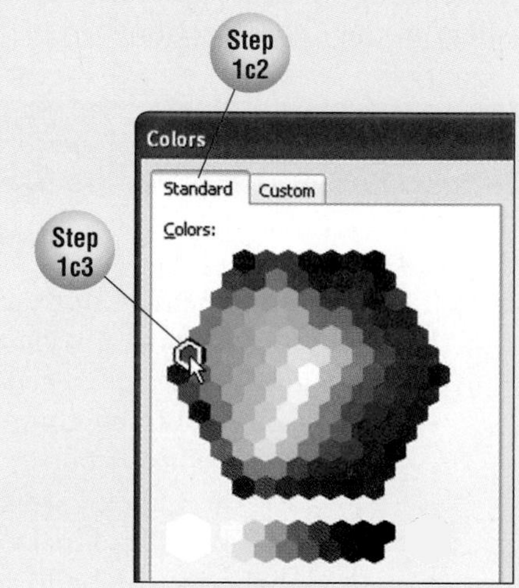

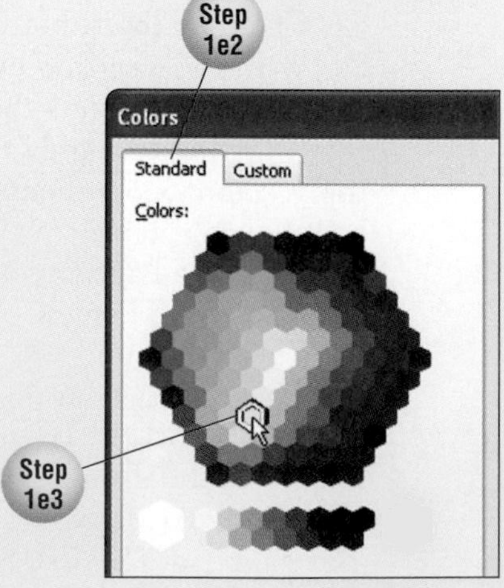

f. Change the *Accent 6* color by completing the following steps:
   1) Click the *Accent 6* color button and then click the *More Colors* option.
   2) At the Colors dialog box, click the Custom tab if necessary.
   3) Select the number in the *Red* text box and then type **0**.
   4) Select the number in the *Green* text box and then type **168**.
   5) Select the number in the *Blue* text box and then type **0**.
   6) Click OK to close the Colors dialog box.
2. Save the custom theme colors by completing the following steps:
   a. Select the text in the *Name* text box.
   b. Type **C23CustomColors02** and then type your last name.
   c. Click the Save button.
3. Close the document without saving it.
4. Open **C23Ex01.docx**.
5. Apply the custom theme colors by completing the following steps:
   a. Click the Page Layout tab.
   b. Click the Theme Colors button in the Themes group.
   c. Click the theme colors option that you named in Step 2 (*C23CustomColors02LastName*) that displays toward the top of the drop-down gallery in the *Custom* group.
6. Save **C23Ex01.docx**.
7. Print page 1 of **C23Ex01.docx** and then close the document.

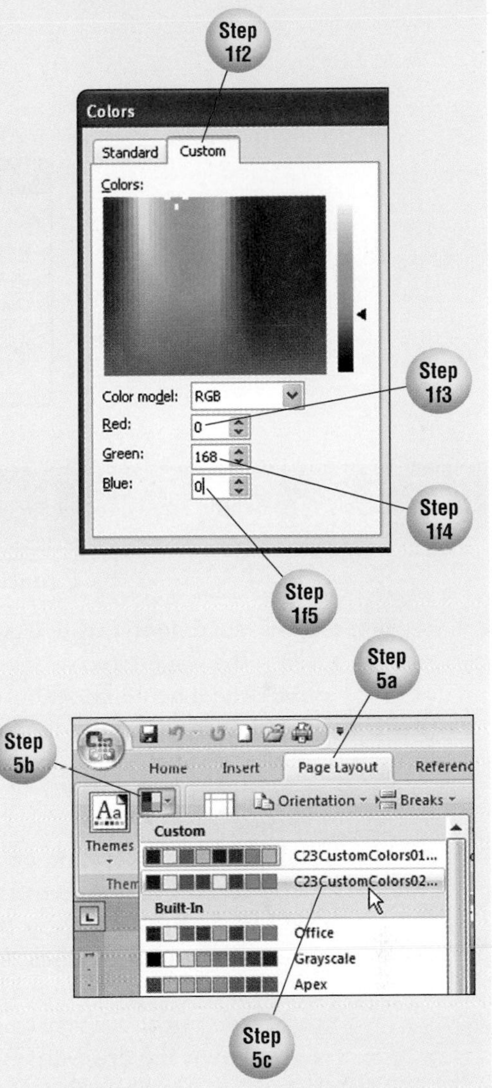

Creating Custom Theme Fonts

Create Custom Theme Fonts
1. Click Page Layout tab.
2. Click Theme Fonts button.
3. Click *Create New Theme Fonts.*
4. Choose desired fonts.
5. Type name for custom theme fonts.
6. Click Save button.

To create custom theme fonts, click the Page Layout tab, click the Theme Fonts button, and then click *Create New Theme Fonts* at the drop-down gallery. This displays the Create New Theme Fonts dialog box, shown in Figure 23.3. At this dialog box, choose a heading font and a body font. Type a name for the custom theme fonts in the *Name* box and then click the Save button.

Figure 23.3 **Create New Theme Fonts Dialog Box**

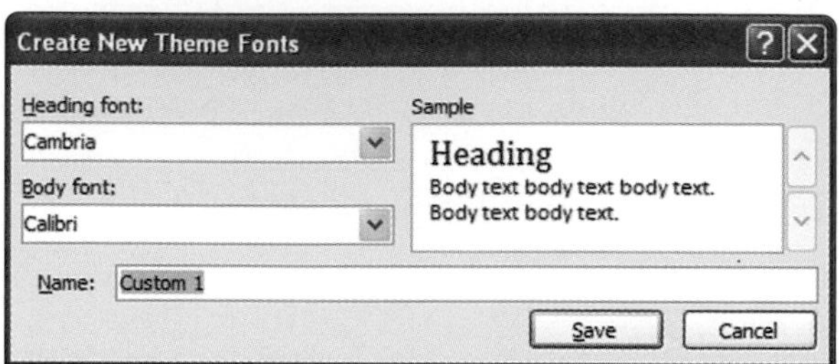

Exercise 2A

Creating Custom Theme Fonts

1. At a blank document, create custom theme fonts by completing the following steps:
   a. Click the Page Layout tab.
   b. Click the Theme Fonts button in the Themes group and then click the *Create New Theme Fonts* option at the drop-down gallery.
   c. At the Create New Theme Fonts dialog box, click the down-pointing arrow at the right side of the *Heading font* option box, scroll up the drop-down list, and then click *Arial.*
   d. Click the down-pointing arrow at the right side of the *Body font* option box, scroll down the drop-down list, and then click *Times New Roman*.
2. Save the custom fonts by completing the following steps:
   a. Select the text in the *Name* text box.
   b. Type **C23CustomFonts01** and then type your last name.
   c. Click the Save button.
3. Close the document without saving it.

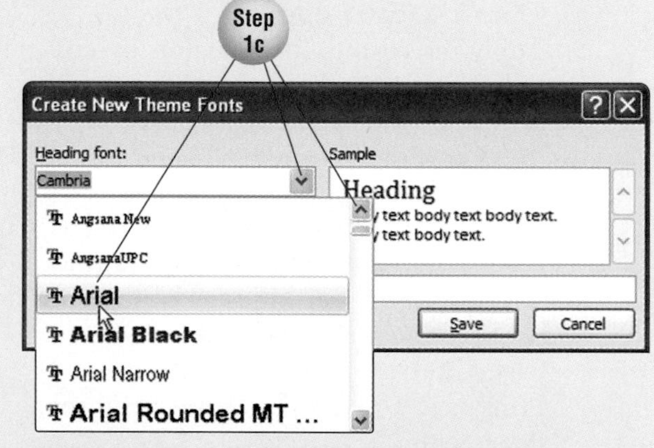

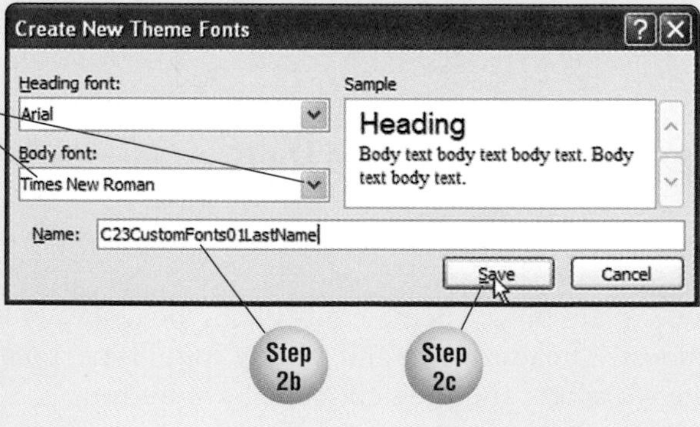

Applying Theme Effects

With options in the Theme Effects button drop-down gallery, you can apply line sets and fill effects to text. You cannot create your own theme effects, but you can apply a theme effect and then save the formatting as your own document theme.

Saving a Document Theme

When you have customized theme colors and fonts and applied theme effects to a document, you can save these in a custom document theme. To do this, click the Themes button in the Themes group in the Page Layout tab and then click *Save Current Theme* at the drop-down gallery. This displays the Save Current Theme dialog box, which has many of the same options that are available in the Save As dialog box. Type a name for your custom document theme in the *File name* text box and then click the Save button.

QUICK STEPS

Save a Document Theme
1. Click Page Layout tab.
2. Click Themes button.
3. Click *Save Current Theme.*
4. Type name for custom theme.
5. Click Save button.

Exercise 2B

Applying Theme Effects and Saving a Document Theme

1. At a blank document, create custom theme colors by completing the following steps:
   a. Click the Page Layout tab.
   b. Click the Theme Colors button and then click *Create New Theme Colors* at the bottom of the drop-down gallery.
   c. At the Create New Theme Colors dialog box, click the *Text/Background - Dark 2* color button and then click Blue in the color palette (the third color from the right in the *Standard Colors* section).

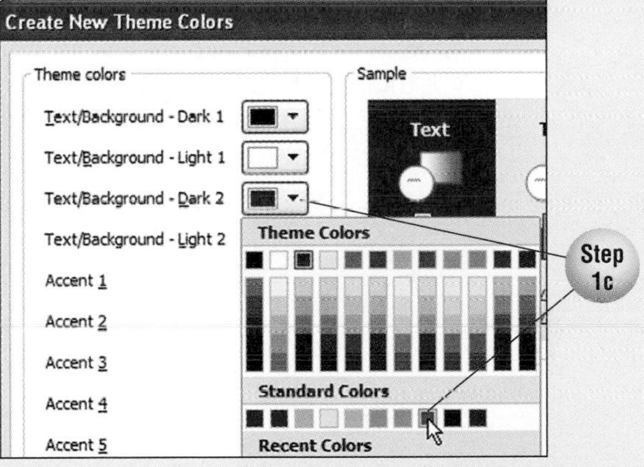

   d. Change the *Accent 1* color by completing the following steps:
      1) Click the color button that displays at the right side of the *Accent 1* option.
      2) Click the More Colors button in the color palette.
      3) At the Colors dialog box, click the Standard tab if necessary.
      4) Click the dark green color at the left of the honeycomb, as shown at the right.
      5) Click OK to close the dialog box.

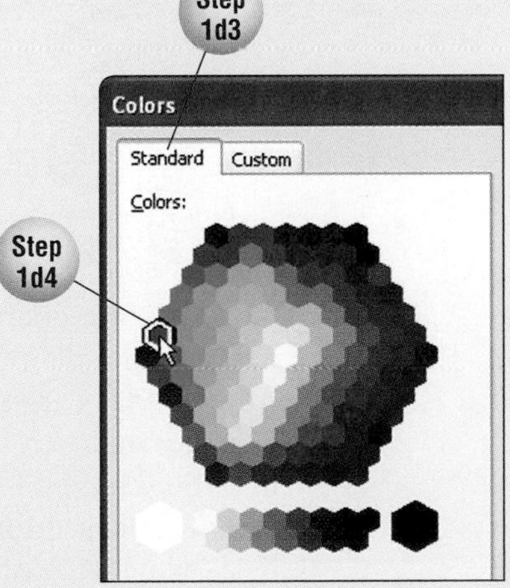

   e. Save the custom colors with the name *C23CustomColors03LastName*.
2. Close the document without saving it.
3. Open **NSSServices.docx** and save the document with the name **C23Ex02**.
4. Make the following changes to the document:
   a. Apply the Title style to the company name, *Northland Security Systems,* located to the right of the image.
   b. Apply the Heading 1 style to the heading *Northland Security Systems Mission*.
   c. Apply the Heading 2 style to the headings *Security Services* and *Security Software*.

5. Apply the custom theme colors you saved by completing the following steps:
   a. Click the Page Layout tab.
   b. Click the Theme Colors button in the Themes group.
   c. Click the *C23CustomColors03LastName* option that displays toward the top of the drop-down gallery in the *Custom* group.

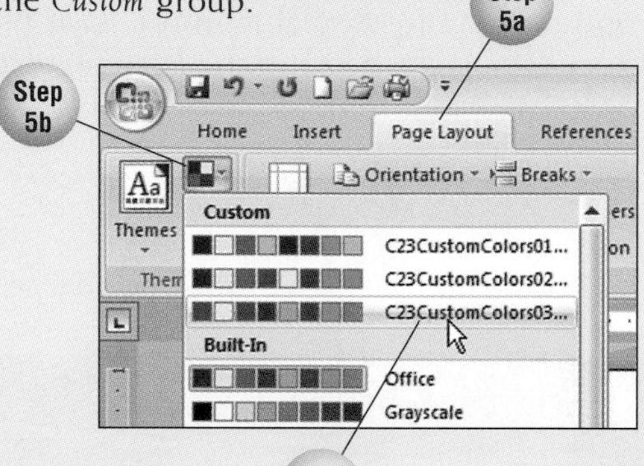

6. Apply the custom theme fonts you saved by clicking the Theme Fonts button in the Themes group and then clicking the *C23CustomFonts01LastName* option that displays toward the top of the drop-down gallery in the *Custom* group.

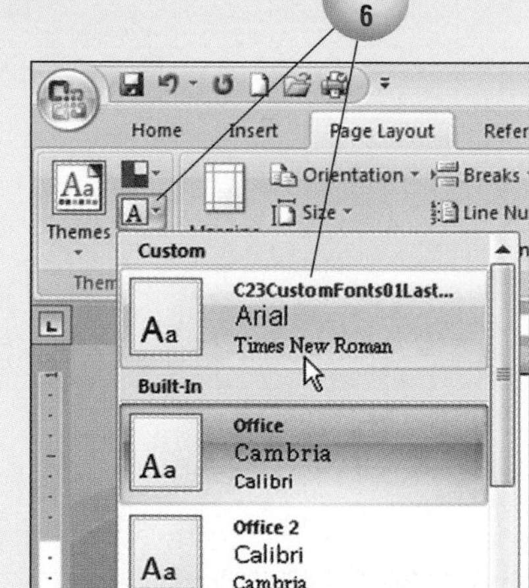

7. Apply a theme effect by clicking the Theme Effects button in the Themes group and then clicking *Concourse* at the drop-down gallery.

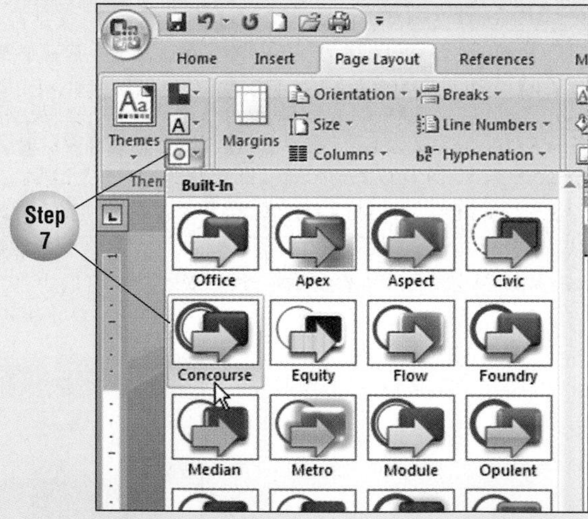

8. Make the following changes to the SmartArt diagram:
   a. Click near the diagram to select it. (When the diagram is selected, a light turquoise border displays around it.)
   b. Click the SmartArt Tools Design tab.
   c. Click the Change Colors button and then click the third color option from the left in the *Colorful* section (*Colorful Range - Accent Colors 3 to 4*).
   d. Click the More button at the right side of the SmartArt Styles group and then click the third option from the left in the top row in the *3-D* section (*Cartoon*).
   e. Click outside the diagram to deselect it.

9. Save the custom theme colors and fonts as well as the Concourse theme effect into a custom document theme by completing the following steps:
   a. Click the Page Layout tab.
   b. Click the Themes button in the Themes group.
   c. Click the *Save Current Theme* option that displays at the bottom of the drop-down gallery.
   d. At the Save Current Theme dialog box, type **C23CustomTheme01** and then type your last name in the *File name* text box.
   e. Click the Save button.

Step 9d

File name: C23CustomTheme01LastName

Save as type: Office Theme (*.thmx)

Save Cancel

Step 9e

10. Save and then print **C23Ex02.docx**.

Editing Custom Themes

Edit Custom Theme Colors
1. Click Page Layout tab.
2. Click Theme Colors button.
3. Right-click desired custom theme.
4. Click *Edit*.
5. Make desired changes.
6. Click Save button.

Edit Custom Theme Fonts
1. Click Page Layout tab.
2. Click Theme Fonts button.
3. Right-click desired custom theme.
4. Click *Edit*.
5. Make desired changes.
6. Click Save button.

You can edit custom theme colors and custom theme fonts. To edit custom theme colors, click the Page Layout tab and then click the Theme Colors button in the Themes group. At the drop-down gallery of custom and built-in themes, right-click your custom theme and then click Edit at the shortcut menu. This displays the Edit Theme Colors dialog box, which contains the same options that are available at the Create New Theme Colors dialog box, shown in Figure 23.1. Make the desired changes to theme colors and then click the Save button.

To edit custom theme fonts, click the Theme Fonts button in the Themes group in the Page Layout tab, right-click your custom theme fonts, and then click Edit at the shortcut menu. This displays the Edit Theme Fonts dialog box, which contains the same options that are available at the Create New Theme Fonts dialog box, shown in Figure 23.3. Make the desired changes and then click the Save button.

Exercise 2C

Editing Custom Themes

1. With **C23Ex02.docx** open, edit the custom theme colors by completing the following steps:
   a. Click the Page Layout tab.
   b. Click the Theme Colors button.
   c. Right-click the *C23CustomColors03LastName* theme and then click Edit at the shortcut menu.

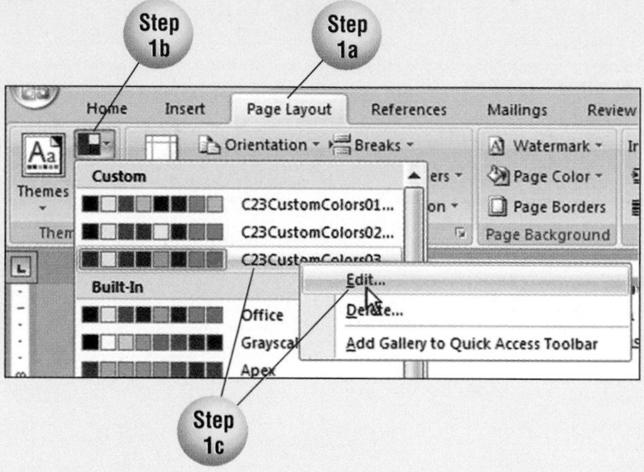

   d. At the Edit Theme Colors dialog box, click the *Text/Background - Dark 2* color button.
   e. Click the More Colors button in the color palette.
   f. At the Colors dialog box, click the Standard tab if necessary.
   g. Click the dark green color at the left edge of the honeycomb, as shown at the right.
   h. Click OK to close the dialog box.
   i. Click the Save button.

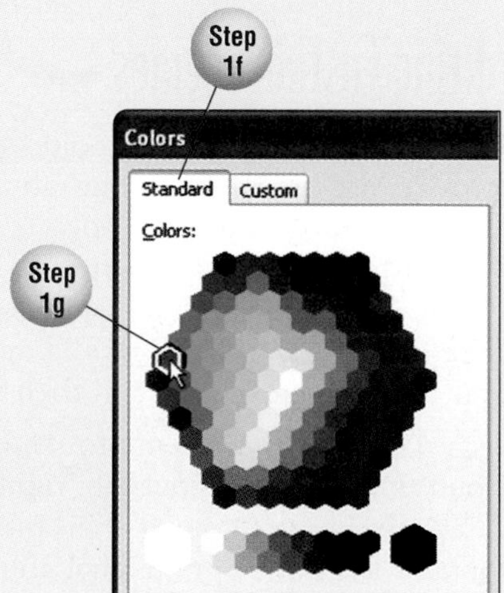

2. Edit the custom theme fonts by completing the following steps:
   a. Click the Theme Fonts button in the Themes group.
   b. Right-click the *C23CustomFonts01LastName* theme and then click *Edit* at the shortcut menu.
   c. At the Edit Theme Fonts dialog box, click the down-pointing arrow at the right side of the *Body font* option box, scroll up the drop-down list, and then click *Constantia*.
   d. Click the Save button.
3. Apply a different theme effect by clicking the Theme Effects button in the Themes group and then clicking *Apex* at the drop-down gallery. (This effect applies a shadow behind the shapes.)
4. Save the changes to the custom theme by completing the following steps:
   a. Click the Themes button and then click *Save Current Theme* at the drop-down gallery.
   b. At the Save Current Theme dialog box, click the *C23CustomTheme01LastName* theme document.
   c. Click the Save button.
   d. At the replace question, click Yes.
5. Save, print, and then close **C23Ex02.docx**.

Resetting to Template Theme

If you apply a built-in theme other than the *Office* default or if you apply a custom theme, you can reset the theme back to the template default. To do this, click the Themes button and then click the *Reset to Theme from Template* at the drop-down gallery. If you are working in the default template provided by Word, clicking this option resets the theme to *Office*.

Reset Template Theme
1. Click Page Layout tab.
2. Click Themes button.
3. Click *Reset to Theme from Template.*

Exercise 3A

Applying Themes and Resetting to the Template Themes

1. Open **NSSSecurity.docx** and save the document with the name **C23Ex03**.
2. Apply the Title style to the company name and the Heading 1 style to the two headings in the document.
3. Apply your custom theme by completing the following steps:
   a. Click the Page Layout tab.
   b. Click the Themes button.
   c. Click the *C23CustomTheme01LastName* custom theme that displays at the top of the drop-down gallery in the *Custom* section.
4. Save and then print **C23Ex03.docx**.
5. Reset the theme to the *Office* default by clicking the Themes button and then clicking *Reset to Theme from Template* at the drop-down gallery. (This returns the theme to the *Office* default.)
6. Save and then close **C23Ex03.docx**.

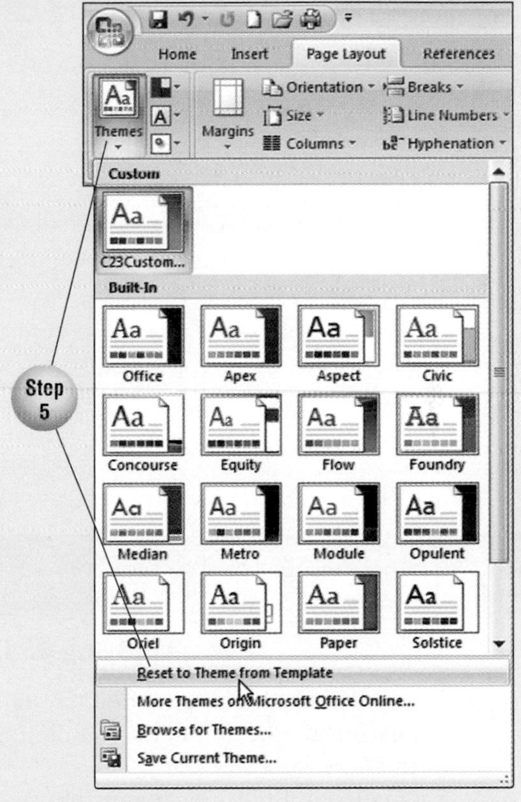

QUICK STEPS

Delete Custom Theme Colors
1. Click Page Layout tab.
2. Click Theme Colors button.
3. Right-click desired custom theme.
4. Click *Delete*.
5. Click Yes.

Delete Custom Theme Fonts
1. Click Page Layout tab.
2. Click Theme Fonts button.
3. Right-click desired custom theme.
4. Click *Delete*.
5. Click Yes.

Delete Custom Theme
1. Click Page Layout tab.
2. Click Themes button.
3. Click *Save Current Theme*.
4. Click custom theme.
5. Click *Delete*.
6. Click Yes.

Deleting Custom Themes

You can delete custom theme colors from the Theme Colors button drop-down gallery, custom theme fonts from the Theme Fonts drop-down gallery, and custom themes from the Save Current Theme dialog box.

To delete custom theme colors, click the Theme Colors button, right-click the theme you want to delete, and then click Delete at the shortcut menu. At the message asking if you want to delete the theme colors, click Yes. To delete custom theme fonts, click the Theme Fonts button, right-click the theme you want to delete, and then click Delete at the shortcut menu. At the message asking if you want to delete the theme fonts, click Yes.

Delete a custom theme (which includes custom colors, fonts, and effects) at the Save Current Theme dialog box. To display this dialog box, click the Themes button and then click *Save Current Theme* at the drop-down gallery. At the dialog box, click the custom theme document name and then click the Delete button on the dialog box toolbar. At the message asking if you are sure you want to send the theme document to the Recycle Bin, click Yes.

Exercise 3B

Applying and Deleting Custom Themes

1. At a blank document, delete the custom theme colors by completing the following steps:
   a. Click the Page Layout tab.
   b. Click the Theme Colors button in the Themes group.
   c. Right-click the *C23CustomColors01LastName* custom theme colors.
   d. Click Delete at the shortcut menu.
   e. At the question asking if you want to delete the theme colors, click Yes.

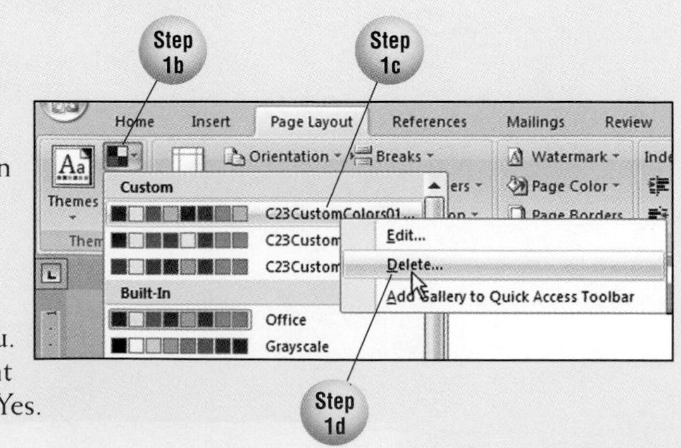

2. Complete steps similar to those in Step 1 to delete the *C23CustomColors02LastName* custom theme colors and the *C23CustomColors03LastName* custom theme colors.
3. Delete the custom theme fonts by completing the following steps:
   a. Click the Theme Fonts button in the Themes group.
   b. Right-click the *C23CustomFonts01LastName* custom theme fonts.
   c. Click Delete at the shortcut menu.
   d. At the question asking if you want to delete the theme fonts, click Yes.
4. Delete the custom theme by completing the following steps:
   a. Click the Themes button.
   b. Click *Save Current Theme* located toward the bottom of the drop-down gallery.
   c. At the Save Current Theme dialog box, click the *C23CustomTheme01LastName* theme document in the list box.
   d. Click the Delete button on the dialog box toolbar.

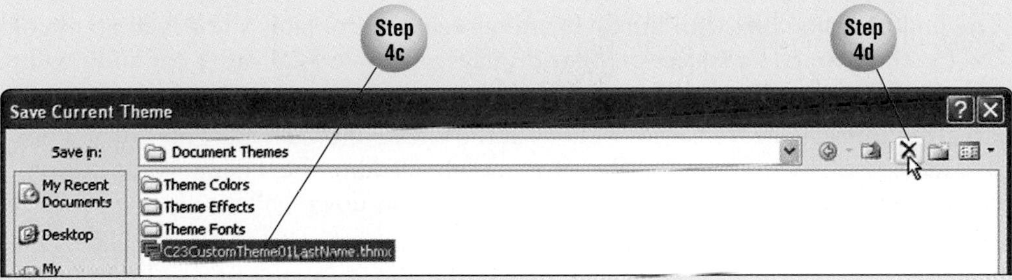

   e. At the message asking if you are sure you want to send the theme to the Recycle Bin, click Yes.
   f. Click the Cancel button to close the dialog box.
5. Close the document without saving it.

Chapter Summary

- Create custom theme colors with options at the Create New Theme Colors dialog box.
- Click the Reset button in the Create New Theme Colors dialog box to reset colors back to the default *Office* template colors.
- Apply custom theme colors by clicking the Page Layout tab, clicking the Theme Colors button, and then clicking the custom theme colors in the *Custom* section of the drop-down gallery.
- Additional color options are available at the Colors dialog box with the Standard tab or the Custom tab selected. Display this dialog box by clicking a color button in the Create New Theme Colors dialog box and then clicking the *More Colors* option.
- The Colors dialog box with the Standard tab selected contains a honeycomb of colors. Click the Custom tab, and a square of color displays with a vertical slider bar and text boxes for specifying percentages of red, green, and blue.
- Create custom theme fonts with options at the Create New Theme Fonts dialog box. Display this dialog box by clicking the Page Layout tab, clicking the Theme Fonts button, and then clicking the *Create New Theme Fonts* option at the drop-down gallery.
- Apply custom theme fonts by clicking the Page Layout tab, clicking the Theme Fonts button, and then clicking the custom theme fonts in the *Custom* section of the drop-down gallery.
- Create custom theme colors and custom theme fonts, apply a theme effect, and then save the changes in a custom theme.
- Save a custom theme at the Save Current Theme dialog box. Display this dialog box by clicking the Themes button in the Themes group and then clicking *Save Current Theme* at the drop-down gallery.
- Edit custom theme colors with options at the Edit Theme Colors dialog box. Display this dialog box by clicking the Theme Colors button, right-clicking the custom theme, and then clicking the *Edit* option.
- Edit custom theme fonts with options at the Edit Theme Fonts dialog box. Display this dialog box by clicking the Theme Fonts button, right-clicking the custom theme, and then clicking the *Edit* option.
- Click the *Reset to Theme from Template* at the Themes button drop-down gallery to reset the theme to the template default.
- Delete custom theme colors by clicking the Theme Colors button, right-clicking the custom theme, and then clicking the *Delete* option.
- Delete custom theme fonts by clicking the Theme Fonts button, right-clicking the custom theme, and then clicking the *Delete* option.
- Delete a custom theme at the Save Current Theme dialog box. Display this dialog box by clicking the Themes button and then clicking *Save Current Theme* at the drop-down gallery. Click the custom theme document name and then click the Delete button on the dialog box toolbar.

Commands review

FEATURE	RIBBON TAB, GROUP	BUTTON, OPTION
Create New Theme Colors dialog box	Page Layout, Themes	, Create New Theme Colors
Create New Theme Fonts dialog box	Page Layout, Themes	, Create New Theme Fonts
Theme effects	Page Layout, Themes	
Save Current Theme dialog box	Page Layout, Themes	, Save Current Theme

Reviewing key points

Completion: In the space provided at the right, indicate the correct term, symbol, or command.

1. The Themes button is located in this tab. ______________________
2. This is the name of the default theme. ______________________
3. Create custom theme colors with options at this dialog box. ______________________
4. Custom theme colors you create display in this section of the Theme Colors button drop-down gallery. ______________________
5. The Colors dialog box with this tab selected displays a honeycomb of color options. ______________________
6. The Colors dialog box with this tab selected displays the *Red*, *Green*, and *Blue* text boxes. ______________________
7. Create custom theme fonts with options at this dialog box. ______________________
8. To edit custom theme fonts, click the Theme Fonts button, do this to the custom theme, and then click Edit at the shortcut menu. ______________________
9. Click this option at the Themes button drop-down gallery to set the theme back to the template default. ______________________
10. Delete custom themes at this dialog box. ______________________

Applying your skills

Assessment 1 Create and Apply Custom Themes to a Medical Plans Document

1. At a blank document, create custom theme colors named *C23CustomColors01* followed by your initials that makes the following color changes:
   a. Change the *Accent 2* color to *Dark Blue* (the second option from the right in the *Standard Colors* section).
   b. Change the *Accent 5* color to *Olive Green, Accent 3, Darker 50%* (the bottom option in the seventh column in the *Theme Colors* section).
2. Click the Theme Effects button and then click *Paper* at the drop-down gallery.
3. Save the custom theme and name it *C23CustomTheme01* followed by your initials. *(Hint: Do this with the* Save Current Theme *option at the* Themes *drop-down gallery.)*
4. Close the document without saving the changes.
5. Open **Document28.docx** and save the document with the name **C23A01**.
6. Make the following changes to the document:
   a. Change the style set to *Formal*.
   b. With the insertion point positioned at the beginning of the document, type the title **Key Life Health Plan**.
   c. Apply the Heading 1 style to the title.
   d. Apply the Heading 2 style to the three headings in the document.
7. Move the insertion point to the end of the document and then insert the document **KLHPDiagram.docx**. *(Hint: Do this with the Object button in the Insert tab.)*
8. Apply the custom theme you created by clicking the Page Layout tab, clicking the Themes button, and then clicking the custom theme named *C23CustomTheme* followed by your initials.
9. Save, print, and then close **C23A01.docx**.

Assessment 2 Create and Apply Custom Themes to Real Photography Document

1. At a blank document, create custom theme colors named *C23CustomColors02* followed by your initials that makes the following color changes:
   a. Change the *Text/Background - Dark 2* color to *Orange, Accent 6, Darker 50%*.
   b. Change the *Accent 1* color to a custom color at the Colors dialog box with the Custom tab selected (enter 0 in the *Red* text box, *140* in the *Green* text box, and 0 in the Blue text box).
2. Create custom theme fonts named *C23CustomFonts01* followed by your initials that changes the Heading font to *Harrington*.
3. Click the Theme Effects button and then click *Verve* at the drop-down gallery.
4. Save the custom theme and name it *C23CustomTheme02* followed by your initials. *(Hint: Do this with the* Save Current Theme *option at the* Themes *drop-down gallery.)*
5. Close the document without saving the changes.
6. Open **RPServices.docx** and save the document with the name **C23A02**.
7. Apply your *C23CustomTheme02(initials)* theme to the document.
8. Save, print, and then close **C23A02.docx**.
9. At a blank document, delete the two custom color themes you created as well as the two custom themes and the one custom theme fonts.

Chapter 24

Formatting with Styles

SNAP
Tutorial 24.1
Using Document Styles

Performance Objectives

Upon successful completion of Chapter 24, you will be able to:

- Change the Quick Styles set default
- Apply styles
- Create new styles
- Create styles from existing formatting
- Create styles from existing styles
- Modify styles
- Save and delete a custom Quick Styles set

Along with the themes you learned about in Chapter 23, Word provides a number of predesigned styles, grouped into Quick Styles sets, that you can use to apply consistent formatting to text in documents. If none of these predesigned styles apply the formatting you want, you can create your own styles. In this chapter, you will learn how to apply, create, modify, and delete styles, as well as how to save and delete a custom Quick Styles set.

Note: Before beginning computer exercises for this chapter, copy to your storage medium the Chapter24 folder from the CD that accompanies this textbook and then make Chapter24 the active folder.

Formatting with Styles

A style is a set of formatting instructions that you can apply to text. Word provides a number of predesigned styles and groups those that apply similar formatting into sets called Quick Styles sets. Whereas a theme changes the overall colors, fonts, and effects used in a document, a Quick Styles set changes how the colors, fonts, and effects are combined and which color, font, and effect are dominant. Using the styles within a Quick Styles set, you can apply formatting that gives your document a uniform and professional appearance.

The default Quick Styles set is named *Default,* and the styles in this set are available in the Styles group in the Home tab. Four *Default* styles display as *thumbnails,* or miniature representations. Generally, these four styles are the Normal, No Spacing, Heading 1, and Heading 2 styles. The styles that display as thumbnails change to reflect the styles that have been applied to the active document. Click the More button to the right of the style thumbnails, and a drop-down gallery displays containing all of the styles available in the default set. Hover your mouse over a style in the drop-down gallery to see how the style will format text in your document.

You can also display the styles available in a Quick Styles set by clicking either the down-pointing arrow or up-pointing arrow to the right of the style thumbnails. Clicking the down-pointing arrow scrolls down the style set, displaying the next four styles. Clicking the up-pointing arrow scrolls up the set of styles.

Change Quick Styles Set Default
1. Change desired Quick Styles set, colors, and/or fonts.
2. Click Change Styles button.
3. Click *Set as Default.*

Changing the Quick Styles Set Default

Along with *Default* (the default Quick Styles set), Word provides a number of other Quick Styles sets. You have used some of these sets in previous chapters to apply formatting to your documents. To view all available Quick Styles sets, click the Change Styles button in the Styles group and then point to *Style Set*. Each Quick Styles set has a name, such as *Default*, *Distinctive*, or *Formal*, that provides a general description of the type of formatting the styles apply.

The styles in a Quick Styles set apply formatting that includes colors and fonts. You can change the colors or fonts applied by styles in a set with the *Colors* and *Fonts* options at the Change Styles drop-down list. However, because the styles in a set are designed to complement one another, in most situations you will not change them. To change style set colors, click the Change Styles button, point to *Colors*, and then click the desired theme colors. The theme colors available with the *Colors* option are the same as those available with the Themes button and Theme Colors button. Change style set fonts by clicking the Change Styles button, pointing to *Fonts*, and then clicking the desired theme fonts. The theme fonts available with the *Fonts* option are the same as those available with the Themes button and Theme Fonts button.

Because *Default* is the Quick Styles set default, it is available when you open a blank Word document. If you consistently format your documents with a different Quick Styles set, you may want to make that set the default. To do this, change to the Quick Styles set that you want as the default and make any desired changes to the set colors and fonts. Click the Change Styles button and then click *Set as Default* at the drop-down list. The new default Quick Styles set applies to new documents you create, but it is not the default for any existing documents.

Exercise 1A

Change the Quick Styles Default

Note: If you are running Word 2007 on a computer connected to a network in a public environment such as a school, you may not be able to save styles to the hard drive. Before beginning Exercise 1A, check with your instructor.

1. Suppose you format many of your documents with the *Modern* Quick Styles set using the *Flow* colors and the *Foundry* fonts, and you want to make it the default. To do this, complete the following steps:
   a. At a blank document, click the Change Styles button, point to *Style Set*, and then click *Modern* at the drop-down gallery.
   b. Click the Change Styles button, point to *Colors*, and then click *Flow* at the drop-down gallery.
   c. Click the Change Styles button, point to *Fonts*, scroll down the fonts drop-down gallery, and then click *Foundry*.

d. Click the Change Styles button and then click *Set as Default*.

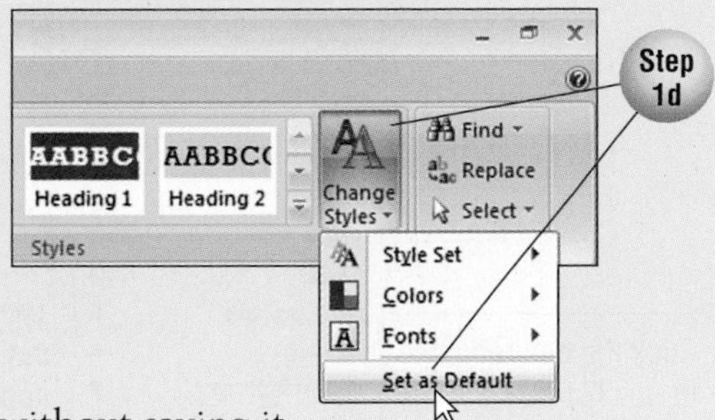

2. Close the document without saving it.
3. Click the New button on the Quick Access toolbar to display a blank document.
4. At the blank document, notice the thumbnails in the Styles group. The formatting reflects the default Quick Styles set, color, and font.
5. Click the Page Layout tab and then notice the Themes group buttons. They reflect the colors and fonts of the default Quick Styles set.
6. Suppose you want a previously created document formatted with the styles in the *Default* Quick Styles set to display with the new default styles applied. To do this, you must insert the file in the current document (rather than open it) by completing the following steps:
   a. Click the Insert tab.
   b. Click the Object button arrow and then click *Text from File*.
   c. Navigate to the Chapter24 folder on your storage medium and then double-click **FCTDocument.docx**. (Notice that the new default Quick Styles set formatting is applied to the document.)
7. Save the document with the name **C24Ex01**.

Applying Styles

You can use a variety of methods to apply styles to text in a document. You can apply a style by clicking the style thumbnail in the Styles group or by clicking the More button and then clicking the style at the drop-down gallery. You can also apply a style with the Quick Styles button on the Mini toolbar. To do this, select the text to which you want the style applied, click the Quick Styles button on the Mini toolbar, and then click the desired style at the drop-down gallery.

Quick Styles

The Styles task pane provides another method for applying a style. Display the Styles task pane, shown in Figure 24.1, by clicking the Styles group dialog box launcher or by pressing Alt + Ctrl + Shift + S. The styles in the currently selected Quick Styles set display in the task pane followed by a paragraph symbol (¶), indicating that the style applies paragraph formatting, or a character symbol (**a**), indicating that the style applies character formatting. If both characters display to the right of a style, the style applies both paragraph and character formatting. In addition to displaying styles that apply formatting, the Styles task pane also displays a *Clear All* style that clears all formatting from the selected text.

Figure 24.1 Styles Task Pane

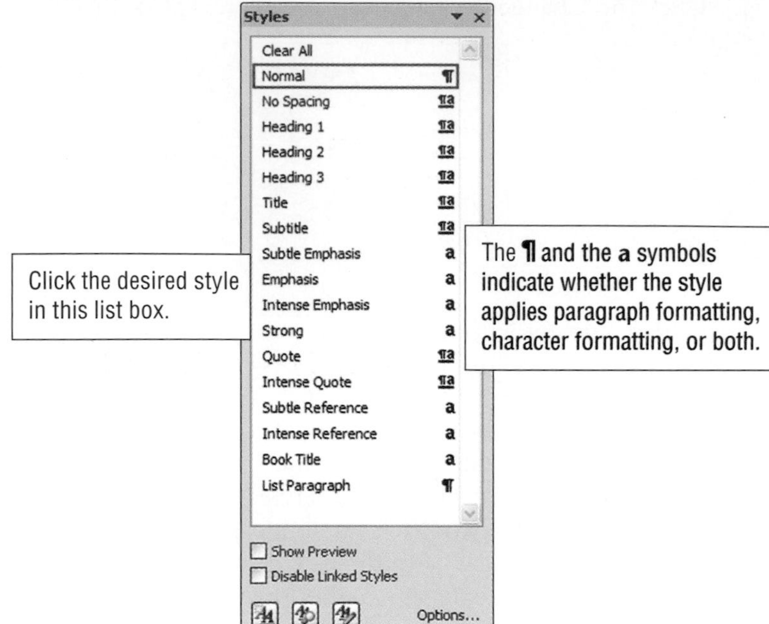

Apply Style
Click style in Styles group.
OR
1. Click More button in Styles group.
2. Click desired style.
OR
1. Select text.
2. Click Quick Styles button on Mini toolbar.
3. Click desired style.
OR
1. Display Styles task pane.
2. Click desired style in task pane.
OR
1. Click More button in Styles group.
2. Click *Apply Style* at drop-down list.
3. Click down-pointing arrow at right of *Style Name* option box.
4. Click desired style at drop-down list.

If you hover the mouse pointer on a style in the Styles task pane, a ScreenTip displays with information about the formatting applied by the style. Apply a style in the Styles task pane by clicking the style. Close the Styles task pane by clicking the Close button located in the upper right corner of the task pane.

You can also apply styles at the Apply Styles window, shown in Figure 24.2. Display this window by clicking the More button in the Styles group and then clicking *Apply Styles* at the drop-down gallery. You can also display the Apply Styles window by pressing Ctrl + Shift + S. Like the Styles task pane, the Apply Styles window contains the styles of the currently selected Quick Styles set. Click the down-pointing arrow at the right side of the *Style Name* option box and then click the desired style at the drop-down list. You can also type the name of the style in the *Style Name* option box and then press Enter.

Figure 24.2 Apply Styles Window

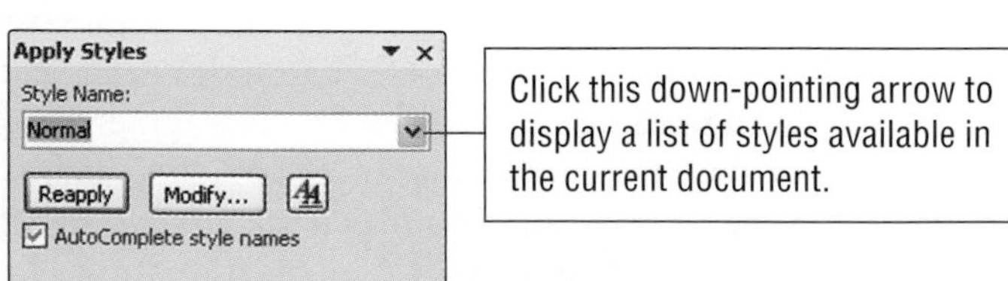

Exercise 1B

Applying Styles

1. With **C24Ex01.docx** open, apply styles using the Mini toolbar by completing the following steps:
   a. Select the heading *SMALL GROUPS*.
   b. Click the Quick Styles button on the Mini toolbar and then click the *Subtle Emphasis* style at the drop-down gallery.

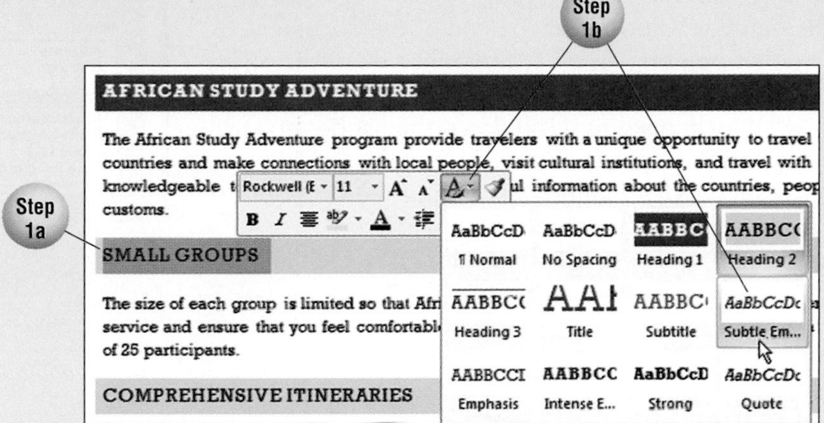

   c. Select the text *COMPREHENSIVE ITINERARIES*.
   d. Click the Quick Styles button on the Mini toolbar and then click the *Subtle Emphasis* style at the drop-down gallery.
2. Apply styles using the Styles task pane by completing the following steps:
   a. Select the heading text *CUSTOM GROUPS*.
   b. Click the Styles group dialog box launcher. (This displays the Styles task pane.)
   c. Click the *Subtle Emphasis* style in the Styles task pane. (Notice that the style is followed by the character symbol (**a**) indicating that the style applies character formatting.)

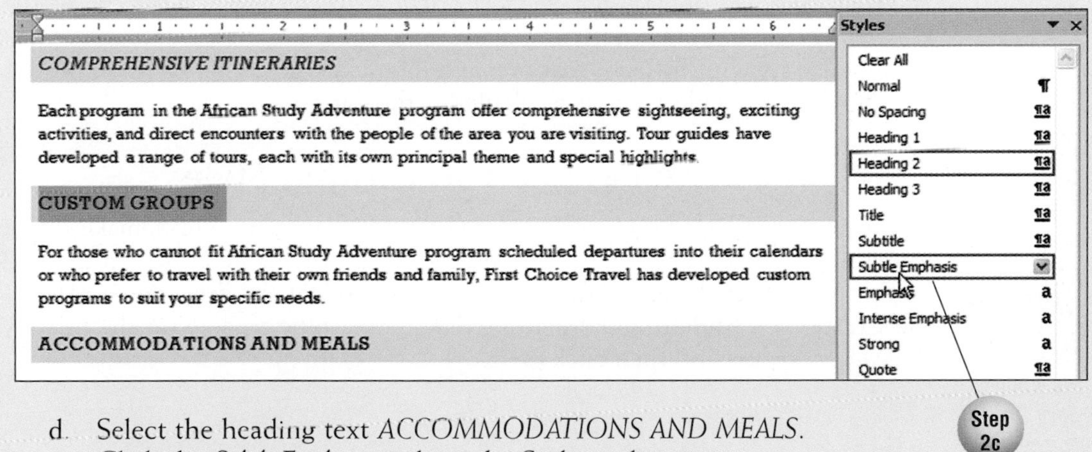

   d. Select the heading text *ACCOMMODATIONS AND MEALS*.
   e. Click the *Subtle Emphasis* style in the Styles task pane.
   f. Select the last line of text in the document (the Mark Twain quote) and then click the *Quote* style in the Styles task pane.
   g. After noticing the formatting of the quote, remove it by making sure the text is selected and then clicking the *Clear All* style located toward the top of the Styles task pane.

h. Click anywhere in the heading *SMALL GROUPS* and notice that the *Subtle Emphasis* style is selected in the Styles task pane. Hover the mouse pointer over the *Subtle Emphasis* style and read the information in the ScreenTip about the formatting applied by the style.

i. Close the Styles task pane by clicking the Close button located in the upper right corner of the task pane.

3. Display the Apply Styles window by clicking the More button in the Styles group and then clicking *Apply Styles* at the drop-down gallery.
4. Select the quote text located at the end of the document, click the down-pointing arrow at the right side of the *Style Name* option box, and then click *Intense Quote* at the drop-down list. (You will need to scroll down the list box to display this option.)
5. Close the Apply Styles window by clicking the Close button located in the upper right corner of the window.
6. Save, print, and then close **C24Ex01.docx**.

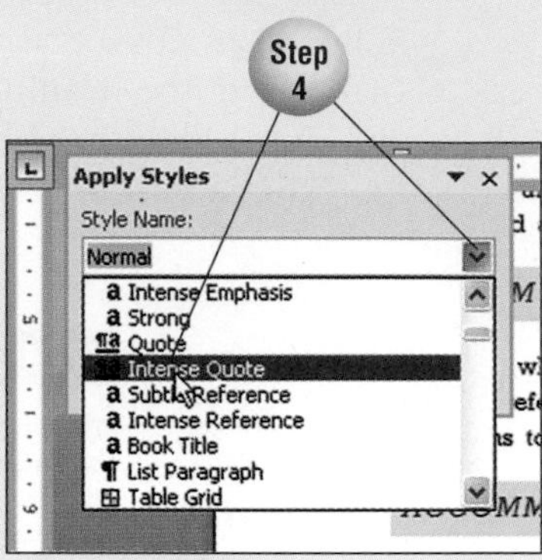

Create Style Based on Existing Formatting
1. Apply desired formatting to text.
2. Select text.
3. Click More button in Styles group.
4. Click *Save Selection as a New Quick Style.*
5. Type name for new style.
6. Click OK.

Create Style Based on Existing Style
1. Apply style to text.
2. Make desired formatting changes.
3. Select text.
4. Click More button in Styles group.
5. Click *Save Selection as a New Quick Style.*
6. Type name for new style.
7. Click OK.

Creating Styles

If none of the predesigned styles provided by Word contain the formatting you desire, you can create your own style. You can create a style based on existing formatting, create a new style and apply all formatting, or modify an existing style.

Creating a Style Based on Existing Formatting

To create a style based on existing formatting, apply the desired formatting to text in a document and then select the text. Click the More button in the Styles group and then click *Save Selection as a New Quick Style* at the drop-down gallery. At the Create New Style from Formatting dialog box, shown in Figure 24.3, type a name for the new style in the *Name* text box and then click OK. The style is inserted in the Quick Styles gallery and is available for the current document.

Creating a Style Based on an Existing Style

To create a style based on an existing style, apply the style to text, make the desired formatting changes, and then select the text. Click the More button in the Styles group and then click *Save Selection as a New Quick Style* at the drop-down gallery. At the Create New Style from Formatting dialog box, type a name for the new style in the *Name* text box and then click OK.

Figure 24.3 Create New Style from Formatting Dialog Box

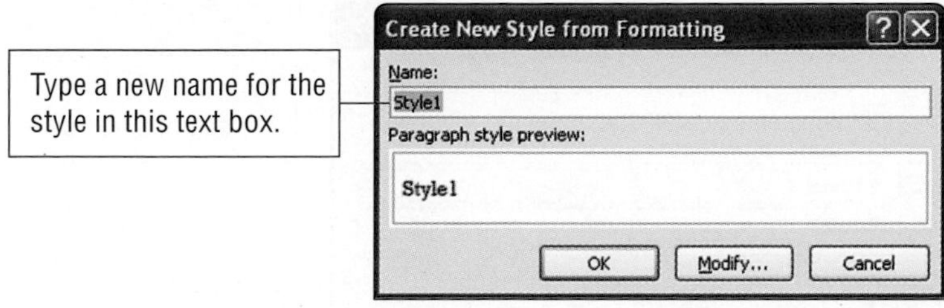

Exercise 2A

Creating a Style from Existing Formatting

1. Open **FCTStyles.docx** and save the document with the name **C24Ex02Styles**.
2. Create a style based on the formatting of *CustomTitle* text by completing the following steps:
   a. Select the text *CustomTitle*. (Make sure you select the paragraph mark (¶) after *Title* to include center alignment paragraph formatting in the style.)
   b. Click the More button in the Styles group.
   c. Click *Save Selection as a New Quick Style.*
   d. At the Create New Style from Formatting dialog box, type your initials followed by **CustomTitle**.
   e. Click OK.
3. Save **C24Ex02Styles.docx**.

Creating a New Style

You can create a style without first applying formatting to text. To do this, click the More button and then click *Save Selection as a New Quick Style* at the drop-down gallery. At the Create New Style from Formatting dialog box, click the Modify button. This displays an expanded Create New Style from Formatting dialog box, shown in Figure 24.4. At this dialog box, type a new name for the style in the *Name* text box and then use the buttons in the *Formatting* section of the dialog box to apply formatting. You can also apply formatting by clicking the Format button that displays in the lower left corner of the screen and then clicking the desired option at the pop-up list. When you have made all desired formatting choices, click OK.

QUICK STEPS

Create New Style
1. Click More button in Styles group.
2. Click *Save Selection as a New Quick Style.*
3. Click Modify button.
4. Type new name for style.
5. Apply desired formatting.
6. Click OK.

Figure 24.4 Expanded Create New Style from Formatting Dialog Box

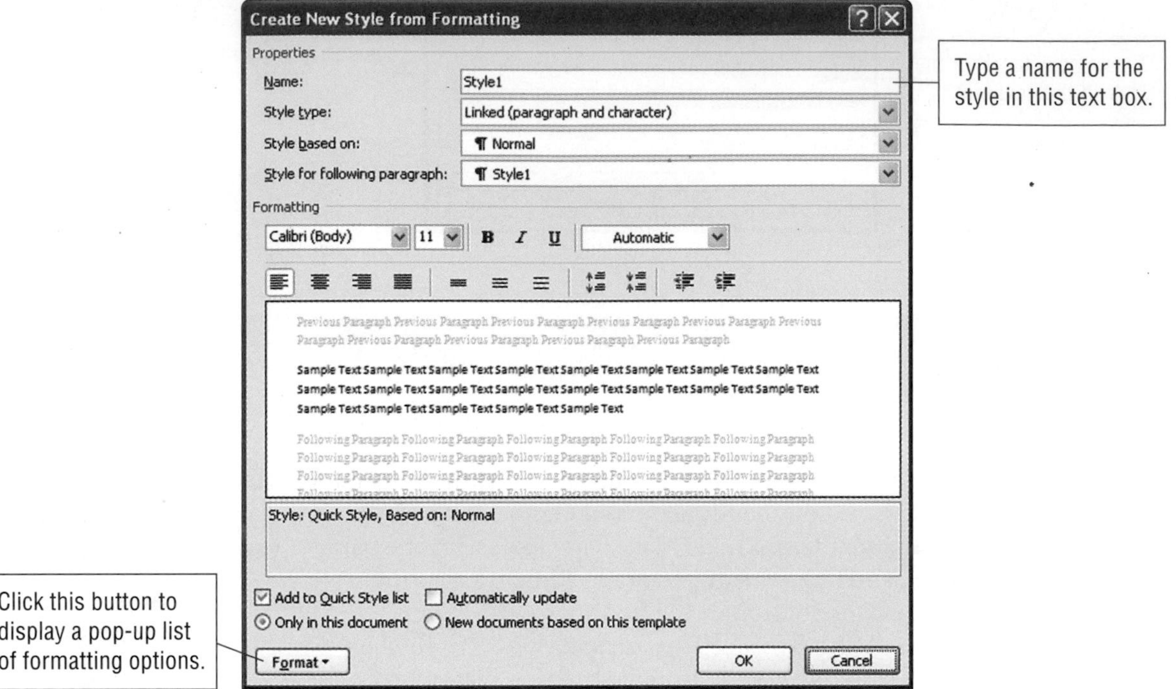

Exercise 2B

Creating a New Style

1. With **C24Ex02Styles.docx** open, press Ctrl + End to move the insertion point to the end of the document.
2. Click the More button in the Styles group.
3. Click *Save Selection as a New Quick Style*.
4. At the Create New Style from Formatting dialog box, type your initials followed by **CustomEmphasis**.
5. Click the Modify button.

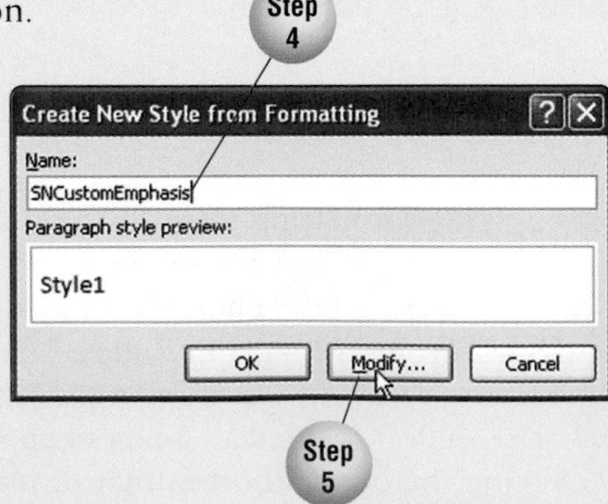

6. At the Create New Style from Formatting expanded dialog box, make the following changes:
   a. Click the down-pointing arrow at the right side of the Font Size button and then click *12*.
   b. Click the Bold button.
   c. Click the down-pointing arrow at the right side of the Font Color button.
   d. Click *More Colors*.
   e. Click the Standard tab.
   f. Click the dark brown color at the lower left edge of the honeycomb, as shown at the right.
   g. Click OK.
   h. Click the Format button located toward the bottom of the Create New Style from Formatting dialog box and then click Font at the pop-up list.
   i. At the Font dialog box, click the *Small Caps* check box to insert a check mark and then click OK to close the dialog box.
   j. Click the Format button and then click Paragraph at the pop-up list.
   k. At the Paragraph dialog box with the Indents and Spacing tab selected, click the up-pointing arrow at the right side of the *Left* measurement box in the *Indentation* section until 0.3" displays.
   l. Select the current measurement in the *After* measurement box in the *Spacing* section and then type **3**.
   m. Click OK to close the Paragraph dialog box.
   n. Click OK to close the Create New Style from Formatting dialog box.
7. Save **C24Ex02Styles.docx**.

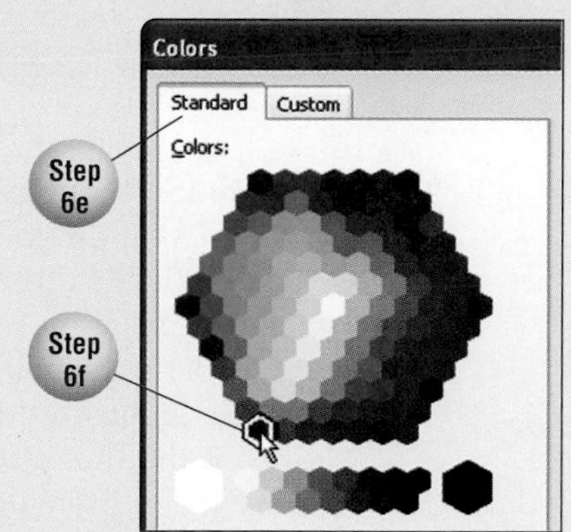

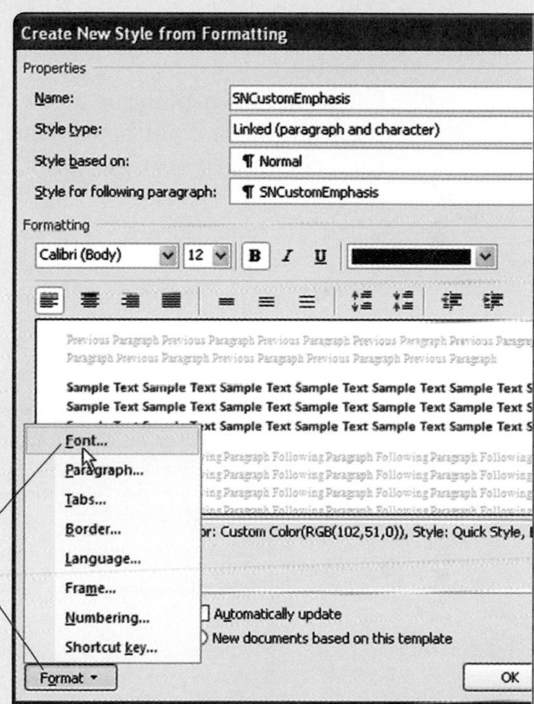

Modifying a Style

If a predesigned style contains most of the formatting you want, you can modify it to create a new style. To do this, right-click the style in the Styles group or the Quick Styles drop-down gallery and then click Modify at the shortcut menu. This displays the Modify Styles dialog box, which contains the same options that are available at the Create New Style from Formatting dialog box. Type a new name in the *Name* text box, make the desired changes, and then click OK.

QUICK STEPS

Modify a Style

1. Right-click desired style in Styles group or Quick Styles drop-down gallery.
2. Click Modify.
3. Type new name for style.
4. Make desired changes.
5. Click OK.

Exercise 2C

Modifying an Existing Style

1. With **C24Ex02Styles.docx** open, modify the Heading 2 style by completing the following steps:
   a. Click the More button in the Styles group.
   b. Right-click the Heading 2 style in the Styles group and then click Modify at the shortcut menu.
   c. At the Modify Style dialog box, type your initials followed by **CustomHeading** in the *Name* text box.
   d. Click the down-pointing arrow at the right of the Font button and then click *Candara* at the drop-down list.
   e. Click the Italic button.
   f. Click the down-pointing arrow at the right side of the Font Color button, and then click *Dark Blue* (the second color from the right in the *Standard Colors* section).

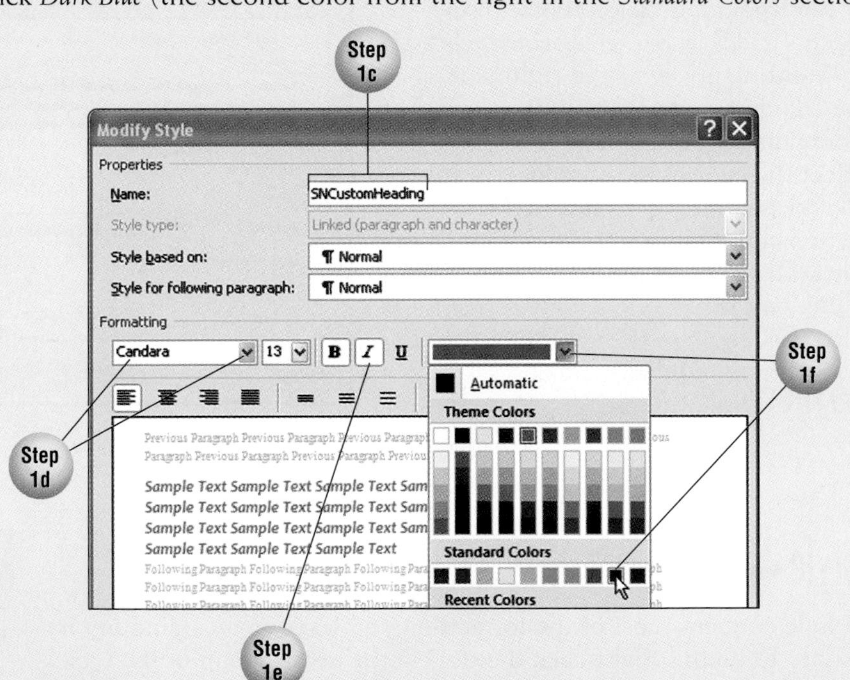

   g. Click OK to close the Modify Style dialog box.
2. Save **C24Ex02Styles.docx**.

Saving a Custom Quick Styles Set

If you want a style that you have created or modified available to apply in other documents, save the style as a custom Quick Styles set. To do this, click the Change Styles button, point to *Style Set*, and then click *Save as Quick Style Set*. At the Save Quick Style Set dialog box, type a name for your Quick Styles set and then click the Save button.

Save a Custom Quick Styles Set

1. Click Change Styles button.
2. Point to *Style Set*.
3. Click *Save as Quick Style Set*.
4. Type name for Quick Styles set.
5. Click Save button.

Exercise 2D

Saving a Custom Quick Styles Set and Applying Custom Styles

1. With **C24Ex02Styles.docx** open, save the styles you created as a Quick Styles set by completing the following steps:
    a. Click the Change Styles button, point to *Style Set*, and then click *Save as Quick Style Set*.
    b. At the Save Quick Style Set dialog box, type your first and last names and then click the Save button.
2. Save and then close **C24Ex02Styles.docx**.
3. Open **FCTZenith.docx** and save the document with the name **C24Ex02**.
4. Change to the Quick Styles set named with your first and last names by clicking the Change Styles button, pointing to *Style Set*, and then clicking the style set named with your first and last names.
5. Apply the custom title style by completing the following steps:
    a. Click on any character in the text *Extreme Adventures*.
    b. Click the custom title style (style that begins with your initials followed by *CustomTitle*) in the Styles group.
    c. Scroll to the end of the document, click on any character in the text *Volunteer Adventures* and then click the custom title style.
6. Apply the custom heading style by completing the following steps:
    a. Click on any character in the text *Antarctic Adventures*.
    b. Click the More button in the Styles group.
    c. Click the custom heading style (style that begins with your initials followed by *CustomHeading*).
    d. Apply the custom heading style to the text *Tall-Ship Adventures* and *Bicycling Adventures*.
7. Apply the custom emphasis style by completing the following steps:
    a. Select the lines of text in the *Antarctic Adventures* section that contain money amounts.
    b. Click the More button in the Styles group and then click the custom emphasis style (style that begins with your initials followed by *CustomEmphasis*).
    c. Apply the custom emphasis style to the lines of text in the *Tall-Ship Adventures* section containing money amounts.
    d. Apply the custom emphasis style to the lines of text in the *Bicycling Adventures* section containing money amounts.
8. Save **C24Ex02.docx**.

Modifying an Applied Style

One of the advantages of applying styles in a document is that if you modify the style formatting, all the text in the document to which that style has been applied is automatically updated. Using styles streamlines formatting and maintains consistency in your documents.

Exercise 2E

Modifying an Applied Style

1. With **C24Ex02.docx** open, edit the style to change the font in the custom title style by completing the following steps:
   a. Right-click the custom title style (style that begins with your initials followed by *CustomTitle*) and then click Modify at the shortcut menu.
   b. At the Modify Style dialog box, change the font to *Candara*, the font size to *18*, and the font color to *Dark Blue*.

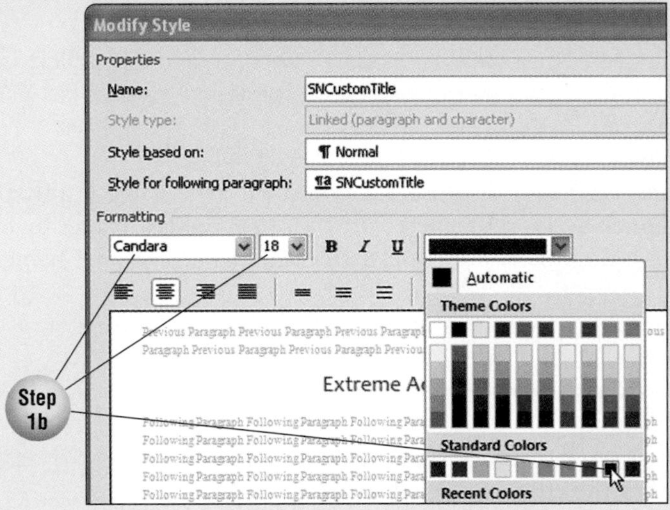

   c. Click the Format button and then click Paragraph at the pop-up list.
   d. At the Paragraph dialog box with the Indents and Spacing tab selected, change the spacing before to 12 points and then click OK to close the dialog box.
   e. Click OK to close the Modify Style dialog box.
2. Scroll through the document and notice the custom title style applied to both titles in the document.
3. Save **C24Ex02.docx**.

Selecting Styles

When styles are applied to text in a document, you can find and select all occurrences of a particular style at one time. With a style selected, you can apply another style, change the formatting, or make other changes. Find and select all occurrences of a particular style by right-clicking the style in the Styles group or in the Quick Styles drop-down gallery and then clicking the *Select All x Instance(s)* (where *x* is the number of instances of the style in the document).

Exercise 2F

Selecting All Occurrences of a Style

1. With **C24Ex02.docx** open, find all occurrences of the custom heading style and then apply the Heading 1 style by completing the following steps:
   a. Click the More button in the Styles group.
   b. Right-click the custom heading style (style that begins with your initials followed by *CustomHeading*) and then click Select All 3 Instance(s) that displays in the shortcut menu.

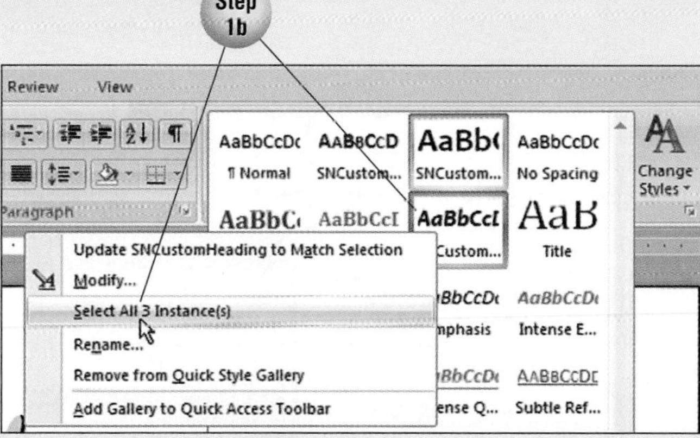

   c. With the three headings selected, click the Heading 1 style in the Styles group. (If the Heading 1 style is not visible, click the More button.)
2. Scroll through the document and notice that the three instances of the custom heading style were replaced with the Heading 1 style.
3. Save **C24Ex02.docx**.

Displaying All Styles

Each Quick Styles set contains a title style, body text style, a number of heading level styles, and other styles that are designed to work together in a single document. Only the styles for the currently selected Quick Styles set display in the Quick Styles drop-down gallery or the Styles task pane. You can display all styles with options at the Style Pane Options dialog box, shown in Figure 24.5. Display this dialog box by clicking the Styles group dialog box launcher and then clicking the <u>Options</u> hyperlink that displays in the lower right corner of the task pane.

Figure 24.5 Style Pane Options Dialog Box

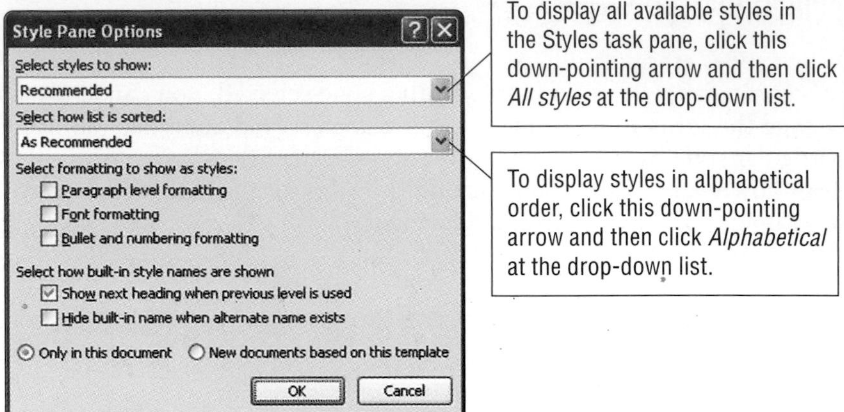

To display all styles, click the down-pointing arrow at the right side of the *Select styles to show* option box and then click *All styles* at the drop-down list. Specify how you want the styles sorted in the Styles task pane with the *Select how list is sorted* option.

Displaying and Selecting Styles

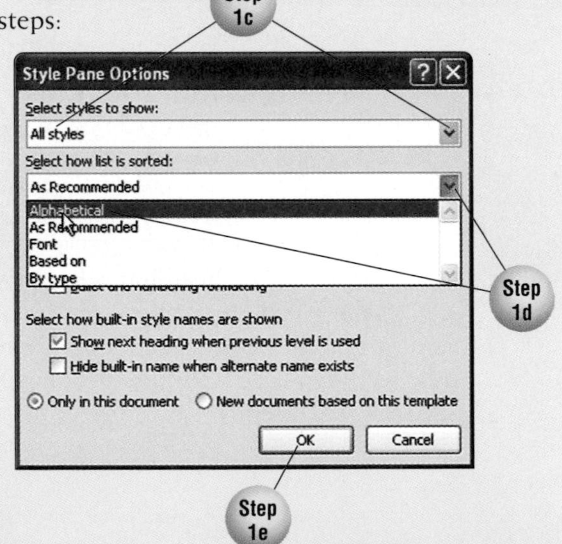

1. With **C24Ex02.docx** open, display all styles in the Styles task pane by completing the following steps:
   a. Click the Styles group dialog box launcher.
   b. Click the Options hyperlink that displays in the lower right corner of the task pane.
   c. At the Style Pane Options dialog box, click the down-pointing arrow at the right side of the *Select styles to show* option and then click *All styles* at the drop-down list.
   d. Click the down-pointing arrow at the right side of the *Select how list is sorted* option and then click *Alphabetical* at the drop-down list.
   e. Click OK to close the dialog box.
2. Apply styles by completing the following steps:

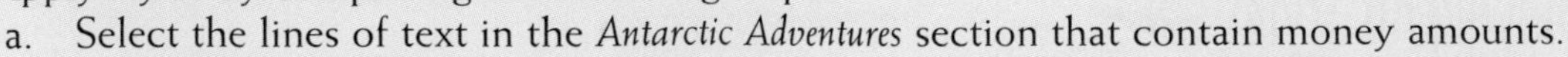

   a. Select the lines of text in the *Antarctic Adventures* section that contain money amounts.
   b. Click the Clear All style that displays at the top of the task pane list box.
   c. Click the Body Text 2 style to see how the style affects the selected text.
   d. Click the Body Text Indent style.
   e. After viewing the body text styles, change them by clicking the Block Text style.
   f. Apply the Block Text style to the other two occurrences of lines of text containing money amounts.
3. Save and then print **C24Ex02.docx**.

Revealing Style Formatting

As you learned earlier, if you hover the mouse over a style in the Styles task pane, a ScreenTip displays with information about the formatting applied by the style. The styles in the Quick Styles gallery display with a visual representation of the formatting applied by the style. You can also display a visual representation of styles by clicking the *Show Preview* check box in the Styles task pane. Another method for displaying the formatting applied by a style is to display the Reveal Formatting task pane. You can display this task pane by pressing Shift + F1 or by inserting a Reveal Formatting button on the Quick Access toolbar and then clicking the button.

Deleting a Custom Quick Styles Set

If you create a custom Quick Styles set and save it in the Save Quick Style Set dialog box, the style set will be available in the Normal template, on which all documents are based. If you no longer need the custom style set, delete it. Do this by clicking the Change Styles button, pointing to *Style Set*, and then clicking *Save as Quick Style Set*. At the Save Quick Style Set dialog box, click the name of the style set you want to delete and then click the Delete button on the dialog box toolbar. At the message asking if you are sure you want to send the document to the Recycle Bin, click Yes.

QUICK STEPS

Delete Custom Quick Styles Set

1. Click Change Styles button.
2. Point to *Style Set*.
3. Click *Save as Quick Style Set*.
4. Click desired style set name.
5. Click *Delete*.
6. Click Yes.

Exercise 2H

Deleting a Quick Styles Set

1. With **C24Ex02.docx** open, view styles in the Styles task pane by completing the following steps:
   a. With the Styles task pane open, click the *Show Preview* check box to insert a check mark.
   b. Scroll through the list box to see how styles display with the preview feature turned on.
   c. Click the *Show Preview* check box to remove the check mark.
   d. Close the Styles task pane by clicking the Close button in the upper right corner of the task pane.
2. Display style formatting in the Reveal Formatting task pane by completing the following steps:
   a. Press Shift + F1 to turn on the display of the Reveal Formatting task pane.
   b. Click the *Distinguish style source* check box to insert a check mark.
   c. Click the title of the document and notice in the Reveal Formatting task pane the formatting applied by the style.
   d. Click the heading and notice in the Reveal Formatting task pane the formatting applied by the style.

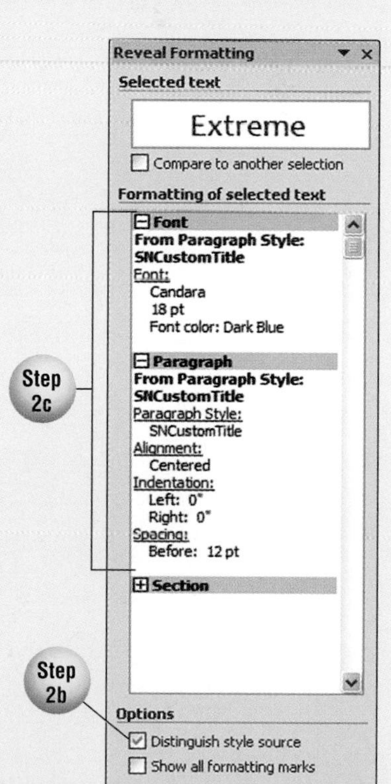

e. Click on other text in the document and view the formatting.
f. Click the *Distinguish style source* check box to remove the check mark.
g. Press Shift + F1 to turn off the display of the Reveal Formatting task pane.

3. Save and then close **C24Ex02.docx**.
4. Delete the custom Quick Styles set you created by completing the following steps:
   a. At a blank document, click the Change Styles button, point to *Style Set*, and then click *Save as Quick Style Set*.
   b. At the Save Quick Style Set dialog box, click the style set named with your first and last names.
   c. Click the Delete button on the dialog box toolbar.
   d. At the message asking if you are sure you want to send the document to the Recycle Bin, click Yes.
   e. Click the Cancel button to close the Save Quick Style Set dialog box.
5. Change back to the default Quick Styles set, colors, and fonts by completing the following steps:
   a. Click the Change Styles button, point to *Style Set*, and then click *Word 2007*.
   b. Click the Change Styles button, point to *Colors*, and then click *Office*.
   c. Click the Change Styles button, point to *Fonts*, and then click *Office*.
   d. Click the Change Styles button and then click *Set as Default*.
6. Close the document without saving it.

Chapter Summary

- Styles within the currently selected Quick Styles set are available in the Styles group in the Home tab.
- To change the Quick Styles set, click the Change Styles button in the Styles group in the Home tab, point to *Style Set*, and then click the desired style set at the drop-down gallery.
- You can change the colors and/or fonts applied by styles in a style set.
- *Default* is the default Quick Styles set. To change this default, change to the Quick Styles set you want as the default, click the Change Styles button again, and then click *Set as Default*.
- Apply styles in five ways: click the style thumbnail in the Styles group, click the More button and then click the style at the drop-down gallery, use the Quick Styles button on the Mini toolbar, use options at the Styles task pane, or use options at the Apply Styles window.
- Click the Styles group dialog box launcher to display the Styles task pane.
- Display the Apply Styles window by clicking the More button in the Styles group and then clicking *Apply Style* at the drop-down gallery.
- You can create a style based on existing formatting or on style formatting or by modifying an existing style. You can also create a new style without first applying formatting to text.
- Save styles you create as a custom Quick Styles set with options at the Save Quick Style Set dialog box.
- An advantage of applying styles is that when you modify a style all text in the document to which that style has been applied is automatically updated.
- You can find and select all occurrences of a particular style at one time.
- Display all available styles in the Styles task pane by changing the *Select styles to show* option at the Style Pane Options dialog box to *All styles*.
- Reveal style formatting by hovering the mouse over a style in the Styles task pane, clicking the *Show Preview* check box in the Styles task pane, or by turning on the display of the Reveal Formatting task pane.
- Delete a custom Quick Styles set at the Save Quick Style Set dialog box.

Commands review

FEATURE	RIBBON TAB, GROUP	BUTTON, OPTION	KEYBOARD SHORTCUT
Styles task pane	Home, Styles		Alt + Ctrl + Shift + S
Apply Styles window	Home, Styles	, Apply Styles	Ctrl + Shift + S
Create New Style from Formatting dialog box	Home, Styles	, Save Selection as a New Quick Style	
Styles Pane Options dialog box	Home, Styles	, Options	
Reveal Formatting task pane			Shift + F1

Reviewing key points

Completion: In the space provided at the right, indicate the correct term, symbol, or command.

1. This is the name of the default Quick Styles set. ________________
2. To view available Quick Styles sets, click the Change Styles button and then click this option. ________________
3. To set a Quick Styles set as the default, change to the desired Quick Styles set, make any desired changes, click the Change Styles button, and then click this option. ________________
4. You can apply a style with this button on the Mini toolbar. ________________
5. Click this button to display the Styles task pane. ________________
6. If you hover the mouse pointer over a style in the Styles task pane, this displays with information about the formatting applied. ________________
7. To create a style based on text with existing formatting, select the text, click the More button, and then click this option at the drop-down gallery. ________________

8. To modify an existing style, do this to the style in the Styles group and then click Modify at the shortcut menu. ____________
9. Display all styles in the Styles task pane by changing the *Select styles to show* option to *All styles* at this dialog box. ____________
10. Press these keys on the keyboard to display the Reveal Formatting task pane. ____________

Applying your skills

Assessment 1 Create and Apply Styles to a Committee Report

1. Open **DeeringStyles.docx** and save the document with the name **C24A01Styles**.
2. Create a style based on the formatting of *DeeringTitle* text and name it with your initials followed by *DeeringTitle*. (Make sure you select the paragraph symbol.)
3. Press Ctrl + End to move the insertion point to the end of the document and then create a new style at the Create New Style from Formatting dialog box. Name it with your initials followed by *DeeringQuote*. Make the following changes at the Create New Style from Formatting expanded dialog box:
   a. Change the left and right indent to 0.5 inch and the spacing after to 12 points.
   b. Click the Italic button.
   c. Insert a single line top border and a single-line bottom border in *Orange, Accent 6, Darker 50%* (the bottom color in the far right column in the Theme Colors group).
4. Modify the Heading 2 style and name it with your initials followed by *DeeringHeading* and make the following formatting changes:
   a. Change the font to 11-point Copperplate Gothic Bold.
   b. Change the font color to *Orange, Accent 6, Darker 50%*.
5. Save the styles you created as a Quick Styles set named with your initials followed by *Deering*.
6. Save and then close **C24A01Styles.docx**.
7. Open **DeeringReport.docx** and save the document with the name **C24A01**.
8. Change to the Quick Styles set named with your initials followed by *Deering*.
9. Apply the DeeringTitle style that is preceded by your initials to the two titles in the document *Audit Committee Report* and *Compensation Committee Report*.
10. Apply the DeeringHeading style that is preceded by your initials to the headings in the report: *Committee Responsibilities*, *Fees to Independent Auditors*, *Compensation Philosophy*, and *Competitive Compensation*.
11. Apply the DeeringQuote style that is preceded by your initials to the second paragraph of text in the document. (The paragraph that begins *Assist the company's Board of Directors . . .*)
12. Edit the DeeringTitle style that is preceded by your initials so it underlines text.
13. Turn on the display of the Styles task pane and then display all styles in alphabetical order. Apply the Block Text style to the bulleted paragraphs in the *Committee Responsibilities* section and the *Compensation Philosophy* section.
14. Delete the *Deering* Quick Styles set you created that is preceded by your initials.
15. Save, print, and then close **C24A01.docx**.

Assessment 2 Create and Apply Styles in a Photography Document

1. At a blank document, create a new style at the Create New Style from Formatting dialog box. Name it with your initials followed by RPQuote. Make the following changes at the Create New Style from Formatting expanded dialog box:
   a. Change the font to 10-point Constantia bold italic and change the font color to *Red, Accent 2, Darker 25%*.
   b. Change the left and right indent to 0.25 inch.
2. Create a new style at the Create New Style from Formatting dialog box. Name it with your initials followed by RPHeading1. Make the following changes at the Create New Style from Formatting expanded dialog box:
   a. Change the font to 18-point Constantia bold italic and change the font color to dark green (choose a dark green at the Colors dialog box with the Standard tab selected).
   b. Insert a bottom border (choose the fifth border style from the bottom of the list) and change the color to dark green.
3. Modify the Intense Reference style and name it with your initials followed by RPHeading2 and make the following formatting changes:
   a. Change the font to 11-point Copperplate Gothic Bold.
   b. Change the font color to *Orange, Accent 6, Darker 50%*.
4. Save the styles you created as a Quick Styles set named with your initials followed by RPStyles.
5. Save the document with the name **C24A02Styles**.
6. Close **C24A02Styles.docx**.
7. Open **RPDocument.docx** and save the document with the name **C24A02**.
8. Change to the Quick Styles set named with your initials followed by *RPStyles*.
9. Apply the RPHeading1 style that is preceded by your initials to the three headings in the document: *Photography*, *Camera Basics*, and *Digital Cameras*.
10. Apply the RPHeading2 style that is preceded by your initials to the three subheadings in the document: *Pixels*, *Aspect Ratio*, and *White Balance*.
11. Apply the RPQuote style that is preceded by your initials to the first paragraph in the document and the last paragraph in the document.
12. Edit the *RPHeading1* style that is preceded by your initials so the bottom border is a double thick-thin line in dark green.
13. Edit the RPQuote style so it indents text 0.5 inch from the left and right margins and changes the color to dark green.
14. Delete the RPStyles Quick Styles set you created that is preceded by your initials.
15. Save, print, and then close **C24A02.docx**.

Chapter 25

Protecting and Preparing Documents

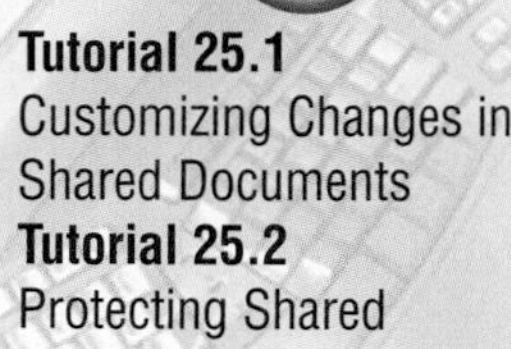

Tutorial 25.1
Customizing Changes in Shared Documents
Tutorial 25.2
Protecting Shared Documents

Performance Objectives

Upon successful completion of Chapter 25, you will be able to:

- Restrict formatting and editing in a document and allow exceptions to restrictions
- Protect a document with a password
- Save a document as read-only
- Modify document properties
- Inspect and encrypt a document
- Restrict permission to a document
- Create and apply a digital signature
- Insert a signature line
- Mark a document as final
- Run the compatibility checker

In Chapter 20, you learned to perform workgroup activities such as inserting comments into a document, tracking changes made by other users, comparing documents, and combining documents from multiple users. In this chapter, you will learn how to protect the integrity of shared documents, limit the formatting or editing changes that other users can make, and prepare documents for distribution.

Note: Before beginning computer exercises for this chapter, copy to your storage medium the Chapter25 folder from the CD that accompanies this textbook and then make Chapter25 the active folder.

Protecting Documents

In a company or organization, you may want to distribute copies of documents you create among members of your workgroup. In some situations, you may want to protect a document and limit the changes that can be made to it. If you create a document that contains sensitive, restricted, or private information, consider protecting it by saving it as a read-only document or securing it with a password.

You can limit the formatting and editing that other users can do in a document with options at the Restrict Formatting and Editing task pane. Limiting formatting and editing changes can be especially useful when a number of people in an organization will be reviewing and editing the same document. For example, suppose you are responsible for preparing the yearly corporate report for your company. This report integrates information from a variety of departments, such as Finance, Human Resources, and Sales and Marketing. You can prepare the report and then specify the portion of it that a given individual is allowed to edit. For example, you can specify that a person from the Finance Department is able to edit only financial information and a person from Human Resources is able to edit only data pertinent to the Human Resources Department. In this way, you can protect the integrity of the document.

To protect a document, display the Restrict Formatting and Editing task pane, shown in Figure 25.1, by clicking the Review tab and then clicking the Protect Document button in the Protect group. Use options in the *Formatting restrictions* section to limit formatting to specific styles and use options in the *Editing restrictions* section to specify the type of editing allowed in the document.

Figure 25.1 Restrict Formatting and Editing Task Pane

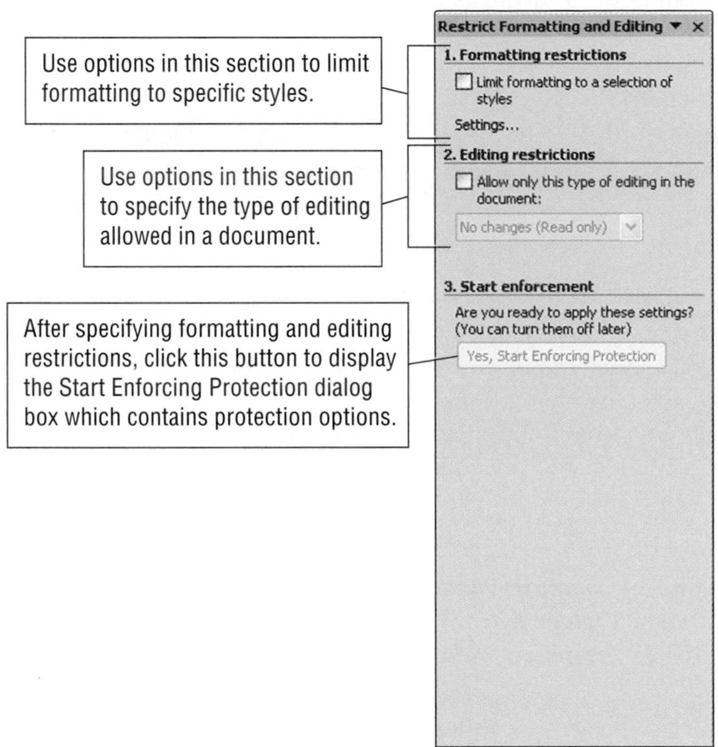

Display Formatting Restrictions Dialog Box

1. Click Review tab.
2. Click Protect Document button.
3. Click the Settings hyperlink in Restrict Formatting and Editing task pane.

Restricting Formatting

With options in the *Formatting restrictions* section of the Restrict Formatting and Editing task pane, you can lock specific styles used in a document, thus allowing the use of only those styles and prohibiting a user from making other formatting changes. Click the Settings hyperlink in the *Formatting restrictions* section, and the Formatting Restrictions dialog box displays, as shown in Figure 25.2.

Figure 25.2 Formatting Restrictions Dialog Box

Insert a check mark in the check boxes preceding those styles you want to allow and remove the check mark from the check boxes preceding styles you do not want to allow.

If you insert a check mark in the *Limit formatting to a selection of styles* check box, a list of styles becomes available in the *Checked styles are currently allowed* list box. In this list box, insert check marks in the check boxes that precede styles you want to allow and remove check marks in the check boxes that precede styles you do not want to allow. You can limit formatting to a minimum number of styles by clicking the Recommended Minimum button. Clicking this button allows formatting with styles that Word uses for certain features such as bulleted or numbered lists. Click the None button to remove all check marks and allow no styles to be used in the document. Click the All button to insert a check mark in all the check boxes and allow all styles to be used in the document.

With options in the *Formatting* section of the dialog box, you can allow or not allow AutoFormat to make changes in a document and allow or not allow users to switch themes or Quick Styles sets.

Exercise 1A

Restricting Formatting of a Document

1. Open **AnnualReport.docx** and save the document with the name **C25Ex01**.
2. Restrict formatting to recommended styles and the Heading 1 and Heading 2 styles by completing the following steps:
   a. Click the Review tab.
   b. Click the Protect Document button in the Protect group.

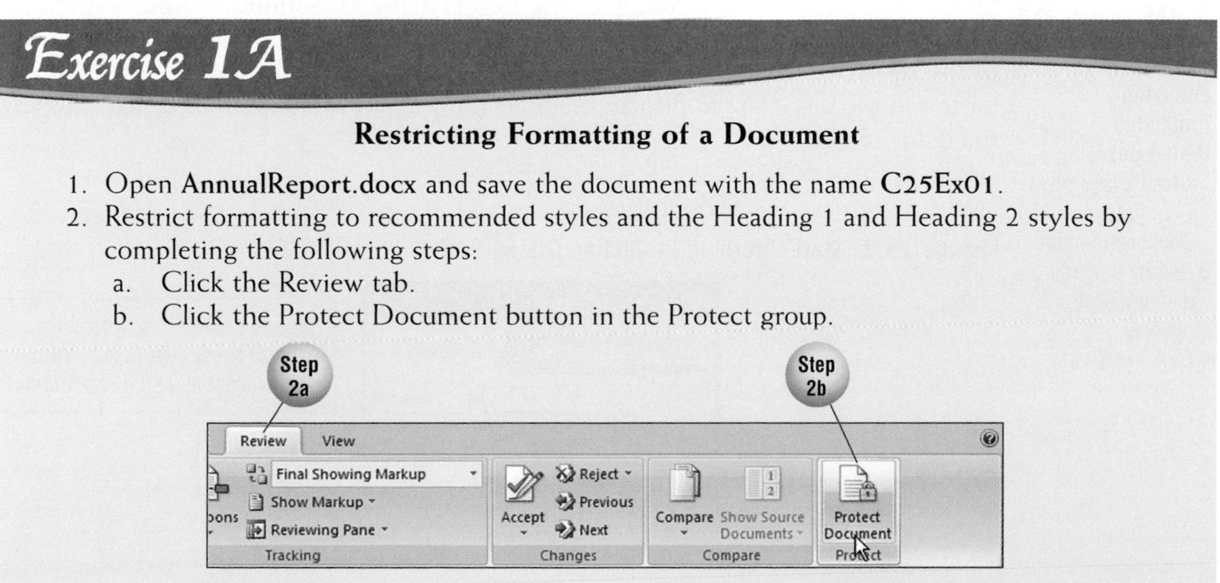

c. At the Restrict Formatting and Editing task pane, click the *Limit formatting to a selection of styles* check box to insert a check mark. (Skip this step if the check box already contains a check mark.)
d. Click the Settings hyperlink.
e. At the Formatting Restrictions dialog box, click the None button.
f. Scroll down the list box and then insert a check mark in the *Heading 1* check box and also the *Heading 2* check box.

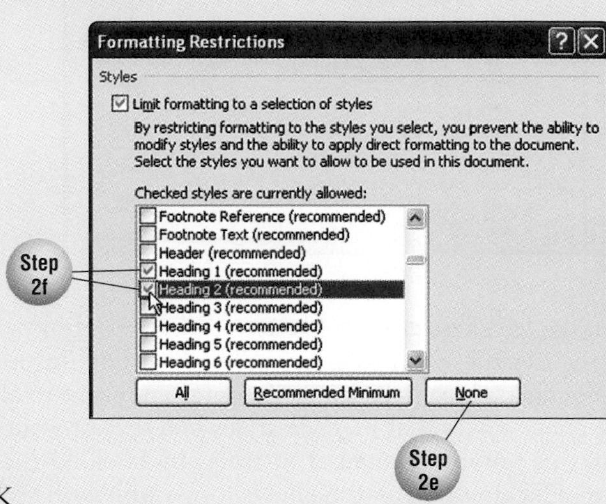

g. Click OK.
h. At the message telling you that the document may contain formatting or styles that are not allowed and asking if you want to remove them, click Yes.

3. Save **C25Ex01.docx**.

Display Start Enforcing Protection Dialog Box
1. Click Review tab.
2. Click Protect Document button.
3. Specify formatting and/or editing options.
4. Click Yes, Start Enforcing Protection button.

Enforcing Restrictions

Specifying formatting and editing restrictions and any exceptions to those restrictions is the first step to protecting your document. The next step is to start the enforcement of the restrictions you have specified. Click the Yes, Start Enforcing Protection button in the task pane to display the Start Enforcing Protection dialog box, shown in Figure 25.3.

Figure 25.3 Start Enforcing Protection Dialog Box

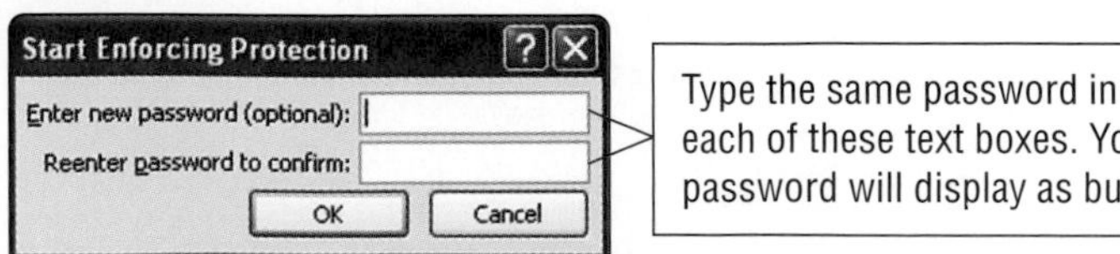

At the Start Enforcing Protection dialog box, the *Password* option is selected automatically. To add a password, type what you want to use as the password in the *Enter new password (optional)* text box. Click in the *Reenter password to confirm* text box and then type the same password again. Choose the *User authentication* option if you want to encrypt the password and use SSL-secured authentication to prevent any unauthorized changes.

Exercise 1B

Protecting a Document

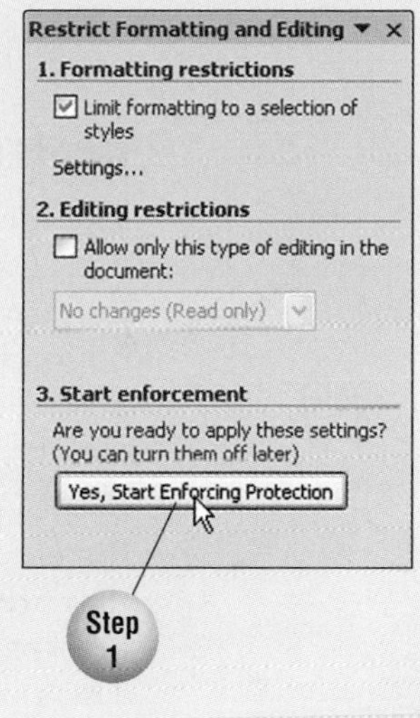

1. With **C25Ex01.docx** open, click the Yes, Start Enforcing Protection button (located toward the bottom of the Restrict Formatting and Editing task pane).
2. At the Start Enforcing Protection dialog box, type **formatting** in the *Enter new password (optional)* text box. (Bullets will display in the text box rather than the letters you type.)
3. Press the Tab key (this moves the insertion point to the *Reenter password to confirm* text box) and then type **formatting**. (Bullets will display in the text box rather than the letters you type.)
4. Click OK to close the dialog box.

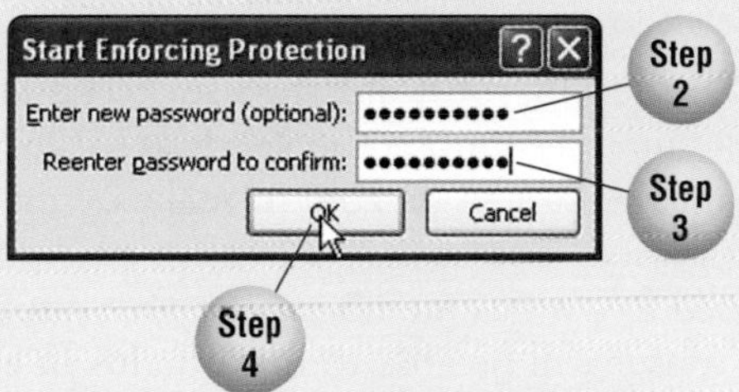

5. Close the Restrict Formatting and Editing task pane by clicking the Close button in the upper right corner of the task pane.
6. Save and then close **C25Ex01.docx**.
7. Open **C25Ex01.docx**.
8. Display the Restrict Formatting and Editing task pane by clicking the Review tab and then clicking the Protect Document button.
9. Read the information that displays in the task pane telling you that the document is protected, special restrictions are in effect, and you may format text with certain styles only. Click the Available styles hyperlink. (This displays the Styles task pane with only four styles in the *Pick formatting to apply* list box: *Clear All, Normal, Heading 1,* and *Heading 2*.)
10. Apply the Heading 1 style to the title TERRA ENERGY CORPORATION and apply the Heading 2 style to the following headings: *Overview, Research and Development, Manufacturing,* and *Sales and Marketing*.

11. Close the Styles task pane.
12. Change the style set to *Formal*.
13. At the message indicating that some of the Quick Styles could not be updated, click OK.
14. Save the document and then print only page 1.
15. Remove the password protection from the document by completing the following steps:
    a. Click the Stop Protection button located toward the bottom of the task pane.
    b. At the Unprotect Document dialog box, type **formatting** in the text box.
    c. Click OK.
16. Save **C25Ex01.docx**.

Restricting Editing

Use the *Editing restrictions* option at the Restrict Formatting and Editing task pane to limit the types of changes a user can make to a document. Insert a check mark in the *Allow only this type of editing in the document* option, and the drop-down list below the option becomes active. Click the down-pointing arrow at the right of the option box, and these options are available: *Tracked changes*, *Comments*, *Filling in forms*, and *No changes (Read only)*.

If you do not want a user to be able to make any changes to a document, choose the *No changes (Read only)* option. If you want the user to be able to make changes that are tracked in the document, choose the *Tracked changes* option. Choose the *Comments* option if you want the user to be able to make comments in a document. The *Tracked Changes* and *Comments* options are useful in a workgroup environment where a document is routed to various members of a group for review. If you choose the *Filling in forms* option, a user will be able to fill in fields in a form but will not be able to make any other editing changes.

Exercise 1C

Restricting Editing of a Document

1. With **C25Ex01.docx** open, restrict editing to comments only by completing the following steps:
    a. Make sure the Restrict Formatting and Editing task pane displays.
    b. Click the *Allow only this type of editing in the document* check box to insert a check mark.
    c. Click the down-pointing arrow at the right of the option box below the *Allow only this type of editing in the document* and then click *Comments* at the drop-down list.

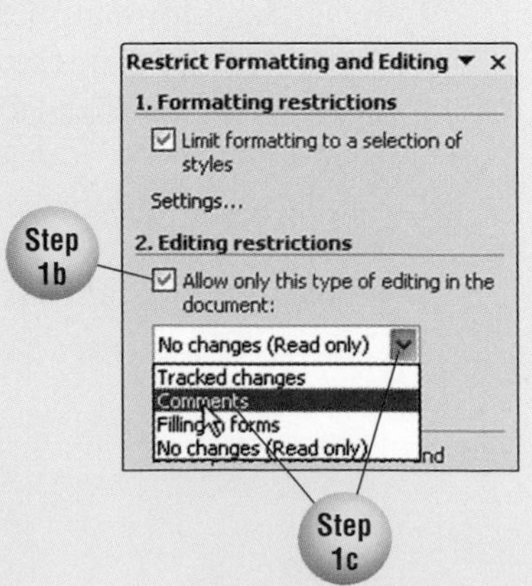

2. Click the Yes, Start Enforcing Protection button located toward the bottom of the task pane.
3. At the Start Enforcing Protection dialog box, click OK. (Adding a password is optional.)
4. Save and then close **C25Ex01.docx**.
5. Open **C25Ex01.docx**.
6. Make sure the Restrict Formatting and Editing task pane displays.
7. Read the information in the task pane that tells you the document is protected and you may only insert comments.
8. Click each of the ribbon tabs and notice the buttons and options that are dimmed and unavailable.
9. Insert a comment by completing the following steps:
   a. Move the insertion point immediately right of the period that ends the last sentence in the second paragraph of the *Overview* section.
   b. Click the Review tab (if necessary), click the Balloons button in the Tracking group, and then click the *Show All Revisions Inline* option.
   c. If necessary, click the Reviewing Pane button to turn on the display of the Reviewing pane.
   d. Click the New Comment button in the Comments group.
   e. Type the following in the Reviewing pane: **Include additional information on the impact of this purchase.**
   f. Close the Reviewing pane.
   g. Click the Stop Protection button located toward the bottom of the Restrict Formatting and Editing task pane.
   h. Close the Restrict Formatting and Editing task pane.
10. Print only the comment. (To do this, display the Print dialog box, change the *Print what* option to *List of markup*, and then click OK.)
11. Save and then close **C25Ex01.docx**.

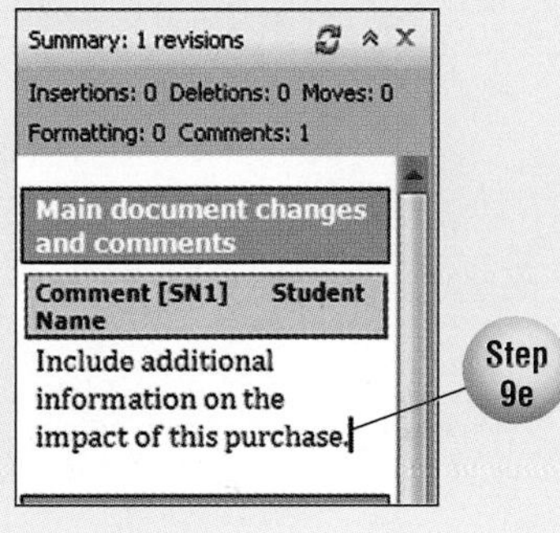

Protecting a Document with a Password

In a previous section of this chapter, you learned how to protect a document with a password by using options at the Start Enforcing Protection dialog box. You can also protect a document with a password by using options at the General Options dialog box, shown in Figure 25.4. To display this dialog box, click the Office button and then click Save As. At the Save As dialog box, click the Tools button located in the lower left corner of the dialog box and then click General Options at the pop-up list.

At the General Options dialog box, you can assign a password to open the document, modify the document, or both. To insert a password to open the document, click in the *Password to open* text box and then type the password. A password should be at least eight characters in length, can contain up to 15 characters, and is case sensitive. Consider combining uppercase letters, lowercase letters, numbers, and symbols in your password to make it more secure. Use the *Password to modify* option to create a password that a person must enter before being able to make edits to the document.

Add a Password to a Document
1. Click Office button, *Save As*.
2. Click Tools button, General Options.
3. Type a password in the *Password to modify* text box.
4. Press Enter.
5. Type the same password again.
6. Press Enter.

Figure 25.4 General Options Dialog Box

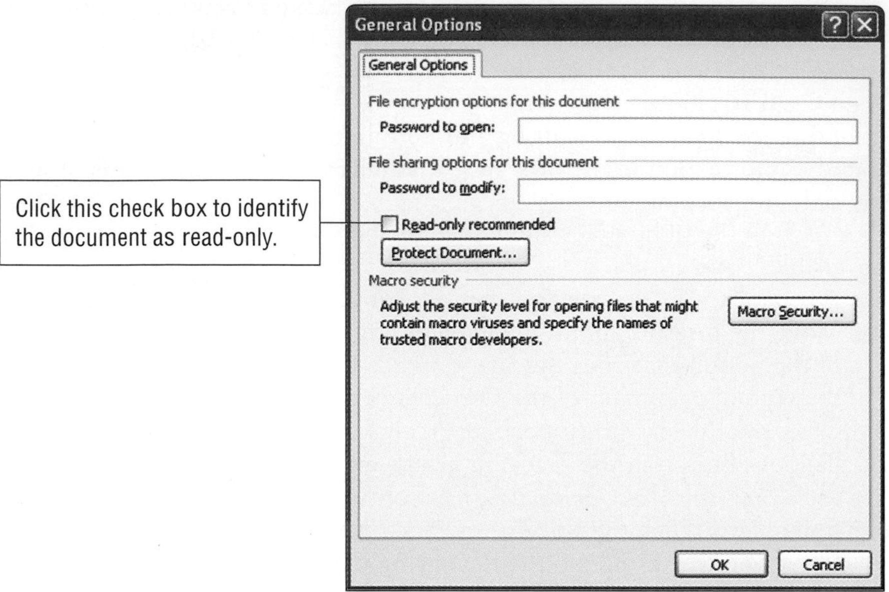

Exercise 2A

Protecting a Document with a Password

1. Open **Contract01.docx**.
2. Save the document and protect it with a password by completing the following steps:
   a. Click the Office button and then click *Save As*.
   b. At the Save As dialog box, click the Tools button located in the lower left corner of the dialog box and then click General Options at the pop-up list.
   c. At the General Options dialog box, type your first name in the *Password to open* text box. (If it is longer than 15 characters, abbreviate it. You will not see your name; instead Word inserts bullets.)

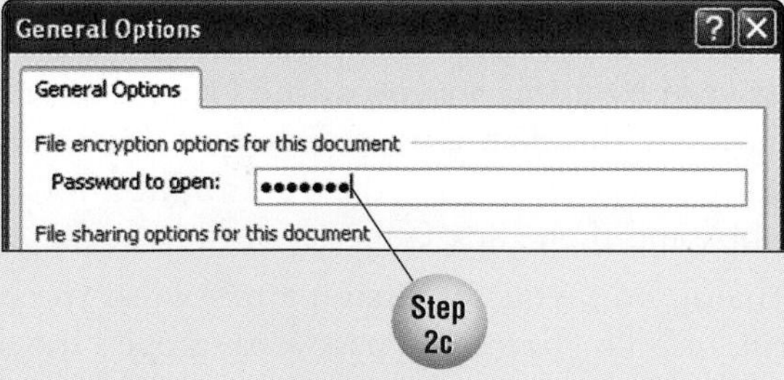

   d. After typing your name, press the Enter key.
   e. At the Confirm Password dialog box, type your name again (be sure to type it exactly as you did in the *Password to open* text box, including upper or lowercase letters), and then press Enter.

3. Select the current name in the *File name* text box, type **C25Ex02a** and then click the Save button.
4. Close **C25Ex02a.docx**.
5. Open **C25Ex02a.docx** and type your password when prompted.
6. Close **C25Ex02a.docx**.

Identifying a Document as Read-Only

Identify Document as Read-Only
1. Click Office button, *Save As*.
2. Click Tools button, *General Options*.
3. Click *Read-only recommended* check box.
4. Click OK.

A read-only document can be opened. You can also make changes to a read-only document, but you cannot save those changes with the same name. Word protects the original document and does not allow you to save the changed document with the same name. You can, however, open a document as read-only, make changes to it, and then save the document with a different name.

To identify the document as read-only, display the Save As dialog box, click the Tools button, and then click General Options at the pop-up list. At the General Options dialog box, click *Read-only recommended* to insert a check mark in the check box. When a person opens the document, a message displays asking whether he or she wants to open the file as read-only.

Exercise 2B

Identifying a Document as Read-Only

1. Open **Notice04.docx**.
2. Click the Office button and then click *Save As*.
3. At the Save As dialog box, click the Tools button and then click General Options at the pop-up list.
4. At the General Options dialog box, click the *Read-only recommended* check box to insert a check mark.

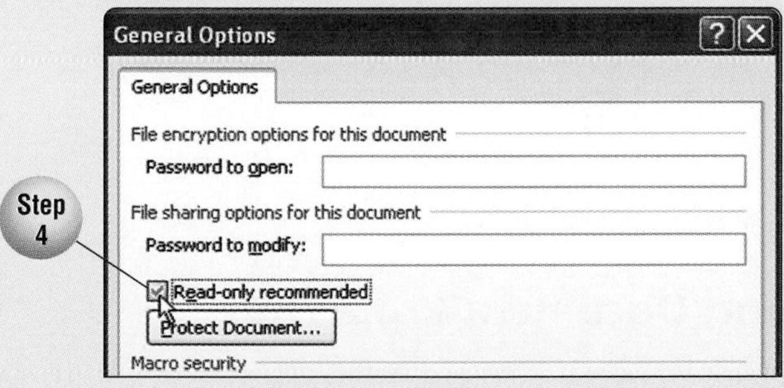

5. Click OK to close the General Options dialog box.
6. Select the text in the *File name* text box and then type **Training**.
7. Click the Save button.
8. Close **Training.docx**.
9. Open **Training.docx** and when the message displays asking if you want to open the document as read-only, click the Yes button.

10. Make the following changes to the document:
    a. Change *Word* to *PowerPoint*.
    b. Change *Thursday, September 24* to *Friday, October 9*.
11. Save the document by completing the following steps:
    a. Click the Save button on the Quick Access toolbar.
    b. At the Save As dialog box, type **C25Ex02b** and then press Enter.
12. Print and then close **C25Ex02b.docx**.

Preparing a Document for Distribution

You can prepare a document for distribution to other employees or colleagues with options at the Office button Prepare side menu, shown in Figure 25.5. To display this side menu, click the Office button and then point to *Prepare*.

Figure 25.5 Office Button Prepare Side Menu

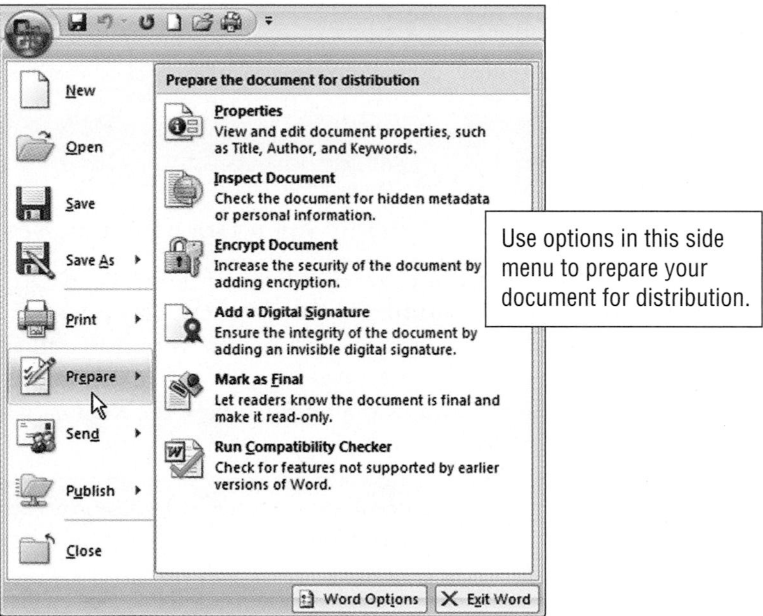

Modify Document Properties
1. Click Office button, *Prepare*, *Properties*.
2. Type, edit, or delete property information.
3. Click Close button.

Modifying Document Properties

Each document you create has properties associated with it, such as the type of document; its location; and when it was created, modified, and accessed. You can add additional information to a document's properties, such as a document title, subject, category, and keywords, at the document information panel, shown in Figure 25.6. Display this panel by clicking the Office button, pointing to *Prepare*, and then clicking the *Properties* option at the side menu.

Figure 25.6 Document Information Panel

Type document information in the text boxes in the document information panel.

Document Properties ▾ Location: Not saved * Required field ×

Author: Title: Subject: Keywords: Category: Status:

Comments:

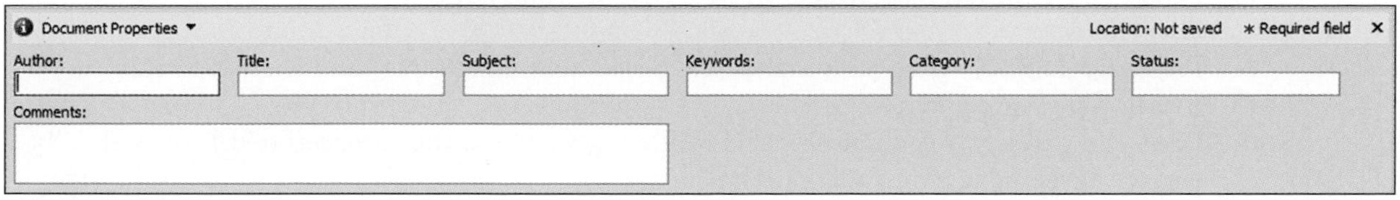

By typing specific information in each of the text boxes in the properties window, you can describe a document. To move the insertion point to the next text box, press the Tab key. To move the insertion point to the preceding text box, press Shift + Tab. Inserting text in some of the text boxes in the document information panel can help you organize and identify your documents. For example, insert specific words contained in the document in the *Keywords* text box, and you can search for all documents containing the specific keywords.

You can print information about a document's properties by using the *Print what* option at the Print dialog box. To do this, display the Print dialog box, click the down-pointing arrow at the right side of the *Print what* option, and then click *Document properties* at the drop-down menu. Click OK to close the Print dialog box.

In addition to inserting information about document properties at the document information panel, you can insert specific information with options at the Properties dialog box. To display this dialog box, click the Document Properties button that displays in the upper left corner of the document information panel and then click *Advanced Properties*. At the Properties dialog box, click a specific tab and then insert the desired information.

Exercise 3A

Inserting Document Properties

1. Open **Agreement02.docx** and save the document with the name **C25Ex03**.
2. Make the following changes to the document.
   a. Search for all occurrences of dark red, 14-point Tahoma bold text and replace with black, 12-point Calibri bold.
   b. Insert a header that prints the page number at the right side of each page.
   c. Insert a footer that prints the document name centered on each page.

3. Customize document properties by completing the following steps:
   a. Display the document information panel by clicking the Office button, pointing to *Prepare*, and then clicking *Properties* at the side menu.
   b. Select any text that may appear in the *Author* text box and then type your first and last names.
   c. Press the Tab key twice (this makes the *Subject* text box active) and then type **Real Estate Sale Agreement**.
   d. Press the Tab key and then type the following words in the *Keywords* text box: **real estate, agreement, contract, purchasing**.
   e. Press the Tab key and then type **Agreement** in the *Category* text box.
   f. Press the Tab key twice and then type the following text in the *Comments* text box: **This is a real estate sale agreement between two parties.**

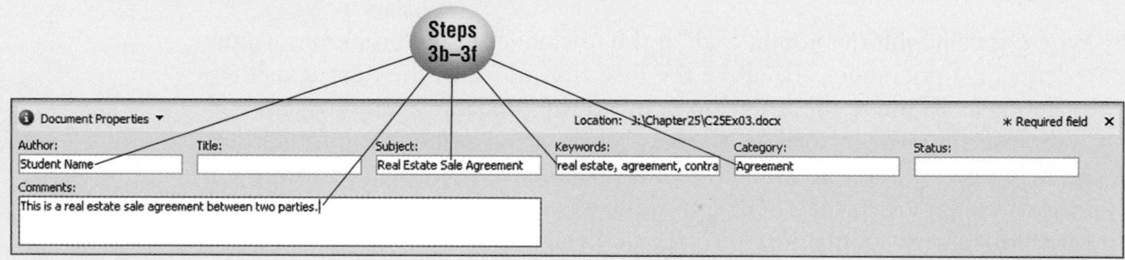

   g. Click the Document Properties button that displays in the upper left corner of the document information panel and then click *Advanced Properties* at the drop-down list.
   h. Click the Summary tab and then type **C25Ex03.docx** in the *Title* text box.

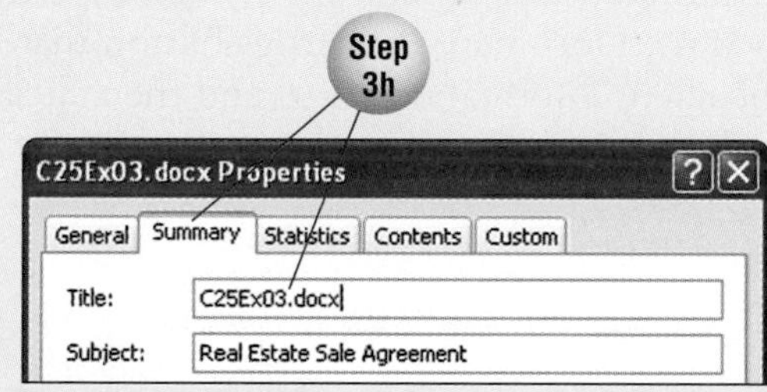

   i. Click each of the remaining tabs and read the information that displays.
   j. Click OK to close the Properties dialog box.
   k. Close the document information panel by clicking the Close button that displays in the upper right corner of the panel.
4. Click the Save button on the Quick Access toolbar.
5. Print only the properties information by completing the following steps:
   a. Click the Office button and then click *Print*.
   b. At the Print dialog box, click the down-pointing arrow at the right side of the *Print what* option and then click *Document properties*.
   c. Click OK.
6. Save **C25Ex03.docx**.

Inspecting a Document

Inspect a Document
1. Click Office button, *Prepare, Inspect Document.*
2. Remove check marks from items you do not want inspected.
3. Click Inspect.

Word includes a document inspection feature you can use to inspect your document for personal data, hidden data, and metadata. Metadata is data that describes other data, such as document properties information. You may want to remove some personal or hidden data before you share a document with other people. To check your document for personal or hidden data, click the Office button, point to *Prepare*, and then click *Inspect Document* at the side menu. This displays the Document Inspector dialog box, shown in Figure 25.7.

Figure 25.7 Document Inspector Dialog Box

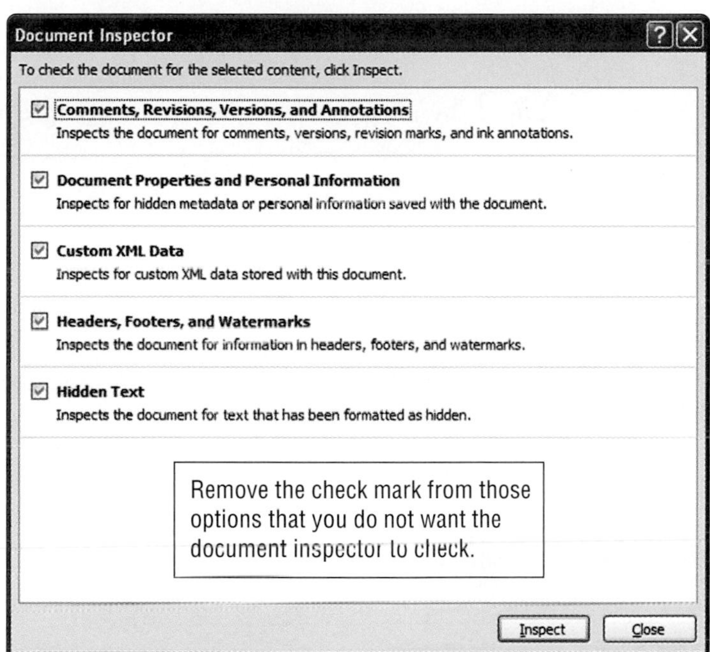

By default, the document inspector checks all of the items listed in the dialog box. If you do not want the inspector to check a specific item in your document, remove the check mark preceding the item. For example, if you know your document has headers and footers and you do not need to check them, click the *Headers, Footers, and Watermark* check box to remove the check mark. Click the Inspect button located toward the bottom of the dialog box, and the document inspector scans the document to identify information.

When the inspection is complete, the results display in the dialog box. A check mark before an option indicates that the inspector did not find the specific items. If an exclamation point is inserted before an option, the inspector found items and displays a list of the items. If you want to remove the found items, click the Remove All button that displays at the right side of the desired option. Click the Reinspect button to ensure that the specific items were removed and then click the Close button.

Exercise 3B

Inspecting a Document

1. With **C25Ex03.docx** open, turn on Track Changes and then make the following editing changes:
   a. Select the title *REAL ESTATE SALE AGREEMENT* and then change the font size to 14 points.
   b. Delete the text *five (5)* that displays in the *Title insurance* paragraph and then type **ten (10)**.
   c. Move the insertion point to the beginning of the text *IN WITNESS WHEREOF* (located on the second page) and then press the Enter key.
   d. Turn off Track Changes.
2. Hide text by completing the following steps:
   a. Move the insertion point to the end of the first paragraph of text in the document and then press the Enter key.
   b. Type **The entire legal description of the property is required for this agreement to be valid.**
   c. Select the text you just typed.
   d. Click the Home tab.
   e. Click the Font group dialog box launcher.
   f. At the Font dialog box, click the *Hidden* option in the *Effects* section.
   g. Click OK to close the dialog box.
3. Click the Save button on the Quick Access toolbar.
4. Inspect the document by completing the following steps:
   a. Click the Office button, point to *Prepare*, and then click *Inspect Document*.
   b. At the Document Inspector dialog box, tell Document Inspector not to check the document for XML data by clicking the *Custom XML Data* check box to remove the check mark.

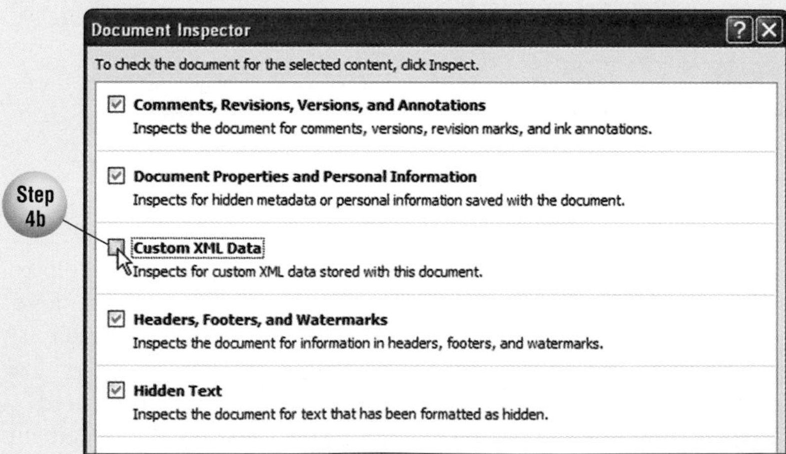

c. Click the Inspect button.
d. Read through the inspection results and then remove all hidden text by clicking the Remove All button that displays at the right side of the *Hidden Text* section. (Make sure a message displays below *Hidden Text* indicating that the text was successfully removed.)

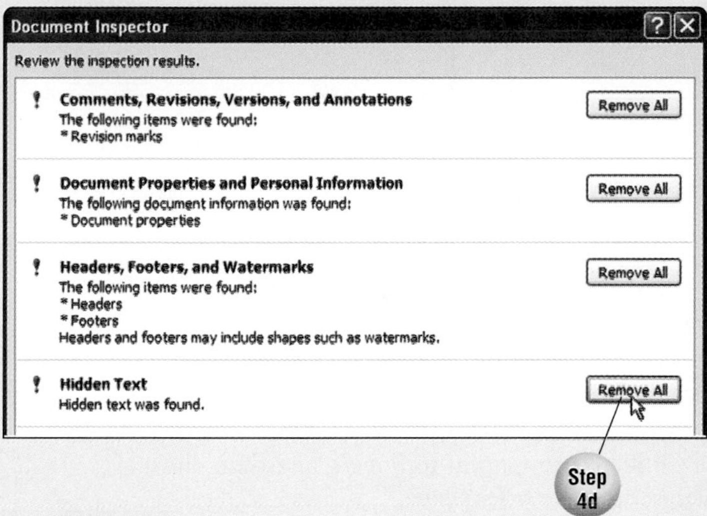

e. Click the Reinspect button.
f. To keep the header and footer text in the document, click the *Headers, Footers, and Watermarks* check box to remove the check mark.
g. Click the Inspect button.
h. Read through the inspection results and then remove all revisions by clicking the Remove All button that displays at the right side of the *Comments, Revisions, Versions, and Annotations* section.
i. Click the Reinspect button.
j. To leave the remaining items in the document, click the Close button.

5. Save **C25Ex03.docx**.

Encrypting a Document

You can insert a password in a document to ensure that the document is opened only by someone who knows the password. You can protect a document with a password in a number of ways: through the Restrict Formatting and Editing task pane, with options at the General Options dialog box, and with the *Encrypt Document* option at the Office button Prepare side menu. Click the Office button, point to *Prepare,* and then click the *Encrypt Document* option. At the Encrypt Document dialog box, shown in Figure 25.8, type a password and then press the Enter key. At the Confirm Password dialog box, type the password again and then click OK.

Encrypt a Document
1. Click Office button, *Prepare, Encrypt Document.*
2. Type a password.
3. Press Enter.
4. Type same password again.
5. Click OK.

Figure 25.8 Encrypt Document Dialog Box

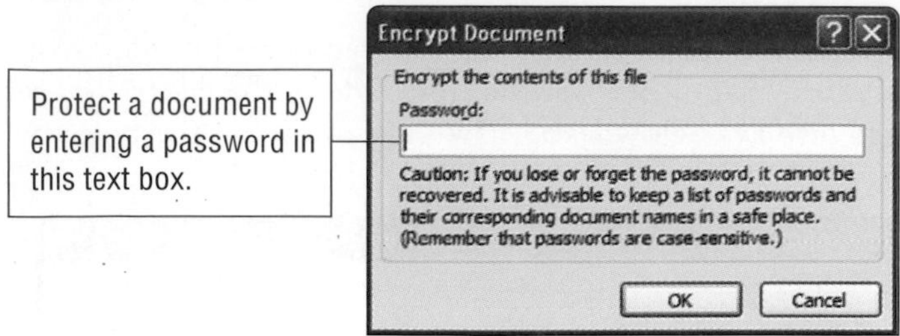

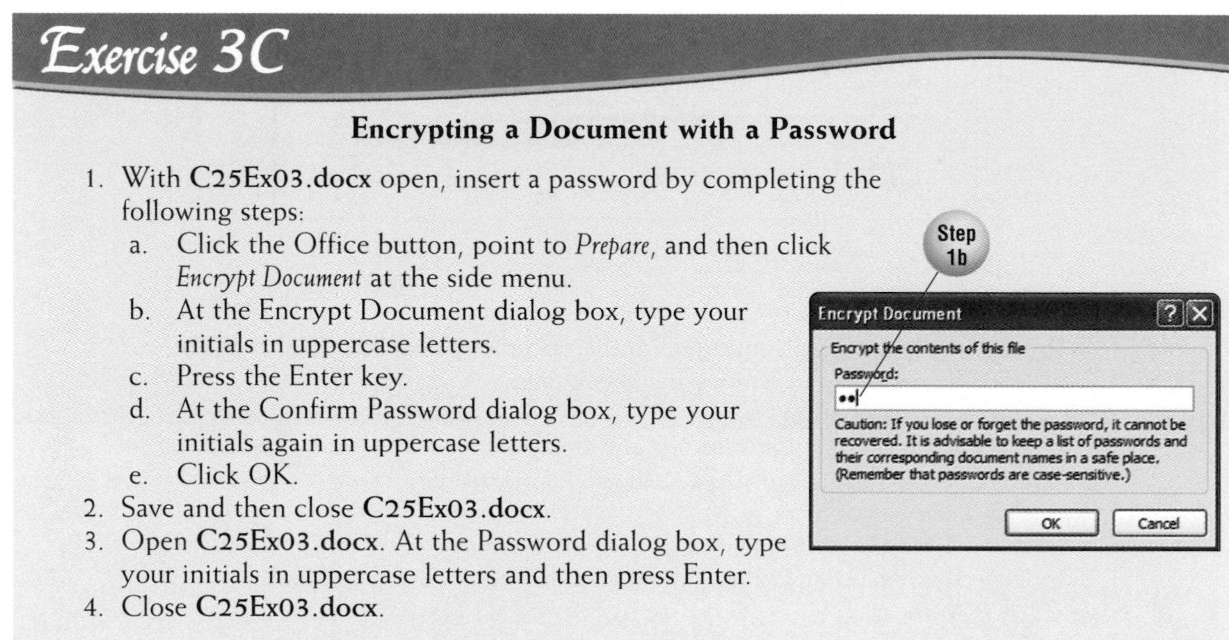

Exercise 3C

Encrypting a Document with a Password

1. With **C25Ex03.docx** open, insert a password by completing the following steps:
   a. Click the Office button, point to *Prepare*, and then click *Encrypt Document* at the side menu.
   b. At the Encrypt Document dialog box, type your initials in uppercase letters.
   c. Press the Enter key.
   d. At the Confirm Password dialog box, type your initials again in uppercase letters.
   e. Click OK.
2. Save and then close **C25Ex03.docx**.
3. Open **C25Ex03.docx**. At the Password dialog box, type your initials in uppercase letters and then press Enter.
4. Close **C25Ex03.docx**.

Restricting Permission

In a previous section of this chapter, you learned how to use options at the Restrict Formatting and Editing task pane to restrict users from formatting or editing documents or sections of documents. You can also use Information Rights Management (IRM) to restrict access to documents. With IRM, you can restrict access to Word documents, Excel workbooks, and PowerPoint presentations. With IRM you can prevent sensitive information from being printed or copied by unauthorized people.

To use IRM, subscribe to the free trial provided by Microsoft. After you have subscribed to IRM, you can use it to restrict access to an open document by clicking the Office button, pointing to *Prepare*, clicking *Restrict Permission*, and then clicking *Restricted Access*. Check with your instructor to determine if this software is available for you to use.

Using a Digital Signature

You can apply a digital signature to a document to authenticate it and indicate that you agree with its contents. When you apply a digital signature, the document is locked so that it cannot be edited or changed unless you remove the digital signature. A digital signature is an electronic stamp that vouches for a document's authenticity. Before applying a digital signature, you must obtain one. You can obtain a digital signature from a commercial certification authority, or you can create your own digital signature. When you create a digital signature, it is saved on the hard drive or the network. Depending on how your system is set up, you might be prevented from using a certificate.

To create a digital signature, click the Office button, point to *Prepare*, and then click *Add a Digital Signature* at the side menu. At the Microsoft Office Word digital signature information message, click OK. At the Get a Digital ID dialog box, click the *Create your own digital ID* option and then click OK. At the Create a Digital ID dialog box, shown in Figure 25.9, insert information and then click OK.

QUICK STEPS

Insert a Digital Signature
1. Save document.
2. Click Office button, *Prepare, Add a Digital Signature.*
3. Type purpose for signing document.
4. Click Sign.
5. Click OK.

Figure 25.9 Create a Digital ID Dialog Box

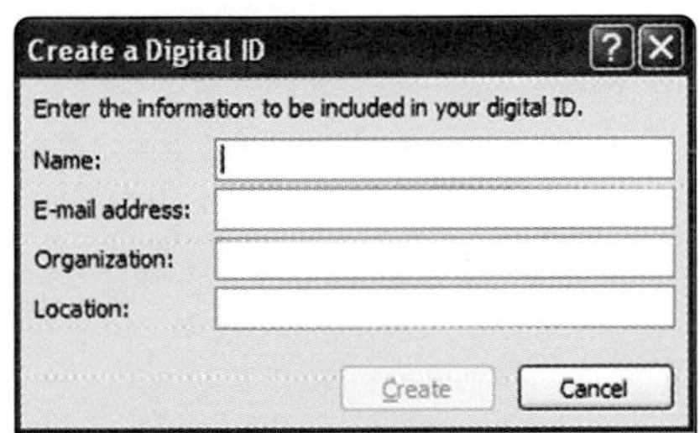

Insert information in the text boxes to identify your digital signature.

Exercise 4A

Creating, Applying, and Viewing a Digital Signature

Note: Check with your instructor before completing this exercise. You may not be able to create a digital signature.

1. Open **Lease01.docx** and save the document with the name **C25Ex04**.
2. Create and apply a digital signature by completing the following steps:
   a. Click the Office button, point to *Prepare*, and then click *Add a Digital Signature* at the side menu.
   b. At the Microsoft Office Word digital signature information message, click OK.
   c. At the Get a Digital ID dialog box, click the *Create your own digital ID* option and then click OK.
   d. At the Create a Digital ID dialog box, insert the following information:
      1) Type your name in the *Name* text box.
      2) Type your actual e-mail address or a fictitious e-mail address in the *E-mail address* text box.
      3) Type your school's name in the *Organization* text box.
      4) Type the city in which your school is located in the *Location* text box.
      5) Click the Create button.

e. At the Sign dialog box, type Agreeing to the terms of the lease. in the *Purpose for signing this document* text box.
f. Click the Sign button.
g. At the message saying your signature has been successfully saved, click OK.

3. Click each of the ribbon tabs and notice the commands and buttons that are inactive or dimmed.
4. View the invisible digital signature details by hovering the mouse pointer over your name in the Signatures task pane, clicking the down-pointing arrow that displays to the right of your name, and then clicking *Signature Details* at the drop-down list.
5. Notice the signature details, including the information on the inserted digital signature and the purpose of the signature.
6. Click the Close button to close the Signature Details dialog box.
7. Close the Signatures task pane by clicking the Close button located in the upper right corner of the task pane.

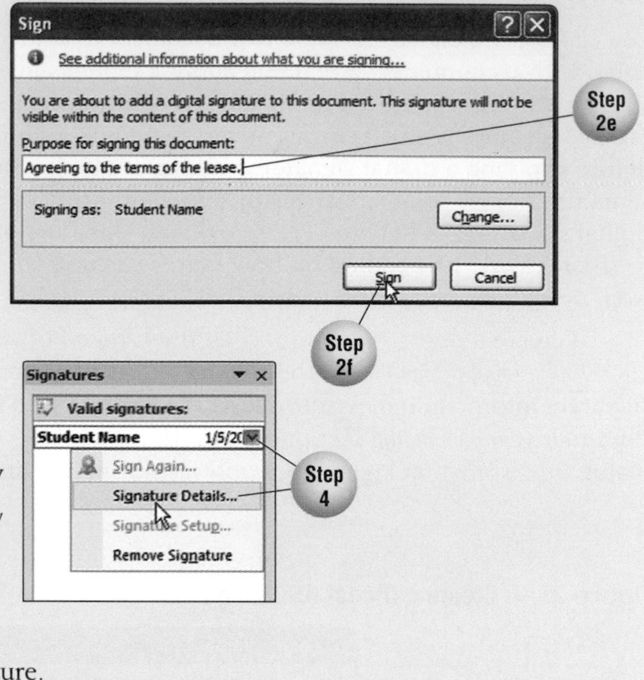

QUICK STEPS

Remove a Digital Signature
1. Click Signatures button at left side of Status bar.
2. Hover mouse pointer over signature in Signatures task pane.
3. Click down-pointing arrow at right of signature.
4. Click *Remove Signature* at drop-down list.

Signatures

Removing a Digital Signature

You can remove a digital signature from a document. When you remove the signature, the document is no longer authenticated, and it is available for formatting and editing. Remove the digital signature at the Signatures task pane. Display the Signatures task pane by clicking the Signatures button that displays toward the left side of the Status bar. This button indicates that a digital signature has been applied to the document.

Exercise 4B

Removing a Digital Signature

1. With **C25Ex04.docx** open, remove the digital signature by completing the following steps:
   a. Click the Signatures button located toward the left side of the Status bar. (This displays the Signatures task pane at the right side of the screen.)

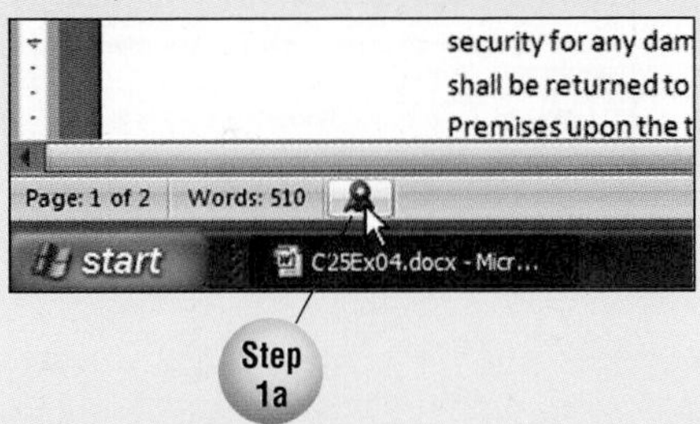

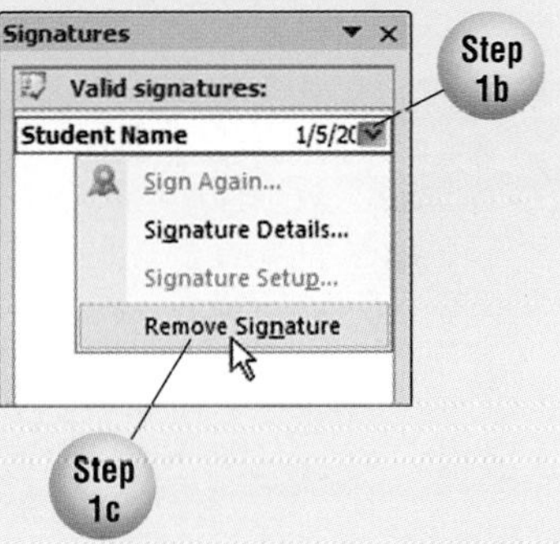

   b. Hover the mouse pointer over your name in the Signatures task pane and then click the down-pointing arrow that displays to the right of your name
   c. Click *Remove Signature* at the drop-down list.
   d. At the message asking if you want to permanently remove the signature, click Yes.
   e. At the message telling you the signature has been removed and the document has been saved, click OK.
2. Close the Signatures task pane.

Inserting a Signature Line

Insert a Signature Line
1. Click Insert tab.
2. Click Signature Line button.
3. Type desired signature information.
4. Click OK.

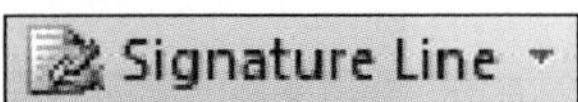

You can insert a signature line in a document that specifies who should sign it. The signature line can include information about the intended signer, such as the person's name, title, and e-mail address. It can also provide instructions for the intended signer. If you send an electronic copy of the document to the intended signer, the person sees the signature line as well as the instructions.

To add a signature line in a document, position the insertion point where you want the signature line to display, click the Insert tab, and then click the Signature Line button in the Text group. At the Signature Setup dialog box, shown in Figure 25.10, type the desired information about the intended signer and then click OK to close the dialog box.

Figure 25.10 Signature Setup Dialog Box

Insert information in this dialog box to insert the signature signer's name and title and to provide instructions to the signer.

Exercise 4C

Inserting a Signature Line

1. With **C25Ex04.docx** open, insert a signature line at the end of the document by completing the following steps:
   a. Press Ctrl + End and then press the Enter key.
   b. Click the Insert tab.
   c. Click the Signature Line button in the Text group.
   d. At the Microsoft Office Word digital signature information message, click OK.
   e. At the Signature Setup dialog box, type your first and last names in the *Suggested signer* text box and then press the Tab key.
   f. Type **Assistant Manager** in the *Suggested signer's title* text box.
   g. Click OK.

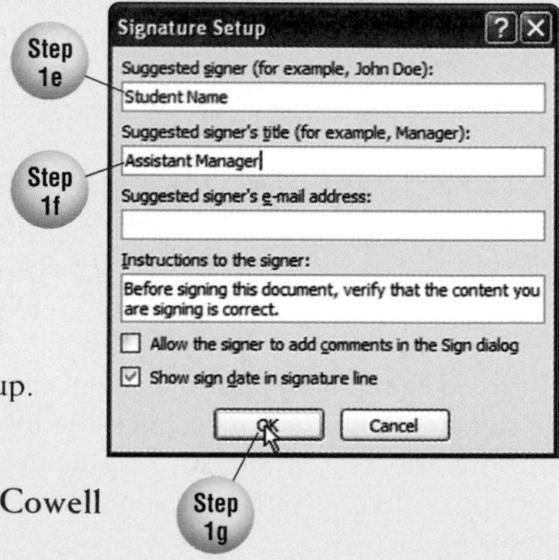

2. Insert a second signature for a lessee to sign by completing the following steps:
   a. Press the Enter key.
   b. If necessary, click the Insert tab.
   c. Click the Signature Line button in the Text group.
   d. At the Microsoft Office Word digital signature information message, click OK.
   e. At the Signature Setup dialog box, type **Jaden Cowell** and then press the Tab key.
   f. Type **Lessee** in the *Suggested signer's title* text box.
   g. Click OK.
3. Save **C25Ex04.docx**.

Inserting a Signature on a Signature Line

When you insert a signature line, the signer can type his or her name on the line, select a digital image of his or her signature, or write a signature using a Tablet PC. When the signer signs the document, a digital signature is added simultaneously that authenticates the identity of the signer. When the document is signed, it becomes a read-only document.

Insert Signature on Signature Line
1. Double-click signature line.
2. Type signature in Sign dialog box.
3. Click Sign.
4. Click OK.

Exercise 4D

Inserting a Signature

1. With **C25Ex04.docx** open, insert a signature on the top signature line by completing the following steps:
   a. Double-click the top signature line.
   b. At the Microsoft Office Word digital signature information message, click OK.
   c. At the Sign dialog box, type your first and last names in the text box following the X.
   d. Click the Sign button.

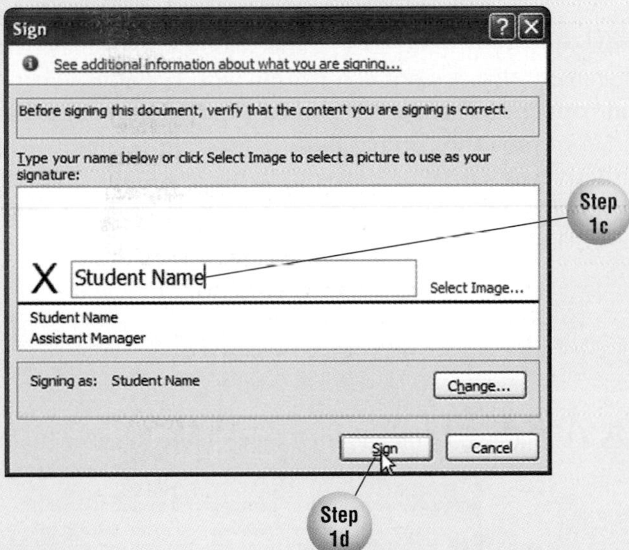

   e. At the message telling you that your signature has been successfully saved, click OK.
2. If an Invalid Signature message displays in the upper left corner of your signature box, complete the following steps to make your signature valid:
   a. Double-click in the signature placeholder.
   b. At the Signature Details dialog box, click the Click here to trust this user's identity hyperlink.
   c. At the Signature Details dialog box, click Close.
3. Close the Signatures task pane.
4. Print and then close **C25Ex04.docx**.

QUICK STEPS

Mark a Document as Final

1. Click Office button, *Prepare, Mark as Final.*
2. Click OK.
3. Click OK.

Run the Compatibility Checker

1. Click Office button, *Prepare, Run Compatibility Checker.*
2. At Microsoft Office Word Compatibility Checker dialog box, click OK.

Marking a Document as Final

You can save a document as read-only and mark it as final with the *Mark as Final* option at the Office button Prepare side menu. To use this feature, click the Office button, point to *Prepare*, and then click *Mark as Final*. At the message saying the document will be marked as final and then saved, click OK. A message box displays telling you that the document has been marked as final to indicate that editing is complete and that it is the final version of the document. The message further indicates that when a document is marked as final, the status property is set to "Final" and typing, editing commands, and proofing marks are turned off; and that a document marked as final can be identified by the Mark As Final icon, which displays toward the left side of the Status bar. At this message, click OK.

Running the Compatibility Checker

Word includes a compatibility checker that checks your documents to identify elements that either are not supported or will act differently in previous versions of Word, from Word 97 through Word 2003. Some features not supported by previous versions of Word include building blocks, citations and bibliographies, tracked moves, and SmartArt. For example, if you save a Word 2007 document containing a SmartArt diagram as a Word 2003 document, the diagram will be converted into a single object that cannot be edited in the previous version.

To determine how compatible the features in your document are with previous versions of Word, click the Office button, point to *Prepare*, and then click *Run Compatibility Checker*. This displays the Microsoft Office Word Compatibility Checker dialog box, shown in Figure 25.11. This dialog box displays a summary of the elements in the document that are not compatible with previous versions of Word and indicates what will happen to them when the document is saved and then opened in a previous version. Word runs the compatibility checker by default when you save a document in an earlier version of Word. If you do not want the compatibility checker to check your documents, remove the check mark from the *Check compatibility when saving in Word 97-2003 formats* option at the Microsoft Office Word Compatibility Checker dialog box.

Figure 25.11 Microsoft Office Word Compatibility Checker Dialog Box

This dialog box displays information on what will happen to text or elements in a document that is saved in a previous version of Word.

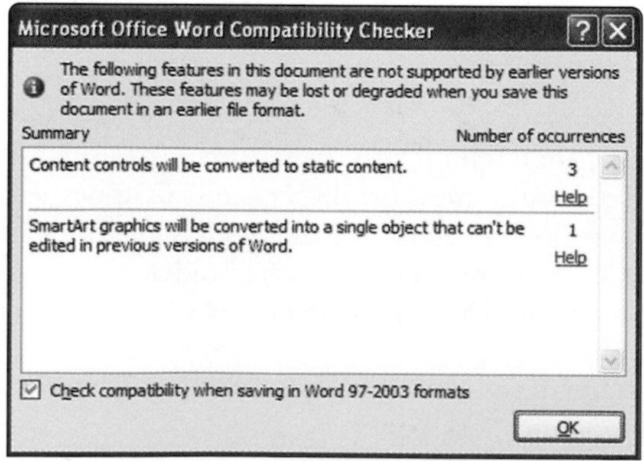

Exercise 5

Checking the Compatibility of Elements

1. Open **KLHPDocument.docx** and then save the document and name it **C25Ex05**.
2. Check how compatible this document would be if you sent it to a colleague who is using Microsoft Word 2003 and determine what would happen to elements not supported by the 2003 version. Run the compatibility checker by completing the following steps:
   a. Click the Office button, point to *Prepare*, and then click *Run Compatibility Checker* at the side menu.
   b. At the Microsoft Office Word Compatibility Checker dialog box, read the information about the elements not supported by 2003 and what will happen to the elements.
   c. Click OK to close the dialog box.
3. Save the document in the 2003 format by completing the following steps:
   a. Click the Office button and then click *Save As*.
   b. At the Save As dialog box, click the down-pointing arrow at the right side of the *Save as type* list box and then click *Word 97-2003 Document (*.doc)* at the drop-down list.
   c. Select the text in the *File name* text box and then type **C25Ex05_2003format**.
   d. Click the Save button.

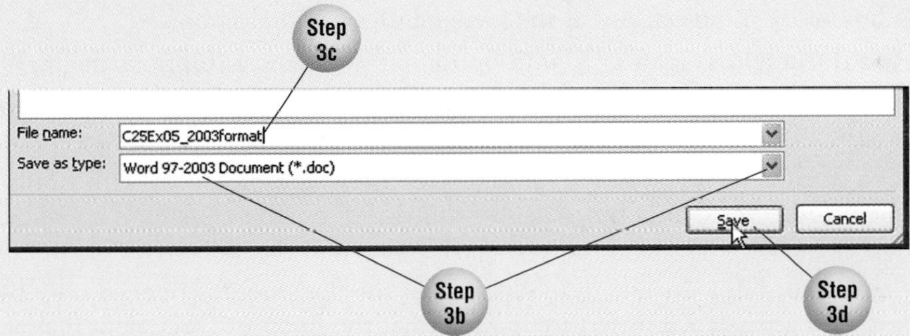

   e. At the Microsoft Office Word Compatibility Checker dialog box, click Continue.
4. Close **C25Ex05_2003format.doc**.
5. Open **C25Ex05.docx** and then mark it as final by completing the following steps:
   a. Click the Office button, point to *Prepare*, and then click *Mark as Final*.
   b. At the message telling you that the document will be marked as final and then saved, click OK.
   c. At the message telling you that the document has been marked as final, click OK.
   d. Click each of the tabs in the ribbon and notice the buttons and options that are available and unavailable.
6. Close **C25Ex05.docx**.

Chapter Summary

- Restrict formatting and editing in a document and apply a password to it with options at the Restrict Formatting and Editing task pane. Display this task pane by clicking the Review tab and then clicking the Protect Document button in the Protect group.
- Restrict formatting by specifying styles that are allowed and not allowed in a document. Do this at the Formatting Restrictions dialog box. Display this dialog box by clicking the Settings hyperlink in the Restrict Formatting and Editing task pane.
- To restrict editing in a document, click the *Allow only this type of editing in the document* option at the Restrict Formatting and Editing task pane, click the down-pointing arrow at the right of the options box, and then click the desired option.
- Enforce editing and formatting restrictions by clicking the Yes, Start Enforcing Protection button in the Restrict Formatting and Editing task pane and make changes to what is allowed at the Start Enforcing Protection dialog box.
- Protect a document with a password by using options at the Start Enforcing Protection dialog box or by using options at the General Options dialog box.
- Specify a document as read-only with options at the General Options dialog box.
- Modify document properties at the document information panel. Display this panel by clicking the Office button, pointing to *Prepare*, and then clicking *Properties*.
- Inspect a document for personal data, hidden data, and metadata with options at the Document Inspector dialog box. Display this dialog box by clicking the Office button, pointing to *Prepare*, and then clicking *Inspect Document* at the side menu.
- Insert a password in a document to ensure that the document is opened only by someone who knows the password. Insert the password at the Encrypt Document dialog box, which you can display by clicking the Office button, pointing to *Prepare*, and then clicking *Encrypt Document*.
- Apply a digital signature to a document to vouch for its authenticity. Once a digital signature is applied to a document, the document is locked and cannot be edited or changed without first removing the digital signature.
- Insert a signature line in a document to specify who should sign the document. Insert a signature line with options at the Signature Setup dialog box. To display this dialog box, click the Insert tab and then click the Signature Line button in the Text group.
- Mark a document as final by saving it as a read-only file. To do this, click the Office button, point to *Prepare*, and then click *Mark as Final*. Typing, editing commands, and proofing marks are turned off when a document is marked as final.
- Run the compatibility checker to check your document and identify elements that are not supported or will act differently in previous versions of Word. To determine the compatibility of the features in your document, click the Office button, point to *Prepare*, and then click *Run Compatibility Checker* at the side menu.

Commands review

FEATURE	RIBBON TAB, GROUP	BUTTON, OPTION
Restrict Formatting and Editing task pane	Review, Protect	
General Options dialog box		, Save As, Tools, General Options
Document information panel		, Prepare, Properties
Document Inspector dialog box		, Prepare, Inspect Document
Encrypt Document dialog box		, Prepare, Encrypt Document
Digital signature		, Prepare, Add a Digital Signature
Signature Setup dialog box	Insert, Text	Signature Line
Microsoft Office Word Compatibility Checker dialog box		, Prepare, Run Compatibility Checker

Reviewing key points

Completion: In the space provided at the right, indicate the correct term, command, or number.

1. Limit the formatting users can apply to text in a document with options in this section of the Restrict Formatting and Editing task pane. ____________________
2. Use options in this section of the Restrict Formatting and Editing task pane to limit the types of changes a user can make to a document. ____________________
3. Protect a document with a password using options at the Start Enforcing Protection dialog box or with options at this dialog box. ____________________
4. Click this button in the Restrict Formatting and Editing task pane to display the Start Enforcing Protection dialog box. ____________________

5. Protect a document with a password with options at the General Options dialog box or at this dialog box. ______________
6. Add document properties information at this panel. ______________
7. This feature checks your document for personal data, hidden data, and metadata. ______________
8. Apply this type of signature to a document to vouch for the authenticity of the document. ______________
9. Insert a signature line into a document with options at this dialog box. ______________
10. Use this feature to check your document and identify elements that are not supported in previous versions of Word. ______________

Applying your skills

Assessment 1 Restrict Formatting in a Computer Report

1. Open **Report01.docx** and save the document with the name **C25A01**.
2. Display the Restrict Formatting and Editing task pane and then restrict formatting to *Heading 2* and *Heading 3* style.
3. Enforce the protection and include the password *computers*.
4. Save and then close **C25A01.docx**.
5. Open **C25A01.docx**.
6. Make sure the Restrict Formatting and Editing task pane displays.
7. Click the Available styles hyperlink.
8. Apply the Heading 2 style to the title *THE COMPUTER ADVANTAGE*. (The Heading 3 style may not display until you apply the Heading 2 style to the first title.)
9. Apply the Heading 3 style to the five headings in the document.
10. Close the Styles task pane and then close the Restrict Formatting and Editing task pane.
11. Save the document and then print only page 1.
12. Close **C25A01.docx**.

Assessment 2 Restrict Editing to Comments in a Software Life Cycle Document

1. Open **Document23.docx** and save the document with the name **C25A02**.
2. Display the Restrict Formatting and Editing task pane, restrict editing to only comments, and then start enforcing the protection (do not include a password).
3. Save and then close **C25A02.docx**.
4. Open **C25A02.docx**.
5. Insert the comment **Create a SmartArt diagram that illustrates the software life cycle.** at the end of the first paragraph of text in the document.
6. Insert the comment **Include the problem-solving steps.** at the end of the paragraph in the *Design* section.

7. Insert the comment **Describe a typical beta testing cycle.** at the end of the paragraph in the *Testing* section.
8. Close the Reviewing pane and the Restrict Formatting and Editing task pane.
9. Print only the comments.
10. Save and then close **C25A02.docx**.

Assessment 3 Insert Document Properties and Save a Software Document in a Different Format

1. Open **Report13.docx** and save the document with the name **C25A03**.
2. Make the following changes to the document:
   a. Apply the Heading 1 style to the title *Developing an Information System*.
   b. Apply the Heading 2 style to the five headings in the document.
   c. Change the style set to *Formal*.
   d. Apply the *Median* theme.
   e. Insert the Alphabet footer and type the name of the document in the text placeholder.
   f. Insert the DRAFT 1 watermark in the document.
3. Move the insertion point to the end of the paragraph in the *Project Team* section, press the Enter key twice, and then insert a hard page break.
4. Press the Up Arrow key to move the insertion point to the end of page 1 and then insert the document named **CycleDiagram.docx**.
5. Display the document information panel and then type the following in the specified text boxes:
   a. Title = **Developing an Information System**
   b. Subject = **Software Development**
   c. Keywords = **software, design, plan**
   d. Category = **Software**
   e. Comments = **This document describes the four steps involved in developing a software system.**
   f. Close the document information panel.
6. Save the document and then print only the document properties.
7. Inspect the document and remove any hidden text.
8. Save and then print **C25A03.docx**.
9. Run the compatibility checker to determine what features are not supported by earlier versions of Word.
10. Save the document in the *Word 97-2003 Document (*.doc)* format and name it **C25A03_2003format**.
11. Save, print, and then close the document.

Performance Assessments

UNIT 5

UNIT05

Customizing Documents and Features

ASSESSING PROFICIENCIES

In this unit, you have learned how to insert, modify, and delete building blocks and how to customize AutoCorrect, Word options, themes, and Quick Styles sets. You also learned how to create, edit, and modify styles, apply styles to text in documents, and protect and prepare a document for distribution.

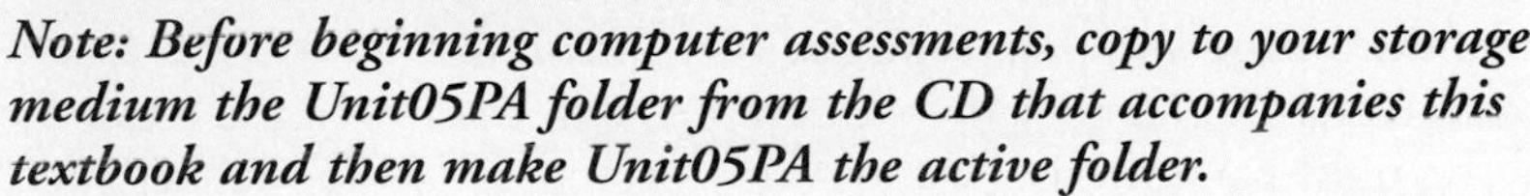

Note: Before beginning computer assessments, copy to your storage medium the Unit05PA folder from the CD that accompanies this textbook and then make Unit05PA the active folder.

Assessment 1 Format and Insert Fields in a Computer Report

1. Open **Report11.docx** and save the document with the name **U05PA01**.
2. With the insertion point positioned at the beginning of the document, press Ctrl + Enter to insert a page break.
3. Apply the Heading 1 style to the two titles in the document *COMPUTER INPUT DEVICES* and *COMPUTER OUTPUT DEVICES*.
4. Apply the Heading 2 style to the six headings in the document.
5. Change the style set to *Traditional*.
6. Change the theme colors to *Trek*.
7. Insert the Transcend (Even Page) footer building block.
8. Double-click in the document, press Ctrl + Home to move the insertion point to the beginning of the document, and then insert the *Automatic Table 1* table of contents building block.
9. Press Ctrl + End to move the insertion point to the end of the document, press the Enter key twice, Press Ctrl + Q, press the Backspace key, and then insert a field that will insert the file name.
10. Press Enter and then insert a field that will insert the current date and time.
11. Save, print, and then close **U05PA01.docx**.

Assessment 2 Create and Apply Custom Themes and AutoCorrect Entries to a Rental Form

1. At a blank document, create custom theme colors named with your initials that make the following color changes:
   a. Change the *Text/Background - Dark 2* color to *Tan, Text 2, Darker 75%*.
   b. Change the *Accent 1* color to *Olive Green, Accent 3, Darker 50%*.
2. Create custom theme fonts named with your initials that apply Verdana to headings and Cambria to body text.
3. Save the custom theme and name it with your initials. (Do this with the *Save Current Theme* option at the Themes drop-down gallery.)
4. Close the document without saving the changes.
5. Open **TRCRentalForm.docx** and save the document with the name **U05PA02**.
6. Search for all occurrences of trc and replace with Tennison Rental Company.
7. Add the following text to AutoCorrect:
   a. Insert *trc* in the *Replace* text box and insert *Tennison Rental Company* in the *With* text box.
   b. Insert *cera* in the *Replace* text box and insert *Construction Equipment Rental Agreement* in the *With* text box.
8. Move the insertion point to the blank line above the *Further Assurances* paragraph located on the third page and then type the text shown in Figure U5.1. Use the Numbering feature to number the paragraphs with the lowercase letter followed by the right parenthesis. (If the AutoCorrect feature capitalizes the first word after the letter and right parenthesis, use the AutoCorrect Options button to return the letter to lowercase.)
9. Apply the Heading 1 style to the title *Construction Equipment Rental Agreement* and apply the Heading 2 style to the headings in the document (*Lease*, *Rent*, *Use and Operation of Equipment*, *Insurance*, *Risk of Loss*, *Maintenance*, *Return of Equipment*, *Warranties of Lessee*, *Default*, and *Further Assurances*).
10. Apply your custom theme to the document.
11. Insert a building block that inserts the word *SAMPLE* as a watermark.
12. Insert a footer that prints the page number at the bottom of each page.
13. Save, print, and then close **U05PA02.docx**.
14. At a blank document, delete your custom theme, custom theme colors, and custom theme fonts. Delete the *trc* and *cera* AutoCorrect entries.

Figure U5.1 Assessment 2

Default

Upon the occurrence of default, trc may without any further notice exercise any one or more of the following remedies:

a) declare all unpaid Rentals under this cera to be immediately due and payable;
b) terminate this cera as to any or all items of Equipment;
c) take possession of the Equipment, and for this purpose enter upon any premises of Lessee and remove the Equipment, without any liability, suit, action, or other proceeding by Lessee;
d) cause Lessee at his/her expense to promptly return the Equipment to trc in the condition set forth in this cera;
e) use, hold, sell, lease, or otherwise dispose of the Equipment or any item of it on the premises of Lessee or any other location without affecting the obligations of Lessee as provided in this cera;
f) proceed by appropriate action either at law or in equity to enforce performance by Lessee of the applicable covenants of this cera or to recover damages for the breach of them; or
g) exercise any other rights accruing to trc under any applicable law upon a default by a lessee.

Assessment 3 Create and Apply Styles to a Business Conduct Report

1. Open **TRCStyles.docx**.
2. Select the clip art image and the text *Tennison Rental Company* and then create a building block named with your initials followed by TRCHeader.
3. Select the horizontal line and the address and telephone number below it and then create a building block named with your initials followed by TRCFooter.
4. Select the *Title* text (including the paragraph mark after the text) and then create a style named with your initials followed by TRCTitle.
5. Select the *Heading 1* text and then create a style named with your initials followed by TRCHeading1.
6. Select the *Heading 2* text and then create a style named with your initials followed by TRCHeading2.
7. Save the styles you created as a Quick Styles set named with your initials followed by Tennison.
8. Close **TRCStyles.docx** without saving the changes.
9. Open **TRCCode.docx** and save the document with the name **U05PA03**.
10. Change to the Quick Styles set named with your initials followed by Tennison.

11. Apply your custom title style to the title *Code of Business Conduct*; apply your custom heading 1 style to the headings in all uppercase letters; and apply your custom heading 2 style to the headings with only the first letter in uppercase.
12. Insert the TRCHeader building block as a header.
13. Insert the TRCFooter building block as a footer.
14. Delete the custom Quick Styles set you created that is preceded by your initials.
15. Save, print, and then close **U05PA03.docx**.
16. Delete the building blocks you created.

Assessment 4 Restrict Formatting in a Report

1. Open **Report14.docx** and save the document with the name **U05PA04**.
2. Select the entire document and then change the line spacing to 1.15.
3. Display the Restrict Formatting and Editing task pane and then restrict formatting to Heading 1 and Heading 2 styles.
4. Enforce the protection and include the password *report*.
5. Save and then close **U05PA04.docx**.
6. Open **U05PA04.docx**.
7. Make sure the Restrict Formatting and Editing task pane displays and then click the Available styles hyperlink.
8. Apply the Heading 1 style to the title of the report and apply the Heading 2 style to the four headings in the report.
9. Close the Styles task pane.
10. Close the Restrict Formatting and Editing task pane.
11. Save the document and then print only page 1.
12. Close **U05PA04.docx**.

Assessment 5 Insert Document Properties and Save a Document in a Previous Version of Word

1. Open **Document28.docx** and save the document with the name **U05PA05**.
2. Make the following changes to the document:
   a. Apply the Heading 1 style to the three headings in the document (*Plan Highlights*, *Quality Assessment*, and *Provider Network*).
   b. Change the style set to *Modern*.
   c. Apply *Foundry* theme colors.
3. Move the insertion point to the end of the document and then insert the document named **KLHPDiagram.docx**.
4. Display the document information panel and then type the following information in the specified text boxes:
   a. Title = **Key Life Health Plan**
   b. Subject = **Company Health Plan**
   c. Keywords = **health, plan, network**
   d. Category = **Health Plan**
   e. Comments = **This document describes highlights of the Key Life Health Plan.**
   f. Close the document information panel.
5. Save the document and then print only the document properties.
6. Inspect the document and remove any hidden text.
7. Save and then print **U05PA05.docx**.

8. Assume that the document will be read by a colleague with Word 2003 and run the compatibility checker to determine what features are not supported by earlier versions of Word.
9. Save the document in the *Word 97-2003 Document (*.doc)* format and name it **U05PA05_2003format**.
10. Save, print, and then close the document.

CREATING ORIGINAL DOCUMENTS

The activity in Assessment 6 gives you the opportunity to practice your writing skills as well as demonstrate your mastery of some of the important Word features presented in this unit. When you compose the document, use correct grammar, precise word choices, and clear sentence construction.

Assessment 6 Design and Apply Building Blocks

Situation: You have been hired as the office manager for Highland Construction Company. The address of the company is 9025 Palmer Park Boulevard, Colorado Springs, CO 80904, and the telephone number is (719) 555-4575. You are responsible for designing business documents that maintain a common appearance and formatting. You decide your first task is to create a letterhead document using the company name, address, telephone number, and a clip art image or other elements to add visual interest. Save the completed letterhead document with the name **HCCLetterhead**. Using the text and elements in the letterhead document, create a building block and name it with your initials followed by *HCCLetterhead*. Save, print, and then close **HCCLetterhead.docx**. Create the following additional building blocks for your company (you decide the building block names but use your initials in each):

- Create a building block footer that contains a border line (in a color matching the colors in the letterhead) and the company slogan "Building Dreams Since 1985."
- Create the following complimentary close building block:

  Sincerely,

  Your Name
  Office Manager
- Create the following company name and address building block:

  Mr. Eric Rashad
  Roswell Industries
  1020 Wasatch Street
  Colorado Springs, CO 80902
- Create the following company name and address building block:

  Ms. Claudia Sanborn
  S & S Supplies
  537 Constitution Avenue
  Colorado Springs, CO 80911

At a blank document, create a letter to Eric Rashad by inserting the company letterhead (the building block that begins with your initials followed by HCCLetterhead). Type today's date, press the Enter key twice, and then insert the Eric Rashad building block. Insert the file named **HCCLetter01.docx** and then insert your complimentary close building block. Finally, insert the footer building block you created for the company. Save the letter with the name **U05PA06Ltr01**. Print and then close the letter. Complete similar steps to create a letter to Claudia Sanborn. Save the completed letter with the name **U05PA06Ltr02**. Print and then close the letter.

Assessment 7 Create AutoCorrect Entries and Format an Agreement Document

Situation: As the office manager at Highland Construction Company, you are responsible for preparing construction agreements. Create an AutoCorrect entry that will replace hcc with Highland Construction Company and bca with Building Construction Agreement. Open **HCCAgreement01.docx** and then type the text shown in Figure U5.2 at the beginning of the document.

Figure U5.2 **Assessment 7**

bca

THIS bca made this ___day of _______________, 2010 by and between hcc and ___________________, hereinafter referred to as "owner," for the considerations hereinafter named, hcc and owner agree as follows:

Financing Arrangements: The Owner will obtain a construction loan to finance construction under this bca. If adequate financing has not been arranged within 30 days of the date of this bca, or the owner cannot provide evidence to hcc of other financial ability to pay the full amount, then hcc may treat this bca as null and void and retain the down payment made on the execution of this bca.

Insert the following in the document:

- Insert at the end of the document a date printed field and a file name field.
- Insert your footer building block as a footer
- Insert a cover page

Add or apply any other enhancements to improve the visual appeal of the document and then save the document with the name **U05PA07.docx**. Print and then close the document.

Delete the building blocks you created and then delete the AutoCorrect entries *hcc* and *bca*.

Unit 6

Referencing Data

- Inserting Endnotes, Footnotes, and References
- Creating Indexes
- Creating Specialized Tables
- Creating Forms
- Creating Forms with Legacy Tools
- Unit 6 Performance Assessments

Signature Microsoft® Word 2007

Microsoft Certified Application Specialist Skills—Unit 6

Reference No.	Skill	Pages
1	**Creating and customizing documents**	
1.1	Create and format documents	
1.1.1	Work with templates	734-738
1.3	Make documents and content easier to find	
1.3.1	Create, modify, and update tables of contents	709-717
1.3.2	Create, modify, and update indexes	689-703
4	**Organizing Content**	
4.4	Insert and format references and captions	
4.4.1	Create and modify sources	671-683
4.4.2	Insert citations and captions	672-675
4.4.3	Insert and modify bibliographies	679-683
4.4.4	Select reference styles	682-683
4.4.5	Create, modify, and update tables of figures and tables of authorities	719-727

Chapter 26

Inserting Endnotes, Footnotes, and References

Tutorial 26.1
Creating and Editing Footnotes and Endnotes

Performance Objectives

Upon successful completion of Chapter 26, you will be able to:

- Create footnotes
- Create endnotes
- Insert and modify sources and citations
- Insert, modify, and format bibliographies

When you write a research paper or report, you may need to include references to identify the sources of information you used. Word provides a variety of methods for citing references including footnotes, endnotes, citations, and bibliographies. You will learn how to cite documents with these reference features as well as how to edit, modify, and delete references.

Note: Before beginning computer exercises for this chapter, copy to your storage medium the Chapter26 folder from the CD that accompanies this textbook and then make Chapter26 the active folder.

Insert Footnote
1. Click References tab.
2. Click Insert Footnote button.
3. Type footnote text.

Insert Endnote
1. Click References tab.
2. Click Insert Endnote button.
3. Type endnote text.

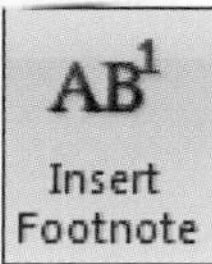

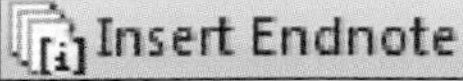

Creating Footnotes and Endnotes

Research papers and reports generally contain information from a variety of sources. To acknowledge and credit these sources, you can insert footnotes or endnotes in a document. A footnote is an explanatory note or reference that is placed at the bottom of the page on which a source is referenced. An endnote is also an explanatory note or reference, but it is placed at the end of a document.

Two steps are involved in creating a footnote or an endnote. The first step is to insert a reference number for the footnote or endnote in the document where the source is referenced. The second step is to type the bibliographic information about the source. In Word, you create footnotes and endnotes in a similar manner. To create a footnote, position the insertion point where you want the reference number to appear, click the References tab, and then click the Insert Footnote button in the Footnotes group. This inserts a superscript number in the document and also inserts a separator line at the bottom of the page with a superscript number below. With the insertion point positioned immediately right of the superscript number beneath the separator line, type the footnote entry text. Word automatically numbers footnotes with superscript Arabic numbers and endnotes with superscript lowercase Roman numerals.

Exercise 1A

Creating Footnotes

1. Open **Report14.docx** and save the document with the name **C26Ex01a**.
2. Create the first footnote shown in Figure 26.1 by completing the following steps:
   a. Position the insertion point at the end of the first paragraph of text in the document.
   b. Click the References tab.
   c. Click the Insert Footnote button in the Footnotes group.

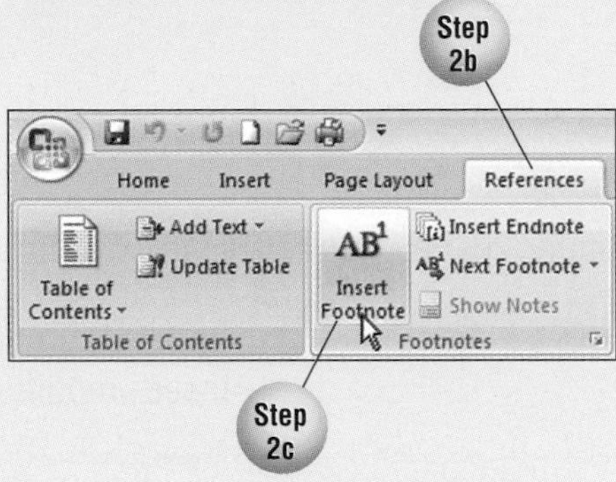

   d. With the insertion point positioned at the bottom of the page immediately following the superscript number, type the first footnote shown in Figure 26.1.

Programmers can look forward to a human language computer interface. With

better interfaces, programmers may be able to describe what they want using natural

---

[1] Curtis, Ray, *Artificial Intelligence*, Home Town Publishing, 2010, pages 45-51.

Step 2d

3. Move the insertion point to the end of the paragraph in the *Speech Recognition* section and then create the second footnote shown in Figure 26.1.
4. Move the insertion point to the end of the second paragraph in the *Natural-Language Interface* section and then create the third footnote shown in Figure 26.1.
5. Move the insertion point to the end of the paragraph in the *Virtual Reality* section and then create the fourth footnote shown in Figure 26.1.
6. Move the insertion point to the end of the last paragraph in the document and then create the fifth footnote shown in Figure 26.1.
7. Save and then close **C26Ex01a.docx**.

Figure 26.1 Exercise 1A

Curtis, Ray, *Artificial Intelligence*, Home Town Publishing, 2010, pages 45-51.

Clemens, Heather, and Reyes, Nicolas, "Integrating Speech Recognition," *Design Technologies*, January/February 2009, pages 12-14.

Glenovich, Daniel, "Language Interfaces," *Corporate Computing*, November 2009, pages 8-14.

Novak, William, *Virtual Reality Worlds*, Lilly-Harris Publishers, 2010, pages 46-58.

Beal, Kathleen, "Challenges of Artificial Intelligence," *Interface Designs*, April 2010, pages 16-22.

Printing Footnotes and Endnotes

When you print a document that contains footnotes, Word automatically reduces the number of text lines on a page by the number of lines in the footnote(s) plus the line separating the footnotes from the document text. (Word separates footnotes from document text with a 2-inch separator line that begins at the left margin.) If the page does not contain enough space, the footnote numbers and bibliographic text are moved to the next page. When you create endnotes in a document, Word prints all endnote references at the end of the document, separated from the text by a 2-inch separator line.

Exercise 1B

Creating Endnotes

1. Open **Report18.docx** and save the document with the name **C26Ex01b**.
2. Change the style set to *Simple*.
3. Create the first endnote shown in Figure 26.2 by completing the following steps:
   a. Position the insertion point at the end of the paragraph in the *Satellite Internet Connections* section.
   b. Click the References tab.
   c. Click the Insert Endnote button.
   d. Type the first endnote shown in Figure 26.2.

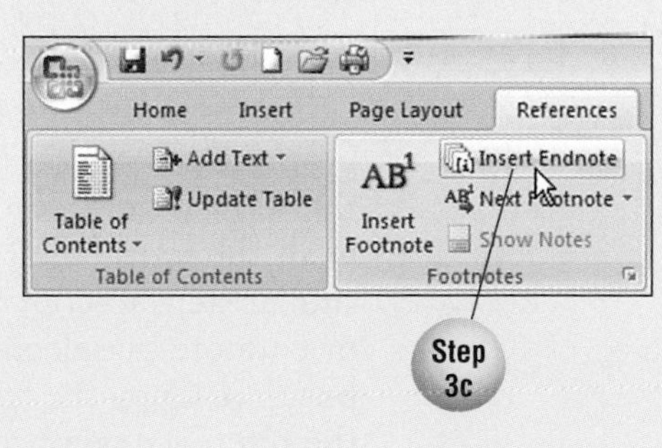

4. Move the insertion point to the end of the second paragraph in the *Second Internet* section and then type the second endnote shown in Figure 26.2.
5. Move the insertion point to the end of the paragraph in the *Internet Services for a Fee* section and then type the third endnote shown in Figure 26.2.
6. Save, print, and then close **C26Ex01b.docx**.

Figure 26.2 **Exercise 1B**

Dossa, Aileen, *Satellite Systems*, Robison Publishing House, 2010, pages 15-38.

Ventrella, Terry, "Future of the Internet," *Computing Today*, October 2010, pages 33-44.

Fuzak, Jolene, "Fee-Based Internet Services," *Connections*, March/April 2010, pages 2-6.

Viewing and Showing Footnotes and Endnotes

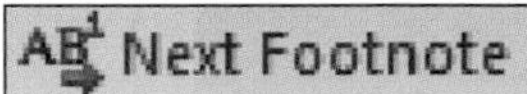

To view footnotes in a document, click the Next Footnote button in the Footnotes group in the References tab. Clicking the Next Footnote button moves the insertion point to the first footnote reference number beyond the insertion point's current location. For example, if the insertion point is located at the beginning of a document, clicking the Next Footnote button moves the insertion point to the location of footnote reference number 1. If the insertion point is located to the right of footnote reference number 2, clicking the Next Footnote button moves the insertion point to the location of footnote reference number 3. Click the Next Footnote button arrow, and a drop-down list displays with options for viewing the previous footnote and for viewing endnotes.

You can move the insertion point to the bibliographic text of a specific footnote with the Show Notes button. Click the Next Footnote button to move the insertion point to the next footnote reference number and then click the Show Notes button. This moves the insertion point to the specific footnote bibliographic text at the bottom of the page. Click the Show Notes button again, and the insertion point moves back to the footnote reference number. You can also view a footnote or endnote by hovering the mouse pointer over the footnote or endnote reference number in the document. This displays the footnote or endnote text in a box above the reference number.

Moving, Copying, and Deleting Footnotes or Endnotes

You can move, copy, or delete footnote or endnote reference numbers. If a footnote or endnote reference number is moved, copied, or deleted, all subsequent footnotes or endnotes remaining in the document are automatically renumbered. To move a footnote or endnote, select the reference number and then click the Cut button in the Clipboard group in the Home tab. Position the insertion point where you want the footnote or endnote inserted and then click the Paste button. Complete similar steps to copy and paste footnotes or endnotes. You can also move a footnote or endnote by selecting the reference number and then dragging it to the desired position. Copy the footnote or endnote by holding down the Ctrl key when dragging the reference number. To delete a footnote or endnote, select the reference number and then press the Delete key. When the reference number is deleted, the entry text is also deleted.

Exercise 1C

Editing and Deleting Footnotes

1. Open **C26Ex01a.docx** and navigate to footnote reference numbers and footnote bibliographic text by completing the following steps:
   a. Click the References tab.
   b. Click the Next Footnote button.
   c. Click the Next Footnote button again.
   d. Click the Next Footnote button arrow and then click *Previous Footnote* at the drop-down list.
   e. Click the Show Notes button to display the first footnote text located at the bottom of the page.

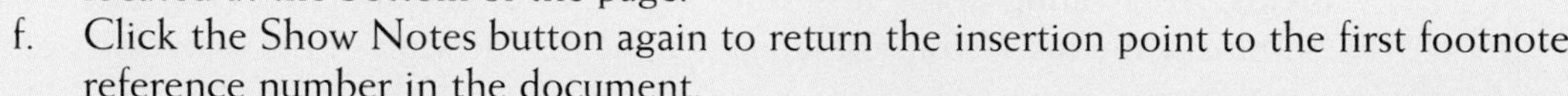

   f. Click the Show Notes button again to return the insertion point to the first footnote reference number in the document.
2. Select the entire document and then change the font to Constantia. (Footnote text is not selected.)
3. Change the font for the footnotes by completing the following steps:
   a. Press Ctrl + Home.
   b. Click the References tab, click the Next Footnote button, and then click the Show Notes button.
   c. Press Ctrl + A. (This selects all footnote entry text on every page.)
   d. Change the font to Constantia.
   e. Click in the document to deselect the text.
4. Delete the fourth footnote by completing the following steps:
   a. Press Ctrl + Home.
   b. Click the Next Footnote button four times.
   c. Select the fourth footnote reference number (superscript number).
   d. Press the Delete key.
5. Save, print, and then close **C26Ex01a.docx**.

Creating Citations and Bibliographies

In addition to using footnotes and endnotes to credit sources in a research paper or manuscript, consider inserting in-text citations and a bibliography to identify sources of quotations, ideas, and borrowed or summarized material. An in-text citation acknowledges that you are borrowing information from a source rather than plagiarizing (stealing) the words or ideas of another.

Word provides three commonly used editorial styles for citing references in research papers and reports: the American Psychological Association (APA) reference style, which is generally used in the social sciences and research fields; the Modern Language Association (MLA) style, which is generally used in the humanities and English composition; and the Chicago Manual of Style (CMS), which is used both in the humanities and social sciences and is considered more complex than either the APA or MLA style.

If you prepare a research paper or report in APA or MLA style, format your document according to the following general guidelines. Use standard-sized paper

(8.5 × 11 inches); set one-inch top, bottom, left, and right margins; double-space text; indent the first line of each paragraph one-half inch; and insert page numbers in the upper right corner of pages.

Insert New Citation

1. Click References tab.
2. Click Insert Citation button.
3. Click *Add New Source* at drop-down list.
4. Type necessary reference information.
5. Click OK.

Inserting Sources and Citations

When you create an in-text citation, Word requires you to enter information about the source in required fields at the Create Source dialog box. To insert a citation in a Word document, click the References tab, click the Insert Citation button in the Citations & Bibliography group, and then click *Add New Source* at the drop-down list. At the Create Source dialog box, shown in Figure 26.3, select the type of reference you want to cite, such as a book, journal article, or report, and then type the bibliographic information in the required fields. If you want to include more information than required in the displayed fields, click the *Show All Bibliography Fields* check box to insert a check mark and then type additional bibliographic information in the extra fields. After filling in the necessary source information, click OK. The citation is automatically inserted in the document at the location of the insertion point.

Figure 26.3 Create Source Dialog Box

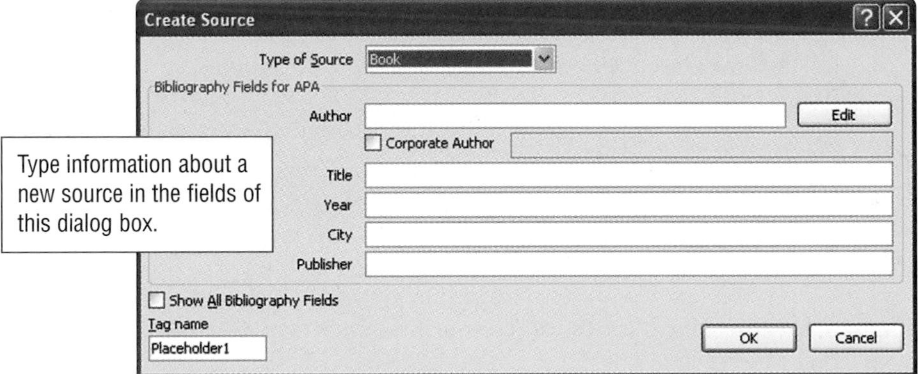

Exercise 2A

Inserting Sources and Citations

1. Open **Reference01.docx** and save the document with the name **C26Ex02**.
2. Press Ctrl + End to move the insertion point to the end of the document and then type the text shown in Figure 26.4 up to the first citation (the text (*Weston,* 2010)). To insert the citation, complete these steps:
   a. Press the spacebar once after typing the text *today*.
   b. Click the References tab.
   c. Click the Insert Citation button in the Citations & Bibliography group and then click *Add New Source* at the drop-down list.

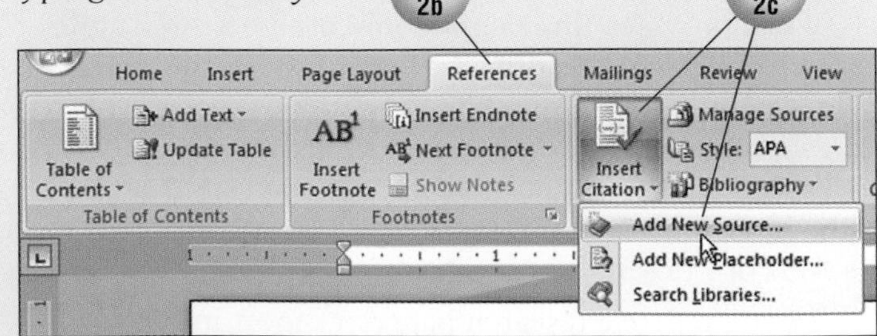

d. At the Create Source dialog box, click the down-pointing arrow at the right of the *Type of Source* option and then click *Journal Article* at the drop-down list.
e. Click in the *Author* text box, type **Scott Weston**, and then press the Tab key three times.
f. Type **Popular Computer Software** in the *Title* text box and then press the Tab key.
g. Type **Computer Education** in the *Journal Name* text box and then press the Tab key.
h. Type **2010** in the *Year* text box and then press the Tab key.
i. Type **10-18** in the *Pages* text box.
j. Click OK.

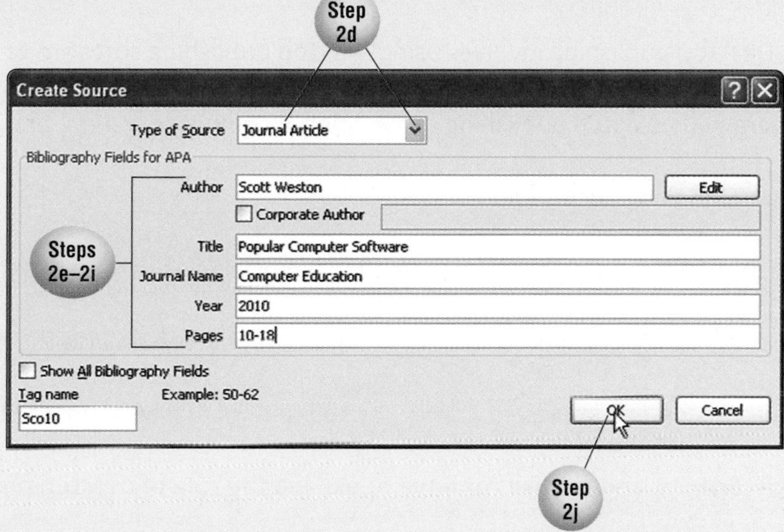

k. Type the period to end the sentence.

3. Continue typing the text up to the next citation (the text (*Prasad,* 2010)) and insert the following source information from a book (click the down-pointing arrow at the right of the *Type of Source* option and then click *Book* at the drop-down list):
   Author = **Allen Prasad**
   Title = **Desktop Publishing in Education**
   Year = **2010**
   City = **Chicago**
   Publisher = **Great Lakes Publishing House**
4. Continue typing the text up to the next citation (the text (*Nakamura,* 2009)) and insert the following source information from a journal article (make sure you change the *Type of Source* to *Journal Article*):
   Author = **Janet Nakamura**
   Title = **Computers and Publishing**
   Journal Name = **Technology Times**
   Year = **2009**
   Pages = **20-28**
   Volume = **6** (Display the *Volume* field by clicking the *Show All Bibliography Fields* check box and then scroll down the options list.)
5. Type the remaining text in Figure 26.4.
6. Save and then print **C26Ex02.docx**.

Figure 26.4 Exercise 2A

During the early 1990s, another type of software program called desktop publishing gained popularity among microcomputer users. With the introduction of the laser printer and its ability to produce high quality documents, desktop publishing software became the fastest growing microcomputer application of the 1990s, and its widespread use continues today (Weston, 2010). Desktop publishing involves using desktop publishing software or word processing software with desktop publishing capabilities, a computer system, and a printer to produce professional-looking documents (Prasad, 2010).

Until the mid-1980s, graphic design depended almost exclusively on design professionals. However, desktop publishing changed all that by bringing graphic design into the office and home. Faster microprocessors, improved printer capabilities, increased supply of clip art, increased storage capacity, and the like continue to expand the role of desktop publishing (Nakamura, 2009). Everything from a flyer to a newsletter can be designed, created, and produced at a computer.

Insert Citation with Existing Source
1. Click References tab.
2. Click Insert Citation button.
3. Click desired reference at drop-down list.

Inserting a Citation with an Existing Source

Once you insert source information at the Create Source dialog box, Word automatically saves it. To insert a citation in a document for source information that has already been saved, click the Insert Citation button in the Citations & Bibliography group and then click the desired reference at the drop-down list.

Exercise 2B

Inserting an Existing Source

1. With **C26Ex02.docx** open, press Ctrl + End to move the insertion point to the end of the document and then press the Enter key once.
2. Type the text in Figure 26.5 up to the citation text (*Weston,* 2010) and insert a citation from an existing source by completing the following steps:
   a. If necessary, click the References tab.
   b. Click the Insert Citation button in the Citations & Bibliography group.
   c. Click the Scott Weston reference at the drop-down list.

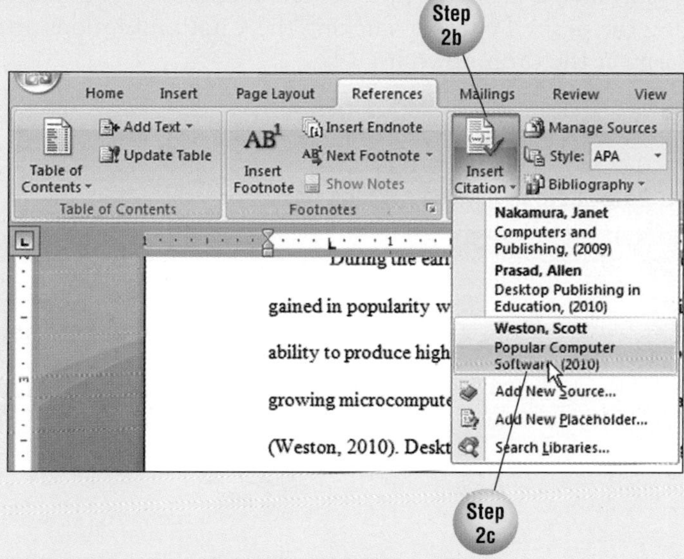

3. Type the remaining text in Figure 26.5 and complete steps similar to those in Step 2 to insert a citation for the existing source by Janet Nakamura.
4. Save and then print **C26Ex02.docx**.

Figure 26.5 Exercise 2B

In traditional publishing, several people may be involved in completing the publication project, which may be costly and time-consuming (Weston, 2010). With the use of desktop publishing software, one person may be performing all of the tasks necessary to complete a project, greatly reducing the costs of publishing documents (Nakamura, 2009). The two approaches have a great deal in common.

Modify Sources
1. Click References tab.
2. Click Manage Sources button.
3. Edit, add, and/or delete references.
4. Click Close.

Modifying Sources

After you have inserted information about a source into a document, you may need to modify the citation to correct errors or change data. To modify source information, click the References tab and then click the Manage Sources button in the Citations & Bibliography group. This displays the Source Manager dialog box, shown in Figure 26.6. In the *Master List* section, the Source Manager dialog box displays all of the citations you have created in Word. The *Current List* section of the dialog box displays all of the citations included in the currently open document. At the Source Manager dialog box, click the desired source in the *Current List* section. Click the Edit button that displays between the list boxes and then make any desired changes at the Edit Source dialog box. The Edit Source dialog box contains the same options that are available at the Create Source dialog box. You can also edit a source by clicking the desired citation, clicking the Citation Options arrow, and then clicking *Edit Source* at the drop-down list.

Figure 26.6 Source Manager Dialog Box

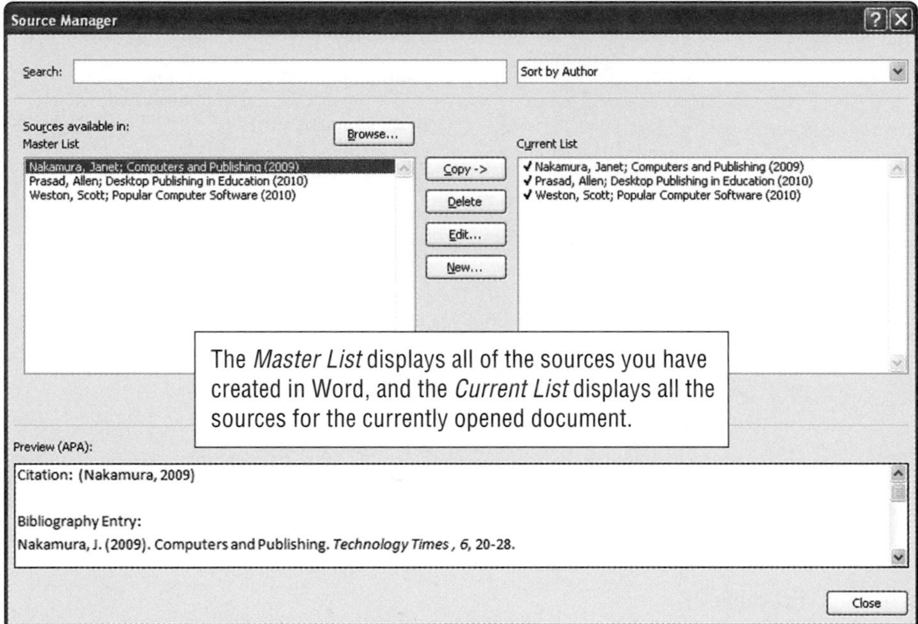

You may also want to add new sources or delete existing sources in a document. To insert a new source, click the New button at the Source Manager dialog box and then insert the source information in the required fields. To delete a source from a document, click the source you wish to delete in the *Current List* section and then click the Delete button.

Inserting Page Numbers in a Citation

If you include a direct quote from a source, you will want to include quotation marks around all of the text borrowed from that source and insert in the citation the page number(s) of the quoted material. To insert specific page numbers into a citation, click the citation in the document to select the citation placeholder. Click the Citation Options arrow and then click *Edit Citation* at the drop-down list. At the Edit Citation dialog box, type in the page or page numbers of the source where the quote was borrowed.

Insert Page Number in Citation

1. Click citation to display placeholder.
2. Click Citation Options arrow.
3. Click *Edit Citation.*
4. Type page number(s).
5. Click OK.

Exercise 2C

Modifying Sources

1. With **C26Ex02.docx** open, edit a source by completing the following steps:
   a. Click the References tab.
   b. Click the Manage Sources button in the Citations & Bibliography group.
   c. At the Source Manager dialog box, click the source entry for Scott Weston in the *Master List* section.
   d. Click the Edit button.

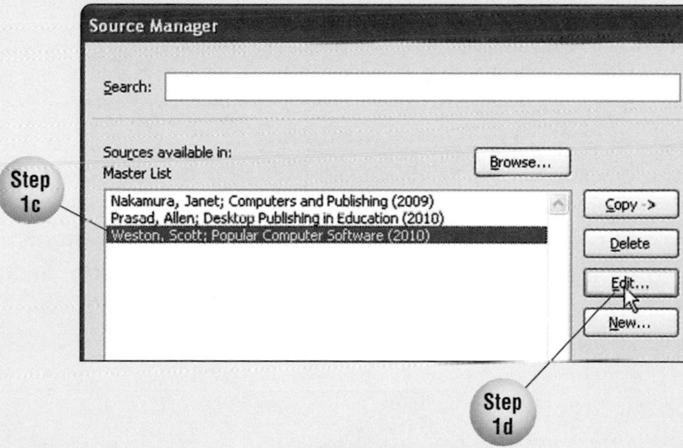

   e. At the Edit Source dialog box, delete the text in the *Year* text box and then type **2009**.
   f. Click OK to close the Edit Source dialog box.
   g. At the message asking if you want to update both the master list and the current list with the changes, click Yes.
   h. Click the Close button to close the Source Manager dialog box. (Notice the year has changed in both of the Weston citations to reflect the edit.)
2. Delete a source by completing the following steps:
   a. Select and then delete the last sentence in the second paragraph in the document, including the citation (the sentence that begins *Desktop publishing involves using . . .*).
   b. Click the Manage Sources button in the Citations & Bibliography group in the References tab.

c. At the Source Manager dialog box, click the Allen Prasad entry in the *Current List* section. (This entry in the list will not contain a check mark because you deleted the citation from the document.)
d. Click the Delete button.

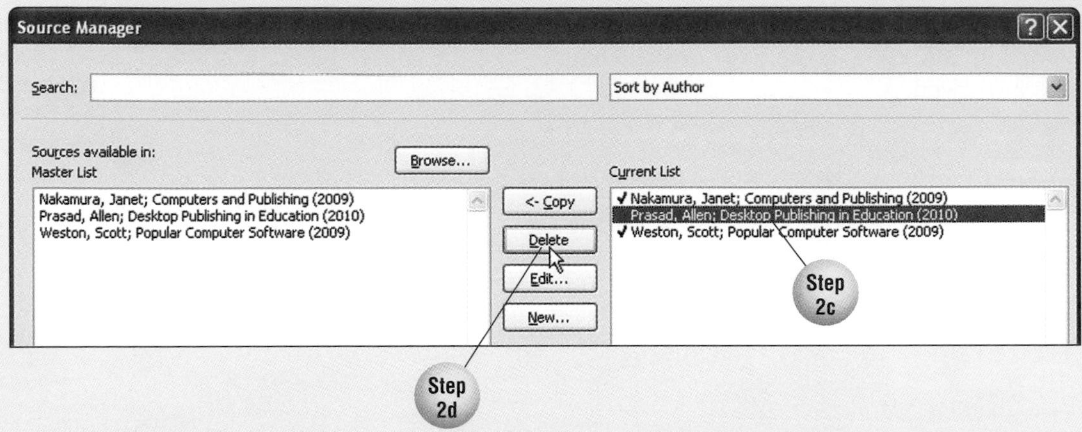

e. Click the Close button to close the Source Manager dialog box.

3. Create and insert a new source in the document by completing the following steps:
   a. Click the Manage Sources button in the Citations & Bibliography group in the References tab.
   b. Click the New button in the Source Manager dialog box.
   c. Type the following book information in the Create Source dialog box:
      Author = **Elena Corsini**
      Title = **Computers in the Education World**
      Year = **2010**
      City = **Houston**
      Publisher = **Rio Grande Publishing**
   d. Click OK to close the Create Source dialog box.
   e. Click the Close button to close the Source Manager dialog box.
   f. Position the insertion point one space after the period that ends the last sentence in the document and then type the sentence, "**Both approaches involve setting goals, planning and organizing content, analyzing layout and design, arranging design elements, typesetting, printing, and distributing the project**" (press the spacebar once after typing the quote marks after *project*.)
   g. Insert a citation at the end of the sentence for Elena Corsini by clicking the Insert Citation button in the Citations & Bibliography group and then clicking the Elena Corsini reference at the drop-down list.
   h. Type the period to end the sentence.

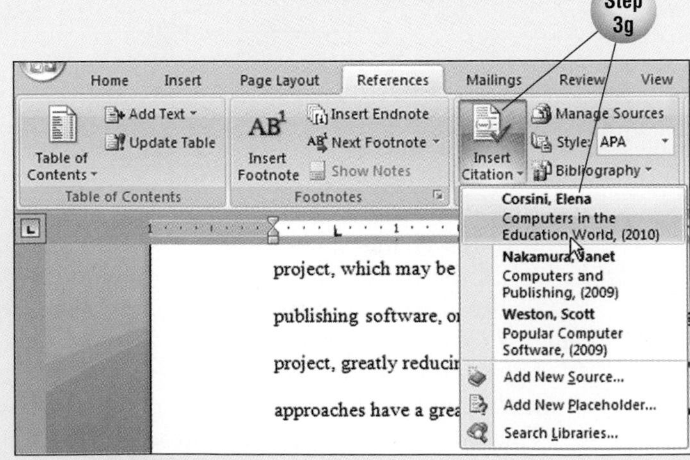

4. Because you inserted a direct quote from Elena Corsini, you will need to include the page number of the book where you found the quote. Insert the page number within the citation by completing the following steps:
   a. Click on any character in the Corsini citation. (This displays the citation placeholder.)
   b. Click the Citation Options arrow that displays at the right side of the citation placeholder and then click *Edit Citation* at the drop-down list.

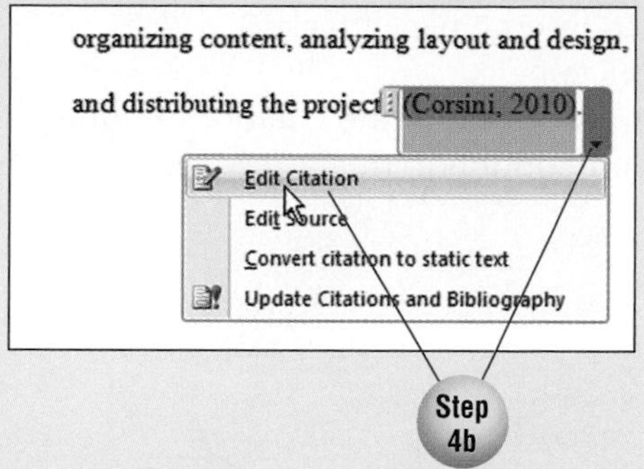

   c. At the Edit Citation dialog box, type **28** in the *Pages* text box.
   d. Click OK.
5. Save **C26Ex02.docx**.

Inserting Bibliographies

If you include citations in a report or research paper, you need to insert as a separate page a bibliography or works cited page at the end of the document. A bibliography or works cited page is an alphabetic list of the books, journal articles, reports, or other sources referenced in the document. When you type source information for citations, Word automatically saves information from all of the fields into a bibliography and works cited list, alphabetized by author's last name or the title of the work. To insert a bibliography, click the References tab and then click the Bibliography button in the Citations & Bibliography group. At the Bibliography drop-down list, click a predesigned built-in bibliography.

Insert Bibliography
1. Click References tab.
2. Click Bibliography button.
3. Click predesigned bibliography at drop-down list.

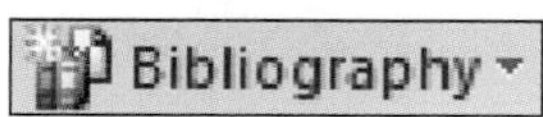

Exercise 2D

Inserting Bibliographies

1. With **C26Ex02.docx** open, insert a bibliography at the end of the document by completing these steps:
   a. Press Ctrl + End to move the insertion point to the end of the document.
   b. Press Ctrl + Enter to insert a page break.
   c. Click the References tab.
   d. Click the Bibliography button in the Citations & Bibliography group.
   e. Click the Bibliography option in the *Built-In* section of the drop-down list.

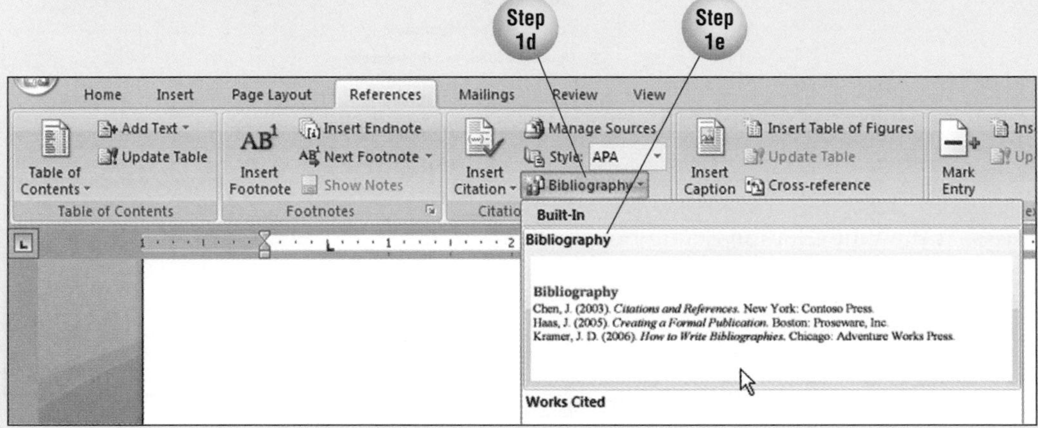

2. Save and then print **C26Ex02.docx**.

Update Bibliography
1. Click on any character in the bibliography.
2. Click Update Citations and Bibliography tab.

Modifying and Updating Bibliographies

If you insert a new source at the Source Manager dialog box or modify an existing source, Word automatically inserts the source information in the bibliography. If you insert a new citation, which requires you to add a new source, Word will not automatically update the bibliography. To update the bibliography, click anywhere in the bibliography and then click the Update Citations and Bibliography tab. The updated bibliography will reflect any changes made to the citations and source information in the document.

Exercise 2E

Modifying and Updating Bibliography

1. With **C26Ex02.docx** open, create a new source and citation by completing the following steps:
   a. Position the insertion point immediately left of the period that ends the last sentence in the first paragraph of the document.
   b. Press the spacebar once.
   c. Click the References tab.
   d. Click the Insert Citation button in the Citations & Bibliography group and then click *Add New Source* at the drop-down list.
   e. At the Create Source dialog box, insert the following source information from a Web site:
      Author = **Barbara Schueller**
      Name of Webpage = **The Past, Present and Future of Desktop Publishing**
      Name of Website = **Computer Applications Forum**
      Year = **2009**
      Month = **April**
      Day = **18**
      Year Accessed = (type current year)
      Month Accessed = (type current month)
      Day Accessed = (type current day)
      URL = **www.emcp.org**
   f. Click OK to close the Create Source dialog box.
2. Update the bibliography to include the new source by completing the following steps:
   a. Click on any character in the bibliography text.
   b. Click the Update Citations and Bibliography tab. (Notice that the updated bibliography includes the Schueller reference.)
3. Save **C26Ex02.docx**.

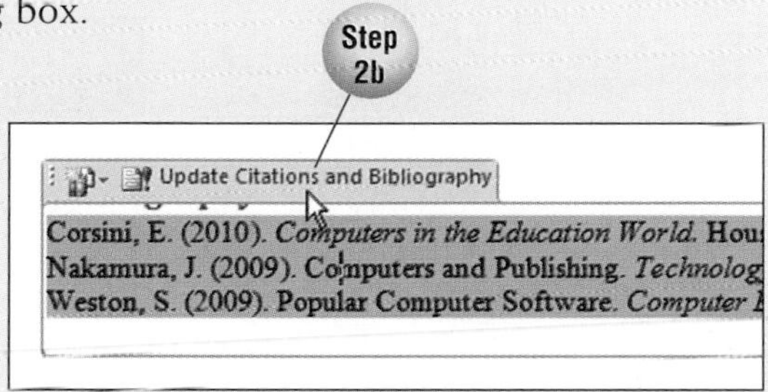

Formatting Bibliographies

Reference styles have specific formatting guidelines. The formatting applied by Word to the bibliography or works cited page may need to be changed to meet specific guidelines of the APA, MLA, or Chicago style. For example, APA and MLA styles require the following formatting guidelines for the bibliography or works cited page:

- Begin bibliography or work cited on a separate page after the text of the report.
- Include the title "Bibliography" or "Work Cited" and center the title.
- Double space between and within entries.
- Begin each entry at the left margin and hang indent second and subsequent lines in each entry.
- Alphabetize the entries.

The general formatting requirements for the Chicago style are similar except entries are single spaced within and double spaced between.

Exercise 2F

Formatting the Bibliography

1. With **C26Ex02.docx** open, make the following formatting changes to the bibliography:
   a. Click on any character in the title *Bibliography*. (The placeholder tab will display over the *Bibliography* title.)
   b. Press Ctrl + E to center the title.
   c. Select the *Bibliography* heading and the entries below the heading.
   d. Click the Home tab.
   e. Click the Line spacing button in the Paragraph group and then click 2.0 at the drop-down list.

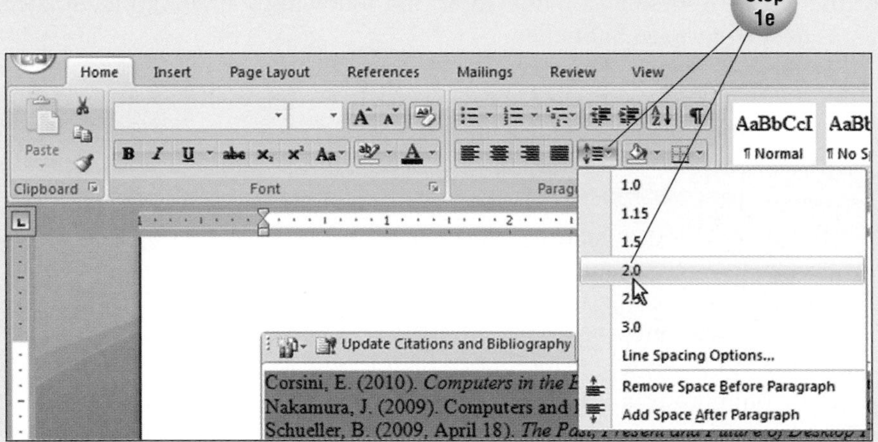

   f. Select only the bibliography entries and then press Ctrl + T. (This hang indents the entries.)
2. Save and then print **C26Ex02.docx**.

Change Citation Style

1. Click References tab.
2. Click down-pointing arrow at right of *Style* option.
3. Click desired style.

Choosing a Citation Style

Instructors or professors may require different forms of citation or reference styles. You can change the citation or reference style before beginning a new document or in an existing document. To do this, click the References tab, click the down-pointing arrow at the right side of the *Style* option, and then click the desired style at the drop-down list.

Exercise 2G

Choosing Citation Styles

1. With **C26Ex02.docx** open, change the document and bibliography from APA style to MLA style by completing the following steps:
   a. Press Ctrl + Home to move the insertion point to the beginning of the document.
   b. Click the References tab.
   c. Click the down-pointing arrow at the right side of the *Style* option in the Citations & Bibliography group and then click *MLA* at the drop-down list.

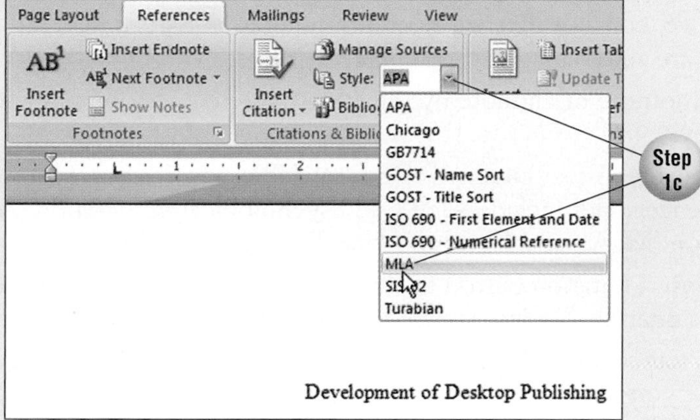

   d. Scroll through the document and notice the changes in the style of the citations and the bibliography.
2. Save **C26Ex02.docx** and then print only the page containing the Bibliography.
3. Change the citation and bibliography style to Chicago by clicking the down-pointing arrow at the right side of the *Style* option and then clicking *Chicago* at the drop-down list.
4. Scroll through the document and notice the changes in the style of the citations and the bibliography.
5. Print page 3 of **C26Ex02.docx**.
6. Save and then close the document.
7. Display a blank document, click the References tab, change the style to *APA*, and then close the document without saving it.

Chapter Summary

- Footnotes and endnotes are explanatory notes or references. Footnotes are inserted and printed at the bottom of the page, and endnotes are printed at the end of the document. Type bibliographic text for footnotes or endnotes at the footnote or endnote pane.
- By default, Word numbers footnotes with Arabic numbers and endnotes with lowercase Roman numerals.
- If you move, copy, or delete a reference number in a document, all other footnotes or endnotes are automatically renumbered.
- Delete a footnote or endnote by selecting the reference number and then pressing the Delete key.
- Consider using in-text citations to acknowledge sources in a paper. Commonly used citation and reference styles include American Psychological Association (APA), Modern Language Association (MLA), and Chicago Manual of Style (CMS).
- Use the Insert Citation button in the Citations & Bibliography group in the References tab to insert a citation. Specify source information at the Create Source dialog box.
- Modify a source by clicking the References tab, clicking the Manage Sources button, clicking the source you want to modify in the Source Manager dialog box, clicking the Edit button, and then making any desired changes at the Edit Source dialog box.
- To insert a new source, click the New button at the Source Manager dialog box and then insert the information in the required fields. To delete a source, click the source in the *Current List* section in the Source Manager dialog box and then click the Delete button.
- After including citations in a report or paper, insert a bibliography or works cited page at the end of the document on a separate page. Insert a bibliography or works cited page with the Bibliography button in the Citations & Bibliography group in the References tab.
- To update a bibliography, click in the bibliography and then click the Update Citations and Bibliography tab.

Commands review

FEATURE	RIBBON TAB, GROUP	BUTTON	KEYBOARD SHORTCUT
Footnote	References, Footnotes	AB¹	Alt + Ctrl + F
Endnote	References, Footnotes	Insert Endnote	Alt + Ctrl + D
Hide/Display Notes	References, Footnotes	Show Notes	
Create Source dialog box	References, Citations & Bibliography		
Source Manager dialog box	References, Citations & Bibliography	Manage Sources	
Bibliography	References, Citations & Bibliography	Bibliography	
Style	References, Citations & Bibliography	Style: APA	

Reviewing key points

Completion: In the space provided at the right, indicate the correct term, symbol, or command.

1. Footnotes are inserted at the end of a page while endnotes are inserted here. ____________
2. Word numbers footnotes with this type of number. ____________
3. Word numbers endnotes with this type of number. ____________
4. View footnotes in a document by clicking this button in the Footnotes group. ____________
5. Two of the most popular styles for preparing a report are APA (American Psychological Association) and this. ____________
6. Click this tab to display the Citations & Bibliography group. ____________
7. Create a new source for a document with options at this dialog box. ____________
8. To modify a source, click this button in the Citations & Bibliography group. ____________

9. To update a bibliography, click anywhere in the bibliography and then click this tab. ____________
10. Change citation and reference styles with this option. ____________

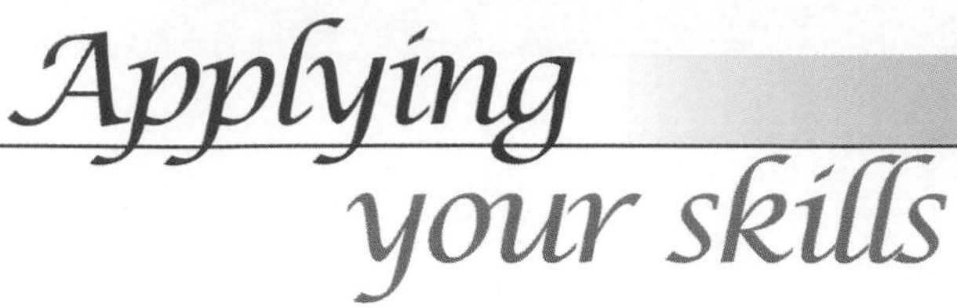

Assessment 1 Insert Footnotes in a Designing Newsletter Report

1. Open **Report17.docx** and save the document with the name **C26A01**.
2. Create the first footnote shown in Figure 26.7 at the end of the first paragraph in the *Applying Guidelines* section.
3. Create the second footnote shown in Figure 26.7 at the end of the third paragraph in the *Applying Guidelines* section.
4. Create the third footnote shown in Figure 26.7 at the end of the last paragraph in the *Applying Guidelines* section.
5. Create the fourth footnote shown in Figure 26.7 at the end of the only paragraph in the *Choose Paper Size and Type* section.
6. Create the fifth footnote shown in Figure 26.7 at the end of the only paragraph in the *Choosing Paper Weight* section.
7. Save and then print **C26A01.docx**.
8. Select the entire document and then change the font to Constantia.
9. Select all of the footnotes and change the font to Constantia.
10. Delete the third footnote.
11. Save, print, and then close **C26A01.docx**.

Figure 26.7 Assessment 1

Habermann, James, "Designing a Newsletter," *Desktop Designs*, January/February 2010, pages 23-29.

Pilante, Shirley G., "Adding Pizzazz to Your Newsletter," *Desktop Publisher*, September 2009, pages 32-39.

Maddock, Arlita G., "Guidelines for a Better Newsletter," *Business Computing*, June 2010, pages 9-14.

Alverso, Monica, "Paper Styles for Newsletters," *Design Technologies*, March 14, 2009, pages 45-51.

Sutton, Keith, "Choosing Paper Styles," *Design Techniques*, March/April, 2009, pages 8-11.

Assessment 2 Insert Sources and Citations in a Privacy Rights Report

1. Open **Reference02.docx** and save the document with the name **C26A02**.
2. Press Ctrl + End to move the insertion point to the end of the document and then type the text shown in Figure 26.8 up to the first citation (the text *(Hartley, 2008)*). Insert the source information from a journal article written by Kenneth Hartley using the following information:
    Author = **Kenneth Hartley**
    Title = **Privacy Laws**
    Journal Name = **Business World**
    Year = **2008**
    Pages = **24-46**
    Volume = **12**
3. Continue typing the text up to the next citation (the text *(Ferraro, 2010)*) and insert the following source information from a book:
    Author = **Ramona Ferraro**
    Title = **Business Employee Rights**
    Year = **2010**
    City = **Tallahassee**
    Publisher = **Everglades Publishing House**
4. Continue typing the text up to the next citation (the text *(Aldrich, 2010)*) and insert the following information from a periodical article:
    Author = **Kelly Aldrich**
    Title = **What Rights Do Employees Have?**
    Periodical Title = **Great Plains Times**
    Year = **2008**
    Month = **May**
    Day = **6**
    Pages = **18-22**
5. Insert the page number in the Kelly Aldrich citation using the Edit Citation dialog box.
6. Type the remaining text in Figure 26.8.
7. Edit the Kenneth Hartley source title to read *Small Business Privacy Laws* in the *Master List* section of the Source Manager dialog box.
8. Select and delete the last two sentences in the second paragraph and then delete the Ramona Ferraro source in the *Current List* section of the Source Manager dialog box.
9. Insert a bibliography at the end of the document on a separate page.
10. Create a new source in the document using the Source Manager dialog box and include the following source information for an article at a Web site:
    Author = **Harold Jefferson**
    Name of Webpage = **Small Business Policies and Procedures**
    Name of Website = **Small Business Administration**
    Year = **2009**
    Month = **December**
    Day = **12**
    Year Accessed = (type current year)
    Month Accessed = (type current month)
    Day Accessed = (type current day)
    URL = **www.emcp.org**
11. Insert a citation for Harold Jefferson at the end of the last sentence in the first paragraph.
12. Update the bibliography.

13. Format the bibliography to meet APA requirements with the following changes:
    a. Center the title *Bibliography*.
    b. Select the Bibliography title and the entries below the title and change the line spacing to 2.0.
    c. Change the spacing after to *0 pt*.
    d. Hang indent the bibliography entries.
14. Save and then print **C26A02.docx**.
15. Change the document and bibliography from APA style to MLA style.
16. Save, print page 2, and then close **C26A02.docx**.

Figure 26.8 Assessment 2

An exception to the ability of companies to monitor their employees does exist. If the company has pledged to respect any aspect of employee privacy, it must keep that pledge. For example, if a business states that it will not monitor employee e-mail or phone calls, by law, it must follow this stated policy (Hartley, 2008). However, no legal requirement exists mandating that companies notify their employees when and if monitoring takes place (Ferraro, 2010). Therefore, employees should assume they are always monitored and act accordingly.

Privacy advocates are calling for this situation to change. "They acknowledge that employers have the right to ensure that their employees are doing their jobs, but they question the need to monitor employees without warning and without limit" (Aldrich, 2010, p. 20). The American Civil Liberties Union has, in fact, proposed a Fair Electronic Monitoring Policy to prevent abuses of employee privacy.

Chapter 27

CHAPTER27

Creating Indexes

SNAP

Tutorial 27.1
Creating an Index

Performance Objectives

Upon successful completion of Chapter 27, you will be able to:

- Create an index
- Mark entries for an index
- Insert an index
- Mark text for an index entry that spans a range of pages
- Mark an index entry as a cross-reference
- Create a concordance file
- Update and delete an index

An index is a list of topics contained in a publication and the pages on which those topics are discussed. Creating an index manually can be tedious. With Word, you can automate the process. In this chapter you will learn the steps to mark text for inclusion in an index and the steps to insert, update, and delete an index.

Note: Before beginning computer exercises for this chapter, copy to your storage medium the Chapter27 folder from the CD that accompanies this textbook and then make Chapter27 the active folder.

Creating an Index

Word automates the process for creating an index and, as you will learn in the next chapter, a table of contents, both in a similar manner. Although Word can automate the process, creating an index still takes thought and consideration. The author of a book, manuscript, or report must determine which topics should be listed as main entries and which should be listed as subentries under a main entry. An index may include such items as the main idea of a document, the main subject of a chapter or section, variations of a heading or subheading, and abbreviations. Figure 27.1 shows an example of an index.

Figure 27.1 **Sample Index**

INDEX

A
Alignment, 12, 16
ASCII, 22, 24, 35
    data processing, 41
    word processing, 39

B
Backmatter, 120
    page numbering, 123
Balance, 67-69
Banners, 14

C
Callout, 78
Captions, 156
Color, 192-195
    ink for offset printing, 193

D
Databases, 124-129
    fields, 124
    records, 124
Directional flow, 70-71

QUICK STEPS

Mark Text for an Index

1. Select text.
2. Click References tab.
3. Click Mark Entry button.
4. Make desired changes.
5. Click Mark button.
6. Click Close button.

OR

1. Select text.
2. Press Alt + Shift + X.
3. Make desired changes.
4. Click Mark All button.
5. Click Close button.

Marking Text for an Index

When you create an index in Word, you electronically mark the words that you want to include as entries. Before marking the words though, you need to determine what main entries and subentries you want to include. You mark text as an index entry at the Mark Index Entry dialog box.

To mark text for inclusion in an index, select the word or words, click the References tab, and then click the Mark Entry button in the Index group. You can also press Alt + Shift + X. At the Mark Index Entry dialog box, shown in Figure 27.2, the selected word(s) appears in the *Main entry* text box. If you want the text to be listed as a main entry, leave it as displayed and then click the Mark button. This turns on the display of nonprinting characters in the document and inserts a field code immediately after the selected text. When you mark the word *software* in Exercise 1A for inclusion in an index, Word inserts the code *{XE "software"}* immediately after the word. When you mark the words *word processing* as a subentry and *software* as the main entry, Word inserts the code *{XE "software:word processing"}* immediately after the words. Click the Close button to close the Mark Index Entry dialog box.

Figure 27.2 **Mark Index Entry Dialog Box**

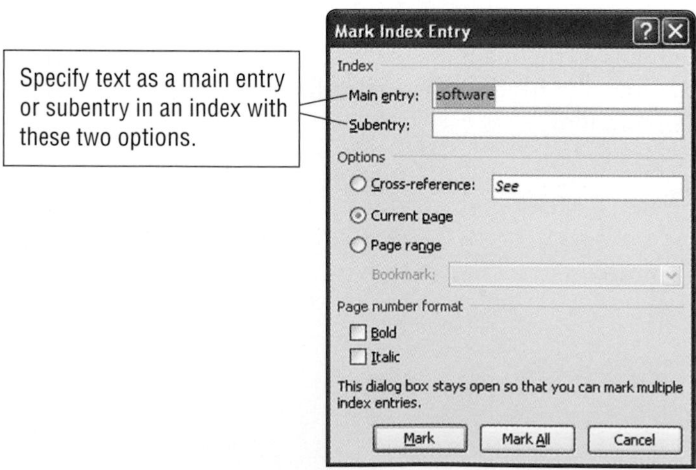

If you want the text that you selected to be listed as a subentry, you will have to make the following changes at the Mark Index Entry dialog box: type the main entry in the *Main entry* text box, click in the *Subentry* text box, and then type the selected text. For example, suppose a publication includes the terms *Page layout* and *Portrait*. The words *Page layout* are to be marked as a main entry for the index and *Portrait* is to be marked as a subentry below *Page layout*. To mark these words for inclusion in an index, you would complete the following steps:

1. Select *Page layout*.
2. Click the References tab and then click the Mark Entry button or press Alt + Shift + X.
3. At the Mark Index Entry dialog box, click the Mark button or the Mark All button. (This turns on the display of nonprinting symbols.)
4. With the Mark Index Entry dialog box still displayed on the screen, click in the document to make the document active, and then select *Portrait*.
5. Click the Mark Index Entry dialog box title bar to make it active.
6. Select *Portrait* in the *Main entry* text box and then type **Page layout**.
7. Click in the *Subentry* text box and then type **Portrait**.
8. Click the Mark button.
9. Click the Close button.

The main entry and subentry do not have to be the same as the selected text. You can select text for an index, type the text you want to display in the *Main entry* or *Subentry* text box, and then click the Mark button. At the Mark Index Entry dialog box, you can apply bold and/or italic formatting to the page numbers that will appear in the index. To apply formatting, click *Bold* and/or *Italic* to insert a check mark in the check box.

The *Options* section of the Mark Index Entry dialog box contains three options, and the *Current page* option is the default. At this setting, the current page number will be listed in the index for the main entry or subentry displayed. Click the *Cross reference* option if you want to cross-reference the main entry or subentry. Type the text you want to use as a cross-reference for that entry in the *Cross-reference* text box. For example, you could mark the word *Serif* and cross reference it to *Typefaces*.

Click the Mark All button at the Mark Index Entry dialog box to mark all occurrences of the text in the document as index entries. Word marks occurrences of the text only if the uppercase and lowercase letters exactly match the index entry.

Exercise 1A

Marking Words for an Index

1. Open **Report15.docx** and save the document with the name **C27Ex01**.
2. Number pages at the bottom center of each page.

3. Mark the word *software* in the first paragraph for the index as a main entry and mark *word processing* in the first paragraph as a subentry below *software* by completing the following steps:
   a. Select *software* (located in the second sentence of the first paragraph).
   b. Click the References tab and then click the Mark Entry button in the Index group.
   c. At the Mark Index Entry dialog box, click the Mark All button. (This turns on the display of nonprinting symbols.)
   d. With the Mark Index Entry dialog box still displayed, click in the document to make the document active and then select *word processing*, located in the last sentence of the first paragraph. (You may want to drag the dialog box down the screen so more of the document text is visible.)
   e. Click the Mark Index Entry dialog box title bar to make the dialog box active.
   f. Select *word processing* in the *Main entry* text box and then type **software**.
   g. Click in the *Subentry* text box and then type **word processing**.
   h. Click the Mark All button.

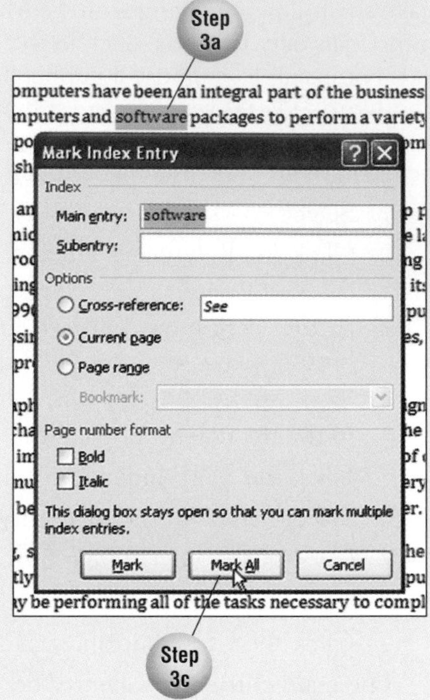

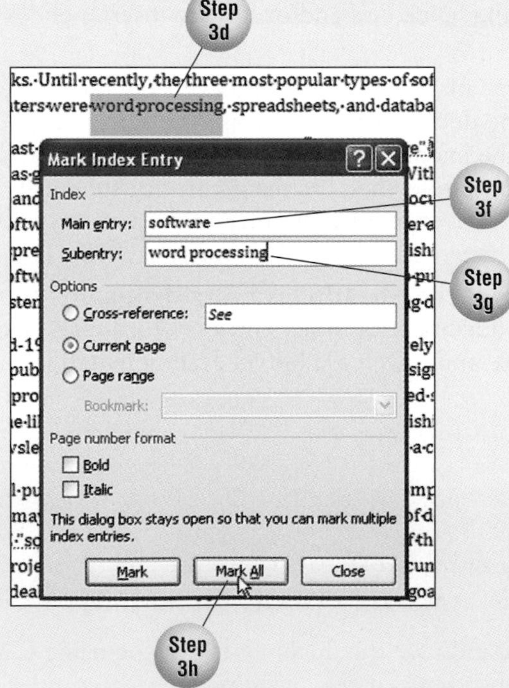

i. With the Mark Index Entry dialog box still displayed, complete steps similar to those in 3d through 3h to mark the *first* occurrence of the following words as main entries or subentries for the index:

In the first paragraph in the Defining Desktop Publishing section:

spreadsheets = subentry (main entry = *software*)
database = subentry (main entry = *software*)

In the second paragraph in the Defining Desktop Publishing section:

publishing = main entry
desktop = subentry (main entry = *publishing*)
printer = main entry
laser = subentry (main entry = *printer*)

In the third paragraph in the Defining Desktop Publishing section:

design = main entry

In the fourth paragraph in the Defining Desktop Publishing section:

traditional = subentry (main entry = *publishing*)

In the first paragraph in the Initiating the Process section:

publication = main entry
planning = subentry (main entry = *publication*)
creating = subentry (main entry = *publication*)
intended audience = subentry (main entry = *publication*)
content = subentry (main entry = *publication*)

In the third paragraph in the Planning the Publication section:

message = main entry

j. Click Close to close the Mark Index Entry dialog box.

4. Turn off the display of nonprinting characters.
5. Save **C27Ex01.docx**.

Inserting an Index

After you have marked all of the words that you want to include in an index as either main entries or subentries, the next step is to insert the index in the document. An index should appear at the end of a document, generally beginning on a separate page. To insert the index, position the insertion point at the end of the document and then insert a page break. With the insertion point positioned below the page break, type **INDEX** and then press the Enter key. With the insertion point positioned at the left margin, click the References tab and then click the Insert Index button in the Index group. At the Index dialog box, shown in Figure 27.3, select any desired formatting and then click OK. Word inserts the index, with the formatting you selected at the Index dialog box, at the location of the insertion point. Word also inserts a section break above and below the index text.

Insert an Index
1. Click References tab.
2. Click Insert Index button.
3. Select desired format.
4. Click OK.

Figure 27.3 Index Dialog Box

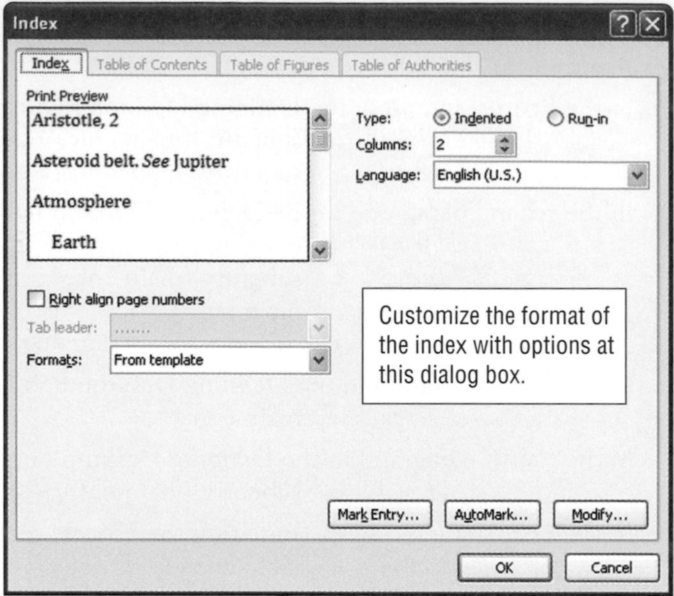

At the Index dialog box, you can customize the format of the index, specifying how the entries will appear. The Print Preview section shows how the index will display in the document. The *Columns* option has a default setting of 2. At this setting, the index will display in two newspaper columns. You can increase or decrease this number.

By default, Word right-aligns numbers in an index. If you do not want numbers right-aligned, click the *Right align page numbers* check box to remove the check mark. The *Tab leader* option is dimmed for all formats except *Formal*. If you click *Formal* in the *Formats* option box, the *Tab leader* option displays in black. The default tab leader character is a period. To change to a different character, click the down-pointing arrow at the right of the text box and then click the desired character.

In the *Type* section, the *Indented* option is the default. At this setting, subentries appear indented below main entries. If you click *Run-in*, subentries display on the same line as main entries.

Click the down-pointing arrow at the right side of the *Formats* option box, and a list of seven formatting choices displays. At this list, click the format you want, and the *Print Preview* box displays how the index will appear in the document with that formatting applied.

Exercise 1B

Inserting an Index

1. With **C27Ex01.docx** open, insert the index in the document by completing the following steps:
   a. Position the insertion point at the end of the document.
   b. Insert a page break.
   c. With the insertion point positioned below the page break, press Ctrl + E and then type INDEX.
   d. Press the Enter key and then change the paragraph alignment back to left.
   e. Click the References tab.
   f. Click the Insert Index button in the Index group.
   g. At the Index dialog box, click the down-pointing arrow at the right side of the *Formats* option box and then click *Modern* at the drop-down list.
   h. Click OK to close the dialog box.
   i. Apply the Heading 1 style to the title *INDEX*.
2. Save and then print the last page (the Index page) of the document.
3. Close **C27Ex01.docx**.

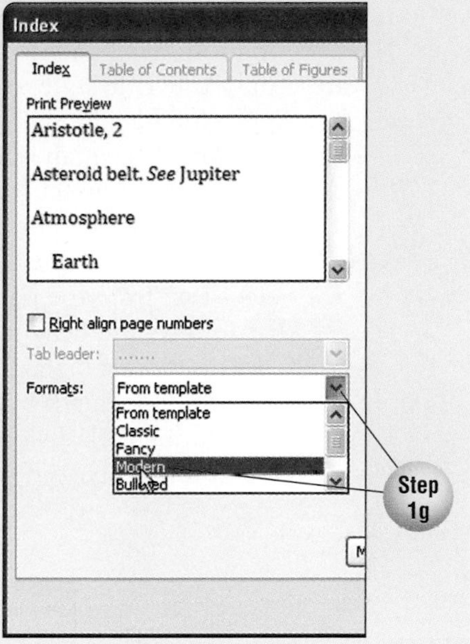

Marking Text that Spans a Range of Pages

If you want to use more than a few words as a single index entry, consider identifying the text as a bookmark and then marking the bookmark as the index entry. This option is especially useful when the text for an entry spans a range of pages. To mark text that you have identified as a bookmark, position the insertion point at the end of the text, click the References tab, and then click the Mark Entry button in the Index group. At the Mark Index Entry dialog box, type the index entry for the text and then click the *Page range* option in the *Options* section. Click the down-pointing arrow at the right side of the *Bookmark* option box and then click the bookmark name at the drop-down list. Click the Mark button to mark the bookmark text and close the dialog box.

Marking an Entry as a Cross-Reference

In some situations, you may want to mark for inclusion in an index text that refers the reader to another entry. For example, if you use the initials MIS in a document to refer to *Management Information Systems*, you can mark MIS as an index entry that refers the reader to the entry for Management Information Systems. To do this, you would select MIS, click the References tab, and then click the Mark Entry button in the Index group. At the Mark Index Entry dialog box, you would click *Cross-reference* in the *Options* section of the dialog box (to move the insertion point inside the text box), type **Management Information Systems**, and then click the Mark button.

Exercise 2

Marking Entries and Inserting an Index

1. Open **Report01.docx** and save the document with the name **C27Ex02**.
2. Make the following changes to the document:
   a. Apply the Title style to the title *THE COMPUTER ADVANTAGE*.
   b. Apply the Heading 2 style to the five headings in the document (*Speed*, *Accuracy*, *Versatility*, *Storage*, and *Communications*).
   c. Change the style set to *Formal*.
   d. Change the theme fonts to *Foundry*.
3. Create a bookmark for the *Speed* section of the document by completing the following steps:
   a. Select text from the beginning of the heading *Speed* through the paragraph of text that follows the heading.
   b. Click the Insert tab.
   c. Click the Bookmark button in the Links group.
   d. At the Bookmark dialog box, type **Speed** in the *Bookmark name* text box.
   e. Click the Add button.

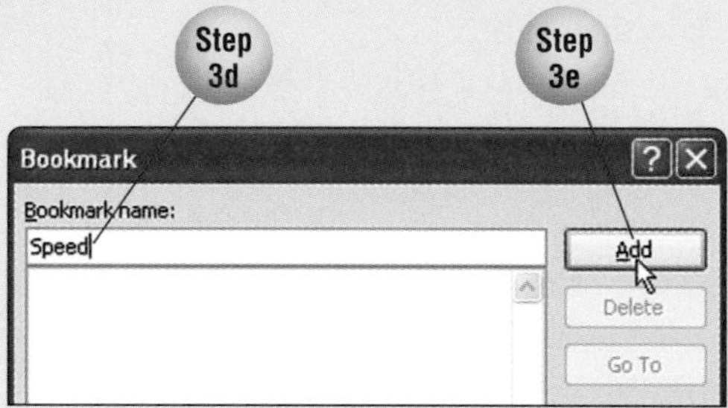

4. Complete steps similar to those in Step 3 to create the following bookmarks:
   a. Select text from the beginning of the *Accuracy* heading through the paragraph of text that follows the heading and then create a bookmark named *Accuracy*.
   b. Select text from the beginning of the *Versatility* heading through the paragraph of text that follows the heading and then create a bookmark named *Versatility*.
   c. Select text from the beginning of the *Storage* heading through the paragraph of text that follows the heading and then create a bookmark named *Storage*.
   d. Select text from the beginning of the *Communications* heading through the two paragraphs of text that follow the heading and then create a bookmark named *Communications*.
5. Mark the *Speed* bookmark as an index entry that spans pages by completing the following steps:
   a. Move the insertion point so it is positioned immediately following the only paragraph of text in the *Speed* section.
   b. Click the References tab.
   c. Click the Mark Entry button in the Index group.

d. At the Mark Index Entry dialog box, type **Speed** in the *Main entry* text box.
e. Click the *Page range* option.
f. Click the down-pointing arrow at the right side of the *Bookmark* option box and then click *Speed* at the drop-down list.
g. Click the Mark button.

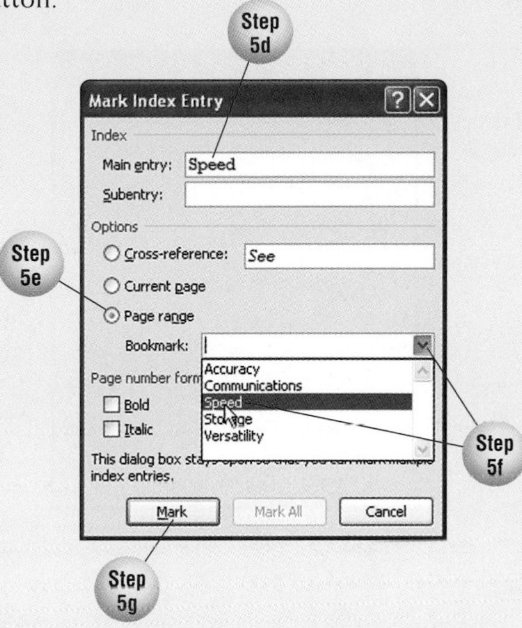

6. Complete steps similar to those in Step 5 to mark the following bookmarks as index entries: *Accuracy*, *Versatility*, *Storage*, and *Communications*.
7. With the Mark Index Entry dialog box open, mark the *first* occurrence of the following words (click the Mark All button) as main entries or subentries for the index:
   a. Mark *computers* located in the first sentence of the first paragraph of text in the document as a main entry.
   b. Mark *personal computers* in the second paragraph of text in the document as a main entry.
   c. Mark *supercomputers* in the *Speed* section of the document as a main entry.
   d. Mark *GIGO* in the *Accuracy* section of the document as a main entry.
   e. Mark the following text located in the *Versatility* section:
      Human Genome Project = main entry
      DNA = main entry
   f. Mark the following text located in the *Communications* section:
      wireless devices = main entry
      personal digital assistants = subentry (main entry = *wireless devices*)
      notebook computers = subentry (main entry = *wireless devices*)
      cell phones = subentry (main entry = *wireless devices*)
      pagers = subentry (main entry = *wireless devices*)
      local area network = main entry
      wide area network = main entry
   g. Click the Close button to close the Mark Index Entry dialog box.
8. Mark *microcomputers* as a cross-reference by completing the following steps:
   a. Press Ctrl + Home to move the insertion point to the beginning of the document.
   b. Select the word *microcomputers* that is located in the first sentence of the second paragraph of text.

c. If necessary, click the References tab.
d. Click the Mark Entry button in the Index group.
e. At the Mark Index Entry dialog box, click the *Cross-reference* option in the *Options* section and then type **personal computers**.
f. Click the Mark button.

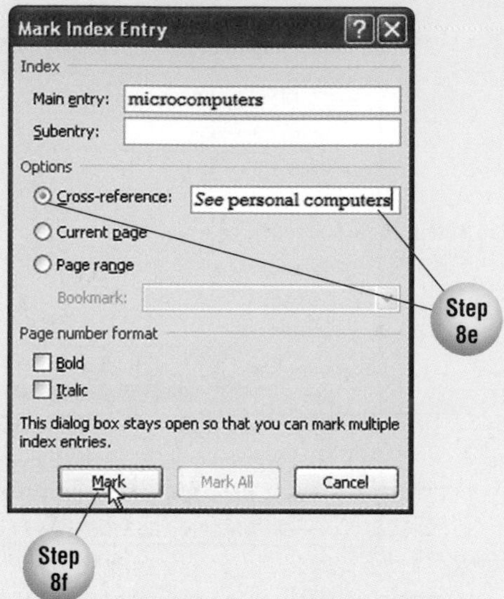

g. Click the Close button to close the Mark Index Entry dialog box.

9. Complete steps similar to those in Steps 8a through 8f to mark the following text as cross references:
   a. Select LAN in the second paragraph of text in the *Communications* section and cross reference it to *local area network*.
   b. Select WAN in the second paragraph of text in the *Communications* section and cross reference it to *wide area network*.
10. Turn off the display of nonprinting characters.
11. Insert the index in the document by completing the following steps:
    a. Position the insertion point at the end of the document.
    b. Insert a page break.
    c. With the insertion point positioned below the page break, press Ctrl + E and then type **INDEX**.
    d. Press the Enter key and then change the paragraph alignment back to left.
    e. Click the References tab.
    f. Click the Insert Index button in the Index group.
    g. At the Index dialog box, click the down-pointing arrow at the right side of the *Formats* option box, scroll down the drop-down list, and then click *Formal*.
    h. Click OK to close the dialog box.
    i. Select the title *INDEX* and then apply the Heading 1 style.

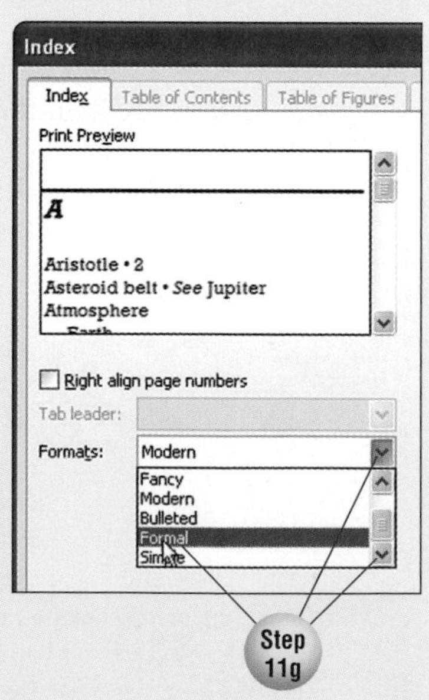

12. Save and then print the last page (the Index page) of the document.
13. Close **C27Ex02.docx**.

Creating a Concordance File

You can save words that appear frequently in a document as a concordance file. Doing this saves you from having to mark references in a document. A concordance file is a Word document that contains a single, two-column table and no text outside the table. In the first column of the table, you enter words you want to index. In the second column, you enter the main entry and subentry that should appear in the index. To create a subentry, separate each main entry from a subentry with a colon. Figure 27.4 shows an example of a completed concordance file.

Create a Concordance File
1. Click Insert tab.
2. Click Table button and drag to create table.
3. In first column, type words you want in index.
4. In second column, type the main entry and subentry.
5. Save document.

Figure 27.4 Concordance File

World War I	World War I
technology	Technology
teletypewriters	Technology: teletypewriters
motion pictures	Technology: motion pictures
television	Technology: television
Radio Corporation of America	Radio Corporation of America
coaxial cable	Coaxial cable
telephone	Technology: telephone
Communications Act of 1934	Communications Act of 1934
World War II	World War II
radar system	Technology: radar system
computer	Computer
Atanasoff Berry Computer	Computer: Atanasoff Berry Computer
Korean War	Korean War
Columbia Broadcasting System	Columbia Broadcasting System
Cold War	Cold War
Vietnam	Vietnam
artificial satellite	Technology: artificial satellite
Communications Satellite Act of 1962	Communications Satellite Act of 1962

In Figure 27.4, the first column of the concordance file lists words as they appear in the document (for example, *World War I*, *technology*, and *television*). The second column lists the text as it should appear in the index, specifying whether it is a main entry or subentry. For example, the text *motion pictures* listed in the first column will appear in the index as a subentry under the main entry *Technology*.

After you have created a concordance file, you can use it to quickly mark text in a document for inclusion in an index. To do this, open the document containing text that you want marked for an index, display the Index dialog box, and then click the AutoMark button. At the Open Index AutoMark File dialog box, double-click the concordance file name in the list box. When you double-click the file name, Word turns on the display of nonprinting symbols, searches through the document for text that matches the text in the first column of the concordance file, and then marks it as specified in the second column. After marking text for the index, you can insert the index in the document as described earlier.

As you create the concordance file in Exercise 3A, Word's AutoCorrect feature will automatically capitalize the first letter of the first word entered in each cell. In Figure 27.4, you can see that several of the first words in the first column do not begin with a capital letter. Before you begin the exercise, consider turning off this AutoCorrect capitalization feature. To do this, click the Office button and then click the Word Options button at the drop-down list. At the Word Options dialog box, click *Proofing* at the left side of the dialog box and then click the AutoCorrect Options button. At the AutoCorrect dialog box with the AutoCorrect tab selected, click the *Capitalize first letter of table cells* check box to remove the check mark. Click OK to close the dialog box and then click OK to close the Word Options dialog box.

Exercise 3A

Creating a Concordance File

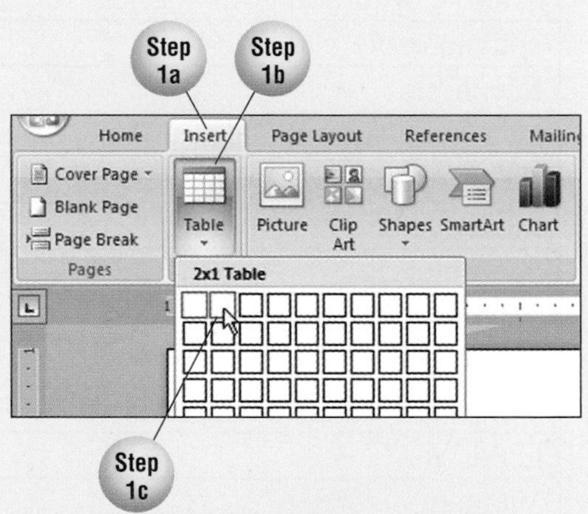

1. At a blank document, create the text shown in Figure 27.5 as a concordance file by completing the following steps:
   a. Click the Insert tab.
   b. Click the Table button in the Tables group.
   c. Drag down and to the right until 2 × *1 Table* displays at the top of the grid and then click the left mouse button.
   d. Type the text in the cells as shown in Figure 27.5. Press the Tab key to move to the next cell. (If you did not remove the check mark before the *Capitalize first letter of table cells* option at the AutoCorrect dialog box, the *n* in the first word in the first cell *newsletters* is automatically capitalized. Hover the mouse over the capital N until the blue rectangle displays, click the AutoCorrect Options button that displays, and then click *Stop Auto-capitalizing First Letter of Table Cells* at the drop-down list.)
2. Save the document with the name **C27Ex03CFile**.
3. Print and then close **C27Ex03CFile.docx**.

Figure 27.5 Exercise 3A

newsletters	Newsletters
software	Software
desktop publishing	Software: desktop publishing
word processing	Software: word processing
printers	Printers
laser	Printers: laser
design	Design
communication	Communication
consistency	Design: consistency
elements	Elements
Nameplate	Elements: nameplate
Logo	Elements: logo
Subtitle	Elements: subtitle
Folio	Elements: folio
Headlines	Elements: headlines
Subheads	Elements: subheads
Byline	Elements: byline
Body Copy	Elements: body copy
Graphics Images	Elements: graphics images
audience	Newsletters: audience
purpose	Newsletters: purpose
focal point	Newsletters: focal point

If you removed the check mark before the *Capitalize first letter of table cells* option at the AutoCorrect dialog box, you may need to turn this feature back on. To do this, click the Office button and then click the Word Options button at the drop-down list. At the Word Options dialog box, click *Proofing* at the left side of the dialog box and then click the AutoCorrect Options button. At the AutoCorrect dialog box with the AutoCorrect tab selected, click the *Capitalize first letter of table cells* check box to insert the check mark. Click OK to close the dialog box and then click OK to close the Word Options dialog box.

Exercise 3B

Inserting an Index Using a Concordance File

1. Open **Report16.docx** and save the document with the name **C27Ex03**.
2. Mark text to include in the index using the concordance file by completing the following steps:
   a. Click the References tab.
   b. Click the Insert Index button in the Index group.

c. At the Index dialog box, click the AutoMark button.

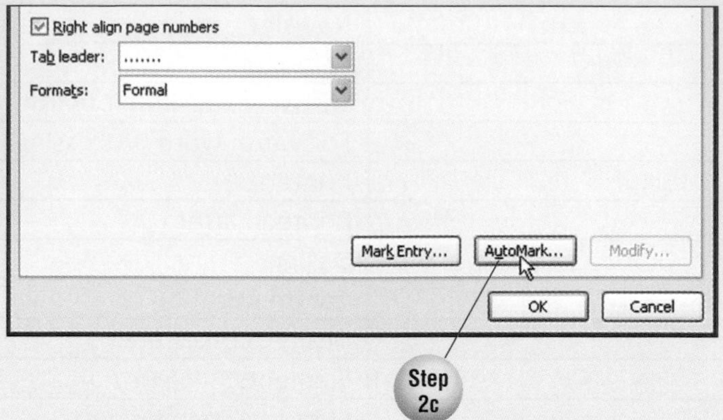

d. At the Open Index AutoMark File dialog box, click the down-pointing arrow at the right side of the *Files of type* option box and then click *All Files (*.*)* at the drop-down list.
e. Double-click **C27Ex03CFile.docx** in the list box. (This turns on the display of the nonprinting symbols.)

3. Insert the index in the document by completing the following steps:
   a. Position the insertion point at the end of the document.
   b. Insert a page break.
   c. Press Ctrl + E and then type **INDEX**.
   d. Press the Enter key and then press Ctrl + L to return the paragraph alignment to left.
   e. Click the Insert Index button in the Index group.
   f. At the Index dialog box, click the down-pointing arrow at the right side of the *Formats* option box and then click *Formal* at the drop-down list.
   g. Click OK to close the dialog box.
4. Apply the Heading 1 style to the *INDEX* title.
5. Turn off the display of nonprinting characters.
6. Save **C27Ex03.docx** and then print only the Index page.

Update an Index
1. Click in index.
2. Click Update Index button or press F9.

Delete an Index
1. Select entire index.
2. Press Delete key.

Updating and Deleting an Index

If you make changes to a document after you have inserted an index, update the index. To do this, click anywhere within the index and then click the Update Index button in the Index group or press F9. To delete an index, select the entire index using either the mouse or the keyboard and then press the Delete key.

Exercise 3C

Updating an Index

1. With **C27Ex03.docx** open, insert a page break at the beginning of the title *PLANNING A NEWSLETTER*.
2. Update the index by clicking anywhere in the index, clicking the References tab, and then clicking the Update Index button in the Index group.

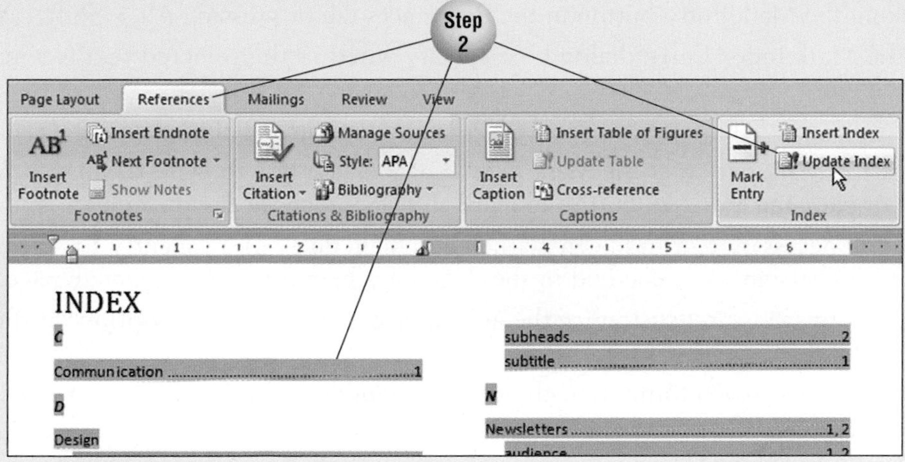

3. Save **C27Ex03.docx** and then print only the Index page.
4. Close **C27Ex03.docx**.

Chapter Summary

- An index is a list of topics contained in a publication and the pages on which those topics are discussed. Word lets you automate the process of creating an index. Mark text for inclusion in an index at the Mark Index Entry dialog box. Display this dialog box by clicking the Mark Entry button in the References tab or pressing Alt + Shift + X.
- At the Mark Index Entry dialog box, specify whether the selected text is a main entry or a subentry.
- The main entry and subentry do not have to be the same as the selected text.
- Click the Mark button at the Mark Index Entry dialog box to mark the currently selected text or click the Mark All button to mark all occurrences in the document.
- After all necessary text has been marked as a main entry or a subentry for the index, insert the index, placing it at the end of the document beginning on a separate page.
- Apply formatting and customize the appearance of an index with options at the Index dialog box.
- Word provides seven formatting choices for an index at the *Formats* option box in the Index dialog box.
- You can identify text as a bookmark and then mark the bookmark as an index entry. Doing this is especially useful when text for an entry spans a range of pages.
- Mark text for the index as a cross-reference if you want the text to refer the reader to another index entry.
- Words that appear frequently in a document can be saved as a concordance file so you do not need to mark each reference. A concordance file is a Word document that contains a single, two-column table.
- Use a concordance file to mark text by displaying the Index dialog box and then clicking the AutoMark button. At the Open Index AutoMark File dialog box, double-click the concordance file name.
- Update an index by clicking the index and then clicking the Update Index button in the Index group or pressing F9.

Commands review

FEATURE	RIBBON TAB, GROUP	BUTTON, OPTION	KEYBOARD SHORTCUT
Mark Index Entry dialog box	References, Index		Alt + Shift + X
Index dialog box	References, Index	Insert Index	
Open Index AutoMark File dialog box	References, Index	Insert Index, AutoMark	
Update index	References, Index	Update Index	F9

Reviewing key points

Completion: In the space provided at the right, indicate the correct term, symbol, or command.

1. An index generally appears at this location in the document. ________________
2. The Mark Entry button is located in the Index group in this tab. ________________
3. This is the keyboard shortcut to display the Mark Index Entry dialog box. ________________
4. When you mark a word for the index, the selected word displays in this text box in the Mark Index Entry dialog box. ________________
5. Click this button at the Mark Index Entry dialog box to mark all of the occurrences of the text in the document as index entries. ________________
6. If you want to mark more than a few words or a phrase for an index entry, consider identifying the text as this. ________________
7. Mark text for the index as this if you want the text to refer the reader to another index entry. ________________
8. Create this type of file and then use it to save time when marking text for an index. ________________
9. Click this button at the Index dialog box to display the Open Index AutoMark File dialog box. ________________
10. This is the keyboard shortcut to update an index. ________________

Applying your skills

Assessment 1 Create an Index for a Natural Interface Report

1. Open **Report14.docx** and save the document with the name **C27A01**.
2. Make the following changes to the document:
   a. Apply the Heading 1 style to the title *NATURAL INTERFACE APPLICATIONS*.
   b. Apply the Heading 2 style to the four headings in the document.
   c. Change the style set to *Modern*.
3. Create the following bookmarks:
   a. Create a bookmark for the *SPEECH RECOGNITION* section and name the bookmark *Speech*.
   b. Create a bookmark for the *NATURAL-LANGUAGE INTERFACE* section and name the bookmark *NLInterface*.
   c. Create a bookmark for the *VIRTUAL REALITY* section and name the bookmark *VReality*.
   d. Create a bookmark for the *MENTAL INTERFACE* section and name the bookmark *MInterface*.
4. Mark the following bookmarks as index entries that span pages:
   a. Mark the *Speech* bookmark as an index entry that spans pages and type **Speech recognition** in the *Main entry* text box.
   b. Mark the *NLInterface* bookmark as an index entry that spans pages and type **Natural-language interface** in the *Main entry* text box.
   c. Mark the *VReality* bookmark as an index entry that spans pages and type **Virtual reality** in the *Main entry* text box.
   d. Mark the *MInterface* bookmark as an index entry that spans pages and type **Mental interface** in the *Main entry* text box.
5. Mark *VR* (located in the *VIRTUAL REALITY* section) as an index entry and cross reference *VR* to *Virtual reality*.
6. Mark the first occurrence of the following words as main entries or subentries for the index:
   a. Mark *artificial intelligence* located in the first sentence of the first paragraph of text in the document as a main entry.
   b. Mark the following text located in the *SPEECH RECOGNITION* section:

      computer = main entry
      voice commands = main entry
      speed = subentry (main entry = *computer*)
      capacity = subentry (main entry = *computer*)

   c. Mark the following text located in the *NATURAL-LANGUAGE INTERFACE* section:

      languages = main entry
      translators = subentry (main entry = *languages*)
7. Insert the index at the end of the document on a separate page and change the *Formats* option at the Index dialog box to *Modern*.
8. Apply the Heading 1 style to the Index heading.
9. Center the two titles in the document *NATURAL INTERFACE APPLICATIONS* and *INDEX*.
10. Save and then print the last page of the document.
11. Close **C27A01.docx**.

Assessment 2 Create an Index Using a Concordance File

1. At a blank document, create the text shown in Figure 27.6 as a concordance file.
2. Save the document with the name **C27A02CFile**.
3. Print and then close **C27A02CFile.docx**.
4. Open **Report17.docx**.
5. Save the document with Save As and name it **C27A02**.
6. Make the following changes to the document:
   a. Mark text for an index using the concordance file **C27A02CFile.docx**.
   b. Insert the index at the end of the document.
   c. Apply the Heading 2 style to the *Index* title and then center the title.
7. Number the pages at the bottom center of each page.
8. Change the style set to *Manuscript*.
9. Insert a page break at the beginning of the title *SECTION 2: CREATING NEWSLETTER LAYOUT*.
10. Update the index.
11. Save the document again, print the index, and then close **C27A02.docx**.

Figure 27.6 Assessment 2

NEWSLETTER	Newsletter
newsletter	Newsletter
consistency	Newsletter: consistency
element	Elements
margins	Elements: margins
column layout	Elements: column layout
nameplate	Elements: nameplate
location	Elements: location
logos	Elements: logo
color	Elements: color
ruled lines	Elements: ruled lines
Focus	Elements: focus
balance	Elements: balance
graphics images	Graphics images
photos	Photos
Headlines	Newsletter: headlines
subheads	Newsletter: subheads
White space	White space
directional flow	Newsletter: directional flow
paper	Paper
size	Paper: size
type	Paper: type
weight	Paper: weight
stock	Paper: stock
margin size	Newsletter: margin size

Chapter 28

Creating Specialized Tables

Tutorial 28.1
Tables of Contents, Figures, and Authorities

Performance Objectives

Upon successful completion of Chapter 28, you will be able to:

- Create, insert, and update a table of contents
- Create, insert, and update a table of figures
- Create, insert, and update a table of authorities

Books, textbooks, reports, and manuscripts often include specialized tables, such as a table of contents, table of figures, or table of authorities. Creating these tables manually can be tedious. With Word, the steps and tasks required, like those required to create an index, can be automated, allowing you to create specialized tables quickly and easily. In this chapter, you will learn the steps to mark text for inclusion in a table of contents, table of figures, or table of authorities and steps to insert the table or list.

Note: Before beginning computer exercises for this chapter, copy to your storage medium the Chapter28 folder from the CD that accompanies this textbook and then make Chapter28 the active folder.

Creating a Table of Contents

A table of contents appears at the beginning of a book, manuscript, or report and contains headings and subheadings with page numbers. In an earlier chapter, you created a table of contents using the Quick Parts button in the Text group in the Insert tab. You can also create a table of contents using the Table of Contents button in the Table of Contents group in the References tab. You can identify text to be included in the table by applying built-in or custom heading styles, assigning levels, or marking text.

Applying Styles

To create a table of contents by applying built-in or custom styles, open the document and then apply the styles you want to use. Word uses text with Heading 1 style applied as the first level of the table of contents text, Heading 2 text for the second level, and so on. Apply the built-in or custom styles with options in the Styles group in the Home tab.

Insert a Table of Contents
1. Apply heading styles.
2. Click References tab.
3. Click Table of Contents button.
4. Click desired options at drop-down list.

Number Table of Contents Page
1. Click Insert tab.
2. Click Page Number button.
3. Click *Format Page Numbers* at drop-down list.
4. Change number format to lowercase Roman numerals.
5. Click OK.

Inserting a Table of Contents

After you have applied styles to the headings in a document, insert the table of contents. To do this, position the insertion point where you want the table to appear in the document, click the References tab, click the Table of Contents button, and then click the desired option at the drop-down list.

Numbering Table of Contents Pages

Generally, the pages in a table of contents are numbered with lowercase Roman numerals (*i, ii, iii*). You can change the page number format to lowercase Roman numerals at the Page Number Format dialog box, shown in Figure 28.1. Display this dialog box by clicking the Insert tab, clicking the Page Number button in the Header & Footer group, and then clicking *Format Page Numbers* at the drop-down list. Numbering on the first page of the document, excluding the Table of Contents page(s), should begin with number 1. To insert two page numbering formats, separate the Table of Contents from the beginning of the document with a section break that begins a new page.

Figure 28.1 Page Number Format Dialog Box

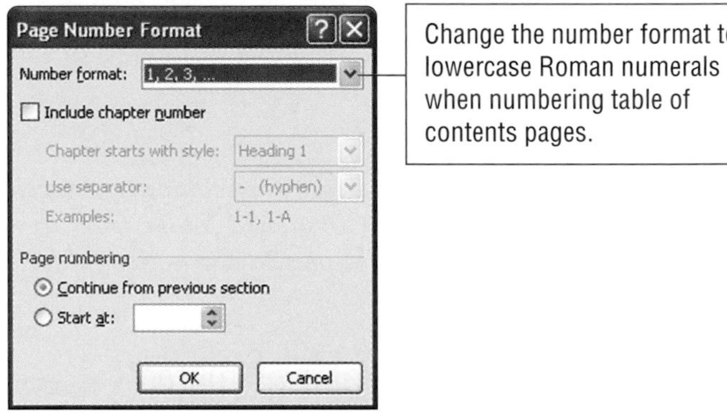

Navigating using a Table of Contents

When you insert a table of contents in a document, you can use the table of contents headings to navigate in a document. Table of contents headings are hyperlinks that are connected to the heading in the document. To navigate in a document using table of contents headings, click in the table of contents to select it. Position the mouse pointer over the desired heading and a box will display with the path and file name as well as the text *Ctrl+Click to follow link*. Hold down the Ctrl key and then click the left mouse button and the insertion point is positioned in the document at the location of the heading.

Exercise 1A

Applying Styles and Inserting a Table of Contents

1. Open **Report05.docx** and save the document with the name **C28Ex01**.
2. With the insertion point positioned immediately left of the *R* in *ROBOTS AS ANDROIDS*, insert a section break by completing the following steps:
   a. Click the Page Layout tab.
   b. Click the Breaks button in the Page Setup group.
   c. Click the *Next Page* option in the *Section Breaks* section.

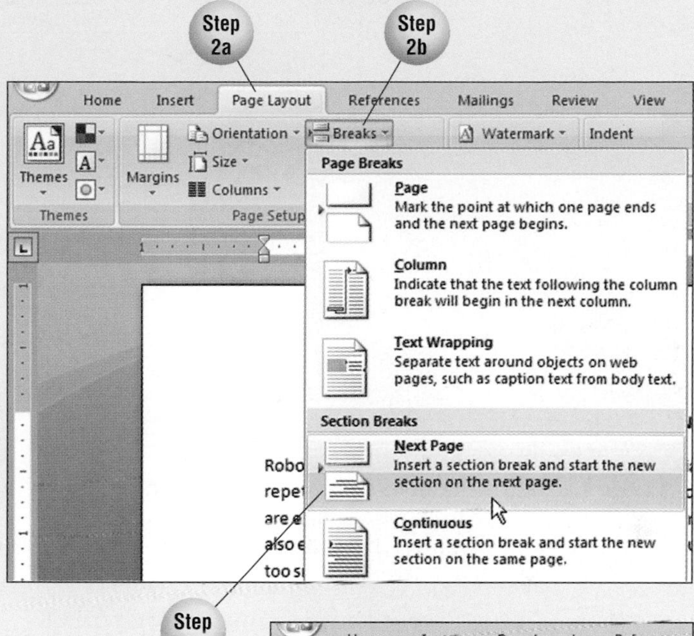

3. With the insertion point positioned below the section break, insert page numbering and change the beginning number to 1 by completing the following steps:
   a. Click the Insert tab.
   b. Click the Page Number button in the Header & Footer group, point to *Bottom of Page*, and then click *Plain Number 2*.
   c. Click the Page Number button and then click *Format Page Numbers* at the drop-down list.

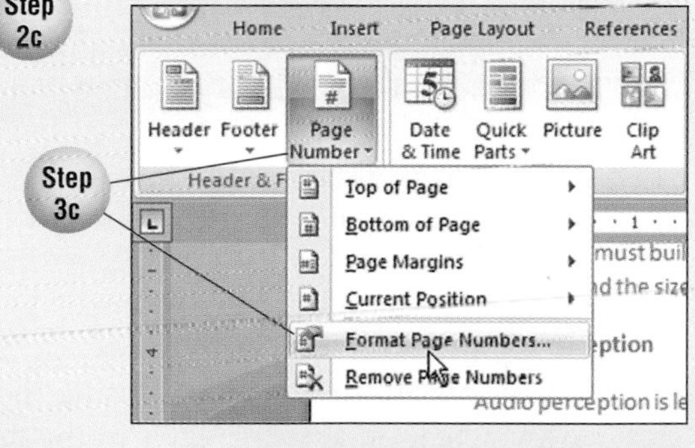

   d. At the Page Number Format dialog box, click *Start at* in the *Page numbering* section. (This inserts a 1 in the *Start at* text box.)
   e. Click OK to close the Page Number Format dialog box.
   f. Double-click in the document to make it active.

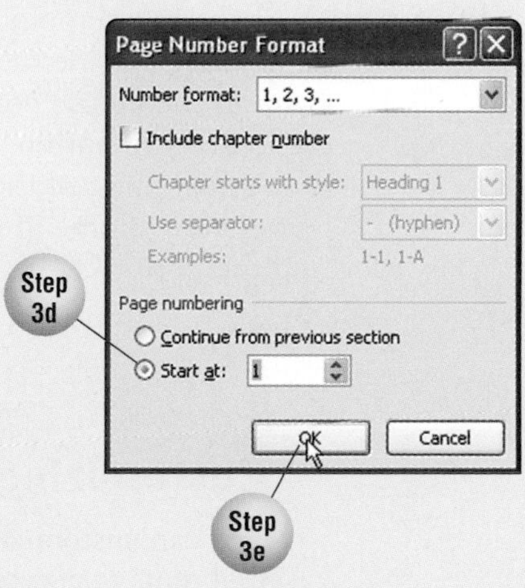

4. Apply the Heading 1 style to the title *ROBOTS AS ANDROIDS*.
5. Apply the Heading 2 style to the five headings in the document (*Visual Perceptions*, *Audio Perception*, *Tactile Perception*, *Locomotion*, and *Navigation*).
6. Insert a table of contents at the beginning of the document by completing the following steps:
   a. Press Ctrl + Home to move the insertion point to the blank page at the beginning of the document.

b. Click the References tab.
c. Click the Table of Contents button and then click the *Automatic Table 1* option in the *Built-In* section of the drop-down list.

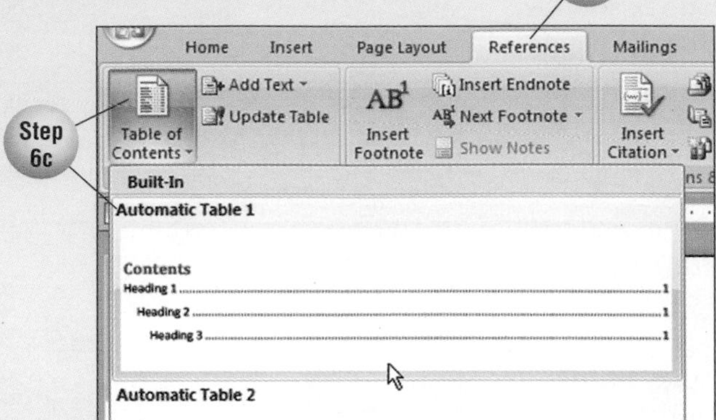

7. Insert page numbering in the Table of Contents page by completing the following steps:
   a. With the insertion point positioned on any character in the table, click the Insert tab.
   b. Click the Page Number button and then click *Format Page Numbers* at the drop-down list.
   c. At the Page Number Format dialog box, click the down-pointing arrow at the right side of the *Number format* option box and then click *i, ii, iii, …* at the drop-down list.
   d. Click OK to close the dialog box.
   e. Double-click in the document to make it active.

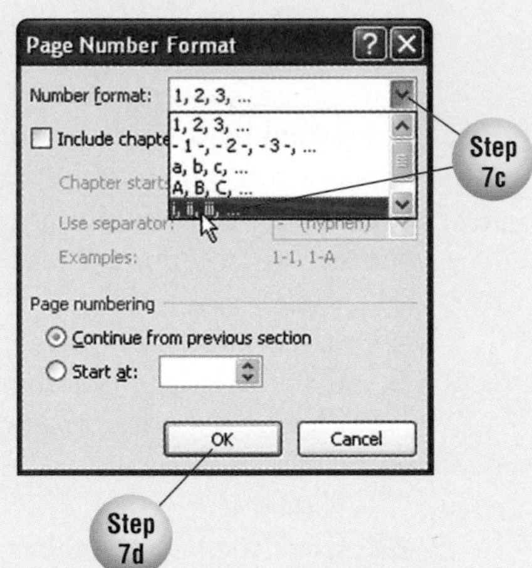

8. Change the style set to *Modern*.
9. Change the theme fonts to *Solstice*.
10. Navigate in the documents using the table of contents by completing the following steps:
    a. Click on any character in the table of contents.
    b. Move the mouse pointer outside the table of contents and then move the mouse pointer back inside the table of contents.
    c. Position the mouse pointer on the *Locomotion* heading, hold down the Ctrl key, click the left mouse button, and then release the Ctrl key. (This moves the insertion point to the beginning of the *Locomotion* heading in the document.)
    d. Press Ctrl + Home to move the insertion point to the beginning of the document.
11. Save and then print **C28Ex01.docx**.

Customizing the Table of Contents

You can customize a table of contents in a document with options at the Table of Contents dialog box, shown in Figure 28.2. Display this dialog box by clicking the Table of Contents button in the References tab and then clicking *Insert Table of Contents* at the drop-down list.

Figure 28.2 Table of Contents Dialog Box

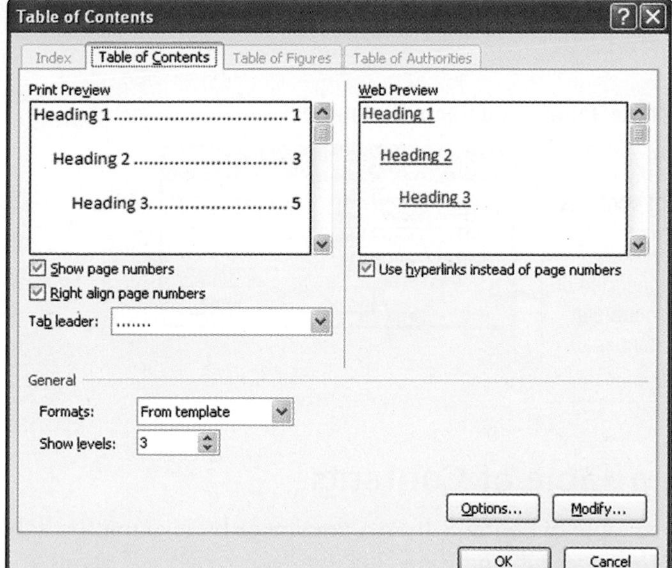

Customize the format of the table of contents with options at this dialog box.

At the Table of Contents dialog box, a sample table displays in the *Print Preview* section. You can change the format of the table by clicking the down-pointing arrow at the right side of the *Formats* option box (located in the *General* section). At the drop-down list that displays, click the format you want to apply. When you select a different format, that format displays in the *Print Preview* section. Page numbers in a table of contents display after the text or aligned at the right margin depending on which options you select. The number of levels that display depends on the number of heading levels you specify in the document.

Tab leaders help guide a reader's eyes from headings in the table to the page numbers. The default tab leader is a period. To choose a different leader, click the down-pointing arrow at the right side of the *Tab leader* text box and then click the leader character that you want to use from the drop-down list.

Word automatically identifies headings in a table of contents as hyperlinks and inserts page numbers. You can use these hyperlinks to move the insertion point to a specific location in the document. To move the insertion point to a specific section, position the mouse pointer on the corresponding heading in the table of contents, hold down the Ctrl key (the mouse pointer turns into a hand), and then click the left mouse button. If you are going to post your document to the Web, consider removing the page numbers because the reader will need only to click the hyperlink to view a specific page.

If you change options at the Table of Contents dialog box and then click OK, a message will display asking if you want to replace the selected table of contents. At this message, click Yes.

Update Table of Contents

1. Click anywhere within table of contents.
2. Click References tab.
3. Click Update Table button.
4. Select *Update page numbers only* or *Update entire table* at Update Table of Contents dialog box.
5. Click OK.

Remove Table of Contents

1. Click References tab.
2. Click Table of Contents button.
3. Click *Remove Table of Contents* at drop-down list.

OR

1. Click on any character in table of contents.
2. Click the Table of Contents tab.
3. Click *Remove Table of Contents* at drop-down list.

Updating a Table of Contents

If you add, delete, move, or edit headings or other text in a document after you have inserted a table of contents, update the table. To do this, click anywhere in the table and then click the Update Table button or press F9 (the Update Field key). At the Update Table of Contents dialog box, shown in Figure 28.3, click *Update page numbers*

only if the changes you made were to the page numbers only, or click *Update entire table* if you made changes to headings or subheadings within the document. Click OK or press Enter to close the dialog box.

Figure 28.3 Update Table of Contents Dialog Box

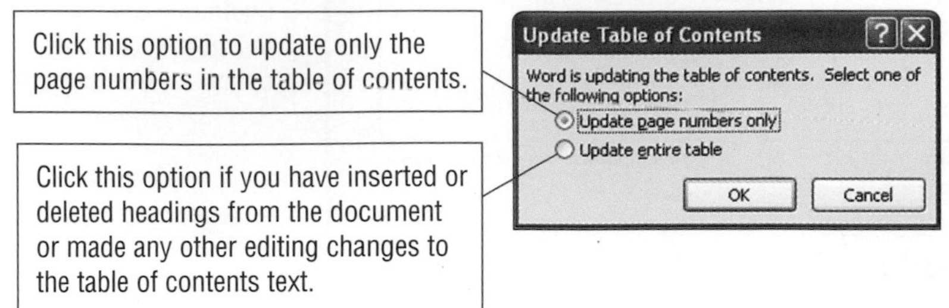

Removing a Table of Contents

You can remove a table of contents from a document by clicking the Table of Contents button in the References tab and then clicking *Remove Table of Contents* at the drop-down list. You can also remove a contents table by clicking on any character in the table, clicking the Table of Contents tab located in the upper left corner of the table of contents (immediately left of the Update Table tab), and then clicking *Remove Table of Contents* at the drop-down list.

Exercise 1B

Customizing and Updating the Table of Contents

1. With **C28Ex01.docx** open, customize the table of contents by completing the following steps:
   a. Click the References tab.
   b. Click the Table of Contents button and then click *Insert Table of Contents* at the drop-down list.
   c. At the Table of Contents dialog box, click the down-pointing arrow at the right side of the *Formats* option in the *General* section and then click *Formal* at the drop-down list.
   d. Click the down-pointing arrow at the right side of the *Tab leader* option box and then click the solid line option (bottom option) at the drop-down list.
   e. Click OK to close the dialog box.

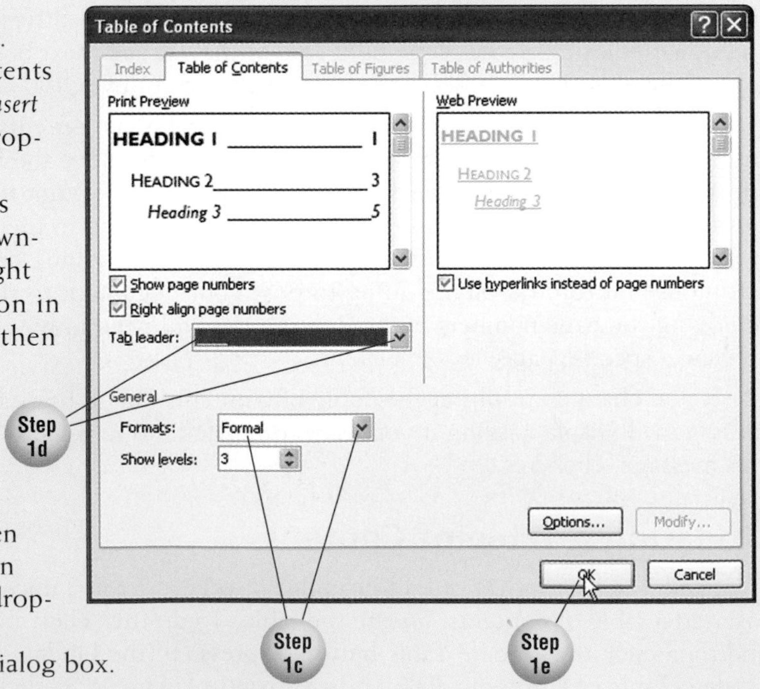

f. At the message asking if you want to replace the selected table of contents, click Yes.
2. Insert a command to keep lines of text together by completing the following steps:
   a. Move the insertion point so it is positioned at the beginning of the *LOCOMOTION* heading.
   b. Click the Home tab.
   c. Click the Paragraph group dialog box launcher.
   d. At the Paragraph dialog box, click the Line and Page Breaks tab.
   e. Click the *Keep with next* check box to insert a check mark.
   f. Click OK to close the dialog box.
3. Update the table of contents by completing the following steps:
   a. Click on any character in the table.
   b. Click the Update Table tab.
   c. At the Update Table of Contents dialog box, make sure *Update page numbers only* is selected and then click OK.

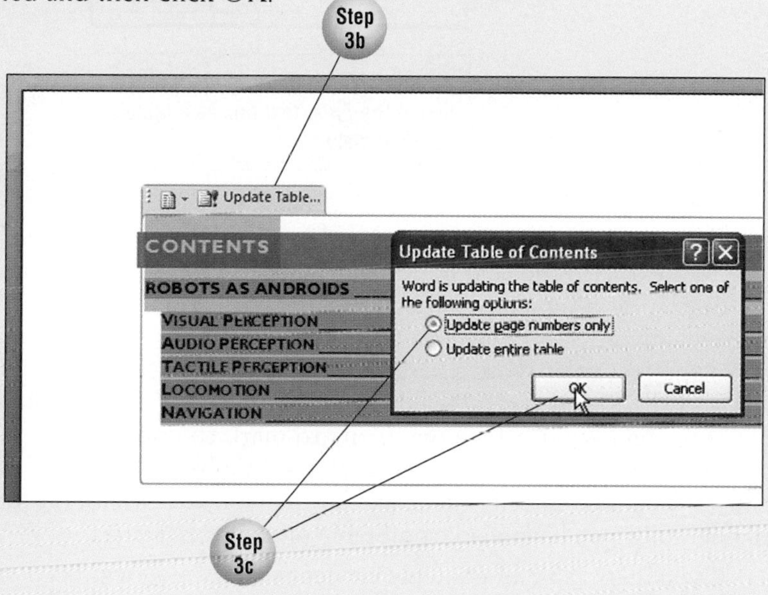

4. Save **C28Ex01.docx** and then print only the table of contents page.
5. Close **C28Ex01.docx**.

Assigning Levels to Table of Contents Entries

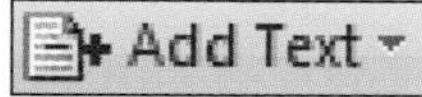

Another method for creating a table of contents is to assign a level to text to be included using the Add Text button in the Table of Contents group in the References tab. Click this button, and a drop-down list of level options displays. Click a level option to assign it to text you have selected. After you have specified levels for all the text you want to include in the table, insert the table of contents by clicking the Table of Contents button and then clicking the desired option at the drop-down list.

Marking Table of Contents Entries as Fields

When you apply styles to text, you apply specific formatting. If you want to identify titles or headings to use in a table of contents, but you do not want heading style formatting applied in the document, mark the text as a field entry. To do this, select the text you want to include in the table of contents and then press Alt + Shift + O. This displays the Mark Table of Contents Entry dialog box, shown in Figure 28.4.

Figure 28.4 Mark Table of Contents Entry Dialog Box

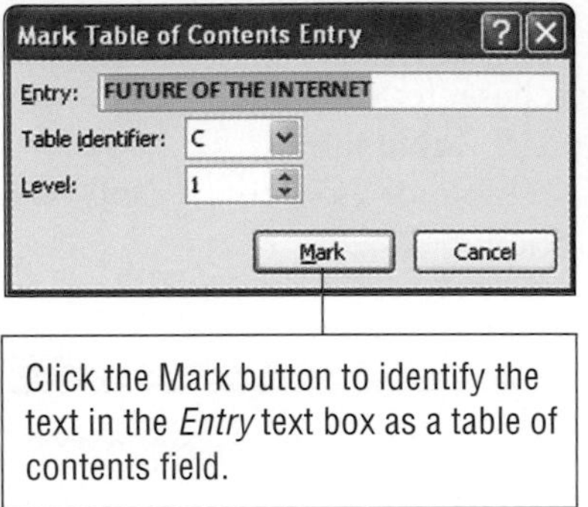

Click the Mark button to identify the text in the *Entry* text box as a table of contents field.

The text you selected displays in the *Entry* text box. Specify the level for the selected text with the *Level* option, and then click the Mark button. This turns on the display of nonprinting characters in the document and inserts a field code immediately after the selected text. As you will see in Exercise 2A, when you select the first title, Word inserts the following code immediately after the title: { TC "FUTURE OF THE INTERNET" \f C \l " 1 " }. The Mark Table of Contents Entry dialog box also remains open. To mark the next entry for the table of contents, select the text and then click the title bar of the Mark Table of Contents Entry dialog box. Specify the level and then click the Mark button. Continue in this manner until you have marked all table of contents entries.

If you mark table of contents entries as fields, you will need to activate the *Table entry fields* option when you insert the table in the document. To do this, display the Table of Contents dialog box and then click the Options button. At the Table of Contents Options dialog box, shown in Figure 28.5, click the *Table entry fields* check box to insert a check mark and then click OK.

Figure 28.5 Table of Contents Options Dialog Box

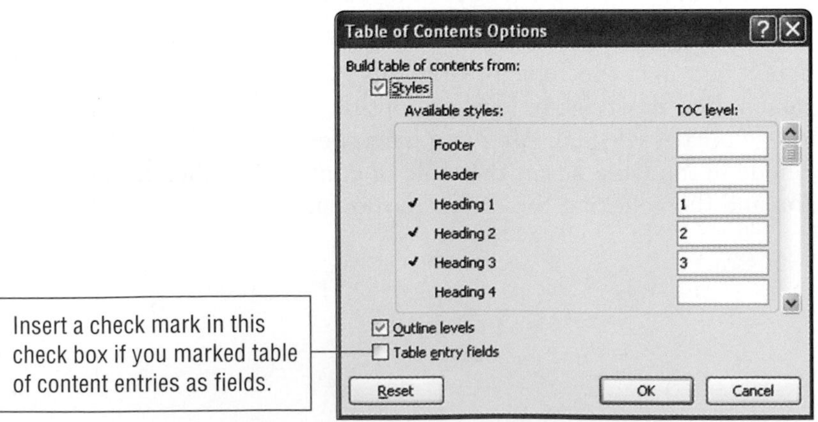

Insert a check mark in this check box if you marked table of content entries as fields.

Exercise 2A

Marking Headings as Fields

1. Open **Report18.docx** and save the document with the name **C28Ex02**.
2. With the insertion point positioned immediately left of the *F* in the title *FUTURE OF THE INTERNET*, insert a section break that begins a new page. *(Hint: Refer to Exercise 1A, Step 3.)*
3. Mark the titles and headings as fields for insertion in a table of contents by completing the following steps:
   a. Select the title *FUTURE OF THE INTERNET*.
   b. Press Alt + Shift + O.
   c. At the Mark Table of Contents Entry dialog box, make sure the *Level* is set at *1* and then click the Mark button. (This turns on the display of nonprinting characters.)
   d. Click in the document and then select the heading *Satellite Internet Connections*.
   e. Click the up-pointing arrow at the right side of the *Level* text box in the Mark Table of Contents Entry dialog box until 2 displays.
   f. Click the Mark button.
   g. Mark the following headings as level 2:
      Second Internet
      Internet Services for a Fee
      Internet 2030
   h. Click the Close button to close the Mark Table of Contents Entry dialog box.

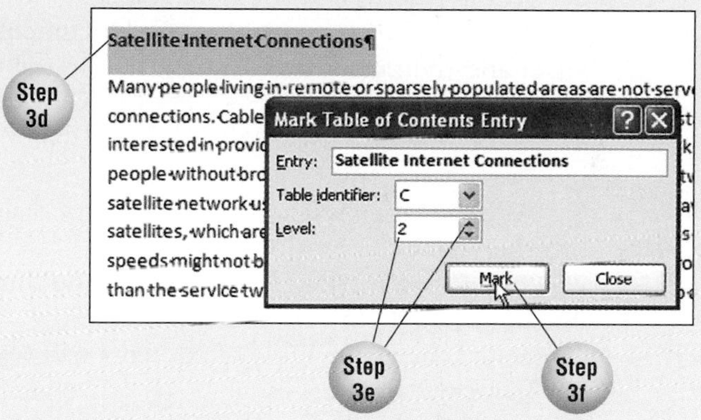

4. With the insertion point positioned below the section break, insert page numbering at the bottom center of each page of the section and change the starting number to 1. *(Hint: Refer to Exercise 1A, Step 6.)*
5. Insert a table of contents at the beginning of the document by completing the following steps:
   a. Position the insertion point at the beginning of the document (on the new page).
   b. Type the title *TABLE OF CONTENTS*, centered and bolded, and then press the Enter key. (The insertion point may not move down to the next line.)
   c. Click the References tab.
   d. Click the Table of Contents button and then click *Insert Table of Contents* at the drop-down list.
   e. At the Table of Contents dialog box, click the Options button.
   f. At the Table of Contents Options dialog box, click *Table entry fields* to insert a check mark in the check box. (This option is located in the bottom left corner of the dialog box.)
   g. Click OK to close the Table of Contents Options dialog box.
   h. Click OK to close the Table of Contents dialog box.
6. Insert lowercase Roman numeral page numbering on the Table of Contents page. *(Hint: Refer to Exercise 1A, Step 7.)*
7. Turn off the display of nonprinting characters.
8. Save and then print **C28Ex02.docx**.

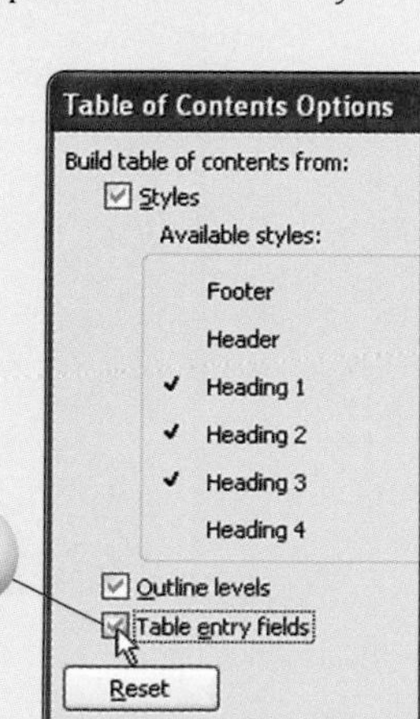

You can insert additional information in a document and update the table. To do this, insert the text and then mark the text with options at the Mark Table of Contents Entry dialog box. Click anywhere in the table of contents and then click the Update Table tab. At the Update Table of Contents dialog box, click the *Update entire table* option and then click OK.

Exercise 2B

Updating the Entire Table of Contents

1. With **C28Ex02.docx** open, insert a file into the document by completing the following steps:
   a. Press Ctrl + End to move the insertion point to the end of the document.
   b. Click the Insert tab.
   c. Click the Object button arrow in the Text group and then click *Text from File* at the drop-down list.
   d. At the Insert File dialog box, navigate to the Chapter28 folder on your storage medium and then double-click **Document29.docx**.
2. Select and then mark text for inclusion in the table of contents by completing the following steps:
   a. Select the title *INTERNET COMMUNITY ISSUES*.
   b. Press Alt + Shift + O.
   c. At the Mark Table of Contents Entry dialog box, make sure the *Level* is set at *1* and then click the Mark button.
3. Select and then mark as level 2 entries the three headings in the document.
4. Update the table of contents by completing the following steps:
   a. Select the entire table of contents text (excluding the title).
   b. Click the References tab.
   c. Click the Update Table button in the Table of Contents group.
   d. At the Update Table of Contents dialog box, click the *Update entire table* option.
   e. Click OK.

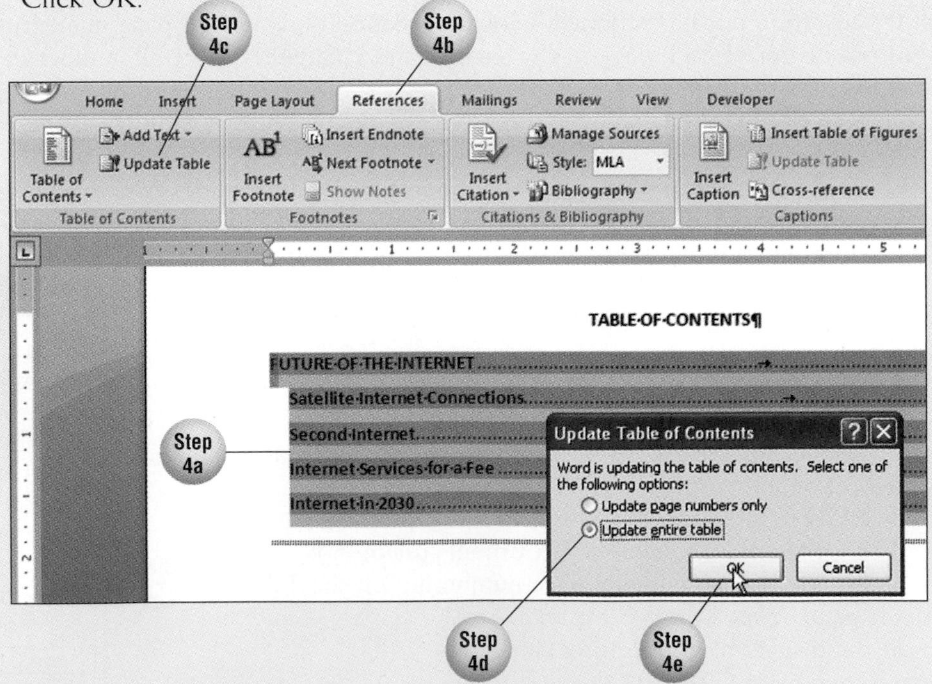

5. Turn off the display of nonprinting characters.
6. Save the document and then print only the table of contents page.
7. Close **C28Ex02.docx**.

Creating a Table of Figures

A document that contains figures should include a list (table) of figures so a reader can quickly locate a specific figure. Figure 28.6 shows an example of a table of figures. You can create a table of figures by marking figures or images as captions and then using the caption names to create the table of figures.

Figure 28.6 Table of Figures

TABLE OF FIGURES

FIGURE 1 SCANNED LINE ART 3
FIGURE 2 DIGITAL HALFTONE 8
FIGURE 3 BAR 12
FIGURE 4 LINE CHARTS 15
FIGURE 5 DETAIL VS. WEIGHT 18

Creating Captions

Create a Caption
1. Select text or image.
2. Click References tab.
3. Click Insert Caption button.
4. Type caption name.
5. Click OK.

A caption is text that describes a figure or picture, and generally displays below the element. You can create a caption by selecting the figure name or image, clicking the References tab, and then clicking the Insert Caption button in the Captions group. This displays the Caption dialog box, shown in Figure 28.7. At the dialog box, make sure *Figure 1* displays in the *Caption* text box and the insertion point is positioned after *Figure 1*. Type a name for the caption, and then press Enter. Word inserts *Figure 1 (caption name)* below the selected text or image. Click the down-pointing arrow at the right side of the *Label* option to specify the caption label. The default is *Figure*, which you can change to *Equation* or *Table*.

Figure 28.7 Caption Dialog Box

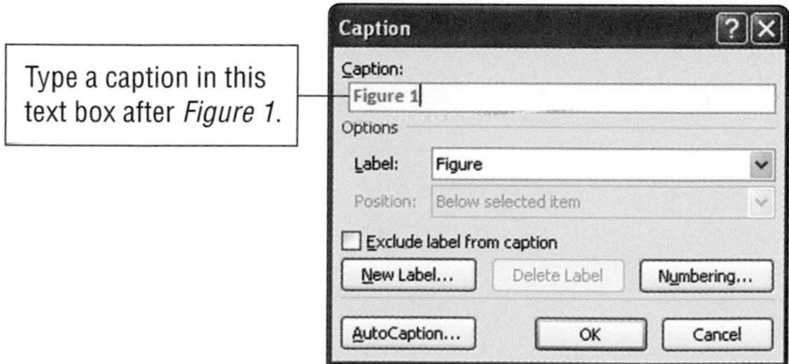

Insert a Table of Figures

1. Click References tab.
2. Click Insert Table of Figures button.
3. Select desired format.
4. Click OK.

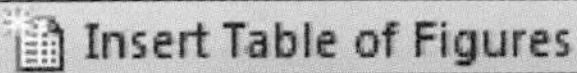

Inserting a Table of Figures

After you have marked the figure text or images in a document as captions, insert the table of figures. A table of figures generally displays at the beginning of a document, after the table of contents and on a separate page. To insert the table of figures, click the Insert Table of Figures button in the Captions group in the References tab. At the Table of Figures dialog box, shown in Figure 28.8, make any necessary changes and then click OK.

Figure 28.8 Table of Figures Dialog Box

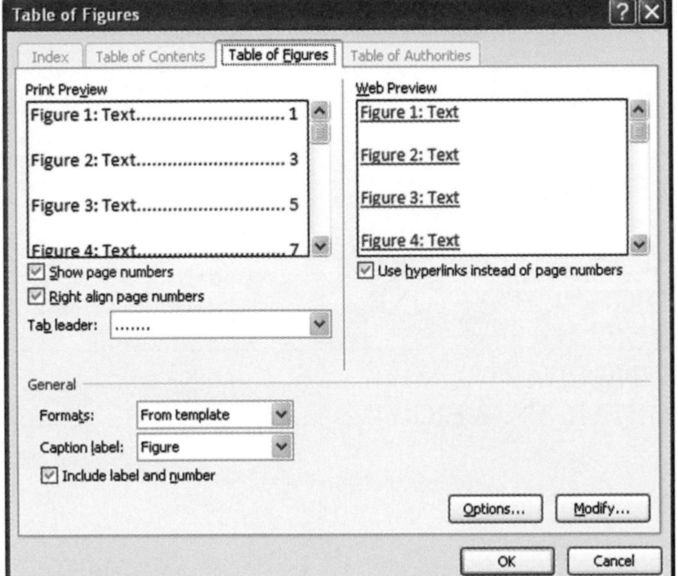

Customize the format of the table of figures with options at this dialog box.

The options available at the Table of Figures dialog box are similar to those available at the Table of Contents dialog box. For example, you can choose a format for the table of figures from the drop-down list at the *Formats* option box, change the alignment of the page numbers, or add leaders before page numbers.

Exercise 3A

Creating a List of Figures

1. Open **Report19.docx** and save the document with the name **C28Ex03**.
2. Add the caption *Figure 1 CRT Monitor* to the CRT monitor image by completing the following steps:
   a. Click the image of the CRT monitor (as shown below).
   b. Click the References tab.
   c. Click the Insert Caption button in the Captions group.
   d. At the Caption dialog box, press the spacebar once and then type **CRT Monitor**.
   e. Click OK or press Enter.

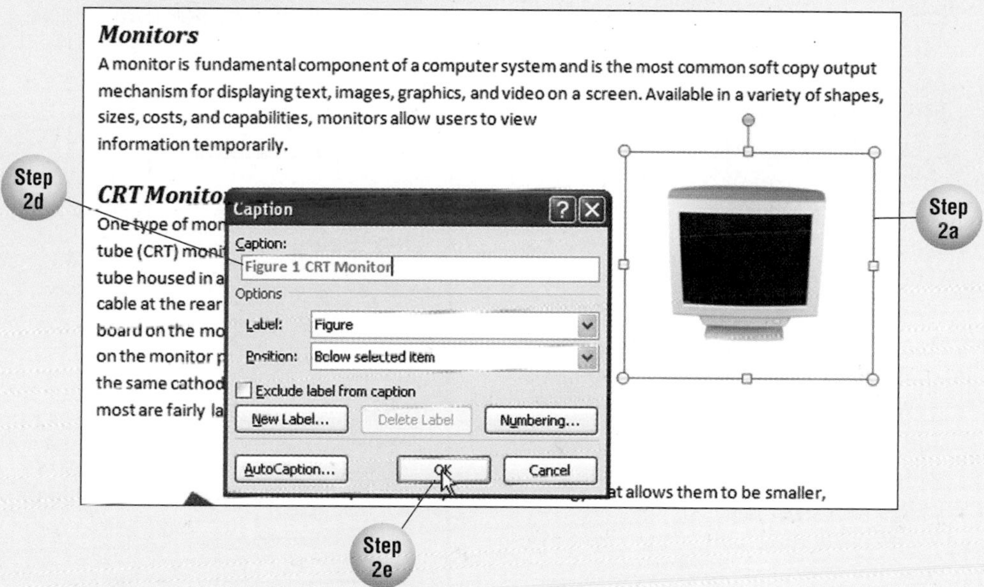

3. Complete steps similar to those in Step 2 to create the caption *Figure 2 Flat-Panel Monitor* for the flat-panel display image.
4. Complete steps similar to those in Step 2 to create the caption *Figure 3 Ink-Jet Printer* for the ink-jet printer image.
5. Complete steps similar to those in Step 2 to create the caption *Figure 4 Laser Printer*.
6. Size and move a figure text box by completing the following steps:
   a. Click the *Figure 1 CRT Monitor* text box. (This inserts a dashed blue line around the text.)
   b. Decrease the size of the right side of the text box so it is positioned closer to the text.
   c. Drag the text box so it is located as shown at the right. (To drag the text box, position the mouse pointer on the border line until the pointer turns into a four-headed arrow. Hold down the left mouse button and then drag the text box.)

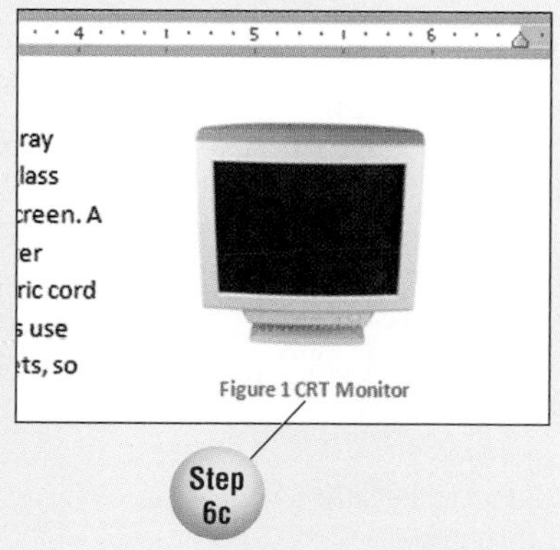

7. Move the text box below the flat-panel monitor image so it is located as shown at the right.
8. Move the text boxes below the remaining two images so they are centered below the images.
9. Insert a table of figures at the beginning of the document by completing the following steps:
   a. Press Ctrl + Home to move the insertion point to the beginning of the document.
   b. Press Ctrl + Enter to insert a page break.
   c. Move the insertion point above the page break and then type **TABLE OF FIGURES** bolded and centered.
   d. Press the Enter key, turn off bold, and then change the paragraph alignment back to left.
   e. Click the References tab.
   f. Click the Insert Table of Figures button in the Captions group.
   g. At the Table of Figures dialog box, click the down-pointing arrow at the right side of the *Formats* option box and then click *Formal* at the drop-down list.
   h. Click OK or press Enter.
10. Save **C28Ex03.docx** and then print the first page.

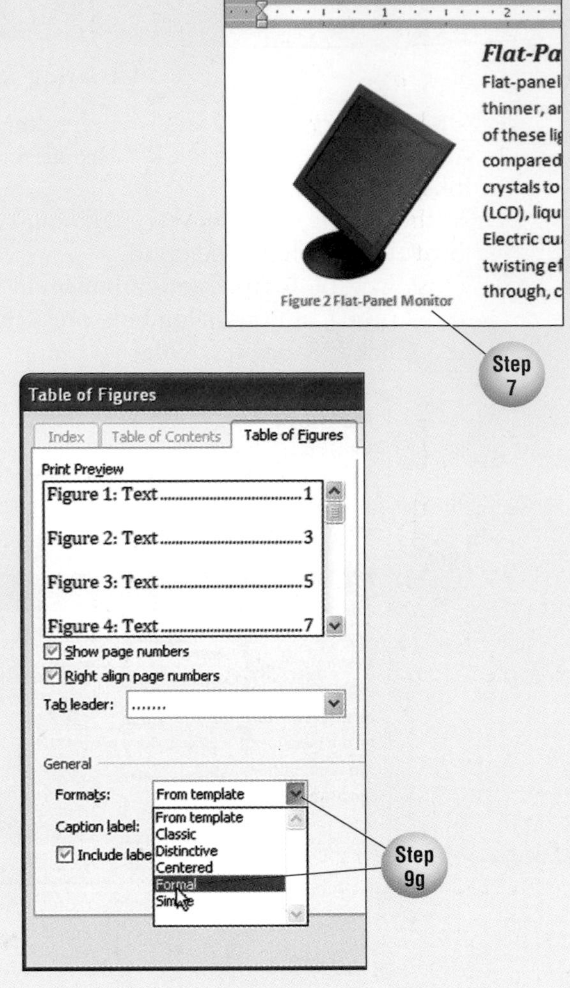

Update Table of Figures
1. Click in table of figures.
2. Click References tab.
3. Click Update Table button or press F9.
4. Click OK at the Update Table of Figures dialog box.

Delete Table of Figures
1. Select entire table of figures.
2. Press Delete key.

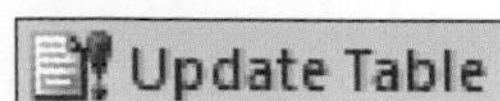

Updating or Deleting a Table of Figures

If you make changes to a document after you have inserted a table of figures, update the table. To do this, click anywhere within the table and then click the Update Table button in the Captions group in the References tab or press F9. At the Update Table of Figures dialog box, click *Update page numbers only* if the changes you made were to the page numbers only, or click *Update entire table* if you made changes to the caption text. Click OK or press Enter to close the dialog box. To delete a table of figures, select the entire table using either the mouse or the keyboard and then press the Delete key.

Exercise 3B

Updating the Table of Figures

1. With **C28Ex03.docx** open, insert a page break at the beginning of the heading *Laser Printers*.
2. Click on any character in the table of figures.
3. Press F9.
4. At the Update Table of Figures dialog box, click OK.
5. Print the first page.
6. Close **C28Ex03.docx** without saving the changes.

Creating a Table of Authorities

A table of authorities is a list of citations that appears in a legal brief or other legal document and the page numbers on which the citations appear. Word provides many common categories under which citations can be organized: Cases, Statutes, Other Authorities, Rules, Treatises, Regulations, and Constitutional Provisions. Within each category, Word alphabetizes the citations. Figure 28.9 shows an example of a table of authorities.

Figure 28.9 Table of Authorities

TABLE OF AUTHORITIES

CASES

Mansfield v. Rydell, 72 Wn.2d 200, 433 P.2d 723 (1993) 3
State v. Fletcher, 73 Wn.2d 332, 124 P.2d 503 (1999) 5
Yang v. Buchwald, 21 Wn.2d 385, 233 P.2d 609 (2002) 7

STATUTES

RCW 8.12.230(2) 4
RCW 6.23.590 7
RCW 5.23.103(3) 10

Creating a table of authorities requires thought and planning. Before you mark any text in a legal document for inclusion in such a table, you need to determine what section headings you want to use and what listings should be contained in each section. When you mark text for the table, you need to find the first occurrence of each citation, mark it as a full citation with the complete name, and then specify a short citation. To mark a citation for a table of authorities, complete the following steps:

Mark Citation for a Table of Authorities
1. Select first occurrence of citation.
2. Press Alt + Shift + I.
3. At Mark Citation dialog box, edit and format text.
4. Specify the category.
5. Click the Mark All button.

1. Select the first occurrence of the citation.
2. Click the References tab and then click the Mark Citation button or press Alt + Shift + I.
3. At the Mark Citation dialog box, shown in Figure 28.10, edit and format the text in the *Selected text* box as you want it to appear in the table of authorities. Edit and format the text in the *Short citation* text box so it matches the short citation you want Word to search for in the document.
4. Click the down-pointing arrow at the right of the *Category* text box and then click the category from the drop-down list that applies to the citation.
5. Click the Mark button to mark the selected citation or click the Mark All button if you want Word to mark all long and short citations in the document that match those displayed in the Mark Citation dialog box.
6. The Mark Citation dialog box remains open so you can mark other citations. To find the next citation in a document, click the Next Citation button. (This prompts Word to search through the document for the next occurrence of text commonly found in a citation such as *in re* or *v.*)
7. Select the text for the next citation and then complete Steps 3 through 5.
8. After marking all citations, click the Close button to close the Mark Citations dialog box.

Figure 28.10 Mark Citation Dialog Box

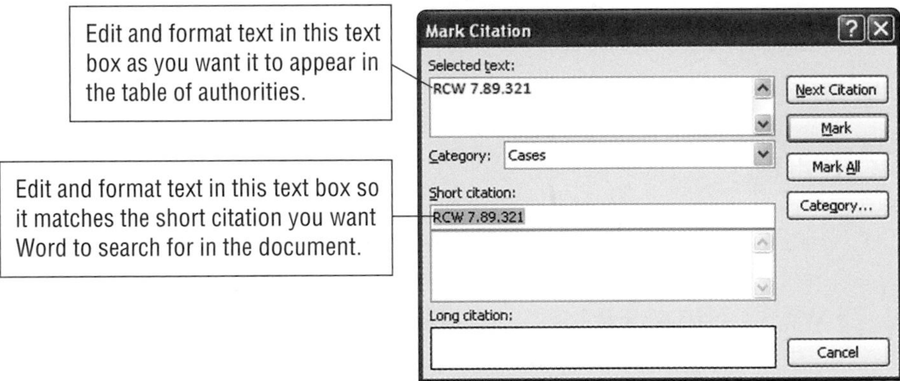

Insert a Table of Authorities
1. Click References tab.
2. Click Insert Table of Authorities button.
3. Select desired format.
4. Click OK.

Insert Table of Authorities

Inserting a Table of Authorities

Once you have marked the citations in a document, you can insert the table of authorities. A table of authorities is inserted in a document in a manner similar to that used to insert a table of contents or figures. A table of authorities generally displays at the beginning of a document. To insert a table of authorities in a document that contains text marked as citations, click the References tab and then click the Insert Table of Authorities button. This displays the Table of Authorities dialog box, shown in Figure 28.11. At this dialog box, make any necessary changes and then click OK to close the dialog box.

Like the Table of Contents dialog box and the Table of Figures dialog box, the Table of Authorities dialog box contains options for formatting a table of authorities. The *Use passim* option is active by default (the check box contains a check mark), which tells Word to replace five or more page references to the same authority with *passim*. With the *Keep original formatting* check box active, Word retains the formatting of the citation as it appears in the document. Click the *Tab leader* option if you want to change the leader character. When you insert a table of authorities, Word includes a heading for each of the seven categories by default. If you want to insert citations for a specific category only, select that category at the *Category* drop-down list.

Figure 28.11 Table of Authorities Dialog Box

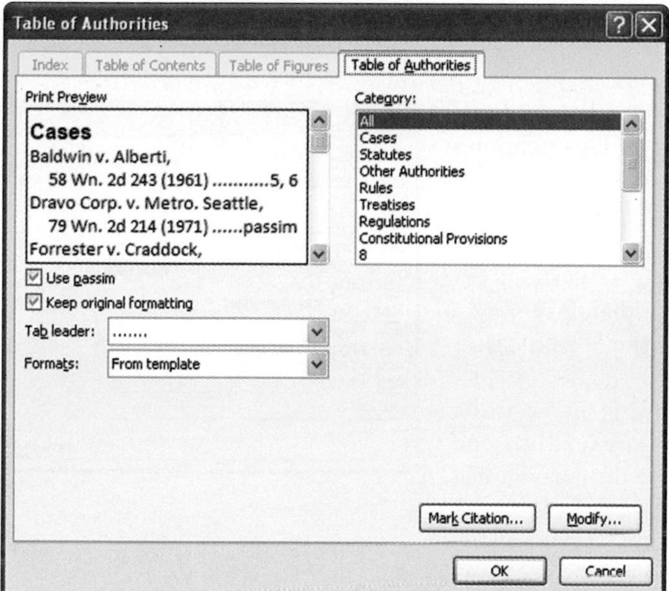

Customize the format of the table of authorities with options at this dialog box.

Exercise 4

Inserting a Table of Authorities

1. Open **LegalBrief.docx** and save the document with the name **C28Ex04**.
2. Mark *RCW 7.89.321* as a statute citation by completing the following steps:
   a. Select *RCW 7.89.321*. (This citation is located toward the middle of the second page. *Hint: Use the Find feature to help you locate this citation.*)
   b. Click the References tab.
   c. Click the Mark Citation button in the Table of Authorities group.
   d. At the Mark Citation dialog box, click the down-pointing arrow at the right side of the *Category* text box and then click *Statutes* at the drop-down list.
   e. Click the Mark All button. (This turns on the display of nonprinting characters.)
   f. Click the Close button to close the Mark Citation dialog box.

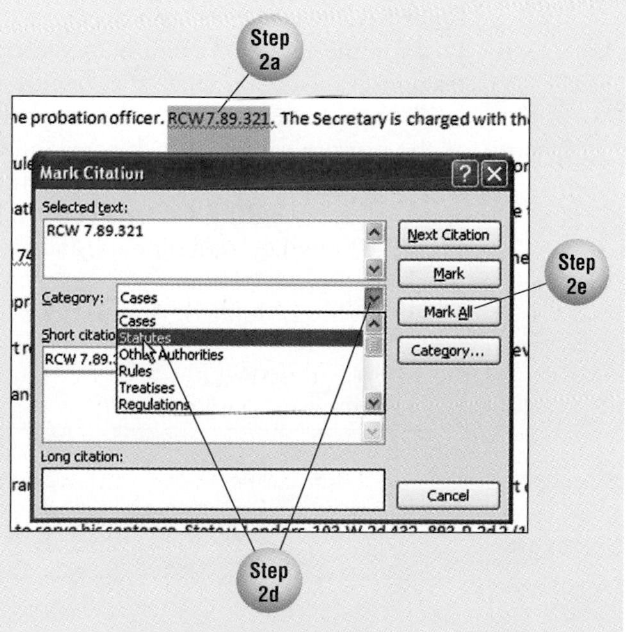

3. Complete steps similar to those in Step 2 to mark *RCW 7.53.443* as a statute citation. (This citation is located toward the middle of the second page.)
4. Complete steps similar to those in Step 2 to mark *RCW 7.72A.432(2)* as a statute citation. (This citation is located toward the bottom of the second page.)
5. Complete steps similar to those in Step 2 to mark *RCW 7.42A.429(1)* as a statute citation. (This citation is located toward the bottom of the second page.)
6. Mark *State v. Connors*, *73 W.2d 743, 430 P.2d 199 (1974)* as a case citation by completing the following steps:
   a. Select *State v. Connors*, *73 W.2d 743, 430 P.2d 199 (1974)*. (This citation is located toward the middle of the second page. *Hint: Use the Find feature to help you locate this citation.*)
   b. Press Alt + Shift + I.
   c. At the Mark Citation dialog box, type **State v. Connors** in the *Short citation* text box.
   d. Click the down-pointing arrow at the right side of the *Category* text box and then click *Cases* at the drop-down list.
   e. Click the Mark All button.
   f. Click the Close button to close the Mark Citation dialog box.

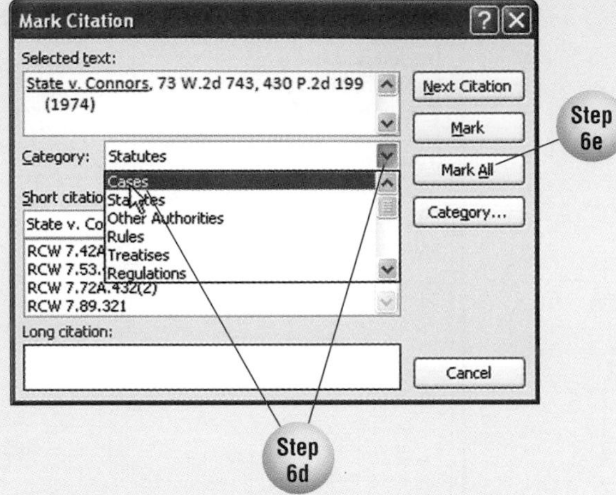

7. Complete steps similar to those in Step 6 to mark *State v. Bertelli*, *63 W.2d 77, 542 P.2d 751 (1971)*. Enter **State v. Bertelli** as the short citation. (This citation is located toward the middle of the second page.)
8. Complete steps similar to those in Step 6 to mark *State v. Landers*, *103 W.2d 432, 893 P.2d 2 (1984)*. Enter **State v. Landers** as the short citation. (This citation is located toward the bottom of the second page.)
9. Insert page numbering and the table of authorities by completing the following steps:
   a. Position the insertion point at the beginning of the document and then press the Enter key once.
   b. Position the insertion point immediately left of the *S* in *STATEMENT OF CASE* and then insert a section break that begins a new page.
   c. With the insertion point positioned below the section break, insert page numbering at the bottom center of each page and change the starting number to 1.
   d. Press Ctrl + Home to move the insertion point to the beginning of the document and then type **TABLE OF AUTHORITIES** centered and bolded.
   e. Press the Enter key, turn off bold, and then change the paragraph alignment back to left.
   f. Click the References tab.
   g. Click the Insert Table of Authorities button.

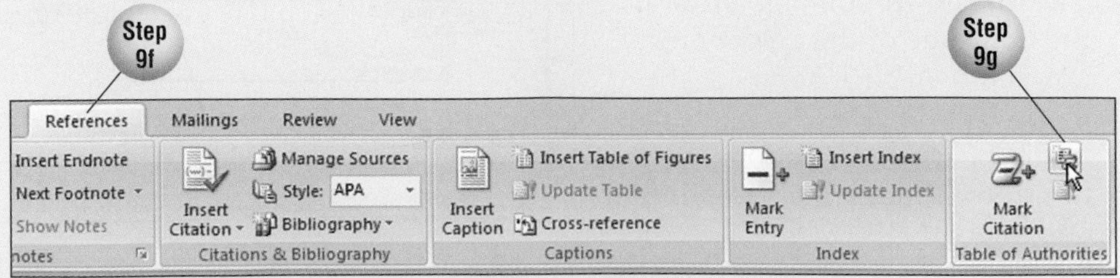

h. At the Table of Authorities dialog box, click the down-pointing arrow at the right side of the *Formats* option box and then click *Formal* at the drop-down list.
i. Click OK or press Enter.

10. With the insertion point positioned anywhere in the table of authorities, change the numbering format to lowercase Roman numerals.
11. Turn off the display of nonprinting characters.
12. Save **C28Ex04.docx** and then print the table of authorities page.
13. Close **C28Ex04.docx**.

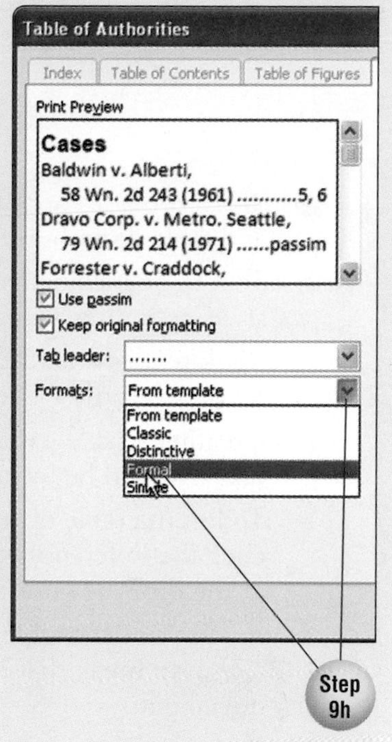

Updating or Deleting a Table of Authorities

Update a Table of Authorities
1. Click in table of authorities.
2. Click References tab.
3. Click Update Table of Authorities button or press F9.

Delete a Table of Authorities
1. Select the entire table of authorities.
2. Press Delete key.

Update Table of Authorities

If you make changes to a document after you have inserted a table of authorities, update the table. To do this, click anywhere within the table and then click the Update Table of Authorities button or press F9. If you need to edit a citation, edit it in the document and not in the table of authorities. If you edit a citation in the table of authorities, your changes will be lost the next time you update the table. To delete a table of authorities, select the entire table of authorities using either the mouse or the keyboard and then press the Delete key.

Chapter Summary

- Word provides options for automating the creation of a table of contents, table of figures, and table of authorities.
- Text to be included in a table of contents can be identified three ways: by applying a heading style, assigning a level, or marking text as a field entry.
- Mark text as a field entry at the Mark Table of Contents dialog box. Display this dialog box by pressing Alt + Shift + O.
- Creating a table of contents involves two steps: applying the appropriate styles to or marking text that will be included and inserting the table of contents in the document.
- To insert a table of contents, position the insertion point where you want the table to appear, click the References tab, click the Table of Contents button, and then click the desired option at the drop-down list.
- If you want the table of contents to print on a page separate from the document text, insert a section break that begins a new page between the table of contents and the title of the document.
- If you make changes to a document after inserting a table of contents, update the table by clicking anywhere in it and then clicking the Update Table button in the References tab or pressing F9. Update a table of figures or table of authorities in a similar manner.
- Remove a table of contents by clicking the Table of Contents button in the References tab and then clicking *Remove Table of Contents* at the drop-down list.
- Create a table of figures by marking specific text or images as captions and then using the caption names to create the table. Mark captions at the Caption dialog box. Display this dialog box by clicking the Insert Caption button in the References tab.
- Insert a table of figures in a document in a manner similar to that used to insert a table of contents. A table of figures generally displays at the beginning of a document, after the table of contents.
- A table of authorities is a list of the citations in a legal brief or other legal document and pages on which the citations appear.
- When you mark text for a table of authorities, find the first occurrence of a citation, mark it as a full citation with the complete name, and then specify a short citation at the Mark Citation dialog box. Display this dialog box by clicking the Mark Citation button on the References tab or pressing Alt + Shift + I.
- Insert a table of authorities in a document in a manner similar to that used to insert a table of contents or figures. A table of authorities generally displays at the beginning of a document.
- Delete a table of figures or a table of authorities by selecting the entire table and then pressing the Delete key.

Commands review

FEATURE	RIBBON TAB, GROUP	BUTTON, OPTION	KEYBOARD SHORTCUT
Page Number Format dialog box	Insert, Header & Footer	, Format Page Numbers	
Table of Contents dialog box	References, Table of Contents	, Insert Table of Contents	
Update Table of Contents Update Table of Figures	References, Table of Contents	Update Table	F9
Mark Table of Contents Entry dialog box			Alt + Shift + O
Table of Contents Options dialog box	References, Table of Contents	, Insert Table of Contents, Options	
Caption dialog box	References, Captions		
Table of Figures dialog box	References, Captions	Insert Table of Figures	
Mark Citation dialog box	References, Table of Authorities		Alt + Shift + I
Table of Authorities dialog box	References, Table of Authorities		
Update Table of Authorities	References, Table of Authorities		

Reviewing key points

Completion: In the space provided at the right, indicate the correct term, symbol, or command.

1. In a built-in table of contents, Word uses text with this heading applied to it as the first level. __________
2. A table of contents generally appears in this location in the document. __________
3. A table of contents is generally numbered with this type of numbers. __________
4. This is the keyboard shortcut to update a table of contents. __________
5. Delete a table of contents by clicking the Table of Contents button in the References tab and then clicking this option. __________
6. This is the keyboard shortcut to display the Mark Table of Contents Entry dialog box. __________
7. If you mark table of contents entries as fields, you will need to activate this option at the Table of Contents Options dialog box. __________
8. Create a table of figures by marking figure names as these. __________
9. This is a list identifying the pages on which citations appear in a legal brief or other legal document. __________
10. This is the keyboard shortcut to display the Mark Citation dialog box. __________

Applying your skills

Assessment 1 Insert a Table of Contents in a Computer Report

1. Open **Report02.docx** and save the document with the name **C28A01**.
2. With the insertion point positioned at the beginning of the document, press Ctrl + Enter to insert a page break.
3. Apply the Heading 1 style to the three titles in the document and apply the Heading 2 style to the five headings.
4. Insert a continuous section break at the beginning of the title *COMPUTERS IN COMMUNICATIONS*.
5. With the insertion point positioned below the section break, insert page numbering and change the beginning number to 1.
6. Insert a table of contents at the beginning of the document with the *Automatic Table 1* option.
7. In the Table of Contents page, change the page numbering style to lowercase Roman numerals.
8. Change the style set to *Distinctive*.
9. Save and then print **C28A01.docx**.
10. Insert a page break at the beginning of the title *COMPUTERS IN ENTERTAINMENT*.
11. Update the table of contents.
12. Print only the table of contents page.
13. Save and then close **C28A01.docx**.

Assessment 2 Insert a Table of Contents in a Computer Viruses Report

1. At a blank document, press the Enter key once and then press Ctrl + Enter to insert a page break.
2. Insert **Report06.docx**. (Do this with the Object button in the Insert tab.)
3. Move the insertion point to the end of the document, press the Backspace key once, and then insert **Report09.docx**.
4. Select the entire document and then change the line spacing to 1.5.
5. Insert a continuous section break at the beginning of the first title (*CHAPTER 1: COMPUTER VIRUSES*).
6. With the insertion point positioned below the section break, insert page numbering and change the beginning number to 1.
7. Insert a table of contents at the beginning of the document with the *Automatic Table 1* option.
8. Apply the Heading 1 style to the Contents heading.
9. In the Table of Contents page, change the page numbering style to lowercase Roman numerals.
10. Save the document with the name **C28A02**.
11. Print **C28A02.docx**.
12. Insert a page break at the beginning of the chapter 2 and the chapter 3 titles.
13. Update the table of contents.
14. Print only the table of contents page.
15. Save and then close **C28A02.docx**.

Assessment 3 Insert Captions and a Table of Figures in a Report

1. Open **Report20.docx** and save the document with the name **C28A03**.
2. Insert a caption for each of the three images in the document. (You determine the name of the caption.)
3. Press Ctrl + Home and then insert a section break that begins a new page.
4. With the insertion point positioned below the section break, insert page numbering and change the beginning page number to 1.
5. Insert a table of figures at the beginning of the document with the title *TABLE OF FIGURES*. Apply the Heading 1 style to the title and center the title.
6. In the TABLE OF FIGURES page, change the page numbering style to lowercase Roman numerals.
7. Save, print, and then close **C28A03.docx**.

Chapter 29

CHAPTER29

Creating Forms

SNAP

Tutorial 29.1
Creating and Customizing Forms

Performance Objectives

Upon successful completion of Chapter 29, you will be able to:

- Insert content controls
- Design a form
- Create a form template
- Insert text, picture, and date drop-down content controls
- Insert instructional text
- Customize content controls
- Protect, print, edit, and customize a template form
- Fill in a form

Many businesses use preprinted forms that generally are filled in by hand or by using a computer. Preprinted forms cost a company money to print and space for storage. With Word 2007, you can create your own forms and eliminate the need to buy and store preprinted forms. In this chapter, you will learn to use ***content controls,*** including plain text, picture, date picker, and drop-down list content controls, to create basic forms. (For information on how to create advanced forms, you will need to refer to Word's Help feature or visit Microsoft's Web site.) You will learn to save your forms as protected documents, create documents from the forms, and enter the requested information.

Note: Before beginning computer exercises for this chapter, copy to your storage medium the Chapter29 folder from the CD that accompanies this textbook and then make Chapter29 the active folder.

Creating a Form

In Word, a ***form*** is a protected document that includes user-defined sections into which a respondent enters information. These user-defined sections are made up of ***content controls*** and ***form fields.*** Content controls limit response options to ensure the collection of desired data. Three types of content controls are available: drop-down boxes, check boxes, or date pickers. Form fields are spaces allotted for a respondent to enter specific text.

The Developer tab, shown in Figure 29.1, contains options for inserting content controls. The Developer tab also contains options that allow you to create forms with legacy tools, which are tools for developing forms that were available in earlier versions of Word. They, too, include options called ***form fields.*** You will create forms with legacy tools in Chapter 30. For the purpose of this chapter and Chapter 30, the term ***data field*** will be used to describe either a content control or a form field.

Figure 29.1 Developer Tab

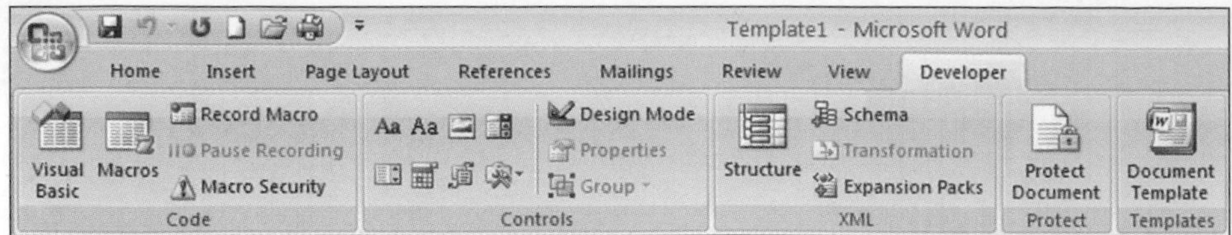

Designing a Form

The goal in creating a form is twofold: to gather all the information necessary to meet your objective and to gather information that is useful and accurate. Thus, the first step in creating a form is to determine the form's purpose. Make a list of all of the information you need to meet your objective. Be careful not to include unnecessary or redundant information, which will frustrate the person who is filling out the form and clutter the form's appearance.

The next step is to plan the layout of the form. The simplest way to design a form is to find an existing form that requests similar information or serves a similar purpose and mimic it. Finding a similar form is not always easy, however, and much of the time you will need to design your form from scratch. If this is the case, you should first sketch your form out on paper. This will give you a guide to follow as you create the form in Word. Some points to consider when designing your form include the following:

- Group like items together in the form. This makes providing complete and accurate information easier for the person filling in the form.
- Place the most important information at the top of the form to increase the likelihood of obtaining the information you desire most. Often a person who is filling in a form fails to complete it entirely before giving it to you.
- Use fonts, colors, lines, and graphics purposefully and sparingly. Overuses of such design elements tend to clutter a form and make it difficult to read.
- Use white space and lines to separate sections of the form. Each section should be clearly defined.

Create a Form Template

1. Click Office button, *New*.
2. Click *My templates...* in *Templates* section.
3. Click Blank Document template.
4. Click *Template* option in *Create New* section.
5. Click OK.

Creating a Form Template

A form is created as a template so a respondent who fills in the form is working on a copy of the form rather than the original. The original is the template form document that is saved as a protected document. In this way, a form can be used over and over again without changing the original. When a form is created from a protected template form document, information can be typed only into the fields designated when the form was created.

Figure 29.2 shows an example of a form document created with the form feature. (You will create this form, shown on p. 738, in Exercise 1A.) You can create forms that contain data fields for text, such as the fields *First Name:*, *Last Name:*, *Address:*, and so on. You can also create forms that contain drop-down lists, dates, or pictures.

To create a new template, click the Office button and then click *New* at the drop-down list. At the New Document dialog box, click *My templates...* in the *Templates* section. At the New dialog box, click the Blank Document template in the list box. Click the *Template* option in the *Create New* section of the dialog box and then click OK. This displays the new template screen where you can type the form and specify data fields.

Displaying the Developer Tab

As noted earlier, the Developer tab contains buttons for inserting data fields into your template form document. To display the Developer tab, click the Office button and then click the Word Options button located toward the bottom of the drop-down list. With *Popular* selected in the Word Options dialog box, click the *Show Developer tab in the Ribbon* check box to insert a check mark and then click OK to close the dialog box. The Developer tab is positioned to the right of the View tab.

QUICK STEPS

Display Developer Tab

1. Click Office button, Word Options.
2. Click *Show Developer tab in the Ribbon* check box.
3. Click OK.

Protect a Template

1. Click Developer tab.
2. Click Protect Document button.
3. Click *Allow only this type of editing in the document* check box.
4. Click down-pointing arrow at right of *Editing restrictions* and then click *Filling in forms.*
5. Click Yes, Start Enforcing Protection button.

Inserting Text Controls

The Controls group in the Developer tab contains two text control buttons, the Rich Text button and the Text button. The Text button inserts a plain text content control that takes on the format of the text that surrounds it. The Rich Text button inserts a content control that supports unique formatting for the content control but is most commonly used when the data that is entered will be used in or linked to another file or document. In this chapter, you will use only plain text content controls.

Protecting a Template

If you want users to enter information in a template but not edit the template itself, protect the template. To do this, click the Protect Document button in the Protect group in the Developer tab. This displays the Restrict Formatting and Editing task pane, shown in Figure 29.3. At this task pane, click in the *Allow only this type of editing in the document* check box to insert a check mark. Click the down-pointing arrow at the right side of the option box in the *Editing restrictions* section and then click *Filling in forms* at the drop-down list. Click the Yes, Start Enforcing Protection button in the

Figure 29.3 Restrict Formatting and Editing Task Pane

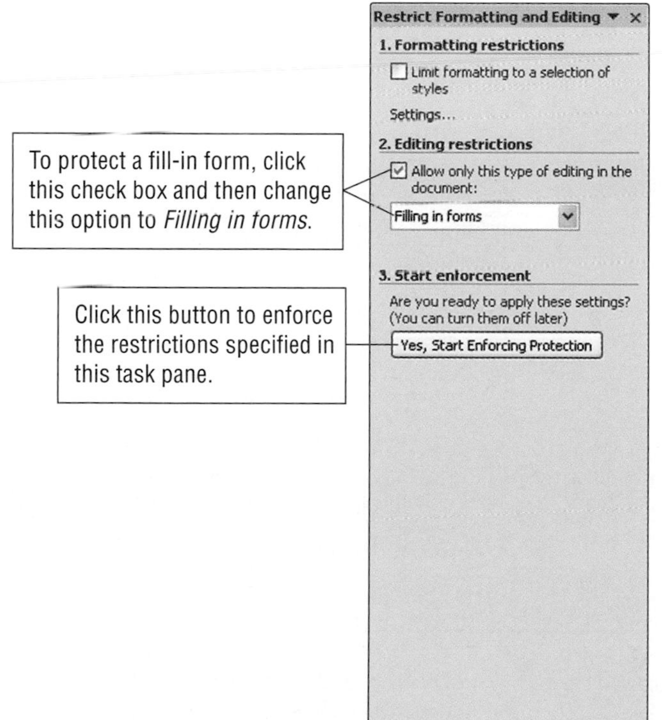

task pane. At the Start Enforcing Protection dialog box, type a password and then close the dialog box. A password is not required to protect a form. If you do not want to password-protect the template, click OK at the Start Enforcing Protection dialog box without entering a password.

Exercise 1A

Creating a Mailing List Template Form

1. Display the Developer tab by completing the following steps:
   a. Click the Office button and then click the Word Options button located toward the bottom of the drop-down list.
   b. With *Popular* selected in the Word Options dialog box, click the *Show Developer tab in the Ribbon* check box to insert a check mark.
   c. Click OK to close the dialog box.

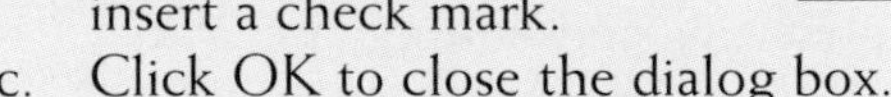

2. Create the form shown in Figure 29.2 (on page 738). To begin, create a template by completing the following steps:
   a. Click the Office button and then click *New*.
   b. At the New Document dialog box, click *My templates...* in the *Templates* section.
   c. At the New dialog box, if necessary, click the Blank Document template in the list box.
   d. Click the *Template* option in the *Create New* section of the dialog box and then click OK.

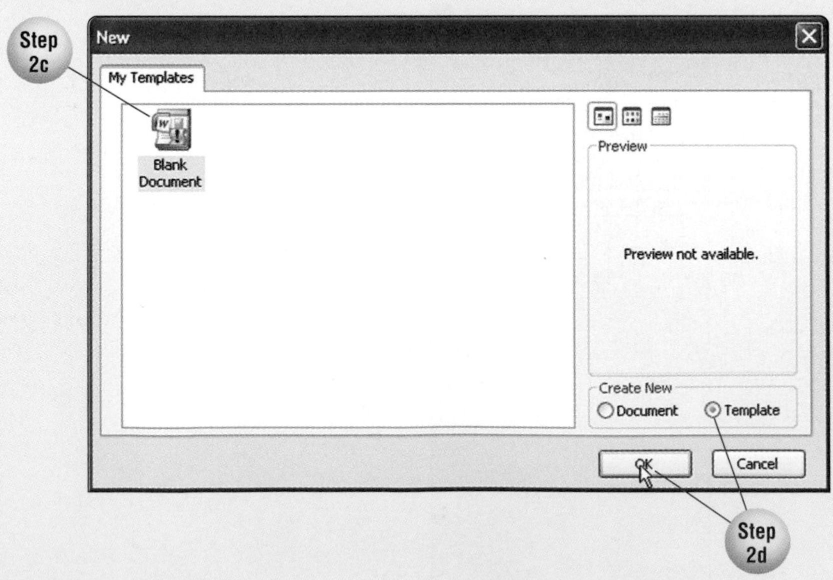

3. At the new template, type the beginning portion of the form shown in Figure 29.2 up to the colon after *First Name:* by completing the following steps:
   a. Click the Page Layout tab and then click the down-pointing arrow at the right side of the *Spacing After* option in the Paragraph group until *0 pt* displays in the measurement box.
   b. Click the Home tab, turn on bold, and then change the font to Arial and the font size to 14 points.
   c. Click the Center button in the Paragraph group, type **STORYTELLER BOOKS**, and then press Enter.
   d. Type **Mailing List Request** and then press Enter twice.
   e. Click the Align Text Left button in the Paragraph group and change the font size to 12 points.
   f. Set left tabs at the 3-inch mark and the 4.5-inch mark on the Ruler.
   g. Type **First Name:** and then turn off bold.
   h. Press the spacebar once.

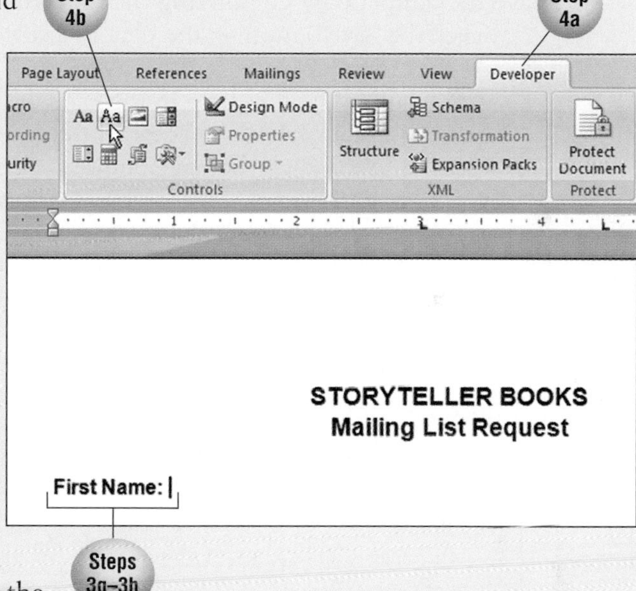

4. Insert a text content control by completing the following steps:
   a. Click the Developer tab.
   b. Click the Text button in the Controls group. (This inserts a plain text content control in the document.)
   c. Press the Right Arrow key to deselect the control.
5. Press the Tab key to move the insertion point to the tab at the 3-inch mark.
6. Turn on bold, type **Last Name:**, and then turn off bold.
7. Press the spacebar once and then click the Text button in the Controls group.
8. Press the Right Arrow key to deselect the control.
9. Press Enter twice.
10. Continue to enter the text and content controls as displayed in Figure 29.2. Remember to turn off bold before inserting the plain text content control. (When you enter the line that contains *City:*, *State:*, and *ZIP Code:*, press Tab to align each item at the tab settings. As you type, content controls and text appear crowded and wrap to the next line. The content controls will not print when you create a document from this template.)
11. Position the insertion point a double space below the last line of the form.
12. Insert the horizontal line by pressing Shift + - (the hyphen key) three times and then pressing the Enter key. (AutoFormat will automatically change the hyphens to a vertical line.)
13. Change the font to 10-point Arial and then type the paragraph of text below the horizontal line as shown in Figure 29.2.
14. Protect the template by completing the following steps:
    a. Click the Developer tab.
    b. Click the Protect Document button in the Protect group.

c. Click the *Allow only this type of editing in the document* check box in the Restrict Formatting and Editing task pane.
d. Click the down-pointing arrow at the right side of the option box in the *Editing restrictions* section of the task pane and then click *Filling in forms* at the drop-down list.
e. Click the Yes, Start Enforcing Protection button.
f. At the Start Enforcing Protection dialog box, click OK. (Creating a password is optional.)
g. Close the Restrict Formatting and Editing task pane.

15. Save the template by completing the following steps:
    a. Click the Save button on the Quick Access toolbar.
    b. At the Templates dialog box, type **XXXMailingListTemplate** in the *File name* text box. (Use your initials in place of the *XXX*.)
    c. Press Enter or click the Save button. (This saves your template with the *.dotx* file extension.)
16. Print and then close **XXXMailingListTemplate.dotx**.

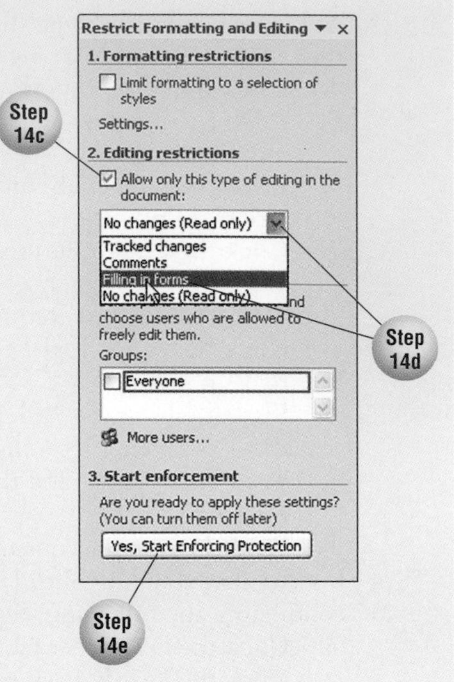

Figure 29.2 Exercise 1A

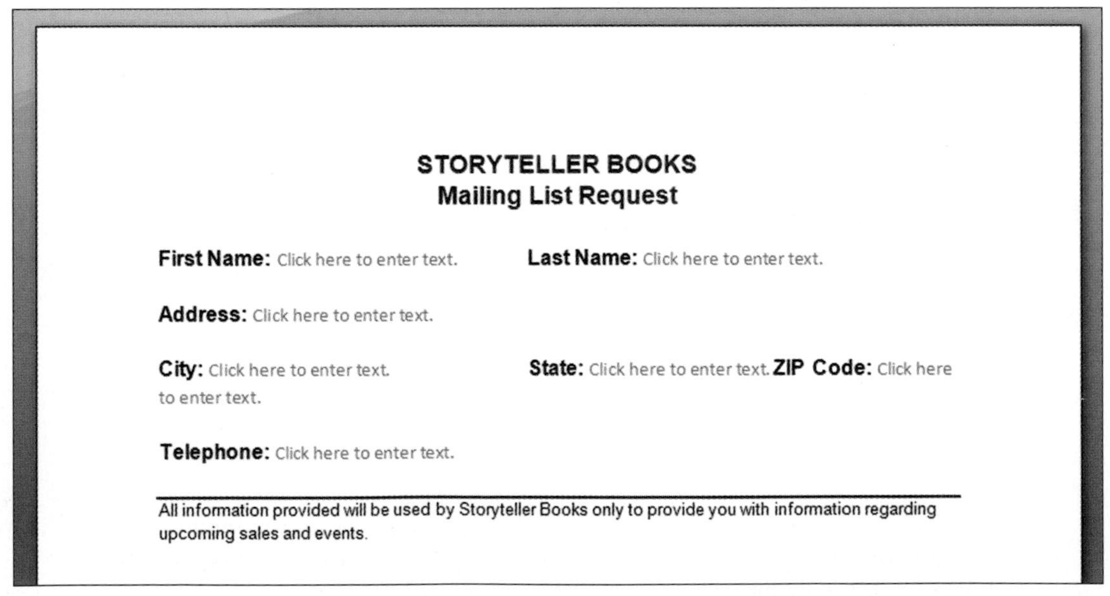

STORYTELLER BOOKS
Mailing List Request

First Name: Click here to enter text. **Last Name:** Click here to enter text.

Address: Click here to enter text.

City: Click here to enter text. **State:** Click here to enter text. **ZIP Code:** Click here to enter text.

Telephone: Click here to enter text.

All information provided will be used by Storyteller Books only to provide you with information regarding upcoming sales and events.

Filling in a Form Document

After you create, protect, and save a template form document, you can use the template to create a personalized document that provides for easy data entry. To fill in a form, open the protected form template document by clicking the Office button and then clicking *New* at the drop-down list. At the New Document dialog box, click *My templates...* in the *Templates* section. At the New dialog box, click the desired template in the list box, make sure *Document* is selected in the *Create New* section, and then click OK.

When you open a protected form template document, the insertion point is automatically inserted in the first data field. To fill in the form, type the information for that data field and then press the Tab key to move the insertion point to the next data field or press Shift + Tab to move the insertion point to the preceding data field.

QUICK STEPS

Fill in a Form Document

1. Click Office button, *New*.
2. Click *My templates...* in *Templates* section.
3. Click desired template.
4. Click OK.

Exercise 1B

Filling in the Mailing List Form

1. Create a form document from the **XXXMailingListTemplate** template. To begin, click the Office button and then click *New* at the drop-down list.
2. At the New Document dialog box, click *My templates...* in the *Templates* section.
3. At the New dialog box, click **XXXMailingListTemplate.dotx**, make sure *Document* is selected in the *Create New* section, and then click OK.

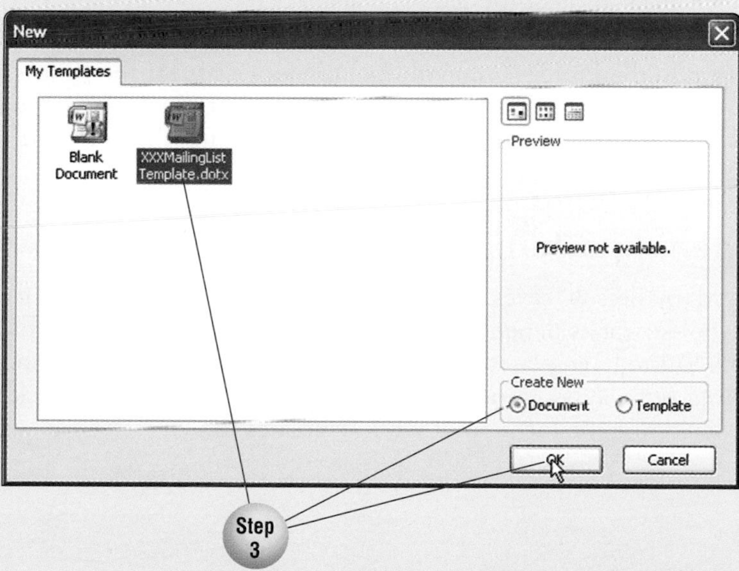

4. With the first text content control selected (the one that displays after *First Name:*), type **Holly**.
5. Press Tab to advance to the next data field and continue entering the information as displayed in Figure 29.4. Make sure the labels are bold and the data field text is not.
6. Save the document by completing the following steps:
   a. Click the Save button on the Quick Access toolbar.
   b. At the Save As dialog box, navigate to the Chapter29 folder on your storage medium.
   c. Type **C29Ex01b** in the *File name* text box and then press Enter.
7. Print and then close **C29Ex01b.docx**.

Figure 29.4 **Exercise 1B**

STORYTELLER BOOKS
Mailing List Request

First Name: Holly **Last Name:** Desmond

Address: 1542 Windett Lane

City: Geneva **State:** IL **ZIP Code:** 60123

Telephone: 630-555-1443

All information provided will be used by Storyteller Books only to provide you with information regarding upcoming sales and events.

QUICK STEPS

Edit a Form Template

1. Click Developer tab.
2. Click Protect Document button.
3. Click Stop Protection button in Restrict Formatting and Editing task pane.
4. Make desired changes.
5. Click Yes, Start Enforcing Protection button.

Editing a Form Template

When you create and then protect a form template, the text in the template cannot be changed. If you need to make changes to a form template, you must open the template document, turn off the protection, and then make the changes. After making the changes, protect the template again before you save it.

To turn off the protection of a template document, click the Protect Document button in the Protect group in the Developer tab. At the Restrict Formatting and Editing task pane, click the Stop Protection button. Make any necessary changes to the document and then protect it again by clicking the Yes, Start Enforcing Protection button.

Opening a Template

Word, by default, saves a template document in the Templates folder. The location of this folder varies depending on your system configuration. In Exercise 1C, you will click Trusted Templates in the *Look in* panel at the left side of the Open dialog box. If your template does not display in the Templates folder, check with your instructor to determine the location of your Templates folder.

Exercise 1C

Editing the Mailing List Template Form

1. Edit the **XXXMailingListTemplate.dotx** as shown in Figure 29.5. To begin, click the Open button on the Quick Access toolbar.
2. Click the Trusted Templates option in the *Look in* panel located at the left side of the Open dialog box.
3. Double-click **XXXMailingListTemplate.dotx** in the dialog box list box.

4. Unprotect the template by completing the following steps:
   a. Click the Developer tab.
   b. Click the Protect Document button in the Protect group.
   c. At the Restrict Formatting and Editing task pane, click the Stop Protection button located toward the bottom of the task pane.
   d. Close the Restrict Formatting and Editing task pane.

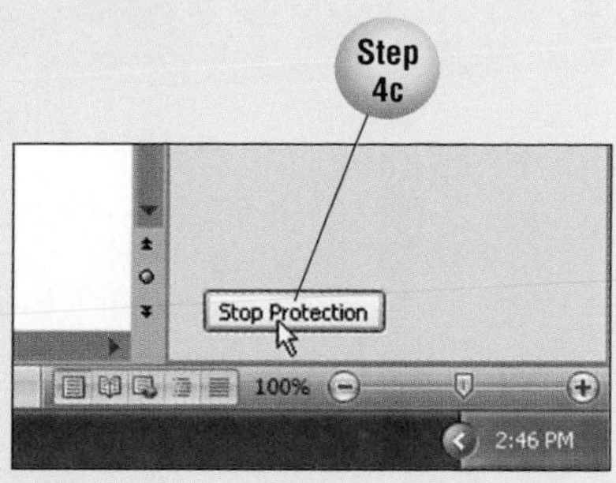

5. Edit a content control and insert another content control by completing the following steps:
   a. Edit the word *Telephone* so it displays as *Home Phone*.
   b. Move the insertion point to the right of the Home Phone text content control.
   c. Press the Tab key.
   d. Turn on bold, type **Cell Phone:**, turn off bold, and then press the spacebar.
   e. Click the Text button in the Controls group.
   f. Move the insertion point so it is positioned at the right side of the *Cell Phone:* content control.
   g. Press the Enter key twice.
   h. Turn on bold, type **E-mail Address:**, turn off bold, and then press the spacebar.
   i. Click the Text button in the Controls group.
6. Protect the document by completing the following steps:
   a. With the Developer tab selected, click the Protect Document button in the Protect group.
   b. Click the Yes, Start Enforcing Protection button.
   c. At the Start Enforcing Protection dialog box, click OK.
   d. Close the Restrict Formatting and Editing task pane.
7. Save and then close **XXXMailingListTemplate.dotx**.

Figure 29.5 Exercise 1C

STORYTELLER BOOKS
Mailing List Request

First Name: Click here to enter text. **Last Name:** Click here to enter text.

Address: Click here to enter text.

City: Click here to enter text. **State:** Click here to enter text. **ZIP Code:** Click here to enter text.

Home Phone: Click here to enter text. **Cell Phone:** Click here to enter text.

E-mail Address: Click here to enter text.

All information provided will be used by Storyteller Books only to provide you with information regarding upcoming sales and events.

Exercise 1D

Filling in the Edited Mailing List Form

1. Create a form document from the **XXXMailingListTemplate.dotx** template by completing the following steps:
   a. Click the Office button and then click *New* at the drop-down list.
   b. At the New Document dialog box, click *My templates...* in the *Templates* section.
   c. At the New dialog box, click **XXXMailingListTemplate.dotx**, make sure *Document* is selected in the *Create New* section, and then click OK.
   d. Type the following text in the specified data fields:
      First Name: **Val**
      Last Name: **Pierobon**
      Address: **1550 South Meridian Street**
      City: **St. Charles**
      State: **IL**
      ZIP: **60123**
      Home Phone: **630-555-0098**
      Cell Phone: **630-555-3423**
      E-mail Address: **vpierobon@emcp.net**

STORYTELLER BOOKS
Mailing List Request

Step 1d

First Name: Val **Last Name:** Pierobon

Address: 1550 South Meridian Street

City: St. Charles **State:** IL **ZIP Code:** 60123

Home Phone: 630-555-0098 **Cell Phone:** 630-555-3423

E-mail Address: vpierobon@emcp.net

All information provided will be used by Storyteller Books only to provide you with information regarding upcoming sales and events.

2. Save the document in the Chapter29 folder on your storage medium with the name **C29Ex01d**.
3. Print and then close **C29Ex01d.docx**.

Creating Forms Using Tables

Word's Table feature is an efficient tool for designing and creating forms. Using tables allows you to set up the framework for your form and provides spaces to enter data fields. Using tables also allows for easy alignment and placement of the elements of the form.

Inserting Instructional Text

Providing respondents who are filling in a form with instructional text can aid in obtaining accurate information. When you create a form, you can add text to each data field, providing specific directions on what information to enter. The instructional text is replaced with the data entered by the respondent.

To insert instructional text, type the instructions at the location where you will insert the text content control. Select the text and then click the Text button in the Controls group in the Developer tab. The instructions are selected and become part of the data field.

Insert Instructional Text
1. Type instructions.
2. Select text.
3. Click Developer tab.
4. Click Text button.

Text

Exercise 2A

Inserting Controls in a Fax Template

1. Create a template by completing the following steps:
   a. Click the Office button and then click *New* at the drop-down list.
   b. At the New Document dialog box, click the *My templates...* option in the Templates section.
   c. At the New dialog box, click *Blank Document* in the list box, click the *Template* option, and then click OK.
2. At the template, insert the **Table13.docx** document by completing the following steps:
   a. Click the Insert tab.
   b. Click the Object button arrow in the Text group and then click *Text from File* at the drop-down list.
   c. At the Insert File dialog box, navigate to the Chapter29 folder on your storage medium and then double-click **Table13.docx**.
3. If the table does not contain blue dashed gridlines between the two cells in the first row (and between other cells and rows in the table), turn on the display of nonprinting table gridlines by completing the following steps:
   a. Click in any cell in the table.
   b. Click the Table Tools Design tab.
   c. Click the Borders button arrow and then click *View Gridlines* at the drop-down list.
4. Insert in the *To:* cell instructional text and a text content control by completing the following steps:
   a. Click the Developer tab.
   b. Click in the *To:* text box and then move the insertion point so it is positioned one space to the right of the colon.
   c. Type **Receiver's name**.
   d. Select *Receiver's name* and then click the Text button in the Controls group.

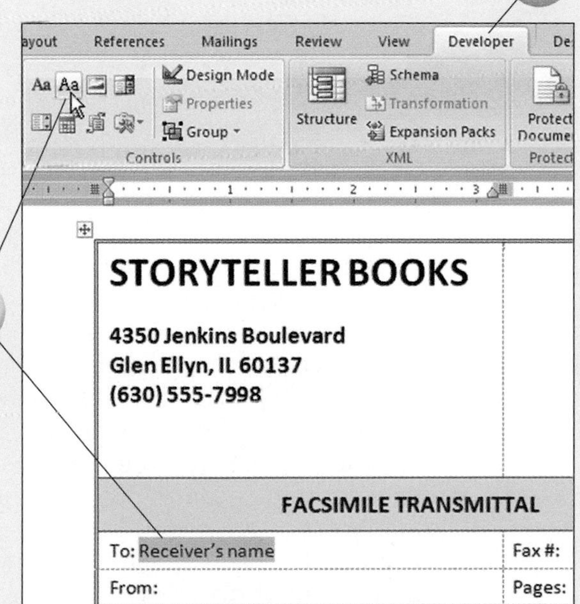

5. Complete steps similar to those in Step 4 to insert the instructional text and text content control in the *Fax #:*, *From:*, *Pages:*, and *Notes:* cells as shown in Figure 29.6.
6. Save the template and name it **XXXFaxTemplate**.

Insert a Picture
1. Click Developer tab.
2. Click Picture Content Control button.
3. Click picture icon.
4. Navigate to desired folder and double-click desired picture file.

Insert a Date Content Control
1. Click Developer tab.
2. Click Date Picker button.

Picture Content Control

Date Picker

Inserting Pictures

You can insert a picture content control that displays a picture, clip art image, drawing, shape, chart, table, or SmartArt diagram. Insert a picture or other visual element in a form using the Picture Content Control button in the Controls group in the Developer tab. Click this button, and a picture frame containing a picture icon is inserted where the insertion point is located. Click the picture icon, and the Insert Picture dialog box displays. At this dialog box, navigate to the folder containing the picture you want to insert and then double-click the picture file. The picture image fills the picture content control.

Using the Date Picker

You can insert a date content control that displays a calendar when a user clicks the down-pointing arrow at the right side of the control. The user can navigate to the desired month and year and then click the date. To insert a date content control, click the Date Picker button in the Controls group in the Developer tab.

Exercise 2B

Inserting a Picture and a Date Picker Content Control

1. With **XXXFaxTemplate.dotx** open, insert a picture content control by completing the following steps:
   a. Click in the upper right corner of the table (this moves the insertion point to the right cell in the first row).
   b. If necessary, click the Developer tab.
   c. Click the Picture Content Control button in the Controls group.
   d. Click the picture icon that displays in the middle of the picture content control in the cell.
   e. At the Insert Picture dialog box, navigate to the Chapter29 folder on your storage medium and then double-click **Books.jpg**.

2. Insert a date content control by completing the following steps:
   a. Click in the *Date:* cell and then move the insertion point so it is positioned one space to the right of the colon.

b. Click the Date Picker button in the Controls group.
3. Protect the template by completing the following steps:
   a. Click the Protect Document button in the Protect group.
   b. Click the *Allow only this type of editing in the document* check box in the Restrict Formatting and Editing task pane.
   c. Click the down-pointing arrow at the right side of the option box in the *Editing restrictions* section of the task pane and then click *Filling in forms* at the drop-down list.
   d. Click the Yes, Start Enforcing Protection button.
   e. At the Start Enforcing Protection dialog box, click OK.
   f. Close the Restrict Formatting and Editing task pane.
4. Save and then close **XXXFaxTemplate.dotx**.

Figure 29.6 Exercises 2A and 2B

STORYTELLER BOOKS

4350 Jenkins Boulevard
Glen Ellyn, IL 60137
(630) 555-7998

FACSIMILE TRANSMITTAL

To: Receiver's name	Fax #: Fax number
From: Sender's name	Pages: # of pages
Date: Click here to enter a date.	
Notes: Enter notes	

Exercise 2C

Filling in the Fax Form

1. Create a form document from the **XXXFaxTemplate.dotx** template by completing the following steps:
   a. Click the Office button and then click *New* at the drop-down list.
   b. At the New Document dialog box, click *My templates...* in the *Templates* section.
   c. At the New dialog box, click **XXXFaxTemplate.dotx**, make sure *Document* is selected in the *Create New* section, and then click OK.

d. Click the *To:* text. (This selects the content control text in the cell.)
e. Type **Wilma Sell** and then press the Tab key.
f. Type **701-555-9876** and then press the Tab key.
g. Type **Jim Trueman** and then press the Tab key.
h. Type **3 including cover** and then press the Tab key.
i. With the *Date:* content control text selected, click the down-pointing arrow at the right side of the content control and then click the Today button that displays below the calendar.
j. Press the Tab key.
k. Type **Please review these documents for information regarding the completion of the User's Center. I will contact you next week for comment.**

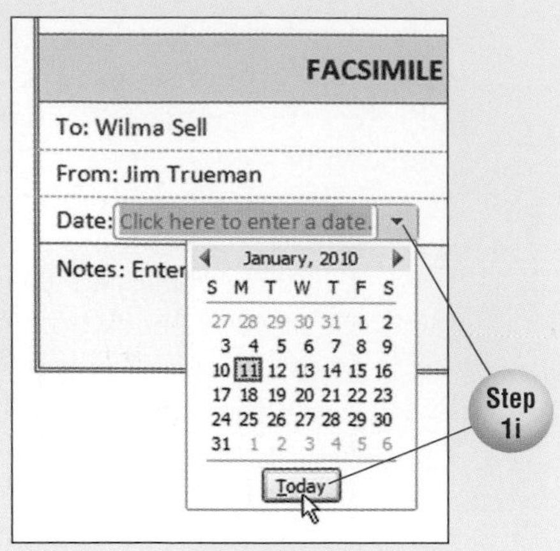

2. Save the document in the Chapter29 folder on your storage medium and name it **C29Ex02**.
3. Print and then close **C29Ex02.docx**.

Create a Drop-Down List
1. Create a template form document.
2. Type field label.
3. Click Developer tab.
4. Click Drop-Down List button.

Specify Drop-Down List Properties
1. Select drop-down list content control.
2. Click Developer tab.
3. Click Properties button.
4. Click Add button.
5. Type desired choice.
6. Click OK.
7. Continue clicking Add and typing desired choices.
8. Click OK to close Control Properties dialog box.

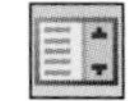
Drop-Down List

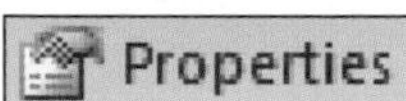

Creating Drop-Down Lists

When you create a form, you may want the respondent to choose from specific options rather than type data into the data field. To make only specific options available, create a data field with a drop-down list. To create a drop-down list, create a template form document, type the field label, and then click the Drop-Down List button in the Controls group in the Developer tab.

Specifying Drop-Down List Properties

To create the list of items from which a respondent will choose, select the control and then click the Properties button in the Controls group in the Developer tab. This displays the Content Control Properties dialog box, shown in Figure 29.7. Each content control includes properties you can change with options at the Content Control Properties dialog box. The content of the dialog box varies depending on the control selected.

To add drop-down list choices, click the Add button in the dialog box. At the Add Choice dialog box, type the first choice in the *Display Name* text box and then click OK. At the Content Control Properties dialog box, click the Add button and then continue until you have entered all choices.

Figure 29.7 Content Control Properties Dialog Box for Drop-Down List Content Control

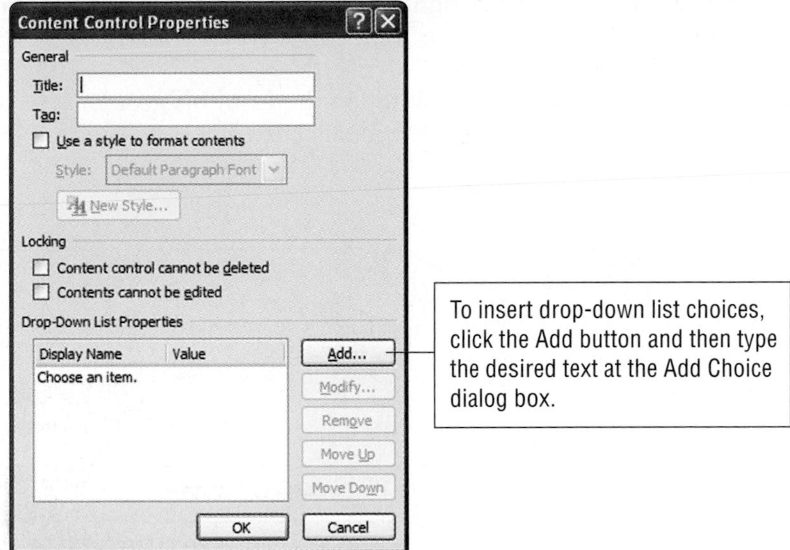

You can modify the list by clicking the desired option in the *Drop-Down List Properties* section and then clicking the Modify button. You can also rearrange the position of an item in the list by selecting the desired item and then clicking either the Move Up or the Move Down button. You can remove an item from the list by selecting the item and then clicking the Remove button.

To fill in a form with a drop-down list data field, select the drop-down list content control, click the down-pointing arrow at the right side of the data field, and then click the desired option. You can also hold down the Alt key, press the Down Arrow key until the desired option is selected, and then press the Enter key.

Word also provides the Combo Box button in the Controls group in the Developer tab. A combo box is similar to a drop-down list but allows the respondent to edit or change the choices in the list. For information on using combo boxes, refer to Word's Help feature.

Exercise 3A

Inserting Controls in a Survey Template

1. Create a template by completing the following steps:
   a. Click the Office button and then click *New* at the drop-down list.
   b. At the New Document dialog box, click the *My templates...* option in the *Templates* section.
   c. At the New dialog box, click *Blank Document* in the list box, click the *Template* option, and then click OK.
2. At the template, insert the **Table14.docx** document. (Use the Object button in the Insert tab.)

3. Click in the cell immediately right of the *How often do you read?* cell and then insert a drop-down list by completing the following steps:
   a. Click the Developer tab.
   b. Click the Drop-Down List button in the Controls group.
   c. With the content control selected, click the Properties button in the Controls group.

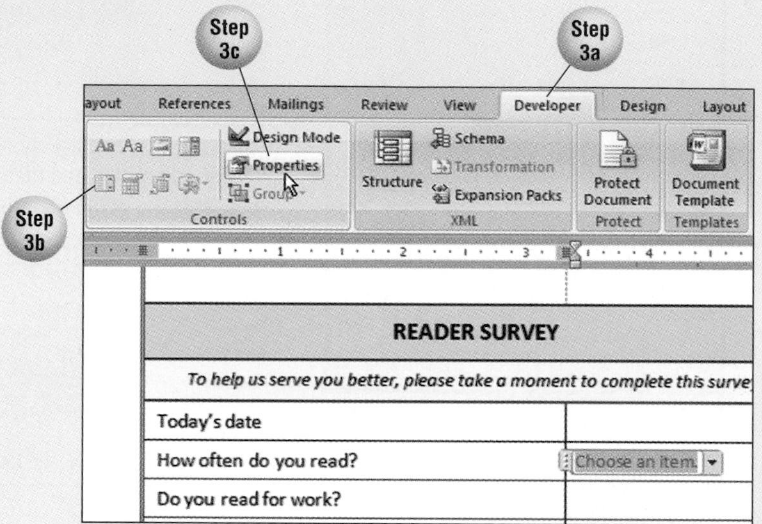

   d. At the Content Control Properties dialog box, click the Add button.
   e. At the Add Choice dialog box, type **Daily** in the *Display Name* text box and then click OK.

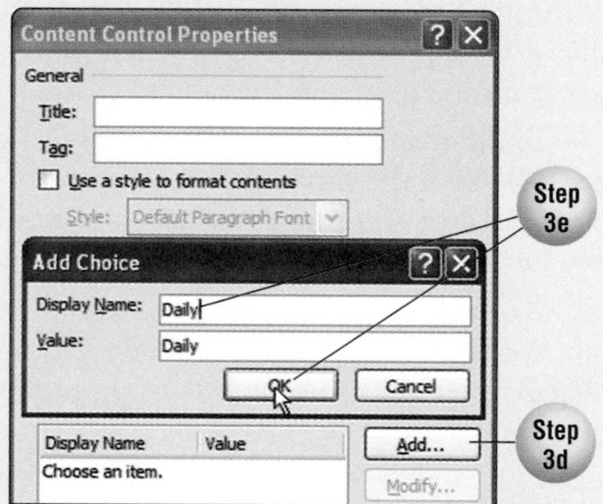

4. Complete steps similar to those in Steps 3d and 3e to insert the remaining drop-down list choices:
   Weekly
   Monthly
   I don't read.
5. Click OK to close the Content Control Properties dialog box.
6. Click in the cell immediately right of the *Do you read for work?* cell and then insert a drop-down list with the following choices:
   Yes
   No
   Sometimes
7. Click in the cell immediately right of the *Do you read for pleasure or entertainment?* cell and then insert a drop-down list with the following choices:
   Yes
   No
   Sometimes
8. Click in the cell immediately right of the *What do you prefer to read for work?* cell and then insert a drop-down list with the following choices:
   Manuals
   Journals
   Textbooks

9. Click in the cell immediately right of the *What do you prefer to read for entertainment?* cell and then insert a drop-down list with the following choices:
   Books
   Magazines
   Newspapers
10. Click in the cell immediately right of the *Where do you prefer to shop?* cell and then insert a drop-down list with the following choices:
    In store
    Online
11. Insert a content control in the *Comments:* cell by completing the following steps:
    a. Click in the *Comments:* cell and then move the insertion point so it is positioned one space to the right of the colon.
    b. Type **Type comments here.**
    c. Select *Type comments here.* and then click the Text button in the Controls group.
    d. Click in a different cell to deselect the content control.
12. Save the template and name it **XXXSurveyTemplate**.

Customizing Picture Content Control Properties

When you use a picture control in a form template, consider locking the picture. With the picture locked, the insertion point does not stop at the picture data field when the respondent presses the Tab key to move to the next data field. Lock a picture by selecting the picture data field and then clicking the Properties button in the Controls group in the Developer tab. At the Content Control Properties dialog box, shown in Figure 29.8, insert a check mark in the *Contents cannot be edited* check box. If you do not want the picture content control to be deleted, insert a check mark in the *Content control cannot be deleted* check box.

Figure 29.8 Content Control Properties Dialog Box for Picture Content Control

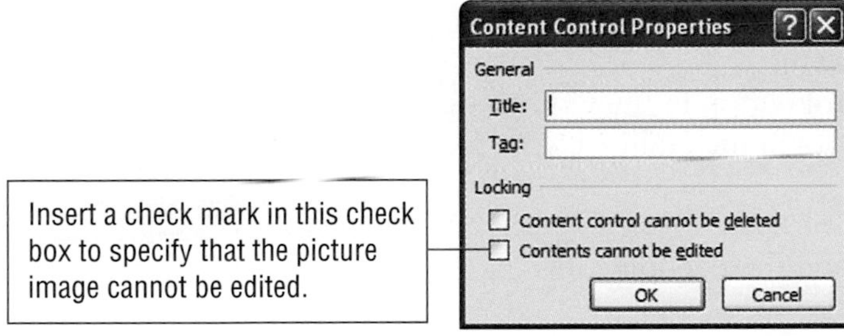

Customizing Date Picker Content Control Properties

The date picker content control has a default format of *m/d/yyyy* for inserting the date. You can customize the date format with options at the Content Control Properties dialog box, shown in Figure 29.9. Choose the desired date format in the list box in the *Date Picker Properties* section of the dialog box and then click OK.

Figure 29.9 Content Control Properties Dialog Box for Date Picker Content Control

Specify the date format by choosing an option in this list box.

Exercise 3B

Customizing Picture and Date Picker Content Control Properties

1. With **XXXSurveyTemplate.dotx** open, insert a picture content control and lock the control by completing the following steps:
   a. Click in the cell in the upper right corner of the table.
   b. If necessary, click the Developer tab.
   c. Click the Picture Content Control button in the Controls group.
   d. Click the picture icon that displays in the middle of the picture content control in the cell.
   e. At the Insert Picture dialog box, navigate to the Chapter29 folder on your storage medium and then double-click **Books.jpg**.
   f. Click the Properties button in the Controls group.
   g. At the Content Control Properties dialog box, click the *Contents cannot be edited* check box to insert a check mark.
   h. Click OK to close the dialog box.

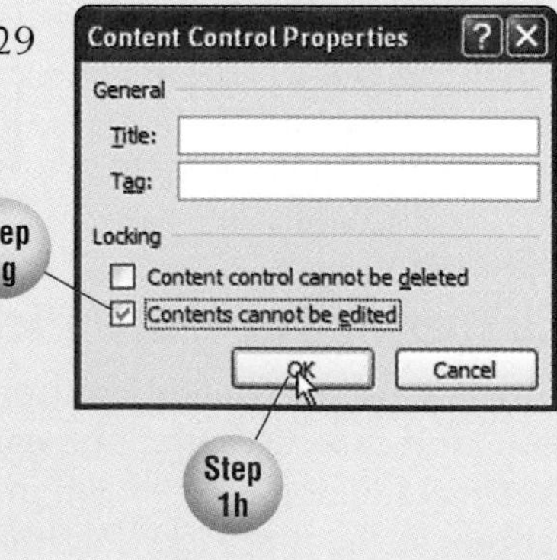

2. Insert a date content control and customize the control by completing the following steps:
   a. Click in the cell immediately right of the *Today's date* cell.
   b. If necessary, click the Developer tab.

c. Click the Date Picker button in the Controls group.
d. Click the Properties button in the Controls group.
e. Click the third option from the top in the list box in the *Date Picker Properties* section of the Content Control Properties dialog box.
f. Click OK to close the dialog box.

3. Protect the template by completing the following steps:
   a. Click the Protect Document button in the Protect group.
   b. Click the *Allow only this type of editing in the document* check box in the Restrict Formatting and Editing task pane.
   c. Click the down-pointing arrow at the right side of the option box in the *Editing restrictions* section of the task pane and then click *Filling in forms* at the drop-down list.
   d. Click the Yes, Start Enforcing Protection button.
   e. At the Start Enforcing Protection dialog box, click OK.
   f. Close the Restrict Formatting and Editing task pane.
4. Save and then close **XXXSurveyTemplate.dotx**.

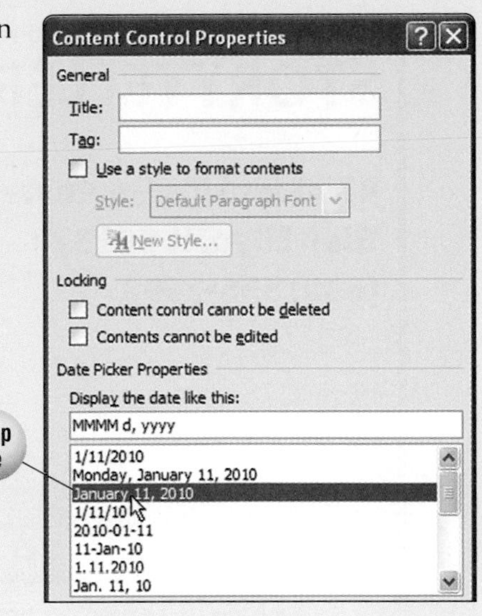

Exercise 3C

Filling in the Survey Form

1. Create a form document from the **XXXSurveyTemplate.dotx** template by completing the following steps:
   a. Click the Office button and then click *New* at the drop-down list.
   b. At the New Document dialog box, click *My templates...* in the *Templates* section.
   c. At the New dialog box, click **XXXSurveyTemplate.dotx**, make sure *Document* is selected in the *Create New* section, and then click OK.
2. With the *Date:* content control text selected, click the down-pointing arrow at the right side of the content control and then click the Today button that displays below the calendar.
3. Press the Tab key. (This selects the drop-down list content control in the cell immediately right of *How often do you read?*)
4. Choose an option from the drop-down list by clicking the down-pointing arrow at the right side of the drop-down list content control and then clicking *Daily*.
5. Fill in the remainder of the form with options as shown in Figure 29.10.
6. Save the document in the Chapter29 folder on your storage medium with the name **C29Ex03**.
7. Print and then close **C29Ex03.docx**.

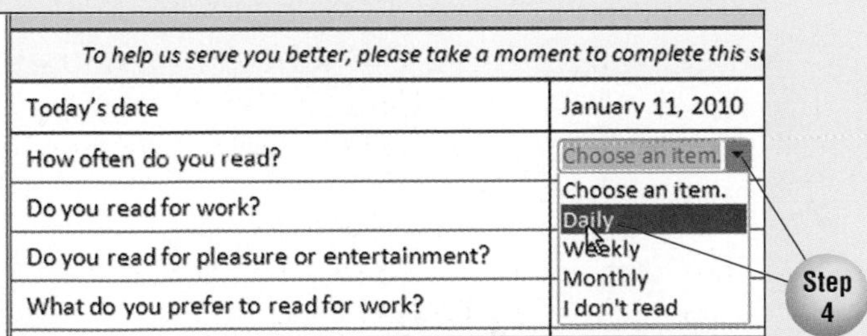

Figure 29.10 Exercise 3C

STORYTELLER BOOKS **4350 Jenkins Boulevard** **Glen Ellyn, IL 60137** **(630) 555-7998**	
READER SURVEY	
To help us serve you better, please take a moment to complete this survey.	
Today's date	(Current date)
How often do you read?	Daily
Do you read for work?	Yes
Do you read for pleasure or entertainment?	Yes
What do you prefer to read for work?	Journals
What do you prefer to read for entertainment?	Books
Where do you shop?	In store
Comments: I do most of my shopping in the store, but I am going to start ordering online in the near future.	

Chapter Summary

- A form is created as a template document with data fields that can be filled in with different information each time the template document is used.
- Three basic steps are involved in creating a form: 1) designing the form document based on a template and building the structure of the form; 2) inserting data fields where information is to be entered with the keyboard; and 3) saving the form as a protected document.
- Create a new template by clicking the Office button and then clicking *New*. Click *My templates...* in the *Templates* section of the New Document dialog box. At the New dialog box, click the Blank Document template in the list box, click the *Template* option in the *Create New* section, and then click OK.
- Insert content controls in a form with buttons in the Developer tab. Display the Developer tab by clicking the Office button and then clicking Word Options. At the Word Options dialog box with *Popular* selected, click the *Show Developer tab in the Ribbon* check box and then click OK.
- Word saves template documents in the Templates subfolder within the Microsoft Office program.
- Use the Text button in the Controls group in the Developer tab to insert a plain text content control.
- Use options at the Restrict Formatting and Editing task pane to protect a template. You can protect a template so a respondent can enter information in the form but cannot edit the form.
- Display the Restrict Formatting and Editing task pane by clicking the Protect Document button in the Protect group in the Developer tab.
- Fill in a form by typing information in the desired field and then pressing the Tab key to move to the next data field or pressing Shift + Tab to move to the previous data field.
- Open a template for editing at the Templates dialog box. Display this dialog box by clicking Trusted Templates in the *Look in* panel in the Open dialog box.
- To edit a form template, stop protection of the template, make any desired changes, and then protect the template.
- You can include instructional text in a content control. To do this, type the instructional text, select the text, and then click the Text button in the Controls group in the Developer tab.
- Use the Picture Content Control button in the Controls group in the Developer tab to insert a picture content control in a form.
- Use the Date Picker button in the Controls group in the Developer tab to insert a date content control in a form.
- Create a drop-down list of choices for a data field with the Drop-Down List button in the Controls group in the Developer tab.
- Click the Properties button in the Controls group in the Developer tab to change the properties of the selected content control. This displays the Content Control Properties dialog box. The contents of the dialog box vary depending on what content control is selected.

Commands review

FEATURE	RIBBON TAB, GROUP	BUTTON, OPTION	KEYBOARD SHORTCUT
Plain Text Content Control	Developer, Controls	Aa	
Restrict Formatting and Editing task pane	Developer, Protect		
Next data field			Tab
Previous data field			Shift + Tab
Templates folder		, Open, Trusted Templates	
Picture Content Control	Developer, Controls		
Date Picker Content Control	Developer, Controls		
Drop-Down List	Developer, Controls		
Content Control Properties	Developer, Controls	Properties	

Reviewing key points

Completion: In the space provided at the right, indicate the correct term, command, or number.

1. By default, Word saves template documents in this folder. ________________
2. This group in the Developer tab contains content control buttons. ________________
3. Use this button in the Developer tab to insert a plain text content control. ________________
4. Click the Protect Document button in the Developer tab, and this task pane displays. ________________
5. When filling in a form, press this key to move to the next data field. ________________
6. To display the default Templates folder, click this option in the *Look in* panel at the Open dialog box. ________________

7. Click this button in the Developer tab to insert a picture frame containing a picture icon. ____________________
8. Click this button in the Developer tab to insert a date content control. ____________________
9. Insert this type of control in a form if you want the respondent to choose from a specific list of options. ____________________
10. Customize a date content control with options at this dialog box. ____________________

Applying your skills

Assessment 1 Create and Fill in a Book Order Form

1. Create the form shown in Figure 29.11 with the following specifications:
   a. Create the form as a template by clicking the Office button and then clicking *New*. At the New Document dialog box, click *My templates...* in the *Templates* section. At the New dialog box, click the Blank Document template in the list box. Click the *Template* option in the *Create New* section of the dialog box and then click OK.
   b. At the template, change the line spacing to single and the spacing after paragraphs to zero.
   c. Insert the **Books.jpg** image using the Picture button in the Insert tab. Size and move the image so it displays as shown in Figure 29.11. Change the text wrapping of the image to *Behind Text*.
   d. Set the company name STORYTELLER BOOKS in 24-point Calibri bold and set the remainder of the text in 11-point Calibri bold. Insert the book symbol at the Symbol dialog box with the *Wingdings* font selected. (The book symbol is in the first row of the symbol list box.)
   e. Insert plain text content controls one space after the colon in each of the following: *Name:*, *Book Title:*, *Author:*, *E-mail:*, *Telephone:*, and *Notes:*.
   f. Insert the horizontal line by holding down the Shift key, pressing the hyphen key three times, and then pressing the Enter key.
2. Protect the template (you do not need to enter a password).
3. Save the template and name it **XXXBookRequestTemplate**.
4. Print and then close **XXXBookRequestTemplate.dotx**.

Table 31.1 **Outlining Tab Buttons**

Button	Name	Action
	Promote to Heading 1	Promotes text to highest level of the outline.
	Promote	Promotes heading (and its body text) by one level; promotes body text to the heading level of the preceding heading.
Level 1	Outline Level	Assigns and displays current level of text.
	Demote	Demotes heading by one level; demotes body text to the heading level below the preceding heading.
	Demote to Body Text	Demotes heading to body text.
	Move Up	Moves selected paragraph(s) to appear after first visible paragraph that follows selected paragraph(s).
	Expand	Expands first heading level below currently selected heading.
	Collapse	Collapses body text into heading and then collapses lowest heading levels into higher heading levels.
Show Level: All Levels	Show Level	Displays all headings through lowest level chosen.
Show Text Formatting	Show Text Formatting	Displays outline with or without character formatting.
Show First Line Only	Show First Line Only	Switches between displaying all body text or only first line of each paragraph.

To change a heading that is identified as normal text to a level 1 heading, position the insertion point on any character in the heading and then click the Promote to Heading 1 button in the Outline Tools group in the Outlining tab. This applies the Heading 1 style to the heading. To change a paragraph to a level 2 heading, position the insertion point anywhere within the text and then click the Demote button. This applies the Heading 2 style to the text.

Exercise 1A

Applying Level Formatting in Outline View

1. Open the **OutlineReport01.docx** document located in the Chapter31 folder on your storage medium and then save the document and name it **C31Ex01**.
2. Change to the Outline view by clicking the View tab and then clicking the Outline button in the Document Views group.

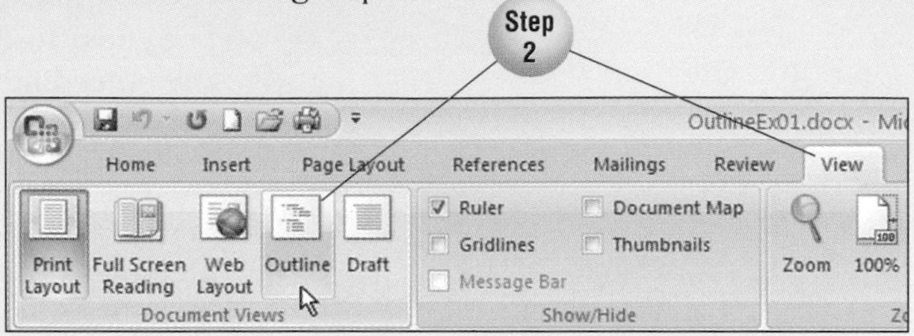

3. Promote and demote heading levels by completing the following steps:
   a. Position the insertion point anywhere in the title *UNAUTHORIZED ACCESS* and then click the Promote to Heading 1 button in the Outline Tools group in the Outlining tab. (This displays *Level 1* in the Outline Level button.)

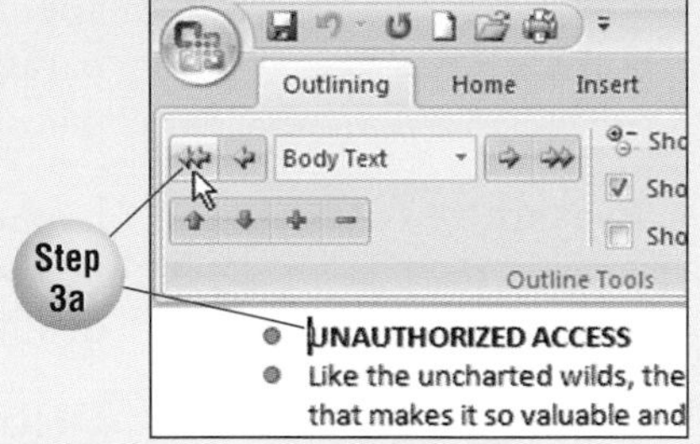

   b. Position the insertion point anywhere in the heading *User IDs and Passwords* and then click the Demote button in the Outline Tools group. (This displays *Level 2* in the Outline Level button.)
   c. Position the insertion point anywhere in the heading *System Backdoors* and then click the Promote button in the Outline Tools group.
   d. Position the insertion point anywhere in the heading *Spoofing* and then click the Promote button in the Outline Tools group.
   e. Position the insertion point anywhere in the heading *Spyware* and then click the Promote button.
4. Save **C31Ex01.docx**.

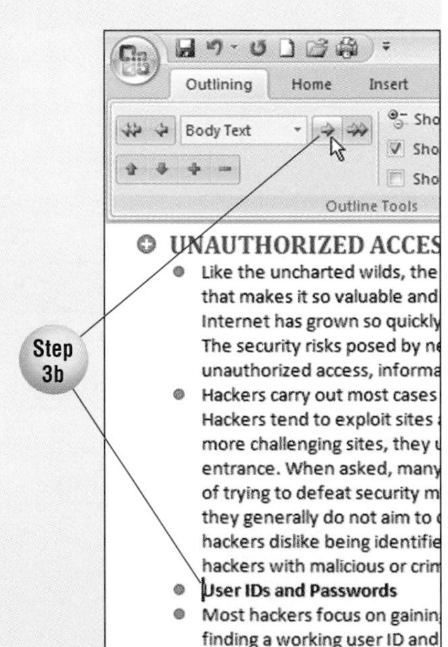

You can also promote or demote a heading in the Outline view by dragging the selection symbol that displays before the heading to the left or right 0.5 inch. The selection symbol for a level heading displays as a circle containing a plus symbol and the selection symbol for body text displays as a circle. For example, to demote text identified as level 1 to level 2, position the arrow pointer on the selection symbol (circle containing a plus symbol) that displays before the level 1 text until the pointer turns into a four-headed arrow. Hold down the left mouse button, drag the mouse to the right until a gray vertical line displays down the screen, and then release the mouse button. Complete similar steps to promote a heading.

Exercise 1B

Promoting and Demoting Headings in a Document

1. With **C31Ex01.docx** open and displayed in Outline view, promote the section 2 title to level 1 by completing the following steps:
   a. Position the mouse pointer on the selection symbol (small, gray circle) that displays before the title *INFORMATION THEFT* until the mouse pointer turns into a four-headed arrow.
   b. Hold down the left mouse button, drag the mouse to the left until a gray vertical line displays toward the left side of the page as shown in the image at the right, and then release the mouse button. (Check to make sure *Level 1* displays in the Outline Level button.)
2. Promote the *Device Security* heading to level 2 by completing the following steps:
   a. Position the mouse pointer on the selection symbol (small, gray circle) that displays before the *Device Security* heading until the mouse pointer turns into a four-headed arrow.
   b. Hold down the left mouse button, drag the mouse to the right until a gray vertical line displays as shown in the image at the right, and then release the mouse button. (Check to make sure *Level 2* displays in the Outline Level button.)
3. Promote the heading *Data Browsing* to level 2 by completing the following steps:
   a. Position the mouse pointer on the selection symbol that displays before the heading *Data Browsing* until the mouse pointer turns into a four-headed arrow.
   b. Hold down the left mouse button, drag the mouse to the left, and then release the mouse button. (Check to make sure *Level 2* displays in the Outline Level button.)
4. Save **C31Ex01.docx**.

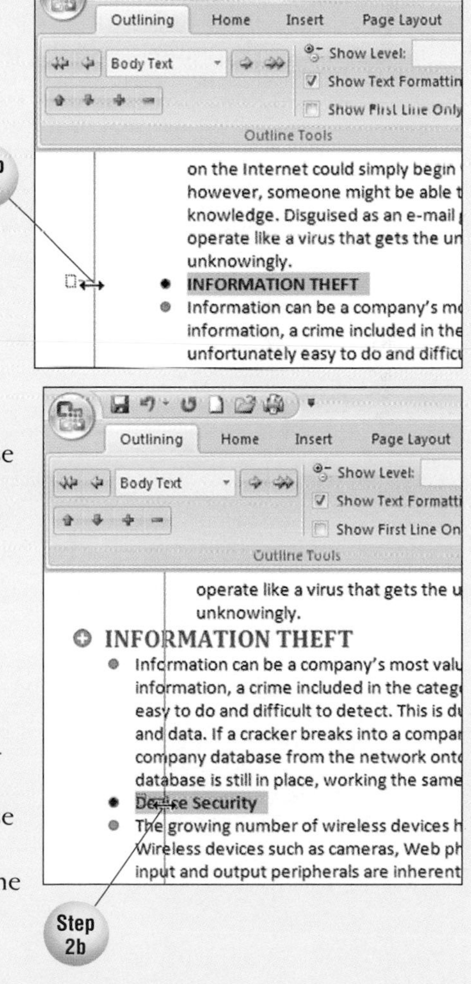

Collapsing and Expanding a Document

One of the major benefits of working in the Outline view is the ability to see a condensed outline of your document without all of the text in between titles, headings, or subheadings. Word lets you collapse a level in an outline so any text or subsequent lower levels disappear temporarily. When you collapse levels, viewing the outline of a document is much easier. For example, when an outline is collapsed, you can see an overview of the entire document and move easily to different locations in the document. You can also move titles and headings and their subordinate headings to new locations in the outline.

The ability to collapse and expand headings in an outline provides flexibility in using Word's Outline feature. One popular use of this capability is to move quickly from one portion of a document to another. For example, if you are working at the beginning of a lengthy document and want to move to a particular section, but you cannot remember the name of the heading in that section or the page number on which it is located, switch to the Outline view, collapse the entire outline, position the insertion point in the desired heading, and then expand the outline.

Another popular use of the collapse and expand feature is in maintaining consistency between various headings. While creating a particular heading, you may need to refer to the previous heading. To do this, switch to the Outline view, collapse the outline, and the previous heading is visible.

To collapse the entire document, click the down-pointing arrow at the right side of the Show Level button in the Outline Tools group in the Outlining tab and then click the level desired at the drop-down list. For example, if the document contains three levels, click *Level 3* at the drop-down list. Figure 31.2 shows the **C31Ex01.docx** document collapsed so only titles and headings display. When a title or heading containing text below it is collapsed, a gray horizontal line displays beneath the heading (as shown in Figure 31.2).

Figure 31.2 Collapsed Document

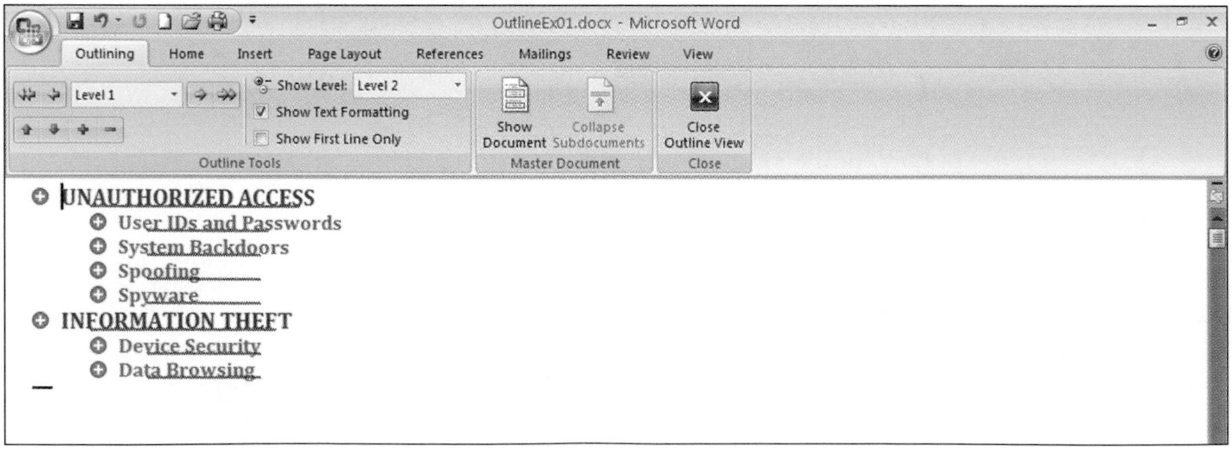

Exercise 1C

Collapsing a Document

1. With **C31Ex01.docx** open, make sure the document displays in Outline view and then press Ctrl + Home to move the insertion point to the beginning of the document.
2. Click the down-pointing arrow at the right side of the Show Level button in the Outline Tools group and then click *Level 2* at the drop-down list.

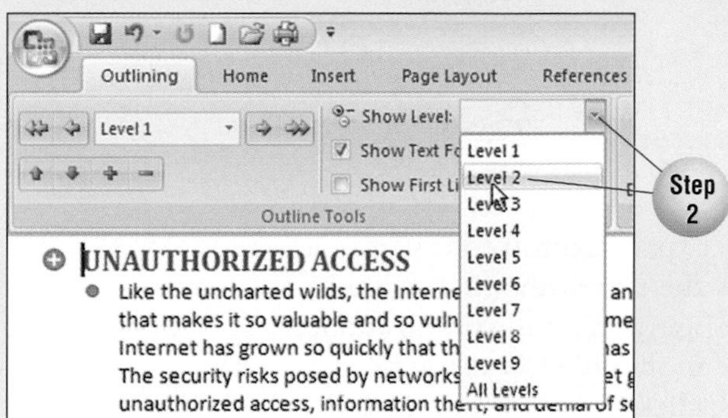

3. With the outline collapsed, click the selection symbol that displays before *Spoofing* and then press the Delete key. (This deletes the heading and text below the heading.)
4. Save and then print **C31Ex01.docx**. (This will print the collapsed outline, not the entire document.)
5. Click the Close Outline View button.
6. Close **C31Ex01.docx**.

To collapse all of the text beneath a particular heading (including the text following any subsequent headings), position the insertion point within the heading, and then click the Collapse button in the Outline Tools group in the Outlining tab. To make the text appear again, click the Expand button in the Outline Tools group.

Exercise 2A

Collapsing and Expanding an Outline

1. Open the **OutlineReport02.docx** document located in the Chapter31 folder on your storage medium and then save the document and name it **C31Ex02**.
2. Click the View tab and then click the Outline button in the Document Views group.
3. Promote the title *COMPUTER VIRUSES* to level 1.
4. Demote the heading *Types of Viruses* to level 2.
5. Promote the heading *Methods of Virus Operation* to level 2.
6. Promote the title *HARDWARE AND SOFTWARE SECURITY RISKS* to level 1.
7. Demote the heading *Systems Failure* to level 2.
8. Promote the heading *Employee Theft* to level 2.
9. Promote the heading *Cracking Software* to level 2.

10. Collapse and expand the document by completing the following steps:
    a. Position the insertion point anywhere in the title *COMPUTER VIRUSES* and then click the Collapse button in the Outline Tools group in the Outlining tab. (This collapses the text in the first section so only the title and headings display.)

    b. Click the Expand button to expand the display of the text in the first section.
    c. With the insertion point still positioned anywhere in the title *COMPUTER VIRUSES*, click the down-pointing arrow at the right side of the Show Level button and then click *Level 1* at the drop-down list. (This displays only the two titles.)

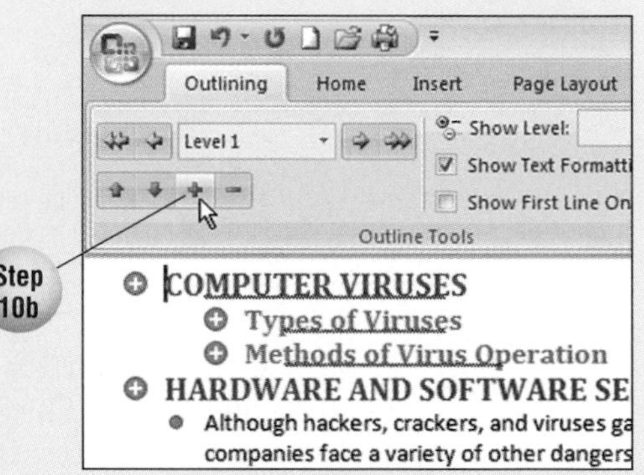

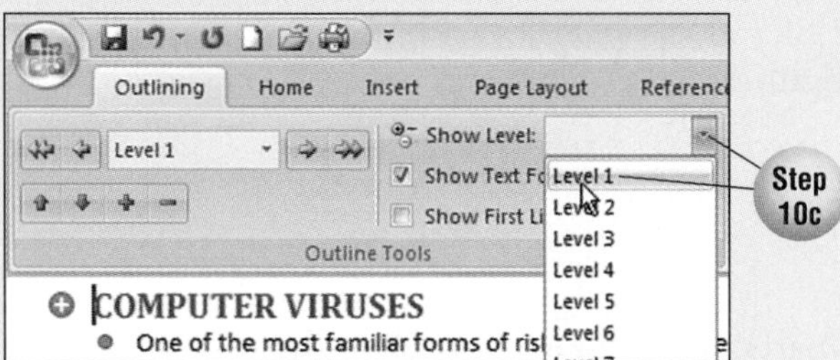

    d. Click the down-pointing arrow at the right side of the Show Level button and then click *Level 2* at the drop-down list. (This displays the titles and headings.)
    e. Click the Expand button in the Outline Tools group.
    f. Click the *Show First Line Only* check box in the Outline Tools group. (This displays only the level headings and the first line of each paragraph in the document.)
    g. Click the *Show First Line Only* check box to remove the check mark.
    h. Click the down-pointing arrow at the right side of the Show Level button and then click *Level 2* at the drop-down list. (This displays the titles and headings.)

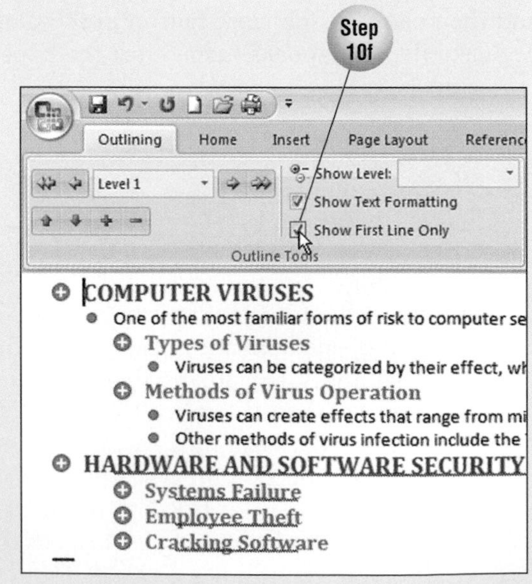

i. Click the selection symbol that precedes *Employee Theft*.
j. With the heading selected, press the Delete key. (This deletes the heading and all text below the heading.)
k. Save and then print the document. (This will print the collapsed outline, not the entire document.)
l. Click the down-pointing arrow at the right side of the Show Level button and then click *All Levels* at the drop-down list. (This displays the entire document.)

11. Save **C31Ex02.docx**.

Organizing an Outline

Collapsing and expanding headings within an outline is only part of the versatility offered by Word's Outline feature. It also offers you the ability to rearrange an entire document by reorganizing an outline. Whole sections of a document can quickly be rearranged by moving the headings at the beginning of those sections. The text that is collapsed beneath the headings is moved at the same time.

For example, to move a level 2 heading below other level 2 headings, you would collapse the outline, select the level 2 heading to be moved, and then click the Move Down button in the Outline Tools group until the level 2 heading is in the desired position.

If headings are collapsed, you only need to select the heading and move it to the desired location. Any subsequent text that is hidden is moved automatically. You can also move headings in a document by positioning the mouse pointer on the selection symbol that displays before the desired heading until the pointer turns into a four-headed arrow. Hold down the mouse, drag the heading to the desired location, and then release the mouse button. As you drag the mouse, a gray horizontal line displays in the document with an arrow attached. Use this horizontal line to help you move the heading to the desired location.

Exercise 2B

Moving Headings in a Document

1. With **C31Ex02.docx** open, make sure the document displays in Outline view, and then press Ctrl + Home to move the insertion point to the beginning of the document.
2. Click the down-pointing arrow at the right side of the Show Level button and then click *Level 1* at the drop-down list.
3. Move the *HARDWARE AND SOFTWARE SECURITY RISKS* section to the beginning of the document by completing the following steps:
   a. Click any character in the title *HARDWARE AND SOFTWARE SECURITY RISKS*.
   b. Click the Move Up button in the Outline Tools group in the Outlining tab.

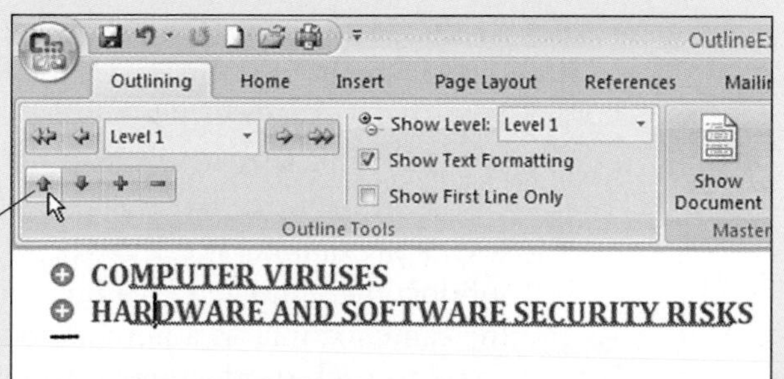

4. Move the heading *Systems Failure* below *Cracking Software* by completing the following steps:
   a. Click the down-pointing arrow at the right side of the Show Level button and then click *Level 2* at the drop-down list.
   b. Position the mouse pointer on the selection symbol that precedes the heading *Systems Failure* until the pointer turns into a four-headed arrow.
   c. Hold down the left mouse button, drag the mouse down until the gray horizontal line with the arrow attached is positioned below *Cracking Software*, and then release the mouse button.
   d. Deselect the text.
5. Save and then print **C31Ex02.docx**. (This will print the collapsed outline, not the entire document.)
6. Click the down-pointing arrow at the right side of the Show Level button and then click *All Levels* at the drop-down list.
7. Click the Close Outline View button.
8. Save and then close **C31Ex02.docx**.

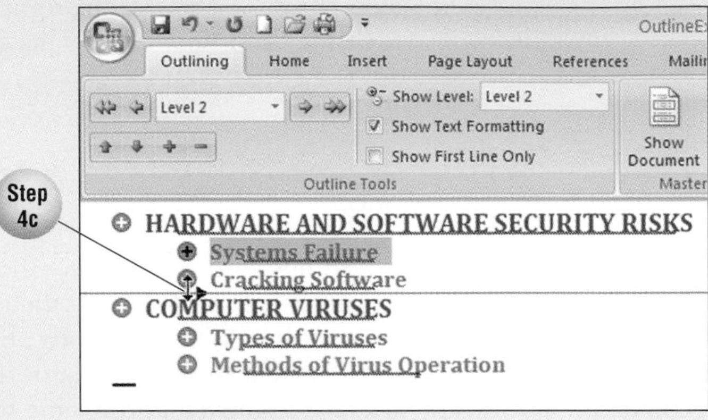

Creating a Master Document and Subdocuments

For projects containing a variety of parts or sections such as a reference guide or book, consider using a *master document*. A master document contains a number of separate documents referred to as *subdocuments*. A master document might be useful in a situation where several people are working on one project. Each person prepares a document for his or her part of the project and then the documents are included in a master document. A master document allows for easier editing of subdocuments. Rather than opening a large document for editing, you can open a subdocument, make changes, and those changes are reflected in the master document. Create a new master document or format an existing document as a master document with buttons in the Master Document group in the Outlining tab.

Creating a Master Document

To create a master document, change to the Outline view, assign heading levels to titles and headings in the document, and then click the Show Document button in the Master Document group. Select the headings and text to be divided into a subdocument and then click the Create button in the Master Document group. Text specified as a subdocument displays surrounded by a thin gray line border and a subdocument icon displays in the upper left corner of the border.

Word creates a subdocument for each heading at the top level within the selected text. For example, if selected text begins with Heading 1 text, Word creates a new subdocument at each Heading 1 in the selected text. Save the master document in the same manner as a normal document. Word automatically assigns a document name to each subdocument using the first characters in the subdocument heading.

Opening and Closing a Master Document and Subdocument

Open a master document at the Open dialog box in the same manner as a normal document. Subdocuments in a master document display collapsed in the master document as shown in Figure 31.3. This figure displays the master document named **C31Ex03.docx** you will create in Exercise 3A. Notice that Word automatically converts subdocument names into hyperlinks. To open a subdocument, hold down the Ctrl key and then click the subdocument hyperlink.

Figure 31.3 C31Ex03.docx

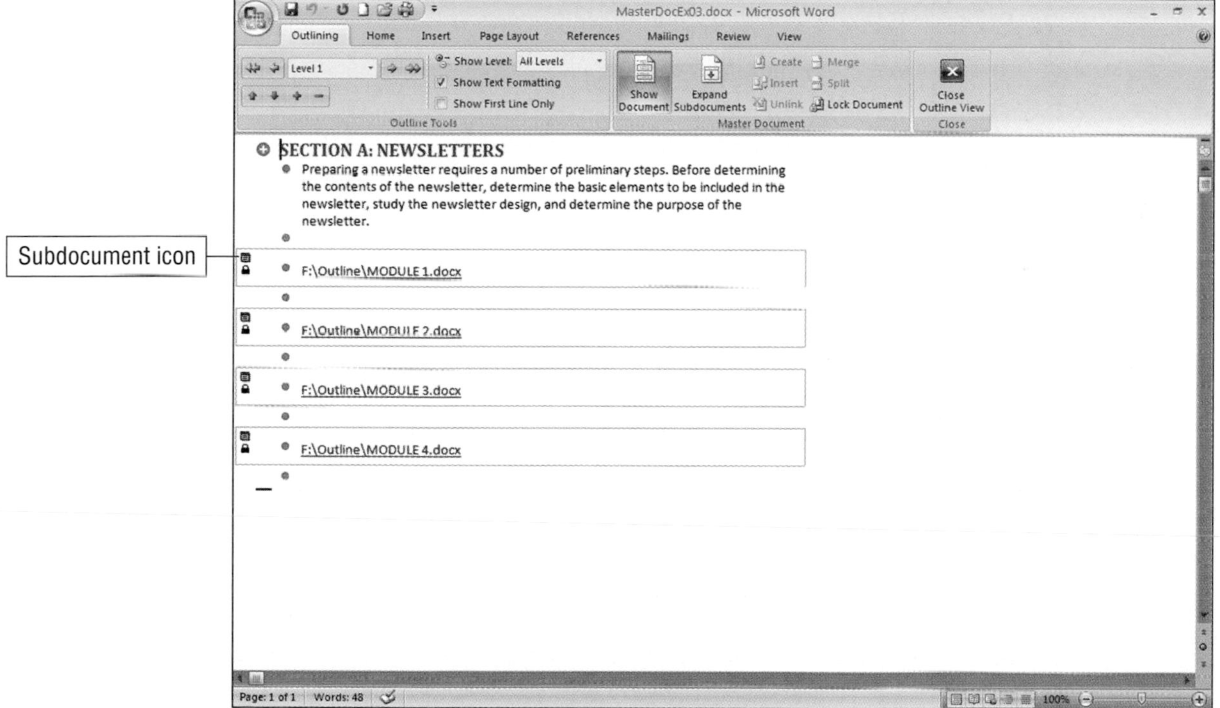

Close a subdocument in the normal manner and, if you made any changes, you will be asked if you want to save the changes. Closing a subdocument redisplays the master document and the subdocument hyperlink displays in a different color (identifying that the hyperlink has been used).

Expanding/Collapsing Subdocuments

Open a master document and subdocuments are automatically collapsed. To expand subdocuments, click the Expand Subdocuments button in the Master Document group in the Outlining tab. This expands the subdocuments and also changes the Expand Subdocuments button to the Collapse Subdocuments button.

Exercise 3A

Creating a Master Document and Expanding/Collapsing Subdocuments

1. At a blank document, type the text shown in Figure 31.4. (Press the Enter key after typing the text.)
2. With the insertion point positioned at the end of the document, insert the document named **MasterDocReport04.docx** located in the Outline folder on your storage medium. (Do this with the Object button in the Insert tab.)
3. With the insertion point positioned at the end of the document, insert the document named **MasterDocReport05.docx**. (Do this with the Object button in the Insert tab.)
4. Move the insertion point to the beginning of the document.
5. Change to Outline view.
6. Promote or demote the headings in the document as identified below:

SECTION A: NEWSLETTERS	=	Level 1
MODULE 1: DEFINING NEWSLETTER ELEMENTS	=	Level 2
Designing a Newsletter	=	Level 3
Defining Basic Newsletter Elements	=	Level 3
MODULE 2: PLANNING A NEWSLETTER	=	Level 2
Defining the Purpose of a Newsletter	=	Level 3
MODULE 3: DESIGNING A NEWSLETTER	=	Level 2
Applying Desktop Publishing Guidelines	=	Level 3
MODULE 4: CREATING NEWSLETTER LAYOUT	=	Level 2
Choosing Paper Size and Type	=	Level 3
Choosing Paper Weight	=	Level 3
Creating Margins for Newsletters	=	Level 3

7. Save the document and name it **C31Ex03**.
8. Create subdocuments with the module text by completing the following steps:
   a. Position the mouse pointer on the selection symbol that displays immediately left of the heading *MODULE 1: DEFINING NEWSLETTER ELEMENTS* until the pointer turns into a four-headed arrow and then click the left mouse button.
   b. Scroll through the document until the *MODULE 4: CREATING NEWSLETTER LAYOUT* heading displays.
   c. Hold down the Shift key, position the mouse pointer on the selection symbol immediately left of the title until the pointer turns into a four-headed arrow, and then click the left mouse button. (This selects all of the text in modules 1, 2, 3, and 4.)

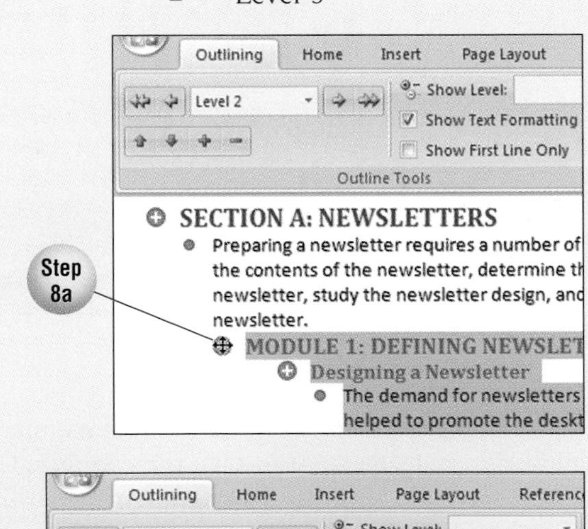

d. With the text selected, click the Show Document button in the Master Document group in the Outlining tab.
e. Click the Create button in the Master Document group.

9. Save and then close **C31Ex03.docx**.
10. Open **C31Ex03.docx**.
11. Print **C31Ex03.docx** by completing the following steps:
    a. Click the Quick Print button on the Quick Access toolbar.
    b. At the question asking if you want to open the subdocuments, click No. (The document will print collapsed as shown in the document screen.)
12. Edit the MODULE 1 subdocument by completing the following steps:
    a. Hold down the Ctrl key and then click the F:\Chapter31\MODULE 1.docx hyperlink.
    b. With the **MODULE 1.docx** document displayed, edit the title so it reads *MODULE 1: DEFINING ELEMENTS*.
    c. Change the heading *Designing a Newsletter* so it displays as *Designing*.
    d. Change the heading *Defining Basic Newsletter Elements* so it displays as *Defining Basic Elements*.
13. Save the subdocument by clicking the Save button on the Quick Access toolbar.
14. Close the subdocument.
15. Expand the subdocuments by clicking the Expand Subdocuments button in the Master Document group in the Outlining tab.
16. Print page 1 of the master document.
17. Collapse the subdocuments by clicking the Collapse Subdocuments button in the Master Document group in the Outlining tab.
18. Save and then close **C31Ex03.docx**.

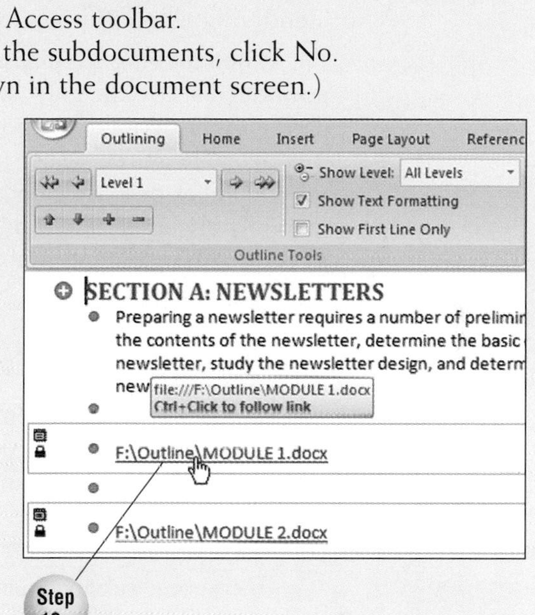

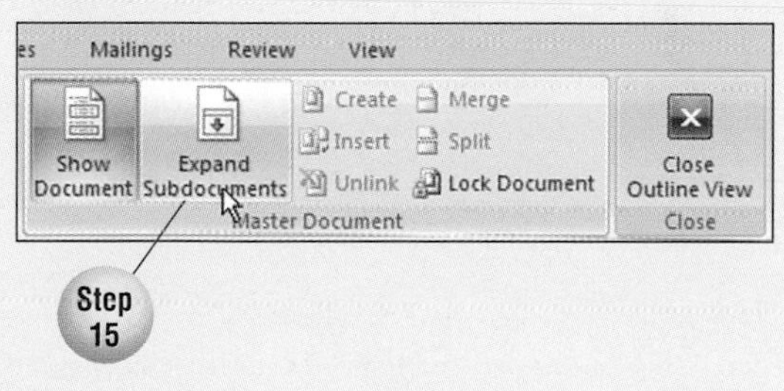

Figure 31.4 **Exercise 3**

SECTION A: NEWSLETTERS

Preparing a newsletter requires a number of preliminary steps. Before determining the contents of the newsletter, determine the basic elements to be included in the newsletter, study newsletter design, and determine the purpose of the newsletter.

Rearranging Subdocuments

Many of the features of a master document are similar to an outline. For example, expanding and collapsing an outline is very similar to expanding and collapsing subdocuments. Also, like headings in an outline, you can move or rearrange subdocuments in a master document.

To rearrange the order of a subdocument, collapse the subdocuments. Position the mouse pointer on the subdocument icon, hold down the left mouse button (mouse pointer turns into a four-headed arrow), drag to the desired location, and then release the mouse button. As you drag with the mouse, a dark gray horizontal line displays identifying where the subdocument will be inserted.

When moving a collapsed subdocument, the dark gray horizontal line must be positioned above the gray circle that displays above a subdocument. If you position the dark gray horizontal line between the gray circle and the top border of a collapsed subdocument, Word will display a message telling you that you cannot change a locked subdocument or master document. With the dark gray horizontal line positioned immediately above the subdocument border, Word assumes you want to insert the selected subdocument into the subdocument. Word will not allow this because subdocuments are locked.

Splitting/Combining Subdocuments

You can split a subdocument into smaller subdocuments or combine subdocuments into one. To split a subdocument, expand subdocuments, select the specific text within the subdocument, and then click the Split button in the Master Document group in the Outlining tab. Word assigns a document name based on the first characters in the subdocument heading.

To combine subdocuments, expand subdocuments and then click the subdocument icon of the first subdocument to be combined. Hold down the Shift key and then click the subdocument icon of the last subdocument (subdocuments must be adjacent). With the subdocuments selected, click the Merge button in the Master Document group. Word saves the combined subdocuments with the name of the first subdocument.

Exercise 3B

Rearranging and Splitting Subdocuments

1. Open **C31Ex03.docx**.
2. Move the Module 4 subdocument above the Module 3 subdocument by completing the following steps:
   a. Position the arrow pointer on the subdocument icon that displays to the left of the F:\Chapter31\MODULE 4.docx subdocument. (The pointer turns into an arrow pointing up and to the right.)

b. Hold down the left mouse button, drag up so the dark gray horizontal line displays between the MODULE 2 and MODULE 3 subdocuments (above the gray circle between the modules), and then release the mouse button.

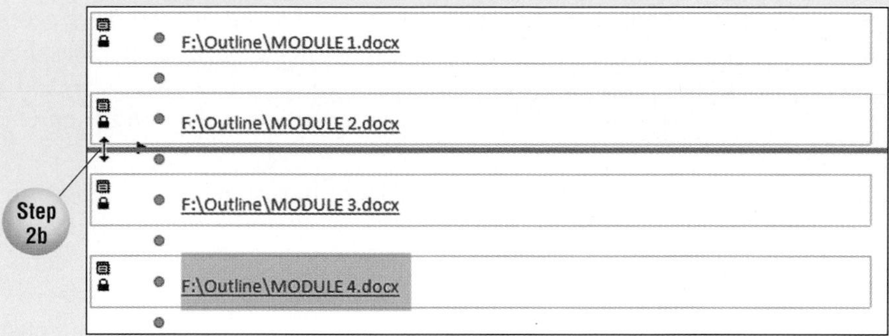

3. Print **C31Ex03.docx**. (At the prompt asking if you want to open the subdocuments, click No.)
4. Delete the F:\Chapter31\MODULE 3.docx subdocument by completing the following steps:
   a. Click the subdocument icon that displays to the left of the F:\Chapter31\MODULE 3.docx subdocument.
   b. Press the Delete key.
5. Split the MODULE 1 subdocument by completing the following steps:
   a. Click the Expand Subdocuments button in the Document View group in the Outlining tab.
   b. Move the insertion point to the MODULE 1 subdocument.
   c. In the MODULE 1 subdocument, edit the heading *Defining Basic Elements* so it displays as *MODULE 2: DEFINING BASIC ELEMENTS*. (You may need to scroll down the document to display this heading.)
   d. Change the level of the heading *MODULE 2: DEFINING BASIC ELEMENTS* from level 3 to level 2.
   e. Position the mouse pointer on the selection symbol that displays immediately left of the heading *MODULE 2: DEFINING BASIC ELEMENTS* until the pointer turns into a four-headed arrow and then click the left mouse button.

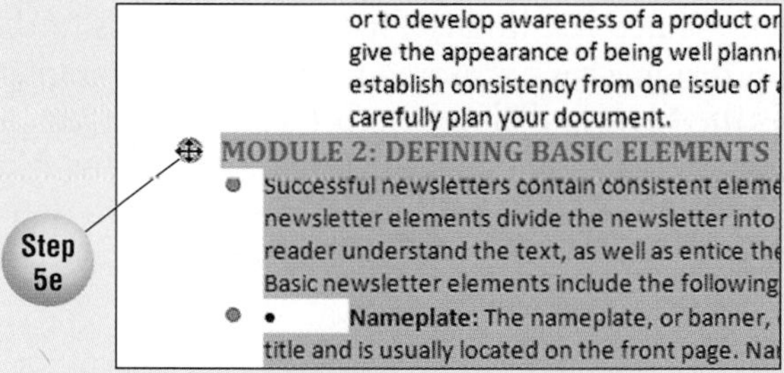

   f. With the text selected, click the Split button in the Master Document group in the Outlining tab.
   g. Click the Collapse Subdocuments button in the Master Document group. At the question asking if you want to save the changes to the master document, click OK.

6. Save and then print **C31Ex03.docx**. (The master document will print with the subdocuments collapsed.)
7. Close **C31Ex03.docx**.

Recording a Macro

Recording a macro involves turning on the macro recorder, performing the steps to be recorded, and then turning off the recorder. Both the View tab and the Developer tab contain buttons for recording a macro. If the Developer tab does not display in the Ribbon, turn on the display by inserting a check mark in the *Show Developer tab in the Ribbon* option in the Word Options dialog box with *Popular* selected in the left panel. (Display this dialog box by clicking the Office button and then clicking the Word Options button.)

To record a macro, click the Record Macro button in the Code group in the Developer tab. You can also click the View tab, click the Macros button arrow in the Macros group, and then click *Record Macro* at the drop-down list. This displays the Record Macro dialog box shown in Figure 31.5. At the Record Macro dialog box, type a name for the macro in the *Macro name* text box. A macro name must begin with a letter and can contain only letters and numbers. Type a description for the macro in the *Description* text box located at the bottom of the dialog box. A macro description can contain a maximum of 255 characters and may include spaces.

By default, Word stores a macro in the Normal template document. Macros stored in this template are available for any document based on the Normal template. In a company or school setting where computers may be networked, consider storing macros in personalized documents or templates. Specify the location for macros with the *Store macro in* option at the Record Macro dialog box (refer to Figure 31.5).

After typing the macro name, specifying where the macro is to be stored, and typing a description, click OK or press Enter to close the Record Macro dialog box. This displays the document screen, a macro icon displays toward the left side of the Status bar, and the mouse displays with a cassette icon attached. In the document, perform the actions to be recorded and when the steps are complete, click the Stop Recording button (previously the Record Macro button) located in the Code group in the Developer tab or click the macro icon that displays toward the left side of the Status bar.

When you record macros in exercises, you will be instructed to name the macros beginning with your initials. An exercise step may instruct you, for example, to "record a macro named XXXInd01." Insert your initials in the macro name instead of the *XXX*. Recorded macros are stored in the Normal template document by default and display at the Macros dialog box. If the computer you are using is networked, macros recorded by other students will also display at the Macros dialog box. Naming a macro with your initials will enable you to distinguish your macros from the macros of other users.

Figure 31.5 Record Macro Dialog Box

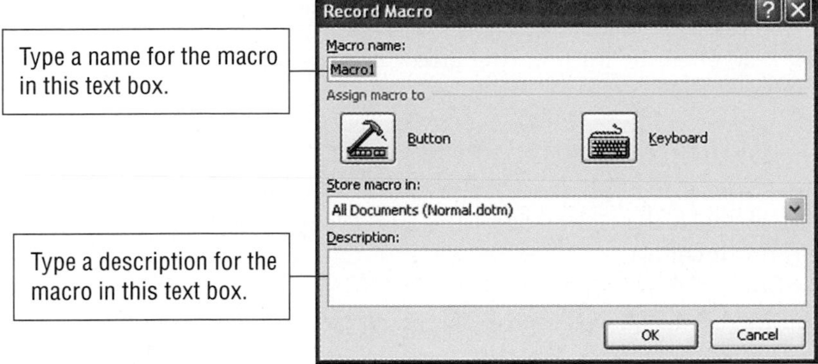

Exercise 4A

Recording Macros

1. Turn on the display of the Developer tab by completing the following steps (skip these steps if the Developer tab is visible):
   a. Click the Office button and then click Word Options at the drop-down list.
   b. Click the *Show Developer tab in the Ribbon* check box to insert a check mark.
   c. Click OK.

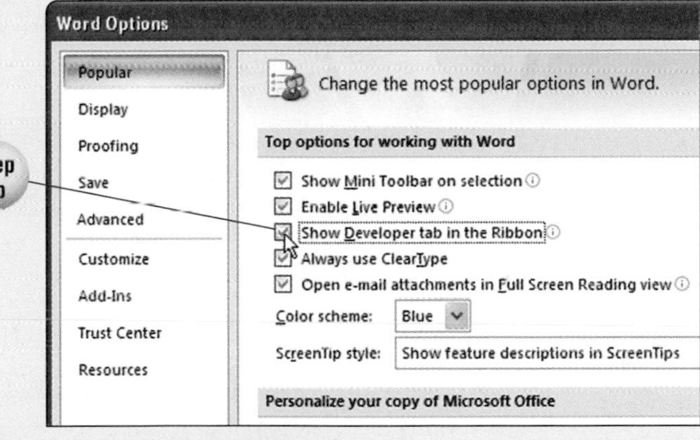

2. Record a macro named XXXInd01 (where your initials are used instead of *XXX*) that indents text in a paragraph 0.5 inch and hang indents second and subsequent lines of the paragraph by completing the following steps:
   a. At a blank document, click the Developer tab.
   b. Click the Record Macro button in the Code group in the Developer tab.
   c. At the Record Macro dialog box, type **XXXInd01** in the *Macro name* text box.
   d. Click inside the *Description* text box and then type **Indent text 0.5 inch and hang indent text.** (If text displays in the *Description* text box, select the text first, and then type the description.)
   e. Click OK.

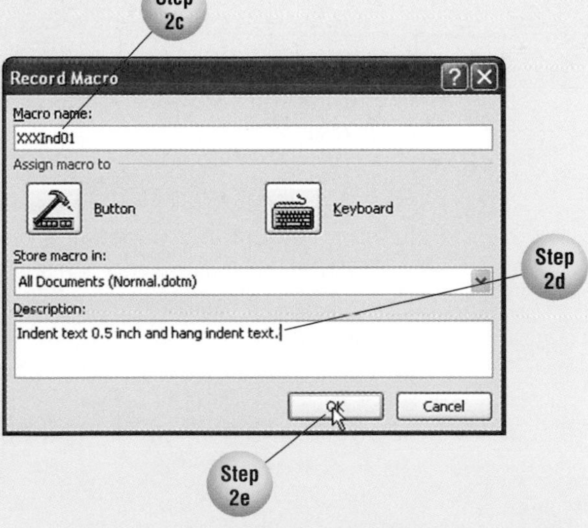

f. At the document, click the Home tab.
g. Click the Paragraph group dialog box launcher.
h. At the Paragraph dialog box, click the up-pointing arrow at the right side of the *Left* option until *0.5"* displays.
i. Click the down-pointing arrow at the right side of the *Special* option box and then click *Hanging* at the drop-down list.
j. Click the down-pointing arrow at the right side of the *After* text box until *0 pt* displays.
k. Click the down-pointing arrow at the right side of the *Line spacing* option box and then click *Single* at the drop-down list.
l. Click OK.
m. Click the macro icon on the Status bar to turn off the macro recording.

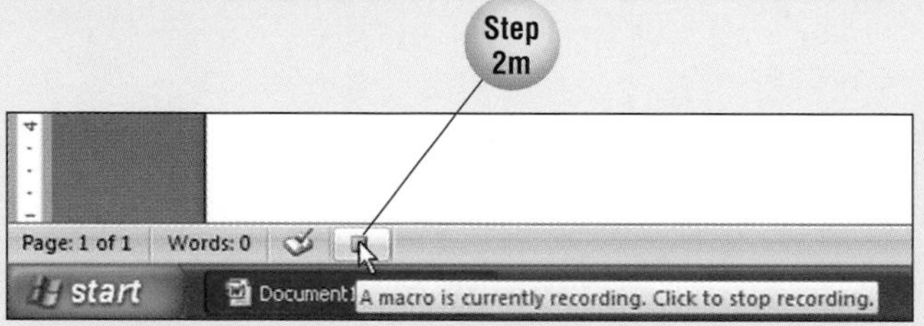

3. Record a macro named XXXInd02 that indents text in a paragraph 1 inch and hang indents second and subsequent lines of the paragraph by completing the following steps:
   a. Click the View tab.
   b. Click the Macros button arrow and then click *Record Macro* at the drop-down list.

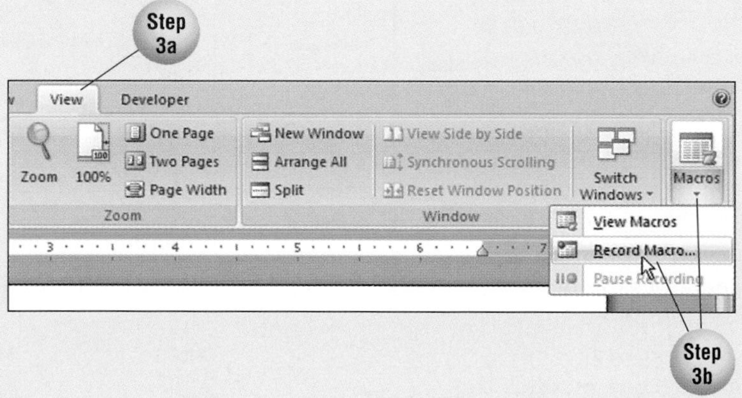

   c. At the Record Macro dialog box, type **XXXInd02** in the *Macro name* text box.
   d. Click inside the *Description* text box and then type **Indent text 1 inch and hang indent text.**
   e. Click OK.
   f. At the document, click the Home tab.
   g. Click the Paragraph group dialog box launcher.
   h. At the Paragraph dialog box, click the up-pointing arrow at the right side of the *Left* option until *1"* displays.
   i. Make sure the *Special* option box displays with *Hanging*, the *After* option is set at *0 pt*, and the *Line spacing* option is set at *Single*.
   j. Click OK.
   k. Click the macro icon on the Status bar to turn off the macro recording.

4. Record a macro that changes the top, left, and right margins by completing the following steps:
    a. Click the Developer tab.
    b. Click the Record Macro button in the Code group.
    c. At the Record Macro dialog box, type **XXXFormat01** in the *Macro name* text box.
    d. Click inside the *Description* text box and then type **Change top, left, and right margin measurements.**
    e. Click OK.
    f. At the document, click the Page Layout tab.
    g. Click the Margins button in the Page Setup group and then click *Custom Margins* at the drop-down list.
    h. At the Page Setup dialog box with the Margins tab selected, change the top margin to *1.5"* and the left and right margins to *1.25"*.
    i. Click OK to close the dialog box.
    j. Click the macro icon on the Status bar to turn off the macro recording.
5. Close the document without saving it.

Running a Macro

To run a recorded macro, click the Macros button in the Code group in the Developer tab or click the Macros button in the View tab. This displays the Macros dialog box shown in Figure 31.6. At this dialog box, double-click the desired macro in the list box or click the macro and then click the Run button.

Figure 31.6 Macros Dialog Box

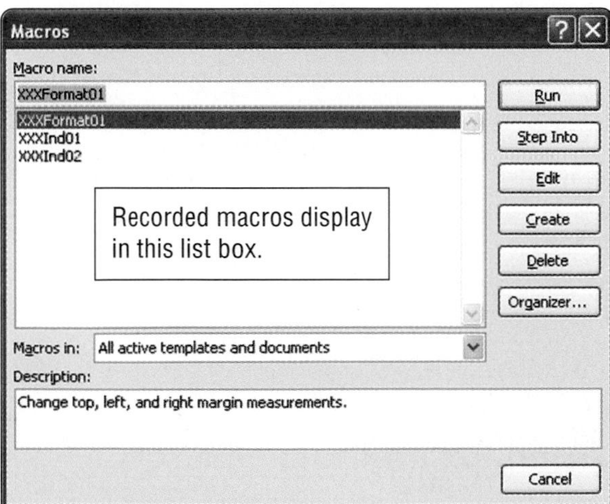

Exercise 4B

Running Macros

1. Open the **MacrosSurvey.docx** located in the Chapter31 folder on your storage medium and then save the document and name it **C31Ex04**.
2. Run the XXXFormat01 macro by completing the following steps:
   a. Click the View tab.
   b. Click the Macros button in the Macros group.
   c. At the Macros dialog box, click ***XXXFormat01*** in the list box.
   d. Click the Run button.

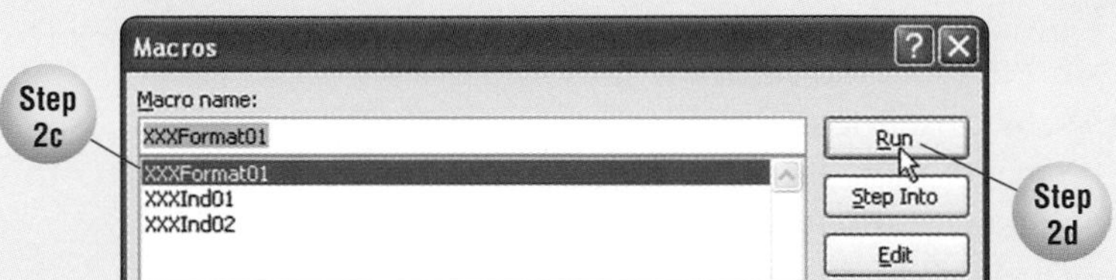

3. Run the XXXInd01 macro for the first numbered paragraph by completing the following steps:
   a. Position the insertion point anywhere in the paragraph that begins with *1*.
   b. Click the Developer tab.
   c. Click the Macros button in the Code group.
   d. At the Macros dialog box, double-click ***XXXInd01*** in the list box.

4. Complete steps similar to those in Step 3 to run the macro for each of the numbered paragraphs (just the numbered paragraphs, not the lettered paragraphs).
5. Complete the following steps to run the XXXInd02 macro:
   a. Select paragraphs *a* through *d* below the first numbered paragraph.
   b. Click the Macros button in the Code group in the Developer tab.
   c. At the Macros dialog box, double-click ***XXXInd02*** in the list box.
6. Complete steps similar to those in 5a through 5c to run the macro for the lettered paragraphs below each of the numbered paragraphs.
7. Save, print, and then close **C31Ex04.docx**.

Pausing and Then Resuming a Macro

When recording a macro, you can temporarily suspend the recording, perform actions that are not recorded, and then resume recording the macro. To pause the recording of a macro, click the Pause Recording button in the Code group in the Developer tab. To resume recording the macro, click the Resume Recorder button (previously the Pause Recording button).

Deleting a Macro

If you no longer need a macro that has been recorded, it can be deleted. To delete a macro, display the Macros dialog box, click the macro name in the list box, and then click the Delete button. At the message asking if you want to delete the macro, click Yes. Click the Close button to close the Macros dialog box.

Exercise 4C

Deleting a Macro

1. At a blank document, delete the XXXFormat01 macro by completing the following steps:
   a. Click the Developer tab and then click the Macros button in the Code group.
   b. At the Macros dialog box, click *XXXFormat01* in the list box.
   c. Click the Delete button.
   d. At the message asking if you want to delete the macro, click Yes.

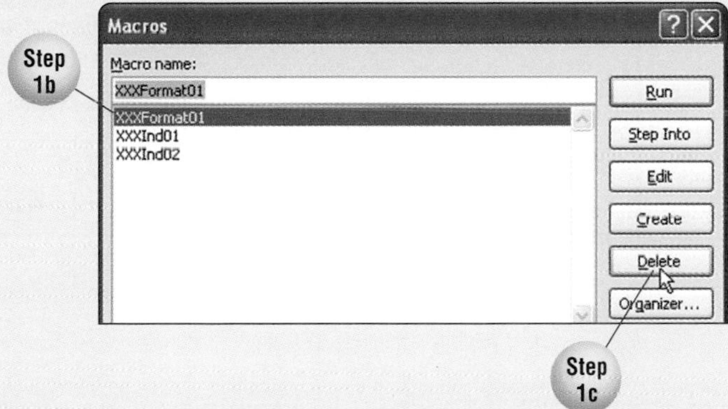

   e. Click the Close button to close the Macros dialog box.
2. Close the document.

Assigning a Macro

Consider assigning macros you use regularly either a shortcut command or to a toolbar. To run a macro that has been assigned to a keyboard command, just press the keys assigned to the macro. To run a macro assigned to a toolbar, just click the button.

Assigning a Macro a Keyboard Command

A macro can be assigned a keyboard command with a letter plus Alt + Ctrl or Alt + Shift. Word has already used many combinations for Word functions. For example, pressing Alt + Ctrl + C inserts the copyright symbol. With the Alt + Ctrl combination, the following letters are available for assigning to a macro: A, B, G, J, Q, W, and X. With the Alt + Shift combination, the following letters are available for assigning to a macro: B, G, H, J, Q, S, V, W, Y, and Z.

Assign a keyboard command to a macro at the Customize Keyboard dialog box shown in Figure 31.7. In Exercise 5 you will record a macro and then assign the macro to a keyboard command. If you delete the macro, the keyboard command is also deleted. This allows you to use the key combination again.

Figure 31.7 Customize Keyboard Dialog Box

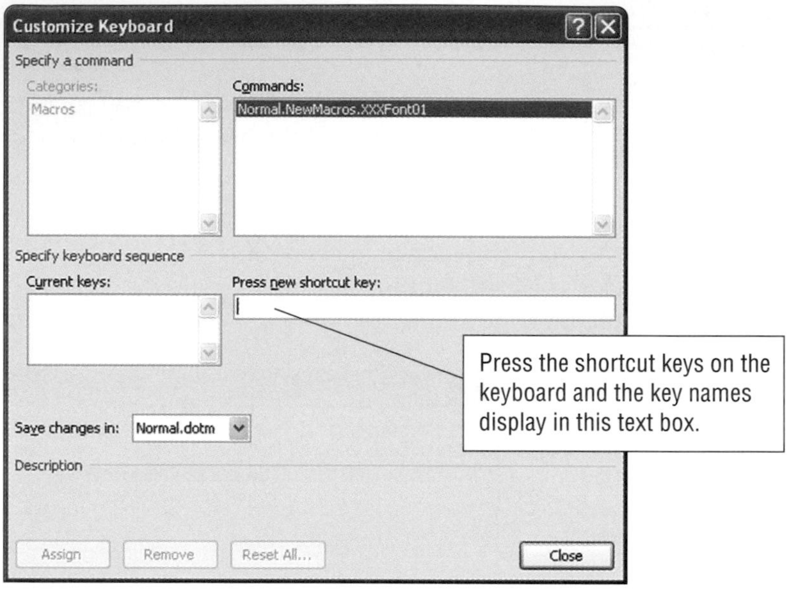

Exercise 5

Recording and Assigning a Keyboard Command to a Macro

1. Record a macro named XXXFont01 that selects text and applies font formatting and assign it the keyboard command Alt + Ctrl + A by completing the following steps:
   a. At a blank document, click the Developer tab and then click the Record Macro button in the Code group in the Developer tab.
   b. At the Record Macro dialog box, type **XXXFont01** in the *Macro name* text box.
   c. Click inside the *Description* text box and then type **Select text and change the font, font size, and font color.**
   d. Click the Keyboard button.

e. At the Customize Keyboard dialog box with the insertion point positioned in the *Press new shortcut key* text box, press Alt + Ctrl + A.
f. Click the Assign button.
g. Click the Close button.
h. At the document, click the Home tab.
i. Press Ctrl + A.
j. Click the Font group dialog box launcher.
k. At the Font dialog box, click *Cambria* in the *Font* list box, click *12* in the *Font Size* list box, and change the *Font color* to Dark Blue.
l. Click OK to close the Font dialog box.
m. At the document, press the Down Arrow on the keyboard.
n. Click the macro icon on the Status bar to turn off the macro recording.

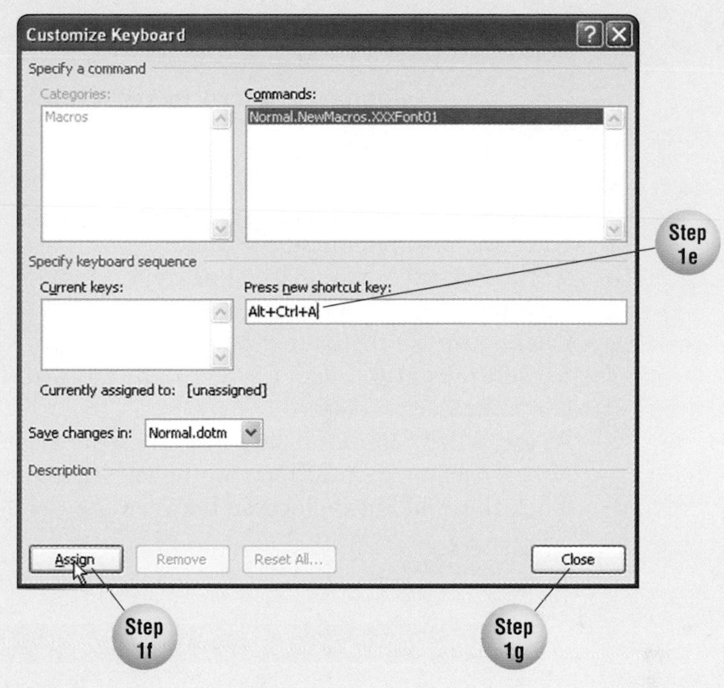

2. Close the document without saving it.
3. Open the document **MacrosLetter.docx** located in the Chapter31 folder on your storage medium and then save the document and name it **C31Ex05**.
4. Run the XXXFont01 macro by pressing Alt + Ctrl + A.
5. Run the XXXInd01 macro for the numbered paragraphs and the XXXInd02 macro for the lettered paragraphs.
6. Save, print, and then close **C31Ex05.docx**.

Assigning a Macro to the Quick Access Toolbar

A macro that you use regularly can be added to the Quick Access toolbar. To run a macro from the Quick Access toolbar, just click the button. To assign a macro to the toolbar, click the Button button at the Record Macro dialog box. This displays the Word Options dialog box with the Customize option selected in the left panel. Click the macro name in the left list box and then click the Add button that displays between the two list boxes. This adds the macro name in the left list box. Click the OK button and the Word Options dialog box closes and a macro button is inserted on the Quick Access toolbar. To remove a macro button from the Quick Access toolbar, right-click the button on the toolbar and then click *Remove from Quick Access Toolbar* option at the shortcut menu.

Exercise 6

Assigning a Macro to the Quick Access Toolbar

1. At a blank document, create a macro named XXXTab01 and assign it to the Quick Access toolbar by completing the following steps:
   a. Click the macro icon on the Status bar.
   b. At the Record Macro dialog box, type **XXXTab01** in the *Macro name* text box.
   c. Click in the *Description* text box and then type **Set left tabs at 0.5 and 1.0 and right tab with leaders at 5.5.**
   d. Click the Button button.
   e. At the Word Options dialog box, click the macro named *Normal.NewMacros.XXXTab01* in the left list box.
   f. Click the Add button located between the two list boxes.

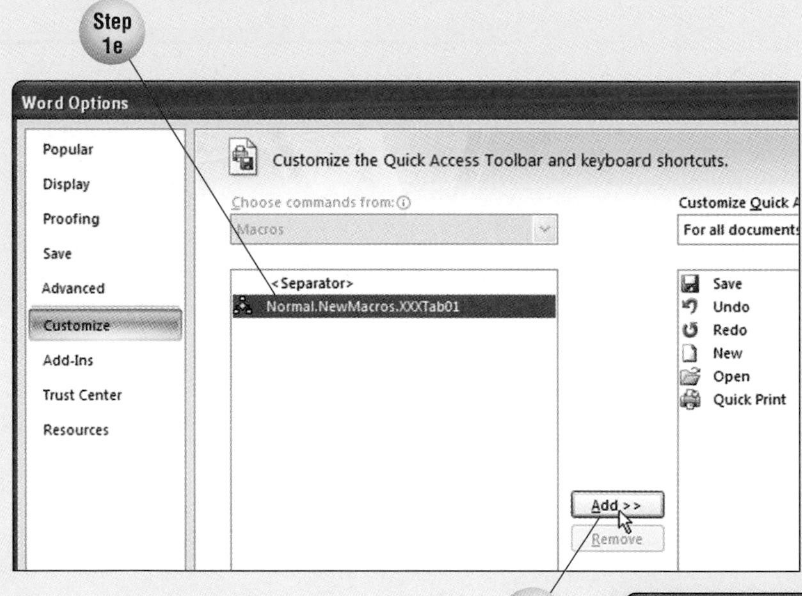

   g. Click OK.
   h. At the blank document, click the Home tab and then click the Paragraph group dialog box launcher.
   i. At the Paragraph dialog box, click the Tabs button located in the lower left corner of the dialog box.
   j. At the Tabs dialog box, type 0.5 and then click the Set button.
   k. Type 1 and then click the Set button.
   l. Type 5.5, click the *Right* option in the *Alignment* section, click 2 .... in the *Leaders* section, and then click the Set button.
   m. Click OK to close the dialog box.

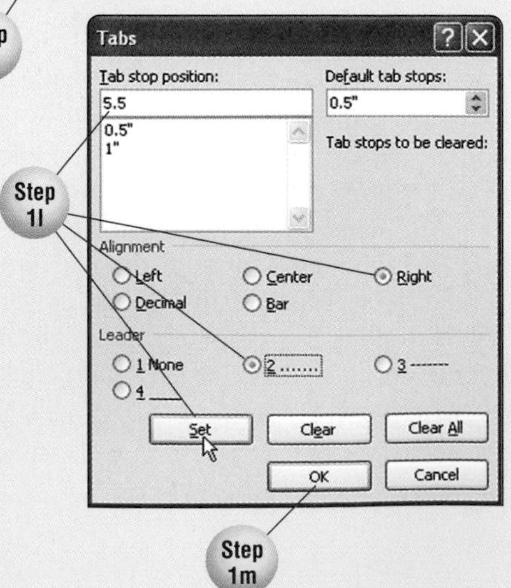

n. At the blank document, click the macro icon on the Status bar to turn off recording.

2. Close the document without saving it.
3. At a blank document, create the document shown in Figure 31.8 by completing the following steps:
   a. Click the macro button on the Quick Access toolbar.
   b. Type the text as shown in Figure 31.8. (Type the first column of text at the first tab stop, not the left margin.)
4. After typing the text, run the XXXFont01 macro by pressing Alt + Ctrl + A.
5. Select the title *COMPUTER CONCEPTS* and then turn on bold.
6. Save the document and name it **C31Ex06**.
7. Print and then close **C31Ex06.docx**.
8. Remove the macro button from the Quick Access toolbar by right-clicking the button and then clicking *Remove from Quick Access Toolbar* at the shortcut menu.

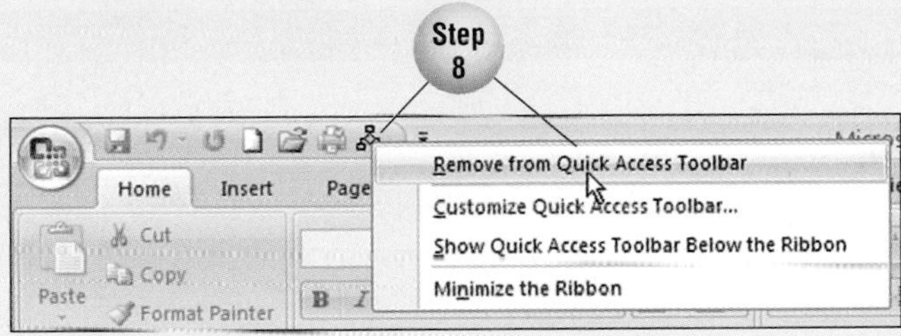

Figure 31.8 Exercise 6

COMPUTER CONCEPTS

Computer Hardware 3

    Types of Computers 4

    Hardware Components 8

Computer Software 14

    Operating Systems 16

    Application Software 20

Networking 25

    Types of Networks 27

    Uses of Networks 30

    Network Topologies 34

Recording a Macro with Fill-in Fields

In Chapter 16, you inserted a Fill-in field in a document that prompted the operator to insert information at the keyboard during a merge. You can also insert a Fill-in field in a macro that requires input from the keyboard. To insert a Fill-in field in a macro, begin the recording of the macro. At the point where the Fill-in field is to be inserted, click the Insert tab, click the Quick Parts button in the Text group, and then click *Field* at the drop-down list. At the Field dialog box with *(All)* selected in the *Categories* list box as shown in Figure 31.9, scroll down the *Field names* and then click the *Fill-in* field. Add information telling the operator what text to enter at the keyboard by clicking in the *Prompt:* text box and then typing the desired message. When you run the macro, type the desired text specified by the prompt message.

Figure 31.9 Field Dialog Box

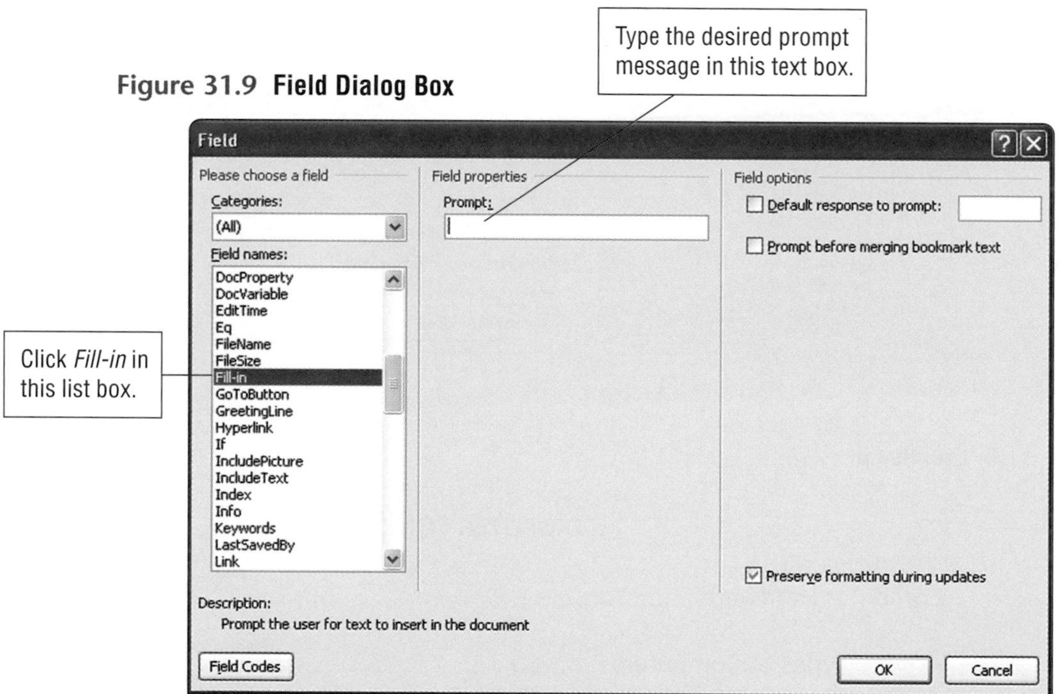

Exercise 7A

Recording a Macro with Fill-in Fields

1. At a blank document, record a macro for inserting notary signature. Begin by clicking the View tab, clicking the Macros button arrow, and then clicking *Record Macro* at the drop-down list.
2. At the Record Macro dialog box, type **XXXNotary** (where your initials are used instead of the *XXX*) in the *Macro name* text box.
3. Click in the *Description* text box and then type **Notary signature information.**
4. Click the Keyboard button.
5. At the Customize Keyboard dialog box with the insertion point positioned in the *Press new shortcut key* text box, press Alt + Shift + S.

6. Click the Assign button.
7. Click the Close button.
8. At the blank document, click the Home tab and then click the No Spacing heading in the Styles group.
9. Set two left tabs by completing the following steps:
   a. Make sure the alignment button at the left side of the Ruler displays with the Left Tab icon.
   b. Click on the 0.5-inch mark on the Ruler.
   c. Click on the 2-inch mark on the Ruler.
   d. Click on the 2.5-inch mark on the Ruler.
10. Type the text shown in Figure 31.10 up to the text *(name of person)*. (Do not type the text *(name of person)*.)
11. Insert a Fill-in field by completing the following steps:
   a. Click the Insert tab.
   b. Click the Quick Parts button in the Text group and then click *Field* at the drop-down list.
   c. At the Field dialog box with *(All)* selected in the *Categories* list box, scroll down the list and then click *Fill-in*.
   d. Click in the *Prompt:* text box and then type **Type name of person signing.**
   e. Click the OK button.

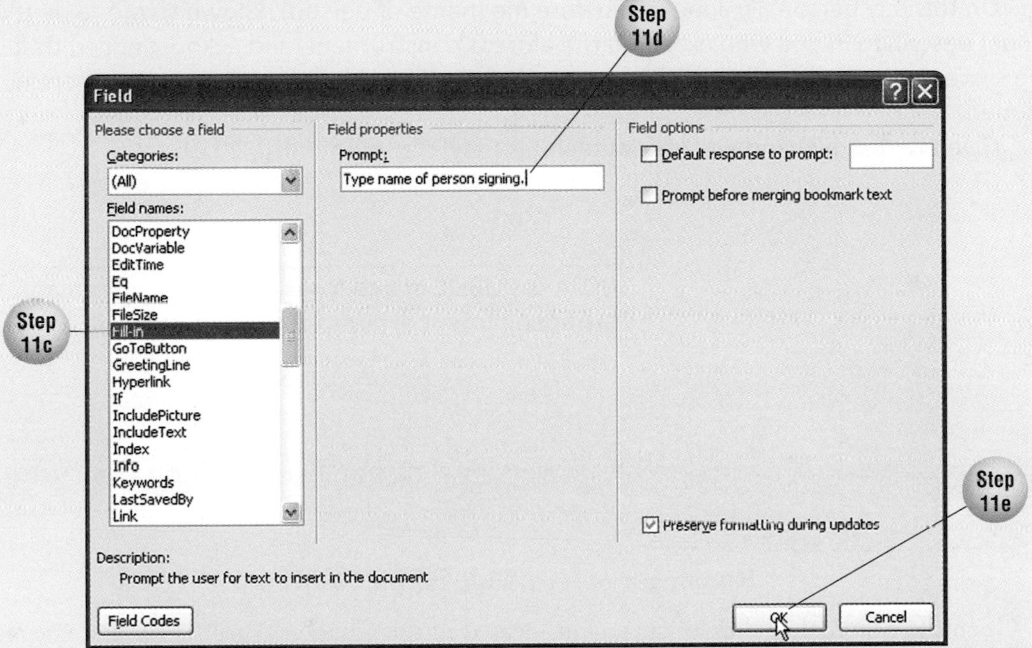

   f. At the Microsoft Word dialog box, type **(name of person)** in the text box and then click OK.

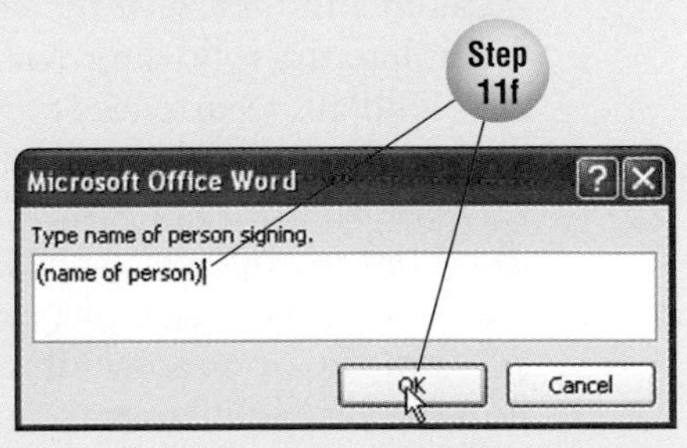

12. Continue typing the notary signature information shown in Figure 31.10 up to the text *(day)* and then insert a Fill-in field by completing steps similar to those in Step 11 that tell the operator to type the current day.

13. Continue typing the notary signature information shown in Figure 31.10 up to the text *(month)* and then insert a Fill-in field by completing steps similar to those in Step 11 that tell the operator to type the current month.
14. Continue typing the notary signature information shown in Figure 31.10 up to the text *(expiration date)* and then insert a Fill-in field by completing steps similar to those in Step 11 that tell the operator to type the expiration date.
15. After inserting the expiration date information, press the Enter key once.
16. End the recording by clicking the macro icon on the Status bar.
17. Close the document without saving it.

Figure 31.10 Exercise 7A

STATE OF CALIFORNIA)
) ss.
COUNTY OF LOS ANGELES)

On this day personally appeared before me (name of person), known to me to be the individual described in and who executed the aforesaid instrument, and acknowledged that he/she signed as his/her free and voluntary act and deed for the uses and purposes therein mentioned.

Given under my hand and official seal this (day) day of (month), 2010.

NOTARY PUBLIC in and for the State of California
My appointment expires (expiration date)

Exercise 7B

Running a Macro with Fill-in Fields

1. Open the **MacrosLegal.docx** document located in the Chapter31 folder on your storage medium and then save the document and name it **C31Ex07**.
2. Complete the following find and replaces:
   a. Find all occurrences of *NAME* and replace with *LOREN HOUSTON*. (Be sure to replace only the occurrences of *NAME* in all uppercase letters. *Hint: Expand the Find and Replace dialog box and insert a check mark in the* Match case *option.*)
   b. Find the one occurrence of *ADDRESS* and replace with *102 Marine Drive, Los Angeles, CA*. (Be sure to replace only the occurrence of *ADDRESS* in all uppercase letters and not the occurrence of *address* in all lowercase letters.)
3. Run the XXXInd01 macro for the numbered paragraphs and run the XXXInd02 macro for the lettered paragraphs.

4. Move the insertion point to the end of the document a double space below the text and then run the XXXNotary macro by completing the following steps:
   a. Press Alt + Shift + S.
   b. When the macro stops and prompts you for the name of person, type **SYLVIA WHITT** and then click OK.

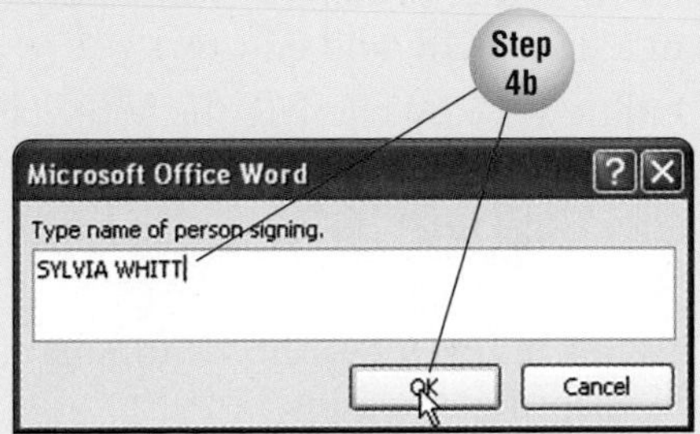

   c. When the macro stops and prompts you for the day, type **10th** and then click OK.
   d. When the macro stops and prompts you for the month, type **March** and then click OK.
   e. When the macro stops and prompts you for the expiration date, type **12/31/2010** and then click OK.
5. Save, print, and then close **C31Ex07.docx**.

Chapter Summary

- Use Word's Outline feature to format headings within a document, view formatted titles, headings, and body text in a document, and edit text.
- Display a document in Outline view by clicking the View tab and then clicking the Outline button in the Document Views group.
- In Outline view, identify particular titles, headings, and subheadings within a document as certain levels.
- When a document displays in Outline view, the Outlining tab contains buttons for assigning levels and expanding and collapsing an outline.
- When a paragraph is identified as a level 1 heading, the Heading 1 style is applied to that paragraph. Heading 2 style is applied to a paragraph identified as a level 2 heading.
- You can promote or demote a heading in Outline view by dragging the selection symbol that displays before a title or heading.
- The advantage of working in Outline view is the ability to see a condensed outline of your document without all of the text in between titles, headings, or subheadings. Another benefit of working in Outline view is in maintaining consistency between various titles and headings.
- To collapse all text beneath a particular heading, click the Collapse button in the Outline Tools group in the Outlining tab. Click the Expand button to display all text.
- In Outline view, you can rearrange the contents of a document. To move a heading and the body text below the heading, select the heading and then click the Move Down or Move Up button in the Outline Tools group. You can also move a heading and the body text below it by dragging the selection symbol that displays before the heading to the desired position.
- A master document contains a number of separate documents called subdocuments. Create a master document or format an existing document as a master document in the Outline view.
- The Outlining tab in the Outline view contains buttons for working with master documents and subdocuments. Clicking the Show Document button and then clicking the Create button both located in the Master Document group in the Outlining tab causes Word to create a subdocument for each heading at the top level within the selected text.
- Save a master document in the normal manner. Word automatically assigns a document name to each subdocument using the first characters in the subdocument heading.
- You can rearrange subdocuments in a master document by dragging the subdocument icon to the desired position.
- Use buttons in the Master Document group in the Outlining tab to create, expand, collapse, merge, and split subdocuments.
- Use Word's Macros feature to execute a series of commands or apply formatting.
- Recording a macro involves turning on the macro recorder, performing the steps to be recorded, and then turning off the recorder.
- Run a macro by displaying the Macros dialog box and then double-clicking the desired macro name.
- You can temporarily suspend the recording of a macro by clicking the Pause Recording button in the Code group in the Developer tab.

- Delete a macro by displaying the Macros dialog box, clicking the macro name to be deleted, and then clicking the Delete button.
- Assign a keyboard command to a macro at the Record Macro dialog box.
- To run a macro that has been assigned a keyboard command, press the keys assigned to the macro.
- You can add a macro to the Quick Access toolbar and then run the macro by clicking the macro button on the toolbar.
- Insert a Fill-in field in a macro that requires keyboard entry while running the macro.

Commands review

FEATURE	RIBBON TAB, GROUP	BUTTON, OPTION	KEYBOARD SHORTCUT
Outline view	View, Document Views		Alt + Ctrl + O
Collapse outline	Outlining, Outline Tools		Alt + Shift + _
Expand outline	Outlining, Outline Tools		Alt + Shift + +
Move up outline level	Outlining, Outline Tools		Alt + Shift + Up
Move down outline level	Outlining, Outline Tools		Alt + Shift + Down
Master Document	Outlining, Master Document		
Collapse subdocuments	Outlining, Master Document		
Expand subdocuments	Outlining, Master Document		
Macros dialog box	Developer, Code OR View, Macros		Alt + F8
Record Macro dialog box	Developer, Code OR View, Macros	Record Macro	
Field dialog box	Insert, Text	Field...	

Reviewing key points

Completion: In the space provided at the right, indicate the correct term, command, or number.

1. The Outline button is located in this tab. __________
2. Click this button to promote a title or heading to level 1. __________
3. Use this button in the Outlining tab to switch between displaying all headings through the lowest level chosen. __________
4. You can promote or demote a heading in the Outline view by dragging this symbol that displays before a heading. __________
5. Click this button in the Outlining tab to collapse all of the text beneath a particular heading. __________
6. To move a level 1 heading below other level 1 headings, select the level 1 heading to be moved and then click this button until the heading is in the desired position. __________
7. The Show Document button is located in this group in the Outlining tab. __________
8. Click the Expand Subdocuments button and the name of the button changes to this. __________
9. This tab contains the Record Macro button in the Code group. __________
10. A macro name must begin with a letter and can contain only letters and these. __________
11. When macro recording is turned on, a macro icon displays on this. __________
12. Delete a macro at this dialog box. __________
13. Assign a keyboard command to a macro at this dialog box. __________
14. You can add a button on this toolbar representing a recorded macro. __________
15. Insert this field in a macro that requires input from the keyboard. __________

Applying your skills

Assessment 1 Assign Levels in Outline View

1. Open the **OutlineReport03.docx** document located in the Chapter31 folder on your storage medium and then save the document and name it **C31A01**.
2. Change to the Outline view and then promote or demote titles and headings as identified below:

COMPUTERS IN COMMUNICATION	=	Level 1
Telecommunications	=	Level 2
Publishing	=	Level 2
News Services	=	Level 2
COMPUTERS IN ENTERTAINMENT	=	Level 1
Television and Film	=	Level 2
Home Entertainment	=	Level 2

3. Collapse the outline so only the two levels display.
4. Save and then print **C31A01.docx**. (This will print the collapsed outline, not the entire document.)

Assessment 2 Move and Delete Headings in a Collapsed Outline

1. With **C31A01.docx** open, make sure the document displays in Outline view and then make the following changes:
   a. Change the Show Level button to *Level 1*.
   b. Move the *COMPUTERS IN COMMUNICATIONS* title below the title *COMMUNICATIONS IN ENTERTAINMENT*.
   c. Change the Show Level button to *Level 2*.
   d. Move the heading *Publishing* below the heading *News Services*.
   e. Delete the *Telecommunications* heading.
2. Save and then print **C31A01.docx**.
3. Display the entire document and then close Outline view.
4. Save and then close **C31A01.docx**.

Assessment 3 Create and Arrange a Master Document

1. Open the **MasterDocReport06.docx** document located in the Chapter31 folder on your storage medium and then save the document and name it **C31A03**.
2. Change to Outline view.
3. Assign to level 1 the following headings:
   Defining Desktop Publishing
   Initiating the Process
   Planning the Publication
   Creating the Content
4. Click the Show Document button in the Master Document group in the Outlining tab.
5. Create subdocuments by selecting the entire document and then clicking the Create button in the Master Document group.
6. Save and then close **C31A03.docx**.
7. Open **C31A03.docx** and then print the document. (Subdocuments will be collapsed.)

8. Make the following changes to the document:
   a. Move the *Planning the Publication* subdocument above the *Initiating the Process* subdocument. (Make sure the dark gray horizontal line is positioned above the gray circle above the *Initiating the Process* subdocument before you release the mouse button.)
   b. Delete the *Creating the Content* subdocument.
9. Save, print, and then close **C31A03.docx**.

Assessment 4 Record and Run a Formatting Macro

1. At a blank document, create a macro with the following specifications:
   a. Name the macro XXXFormat02.
   b. Type **Apply character and paragraph formatting.** as the description.
   c. When recording the macro, press Ctrl + A to select the entire document.
   d. Change the font to 18-point Candara bold and change the font color to Aqua, Accent 5, Darker 25%.
   e. Click the Center button in the Paragraph group.
   f. Display the Page Setup dialog box with the Layout tab selected and then change the *Vertical alignment* option to *Center*. *(Hint: To display the Page Setup dialog box, click the Page Layout tab and then click the Page Setup group dialog box launcher.)*
   g. Press the Down Arrow key and then stop the recording of the macro.
   h. Close the document without saving it.
2. Open the document named **MacrosAnnouncement.docx** located in the Chapter31 folder on your storage medium and then save the document and name it **C31A04A**.
3. Run the XXXFormat02 macro.
4. Save, print, and then close **C31A04A**.
5. Open the document named **MacrosMenu.docx** located in the Chapter31 folder on your storage medium and then save the document and name it **C31A04B**.
6. Run the XXXFormat02 macro.
7. Save, print, and then close **C31A04B.docx**.

Assessment 5 Record and Run a Macro that Sets Tabs

1. At a blank document, run the XXXTab01 macro and then create the document shown in Figure 31.11. (Type the text in the first column at the first tab stop, not the left margin.)
2. Save the completed document and name it **C31A05**.
3. Print and then close **C31A05.docx**.

Figure 31.11 Assessment 5

McCORMACK FUNDS CORPORATION

Public Relations Department, Extension Numbers

Roger Maldon 129

Kimberly Holland..143

Richard Perez 317

Sharon Rawlins 211

Earl Warnberg 339

Susan Fanning 122

Assessment 6 Record and Run a Macro with Fill-in Fields

1. At a blank document, record a macro named XXXNotSig that includes the information shown in Figure 31.12. Set left tabs at the 0.5-inch mark, the 1.5-inch mark, and the 3-inch mark on the Ruler. Include Fill-in fields in the macro where you see the text in parentheses. After inserting the *(county)* Fill-in field, press the Enter key and then end the macro recording.
2. Close the document without saving it.
3. Open **MacrosContract.docx**, save the document, and then name it **C31A06**.
4. Move the insertion point to the end of the document and then run the XXXNotSig macro and insert the following information when prompted:
   (name 1) = LLOYD KOVICH
   (name 2) = JOANNE MILNER
   (county) = Ramsey County
5. Save, print, and then close **C31A06.docx**.

Figure 31.12 Assessment 6

STATE OF MINNESOTA)
) ss.
COUNTY OF RAMSEY)

I certify that I know or have satisfactory evidence that (name 1) and (name 2) are the persons who appeared before me, and said persons acknowledge that they signed the foregoing Contract and acknowledged it to be their free and voluntary act for the uses and purposes therein mentioned.

____
NOTARY PUBLIC in and for the State of
Minnesota residing in (county)

Performance Assessments

UNIT

Referencing Data

ASSESSING PROFICIENCIES

In this unit, you have learned how to reference data with footnotes, endnotes, citations, and bibliographies. You have learned to create an index, table of contents, table of figures, and table of authorities, and you have learned to create forms with content controls and form fields. The following assessments address these skills. The content of Optional Chapter 31, however, is not included in the assessments.

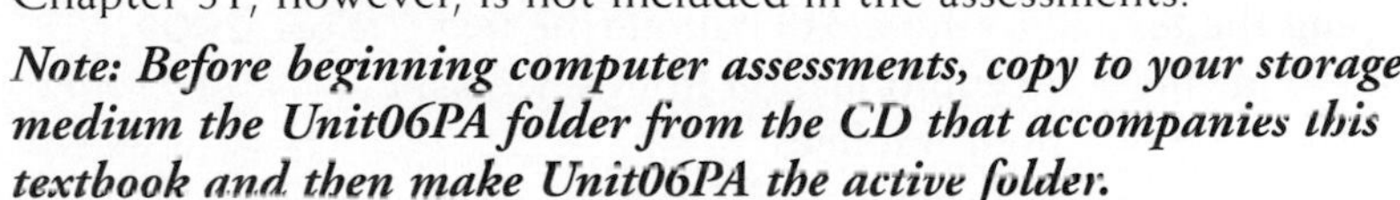

Note: Before beginning computer assessments, copy to your storage medium the Unit06PA folder from the CD that accompanies this textbook and then make Unit06PA the active folder.

Assessment 1 **Insert Footnotes in a Report**

1. Open **Report15.docx** and save the document with the name **U06PA01**.
2. Create the first footnote shown in Figure U6.1 at the end of the second paragraph in the *Defining Desktop Publishing* section.
3. Create the second footnote shown in Figure U6.1 at the end of the fourth paragraph in the *Defining Desktop Publishing* section.
4. Create the third footnote shown in Figure U6.1 at the end of the second paragraph in the *Planning the Publication* section.
5. Create the fourth footnote shown in Figure U6.1 at the end of the last paragraph in the document.

Figure U6.1 **Assessment 1**

Raines, Charlotte, *Desktop Publishing Design*, Cornwall & Lewis Publishing, 2009, pages 67-72.

Sutton, Terrence, "The Desktop Publishing Approach," *Desktop Publishing*, August 2009, pages 3-6.

Chun, Rebecca, *Desktop Publishing with Style*, Monroe-Ackerman Publishing, 2009, pages 89-93.

Castillo, Carlos, *Desktop Publishing Tips and Tricks*, Aurora Publishing House, 2010, pages 103-106.

6. Save and then print **U06PA01.docx**.
7. Select the entire document and then change the font to Constantia.
8. Select all of the footnotes and change the font to Constantia.
9. Delete the third footnote.
10. Save, print, and then close **U06PA01.docx**.

Assessment 2 Create Citations and Prepare a Bibliography for a Report

1. Open **Reference03.docx** and save the document with the name **U06PA02**.
2. Press Ctrl + End to move the insertion point to the end of the document and then type the text shown in Figure U6.2 (in APA style) up to the first citation (the text *(Mercado, 2010)*). Insert the source information from a journal article written by Claudia Mercado using the following information:
   Author = **Claudia Mercado**
   Title = **Connecting a Web Page**
   Journal Name = **Connections**
   Year = **2010**
   Pages = **12-21**
   Volume = **5**
3. Continue typing the text up to the next citation (the text *(Holmes, 2009)*) and insert the following source information from a Web site:
   Author = **Brent Holmes**
   Name of Web page = **Hosting Your Web Page**
   Name of Web site = **Design Guru**
   Year = **2009**
   Month = **September**
   Day = **28**
   Year Accessed = (type current year)
   Month Accessed = (type current month)
   Day Accessed = (type current day)
   URL = **www.emcp.net**
4. Continue typing the text up to the next citation (the text *(Vukovich, 2008)*) and insert the following information from a book:
   Author = **Ivan Vukovich**
   Title = **Computer Technology in the Business Environment**
   Year = **2008**
   City = **San Francisco**
   Publisher = **Gold Coast Publishing**
5. Insert the page number in the citation by Ivan Vukovich using the Edit Citation dialog box.
6. Type the remaining text in Figure U6.2.
7. Edit the Ivan Vukovich source last name to *Vulkovich* in the *Master List* section of the Source Manager dialog box.
8. Create a new source in the document using the Source Manager dialog box and include the following source information for a journal article:
   Author = **Sonia Jaquez**
   Title = **Organizing a Web Page**
   Journal Name = **Design Techniques**
   Year = **2010**
   Pages = **32-44**
   Volume = **9**

9. Insert at the end of the last paragraph in the document the sentence **Browsers look for pages with these names first when a specific file at a Web site is requested, and index pages display by default if no other page is specified.**
10. Insert a citation for Sonia Jaquez at the end of the sentence you just typed.
11. Insert a citation for Claudia Mercado following the second sentence in the first paragraph of the document.
12. Insert a bibliography at the end of the document on a separate page.
13. Format the bibliography to meet APA requirements with the following changes:
    a. Center the title *Bibliography*.
    b. Select the Bibliography title and the entries below the title and change the line spacing to 2.0.
    c. Change the spacing after paragraphs to *0 points*.
    d. Hang indent the bibliography entries.
14. Save and then print **U06PA02.docx**.
15. Change the document and bibliography from APA style to MLA style.
16. Save, print page 3, and then close **U06PA02.docx**.

Figure U6.2 **Assessment 2**

Choosing a Host

One of the first tasks in Web site development is finding a good host for the site. Essentially, a Web host lets you store a copy of your Web pages on the hard drive of a powerful computer connected to the Internet with a fast connection that can handle thousands of users (Mercado, 2010). Hosting your own Web site is possible but is only feasible if you own an extra computer that can be dedicated to the role of a Web server, have a high-speed Internet connection, and feel confident about handling the job of network security and routing (Holmes, 2009). Most people's situations do not fit those criteria. Fortunately, several free and fee-based Web hosting services are available.

Organizing the Site

As you plan a Web site, decide what types of content you will include and think about how all of the pages should link together. Most Web sites have a home page that provides the starting point for users entering the site. "Like the top of a pyramid or the table of contents of a book, the home page leads to other Web pages via hyperlinks" (Vukovich, 2008, p. 26). Most home pages have the default name of index.html (or sometimes index.htm).

Assessment 3 Create an Index and Table of Contents for a Report

1. At a blank document, create the text shown in Figure U6.3 as a concordance file.
2. Save the document with the name **U06PA03CF**.
3. Print and then close **U06PA03CF.docx**.
4. Open **Report21.docx** and save the document with the name **U06PA03**.
5. Make the following changes to the document:
   a. Apply the Heading 1 style to the title and apply the Heading 2 style to the two headings in the report.
   b. Change the style set to *Simple*.
   c. Mark text for an index using the concordance file **U06PA03CF.docx**.
   d. Compile the index at the end of the document.
   e. Apply the Heading 1 style to the title of the index.
   f. Insert a table of contents at the beginning of the document.
   g. Number the table of contents page with a lowercase Roman numeral.

Figure U6.3 **Assessment 3**

message	Message
publication	Publication
Design	Design
flyer	Flyer
letterhead	Letterhead
newsletter	Newsletter
intent	Design: intent
audience	Design: audience
layout	Design: layout
thumbnail	Thumbnail
principles	Design: principles
Focus	Design: focus
focus	Design: focus
balance	Design: balance
proportion	Design: proportion
contrast	Design: contrast
directional flow	Design: directional flow
consistency	Design: consistency
color	Design: color
White space	White space
white space	White space
Legibility	Legibility
headline	Headline
Subheads	Subheads
subheads	Subheads

h. Number the other pages in the report with Arabic numbers and start the numbering with 1 on the page containing the report title.
6. Make sure the table of contents displays the correct page numbers. If not, update the table of contents.
7. Save, print, and then close **U06PA03.docx**.

Assessment 4 Create Captions and Insert a Table of Figures in a Report

1. Open **Report22.docx** and save the document with the name **U06PA04**.
2. Insert the following captions:

   First image = Mainframe
   Second image = Microcomputer
   Third image = DNA Strand
   Fourth image = PDA

3. Move the insertion point to the beginning of the title *COMPUTING ADVANTAGE* and then insert a section break that begins a new page. Move the insertion point to the beginning of the document (on the blank page) and then insert a table of figures with the title *TABLE OF FIGURES*. Apply the Heading 1 style to the title, change the font size to 14 points, and center the title.
4. Save, print, and then close **U06PA04.docx**.

Assessment 5 Create and Fill in a Purchase Order Form

1. Create the form shown in Figure U6.4 as a template and use the Table feature to create the columns and rows. Include the following elements:
   a. Apply border and shading formatting as shown in the figure.
   b. Insert a picture content control, a date picker content control, and plain text content controls in the appropriate cells. Lock the picture content control so it cannot be edited.
   c. Insert a drop-down list content control for *Company Status* with the following choices: *Bronze*, *Silver*, and *Gold*.
2. Protect the template.
3. Save the template with the name **XXXSBPOTemplate**.
4. Print and then close **XXXSBPOTemplate.dotx**.
5. Create a form document from the **XXXSBPOTemplate** template with the following information:

   Company Name: = **John's Corner Market**
   Date: = *(Insert current date.)*
   Company Status: *Choose the* Gold *option.*
   Description: = **Sales Insight**
   Quantity: = **5**
   Cost: = **$20.50**
   Description: = **Strategic Marketing**
   Quantity: = **2**
   Cost: = **$134.50**
   Description: = **Advertising**
   Quantity: = **3**
   Cost: = **$201.00**

6. Save the document with the name **U06PA05**.
7. Print and then close **U06PA05.docx**.

Figure U6.4 **Assessment 5**

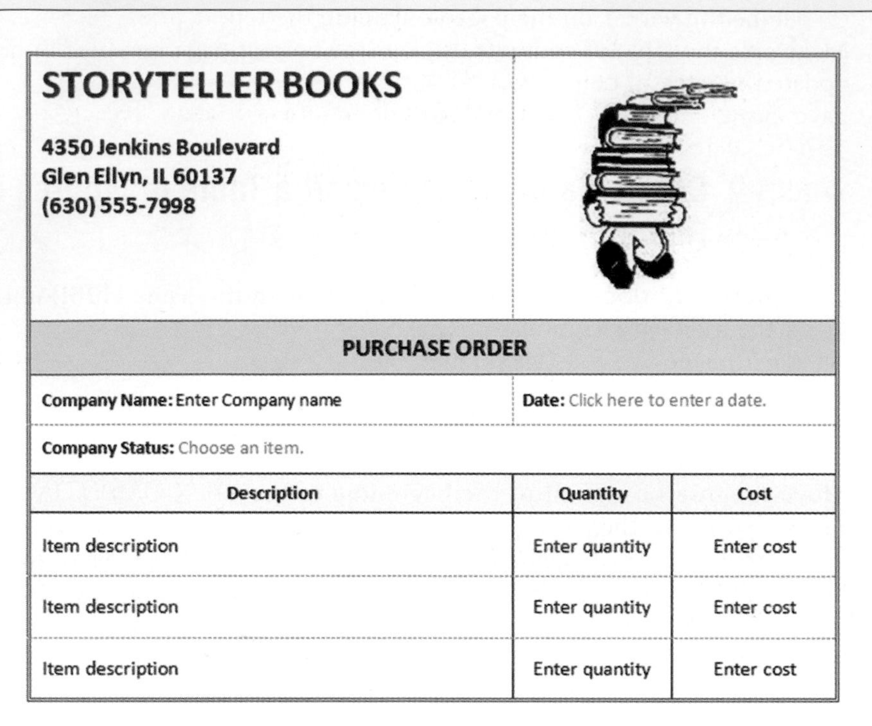

STORYTELLER BOOKS 4350 Jenkins Boulevard Glen Ellyn, IL 60137 (630) 555-7998		
PURCHASE ORDER		
Company Name: Enter Company name	**Date:** Click here to enter a date.	
Company Status: Choose an item.		
Description	**Quantity**	**Cost**
Item description	Enter quantity	Enter cost
Item description	Enter quantity	Enter cost
Item description	Enter quantity	Enter cost

Assessment 6 Create and Fill in an Insurance Application Form

1. Create a template, insert a file, and then insert form fields in the template as shown in Figure U6.5 with the following specifications:
   a. Create the form as a template.
   b. At the template document screen, insert the document named **LAApplication04.docx**.
   c. Insert a text form field for *Client Number:* that specifies a maximum length of 6.
   d. Insert a text form field for *Type of Deduction:* that specifies *Flat* as the default text.
   e. Insert a drop-down form field for *Deduction Amount:* that includes the following four choices: *None*, *$1,000*, *$2,500*, and *$5,000*.
   f. Insert a check box form field in the cell immediately left of *AANA* that is checked by default.
   g. Insert the remaining text and check box form fields as shown in Figure U6.5.
2. Protect the template.
3. Save the template with the name **XXXLAProfAppTemplate**.
4. Print and then close **XXXLAProfAppTemplate.dotx**.
5. Create a form document from the **XXXLAProfAppTemplate.dotx** template and then insert the following information in the specified data field:

First Name:	=	**Rachel**
Middle Name:	=	**Brianne**
Last Name:	=	**Hayward**
Address:	=	**12091 South 234th Street, Fairbanks, AK 99704**
Date of Birth:	=	**01/18/1982**

Client Number: = 10-541
Current Date: = *(Insert the current date.)*
Type of Deduction: = Flat
Deduction Amount: = $5,000
(Leave the check mark in the AANA *check box and also insert a check mark in the* APTA-PPS *check box.)*
(Insert a check mark in the Occupational Therapist *check box.)*

6. Save the document with the name **U06PA06**.
7. Print and then close **U06PA06.docx**.

Figure U6.5 **Assessment 6**

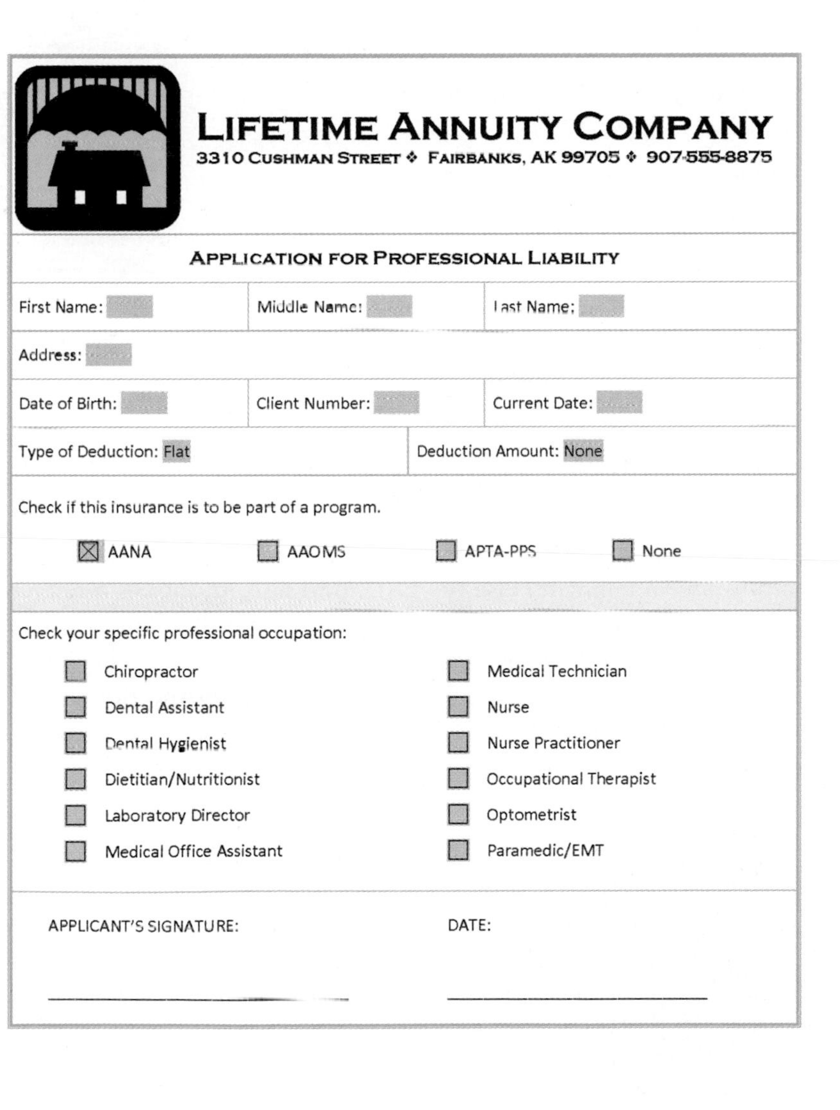

LIFETIME ANNUITY COMPANY
3310 CUSHMAN STREET ❖ FAIRBANKS, AK 99705 ❖ 907-555-8875

APPLICATION FOR PROFESSIONAL LIABILITY

First Name: | Middle Name: | Last Name:
Address:
Date of Birth: | Client Number: | Current Date:
Type of Deduction: Flat | Deduction Amount: None

Check if this insurance is to be part of a program.
☒ AANA ☐ AAOMS ☐ APTA-PPS ☐ None

Check your specific professional occupation:
☐ Chiropractor ☐ Medical Technician
☐ Dental Assistant ☐ Nurse
☐ Dental Hygienist ☐ Nurse Practitioner
☐ Dietitian/Nutritionist ☐ Occupational Therapist
☐ Laboratory Director ☐ Optometrist
☐ Medical Office Assistant ☐ Paramedic/EMT

APPLICANT'S SIGNATURE: DATE:

CREATING ORIGINAL DOCUMENTS

The activities in Assessment 7 and Assessment 8 give you the opportunity to practice your writing skills as well as demonstrate your mastery of some of the important Word features presented in this unit. When you compose the documents, use correct grammar, precise word choices, and clear sentence construction.

Assessment 7 Format an Employee Handbook

Situation: You work in the Human Resources Department at Brennan Distributors where you are responsible for preparing an employee handbook. Open the **BDHandbook.docx** document and save it with the name **U06PA07**. Make the following changes to the document:

- Insert page breaks before each of the centered titles (except the first title *Introduction*).
- Apply heading styles to the titles and headings.
- Change to a style set of your choosing.
- Apply a theme that makes the handbook easy to read.
- Insert a table of contents.
- Create a concordance file and then insert an index.
- Insert appropriate page numbering in the document.
- Insert a cover page.
- Add any other elements to improve the visual appeal of the document.

Save, print, and then close **U06PA07.docx**.

Assessment 8 Create a Contact Information Form

Situation: You work for the Evergreen Regional Center where you are responsible for creating fill-in forms for the Records Department. Your supervisor has asked you to create a fill-in form template. Use the **ERCFundingApp.docx** as a reference (for the clip art image, font face, and colors) and create a form that includes the following specifications (you determine the layout of the form and the types of form fields used):

- Use the information in the first cell in the **ERCFundingApp.docx** document for the first cell in the template you design.
- Title the form *Contact Information*.
- Include the following fields:
    - Name
    - Birth date
    - Marital status
    - Gender
    - Address
    - Email address
    - Occupation
    - Emergency contact

After creating the form template, save the template document with the name **XXXU06PA08**. Use the **XXXU06PA08.dotx** form template to create a filled-in form. You make up the information to insert in the form. Save the completed form document with the name **U06PA08**. Print and then close **U0PA08.docx**.

Appendix A

Proofreaders' Marks

	Proofreaders' Mark		Example	Revised
#	Insert space		lettertothe	letter to the
℘	Delete		the commands is	the command is
lc /	Lowercase	lc	he is Branch Manager	he is branch manager
(cap) or uc ≡	Uppercase	(cap)	Margaret simpson	Margaret Simpson
¶	New paragraph	¶	The new product	The new product
no ¶	No paragraph	no ¶	the meeting. Bring the	the meeting. Bring the
∧	Insert		pens, and clips	pens, and clips
⊙	Insert period		a global search⊙	a global search.
⊐	Move right	⊐	With the papers	With the papers
⊏	Move left		⊏access the code	access the code
⊐⊏	Center		⊐ Chapter Six ⊏	Chapter Six
∽	Transpose		It is raesonable	It is reasonable
(sp)	Spell out	(sp)	475 Mill (Ave.)	475 Mill Avenue
• • •	Stet (do not delete)		I am very pleased	I am very pleased
⁀	Close up		regret fully	regretfully
ss	Single-space		The margin top ss is 1 inch.	The margin top is 1 inch.
ds	Double-space	ds	Paper length is set for 11 inches.	Paper length is set for 11 inches.
ts	Triple-space	ts	The F8 function key turns on Extend	The F8 function key turns on Extend
bf	Boldface	bf	Boldface type provides emphasis.	**Boldface** type provides emphasis.
(ital)	Italics	(ital)	Use italics for terms to be defined.	Use *italics* for terms to be defined.

Appendix B

Formatting a Memo

The formatting for an interoffice correspondence, referred to as a *memo* (short for *memorandum*) can vary from company to company. However, the content of a memo should be brief and to the point, and the format should support quick reading, easy distribution, and efficient filing. In some exercises in this textbook, you will be required to type and format a memo. When asked to format a memo, use the formatting shown below. Include reference initials at the end of the memo as shown below, along with the document name. The reference initials are indicated by the *XX*. In this textbook, insert your own initials instead of the *XX*.

DATE: → February 15, 2010

Tab twice

TO: → Jim Everson, Resources Coordinator

Tab twice

FROM: → Isabelle Brown, Training Coordinator

Tab twice

SUBJECT: → Network and Internet Books

Tab once

While attending the Southern Computer Technology Conference earlier this month, I discovered several excellent network and Internet security reference books. I would like you to order *Managing Network Security* by Douglas Baker and published by Evergreen Publishing House and *Network Management* by Geraldine Kingston and published by Bonari & Jenkins. Please make these books available in the business section of the library. The books retail for approximately $35. If you have enough in your budget, please order two copies of both books.

I would also like you to order fifteen copies of *Internet Security* by Jeong Pak and published by Meridian Publishers and twenty copies of *Protecting and Securing Data* by Glenn Rowan and published by Canon Beach Publishing. The technical support team needs these books for training that will take place in April.

XX:Memo01.docx

Appendix C

Formatting a Business Letter

When you create a business letter, consider formatting the letter in ***full block*** style, a common business letter format. In full block style, all elements of the letter are aligned at the left margin, creating a clean, businesslike look. The spacing in a block-style letter varies depending on the spacing in your document. If you retain the default line and paragraph spacing (1.15-point line spacing and 10 points of spacing after paragraphs), format your business letter in a manner similar to that shown below. If you change the line spacing to 1 and remove the spacing after paragraphs, format your business letter in a manner similar to that shown on the next page. The business letters contain standard punctuation, which includes a colon after the salutation (Dear Mrs. Cardoza:) and a comma after the complimentary close (Sincerely,).

2-inch top margin

April 6, 2010

3 Enters

Mrs. Tina Cardoza *(press Shift + Enter)*
2314 Magnolia Drive *(press Shift + Enter)*
P.O. Box 231 *(press Shift + Enter)*
Augusta, ME 04336

Dear Mrs. Cardoza:

Now is the time to sign up for a sun-filled, fun-filled family vacation. We are offering three-day, seven-day, and ten-day fun-in-the-sun vacation packages to several southern destinations, including Los Angeles, Orlando, Miami, New Orleans, and Maui. Limited by a budget? No problem. We can find the perfect vacation for you and your family that fits within your budget.

We know we can create a vacation package that is as exciting and adventurous as your previous vacation. Right now, you can spend seven days and six nights in beautiful and tropical Maui, Hawaii, at the Pacific Beach Cabanas for under $700 per person including airfare! We also have a four-day, three-night vacation package to Orlando, Florida for less than $400 per person. To find out about these fabulous and affordable vacations, stop by our office and talk to a travel consultant or give us a call and book your next fun-and-sun family vacation.

Sincerely,

2 Enters

Megan Arigala

XX:BlockLetter

2-inch top margin

April 6, 2010

5 Enters

Mrs. Tina Cardoza
2314 Magnolia Drive
P.O. Box 231
Augusta, ME 04336

ds

Dear Mrs. Cardoza:

ds

Now is the time to sign up for a sun-filled, fun-filled family vacation. We are offering three-day, seven-day, and ten-day fun-in-the-sun vacation packages to several southern destinations, including Los Angeles, Orlando, Miami, New Orleans, and Maui. Limited by a budget? No problem. We can find the perfect vacation for you and your family that fits within your budget.

ds

We know we can create a vacation package that is as exciting and adventurous as your previous vacation. Right now, you can spend seven days and six nights in beautiful and tropical Maui, Hawaii, at the Pacific Beach Cabanas for under $700 per person including airfare! We also have a four-day, three-night vacation package to Orlando, Florida for less than $400 per person. To find out about these fabulous and affordable vacations, stop by our office and talk to a travel consultant or give us a call and book your next fun-and-sun family vacation.

ds

Sincerely,

4 Enters

Megan Arigala

ds

XX:BlockLetter

Index

C

D

G

H

I

J

K

L

M

N

O

P

Q

R

S

T

U

V

W

X

Y

Z